2010 | WORLD DEVELOPMENT INDICATORS

Photo credits: Front cover, Joerg Boethling/Peter Arnold, Inc.; page xxiv, Curt Carnemark/World Bank; page 52, Curt
Carnemark/World Bank; page 148, Scott Wallace/World Bank; page 216, Curt Carnemark/World Bank; page 286,
Scott Wallace/World Bank; page 344, Curt Carnemark/World Bank.

If you have questions or comments about this product, please contact:

Development Data Group
The World Bank
1818 H Street NW, Room MC2-812, Washington, D.C. 20433 USA
Hotline: 800 590 1906 or 202 473 7824; fax 202 522 1498
Email: data@worldbank.org
Web site: www.worldbank.org or www.worldbank.org/data

ISBN 978-0-8213-8232-5

ECO-AUDIT
Environmental Benefits Statement
The World Bank is committed to preserving endangered forests and natural resources. The Office of the Publisher
has chosen to print *World Development Indicators 2010* on recycled paper with 50 percent post-consumer fiber in
accordance with the recommended standards for paper usage set by the Green Press Initiative, a nonprofit program
supporting publishers in using fiber that is not sourced from endangered forests. For more information, visit www.
greenpressinitiative.org.

Saved:
116 trees
37 million Btu of total energy
11,069 pounds of net greenhouse gases
53,312 gallons of waste water
3,237 pounds of solid waste

2010 | WORLD DEVELOPMENT INDICATORS

 THE WORLD BANK

PREFACE

The 1998 edition of *World Development Indicators* initiated a series of annual reports on progress toward the International Development Goals. In the foreword then–World Bank President James D. Wolfensohn recognized that "by reporting regularly and systematically on progress toward the targets the international community has set for itself, we will focus attention on the task ahead and make those responsible for advancing the development agenda accountable for results." The same vision inspired world leaders to commit themselves to the Millennium Development Goals. On this, the 10th anniversary of the Millennium Declaration, *World Development Indicators 2010* focuses on progress toward the Millennium Development Goals and the challenges of meeting them.

There has been remarkable progress.

Despite the global financial crisis, poverty rates in developing countries continue to fall, with every likelihood of reaching and then exceeding the Millennium Development Goals target in most regions of the world. Since the turn of the century, 37 million more children have enrolled in primary school. Measles immunization rates have risen to 81 percent, with similar progress in other vaccination programs and health-related services. Since 2000 the number of children dying before age 5 has fallen from more than 10 million a year to 8.8 million.

So, much progress. But we still have far to go. Global and regional averages cannot disguise the large differences between countries. Average annual incomes range from $280 to more than $60,000 per person. Life expectancy ranges from 44 years to 83 years. And differences within countries can be even greater. But we should not be discouraged. Nor should we conclude that the effort has failed just because some countries will fall short of the targets. The Millennium Development Goals have helped to focus development efforts where they will do the most good and have created new demand for good statistics.

Responding to the demand for statistics to monitor progress on the Millennium Development Goals, developing countries and donor agencies have invested in statistical systems, conducted more frequent surveys, and improved methodologies. And the results are beginning to show in the pages of *World Development Indicators*. But here too our success makes us keenly aware of the need to do more to enrich the quality of development statistics.

And we are just as committed to making them more widely available. With the release of the 2010 edition of *World Development Indicators,* the World Bank is redesigning its Web sites and making its development databases freely and fully accessible. As always, we invite your ideas and innovations in putting statistics in service to people.

Shaida Badiee
Director
Development Economics Data Group

ACKNOWLEDGMENTS

This book and its companion volumes, *The Little Data Book* and *The Little Green Data Book,* are prepared by a team led by Soong Sup Lee under the supervision of Eric Swanson and comprising Awatif Abuzeid, Mehdi Akhlaghi, Azita Amjadi, Uranbileg Batjargal, David Cieslikowski, Loveena Dookhony, Richard Fix, Shota Hatakeyama, Masako Hiraga, Kiyomi Horiuchi, Bala Bhaskar Naidu Kalimili, Buyant Erdene Khaltarkhuu, Alison Kwong, K. Sarwar Lateef, Ibrahim Levent, Raymond Muhula, Changqing Sun, K.M. Vijayalakshmi, and Estela Zamora, working closely with other teams in the Development Economics Vice Presidency's Development Data Group. The electronic products were prepared with contributions from Azita Amjadi, Ramvel Chandrasekaran, Ying Chi, Jean-Pierre Djomalieu, Ramgopal Erabelly, Reza Farivari, Shelley Fu, Gytis Kanchas, Buyant Erdene Khaltarkhuu, Ugendran Makhachkala, Vilas Mandlekar, Nacer Megherbi, Parastoo Oloumi, Abarna Panchapakesan, William Prince, Sujay Ramasamy, Malarvizhi Veerappan, and Vera Wen. The work was carried out under the management of Shaida Badiee. Valuable advice was provided by Shahrokh Fardoust.

The choice of indicators and text content was shaped through close consultation with and substantial contributions from staff in the World Bank's four thematic networks—Sustainable Development, Human Development, Poverty Reduction and Economic Management, and Financial and Private Sector Development—and staff of the International Finance Corporation and the Multilateral Investment Guarantee Agency. Most important, the team received substantial help, guidance, and data from external partners. For individual acknowledgments of contributions to the book's content, please see *Credits.* For a listing of our key partners, see *Partners.*

Communications Development Incorporated provided overall design direction, editing, and layout, led by Meta de Coquereaumont, Bruce Ross-Larson, and Christopher Trott. Elaine Wilson created the cover and graphics and typeset the book. Joseph Caponio provided production assistance. Communications Development's London partner, Peter Grundy of Peter Grundy Art & Design, designed the report. Staff from External Affairs oversaw printing and dissemination of the book.

TABLE OF CONTENTS

FRONT

1. WORLD VIEW

2. PEOPLE

3. ENVIRONMENT

TABLE OF CONTENTS

4. ECONOMY

5. STATES AND MARKETS

6. GLOBAL LINKS

BACK

PARTNERS

Defining, gathering, and disseminating international statistics is a collective effort of many people and organizations. The indicators presented in *World Development Indicators* are the fruit of decades of work at many levels, from the field workers who administer censuses and household surveys to the committees and working parties of the national and international statistical agencies that develop the nomenclature, classifications, and standards fundamental to an international statistical system. Nongovernmental organizations and the private sector have also made important contributions, both in gathering primary data and in organizing and publishing their results. And academic researchers have played a crucial role in developing statistical methods and carrying on a continuing dialogue about the quality and interpretation of statistical indicators. All these contributors have a strong belief that available, accurate data will improve the quality of public and private decisionmaking.

The organizations listed here have made *World Development Indicators* possible by sharing their data and their expertise with us. More important, their collaboration contributes to the World Bank's efforts, and to those of many others, to improve the quality of life of the world's people. We acknowledge our debt and gratitude to all who have helped to build a base of comprehensive, quantitative information about the world and its people.

For easy reference, Web addresses are included for each listed organization. The addresses shown were active on March 1, 2010. Information about the World Bank is also provided.

International and government agencies

Carbon Dioxide Information Analysis Center

The Carbon Dioxide Information Analysis Center (CDIAC) is the primary global climate change data and information analysis center of the U.S. Department of Energy. The CDIAC's scope includes anything that would potentially be of value to those concerned with the greenhouse effect and global climate change, including concentrations of carbon dioxide and other radiatively active gases in the atmosphere, the role of the terrestrial biosphere and the oceans in the biogeochemical cycles of greenhouse gases, emissions of carbon dioxide to the atmosphere, long-term climate trends, the effects of elevated carbon dioxide on vegetation, and the vulnerability of coastal areas to rising sea levels.

For more information, see http://cdiac.esd.ornl.gov/.

Deutsche Gesellschaft für Technische Zusammenarbeit

The Deutsche Gesellschaft für Technische Zusammenarbeit (GTZ) GmbH is a German government-owned corporation for international cooperation with worldwide operations. GTZ's aim is to positively shape political, economic, ecological, and social development in partner countries, thereby improving people's living conditions and prospects.

For more information, see www.gtz.de/.

Food and Agriculture Organization

The Food and Agriculture Organization, a specialized agency of the United Nations, was founded in October 1945 with a mandate to raise nutrition levels and living standards, to increase agricultural productivity, and to better the condition of rural populations. The organization provides direct development assistance;

collects, analyzes, and disseminates information; offers policy and planning advice to governments; and serves as an international forum for debate on food and agricultural issues.

For more information, see www.fao.org/.

Internal Displacement Monitoring Centre

The Internal Displacement Monitoring Centre was established in 1998 by the Norwegian Refugee Council and is the leading international body monitoring conflict-induced internal displacement worldwide. The center contributes to improving national and international capacities to protect and assist the millions of people around the globe who have been displaced within their own country as a result of conflicts or human rights violations.

For more information, see www.internal-displacement.org/.

International Civil Aviation Organization

The International Civil Aviation Organization (ICAO), a specialized agency of the United Nations, is responsible for establishing international standards and recommended practices and procedures for the technical, economic, and legal aspects of international civil aviation operations. ICAO's strategic objectives include enhancing global aviation safety and security and the efficiency of aviation operations, minimizing the adverse effect of global civil aviation on the environment, maintaining the continuity of aviation operations, and strengthening laws governing international civil aviation.

For more information, see www.icao.int/.

International Labour Organization

The International Labour Organization (ILO), a specialized agency of the United Nations, seeks the promotion of social justice and internationally recognized human and labor rights. ILO helps advance the creation of decent jobs and the kinds of economic and working conditions that give working people and business people a stake in lasting peace, prosperity, and progress. As part of its mandate, the ILO maintains an extensive statistical publication program.

For more information, see www.ilo.org/.

International Monetary Fund

The International Monetary Fund (IMF) is an international organization of 186 member countries established to promote international monetary cooperation, a stable system of exchange rates, and the balanced expansion of international trade and to foster economic growth and high levels of employment. The IMF reviews national, regional, and global economic and financial developments; provides policy advice to member countries; and serves as a forum where they can discuss the national, regional, and global consequences of their policies.

The IMF also makes financing temporarily available to member countries to help them address balance of payments problems. Among the IMF's core missions are the collection and dissemination of high-quality macroeconomic and financial statistics as an essential prerequisite for formulating appropriate policies. The

PARTNERS

IMF provides technical assistance and training to member countries in areas of its core expertise, including the development of economic and financial data in accordance with international standards.

For more information, see www.imf.org/.

International Telecommunication Union

The International Telecommunication Union (ITU) is the leading UN agency for information and communication technologies. ITU's mission is to enable the growth and sustained development of telecommunications and information networks and to facilitate universal access so that people everywhere can participate in, and benefit from, the emerging information society and global economy. A key priority lies in bridging the so-called Digital Divide by building information and communication infrastructure, promoting adequate capacity building, and developing confidence in the use of cyberspace through enhanced online security. ITU also concentrates on strengthening emergency communications for disaster prevention and mitigation.

For more information, see www.itu.int/.

KPMG

KPMG operates as an international network of member firms in more than 140 countries offering audit, tax, and advisory services. It works closely with clients, helping them to mitigate risks and perform in the dynamic and challenging environment in which they do business.

For more information, see www.kpmg.com/Global.

National Science Foundation

The National Science Foundation (NSF) is an independent U.S. government agency whose mission is to promote the progress of science; to advance the national health, prosperity, and welfare; and to secure the national defense. NSF's goals—discovery, learning, research infrastructure, and stewardship—provide an integrated strategy to advance the frontiers of knowledge, cultivate a world-class, broadly inclusive science and engineering workforce, expand the scientific literacy of all citizens, build the nation's research capability through investments in advanced instrumentation and facilities, and support excellence in science and engineering research and education through a capable and responsive organization.

For more information, see www.nsf.gov/.

Organisation for Economic Co-operation and Development

The Organisation for Economic Co-operation and Development (OECD) includes 30 member countries sharing a commitment to democratic government and the market economy to support sustainable economic growth, boost employment, raise living standards, maintain financial stability, assist other countries' economic development, and contribute to growth in world trade. With active relationships with some 100 other countries, it has a global reach. It is best known for its publications and statistics, which cover economic and social issues from macroeconomics to trade, education, development, and science and innovation.

The Development Assistance Committee (DAC, www.oecd.org/dac/) is one of the principal bodies through which the OECD deals with issues related to cooperation with developing countries. The DAC is a key forum of major bilateral donors, who work together to increase the effectiveness of their common efforts to support sustainable development. The DAC concentrates on two key areas: the contribution of international development to the capacity of developing countries to participate in the global economy and the capacity of people to overcome poverty and participate fully in their societies.

For more information, see www.oecd.org/.

Stockholm International Peace Research Institute

The Stockholm International Peace Research Institute (SIPRI) conducts research on questions of conflict and cooperation of importance for international peace and security, with the aim of contributing to an understanding of the conditions for peaceful solutions to international conflicts and for a stable peace. SIPRI's main publication, *SIPRI Yearbook,* is an authoritive and independent source on armaments and arms control and other conflict and security issues.

For more information, see www.sipri.org/.

Understanding Children's Work

As part of broader efforts to develop effective and long-term solutions to child labor, the International Labour Organization, the United Nations Children's Fund (UNICEF), and the World Bank initiated the joint interagency research program "Understanding Children's Work and Its Impact" in December 2000. The Understanding Children's Work (UCW) project was located at UNICEF's Innocenti Research Centre in Florence, Italy, until June 2004, when it moved to the Centre for International Studies on Economic Growth in Rome.

The UCW project addresses the crucial need for more and better data on child labor. UCW's online database contains data by country on child labor and the status of children.

For more information, see www.ucw-project.org/.

United Nations

The United Nations currently has 192 member states. The purposes of the United Nations, as set forth in its charter, are to maintain international peace and security; to develop friendly relations among nations; to cooperate in solving international economic, social, cultural, and humanitarian problems and in promoting respect for human rights and fundamental freedoms; and to be a center for harmonizing the actions of nations in attaining these ends.

For more information, see www.un.org/.

United Nations Centre for Human Settlements, Global Urban Observatory

The Urban Indicators Programme of the United Nations Human Settlements Programme was established to address the urgent global need to improve the urban knowledge base by helping countries and cities design, collect, and apply policy-oriented indicators related to development at the city level.

With the Urban Indicators and Best Practices programs, the Global Urban Observatory is establishing a worldwide information, assessment, and capacity-building network to help governments, local authorities, the private sector, and nongovernmental and other civil society organizations.

For more information, see www.unhabitat.org/.

PARTNERS

United Nations Children's Fund

The United Nations Children's Fund (UNICEF) works with other UN bodies and with governments and non-governmental organizations to improve children's lives in more than 190 countries through various programs in education and health. UNICEF focuses primarily on five areas: child survival and development, basic education and gender equality (including girls' education), child protection, HIV/AIDS, and policy advocacy and partnerships.

For more information, see www.unicef.org/.

United Nations Conference on Trade and Development

The United Nations Conference on Trade and Development (UNCTAD) is the principal organ of the United Nations General Assembly in the field of trade and development. Its mandate is to accelerate economic growth and development, particularly in developing countries. UNCTAD discharges its mandate through policy analysis; intergovernmental deliberations, consensus building, and negotiation; monitoring, implementation, and follow-up; and technical cooperation.

For more information, see www.unctad.org/.

United Nations Department of Peacekeeping Operations

The United Nations Department of Peacekeeping Operations contributes to the most important function of the United Nations—maintaining international peace and security. The department helps countries torn by conflict to create the conditions for lasting peace. The first peacekeeping mission was established in 1948 and has evolved to meet the demands of different conflicts and a changing political landscape. Today's peacekeepers undertake a wide variety of complex tasks, from helping build sustainable institutions of governance, to monitoring human rights, to assisting in security sector reform, to disarmaming, demobilizing, and reintegrating former combatants.

For more information, see www.un.org/en/peacekeeping/.

United Nations Educational, Scientific, and Cultural Organization, Institute for Statistics

The United Nations Educational, Scientific, and Cultural Organization (UNESCO) is a specialized agency of the United Nations that promotes international cooperation among member states and associate members in education, science, culture, and communications. The UNESCO Institute for Statistics is the organization's statistical branch, established in July 1999 to meet the growing needs of UNESCO member states and the international community for a wider range of policy-relevant, timely, and reliable statistics on these topics.

For more information, see www.uis.unesco.org/.

United Nations Environment Programme

The mandate of the United Nations Environment Programme is to provide leadership and encourage partnership in caring for the environment by inspiring, informing, and enabling nations and people to improve their quality of life without compromising that of future generations.

For more information, see www.unep.org/.

United Nations Industrial Development Organization

The United Nations Industrial Development Organization was established to act as the central coordinating body for industrial activities and to promote industrial development and cooperation at the global, regional, national, and sectoral levels. Its mandate is to help develop scientific and technological plans and programs for industrialization in the public, cooperative, and private sectors.

For more information, see www.unido.org/.

United Nations Office on Drugs and Crime

The United Nations Office on Drugs and Crime was established in 1977 and is a global leader in the fight against illicit drugs and international crime. The office assists member states in their struggle against illicit drugs, crime, and terrorism by helping build capacity, conducting research and analytical work, and assisting in the ratification and implementation of relevant international treaties and domestic legislation related to drugs, crime, and terrorism.

For more information, see www.unodc.org/.

The UN Refugee Agency

The UN Refugee Agency (UNHCR) is mandated to lead and coordinate international action to protect refugees and resolve refugee problems worldwide. Its primary purpose is to safeguard the rights and well-being of refugees. UNHCR also collects and disseminates statistics on refugees.

For more information, see www.unhcr.org

Upsalla Conflict Data Program

The Upsalla Conflict Data Program has collected information on armed violence since 1946 and is one of the most accurate and well used data sources on global armed conflicts. Its definition of armed conflict is becoming a standard in how conflicts are systematically defined and studied. In addition to data collection on armed violence, its researchers conduct theoretically and empirically based analyses of the causes, escalation, spread, prevention, and resolution of armed conflict.

For more information, see www.pcr.uu.se/research/UCDP/.

World Bank

The World Bank is a vital source of financial and technical assistance for developing countries. The World Bank is made up of two unique development institutions owned by 186 member countries—the International Bank for Reconstruction and Development (IBRD) and the International Development Association (IDA). These institutions play different but collaborative roles to advance the vision of an inclusive and sustainable globalization. The IBRD focuses on middle-income and creditworthy poor countries, while IDA focuses on the poorest countries. Together they provide low-interest loans, interest-free credits, and grants to developing countries for a wide array of purposes, including investments in education, health, public administration, infrastructure, financial and private sector development, agriculture, and environmental and natural resource management. The World Bank's work focuses on achieving the Millennium Development Goals by working with partners to alleviate poverty.

For more information, see www.worldbank.org/data/.

PARTNERS

World Health Organization

The objective of the World Health Organization (WHO), a specialized agency of the United Nations, is the attainment by all people of the highest possible level of health. It is responsible for providing leadership on global health matters, shaping the health research agenda, setting norms and standards, articulating evidence-based policy options, providing technical support to countries, and monitoring and assessing health trends.

For more information, see www.who.int/.

World Intellectual Property Organization

The World Intellectual Property Organization (WIPO) is a specialized agency of the United Nations dedicated to developing a balanced and accessible international intellectual property (IP) system, which rewards creativity, stimulates innovation, and contributes to economic development while safeguarding the public interest. WIPO carries out a wide variety of tasks related to the protection of IP rights. These include developing international IP laws and standards, delivering global IP protection services, encouraging the use of IP for economic development, promoting better understanding of IP, and providing a forum for debate.

For more information, see www.wipo.int/.

World Tourism Organization

The World Tourism Organization is an intergovernmental body entrusted by the United Nations with promoting and developing tourism. It serves as a global forum for tourism policy issues and a source of tourism know-how.

For more information, see www.unwto.org/.

World Trade Organization

The World Trade Organization (WTO) is the only international organization dealing with the global rules of trade between nations. Its main function is to ensure that trade flows as smoothly, predictably, and freely as possible. It does this by administering trade agreements, acting as a forum for trade negotiations, settling trade disputes, reviewing national trade policies, assisting developing countries in trade policy issues—through technical assistance and training programs—and cooperating with other international organizations. At the heart of the system—known as the multilateral trading system—are the WTO's agreements, negotiated and signed by a large majority of the world's trading nations and ratified by their parliaments.

For more information, see www.wto.org/.

Private and nongovernmental organizations

Containerisation International

Containerisation International Yearbook is one of the most authoritative reference books on the container industry. The information can be accessed on the Containerisation International Web site, which also provides a comprehensive online daily business news and information service for the container industry.

For more information, see www.ci-online.co.uk/.

DHL

DHL provides shipping and customized transportation solutions for customers in more than 220 countries and territories. It offers expertise in express, air, and ocean freight; overland transport; contract logistics solutions; and international mail services.

For more information, see www.dhl.com/.

International Institute for Strategic Studies

The International Institute for Strategic Studies (IISS) provides information and analysis on strategic trends and facilitates contacts between government leaders, business people, and analysts that could lead to better public policy in international security and international relations. The IISS is a primary source of accurate, objective information on international strategic issues.

For more information, see www.iiss.org/.

International Road Federation

The International Road Federation (IRF) is a nongovernmental, not-for-profit organization whose mission is to encourage and promote development and maintenance of better, safer, and more sustainable roads and road networks. Working together with its members and associates, the IRF promotes social and economic benefits that flow from well planned and environmentally sound road transport networks. It helps put in place technological solutions and management practices that provide maximum economic and social returns from national road investments. The IRF works in all aspects of road policy and development worldwide with governments and financial institutions, members, and the community of road professionals.

For more information, see www.irfnet.org/.

Netcraft

Netcraft provides Internet security services such as antifraud and antiphishing services, application testing, code reviews, and automated penetration testing. Netcraft also provides research data and analysis on many aspects of the Internet and is a respected authority on the market share of web servers, operating systems, hosting providers, Internet service providers, encrypted transactions, electronic commerce, scripting languages, and content technologies on the Internet.

For more information, see http://news.netcraft.com/.

PARTNERS

PricewaterhouseCoopers

PricewaterhouseCoopers provides industry-focused services in the fields of assurance, tax, human resources, transactions, performance improvement, and crisis management services to help address client and stakeholder issues.

For more information, see www.pwc.com/.

Standard & Poor's

Standard & Poor's is the world's foremost provider of independent credit ratings, indexes, risk evaluation, investment research, and data. S&P's *Global Stock Markets Factbook* draws on data from S&P's Emerging Markets Database (EMDB) and other sources covering data on more than 100 markets with comprehensive market profiles for 82 countries. Drawing a sample of stocks in each EMDB market, Standard & Poor's calculates indexes to serve as benchmarks that are consistent across national boundaries.

For more information, see www.standardandpoors.com/.

World Conservation Monitoring Centre

The World Conservation Monitoring Centre provides information on the conservation and sustainable use of the world's living resources and helps others to develop information systems of their own. It works in close collaboration with a wide range of people and organizations to increase access to the information needed for wise management of the world's living resources.

For more information, see www.unep-wcmc.org/.

World Economic Forum

The World Economic Forum (WEF) is an independent international organization committed to improving the state of the world by engaging leaders in partnerships to shape global, regional, and industry agendas. Economic research at the WEF—led by the Global Competitiveness Programme—focuses on identifying the impediments to growth so that strategies to achieve sustainable economic progress, reduce poverty, and increase prosperity can be developed. The WEF's competitiveness reports range from global coverage, such as *Global Competitiveness Report,* to regional and topical coverage, such as *Africa Competitiveness Report, The Lisbon Review,* and *Global Information Technology Report.*

For more information, see: www.weforum.org/.

World Information Technology and Services Alliance

The World Information Technology and Services Alliance (WITSA) is a consortium of more than 60 information technology (IT) industry associations from economies around the world. WITSA members represent over 90 percent of the world IT market. As the global voice of the IT industry, WITSA has an active role in international public policy issues affecting the creation of a robust global information infrastructure, including advocating policies that advance the industry's growth and development, facilitating international trade and investment in IT products and services, increasing competition through open markets and regulatory reform, strengthening national industry associations through the sharing of knowledge, protecting intellectual property, encouraging cross-industry and government cooperation to enhance information security, bridging the education and skills gap, and safeguarding the viability and continued growth of the Internet and electronic commerce.

For more information, see www.witsa.org/.

World Resources Institute

The World Resources Institute is an independent center for policy research and technical assistance on global environmental and development issues. The institute provides—and helps other institutions provide—objective information and practical proposals for policy and institutional change that will foster environmentally sound, socially equitable development. The institute's current areas of work include trade, forests, energy, economics, technology, biodiversity, human health, climate change, sustainable agriculture, resource and environmental information, and national strategies for environmental and resource management.

For more information, see www.wri.org/.

USERS GUIDE

Tables

The tables are numbered by section and display the identifying icon of the section. Countries and economies are listed alphabetically (except for Hong Kong SAR, China, which appears after China). Data are shown for 155 economies with populations of more than 1 million, as well as for Taiwan, China, in selected tables. Table 1.6 presents selected indicators for 55 other economies—small economies with populations between 30,000 and 1 million and smaller economies if they are members of the International Bank for Reconstruction and Development or, as it is commonly known, the World Bank. A complete set of indicators for these economies is available on the *World Development Indicators* CD-ROM and in *WDI Online.* The term *country,* used interchangeably with *economy,* does not imply political independence, but refers to any territory for which authorities report separate social or economic statistics. When available, aggregate measures for income and regional groups appear at the end of each table.

Indicators are shown for the most recent year or period for which data are available and, in most tables, for an earlier year or period (usually 1990 or 1995 in this edition). Time-series data for all 210 economies are available on the *World Development Indicators* CD-ROM and in *WDI Online.*

Known deviations from standard definitions or breaks in comparability over time or across countries are either footnoted in the tables or noted in *About the data.* When available data are deemed to be too weak to provide reliable measures of levels and trends or do not adequately adhere to international standards, the data are not shown.

Aggregate measures for income groups

The aggregate measures for income groups include 210 economies (the economies listed in the main tables plus those in table 1.6) whenever data are available. To maintain consistency in the aggregate measures over time and between tables, missing data are imputed where possible. The aggregates are totals (designated by a *t* if the aggregates include gap-filled estimates for missing data and by an *s,* for

simple totals, where they do not), median values (*m*), weighted averages (*w*), or simple (unweighted) averages (*u*). Gap filling of amounts not allocated to countries may result in discrepancies between subgroup aggregates and overall totals. For further discussion of aggregation methods, see *Statistical methods.*

Aggregate measures for regions

The aggregate measures for regions cover only low- and middle-income economies, including economies with populations of less than 1 million listed in table 1.6.

The country composition of regions is based on the World Bank's analytical regions and may differ from common geographic usage. For regional classifications, see the map on the inside back cover and the list on the back cover flap. For further discussion of aggregation methods, see *Statistical methods.*

Statistics

Data are shown for economies as they were constituted in 2008, and historical data are revised to reflect current political arrangements. Exceptions are noted throughout the tables.

Additional information about the data is provided in *Primary data documentation.* That section summarizes national and international efforts to improve basic data collection and gives country-level information on primary sources, census years, fiscal years, statistical methods and concepts used, and other background information. *Statistical methods* provides technical information on some of the general calculations and formulas used throughout the book.

Data consistency, reliability, and comparability

Considerable effort has been made to standardize the data, but full comparability cannot be assured, and care must be taken in interpreting the indicators. Many factors affect data availability, comparability, and reliability: statistical systems in many developing economies are still weak; statistical methods, coverage, practices, and definitions differ widely; and cross-country and intertemporal comparisons involve complex technical and conceptual problems that cannot be resolved unequivocally. Data coverage may

not be complete because of special circumstances affecting the collection and reporting of data, such as problems stemming from conflicts.

For these reasons, although data are drawn from the sources thought to be most authoritative, they should be construed only as indicating trends and characterizing major differences among economies rather than as offering precise quantitative measures of those differences. Discrepancies in data presented in different editions of *World Development Indicators* reflect updates by countries as well as revisions to historical series and changes in methodology. Thus readers are advised not to compare data series between editions of *World Development Indicators* or between different World Bank publications. Consistent time-series data for 1960–2008 are available on the *World Development Indicators* CD-ROM and in *WDI Online.*

Except where otherwise noted, growth rates are in real terms. (See *Statistical methods* for information on the methods used to calculate growth rates.) Data for some economic indicators for some economies are presented in fiscal years rather than calendar years; see *Primary data documentation.* All dollar figures are current U.S. dollars unless otherwise stated. The methods used for converting national currencies are described in *Statistical methods.*

Country notes

- Unless otherwise noted, data for China do not include data for Hong Kong SAR, China; Macao SAR, China; or Taiwan, China.
- Data for Indonesia include Timor-Leste through 1999 unless otherwise noted
- Montenegro declared independence from Serbia and Montenegro on June 3, 2006. When available, data for each country are shown separately. However, some indicators for Serbia continue to include data for Montenegro through 2005; these data are footnoted in the tables. Moreover, data for most indicators from 1999 onward for Serbia exclude data for Kosovo, which in 1999 became a territory under international administration pursuant to UN Security Council Resolution 1244 (1999);

any exceptions are noted. Kosovo became a World Bank member on June 29, 2009, and its data are shown in the tables when available.

Classification of economies

For operational and analytical purposes the World Bank's main criterion for classifying economies is gross national income (GNI) per capita (calculated by the *World Bank Atlas* method). Every economy is classified as low income, middle income (subdivided into lower middle and upper middle), or high income. For income classifications see the map on the inside front cover and the list on the front cover flap. Low- and middle-income economies are sometimes referred to as developing economies. The term is used for convenience; it is not intended to imply that all economies in the group are experiencing similar development or that other economies have reached a preferred or final stage of development. Note that classification by income does not necessarily reflect development status. Because GNI per capita changes over time, the country composition of income groups may change from one edition of *World Development Indicators* to the next. Once the classification is fixed for an edition, based on GNI per capita in the most recent year for which data are available (2008 in this edition), all historical data presented are based on the same country grouping.

Low-income economies are those with a GNI per capita of $975 or less in 2008. Middle-income economies are those with a GNI per capita of more than $975 but less than $11,906. Lower middle-income and upper middle-income economies are separated at a GNI per capita of $3,855. High-income economies are those with a GNI per capita of $11,906 or more. The 16 participating member countries of the euro area are presented as a subgroup under high-income economies.

Symbols

..

means that data are not available or that aggregates cannot be calculated because of missing data in the years shown.

0 or 0.0

means zero or small enough that the number would round to zero at the displayed number of decimal places.

/

in dates, as in 2003/04, means that the period of time, usually 12 months, straddles two calendar years and refers to a crop year, a survey year, or a fiscal year.

$

means current U.S. dollars unless otherwise noted.

>

means more than.

<

means less than.

Data presentation conventions

- A blank means not applicable or, for an aggregate, not analytically meaningful.
- A billion is 1,000 million.
- A trillion is 1,000 billion.
- Figures in italics refer to years or periods other than those specified or to growth rates calculated for less than the full period specified.
- Data for years that are more than three years from the range shown are footnoted.

The cutoff date for data is February 1, 2010.

WORLD
VIEW

The Millennium Declaration, adopted unanimously by world leaders at the United Nations in September 2000, was not the first effort to mobilize global action to end poverty. The First United Nations Development Decade, proclaimed in 1961, drew attention to the great differences among development outcomes and called for accelerating growth. Subsequent Development Decades formulated new development strategies. But not until the 1990s did a consensus emerge that eliminating poverty, broadly defined, should be at the center of development efforts. Analytical work at the World Bank (World Bank 1990) and the United Nations Development Programme (UNDP 1990) shaped a view of poverty as multifaceted, not just about income or consumption, and envisioned development as a means to empower the poor by increasing their access to employment and to health, education, and other social services. This consensus was reflected in a series of UN summits in the early 1990s that culminated in the 1995 World Summit on Social Development, which endorsed the goal of eradicating poverty.

The Millennium Development Goals: countdown to 2015

Inspired by the lofty goals announced at these summits, a high-level meeting of the Development Assistance Committee in 1996 endorsed seven International Development Goals and accompanying indicators for assessing aid efforts (OECD DAC 1996). Despite the goals' origins in UN summits and conferences, some viewed them with suspicion because they had been promulgated by rich donors. Nevertheless, the goals helped focus attention on the need to measure development outcomes. And most were incorporated into the Millennium Declaration, which was adopted unanimously at the United Nations Millennium Summit in 2000. A year later the UN Secretary-General's *Road Map towards the Implementation of the Millennium Declaration* (UN 2001) formally unveiled eight goals, supported by 18 quantified and time-bound targets and 48 indicators, which became the Millennium Development Goals (MDGs).

Like the International Development Goals, the MDGs took 1990 as their benchmark and 2015 as the completion date. An important difference is the inclusion in the MDGs of an eighth goal defining a global partnership for development between rich countries and developing countries. The partnership is intended to achieve the seven other goals by creating a fair and rule-based financial and trading system, increasing aid for the poorest and most isolated countries, and improving access to new technologies.

A decade has passed since the Millennium Declaration, and the countdown to 2015 has begun. *World Development Indicators 2010* takes a comprehensive look at the issues facing developing countries as they attempt to meet the targets set for 2015. This section looks at progress through 2008 and examines such cross-cutting issues as inequality in outcomes; tension between quantitative targets and quality outcomes; impact of the quality of governance on implementation of the MDGs, particularly in fragile states; and progress in data availability and quality.

An overview of progress on the Millennium Development Goals

Opinion is divided on whether the MDGs were intended as global targets and whether each country was intended to adopt or adapt them. The Millennium Declaration enunciated global targets, but the UN Secretary-General's road map saw the targets as operational goals for member states. For countries already making strong development progress, the targets were relatively easy. Economic growth is closely associated with progress on the MDGs (see section 4). Where economic growth was rapid, poverty reduction and social indicators improved; where growth was slow and institutional deficits large, the going was more difficult. What worked in one setting did not always work in others. Responses to policy initiatives depend on constraints imposed by local culture, the resources at society's disposal, and the local environment.

Progress has been considerable. Despite the current crisis, the target to reduce by half the proportion of people living in extreme poverty is within reach at a global level. Rapid growth in East Asia and Pacific and falling poverty rates in South Asia, the two regions with the most people living on less than $1.25 a day, account for this remarkable achievement.

But progress has been uneven at the country level (figure 1a). Only 49 of 87 countries with data are on track to achieve the poverty target. Some 47 percent of the people in low- and middle-income countries live in countries that have already attained the target or are on track to do so, while 41 percent live in countries that are off track or seriously off track (figure 1b). And 12 percent live in the 60 countries for which there are insufficient data to assess progress.

Progress on the human development indicators is mixed. In absolute terms progress has been impressive. Since 2000 some 37 million more children have been able to attend and complete primary school. More than 14 million children have been vaccinated against measles, with similar progress in other vaccination programs and health-related services. Since 2000 the number of children dying before age 5 has fallen from more than 10 million a year to 8.8 million.

The greatest progress has been toward the targets for primary school attendance, gender equality in primary and secondary school, and access to safe drinking water:

- Seven of ten people in developing countries live in countries that have already attained universal primary school completion or are on track to do so. But only two in five developing countries will have done so, while more than one in three countries is off track or seriously off track.

- Four of five people in developing countries live in countries that have attained or are likely to attain gender equality in primary and secondary education. Some 81 of 144 countries have attained this goal, and another 10 are on track to do so.

- Seven of ten people in developing countries live in countries that have halved the proportion of people without sustainable access to improved water, though more than half of developing countries have not achieved the target. Progress in sanitation has been much slower, among the worst for the MDGs. Only 16 percent of the population in developing countries live in countries that have managed to halve the proportion of people with sustainable access to basic sanitation, and only one in five countries has succeeded in doing so. Nearly 7 of 10 countries are off track or seriously off track on this goal.

Progress has been slowest in reducing child malnutrition and child mortality.

- Standards for measuring malnutrition (weight for age) among children have been revised. Under the new methodology 25 of the 55 countries with data have met or are on track to meet this goal, while 30 are not.

- Some 45 percent of people in developing countries live in countries that have reduced or are on track to reduce the under-five mortality rate by two-thirds, while some 56

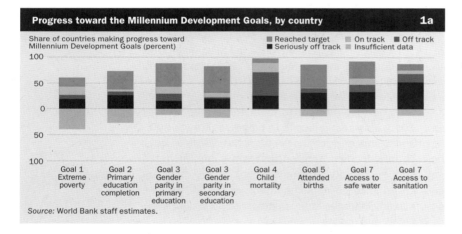

Progress toward the Millennium Development Goals, by country 1a

Share of countries making progress toward Millennium Development Goals (percent)

Legend: ■ Reached target ■ On track ■ Off track ■ Seriously off track ■ Insufficient data

Goals: Goal 1 Extreme poverty; Goal 2 Primary education completion; Goal 3 Gender parity in primary education; Goal 3 Gender parity in secondary education; Goal 4 Child mortality; Goal 5 Attended births; Goal 7 Access to safe water; Goal 7 Access to sanitation

Source: World Bank staff estimates.

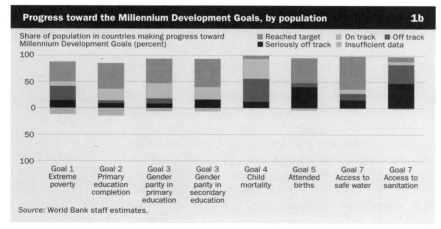

Progress toward the Millennium Development Goals, by population 1b

Share of population in countries making progress toward Millennium Development Goals (percent)

Legend: ■ Reached target ■ On track ■ Off track ■ Seriously off track ■ Insufficient data

Goals: Goal 1 Extreme poverty; Goal 2 Primary education completion; Goal 3 Gender parity in primary education; Goal 3 Gender parity in secondary education; Goal 4 Child mortality; Goal 5 Attended births; Goal 7 Access to safe water; Goal 7 Access to sanitation

Source: World Bank staff estimates.

percent live in the 102 of 144 countries that are unlikely to attain this goal.

Progress by income group

The first edition of *World Development Indicators* (in 1997) reported a developing country population in 1995 of 4.8 billion, two-thirds in low-income countries. China and India together had 2.1 billion people. This edition reports a developing country population in 2008 of 5.6 billion, two-thirds of whom live in lower middle-income countries. This massive shift reflects the advance of China and India from low-income to lower middle-income status. Today, 43 low-income countries account for just under 1 billion people, and 46 upper middle-income countries account for about 950 million. Some 3.7 billion people live in 55 lower middle-income countries, two-thirds of them in China and India.

Progress on the MDGs among low-income countries has generally been poor (figure 1c). This is not surprising considering the domination of this group by states in fragile situations. With the exception of gender equality in primary schools (61 percent of low-income countries expect to ensure gender equality in primary schools but only 30 percent in secondary schools) and access to water (35 percent of countries expect to reach this goal), no more than one in five countries has reached or is on track to reach the goals.

Middle-income countries generally do much better (figure 1d). Progress for upper middle-income countries is more difficult when the goal involves a large reduction from already advanced levels attained (figure 1e). Thus, for example, child mortality rates in upper middle-income countries averaged 47 per 1,000 in 1990 (four times the average for high-income countries) and have fallen to 24 (compared with 7 for high-income countries). A two-thirds reduction would require the rate to fall to 16. Still, a majority of these countries are expected to attain most of the goals.

Lower middle-income countries also do much better than low-income countries, though they still face serious challenges in meeting human development–related goals. A third expect to reach the poverty reduction goal, and 38 percent have already attained the primary school completion goal and 7 percent are on track to do so. Two of three countries in this group have attained or expect to attain gender equality in secondary schools.

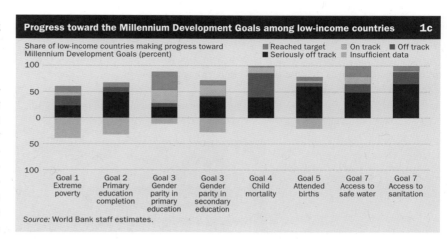

Progress toward the Millennium Development Goals among low-income countries 1c

Share of low-income countries making progress toward Millennium Development Goals (percent)

■ Reached target ■ On track ■ Off track ■ Seriously off track ■ Insufficient data

Goal 1 Extreme poverty · Goal 2 Primary education completion · Goal 3 Gender parity in primary education · Goal 3 Gender parity in secondary education · Goal 4 Child mortality · Goal 5 Attended births · Goal 7 Access to safe water · Goal 7 Access to sanitation

Source: World Bank staff estimates.

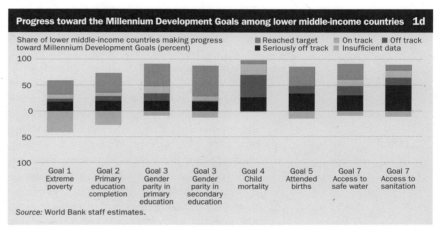

Progress toward the Millennium Development Goals among lower middle-income countries 1d

Share of lower middle-income countries making progress toward Millennium Development Goals (percent)

■ Reached target ■ On track ■ Off track ■ Seriously off track ■ Insufficient data

Goal 1 Extreme poverty · Goal 2 Primary education completion · Goal 3 Gender parity in primary education · Goal 3 Gender parity in secondary education · Goal 4 Child mortality · Goal 5 Attended births · Goal 7 Access to safe water · Goal 7 Access to sanitation

Source: World Bank staff estimates.

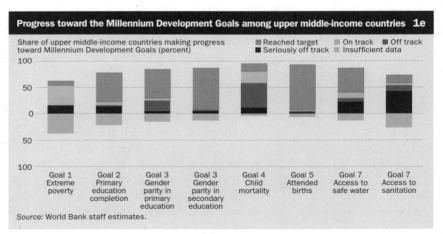

Progress toward the Millennium Development Goals among upper middle-income countries 1e

Share of upper middle-income countries making progress toward Millennium Development Goals (percent)

■ Reached target ■ On track ■ Off track ■ Seriously off track ■ Insufficient data

Goal 1 Extreme poverty · Goal 2 Primary education completion · Goal 3 Gender parity in primary education · Goal 3 Gender parity in secondary education · Goal 4 Child mortality · Goal 5 Attended births · Goal 7 Access to safe water · Goal 7 Access to sanitation

Source: World Bank staff estimates.

And 43 percent expect to attain access to the water goal. The two areas where lower middle-income countries do poorly are child mortality and access to sanitation, with 7 of 10 countries not expected to attain the child mortality reduction goal and 2 of 3 countries the sanitation goal. Many of these countries have large concentrations of poverty reflecting high levels of income inequality.

Goal 1   Eradicate poverty and hunger

We will spare no effort to free our fellow men, women and children from the abject and dehumanizing conditions of extreme poverty . . . We resolve further to halve, by the year 2015, the proportion of the world's people whose income is less than one dollar a day.

—United Nations Millennium Declaration (2000)

> **Target 1A**
> **Halve, between 1990 and 2015, the proportion of people whose income is less than $1.25 a day**

Defined as average daily consumption of $1.25 or less, extreme poverty means living on the edge of subsistence. The number of people living in extreme poverty has been falling since 1990, slowly at first and more rapidly since the turn of the century. The largest reduction has occurred in East Asia and Pacific, where China has made great strides. In South Asia accelerated growth in India could lift millions more out of poverty. Sub-Saharan Africa, which stagnated through most of the 1990s, has begun to reduce the number of people in extreme poverty. Although the decline was slowed by the global financial crisis, the number of people living in extreme poverty is expected to fall to around 900 million by 2015, even as the population living in developing countries rises to 5.8 billion. Still, an additional 1.1 billion people will live on less than $2 a day.

Most regions on track

The international poverty line was revalued from $1.08 a day (in 1993 prices) to $1.25 (in 2005 prices), using new estimates of the cost of living derived from the 2005 International Comparison Program. Although the new estimates increased the number and proportion of people living in extreme poverty, the reduction in poverty rates remained the same. East Asia and Pacific will exceed the target set by the Millennium Declaration, reducing extreme poverty rates almost 90 percent from 1990 to 2015. South Asia, which made slower progress through the early part of the 21st century, will also reach the target if growth continues, as will the Middle East and North Africa and Latin America and the Caribbean. Sub-Saharan Africa will be the only region with a sizable number of people in extreme poverty that fails to reach the target.

Uneven progress

Global and regional averages disguise large differences among countries. Since 2000, 49 countries have attained the rate of poverty reduction needed to cut 1990 poverty rates by half and achieve the target. Thirty-eight remain off track and unlikely to reach the target. And 57 countries—22 of them in Sub-Saharan Africa—lack sufficient survey data to measure progress since 1990.

Living below the poverty line

Poverty lines in poor countries are usually set at the level needed to obtain a basic supply of food and the bare necessities of life. Many poor people subsist on far less than that. The average daily expenditure of the poor is derived from the poverty gap ratio—the average shortfall of the total population from the poverty line as a percentage of the poverty line. But averages are only that: many more live on even less. To overcome extreme poverty, everyone must first get to the poverty line.

Monitoring inequality

The share of income or consumption received by the poorest 20 percent of the population was incorporated in the Millennium Development Goals as a basic measure of equity. In a typical developing country the poorest 20 percent of the population accounts for just 6 percent of total income or consumption. Since 1990 that share has increased most in low-income countries and has tended to shrink in upper middle-income countries. Many factors affect the distribution of income or consumption, and there is no clear link between economic growth and changes in income distribution.

All regions but Sub-Saharan Africa are on track to reach the poverty reduction target

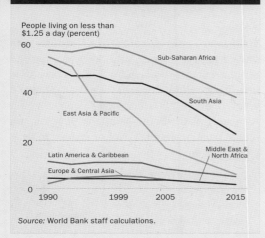

People living on less than $1.25 a day (percent)

Source: World Bank staff calculations.

The number of people living in extreme poverty has been falling since 1990

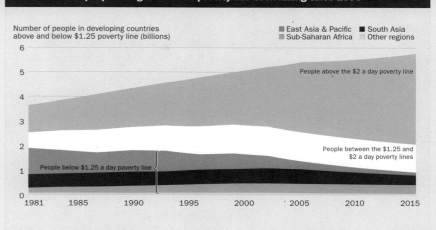

Number of people in developing countries above and below $1.25 poverty line (billions)

■ East Asia & Pacific   ■ South Asia
■ Sub-Saharan Africa   □ Other regions

People above the $2 a day poverty line

People below $1.25 a day poverty line

People between the $1.25 and $2 a day poverty lines

Source: World Bank staff calculations.

Progress in reducing poverty

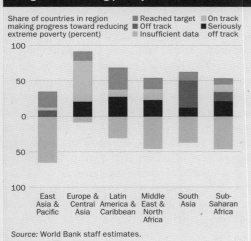

Share of countries in region making progress toward reducing extreme poverty (percent)

■ Reached target   □ On track
■ Off track   ■ Seriously off track
■ Insufficient data

Source: World Bank staff estimates.

More gainers than losers

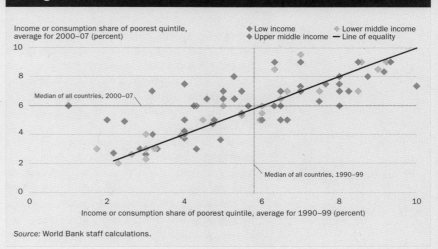

Income or consumption share of poorest quintile, average for 2000–07 (percent)

◆ Low income   ◆ Lower middle income
◆ Upper middle income   — Line of equality

Median of all countries, 2000–07

Median of all countries, 1990–99

Income or consumption share of poorest quintile, average for 1990–99 (percent)

Source: World Bank staff calculations.

Living below the poverty line—poorer than poor

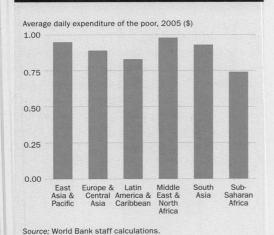

Average daily expenditure of the poor, 2005 ($)

Source: World Bank staff calculations.

We strongly support fair globalization and resolve to make the goals of full and productive employment and decent work for all, including for women and young people . . . part of our efforts to achieve the Millennium Development Goals.
—United Nations World Summit Outcome (2005)

Target 1B
Achieve full and productive employment and decent work for all, including women and young people

Recognizing the importance of productive employment for creating the means for poverty reduction, the UN General Assembly adopted a new target at its 2005 high-level review of the Millennium Development Goals. Because employment patterns change as economies develop, the target does not specify values to be achieved. But time trends and differences between regions provide evidence of structural change—and progress toward the Millennium Development Goals.

Full employment
Labor time lost can never be recovered, so maintaining full employment is important for sustaining growth and income generation. But over the long run employment to population ratios tend to fall as economies become wealthier, young people stay in school longer, and people live longer past their working years.

Raising productivity
Increasing productivity is the key to raising incomes and reducing poverty. Over the past two decades output per worker has grown faster in Asia and Eastern Europe than in high-income economies. East Asia and Pacific, starting from a low level, has made the largest gains but has still not caught up with the middle-income economies of Europe and Central Asia, Latin America and the Caribbean, and the Middle East and North Africa. Average productivity in Sub-Saharan Africa remains very low, roughly at the level in East Asia and Pacific in 1999.

Workers at risk
Vulnerable employment—own-account and unpaid family workers, who are least likely to be protected by labor laws and social safety nets—accounted for just over half of world employment in 2007 and remains high in East Asia and Pacific, South Asia, and Sub-Saharan Africa. Women are more likely than men to be in vulnerable employment.

Target 1C
Halve, between 1990 and 2015, the proportion of people who suffer from hunger

A calorie shortfall
Undernourishment measures the availability of food to meet people's basic energy needs. Rising agricultural production has kept ahead of population growth in most regions, but rising prices and the diversion of food crops to fuel production have reversed the declining rate of undernourishment since 2004–06. The Food and Agriculture Organization of the United Nations estimates that the number of people worldwide who receive less than 2,100 calories a day rose from 873 million in 2004–06 to 915 million in 2006–08 and could rise further in the next two years (FAO 2009b).

Underweight children
A shortfall in food calories is only one cause of malnutrition. The distribution of food within families, a person's health, and the availability of micronutrients (minerals and vitamins) also affect nutritional outcomes. Women and children are the most vulnerable. Even before the recent food crisis, about a quarter of children in Sub-Saharan Africa and two-fifths in South Asia were underweight. And children in the poorest households in developing countries are more than twice as likely to be underweight as those in the richest households.

Labor productivity has increased . . .

Average annual growth in output per
employed person, 1991–2008 (percent)

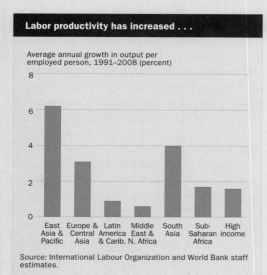

Source: International Labour Organization and World Bank staff
estimates.

. . . but large differences remain

Output per employed person (2005 purchasing power parity $, thousands)   ■ 1991 ■ 2000 ■ 2008

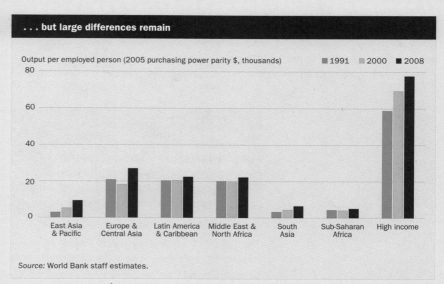

Source: World Bank staff estimates.

Employment ratios tend to fall as income increases

Employment to population ratio, 2008 (percent)

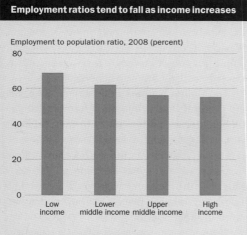

Source: International Labour Organization, Key Indicators of the
Labour Market database.

Workers in vulnerable employment lack safety nets

Vulnerable employment as share of total employment (percent)   ■ 2000 ■ 2008

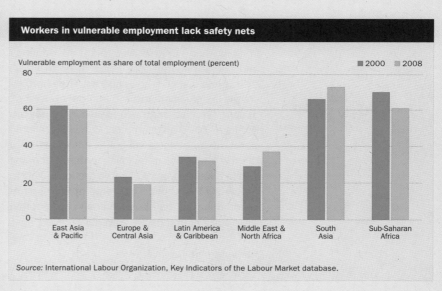

Source: International Labour Organization, Key Indicators of the Labour Market database.

People with insufficient daily nourishment

Prevalance of undernourishment
(percent of population)   ■ 1990–92 ■ 2004–06

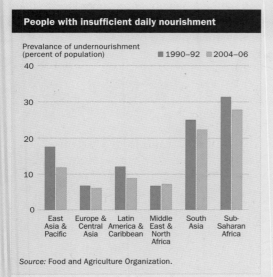

Source: Food and Agriculture Organization.

Child malnutrition rates remain high in South Asia and Sub-Saharan Africa

Share of children under age 5 under weight for age (percent)   ■ 2000 ■ 2008

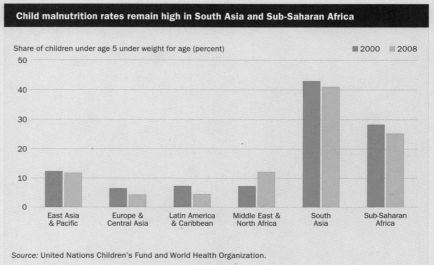

Source: United Nations Children's Fund and World Health Organization.

Goal 2 Achieve universal primary education

Every person—child, youth and adult—shall be able to benefit from educational opportunities designed to meet their basic learning needs.
— World Declaration on Education for All, Jomtien, Thailand (1990)

> ## Target 2C
> ## Ensure that by 2015 children everywhere, boys and girls alike, will be able to complete a full course of primary schooling

The goal of educating every child at least through primary school was announced in 1990 by the Jomtien Conference on Education for All. Progress in the least developed countries, slow through the 1990s, has accelerated since 2000. Countries in three regions—East Asia and Pacific, Europe and Central Asia, and Latin America and the Caribbean—are close to enrolling all their primary-school-age children. The sharp increase in enrollment rates in Sub-Saharan Africa despite population growth is also encouraging. But as of 2006 an estimated 72 million children worldwide were not in school—and about half of them will have no contact with formal education. Within countries, poor children are less likely to be enrolled in school, but large proportions of children in wealthier households in the poorest developing countries are also not enrolled.

Keeping children in school
For all children to complete a course of primary education, they must be enrolled in school. Although enrollments in grade 1 have been increasing, many children drop out of primary school because their families do not see the value of education. Many things discourage children and their parents: absent or indifferent teachers, inadequate or dangerous facilities, and demand for children's labor at home or in the market. Enrolling all children and keeping them in school will require continuing reforms and increased investment.

Progress toward education for all
Based on available data, 50 developing countries have achieved universal primary education, and 7 more are on track to do so. Countries in Europe and Central Asia and Latin America and the Caribbean have been most successful in reaching the target. Thirty-eight countries, most of them in Sub-Saharan Africa, are seriously off track and unlikely to reach the target.

The literacy challenge
Literacy comes closest to a general measure of the quality of education outcomes. Throughout developing countries youth literacy rates are higher than adult literacy rates—a result of expanded access to formal schooling.

The United Nations Educational, Scientific, and Cultural Organization Institute of Statistics defines literacy as the ability to read and write with understanding a short, simple sentence about everyday life. In many countries national assessment tests are enabling ministries of education to monitor progress. But practices differ, and in some places literacy is assessed simply by school attendance.

Dramatic improvements have occurred in the Middle East and North Africa and South Asia. But in every region except Latin America and the Caribbean boys are more literate than girls, a difference seen most starkly in South Asia and Sub-Saharan Africa.

Progress toward universal primary education

Share of countries in region making progress toward universal primary education (percent)

■ Reached target ■ On track
■ Off track ■ Seriously off track
■ Insufficient data

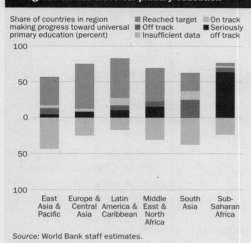

Source: World Bank staff estimates.

To reach the goal of universal primary education, children must remain in school

Share of students starting grade 1 who reach the last grade of primary education (percent)

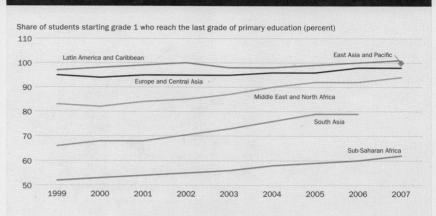

Source: United Nations Educational, Scientific, and Cultural Organization Institute for Statistics.

Youth literacy is on the rise . . .

Youth literacy rate (percent)

■ 1990 ■ 2008

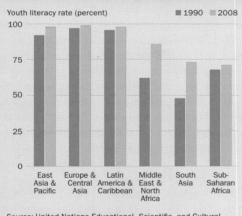

Source: United Nations Educational, Scientific, and Cultural Organization Institute for Statistics.

Primary school enrollments are rising

Net primary enrollment rate (percent)

■ 2000 ■ 2007

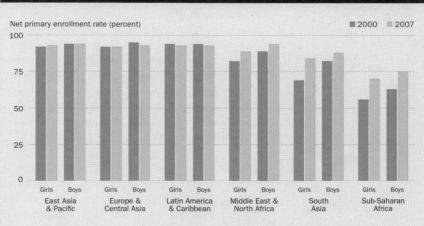

Source: United Nations Educational, Scientific, and Cultural Organization Institute for Statistics.

. . . but in most regions girls lag behind boys

Youth literacy rate, 2008 (percent)

■ Female ■ Male

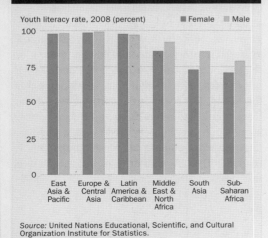

Source: United Nations Educational, Scientific, and Cultural Organization Institute for Statistics.

Goal 3 Promote gender equality and empower women

We also resolve . . . to promote gender equality and the empowerment of women as effective ways to combat poverty, hunger and disease and to stimulate development that is truly sustainable.

—United Nations Millennium Declaration (2000)

> ## Target 3A
> ## Eliminate gender disparity in primary and secondary education, preferably by 2005, and in all levels of education no later than 2015

Education opportunities for girls have expanded. Patterns of enrollment in upper middle-income countries now resemble those in high-income countries, while those in lower middle-income countries are nearing equity. But gender gaps remain large in low-income countries, especially at the primary and secondary levels. Girls born in poor households and living in rural communities are least likely to be enrolled in school. Cultural attitudes and practices that promote early marriage, the seclusion of girls, and the education of boys over girls continue to present formidable barriers to gender parity.

Progress toward gender parity in education
Developing countries continue to make progress toward gender parity in primary and secondary education. Sixty-four countries, many of them in Europe and Central Asia and Latin America and the Caribbean, have achieved gender parity in enrollment, and another twenty are on track to do so by 2015. But 22 countries are seriously off track, the majority of them in Sub-Saharan Africa.

Patterns of progress at the secondary level are similar to those at the primary level: 73 countries have achieved gender parity, and another 14 are on track. Latin America and the Caribbean and Europe and Central Asia have made the most progress. However, 29 countries, more than two-thirds of them in Sub-Saharan Africa, are seriously off track and are unlikely to achieve parity if current trends continue. In most regions, progress toward gender parity has been faster in secondary schools than in primary schools. In Latin America and the Caribbean, for example, four of five countries have reached the target at the secondary level, while only slightly more than half have reached the target or are on track to do so at the primary level. These patterns imply that boys are leaving secondary school in disproportionate numbers—not a good solution to achieving gender parity.

Data for tertiary education are not widely reported. Most countries with data have made progress toward gender parity, but countries in South Asia and Sub-Saharan Africa lag behind.

Where and how women work
Women's share in paid employment in the nonagricultural sector has risen marginally in some regions but remains less than 20 percent in South Asia and Sub-Saharan Africa. There are more men than women in wage and salaried employment in all regions but Europe and Central Asia and Latin America and the Caribbean. In Sub-Saharan Africa there are almost twice as many men as women in salaried and wage employment. Women are also clearly segregated in sectors that are generally known to be lower paid. And in the sectors where women dominate, such as health care, women rarely hold upper-level management jobs.

Women in government
The proportion of parliamentary seats held by women has increased steadily since the 1990s. The most impressive gains have come in Latin America and the Caribbean, the Middle East and North Africa, and South Asia, where women's representation rose 30–50 percent over 1990–2009. But while countries in the Middle East and North Africa made substantial gains, women still hold less than 10 percent of parliamentary seats, the lowest among all regions. Latin America and the Caribbean is out in front, with women holding 23 percent of the seats. But Rwanda leads the way, making history in 2008 when it elected 56 percent of women to its parliament. Worldwide, women are entering more political leadership positions. In March 2009, 15 women were heads of state, up from 9 in 2000.

Progress toward gender parity in primary education

Share of countries in region making progress toward gender parity in primary education (percent)

■ Reached target ■ On track
■ Off track ■ Seriously
■ Insufficient data off track

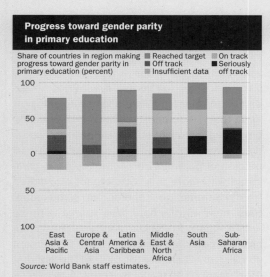

Source: World Bank staff estimates.

As income rises, so does female enrollment

Ratio of female to male enrollment rates, 2007 (percent)

■ Primary ■ Secondary ■ Tertiary

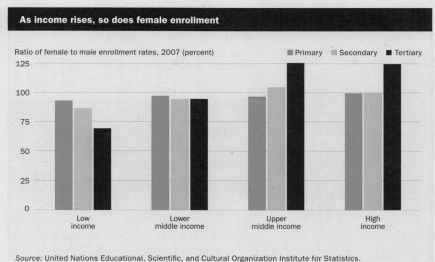

Source: United Nations Educational, Scientific, and Cultural Organization Institute for Statistics.

Progress toward gender parity in secondary education

Share of countries in region making progress toward gender parity in secondary education (percent)

■ Reached target ■ On track
■ Off track ■ Seriously
■ Insufficient data off track

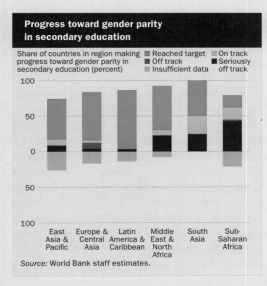

Source: World Bank staff estimates.

Women's share in nonagricultural work has barely changed

Share of women employed in nonagricultural sector (percent)

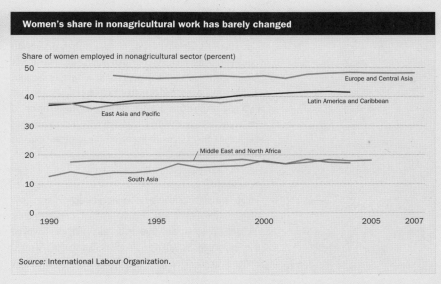

Source: International Labour Organization.

Progress toward gender parity in tertiary education

Share of countries in region making progress toward gender parity in tertiary education (percent)

■ Reached target ■ On track
■ Off track ■ Seriously
■ Insufficient data off track

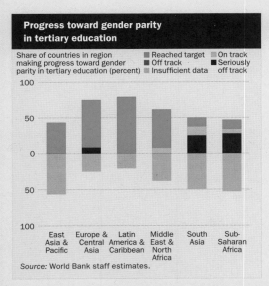

Source: World Bank staff estimates.

Women's political representation is growing

Share of seats held by women in national parliaments (percent)

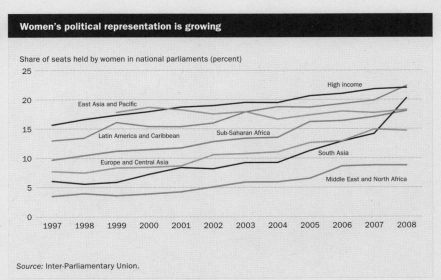

Source: Inter-Parliamentary Union.

Goal 4 Reduce child mortality

As leaders we have a duty therefore to all the world's people, especially the most vulnerable and, in particular, the children of the world, to whom the future belongs.

—United Nations Millennium Declaration (2000)

> **Target 4A**
> **Reduce by two-thirds, between 1990 and 2015, the under-five mortality rate**

Deaths of children under age 5 have been declining since 1990. In 2006, for the first time, the number of children who died before their fifth birthday fell below 10 million. In developing countries child mortality declined about 25 percent, from 101 per 1,000 in 1990 to 73 in 2008. Still, many countries in Sub-Saharan Africa have made little progress—there, one child in seven dies before the fifth birthday. The odds are slightly better in South Asia, where one child in thirteen dies before the fifth birthday. These two regions remain overriding priorities for child survival interventions such as immunizations, exclusive breastfeeding, and insecticide-treated nets.

Measuring progress

Thirty-nine countries have achieved or are now on track to achieve the target of a two-thirds reduction in under-five mortality rates. Two of the poorest countries in Sub-Saharan Africa, Eritrea and Malawi, have made remarkable progress. Successful countries now account for half the population of low- and middle-income economies.

Preventing child deaths

Immunizations for measles continue to expand worldwide. In all regions coverage is now more than 70 percent, resulting in marked improvements in child survival. However, severe disparities remain within countries. Only 40 percent of poor children are immunized, compared with more than 60 percent of children from wealthier households. In some countries, however, the poor have shared in these health improvements. In Mozambique immunization coverage increased from 58 percent in 1997 to 77 percent in 2003. The poorest 40 percent of households were the beneficiaries of most of this increase. Despite all these improvements, measles remains one of the leading causes of vaccine-preventable child mortality.

Life expectancy begins at birth

Infant mortality—child deaths before age 1—is the primary contributor to child mortality. Improvements in infant and child mortality are the major contributors to increasing life expectancy in developing countries. Success in reducing infant mortality may be viewed as a general indicator of progress toward the human development outcomes in the Millennium Development Goals: access to medicines, health facilities, water, and sanitation; fertility patterns; maternal health; maternal and infant nutrition; maternal and infant disease exposure; and female literacy (Mishra and Newhouse 2007).

Progress toward reducing child mortality

Share of countries in region making progress toward reducing child mortality (percent)

Reached target · On track
Off track · Seriously off track
Insufficient data

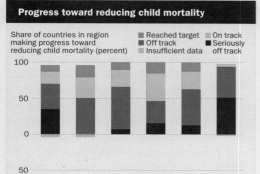

Source: World Bank staff estimates.

Child mortality rates have fallen by as much as 57 percent since 1990

Under-five mortality rate (per 1,000)

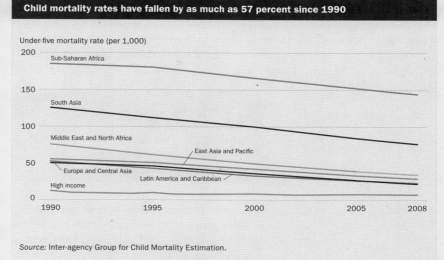

Source: Inter-agency Group for Child Mortality Estimation.

Progress toward measles immunization

Share of countries in region making progress toward measles immunization (percent)

Reached target · On track
Off track · Seriously off track
Insufficient data

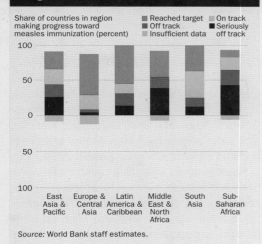

Source: World Bank staff estimates.

Measles is the leading cause of vaccine-preventable deaths in children

Measles immunization rate (percent)

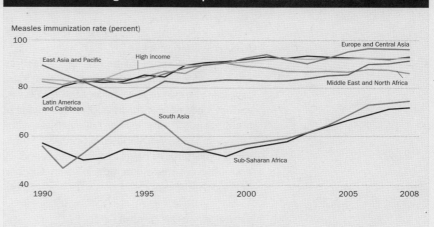

Source: United Nations Children's Fund and World Health Organization.

Infant mortality rates are falling

Reduction of infant mortality rate, 1990–2008 (percent)

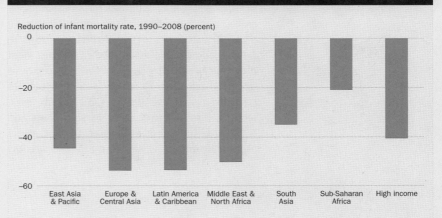

Source: World Bank staff estimates.

Goal 5 Improve maternal health

[W]e resolve to promote gender equality and eliminate pervasive gender discrimination by . . . ensuring equal access to reproductive health.
—United Nations World Summit Outcome (2005)

Target 5A
Reduce by three-quarters, between 1990 and 2015, the maternal mortality ratio

Every year more than 500,000 women die from complications of pregnancy or childbirth, almost all of them (99 percent) in developing countries. For each woman who dies, 30–50 women suffer injury, infection, or disease. Pregnancy-related complications are among the leading causes of death and disability for women ages 15–49 in developing countries.

Dangerous for mothers
About half of maternal deaths occur in Sub-Saharan Africa, and about a third in South Asia. Together the two regions accounted for 85 percent of maternal deaths in 2005. The causes of maternal death vary. Hemorrhage is the leading cause in South Asia and Sub-Saharan Africa, while hypertensive disorders during pregnancy and labor are more common in Latin America and the Caribbean.

Providing care to mothers
Skilled attendance at delivery is critical for reducing maternal mortality. Since 1990 every region has made some progress in improving the availability of skilled health personnel at childbirth. In developing countries births attended by skilled health staff rose from about 50 percent in 1990 to 66 percent in 2008. Countries in Europe and Central Asia have made the most progress in ensuring safe deliveries. Most have achieved universal coverage, and the rest are on track to achieve it by 2015. But the overall picture remains sobering. In South Asia and Sub-Saharan Africa more than half of births are not attended by skilled staff. And wealthy women are more than twice as likely as the poorest women to have access to skilled health staff at childbirth.

Many health problems among pregnant women are preventable and treatable through visits with trained health workers before childbirth. At least four visits would enable women to receive important services such as tetanus vaccinations, treatment of infections, and treatment for life-threatening complications. The proportion of pregnant women who had at least one antenatal visit rose from about 64 percent in 1990 to 79 percent in 2008. But the proportion who had four or more visits is still less than 50 percent in South Asia and Sub-Saharan Africa, where the majority of maternal deaths occur. The provision of reproductive health services is advancing very slowly in these regions.

Target 5B
Achieve, by 2015, universal access to reproductive health

High risks for young mothers and their children
In developing countries women continue to die because they lack access to contraception. And early pregnancy multiplies the chance of dying in childbirth. Contraceptive use has increased in most developing countries for which data are available, generally accompanied by reductions in fertility. In almost all regions more than half of women who are married or in union use some method of birth control. The exception is Sub-Saharan Africa, where contraceptive prevalence has remained at a little over 20 percent.

More than 200 million women want to delay or cease childbearing—roughly one in six women of reproductive age. Substantial proportions of women in every country—more than half in some—say that their last birth was unwanted or mistimed. More than a quarter of these pregnancies, about 52 million annually, end in abortion. About 13 percent of maternal deaths are attributed to unsafe abortions, and young women are especially vulnerable.

Skilled care at birth can prevent complications from becoming fatalities

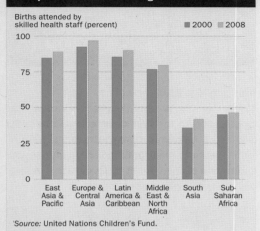

Births attended by skilled health staff (percent) ■ 2000 ■ 2008

Source: United Nations Children's Fund.

Most deaths from complications of childbirth are in Sub-Saharan Africa and South Asia

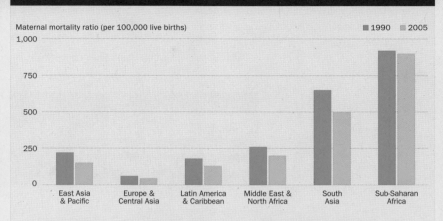

Maternal mortality ratio (per 100,000 live births) ■ 1990 ■ 2005

Source: Estimates developed by World Health Organization, United Nations Children's Fund, United Nations Population Fund, and World Bank.

Contraceptive use has increased, but many women are still unable to get family planning services

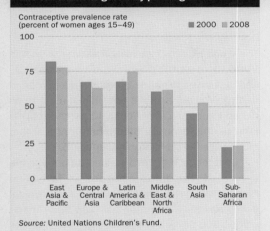

Contraceptive prevalence rate (percent of women ages 15–49) ■ 2000 ■ 2008

Source: United Nations Children's Fund.

The risks are higher for both mother and child when births occur frequently and at young ages

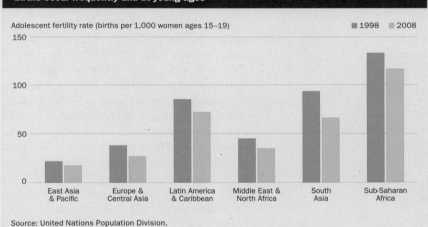

Adolescent fertility rate (births per 1,000 women ages 15–19) ■ 1998 ■ 2008

Source: United Nations Population Division.

Progress in providing care to mothers

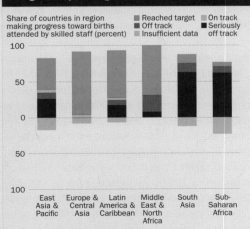

Share of countries in region making progress toward births attended by skilled staff (percent)

■ Reached target ■ On track ■ Off track ■ Seriously off track ■ Insufficient data

Source: World Bank staff estimates.

Care before delivery reduces risks for mothers and children

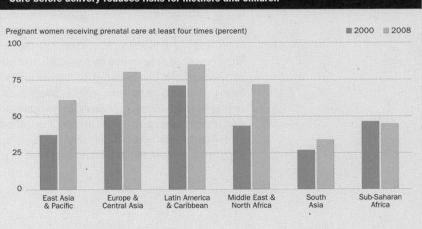

Pregnant women receiving prenatal care at least four times (percent) ■ 2000 ■ 2008

Source: United Nations Children's Fund.

Goal 6 Combat HIV/AIDS, malaria, and other diseases

We recognize that HIV/AIDS, malaria, tuberculosis and other infectious diseases pose severe risks for the entire world and serious challenges to the achievement of development goals.

—United Nations World Summit Outcome (2005)

Target 6A
Have halted by 2015 and begun to reverse the spread of HIV/AIDS

Living with HIV/AIDS

Worldwide, some 33.4 million people—two-thirds of them in Sub-Saharan Africa and most of them women—are living with HIV/AIDS, but the prevalence rate has remained constant since 2000. There were 2.7 million new HIV infections in 2008, a 17 percent decline over eight years. In 14 of 17 African countries with adequate survey data the proportion of pregnant women ages 15–24 living with HIV/AIDS has declined since 2000–01. Some of the most worrisome increases in new infections are now occurring in populous countries in other regions, such as Indonesia, the Russian Federation, and some high-income countries. Even more worrisome, an estimated 370,000 children younger than age 15 became infected with HIV in 2007. Globally, the number rose from 1.6 million in 2001 to 2.0 million in 2007. Most of these children (90 percent) live in Sub-Saharan Africa.

Orphaned and vulnerable

Worldwide in 2008 some 17.5 million children had lost one or both parents to AIDS, including nearly 14.1 million children in Sub-Saharan Africa. A key indicator of progress in HIV/AIDS treatment and the situation of children affected by AIDS is school attendance by orphans. Orphans and vulnerable children are at higher risk of missing out on schooling, live in households with less food security, and are in greater danger of exposure to HIV. The disparity in school attendance between orphans and nonorphans appears to be shrinking in many countries.

Target 6B
Achieve by 2010 universal access to treatment for HIV/AIDS for all those who need it

Treating HIV/AIDS

Wider access to antiretroviral treatment has contributed to the first decline in AIDS deaths since the epidemic began. Coverage has improved substantially in Sub-Saharan Africa, but more than 60 percent of the population in need still do not have access to treatment.

Target 6C
Have halted by 2015 and begun to reverse the incidence of malaria and other diseases

Curbing the toll of malaria

The World Health Organization estimates that in 2006 there were 190–330 million malaria episodes, leading to nearly 1 million malaria-related deaths. While malaria is endemic in most tropical and subtropical regions, 90 percent of malaria deaths occur in Sub-Saharan Africa, and most are among children under age 5.

Children who survive malaria do not escape unharmed. Repeated episodes of fever and anemia take a toll on their mental and physical development. Much progress has been made across Sub-Saharan Africa in scaling up insecticide-treated net use among children, which rose from 2 percent in 2000 to 20 percent in 2006. In countries with trend data, 19 of 22 countries showed at least a threefold increase over 2000–06, and 17 showed a fivefold increase.

Tuberculosis rates falling, but not fast enough

The number of new tuberculosis cases globally peaked in 2004 and is leveling off. Tuberculosis prevalence (cases per 100,000 people) has fallen, but the target of halving 1990 prevalence and death rates by 2015 is unlikely to be met in all regions. Prevalence is still high in Sub-Saharan Africa, and South Asian countries appear to have just returned to 1990 prevalence levels in 2007. In 2007 there were 13.7 million cases globally, down only slightly from the 13.9 million in 2006, when 1.3 million infected people died. An estimated half million people who died were also HIV positive.

Tuberculosis prevalence and mortality are falling, but resistant strains remain a challenge

Deaths from tuberculosis (per 100,000 people)

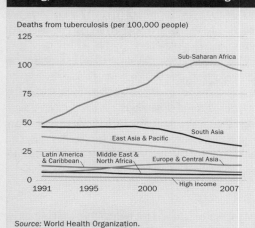

Source: World Health Organization.

Two-thirds of young people living with HIV/AIDS are in Sub-Saharan Africa, most of them women

HIV prevalence among people ages 15–24, 2007 (percent)

■ Male   ■ Female

Source: Joint United Nations Programme on HIV/AIDS and World Health Organization.

Use of insecticide-treated nets by children is rising

■ 1999–2005   ■ 2005–08

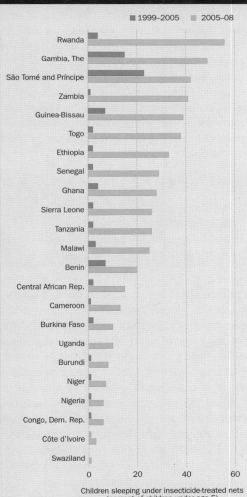

Children sleeping under insecticide-treated nets
(percent of children under age 5)

Source: United Nations Children's Fund.

Orphaned children are less likely to attend school

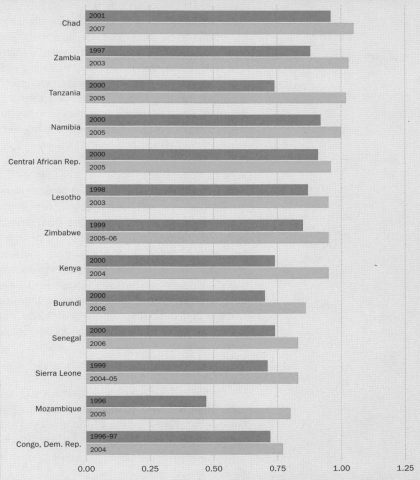

Ratio of school attendance of orphans to school attendance of nonorphans, 2000–07

Source: United Nations Children's Fund.

Goal 7 Ensure environmental sustainability

We must spare no effort to free all of humanity, and above all our children and grandchildren, from the threat of living on a planet irredeemably spoilt by human activities, and whose resources would no longer be sufficient for their needs.

—United Nations Millennium Declaration (2000)

Target 7A
Integrate the principles of sustainable development into country policies and programs and reverse the loss of environmental resources

International concern for the loss of environmental resources and the impact on human welfare was first expressed in 1972 at the UN Conference on the Human Environment. The 1992 "Earth Summit" in Rio de Janeiro adopted Agenda 21, a comprehensive blueprint of actions to be taken globally, nationally, and locally in every area in which humans directly affect the environment. Agenda 21 was incorporated into the Millennium Declaration along with a commitment to embark on the reductions in greenhouse gas emissions required under the Kyoto Protocol and to implement the conventions on biodiversity and desertification.

Forests lost
Loss of forests is one of the most tangible measures of environmental destruction. Many of the world's poor people depend on forests. The loss of forests threatens their livelihoods, destroys habitat that harbors biodiversity, and eliminates an important carbon sink that helps to moderate the climate. Net losses since 1990 have been substantial, especially in Latin America and the Caribbean and Sub-Saharan Africa, but recent data show a slowing in the global rate of deforestation.

Rising greenhouse gas emissions
The United Nations Framework Convention on Climate Change (UNFCCC) was agreed at the 1972 Earth Summit. Neither the UNFCCC nor the Millennium Development Goals commit countries to specific targets for reducing emissions of greenhouse gases. And despite the commitments made by the 37 industrial countries that are parties to the 1997 Kyoto Protocol, emissions of greenhouse gases have continued to rise.

As economies develop, their use of energy derived from fossil fuels increases. Even with improved energy efficiency, which has lowered carbon dioxide emissions per unit of GDP, average emissions per person continue to rise. Without agreed and enforceable targets for reduced emissions, little progress will be made in reducing the threat of global climate change.

Greater demands on water resources
Most water is used for agriculture and industry, with only a small part going to domestic consumption. Growing economies and populations are putting greater demands on the world's freshwater resources. In 2007 there were 62 economies with less than 1,700 cubic meters of freshwater resources per person, a level associated with water stress. Of these, 41 were in water scarcity, with less than 1,000 cubic meters per person. Water pollution and wasteful practices further reduce available water. In some economies, especially in the Middle East and North Africa, withdrawals exceed available resources, and the difference is made up by desalinization of sea water.

Target 7B
Reduce biodiversity loss, achieving, by 2010, a significant reduction in the rate of loss

The loss of habitat for animal and plant species has led to widespread extinctions. Developing economies, especially those near the equator, contain some of the most important regions of biodiversity.

Preservation of habitat through the designation of protected areas is an important practical step to ensure sustainable development. The number and size of protected areas have increased, but there is no direct evidence that the rate of biodiversity loss has slowed.

Demands on the world's freshwater resources are rising

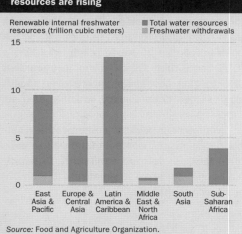

Renewable internal freshwater resources (trillion cubic meters)

■ Total water resources
■ Freshwater withdrawals

Source: Food and Agriculture Organization.

The world has lost more than 1.4 million square kilometers of forest since 1990

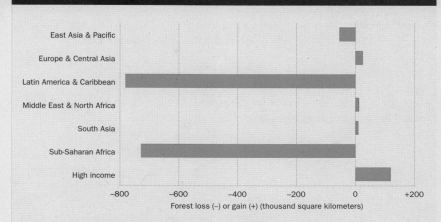

Forest loss (–) or gain (+) (thousand square kilometers)

Source: Food and Agriculture Organization.

Some 18 million square kilometers of land have been protected . . .

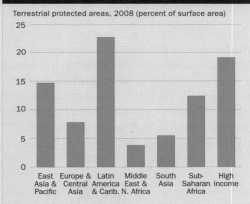

Terrestrial protected areas, 2008 (percent of surface area)

Source: United Nations Environment Programme, World Conservation Monitoring Centre.

Lowering the carbon footprint of GDP

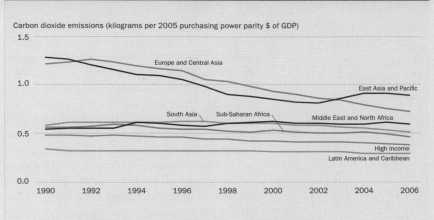

Carbon dioxide emissions (kilograms per 2005 purchasing power parity $ of GDP)

Source: Carbon Dioxide Information Analysis Center and World Bank staff calculations.

. . . but only 3 million square kilometers of marine areas are protected

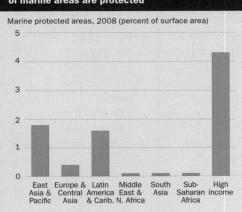

Marine protected areas, 2008 (percent of surface area)

Source: United Nations Environment Programme, World Conservation Monitoring Centre.

Carbon dioxide emissions continue to rise

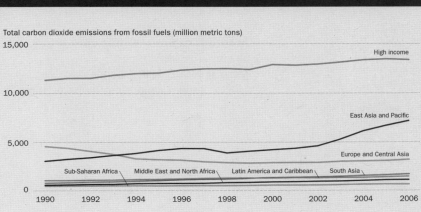

Total carbon dioxide emissions from fossil fuels (million metric tons)

Source: Carbon Dioxide Information Analysis Center.

We will put into place policies to ensure adequate investment in a sustainable manner in health, clean water and sanitation . . .
—United Nations World Summit Outcome (2005)

. . . recognizing the urgent need for the provision of increased resources for affordable housing and housing-related infrastructure . . .
—United Nations World Summit Outcome (2005)

Target 7C
Halve by 2015 the proportion of people without sustainable access to safe drinking water and basic sanitation

More people have access to an improved water source

In 1990 almost 1 billion people in developing countries lacked convenient access to an adequate daily supply of water from an improved source. The numbers lacking access have been declining. At least 65 developing countries are on track to reduce by half the proportion of people lacking access to an improved water source, and others could still reach the target by 2015.

But an "improved source" does not always mean a source of safe water. Water from improved sources, such as public taps or hand pumps and tubewells, may not meet standards of water quality set by the World Health Organization. Such sources may also require much fetching and carrying of water: many people, especially in rural areas, still do not have the convenience of piped water in their homes.

Access to improved sanitation has proved more difficult

More than 1.5 billion people lack access to toilets, latrines, and other forms of improved sanitation, a number that has barely changed since 1990. In developing countries the proportion of the population without access to improved sanitation fell from 55 percent in 1990 to 45 percent in 2006. To reach the target in 2015, more than 1.1 billion more people will have to gain access to an improved facility. Progress has been slowest in South Asia and Sub-Saharan Africa.

Even as countries try to improve their sanitation systems, 18 percent of the world's population lack any form of sanitation. They practice open defecation, at great risk to their own health and to that of others around them.

Target 7D
Achieve by 2020 a significant improvement in the lives of at least 100 million slum dwellers

A growing need for urban housing

The Millennium Declaration adopted the goal of the "Cities without Slums" initiative, to improve the lives of 100 million slum dwellers, although at the time there was no standard definition of a slum. Since then work by the United Nations Human Settlements Programme (UN-HABITAT) has helped quantify the number of people living in urban slums. That evidence suggests that more than 200 million urban dwellers have enjoyed improved living conditions, but the number of people moving into urban areas has grown even faster. UN-HABITAT estimates that more than 825 million people are now living in dwellings that lack access to an improved drinking water source, improved sanitation facilities, sufficient living area, durable structure, or security of tenure. In Sub-Saharan Africa more than half the urban population lives in slum conditions.

Progress on access to an improved water source

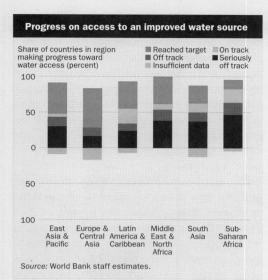

Share of countries in region making progress toward water access (percent)

■ Reached target ■ On track
■ Off track ■ Seriously
■ Insufficient data off track

Source: World Bank staff estimates.

Most regions will achieve the 2015 target for access to an improved water source

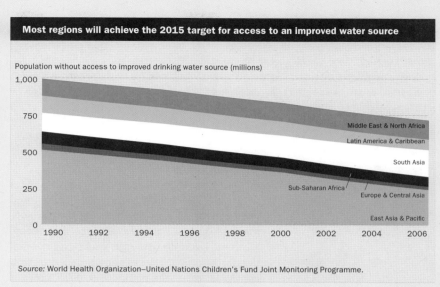

Population without access to improved drinking water source (millions)

Source: World Health Organization–United Nations Children's Fund Joint Monitoring Programme.

Progress on access to improved sanitation

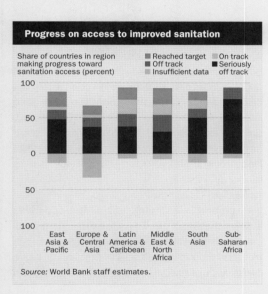

Share of countries in region making progress toward sanitation access (percent)

■ Reached target ■ On track
■ Off track ■ Seriously
■ Insufficient data off track

Source: World Bank staff estimates.

More than 1.5 billion people still lack sanitation facilities

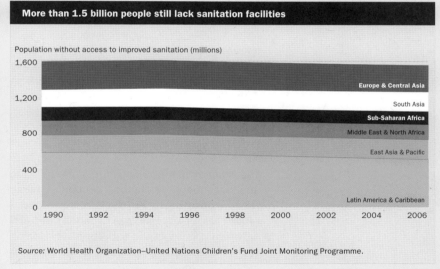

Population without access to improved sanitation (millions)

Source: World Health Organization–United Nations Children's Fund Joint Monitoring Programme.

The original housing target has been met, but millions still live in slum conditions

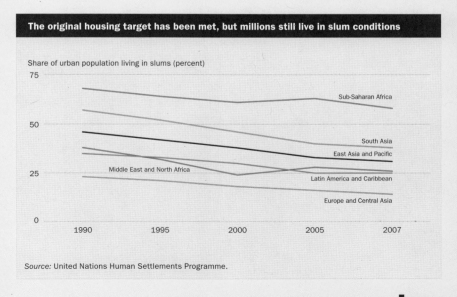

Share of urban population living in slums (percent)

Source: United Nations Human Settlements Programme.

Goal 8   Develop a global partnership for development

Success in meeting these objectives depends, inter alia, *on good governance within each country. It also depends on good governance at the international level and on transparency in the financial, monetary and trading systems. We are committed to an open, equitable, rule-based, predictable and nondiscriminatory multilateral trading and financial system.*

—United Nations Millennium Declaration (2000)

Official development assistance

Following the Millennium Summit, world leaders meeting at Monterrey, Mexico, in 2002 agreed on the need to provide financing for development through a coherent process that recognized the need for domestic as well as international resources. These leaders called on rich countries to increase aid levels to 0.7 percent of their gross national income (GNI), but only a few have. Three years later, the leaders of the Group of Eight industrialized countries meeting in Gleneagles, Scotland, made specific commitments to increase aid flows to Africa. Aid flows have increased substantially since 2000—from $69 billion in 2000 to $122 billion in 2008 (in 2007 dollars). While aid flows to Africa have increased, at $38 billion in 2008 they have fallen well short of the Gleneagles commitments.

Market access

The world economy is bound together by trade and investment. To improve the opportunities for developing countries, the Millennium Declaration calls for rich countries to permit tariff- and duty-free access of the exports of developing countries and draws attention to the need for assistance to improve countries' capacity to export.

Average tariffs levied by rich countries have been falling, but many obstacles remain for developing country exporters. The averages disguise high peak tariffs applied selectively to certain goods. Arcane rules of origin may also prevent countries from qualifying for duty-free access. And subsidies paid by rich countries to agricultural producers make it hard for developing countries to compete. Though falling, subsidies are still much higher than the level of aid provided by the same counties.

Debt sustainability

Better debt management, trade expansion, and, for the poorest countries, substantial debt relief have reduced the burden of debt service. The slowdown in the global economy since 2007 is likely to reverse these trends in the near term and increase the difficulties of servicing debt or borrowing to finance balance of payments deficits, especially for countries with above average debt levels. Debt relief under the Heavily Indebted Poor Countries Initiative has reduced future debt payments by $57 billion (in end-2008 net present value terms) for 35 countries that have reached their decision point. And 28 countries that have also reached the completion point have received additional assistance of $25 billion (in end-2008 net present value terms) under the Multilateral Debt Relief Initiative.

Access to technology

If trade and investment provide the economic sinews that bind the world together, communications is the nerve tissue, relaying messages from the most remote parts of the planet. While the growth of fixed-line systems has peaked in high-income economies and slowed appreciably in developing countries, mobile cellular subscriptions continue to grow at a rapid pace, and Internet use, barely under way in 2000, is now spreading through many developing countries.

The burden of debt service has been falling for developing countries

Debt service as share of exports (percent)

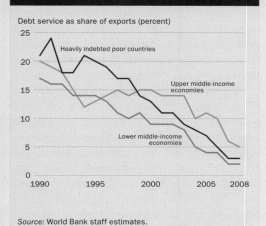

Source: World Bank staff estimates.

Aid efforts by DAC donors have increased, but most fall short of their commitments

Official development assistance as share of GNI (percent)

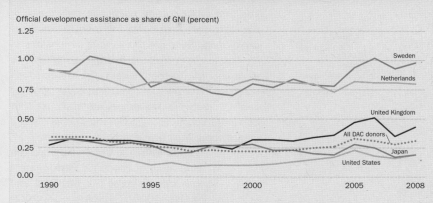

Source: Organisation for Economic Co-operation and Development, Development Assistance Committee.

Developing countries have easier access to OECD markets . . .

Share of goods (excluding arms) admitted free of tariffs from developing countries (percent)

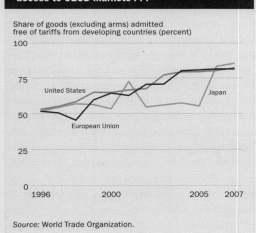

Source: World Trade Organization.

Growth of fixed telephone lines has slowed, but cellular phone use is rising rapidly

Telephone subscriptions (per 100 people)

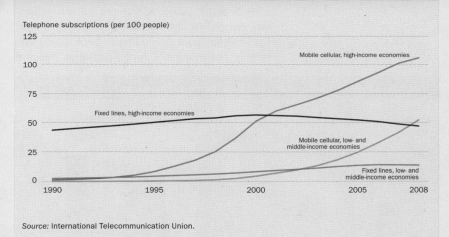

Source: International Telecommunication Union.

. . . but agricultural subsidies by OECD members exceed their net official development assistance

Percent

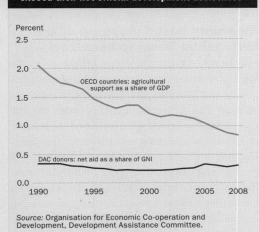

Source: Organisation for Economic Co-operation and Development, Development Assistance Committee.

Internet use in developing countries is beginning to take off

Internet users (per 100 people)

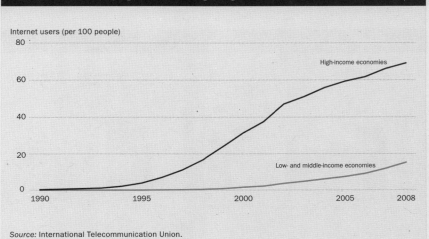

Source: International Telecommunication Union.

Millennium Development Goals and inequality

The first cross-cutting challenge for quality of life indicators is to detail the inequalities in individual conditions in the various dimensions of life, rather than just the average conditions in each country. To some extent, the failure to account for these inequalities explains the "growing gap" . . . between the aggregate statistics that dominate policy discussions and people's sentiments about their own condition.

Report by the Commission on the Measurement of Economic Performance and Social Progress (Stiglitz, Sen, and Fitoussi 2009), September 14, 2009

Although goal 1 includes a measure of income inequality, the MDGs do not directly address differences in outcome associated with socioeconomic status, race, religion, or ethnic identity, although goal 3 addresses gender inequality. For nearly all the goals, the indicators used to monitor them may conceal large disparities within populations. Country averages obscure differences between urban and rural areas, among religions and ethnic groups, between the sexes (figure 1f), and almost always between the rich and the poor. The degree of inequality varies from country to country, but within each country it is usually the poor who fare the worst (World Bank and IMF 2007).

Child death rates have fallen in low- and middle-income countries from 100 per 1,000 live births in 1990 to 75 in 2008, but they are falling less rapidly for the very poor (figure 1g). Poor people have less access to health services. They are more exposed to health risks because of malnutrition, high treatment costs, and long distances to health clinics. Some programs can be targeted to reach the most needy—oral rehydration therapy has been successful in reaching poor children and Brazil has improved income distribution (box 1h)—but large disparities remain. More midwives attend births in richer than in poorer areas of countries (Watkins 2008). Similarly, while primary school completion rates rose between 1991 and 2008 in low- and middle-income countries from an average of 78 percent to 86 percent (see table 1.2), in 36 countries primary completion rates were 20 or more percentage points higher for the richest quintile than the poorest (see table 2.15).The probability that a poor Tanzanian child will complete primary school is less than one in three, whereas almost all rich Tanzanian children complete primary school. Large gaps persist between the rich and the poor in the gross intake rate in grade 1, average years of schooling, and out of school children (see table 2.15). In Mali nearly 7 of 10 children ages 6–11 in the poorest 20 percent of the population are out of school, compared with 2 of 10 in the richest 20 percent.

An equity-based measure of the Millennium Development Goals

In a world of great inequality progress on the MDG indicators does not guarantee that poor people will be better off. Some countries could attain the MDG targets largely by improving outcomes for the richest 60 percent of the population, without improving conditions for the poor.

Until the late 1990s difficulties measuring income and consumption had inhibited assessment of economic inequalities. Then researchers found that information about readily observable household characteristics such as the type of roof or possessions such as radios and bicycles

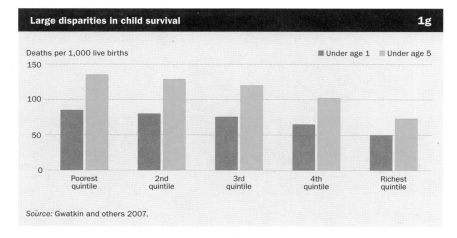

Inequalities for school completion rates persist for men and women   **1f**

School completion rate (percent)   ■ Female   ■ Male

Source: Gwatkin and others 2007.

Large disparities in child survival   **1g**

Deaths per 1,000 live births   ■ Under age 1   ■ Under age 5

Source: Gwatkin and others 2007.

Brazil improves income distribution 1h

While income inequalities have worsened in most middle-income countries, Brazil has seen dramatic improvements in both poverty and income distribution. Brazil's poverty rate fell from 41 percent in the early 1990s to 33–34 percent in 1995, where it stayed until 2003, when a steady decline began that lowered the poverty rate to 25.6 percent by 2006. Extreme poverty rates followed a similar path, falling from 14.5 percent in 2003 to 9.1 percent in 2006. Using the World Bank's global definition of poverty of living on less than $1 a day, the poverty headcount ratio dropped steadily from 14 percent in 1990 to 8 percent in 2004. Reductions in the number of people living in poverty have been accompanied by a decline in income inequality as measured by the Gini index, from 0.60 in 2002 to 0.54 in 2006. Income growth for the poorest 10 percent outstripped income growth for the richest 10 percent (see figure).

Lower poverty and more equitable income distribution have been fueled by low inflation, a targeted transfer program (including Bolsa Famillia, a conditional cash transfer program), improvements in labor productivity following gains in schooling, and better integration of labor markets across Brazil. Inequality remains among the highest in the world, but recent improvements show that inequality does not inevitably accompany development. Social indicators have improved as well. Child mortality rates fell sharply, from 56 per 1,000 in 1990 to 22 in 2008, in part reflecting better immunization rates. Births attended by skilled health staff rose to 97 percent. Primary completion rates rose 90 percent in 1990 to universal coverage.

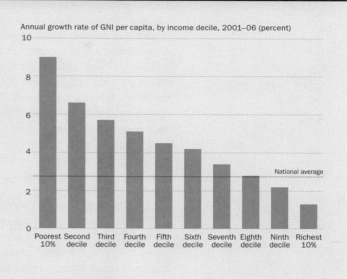

Annual growth rate of GNI per capita, by income decile, 2001–06 (percent)

Source: World Bank 2008a.

could provide a reliable measure of household wealth and a reasonable proxy for household income and consumption data. An index constructed from these physical indicators is now widely used to analyze data from Demographic and Health Surveys and Multiple Indicator Cluster Surveys wealth quintiles. Jan Vandermoortele (2009) has suggested adjusting national averages by assigning greater weight to the scores of the poor. Giving a score of 30 instead of 20 to the poorest quintile and 10 instead of 20 to the richest quintile, with intermediate quintile scores of 25, 20, and 15, enables the weighted average to better measure progress by the poorer quintiles. Figure 1i shows how average child mortality rates would be adjusted for selected countries. The adjusted measure would credit countries making more rapid progress in improving the outcomes of the poor with making faster progress toward the MDG targets. This or other methods of adjusting for distributional patterns are worth exploring for future use.

Progress in service quality

Inequality in access to health and education services is mirrored by unevenness in the quality of services delivered. Education quality has lagged behind the substantial quantitative progress in access to schools. Quality as measured by differences in cognitive skills is not just a rich-poor issue in developing countries: it is also a source of huge disparities between developed

Child mortality rates rise when adjusted for equity 1i

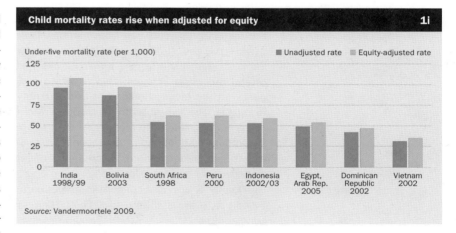

Under-five mortality rate (per 1,000)   ■ Unadjusted rate   ■ Equity-adjusted rate

Source: Vandermoortele 2009.

and developing countries. The duration and curriculum of primary schooling reflect the need for children to acquire competencies in basic knowledge, skills, values, and behavior. Thus the importance of ensuring that all children complete at least the primary stage of schooling.

Yet the evidence suggests that merely attaining 100 percent primary completion rates, which many developing countries are on track to do, will not ensure that children acquire the necessary competencies. The expansion of education systems, including the building of schools and hiring and training of teachers, is a popular and appropriate strategy for meeting the MDG target. But promoting learning and the acquisition of competencies is a much more difficult challenge. Reading comprehension tests organized under the Programme for International Student Assessment show that on a scale of 1 (low) to 5 (high), some 15 percent of students in rich countries scored below level 1, while 45 percent of students in Asian countries and 54 percent in Latin American and Caribbean countries did (Watkins 2008). In a recent survey of students in grades 6–8 in government schools in India, 31 percent of students who had completed primary education could not read a simple story and 29 percent could not do two-digit subtraction—competencies they should have acquired by grade 2. Similar results emerge from other testing.

Low education quality reflects resource constraints and weak management. These lead to poor infrastructure, high pupil–teacher ratios, and poorly trained, paid, and motivated teachers, resulting in teacher absenteeism and low-quality teaching. This erodes the implicit MDG target of achieving universal competencies. Low-quality schooling also leads to high levels of repetition and drop-out and weakens the demand for education from parents. Poor people pay the greatest price for low quality because their children are the most likely to attend the worst schools. This is not to suggest that the focus should shift from quantity to quality. The two need to go together. More effort is also needed to monitor student learning through national and international assessments and benchmarking to create stronger incentives for better performance.

Quality is of equal concern in health care, though data are still hard to collect. There is considerable evidence of widespread misdiagnosis of ailments and failure to adhere to recommended protocols or checklists for treatment of major diseases. High maternal mortality ratios through much of South Asia and Sub-Saharan Africa reflect poor-quality care that is not directly measured in the MDGs. The number of antenatal visits is measured but not their quality. The proportions of births attended by skilled attendants are monitored, but not the practices followed. This poor state of health information systems has resulted in a dependence on surveys, which take place at long intervals and do not capture moment of care data (Shankar and others 2008). An upgrade in locally based health information systems is needed to provide real-time data on delivery practices, care, and outcome to improve practices and reduce maternal and infant mortality.

Governance and fragility

Reaching poor people and ensuring that the services they receive improve human outcomes depend on governments discharging their responsibility to their citizens. This is more than a matter of ensuring economic growth, although growth and per capita incomes are closely associated with improved education and health outcomes. And it is more than a matter of public spending, although financing is a critical input. It is also a matter of ensuring that the money is well spent and achieves the intended objectives. And that requires strong governance and public accountability between citizens and their elected governments, between governments and service providers, and between service providers and citizens. To meet the MDGs, governments need to provide the physical and human infrastructure to improve access to schools and public health facilities, but they also need to provide incentives for the efficient delivery of services and to be responsive to public complaints about service provision.

Countries that underperform on health and education outcomes often have poor governance. Cameroon, for example, is a lower middle-income country whose pattern of health outcomes matches that of countries that are far poorer. Its under-five mortality rate of 131 per 1,000 is above the average for low-income countries and almost double the average for lower middle-income countries, while the under-five mortality rate for the poorest 20 percent (189 per 1,000) was more than twice the average for the richest (88) in 2006. The maternal mortality ratio is also high (669 per 100,000) despite improving indicators for prenatal care and births attended by skilled health staff. These poor health outcomes reflect in part low public spending: less than 1 percent of GDP in 2007, compared with an average of 2.4 percent for Sub-Saharan Africa and 1.8 percent for lower middle-income countries (see table 2.16). Resources are also poorly allocated, directed at centralized administration rather than front-line workers. But poor governance drives many of these outcomes as well. As in many developing countries citizens needing health care must pay high "informal payments." Drugs and procurement are major sources of illegally diverted funds.

Measuring governance is not easy, involving many institutions and formal and informal rules that guide their operation. Formal rules are easier to observe and measure. Informal rules, steeped in a country's culture and history, are less easy to observe but may have a greater impact. Efforts are being made to measure governance. The World Bank's Country Policy and Institutional Assessment measure (see table 5.9) provides two sets of indicators of the relationship between governance and social indicators. One set captures dimensions of governance that influence social outcomes, such as the quality of budgetary and financial management, the efficiency of revenue mobilization, the quality of public administration, and corruption. Another set captures policies for social inclusion and equity directed at such outcomes as gender equality, equity of public resource use, human capacity building, social protection and labor, and policies for environmental sustainability. The relationship between the two indicator sets is close (figure 1j). While some countries appear to have strong social policies and outcomes despite poor governance (Bangladesh is an example), in most cases better governance goes with better policies and outcomes.

Countries facing particularly severe development challenges—weak institutional capacity, poor governance, political instability, and conflict—are sometimes referred to as fragile states. They are least likely to achieve the MDGs. The 2010 list of core fragile states accounts for only 6 percent of the population of developing countries but for more than 12 percent of the extreme poor. They account for 21 percent of child deaths in developing countries and 20 percent of children who did not complete primary school on time. Fragile states make up a majority of the low-income countries that will not achieve the goal of gender parity in primary and secondary schools. This lack of progress reflects weak governance, low institutional capacity, and frequent internal and sometimes external conflicts.

This is not to suggest that fragile states have a uniformly poor record on the MDGs. The performance of 20 large (more than 1 million population) fragile states on under-five mortality shows that child mortality increased in 3 countries and showed little or no progress in 9, but improved in 8 to a level below the average for low-income countries (figure 1k).

Building capacity for better data

The second half of the 1990s saw a marked increase in demand for reliable data to design poverty reduction programs and demonstrate their effectiveness. Developing country governments faced both domestic and external

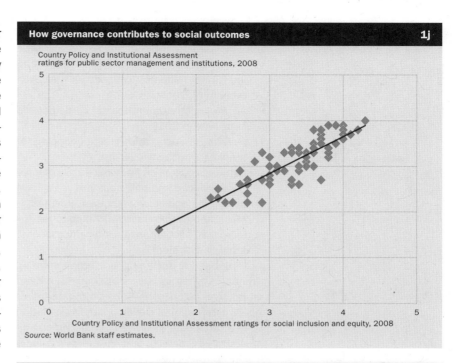

How governance contributes to social outcomes 1j

Country Policy and Institutional Assessment ratings for public sector management and institutions, 2008

Country Policy and Institutional Assessment ratings for social inclusion and equity, 2008

Source: World Bank staff estimates.

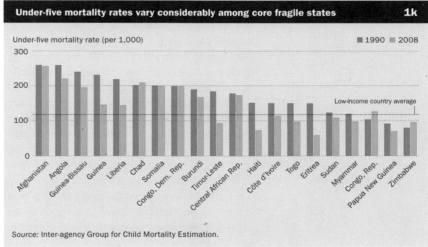

Under-five mortality rates vary considerably among core fragile states 1k

Under-five mortality rate (per 1,000)   ■ 1990 ■ 2008

Low-income country average

Afghanistan, Angola, Guinea-Bissau, Guinea, Liberia, Chad, Somalia, Congo, Dem. Rep., Burundi, Timor-Leste, Central African Rep., Haiti, Côte d'Ivoire, Togo, Eritrea, Sudan, Myanmar, Congo, Rep., Papua New Guinea, Zimbabwe

Source: Inter-agency Group for Child Mortality Estimation.

pressure to produce better data and monitor development outcomes more systematically. Increasingly, the need for improved statistical capacity building began to emerge from poverty reduction strategies supported by grants and concessional funding from the International Monetary Fund and the World Bank, and United Nations development assistance frameworks. In response, the Partnership in Statistics for Development in the 21st Century (PARIS21) was created in November 1999 to bring together donors and developing countries to promote statistical capacity-building programs.

Adoption of the MDGs gave new momentum to the demand for better data. A series of

Managing for Development Results conferences produced a Marrakech Action Plan calling for:

- All low-income countries to develop and implement national strategies for the development of statistics.
- All low-income countries to participate in censuses in 2010.
- Greater domestic and foreign financing for statistical capacity building.
- Establishment of an International Household Survey Network to help countries learn from each other and benchmark their progress.
- Major improvements in MDG monitoring.
- Increased accountability of the international statistical system.

Progress in designing and implementing national strategies for statistics has been impressive (figure 1l). Some 42 percent of the 78 International Development Association (IDA)–eligible countries are already implementing a strategy, and 32 percent are designing a strategy or awaiting its adoption.

Measuring progress in statistical capacity building

Developing a strategy is only the beginning. Implementation calls for increased investment to address structural and capacity constraints. Strategies must be effectively linked to government budgets and action plans. Progress in improving institutional capacity through better practices and better data collection was modest over the decade (table 1m). The major area of improvement was in the availability of data. Countries in Europe and Central Asia and Latin America and the Caribbean also greatly improved their scores on practice and collection and South Asia on collection.

To ensure that the increased efforts and donor financing for statistical capacity development are producing results, the World Bank launched a statistical capacity indicator in 2004 based on information that is easily collected and publicly available in most countries. The indicator combines three measures of statistical capacity:

- *Practice,* a measure of a country's capacity to meet international standards, methods, and data reporting practices in economic and social statistics.
- *Collection,* a measure of a country's ability to collect data at recommended intervals.
- *Availability,* a measure of a country's capacity to make data available and accessible to users in international data sources such as *World Development Indicators.*

Over 1999–2009 the statistical capacity index for 117 World Bank borrower countries rose from 52 to 65. Progress was faster in non-Sub-Saharan IDA countries (up 20 percentage points) than in Sub-Saharan IDA countries (up 6 percentage points). Of 42 Sub-Saharan African countries with statistical capacity data for both 1999 and 2009, 12 saw a decline and 8 barely improved. However, several Sub-Saharan countries recorded substantial improvements. The predominance of core fragile states in Sub-Saharan Africa contributed to the poor scores. Some 16 core fragile states saw a modest improvement over the decade (up 6 percentage points). A few exceptions—Afghanistan, Burundi, Republic of Congo, and Liberia—saw substantial increases in their statistical capacity index, albeit from a low base (figure 1n).

Data availability improves

Data availability has improved considerably. The United Nations Educational, Scientific, and Cultural Organization has reported a substantial increase in the availability of enrollment data. The number of countries conducting health-related surveys at least every three years has doubled.

Thus, MDG-related data are becoming more available. In 2003 only 4 countries had two data points for 16 or more of the 22 MDG indicators. Today, some 118 countries (72 percent) have two data points for the 16–22 indicators grouping (figure 1o). Improvements in statistical capacity have been accompanied by improvements in reporting to international agencies and increased access and understanding in these agencies of national sources (PARIS21 2009).

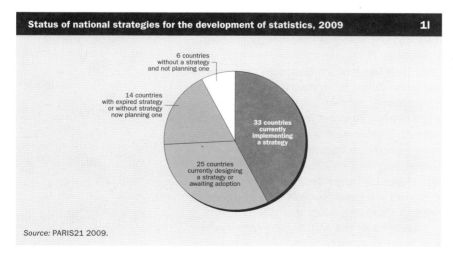

Status of national strategies for the development of statistics, 2009   **1l**

6 countries without a strategy and not planning one

14 countries with expired strategy or without strategy now planning one

33 countries currently implementing a strategy

25 countries currently designing a strategy or awaiting adoption

Source: PARIS21 2009.

Statistical capacity indicators by region and areas of performance 1m

Statistical capacity index component	All countries		East Asia		Europe and Central Asia		Latin America and the Caribbean		Middle East and North Africa		South Asia		Sub-Saharan Africa	
	1999	2009	1999	2009	1999	2009	1999	2009	1999	2009	1999	2009	1999	2009
Overall	52	65	55	68	55	79	62	75	49	59	50	68	47	54
Practice	45	56	50	63	51	76	53	68	46	55	43	58	36	38
Collection	53	63	56	65	63	81	65	75	45	55	50	72	45	48
Availability	59	77	59	76	50	80	68	84	55	68	56	73	61	75

Source: World Bank staff estimates.

The effort to get low-income countries to participate in 2010 censuses promises to greatly improve global coverage. Only nine countries have not yet scheduled a census (seven also did not participate in 2000). PARIS21 (2009) estimates that some 140 million people will not be covered by the 2010 censuses, well down from the 550 million in the 2000 censuses.

Data quality remains uncertain

Despite this impressive progress, data quality remains a concern. "Far too much of the growing amount of data cited in high-level reports is still based on poor quality information, extrapolation, and guesswork" (Manning 2009, p. 38). Strengthening national statistical systems must go beyond producing a few high-profile statistics to improving the underlying processes. This includes the sectoral agencies responsible for delivering services and collecting data on the population served. A heavy reliance on household surveys—which can produce high-quality data but at greater cost and lower frequency than national statistical systems—may be necessary to compensate for a lack of vital registration systems and reliable administrative systems. But if the main source of information is surveys that take place only every three to five years, it is difficult to reward good performance or correct poor performance. There is a "growing mismatch between the multiple demands for monitoring and the ability of local systems to generate credible data" (Manning 2009, p. 38).

The best assurance of high-quality data is an independent and well managed statistical system that adheres to recognized standards, uses a variety of instruments (surveys, censuses, and administrative records), documents its processes, and publishes its results. High-quality systems do not exist in a vacuum. Users must demand reliable data and recognize their

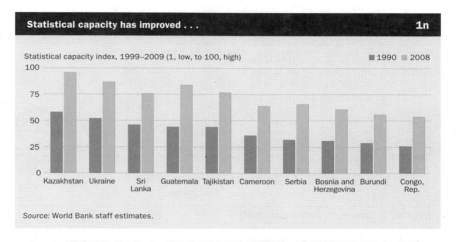

Statistical capacity has improved . . . 1n

Statistical capacity index, 1999–2009 (1, low, to 100, high) ■ 1990 ■ 2008

Source: World Bank staff estimates.

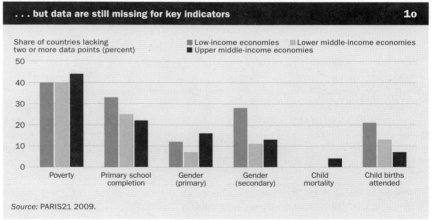

. . . but data are still missing for key indicators 1o

Share of countries lacking two or more data points (percent) ■ Low-income economies ■ Lower middle-income economies ■ Upper middle-income economies

Source: PARIS21 2009.

value. And someone—usually the government—must be willing to pay for them. Statistics are the classic example of a public good, which can be shared by many without loss to any—but they are still costly to produce. The MDGs have helped to raise the profile of statistics and the agencies that produce them, but the achievements of the last two decades are far from secure. Without continuous improvement and a strong commitment to producing useful, high-quality data, statistical systems will languish. Public and private sectors will be the poorer for it.

Millennium Development Goals

Goals and targets from the Millennium Declaration Indicators for monitoring progress

Goal 1	**Eradicate extreme poverty and hunger**		
Target 1.A	Halve, between 1990 and 2015, the proportion of people whose income is less than $1 a day	1.1	Proportion of population below $1 purchasing power parity (PPP) a day[1]
		1.2	Poverty gap ratio [incidence × depth of poverty]
		1.3	Share of poorest quintile in national consumption
Target 1.B	Achieve full and productive employment and decent work for all, including women and young people	1.4	Growth rate of GDP per person employed
		1.5	Employment to population ratio
		1.6	Proportion of employed people living below $1 (PPP) a day
		1.7	Proportion of own-account and contributing family workers in total employment
Target 1.C	Halve, between 1990 and 2015, the proportion of people who suffer from hunger	1.8	Prevalence of underweight children under five years of age
		1.9	Proportion of population below minimum level of dietary energy consumption

Goal 2	**Achieve universal primary education**		
Target 2.A	Ensure that by 2015 children everywhere, boys and girls alike, will be able to complete a full course of primary schooling	2.1	Net enrollment ratio in primary education
		2.2	Proportion of pupils starting grade 1 who reach last grade of primary education
		2.3	Literacy rate of 15- to 24-year-olds, women and men

Goal 3	**Promote gender equality and empower women**		
Target 3.A	Eliminate gender disparity in primary and secondary education, preferably by 2005, and in all levels of education no later than 2015	3.1	Ratios of girls to boys in primary, secondary, and tertiary education
		3.2	Share of women in wage employment in the nonagricultural sector
		3.3	Proportion of seats held by women in national parliament

Goal 4	**Reduce child mortality**		
Target 4.A	Reduce by two-thirds, between 1990 and 2015, the under-five mortality rate	4.1	Under-five mortality rate
		4.2	Infant mortality rate
		4.3	Proportion of one-year-old children immunized against measles

Goal 5	**Improve maternal health**		
Target 5.A	Reduce by three-quarters, between 1990 and 2015, the maternal mortality ratio	5.1	Maternal mortality ratio
		5.2	Proportion of births attended by skilled health personnel
Target 5.B	Achieve by 2015 universal access to reproductive health	5.3	Contraceptive prevalence rate
		5.4	Adolescent birth rate
		5.5	Antenatal care coverage (at least one visit and at least four visits)
		5.6	Unmet need for family planning

Goal 6	**Combat HIV/AIDS, malaria, and other diseases**		
Target 6.A	Have halted by 2015 and begun to reverse the spread of HIV/AIDS	6.1	HIV prevalence among population ages 15–24 years
		6.2	Condom use at last high-risk sex
		6.3	Proportion of population ages 15–24 years with comprehensive, correct knowledge of HIV/AIDS
		6.4	Ratio of school attendance of orphans to school attendance of nonorphans ages 10–14 years
Target 6.B	Achieve by 2010 universal access to treatment for HIV/AIDS for all those who need it	6.5	Proportion of population with advanced HIV infection with access to antiretroviral drugs
Target 6.C	Have halted by 2015 and begun to reverse the incidence of malaria and other major diseases	6.6	Incidence and death rates associated with malaria
		6.7	Proportion of children under age five sleeping under insecticide-treated bednets
		6.8	Proportion of children under age five with fever who are treated with appropriate antimalarial drugs
		6.9	Incidence, prevalence, and death rates associated with tuberculosis
		6.10	Proportion of tuberculosis cases detected and cured under directly observed treatment short course

The Millennium Development Goals and targets come from the Millennium Declaration, signed by 189 countries, including 147 heads of state and government, in September 2000 (www.un.org/millennium/declaration/ares552e.htm) as updated by the 60th UN General Assembly in September 2005. The revised Millennium Development Goal (MDG) monitoring framework shown here, including new targets and indicators, was presented to the 62nd General Assembly, with new numbering as recommended by the Inter-agency and Expert Group on MDG Indicators at its 12th meeting on 14 November 2007. The goals and targets are interrelated and should be seen as a whole. They represent a partnership between the developed countries and the developing countries "to create an environment—at the national and global levels alike—which is conducive to development and the elimination of poverty." All indicators should be disaggregated by sex and urban-rural location as far as possible.

Goals and targets from the Millennium Declaration   Indicators for monitoring progress

Goal 7	**Ensure environmental sustainability**

Target 7.A Integrate the principles of sustainable development into country policies and programs and reverse the loss of environmental resources	7.1 Proportion of land area covered by forest 7.2 Carbon dioxide emissions, total, per capita and per $1 GDP (PPP)
	7.3 Consumption of ozone-depleting substances
Target 7.B Reduce biodiversity loss, achieving, by 2010, a significant reduction in the rate of loss	7.4 Proportion of fish stocks within safe biological limits 7.5 Proportion of total water resources used 7.6 Proportion of terrestrial and marine areas protected 7.7 Proportion of species threatened with extinction
Target 7.C Halve by 2015 the proportion of people without sustainable access to safe drinking water and basic sanitation	7.8 Proportion of population using an improved drinking water source 7.9 Proportion of population using an improved sanitation facility
Target 7.D Achieve by 2020 a significant improvement in the lives of at least 100 million slum dwellers	7.10 Proportion of urban population living in slums[2]

Goal 8	**Develop a global partnership for development**

Target 8.A Develop further an open, rule-based, predictable, nondiscriminatory trading and financial system (Includes a commitment to good governance, development, and poverty reduction—both nationally and internationally.)	Some of the indicators listed below are monitored separately for the least developed countries (LDCs), Africa, landlocked developing countries, and small island developing states. **Official development assistance (ODA)** 8.1 Net ODA, total and to the least developed countries, as percentage of OECD/DAC donors' gross national income 8.2 Proportion of total bilateral, sector-allocable ODA of OECD/DAC donors to basic social services (basic education, primary health care, nutrition, safe water, and sanitation)
Target 8.B Address the special needs of the least developed countries (Includes tariff and quota-free access for the least developed countries' exports; enhanced program of debt relief for heavily indebted poor countries (HIPC) and cancellation of official bilateral debt; and more generous ODA for countries committed to poverty reduction.)	8.3 Proportion of bilateral official development assistance of OECD/DAC donors that is untied 8.4 ODA received in landlocked developing countries as a proportion of their gross national incomes 8.5 ODA received in small island developing states as a proportion of their gross national incomes
Target 8.C Address the special needs of landlocked developing countries and small island developing states (through the Programme of Action for the Sustainable Development of Small Island Developing States and the outcome of the 22nd special session of the General Assembly)	**Market access** 8.6 Proportion of total developed country imports (by value and excluding arms) from developing countries and least developed countries, admitted free of duty 8.7 Average tariffs imposed by developed countries on agricultural products and textiles and clothing from developing countries 8.8 Agricultural support estimate for OECD countries as a percentage of their GDP 8.9 Proportion of ODA provided to help build trade capacity
Target 8.D Deal comprehensively with the debt problems of developing countries through national and international measures in order to make debt sustainable in the long term	**Debt sustainability** 8.10 Total number of countries that have reached their HIPC decision points and number that have reached their HIPC completion points (cumulative) 8.11 Debt relief committed under HIPC Initiative and Multilateral Debt Relief Initiative (MDRI) 8.12 Debt service as a percentage of exports of goods and services
Target 8.E In cooperation with pharmaceutical companies, provide access to affordable essential drugs in developing countries	8.13 Proportion of population with access to affordable essential drugs on a sustainable basis
Target 8.F In cooperation with the private sector, make available the benefits of new technologies, especially information and communications	8.14 Telephone lines per 100 population 8.15 Cellular subscribers per 100 population 8.16 Internet users per 100 population

1. Where available, indicators based on national poverty lines should be used for monitoring country poverty trends.

2. The proportion of people living in slums is measured by a proxy, represented by the urban population living in households with at least one of these characteristics: lack of access to improved water supply, lack of access to improved sanitation, overcrowding (3 or more persons per room), and dwellings made of nondurable material.

1.1 Size of the economy

	Population	Surface area	Population density	Gross national income, *Atlas* method		Gross national income per capita, *Atlas* method		Purchasing power parity gross national income			Gross domestic product	
									Per capita			Per capita
	millions	thousand sq. km	people per sq. km	$ billions	Rank	$	Rank	$ billions	$	Rank	% growth	% growth
	2008	2008	2008	2008	2008	2008	2008	2008	2008	2008	2007–08	2007–08
Afghanistan	29	652	44	10.6	121	370	198	32.0[a]	1,100[a]	192	2.3	−0.4
Albania	3	29	115	12.1	114	3,840	113	23.6	7,520	112	6.0	5.6
Algeria	34	2,382	14	144.2	50	4,190	109	270.9[a]	7,880[a]	107	3.0	1.5
Angola	18	1,247	14	60.2	63	3,340	124	86.9	4,820	130	13.2	10.2
Argentina	40	2,780	15	286.6	28	7,190	85	557.9	13,990	76	6.8[b]	5.7[b]
Armenia	3	30	109	10.3	122	3,350	123	19.4	6,310	119	6.8	6.6
Australia	21	7,741	3	862.5	15	40,240	29	798.3	37,250	26	3.7	0.6
Austria	8	84	101	382.7	25	45,900	19	311.5	37,360	25	1.8	1.3
Azerbaijan	9	87	105	33.2	80	3,830	114	67.4	7,770	109	10.8	9.5
Bangladesh	160	144	1,229	83.4	58	520	186	232.4	1,450	179	6.2	4.7
Belarus	10	208	48	51.9	66	5,360	98	117.2	12,110	88	10.0	10.3
Belgium	11	31	354	477.3	18	44,570	21	378.9	35,380	31	1.1	0.3
Benin	9	113	78	6.1	140	700	178	12.7	1,470	178	5.1	1.8
Bolivia	10	1,099	9	14.1	106	1,460	152	40.1	4,140	141	6.1	4.3
Bosnia and Herzegovina	4	51	74	17.1	102	4,520	106	31.5	8,360	104	5.4	5.6
Botswana	2	582	3	12.8	112	6,640	90	25.6	13,300	81	2.9	1.4
Brazil	192	8,515	23	1,401.3	10	7,300	83	1,933.0	10,070	95	5.1	4.1
Bulgaria	8	111	70	41.8	73	5,490	96	86.7	11,370	91	6.0	6.5
Burkina Faso	15	274	56	7.3	135	480	187	17.6	1,160	188	4.5	1.0
Burundi	8	28	314	1.1	188	140	210	3.1	380	208	4.5	1.4
Cambodia	15	181	82	9.3	125	640	179	27.2	1,860	172	6.7	5.0
Cameroon	19	475	40	21.9	92	1,150	156	41.4	2,170	163	3.9	1.6
Canada	33	9,985	4	1,453.8	9	43,640	22	1,289.5	38,710	21	0.4	−0.6
Central African Republic	4	623	7	1.8	175	410	192	3.2	730	202	2.2	0.3
Chad	11	1,284	9	5.9	141	540	185	11.7	1,070	194	−0.2	−2.9
Chile	17	756	23	157.5	46	9,370	76	222.4	13,240	82	3.2	2.1
China	1,325	9,598	142	3,888.1	3	2,940	127	7,960.7	6,010	122	9.0	8.4
Hong Kong SAR, China	7	1	6,696	219.3	36	31,420	37	306.8	43,960	15	2.4	1.6
Colombia	45	1,142	41	207.9	37	4,620	104	379.4	8,430	102	2.5	1.0
Congo, Dem. Rep.	64	2,345	28	9.8	124	150	209	18.0	280	210	6.2	3.3
Congo, Rep.	4	342	11	6.5	137	1,790	147	10.1	2,800	155	5.6	3.7
Costa Rica	5	51	89	27.4	85	6,060	92	49.5[a]	10,950[a]	93	2.6	1.2
Côte d'Ivoire	21	322	65	20.3	97	980	166	32.6	1,580	176	2.2	−0.1
Croatia	4	57	82	60.2	64	13,580	63	75.6	17,050	68	2.4	2.4
Cuba	11	111	102	..		..[c]		..	..		..	..
Czech Republic	10	79	135	173.6	43	16,650	55	238.6	22,890	55	2.5	1.6
Denmark	5	43	129	323.0	26	58,800	7	206.2	37,530	24	−1.1	−1.7
Dominican Republic	10	49	206	43.1	71	4,330	107	77.6[a]	7,800[a]	108	5.3	3.8
Ecuador	13	284	49	49.8	67	3,690	116	104.8	7,770	109	6.5	5.4
Egypt, Arab Rep.	82	1,001	82	146.8	49	1,800	146	445.7	5,470	125	7.2	5.2
El Salvador	6	21	296	21.2	95	3,460	122	40.7[a]	6,630[a]	118	2.5	2.1
Eritrea	5	118	49	1.5	179	300	202	3.1[a]	640[a]	205	2.0	−1.0
Estonia	1	45	32	19.5	100	14,570	62	25.9	19,320	65	−3.6	−3.5
Ethiopia	81	1,104	81	22.4	89	280	204	70.2	870	197	11.3	8.5
Finland	5	338	17	252.9	32	47,600	16	191.0	35,940	29	0.9	0.5
France	62[d]	549[d]	114[d]	2,695.6	6	42,000	25	2,135.8	33,280	36	0.4	−0.1
Gabon	1	268	6	10.6	120	7,320	82	17.9	12,390	87	2.3	0.5
Gambia, The	2	11	166	0.7	194	400	194	2.1	1,280	183	5.9	3.0
Georgia	4	70	62	10.8	118	2,500	135	21.2	4,920	129	2.0	3.2
Germany	82	357	235	3,506.9	4	42,710	23	2,951.8	35,950	28	1.3	1.5
Ghana	23	239	103	14.7	104	630	180	30.9	1,320	182	7.3	5.1
Greece	11	132	87	319.2	27	28,400	40	318.0	28,300	42	2.9	2.5
Guatemala	14	109	128	36.6	76	2,680	132	64.2[a]	4,690[a]	132	4.0	1.5
Guinea	10	246	40	3.5	159	350	199	9.5	970	196	4.7	2.4
Guinea-Bissau	2	36	56	0.4	203	250	206	0.8	520	206	3.3	1.0
Haiti	10	28	358	..		..[e]		..	..		1.3	−0.3
Honduras	7	112	65	12.7	113	1,740	149	28.0[a]	3,830[a]	144	4.0	1.9

	Population	Surface area	Population density	Gross national income, *Atlas* method		Gross national income per capita, *Atlas* method		Purchasing power parity gross national income			Gross domestic product	
	millions	thousand sq. km	people per sq. km	$ billions	Rank	$	Rank	$ billions	Per capita $	Rank	% growth	Per capita % growth
	2008	**2008**	**2008**	**2008**	**2008**	**2008**	**2008**	**2008**	**2008**	**2008**	**2007–08**	**2007–08**
Hungary	10	93	112	128.6	52	12,810	66	182.8	18,210	66	0.6	0.8
India	1,140	3,287	383	1,186.7	12	1,040	162	3,339.3	2,930	153	6.1	4.7
Indonesia	227	1,905	125	426.8	22	1,880	145	816.9	3,590	147	6.1	4.8
Iran, Islamic Rep.	72	1,745	44	*251.5*	30	*3,540*	117	*769.7*	*10,840*	92	*7.8*	*6.4*
Iraq	31	438	70	..		..[f]		..	..		..	..
Ireland	4	70	64	220.3	34	49,770	12	158.0	35,710	30	–3.0	–4.5
Israel	7	22	338	180.6	40	24,720	45	200.6	27,450	44	4.0	2.2
Italy	60	301	203	2,121.6	7	35,460	32	1,843.0	30,800	39	–1.0	–1.8
Jamaica	3	11	248	12.9	110	4,800	101	19.8[a]	7,360[a]	114	–1.3	–1.7
Japan	128	378	350	4,869.1	2	38,130	31	4,493.7	35,190	33	–0.7	–0.6
Jordan	6	89	67	20.5	96	3,470	121	33.8	5,710	124	7.9	4.5
Kazakhstan	16	2,725	6	96.6	55	6,160	91	152.2	9,710	97	3.2	1.9
Kenya	39	580	68	28.4	83	730	177	60.3	1,550	177	1.7	–1.0
Korea, Dem. Rep.	24	121	198	..		..[e]		..	..		..	..
Korea, Rep.	49	100	502	1,046.3	14	21,530	49	1,353.2	27,840	43	2.2	1.9
Kosovo	2	11	165	..		..[f]		..	..		..	..
Kuwait	3	18	153	*117.0*	51	*43,930*	14	*142.3*	*53,430*	4	*4.4*	*1.9*
Kyrgyz Republic	5	200	28	4.1	155	780	174	11.4	2,150	164	7.6	6.7
Lao PDR	6	237	27	4.7	147	760	175	12.7	2,050	167	7.5	5.5
Latvia	2	65	36	26.9	86	11,860	69	36.3	16,010	71	–4.6	–4.2
Lebanon	4	10	410	28.4	82	6,780	86	49.2	11,740	90	8.5	7.7
Lesotho	2	30	68	2.2	173	1,060	160	4.0	1,970	170	3.9	3.0
Liberia	4	111	39	0.7	195	170	208	1.2	310	209	7.1	2.4
Libya	6	1,760	4	77.9	60	12,380[g]	67	102.4[a]	16,260[a]	70	3.8	1.7
Lithuania	3	65	54	39.9	75	11,870	68	57.7	17,170	67	3.0	3.6
Macedonia, FYR	2	26	80	8.4	129	4,130	110	18.9	9,250	99	5.0	4.9
Madagascar	19	587	33	7.9	131	420	190	20.0	1,050	195	7.3	4.5
Malawi	15	118	158	4.2	152	280	204	12.1	810	199	9.7	6.7
Malaysia	27	330	82	196.0	39	7,250	84	370.8	13,730	77	4.6	2.9
Mali	13	1,240	10	7.4	134	580	184	13.9	1,090	193	5.0	2.5
Mauritania	3	1,031	3	*2.6*	164	*840*	169	*6.3*	*1,990*	166	*1.9*	–0.6
Mauritius	1	2	625	8.5	127	6,700	87	16.0	12,570	85	4.5	3.9
Mexico	106	1,964	55	1,062.4	13	9,990	74	1,525.4	14,340	75	1.8	0.7
Moldova	4	34	110	5.3[h]	144	1,500[h]	151	11.7[h]	3,270[h]	149	7.2[h]	7.4[h]
Mongolia	3	1,564	2	4.4	149	1,670	150	9.2	3,470	148	8.9	7.6
Morocco	32	447	71	80.8[i]	59	2,520[i]	134	134.3[i]	4,180[i]	140	5.6[i]	4.3[i]
Mozambique	22	799	28	8.4	130	380	197	17.2	770	200	6.8	4.3
Myanmar	50	677	76	..		..[e]		..	..		12.7	11.8
Namibia	2	824	3	9.0	126	4,210	108	13.3	6,240	120	2.9	0.9
Nepal	29	147	201	11.5	117	400	194	32.1	1,110	190	5.3	3.4
Netherlands	16	42	487	811.4	16	49,340	13	667.9	40,620	17	2.1	1.7
New Zealand	4	268	16	118.8	53	27,830	41	107.6	25,200	49	–1.1	–2.0
Nicaragua	6	130	47	6.1	138	1,080	159	14.9[a]	2,620[a]	158	3.5	2.2
Niger	15	1,267	12	4.8	146	330	200	10.0	680	204	9.5	5.3
Nigeria	151	924	166	177.4	42	1,170	155	298.8	1,980	169	6.0	3.6
Norway	5	324	16	416.4	24	87,340	2	282.5	59,250	3	2.1	0.9
Oman	3	310	9	*39.1*	72	*14,330*	59	60.4	*22,150*	54	*7.7*	5.5
Pakistan	166	796	215	157.3	47	950[j]	169	429.9	2,590	159	2.0	–0.2
Panama	3	75	46	22.7	88	6,690	88	42.9[a]	12,620[a]	84	9.2	7.4
Papua New Guinea	7	463	15	6.8	136	1,040	162	13.3[a]	2,030[a]	168	6.6	4.1
Paraguay	6	407	16	13.1	108	2,110	141	29.0	4,660	134	5.8	3.9
Peru	29	1,285	23	115.1	54	3,990	112	229.1	7,940	106	9.8	8.5
Philippines	90	300	303	170.4	44	1,890	144	352.4	3,900	143	3.8	2.0
Poland	38	313	125	447.1	20	11,730	70	637.0	16,710	69	4.9	4.9
Portugal	11	92	116	219.6	35	20,680	50	237.2	22,330	56	0.0	–0.2
Puerto Rico	4	9	446	..		..[k]		..	..		..	..
Qatar	1	12	111	..		..[k]		..	..		*12.2*	–0.7

	Population	Surface area	Population density	Gross national income, *Atlas* method		Gross national income per capita, *Atlas* method		Purchasing power parity gross national income			Gross domestic product	
	millions	thousand sq. km	people per sq. km	$ billions	Rank	$	Rank	$ billions	Per capita $	Rank	% growth	Per capita % growth
	2008	**2008**	**2008**	**2008**	**2008**	**2008**	**2008**	**2008**	**2008**	**2008**	**2007–08**	**2007–08**
Romania	22	238	94	178.1	41	8,280	80	287.9	13,380	80	9.4	9.6
Russian Federation	142	17,098	9	1,371.2	11	9,660	75	2,192.2	15,440	73	5.6	5.7
Rwanda	10	26	394	4.3	150	440	188	10.8	1,110	190	11.2	8.2
Saudi Arabia	25	2,000[l]	12	440.5	21	17,870	54	603.5	24,490	52	4.4	2.4
Senegal	12	197	63	11.9	116	980[m]	166	21.7	1,780	175	3.3	0.6
Serbia	7	88	83	41.1	74	5,590	95	76.3	10,380	94	1.2	1.7
Sierra Leone	6	72	78	1.8	176	320	201	4.3	770	200	5.5	2.9
Singapore	5	1	6,943	168.2	45	34,760	33	232.0	47,940	12	1.1	−4.1
Slovak Republic	5	49	112	89.7	56	16,590	56	116.0	21,460	60	6.2	6.0
Slovenia	2	20	100	49.0	68	24,230	46	54.9	27,160	45	3.5	3.4
Somalia	9	638	14	..		..[e]		..	..		..	..
South Africa	49	1,219	40	283.2	29	5,820	94	476.2	9,780	96	3.1	1.3
Spain	46	505	91	1,454.8	8	31,930	36	1,404.4	30,830	38	1.2	−0.3
Sri Lanka	20	66	312	35.8	78	1,780	148	89.9	4,460	136	6.0	5.2
Sudan	41	2,506	17	45.7	69	1,100	158	79.4	1,920	171	8.3	5.9
Swaziland	1	17	68	3.0	165	2,600	133	5.8	5,000	128	2.4	1.0
Sweden	9	450	22	469.4	19	50,910	10	348.3	37,780	23	−0.2	−0.9
Switzerland	8	41	191	424.5	23	55,510	8	299.8	39,210	20	1.8	0.5
Syrian Arab Republic	21	185	112	44.4	70	2,160	140	92.4	4,490	135	5.2	2.7
Tajikistan	7	143	49	4.1	156	600	183	12.7	1,860	172	7.9	6.2
Tanzania	42	947	48	18.4[n]	101	440[n]	188	52.0[n]	1,260[n]	184	7.5[n]	4.4[n]
Thailand	67	513	132	247.2	33	3,670	118	523.1	7,760	111	2.5	1.8
Timor-Leste	1	15	74	2.7	166	2,460	136	5.2[a]	4,690[a]	132	13.2	9.6
Togo	6	57	119	2.6	167	410	192	5.3	830	198	1.1	−1.4
Trinidad and Tobago	1	5	260	22.1	90	16,590	56	32.3[a]	24,230[a]	53	3.5	3.1
Tunisia	10	164	66	36.0	77	3,480	120	77.0	7,450	113	4.5	3.5
Turkey	74	784	96	666.6	17	9,020	78	991.7	13,420	78	0.9	−0.3
Turkmenistan	5	488	11	14.4	105	2,840	128	30.9[a]	6,120[a]	121	9.8	8.4
Uganda	32	241	161	13.3	107	420	190	36.1	1,140	189	9.5	6.0
Ukraine	46	604	80	148.6	48	3,210	126	333.5	7,210	116	2.1	2.7
United Arab Emirates	4	84	54	..		..[k]		..	..		6.3	*3.1*
United Kingdom	61	244	254	2,827.3	5	46,040	18	2,225.5	36,240	27	0.7	0.0
United States	304	9,632	33	14,572.9	1	47,930	15	14,724.7	48,430	11	0.4	−0.5
Uruguay	3	176	19	27.5	84	8,260	81	41.8	12,540	86	8.9	8.6
Uzbekistan	27	447	64	24.7	87	910	172	72.6[a]	2,660[a]	157	9.0	7.2
Venezuela, RB	28	912	32	257.9	31	9,230	77	358.6	12,840	83	4.8	3.1
Vietnam	86	331	278	76.8	61	890	173	232.2	2,690	156	6.2	4.9
West Bank and Gaza	4	6	654	..		..[f]		..	..		..	..
Yemen, Rep.	23	528	43	21.9	91	960	168	50.9	2,220	162	3.9	1.0
Zambia	13	753	17	12.0	115	950	169	15.5	1,230	185	6.0	3.4
Zimbabwe	12	391	32	..		..[e]		..	..		..	..
World	**6,697 s**	**134,097 s**	**52 w**	**57,960.4 t**		**8,654 w**		**69,749.6 t**	**10,415 w**		**1.7 w**	**0.5 w**
Low income	976	19,313	52	510.5		523		1,321.9	1,354		6.3	4.1
Middle income	4,652	79,485	60	15,123.0		3,251		28,533.4	6,133		5.8	4.7
Lower middle income	3,703	32,309	119	7,674.5		2,073		16,994.4	4,589		7.4	6.1
Upper middle income	949	47,176	21	7,454.1		7,852		11,589.1	12,208		4.2	3.3
Low & middle income	5,629	98,797	59	15,648.9		2,780		29,847.2	5,303		5.8	4.5
East Asia & Pacific	1,930	16,299	122	5,102.0		2,644		10,461.1	5,421		8.0	7.2
Europe & Central Asia	443	23,926	19	3,258.0		7,350		5,298.2	11,953		4.1	3.8
Latin America & Carib.	566	20,421	28	3,831.0		6,768		5,837.8	10,312		4.3	3.2
Middle East & N. Africa	325	8,778	38	1,052.6		3,237		2,345.5	7,343		5.5	3.7
South Asia	1,545	5,131	324	1,487.5		963		4,163.4	2,695		5.6	4.1
Sub-Saharan Africa	819	24,242	35	882.6		1,077		1,596.5	1,949		5.1	2.5
High income	1,069	35,299	32	42,415.0		39,687		40,253.8	37,665		0.5	−0.2
Euro area	326	2,583	130	12,663.5		38,839		10,822.7	33,193		0.7	0.2

a. Based on regression; others are extrapolated from the 2005 International Comparison Program benchmark estimates. b. Private analysts estimate that GDP volume growth has been significantly lower than official reports have shown since the last quarter of 2008. c. Estimated to be upper middle income ($3,856–$11,905). d. Excludes the French overseas departments of French Guiana, Guadeloupe, Martinique, and Réunion. e. Estimated to be low income ($975 or less). f. Estimated to be lower middle income ($976–$3,855). g. Included in the aggregates for upper middle-income economies based on earlier data. h. Excludes Transnistria. i. Includes Former Spanish Sahara. j. Included in the aggregates for lower middle-income economies based on earlier data. k. Estimated to be high income ($11,906 or more). l. Provisional estimate. m. Included in the aggregates for low-income economies based on earlier data. n. Covers mainland Tanzania only.

About the data

Population, land area, income, and output are basic measures of the size of an economy. They also provide a broad indication of actual and potential resources. Population, land area, income (as measured by gross national income, GNI), and output (as measured by gross domestic product, GDP) are therefore used throughout *World Development Indicators* to normalize other indicators.

Population estimates are generally based on extrapolations from the most recent national census. For further discussion of the measurement of population and population growth, see *About the data* for table 2.1.

The surface area of an economy includes inland bodies of water and some coastal waterways. Surface area thus differs from land area, which excludes bodies of water, and from gross area, which may include offshore territorial waters. Land area is particularly important for understanding an economy's agricultural capacity and the environmental effects of human activity. (For measures of land area and data on rural population density, land use, and agricultural productivity, see tables 3.1–3.3.) Innovations in satellite mapping and computer databases have resulted in more precise measurements of land and water areas.

GNI measures total domestic and foreign value added claimed by residents. GNI comprises GDP plus net receipts of primary income (compensation of employees and property income) from nonresident sources. The World Bank uses GNI per capita in U.S. dollars to classify countries for analytical purposes and to determine borrowing eligibility. For definitions of the income groups in *World Development Indicators,* see *Users guide.* For discussion of the usefulness of national income and output as measures of productivity or welfare, see *About the data* for tables 4.1 and 4.2.

When calculating GNI in U.S. dollars from GNI reported in national currencies, the World Bank follows the *World Bank Atlas* conversion method, using a three-year average of exchange rates to smooth the effects of transitory fluctuations in exchange rates. (For further discussion of the *World Bank Atlas* method, see *Statistical methods.*)

Because exchange rates do not always reflect differences in price levels between countries, the table also converts GNI and GNI per capita estimates into international dollars using purchasing power parity (PPP) rates. PPP rates provide a standard measure allowing comparison of real levels of expenditure between countries, just as conventional price indexes allow comparison of real values over time.

PPP rates are calculated by simultaneously comparing the prices of similar goods and services among a large number of countries. In the most recent round of price surveys conducted by the International Comparison Program (ICP), 146 countries and territories participated in the data collection, including China for the first time, India for the first time since 1985, and almost all African countries. The PPP conversion factors presented in the table come from three sources. For 45 high- and upper middle-income countries conversion factors are provided by Eurostat and the Organisation for Economic Co-operation and Development (OECD), with PPP estimates for 34 European countries incorporating new price data collected since 2005. For the remaining 2005 ICP countries the PPP estimates are extrapolated from the 2005 ICP benchmark results, which account for relative price changes between each economy and the United States. For countries that did not participate in the 2005 ICP round, the PPP estimates are imputed using a statistical model.

More information on the results of the 2005 ICP is available at www.worldbank.org/data/icp.

All 210 economies shown in *World Development Indicators* are ranked by size, including those that appear in table 1.6. The ranks are shown only in table 1.1. No rank is shown for economies for which numerical estimates of GNI per capita are not published. Economies with missing data are included in the ranking at their approximate level, so that the relative order of other economies remains consistent.

Definitions

• **Population** is based on the de facto definition of population, which counts all residents regardless of legal status or citizenship—except for refugees not permanently settled in the country of asylum, who are generally considered part of the population of their country of origin. The values shown are midyear estimates. See also table 2.1. • **Surface area** is a country's total area, including areas under inland bodies of water and some coastal waterways. • **Population density** is midyear population divided by land area in square kilometers. • **Gross national income (GNI)** is the sum of value added by all resident producers plus any product taxes (less subsidies) not included in the valuation of output plus net receipts of primary income (compensation of employees and property income) from abroad. Data are in current U.S. dollars converted using the *World Bank Atlas* method (see *Statistical methods*). • **GNI per capita** is GNI divided by midyear population. GNI per capita in U.S. dollars is converted using the *World Bank Atlas* method. • **Purchasing power parity (PPP) GNI** is GNI converted to international dollars using PPP rates. An international dollar has the same purchasing power over GNI that a U.S. dollar has in the United States. • **Gross domestic product (GDP)** is the sum of value added by all resident producers plus any product taxes (less subsidies) not included in the valuation of output. Growth is calculated from constant price GDP data in local currency. • **GDP per capita** is GDP divided by midyear population.

Data sources

Population estimates are prepared by World Bank staff from a variety of sources (see *Data sources* for table 2.1). Data on surface and land area are from the Food and Agriculture Organization (see *Data sources* for table 3.1). GNI, GNI per capita, GDP growth, and GDP per capita growth are estimated by World Bank staff based on national accounts data collected by World Bank staff during economic missions or reported by national statistical offices to other international organizations such as the OECD. PPP conversion factors are estimates by Eurostat/OECD and by World Bank staff based on data collected by the ICP.

	Eradicate extreme poverty and hunger					Achieve universal primary education		Promote gender equality		Reduce child mortality	
	Share of poorest quintile in national consumption or income % 1995–2008[a,b]	Vulnerable employment Unpaid family workers and own-account workers % of total employment		Prevalence of malnutrition Underweight % of children under age 5		Primary completion rate %		Ratio of girls to boys enrollments in primary and secondary school %		Under-five mortality rate per 1,000	
		1990	2008	1990	2000–08[a]	1991	2008[c]	1991	2008[c]	1990	2008
Afghanistan	..	..	..	..	32.9	..	..	54	58	260	257
Albania	7.8	..	..	..	6.6	..	..	96	..	46	14
Algeria	6.9	..	..	..	11.1	80	114	83	..	64	41
Angola	2.0	..	..	..	27.5	34	..	..	..	260	220
Argentina	3.6[d]	..	20[e,f]	..	2.3	..	100	..	104	29	16
Armenia	8.6	..	..	..	4.2	..	98	..	104	56	23
Australia	..	10	9	..	..	..	..	101	98	9	6
Austria	8.6	..	9	..	..	..	102	95	97	9	4
Azerbaijan	13.3	..	53	..	8.4	..	121	100	98	98	36
Bangladesh	9.4	..	..	64.3	41.3	..	58	..	106	149	54
Belarus	8.8	..	..	..	1.3	94	96	..	101	24	13
Belgium	8.5	16	10	..	..	79	86	101	98	10	5
Benin	6.9	..	..	..	20.2	22	65	50	..	184	121
Bolivia	2.7	40[e]	..	8.9	5.9	71	98	..	99	122	54
Bosnia and Herzegovina	6.7	..	..	..	1.6	..	..	..	100	23	15
Botswana	3.1	..	..	..	10.7	90	99	109	100	50	31
Brazil	3.0	29[e]	27	..	2.2	..	..	..	102	56	22
Bulgaria	8.7	..	9	..	1.6	101	98	99	97	18	11
Burkina Faso	7.0	..	..	..	37.4	20	38	62	85[f]	201	169
Burundi	9.0	..	..	..	38.9	46	45	82	91	189	168
Cambodia	6.5	..	..	..	28.8	..	79	73	90	117	90
Cameroon	5.6	..	..	18.0	16.6	53	73	83	84	149	131
Canada	7.2	..	10[e]	..	..	..	96	99	99	8	6
Central African Republic	5.2	..	..	..	21.8	28	33	61	..	178	173
Chad	6.3	..	..	..	33.9	18	31	42	64	201	209
Chile	4.1	..	24	..	0.5	..	96	100	99	22	9
China	5.7	..	..	..	6.8	107	99	86	103	46	21
Hong Kong SAR, China	5.3	..	7	..	..	102	..	103	100	..	..
Colombia	2.3	28[e]	46	..	5.1	73	110	108	104	35	20
Congo, Dem. Rep.	5.5	..	..	..	28.2	48	53	..	76	199	199
Congo, Rep.	5.0	..	..	..	11.8	54	73	86	..	104	127
Costa Rica	4.4	25	20	..	..	79	93	101	102	22	11
Côte d'Ivoire	5.0	..	..	..	16.7	42	48	65	..	150	114
Croatia	8.8	..	16[e]	..	..	..	102	..	102	13	6
Cuba	..	..	..	..	..	99	90	106	99	14	6
Czech Republic	10.2	..	13	..	2.1	..	94	98	101	12	4
Denmark	8.3	7	5	..	..	98	101	101	102	9	4
Dominican Republic	4.4	39	42	8.4	3.4	..	91	..	103	62	33
Ecuador	3.4	36[e]	34[e]	..	6.2	..	106	..	100	53	25
Egypt, Arab Rep.	9.0	..	25	11.6	6.8	..	95	81	..	90	23
El Salvador	4.3	..	36	11.1	6.1	65	89	101	98	62	18
Eritrea	..	..	..	..	34.5	..	47	..	77	150	58
Estonia	6.8	2	6	..	..	..	100	103	101	18	6
Ethiopia	9.3	..	52[e]	..	34.6	..	52	68	85	210	109
Finland	9.6	..	9	..	..	97	98	109	102	7	3
France	7.2	11	6	..	..	106	..	102	100	9	4
Gabon	6.1	..	..	..	8.8	..	..	..	..	92	77
Gambia, The	4.8	..	..	..	15.8	..	79	64	102	153	106
Georgia	5.4	..	62	..	2.3	..	100	98	96	47	30
Germany	8.5	..	7	..	1.1	..	105	99	98	9	4
Ghana	5.2	..	..	24.1	13.9	64	79	79	96	118	76
Greece	6.7	..	27	..	..	..	101	99	97	11	4
Guatemala	3.4	..	..	..	17.7	..	80	..	94	77	35
Guinea	5.8	..	..	..	22.5	17	55	45	77	231	146
Guinea-Bissau	7.2	..	..	..	17.4	..	..	..	..	240	195
Haiti	2.5	..	..	..	18.9	27	..	94	..	151	72
Honduras	2.5	49[e]	..	..	8.6	64	90	106	107	55	31

	Eradicate extreme poverty and hunger				Achieve universal primary education		Promote gender equality		Reduce child mortality	
	Share of poorest quintile in national consumption or income % 1995–2008[a,b]	Vulnerable employment Unpaid family workers and own-account workers % of total employment		Prevalence of malnutrition Underweight % of children under age 5		Primary completion rate %		Ratio of girls to boys enrollments in primary and secondary school %		Under-five mortality rate per 1,000	
		1990	2008	1990	2000–08[a]	1991	2008[c]	1991	2008[c]	1990	2008
Hungary	8.6	7	7	2.3	..	94	95	100	99	17	7
India	8.1	..	..	..	43.5	63	94	70	92	116	69
Indonesia	7.4	..	63	31.0	19.6	93	108	93	98	86	41
Iran, Islamic Rep.	6.4	..	43	..	..	88	117	85	116	73	32
Iraq	..	..	..	..	7.1	..	..	78	..	53	44
Ireland	7.4	20	12	..	..	..	97	104	103	9	4
Israel	5.7	..	7	..	..	..	102	105	101	11	5
Italy	6.5	27	19	..	..	98	101	100	99	10	4
Jamaica	5.2	42	35	..	2.2	94	89	101	100	33	31
Japan	..	19	11	..	..	102	..	101	100	6	4
Jordan	7.2	..	..	4.8	3.6	95	99	101	103	38	20
Kazakhstan	8.7	..	..	..	4.9	..	105[f]	102	98[f]	60	30
Kenya	4.7	..	..	..	16.5	..	80	94	96	105	128
Korea, Dem. Rep.	..	..	..	..	17.8	..	..	..	..	55	55
Korea, Rep.	7.9	..	25	..	..	98	99	99	97	9	5
Kosovo	..	..	..	..	..	..	..	..	..	..	..
Kuwait	..	..	..	..	..	..	98	97	100	15	11
Kyrgyz Republic	8.8	..	47	..	2.7	..	92	..	100	75	38
Lao PDR	8.5	..	..	..	31.6	45	75	76	87	157	61
Latvia	6.7	..	7	..	..	..	95	101	100	17	9
Lebanon	..	..	..	..	4.2	..	87	..	103	40	13
Lesotho	3.0	..	..	..	16.6	59	73	124	105	101	79
Liberia	6.4	..	..	..	20.4	..	58	..	86	219	145
Libya	..	..	..	..	5.6	..	..	..	105	38	17
Lithuania	6.8	..	9	..	..	..	96	..	100	16	7
Macedonia, FYR	5.2	..	22	..	1.8	..	92	..	98	36	11
Madagascar	6.2	..	..	35.5	36.8	36	71	98	97	167	106
Malawi	7.0	..	..	24.4	15.5	28	54	81	99	225	100
Malaysia	6.4	29	22	..	..	91	96	101	..	18	6
Mali	6.5	..	..	..	27.9	12	57	58	78	250	194
Mauritania	6.2	..	..	..	23.2	33	64	71	104	129	118
Mauritius	..	12	17	..	..	115	90	102	100	24	17
Mexico	3.8	26	30	13.9	3.4	88	104	97	101	45	17
Moldova	6.7	..	32	..	3.2	..	84	105	102	37	17
Mongolia	7.1	..	..	..	5.3	..	93	109	104	98	41
Morocco	6.5	..	51	8.1	9.9	48	81	70	88	88	36
Mozambique	5.4	..	..	..	21.2	26	59	71	87	249	130
Myanmar	..	..	..	..	29.6	..	97	95	99	120	98
Namibia	..	..	..	21.5	17.5	..	81	106	104	72	42
Nepal	6.1	..	..	..	38.8	50	76	59	93	142	51
Netherlands	7.6	8	9	..	..	..	..	97	98	8	5
New Zealand	6.4	13	12	..	..	103	..	100	102	11	6
Nicaragua	3.8	..	45	..	4.3	42	75	109	102	68	27
Niger	5.9	..	..	41.0	39.9	17	40[f]	53	74	305	167
Nigeria	5.1	..	..	35.1	27.2	..	..	78	85	230	186
Norway	9.6	..	6	..	..	100	96	102	99	9	4
Oman	..	..	..	..	..	65	80	89	99	31	12
Pakistan	9.1	..	62	39.0	31.3	..	60	..	80	130	89
Panama	2.5	34	28	..	..	..	102	..	101	31	23
Papua New Guinea	4.5	..	..	..	18.1	46	..	80	..	91	69
Paraguay	3.4	23[e]	47	2.8	..	68	95	98	99	42	28
Peru	3.6	36[e]	40[e]	8.8	5.4	..	103	96	101	81	24
Philippines	5.6	..	45	..	26.2	88	92	100	102	61	32
Poland	7.3	..	19	..	..	98	96	100	99	17	7
Portugal	5.8	25	19	..	..	95	..	103	101	15	4
Puerto Rico	..	..	..	..	..	..	..	..	..	..	..
Qatar	3.9	..	..	..	..	71	115	98	120	20	10

	Eradicate extreme poverty and hunger					Achieve universal primary education		Promote gender equality		Reduce child mortality	
	Share of poorest quintile in national consumption or income % 1995–2008[a,b]	Vulnerable employment Unpaid family workers and own-account workers % of total employment		Prevalence of malnutrition Underweight % of children under age 5		Primary completion rate %		Ratio of girls to boys enrollments in primary and secondary school %		Under-five mortality rate per 1,000	
		1990	2008	1990	2000–08[a]	1991	2008[c]	1991	2008[c]	1990	2008
Romania	7.9	27	31	..	3.5	100	120	99	99	32	14
Russian Federation	5.6	1	6	..	..	..	94	104	98	27	13
Rwanda	5.4	..	..	24.3	18.0	35	54	95	100	174	112
Saudi Arabia	..	..	..	..	5.3	55	95	84	91	43	21
Senegal	6.2	83	..	..	14.5	43	56	68	96	149	108
Serbia	9.1	..	23	..	1.8	..	104	..	102	29	7
Sierra Leone	6.1	..	..	..	28.3	..	88	64	84	278	194
Singapore	5.0	8	10	..	3.3	..	..	..	..	7	3
Slovak Republic	8.8	..	11	..	..	..	94	..	100	15	8
Slovenia	8.2	..	11	..	..	..	..	..	99	10	4
Somalia	..	..	..	..	32.8	..	..	..	..	200	200
South Africa	3.1	..	3	..	..	76	86	104	100	56	67
Spain	7.0	22	12	..	..	103	98	104	103	9	4
Sri Lanka	6.8	..	41[e]	..	21.1	101	105	102	..	29	15
Sudan	..	..	..	..	31.7	40	57[f]	78	89[f]	124	109
Swaziland	4.5	..	..	..	6.1	61	72	98	92	84	83
Sweden	9.1	..	7	..	..	96	95	102	99	7	3
Switzerland	7.6	9	10	..	..	53	93	97	97	8	5
Syrian Arab Republic	..	..	..	..	10.0	89	114	85	97	37	16
Tajikistan	7.8	..	..	..	14.9	..	98	..	91	117	64
Tanzania	7.3	..	88[e]	25.1	16.7	63	83	97	..	157	104
Thailand	6.1	70	53	..	7.0	..	..	..	..	32	14
Timor-Leste	8.9	..	..	..	40.6	..	80	..	..	184	93
Togo	5.4	..	..	21.2	22.3	35	61	59	75	150	98
Trinidad and Tobago	..	22	..	..	4.4	102	92	101	101	34	35
Tunisia	5.9	..	..	8.5	3.3	74	102	86	103	50	21
Turkey	5.4	..	35	..	3.5	90	99	81	89	84	22
Turkmenistan	6.0	..	..	..	..	..	..	..	..	99	48
Uganda	6.1	..	..	19.7	16.4	..	56	82	99	186	135
Ukraine	9.4	..	..	..	4.1	94	99	..	99	21	16
United Arab Emirates	..	..	..	..	..	103	105	104	101	17	8
United Kingdom	6.1	10	11	..	..	..	..	102	102	9	6
United States	5.4	..	..	..	1.3	..	96	100	100	11	8
Uruguay	4.3	..	25	..	6.0	94	104	..	98	24	14
Uzbekistan	7.1	..	..	..	4.4	..	96	94	98	74	38
Venezuela, RB	4.9	..	30	..	..	79	95	105	102	32	18
Vietnam	7.1	..	..	..	20.2	..	..	..	..	56	14
West Bank and Gaza	..	..	36	..	2.2	..	83	..	104	38	27
Yemen, Rep.	7.2	..	..	..	43.1	..	61	..	..	127	69
Zambia	3.6	65	..	21.2	14.9	..	93	..	95	172	148
Zimbabwe	4.6	..	..	8.0	14.0	97	..	92	97	79	96
World	.. w	.. w	.. w		22.4 w	79 w	89 w	87 w	96 w	92 w	67 w
Low income		..	..	..	27.5	44	66	80	91	160	118
Middle income		..	..	..	22.2	83	94	85	97	85	57
Lower middle income		..	..	..	25.1	82	92	81	96	93	64
Upper middle income		..	24	..	3.8	88	100	98	100	47	23
Low & middle income		..	..	..	23.5	78	88	84	96	101	73
East Asia & Pacific		..	..	..	11.9	101	100	89	102	55	29
Europe & Central Asia		..	19	..	..	93	98	98	97	50	22
Latin America & Carib.		..	31	..	4.5	84	101	99	102	53	23
Middle East & N. Africa		..	37	..	12.2	..	94	80	96	76	34
South Asia		..	..	..	41.1	62	79	69	91	125	76
Sub-Saharan Africa		..	..	..	25.3	51	62	82	88	185	144
High income		..	..	..	..	..	..	100	99	12	7
Euro area		..	12	..	..	101	..	..	..	9	4

a. Data are for the most recent year available. b. See table 2.9 for survey year and whether share is based on income or consumption expenditure. c. Provisional data. d. Urban data. e. Limited coverage. f. Data are for 2009.

About the data

Tables 1.2–1.4 present indicators for 17 of the 21 targets specified by the Millennium Development Goals. Each of the eight goals includes one or more targets, and each target has several associated indicators for monitoring progress toward the target. Most of the targets are set as a value of a specific indicator to be attained by a certain date. In some cases the target value is set relative to a level in 1990. In others it is set at an absolute level. Some of the targets for goals 7 and 8 have not yet been quantified.

The indicators in this table relate to goals 1–4. Goal 1 has three targets between 1990 and 2015: to halve the proportion of people whose income is less than $1.25 a day, to achieve full and productive employment and decent work for all, and to halve the proportion of people who suffer from hunger. Estimates of poverty rates are in tables 2.7 and 2.8. The indicator shown here, the share of the poorest quintile in national consumption or income, is a distributional measure. Countries with more unequal distributions of consumption (or income) have a higher rate of poverty for a given average income. Vulnerable employment measures the portion of the labor force that receives the lowest wages and least security in employment. No single indicator captures the concept of suffering from hunger. Child malnutrition is a symptom of inadequate food supply, lack of essential nutrients, illnesses that deplete these

nutrients, and undernourished mothers who give birth to underweight children.

Progress toward universal primary education is measured by the primary completion rate. Because many school systems do not record school completion on a consistent basis, it is estimated from the gross enrollment rate in the final grade of primary school, adjusted for repetition. Official enrollments sometimes differ significantly from attendance, and even school systems with high average enrollment ratios may have poor completion rates.

Eliminating gender disparities in education would help increase the status and capabilities of women. The ratio of female to male enrollments in primary and secondary school provides an imperfect measure of the relative accessibility of schooling for girls.

The targets for reducing under-five mortality rates are among the most challenging. Under-five mortality rates are harmonized estimates produced by a weighted least squares regression model and are available at regular intervals for most countries.

Most of the 60 indicators relating to the Millennium Development Goals can be found in *World Development Indicators*. Table 1.2a shows where to find the indicators for the first four goals. For more information about data collection methods and limitations, see *About the data* for the tables listed there. For information about the indicators for goals 5–8, see *About the data* for tables 1.3 and 1.4.

Definitions

• **Share of poorest quintile in national consumption or income** is the share of the poorest 20 percent of the population in consumption or, in some cases, income. • **Vulnerable employment** is the sum of unpaid family workers and own-account workers as a percentage of total employment. • **Prevalence of malnutrition** is the percentage of children under age 5 whose weight for age is more than two standard deviations below the median for the international reference population ages 0–59 months. The data are based on the new international child growth standards for infants and young children, called the Child Growth Standards, released in 2006 by the World Health Organization. • **Primary completion rate** is the percentage of students completing the last year of primary school. It is calculated as the total number of students in the last grade of primary school, minus the number of repeaters in that grade, divided by the total number of children of official graduation age. • **Ratio of girls to boys enrollments in primary and secondary school** is the ratio of the female to male gross enrollment rate in primary and secondary school. • **Under-five mortality rate** is the probability that a newborn baby will die before reaching age 5, if subject to current age-specific mortality rates. The probability is expressed as a rate per 1,000.

Location of indicators for Millennium Development Goals 1–4	1.2a
Goal 1. Eradicate extreme poverty and hunger	**Table**
1.1 Proportion of population below $1.25 a day	2.8
1.2 Poverty gap ratio	2.7, 2.8
1.3 Share of poorest quintile in national consumption	1.2, 2.9
1.4 Growth rate of GDP per person employed	2.4
1.5 Employment to population ratio	2.4
1.6 Proportion of employed people living below $1 per day	—
1.7 Proportion of own-account and unpaid family workers in total employment	1.2, 2.4
1.8 Prevalence of underweight in children under age five	1.2, 2.20
1.9 Proportion of population below minimum level of dietary energy consumption	2.20
Goal 2. Achieve universal primary education	
2.1 Net enrollment ratio in primary education	2.12
2.2 Proportion of pupils starting grade 1 who reach last grade of primary	2.13
2.3 Literacy rate of 15- to 24-year-olds	2.14
Goal 3. Promote gender equality and empower women	
3.1 Ratio of girls to boys in primary, secondary, and tertiary education	1.2, 2.12*
3.2 Share of women in wage employment in the nonagricultural sector	1.5, 2.3*
3.3 Proportion of seats held by women in national parliament	1.5
Goal 4. Reduce child mortality	
4.1 Under-five mortality rate	1.2, 2.22
4.2 Infant mortality rate	2.22
4.3 Proportion of one-year-old children immunized against measles	2.18

— No data are available in the World Development Indicators database. * Table shows information on related indicators.

Data sources

The indicators here and throughout this book have been compiled by World Bank staff from primary and secondary sources. Efforts have been made to harmonize the data series used to compile this table with those published on the United Nations Millennium Development Goals Web site (www.un.org/millenniumgoals), but some differences in timing, sources, and definitions remain. For more information see the data sources for the indicators listed in table 1.2a.

	Improve maternal health			Combat HIV/AIDS and other diseases		Ensure environmental sustainability					Develop a global partnership for development
	Maternal mortality ratio Modeled estimate per 100,000 live births	Contraceptive prevalence rate % of married women ages 15–49		HIV prevalence % of population ages 15–49	Incidence of tuberculosis per 100,000 people	Carbon dioxide emissions per capita metric tons		Proportion of species threatened with extinction %	Access to improved sanitation facilities % of population		Internet users per 100 people[a]
	2005	1990	2003–08[b]	2007	2008	1990	2006	2008	1990	2006	2008
Afghanistan	1,800	..	15	..	189	0.1	0.0	0.7	..	30	1.7
Albania	92	..	60	..	16	2.3	1.4	1.5	..	97	23.9
Algeria	180	47	61	0.1	58	3.1	4.0	2.1	88	94	11.9
Angola	1,400	..	..	2.1	292	0.4	0.6	1.4	26	50	3.1
Argentina	77	..	..	0.5	30	3.5	4.4	1.9	81	91	28.1
Armenia	76	..	53	0.1	73	1.1	1.4	0.9	..	91	6.2
Australia	4	..	..	0.2	7	17.2	18.0	4.7	100	100	70.8
Austria	4	..	..	0.2	0	7.9	8.7	1.9	100	100	71.2
Azerbaijan	82	..	51	0.2	110	6.0	4.1	0.8	..	80	28.2
Bangladesh	570	40	56	..	225	0.1	0.3	1.9	26	36	0.3
Belarus	18	..	73	0.2	43	9.6	7.1	0.7	..	93	32.1
Belgium	8	78	..	0.2	9	10.8	10.2	1.3	..	..	68.1
Benin	840	..	17	1.2	92	0.1	0.4	1.5	12	30	1.8
Bolivia	290	30	61	0.2	144	0.8	1.2	0.8	33	43	10.8
Bosnia and Herzegovina	3	..	36	<0.1	51	1.2	7.3	13.1	..	95	34.7
Botswana	380	33	..	23.9	712	1.6	2.6	0.5	38	47	6.2
Brazil	110	59	81	0.6	46	1.4	1.9	1.3	71	77	37.5
Bulgaria	11	..	..	..	43	8.8	6.2	1.1	99	99	34.7
Burkina Faso	700	..	17	1.6	220	0.1	0.1	1.0	5	13	0.9
Burundi	1,100	..	9	2.0	357	0.1	0.0	1.5	44	41	0.8
Cambodia	540	..	40	0.8	490	0.0	0.3	29.8	8	28	0.5
Cameroon	1,000	16	29	5.1	187	0.1	0.2	5.4	39	51	3.8
Canada	7	..	..	0.4	5	16.2	16.7	1.8	100	100	75.3
Central African Republic	980	..	19	6.3	336	0.1	0.1	0.6	11	31	0.4
Chad	1,500	..	3	3.5	291	0.0	0.0	1.0	5	9	1.2
Chile	16	56	58	0.3	11	2.7	3.7	2.4	84	94	32.5
China	45	85	85	0.1	97	2.1	4.7	2.4	48	65	22.5
Hong Kong SAR, China	..	86	..	..	91	4.8	5.7	13.2	..	..	67.0
Colombia	130	66	78	0.6	36	1.7	1.5	1.2	68	78	38.5
Congo, Dem. Rep.	1,100	8	21	..	382	0.1	0.0	2.5	15	31	..
Congo, Rep.	740	..	44	3.5	393	0.5	0.4	1.0	..	20	4.3
Costa Rica	30	..	96	0.4	11	1.0	1.8	1.9	94	96	32.3
Côte d'Ivoire	810	..	13	3.9	410	0.5	0.3	3.9	20	24	3.2
Croatia	7	..	..	<0.1	25	3.8	5.3	1.8	99	99	50.5
Cuba	45	..	77	0.1	6	3.1	2.6	4.2	98	98	12.9
Czech Republic	4	78	..	..	9	12.7	11.2	1.5	100	99	57.8
Denmark	3	78	..	0.2	7	9.8	9.9	1.6	100	100	83.3
Dominican Republic	150	56	73	1.1	73	1.3	2.1	2.1	68	79	21.6
Ecuador	210	53	73	0.3	72	1.6	2.4	10.4	71	84	28.8
Egypt, Arab Rep.	130	47	60	..	20	1.3	2.1	4.1	50	66	16.6
El Salvador	170	47	73	0.8	32	0.5	1.1	1.8	73	86	10.6
Eritrea	450	..	..	1.3	97	..	0.1	15.0	3	5	4.1
Estonia	25	..	..	1.3	34	16.3	13.0	0.6	95	95	66.2
Ethiopia	720	4	15	2.1	368	0.1	0.1	1.3	4	11	0.4
Finland	7	77	..	0.1	7	10.2	12.7	1.3	100	100	82.5
France	8	81	..	0.4	6	7.0	6.2	2.5	..	..	67.9
Gabon	520	..	..	5.9	452	6.6	1.5	2.1	..	36	6.2
Gambia, The	690	12	..	0.9	263	0.2	0.2	2.2	..	52	6.9
Georgia	66	..	47	0.1	107	2.9	1.2	1.0	94	93	23.8
Germany	4	75	..	0.1	5	12.0	9.8	2.2	100	100	75.5
Ghana	560	13	24	1.9	202	0.3	0.4	3.7	6	10	4.3
Greece	3	..	..	0.2	6	7.2	8.6	2.1	97	98	43.1
Guatemala	290	..	..	0.8	63	0.6	0.9	2.4	70	84	14.3
Guinea	910	..	9	1.6	302	0.2	0.1	2.2	13	19	0.9
Guinea-Bissau	1,100	..	10	1.8	224	0.2	0.2	2.4	..	33	2.4
Haiti	670	10	32	2.2	246	0.1	0.2	2.3	29	19	10.1
Honduras	280	47	65	0.7	64	0.5	1.0	3.5	45	66	13.1

	Improve maternal health			Combat HIV/AIDS and other diseases		Ensure environmental sustainability					Develop a global partnership for development
	Maternal mortality ratio Modeled estimate per 100,000 live births	Contraceptive prevalence rate % of married women ages 15–49		HIV prevalence % of population ages 15–49	Incidence of tuberculosis per 100,000 people	Carbon dioxide emissions per capita metric tons		Proportion of species threatened with extinction %	Access to improved sanitation facilities % of population		Internet users per 100 people[a]
	2005	1990	2003–08[b]	2007	2008	1990	2006	2008	1990	2006	2008
Hungary	6	..	..	0.1	16	6.0	5.7	1.8	100	100	58.5
India	450	43	56	0.3	168	0.8	1.4	3.3	14	28	4.5
Indonesia	420	50	61	0.2	189	0.8	1.5	3.4	51	52	7.9
Iran, Islamic Rep.	140	49	79	0.2	20	4.2	6.7	1.0	83	..	32.0
Iraq	300	14	50	..	64	2.8	3.2	11.0	..	76	1.0
Ireland	1	60	..	0.2	9	8.8	10.3	1.8	..	..	62.7
Israel	4	68	..	0.1	6	7.2	10.0	4.3	..	..	47.9
Italy	3	..	..	0.4	7	7.5	8.0	2.2	..	..	41.8
Jamaica	170	55	..	1.6	7	3.3	4.6	7.7	83	83	57.3
Japan	6	58	..	..	22	9.5	10.1	4.9	100	100	75.2
Jordan	62	40	57	..	6	3.3	3.7	3.4	..	85	27.0
Kazakhstan	140	..	51	0.1	175	15.9	12.6	1.1	97	97	10.9
Kenya	560	27	39	..	328	0.2	0.3	3.9	39	42	8.7
Korea, Dem. Rep.	370	62	..	..	344	12.1	3.6	1.3	..	..	0.0
Korea, Rep.	14	79	..	<0.1	88	5.6	9.8	1.7	..	..	75.8
Kosovo	..	..	..	..	..	..	..	..	..	..	..
Kuwait	4	..	..	..	34	19.2	33.3	6.3	..	..	36.7
Kyrgyz Republic	150	..	48	0.1	159	2.4	1.1	0.8	..	93	16.1
Lao PDR	660	..	38	0.2	150	0.1	0.2	1.2	..	48	8.5
Latvia	10	..	..	0.8	50	5.1	3.3	1.4	..	78	60.4
Lebanon	150	..	58	0.1	14	3.1	3.8	1.2	..	..	22.5
Lesotho	960	23	37	23.2	635	..	..	0.6	..	36	3.6
Liberia	1,200	..	11	1.7	283	0.2	0.2	3.8	40	32	0.5
Libya	97	..	..	..	17	9.2	9.2	1.6	97	97	5.1
Lithuania	11	..	..	0.1	71	6.0	4.2	0.9	..	..	54.4
Macedonia, FYR	10	..	14	<0.1	24	5.6	5.3	0.9	..	89	41.5
Madagascar	510	17	27	0.1	256	0.1	0.2	6.4	8	12	1.7
Malawi	1,100	13	41	11.9	324	0.1	0.1	3.3	46	60	2.1
Malaysia	62	50	..	0.5	102	3.1	7.2	6.9	..	94	55.8
Mali	970	..	8	1.5	322	0.0	0.0	1.0	35	45	1.6
Mauritania	820	3	9	0.8	324	1.3	0.5	2.9	20	24	1.9
Mauritius	15	75	..	1.7	22	1.4	3.1	24.3	94	94	22.2
Mexico	60	..	71	0.3	19	4.6	4.2	3.2	56	81	22.2
Moldova	22	..	68	0.4	175	4.8	2.1	1.3	..	79	23.4
Mongolia	46	..	66	0.1	205	4.5	3.7	1.1	..	50	12.5
Morocco	240	42	63	0.1	116	0.9	1.5	1.9	52	72	33.0
Mozambique	520	..	16	12.5	420	0.1	0.1	2.9	20	31	1.6
Myanmar	380	17	34	0.7	404	0.1	0.2	2.7	23	82	0.2
Namibia	210	29	55	15.3	747	0.0	1.4	2.1	26	35	5.3
Nepal	830	23	48	0.5	163	0.0	0.1	1.1	9	27	1.7
Netherlands	6	76	..	0.2	7	11.2	10.3	1.3	100	100	87.0
New Zealand	9	..	..	0.1	8	6.6	7.3	5.1	..	..	71.4
Nicaragua	170	..	72	0.2	46	0.6	0.8	1.3	42	48	3.3
Niger	1,800	4	11	0.8	178	0.1	0.1	1.0	3	7	0.5
Nigeria	1,100	6	15	3.1	303	0.5	0.7	4.3	26	30	15.9
Norway	7	74	..	0.1	6	7.4	8.6	1.5	..	..	82.5
Oman	64	9	..	..	14	5.6	15.5	4.2	85	..	20.0
Pakistan	320	15	30	0.1	231	0.6	0.9	1.7	33	58	11.1
Panama	130	..	..	1.0	47	1.3	2.0	2.9	..	74	27.5
Papua New Guinea	470	..	32	1.5	250	0.5	0.7	3.6	44	45	1.8
Paraguay	150	48	79	0.6	47	0.5	0.7	0.5	60	70	14.3
Peru	240	59	71	0.5	119	1.0	1.4	2.8	55	72	24.7
Philippines	230	36	51	..	285	0.7	0.8	6.6	58	78	6.2
Poland	8	49	..	0.1	25	9.1	8.3	1.2	..	..	49.0
Portugal	11	..	..	0.5	30	4.5	5.7	2.8	92	99	42.1
Puerto Rico	18	..	..	..	3	..	..	3.6	..	..	25.3
Qatar	12	..	..	..	55	25.2	46.1	..	100	100	34.0

	Improve maternal health			Combat HIV/AIDS and other diseases		Ensure environmental sustainability					Develop a global partnership for development
	Maternal mortality ratio Modeled estimate per 100,000 live births	Contraceptive prevalence rate % of married women ages 15–49		HIV prevalence % of population ages 15–49	Incidence of tuberculosis per 100,000 people	Carbon dioxide emissions per capita metric tons		Proportion of species threatened with extinction %	Access to improved sanitation facilities % of population		Internet users per 100 people[a]
	2005	1990	2003–08[b]	2007	2008	1990	2006	2008	1990	2006	2008
Romania	24	..	70	0.1	134	6.8	4.6	1.6	72	72	28.8
Russian Federation	28	*34*	..	1.1	107	*13.9*	11.0	1.3	87	87	31.9
Rwanda	1,300	*21*	36	2.8	387	0.1	0.1	1.6	29	23	3.1
Saudi Arabia	18	..	..	..	19	13.2	16.1	3.8	91	99	31.5
Senegal	980	..	12	1.0	277	0.4	0.4	2.2	26	28	8.4
Serbia	14[c]	..	41	0.1	18	..	..	..	..	92	44.9
Sierra Leone	2,100	..	8	1.7	608	0.1	0.2	3.2	..	11	0.3
Singapore	14	*65*	..	0.2	39	15.4	12.8	9.7	100	100	69.6
Slovak Republic	6	*74*	..	<0.1	12	8.4	6.9	1.1	100	100	66.0
Slovenia	6	..	..	<0.1	12	6.2	7.6	2.1	..	..	55.7
Somalia	1,400	*1*	15	0.5	388	0.0	0.0	3.2	..	23	1.1
South Africa	400	*57*	60	18.1	960	9.5	8.7	1.6	55	59	8.6
Spain	4	..	..	0.5	17	5.9	8.0	3.8	100	100	55.4
Sri Lanka	58	..	68	..	66	0.2	0.6	14.0	71	86	5.8
Sudan	450	*9*	8	1.4	119	0.2	0.3	2.4	33	35	10.2
Swaziland	390	*20*	51	26.1	1,227	0.5	0.9	0.8	..	50	6.9
Sweden	3	..	..	0.1	6	6.0	5.6	1.4	100	100	87.7
Switzerland	5	..	..	0.6	5	6.4	5.6	1.4	100	100	75.9
Syrian Arab Republic	130	..	58	..	22	2.9	3.5	2.0	81	92	17.3
Tajikistan	170	..	37	0.3	199	3.9	1.0	0.8	..	92	8.8
Tanzania	950	*10*	26	6.2	190	0.1	0.1	5.1	35	33	1.2
Thailand	110	..	77	1.4	137	1.7	4.1	3.4	78	96	23.9
Timor-Leste	380	..	20	..	498	..	0.2	..	..	41	..
Togo	510	*34*	17	3.3	438	0.2	0.2	1.2	13	12	5.4
Trinidad and Tobago	45	..	43	1.5	24	13.9	25.3	1.7	93	92	17.0
Tunisia	100	*50*	60	0.1	24	1.6	2.3	2.1	74	85	27.1
Turkey	44	*63*	73	..	30	2.6	3.7	1.4	85	88	34.4
Turkmenistan	130	..	48	<0.1	68	*7.2*	9.0	10.7	..	..	1.5
Uganda	550	*5*	24	5.4	311	0.0	0.1	2.5	29	33	7.9
Ukraine	18	..	67	1.6	102	*11.7*	6.8	1.1	96	93	10.5
United Arab Emirates	37	..	..	..	6	29.3	32.8	14.1	97	97	65.2
United Kingdom	8	..	..	0.2	12	10.0	9.4	2.8	..	..	76.0
United States	11	*71*	..	0.6	5	19.5	19.3	5.7	100	100	75.9
Uruguay	20	..	..	0.6	22	1.3	2.1	2.6	100	100	40.2
Uzbekistan	24	..	65	0.1	128	5.3	4.4	1.0	93	96	9.0
Venezuela, RB	57	..	..	..	33	6.2	6.3	1.1	83	..	25.7
Vietnam	150	*53*	76	0.5	200	0.3	1.3	3.5	29	65	24.2
West Bank and Gaza	..	..	50	..	19	..	0.8	..	..	80	9.0
Yemen, Rep.	430	*10*	28	..	88	..	1.0	12.6	28	46	1.6
Zambia	830	*15*	41	15.2	468	0.3	0.2	0.7	42	52	5.5
Zimbabwe	880	*43*	60	15.3	762	1.6	0.9	0.9	44	46	11.4
World	**400 w**	**57 w**	**61 w**	**0.8 w**	**139 w**	**4.3[d] w**	**4.4[d] w**		**51 w**	**60 w**	**23.9 w**
Low income	790	26	38	2.3	282	0.6	0.5		25	38	4.6
Middle income	320	58	66	0.6	137	1.8	3.3		47	58	17.3
Lower middle income	370	60	65	0.4	145	1.4	2.8		39	52	13.9
Upper middle income	110	52	72	1.5	106	3.8	5.2		76	82	30.6
Low & middle income	440	54	61	0.9	162	1.6	2.8		43	55	15.3
East Asia & Pacific	150	75	77	0.2	138	1.9	3.8		48	66	19.4
Europe & Central Asia	45	..	..	0.6	87	9.4	7.3		88	89	28.6
Latin America & Carib.	130	56	75	0.5	47	2.4	2.6		68	78	28.9
Middle East & N. Africa	200	42	62	0.1	44	2.5	3.5		67	74	18.9
South Asia	500	40	53	0.3	180	0.7	1.1		18	33	4.7
Sub-Saharan Africa	900	15	23	5.0	352	0.9	0.8		26	31	6.5
High income	10	72	..	0.3	14	12.1	12.7		99	100	69.1
Euro area	5	..	..	0.3	8	7.5	8.4		..	..	62.6

a. Data are from the International Telecommunication Union's (ITU) World Telecommunication Development Report database. Please cite ITU for third-party use of these data. b. Data are for the most recent year available. c. Includes Montenegro. d. Includes emissions not allocated to specific countries.

The Millennium Development Goals address concerns common to all economies. Diseases and environmental degradation do not respect national boundaries. Epidemic diseases, wherever they occur, pose a threat to people everywhere. And environmental damage in one location may affect the well-being of plants, animals, and humans far away. The indicators in the table relate to goals 5, 6, and 7 and the targets of goal 8 that address access to new technologies. For the other targets of goal 8, see table 1.4.

The target of achieving universal access to reproductive health has been added to goal 5 to address the importance of family planning and health services in improving maternal health and preventing maternal death. Women with multiple pregnancies are more likely to die in childbirth. Access to contraception is an important way to limit and space births.

Measuring disease prevalence or incidence can be difficult. Most developing economies lack reporting systems for monitoring diseases. Estimates are often derived from survey data and report data from sentinel sites, extrapolated to the general population. Tracking diseases such as HIV/AIDS, which has a long latency

between contraction of the virus and the appearance of symptoms, or malaria, which has periods of dormancy, can be particularly difficult. The table shows the estimated prevalence of HIV among adults ages 15–49. Prevalence among older populations can be affected by life-prolonging treatment. The incidence of tuberculosis is based on case notifications and estimates of cases detected in the population.

Carbon dioxide emissions are the primary source of greenhouse gases, which contribute to global warming, threatening human and natural habitats. In recognition of the vulnerability of animal and plant species, a new target of reducing biodiversity loss has been added to goal 7.

Access to reliable supplies of safe drinking water and sanitary disposal of excreta are two of the most important means of improving human health and protecting the environment. Improved sanitation facilities prevent human, animal, and insect contact with excreta.

Internet use includes narrowband and broadband Internet. Narrowband is often limited to basic applications; broadband is essential to promote e-business, e-learning, e-government, and e-health.

• **Maternal mortality ratio** is the number of women who die from pregnancy-related causes during pregnancy and childbirth, per 100,000 live births. Data are from various years and adjusted to a common 2005 base year. The values are modeled estimates (see *About the data* for table 2.19). • **Contraceptive prevalence rate** is the percentage of women ages 15–49 married or in union who are practicing, or whose sexual partners are practicing, any form of contraception. • **HIV prevalence** is the percentage of people ages 15–49 who are infected with HIV. • **Incidence of tuberculosis** is the estimated number of new tuberculosis cases (pulmonary, smear positive, and extrapulmonary). • **Carbon dioxide emissions** are those stemming from the burning of fossil fuels and the manufacture of cement. They include emissions produced during consumption of solid, liquid, and gas fuels and gas flaring (see table 3.8). • **Proportion of species threatened with extinction** is the total number of threatened mammal (excluding whales and porpoises), bird, and higher native, vascular plant species as a percentage of the total number of known species of the same categories. • **Access to improved sanitation facilities** is the percentage of the population with at least adequate access to excreta disposal facilities (private or shared, but not public) that can effectively prevent human, animal, and insect contact with excreta (facilities do not have to include treatment to render sewage outflows innocuous). Improved facilities range from simple but protected pit latrines to flush toilets with a sewerage connection. To be effective, facilities must be correctly constructed and properly maintained. • **Internet users** are people with access to the worldwide network.

Location of indicators for Millennium Development Goals 5–7 — 1.3a

Goal 5. Improve maternal health	Table
5.1 Maternal mortality ratio	1.3, 2.19
5.2 Proportion of births attended by skilled health personnel	2.19
5.3 Contraceptive prevalence rate	1.3, 2.19
5.4 Adolescent fertility rate	2.19
5.5 Antenatal care coverage	1.5, 2.19
5.6 Unmet need for family planning	2.19
Goal 6. Combat HIV/AIDS, malaria, and other diseases	
6.1 HIV prevalence among population ages 15–24	1.3*, 2.21*
6.2 Condom use at last high-risk sex	2.21*
6.3 Proportion of population ages 15–24 with comprehensive, correct knowledge of HIV/AIDS	—
6.4 Ratio of school attendance of orphans to school attendance of nonorphans ages 10–14	—
6.5 Proportion of population with advanced HIV infection with access to antiretroviral drugs	—
6.6 Incidence and death rates associated with malaria	—
6.7 Proportion of children under age 5 sleeping under insecticide-treated bednets	2.18
6.8 Proportion of children under age 5 with fever who are treated with appropriate antimalarial drugs	2.18
6.9 Incidence, prevalence, and death rates associated with tuberculosis	1.3, 2.21
6.10 Proportion of tuberculosis cases detected and cured under directly observed treatment short course	2.18
Goal 7. Ensure environmental sustainability	
7.1 Proportion of land area covered by forest	3.1
7.2 Carbon dioxide emissions, total, per capita, and per $1 purchasing power parity GDP	3.8
7.3 Consumption of ozone-depleting substances	3.9*
7.4 Proportion of fish stocks within safe biological limits	—
7.5 Proportion of total water resources used	3.5
7.6 Proportion of terrestrial and marine areas protected	—
7.7 Proportion of species threatened with extinction	1.3
7.8 Proportion of population using an improved drinking water source	1.3, 2.18, 3.5
7.9 Proportion of population using an improved sanitation facility	1.3, 2.18, 3.11
7.10 Proportion of urban population living in slums	—

— No data are available in the World Development Indicators database. * Table shows information on related indicators.

The indicators here and throughout this book have been compiled by World Bank staff from primary and secondary sources. Efforts have been made to harmonize the data series used to compile this table with those published on the United Nations Millennium Development Goals Web site (www.un.org/millenniumgoals), but some differences in timing, sources, and definitions remain. For more information see the data sources for the indicators listed in table 1.3a.

Development Assistance Committee members

	Net official development assistance (ODA) by donor		Least developed countries' access to high-income markets							Support to agriculture
	% of donor GNI	For basic social services[a] % of total sector-allocable ODA	Goods (excluding arms) admitted free of tariffs % of exports from least developed countries		Average tariff on exports of least developed countries %						% of GDP
					Agricultural products		Textiles		Clothing		
	2008	2008	2001	2007	2001	2007	2001	2007	2001	2007	2008[b]
Australia	0.34	15.6	94.5	100.0	0.2	0.0	5.0	0.0	19.6	0.0	0.29
Canada	0.32	16.2	48.3	99.9	0.3	0.1	5.8	0.2	18.8	1.7	0.55
European Union			99.8	98.2	1.7	1.5	0.0	0.1	0.0	1.2	0.91
Austria	0.42	4.7									
Belgium	0.47	17.6									
Denmark	0.82	12.6									
Finland	0.43	10.9									
France	0.39	10.2									
Germany	0.38	7.7									
Greece	0.20	3.7									
Ireland	0.58	27.6									
Italy	0.20	8.8									
Luxembourg	0.92	34.4									
Netherlands	0.80	20.9									
Portugal	0.27	3.0									
Spain	0.43	20.5									
Sweden	0.98	11.7									
United Kingdom	0.43	20.9									
Japan	0.18	2.4	82.2	99.6	4.9	1.3	0.2	2.6	0.0	0.1	1.06
New Zealand[c]	0.30	22.7	64.2	99.2	0.0	0.0	9.3	0.0	12.9	0.0	0.23
Norway	0.88	13.1	97.6	99.8	3.1	0.2	4.5	0.0	1.4	1.0	0.95
Switzerland	0.41	9.4	93.3	95.0	6.0	2.8	0.0	0.0	0.0	0.0	1.24
United States	0.18	32.1	46.2	76.8	6.3	6.0	6.8	5.6	13.9	11.3	0.67

Heavily indebted poor countries (HIPCs)

| | HIPC decision point[d] | HIPC completion point[d] | HIPC Initiative assistance | MDRI assistance | | HIPC decision point[d] | HIPC completion point[d] | HIPC Initiative assistance | MDRI assistance |
			end-2008 net present value $ millions					end-2008 net present value $ millions	
Afghanistan	Jul. 2007	Jan. 2010	600	38[e]	Honduras	Jul. 2000	Apr. 2005	822	1,599
Benin	Jul. 2000	Mar. 2003	388	633	Liberia	Mar. 2008	Floating	2,988	..
Bolivia[f]	Feb. 2000	Jun. 2001	1,967	1,655	Madagascar	Dec. 2000	Oct. 2004	1,236	1,351
Burkina Faso[f,g]	Jul. 2000	Apr. 2002	818	638	Malawi[g]	Dec. 2000	Aug. 2006	1,388	733
Burundi	Aug. 2005	Jan. 2009	964	70[h]	Mali[f]	Sep. 2000	Mar. 2003	797	1,097
Cameroon	Oct. 2000	Apr. 2006	1,874	778	Mauritania	Feb. 2000	Jun. 2002	920	465
Central African Republic	Sep. 2007	Jun. 2009	638	146	Mozambique[f]	Apr. 2000	Sep. 2001	3,169	1,107
Chad	May 2001	Floating	240	..	Nicaragua	Dec. 2000	Jan. 2004	4,894	985
Congo, Dem. Rep.	Jul. 2003	Floating	8,061	..	Niger[g]	Dec. 2000	Apr.2004	953	542
Congo, Rep.	Mar. 2006	Jan. 2010	1,945	201[e]	Rwanda[g]	Dec. 2000	Apr. 2005	963	234
Côte d'Ivoire	Mar. 2009	Floating	3,005	..	São Tomé & Príncipe[g]	Dec. 2000	Mar. 2007	173	27
Ethiopia[g]	Nov. 2001	Apr. 2004	2,726	1,512	Senegal	Jun. 2000	Apr. 2004	722	1,435
Gambia, The	Dec. 2000	Dec. 2007	99	191	Sierra Leone	Mar. 2002	Dec. 2006	906	368
Ghana	Feb. 2002	Jul. 2004	3,080	2,181	Tanzania	Apr. 2000	Nov. 2001	2,997	2,124
Guinea	Dec. 2000	Floating	807	..	Togo	Nov. 2008	Floating	270	..
Guinea-Bissau	Dec. 2000	Floating	615	..	Uganda[f]	Feb. 2000	May 2000	1,520	1,879
Guyana[f]	Nov. 2000	Dec. 2003	903	416	Zambia	Dec. 2000	Apr. 2005	3,697	1,701
Haiti	Nov. 2006	Jun. 2009	155	557					

a. Includes primary education, basic life skills for youth, adult and early childhood education, basic health care, basic health infrastructure, basic nutrition, infectious disease control, health education, health personnel development, population policy and administrative management, reproductive health care, family planning, sexually transmitted disease control including HIV/AIDS, personnel development for population and reproductive health, basic drinking water supply and basic sanitation, and multisector aid for basic social services.
b. Provisional data. c. Calculated by World Bank staff using the World Integrated Trade Solution based on the United Nations Conference on Trade and Development's Trade Analysis and Information Systems database. d. Refers to the Enhanced HIPC Initiative. e. Data are in nominal terms because data in end-2008 net present value terms are unavailable. f. Also reached completion point under the original HIPC Initiative. The assistance includes original debt relief. g. Assistance includes topping up at completion point. h. Includes $15 million (in nominal terms) of committed debt relief by the International Monetary Fund, converted to end-2008 net present value terms.

About the data

Achieving the Millennium Development Goals requires an open, rule-based global economy in which all countries, rich and poor, participate. Many poor countries, lacking the resources to finance development, burdened by unsustainable debt, and unable to compete globally, need assistance from rich countries. For goal 8—develop a global partnership for development—many indicators therefore monitor the actions of members of the Organisation for Economic Co-operation and Development's (OECD) Development Assistance Committee (DAC).

Official development assistance (ODA) has risen in recent years as a share of donor countries' gross national income (GNI), but the poorest economies need additional assistance to achieve the Millennium Development Goals. Net ODA disbursements from DAC donors reached $120 billion in 2008—the highest level ever—representing a 16 percent increase in nominal terms from the 2007 level.

One important action that high-income economies can take is to reduce barriers to exports from low- and middle-income economies. The European Union has begun to eliminate tariffs on developing economy exports of "everything but arms," and the United States offers special concessions to Sub-Saharan African exports. However, these programs still have many restrictions.

Average tariffs in the table reflect high-income OECD member tariff schedules for exports of countries designated least developed countries by the United Nations. Although average tariffs have been falling, averages may disguise high tariffs on specific goods (see table 6.8 for each country's share of tariff lines with "international peaks"). The averages in the table include ad valorem duties and equivalents.

Subsidies to agricultural producers and exporters in OECD countries are another barrier to developing economies' exports. Agricultural subsidies in OECD economies are estimated at $376 billion in 2008.

The Debt Initiative for Heavily Indebted Poor Countries (HIPCs), an important step in placing debt relief within the framework of poverty reduction, is the first comprehensive approach to reducing the external debt of the world's poorest, most heavily indebted countries. A 1999 review led to an enhancement of the framework. In 2005, to further reduce the debt of HIPCs and provide resources for meeting the Millennium Development Goals, the Multilateral Debt Relief Initiative (MDRI), proposed by the Group of Eight countries, was launched.

Under the MDRI four multilateral institutions—the International Development Association (IDA), International Monetary Fund (IMF), African Development Fund (AfDF), and Inter-American Development Bank (IDB)—provide 100 percent debt relief on eligible debts due to them from countries having completed the HIPC Initiative process. Data in the table refer to status as of February 2010 and might not show countries that have since reached the decision or completion point. Debt relief under the HIPC Initiative has reduced future debt payments by $57 billion (in end-2008 net present value terms) for 35 countries that have reached the decision point. And 28 countries that have reached the completion point have received additional assistance of $25 billion (in end-2008 net present value terms) under the MDRI.

Definitions

• **Net official development assistance (ODA)** is grants and loans (net of repayments of principal) that meet the DAC definition of ODA and are made to countries on the DAC list of recipients. • **ODA for basic social services** is aid reported by DAC donors for basic education, primary health care, nutrition, population policies and programs, reproductive health, and water and sanitation services. • **Goods admitted free of tariffs** are exports of goods (excluding arms) from least developed countries admitted without tariff. • **Average tariff** is the unweighted average of the effectively applied rates for all products subject to tariffs. • **Agricultural products** are plant and animal products, including tree crops but excluding timber and fish products. • **Textiles** and **clothing** are natural and synthetic fibers and fabrics and articles of clothing made from them. • **Support to agriculture** is the value of gross transfers from taxpayers and consumers arising from policy measures, net of associated budgetary receipts, regardless of their objectives and impacts on farm production and income or consumption of farm products. • **HIPC decision point** is the date when a heavily indebted poor country with an established track record of good performance under adjustment programs supported by the IMF and the World Bank commits to additional reforms and a poverty reduction strategy and starts receiving debt relief. • **HIPC completion point** is the date when a country successfully completes the key structural reforms agreed on at the decision point, including implementing a poverty reduction strategy. The country then receives full debt relief under the HIPC Initiative without further policy conditions. • **HIPC Initiative assistance** is the debt relief committed as of the decision point (assuming full participation of creditors). Topping-up assistance and assistance provided under the original HIPC Initiative were committed in net present value terms as of the decision point and are converted to end-2008 terms. • **MDRI assistance** is 100 percent debt relief on eligible debt from IDA, IMF, AfDF, and IDB, delivered in full to countries having reached the HIPC completion point.

Location of indicators for Millennium Development Goal 8 — 1.4a

Goal 8. Develop a global partnership for development	Table
8.1 Net ODA as a percentage of DAC donors' gross national income	1.4, 6.14
8.2 Proportion of ODA for basic social services	1.4
8.3 Proportion of ODA that is untied	6.15b
8.4 Proportion of ODA received in landlocked countries as a percentage of GNI	—
8.5 Proportion of ODA received in small island developing states as a percentage of GNI	—
8.6 Proportion of total developed country imports (by value, excluding arms) from least developed countries admitted free of duty	1.4
8.7 Average tariffs imposed by developed countries on agricultural products and textiles and clothing from least developed countries	1.4, 6.8*
8.8 Agricultural support estimate for OECD countries as a percentage of GDP	1.4
8.9 Proportion of ODA provided to help build trade capacity	—
8.10 Number of countries reaching HIPC decision and completion points	1.4
8.11 Debt relief committed under new HIPC initiative	1.4
8.12 Debt services as a percentage of exports of goods and services	6.11*
8.13 Proportion of population with access to affordable, essential drugs on a sustainable basis	—
8.14 Telephone lines per 100 people	1.3*, 5.11
8.15 Cellular subscribers per 100 people	1.3*, 5.11
8.16 Internet users per 100 people	5.12

— No data are available in the World Development Indicators database. * Table shows information on related indicators.

Data sources

Data on ODA are from the OECD. Data on goods admitted free of tariffs and average tariffs are from the World Trade Organization, in collaboration with the United Nations Conference on Trade and Development and the International Trade Centre. These data are available at www.mdg-trade.org. Data on subsidies to agriculture are from the OECD's *Producer and Consumer Support Estimates, OECD Database 1986–2008*. Data on the HIPC Initiative and MDRI are from the World Bank's Economic Policy and Debt Department.

	Female population	Life expectancy at birth		Pregnant women receiving prenatal care	Teenage mothers	Women in wage employment in nonagricultural sector	Unpaid family workers		Women in parliaments	
		years					Male	Female		
	% of total	Male	Female	%	% of women ages 15–19	% of nonagricultural wage employment	% of male employment	% of female employment	% of total seats	
	2008	2008	2008	2003–08[a]	2003–08[a]	2007	2003–08[a]	2003–08[a]	1990	2009
Afghanistan	48.2	44	44	36	..	..	..	..	4	28
Albania	50.6	74	80	97	..	..	..	..	29	16
Algeria	49.5	71	74	89	..	..	7.1	13.6	2	8
Angola	50.7	45	49	80	29	..	..	..	15	37
Argentina	51.0	72	79	99	..	45	0.7[b]	1.6[b]	6	42
Armenia	53.4	70	77	93	5	46	..	..	36	8
Australia	50.3	79	84	..	..	47	0.2	0.4	6	27
Austria	51.3	78	83	..	..	46	2.0	2.7	12	28
Azerbaijan	51.2	68	73	77	6	50	0.0	0.0	..	11
Bangladesh	49.4	65	67	51	33	20	9.7	60.1	10	19
Belarus	53.5	65	77	99	..	56	..	..	..	32
Belgium	51.0	77	83	..	..	46	0.4	2.2	9	35
Benin	49.6	60	63	84	21	..	..	..	3	11
Bolivia	50.1	64	68	77	16	..	..	..	9	17
Bosnia and Herzegovina	51.9	73	78	99	..	35	2.0	8.9	..	12
Botswana	50.1	54	54	..	..	42	2.2	2.2	5	11
Brazil	50.7	69	76	98	..	..	4.6	8.1	5	9
Bulgaria	51.6	70	77	..	..	52	0.6	1.5	21	21
Burkina Faso	50.1	52	54	85	23	..	..	..	..	15
Burundi	51.0	49	52	92	..	..	..	..	..	31
Cambodia	51.1	59	63	69	8	..	..	..	..	16
Cameroon	50.0	51	52	82	28	..	..	..	14	14
Canada	50.5	79	83	..	..	50	0.1[b]	0.2[b]	13	22
Central African Republic	50.9	45	49	69	..	..	..	..	4	11
Chad	50.3	47	50	39	37	..	..	..	..	5
Chile	50.5	76	82	..	..	37	0.9	2.8	..	15
China	48.1[c]	71[c]	75[c]	91	..	..	..	..	21	21
Hong Kong SAR, China	52.5	79	86	..	..	48	0.1	1.1	..	..
Colombia	50.8	69	77	94	21	49	2.7	6.3	5	8
Congo, Dem. Rep.	50.5	46	49	85	24	..	..	..	5	8
Congo, Rep.	50.1	53	55	86	27	..	..	..	14	7
Costa Rica	49.2	77	81	90	..	41	1.3	2.8	11	37
Côte d'Ivoire	49.0	56	59	85	..	..	..	..	6	9
Croatia	51.8	72	80	100	4	46	1.1[b]	3.7[b]	..	21
Cuba	49.9	77	81	100	..	44	..	..	34	43
Czech Republic	51.0	74	81	..	..	46	0.3	1.0	..	16
Denmark	50.5	77	81	..	..	49	0.3	0.5	31	38
Dominican Republic	49.7	70	75	99	21	39	2.9	3.4	8	20
Ecuador	49.9	72	78	84	..	37	4.4[b]	11.1[b]	5	32
Egypt, Arab Rep.	49.7	68	72	74	9	18	8.6	32.6	4	2
El Salvador	52.7	67	76	94	..	49	8.8	9.9	12	19
Eritrea	50.9	57	62	..	..	..	..	..	..	22
Estonia	53.9	69	80	..	..	52	0.0	0.0	..	21
Ethiopia	50.3	54	57	28	17	47	7.8[b]	12.7[b]	..	22
Finland	51.0	76	83	..	..	51	0.6	0.4	32	42
France	51.4	78	85	..	..	49	0.3	0.9	7	18
Gabon	50.1	59	62	..	..	..	..	..	13	17
Gambia, The	50.4	54	58	98	..	..	..	..	8	9
Georgia	52.9	68	75	94	..	49	19.0	39.0	..	5
Germany	51.0	78	83	..	..	47	0.4	1.5	..	33
Ghana	49.3	56	58	95	13	..	..	..	..	8
Greece	50.4	78	82	..	..	42	3.4	9.8	7	15
Guatemala	51.3	67	74	..	..	43	..	..	7	12
Guinea	49.5	56	60	88	32	..	..	..	..	19
Guinea-Bissau	50.5	46	49	78	..	..	..	..	20	10
Haiti	50.6	59	63	85	14	..	..	..	..	4
Honduras	50.1	70	75	92	22	33	12.1[b]	8.3[b]	10	23

	Female population	Life expectancy at birth		Pregnant women receiving prenatal care	Teenage mothers	Women in wage employment in nonagricultural sector	Unpaid family workers		Women in parliaments	
		years					Male % of male employment	Female % of female employment		
	% of total 2008	Male 2008	Female 2008	% 2003–08[a]	% of women ages 15–19 2003–08[a]	% of nonagricultural wage employment 2007	2003–08[a]	2003–08[a]	% of total seats 1990	2009
Hungary	52.5	70	78	..	..	48	0.3	0.5	21	11
India	48.3	62	65	74	16	*18*	..	..	5	11
Indonesia	50.1	69	73	93	9	31	7.8	33.6	12	18
Iran, Islamic Rep.	49.1	70	73	98	..	*16*	5.4	32.7	2	3
Iraq	49.4	64	72	84	..	..	..	..	11	26
Ireland	49.9	78	82	..	..	48	0.6	0.8	8	13
Israel	50.4	79	83	..	..	49	0.1	0.4	7	18
Italy	51.4	79	85	..	..	43	1.2	2.5	13	21
Jamaica	51.1	69	75	91	..	*46*	0.5	2.2	5	13
Japan	51.3	79	86	..	..	42	1.1	7.3	1	11
Jordan	48.7	71	75	99	4	*26*	..	..	0	6
Kazakhstan	52.3	61	72	100	7	..	1.0	1.3	..	*16*
Kenya	50.0	54	55	88	23	..	..	..	1	10
Korea, Dem. Rep.	50.6	65	69	..	..	..	..	..	21	16
Korea, Rep.	50.5	77	83	..	..	42	1.2	12.7	2	14
Kosovo	..	67	72	..	..	..	..	..	..	..
Kuwait	40.3	76	80	..	..	..	..	..	..	8
Kyrgyz Republic	50.7	63	72	97	..	51	8.8	19.3	..	26
Lao PDR	50.1	64	66	35	..	*50*	..	..	6	25
Latvia	53.9	67	78	..	..	52	1.4	1.2	..	20
Lebanon	51.0	70	74	96	..	..	..	..	0	3
Lesotho	52.9	44	46	90	20	..	..	..	..	25
Liberia	50.3	57	60	79	32	..	..	..	..	13
Libya	48.3	72	77	..	..	..	..	..	..	8
Lithuania	53.3	66	78	..	..	53	1.0	2.0	..	18
Macedonia, FYR	50.1	72	77	94	..	42	7.0	14.9	..	28
Madagascar	50.2	59	62	80	34	*38*	32.1	73.0	7	8
Malawi	50.3	52	54	92	34	..	..	..	10	21
Malaysia	49.2	72	77	79	..	39	2.7	8.8	5	11
Mali	50.6	48	49	70	36	..	18.4	10.2	..	10
Mauritania	49.3	55	59	75	..	..	..	..	..	22
Mauritius	50.4	69	76	..	..	37	0.9	4.7	7	17
Mexico	50.7	73	78	94	..	39	4.9	10.0	12	28
Moldova	52.5	65	72	98	6	55	1.3	3.4	..	26
Mongolia	50.5	63	70	89	..	53	18.4	31.7	25	4
Morocco	50.9	69	74	68	7	28	16.5	51.8	0	11
Mozambique	51.4	47	49	89	41	..	..	..	16	35
Myanmar	51.1	59	64	..	..	..	..	..	..	..
Namibia	50.7	60	62	95	15	..	3.2	5.8	7	27
Nepal	50.3	66	67	44	19	..	..	..	6	33
Netherlands	50.5	78	82	..	..	47	0.2	0.8	21	41
New Zealand	50.6	78	82	..	..	49	0.8	1.5	14	34
Nicaragua	50.5	70	76	90	..	*39*	12.2	9.1	15	19
Niger	49.9	51	52	46	39	..	..	..	5	12
Nigeria	49.9	47	48	58	25	*21*	..	..	..	7
Norway	50.3	78	83	..	..	49	0.2	0.4	36	*36*
Oman	43.5	74	78	..	..	..	..	..	..	0
Pakistan	48.5	66	67	61	9	13	18.6	61.9	10	23
Panama	49.6	73	78	..	..	43	2.3	4.0	8	9
Papua New Guinea	49.2	59	63	79	..	..	..	..	0	1
Paraguay	49.5	70	74	96	..	40	10.8	8.9	6	13
Peru	49.9	71	76	91	26	43	4.7[b]	9.9[b]	6	28
Philippines	49.6	70	74	91	8	42	9.0	18.0	9	21
Poland	51.7	71	80	..	..	47	2.7	5.9	14	20
Portugal	51.6	76	82	..	..	48	0.7	1.2	8	*28*
Puerto Rico	52.0	75	83	..	..	42	0.0	0.0	..	..
Qatar	24.8	75	77	..	..	..	0.0	0.0	..	0

	Female population	Life expectancy at birth		Pregnant women receiving prenatal care	Teenage mothers	Women in wage employment in nonagricultural sector	Unpaid family workers		Women in parliaments	
		years					Male % of male employment	Female % of female employment	% of total seats	
	% of total 2008	Male 2008	Female 2008	% 2003–08[a]	% of women ages 15–19 2003–08[a]	% of nonagricultural wage employment 2007	2003–08[a]	2003–08[a]	1990	2009
Romania	51.4	70	77	94	..	46	6.0	18.9	34	11
Russian Federation	53.8	62	74	..	..	51	0.1	0.1	..	14
Rwanda	51.6	48	52	96	4	..	..	..	17	56
Saudi Arabia	45.1	71	75	..	..	15	..	..	..	0
Senegal	50.4	54	57	87	19	..	..	..	13	22
Serbia	50.5	71	76	98	..	14[d]	3.1	11.9	..	22
Sierra Leone	51.3	46	49	81	..	..	14.8	21.6	..	13
Singapore	49.7	78	83	..	..	45	0.4	1.3	5	25
Slovak Republic	51.5	71	79	..	..	50	0.1	0.2	..	19
Slovenia	51.2	76	83	..	..	47	3.2	5.4	..	13
Somalia	50.4	48	51	26	..	..	..	..	4	6
South Africa	50.7	50	53	92	..	44	0.3	0.6	3	45
Spain	50.7	78	84	..	..	44	0.8	1.4	15	36
Sri Lanka	50.7	70	78	99	..	31	4.4[b]	21.7[b]	5	6
Sudan	49.7	57	60	64	..	..	..	..	..	18
Swaziland	51.2	46	45	85	23	..	..	..	4	14
Sweden	50.4	79	83	..	..	50	0.2	0.3	38	47
Switzerland	51.1	80	85	..	..	47	1.7	3.2	14	29
Syrian Arab Republic	49.5	72	76	84	..	..	..	..	9	12
Tajikistan	50.6	64	69	80	..	37	..	..	..	18
Tanzania	50.2	55	56	76	26	31	9.7[b]	13.0[b]	..	30
Thailand	50.8	66	72	98	..	45	14.0	29.9	3	12
Timor-Leste	49.1	60	62	61	..	..	..	..	..	29
Togo	50.5	61	64	84	..	..	..	..	5	11
Trinidad and Tobago	51.4	66	73	96	..	44	0.3	1.7	17	27
Tunisia	49.7	72	76	96	..	..	..	..	4	23
Turkey	49.8	70	74	54	..	21	5.3	37.7	1	9
Turkmenistan	50.7	61	69	99	..	..	..	..	26	17
Uganda	49.9	52	53	94	25	..	10.3[b]	40.5[b]	12	31
Ukraine	53.9	63	74	99	4	55	0.4	0.3	..	8
United Arab Emirates	32.5	77	79	..	..	14	0.0	0.0	0	23
United Kingdom	51.0	78	82	..	..	52	0.2	0.5	6	20
United States	50.7	76	81	..	..	47	0.1	0.1	7	17
Uruguay	51.8	72	80	97	..	46	0.9[b]	3.0[b]	6	12
Uzbekistan	50.3	65	71	99	..	..	..	..	..	18
Venezuela, RB	49.8	71	77	..	..	41	0.6	1.6	10	19
Vietnam	50.7	72	76	91	..	..	18.9	47.2	18	26
West Bank and Gaza	49.1	72	75	99	..	17	6.6	31.5	..	..
Yemen, Rep.	49.4	61	65	47	..	..	..	..	4	0[e]
Zambia	50.1	45	46	94	28	..	..	..	7	15
Zimbabwe	51.7	44	45	94	21	..	..	..	11	15
World	**49.6 w**	**67 w**	**71 w**	**82 w**		**.. w**	**.. w**	**.. w**	**13 w**	**19 w**
Low income	50.2	58	60	69			..	..	..	19
Middle income	49.2	67	71	84		..	..	..	13	17
Lower middle income	48.8	66	70	83		..	..	..	14	16
Upper middle income	51.1	68	75	90		45	3.4	7.3	12	20
Low & middle income	49.4	65	69	82		..	..	..	13	18
East Asia & Pacific	48.8	70	74	91		..	..	..	17	18
Europe & Central Asia	52.2	66	75	..		48	2.0	5.4	..	15
Latin America & Carib.	50.6	70	77	95		..	4.0	7.5	12	23
Middle East & N. Africa	49.6	69	73	83		..	..	..	4	9
South Asia	48.5	63	65	69		18	..	..	6	20
Sub-Saharan Africa	50.2	51	53	72		..	..	..	..	18
High income	50.6	77	83	..		46	0.5	2.3	12	22
Euro area	51.1	78	84	..		46	0.8	1.8	12	25

a. Data are for the most recent year available. b. Limited coverage. c. Includes Taiwan, China. d. Data are for 2008. e. Less than 0.5.

About the data

Despite much progress in recent decades, gender inequalities remain pervasive in many dimensions of life—worldwide. But while disparities exist throughout the world, they are most prevalent in developing countries. Gender inequalities in the allocation of such resources as education, health care, nutrition, and political voice matter because of the strong association with well-being, productivity, and economic growth. These patterns of inequality begin at an early age, with boys routinely receiving a larger share of education and health spending than do girls, for example.

Because of biological differences girls are expected to experience lower infant and child mortality rates and to have a longer life expectancy than boys. This biological advantage may be overshadowed, however, by gender inequalities in nutrition and medical interventions and by inadequate care during pregnancy and delivery, so that female rates of illness and death sometimes exceed male rates, particularly during early childhood and the reproductive years. In high-income countries women tend to outlive men by four to eight years on average, while in low-income countries the difference is narrower—about two to three years. The difference in child mortality rates (table 2.22) is another good indicator of female social disadvantage because nutrition and medical interventions are particularly important for the 1–4 age group. Female child mortality rates that are as high as or higher than male child mortality rates may indicate discrimination against girls.

Having a child during the teenage years limits girls' opportunities for better education, jobs, and income. Pregnancy is more likely to be unintended during the teenage years, and births are more likely to be premature and are associated with greater risks of complications during delivery and of death. In many countries maternal mortality (tables 1.3 and 2.19) is a leading cause of death among women of reproductive age. Most maternal deaths result from preventable causes—hemorrhage, infection, and complications from unsafe abortions. Prenatal care is essential for recognizing, diagnosing, and promptly treating complications that arise during pregnancy. In high-income countries most women have access to health care during pregnancy, but in developing countries many women suffer pregnancy-related complications, and over half a million die every year (Glasier and others 2006). This is reflected in the differences in maternal mortality ratios between high- and low-income countries.

Women's wage work is important for economic growth and the well-being of families. But women often face such obstacles as restricted access to education and vocational training, heavy workloads at home and in unpaid domestic and market activities, and labor market discrimination. These obstacles force women to limit their participation in paid economic activities. And even when women work, these obstacles cause women to be less productive and to receive lower wages. When women are in paid employment, they tend to be concentrated in the nonagricultural sector. However, in many developing countries women are a large part of agricultural employment, often as unpaid family workers. Among people who are unsalaried, women are more likely than men to be unpaid family workers, while men are more likely than women to be self-employed or employers. There are several reasons for this.

Few women have access to credit markets, capital, land, training, and education, which may be required to start a business. Cultural norms may prevent women from working on their own or from supervising other workers. Also, women may face time constraints due to their traditional family responsibilities. Because of biases and misclassification substantial numbers of employed women may be underestimated or reported as unpaid family workers even when they work in association or equally with their husbands in the family enterprise.

Women are vastly underrepresented in decision-making positions in government, although there is some evidence of recent improvement. Gender parity in parliamentary representation is still far from being realized. In 2009 women accounted for 19 percent of parliamentarians worldwide, compared with 9 percent in 1987. Without representation at this level, it is difficult for women to influence policy.

For information on other aspects of gender, see tables 1.2 (Millennium Development Goals: eradicating poverty and saving lives), 1.3 (Millennium Development Goals: protecting our common environment), 2.3 (Employment by economic activity), 2.4 (Decent work and productive employment), 2.5 (Unemployment), 2.6 (Children at work), 2.10 (Assessing vulnerability and security), 2.13 (Education efficiency), 2.14 (Education completion and outcomes), 2.15 (Education gaps by income and gender), 2.19 (Reproductive health), 2.21 (Health risk factors and future challenges), and 2.22 (Mortality).

Definitions

• **Female population** is the percentage of the population that is female. • **Life expectancy at birth** is the number of years a newborn infant would live if prevailing patterns of mortality at the time of its birth were to stay the same throughout its life. • **Pregnant women receiving prenatal care** are the percentage of women attended at least once during pregnancy by skilled health personnel for reasons related to pregnancy. • **Teenage mothers** are the percentage of women ages 15–19 who already have children or are currently pregnant. • **Women in wage employment in nonagricultural sector** are female wage employees in the nonagricultural sector as a percentage of total nonagricultural wage employment. • **Unpaid family workers** are those who work without pay in a market-oriented establishment or activity operated by a related person living in the same household. • **Women in parliaments** are the percentage of parliamentary seats in a single or lower chamber held by women.

Data sources

Data on female population are from the United Nations Population Division's *World Population Prospects: The 2008 Revision,* and data on life expectancy for more than half the countries in the table (most of them developing countries) are from its *World Population Prospects: The 2008 Revision,* with additional data from census reports, other statistical publications from national statistical offices, Eurostat's *Demographic Statistics,* the Secretariat of the Pacific Community's Statistics and Demography Programme, and the U.S. Bureau of the Census International Data Base. Data on pregnant women receiving prenatal care are from household surveys, including Demographic and Health Surveys by Macro International and Multiple Indicator Cluster Surveys by the United Nations Children's Fund (UNICEF), and UNICEF's *The State of the World's Children 2010.* Data on teenage mothers are from Demographic and Health Surveys by Macro International. Data on labor force and employment are from the International Labour Organization's *Key Indicators of the Labour Market,* 6th edition. Data on women in parliaments are from the Inter-Parliamentary Union.

	Population	Surface area	Population density	Gross national income				Gross domestic product		Life expectancy at birth	Adult literacy rate	Carbon dioxide emissions
				Atlas method		Purchasing power parity						
					Per capita		Per capita		Per capita		% ages 15	thousand
	thousands	thousand sq. km	people per sq. km	$ millions	$	$ millions	$	% growth	% growth	years	and older	metric tons
	2008	2008	2008	2008	2008	2008	2008	2007–08	2007–08	2008	2008	2006
American Samoa	66	0.2	331	..	..[a]	..	..	..	..	..	..	..
Andorra	84	0.5	178	*3,038*	*36,970*	..	..	1.4	−1.4	..	..	..
Antigua and Barbuda	87	0.4	197	1,143	13,200	1,702[b]	19,650[b]	2.5	1.3	..	..	410
Aruba	105	0.2	586	..	..[c]	..	..	..	..	75	98	2,308
Bahamas, The	338	13.9	34	*7,136*	*21,390*	..	..	2.8	1.5	73	..	2,107
Bahrain	776	0.7	1,092	19,713	25,420	25,906	33,400	6.3	4.1	76	91	19,668
Barbados	255	0.4	593	..	..[c]	..	..	..	..	77	..	1,315
Belize	322	23.0	14	1,205	3,740	1,913[b]	5,940[b]	3.8	0.4	76	..	817
Bermuda	64	0.1	1,284	..	..[c]	..	..	4.6	4.3	79	..	564
Bhutan	687	38.4	18	1,307	1,900	3,310	4,820	13.8	12.0	66	..	392
Brunei Darussalam	392	5.8	74	*10,211*	*27,050*	19,540	50,770	0.6	−1.3	77	95	5,903
Cape Verde	499	4.0	124	1,399	2,800	1,537	3,080	2.8	1.4	71	84	297
Cayman Islands	54	0.3	209	..	..[c]	..	..	..	..	..	99	502
Channel Islands	150	0.2	787	*10,242*	*68,610*	..	..	5.9	5.7	79	..	..
Comoros	644	1.9	346	483	750	754	1,170	1.0	−1.4	65	74	88
Cyprus	862	9.3	93	21,367[d]	26,940[d]	19,811[d]	24,980[d]	3.6[d]	2.4[d]	80	98	7,497
Djibouti	849	23.2	37	957	1,130	1,972	2,320	3.9	2.0	55	..	473
Dominica	73	0.8	98	348	4,750	607[b]	8,290[b]	4.3	3.7	..	..	114
Equatorial Guinea	659	28.1	24	9,875	14,980	14,305	21,700	11.3	8.4	50	93	4,338
Faeroe Islands	49	1.4	35	..	..[c]	..	..	..	..	79	..	678
Fiji	844	18.3	46	3,382	4,010	3,647	4,320	0.2	−0.4	69	..	1,663
French Polynesia	266	4.0	73	..	..[c]	..	..	..	..	74	..	854
Greenland	56	410.5	0[e]	*1,682*	*29,740*	..	..	0.7	1.1	68	..	557
Grenada	104	0.3	305	609	5,880	873[b]	8,430[b]	2.1	1.7	75	..	234
Guam	176	0.5	325	..	..[c]	..	..	..	..	76	..	..
Guyana	763	215.0	4	1,107	1,450	2,308[b]	3,020[b]	3.0	3.1	67	..	1,491
Iceland	317	103.0	3	12,839	40,450	8,031	25,300	0.3	−1.5	82	..	2,184
Isle of Man	81	0.6	141	*3,972*	*49,310*	..	..	7.5	7.4	..	..	..

About the data

The table shows data for 55 economies with populations between 30,000 and 1 million and for smaller economies if they are members of the World Bank. Where data on gross national income (GNI) per capita are not available, the estimated range is given. For more information on the calculation of GNI and purchasing power parity (PPP) conversion factors, see *About the data* for table 1.1. Additional data for the economies in the table are available on the *World Development Indicators* CD-ROM or in *WDI Online*.

Definitions

• **Population** is based on the de facto definition of population, which counts all residents regardless of legal status or citizenship—except for refugees not permanently settled in the country of asylum, who are generally considered part of the population of their country of origin. The values shown are midyear estimates. For more information, see *About the data* for table 2.1. • **Surface area** is a country's total area, including areas under inland bodies of water and some coastal waterways. • **Population density** is midyear population divided by land area in square kilometers. • **Gross national income (GNI), *Atlas* method,** is the sum of value added by all resident producers plus any product taxes (less subsidies) not

included in the valuation of output plus net receipts of primary income (compensation of employees and property income) from abroad. Data are in current U.S. dollars converted using the *World Bank Atlas* method (see *Statistical methods*). • **Purchasing power parity (PPP) GNI** is GNI converted to international dollars using PPP rates. An international dollar has the same purchasing power over GNI that a U.S. dollar has in the United States. • **GNI per capita** is GNI divided by midyear population. • **Gross domestic product (GDP)** is the sum of value added by all resident producers plus any product taxes (less subsidies) not included in the valuation of output. Growth is calculated from constant price GDP data in local

	Population	Surface area	Population density	Gross national income				Gross domestic product		Life expectancy at birth	Adult literacy rate	Carbon dioxide emissions
				Atlas method		Purchasing power parity						
	thousands **2008**	thousand sq. km **2008**	people per sq. km **2008**	$ millions **2008**	Per capita $ **2008**	$ millions **2008**	Per capita $ **2008**	% growth **2007–08**	Per capita % growth **2007–08**	years **2008**	% ages 15 and older **2008**	thousand metric tons **2006**
Kiribati	97	0.8	119	197	2,040	349[b]	3,610[b]	3.0	1.4	..	..	26
Liechtenstein	36	0.2	223	*3,463*	*97,990*	..	..	3.1	2.2	83	..	..
Luxembourg	489	2.6	189	33,960	69,390	25,785	52,770	–0.9	–2.7	81	..	11,318
Macau SAR, China	526	0.0	18,659	*18,142*	*35,360*	*26,811*	*52,260*	13.2	10.4	81	93	2,308
Maldives	305	0.3	1,017	1,110	3,640	1,613	5,290	5.2	3.7	72	98	678
Malta	412	0.3	1,287	*6,825*	*16,690*	*8,418*	*20,580*	3.8	*3.1*	80	..	2,587
Marshall Islands	60	0.2	331	195	3,270	..	..	1.5	–0.8	..	..	84
Mayotte	191	0.4	511	..	..[a]	..	..	..	..	76	..	..
Micronesia, Fed. Sts.	110	0.7	158	272	2,460	361[b]	3,270[b]	–2.9	–3.1	69	..	..
Monaco	33	0.0	16,358	..	..[c]	..	..	..	..	..	..	..
Montenegro	622	13.8	46	4,146	6,660	8,350	13,420	8.1	7.9	74	..	..
Netherlands Antilles	195	0.8	244	..	..[c]	..	..	..	..	76	96	3,752
New Caledonia	247	18.6	13	..	..[c]	..	..	..	..	76	96	2,799
Northern Mariana Islands	85	0.5	186	..	..[c]	..	..	..	..	..	..	..
Palau	20	0.5	44	175	8,630	..	..	–1.0	–1.6	..	..	117
Samoa	179	2.8	63	504	2,820	789[b]	4,410[b]	–3.4	–3.4	72	99	158
San Marino	31	0.1	517	*1,430*	*46,770*	..	..	4.5	*3.1*	82	..	..
São Tomé and Príncipe	160	1.0	167	164	1,030	286	1,790	5.8	4.1	66	88	103
Seychelles	87	0.5	189	889	10,220	1,707[b]	19,630[b]	2.8	0.5	73	..	696
Solomon Islands	511	28.9	18	518	1,010	1,090[b]	2,130[b]	6.9	4.3	66	..	180
St. Kitts and Nevis	49	0.3	189	535	10,870	761[b]	15,480[b]	8.2	7.4	..	..	136
St. Lucia	170	0.6	279	921	5,410	1,535[b]	9,020[b]	0.5	–0.6	..	..	374
St. Vincent & Grenadines	109	0.4	280	551	5,050	934[b]	8,560[b]	–1.1	–1.2	72	..	194
Suriname	515	163.8	3	2,454	4,760	3,439[b]	6,680[b]	5.1	4.2	69	91	2,378
Tonga	104	0.8	144	279	2,690	412[b]	3,980[b]	0.8	0.4	72	99	132
Vanuatu	234	12.2	19	*442*	*1,940*	793[b]	3,480[b]	6.6	3.9	70	81	88
Virgin Islands (U.S.)	110	0.4	314	..	..[c]	..	..	..	..	79	..	..

a. Estimated to be upper middle income ($3,856–$11,905). b. Based on regression; others are extrapolated from the 2005 International Comparison Program benchmark estimates.
c. Estimated to be high income ($11,906 or more). d. Data are for the area controlled by the government of the Republic of Cyprus. e. Less than 0.5.

currency. • **GDP per capita** is GDP divided by midyear population. • **Life expectancy at birth** is the number of years a newborn infant would live if prevailing patterns of mortality at the time of its birth were to stay the same throughout its life. • **Adult literacy rate** is the percentage of adults ages 15 and older who can, with understanding, read and write a short, simple statement about their everyday life. • **Carbon dioxide emissions** are those stemming from the burning of fossil fuels and the manufacture of cement. They include carbon dioxide produced during consumption of solid, liquid, and gas fuels and gas flaring.

Data sources

The indicators here and throughout the book are compiled by World Bank staff from primary and secondary sources. More information about the indicators and their sources can be found in the *About the data, Definitions,* and *Data sources* entries that accompany each table in subsequent sections.

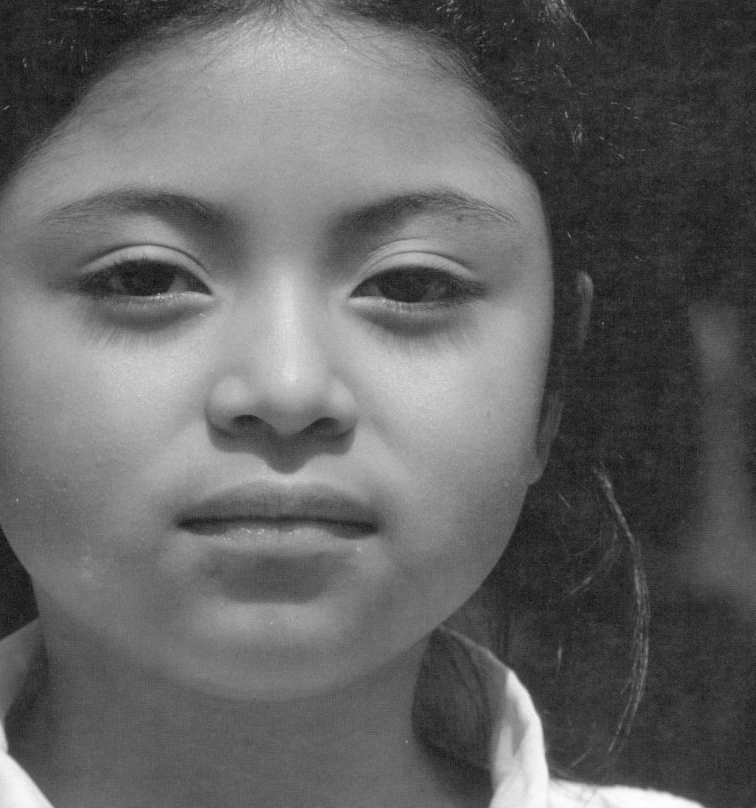

PEOPLE

Achieving the Millennium Development Goals (MDGs) promises a better life for millions: lives saved; women empowered; illiteracy, hunger, and malnutrition reduced or eliminated; and children ensured access to high-quality education and health services. Because the MDGs are so important, countries have been striving to effectively monitor progress toward achieving them. Though the world overall has made progress, many countries remain off track—particularly fragile states and countries emerging from conflict. The global financial crisis could push an estimated 50 million people into poverty, with serious consequences for human development. Poor families cut short their children's schooling, prolonging poverty into the next generation because dropouts earn less as adults. Families are also likely to have to cut back on consumption as recent increases in food prices put pressures on budgets, damaging children's nutrition and health. But the story is not all bleak.

Monitoring the Millennium Development Goals: what do the available data tell us?

Many countries and regions have made remarkable progress. Deaths of children under age 5 have declined steadily in developing countries, falling from 101 per 1,000 live births in 1990 to 73 in 2008, despite population growth. But many countries have made little progress, especially in Sub-Saharan Africa, and large disparities persist between the richest and poorest children in countries across all regions (figure 2a).

Interventions that could yield breakthroughs for children show mixed success. One child in four in developing countries is underweight—even more in low-income countries (figure 2b). But distribution of insecticide-treated nets has reduced the toll of malaria—a major killer of children—and higher immunization rates are making advances against measles (United Nations 2009a).

Healthy births continue to be a privilege of the rich. Developed countries report 10 maternal deaths per 100,000 live births, compared with 440 in developing countries—and 14 developing countries have maternal mortality ratios of 1,000 or higher (United Nations 2009a). Interventions to prevent maternal deaths, such as prenatal care, have improved in all regions, but poor women in the world's poorest countries have the least access to them (figure 2c). Access to contraception is increasing in all regions, but unmet need remains high at 11 percent (United Nations 2009a).

Major accomplishments have also been made in education. Enrollment in primary school reached

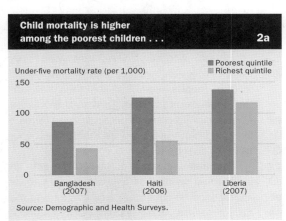

Child mortality is higher among the poorest children . . . 2a

Under-five mortality rate (per 1,000)

■ Poorest quintile
■ Richest quintile

Bangladesh (2007), Haiti (2006), Liberia (2007)

Source: Demographic and Health Surveys.

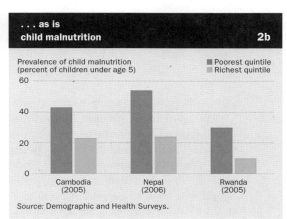

. . . as is child malnutrition 2b

Prevalence of child malnutrition (percent of children under age 5)

■ Poorest quintile
■ Richest quintile

Cambodia (2005), Nepal (2006), Rwanda (2005)

Source: Demographic and Health Surveys.

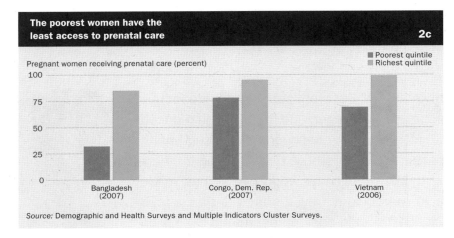

The poorest women have the least access to prenatal care

2c

Pregnant women receiving prenatal care (percent)

■ Poorest quintile
■ Richest quintile

Bangladesh (2007) · Congo, Dem. Rep. (2007) · Vietnam (2006)

Source: Demographic and Health Surveys and Multiple Indicators Cluster Surveys.

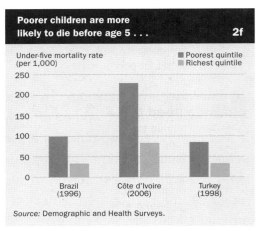

Poorer children are more likely to die before age 5 . . .

2f

Under-five mortality rate (per 1,000)

■ Poorest quintile
■ Richest quintile

Brazil (1996) · Côte d'Ivoire (2006) · Turkey (1998)

Source: Demographic and Health Surveys.

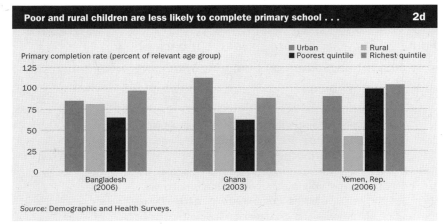

Poor and rural children are less likely to complete primary school . . .

2d

Primary completion rate (percent of relevant age group)

■ Urban   ■ Rural
■ Poorest quintile   ■ Richest quintile

Bangladesh (2006) · Ghana (2003) · Yemen, Rep. (2006)

Source: Demographic and Health Surveys.

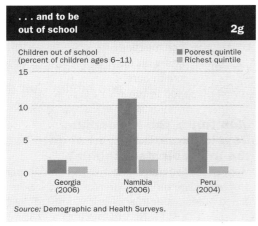

. . . and to be out of school

2g

Children out of school (percent of children ages 6–11)

■ Poorest quintile
■ Richest quintile

Georgia (2006) · Namibia (2006) · Peru (2004)

Source: Demographic and Health Surveys.

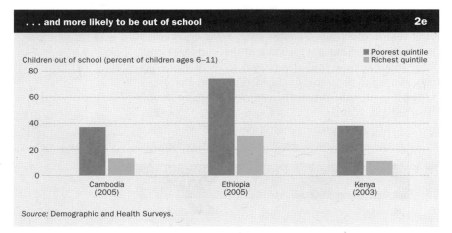

. . . and more likely to be out of school

2e

Children out of school (percent of children ages 6–11)

■ Poorest quintile
■ Richest quintile

Cambodia (2005) · Ethiopia (2005) · Kenya (2003)

Source: Demographic and Health Surveys.

86 percent in developing countries overall in 2007, up from 81 percent in 2000. Most of the progress was in regions lagging furthest behind—Sub-Saharan Africa (up 14 percentage points) and South Asia (up 10 percentage points). Primary school completion rates also improved, from 80 percent in 2000 to 88 percent in 2007, with the greatest improvements in the Middle East and North Africa. But the improvement was not uniformly distributed: children from poorer households and rural areas are less likely to complete their primary education (figure 2d).

In many countries and regions universal primary education (Millennium Development Goal 2) is jeopardized by the number of children who are out of school. In 2007 an estimated 72 million children were out of school, almost half of them in Sub-Saharan Africa and 18 million of them in South Asia. Nearly half of children out of school have had no contact with formal education. Another 23 percent were previously enrolled but dropped out (United Nations 2009a). Inequalities within countries mean that the poor are most likely to lose out: children from poor households are two to three times as likely to be out of school as their richest counterparts (figure 2e).

And although some of the MDG targets and indicators may be less relevant for many upper middle-income countries, they continue to matter for others. Wide disparities in well-being and achievement between the poorest and the wealthiest populations persist, impeding countries' ability to meet their targets (figures 2f and 2g). Under-five mortality for richer children is less than half that for poorer children.

Beyond data: what more do countries need to do?

The MDGs continue to provide a focus for country efforts, along with the need to strengthen data collection and analysis to assess progress. At the same time governments need to concentrate on interventions that improve access to quality health and education services that can produce favorable outcomes for the MDGs.

Health

Slow progress on meeting the health MDGs has been associated with disappointing advances in access to health care. Many health systems are not equipped to provide health care for all, reflecting the inability of governments and societies to mobilize the requisite resources and institutions. In particular, countries need to improve three areas of service delivery that focus on people's needs: infrastructure, available staff to deliver services, and adequate and effective funding (Gauthier and others 2009).

Infrastructure. The quality of health services depends on the availability of basic infrastructure services such as electricity and water. Electricity —limited in many poor countries—is necessary for operating medical equipment and facilities. Because unclean water is an important vector of sickness, clean running water is fundamental to service quality. Yet data indicate that first-line facilities in many countries lack these basic services (figure 2h). And in some countries infrastructure is deteriorating (figure 2i).

The accessibility and quality of health care services are often constrained by the unavailability of basic medical services and equipment (figure 2j). Poor countries often have fewer than 1.1 doctors and 0.9 nurse per 1,000 people, with access unevenly distributed across income groups. Wealthy people are better able to get to well staffed facilities and can afford to be seen by doctors (figure 2k).

Staffing. In many developing countries staff absenteeism is high, reflecting inadequate incentives and weak local accountability. For example, on an average day 40 percent of primary

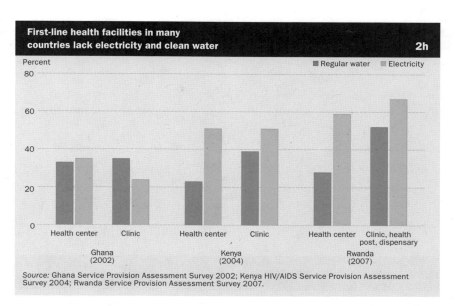

First-line health facilities in many countries lack electricity and clean water · 2h

Percent

Legend: ■ Regular water ■ Electricity

Ghana (2002): Health center, Clinic
Kenya (2004): Health center, Clinic
Rwanda (2007): Health center, Clinic, health post, dispensary

Source: Ghana Service Provision Assessment Survey 2002; Kenya HIV/AIDS Service Provision Assessment Survey 2004; Rwanda Service Provision Assessment Survey 2007.

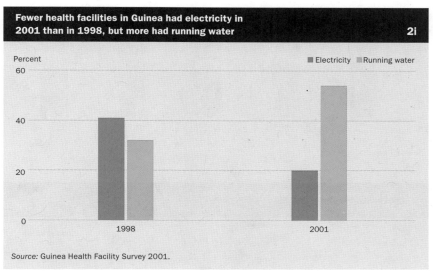

Fewer health facilities in Guinea had electricity in 2001 than in 1998, but more had running water · 2i

Percent

Legend: ■ Electricity ■ Running water

1998, 2001

Source: Guinea Health Facility Survey 2001.

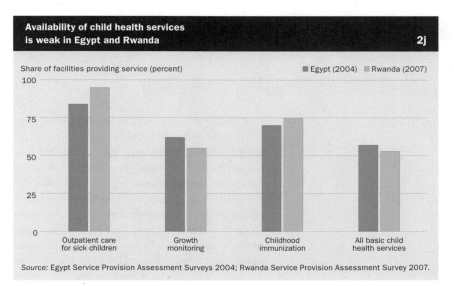

Availability of child health services is weak in Egypt and Rwanda · 2j

Share of facilities providing service (percent)

Legend: ■ Egypt (2004) ■ Rwanda (2007)

Outpatient care for sick children, Growth monitoring, Childhood immunization, All basic child health services

Source: Egypt Service Provision Assessment Surveys 2004; Rwanda Service Provision Assessment Survey 2007.

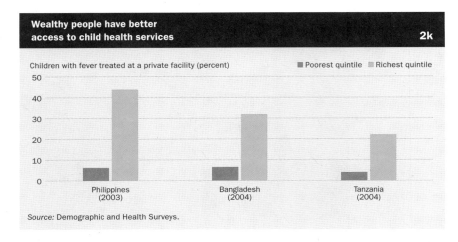

Wealthy people have better access to child health services `2k`

Children with fever treated at a private facility (percent)

■ Poorest quintile ■ Richest quintile

Source: Demographic and Health Surveys.

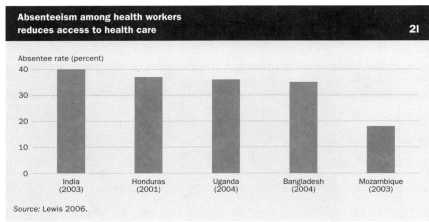

Absenteeism among health workers reduces access to health care `2l`

Absentee rate (percent)

India (2003), Honduras (2001), Uganda (2004), Bangladesh (2004), Mozambique (2003)

Source: Lewis 2006.

Distribution of health workers in Zambia, 2004 (per 100,000 people) `2m`

Classification	National	Rural	Urban	Ratio of urban to rural
Doctors	6.4	5.2	36.1	6.9
Nurses	41.6	17.7	44.7	2.5
Pharmacists/technicians	1.2	1.1	5.5	5.0
Laboratory technicians	2.7	2.5	7.9	3.2
All health workers	119.8	115.0	234.6	2.0

Source: Zambian Ministry of Health and WHO 2005.

health care workers in India are not at work (figure 2l). Because most people have to travel far to get to a health center, a high probability that the clinic will not be staffed may discourage patients from seeking care.

Uneven distribution of health workers is a major problem in several countries, especially in rural and poorer areas. For example, Zambia has twice as many health workers in urban areas as in rural areas (table 2m). Distribution of doctors is most uneven—they are seven

times more common in urban areas—followed by pharmacists.

Funding. As a country's income grows, total spending on health care rises. In 2007 high-income economies spent an average of 11 percent of GDP on health services and developing economies 5 percent. Funding for front-line service providers is low in many developing countries because of leakages and allocation rules that favor other purposes. Industrialized countries have shown that the disproportionate focus on hospitals and tertiary care, which dominated practice worldwide for much of the last two decades of the 20th century, has been a major source of inefficiency and inequality. For example, less than 20 percent of doctors in Thailand were specialists 30 years ago; by 2003, 70 percent were (World Health Organization, *World Health Report 2008*).

Education

In 2002 the World Bank and development partners launched the Education for All Fast Track Initiative, a global partnership to help low-income countries meet the MDG target of universal primary education and the Education for All goal that all children complete a full cycle of primary education by 2015. The initiative encourages countries to design sound education plans and provides additional indicators for tracking progress toward the education MDG, including indicators to monitor infrastructure and capacity at the primary school level, availability and presence in the classroom of qualified teachers, and expenditures on primary education.

At the school. Many schools lack the most basic infrastructure elements that are taken for granted in developed countries (figure 2n). For example, a 2008 survey of primary schools in Asia, Latin America, and North Africa found that more than one student in five in Paraguay, the Philippines, and Sri Lanka was in a school that lacked running water (UNESCO Institute for Statistics 2008b). No country in the survey had a library in every school. In India, Paraguay, Peru, the Philippines, Sri Lanka, and Tunisia, less than half the students were in schools with a telephone.

The survey also showed major gaps in resources between urban and rural schools. In four states of India 27 percent of village schools have electricity while 76 percent of schools in towns and cities do. Only about half these rural schools have enough toilets for girls, and less than 4 percent have a telephone. In Peru less than half of village schools have electricity, a library, or toilets for boys or girls; nearly all urban schools have electricity, 65 percent have enough lavatories, and 74 percent have libraries.

Teachers. To achieve Education for All goals, few inputs are more essential than having a teacher in the classroom. It is obvious that teacher absence will affect education quality. But teacher absence can also affect education access and school completion rates because poor quality discourages parents from making the sacrifices necessary to send their children to school. More important, high rates of teacher absence often signal deeper problems of accountability and governance that are themselves barriers to educational progress.

How prevalent is the problem of teacher absence? One difficulty in studying teacher absence is that administrative records of teachers' attendance may not be accurate. In countries with the highest absence rates, administrative records may be an especially poor guide to teacher attendance. If poor governance and low levels of accountability undermine teachers' incentives to attend school, those same factors are likely to reduce the accuracy of official attendance records. A study that measured attendance through direct observation of teachers during surprise visits to primary schools in six poor countries in 2002–03 found that teachers were absent about 19 percent of the time on average (Abadzi 2007; figure 2o). On an average day 27 percent of the teachers in Uganda were not at work compared with 5 percent in New York State.

Few teachers face serious threats of being fired for excessive absences. In a survey of 3,000 Indian government schools only one teacher was fired for poor attendance (Abdul Latif Jameel Poverty Action Lab 2009). Even in private schools, where teachers are less protected and schools have financial incentives to provide better service, only 35 of 600 schools reported a teacher being fired for poor attendance.

Funding. Adequate resources are critical for ensuring good quality outcomes in education. Studies have repeatedly stressed the need to ensure adequate and stable funding for education (Bruns, Mingat, and Rakotomalala 2003).

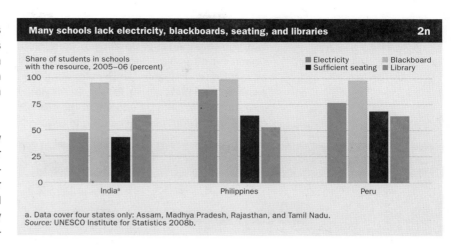

Many schools lack electricity, blackboards, seating, and libraries 2n

Share of students in schools with the resource, 2005–06 (percent)

Legend: Electricity, Blackboard, Sufficient seating, Library

a. Data cover four states only: Assam, Madhya Pradesh, Rajasthan, and Tamil Nadu.
Source: UNESCO Institute for Statistics 2008b.

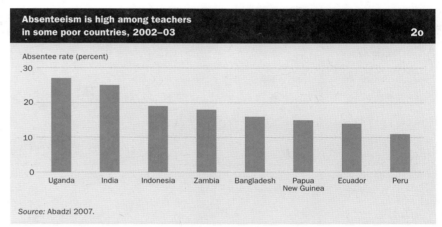

Absenteeism is high among teachers in some poor countries, 2002–03 2o

Absentee rate (percent)

Source: Abadzi 2007.

The cost of education 2p

The allocation of public budgets is ultimately the result of competing demands for limited resources. Countries with rising demand for education and limited funding need to keep costs per student low. In 2005 in Sub-Saharan Africa average spending per primary school student was almost 13 percent of per capita GDP, though spending ranged from 4 percent in the Republic of Congo to 35 percent in Burkina Faso. In East Asia and Pacific average spending per primary school student was 15 percent, yet two countries reported the lowest spending levels in the world (Indonesia and Myanmar, at just 3 percent). By contrast, countries in North America and Western Europe tend to spend an average of about 22 percent and those in Central and Eastern Europe around 17 percent.

Source: UNESCO Institute for Statistics, *Global Education Digest 2007.*

Countries with higher primary gross enrollment ratios and primary completion rates tend to devote a greater share of national income or government budgets to public primary education.

Governments struggle to fund free basic education for all (box 2p). Almost a third of education funding worldwide is allocated to the primary level ($741 billion, or 1.3 percent of global GDP in purchasing power parity terms; table 2q). Sub-Saharan Africa invests the greatest share (2.1 percent of GDP), followed by the Arab States (1.8 percent) and

Latin America and the Caribbean (1.6 percent). In Burkina Faso, Cambodia, Cameroon, Dominican Republic, and Kenya the share of education funding going to primary education exceeded 60 percent in 2005. These large investments in primary education may reflect efforts to provide basic education to relatively large school-age populations—or they may indicate that few students pursue higher levels of education.

Achievements and gaps in data availability

Attention to the MDGs has been accompanied by substantial increases in the availability of health and education statistics. But data availability remains inadequate in some countries, and some countries still lack sufficient information (two or more data points) to assess progress (figure 2r). Efforts to expand and improve statistical output have benefited from programs to strengthen institutions and individual skills within national statistical systems. Where administrative sources are weak, progress in closing data gaps has been made by mounting household surveys to supplement available data.

One of the most serious gaps is the lack of reliable information on births and deaths in poor countries that lack vital registration systems. On average, only half the births in developing countries were reported from civil registration systems to the United Nations Statistics Division during 2000–07, with coverage especially low in South Asia and Sub-Saharan

	Public expenditures on primary education, by region, 2004		2q
Region	Total expenditure on education (percent of GDP)	Expenditure on primary education (percent of GDP)	Expenditure on primary education as share of total expenditure on education (percent)
Arab states	4.9	1.8	37
Central Asia	2.8	0.6	21
Central and Eastern Europe	4.2	1.1	26
East Asia and Pacific	2.8	1.0	36
Latin America and Caribbean	4.4	1.6	36
North America and Western Europe	5.6	1.5	27
South and West Asia	3.6	1.2	33
Sub-Saharan Africa	4.5	2.1	47
World	4.3	1.3	30

Note: Data are classified by United Nations Education, Scientific, and Cultural Organization regions.
Source: UNESCO Institute for Statistics, *Global Education Digest 2007.*

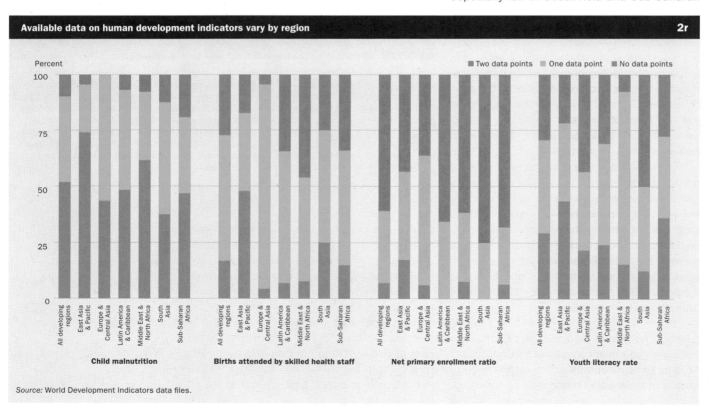

Available data on human development indicators vary by region 2r

Source: World Development Indicators data files.

Africa (figure 2s). Reporting of infant deaths is even lower: fewer than a third of infant deaths in developing countries were reported, with low coverage in all regions except Europe and Central Asia and Latin America and the Caribbean (figure 2t).

For countries lacking vital registration systems, household surveys and censuses are important sources of fertility and mortality data. The 2010 round of censuses, covering 1996–2014, promises to be far more successful than the previous round. More than 500 million people in 27 countries and areas were not included in the 2000 census round. For 2010 only nine countries have not yet scheduled a census, reducing the number of people not enumerated to about 140 million, a drop of 75 percent from the previous census round.

In education, despite improved reporting of school enrollment and completion rates, difficulties remain in measuring dropouts and out of school children. Many children have had some contact with schooling (figure 2u), but there is still a lack of conceptual clarity in the definitions of the school-age population and school participation. Data from school censuses may overestimate enrollment rates because registered children may not show up or may drop out during the school year. Or the data may undercount students because some students who did not register or officially enroll did attend school. Likewise, household surveys may not use consistent definitions of school attendance or may fail to correct for seasonal variation in attendance.

Another problem is inaccuracies in data for school-age populations (the denominator in calculations of enrollment rates). Different compilers may use different estimates of population size, or ministries of educations may use outdated population estimates. For example, some population estimates or enrollment numbers may include migrants while others exclude them. If the school enrollment data include migrant children while the population estimates exclude them, the resulting enrollment rates will not be accurate. Most critical is the problem of going from sample statistics to estimates for the universe if the sample frame or sample design is not accurate. Censuses, which will become available for virtually all developing countries, remain an important source of information on the age-sex structure of populations.

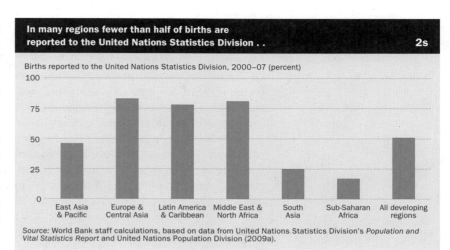

In many regions fewer than half of births are reported to the United Nations Statistics Division . . 2s

Births reported to the United Nations Statistics Division, 2000–07 (percent)

Source: World Bank staff calculations, based on data from United Nations Statistics Division's *Population and Vital Statistics Report* and United Nations Population Division (2009a).

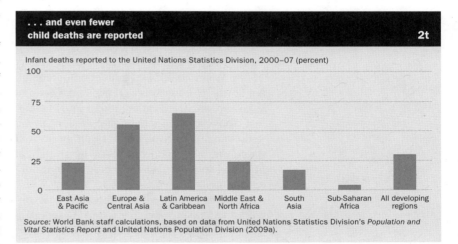

. . . and even fewer child deaths are reported 2t

Infant deaths reported to the United Nations Statistics Division, 2000–07 (percent)

Source: World Bank staff calculations, based on data from United Nations Statistics Division's *Population and Vital Statistics Report* and United Nations Population Division (2009a).

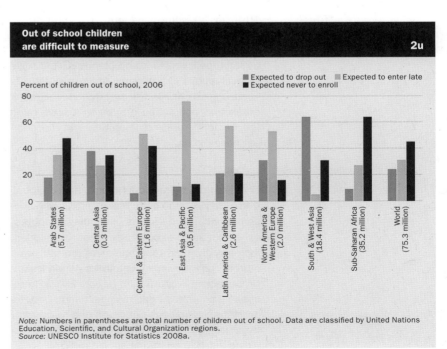

Out of school children are difficult to measure 2u

Percent of children out of school, 2006

■ Expected to drop out ■ Expected to enter late ■ Expected never to enroll

Note: Numbers in parentheses are total number of children out of school. Data are classified by United Nations Education, Scientific, and Cultural Organization regions.
Source: UNESCO Institute for Statistics 2008a.

Beyond the Millennium Development Goals: monitoring emerging challenges

On the whole, people are healthier and better educated than they were 30 years ago, but progress has been deeply unequal. And the nature of some problems is changing at a rate that is wholly unexpected. Thirty years ago about 38 percent of the world's population lived in cities. By 2008 more than 50 percent (3.3 billion people) did. A third of urban dwellers (more than 1 billion people) live in slum areas that lack basic social services. By 2030, 60 percent of the world's population (almost 5 billion people) are projected to live in urban areas, and most of this growth will be concentrated in smaller cities in developing countries and in megacities of unprecedented size in Southern and Eastern Asia (World Health Organization, *World Health Report 2008*). While health and education outcomes are better in urban areas on average, economic and social stratification perpetuates inequities. These and other emerging challenges will raise demand for types of data different from those routinely collected today by statistical offices—and will call for increased national accountability.

Experience shows that targeted interventions and funding have succeeded in expanding programs to deliver services to those most in need. But achieving the MDGs will also require stronger accountability and a clearer focus on data and statistics, analytic methods for new data collection, improved use of data by national policymakers and planners, and regular evaluations of programs and new initiatives. Achieving the MDGs will also require targeting areas and population groups that have been left behind—rural communities and the poorest households.

Health

Urbanization, aging populations, and a globalized lifestyle combine to make chronic and noncommunicable diseases, including diabetes, cancers, cardiovascular diseases, and injuries, increasingly important causes of mortality and morbidity in developing countries (World Health Organization, *World Health Report 2008*). In response, countries need to collect and strengthen statistics on cause of death and move away from fragmented attention to the needs of single-disease programs such as HIV/AIDS.

The increase in noncommunicable diseases, accompanied by a shift in the distribution of death and disease from younger to older people as the population ages, will affect service delivery and the allocation of health budgets. Among the economically and socially deprived populations of poor countries, these changes are most likely to affect children and young adults, especially women. And this rise in chronic, noncommunicable diseases comes on top of an unfinished agenda on communicable diseases and maternal and child health.

In addition to the shifting epidemiological burden of diseases, developing countries, especially low-income countries, continue to struggle with low access to health services. For people in these countries, out-of-pocket expenses make up more than half of health care costs, depriving many families of needed care because they cannot afford it (figure 2v). Also, more than 100 million people worldwide are pushed into poverty each year because of catastrophic health care expenditures (World Health Organization,

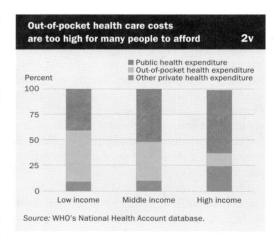

Out-of-pocket health care costs are too high for many people to afford 2v

Source: WHO's National Health Account database.

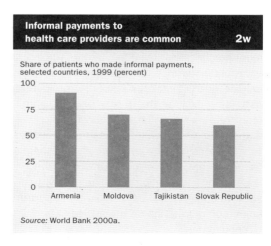

Informal payments to health care providers are common 2w

Source: World Bank 2000a.

World Health Report 2008). Compounding problems of access and equity is weak governance in the delivery of health services. In developing and transition economies, informal payments to health care providers are high (figure 2w).

Reliable mortality statistics, the cornerstone of national health information systems, are necessary for assessing population health, planning health policies and health services, and evaluating epidemiological and other health system programs. And the data are essential for monitoring progress toward the health-related MDGs of reducing maternal and child mortality and mortality from HIV/AIDS, tuberculosis, and malaria. Yet in 2007 only 61 percent of developing countries had complete registration systems, and among these only a handful had reliable cause of death statistics. Few efforts have been made to systematically build or strengthen country capacities to collect and use data. The pace needs to quicken.

Education

Achieving universal primary education (Goal 2) is vital to meeting all the other MDGs. The steady increase in primary school enrollment in nearly all regions is an encouraging sign. But countries still need to translate these enrollment rates into opportunities for learning.

Enrollment is not a sufficient measure of learning. Because school attendance is a better predictor of learning outcomes (Abadzi 2007), monitoring of student attendance needs to be strengthened. Many students enrolled on the first day of school do not actually attend during some or part of the year (table 2x). Retaining all enrolled children in school is a challenge for most countries, requiring varied strategies, concerted effort, and investment. And school retention should translate into instructional time for children, so that they can develop cognitive skills and knowledge. Instructional time varies greatly by country (figure 2y), and few countries systematically monitor learning outcomes by assessing student achievement or participating in regional or international assessments. Countries must shift their focus from access to achievement, making learning outcomes a central part of the education agenda.

Primary school enrollment and attendance, 2003–08 — 2x

Economy or group	Primary school net enrollment rate (percent)		Primary school net attendance rate (percent)	
	Male	Female	Male	Female
Africa	79	74	69	66
Sub-Saharan Africa	76	70	65	63
Eastern and Southern Africa	83	82	69	70
West and Central Africa	68	58	63	58
Middle East and North Africa	92	88	85	81
Asia	92	89	84	81[a]
South Asia	87	82	83	79
East Asia and Pacific	98	97	88	88[a]
Latin America and Caribbean	95	95	92	93
CEE/CIS	92	90	94	92
Developed economies	94	95	..	..
Developing economies	89	86	80	78[a]
Least developed countries	81	76	67	65
World	90	87	81	78[a]

Note: CEE/CIS is Central and Eastern Europe and Commonwealth of Independent States.
a. Excludes China.
Source: UNICEF, *The State of the World's Children 2010.*

Instructional time for children varies considerably by country, 2004–06 — 2y

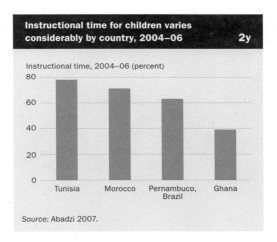

Instructional time, 2004–06 (percent)

Source: Abadzi 2007.

2.1 | Population dynamics

	Population			Average annual population growth		Population age composition			Dependency ratio		Crude death rate	Crude birth rate
							%		% of working-age population		per 1,000 people	per 1,000 people
						Ages 0–14	Ages 15–64	Ages 65+	Young	Old		
		millions		%								
	1990	2008	2015	1990–2008	2008–15	2008	2008	2008	2008	2008	2008	2008
Afghanistan	18.6	29.0	35.0	2.5	2.7	46	51	2	90	4	20	47
Albania	3.3	3.1	3.3	−0.3	0.5	24	66	9	36	14	6	15
Algeria	25.3	34.4	38.1	1.7	1.5	28	68	5	41	7	5	21
Angola	10.7	18.0	21.7	2.9	2.6	45	52	2	87	5	17	43
Argentina	32.5	39.9	42.4	1.1	0.9	25	64	11	40	16	8	17
Armenia	3.5	3.1	3.1	−0.8	0.2	21	68	12	30	17	9	15
Australia	17.1	21.4	23.4	1.3	1.3	19	67	13	28	20	7	14
Austria	7.7	8.3	8.4	0.4	0.2	15	68	17	22	25	9	9
Azerbaijan	7.2	8.7	9.4	1.1	1.1	25	69	7	36	10	6	18
Bangladesh	115.6	160.0	176.3	1.8	1.4	32	64	4	50	6	7	21
Belarus	10.2	9.7	9.4	−0.3	−0.4	15	71	14	21	19	14	11
Belgium	10	10.7	11.0	0.4	0.4	17	66	17	26	26	9	12
Benin	4.8	8.7	10.6	3.3	2.9	43	54	3	81	6	9	39
Bolivia	6.7	9.7	10.8	2.1	1.6	37	59	5	63	8	8	27
Bosnia and Herzegovina	4.3	3.8	3.7	−0.7	−0.2	16	71	14	22	20	10	9
Botswana	1.4	1.9	2.1	2.0	1.3	34	63	4	54	6	12	25
Brazil	149.6	192.0	202.4	1.4	0.8	26	67	7	39	10	6	16
Bulgaria	8.7	7.6	7.3	−0.7	−0.6	13	69	17	19	25	14	10
Burkina Faso	8.8	15.2	19.0	3.0	3.2	46	52	2	89	4	13	47
Burundi	5.7	8.1	9.4	2.0	2.2	39	58	3	67	5	14	34
Cambodia	9.7	14.6	16.4	2.3	1.7	34	62	3	55	5	8	25
Cameroon	12.2	19.1	22.2	2.5	2.1	41	55	4	74	6	14	37
Canada	27.8	33.3	35.7	1.0	1.0	17	70	14	24	20	7	11
Central African Republic	2.9	4.3	4.9	2.2	1.8	41	55	4	74	7	17	35
Chad	6.1	10.9	13.1	3.2	2.6	46	51	3	89	6	17	46
Chile	13.2	16.8	17.9	1.3	0.9	23	68	9	34	13	5	15
China	1,135.2	1,324.7	1,377.7	0.9	0.6	21[a]	72[a]	8[a]	29[a]	11[a]	7	12
Hong Kong SAR, China	5.7	7.0	7.3	1.1	0.7	13	75	13	17	17	6	11
Colombia	33.2	45.0	49.3	1.7	1.3	30	65	5	45	8	6	20
Congo, Dem. Rep.	37	64.3	77.4	3.1	2.7	47	50	3	93	5	17	45
Congo, Rep.	2.4	3.6	4.2	2.2	2.2	41	56	4	73	7	13	35
Costa Rica	3.1	4.5	4.9	2.1	1.3	26	67	6	39	9	4	17
Côte d'Ivoire	12.6	20.6	24.2	2.7	2.3	41	55	4	74	7	11	35
Croatia	4.8	4.4	4.4	−0.4	−0.2	15	68	17	23	25	12	10
Cuba	10.6	11.2	11.2	0.3	0.0	18	70	12	26	16	7	10
Czech Republic	10.4	10.4	10.6	0.0	0.3	14	71	15	20	21	10	11
Denmark	5.1	5.5	5.6	0.4	0.3	18	66	16	28	24	10	12
Dominican Republic	7.4	10.0	10.8	1.7	1.1	32	62	6	51	9	6	23
Ecuador	10.3	13.5	14.6	1.5	1.1	31	62	6	51	10	5	21
Egypt, Arab Rep.	57.8	81.5	91.7	1.9	1.7	32	63	5	52	7	6	25
El Salvador	5.3	6.1	6.4	0.8	0.6	33	60	7	55	12	7	20
Eritrea	3.2	4.9	6.0	2.5	2.8	42	56	2	74	4	8	37
Estonia	1.6	1.3	1.3	−0.9	−0.1	15	68	17	22	25	12	12
Ethiopia	48.3	80.7	96.2	2.9	2.5	44	53	3	83	6	12	38
Finland	5.0	5.3	5.4	0.4	0.3	17	67	17	25	25	9	11
France[b]	56.7	62.3	63.9	0.5	0.4	18	65	17	28	26	9	13
Gabon	0.9	1.4	1.6	2.5	1.8	37	59	4	62	7	10	27
Gambia, The	0.9	1.7	2.0	3.4	2.5	42	55	3	78	5	11	37
Georgia	5.5	4.3	4.1	−1.3	−0.8	17	68	14	25	21	12	12
Germany	79.4	82.1	80.6	0.2	−0.3	14	66	20	21	30	10	8
Ghana	15.0	23.4	26.6	2.5	1.9	39	58	4	67	6	11	32
Greece	10.2	11.2	11.4	0.6	0.2	14	68	18	21	27	10	10
Guatemala	8.9	13.7	16.2	2.4	2.4	42	53	4	79	8	6	33
Guinea	6.1	9.8	11.8	2.6	2.6	43	54	3	80	6	11	40
Guinea-Bissau	1.0	1.6	1.8	2.4	2.3	43	54	3	79	6	17	41
Haiti	7.1	9.9	10.7	1.8	1.1	37	59	4	62	7	9	28
Honduras	4.9	7.3	8.4	2.2	1.9	38	58	4	66	7	5	27

Population dynamics | 2.1

	Population			Average annual population growth		Population age composition			Dependency ratio		Crude death rate	Crude birth rate
							%		% of working-age population			
						Ages 0–14	Ages 15–64	Ages 65+	Young	Old	per 1,000 people	per 1,000 people
	millions			%								
	1990	2008	2015	1990–2008	2008–15	2008	2008	2008	2008	2008	2008	2008
Hungary	10.4	10.0	9.9	−0.2	−0.2	15	69	16	22	23	13	10
India	849.5	1,140.0	1,246.9	1.6	1.3	32	63	5	50	8	7	23
Indonesia	177.4	227.3	247.5	1.4	1.2	27	67	6	41	9	6	19
Iran, Islamic Rep.	54.4	72.0	78.6	1.6	1.3	24	71	5	35	7	6	19
Iraq	18.9	30.7	36.3	2.7	2.4	41	55	3	75	6	6	31
Ireland	3.5	4.4	4.8	1.3	1.0	21	68	11	30	16	6	17
Israel	4.7	7.3	8.2	2.5	1.7	28	62	10	45	16	5	22
Italy	56.7	59.8	60.8	0.3	0.2	14	66	20	22	31	10	10
Jamaica	2.4	2.7	2.8	0.7	0.4	30	62	8	48	12	6	17
Japan	123.5	127.7	125.3	0.2	−0.3	13	65	21	21	33	9	9
Jordan	3.2	5.9	6.8	3.5	2.0	35	61	4	57	6	4	26
Kazakhstan	16.3	15.7	16.9	−0.2	1.0	24	69	7	34	11	10	23
Kenya	23.4	38.8	46.4	2.8	2.6	43	55	3	78	5	12	39
Korea, Dem. Rep.	20.1	23.8	24.4	0.9	0.3	22	68	9	32	14	10	14
Korea, Rep.	42.9	48.6	49.3	0.7	0.2	17	72	10	24	14	5	9
Kosovo	1.9	1.8	1.9	−0.2	0.6	..	..	..	..	..	7	19
Kuwait	2.1	2.7	3.2	1.4	2.1	23	74	2	31	3	2	18
Kyrgyz Republic	4.4	5.3	5.7	1.0	1.2	30	65	5	46	8	7	24
Lao PDR	4.2	6.2	7.0	2.2	1.8	38	58	4	66	6	7	27
Latvia	2.7	2.3	2.2	−0.9	−0.5	14	69	17	20	25	14	11
Lebanon	3.0	4.2	4.4	1.9	0.8	26	67	7	39	11	7	16
Lesotho	1.6	2.0	2.2	1.4	0.8	39	56	5	70	8	17	29
Liberia	2.2	3.8	4.8	3.1	3.3	43	54	3	80	6	10	38
Libya	4.4	6.3	7.2	2.0	1.8	30	66	4	46	6	4	23
Lithuania	3.7	3.4	3.2	−0.5	−0.7	15	69	16	22	23	13	10
Macedonia, FYR	1.9	2.0	2.0	0.4	0.0	18	70	12	26	17	9	11
Madagascar	11.3	19.1	22.8	2.9	2.5	43	54	3	81	6	9	36
Malawi	9.5	14.8	18.0	2.5	2.7	46	50	3	92	6	12	40
Malaysia	18.1	27.0	30.0	2.2	1.5	30	65	5	46	7	4	20
Mali	8.7	12.7	15.4	2.1	2.7	44	53	2	83	4	16	43
Mauritania	2.0	3.2	3.7	2.7	2.1	40	58	3	69	5	10	34
Mauritius	1.1	1.3	1.3	1.0	0.4	23	70	7	33	10	7	13
Mexico	83.2	106.4	113.1	1.4	0.9	29	65	6	45	10	5	18
Moldova	4.4	3.6	3.5	−1.0	−0.7	17	72	11	24	16	13	12
Mongolia	2.2	2.6	2.9	1.0	1.1	27	70	4	38	6	7	19
Morocco	24.8	31.6	34.3	1.3	1.2	29	66	5	44	8	6	20
Mozambique	13.5	22.4	25.9	2.8	2.1	44	53	3	84	6	16	39
Myanmar	40.8	49.6	53.0	1.1	1.0	27	67	5	40	8	10	21
Namibia	1.4	2.1	2.4	2.3	1.8	37	59	4	63	6	9	28
Nepal	19.1	28.8	32.5	2.3	1.7	37	59	4	63	7	6	25
Netherlands	15.0	16.4	16.8	0.5	0.3	18	67	15	27	22	8	11
New Zealand	3.4	4.3	4.6	1.2	1.0	21	67	13	31	19	7	15
Nicaragua	4.1	5.7	6.3	1.7	1.4	36	60	4	60	7	5	25
Niger	7.9	14.7	19.1	3.4	3.8	50	48	2	103	4	15	54
Nigeria	97.3	151.2	178.7	2.4	2.4	43	54	3	79	6	16	40
Norway	4.2	4.8	5.1	0.7	0.9	19	66	15	29	22	9	13
Oman	1.8	2.8	3.2	2.3	2.0	32	65	3	49	4	3	22
Pakistan	108.0	166.1	193.5	2.4	2.2	37	59	4	63	7	7	30
Panama	2.4	3.4	3.8	1.9	1.5	30	64	6	46	10	5	21
Papua New Guinea	4.1	6.6	7.7	2.6	2.2	40	57	2	70	4	8	31
Paraguay	4.2	6.2	7.0	2.1	1.6	34	61	5	57	8	6	25
Peru	21.8	28.8	31.2	1.6	1.1	31	64	6	48	9	5	21
Philippines	62.4	90.3	102.7	2.1	1.8	34	62	4	56	7	5	25
Poland	38.1	38.1	38.0	0.0	−0.1	15	71	13	21	19	10	11
Portugal	9.9	10.6	10.7	0.4	0.0	15	67	18	23	26	10	10
Puerto Rico	3.5	4.0	4.0	0.6	0.3	21	66	13	31	20	8	12
Qatar	0.5	1.3	1.6	5.6c	3.4	16	83	1	20	1	2	12

2.1 | Population dynamics

	Population			Average annual population growth		Population age composition			Dependency ratio		Crude death rate	Crude birth rate
							%		% of working-age population		per 1,000 people	per 1,000 people
		millions		%		Ages 0–14	Ages 15–64	Ages 65+	Young	Old		
	1990	2008	2015	1990–2008	2008–15	2008	2008	2008	2008	2008	2008	2008
Romania	23.2	21.5	21.0	−0.4	−0.4	15	70	15	22	21	12	10
Russian Federation	148.3	142.0	139.0	−0.2	−0.3	15	72	13	20	18	15	12
Rwanda	7.2	9.7	11.7	1.7	2.7	42	55	3	76	5	14	41
Saudi Arabia	16.3	24.6	28.6	2.3	2.1	33	64	3	51	4	4	23
Senegal	7.5	12.2	14.5	2.7	2.5	44	54	2	81	4	11	38
Serbia	7.6	7.4	7.2	−0.2	−0.3	18[d]	68[d]	15[d]	26[d]	21[d]	14	9
Sierra Leone	4.1	5.6	6.6	1.7	2.4	43	55	2	79	3	16	40
Singapore	3.0	4.8	5.4	2.6	1.5	17	73	9	23	13	4	10
Slovak Republic	5.3	5.4	5.4	0.1	0.1	16	72	12	22	17	10	11
Slovenia	2.0	2.0	2.1	0.1	0.4	14	70	16	20	23	9	10
Somalia	6.6	8.9	10.7	1.7	2.6	45	52	3	86	5	16	44
South Africa	35.2	48.7	51.1	1.8	0.7	31	65	4	47	7	15	22
Spain	38.8	45.6	47.9	0.9	0.7	15	68	17	22	25	9	11
Sri Lanka	17.1	20.2	21.2	0.9	0.7	24	68	7	35	11	6	19
Sudan	27.1	41.3	47.7	2.3	2.0	40	57	4	69	6	10	31
Swaziland	0.9	1.2	1.3	1.7	1.4	40	57	3	70	6	16	30
Sweden	8.6	9.2	9.6	0.4	0.6	17	66	18	25	27	10	12
Switzerland	6.7	7.6	7.9	0.7	0.4	16	68	17	23	25	8	10
Syrian Arab Republic	12.7	20.6	24.1	2.7	2.2	35	61	3	58	5	3	28
Tajikistan	5.3	6.8	7.8	1.4	1.8	38	59	4	64	6	6	28
Tanzania	25.5	42.5	52.1	2.8	2.9	45	52	3	85	6	11	42
Thailand	56.7	67.4	69.9	1.0	0.5	22	71	7	31	11	9	15
Timor-Leste	0.7	1.1	1.4	2.2	3.3	45	52	3	87	6	9	40
Togo	3.9	6.5	7.6	2.8	2.3	40	56	3	72	6	8	33
Trinidad and Tobago	1.2	1.3	1.4	0.5	0.3	21	73	7	29	9	8	15
Tunisia	8.2	10.3	11.1	1.3	1.1	24	70	7	34	10	6	18
Turkey	56.1	73.9	79.9	1.5	1.1	27	67	6	41	9	6	18
Turkmenistan	3.7	5.0	5.5	1.8	1.3	30	66	4	46	7	8	22
Uganda	17.7	31.7	39.7	3.2	3.2	49	48	3	101	5	13	46
Ukraine	51.9	46.3	44.4	−0.6	−0.6	14	70	16	20	23	16	11
United Arab Emirates	1.9	4.5	5.2	4.9	2.1	19	80	1	24	1	2	14
United Kingdom	57.2	61.4	63.8	0.4	0.5	18	66	16	27	25	9	13
United States	249.6	304.1	323.5	1.1	0.9	20	67	13	31	19	8	14
Uruguay	3.1	3.3	3.4	0.4	0.3	23	63	14	36	22	9	15
Uzbekistan	20.5	27.3	30.2	1.6	1.5	30	65	5	46	7	5	22
Venezuela, RB	19.8	27.9	31.0	1.9	1.5	30	65	5	47	8	5	21
Vietnam	66.2	86.2	92.8	1.5	1.1	27	67	6	39	9	5	17
West Bank and Gaza	2.0	3.9	4.8	3.8	2.8	45	52	3	87	6	4	36
Yemen, Rep.	12.3	22.9	27.8	3.5	2.8	44	53	2	83	4	7	37
Zambia	7.9	12.6	15.0	2.6	2.4	46	51	3	91	6	17	43
Zimbabwe	10.5	12.5	14.0	1.0	1.7	40	56	4	72	7	16	30
World	**5,278.9 s**	**6,697.3 s**	**7,241.2 s**	**1.3 w**	**1.1 w**	**27 w**	**65 w**	**7 w**	**42 w**	**11 w**	**8 w**	**20 w**
Low income	653.6	976.2	1,127.4	2.2	2.1	38	58	4	66	6	11	32
Middle income	3,685.7	4,652.3	5,006.3	1.3	1.0	27	66	6	41	10	8	19
Lower middle income	2,889.5	3,703.0	4,011.2	1.4	1.1	28	66	6	42	9	8	20
Upper middle income	796.2	949.3	995.1	1.0	0.7	25	67	8	36	12	8	17
Low & middle income	4,339.3	5,628.5	6,133.7	1.4	1.2	29	65	6	45	9	8	21
East Asia & Pacific	1,599.6	1,929.6	2,035.6	1.0	0.8	23	70	7	33	10	7	14
Europe & Central Asia	433.2	443.3	449.2	0.1	0.2	19	70	11	28	16	11	14
Latin America & Carib.	435.5	566.1	606.8	1.5	1.0	29	65	7	44	10	6	19
Middle East & N. Africa	227.4	325.2	366.1	2.0	1.7	31	64	4	49	7	6	24
South Asia	1,128.7	1,545.1	1,706.5	1.7	1.4	33	63	5	52	7	7	24
Sub-Saharan Africa	514.9	819.3	969.5	2.6	2.4	43	54	3	79	6	14	38
High income	939.6	1,068.7	1,107.4	0.7	0.5	18	67	15	26	23	8	12
Euro area	301.6	326.1	331.0	0.4	0.2	15	67	18	23	27	9	10

a. Includes Taiwan, China. b. Excludes the French overseas departments of French Guiana, Guadeloupe, Martinique, and Réunion. c. Increase is due to a surge in the number of migrants since 2004. d. Includes Kosovo.

Population estimates are usually based on national population censuses, but the frequency and quality vary by country. Most countries conduct a complete enumeration no more than once a decade. Estimates for the years before and after the census are interpolations or extrapolations based on demographic models. Errors and undercounting occur even in high-income countries; in developing countries errors may be substantial because of limits in the transport, communications, and other resources required to conduct and analyze a full census.

The quality and reliability of official demographic data are also affected by public trust in the government, government commitment to full and accurate enumeration, confidentiality and protection against misuse of census data, and census agencies' independence from political influence. Moreover, comparability of population indicators is limited by differences in the concepts, definitions, collection procedures, and estimation methods used by national statistical agencies and other organizations that collect the data.

Of the 155 economies in the table and the 55 economies in table 1.6, 180 (about 86 percent) conducted a census during the 2000 census round (1995–2004). As of March 2010, 61 countries have completed a census for the 2010 census round (2005–14). The currentness of a census and the availability of complementary data from surveys or registration systems are objective ways to judge demographic data quality. Some European countries' registration systems offer complete information on population in the absence of a census. See table 2.17 and *Primary data documentation* for the most recent census or survey year and for the completeness of registration.

Current population estimates for developing countries that lack recent census data and pre- and post-census estimates for countries with census data are provided by the United Nations Population Division and other agencies. The cohort component method—a standard estimation method for estimating and projecting population—requires fertility, mortality, and net migration data, often collected from sample surveys, which can be small or limited in coverage. Population estimates are from demographic modeling and so are susceptible to biases and errors from shortcomings in the model and in the data. Because the five-year age group is the cohort unit and five-year period data are used, interpolations to obtain annual data or single age structure may not reflect actual events or age composition.

The growth rate of the total population conceals age-group differences in growth rates. In many developing countries the once rapidly growing under-15

population is shrinking. Previously high fertility rates and declining mortality rates are now reflected in the larger share of the working-age population.

Dependency ratios capture variations in the proportions of children, elderly people, and working-age people in the population that imply the dependency burden that the working-age population bears in relation to children and the elderly. But dependency ratios show only the age composition of a population, not economic dependency. Some children and elderly people are part of the labor force, and many working-age people are not.

Vital rates are based on data from birth and death registration systems, censuses, and sample surveys by national statistical offices and other organizations, or on demographic analysis. Data for 2008 for most high-income countries are provisional estimates based on vital registers. The estimates for many countries are projections based on extrapolations of levels and trends from earlier years or interpolations of population estimates and projections from the United Nations Population Division.

Vital registers are the preferred source for these data, but in many developing countries systems for registering births and deaths are absent or incomplete because of deficiencies in the coverage of events or geographic areas. Many developing countries carry out special household surveys that ask respondents about recent births and deaths. Estimates derived in this way are subject to sampling errors and recall errors.

The United Nations Statistics Division monitors the completeness of vital registration systems. The share of countries with at least 90 percent complete vital registration rose from 45 percent in 1988 to 61 percent in 2007. Still, some of the most populous developing countries—China, India, Indonesia, Brazil, Pakistan, Bangladesh, Nigeria—lack complete vital registration systems. From 2000 to 2007, on average 64 percent of births, 62 percent of deaths, and 45 percent of infant deaths were registered and reported to the United Nations Statistics Division.

International migration is the only other factor besides birth and death rates that directly determines a country's population growth. From 1990 to 2005 the number of migrants in high-income countries rose 40 million. About 195 million people (3 percent of the world population) live outside their home country. Estimating migration is difficult. At any time many people are located outside their home country as tourists, workers, or refugees or for other reasons. Standards for the duration and purpose of international moves that qualify as migration vary, and estimates require information on flows into and out of countries that is difficult to collect.

• **Population** is based on the de facto definition of population, which counts all residents regardless of legal status or citizenship—except for refugees not permanently settled in the country of asylum, who are generally considered part of the population of their country of origin. The values shown are mid-year estimates for 1990 and 2008 and projections for 2015. • **Average annual population growth** is the exponential change for the period indicated. See *Statistical methods* for more information. • **Population age composition** is the percentage of the total population that is in specific age groups. • **Dependency ratio** is the ratio of dependents—people younger than 15 or older than 64—to the working-age population—those ages 15–64. • **Crude death rate** and **crude birth rate** are the number of deaths and the number of live births occurring during the year, per 1,000 people, estimated at midyear. Subtracting the crude death rate from the crude birth rate provides the rate of natural increase, which is equal to the population growth rate in the absence of migration.

Data sources

The World Bank's population estimates are compiled and produced by its Development Data Group in consultation with its Human Development Network, operational staff, and country offices. The United Nations Population Division's *World Population Prospects: The 2008 Revision* is a source of the demographic data for more than half the countries, most of them developing countries, and the source of data on age composition and dependency ratios for all countries. Other important sources are census reports and other statistical publications from national statistical offices; household surveys conducted by national agencies, Macro International, and the U.S. Centers for Disease Control and Prevention; Eurostat's *Demographic Statistics;* Secretariat of the Pacific Community, Statistics and Demography Programme; and U.S. Bureau of the Census, International Data Base.

2.2

Labor force structure

	Labor force participation rate				Labor force				
	% ages 15 and older				Total millions		Ages 15 and older average annual % growth	Female % of labor force	
	Male		Female						
	1990	2008	1990	2008	1990	2008	1990–2008	1990	2008
Afghanistan	87	89	32	33	5.9	9.3	2.5	26.2	26.6
Albania	84	70	51	49	1.4	1.4	0.1	39.9	42.3
Algeria	75	77	23	37	7.0	14.5	4.0	23.4	31.2
Angola	90	89	74	74	4.6	8.0	3.1	46.3	46.8
Argentina	78	75	43	51	13.5	19.1	1.9	36.9	41.1
Armenia	78	67	61	59	1.7	1.6	−0.3	46.3	49.6
Australia	74	70	52	58	8.5	11.3	1.6	41.3	45.3
Austria	68	65	43	53	3.5	4.3	1.1	40.9	45.5
Azerbaijan	78	71	59	61	3.1	4.1	1.6	46.8	50.2
Bangladesh	89	84	61	58	49.5	76.8	2.4	39.9	40.9
Belarus	74	65	60	55	5.3	4.9	−0.4	48.9	49.5
Belgium	59	58	36	47	3.9	4.8	1.1	39.0	44.9
Benin	88	86	57	67	1.9	3.6	3.5	41.1	45.7
Bolivia	85	83	59	62	2.8	4.4	2.6	43.1	43.9
Bosnia and Herzegovina	82	66	53	55	2.0	1.9	0.0[a]	45.2	47.1
Botswana	78	64	64	72	0.5	1.0	3.3	45.5	47.5
Brazil	84	81	45	60	62.6	99.9	2.6	35.1	43.5
Bulgaria	63	55	55	49	4.1	3.7	−0.6	47.9	46.3
Burkina Faso	91	90	77	78	3.9	6.9	3.2	48.0	47.0
Burundi	90	91	91	91	2.8	4.4	2.5	52.5	52.7
Cambodia	85	87	78	73	4.3	7.5	3.1	52.8	48.8
Cameroon	79	75	48	53	4.4	7.5	3.0	37.5	39.8
Canada	75	71	58	62	14.7	18.7	1.3	44.1	46.9
Central African Republic	88	88	69	71	1.3	2.0	2.4	45.6	46.6
Chad	84	77	65	63	2.4	4.2	3.1	45.6	45.3
Chile	77	70	32	44	5.0	7.7	2.4	30.5	37.5
China	85	78	73	68	643.9	776.9	1.0	44.8	44.6
Hong Kong SAR, China	79	67	47	53	2.9	3.7	1.5	36.3	45.8
Colombia	76	78	29	41	11.2	18.6	2.8	28.2	35.7
Congo, Dem. Rep.	86	89	53	56	13.4	24.0	3.2	39.9	40.6
Congo, Rep.	83	82	59	63	1.0	1.6	2.6	42.1	43.5
Costa Rica	84	78	33	45	1.2	2.1	3.3	27.4	35.2
Côte d'Ivoire	89	85	43	51	4.7	8.1	3.1	30.1	36.7
Croatia	74	59	47	46	2.2	2.0	−0.5	42.7	45.5
Cuba	72	68	36	42	4.4	5.1	0.8	33.0	38.0
Czech Republic	79	66	52	49	4.9	5.2	0.3	44.4	43.4
Denmark	74	68	62	61	2.9	3.0	0.1	46.1	46.9
Dominican Republic	82	72	43	51	2.9	4.4	2.3	33.2	38.9
Ecuador	78	78	33	47	3.5	5.7	2.8	29.5	37.9
Egypt, Arab Rep.	74	71	27	23	16.8	26.3	2.5	26.6	23.9
El Salvador	80	75	41	47	1.9	2.5	1.5	35.2	42.2
Eritrea	88	86	55	60	1.2	2.1	3.2	41.4	43.6
Estonia	71	64	63	55	0.8	0.7	−1.0	49.5	49.2
Ethiopia	89	91	72	78	21.5	38.2	3.2	45.1	47.1
Finland	70	63	59	58	2.6	2.7	0.2	47.1	48.1
France	63	59	46	51	25.0	28.6	0.7	43.3	47.0
Gabon	83	79	63	69	0.4	0.7	3.0	44.2	46.4
Gambia, The	86	83	71	71	0.4	0.7	3.4	46.2	46.2
Georgia	82	74	60	55	2.8	2.3	−1.2	46.9	47.0
Germany	71	64	45	53	38.8	42.4	0.5	40.7	45.4
Ghana	74	73	70	74	6.0	10.6	3.2	48.9	49.2
Greece	65	63	36	43	4.2	5.2	1.2	36.2	40.4
Guatemala	89	84	39	48	3.1	5.3	3.0	31.0	37.8
Guinea	90	89	79	79	2.9	4.7	2.7	46.8	46.8
Guinea-Bissau	86	90	59	60	0.4	0.6	2.4	43.0	42.4
Haiti	81	83	57	58	2.8	4.4	2.5	43.0	42.7
Honduras	87	81	41	42	1.7	2.8	2.7	32.3	34.0

Labor force structure | **2.2**

	Labor force participation rate				Labor force				
	% ages 15 and older				Total millions		Ages 15 and older average annual % growth	Female % of labor force	
	Male		Female						
	1990	2008	1990	2008	1990	2008	1990–2008	1990	2008
Hungary	64	57	46	43	4.5	4.3	–0.3	44.5	45.4
India	85	81	34	33	317.8	449.9	1.9	27.1	27.8
Indonesia	81	86	50	52	74.9	112.8	2.3	38.4	38.4
Iran, Islamic Rep.	80	75	22	31	15.5	27.8	3.2	20.1	30.1
Iraq	73	69	11	13	4.3	7.5	3.0	13.1	16.1
Ireland	68	72	35	54	1.3	2.2	2.8	33.9	42.8
Israel	61	59	42	54	1.7	3.1	3.5	40.6	46.0
Italy	64	58	35	38	23.7	25.2	0.3	36.5	40.4
Jamaica	80	73	65	57	1.1	1.2	0.5	46.6	45.1
Japan	77	69	50	49	63.9	66.9	0.3	40.7	41.5
Jordan	68	70	15	23	0.7	1.9	5.2	16.2	22.8
Kazakhstan	78	75	62	66	7.8	8.5	0.4	47.0	50.0
Kenya	90	87	75	76	9.8	18.2	3.4	46.0	46.5
Korea, Dem. Rep.	79	78	55	55	10.0	12.2	1.1	42.6	42.6
Korea, Rep.	73	72	47	50	19.2	24.4	1.3	39.7	41.9
Kosovo	..	..	..	..	..	..	..	..	..
Kuwait	81	81	36	44	0.9	1.4	2.8	22.4	24.3
Kyrgyz Republic	74	75	58	56	1.8	2.5	1.8	46.1	42.6
Lao PDR	83	80	80	78	1.9	3.0	2.4	49.8	50.6
Latvia	76	69	63	56	1.4	1.2	–1.0	49.6	48.9
Lebanon	83	77	20	22	0.9	1.4	2.8	23.3	24.9
Lesotho	85	75	68	70	0.7	0.9	1.9	51.7	52.4
Liberia	86	85	65	67	0.8	1.5	3.3	46.7	47.6
Libya	78	77	15	24	1.2	2.3	3.7	14.8	21.9
Lithuania	73	60	59	51	1.9	1.6	–0.9	48.1	48.9
Macedonia, FYR	73	65	46	43	0.8	0.9	0.6	40.7	39.7
Madagascar	85	89	83	84	5.4	9.4	3.1	48.4	49.2
Malawi	80	80	76	75	3.9	6.1	2.5	50.7	49.9
Malaysia	80	80	43	44	7.0	11.7	2.9	34.5	35.2
Mali	70	66	37	37	2.5	3.7	2.1	36.1	36.8
Mauritania	84	80	53	59	0.7	1.4	3.4	39.8	41.7
Mauritius	82	75	38	42	0.4	0.6	1.4	32.1	36.4
Mexico	84	79	34	43	29.9	46.7	2.5	30.0	36.0
Moldova	73	48	61	47	2.1	1.5	–2.0	48.7	50.7
Mongolia	65	61	63	67	0.9	1.4	2.5	45.6	47.4
Morocco	82	79	25	27	7.8	11.8	2.3	23.7	26.1
Mozambique	84	77	85	85	6.3	10.8	3.0	53.2	52.1
Myanmar	87	86	71	64	20.7	26.8	1.4	45.3	44.5
Namibia	64	60	48	52	0.4	0.8	3.0	44.9	46.7
Nepal	80	76	52	63	7.5	12.9	3.0	38.0	45.4
Netherlands	69	69	43	59	6.9	8.9	1.4	38.8	45.5
New Zealand	73	73	54	62	1.7	2.3	1.7	43.0	46.2
Nicaragua	85	87	39	46	1.4	2.3	2.8	32.3	37.8
Niger	87	88	27	38	2.3	4.6	3.8	24.7	30.8
Nigeria	75	71	36	39	29.4	48.6	2.8	33.0	34.9
Norway	71	69	57	64	2.2	2.6	1.0	44.7	47.6
Oman	81	77	19	25	0.6	1.1	3.4	13.7	18.3
Pakistan	85	85	14	21	31.0	55.8	3.3	12.7	19.2
Panama	81	79	39	49	0.9	1.6	3.0	32.4	36.9
Papua New Guinea	75	73	71	71	1.8	2.9	2.7	46.9	48.9
Paraguay	82	84	47	56	1.7	2.9	3.1	34.9	38.7
Peru	75	82	49	57	8.3	13.3	2.6	39.7	43.3
Philippines	83	80	48	49	24.1	37.9	2.5	36.5	38.2
Poland	71	60	55	47	18.1	17.7	–0.1	45.4	44.8
Portugal	72	68	49	56	4.7	5.6	0.9	42.4	46.8
Puerto Rico	59	56	31	37	1.2	1.5	1.3	35.8	41.7
Qatar	93	90	40	48	0.3	0.9	6.7	13.5	11.6

	Labor force participation rate				Labor force				
	% ages 15 and older				Total millions		Ages 15 and older average annual % growth	Female % of labor force	
	Male		Female						
	1990	**2008**	**1990**	**2008**	**1990**	**2008**	**1990–2008**	**1990**	**2008**
Romania	66	58	60	47	11.8	10.0	−0.9	46.3	44.5
Russian Federation	75	69	60	57	76.8	76.0	−0.1	48.6	49.7
Rwanda	88	80	87	86	3.2	4.8	2.3	52.1	52.8
Saudi Arabia	80	80	15	21	5.0	9.0	3.2	11.5	16.3
Senegal	90	87	62	65	3.0	5.2	3.0	40.8	43.1
Serbia	..	..	..	..	..	..	..	..	..
Sierra Leone	65	67	66	66	1.6	2.1	1.6	50.9	51.4
Singapore	79	75	51	54	1.6	2.6	2.9	39.1	41.7
Slovak Republic	78	68	59	51	2.6	2.7	0.3	46.8	44.7
Slovenia	75	64	47	54	0.8	1.0	1.2	46.8	46.5
Somalia	89	88	58	57	2.6	3.5	1.6	41.8	40.9
South Africa	64	60	36	47	10.4	18.6	3.2	37.5	43.7
Spain	68	66	34	49	15.6	22.8	2.1	34.8	43.0
Sri Lanka	79	74	37	35	6.8	8.3	1.1	31.8	32.7
Sudan	78	72	27	31	8.0	13.1	2.7	26.0	29.5
Swaziland	79	68	45	53	0.3	0.4	2.7	41.2	43.4
Sweden	70	67	63	61	4.7	5.0	0.3	47.7	47.4
Switzerland	77	72	57	61	3.8	4.4	0.8	42.9	46.5
Syrian Arab Republic	81	78	18	21	3.3	6.7	4.0	18.3	20.7
Tajikistan	83	68	59	56	2.1	2.8	1.7	43.3	43.6
Tanzania	93	90	87	86	12.3	20.8	2.9	49.8	49.4
Thailand	87	80	75	66	32.1	38.5	1.0	47.0	46.2
Timor-Leste	81	83	58	59	0.3	0.4	1.7	40.4	40.9
Togo	88	87	56	63	1.5	2.9	3.5	40.1	43.3
Trinidad and Tobago	76	78	39	54	0.5	0.7	2.3	35.0	43.0
Tunisia	75	70	21	26	2.4	3.8	2.5	21.6	26.6
Turkey	81	70	34	25	20.7	25.8	1.2	29.7	26.2
Turkmenistan	74	70	58	61	1.4	2.4	2.8	46.1	46.7
Uganda	91	90	81	78	7.9	13.6	3.0	47.7	46.6
Ukraine	71	64	56	52	25.5	23.1	−0.6	49.2	48.9
United Arab Emirates	92	94	25	42	1.0	2.8	6.0	9.8	15.5
United Kingdom	73	67	52	55	29.0	31.5	0.5	43.2	45.7
United States	75	70	57	59	129.2	158.2	1.1	44.4	46.1
Uruguay	71	73	48	53	1.4	1.6	0.9	40.8	43.7
Uzbekistan	85	70	53	58	7.3	12.3	2.9	45.5	45.9
Venezuela, RB	82	81	36	51	7.2	12.7	3.2	30.5	39.1
Vietnam	81	75	74	68	31.1	45.6	2.1	50.7	48.7
West Bank and Gaza	66	67	11	16	0.4	0.9	4.6	13.8	18.0
Yemen, Rep.	70	66	16	20	2.6	6.0	4.5	18.0	20.8
Zambia	81	81	61	60	3.0	4.7	2.5	44.3	43.8
Zimbabwe	80	78	67	60	4.1	4.9	1.0	46.3	47.8
World	**80 w**	**77 w**	**52 w**	**52 w**	**2,322.0 t**	**3,102.8 t**	**1.6 w**	**39.2 w**	**40.4 w**
Low income	85	83	65	65	276.8	441.4	2.6	44.1	44.5
Middle income	82	78	51	49	1,612.4	2,159.8	1.6	37.8	38.8
Lower middle income	83	79	53	49	1,290.3	1,727.9	1.6	37.7	38.1
Upper middle income	78	73	46	50	322.0	432.0	1.6	38.0	42.0
Low & middle income	83	79	53	52	1,889.1	2,601.3	1.8	38.7	39.8
East Asia & Pacific	84	79	69	64	847.3	1,079.8	1.3	44.1	44.6
Europe & Central Asia	75	67	56	50	199.9	200.0	0.0[a]	45.8	45.2
Latin America & Carib.	81	79	40	52	163.3	264.5	2.7	32.1	41.1
Middle East & N. Africa	77	73	22	26	62.4	111.1	3.2	21.4	26.5
South Asia	85	82	35	35	421.5	618.6	2.1	28.1	29.4
Sub-Saharan Africa	82	80	57	60	194.7	327.2	2.9	42.2	43.6
High income	72	68	49	53	432.9	501.5	0.8	41.1	43.3
Euro area	67	62	42	49	130.4	147.6	0.7	39.4	43.7

a. Less than 0.05.

Labor force structure | 2.2

The labor force is the supply of labor available for producing goods and services in an economy. It includes people who are currently employed and people who are unemployed but seeking work as well as first-time job-seekers. Not everyone who works is included, however. Unpaid workers, family workers, and students are often omitted, and some countries do not count members of the armed forces. Labor force size tends to vary during the year as seasonal workers enter and leave.

Data on the labor force are compiled by the International Labour Organization (ILO) from labor force surveys, censuses, establishment censuses and surveys, and administrative records such as employment exchange registers and unemployment insurance schemes. For some countries a combination of these sources is used. Labor force surveys are the most comprehensive source for internationally comparable labor force data. They can cover all noninstitutionalized civilians, all branches and sectors of the economy, and all categories of workers, including people holding multiple jobs. By contrast, labor force data from population censuses are often based on a limited number of questions on the economic characteristics of individuals, with little scope to probe. The resulting data often differ from labor force survey data and vary considerably by country, depending on the census scope and coverage. Establishment censuses and surveys provide data only on the employed population, not unemployed workers, workers in small establishments, or workers in the informal sector (ILO, *Key Indicators of the Labour Market 2001–2002*).

The reference period of a census or survey is another important source of differences: in some countries data refer to people's status on the day of the census or survey or during a specific period before the inquiry date, while in others data are recorded without reference to any period. In developing countries, where the household is often the basic unit of production and all members contribute to output, but some at low intensity or irregularly, the estimated labor force may be much smaller than the numbers actually working.

Differing definitions of employment age also affect comparability. For most countries the working age is 15 and older, but in some countries children younger than 15 work full- or part-time and are included in the estimates. Similarly, some countries have an upper age limit. As a result, calculations may systematically over- or underestimate actual rates. For

further information on source, reference period, or definition, consult the original source.

The labor force participation rates in the table are from the ILO's Key Indicators of the Labour Market, 6th edition, database. These harmonized estimates use strict data selection criteria and enhanced methods to ensure comparability across countries and over time, including collection and tabulation methodologies and methods applied to such country-specific factors as military service requirements. Estimates are based mainly on labor force surveys, with other sources (population censuses and nationally reported estimates) used only when no survey data are available.

Participation rates indicate the relative size of the labor supply. Beginning in the 2008 edition of *World Development Indicators,* the indicator covers the population ages 15 and older, to include people who continue working past age 65. In previous editions the indicator was for the population ages 15–64, so participation rates are not comparable across editions.

The labor force estimates in the table were calculated by applying labor force participation rates from the ILO database to World Bank population estimates to create a series consistent with these population estimates. This procedure sometimes results in labor force estimates that differ slightly from those in the ILO's *Yearbook of Labour Statistics* and its database Key Indicators of the Labour Market.

Estimates of women in the labor force and employment are generally lower than those of men and are not comparable internationally, reflecting that demographic, social, legal, and cultural trends and norms determine whether women's activities are regarded as economic. In many countries many women work on farms or in other family enterprises without pay, and others work in or near their homes, mixing work and family activities during the day.

• **Labor force participation rate** is the proportion of the population ages 15 and older that is economically active: all people who supply labor for the production of goods and services during a specified period. • **Total labor force** is people ages 15 and older who meet the ILO definition of the economically active population. It includes both the employed and the unemployed. • **Average annual percentage growth of the labor force** is calculated using the exponential endpoint method (see *Statistical methods* for more information). • **Female labor force as as a percentage of the labor force** shows the extent to which women are active in the labor force.

Data on labor force participation rates are from the ILO's Key Indicators of the Labour Market, 6th edition, database. Labor force numbers were calculated by World Bank staff, applying labor force participation rates from the ILO database to population estimates.

Employment by economic activity

	Agriculture				Industry				Services			
	Male % of male employment		Female % of female employment		Male % of male employment		Female % of female employment		Male % of male employment		Female % of female employment	
	1990–92[a]	2004–08[a]	1990–92[a]	2004–08[a]	1990–92[a]	2004–08[a]	1990–92[a]	2004–08[a]	1990–92[a]	2004–08[a]	1990–92[a]	2004–08[a]
Afghanistan	..	..	..	..	..	..	..	..	..	..	..	..
Albania	..	..	..	..	..	..	..	..	..	..	..	..
Algeria	..	20	..	22	..	26	..	28	..	54	..	49
Angola	..	..	..	..	..	..	..	..	..	..	..	..
Argentina	0[b,c]	3[c]	0[b,c]	0[b,c]	40[c]	34[c]	18[c]	11[c]	59[c]	63[c]	81[c]	88[c]
Armenia	..	46	..	46	..	21	..	10	..	33	..	45
Australia	6	4	4	2	32	31	12	9	61	64	84	89
Austria	6	6	8	6	47	37	20	12	46	57	72	82
Azerbaijan	..	40	..	38	..	17	..	9	..	44	..	53
Bangladesh	54	42	85	68	16	15	9	13	25	43	2	19
Belarus	..	..	..	..	..	..	..	..	..	..	..	..
Belgium	3	2	2	1	41	36	16	11	56	61	81	88
Benin	..	..	..	..	..	..	..	..	..	..	..	..
Bolivia	3[c]	..	1[c]	..	42[c]	..	17[c]	..	55[c]	..	82[c]	..
Bosnia and Herzegovina	..	..	..	..	..	..	..	..	..	..	..	..
Botswana	..	35	..	24	..	19	..	11	..	46	..	65
Brazil	31[c]	23	25[c]	15	27[c]	28	10[c]	13	43[c]	50	65[c]	72
Bulgaria	..	9	..	6	..	42	..	29	..	49	..	65
Burkina Faso	..	..	..	..	..	..	..	..	..	..	..	..
Burundi	..	..	..	..	..	..	..	..	..	..	..	..
Cambodia	..	..	..	..	..	..	..	..	..	..	..	..
Cameroon	..	..	..	..	..	..	..	..	..	..	..	..
Canada	6[c]	3[c]	2[c]	2[c]	31[c]	32[c]	11[c]	11[c]	64[c]	65[c]	87[c]	88[c]
Central African Republic	..	..	..	..	..	..	..	..	..	..	..	..
Chad	..	..	..	..	..	..	..	..	..	..	..	..
Chile	24	16	6	6	32	31	15	11	45	53	79	84
China	..	..	..	..	..	..	..	..	..	..	..	..
Hong Kong SAR, China	1	0[b]	0[b]	0[b]	37	21	27	6	63	78	73	94
Colombia	2[c]	27	1[c]	6	35[c]	22	25[c]	16	63[c]	51	74[c]	78
Congo, Dem. Rep.	..	..	..	..	..	..	..	..	..	..	..	..
Congo, Rep.	..	..	..	..	..	..	..	..	..	..	..	..
Costa Rica	32	18	5	5	27	28	25	13	41	54	69	82
Côte d'Ivoire	..	..	..	..	..	..	..	..	..	..	..	..
Croatia	..	12	..	14	..	40	..	18	..	48	..	67
Cuba	..	25	..	9	..	22	..	12	..	54	..	79
Czech Republic	..	4	..	2	..	51	..	27	..	45	..	71
Denmark	7	4	3	1	37	32	16	12	56	64	82	86
Dominican Republic	26	21	3	2	23	26	21	14	52	53	76	84
Ecuador	10[c]	11[c]	2[c]	4[c]	29[c]	28[c]	17[c]	13[c]	62[c]	61[c]	81[c]	83[c]
Egypt, Arab Rep.	35	28	52	43	25	26	10	6	41	46	37	51
El Salvador	48	29	15	5	23	26	23	19	29	45	63	76
Eritrea	..	..	..	..	..	..	..	..	..	..	..	..
Estonia	23	5	13	2	42	48	30	23	36	46	57	75
Ethiopia	..	12[c]	..	6[c]	..	27[c]	..	17[c]	..	61[c]	..	77[c]
Finland	11	6	6	3	38	39	15	11	51	54	78	86
France	7	4	5	2	39	34	17	11	54	61	78	86
Gabon	..	..	..	..	..	..	..	..	..	..	..	..
Gambia, The	..	..	..	..	..	..	..	..	..	..	..	..
Georgia	..	51	..	57	..	17	..	4	..	33	..	39
Germany	4	3	4	2	50	41	24	16	46	56	73	83
Ghana	66	..	59	..	10	..	10	..	23	..	32	..
Greece	20	8	26	9	29	22	17[c]	7	51	44	57[c]	59
Guatemala	19[c]	44	3[c]	16	36[c]	24	27[c]	21	45[c]	32	70[c]	63
Guinea	..	..	..	..	..	..	..	..	..	..	..	..
Guinea-Bissau	..	..	..	..	..	..	..	..	..	..	..	..
Haiti	76	..	50	..	9	..	9	..	13	..	38	..
Honduras	53[c]	51[c]	6[c]	13[c]	18[c]	20[c]	25[c]	23[c]	29[c]	29[c]	69[c]	63[c]

Employment by economic activity | 2.3

	Agriculture				Industry				Services			
	Male % of male employment		Female % of female employment		Male % of male employment		Female % of female employment		Male % of male employment		Female % of female employment	
	1990–92[a]	2004–08[a]	1990–92[a]	2004–08[a]	1990–92[a]	2004–08[a]	1990–92[a]	2004–08[a]	1990–92[a]	2004–08[a]	1990–92[a]	2004–08[a]
Hungary	19	6	13	2	43	42	29	21	38	52	58	77
India	..	..	..	..	..	..	..	..	..	..	..	..
Indonesia	54	41	57	41	15	21	13	15	31	38	31	44
Iran, Islamic Rep.	..	21	..	33	..	33	..	29	..	47	..	38
Iraq	..	14	..	33	..	20	..	7	..	66	..	60
Ireland	19	9	3	2	33	38	18	10	48	53	78	88
Israel	5	3	2	1	38	32	15	11	57	65	83	88
Italy	8	5	9	3	41	39	23	16	52	57	68	81
Jamaica	36	26	16	8	25	27	12	5	39	47	72	87
Japan	6	4	7	4	40	35	27	17	54	59	65	77
Jordan	..	..	..	..	..	..	..	..	..	..	..	..
Kazakhstan	..	35	..	32	..	24	..	10	..	41	..	58
Kenya	..	..	..	..	..	..	..	..	..	..	..	..
Korea, Dem. Rep.	..	..	..	..	..	..	..	..	..	..	..	..
Korea, Rep.	14	7	18	8	40	33	28	16	46	60	54	76
Kosovo	..	..	..	..	..	..	..	..	..	..	..	..
Kuwait	..	..	..	..	..	..	..	..	..	..	..	..
Kyrgyz Republic	..	37	..	35	..	26	..	11	..	37	..	54
Lao PDR	..	..	..	..	..	..	..	..	..	..	..	..
Latvia	..	10	..	6	..	40	..	17	..	49	..	77
Lebanon	..	..	..	..	..	..	..	..	..	..	..	..
Lesotho	..	..	..	..	..	..	..	..	..	..	..	..
Liberia	..	..	..	..	..	..	..	..	..	..	..	..
Libya	..	..	..	..	..	..	..	..	..	..	..	..
Lithuania	..	10	..	6	..	41	..	19	..	49	..	75
Macedonia, FYR	..	19	..	17	..	33	..	29	..	48	..	54
Madagascar	..	82	..	83	..	5	..	2	..	13	..	16
Malawi	..	..	..	..	..	..	..	..	..	..	..	..
Malaysia	23	18	20	10	31	32	32	23	46	51	48	67
Mali	..	50	..	30	..	18	..	15	..	32	..	55
Mauritania	..	..	..	..	..	..	..	..	..	..	..	..
Mauritius	15	10	13	8	36	36	48	26	48	54	39	66
Mexico	34	19	11	4	25	31	19	18	41	50	70	77
Moldova	..	36	..	30	..	25	..	12	..	39	..	58
Mongolia	..	41	..	35	..	21	..	15	..	39	..	50
Morocco	4[c]	37	3[c]	61	33[c]	22	46[c]	15	63[c]	41	51[c]	24
Mozambique	..	..	..	..	..	..	..	..	..	..	..	..
Myanmar	..	..	..	..	..	..	..	..	..	..	..	..
Namibia	45	34	52	25	21	19	8	9	34	47	40	65
Nepal	75	..	91	..	4	..	1	..	20	..	8	..
Netherlands	5	3	2	2	33	27	10	8	60	63	81	85
New Zealand	13[c]	9	8[c]	5	31[c]	32	13[c]	10	56[c]	58	79[c]	85
Nicaragua	..	42	..	8	..	20	..	18	..	38	..	73
Niger	..	..	..	..	..	..	..	..	..	..	..	..
Nigeria	..	..	..	..	..	..	..	..	..	..	..	..
Norway	7	4	3	1	34	33	10	8	58	63	86	90
Oman	..	..	..	..	..	..	..	..	..	..	..	..
Pakistan	45	36	69	72	20	23	15	13	35	41	16	15
Panama	35	21	3	3	20	25	11	10	45	54	85	87
Papua New Guinea	..	..	..	..	..	..	..	..	..	..	..	..
Paraguay	..	31	..	19	..	24	..	10	..	45	..	71
Peru	1[c]	12[c]	0[b,c]	6[c]	30[c]	41[c]	13[c]	43[c]	69[c]	46[c]	87[c]	51[c]
Philippines	53	44	32	24	17	18	14	11	29	39	55	65
Poland	..	15	..	14	..	41	..	18	..	44	..	68
Portugal	10	11	13	12	39	40	24	17	51	49	63	71
Puerto Rico	5	2	0[b]	0[b]	27	26	19	10	67	72	80	89
Qatar	..	4	..	0	..	48	..	4	..	48	..	96

	Agriculture				Industry				Services			
	Male % of male employment		Female % of female employment		Male % of male employment		Female % of female employment		Male % of male employment		Female % of female employment	
	1990–92[a]	2004–08[a]	1990–92[a]	2004–08[a]	1990–92[a]	2004–08[a]	1990–92[a]	2004–08[a]	1990–92[a]	2004–08[a]	1990–92[a]	2004–08[a]
Romania	29	27	38	30	44	38	30	24	28	35	33	46
Russian Federation	..	11	..	7	..	38	..	20	..	51	..	73
Rwanda	..	..	..	..	..	..	..	..	..	..	..	..
Saudi Arabia	..	5	..	0[b]	..	23	..	1	..	72	..	99
Senegal	..	34	..	33	..	20	..	5	..	33	..	42
Serbia	..	24	..	26	..	34	..	16	..	42	..	58
Sierra Leone	..	66	..	71	..	10	..	3	..	23	..	26
Singapore	1	2	0[b]	1	36	26	32	18	63	72	68	82
Slovak Republic	..	6	..	2	..	52	..	24	..	43	..	74
Slovenia	..	10	..	10	..	44	..	23	..	45	..	65
Somalia	..	..	..	..	..	..	..	..	..	..	..	..
South Africa	..	11	..	7	..	35	..	14	..	54	..	80
Spain	11	6	8	3	41	40	17	11	49	55	75	86
Sri Lanka	..	28[c]	..	37[c]	..	26[c]	..	27	..	41	..	34
Sudan	..	..	..	..	..	..	..	..	..	..	..	..
Swaziland	..	..	..	..	..	..	..	..	..	..	..	..
Sweden	5	3	2	1	40	33	12	9	55	64	86	90
Switzerland	5	5	4	3	39	34	15	12	57	62	81	86
Syrian Arab Republic	23	..	54	..	28	..	8	..	49	..	38	..
Tajikistan	..	42	..	75	..	27	..	5	..	31	..	20
Tanzania	..	71	..	78	..	7	..	3	..	22	..	19
Thailand	59	43	62	40	17	22	13	19	24	35	25	41
Timor-Leste	..	..	..	..	..	..	..	..	..	..	..	..
Togo	..	..	..	..	..	..	..	..	..	..	..	..
Trinidad and Tobago	15	6	6	2	34	41	14	16	51	52	80	82
Tunisia	..	..	..	..	..	..	..	..	..	..	..	..
Turkey	33	19	72	46	26	30	11	15	41	51	17	39
Turkmenistan	..	..	..	..	..	..	..	..	..	..	..	..
Uganda	..	..	..	..	..	..	..	..	..	..	..	..
Ukraine	..	..	..	..	..	..	..	..	..	..	..	..
United Arab Emirates	..	6	..	0[b]	..	45	..	6	..	49	..	92
United Kingdom	3	2	1	1	41	32	16	9	55	66	82	90
United States	4	2	1	1	34	30	14	9	62	68	85	90
Uruguay	7[c]	16	1[c]	5	36[c]	29	21[c]	13	57[c]	56	78[c]	83
Uzbekistan	..	..	..	..	..	..	..	..	..	..	..	..
Venezuela, RB	17	13	2	2	32	30	16	12	52	56	82	86
Vietnam	..	56	..	60	..	21	..	14	..	23	..	26
West Bank and Gaza	..	11	..	36	..	27	..	10	..	61	..	53
Yemen, Rep.	44	..	83	..	14	..	2	..	38	..	13	..
Zambia	47	..	56	..	15	..	3	..	22	..	18	..
Zimbabwe	..	..	..	..	..	..	..	..	..	..	..	..
World	.. w	.. w	.. w	.. w	.. w	.. w	.. w	.. w	.. w	.. w	.. w	.. w
Low income	..	..	..	..	..	..	..	..	..	..	..	..
Middle income	..	..	..	..	..	..	..	..	..	..	..	..
Lower middle income	..	..	..	..	..	..	..	..	..	..	..	..
Upper middle income	..	16	..	9	..	33	..	19	..	51	..	72
Low & middle income	..	..	..	..	..	..	..	..	..	..	..	..
East Asia & Pacific	..	..	..	..	..	..	..	..	..	..	..	..
Europe & Central Asia	..	16	..	16	..	35	..	19	..	48	..	65
Latin America & Carib.	21	20	13	9	30	29	14	16	49	51	72	75
Middle East & N. Africa	..	..	..	..	..	..	..	..	..	..	..	..
South Asia	..	..	..	..	..	..	..	..	..	..	..	..
Sub-Saharan Africa	..	..	..	..	..	..	..	..	..	..	..	..
High income	6	4	5	2	38	34	19	12	55	62	76	85
Euro area	7	5	6	3	42	38	20	13	50	56	73	83

Note: Data across sectors may not sum to 100 percent because of workers not classified by sector.
a. Data are for the most recent year available. b. Less than 0.5. c. Limited coverage.

Employment by economic activity **2.3**

About the data

The International Labour Organization (ILO) classifies economic activity using the International Standard Industrial Classification (ISIC) of All Economic Activities, revision 2 (1968) and revision 3 (1990). Because this classification is based on where work is performed (industry) rather than type of work performed (occupation), all of an enterprise's employees are classified under the same industry, regardless of their trade or occupation. The categories should sum to 100 percent. Where they do not, the differences are due to workers who cannot be classified by economic activity.

Data on employment are drawn from labor force surveys, household surveys, official estimates, censuses and administrative records of social insurance schemes, and establishment surveys when no other information is available. The concept of employment generally refers to people above a certain age who worked, or who held a job, during a reference period. Employment data include both full-time and part-time workers.

There are many differences in how countries define and measure employment status, particularly members of the armed forces, self-employed workers, and unpaid family workers. Where members of the armed forces are included, they are allocated to the service sector, causing that sector to be somewhat overstated relative to the service sector in economies where they are excluded. Where data are obtained from establishment surveys, data cover only employees; thus self-employed and unpaid family workers are excluded. In such cases the employment share of the agricultural sector is severely underreported. Caution should be also used where the data refer only to urban areas, which record little or no agricultural work. Moreover, the age group and area covered could differ by country or change over time within a country. For detailed information on breaks in series, consult the original source.

Countries also take different approaches to the treatment of unemployed people. In most countries unemployed people with previous job experience are classified according to their last job. But in some countries the unemployed and people seeking their first job are not classifiable by economic activity. Because of these differences, the size and distribution of employment by economic activity may not be fully comparable across countries.

The ILO's *Yearbook of Labour Statistics* and its database Key Indicators of the Labour Market report data by major divisions of the ISIC revision 2 or revision 3. In the table the reported divisions or categories are aggregated into three broad groups: agriculture, industry, and services. Such broad classification may obscure fundamental shifts within countries' industrial patterns. A slight majority of countries report economic activity according to the ISIC revision 2 instead of revision 3. The use of one classification or the other should not have a significant impact on the information for the three broad sectors presented in the table.

The distribution of economic wealth in the world remains strongly correlated with employment by economic activity. The wealthier economies are those with the largest share of total employment in services, whereas the poorer economies are largely agriculture based.

The distribution of economic activity by gender reveals some clear patterns. Men still make up the majority of people employed in all three sectors, but the gender gap is biggest in industry. Employment in agriculture is also male-dominated, although not as much as industry. Segregating one sex in a narrow range of occupations significantly reduces economic efficiency by reducing labor market flexibility and thus the economy's ability to adapt to change. This segregation is particularly harmful for women, who have a much narrower range of labor market choices and lower levels of pay than men. But it is also detrimental to men when job losses are concentrated in industries dominated by men and job growth is centered in service occupations, where women have better chances, as has been the recent experience in many countries.

There are several explanations for the rising importance of service jobs for women. Many service jobs—such as nursing and social and clerical work—are considered "feminine" because of a perceived similarity to women's traditional roles. Women often do not receive the training needed to take advantage of changing employment opportunities. And the greater availability of part-time work in service industries may lure more women, although it is unclear whether this is a cause or an effect.

Definitions

- **Agriculture** corresponds to division 1 (ISIC revision 2) or tabulation categories A and B (ISIC revision 3) and includes hunting, forestry, and fishing.
- **Industry** corresponds to divisions 2–5 (ISIC revision 2) or tabulation categories C–F (ISIC revision 3) and includes mining and quarrying (including oil production), manufacturing, construction, and public utilities (electricity, gas, and water). • **Services** correspond to divisions 6–9 (ISIC revision 2) or tabulation categories G–P (ISIC revision 3) and include wholesale and retail trade and restaurants and hotels; transport, storage, and communications; financing, insurance, real estate, and business services; and community, social, and personal services.

Data sources

Data on employment are from the ILO's Key Indicators of the Labour Market, 6th edition, database.

Decent work and productive employment

	Employment to population ratio				Gross enrollment ratio, secondary		Vulnerable employment				Labor productivity	
	Total % ages 15 and older		Youth % ages 15–24		% of relevant age group		Unpaid family workers and own-account workers				GDP per person employed % growth	
							Male % of male employment		Female % of female employment			
	1991	2008	1991	2008	1991	2008[a]	1990	2008	1990	2008	1990–92	2003–05
Afghanistan	54	55	45	47	16	29	..	..	..	..	..	..
Albania	49	46	37	36	88	..	..	..	..	..	–17.5	5.4
Algeria	39	49	25	31	60	..	..	..	..	..	–4.0	1.3
Angola	77	76	71	69	10	..	..	..	..	..	–5.0	12.0
Argentina	53	57	42	36	74	85	..	22[b]	..	17[b]	9.0	2.1
Armenia	38	38	24	25	..	88	..	..	..	..	–24.8	12.7
Australia	56	59	58	64	82	148	12	11	9	7	3.3	0.3
Austria	52	55	61	53	102	100	..	9	..	9	0.7	2.4
Azerbaijan	57	60	38	39	88	106	..	41	..	66	–12.6	24.8
Bangladesh	74	68	66	56	20	44	..	..	..	..	1.9	4.2
Belarus	58	52	40	35	93	95	..	..	..	..	–4.0	10.3
Belgium	44	47	31	27	101	110	17	11	15	9	1.6	1.4
Benin	70	72	64	59	11	..	..	..	..	..	..	..
Bolivia	61	71	48	49	44	82	32[b]	..	50[b]	..	2.6	1.0
Bosnia and Herzegovina	42	42	17	18	..	89	..	..	..	..	–14.8	4.6
Botswana	47	46	34	27	49	80	..	..	..	..	..	..
Brazil	56	64	54	53	61	100	29[b]	30	30[b]	24	–0.3	0.4
Bulgaria	45	46	27	27	86	105	..	10	..	8	3.1	3.7
Burkina Faso	82	82	77	74	7	20[c]	..	..	..	..	1.3	2.1
Burundi	85	84	74	73	5	18	..	..	..	..	..	..
Cambodia	77	75	66	68	25	40	..	..	..	..	4.0	6.5
Cameroon	59	59	37	33	26	37	..	..	..	..	–6.7	1.1
Canada	58	61	57	61	101	101	..	12[b]	..	9[b]	0.8	1.4
Central African Republic	73	73	59	58	12	..	..	..	..	..	..	..
Chad	67	70	51	50	7	19	..	..	..	..	..	..
Chile	51	50	34	24	73	94	..	25	..	21	6.6	2.9
China	75	71	71	55	41	74	..	..	..	..	6.8	9.2
Hong Kong SAR, China	62	57	54	38	80	83	..	10	..	4	5.3	5.5
Colombia	52	62	38	43	53	91	30[b]	48	26[b]	46	–0.7	2.2
Congo, Dem. Rep.	68	67	60	62	21	35	..	..	..	..	–12.9	4.2
Congo, Rep.	66	65	49	46	46	..	..	..	..	..	..	..
Costa Rica	56	57	48	43	45	89	26	20	21	20	2.4	1.3
Côte d'Ivoire	63	60	52	45	20	..	..	..	..	..	–3.6	–0.3
Croatia	50	46	27	29	..	94	..	15[b]	..	17[b]	–7.7	3.0
Cuba	52	54	40	32	94	91	..	..	..	..	..	..
Czech Republic	58	54	48	29	91	95	..	15	..	9	–5.2	4.7
Denmark	59	60	65	61	109	119	7	7	6	3	2.5	2.2
Dominican Republic	44	53	28	34	..	75	42	49	30	30	0.7	2.2
Ecuador	52	61	39	40	55	70	33[b]	29[b]	41[b]	41[b]	–0.1	1.9
Egypt, Arab Rep.	43	43	22	23	69	..	..	20	..	44	2.1	1.6
El Salvador	59	54	42	39	38	64	..	29	..	44	..	..
Eritrea	66	66	60	54	..	30	..	..	..	..	..	..
Estonia	61	55	43	29	100	100	2	8	3	4	–9.4	7.4
Ethiopia	71	81	64	74	14	33	..	48[b]	..	56[b]	–8.4	7.3
Finland	57	55	45	44	116	111	..	11	..	7	1.4	2.3
France	47	48	28	29	100	113	11	7	10	5	1.4	1.8
Gabon	58	58	37	33	39	..	..	..	..	..	..	..
Gambia, The	73	72	59	55	19	51	..	..	..	..	..	..
Georgia	57	54	28	22	95	90	..	..	..	17[b]	–25.3	9.8
Germany	54	52	58	44	98	101	..	7	..	6	3.7	0.8
Ghana	68	65	40	40	35	54	..	..	..	..	2.8	3.0
Greece	44	48	31	28	94	102	..	27	..	27	2.4	2.8
Guatemala	55	62	50	52	23	57	..	..	..	..	1.0	2.1
Guinea	82	81	75	73	10	36	..	..	..	..	..	..
Guinea-Bissau	66	67	57	63	6	36	..	..	..	..	..	..
Haiti	56	55	37	47	21	..	..	..	..	..	..	..
Honduras	59	56	49	43	33	65	48[b]	..	50[b]	..	..	..

	Employment to population ratio				Gross enrollment ratio, secondary		Vulnerable employment				Labor productivity	
							Unpaid family workers and own-account workers				GDP per person employed	
	Total % ages 15 and older		Youth % ages 15–24		% of relevant age group		Male % of male employment		Female % of female employment		% growth	
	1991	2008	1991	2008	1991	2008[a]	1990	2008	1990	2008	1990–92	2003–05
Hungary	48	45	37	20	86	97	8	8	7	6	0.3	4.6
India	58	56	46	40	42	57	..	..	..	..	1.0	5.8
Indonesia	63	62	46	41	46	76	..	60	..	68	6.2	4.7
Iran, Islamic Rep.	46	49	33	36	53	80	..	40	..	56	6.5	0.4
Iraq	37	37	27	23	44	..	..	..	..	..	−33.6	17.5
Ireland	44	58	38	44	100	113	25	17	9	5	2.4	1.6
Israel	45	50	25	27	92	91	..	9	..	5	0.0	3.1
Italy	43	44	30	25	79	100	29	21	24	15	0.6	0.6
Jamaica	61	56	40	29	66	90	46	38	37	31	0.7	−0.4
Japan	61	54	43	40	97	101	15	10	26	12	0.7	2.0
Jordan	36	38	25	20	82	86	..	..	..	..	−5.5	3.9
Kazakhstan	63	64	46	42	100	95[c]	..	..	..	..	−15.1	7.5
Kenya	73	73	62	59	46	58	..	..	..	..	−3.9	2.1
Korea, Dem. Rep.	62	64	46	39	..	..	..	..	..	..	..	..
Korea, Rep.	59	58	36	28	90	97	..	23	..	28	5.0	2.8
Kosovo	..	..	..	..	..	..	..	..	..	..	..	..
Kuwait	62	65	29	30	43	91	..	..	..	..	−0.2	1.4
Kyrgyz Republic	58	58	41	40	100	85	..	47	..	47	−13.1	−0.4
Lao PDR	80	78	74	64	23	44	..	..	..	..	..	..
Latvia	58	55	43	35	92	115	..	8	..	6	−19.6	8.1
Lebanon	44	46	31	29	62	82	..	..	..	..	..	..
Lesotho	48	54	40	40	24	40	..	..	..	..	..	..
Liberia	66	66	57	57	..	32	..	..	..	..	..	..
Libya	45	49	28	27	..	93	..	..	..	..	..	..
Lithuania	54	50	36	18	92	99	..	11	..	8	−13.9	6.3
Macedonia, FYR	37	35	17	13	..	84	..	24	..	20	−5.6	4.1
Madagascar	79	83	65	71	18	30	..	..	..	..	−5.9	1.5
Malawi	72	72	48	49	8	29	..	..	..	..	−1.9	1.9
Malaysia	60	61	47	45	57	..	31	23	25	21	6.0	5.1
Mali	49	47	40	35	7	35	..	..	..	..	0.4	1.0
Mauritania	67	47	54	23	13	23	..	..	..	..	..	..
Mauritius	56	54	45	37	55	88	13	18	7	15	..	..
Mexico	57	57	50	42	54	87	29	28	15	32	1.0	1.6
Moldova	58	45	39	17	80	83	..	35	..	30	−22.0	9.0
Mongolia	50	52	39	35	82	95	..	..	..	..	..	..
Morocco	46	46	40	35	36	56	..	46	..	65	−1.7	1.7
Mozambique	80	78	67	66	7	21	..	..	..	..	−3.0	6.2
Myanmar	74	74	62	53	23	49	..	..	..	..	2.0	8.9
Namibia	45	43	24	14	43	66	..	..	..	..	..	..
Nepal	60	62	52	46	33	43	..	..	..	..	..	..
Netherlands	51	59	55	67	120	120	7	10	10	8	0.4	2.3
New Zealand	55	63	55	56	92	120	15	14	10	10	0.5	0.3
Nicaragua	57	58	46	48	43	68	..	45	..	46	..	..
Niger	59	60	50	52	7	11	..	..	..	..	−5.7	0.2
Nigeria	53	52	29	24	23	30	..	..	..	..	−2.9	4.6
Norway	58	62	49	56	103	113	..	8	..	3	3.9	2.4
Oman	53	51	30	29	45	88	..	..	..	..	0.2	3.7
Pakistan	48	52	38	44	23	33	..	58	..	75	6.5	4.4
Panama	50	59	33	40	62	71	44	30	19	24	..	..
Papua New Guinea	70	70	57	54	12	..	..	..	..	..	..	..
Paraguay	61	73	51	58	31	66	17[b]	45	31[b]	50	..	..
Peru	53	69	34	53	67	98	30[b]	33[b]	46[b]	47[b]	−0.8	2.7
Philippines	59	60	42	39	70	81	..	44	..	47	−3.3	2.5
Poland	53	48	31	27	87	100	..	20	..	18	2.8	2.7
Portugal	58	56	53	35	66	101	22	18	30	19	2.2	1.4
Puerto Rico	37	41	21	29	..	..	..	..	..	..	..	..
Qatar	73	77	35	47	84	93	..	..	..	..	0.1	7.4

Decent work and productive employment

	Employment to population ratio				Gross enrollment ratio, secondary		Vulnerable employment				Labor productivity	
	Total % ages 15 and older		Youth % ages 15–24		% of relevant age group		Unpaid family workers and own-account workers Male % of male employment		Female % of female employment		GDP per person employed % growth	
	1991	2008	1991	2008	1991	2008[a]	1990	2008	1990	2008	1990–92	2003–05
Romania	56	48	42	24	92	87	21	31	33	32	–9.3	8.0
Russian Federation	57	57	34	33	93	84	1	6	1	6	–7.9	6.1
Rwanda	87	80	79	64	9	22	..	..	..	..	..	..
Saudi Arabia	50	51	26	25	44	95	..	..	..	..	4.9	1.8
Senegal	67	66	60	55	15	31	77	..	91	..	–1.0	3.4
Serbia	49[d]	47[d]	28[d]	30[d]	..	90	..	20	..	14	..	..
Sierra Leone	64	65	38	42	16	35	..	..	..	..	..	..
Singapore	64	62	56	38	..	..	10	12	6	7	1.5	6.7
Slovak Republic	55	53	43	30	..	93	..	14	..	6	–0.8	5.2
Slovenia	55	54	38	32	89	94	..	12	..	10	–2.3	4.2
Somalia	66	67	59	58	..	..	..	..	..	..	..	..
South Africa	39	41	19	15	69	95	..	2	..	3	–4.5	3.9
Spain	41	49	36	37	105	119	20	13	24	10	2.4	–1.2
Sri Lanka	51	55	31	36	72	..	..	39[b]	..	44[b]	5.5	2.2
Sudan	46	47	29	23	20	38[c]	..	..	..	..	–1.3	–0.2
Swaziland	54	50	34	26	43	53	..	..	..	..	..	..
Sweden	62	58	59	45	90	103	..	9	..	4	1.9	3.9
Switzerland	65	61	69	63	98	96	8	10	11	11	–0.6	2.0
Syrian Arab Republic	47	45	38	32	48	74	..	..	..	..	6.5	0.6
Tajikistan	54	55	36	38	102	84	..	..	..	..	–20.4	2.5
Tanzania	87	78	79	70	5	..	..	82[b]	..	93[b]	–2.4	4.8
Thailand	77	72	70	46	30	..	67	51	74	56	6.8	3.3
Timor-Leste	64	67	51	58	..	..	..	..	..	..	..	..
Togo	66	65	58	53	20	41	..	..	..	..	..	..
Trinidad and Tobago	45	61	33	46	82	89	22	..	21	..	–3.5	4.5
Tunisia	41	41	29	22	45	90	..	..	..	..	2.6	2.1
Turkey	53	42	48	31	48	82	..	30	..	49	1.0	6.7
Turkmenistan	56	58	35	34	..	..	..	..	..	..	–13.0	6.0
Uganda	82	83	73	75	11	25	..	..	..	..	–1.1	3.3
Ukraine	57	54	37	34	94	94	..	..	..	..	–7.9	6.0
United Arab Emirates	71	76	43	46	68	94	..	..	..	..	–3.9	2.2
United Kingdom	56	56	66	56	87	97	13	14	6	7	2.0	1.7
United States	59	59	56	51	92	94	..	..	..	..	1.7	1.9
Uruguay	53	56	42	39	84	92	..	26	..	24	5.2	5.1
Uzbekistan	54	58	36	39	99	102	..	..	..	..	–7.8	4.1
Venezuela, RB	51	61	35	40	53	81	..	28	..	33	4.5	15.0
Vietnam	75	69	75	51	32	..	..	..	..	..	4.6	5.7
West Bank and Gaza	30	30	19	15	..	92	..	34	..	44	..	..
Yemen, Rep.	38	39	23	22	..	..	..	..	..	..	0.9	0.6
Zambia	57	61	40	46	23	52	56	..	81	..	–2.5	3.2
Zimbabwe	70	65	48	50	49	41	..	..	..	..	–4.7	–5.6
World	**62 w**	**60 w**	**52 w**	**45 w**	**50 w**	**66 w**	**.. w**	**.. w**	**.. w**	**.. w**	**0.7 w**	**3.3 w**
Low income	70	69	60	56	26	41	..	..	..	..	–2.8	4.5
Middle income	62	60	52	42	47	67	..	..	..	..	1.3	5.9
Lower middle income	65	62	55	43	42	62	..	..	..	..	3.2	6.7
Upper middle income	54	56	41	38	67	90	..	25	..	24	–2.1	3.9
Low & middle income	63	62	53	45	44	62	..	..	..	..	1.1	5.8
East Asia & Pacific	73	69	67	51	41	73	..	..	..	..	6.5	7.8
Europe & Central Asia	55	52	38	32	85	89	..	19	..	18	–8.0	6.3
Latin America & Carib.	55	61	46	45	57	88	..	32	..	32	1.8	2.5
Middle East & N. Africa	43	45	29	29	54	72	..	33	..	52	1.5	0.9
South Asia	59	57	48	42	37	52	..	..	..	..	3.1	5.5
Sub-Saharan Africa	64	64	50	49	22	33	..	..	..	..	–5.3	3.7
High income	55	55	47	43	91	100	..	..	..	..	2.3	1.8
Euro area	48	50	41	37	..	..	..	12	..	9	2.4	1.0

a. Provisional data. b. Limited coverage. c. Data are for 2009. d. Includes Montenegro.

About the data

Four targets were added to the UN Millennium Declaration at the 2005 World Summit High-Level Plenary Meeting of the 60th Session of the UN General Assembly. One was full and productive employment and decent work for all, which is seen as the main route for people to escape poverty. The four indicators for this target have an economic focus, and three of them are presented in the table.

The employment to population ratio indicates how efficiently an economy provides jobs for people who want to work. A high ratio means that a large proportion of the population is employed. But a lower employment to population ratio can be seen as a positive sign, especially for young people, if it is caused by an increase in their education. This indicator has a gender bias because women who do not consider their work employment or who are not perceived as working tend to be undercounted. This bias has different effects across countries.

Comparability of employment ratios across countries is also affected by variations in definitions of employment and population (see *About the data* for table 2.3). The biggest difference results from the age range used to define labor force activity. The population base for employment ratios can also vary (see table 2.1). Most countries use the resident, noninstitutionalized population of working age living in private households, which excludes members of the armed forces and individuals residing in mental, penal, or other types of institutions. But some countries include members of the armed forces in the population base of their employment ratio while excluding them from employment data (International Labour Organization, *Key Indicators of the Labour Market*, 6th edition).

The proportion of unpaid family workers and own-account workers in total employment is derived from information on status in employment. Each status group faces different economic risks, and unpaid family workers and own-account workers are the most vulnerable—and therefore the most likely to fall into poverty. They are the least likely to have formal work arrangements, are the least likely to have social protection and safety nets to guard against economic shocks, and often are incapable of generating sufficient savings to offset these shocks. A high proportion of unpaid family workers in a country indicates weak development, little job growth, and often a large rural economy.

Data on employment by status are drawn from labor force surveys and household surveys, supplemented by official estimates and censuses for a small group of countries. The labor force survey is the most comprehensive source for internationally comparable employment, but there are still some limitations for comparing data across countries and over time even within a country. Information from labor force surveys is not always consistent in what is included in employment. For example, information provided by the Organisation for Economic Cooperation and Development relates only to civilian employment, which can result in an underestimation of "employees" and "workers not classified by status," especially in countries with large armed forces. While the categories of unpaid family workers and self-employed workers, which include own-account workers, would not be affected, their relative shares would be. Geographic coverage is another factor that can limit cross-country comparisons. The employment by status data for most Latin American countries covers urban areas only. Similarly, in some countries in Sub-Saharan Africa, where limited information is available anyway, the members of producer cooperatives are usually excluded from the self-employed category. For detailed information on definitions and coverage, consult the original source.

Labor productivity is used to assess a country's economic ability to create and sustain decent employment opportunities with fair and equitable remuneration. Productivity increases obtained through investment, trade, technological progress, or changes in work organization can increase social protection and reduce poverty, which in turn reduce vulnerable employment and working poverty. Productivity increases do not guarantee these improvements, but without them—and the economic growth they bring—improvements are highly unlikely. For comparability of individual sectors labor productivity is estimated according to national accounts conventions. However, there are still significant limitations on the availability of reliable data. Information on consistent series of output in both national currencies and purchasing power parity dollars is not easily available, especially in developing countries, because the definition, coverage, and methodology are not always consistent across countries. For example, countries employ different methodologies for estimating the missing values for the nonmarket service sectors and use different definitions of the informal sector.

Definitions

- **Employment to population ratio** is the proportion of a country's population that is employed. People ages 15 and older are generally considered the working-age population. People ages 15–24 are generally considered the youth population. • **Gross enrollment ratio, secondary,** is the ratio of total enrollment in secondary education, regardless of age, to the population of the age group that officially corresponds to secondary education. • **Vulnerable employment** is unpaid family workers and own-account workers as a percentage of total employment. • **Labor productivity** is the growth rate of gross domestic product (GDP) divided by total employment in the economy.

Data sources

Data on employment to population ratio, vulnerable employment, and labor productivity are from the International Labour Organization's Key Indicators of the Labour Market, 6th edition, database. Data on gross enrollment ratios are from the United Nations Educational, Scientific, and Cultural Organization Institute for Statistics.

	Unemployment						Long-term unemployment			Unemployment by educational attainment		
	Total % of total labor force		Male % of male labor force		Female % of female labor force		% of total unemployment			% of total unemployment		
							Total	Male	Female	Primary	Secondary	Tertiary
	1990–92[a]	2005–08[a]	1990–92[a]	2005–08[a]	1990–92[a]	2005–08[a]	2005–08[a]	2005–08[a]	2005–08[a]	2005–08[a]	2005–08[a]	2005–08[a]
Afghanistan	..	8.5	..	7.6	..	9.5	..	..	..	..	..	..
Albania	..	..	..	..	..	..	..	..	..	..	..	..
Algeria	23.0	13.8	24.2	12.9	20.3	18.4	..	..	..	..	..	..
Angola	..	..	..	..	..	..	..	..	..	..	..	..
Argentina	6.7[b]	7.3[b]	6.4[b]	6.0[b]	7.0[b]	8.9[b]	..	..	..	48.1[b]	36.7[b]	15.3[b]
Armenia	..	..	..	..	..	..	..	..	..	5.2	83.0	11.9
Australia	10.8	4.2	11.4	4.0	10.0	4.6	14.9[b]	15.7[b]	13.9[b]	48.0	34.1	17.9
Austria	3.6	3.8	3.5	3.6	3.8	4.1	24.2	25.8	22.6	37.9	52.1	10.0
Azerbaijan	..	6.5	..	7.8	..	5.3	..	..	..	6.3	78.9	14.9
Bangladesh	..	4.3	..	3.4	..	7.0	..	..	..	33.0	24.4	15.9
Belarus	..	..	..	..	..	..	..	..	..	10.0	39.0	51.0
Belgium	6.7	7.0	4.8	6.5	9.5	7.6	52.6	49.9	55.7	42.1	38.2	19.7
Benin	1.5	..	2.2	..	0.6	..	..	..	..	..	..	..
Bolivia	5.5[b]	..	5.5[b]	..	5.6[b]	..	..	..	..	..	..	..
Bosnia and Herzegovina	17.6	29.0	15.5	26.7	21.6	33.0	..	..	..	95.7	..	4.0
Botswana	..	17.6	..	15.3	..	19.9	..	..	..	..	..	..
Brazil	6.4[b]	7.9[b]	5.4[b]	6.1[b]	7.9[b]	10.0[b]	..	..	..	51.6	33.6	3.6
Bulgaria	..	5.7	..	5.5	..	5.8	51.7	50.1	53.5	41.8	49.7	8.6
Burkina Faso	..	..	..	..	..	..	..	..	..	..	..	..
Burundi	0.5	..	0.7	..	0.3	..	..	..	..	..	..	..
Cambodia	..	..	..	..	..	..	..	..	..	..	..	..
Cameroon	..	..	..	..	..	..	..	..	..	..	..	..
Canada	11.2[b]	6.1	12.0[b]	6.6	10.2[b]	5.7	7.1[b]	7.9[b]	6.1[b]	27.7[b]	41.1[b]	31.2[b]
Central African Republic	..	..	..	..	..	..	..	..	..	..	..	..
Chad	..	..	..	..	..	..	..	..	..	..	..	..
Chile	4.4	7.8	3.9	6.8	5.3	9.5	..	..	..	17.8	58.5	23.5
China	2.3[b]	4.2[b]	..	..	..	..	..	..	..	..	..	..
Hong Kong SAR, China	2.0	3.5	2.0	4.5	1.9	3.4	..	..	..	40.8	41.4	16.6
Colombia	9.5[b]	11.7	6.8[b]	8.9	13.0[b]	14.5	..	..	..	76.6	..	20.6
Congo, Dem. Rep.	..	..	..	..	..	..	..	..	..	..	..	..
Congo, Rep.	..	..	..	..	..	..	..	..	..	..	..	..
Costa Rica	4.1	4.6	3.5	3.3	5.4	6.8	..	..	..	65.2	27.3	6.4
Côte d'Ivoire	6.7	..	..	..	..	..	..	..	..	..	..	..
Croatia	..	8.4	..	7.0	..	10.0	61.5	57.2	65.3	20.4	67.8	11.8
Cuba	..	1.8	..	1.7	..	1.9	..	..	..	43.0	52.4	4.6
Czech Republic	..	4.4	..	3.5	..	5.6	50.2	50.4	50.0	26.8	68.8	4.3
Denmark	9.0	3.3	8.3	3.0	9.9	3.7	16.1	19.0	13.9	35.9	35.1	23.0
Dominican Republic	20.7	15.6	12.0	9.3	35.2	25.4	..	..	..	35.0	44.5	16.4
Ecuador	8.9[b]	6.9	6.0[b]	5.6[b]	13.2[b]	10.9[b]	..	..	..	74.0[b]	..	23.6[b]
Egypt, Arab Rep.	9.0	8.7	6.4	5.9	17.0	19.3	..	..	..	..	..	..
El Salvador	7.9[b]	6.6	8.4[b]	8.5	7.2[b]	3.9	..	..	..	..	..	..
Eritrea	..	..	..	..	..	..	..	..	..	..	..	..
Estonia	3.7	5.5	3.9	5.8	3.5	5.2	..	..	..	23.1	57.8	16.6
Ethiopia	..	17.0[b]	..	11.7[b]	..	22.6[b]	..	..	..	35.9	13.3	3.2
Finland	11.6	6.4	13.3	6.1	9.6	6.7	18.2	20.1	16.2	35.5	45.9	18.6
France	10.2	7.4	8.1	6.9	12.8	7.9	37.9	39.3	36.5	39.9	39.6	19.9
Gabon	..	..	..	..	..	..	..	..	..	..	..	..
Gambia, The	..	..	..	..	..	..	..	..	..	..	..	..
Georgia	..	13.3	..	13.9	..	12.6	..	..	..	5.1	52.5	42.3
Germany	6.3	7.5	4.9	7.4	8.2	7.5	53.4	54.0	52.7	33.1	56.3	10.6
Ghana	4.7	..	3.7	..	5.5	..	..	..	..	..	..	..
Greece	7.8	7.7	4.9	5.1	12.9	11.4	49.6	42.8	53.8	29.3	48.4	21.8
Guatemala	..	1.8	..	1.5	..	2.4	..	..	..	..	..	..
Guinea	..	..	..	..	..	..	..	..	..	..	..	..
Guinea-Bissau	..	..	..	..	..	..	..	..	..	..	..	..
Haiti	12.7	..	11.9	..	13.8	..	..	..	..	..	..	..
Honduras	3.2[b]	3.1[b]	3.3[b]	2.5[b]	3.0[b]	4.2[b]	..	..	..	..	..	..

	Unemployment						Long-term unemployment			Unemployment by educational attainment		
	Total % of total labor force		Male % of male labor force		Female % of female labor force			% of total unemployment			% of total unemployment	
	1990–92[a]	2005–08[a]	1990–92[a]	2005–08[a]	1990–92[a]	2005–08[a]	Total 2005–08[a]	Male 2005–08[a]	Female 2005–08[a]	Primary 2005–08[a]	Secondary 2005–08[a]	Tertiary 2005–08[a]
Hungary	9.9	7.8	11.0	7.6	8.7	8.1	47.6	48.8	46.3	33.1	58.7	8.1
India	..	..	..	..	..	..	..	..	..	29.0	37.7	33.3
Indonesia	2.8	8.4	2.7	8.1	3.0	10.8	..	..	..	44.4	40.7	9.6
Iran, Islamic Rep.	11.1	10.5	9.5	9.3	24.4	15.7	..	..	..	41.8	34.7	19.6
Iraq	..	..	..	..	..	..	..	..	..	..	..	..
Ireland	15.0	6.0	14.9	7.0	15.3	4.6	29.4	33.2	21.7	39.8	37.2	18.2
Israel	11.2	6.2[b]	9.2	5.7[b]	13.9	7.0[b]	..	..	..	12.2	12.8	72.5
Italy	9.3	6.7	6.7	5.5	13.9	8.5	47.5	44.9	49.9	46.5	40.6	11.3
Jamaica	15.4	10.6	9.4	7.3	22.2	14.6	..	..	..	9.7	4.3	8.4
Japan	2.2	4.0	2.1	4.1	2.2	3.8	33.3	39.9	23.8	67.2	..	32.8
Jordan	..	12.7	..	10.1	..	24.3	..	..	..	..	..	..
Kazakhstan	..	..	..	..	..	..	..	..	..	..	..	..
Kenya	..	..	..	..	..	..	..	..	..	..	..	..
Korea, Dem. Rep.	..	..	..	..	..	..	..	..	..	..	..	..
Korea, Rep.	2.5	3.2	2.8	3.6	2.1	2.6	2.7	3.7	0.4	15.2	49.7	35.2
Kosovo	..	..	..	..	..	..	..	..	..	..	..	..
Kuwait	..	..	..	..	..	..	..	..	..	19.4	41.4	9.6
Kyrgyz Republic	..	8.3	..	7.7	..	9.0	..	..	..	13.3	77.1	9.6
Lao PDR	..	1.4	..	1.3	..	1.4	..	..	..	..	..	..
Latvia	..	7.5	..	8.0	..	6.9	25.7	44.6	39.7	24.3	59.9	14.6
Lebanon	..	..	..	..	..	..	..	..	..	..	..	..
Lesotho	..	..	..	..	..	..	..	..	..	..	..	..
Liberia	..	5.6	..	6.8	..	4.2	..	..	..	..	..	..
Libya	..	..	..	..	..	..	..	..	..	..	..	..
Lithuania	..	5.8	..	6.1	..	5.6	52.4	54.1	50.8	14.2	70.4	15.4
Macedonia, FYR	..	33.8	..	33.5	..	34.2	..	..	..	..	..	..
Madagascar	..	2.6	..	1.7	..	3.5	..	..	..	43.9	23.8	9.3
Malawi	..	..	..	..	..	..	..	..	..	..	..	..
Malaysia	3.7	3.2	..	3.1	..	3.4	..	..	..	13.3	61.6	25.1
Mali	..	..	..	..	..	..	..	..	..	..	..	..
Mauritania	..	..	..	..	..	..	..	..	..	..	..	..
Mauritius	..	7.3	..	4.1	..	12.8	..	..	..	44.2	48.5	6.4
Mexico	3.1	4.0	2.7	3.9	4.0	4.2	1.7	1.6	1.8	50.7	24.5	22.9
Moldova	..	4.0	..	4.6	..	3.4	..	..	..	..	..	..
Mongolia	..	2.8	..	2.3	..	3.2	..	..	..	..	..	..
Morocco	16.0[b]	9.6	13.0[b]	9.6	25.3[b]	9.8	..	..	..	51.1[b]	22.4[b]	21.6[b]
Mozambique	..	..	..	..	..	..	..	..	..	..	..	..
Myanmar	6.0	..	4.7	..	8.8	..	..	..	..	..	..	..
Namibia	19.0	..	20.0	..	19.0	..	..	..	..	..	..	..
Nepal	..	..	..	..	..	..	..	..	..	..	..	..
Netherlands	5.5	2.8	4.3	2.5	7.3	3.0	36.3	38.3	34.4	41.3	39.7	17.0
New Zealand	10.4[b]	4.1	11.0[b]	4.0	9.6[b]	4.2	4.4[b]	5.5[b]	3.2[b]	30.6	38.8	26.9
Nicaragua	14.4	5.2	11.3	5.4	19.5	4.9	..	..	..	72.8	2.1	18.0
Niger	..	..	..	..	..	..	..	..	..	..	..	..
Nigeria	..	..	..	..	..	..	..	..	..	..	..	..
Norway	5.9	2.6	6.6	2.7	5.1	2.4	6.0	6.0	6.0	25.4	49.2	20.6
Oman	..	..	..	..	..	..	..	..	..	..	..	..
Pakistan	5.2	5.1	3.8	4.2	14.0	8.6	..	..	..	14.3	11.4	26.0
Panama	14.7	6.8	10.8	5.3	22.3	9.3	..	..	..	36.0	39.6	24.0
Papua New Guinea	7.7	..	9.0	..	5.9	..	..	..	..	..	..	..
Paraguay	5.3[b]	5.7	6.4[b]	4.6	3.8[b]	7.4	..	..	..	49.9	38.0	9.9
Peru	9.4[b]	7.0[b]	7.5[b]	5.9[b]	12.5[b]	8.2[b]	..	..	..	30.0[b]	31.9[b]	37.6[b]
Philippines	8.6	7.4	7.9	7.6	9.9	7.1	..	..	..	13.6	46.2	39.4
Poland	13.3	7.1	12.2	6.4	14.7	8.0	29.0	27.3	30.8	16.4	73.2	10.4
Portugal	4.1[b]	7.6	3.5[b]	6.5	5.0[b]	8.8	48.3	49.9	46.9	68.1	15.4	13.2
Puerto Rico	16.9	11.6	19.1	12.0	13.3	9.5	..	..	..	..	..	..
Qatar	..	..	..	..	..	..	..	..	..	..	..	..

	Unemployment						Long-term unemployment			Unemployment by educational attainment		
	Total % of total labor force		Male % of male labor force		Female % of female labor force		% of total unemployment			% of total unemployment		
							Total	Male	Female	Primary	Secondary	Tertiary
	1990–92[a]	2005–08[a]	1990–92[a]	2005–08[a]	1990–92[a]	2005–08[a]	2005–08[a]	2005–08[a]	2005–08[a]	2005–08[a]	2005–08[a]	2005–08[a]
Romania	..	5.8	..	6.7	..	4.7	41.3	43.0	38.4	25.8	66.3	6.1
Russian Federation	5.3	6.2	5.4	6.4	5.2	5.8	..	..	..	13.7	54.2	32.1
Rwanda	0.3	..	0.6	..	0.2	..	..	..	..	..	..	..
Saudi Arabia	..	5.6	..	4.2	..	13.2	..	..	..	26.2	44.6	28.7
Senegal	..	11.1	..	7.9	..	13.6	..	..	..	40.2	6.9	2.5
Serbia	..	13.6	..	11.9	..	15.8	71.1	70.1	72.1	20.3	68.4	11.2
Sierra Leone	..	..	..	..	..	..	..	..	..	..	..	..
Singapore	2.7	3.2	2.7	3.0	2.6	3.5	..	..	..	31.0	25.6	43.2
Slovak Republic	..	9.5	..	8.4	..	10.9	66.1	65.6	66.6	29.2	65.3	5.3
Slovenia	..	4.4	..	4.0	..	4.9	42.2	38.5	40.0	25.0	60.4	12.5
Somalia	..	..	..	..	..	..	..	..	..	..	..	..
South Africa	..	22.9	..	20.0	..	26.3	..	..	..	36.2	56.3	4.5
Spain	18.1	11.3	13.9	10.1	25.8	13.0	23.8	18.8	28.9	54.8	23.6	20.4
Sri Lanka	14.6[b]	5.2[b]	10.6[b]	3.6[b]	21.0[b]	8.0[b]	..	..	..	45.4[b]	22.0[b]	32.6[b]
Sudan	..	..	..	..	..	..	..	..	..	..	..	..
Swaziland	..	28.2	..	..	..	..	..	..	..	..	..	..
Sweden	5.7	6.2	6.7	5.9	4.6	6.6	12.4	13.5	11.3	32.2	46.0	17.1
Switzerland	2.8	3.4	2.3	2.8	3.5	4.0	34.3	27.3	39.9	28.8	53.2	17.9
Syrian Arab Republic	6.8	..	5.2	..	14.0	..	..	..	..	..	..	..
Tajikistan	..	..	..	..	..	..	..	..	..	66.5	28.8	4.6
Tanzania	3.6[b]	4.3	2.8[b]	2.8	4.3[b]	5.8	..	..	..	..	..	..
Thailand	1.4	1.4	1.3	1.5	1.5	1.3	..	..	..	40.5	45.5	0.1
Timor-Leste	..	..	..	..	..	..	..	..	..	..	..	..
Togo	..	..	..	..	..	..	..	..	..	..	..	..
Trinidad and Tobago	19.6	6.5	17.0	4.4	23.9	9.6	..	..	..	..	..	..
Tunisia	..	14.2	..	13.1	..	17.3	..	..	..	41.4	37.7	13.6
Turkey	8.5	9.4	8.8	9.4	7.8	9.4	26.9	24.0	34.4	52.3	28.2	12.7
Turkmenistan	..	..	..	..	..	..	..	..	..	..	..	..
Uganda	..	..	..	..	..	..	..	..	..	..	..	..
Ukraine	..	6.4	..	6.7	..	6.0	..	..	..	8.5	52.2	39.3
United Arab Emirates	..	3.1	..	2.5	..	7.1	..	..	..	24.3	36.0	21.6
United Kingdom	9.8	5.6	11.6	6.1	7.4	5.1	25.5	30.5	18.4	37.3	47.7	14.3
United States	7.5[b]	5.8	7.9[b]	6.0	7.0[b]	5.4	10.6[b]	10.9[b]	10.3[b]	18.7	35.5	45.7
Uruguay	9.0[b]	7.6	6.8[b]	5.4	11.8[b]	10.1	..	..	..	59.1	27.0	13.8
Uzbekistan	..	..	..	..	..	..	..	..	..	..	..	..
Venezuela, RB	7.7	7.4	8.2	7.1	6.8	7.8	..	..	..	..	..	..
Vietnam	..	..	..	..	..	..	..	..	..	..	..	..
West Bank and Gaza	..	26.0	..	26.4	..	23.8	..	..	..	54.3	14.2	23.5
Yemen, Rep.	..	..	..	..	..	..	..	..	..	..	..	..
Zambia	18.9	..	16.3	..	22.4	..	..	..	..	..	..	..
Zimbabwe	..	..	..	..	..	..	..	..	..	..	..	..
World	.. w	.. w	.. w	.. w	.. w	.. w	.. w	.. w	.. w	.. w	.. w	.. w
Low income	..	..	..	..	..	..	..	..	..	..	..	..
Middle income	..	..	..	..	..	..	..	..	..	..	..	..
Lower middle income	..	..	..	..	..	..	..	..	..	..	..	..
Upper middle income	7.2	8.0	6.7	7.3	8.0	10.0	..	..	..	37.3	43.2	17.9
Low & middle income	..	..	..	..	..	..	..	..	..	..	..	..
East Asia & Pacific	2.5	4.7	..	..	..	..	..	..	..	..	..	..
Europe & Central Asia	..	6.9	..	7.9	..	7.2	..	..	..	25.7	52.4	22.8
Latin America & Carib.	6.6	7.3	5.4	5.9	8.3	9.0	..	..	..	51.6	34.5	12.1
Middle East & N. Africa	12.7	10.6	10.8	9.0	21.6	16.2	..	..	..	..	..	..
South Asia	..	..	..	..	..	..	..	..	..	..	..	..
Sub-Saharan Africa	..	..	..	..	..	..	..	..	..	..	..	..
High income	7.2	5.9	6.9	5.8	7.7	6.0	25.2	26.4	23.2	35.3	41.5	26.6
Euro area	9.0	7.5	7.1	6.8	11.9	8.3	42.4	41.6	42.8	41.4	42.9	14.9

a. Data are for the most recent year available. b. Limited coverage.

Unemployment and total employment are the broadest indicators of economic activity as reflected by the labor market. The International Labour Organization (ILO) defines the unemployed as members of the economically active population who are without work but available for and seeking work, including people who have lost their jobs or who have voluntarily left work. Some unemployment is unavoidable. At any time some workers are temporarily unemployed—between jobs as employers look for the right workers and workers search for better jobs. Such unemployment, often called frictional unemployment, results from the normal operation of labor markets.

Changes in unemployment over time may reflect changes in the demand for and supply of labor; they may also reflect changes in reporting practices. Paradoxically, low unemployment rates can disguise substantial poverty in a country, while high unemployment rates can occur in countries with a high level of economic development and low rates of poverty. In countries without unemployment or welfare benefits people eke out a living in vulnerable employment. In countries with well developed safety nets workers can afford to wait for suitable or desirable jobs. But high and sustained unemployment indicates serious inefficiencies in resource allocation.

The ILO definition of unemployment notwithstanding, reference periods, the criteria for people considered to be seeking work, and the treatment of people temporarily laid off or seeking work for the first time vary across countries. In many developing countries it is especially difficult to measure employment and unemployment in agriculture. The timing of a survey, for example, can maximize the effects of seasonal unemployment in agriculture. And informal sector employment is difficult to quantify where informal activities are not tracked.

Data on unemployment are drawn from labor force sample surveys and general household sample surveys, censuses, and official estimates, which are generally based on information from different sources and can be combined in many ways. Administrative records, such as social insurance statistics and employment office statistics, are not included in the table because of their limitations in coverage. Labor force surveys generally yield the most comprehensive data because they include groups not covered in other unemployment statistics, particularly people seeking work for the first time. These surveys generally use a definition of unemployment that follows the international recommendations more closely than that used by other sources and therefore generate statistics that are more comparable internationally. But the age group, geographic coverage, and collection methods could differ by country or change over time within a country. For detailed information, consult the original source.

Women tend to be excluded from the unemployment count for various reasons. Women suffer more from discrimination and from structural, social, and cultural barriers that impede them from seeking work. Also, women are often responsible for the care of children and the elderly and for household affairs. They may not be available for work during the short reference period, as they need to make arrangements before starting work. Furthermore, women are considered to be employed when they are working part-time or in temporary jobs, despite the instability of these jobs or their active search for more secure employment.

Long-term unemployment is measured by the length of time that an unemployed person has been without work and looking for a job. The data in the table are from labor force surveys. The underlying assumption is that shorter periods of joblessness are of less concern, especially when the unemployed are covered by unemployment benefits or similar forms of support. The length of time that a person has been unemployed is difficult to measure, because the ability to recall that time diminishes as the period of joblessness extends. Women's long-term unemployment is likely to be lower in countries where women constitute a large share of the unpaid family workforce.

Unemployment by level of educational attainment provides insights into the relation between the educational attainment of workers and unemployment and may be used to draw inferences about changes in employment demand. Information on educational attainment is the best available indicator of skill levels of the labor force. Besides the limitations to comparability raised for measuring unemployment, the different ways of classifying the education level may also cause inconsistency. Education level is supposed to be classified according to International Standard Classification of Education 1997 (ISCED97). For more information on ISCED97, see *About the data* for table 2.11.

• **Unemployment** is the share of the labor force without work but available for and seeking employment. Definitions of labor force and unemployment may differ by country (see *About the data*). • **Long-term unemployment** is the number of people with continuous periods of unemployment extending for a year or longer, expressed as a percentage of the total unemployed. • **Unemployment by educational attainment** is the unemployed by level of educational attainment as a percentage of the total unemployment. The levels of educational attainment accord with the ISCED97 of the United Nations Educational, Scientific, and Cultural Organization.

Data sources

Data on unemployment are from the ILO's Key Indicators of the Labour Market, 6th edition, database.

	Survey year	Children in employment					Employment by economic activity[a]			Status in employment[a]		
			% of children ages 7–14		% of children ages 7–14 in employment		% of children ages 7–14 in employment			% of children ages 7–14 in employment		
		Total	Male	Female	Work only	Study and work	Agriculture	Manufacturing	Services	Self-employed	Wage	Unpaid family
Afghanistan		..	..	..	..	..	..	..	..	..	..	..
Albania	2000	36.6	41.1	31.8	43.1	56.9	..	..	..	..	1.4	93.1
Algeria		..	..	..	..	..	..	..	..	..	..	..
Angola[b]	2001	30.1	30.0	30.1	26.6	73.4	..	..	..	..	6.2	80.1
Argentina	2004	12.9	15.7	9.8	4.8	95.2	..	..	..	34.2	8.1	56.2
Armenia		..	..	..	..	..	..	..	..	..	..	..
Australia		..	..	..	..	..	..	..	..	..	..	..
Austria		..	..	..	..	..	..	..	..	..	..	..
Azerbaijan	2005	5.2	5.8	4.5	6.3	93.7	91.7	0.7	7.4	4.1	3.8	92.1
Bangladesh	2006	16.2	25.7	6.4	37.8	62.2	..	..	..	–	17.0	77.8
Belarus	2005	11.7	12.1	11.2	0.0	100.0	..	..	..	..	9.2	78.8
Belgium		..	..	..	..	..	..	..	..	..	..	..
Benin	2006	74.4	72.8	76.1	36.1	63.9	..	..	..	..	..	..
Bolivia	2008	32.1	33.0	31.1	5.0	95.0	73.2	6.1	19.2	1.4	8.7	89.9
Bosnia and Herzegovina	2006	10.6	11.7	9.5	0.1	99.9	..	..	..	..	1.6	92.1
Botswana		..	..	..	..	..	..	..	..	..	..	..
Brazil	2007	6.1	8.1	4.0	6.6	93.4	55.5	8.7	33.5	6.8	23.1	70.1
Bulgaria		..	..	..	..	..	..	..	..	..	..	..
Burkina Faso	2006	42.1	49.0	34.5	67.7	32.3	70.9	1.4	24.9	1.9	2.2	95.8
Burundi	2005	11.7	12.5	11.0	38.9	61.1	..	..	25.9	68.6	..	..
Cambodia[c]	2003–04	48.9	49.6	48.1	13.8	86.2	82.3	4.2	12.9	6.0	4.1	89.4
Cameroon	2007	43.6	43.7	43.5	21.9	78.1	88.8	3.2	8.0	2.5	0.8	96.1[d]
Canada		..	..	..	..	..	..	..	..	..	..	..
Central African Republic	2000	67.0	66.5	67.6	54.9	45.1	..	..	..	..	2.0	56.4
Chad	2004	60.4	64.4	56.2	49.1	50.9	..	..	..	..	1.8	77.2
Chile	2003	4.1	5.1	3.1	3.2	96.8	24.1	6.9	66.9	..	..	..
China		..	..	..	..	..	..	..	..	..	..	..
Hong Kong SAR, China		..	..	..	..	..	..	..	..	..	..	..
Colombia	2007	3.9	5.3	2.3	24.8	75.2	41.2	10.8	46.1	22.7	29.1	45.6
Congo, Dem. Rep.[c]	2000	39.8	39.9	39.8	35.7	64.3	..	..	..	..	6.6	76.7
Congo, Rep	2005	30.1	29.9	30.2	9.9	90.1	..	..	..	..	4.2	84.5
Costa Rica[c]	2004	5.7	8.1	3.5	44.6	55.4	40.3	9.5	49.0	15.8	57.7	26.6
Côte d'Ivoire	2006	45.7	47.7	43.6	46.8	53.2	..	..	..	..	2.4	88.0
Croatia		..	..	..	..	..	..	..	..	..	..	..
Cuba		..	..	..	..	..	..	..	..	..	..	..
Czech Republic		..	..	..	..	..	..	..	..	..	..	..
Denmark		..	..	..	..	..	..	..	..	..	..	..
Dominican Republic[c]	2005	5.8	9.0	2.7	6.2	93.8	18.5	9.8	57.5	23.8	19.5	56.2[d]
Ecuador	2006	14.3	16.9	11.6	21.0	79.0	69.3	6.3	22.8	3.6	15.2	81.2
Egypt, Arab Rep.	2005	7.9	11.5	4.3	21.0	79.0	..	..	..	11.4	87.4	..
El Salvador	2007	7.1	10.1	3.8	24.9	75.1	50.1	13.3	35.2	2.2	23.6	74.2
Eritrea		..	..	..	..	..	..	..	..	..	..	..
Estonia		..	..	..	..	..	..	..	..	..	..	..
Ethiopia	2005	56.0	64.3	47.1	69.4	30.6	94.6	1.5	3.7	1.7	2.4	95.8
Finland		..	..	..	..	..	..	..	..	..	..	..
France		..	..	..	..	..	..	..	..	..	..	..
Gabon		..	..	..	..	..	..	..	..	..	..	..
Gambia, The	2005	43.5	33.9	52.3	32.1	67.9	..	..	..	..	1.1	87.3
Georgia		..	..	..	..	..	..	..	..	..	..	..
Germany		..	..	..	..	..	..	..	..	..	..	..
Ghana	2006	48.9	49.9	48.0	18.7	81.3	..	..	..	..	6.1	76.2
Greece		..	..	..	..	..	..	..	..	..	..	..
Guatemala	2006	18.2	24.5	11.7	30.5	69.5	63.7	9.7	24.7	2.0	18.8	79.2
Guinea	1994	48.3	47.2	49.5	98.6	1.4	..	..	..	..	..	..
Guinea-Bissau	2006	50.5	52.8	48.1	36.4	63.6	..	..	..	..	4.0	87.7
Haiti	2005	33.4	37.3	29.6	17.7	82.3	..	..	..	..	1.8	79.4
Honduras	2004	6.8	10.4	3.2	48.6	51.4	63.4	8.3	24.7	2.7	19.9	73.8

	Survey year	Children in employment					Employment by economic activity[a]			Status in employment[a]		
		% of children ages 7–14			% of children ages 7–14 in employment		% of children ages 7–14 in employment			% of children ages 7–14 in employment		
		Total	Male	Female	Work only	Study and work	Agriculture	Manufacturing	Services	Self-employed	Wage	Unpaid family
Hungary		..	..	..	..	..	..	..	..	..	..	..
India	2004–05	4.2	4.2	4.2	84.9	15.2	69.4	16.0	12.4	7.1	6.8	59.3
Indonesia	2000	8.9	8.8	9.1	24.9	75.1	..	..	..	..	17.8	75.8[d]
Iran, Islamic Rep.		..	..	..	..	..	..	..	..	..	..	..
Iraq	2006	14.7	17.9	11.3	32.4	67.6	..	..	..	..	7.0	85.3
Ireland		..	..	..	..	..	..	..	..	..	..	..
Israel		..	..	..	..	..	..	..	..	..	..	..
Italy		..	..	..	..	..	..	..	..	..	..	..
Jamaica	2005	9.8	11.3	8.3	2.5	97.5	..	..	..	..	16.3	74.9
Japan		..	..	..	..	..	..	..	..	..	..	..
Jordan		..	..	..	..	..	..	..	..	..	..	..
Kazakhstan	2006	3.6	4.4	2.8	1.6	98.4	..	..	..	–	4.0	75.0
Kenya	2000	37.7	40.1	35.2	14.1	85.9	..	..	..	..	..	..
Korea, Dem. Rep.		..	..	..	..	..	..	..	..	..	..	..
Korea, Rep.		..	..	..	..	..	..	..	..	..	..	..
Kosovo		..	..	..	..	..	..	..	..	..	..	..
Kuwait		..	..	..	..	..	..	..	..	..	..	..
Kyrgyz Republic	2006	5.2	5.8	4.6	7.9	92.1	..	..	..	–	3.7	81.9
Lao PDR		..	..	..	..	..	..	..	..	..	..	..
Latvia		..	..	..	..	..	..	..	..	..	..	..
Lebanon		..	..	..	..	..	..	..	..	..	..	..
Lesotho	2002	2.6	4.0	1.3	74.4	25.6	58.0	0.0	10.4	3.7	36.6	59.7[e]
Liberia	2007	37.4	37.8	37.1	45.0	55.0	..	..	..	..	1.7	79.3
Libya		..	..	..	..	..	..	..	..	..	..	..
Lithuania		..	..	..	..	..	..	..	..	..	..	..
Macedonia, FYR	2005	11.8	14.8	8.6	2.8	97.2	..	..	..	..	3.9	89.5
Madagascar	2007	26.1	28.0	24.1	40.6	59.4	86.9	2.5	8.6	0.0	10.4	89.6
Malawi	2006	40.3	41.3	39.4	10.5	89.5	..	..	..	..	6.7	75.5
Malaysia		..	..	..	..	..	..	..	..	..	..	..
Mali	2006	49.5	55.0	44.1	59.5	40.5	..	..	..	..	1.6	80.4
Mauritania		..	..	..	..	..	..	..	..	..	..	..
Mauritius		..	..	..	..	..	..	..	..	..	..	..
Mexico	2007	8.3	10.9	5.6	17.2	82.8	36.7	10.8	48.5	3.4	33.7	62.9
Moldova	2000	33.5	34.1	32.8	3.8	96.2	..	..	..	..	2.9	82.0
Mongolia	2006–07	10.1	11.4	8.6	16.4	83.6	91.3	0.3	6.3	5.4	0.2	94.5
Morocco	1998–99	13.2	13.5	12.8	93.2	6.8	60.6	8.3	10.1	2.1	10.0	81.7
Mozambique[c]	1996	1.8	1.9	1.7	100.0	0.0	..	..	..	..	..	..
Myanmar		..	..	..	..	..	..	..	..	..	..	..
Namibia	1999	15.4	16.2	14.7	9.5	90.5	91.5	0.4	8.0	0.1	4.5	95.0
Nepal	1999	47.2	42.2	52.4	35.6	64.4	87.0	1.4	11.1	4.2	3.3	92.4
Netherlands		..	..	..	..	..	..	..	..	..	..	..
New Zealand		..	..	..	..	..	..	..	..	..	..	..
Nicaragua	2005	10.1	16.2	3.9	30.8	69.2	70.5	9.7	19.3	1.2	13.8	85.0[e]
Niger	2006	47.1	49.2	45.0	66.5	33.5	..	..	..	4.8	74.5	..
Nigeria		..	..	..	..	..	..	..	..	..	..	..
Norway		..	..	..	..	..	..	..	..	..	..	..
Oman		..	..	..	..	..	..	..	..	..	..	..
Pakistan		..	..	..	..	..	..	..	..	..	..	..
Panama	2008	8.9	12.1	5.4	14.6	85.4	73.3	2.9	22.9	12.6	11.3	76.1[d]
Papua New Guinea		..	..	..	..	..	..	..	..	..	..	..
Paraguay[c]	2005	15.3	22.6	7.7	24.2	75.7	60.8	6.2	32.1	9.3	24.8	65.8
Peru	2007	42.2	44.8	39.4	4.0	96.0	62.6	5.0	31.2	3.9	6.1	90.0
Philippines	2001	13.3	16.3	10.0	14.8	85.2	64.3	4.1	30.6	4.1	22.8	73.1
Poland		..	..	..	..	..	..	..	..	..	..	..
Portugal	2001	3.6	4.6	2.6	3.6	96.4	48.5	11.2	33.3	..	..	..
Puerto Rico		..	..	..	..	..	..	..	..	..	..	..
Qatar		..	..	..	..	..	..	..	..	..	..	..

	Survey year	Children in employment					Employment by economic activity[a]			Status in employment[a]		
		% of children ages 7–14 in employment			% of children ages 7–14 in employment		% of children ages 7–14 in employment			% of children ages 7–14 in employment		
		Total	Male	Female	Work only	Study and work	Agriculture	Manufacturing	Services	Self-employed	Wage	Unpaid family
Romania	2000	1.4	1.7	1.1	20.7	79.3	97.1	0.0	2.3	4.5	92.9[d]	..
Russian Federation		..	..	..	..	..	..	..	..	..	..	..
Rwanda	2008	7.5	8.0	7.0	18.5	81.5	80.8	0.6	9.4	14.9	12.8	72.4
Saudi Arabia		..	..	..	..	..	..	..	..	..	..	..
Senegal	2005	18.5	24.4	12.6	61.9	38.1	79.1	5.0	14.0	6.3	4.4	84.1
Serbia	2005	6.9	7.2	6.6	2.1	97.9	..	..	..	..	5.2	89.4
Sierra Leone	2005	62.7	63.6	61.8	29.9	70.1	..	..	..	..	1.0	71.1
Singapore		..	..	..	..	..	..	..	..	..	..	..
Slovak Republic		..	..	..	..	..	..	..	..	..	..	..
Slovenia		..	..	..	..	..	..	..	..	..	..	..
Somalia	2006	43.5	45.5	41.5	53.5	46.5	..	..	..	..	1.6	94.8
South Africa	1999	27.7	29.0	26.4	5.1	94.9	..	..	..	7.1	7.1	85.8
Spain		..	..	..	..	..	..	..	..	..	..	..
Sri Lanka	1999	17.0	20.4	13.4	5.4	94.6	71.2	13.1	15.0	2.9	8.3	88.0
Sudan[f]	2000	19.1	21.5	16.8	55.9	44.1	..	..	..	..	7.3	81.3
Swaziland	2000	11.2	11.4	10.9	14.0	86.0	..	..	..	..	10.4	85.9
Sweden		..	..	..	..	..	..	..	..	..	..	..
Switzerland		..	..	..	..	..	..	..	..	..	..	..
Syrian Arab Republic	2006	6.6	8.8	4.3	34.6	65.4	..	..	..	..	21.5	68.8
Tajikistan	2005	8.9	8.7	9.1	9.0	91.0	..	..	..	..	24.2	71.3
Tanzania	2006	31.1	35.0	27.1	28.2	71.8	85.3	0.7	14.0	56.3[g]	0.9	42.8
Thailand	2005	15.1	15.7	14.4	4.2	95.8	..	..	..	..	13.5	80.0
Timor-Leste[c]	2001	7.6	7.1	8.1	26.8	73.2	91.8	0.0	8.2	28.0	0.0	72.0
Togo	2006	38.7	39.8	37.4	29.8	70.2	82.9	1.3	15.1	5.0	1.6	93.4
Trinidad and Tobago	2000	3.9	5.2	2.8	12.8	87.2	..	..	..	..	29.8	64.9
Tunisia		..	..	..	..	..	..	..	..	..	..	..
Turkey[h]	2006	2.6	3.3	1.8	38.8	61.2	57.1	14.3	20.9	2.1	34.1	63.8
Turkmenistan		..	..	..	..	..	..	..	..	..	..	..
Uganda	2005–06	38.2	39.8	36.5	7.7	92.3	95.5	1.4	3.0	1.4	1.5	97.1
Ukraine	2005	17.3	18.0	16.6	0.1	99.9	..	..	..	..	3.1	79.3
United Arab Emirates		..	..	..	..	..	..	..	..	..	..	..
United Kingdom		..	..	..	..	..	..	..	..	..	..	..
United States		..	..	..	..	..	..	..	..	..	..	..
Uruguay		..	..	..	..	..	..	..	..	..	..	..
Uzbekistan		..	..	..	..	..	..	..	..	..	..	..
Venezuela, RB[c]	2006	5.1	6.9	3.3	19.8	80.2	32.3	7.2	55.7	31.6	33.1	35.3
Vietnam	2006	21.3	21.0	21.6	11.9	88.1	..	..	..	..	5.9	91.2
West Bank and Gaza		..	..	..	..	..	..	..	..	..	..	..
Yemen, Rep.	2006	18.3	20.7	15.9	30.9	69.1	..	..	..	..	6.1	86.1
Zambia	2005	47.9	48.9	46.8	25.9	74.1	95.9	0.6	3.5	2.6	0.7	96.5
Zimbabwe	1999	14.3	15.3	13.3	12.0	88.0	..	..	..	3.4	28.4	68.2

a. Shares may not sum to 100 percent because of a residual category not included in the table. b. Covers only Angola-secured territory. c. Covers children ages 10–14. d. Refers to family workers, regardless of whether they are paid. e. Refers to unpaid workers, regardless of whether they are family workers. f. Covers northern Sudan only. g. Includes workers who are self-employed in the nonagricultural sector and workers who are working on their own or family farm or shamba. h. Covers children ages 6–14.

About the data

The data in the table refer to children's work in the sense of "economic activity"—that is, children in employment, a broader concept than child labor (see ILO 2009a for details on this distinction).

In line with the definition of economic activity adopted by the 13th International Conference of Labour Statisticians, the threshold for classifying a person as employed is to have been engaged at least one hour in any activity during the reference period relating to the production of goods and services set by the 1993 UN System of National Accounts. Children seeking work are thus excluded. Economic activity covers all market production and certain nonmarket production, including production of goods for own use. It excludes unpaid household services (commonly called "household chores")—that is, the production of domestic and personal services by household members for own-household consumption.

Data are from household surveys conducted by the International Labor Organization (ILO), the United Nations Children's Fund (UNICEF), the World Bank, and national statistical offices. The surveys yield data on education, employment, health, expenditure, and consumption indicators related to children's work.

Household survey data generally include information on work type—for example, whether a child is working for payment in cash or in kind or is involved in unpaid work, working for someone who is not a member of the household, or involved in any type of family work (on the farm or in a business). Country surveys define the ages for child labor as 5–17. The data in the table have been recalculated to present statistics for children ages 7–14.

Although efforts are made to harmonize the definition of employment and the questions on employment in survey questionnaires, significant differences remain in the survey instruments that collect data on children in employment and in the sampling design underlying the surveys. Differences exist not only across different household surveys in the same country but also across the same type of survey carried out in different countries, so estimates of working children are not fully comparable across countries.

The table aggregates the distribution of children in employment by the industrial categories of the International Standard Industrial Classification (ISIC): agriculture, manufacturing, and services. A residual category—which includes mining and quarrying; electricity, gas, and water; construction; extraterritorial organization; and other inadequately defined activities—is not presented. Both ISIC revision 2 and revision 3 are used, depending on the country's codification for describing economic activity. This does not affect the definition of the groups in the table.

The table also aggregates the distribution of children in employment by status in employment, based on the International Classification of Status in Employment (1993), which shows the distribution in employment by three major categories: self-employed workers, wage workers (also known as employees), and unpaid family workers. A residual category—which includes those not classifiable by status—is not presented.

Definitions

• **Survey year** is the year in which the underlying data were collected. • **Children in employment** are children involved in any economic activity for at least one hour in the reference week of the survey. • **Work only** refers to children who are employed and not attending school. • **Study and work** refer to children attending school in combination with employment. • **Employment by economic activity** is the distribution of children in employment by the major industrial categories (ISIC revision 2 or revision 3). • **Agriculture** corresponds to division 1 (ISIC revision 2) or categories A and B (ISIC revision 3) and includes agriculture and hunting, forestry and logging, and fishing. • **Manufacturing** corresponds to division 3 (ISIC revision 2) or category D (ISIC revision 3). • **Services** correspond to divisions 6–9 (ISIC revision 2) or categories G–P (ISIC revision 3) and include wholesale and retail trade, hotels and restaurants, transport, financial intermediation, real estate, public administration, education, health and social work, other community services, and private household activity. • **Self-employed workers** are people whose remuneration depends directly on the profits derived from the goods and services they produce, with or without other employees, and include employers, own-account workers, and members of producers cooperatives. • **Wage workers** (also known as employees) are people who hold explicit (written or oral) or implicit employment contracts that provide basic remuneration that does not depend directly on the revenue of the unit for which they work. • **Unpaid family workers** are people who work without pay in a market-oriented establishment operated by a related person living in the same household.

Data sources

Data on children at work are estimates produced by the Understanding Children's Work project based on household survey data sets made available by the ILO's International Programme on the Elimination of Child Labour under its Statistical Monitoring Programme on Child Labour, UNICEF under its Multiple Indicator Cluster Survey program, the World Bank under its Living Standards Measurement Study program, and national statistical offices. Information on how the data were collected and some indication of their reliability can be found at www.ilo.org/public/english/standards/ipec/simpoc/, www.childinfo.org, and www.worldbank.org/lsms. Detailed country statistics can be found at www.ucw-project.org.

Brazil has rapidly reduced children's employment and raised school attendance | 2.6a

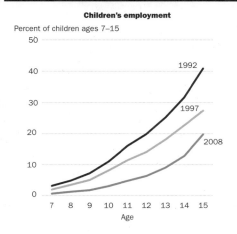

Children's employment

Percent of children ages 7–15

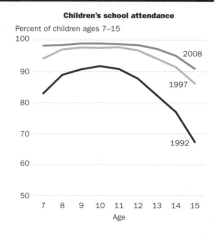

Children's school attendance

Percent of children ages 7–15

Source: Understanding Children's Work project calculations based on Brazilian Pesquisa Nacional por Amostra de Domicílios Surveys.

Poverty rates at national poverty lines

	Population below national poverty line								Poverty gap at national poverty line			
	Survey year	Rural %	Urban %	National %	Survey year	Rural %	Urban %	National %	Survey year	Rural %	Urban %	National %
Afghanistan	2007	45.0	27.0	42.0		..	..	..		..	..	..
Albania	2002	29.6	19.5	25.4	2005	24.2	11.2	18.5	2005	5.3	2.3	4.0
Algeria	1988	16.6	7.3	12.2	1995	30.3	14.7	22.6	1995	4.5	1.8	3.2
Argentina[a]	2001	..	35.9	..		..	..	..		..	..	..
Armenia	1998–99	50.8	58.3	55.1	2001	48.7	51.9	50.9	2001	..	..	15.1
Azerbaijan	1995	..	..	68.1	2001	42.0	55.0	49.6	2001	..	..	15.5
Bangladesh	2000	52.3	35.1	48.9	2005	43.8	28.4	40.0	2005	9.8	6.5	9.0
Belarus	2002	..	..	30.5	2004	..	..	17.4		..	..	..
Benin	1999	33.0	23.3	29.0	2003	46.0	29.0	39.0	2003	14.0	8.0	12.0
Bolivia	2000	75.0	27.9	45.2	2007	63.9	23.7	37.7		..	..	..
Bosnia and Herzegovina	2001–02	19.9	13.8	19.5		..	..	..	2001–02	4.9	2.8	4.6
Brazil	1998	51.4	14.7	22.0	2002–03	41.0	17.5	21.5	2002–03	28.4	17.8	19.6
Bulgaria	1997	..	..	36.0	2001	..	..	12.8	2001	..	..	4.2
Burkina Faso	1998	61.1	22.4	54.6	2003	52.4	19.2	46.4	2003	17.6	5.1	15.3
Burundi	1998	64.6	66.5	68.0		..	..	..		..	..	..
Cambodia	2004	39.2	..	34.7	2007	34.7	..	30.1	2007	8.3	..	7.2
Cameroon[a]	2001	52.1	17.9	40.2	2007	55.0	12.2	39.9	2007	17.5	2.8	13.2
Chad	1995–96	48.6	..	43.4		..	..	..	1995–96	26.3	..	27.5
Chile[a]	2003	..	..	18.7	2006	..	..	13.7		..	..	..
China[a]	2000	3.5	..	..	2005	2.5	..	..		..	..	..
Colombia	2002	70.1	50.4	55.7	2006	62.1	39.1	45.1		..	..	..
Congo, Dem. Rep.	2004–05	75.7	61.5	71.3		..	..	..	2004–05	34.9	26.2	32.2
Congo, Rep.	2005	49.2	..	42.3		..	..	..		..	..	..
Costa Rica	1989	35.8	26.2	31.7	2004	28.3	20.8	23.9	2004	10.8	7.0	8.6
Croatia	2002	..	..	11.2	2004	..	..	11.1		..	..	..
Dominican Republic[a]	2000	50.8	28.9	36.5	2007	54.1	45.4	48.5		..	..	..
Ecuador[a]	1999	75.1	36.4	52.2	2006	61.5	24.9	38.3		..	..	..
Egypt, Arab Rep.	1995–96	23.3	22.5	22.9	1999–2000	..	..	16.7	1999–2000	..	..	3.0
El Salvador[a]	2000	53.7[b]	29.9[b]	38.8[b]	2006	36.0[b]	27.8[b]	30.7[b]		..	..	..
Eritrea	1993–94	..	..	53.0		..	..	..		..	..	..
Estonia	1995	14.7	6.8	8.9		..	..	..	1995	6.6	1.8	3.1
Ethiopia	1995–96	47.0	33.3	45.5	1999–2000	45.0	37.0	44.2	1999–2000	12.0	10.0	12.0
Gambia, The	1998	61.0	48.0	57.6	2003	63.0	57.0	61.3	2003	..	..	25.9
Georgia	2002	55.4	48.5	52.1	2003	52.7	56.2	54.5		..	..	..
Ghana	1998–99	49.6	19.4	39.5	2005–06	39.2	10.8	28.5	2005–06	13.5	3.1	9.6
Guatemala	2000	..	..	56.2	2006	72.0	28.0	51.0		..	..	..
Guinea	1994	..	..	40.0		..	..	..		..	..	..
Guinea-Bissau	2002	..	52.6	65.7		..	..	..	2000	..	17.5	25.7
Haiti	1987	..	..	65.0	1995	66.0	..	..		..	..	..
Honduras	1998–99	71.2	28.6	52.5	2004	70.4	29.5	50.7	2004	34.5	9.1	22.3
Hungary	1993	..	..	14.5	1997	..	..	17.3	1997	4.1	..	..
India	1993–94	37.3	32.4	36.0	1999–2000	30.2	24.7	28.6	1999–2000	5.6	6.9	..
Indonesia	1996	19.8	13.6	17.6	2004	20.1	12.1	16.7	2004	..	..	2.9
Jamaica	1995	37.0	18.7	27.5	2000	25.1	12.8	18.7		..	..	..
Jordan	1997	27.0	19.7	21.3	2002	18.7	12.9	14.2	2002	4.7	2.9	3.3
Kazakhstan	2001	..	..	17.6	2002	..	..	15.4	2002	4.5	2.0	3.1
Kenya	1997	53.0	49.0	52.0	2005/06	49.7	34.4	46.6	2005/06	14.1	2.5	16.6
Kosovo	2003–04	44.2	42.1	43.5	2005–06	49.2	37.4	45.1	2005–06	..	..	13.3
Kyrgyz Republic	2003	57.5	35.7	49.9	2005	50.8	29.8	43.1	2005	12.0	7.0	10.0
Lao PDR	1997–98	41.0	26.9	38.6	2002–03	..	..	33.5	2002–03	..	..	8.0
Latvia	2002	11.6	..	7.5	2004	12.7	..	5.9	2004	..	..	1.2

	Population below national poverty line							Poverty gap at national poverty line			
	Survey year	Rural %	Urban %	National %	Survey year	Rural %	Urban %	National %	Survey year	Rural %	Urban %	National %
Lesotho[a]	1994/95	68.9	36.7	66.6	2002/03	60.5	41.5	56.3		..	..	..
Macedonia, FYR	2002	25.3	..	21.4	2003	22.3	..	21.7	2003	6.5	..	6.7
Madagascar[a]	1999	76.7	52.1	71.3	2005	53.5	52.0	68.7	2005	28.9	19.3	26.8
Malawi	1997–98	66.5	54.9	65.3	2004–05	55.9	25.4	52.4	2004–05	8.6	2.8	8.0
Malaysia	1989	..	..	15.5		..	..	..		..	..	..
Mali	1998	75.9	30.1	63.8		..	..	..		..	..	..
Mauritania	1996	65.5	30.1	50.0	2000	61.2	25.4	46.3		..	..	..
Mauritius	1992	..	..	10.6		..	..	..		..	..	..
Mexico	2002	65.4	41.5	50.6	2004	56.9	41.0	47.0		..	..	..
Moldova	2001	64.1	58.0	62.4	2002	67.2	42.6	48.5	2002	..	..	16.5
Mongolia	1998	32.6	39.4	35.6	2002	43.4	30.3	36.1	2002	13.2	9.2	11.0
Morocco	1990–91	18.0	7.6	13.1	1998–99	27.2	12.0	19.0	1998–99	6.7	2.5	4.4
Mozambique	1996–97	71.3	62.0	69.4	2002–03	54.1	51.6	55.2	2002–03	19.9	18.9	20.4
Myanmar	2004–05	36.0	22.0	32.0		..	..	..	2004–05	7.0	4.0	7.0
Nepal	1995–96	43.3	21.6	41.8	2003–04	34.6	9.6	30.9	2003–04	8.5	2.2	7.5
Nicaragua	1998	68.5	30.5	47.9	2001	64.3	28.7	45.8	2001	25.9	8.7	17.0
Niger	1989–93	66.0	52.0	63.0		..	..	..		..	..	..
Nigeria	1985	49.5	31.7	43.0	1992–93	36.4	30.4	34.1		..	..	..
Pakistan	1993	33.4	17.2	28.6	1998–99	35.9	24.2	32.6	1998–99	7.9	5.0	7.0
Panama	1997	64.9	15.3	37.3	2003	..	..	36.8	1997	32.1	3.9	16.4
Papua New Guinea	1996	41.3	16.1	37.5		..	..	..	1996	13.8	4.3	12.4
Paraguay[c]	1990	28.5	19.7	20.5		..	..	..	1990	10.5	5.6	6.0
Peru	2003	75.7	39.5	52.2	2004	72.5	40.3	51.6	2004	28.3	12.4	18.0
Philippines	1994	45.4	18.6	32.1	1997	36.9	11.9	25.1	1997	10.0	2.6	6.4
Poland	1996	..	..	14.6	2001	..	..	14.8		..	..	..
Romania	1995	..	..	25.4	2002	..	..	28.9	2002	..	..	7.6
Russian Federation	1998	..	..	31.4	2002	..	..	19.6	2002	..	..	5.1
Rwanda[a]	1999–2000	65.7	14.3	60.3	2005–06	62.5	..	56.9		..	..	..
Senegal	1992	40.4	23.7	33.4		..	..	..	1992	16.4	3.1	13.9
Sierra Leone	1989	..	..	82.8	2003–04	79.0	56.4	70.2	2003–04	34.0	..	29.0
Slovak Republic	2004	..	..	16.8		..	..	..	2004	..	..	5.5
South Africa[a]	2000	..	..	38.0	2008	..	..	22.0	2008	..	..	6.0
Sri Lanka	1995–96	27.0	15.0	25.0	2002	7.9	24.7	22.7	2002	5.6	1.7	5.1
Swaziland	2000–01	75.0	49.0	69.2		..	..	..	2000–01	..	..	32.9
Tajikistan	2003	73.8	68.8	72.4	2007	55.0	49.4	53.5	2003	12.4	12.5	12.4
Tanzania	1991	40.8	31.2	38.6	2000–01	38.7	29.5	35.7		..	..	..
Thailand	1994	..	..	9.8	1998	..	..	13.6	1998	..	..	3.0
Timor-Leste	2001	..	..	39.7		..	..	..	2001	..	..	11.9
Togo	1987–89	..	..	32.3		..	..	..	1987–89	..	..	10.0
Trinidad and Tobago	1992	20.0	24.0	21.0		..	..	..	1992	6.2	7.4	7.3
Tunisia	1990	13.1	3.5	7.4	1995	13.9	3.6	7.6	1990	3.3	0.9	1.7
Turkey	1994	..	..	28.3	2002	34.5	22.0	27.0	2002	..	..	0.3
Uganda[a]	2002–03	42.7	14.4	38.8	2005–06	34.2	13.7	31.1	2005–06	9.7	3.5	8.7
Ukraine	2000	34.9	..	31.5	2003	28.4	..	19.5		..	..	..
Uruguay	1994	..	20.2	..	1998	..	24.7	..	1998	..	8.6	..
Uzbekistan	2000–01	33.6	27.8	31.5	2003	29.8	22.6	27.2		..	..	..
Venezuela, RB	1989	..	..	31.3	1997–99	..	..	52.0	1997–99	..	..	24.0
Vietnam	1998	45.5	9.2	37.4	2002	35.6	6.6	28.9	2002	8.7	1.3	6.9
Yemen, Rep.	1998	45.0	30.8	41.8		..	..	..	1998	14.7	8.2	13.2
Zambia	1998	83.1	56.0	72.9	2004	78.0	53.0	68.0	2004	44.0	22.0	36.0
Zimbabwe	1990–91	35.8	3.4	25.8	1995–96	48.0	7.9	34.9		..	..	..

a. Data are from national sources. b. Data refer to share of households rather than share of population. c. Covers Asunción metropolitan area only.

The World Bank periodically prepares poverty assessments of countries in which it has an active program, in close collaboration with national institutions, other development agencies, and civil society groups, including poor people's organizations. Poverty assessments report the extent and causes of poverty and propose strategies to reduce it. Since 1992 the World Bank has conducted about 200 poverty assessments, which are the main source of the poverty estimates presented in the table. Countries report similar assessments as part of their Poverty Reduction Strategies.

The poverty assessments are the best available source of information on poverty estimates using national poverty lines. They often include separate assessments of urban and rural poverty. Data are derived from nationally representative household surveys conducted by national statistical offices or by private agencies under the supervision of government or international agencies and obtained from government statistical offices and World Bank Group country departments.

Some poverty assessments analyze the current poverty status of a country using the latest available household survey data, while others use survey data for several years to analyze poverty trends. Thus, poverty estimates for more than one year might be derived from a single poverty assessment. A poverty assessment might not use all available household surveys, or survey data might become available at a later date even though data were collected before the poverty assessment date. Thus poverty assessments may not fully represent all household survey data.

Many developing countries, particularly middle-income countries, have their own poverty monitoring programs with well documented estimation methodologies. The programs regularly publish what the countries consider official poverty estimates. Such estimates are reviewed by World Bank researchers and included in the table.

Data availability

The number of data sets within two years of any given year rose dramatically, from 13 between 1978 and 1982 to 158 between 2001 and 2006. Data coverage is improving in all regions, but the Middle East and North Africa and Sub-Saharan Africa continue to lag. The database, maintained by a team in the World Bank's Development Research Group, is updated annually as new survey data become available, and a major reassessment of progress against poverty is made about every three years. A complete overview of data availability by year and country is available at http://iresearch.worldbank.org/povcalnet/.

Data quality

Poverty assessments are based on surveys fielded to collect, among other things, information on income or consumption from a sample of households. To be useful for poverty estimates, surveys must be nationally representative and include sufficient information to compute a comprehensive estimate of total household consumption or income (including consumption or income from own production), from which it is possible to construct a correctly weighted distribution of consumption or income per person. There remain many potential problems with household survey data, including selective nonresponse and differences in the menu of consumption items presented and the length of the period over which respondents must recall their expenditures. These issues are discussed in *About the data* for table 2.8.

National poverty lines

National poverty lines are used to make estimates of poverty consistent with the country's specific economic and social circumstances and are not intended for international comparisons of poverty rates. The setting of national poverty lines reflects local perceptions of the level of consumption or income needed not to be poor. The perceived boundary between poor and not poor rises with the average income of a country and so does not provide a uniform measure for comparing poverty rates across countries. Nevertheless, national poverty estimates are clearly the appropriate measure for setting national policies for poverty reduction and for monitoring their results.

Almost all the national poverty lines use a food bundle based on prevailing diets that attains predetermined nutritional requirements for good health and normal activity levels, plus an allowance for nonfood spending. The rise in poverty lines with average income is driven more by the gradient in the nonfood component of the poverty lines than in the food component, although there is still an appreciable share attributable to the gradient in food poverty lines. While nutritional requirements tend to be fairly similar even across countries at different levels of economic development, richer countries tend to use a more expensive food bundle—more meat and vegetables, less starchy staples, and more processed foods generally—for attaining the same nutritional needs.

• **Survey year** is the year in which the underlying data were collected. • **Rural population below national poverty line** is the percentage of the rural population living below the national rural poverty line. • **Urban population below national poverty line** is the percentage of the urban population living below the national urban poverty line. • **National population below national poverty line** is the percentage of the country's population living below the national poverty line. National estimates are based on population-weighted subgroup estimates from household surveys. • **Poverty gap at national poverty line** is the mean shortfall from the poverty line (counting the nonpoor as having zero shortfall) as a percentage of the poverty line. This measure reflects the depth of poverty as well as its incidence.

The poverty measures are prepared by the World Bank's Development Research Group, based on data from World Bank's country poverty assessments and country Poverty Reduction Strategies. Summaries of poverty assessments are available at www.worldbank.org/povertynet, by selecting "Poverty assessments" from the left side bar. Poverty assessment documents are available at www-wds.worldbank.org, under "By topic," "Poverty reduction," "Poverty assessment." Further discussion of how national poverty lines vary across countries can be found in Ravallion, Chen, and Sangraula's "Dollar a Day Revisited" (2008).

Poverty rates at international poverty lines

	International poverty line in local currency			International poverty line								
	$1.25 a day 2005	$2 a day 2005	Survey year	Population below $1.25 a day %	Poverty gap at $1.25 a day %	Population below $2 a day %	Poverty gap at $2 a day %	Survey year	Population below $1.25 a day %	Poverty gap at $1.25 a day %	Population below $2 a day %	Poverty gap at $2 a day %
Albania	75.51	120.82	2002[a]	<2	<0.5	8.7	1.4	2005[a]	<2	<0.5	7.8	1.4
Algeria	48.42[b]	77.48[b]	1988[a]	6.6	1.8	23.8	6.6	1995[a]	6.8	1.4	23.6	6.4
Angola	88.13	141.01	2000[a]	54.3	29.9	70.2	42.3		..	..	..	..
Argentina	1.69	2.71	2005[c,d]	4.5	1.0	11.3	3.6	2006[c,d]	3.4	1.2	7.3	2.7
Armenia	245.24	392.38	2003[a]	10.6	1.9	43.4	11.3	2007[a]	3.7	0.7	21.0	4.6
Azerbaijan	2,170.94	3,473.51	2001[a]	6.3	1.1	27.1	6.8	2005[a]	<2	<0.5	<2	<0.5
Bangladesh	31.87	50.99	2000[a]	57.8[e]	17.3[e]	85.4[e]	38.7[e]	2005[a]	49.6[e]	13.1[e]	81.3[e]	33.8[e]
Belarus	949.53	1,519.25	2005[a]	<2	<0.5	<2	<0.5	2007[a]	<2	<0.5	<2	<0.5
Belize	1.83	2.93	1995[a]	13.4	5.4	23.1	10.3		..	..	..	..
Benin	343.99	550.38	2003[a]	47.3	15.7	75.3	33.5		..	..	..	..
Bhutan	23.08	36.93	2003[a]	26.2	7.0	49.5	18.8		..	..	..	..
Bolivia	3.21	5.14	2005[b]	19.6	9.7	30.3	15.5	2007[b]	11.9	5.6	21.9	9.5
Bosnia and Herzegovina	1.09	1.74	2004[a]	<2	<0.5	<2	<0.5	2007[a]	<2	<0.5	<2	<0.5
Botswana	4.23	6.77	1985–86[a]	35.6	13.8	54.7	25.8	1993–94[a]	31.2	11.0	49.4	22.3
Brazil	1.96	3.14	2005[d]	7.8	1.6	18.3	5.9	2007[d]	5.2	1.3	12.7	4.1
Bulgaria	0.92	1.47	2001[a]	2.6	<0.5	7.8	2.2	2003[a]	<2	<0.5	<2	0.9
Burkina Faso	303.02	484.83	1998[a]	70.0	30.2	87.6	49.1	2003[a]	56.5	20.3	81.2	39.2
Burundi	558.79	894.07	1998[a]	86.4	47.3	95.4	64.1	2006[a]	81.3	36.4	93.4	56.0
Cambodia	2,019.12	3,230.60	2004[a]	40.2	11.3	68.2	28.0	2007[a]	25.8	6.1	57.8	20.1
Cameroon	368.12	588.99	1996[a]	51.5	18.9	74.4	36.0	2001[a]	32.8	10.2	57.7	23.6
Cape Verde	97.72	156.35	2001[a]	20.6	5.9	40.2	14.9		..	..	..	..
Central African Republic	384.33	614.93	1993[a]	82.8	57.0	90.7	68.4	2003[a]	62.4	28.3	81.9	45.3
Chad	409.46	655.14	2002–03[a]	61.9	25.6	83.3	43.9		..	..	..	..
Chile	484.20	774.72	2003[d]	<2	<0.5	5.3	1.3	2006[d]	<2	<0.5	2.4	0.39
China	5.11[f]	8.17[f]	2002[a]	28.4[g]	8.7[g]	51.1[g]	20.6[g]	2005[a]	15.9[g]	4.0[g]	36.3[g]	12.2[g]
Colombia	1,489.68	2,383.48	2003[d]	15.4	6.1	26.3	10.9	2006[d]	16.0	5.7	27.9	11.9
Comoros	368.01	588.82	2004[a]	46.1	20.8	65.0	34.2		..	..	..	..
Congo, Dem. Rep.	395.29	632.46	2005–06[a]	59.2	25.3	79.5	42.4		..	..	..	..
Congo, Rep.	469.46	751.14	2005[a]	54.1	22.8	74.4	38.8		..	..	..	..
Costa Rica	348.70[b]	557.92[b]	2005[d]	2.4	<0.5	8.6	2.3	2007[d]	<2	<0.5	4.3	1.3
Croatia	5.58	8.92	2001[a]	<2	<0.5	<2	<0.5	2005[a]	<2	<0.5	<2	<0.5
Czech Republic	19.00	30.39	1993[d]	<2	<0.5	<2	<0.5	1996[d]	<2	<0.5	<2	<0.5
Côte d'Ivoire	407.26	651.62	1998[a]	24.1	6.7	49.1	18.1	2002[a]	23.3	6.8	46.8	17.6
Djibouti	134.76	215.61	1996[a]	4.8	1.6	15.1	4.5	2002[a]	18.8	5.3	41.2	14.6
Dominican Republic	25.50[b]	40.79[b]	2005[d]	5.0	0.9	15.1	4.3	2007[d]	4.4	1.3	12.3	3.9
Ecuador	0.63	1.00	2005[d]	9.8	3.2	20.4	7.6	2007[d]	4.7	1.2	12.8	4.0
Egypt, Arab Rep.	2.53	4.04	1999–00[a]	<2	<0.5	19.3	3.5	2004–05[a]	<2	<0.5	18.4	3.5
El Salvador	6.02[b]	9.62[b]	2005[d]	11.0	4.8	20.5	8.9	2007[d]	6.4	2.7	13.2	5.3
Estonia	11.04	17.66	2002[a]	<2	<0.5	2.5	0.6	2004[a]	<2	<0.5	<2	<0.5
Ethiopia	3.44	5.50	1999–00[a]	55.6	16.2	86.4	37.9	2005[a]	39.0	9.6	77.5	28.8
Gabon	554.69	887.50	2005[a]	4.8	0.9	19.6	5.0		..	..	..	..
Gambia, The	12.93	20.69	1998[a]	66.7	34.7	82.0	50.0	2003[a]	34.3	12.1	56.7	24.9
Georgia	0.98	1.57	2002[a]	15.1	4.7	34.2	12.2	2005[a]	13.4	4.4	30.4	10.9
Ghana	5,594.78	8,951.64	1998–99[a]	39.1	14.4	63.3	28.5	2006[a]	30.0	10.5	53.6	22.3
Guatemala	5.68[b]	9.08[b]	2002[d]	16.9	6.5	29.8	12.9	2006[d]	11.7	3.5	24.3	8.9
Guinea-Bissau	355.34	568.55	1993[a]	52.1	20.6	75.7	37.4	2002[a]	48.8	16.5	77.9	34.8
Guinea	1,849.46	2,959.13	1994[a]	36.8	11.5	63.8	26.4	2003[a]	70.1	32.2	87.2	50.2
Guyana	131.47[b]	210.35[b]	1993[d]	5.8	2.6	15.0	5.4	1998[d]	7.7	3.9	16.8	6.9
Haiti	24.21[b]	38.73[b]	2001[d]	54.9	28.2	72.1	41.8		..	..	..	..
Honduras	12.08[b]	19.32[b]	2005[d]	22.2	10.2	34.8	16.7	2006[d]	18.2	8.2	29.7	14.2
Hungary	171.90	275.03	2002[a]	<2	<0.5	<2	<0.5	2004[a]	<2	<0.5	<2	<0.5
India	19.50[h]	31.20[h]	1993–94[a]	49.4[g]	14.4[g]	81.7[g]	35.3[g]	2004–05[a]	41.6[g]	10.8[g]	75.6[g]	30.4[g]
Indonesia	5,241.03[h]	8,385.65[h]	2005[a]	21.4[g]	4.6[g]	53.8[g]	17.3[g]	2007[a]	29.4	7.1	60.0	21.8
Iran, Islamic Rep.	3,393.53	5,429.65	1998[a]	<2	<0.5	8.3	1.8	2005[a]	<2	<0.5	8.0	1.8
Jamaica	54.20[b]	86.72[b]	2002[a]	<2	<0.5	8.7	1.6	2004[a]	<2	<0.5	5.8	0.9
Jordan	0.62	0.99	2002–03[a]	<2	<0.5	11.0	2.1	2006[a]	<2	<0.5	3.5	0.6
Kazakhstan	81.21	129.93	2003[a]	3.1	<0.5	17.2	3.9	2007[a]	<2	<0.5	<2	<0.5

	International poverty line in local currency		International poverty line									
	$1.25 a day 2005	$2 a day 2005	Survey year	Population below $1.25 a day %	Poverty gap at $1.25 a day %	Population below $2 a day %	Poverty gap at $2 a day %	Survey year	Population below $1.25 a day %	Poverty gap at $1.25 a day %	Population below $2 a day %	Poverty gap at $2 a day %
Kenya	40.85	65.37	1997[a]	19.6	4.6	42.7	14.7	2005–06[a]	19.7	6.1	39.9	15.1
Kyrgyz Republic	16.25	26.00	2004[a]	21.8	4.4	51.9	16.8	2007[a]	3.4	<0.5	27.5	5.2
Lao PDR	4,677.02	7,483.24	1997–98	49.3[e]	14.9[e]	79.9[e]	34.4[e]	2002–03[a]	44.0[e]	12.1[e]	76.8[e]	31.0[e]
Latvia	0.43	0.69	2004[a]	<2	<0.5	<2	<0.5	2007[a]	<2	<0.5	<2	<0.5
Lesotho	4.28	6.85	1995[a]	47.6	26.7	61.1	37.3	2002–03[a]	43.4	20.8	62.2	33.0
Liberia	0.64	1.02	2007[a]	83.7	40.8	94.8	59.5		..	..	..	..
Lithuania	2.08	3.32	2002[a]	<2	<0.5	<2	<0.5	2004[a]	<2	<0.5	<2	<0.5
Macedonia, FYR	29.47[b]	47.16[b]	2003[a]	<2	<0.5	3.2	0.7	2006[a]	<2	<0.5	5.3	1.3
Madagascar	945.48	1,512.76	2001[a]	76.3	41.4	88.7	57.2	2005[a]	67.8	26.5	89.6	46.9
Malawi	71.15	113.84	1997–98[d]	83.1	46.0	93.5	62.3	2004–05[a,i]	73.9	32.3	90.4	51.8
Malaysia	2.64	4.23	1997[d]	<2	<0.5	6.8	1.3	2004[d]	<2	<0.5	7.8	1.4
Mali	362.10	579.36	2001[a]	61.2	25.8	82.0	43.6	2006[a]	51.4	18.8	77.1	36.5
Mauritania	157.08	251.33	1995–96[a]	23.4	7.1	48.3	17.8	2000[a]	21.2	5.7	44.1	15.9
Mexico	9.56	15.30	2006[a]	<2	<0.5	4.8	1.0	2008[d]	4.0	1.8	8.2	3.3
Moldova	6.03	9.65	2004[a]	8.1	1.7	28.9	7.9	2007[a]	2.4	0.5	11.5	2.7
Mongolia	653.12	1,044.99	2002[a]	15.5	3.6	38.8	12.3	2007–08[a]	2.2	0.4	13.6	2.9
Montenegro	0.62	1.00	2005[a]	<2	<0.5	5.7	1.1	2007[a]	<2	<0.5	<2	<0.5
Morocco	6.89	11.02	2000[a]	6.3	0.9	24.3	6.3	2007[a]	2.5	0.5	14.0	3.1
Mozambique	14,532.12	23,251.39	1996–97[a]	81.3	42.0	92.9	59.4	2002–03[a]	74.7	35.4	90.0	53.5
Namibia	6.33	10.13	1993[d]	49.1	24.6	62.2	36.5		..	..	..	..
Nepal	33.08	52.93	1995–96[a]	68.4	26.7	88.1	46.8	2003–04[a]	55.1	19.7	77.6	37.8
Nicaragua	9.12[b]	14.59[b]	2001[d]	19.4	6.7	37.5	14.4	2005[d]	15.8	5.2	31.8	12.3
Niger	334.16	534.66	1994[a]	78.2	38.6	91.5	56.5	2005[a]	65.9	28.1	85.6	46.6
Nigeria	98.23	157.17	1996–97[a]	68.5	32.1	86.4	49.7	2003–04[a]	64.4	29.6	83.9	46.9
Pakistan	25.89	41.42	2001–02[a]	35.9	7.9	73.9	26.4	2004–05[a]	22.6	4.4	60.3	18.7
Panama	0.76[b]	1.22[b]	2004[d]	9.2	2.7	18.0	6.8	2006[d]	9.5	3.1	17.8	7.1
Papua New Guinea	2.11[b]	3.37[b]	1996[a]	35.8	12.3	57.4	25.5		..	..	..	..
Paraguay	2,659.74	4,255.59	2005[d]	9.3	3.4	18.4	7.3	2007[d]	6.5	2.7	14.2	5.5
Peru	2.07	3.31	2005[d]	8.2	2.0	19.4	6.3	2007[d]	7.7	2.3	17.8	6.2
Philippines	30.22	48.36	2003[a]	22.0	5.5	43.8	16.0	2006[a]	22.6	5.5	45.0	16.3
Poland	2.69	4.31	2002[a]	<2	<0.5	<2	<0.5	2005[a]	<2	<0.5	<2	<0.5
Romania	2.15	3.44	2002[a]	2.9	0.8	13.0	3.2	2007[a]	<2	<0.5	4.1	0.1
Russian Federation	16.74	26.78	2002[a]	<2	<0.5	3.7	0.6	2007[a]	<2	<0.5	<2	<0.5
Rwanda	295.93	473.49	1984–85[a]	63.3	19.7	88.4	41.8	2000[a]	76.6	38.2	90.3	55.7
São Tomé and Príncipe	7,949.55	12,725.55	2000–01[a]	28.4	8.4	56.6	21.6		..	..	..	..
Senegal	372.81	596.49	2001[a]	44.2	14.3	71.3	31.2	2005[a]	33.5	10.8	60.3	24.6
Serbia	42.86	68.62	2003[a]	<2	<0.5	<2	<0.5	2008[a]	<2	<0.5	<2	<0.5
Seychelles	6.53	10.46	1999–00[a]	<2	<0.5	<2	<0.5	2006–07[a]	<2	<0.5	<2	<0.5
Sierra Leone	1,745.26	2,792.42	1989–90[a]	62.8	44.8	75.0	54.0	2003[a]	53.4	20.3	76.1	37.5
Slovak Republic	23.53	37.66	1992[d]	<2	<0.5	<2	<0.5	1996[d]	<2	<0.5	<2	<0.5
Slovenia	198.25	317.20	2002[a]	<2	<0.5	<2	<0.5	2004[a]	<2	<0.5	<2	<0.5
South Africa	5.71	9.14	1995[a]	21.4	5.2	39.9	15.0	2000[a]	26.2	8.2	42.9	18.3
Sri Lanka	50.05	80.08	1995–96[a]	16.3	3.0	46.7	13.7	2002[a]	14.0	2.6	39.7	11.8
St. Lucia	2.37[b]	3.80[b]	1995[d]	20.9	7.2	40.6	15.5		..	..	..	..
Suriname	2.29[b]	3.67[b]	1999[d]	15.5	5.9	27.2	11.7		..	..	..	..
Swaziland	4.66	7.45	1994–95[a]	78.6	47.7	89.3	61.6	2000–01[a]	62.9	29.4	81.0	45.8
Tajikistan	1.16	1.85	2003[a]	36.3	10.3	68.8	26.7	2004[a]	21.5	5.1	50.8	16.8
Tanzania	603.06	964.90	1991–92[a]	72.6	29.7	91.3	50.1	2000–01[a]	88.5	46.8	96.6	64.4
Thailand	21.83	34.93	2002[a]	<2	<0.5	15.1	2.8	2004[a]	<2	<0.5	11.5	2.0
Timor-Leste	0.61[b]	0.98[b]	2001[a]	52.9	19.1	77.5	37.0	2007[a]	37.2	8.7	72.8	27.0
Togo	352.82	564.51	2006[a]	38.7	11.4	69.3	27.9		..	..	..	..
Trinidad and Tobago	5.77[b]	9.23[b]	1988[d]	<2	<0.5	8.6	1.9	1992[d]	4.2	1.1	13.5	3.9
Tunisia	0.87	1.39	1995[a]	6.5	1.3	20.4	5.8	2000[a]	2.6	<0.5	12.8	3.0
Turkey	1.25	2.00	2002[a]	2.0	<0.5	9.6	2.3	2006[a]	2.6	<0.5	8.2	2.4
Turkmenistan	5,961.06[b]	9,537.69[b]	1993[d]	63.5	25.8	85.7	44.8	1998[a]	24.8	7.0	49.6	18.4
Uganda	930.77	1,489.24	2002[a]	57.4	22.7	79.8	40.6	2005[a]	51.5	19.1	75.6	36.4

Poverty rates at international poverty lines

	International poverty line in local currency		International poverty line									
	$1.25 a day **2005**	$2 a day **2005**	Survey year	Population below $1.25 a day %	Poverty gap at $1.25 a day %	Population below $2 a day %	Poverty gap at $2 a day %	Survey year	Population below $1.25 a day %	Poverty gap at $1.25 a day %	Population below $2 a day %	Poverty gap at $2 a day %
Ukraine	2.14	3.42	2005[a]	<2	<0.5	<2	<0.5	2008[a]	<2	<0.5	<2	<0.5
Uruguay	19.14	30.62	2005[c,d]	<2	<0.5	4.5	0.7	2007[d]	<2	<0.5	4.3	1.0
Uzbekistan	470.09[b]	752.14[b]	..	..	..	..	..	..	..	..	..	..
Venezuela, RB	1,563.90	2,502.24	2003[d]	18.4	8.8	31.7	14.6	2006[d]	3.5	1.2	10.2	3.2
Vietnam	7,399.87	11,839.79	2004[a]	24.2	5.1	52.5	17.9	2006[a]	21.5	4.6	48.4	16.2
Yemen, Rep.	113.83	182.12	1998[a]	12.9	3.0	36.3	11.1	2005[a]	17.5	4.2	46.6	14.8
Zambia	3,537.91	5,660.65	2002–03[a]	64.6	27.1	85.1	45.8	2004–05[a]	64.3	32.8	81.5	48.3

a. Expenditure based. b. In purchasing power parity (PPP) dollars imputed using regression. c. Covers urban areas only. d. Income based. e. Adjusted by spatial consumer price index information. f. PPP conversion factor based on urban prices. g. Weighted average of urban and rural estimates. h. Weighted average of urban and rural poverty lines. i. Due to change in survey design, the most recent survey is not strictly comparable with the previous one.

Regional poverty estimates and progress toward the Millennium Development Goals

Global poverty measured at the $1.25 a day poverty line has been decreasing since the 1980s. The share of population living on less than $1.25 a day fell 10 percentage points, to 42 percent, in 1990 and then fell nearly 17 percentage points between 1990 and 2005. The number of people living in extreme poverty fell from 1.9 billion in 1981 to 1.8 billion in 1990 to about 1.4 billion in 2005 (figure 2.8a). This substantial reduction in extreme poverty over the past quarter century, however, disguises large regional differences.

The greatest reduction in poverty occurred in East Asia and Pacific, where the poverty rate declined from 78 percent in 1981 to 17 percent in 2005 and the number of people living on less than $1.25 a day dropped more than 750 million (figure 2.8b). Much of this decline was in China, where poverty fell from 84 percent to 16 percent, leaving 620 million fewer people in poverty.

Over the same period the poverty rate in South Asia fell from 59 percent to 40 percent (table 2.8c). In contrast, the poverty rate fell only slightly in Sub-Saharan Africa—from less than 54 percent in 1981 to more than 58 percent in 1999 then down to 51 percent in 2005. But the number of people living below the poverty line has nearly doubled.

Only East Asia and Pacific is consistently on track to meet the Millennium Development Goal target of reducing 1990 poverty rates by half by 2015. A slight acceleration over historical growth rates could lift Latin America and the Caribbean and South Asia to the target. However, the recent slowdown in the global economy may leave these regions and many countries short of the target. Preliminary estimates for 2009 suggest that lower economic growth rates will likely leave 50 million more people below the $1.25 a day poverty line than had been expected before the crisis.

Most of the people who have escaped extreme poverty remain very poor by the standards of middle-income economies. The median poverty line for developing countries in 2005 was $2.00 a day. The poverty rate for all developing countries measured at this line fell from nearly 70 percent in 1981 to 47 percent in 2005, but the number of people living on less than $2.00 a day has remained nearly constant at 2.5 billion. The largest decrease, both in number and proportion, occurred in East Asia and Pacific, led by China. Elsewhere, the number of people living on less than $2.00 a day increased, and the number of people living between $1.25 and $2.00 a day nearly doubled, to 1.2 billion. In 2009 the global growth deceleration will likely leave 57 million more people below the $2 a day poverty line.

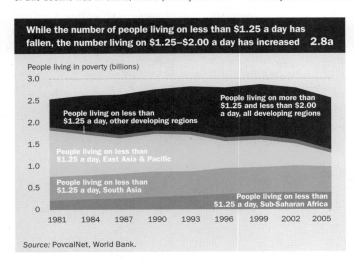

While the number of people living on less than $1.25 a day has fallen, the number living on $1.25–$2.00 a day has increased 2.8a

Source: PovcalNet, World Bank.

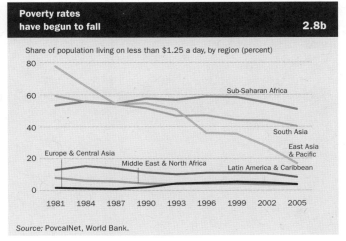

Poverty rates have begun to fall 2.8b

Source: PovcalNet, World Bank.

2.8 Poverty rates at international poverty lines

Regional poverty estimates									2.8c
Region or country	1981	1984	1987	1990	1993	1996	1999	2002	2005
People living on less than 2005 PPP $1.25 a day (millions)									
East Asia & Pacific	1,072	947	822	873	845	622	635	507	316
China	835	720	586	683	633	443	447	363	208
Europe & Central Asia	7	6	5	9	20	22	24	22	17
Latin America & Caribbean	47	59	57	50	47	53	55	57	45
Middle East & North Africa	14	12	12	10	10	11	12	10	11
South Asia	548	548	569	579	559	594	589	616	596
India	420	416	428	436	444	442	447	460	456
Sub-Saharan Africa	211	242	258	297	317	356	383	390	388
Total	1,900	1,814	1,723	1,818	1,799	1,658	1,698	1,601	1,374
Share of people living on less than 2005 PPP $1.25 a day (percent)									
East Asia & Pacific	77.7	65.5	54.2	54.7	50.8	36.0	35.5	27.6	16.8
China	84.0	69.4	54.0	60.2	53.7	36.4	35.6	28.4	15.9
Europe & Central Asia	1.7	1.3	1.1	2.0	4.3	4.6	5.1	4.6	3.7
Latin America & Caribbean	12.9	15.3	13.7	11.3	10.1	10.9	10.9	10.7	8.2
Middle East & North Africa	7.9	6.1	5.7	4.3	4.1	4.1	4.2	3.6	3.6
South Asia	59.4	55.6	54.2	51.7	46.9	47.1	44.1	43.8	40.3
India	59.8	55.5	53.6	51.3	49.4	46.6	44.8	43.9	41.6
Sub-Saharan Africa	53.4	55.8	54.5	57.6	56.9	58.8	58.4	55.0	50.9
Total	51.9	46.7	41.9	41.7	39.2	34.5	33.7	30.5	25.2
People living on less than 2005 PPP $2.00 a day (millions)									
East Asia & Pacific	1,278	1,280	1,238	1,274	1,262	1,108	1,105	954	729
China	972	963	907	961	926	792	770	655	474
Europe & Central Asia	35	28	25	32	49	56	68	57	42
Latin America & Caribbean	90	110	103	96	96	107	111	114	94
Middle East & North Africa	46	44	47	44	48	52	52	51	51
South Asia	799	836	881	926	950	1,009	1,031	1,084	1,092
India	609	635	669	702	735	757	783	813	828
Sub-Saharan Africa	294	328	351	393	423	471	509	536	556
Total	2,542	2,625	2,646	2,765	2,828	2,803	2,875	2,795	2,564
Share of people living on less than 2005 PPP $2.00 a day (percent)									
East Asia & Pacific	92.6	88.5	81.6	79.8	75.8	64.1	61.8	51.9	38.7
China	97.8	92.9	83.7	84.6	78.6	65.1	61.4	51.2	36.3
Europe & Central Asia	8.3	6.5	5.6	6.9	10.3	11.9	14.3	12.0	8.9
Latin America & Caribbean	24.6	28.1	24.9	21.9	20.7	22.0	21.8	21.6	17.1
Middle East & North Africa	26.7	23.1	22.7	19.7	19.8	20.2	19.0	17.6	16.9
South Asia	86.5	84.8	83.9	82.7	79.7	79.9	77.2	77.1	73.9
India	86.6	84.8	83.8	82.6	81.7	79.8	78.4	77.6	75.6
Sub-Saharan Africa	73.8	75.5	74.0	76.1	75.9	77.9	77.6	75.6	72.9
Total	69.4	67.7	64.3	63.4	61.6	58.3	57.1	53.3	47.0

Source: World Bank PovcalNet.

Poverty rates at international poverty lines

About the data

The World Bank produced its first global poverty estimates for developing countries for *World Development Report 1990: Poverty* using household survey data for 22 countries (Ravallion, Datt, and van de Walle 1991). Since then there has been considerable expansion in the number of countries that field household income and expenditure surveys. The World Bank's poverty monitoring database now includes more than 600 surveys representing 115 developing countries. More than 1.2 million randomly sampled households were interviewed in these surveys, representing 96 percent of the population of developing countries.

Data availability

The number of data sets within two years of any given year rose dramatically, from 13 between 1978 and 1982 to 158 between 2001 and 2006. Data coverage is improving in all regions, but the Middle East and North Africa and Sub-Saharan Africa continue to lag. The database, maintained by a team in the World Bank's Development Research Group, is updated annually as new survey data become available, and a major reassessment of progress against poverty is made about every three years. A complete overview of data availability by year and country is available at http://iresearch.worldbank.org/povcalnet/.

Data quality

Besides the frequency and timeliness of survey data, other data quality issues arise in measuring household living standards. The surveys ask detailed questions on sources of income and how it was spent, which must be carefully recorded by trained personnel. Income is generally more difficult to measure accurately, and consumption comes closer to the notion of living standards. And income can vary over time even if living standards do not. But consumption data are not always available: the latest estimates reported here use consumption for about two-thirds of countries.

However, even similar surveys may not be strictly comparable because of differences in timing or in the quality and training of enumerators. Comparisons of countries at different levels of development also pose a potential problem because of differences in the relative importance of the consumption of nonmarket goods. The local market value of all consumption in kind (including own production, particularly important in underdeveloped rural economies) should be included in total consumption expenditure, but may not be. Most survey data now include valuations for consumption or income from own production, but valuation methods vary.

The statistics reported here are based on consumption data or, when unavailable, on income surveys. Analysis of some 20 countries for which income and consumption expenditure data were both available from the same surveys found income to yield a higher mean than consumption but also higher inequality. When poverty measures based on consumption and income were compared, the two effects roughly cancelled each other out: there was no significant statistical difference.

International poverty lines

International comparisons of poverty estimates entail both conceptual and practical problems. Countries have different definitions of poverty, and consistent comparisons across countries can be difficult. Local poverty lines tend to have higher purchasing power in rich countries, where more generous standards are used, than in poor countries.

Poverty measures based on an international poverty line attempt to hold the real value of the poverty line constant across countries, as is done when making comparisons over time. Since *World Development Report 1990* the World Bank has aimed to apply a common standard in measuring extreme poverty, anchored to what *poverty* means in the world's poorest countries. The welfare of people living in different countries can be measured on a common scale by adjusting for differences in the purchasing power of currencies. The commonly used $1 a day standard, measured in 1985 international prices and adjusted to local currency using purchasing power parities (PPPs), was chosen for *World Development Report 1990* because it was typical of the poverty lines in low-income countries at the time.

Early editions of *World Development Indicators* used PPPs from the Penn World Tables to convert values in local currency to equivalent purchasing power measured in U.S dollars. Later editions used 1993 consumption PPP estimates produced by the World Bank. International poverty lines were recently revised using the new data on PPPs compiled in the 2005 round of the International Comparison Program, along with data from an expanded set of household income and expenditure surveys. The new extreme poverty line is set at $1.25 a day in 2005 PPP terms, which represents the mean of the poverty lines found in the poorest 15 countries ranked by per capita consumption. The new poverty line maintains the same standard for extreme poverty—the poverty line typical of the poorest countries in the world—but updates it using the latest information on the cost of living in developing countries.

PPP exchange rates are used to estimate global poverty, because they take into account the local prices of goods and services not traded internationally. But PPP rates were designed for comparing aggregates from national accounts, not for making international poverty comparisons. As a result, there is no certainty that an international poverty line measures the same degree of need or deprivation across countries. So-called poverty PPPs, designed to compare the consumption of the poorest people in the world, might provide a better basis for comparison of poverty across countries. Work on these measures is ongoing.

Definitions

• **International poverty line in local currency** is the international poverty lines of $1.25 and $2.00 a day in 2005 prices, converted to local currency using the PPP conversion factors estimated by the International Comparison Program. • **Survey year** is the year in which the underlying data were collected. • **Population below $1.25 a day** and **population below $2 a day** are the percentages of the population living on less than $1.25 a day and $2.00 a day at 2005 international prices. As a result of revisions in PPP exchange rates, poverty rates for individual countries cannot be compared with poverty rates reported in earlier editions. • **Poverty gap** is the mean shortfall from the poverty line (counting the nonpoor as having zero shortfall), expressed as a percentage of the poverty line. This measure reflects the depth of poverty as well as its incidence.

Data sources

The poverty measures are prepared by the World Bank's Development Research Group. The international poverty lines are based on nationally representative primary household surveys conducted by national statistical offices or by private agencies under the supervision of government or international agencies and obtained from government statistical offices and World Bank Group country departments. The World Bank Group has prepared an annual review of its poverty work since 1993. For details on data sources and methods used in deriving the World Bank's latest estimates, and further discussion of the results, see Shaohua Chen and Martin Ravallion's "The Developing World Is Poorer Than We Thought, but No Less Successful in the Fight against Poverty?" (2008).

	Survey year	Gini index	Lowest 10%	Lowest 20%	Second 20%	Third 20%	Fourth 20%	Highest 20%	Highest 10%
					Percentage share of income or consumption[a]				
Afghanistan		..	..	..	..	..	..	..	..
Albania	2005[b]	33.0	3.2	7.8	12.2	16.6	22.6	40.9	25.9
Algeria	1995[b]	35.3	2.8	6.9	11.5	16.3	22.8	42.4	26.9
Angola	2000[b]	58.6	0.6	2.0	5.7	10.8	19.7	61.9	44.7
Argentina[c]	2006[d]	48.8	1.2	3.6	8.2	13.4	21.7	53.0	36.1
Armenia	2007[b]	30.2	3.6	8.6	13.0	17.1	22.1	39.2	24.5
Australia	1994[d]	35.2	2.0	5.9	12.0	17.2	23.6	41.3	25.4
Austria	2000[d]	29.1	3.3	8.6	13.3	17.4	22.9	37.8	23.0
Azerbaijan	2005[b]	16.8	6.1	13.3	16.2	18.7	21.7	30.2	17.5
Bangladesh	2005[b]	31.0	4.3	9.4	12.6	16.1	21.1	40.8	26.6
Belarus	2007[b]	28.8	3.6	8.8	13.4	17.5	22.6	37.7	23.0
Belgium	2000[d]	33.0	3.4	8.5	13.0	16.3	20.8	41.4	28.1
Belize	1995[b]	59.6	0.6	2.1	5.4	10.4	19.2	62.9	45.8
Benin	2003[b]	38.6	2.9	6.9	10.9	15.1	21.2	45.9	31.0
Bhutan	2003[b]	46.7	2.2	5.4	8.8	12.9	20.0	53.0	37.5
Bolivia	2007[b]	57.2	0.7	2.7	6.5	11.0	18.6	61.2	45.3
Bosnia and Herzegovina	2007[b]	36.3	2.6	6.7	11.4	16.0	22.9	43.1	27.1
Botswana	1993–94[b]	61.0	1.3	3.1	5.8	9.6	16.4	65.0	51.2
Brazil	2007[d]	55.0	1.1	3.0	6.9	11.8	19.6	58.7	43.0
Bulgaria	2003[b]	29.2	3.5	8.7	13.5	17.4	22.3	38.1	23.8
Burkina Faso	2003[b]	39.6	3.0	7.0	10.6	14.7	20.6	47.1	32.4
Burundi	2006[b]	33.3	4.1	9.0	11.9	15.4	21.0	42.8	28.0
Cambodia	2007[b]	44.2	2.7	6.5	9.7	12.9	18.9	52.0	36.9
Cameroon	2001[b]	44.6	2.4	5.6	9.3	13.7	20.5	50.9	35.5
Canada	2000[d]	32.6	2.6	7.2	12.7	17.2	23.0	39.9	24.8
Cape Verde	2001[b]	50.4	1.7	4.5	8.1	12.2	19.1	56.1	40.5
Central African Republic	2003[b]	43.6	2.1	5.2	9.4	14.3	21.7	49.4	33.0
Chad	2002–03[b]	39.8	2.6	6.3	10.4	15.0	21.8	46.6	30.8
Chile	2006[d]	52.0	1.6	4.1	7.7	12.2	19.3	56.8	41.7
China	2005[d]	41.5	2.4	5.7	9.8	14.7	22.0	47.8	31.4
Hong Kong SAR, China	1996[d]	43.4	2.0	5.3	9.4	13.9	20.7	50.7	34.9
Colombia	2006[d]	58.5	0.8	2.3	6.0	11.0	19.1	61.6	45.9
Comoros	2004[b]	64.3	0.9	2.6	5.4	8.9	15.1	68.1	55.0
Congo, Dem. Rep.	2005–06[b]	44.4	2.3	5.5	9.2	13.8	20.9	50.6	34.7
Congo, Rep.	2005[b]	47.3	2.1	5.0	8.4	13.0	20.5	53.1	37.1
Costa Rica	2007[d]	48.9	1.6	4.4	8.5	12.7	19.7	54.6	38.6
Côte d'Ivoire	2002[b]	48.4	2.0	5.0	8.7	12.9	19.3	54.1	39.6
Croatia	2005[b]	29.0	3.6	8.8	13.3	17.3	22.7	37.9	23.1
Cuba		..	..	..	..	..	..	..	..
Czech Republic	1996[d]	25.8	4.3	10.2	14.3	17.5	21.7	36.2	22.7
Denmark	1997[d]	24.7	2.6	8.3	14.7	18.2	22.9	35.8	21.3
Djibouti	2002[b]	39.9	2.3	6.0	10.6	15.1	21.8	46.5	30.8
Dominican Republic	2007[d]	48.4	1.6	4.4	8.5	13.1	20.2	53.8	37.7
Ecuador	2007[d]	54.4	1.2	3.4	7.2	11.8	19.2	58.5	43.3
Egypt, Arab Rep.	2004–05[b]	32.1	3.9	9.0	12.6	16.1	20.9	41.5	27.6
El Salvador	2007[d]	46.9	1.3	4.3	9.2	13.7	20.8	52.0	36.1
Eritrea		..	..	..	..	..	..	..	..
Estonia	2004[b]	36.0	2.7	6.8	11.6	16.2	22.5	43.0	27.7
Ethiopia	2005[b]	29.8	4.1	9.3	13.2	16.8	21.4	39.4	25.6
Finland	2000[d]	26.9	4.0	9.6	14.1	17.5	22.1	36.7	22.6
France	1995[b]	32.7	2.8	7.2	12.6	17.2	22.8	40.2	25.1
Gabon	2005[b]	41.5	2.5	6.1	10.1	14.6	21.2	47.9	32.7
Gambia, The	2003[b]	47.3	2.0	4.8	8.6	13.2	20.6	52.8	36.9
Georgia	2005[b]	40.8	1.9	5.4	10.5	15.3	22.2	46.7	30.6
Germany	2000[d]	28.3	3.2	8.5	13.7	17.8	23.1	36.9	22.1
Ghana	2006[b]	42.8	1.9	5.2	9.8	14.8	21.9	48.3	32.5
Greece	2000[d]	34.3	2.5	6.7	11.9	16.8	23.0	41.5	26.0

Distribution of income or consumption

	Survey year	Gini index	Percentage share of income or consumption[a]						
			Lowest 10%	Lowest 20%	Second 20%	Third 20%	Fourth 20%	Highest 20%	Highest 10%
Guatemala	2006[d]	53.7	1.3	3.4	7.2	12.0	19.5	57.8	42.4
Guinea	2003[b]	43.3	2.4	5.8	9.6	14.1	20.8	49.7	34.4
Guinea-Bissau	2002[b]	35.5	2.9	7.2	11.6	16.0	22.1	43.0	28.0
Guyana	1998[d]	43.2	1.1	4.3	9.8	14.5	21.3	50.1	34.4
Haiti	2001[d]	59.5	0.9	2.5	5.9	10.5	18.1	63.0	47.8
Honduras	2006[d]	55.3	0.7	2.5	6.7	12.1	20.4	58.4	42.2
Hungary	2004[b]	30.0	3.5	8.6	13.1	17.1	22.5	38.7	24.1
India	2004–05[b]	36.8	3.6	8.1	11.3	14.9	20.4	45.3	31.1
Indonesia	2007[b]	37.6	3.1	7.4	11.0	14.9	21.3	45.5	30.1
Iran, Islamic Rep.	2005[b]	38.3	2.6	6.4	10.9	15.6	22.2	45.0	29.6
Iraq		..	..	..	..	..	..	..	..
Ireland	2000[d]	34.3	2.9	7.4	12.3	16.3	21.9	42.0	27.2
Israel	2001[d]	39.2	2.1	5.7	10.5	15.9	23.0	44.9	28.8
Italy	2000[d]	36.0	2.3	6.5	12.0	16.8	22.8	42.0	26.8
Jamaica	2004[b]	45.5	2.1	5.2	9.0	13.8	20.9	51.2	35.6
Japan	1993[d]	24.9	4.8	10.6	14.2	17.6	22.0	35.7	21.7
Jordan	2006[b]	37.7	3.0	7.2	11.1	15.2	21.1	45.4	30.7
Kazakhstan	2007[b]	30.9	3.6	8.7	12.8	16.6	22.0	39.9	25.1
Kenya	2005–06[b]	47.7	1.8	4.7	8.8	13.3	20.3	53.0	37.8
Korea, Dem. Rep.		..	..	..	..	..	..	..	..
Korea, Rep.	1998[d]	31.6	2.9	7.9	13.6	18.0	23.1	37.5	22.5
Kosovo		..	..	..	..	..	..	..	..
Kuwait		..	..	..	..	..	..	..	..
Kyrgyz Republic	2007[b]	33.5	3.9	8.8	11.9	15.1	21.6	42.6	27.6
Lao PDR	2002–03[b]	32.6	3.7	8.5	12.3	16.2	21.6	41.4	27.0
Latvia	2007[b]	36.3	2.6	6.7	11.5	15.9	22.6	43.3	27.8
Lebanon		..	..	..	..	..	..	..	..
Lesotho	2002–03[b]	52.5	1.0	3.0	7.2	12.5	21.0	56.4	39.4
Liberia	2007[b]	52.6	2.4	6.4	11.4	15.7	21.6	45.0	30.1
Libya		..	..	..	..	..	..	..	..
Lithuania	2004[b]	35.8	2.7	6.8	11.5	16.3	22.7	42.8	27.4
Macedonia, FYR	2006[b]	42.8	1.9	5.2	10.0	14.5	21.5	48.8	32.3
Madagascar	2005[b]	47.2	2.6	6.2	9.6	13.1	17.7	53.5	41.5
Malawi	2004–05[b]	39.0	2.9	7.0	10.8	14.9	20.9	46.4	31.7
Malaysia	2004[d]	37.9	2.6	6.4	10.8	15.8	22.8	44.4	28.5
Maldives	2004[b]	37.4	2.6	6.5	10.9	15.6	22.6	44.3	27.9
Mali	2006[b]	39.0	2.7	6.5	10.7	15.2	21.6	46.0	30.5
Mauritania	2000[b]	39.0	2.5	6.2	10.5	15.4	22.3	45.7	29.6
Mauritius		..	..	..	..	..	..	..	..
Mexico	2008[d]	51.6	1.2	3.8	8.1	12.4	19.2	56.4	41.3
Micronesia	2000[b]	0.5	1.6	5.1	10.2	19.0	64.0	47.1	
Moldova	2007[b]	37.4	2.7	6.7	11.1	15.6	22.0	44.6	28.9
Mongolia	2007–08[b]	36.6	2.9	7.1	11.2	15.6	22.1	44.0	28.3
Montenegro	2007[b]	36.9	2.6	6.5	11.4	16.1	22.2	43.7	28.6
Morocco	2007[b]	40.9	2.7	6.5	10.5	14.5	20.6	47.9	33.2
Mozambique	2002–03[b]	47.1	2.1	5.4	9.2	13.1	19.0	53.3	39.2
Myanmar		..	..	..	..	..	..	..	..
Namibia	1993[d]	74.3	0.6	1.5	2.8	5.5	12.0	78.3	65.0
Nepal	2003–04[b]	47.3	2.7	6.1	8.9	12.5	18.4	54.2	40.4
Netherlands	1999[d]	30.9	2.5	7.6	13.2	17.2	23.3	38.7	22.9
New Zealand	1997[d]	36.2	2.2	6.4	11.4	15.8	22.6	43.8	27.8
Nicaragua	2005[d]	52.3	1.4	3.8	7.7	12.3	19.4	56.9	41.8
Niger	2005[d]	43.9	2.3	5.9	9.8	13.9	20.1	50.3	35.7
Nigeria	2003–04[b]	42.9	2.0	5.1	9.7	14.7	21.9	48.6	32.4
Norway	2000[d]	25.8	3.9	9.6	14.0	17.2	22.0	37.2	23.4
Oman		..	..	..	..	..	..	..	..
Pakistan	2004–05[b]	31.2	3.9	9.1	12.8	16.3	21.3	40.5	26.5

2.9 | Distribution of income or consumption

	Survey year	Gini index	Percentage share of income or consumption[a]						
			Lowest 10%	Lowest 20%	Second 20%	Third 20%	Fourth 20%	Highest 20%	Highest 10%
Panama	2006[d]	54.9	0.8	2.5	6.6	12.1	20.8	58.0	41.4
Papua New Guinea	1996[b]	50.9	1.9	4.5	7.7	12.1	19.3	56.4	40.9
Paraguay	2007[d]	53.2	1.1	3.4	7.6	12.2	19.4	57.4	42.3
Peru	2007[d]	50.5	1.3	3.6	7.8	13.0	20.8	54.8	38.4
Philippines	2006[b]	44.0	2.4	5.6	9.1	13.7	21.2	50.4	33.9
Poland	2005[b]	34.9	3.0	7.3	11.7	16.2	22.4	42.4	27.2
Portugal	1997[d]	38.5	2.0	5.8	11.0	15.5	21.9	45.9	29.8
Puerto Rico		..	..	..	..	..	..	..	..
Qatar	2006–07[b]	41.1	1.3	3.9	..	..	..	52.0	35.9
Romania	2007[b]	32.1	3.2	7.9	12.7	16.8	22.3	40.3	25.6
Russian Federation	2007[b]	43.7	2.2	5.6	9.6	13.9	20.7	50.2	34.3
Rwanda	2000[b]	46.7	2.3	5.4	9.0	13.2	19.6	52.8	38.2
São Tomé and Príncipe	2000–01[b]	50.6	2.1	5.2	8.7	12.1	17.6	56.5	43.6
Saudi Arabia		..	..	..	..	..	..	..	..
Senegal	2005[b]	39.2	2.5	6.2	10.6	15.3	22.0	45.9	30.1
Serbia	2008[b]	28.2	3.8	9.1	13.6	17.4	22.5	37.5	22.7
Seychelles	2006–07[b]	1.6	3.7	5.7	8.4	12.4	69.8	60.0	
Sierra Leone	2003[b]	42.5	2.6	6.1	9.7	14.0	20.9	49.3	33.6
Singapore	1998[d]	42.5	1.9	5.0	9.4	14.6	22.0	49.0	32.8
Slovak Republic	1996[d]	25.8	3.1	8.8	14.9	18.6	22.9	34.8	20.8
Slovenia	2004[b]	31.2	3.4	8.2	12.8	17.0	22.6	39.4	24.6
Somalia		..	..	..	..	..	..	..	..
South Africa	2000[b]	57.8	1.3	3.1	5.6	9.9	18.8	62.7	44.9
Spain	2000[d]	34.7	2.6	7.0	12.1	16.4	22.5	42.0	26.6
Sri Lanka	2002[b]	41.1	2.9	6.8	10.4	14.4	20.5	48.0	33.3
St. Lucia	1995[d]	42.6	1.7	5.1	10.3	14.4	21.4	48.8	31.6
Sudan		..	..	..	..	..	..	..	..
Suriname	1999[d]	52.8	1.0	3.1	7.5	12.2	19.9	57.4	40.0
Swaziland	2000–01[b]	50.7	1.8	4.5	8.0	12.3	19.4	55.9	40.8
Sweden	2000[d]	25.0	3.6	9.1	14.0	17.6	22.7	36.6	22.2
Switzerland	2000[d]	33.7	2.9	7.6	12.2	16.3	22.6	41.3	25.9
Syrian Arab Republic		..	..	..	..	..	..	..	..
Tajikistan	2004[b]	33.6	3.2	7.8	12.0	16.4	21.9	41.9	26.6
Tanzania	2000–01[b]	34.6	3.1	7.3	11.8	16.3	22.3	42.3	27.0
Thailand	2004[b]	42.5	2.6	6.1	9.8	14.2	21.0	49.0	33.7
Timor-Leste	2007[b]	31.9	3.9	8.9	12.5	16.0	21.2	41.3	27.0
Togo	2006[b]	34.4	2.0	5.4	10.3	15.2	22.0	47.1	31.3
Trinidad and Tobago	1992[d]	40.3	2.1	5.5	10.3	15.5	22.7	45.9	29.9
Tunisia	2000[b]	40.81	2.4	5.9	10.2	14.9	21.8	47.2	31.6
Turkey	2006[b]	41.2	2.0	5.4	10.3	15.2	22.0	47.1	31.3
Turkmenistan	1998[b]	40.8	2.5	6.0	10.2	14.9	21.7	47.2	31.8
Uganda	2005[b]	42.6	2.6	6.1	9.8	14.1	20.7	49.3	34.1
Ukraine	2008[b]	27.6	3.9	9.4	13.6	17.4	22.6	37.0	22.5
United Arab Emirates		..	..	..	..	..	..	..	..
United Kingdom	1999[d]	36.0	2.1	6.1	11.4	16.0	22.5	44.0	28.5
United States	2000[d]	40.8	1.9	5.4	10.7	15.7	22.4	45.8	29.9
Uruguay	2007[d]	47.1	1.6	4.3	8.6	13.6	21.4	52.1	35.5
Uzbekistan	2003[b]	36.7	2.9	7.1	11.5	15.7	21.5	44.2	29.5
Venezuela, RB	2006[d]	43.4	1.7	4.9	9.6	14.8	22.1	48.6	32.7
Vietnam	2006[b]	37.8	3.1	7.1	10.8	15.2	21.6	45.4	29.8
West Bank and Gaza		..	..	..	..	..	..	..	..
Yemen, Rep.	2005[b]	37.7	2.9	7.2	11.3	15.3	21.0	45.3	30.8
Zambia	2004–05[b]	50.7	1.3	3.6	7.8	12.8	20.6	55.2	38.9
Zimbabwe	1995[b]	50.1	1.8	4.6	8.1	12.2	19.3	55.7	40.3

a. Percentage shares by quintile may not sum to 100 percent because of rounding. b. Refers to expenditure shares by percentiles of population, ranked by per capita expenditure. c. Urban data. d. Refers to income shares by percentiles of population, ranked by per capita income.

Distribution of income or consumption | 2.9

About the data

Inequality in the distribution of income is reflected in the percentage shares of income or consumption accruing to portions of the population ranked by income or consumption levels. The portions ranked lowest by personal income receive the smallest shares of total income. The Gini index provides a convenient summary measure of the degree of inequality. Data on the distribution of income or consumption come from nationally representative household surveys. Where the original data from the household survey were available, they have been used to directly calculate the income or consumption shares by quintile. Otherwise, shares have been estimated from the best available grouped data.

The distribution data have been adjusted for household size, providing a more consistent measure of per capita income or consumption. No adjustment has been made for spatial differences in cost of living within countries, because the data needed for such calculations are generally unavailable. For further details on the estimation method for low- and middle-income economies, see Ravallion and Chen (1996).

Because the underlying household surveys differ in method and type of data collected, the distribution data are not strictly comparable across countries. These problems are diminishing as survey methods improve and become more standardized, but achieving strict comparability is still impossible (see *About the data* for tables 2.7 and 2.8).

Two sources of noncomparability should be noted in particular. First, the surveys can differ in many respects, including whether they use income or consumption expenditure as the living standard indicator. The distribution of income is typically more unequal than the distribution of consumption. In addition, the definitions of income used differ more often among surveys. Consumption is usually a much better welfare indicator, particularly in developing countries. Second, households differ in size (number of members) and in the extent of income sharing among members. And individuals differ in age and consumption needs. Differences among countries in these respects may bias comparisons of distribution.

World Bank staff have made an effort to ensure that the data are as comparable as possible. Wherever possible, consumption has been used rather than income. Income distribution and Gini indexes for high-income economies are calculated directly from the Luxembourg Income Study database, using an estimation method consistent with that applied for developing countries.

Definitions

• **Survey year** is the year in which the underlying data were collected. • **Gini index** measures the extent to which the distribution of income (or consumption expenditure) among individuals or households within an economy deviates from a perfectly equal distribution. A Lorenz curve plots the cumulative percentages of total income received against the cumulative number of recipients, starting with the poorest individual. The Gini index measures the area between the Lorenz curve and a hypothetical line of absolute equality, expressed as a percentage of the maximum area under the line. Thus a Gini index of 0 represents perfect equality, while an index of 100 implies perfect inequality. • **Percentage share of income or consumption** is the share of total income or consumption that accrues to subgroups of population indicated by deciles or quintiles.

The Gini coefficient and ratio of income or consumption of the richest quintile to the poorest quintiles are closely correlated   2.9a

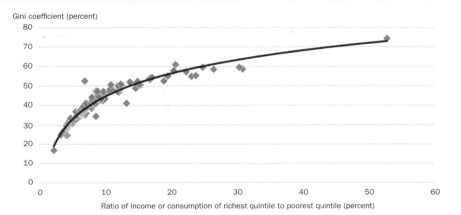

There are many ways to measure income or consumption inequality. The Gini coefficient shows inequality over the entire population; the ratio of income or consumption of the richest quintile to the poorest quintiles shows differences only at the tails of the population distribution. Both measures are closely correlated and provide similar information. At low levels of inequality the Gini coefficient is a more sensitive measure, but above a Gini value of 45–55 percent the inequality ratio rises faster.

Source: World Development Indicators data files.

Data sources

Data on distribution are compiled by the World Bank's Development Research Group using primary household survey data obtained from government statistical agencies and World Bank country departments. Data for high-income economies are from the Luxembourg Income Study database.

Assessing vulnerability and security

	Youth unemployment		Female-headed households	Pension contributors			Public expenditure on pensions			
	Male % of male labor force ages 15–24 **2005–08**[a]	Female % of female labor force ages 15–24 **2005–08**[a]	% of total **2005–08**[a]	Year	% of labor force	% of working-age population	Year	% of GDP	Year	Average pension % of average wage
Afghanistan	..	..	..	2005	..	2.2	2005	0.5		..
Albania	..	..	..	2007	49.8	34.1	2007	5.9		..
Algeria	..	..	..	2002	36.7	22.1	2002	3.2		..
Angola	..	..	25							..
Argentina	16[b]	24[b]	34	2007	42.5	30.8	2007	8.0	2000	43.8
Armenia	..	..	36	2007	88.0	65.7	2006	3.2	2007	20.3
Australia	9[b]	9[b]	..	2005	92.6	69.6	2005	3.5[c]		..
Austria	8	8	..	2005	96.4	68.7	2005	12.6[c]		..
Azerbaijan	18	10	25	2007	36.8	30.2	2006	3.7	2006	24.3
Bangladesh	8	14	13	2004	2.8	2.1	2001	0.5		..
Belarus	..	..	54	2008	94.7	67.0	2008	10.2	2002	41.6
Belgium	17	19	..	2005	94.2	61.6	2005	9.0[c]		..
Benin	..	..	23	1996	4.8	..	2006	1.5		..
Bolivia	..	..	..	2007	11.5	9.2	2000	4.5		..
Bosnia and Herzegovina	55	62	..	2005	35.5	25.5	2005	7.7		..
Botswana	..	..	..	..	..	..	..	..		..
Brazil	..	..	..	2007	51.0	39.2	2004	12.6		..
Bulgaria	14	11	..	2007	83.5	48.3	2007	9.8	2004	42.9
Burkina Faso	..	..	..	1993	3.1	3.0	1992	0.3		..
Burundi	..	..	..	1993	3.3	3.0	1991	0.2		..
Cambodia	..	..	24	..	..	..	..	..		..
Cameroon	..	..	..	1993	13.7	11.5	2001	0.8		..
Canada	12[b]	10[b]	..	2005	90.5	71.4	2005	4.1[c]		..
Central African Republic	..	..	..	2004	1.5	1.3	2004	0.8		..
Chad	..	..	..	1990	1.1	1.0	1997	0.1		..
Chile	17	22	..	2007	57.3	35.5	2001	2.9	2006	53.5
China	..	..	..	2005	20.5	17.2	1996	2.7		..
Hong Kong SAR, China	11	7	..	2008	77.0	55.6				..
Colombia	16	28	19	2007	24.9	19.0	2006	2.7		..
Congo, Dem. Rep.	..	..	21	..	..	..	..	..		..
Congo, Rep.	..	..	23	1992	5.8	5.6	2004	0.9		..
Costa Rica	8	15	..	2004	55.3	37.6	2006	2.4		..
Côte d'Ivoire	..	..	..	1997	9.3	9.1	1997	0.3		..
Croatia	19	27	..	2007	75.2	51.0	2007	11.3	2005	32.4
Cuba	..	..	46	..	..	..	1992	12.6		..
Czech Republic	10	10	..	2008	93.0	66.0	2008	8.1	2005	40.7
Denmark	7	8	..	2007	94.4	86.9	2005	5.4[c]		..
Dominican Republic	21	45	35	2007	21.4	15.1	2000	0.8		..
Ecuador	12[b]	23[b]	..	2004	27.0	20.8	2002	2.5		..
Egypt, Arab Rep.	23	62	12	2004	55.5	27.7	2004	4.1		..
El Salvador	14	10	..	2007	24.0	16.6	2006	1.9		..
Eritrea	..	..	..	..	..	..	2001	0.3		..
Estonia	12	12	..	2004	95.2	68.6	2003	6.0	2007	35.4
Ethiopia	20[b]	29[b]	23	..	..	..	2007	0.3		..
Finland	17	16	..	2005	88.7	67.2	2005	8.4[c]		..
France	18	18	..	2005	89.9	61.4	2005	12.4[c]		..
Gabon	..	..	..	1995	15.0	14.0		..		..
Gambia, The	..	..	..	2003	3.8	2.9		..		..
Georgia	28	37	..	2004	29.9	22.7	2004	3.0	2003	13.0
Germany	11	10	..	2005	88.2	65.5	2005	11.4[c]		..
Ghana	..	..	34	2004	9.1	7.1	2002	1.3		..
Greece	17	29	..	2005	85.2	58.5	2005	11.5[c]		..
Guatemala	..	..	..	2005	24.0	18.0	2005	1.0		..
Guinea	..	..	17	1993	1.5	1.8		..		..
Guinea-Bissau	..	..	..	2004	1.9	1.5	2005	2.1		..
Haiti	..	..	44	..	..	..		..		..
Honduras	5[b]	11[b]	26	2006	16.1	12.4	1994	0.6		..

	Youth unemployment		Female-headed households	Pension contributors			Public expenditure on pensions			
	Male % of male labor force ages 15–24 2005–08[a]	Female % of female labor force ages 15–24 2005–08[a]	% of total 2005–08[a]	Year	% of labor force	% of working- age population	Year	% of GDP	Year	Average pension % of average wage
Hungary	19	21	..	2008	92.0	56.0	2008	10.5	2005	39.8
India	..	..	14	2004	9.0	5.7	2007	2.0		..
Indonesia	24	27	13	2002	15.5	11.3		..		..
Iran, Islamic Rep.	20	30	..	2001	35.1	20.0	2000	1.1		..
Iraq	..	..	11		..	..		..		..
Ireland	15	10	..	2005	88.0	63.9	2005	3.4[c]		..
Israel	15	17	..	1992	82.0	63.0	1996	5.9		..
Italy	19	25	..	2005	92.4	58.4	2005	14.0[c]		..
Jamaica	..	..	..	2004	17.4	12.6	1996	..		..
Japan	8	7	..	2005	95.3	75.0	2005	8.7[c]		..
Jordan	..	..	41	2004	32.2	18.6	2001	2.2		..
Kazakhstan	..	..	..	2004	33.8	26.4	2004	4.9	2003	24.9
Kenya	..	..	..	2005	8.0	6.7	2003	1.1		..
Korea, Dem. Rep.	..	..	..		..	..		..		..
Korea, Rep.	11	7	..	2005	78.0	55.0	2005	1.6[c]		..
Kosovo			..	2005	23.0	..	2005	3.4		..
Kuwait	..	..	..		..	..	1990	3.5		..
Kyrgyz Republic	14	16	25	2006	42.2	28.9	2006	4.8	2003	27.5
Lao PDR	..	..	..		..	..		..		..
Latvia	13	13	..	2003	92.4	66.5	2002	7.5	2005	33.1
Lebanon	..	..	..	2003	33.1	19.9	2003	2.1		..
Lesotho	..	..	..	2005	5.7	3.6		..		..
Liberia	6	4	31		..	..		..		..
Libya	..	..	..	2004	65.5	38.1	2001	2.1		..
Lithuania	13	15	..	2007	..	68.7	2007	6.3	2005	30.9
Macedonia, FYR	57	58	8	2008	48.4	30.4	2008	9.4	2006	55.0
Madagascar	2	3	..	1993	5.4	4.8	1990	0.2		..
Malawi	..	..	..		..	..		..		..
Malaysia	11	12	..	2008	46.9	32.5	1999	6.5		..
Mali	..	..	12	1990	2.5	2.0	1991	0.4		..
Mauritania	..	..	..	1995	5.0	4.0	1992	0.2		..
Mauritius	20	31	..	2000	51.4	33.6	1999	4.4		..
Mexico	6	8	..	2006	36.2	24.3	2005	1.3[c]		..
Moldova	15	14	34	2007	42.0	77.8	2007	7.2	2003	20.9
Mongolia	..	..	29	2005	33.6	21.4	2007	6.5[d]		..
Morocco	18	16	..	2003	22.4	12.8	2003	1.9		..
Mozambique	..	..	..	1995	2.0	2.1	1996	0.0		..
Myanmar	..	..	..		..	..		..		..
Namibia	..	..	44		..	..		..		..
Nepal	..	..	23	2006	3.5	2.5	2003	0.3		..
Netherlands	7	8	..	2005	90.3	70.4	2005	5.0[c]		..
New Zealand	10[b]	10[b]	..	2003	92.7	72.2	2005	4.4[c]		..
Nicaragua	8	10	..	2005	17.9	11.5	1996	2.5		..
Niger	..	..	19	2006	1.3	1.2	2006	0.7		..
Nigeria	..	..	..	2005	1.7	1.2	1991	0.1		..
Norway	8	7	..	2005	90.8	75.7	2005	4.8[c]		..
Oman	..	..	..		..	..		..		..
Pakistan	7	9	10	2004	6.4	4.0	1993	0.9		..
Panama	13	24	..	2008	..	42.0	1996	4.3		..
Papua New Guinea	..	..	..		..	..		..		..
Paraguay	9	18	..	2004	11.6	9.1	2001	1.2		..
Peru	14[b]	15[b]	22	2007	16.5	13.1	2000	2.6		..
Philippines	14	17	19	2007	20.8	15.5	1993	1.0		..
Poland	15	20	..	2005	84.9	54.5	2005	11.4[c]	2007	47.1
Portugal	13	20	..	2005	91.4	71.9	2005	10.2[c]		..
Puerto Rico	24	19	..							..
Qatar	..	..	..		..	..		..		..

	Youth unemployment		Female-headed households	Pension contributors			Public expenditure on pensions			
	Male % of male labor force ages 15–24 2005–08[a]	Female % of female labor force ages 15–24 2005–08[a]	% of total 2005–08[a]	Year	% of labor force	% of working-age population	Year	% of GDP	Year	Average pension % of average wage
Romania	19	18	..	2007	53.4	36.3	2007	5.7	2005	41.5
Russian Federation	14	15	..				2007	4.7	2003	29.2
Rwanda	..	..	34	2004	4.8	4.1				..
Saudi Arabia	..	..	..				1998	0.2		..
Senegal	..	..	23	2003	5.3	3.9	2003	1.3		..
Serbia	41	48	29	2003	46.0[e]	32.2[e]	2007	13.3[e]		..
Sierra Leone	..	..	..	2004	4.6	3.6				
Singapore	7	11	..	2008	62.0	45.3	1996	1.4		
Slovak Republic	19	20	..	2005	85.5	55.3	2005	6.2[c]	2005	44.7
Slovenia	10	11	..	2007	87.3	62.7	2007	11.8	2005	44.3
Somalia	..	..	..		..	..		..		..
South Africa	43	52	..		..	..		..		..
Spain	24	26	..	2005	91.0	63.2	2005	8.1[c]	2006	58.6
Sri Lanka	17[b]	28[b]	..	2004	35.6	22.2	2002	2.0		..
Sudan	..	..	19	1995	12.1	12.0		..		..
Swaziland	..	..	48		..	..		..		..
Sweden	20	21	..	2005	91.0	72.3	2005	7.7[c]		..
Switzerland	7	7	..	2005	100.0	79.1	2005	6.8[c]	2000	40.0
Syrian Arab Republic	..	..	..	2004	17.4	11.4	2004	1.3		..
Tajikistan	..	..	..		..	..	2005	2.4	2003	25.7
Tanzania	7	10	25	2006	4.3	4.1	2006	0.9		..
Thailand	5	4	30	2005	27.2	21.8		..		..
Timor-Leste	..	..	..		..	..		..		..
Togo	..	..	..	1997	15.9	15.0	1997	0.6		..
Trinidad and Tobago	13	22	..	2004	55.6	..	1996	0.6		..
Tunisia	31	29	..	2004	45.3	25.4	2003	4.3		..
Turkey	18	18	..	2007	55.0	30.5	2007	9.6	2007	61.3
Turkmenistan	..	..	..		..	..	1996	2.3		..
Uganda	..	..	30	2004	10.7	9.3	2003	0.3		..
Ukraine	15	14	49	2007	68.2	47.4	2007	15.5	2007	48.3
United Arab Emirates	7	13	..		..	..		..		..
United Kingdom	17	13	..	2005	92.7	71.4	2005	5.7[c]		..
United States	12[b]	9[b]	..	2005	92.5	72.5	2005	6.0[c]	2006	29.2
Uruguay	20	30	..	2004	55.0	44.3	2007	10.0		..
Uzbekistan	..	..	18	2005	86.0	57.0	2005	6.5	2005	40.0
Venezuela, RB	13	17	..	2004	31.8	23.8	2001	2.7		..
Vietnam	..	..	..	2005	13.2	10.8	1998	1.6		..
West Bank and Gaza	34	43	..	2008	17.0	7.8	2008	4.0		..
Yemen, Rep.	..	..	..	2005	10.0	5.5	1999	0.9		..
Zambia	..	..	24	2006	10.9	8.0	2006	1.0		..
Zimbabwe	..	..	38	1995	12.0	10.0	2002	2.3		..
World	.. w	.. w								
Low income	..	..								
Middle income	..	..								
Lower middle income	..	..								
Upper middle income	17	21								
Low & middle income	..	..								
East Asia & Pacific	..	..								
Europe & Central Asia	18	18								
Latin America & Carib.	..	..								
Middle East & N. Africa	..	..								
South Asia	..	..								
Sub-Saharan Africa	..	..								
High income	13	12								
Euro area	16	17								

a. Data are for the most recent year available. b. Limited coverage. c. Includes expenditure on old-age and survivors benefits only. d. Includes old-age, survivors, disability, military, and work accident or disease pensions. e. Includes Montenegro.

As traditionally measured, poverty is a static concept, and vulnerability a dynamic one. Vulnerability reflects a household's resilience in the face of shocks and the likelihood that a shock will lead to a decline in well-being. Thus, it depends primarily on the household's assets and insurance mechanisms. Because poor people have fewer assets and less diversified sources of income than do the better-off, fluctuations in income affect them more.

Enhancing security for poor people means reducing their vulnerability to such risks as ill health, providing them the means to manage risk themselves, and strengthening market or public institutions for managing risk. Tools include microfinance programs, public provision of education and basic health care, and old age assistance (see tables 2.11 and 2.16).

Poor households face many risks, and vulnerability is thus multidimensional. The indicators in the table focus on individual risks—youth unemployment, female-headed households, income insecurity in old age—and the extent to which publicly provided services may be capable of mitigating some of these risks. Poor people face labor market risks, often having to take up precarious, low-quality jobs and to increase their household's labor market participation by sending their children to work (see tables 2.4 and 2.6). Income security is a prime concern for the elderly.

Youth unemployment is an important policy issue for many economies. Experiencing unemployment may permanently impair a young person's productive potential and future employment opportunities. The table presents unemployment among youth ages 15–24, but the lower age limit for young people in a country could be determined by the minimum age for leaving school, so age groups could differ across countries. Also, since this age group is likely to include school leavers, the level of youth unemployment varies considerably over the year as a result of different school opening and closing dates. The youth unemployment rate shares similar limitations on comparability as the general unemployment rate. For further information, see *About the data* for table 2.5 and the original source.

The definition of female-headed household differs greatly across countries, making cross-country comparison difficult. In some cases it is assumed that a woman cannot be the head of any household with an adult male, because of sex-biased stereotype. Caution should be used in interpreting the data.

Pension scheme coverage may be broad or even universal where eligibility is determined by citizenship,

residency, or income status. In contribution-related schemes, however, eligibility is usually restricted to individuals who have contributed for a minimum number of years. Definitional issues—relating to the labor force, for example—may arise in comparing coverage by contribution-related schemes over time and across countries (for country-specific information, see Hinz and others forthcoming). The share of the labor force covered by a pension scheme may be overstated in countries that do not try to count informal sector workers as part of the labor force.

Public interventions and institutions can provide services directly to poor people, although whether these interventions and institutions work well for the poor is debated. State action is often ineffective, in part because governments can influence only a few of the many sources of well-being and in part because of difficulties in delivering goods and services. The effectiveness of public provision is further constrained by the fiscal resources at governments' disposal and the fact that state institutions may not be responsive to the needs of poor people.

The data on public pension spending cover the pension programs of the social insurance schemes for which contributions had previously been made. In many cases noncontributory pensions or social assistance targeted to the elderly and disabled are also included. A country's pattern of spending is correlated with its demographic structure—spending increases as the population ages.

• **Youth unemployment** is the share of the labor force ages 15–24 without work but available for and seeking employment. • **Female-headed households** are the percentage of households with a female head. • **Pension contributors** are the share of the labor force or working-age population (here defined as ages 15 and older) covered by a pension scheme. • **Public expenditure on pensions** is all government expenditures on cash transfers to the elderly, the disabled, and survivors and the administrative costs of these programs. • **Average pension** is the average pension payment of all pensioners of the main pension schemes (including old-age, survivors, disability, military, and work accident or disease pensions) divided by the average wage of all formal sector workers.

Data sources

Data on youth unemployment are from the ILO's Key Indicators of the Labour Market, 6th edition, database. Data on female-headed household are from Demographic and Health Surveys by Macro International. Data on pension contributors and pension spending are from Hinz and others' "International Patterns of Pension Provision II" (forthcoming).

	Public expenditure per student						Public expenditure on education		Trained teachers in primary education	Primary school pupil–teacher ratio
	Primary		% of GDP per capita Secondary		Tertiary		% of GDP	% of total government expenditure	% of total	pupils per teacher
	1999	2008[a]	1999	2008[a]	1999	2008[a]	2008[a]	2008[a]	2008[a]	2008[a]
Afghanistan	..	..	..	..	..	..	..	..	..	43
Albania	..	..	..	..	..	..	..	..	..	..
Algeria	12.0	..	..	..	..	..	..	..	98.9	23
Angola	..	..	..	..	..	80.8	2.6	..	..	..
Argentina	12.9	13.2	18.2	20.3	17.7	14.2	5.5	15.0	..	16
Armenia	..	..	..	..	..	..	3.0	15.0	..	19
Australia	16.9	18.2	15.4	16.2	27.2	24.7	5.2	14.0	..	..
Austria	24.9	..	29.9	..	51.6	..	..	..	..	12
Azerbaijan	6.9	5.2	17.0	8.0	19.1	9.2	1.9	11.9	99.9	11
Bangladesh	..	10.5	13.6	14.3	50.7	39.8	2.4	14.0	54.4	44
Belarus	..	..	..	..	..	18.1	5.2	9.3	99.9	15
Belgium	18.2	20.5	23.7	..	38.3	35.5	6.0	12.4	..	11
Benin	11.9	12.4	24.2	..	157.0	153.4	3.6	15.9	71.8	45
Bolivia	14.2	13.7	11.7	14.5	44.1	..	6.3	..	..	24
Bosnia and Herzegovina	..	..	..	..	..	..	..	..	..	..
Botswana	..	12.6	..	38.3	..	..	8.1	21.0	94.3	25
Brazil	10.8	..	9.5	..	57.1	..	5.0	16.2	..	24
Bulgaria	15.5	23.6	18.8	22.0	17.9	23.2	4.2	11.6	..	16
Burkina Faso	..	29.1	..	30.3	..	308.3	4.6	15.4	87.7	49[b]
Burundi	14.7	18.8	..	58.2	1,051.5	563.9	7.2	22.3	87.4	52
Cambodia	5.9	..	11.5	..	43.7	..	1.6	12.4	98.2	49
Cameroon	..	7.6	..	39.1	..	126.1	3.9	17.0	61.8	46
Canada	..	..	..	..	47.1	..	..	..	..	..
Central African Republic	..	5.5	..	..	..	305.2	1.3	12.0	..	90
Chad	9.2	..	28.3	..	..	..	..	..	35.5	62
Chile	14.4	11.9	14.8	13.4	19.4	11.5	3.4	18.2	..	27
China	..	..	11.6	..	90.1	..	..	..	..	18
Hong Kong SAR, China	12.4	12.7	17.7	15.6	..	47.3	3.3	23.0	95.1	17
Colombia	15.2	12.4	16.1	14.8	37.8	26.0	3.9	14.9	100.0	29
Congo, Dem. Rep.	..	..	..	..	..	..	..	..	93.3	39
Congo, Rep.	15.2	..	..	..	362.2	..	..	..	89.0	52
Costa Rica	16.0	..	23.2	..	55.0	..	5.0	22.8	86.0	19
Côte d'Ivoire	17.9	..	56.1	..	218.9	..	4.6	24.6	100.0	42
Croatia	..	..	..	..	35.8	..	..	..	..	17
Cuba	27.9	51.1	41.4	60.1	86.6	43.5	13.3	18.5	100.0	10
Czech Republic	11.2	13.6	21.7	23.1	33.7	37.4	4.6	10.5	..	19
Denmark	24.6	24.5	38.1	34.4	65.9	53.4	7.9	15.5	..	..
Dominican Republic	7.1	7.4	..	6.5	..	..	2.2	11.0	89.2	20
Ecuador	4.5	..	9.7	..	..	..	..	..	71.6	23
Egypt, Arab Rep.	..	..	..	..	..	..	3.7	12.1	..	27
El Salvador	8.6	8.5	7.5	9.1	8.9	31.5	3.6	13.1	93.2	33
Eritrea	15.1	8.2	37.6	8.1	433.2	..	2.0	..	89.3	47
Estonia	21.0	..	27.3	..	32.0	..	..	..	..	13
Ethiopia	..	12.4	..	8.9	..	642.7	5.5	23.3	89.7	59
Finland	17.4	17.9	25.8	31.5	40.3	33.1	6.1	12.6	..	15
France	17.3	17.1	28.5	26.6	29.7	33.5	5.6	10.6	..	19
Gabon	..	..	..	..	..	..	..	..	..	..
Gambia, The	..	..	..	..	..	..	..	..	..	34
Georgia	..	14.7	..	15.4	..	11.4	2.9	7.2	95.0	9
Germany	14.8	16.1	20.5	20.7	..	..	4.4	9.7	..	14
Ghana	..	17.9	..	28.3	..	..	..	..	49.1	31
Greece	11.7	..	15.5	..	26.2	..	..	..	..	10
Guatemala	6.7	10.3	4.3	5.9	..	19.0	3.0	..	..	29
Guinea	11.4	5.0	..	4.4	..	71.5	1.7	19.2	82.1	44
Guinea-Bissau	..	..	..	..	..	..	..	..	..	62
Haiti	..	..	..	..	..	..	..	..	..	..
Honduras	..	1.1	..	1.1	..	..	..	..	36.4	33

	Public expenditure per student						Public expenditure on education		Trained teachers in primary education	Primary school pupil–teacher ratio
	Primary		% of GDP per capita Secondary		Tertiary		% of GDP	% of total government expenditure	% of total	pupils per teacher
	1999	2008[a]	1999	2008[a]	1999	2008[a]	2008[a]	2008[a]	2008[a]	2008[a]
Hungary	18.0	25.6	19.1	23.2	34.2	23.8	5.4	10.4	..	10
India	11.9	8.9	24.7	16.2	90.8	55.0	3.2	..	..	..
Indonesia	..	..	..	..	..	..	3.5	17.5	..	19
Iran, Islamic Rep.	9.1	13.5	9.9	20.3	34.8	20.7	4.8	20.0	..	20
Iraq	..	..	..	..	..	..	..	..	..	..
Ireland	11.0	15.0	16.8	22.8	28.5	26.4	4.8	14.0	..	16
Israel	20.6	20.2	22.0	20.5	31.1	23.1	6.2	..	..	13
Italy	24.0	25.1	27.7	28.6	27.6	23.4	4.7	9.7	..	10
Jamaica	13.4	17.3	21.0	19.9	70.4	..	5.5	..	..	..
Japan	21.1	21.9	20.9	22.4	15.1	19.1	3.5	9.5	..	18
Jordan	13.7	13.0	15.8	16.5	..	..	..	..	..	..
Kazakhstan	..	..	..	..	..	7.9	2.8	..	..	16[b]
Kenya	22.5	22.3	15.1	22.0	207.8	..	6.6	20.2	98.4	47
Korea, Dem. Rep.	..	..	..	..	..	..	..	..	..	..
Korea, Rep.	18.4	17.2	15.7	22.2	8.4	9.5	4.2	..	..	26
Kosovo	..	..	..	..	..	..	..	..	..	..
Kuwait	19.2	11.1	..	14.6	..	82.8	3.8	12.9	100.0	9
Kyrgyz Republic	..	..	..	..	24.3	22.8	6.6	25.6	64.4	24
Lao PDR	2.2	..	4.5	..	68.6	..	2.3	12.2	96.9	30
Latvia	19.5	37.3	23.7	19.3	27.9	15.9	5.1	13.4	..	12
Lebanon	..	..	..	..	14.2	12.5	2.0	8.1	12.8	14
Lesotho	34.4	22.3	76.6	50.2	1,385.2	1,182.4	12.4	23.7	71.4	37
Liberia	..	5.7	..	8.4	..	..	2.7	12.1	40.2	24
Libya	..	..	..	..	23.9	..	..	..	..	..
Lithuania	..	16.4	..	20.3	34.2	17.0	4.8	14.4	..	13
Macedonia, FYR	..	..	..	..	..	..	4.7	13.3	..	18
Madagascar	8.9	7.4	..	13.0	171.7	137.2	2.9	13.4	52.1	47
Malawi	..	..	..	..	..	..	..	..	..	93
Malaysia	12.5	10.8	21.7	..	81.1	59.7	4.7	..	..	16
Mali	13.5	10.4	53.0	34.5	227.7	114.8	3.8	19.5	50.1	51
Mauritania	11.2	12.8	35.3	36.7	77.8	..	4.4	15.6	100.0	37
Mauritius	9.7	10.3	15.3	17.4	40.4	29.8	3.9	12.7	100.0	22
Mexico	11.7	13.4	14.2	13.8	47.8	35.4	4.8	..	..	28
Moldova	..	34.3	..	32.4	..	38.9	8.2	19.8	..	16
Mongolia	..	14.7	..	14.7	..	..	5.1	..	99.0	30[b]
Morocco	17.0	16.3	44.5	38.3	94.9	72.1	5.5	26.1	100.0	27
Mozambique	..	14.5	..	83.7	..	..	5.0	21.0	67.0	64
Myanmar	..	..	6.8	..	27.5	..	..	..	99.0	29
Namibia	22.1	15.7	36.2	16.0	156.9	117.8	6.5	22.4	95.0	29
Nepal	9.1	15.1	13.1	11.2	141.6	..	3.8	..	66.4	38
Netherlands	15.2	17.8	22.2	25.4	47.4	43.9	5.5	12.0	..	..
New Zealand	20.1	17.6	24.3	19.8	41.6	29.2	6.2	19.7	..	16
Nicaragua	..	9.8	..	4.5	..	..	..	..	72.7	29
Niger	20.2	27.1	60.9	49.6	..	398.0	3.7	15.5	98.0[b]	39[b]
Nigeria	..	..	..	..	..	..	..	..	51.2	46
Norway	19.8	18.2	26.8	..	45.8	44.8	6.5	16.2	..	..
Oman	11.2	..	21.8	..	..	..	4.0	31.1	100.0	12
Pakistan	..	..	..	..	..	..	2.9	11.2	85.1	41
Panama	13.7	7.5	19.1	10.0	33.6	..	3.8	18.0	91.3	24
Papua New Guinea	..	..	..	..	..	..	..	..	..	36
Paraguay	13.6	..	18.4	..	58.9	..	..	..	..	..
Peru	7.6	7.3	10.8	8.9	21.2	10.9	2.5	16.4	..	22
Philippines	12.8	..	11.0	..	15.4	..	..	..	..	34
Poland	..	27.0	16.5	24.9	21.1	18.4	5.7	12.0	..	11
Portugal	19.5	22.4	27.5	34.0	28.1	28.8	5.3	11.3	..	12
Puerto Rico	..	..	..	..	..	..	..	..	..	..
Qatar	..	..	..	..	..	..	..	..	52.3	13

2.11 Education inputs

	Public expenditure per student						Public expenditure on education		Trained teachers in primary education	Primary school pupil–teacher ratio
	Primary		Secondary		Tertiary		% of GDP	% of total government expenditure	% of total	pupils per teacher
			% of GDP per capita							
	1999	**2008ª**	**1999**	**2008ª**	**1999**	**2008ª**	**2008ª**	**2008ª**	**2008ª**	**2008ª**
Romania	8.5	..	16.0	..	32.6	..	..	..	..	17
Russian Federation	..	..	..	..	..	16.0	4.0	11.8	..	17
Rwanda	7.7	8.2	29.4	34.3	680.7	222.8	4.1	20.4	94.2	68
Saudi Arabia	..	18.4	..	18.3	..	..	..	..	91.5	11
Senegal	14.1	17.0	..	31.3	..	207.7	4.8	26.3	..	36
Serbia	..	..	..	..	..	..	..	..	100.0	17
Sierra Leone	..	..	..	..	..	..	..	..	49.4	44
Singapore	..	11.2ᵇ	..	16.6ᵇ	..	26.9ᵇ	3.2ᵇ	11.6ᵇ	97.1	19
Slovak Republic	10.2	15.3	18.4	..	32.9	..	3.8	10.2	..	15
Slovenia	26.3	..	25.7	..	27.9	21.6	5.7	12.9	..	16
Somalia	..	..	..	..	..	..	..	..	..	..
South Africa	14.2	13.7	20.0	16.0	60.7	..	5.1	16.2	..	31
Spain	18.0	19.4	24.4	24.0	19.6	23.5	4.3	11.1	..	13
Sri Lanka	..	..	..	..	..	..	..	..	..	24
Sudan	..	..	..	..	..	..	..	..	59.7ᵇ	38ᵇ
Swaziland	8.4	16.3	23.7	41.1	351.5	347.5	7.9	21.6	94.0	32
Sweden	22.5	24.7	26.2	32.0	52.1	39.5	6.9	12.6	..	10
Switzerland	22.7	23.3	27.3	26.5	53.8	53.5	5.5	16.3	..	..
Syrian Arab Republic	11.2	18.4	21.7	14.0	..	..	4.9	16.7	..	18
Tajikistan	..	..	..	..	..	21.8	3.5	18.7	88.3	23
Tanzania	..	..	..	..	..	..	..	..	100.0	52
Thailand	17.8	..	15.9	..	36.0	30.5	4.0	20.9	..	16
Timor-Leste	..	27.6	..	..	..	..	7.1	7.3	..	41
Togo	8.5	9.4	30.3	19.1	..	155.2	3.7	17.2	14.6	39
Trinidad and Tobago	11.6	..	12.3	..	149.3	..	..	..	86.6	17
Tunisia	15.6	..	27.1	..	89.4	54.0	7.1	20.5	..	18
Turkey	8.2	..	10.4	..	33.5	28.1	..	..	..	..
Turkmenistan	..	..	..	..	..	..	..	..	..	..
Uganda	..	7.5ᵇ	..	20.3ᵇ	..	121.1	3.3ᵇ	15.6ᵇ	89.4	50
Ukraine	..	..	..	..	36.5	25.1	5.3	20.2	99.8	16
United Arab Emirates	8.7	4.9	11.6	6.9	41.5	..	..	..	100.0	17
United Kingdom	14.1	22.1	24.2	27.3	26.0	29.2	5.6	11.9	..	17
United States	17.9	22.2	22.5	24.6	27.0	25.4	5.7	14.8	..	14
Uruguay	7.2	8.5	9.9	10.4	..	18.1	3.9	14.4	..	15
Uzbekistan	..	..	..	..	..	..	..	..	100.0	18
Venezuela, RB	..	9.1	..	8.1	..	..	3.7	..	83.5	16
Vietnam	..	19.7	..	17.3	..	61.7	5.3	..	98.6	20
West Bank and Gaza	..	..	..	..	..	..	..	..	100.0	30
Yemen, Rep.	..	..	..	..	..	..	5.2	16.0	..	..
Zambia	7.2	..	19.4	..	164.6	..	1.4	..	..	61
Zimbabwe	12.7	..	19.3	..	193.0	..	..	..	..	38
World	.. m	.. m	.. m	.. m	.. m	.. m	**4.6 m**	.. m		**24 w**
Low income	..	..	..	..	..	..	..	..		45
Middle income	..	..	..	..	..	..	4.5	..		23
Lower middle income	..	..	..	..	..	..	4.0	..		..
Upper middle income	13.5	..	18.1	..	34.2	18.4	4.6	14.0		22
Low & middle income	..	..	..	..	..	..	4.0	..		27
East Asia & Pacific	..	..	..	..	38.2	..	..	..		19
Europe & Central Asia	..	..	..	..	..	18.4	4.5	14.4		16
Latin America & Carib.	12.7	11.0	13.7	10.7	44.0	..	3.6	..		25
Middle East & N. Africa	..	..	..	..	..	..	5.2	18.5		24
South Asia	..	..	13.6	..	90.8	..	2.9	..		..
Sub-Saharan Africa	..	..	..	..	..	..	..	..		49
High income	17.9	18.2	22.4	23.2	32.9	29.0	5.4	12.6		15
Euro area	17.3	17.8	24.4	26.0	29.1	28.8	5.3	11.3		14

a. Provisional data. b. Data are for 2009.

About the data

Data on education are compiled by the United Nations Educational, Scientific, and Cultural Organization (UNESCO) Institute for Statistics from official responses to surveys and from reports provided by education authorities in each country. The data are used for monitoring, policymaking, and resource allocation. However, coverage and data collection methods vary across countries and over time within countries, so comparisons should be made with caution.

For most countries the data on education spending in the table refer to public spending—government spending on public education plus subsidies for private education—and generally exclude foreign aid for education. They may also exclude spending by religious schools, which play a significant role in many developing countries. Data for some countries and some years refer to ministry of education spending only and exclude education expenditures by other ministries and local authorities.

Many developing countries seek to supplement public funds for education, some with tuition fees to recover part of the cost of providing education services or to encourage development of private schools. Fees raise difficult questions of equity, efficiency, access, and taxation, however, and some governments have used scholarships, vouchers, and other public finance methods to counter criticism. For greater detail, consult the country- and indicator-specific notes in the original source.

The share of public expenditure devoted to education allows an assessment of the priority a government assigns to education relative to other public investments, as well as a government's commitment to investing in human capital development. It also reflects the development status of a country's education system relative to that of others. However, returns on investment to education, especially primary and lower secondary education, cannot be understood simply by comparing current education indicators with national income. It takes a long time before currently enrolled children can productively contribute to the national economy (Hanushek 2002).

Data on education finance are generally of poor quality. This is partly because ministries of education, from which the UNESCO Institute for Statistics collects data, may not be the best source for education finance data. Other agencies, particularly ministries of finance, need to be consulted, but coordination is not easy. It is also difficult to track actual spending from the central government to local institutions. And private spending adds to the complexity of collecting accurate data on public spending.

The share of trained teachers in primary education measures the quality of the teaching staff. It does not take account of competencies acquired by teachers through their professional experience or self-instruction or of such factors as work experience, teaching methods and materials, or classroom conditions, which may affect the quality of teaching. Since the training teachers receive varies greatly (pre-service or in-service), care should be taken in making comparisons across countries.

The primary school pupil–teacher ratio reflects the average number of pupils per teacher. It differs from the average class size because of the different practices countries employ, such as part-time teachers, school shifts, and multigrade classes. The comparability of pupil–teacher ratios across countries is affected by the definition of teachers and by differences in class size by grade and in the number of hours taught, as well as the different practices mentioned above. Moreover, the underlying enrollment levels are subject to a variety of reporting errors (for further discussion of enrollment data, see *About the data* for table 2.12). While the pupil–teacher ratio is often used to compare the quality of schooling across countries, it is often weakly related to the value added of schooling systems.

In 1998 UNESCO introduced the new International Standard Classification of Education 1997 (ISCED 1997). Consistent historical time series with reclassification of the pre–ISCED 1997 series were produced for a selection of indicators in 2008. The full set of the historical series is forthcoming.

In 2006 the UNESCO Institute for Statistics also changed its convention for citing the reference year of education data and indicators to the calendar year in which the academic or financial year ends. Data that used to be listed for 2006, for example, are now listed for 2007. This change was implemented to present the most recent data available and to align the data reporting with that of other international organizations (in particular the Organisation for Economic Co-operation and Development and Eurostat).

Definitions

• **Public expenditure per student** is public current and capital spending on education divided by the number of students by level as a percentage of gross domestic product (GDP) per capita. • **Public expenditure on education** is current and capital public expenditure on education as a percentage of GDP and as a percentage of total government expenditure. • **Trained teachers in primary education** are the percentage of primary school teachers who have received the minimum organized teacher training (pre-service or in-service) required for teaching in their country. • **Primary school pupil–teacher ratio** is the number of pupils enrolled in primary school divided by the number of primary school teachers (regardless of their teaching assignment).

Data sources

Data on education inputs are from the UNESCO Institute for Statistics, which compiles international data on education in cooperation with national commissions and national statistical services.

	Gross enrollment ratio				Net enrollment ratio				Adjusted net enrollment ratio, primary		Children out of school	
		% of relevant age group				% of relevant age group			% of primary-school-age children		thousand primary-school-age children	
	Preprimary	Primary	Secondary	Tertiary	Primary		Secondary		Male	Female	Male	Female
	2008[a]	2008[a]	2008[a]	2008[a]	1991	2008[a]	1999	2008[a]	2008[a]	2008[a]	2008[a]	2008[a]
Afghanistan	..	106	29	..	25	..	..	27	..	..	..	..
Albania	..	..	..	..	..	..	70	..	..	..	..	..
Algeria	23	108	..	24	89	95	..	..	96	95	68	88
Angola	..	..	..	3	49	..	..	..	..	..	..	..
Argentina	67	115	85	68	95	..	76	79	..	..	..	..
Armenia	33	80	88	34	..	74	86	86	73	75	22	18
Australia	101	105	148	75	98	97	90	88	97	98	32	22
Austria	92	101	100	50	88	98	..	..	97	98	5	3
Azerbaijan	26	116	106	16	89	96	75	98	97	95	7	9
Bangladesh	..	94	44	7	70	88	40	41	88	94	1,028	518
Belarus	102	99	95	73	85	94	82	87	94	96	12	7
Belgium	121	102	110	62	96	98	..	87	98	98	8	6
Benin	13	117	..	6	46	93	18	..	99	86	7	91
Bolivia	49	108	82	38	..	94	68	70	95	95	39	32
Bosnia and Herzegovina	11	111	89	34	79	..	..	..	..	..	..	..
Botswana	16	110	80	..	89	86	60	..	..	..	10	2
Brazil	62	130	100	30	..	93	66	77	93	94	465	440
Bulgaria	82	101	105	50	..	95	85	88	97	96	5	5
Burkina Faso	3	79[b]	20[b]	3	27	63[b]	9	15[b]	68[b]	60[b]	392[b]	473[b]
Burundi	3	136	18	3	53	99	..	..	91	89	55	67
Cambodia	13	116	40	7	72	89	15	34	90	87	99	131
Cameroon	25	111	37	8	69	88	..	..	94	82	83	255
Canada	70	99	101	..	98	..	95	..	..	..	..	..
Central African Republic	3	77	..	2	53	59	..	..	68	50	107	168
Chad	..	83	19	2	34	..	7	..	..	..	..	..
Chile	56	105	94	50	89	94	..	85	95	94	41	46
China	42	112	74	22	97	..	..	..	..	..	..	..
Hong Kong SAR, China	..	..	83	34	92	..	74	75	..	..	..	..
Colombia	49	120	91	35	71	90	56	71	93	94	147	138
Congo, Dem. Rep.	3	90	35	5	56	..	..	..	..	..	..	..
Congo, Rep.	12	114	..	..	81	59	..	..	66	62	91	102
Costa Rica	69	110	89	..	87	..	..	..	..	..	..	..
Côte d'Ivoire	3	74	..	8	46	..	18	..	..	..	..	..
Croatia	51	99	94	47	..	90	81	88	98	100	2	0[c]
Cuba	111	102	91	122	94	99	73	84	100	99	2	2
Czech Republic	114	102	95	54	87	92	..	..	91	94	22	14
Denmark	96	99	119	80	98	96	88	90	95	97	10	6
Dominican Republic	35	104	75	..	..	80	38	58	82	83	117	103
Ecuador	100	118	70	35	98	97	46	59	..	..	..	..
Egypt, Arab Rep.	16	100	..	..	81	94	71	..	97	93	137	324
El Salvador	60	115	64	25	..	94	47	55	95	96	23	15
Eritrea	13	52	30	2[b]	15	39	17	26	43	37	173	187
Estonia	95	99	100	65	88	94	84	90	96	97	1	1
Ethiopia	4	98	33	4	24	78	12	25	82	76	1,180	1,552
Finland	64	98	111	94	98	96	95	97	96	97	7	6
France	113	110	113	55	100	99	94	98	99	99	16	13
Gabon	..	..	..	..	91	..	..	..	..	..	..	..
Gambia, The	22	86	51	..	50	69	26	42	69	74	40	33
Georgia	63	107	90	34	97	99	76	81	96	93	6	10
Germany	108	106	101	..	84	98	..	..	..	..	..	..
Ghana	67	102	54	6	56	74	33	46	74	75	460	422
Greece	69	101	102	91	95	99	82	91	99	100	2	0[c]
Guatemala	29	114	57	18	64	95	24	40	98	95	23	55
Guinea	11	90	36	9	27	71	12	28	77	67	175	245
Guinea-Bissau	..	120	36	3	40	..	10	..	..	..	..	..
Haiti	..	..	..	..	21	..	..	..	..	..	..	..
Honduras	40	116	65	19	88	97	..	..	96	98	22	9

	Gross enrollment ratio				Net enrollment ratio				Adjusted net enrollment ratio, primary		Children out of school	
		% of relevant age group				% of relevant age group			% of primary-school-age children		thousand primary-school-age children	
	Preprimary	Primary	Secondary	Tertiary	Primary		Secondary		Male	Female	Male	Female
	2008[a]	2008[a]	2008[a]	2008[a]	1991	2008[a]	1999	2008[a]	2008[a]	2008[a]	2008[a]	2008[a]
Hungary	89	98	97	67	..	89	82	90	95	95	10	10
India	47	113	57	13	..	90	..	..	97	94	1,782	3,781
Indonesia	45	121	76	18	98	95	50	70	..	..	..	..
Iran, Islamic Rep.	52	128	80	36	91	..	..	75	..	..	..	..
Iraq	..	..	..	..	92	..	30	..	..	..	..	..
Ireland	..	105	113	61	90	97	84	88	96	97	8	6
Israel	98	111	91	60	..	97	86	88	97	98	13	8
Italy	101	104	100	67	98	99	88	92	100	99	5	14
Jamaica	89	90	90	..	97	85	83	77	86	85	24	26
Japan	88	102	101	58	100	100	99	98	..	..	..	..
Jordan	33	96	86	38	..	89	79	84	93	94	32	23
Kazakhstan	39[b]	109[b]	95[b]	41[b]	88	89[b]	87	87[b]	99[b]	100[b]	4[b]	2[b]
Kenya	48	112	58	4[b]	..	82	33	49	82	83	563	524
Korea, Dem. Rep.	..	..	..	..	..	..	..	..	..	..	..	..
Korea, Rep.	105	104	97	96	99	99	97	96	100	98	4	41
Kosovo	..	..	..	..	..	..	..	..	..	..	..	..
Kuwait	76	95	91	18	49	88	89	80	94	93	6	8
Kyrgyz Republic	17	95	85	52	92	84	..	80	91	91	19	19
Lao PDR	15	112	44	13	60	82	26	36	84	81	65	76
Latvia	90	97	115	69	94	..	..	..	..	..	..	..
Lebanon	72	101	82	52	66	88	..	75	90	89	25	25
Lesotho	..	108	40	4	72	73	17	25	71	75	54	47
Liberia	84	91	32	..	..	..	20	..	..	..	..	..
Libya	9	110	93	..	..	..	..	..	..	..	..	..
Lithuania	69	96	99	76	..	91	90	92	94	94	4	4
Macedonia, FYR	38	93	84	36	..	87	79	..	91	92	5	4
Madagascar	9	152	30	3	72	98	12	24	99	100	16	3
Malawi	..	120	29	0	48	91	29	25	88	94	155	80
Malaysia	57	98	..	30	93	97	65	..	98	97	39	41
Mali	4	91	35	5	23	72	..	29	81	68	190	316
Mauritania	..	98	23	4	35	80	14	16	78	83	54	40
Mauritius	98	99	88	16[b]	93	93	67	..	93	94	4	4
Mexico	113	113	87	26	98	98	56	71	99	100	52	28
Moldova	72	89	83	40	89	83	80	79	86	85	12	12
Mongolia	57	102	95	50	90	89	58	82	99	99	1	1
Morocco	57	107	56	12	56	89	30	..	92	88	148	217
Mozambique	..	114	21	..	42	80	3	6	82	77	378	486
Myanmar	6	115	49	11	96	..	31	46	..	..	..	..
Namibia	31	112	66	9	84	89	39	54	88	93	22	12
Nepal	35	124	43	..	62	..	..	..	..	..	..	..
Netherlands	101	107	120	60	95	99	91	89	99	98	5	11
New Zealand	93	101	120	79	100	99	90	..	99	100	2	1
Nicaragua	56	117	68	..	70	92	35	45	93	94	29	24
Niger	3[b]	62[b]	11	1[b]	23	54[b]	6	9	60[b]	48[b]	510[b]	636[b]
Nigeria	16	93	30	..	54	61	..	26	66	60	4,023	4,626
Norway	92	98	113	76	100	98	96	97	98	98	4	3
Oman	34	75	88	26	69	68	65	78	71	73	54	48
Pakistan	..	85	33	5	33	66	22	33	72	60	3,060	4,201
Panama	69	111	71	45	92	98	59	66	99	98	2	3
Papua New Guinea	..	55	..	..	66	..	..	..	..	..	..	..
Paraguay	34	108	66	..	94	92	..	58	93	93	31	27
Peru	68	113	98	34	87	97	62	76	..	..	..	..
Philippines	47	108	81	28	96	90	50	60	90	92	635	481
Poland	60	97	100	67	..	96	90	94	95	96	60	49
Portugal	80	115	101	57	98	99	82	88	99	99	2	4
Puerto Rico	..	..	..	..	..	..	..	..	..	..	..	..
Qatar	51	109	93	11	89	..	74	79	..	..	..	..

2.12 Participation in education

	Gross enrollment ratio				Net enrollment ratio				Adjusted net enrollment ratio, primary		Children out of school	
		% of relevant age group				% of relevant age group			% of primary-school-age children		thousand primary-school-age children	
	Preprimary	Primary	Secondary	Tertiary	Primary		Secondary		Male	Female	Male	Female
	2008[a]	2008[a]	2008[a]	2008[a]	1991	2008[a]	1999	2008[a]	2008[a]	2008[a]	2008[a]	2008[a]
Romania	72	105	87	58	81	94	75	73	96	97	16	14
Russian Federation	89	97	84	75	99	..	..	..	..	..	..	..
Rwanda	..	151	22	4	67	96	..	..	95	97	38	22
Saudi Arabia	11	98	95	30	59	85	..	73	85	84	244	259
Senegal	11	84	31	8	45	73	..	25	75	76	248	233
Serbia	57	101	90	49	..	97	..	90	98	98	3	3
Sierra Leone	5	158	35	..	40	..	..	25	..	..	..	..
Singapore	..	..	..	..	..	..	..	..	..	..	..	..
Slovak Republic	94	102	93	50	..	..	..	..	..	..	..	..
Slovenia	80	103	94	85	96	96	90	89	97	96	2	2
Somalia	..	..	..	..	..	..	..	..	..	..	..	..
South Africa	51	105	95	..	90	87	63	72	92	94	284	219
Spain	123	105	119	68	100	100	88	94	100	100	1	5
Sri Lanka	..	105	..	..	83	100	..	..	..	..	..	..
Sudan	28[b]	74[b]	38[b]	..	..	..	..	..	..	..	..	..
Swaziland	..	108	53	4	74	83	32	29	82	84	19	18
Sweden	101	94	103	75	100	94	87	99	94	94	20	20
Switzerland	101	102	96	47	84	93	84	85	98	99	5	3
Syrian Arab Republic	10	124	74	..	91	..	36	68	..	..	..	..
Tajikistan	9	102	84	20	77	97	63	83	99	96	2	15
Tanzania	34	110	..	1	51	99	5	..	96	95	138	179
Thailand	..	..	..	..	..	..	..	..	..	..	..	..
Timor-Leste	..	107	..	15[b]	..	76	23	31	79	76	20	22
Togo	4	105	41	5	65	83	20	..	91	80	44	99
Trinidad and Tobago	82	103	89	..	90	92	70	74	96	95	3	3
Tunisia	..	108	90	32	94	98	69	..	99	100	6	0[c]
Turkey	16	98	82	37	89	94	..	71	95	92	194	313
Turkmenistan	..	..	..	..	..	..	..	..	..	..	..	..
Uganda	19	120	25	4	51	97	8	19	96	99	134	49
Ukraine	98	98	94	79	81	89	91	85	89	90	89	81
United Arab Emirates	87	108	94	25	99	92	69	84	99	99	1	1
United Kingdom	73	104	97	59	98	97	95	91	98	99	42	24
United States	61	98	94	82	97	91	88	88	92	93	1,018	797
Uruguay	81	114	92	64	91	98	..	68	98	98	4	3
Uzbekistan	27	94	102	10	78	90	..	92	94	91	74	98
Venezuela, RB	69	103	81	78	..	90	47	69	92	92	141	123
Vietnam	..	..	..	..	89	..	59	..	..	..	..	..
West Bank and Gaza	30	80	92	47	..	73	77	89	77	78	56	52
Yemen, Rep.	..	85	..	10	..	73	32	..	80	66	395	641
Zambia	..	119	52	..	80	95	17	49	96	98	47	29
Zimbabwe	..	104	41	..	84	90	40	38	90	91	121	103
World	**45 w**	**106 w**	**66 w**	**26 w**	**.. w**	**87 w**	**.. w**	**.. w**	**90 w**	**88 w**		
Low income	..	101	41	6	..	80	..	..	83	79		
Middle income	46	109	67	23	..	88	..	..	92	90		
Lower middle income	41	108	62	18	..	87	..	..	91	89		
Upper middle income	64	110	90	43	..	94	..	..	95	95		
Low & middle income	41	107	62	20	..	86	..	..	90	87		
East Asia & Pacific	42	112	73	..	96	..	..	..	..	..		
Europe & Central Asia	54	98	89	55	90	92	..	..	94	93		
Latin America & Carib.	66	117	88	35	..	94	60	71	94	95		
Middle East & N. Africa	29	106	72	26	..	91	60	..	94	90		
South Asia	47	108	52	11	68	86	..	..	92	86		
Sub-Saharan Africa	16	97	33	6	..	73	..	..	76	71		
High income	79	102	100	69	95	95	..	..	94	95		
Euro area	106	..	..	..	..	..	..	..	..	..		

a. Provisional data. b. Data are for 2009. c. Less than 0.5.

About the data

School enrollment data are reported to the United Nations Educational, Scientific, and Cultural Organization (UNESCO) Institute for Statistics by national education authorities and statistical offices. Enrollment ratios help monitor whether a country is on track to achieve the Millennium Development Goal of universal primary education by 2015, and whether an education system has the capacity to meet the needs of universal primary education, as indicated in part by gross enrollment ratios.

Enrollment ratios, while a useful measure of participation in education, have limitations. They are based on annual school surveys, which are typically conducted at the beginning of the school year and do not reflect actual attendance or dropout rates during the year. And school administrators may exaggerate enrollments, especially if there is a financial incentive to do so.

Also, the gross and net primary enrollment ratios have an inherent weakness: the length of primary education differs across countries, although the International Standard Classification of Education tries to minimize the difference. A shorter duration for primary education tends to increase the ratio; a longer one to decrease it (in part because more older children drop out).

Overage or underage enrollments are frequent, particularly when parents prefer children to start school

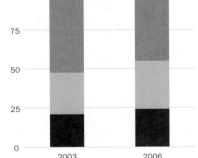

The situations of out of school children vary widely   2.12a

Percent

■ Not expected to enroll
■ Expected to enroll   ■ Drop out

Some children who are out of school can be expected to enter school late, some have already had some contact with schooling but will drop out, and others will never enter school. For countries to reach the goal of education for all, policies that address all three situations will need to be implemented.

Source: UNESCO Institute for Statistics 2008b.

at other than the official age. Age at enrollment may be inaccurately estimated or misstated, especially in communities where registration of births is not strictly enforced.

Other problems of cross-country comparison stem from errors in school-age population estimates. Age-sex structures drawn from censuses or vital registrations, the primary data sources on school-age population, commonly underenumerate (especially young children) to circumvent laws or regulations. Errors are also introduced when parents round children's ages. While census data are often adjusted for age bias, adjustments are rarely made for inadequate vital registration systems. Compounding these problems, pre- and postcensus estimates of school-age children are model interpolations or projections that may miss important demographic events (see discussion of demographic data in *About the data* for table 2.1).

Gross enrollment ratios indicate the capacity of each level of the education system, but a high ratio may reflect a substantial number of overage children enrolled in each grade because of repetition rather than a successful education system. The net enrollment ratio excludes overage and underage students to capture more accurately the system's coverage and internal efficiency but does not account for children who fall outside the official school age because of late or early entry rather than grade repetition. Differences between gross and net enrollment ratios show the incidence of overage and underage enrollments.

Adjusted net primary enrollment (called total net primary enrollment in the 2008 edition), recently added as a Millennium Development Goal indicator, captures primary-school-age children who have progressed to secondary education, which the traditional net enrollment ratio excludes.

Data on children out of school (primary-school-age children not enrolled in school—dropouts, children never enrolled, and children of primary age enrolled in preprimary education) are compiled from administrative data. Large numbers of children out of school create pressure to enroll children and provide classrooms, teachers, and educational materials, a task made difficult in many countries by limited education budgets. However, getting children into school is a high priority for countries and crucial for achieving the Millennium Development Goal of universal primary education.

In 2006 the UNESCO Institute for Statistics changed its convention for citing the reference year. For more information, see *About the data* for table 2.11.

Definitions

- **Gross enrollment ratio** is the ratio of total enrollment, regardless of age, to the population of the age group that officially corresponds to the level of education shown. • **Preprimary education** refers to the initial stage of organized instruction, designed primarily to introduce very young children to a school-type environment. • **Primary education** provides children with basic reading, writing, and mathematics skills along with an elementary understanding of such subjects as history, geography, natural science, social science, art, and music. • **Secondary education** completes the provision of basic education that began at the primary level and aims at laying the foundations for lifelong learning and human development by offering more subject- or skill-oriented instruction using more specialized teachers. • **Tertiary education** refers to a wide range of post-secondary education institutions, including technical and vocational education, colleges, and universities, whether or not leading to an advanced research qualification, that normally require as a minimum condition of admission the successful completion of education at the secondary level. • **Net enrollment ratio** is the ratio of total enrollment of children of official school age based on the International Standard Classification of Education 1997 to the population of the age group that officially corresponds to the level of education shown. • **Adjusted net enrollment ratio, primary,** is the ratio of total enrollment of children of official school age for primary education who are enrolled in primary or secondary education to the total primary-school-age population. • **Children out of school** are the number of primary-school-age children not enrolled in primary or secondary school.

Data sources

Data on gross and net enrollment ratios and out of school children are from the UNESCO Institute for Statistics.

	Gross intake rate in grade 1		Cohort survival rate						Repeaters in primary school		Transition to secondary school	
	% of relevant age group		% of grade 1 students						% of enrollment		%	
			Reaching grade 5				Reaching last grade of primary education					
	Male	Female	Male		Female		Male	Female	Male	Female	Male	Female
	2008[a]	2008[a]	1991	2007[a]	1991	2007[a]	2007[a]	2007[a]	2008[a]	2008[a]	2007[a]	2007[a]
Afghanistan	119	82	..	..	..	..	..	..	0	0	..	..
Albania	..	..	..	..	..	..	..	..	..	..	..	..
Algeria	104	102	95	95	94	97	91	95	10	6	90	92
Angola	..	..	..	..	..	..	..	..	..	..	..	..
Argentina	112	111	..	95	..	97	93	96	8	5	93	95
Armenia	90	93	..	..	..	..	29	27	0[b]	0[b]	100	98
Australia	..	..	98	..	99	..	..	..	..	..	..	..
Austria	106	102	..	..	..	..	97	99	..	..	100	99
Azerbaijan	115	114	..	..	..	..	100	98	0[b]	0[b]	100	99
Bangladesh	97	99	..	52	..	58	52	58	13	13	95	100
Belarus	97	102	..	..	..	..	99	100	0[b]	0[b]	100	100
Belgium	99	101	90	95	92	97	92	95	3	3	100	99
Benin	171	157	54	..	56	..	..	..	14	14	72	70
Bolivia	121	120	..	83	..	83	81	80	3	2	90	90
Bosnia and Herzegovina	..	..	..	..	..	..	..	..	1	0[b]	..	..
Botswana	116	113	81	94	87	95	90	94	6	4	98	98
Brazil	..	..	..	..	..	..	..	..	..	..	..	..
Bulgaria	109	110	..	..	..	..	94	94	3	2	94	95
Burkina Faso	90[c]	83[c]	71	78	68	81	68	71	11	10	54	50
Burundi	151	142	65	59	58	65	51	57	33	34	37	31
Cambodia	129	122	..	60	..	65	52	57	12	10	80	79
Cameroon	127	110	..	63	..	63	57	56	17	16	46	50
Canada	98	98	95	..	98	..	..	..	0	0	..	..
Central African Republic	93	70	24	61	22	57	53	47	26	27	44	51
Chad	114	84	56	41	41	34	33	25	21	23	64	65
Chile	103	102	94	96	91	97	..	..	5	3	..	..
China	92	95	58	..	78	..	..	..	0[b]	0[b]	..	..
Hong Kong SAR, China	..	..	..	100	..	100	100	100	1	1	100	100
Colombia	127	124	..	85	..	93	85	93	4	3	98	99
Congo, Dem. Rep.	105	128	58	80	50	79	82	76	15	16	64	54
Congo, Rep.	107	98	56	76	65	80	70	71	23	22	63	63
Costa Rica	95	95	83	95	85	98	93	96	8	6	100	94
Côte d'Ivoire	81	69	75	83	70	73	83	66	18	18	50	43
Croatia	94	94	..	..	..	..	100	100	0[b]	0[b]	99	100
Cuba	96	98	..	96	..	97	95	97	1	0[b]	98	99
Czech Republic	112	110	..	98	..	99	98	99	1	0[b]	99	99
Denmark	98	99	94	100	94	100	..	..	0	0	97	96
Dominican Republic	110	98	..	70	..	77	64	74	4	3	90	94
Ecuador	141	139	..	46	..	39	38	32	2	1	72	67
Egypt, Arab Rep.	98	96	..	96	..	97	94	96	4	2	..	..
El Salvador	123	119	..	78	..	82	74	78	7	5	92	92
Eritrea	44	37	..	77	..	69	77	69	16	15	84	81
Estonia	100	99	..	98	..	98	99	98	0	0	..	..
Ethiopia	162	144	16	46	23	49	39	42	5	5	88	89
Finland	99	99	100	100	100	100	100	100	1	0[b]	100	100
France	..	..	69	..	95	..	..	..	..	..	..	..
Gabon	..	..	..	..	..	..	..	..	..	..	..	..
Gambia, The	91	96	..	71	..	72	68	72	6	5	84	84
Georgia	114	118	..	94	..	97	94	97	0[b]	0[b]	99	100
Germany	104	102	..	..	..	..	98	99	1	1	99	98
Ghana	109	112	81	..	79	..	..	..	7	6	90	96
Greece	102	103	100	99	100	98	98	98	1	1	100	99
Guatemala	123	121	..	71	..	70	65	64	13	11	93	90
Guinea	97	87	64	74	48	65	60	49	15	16	34	26
Guinea-Bissau	..	..	..	..	..	..	..	..	..	..	..	..
Haiti	..	..	..	..	..	..	..	..	..	..	..	..
Honduras	126	122	..	75	..	80	74	79	6	5	68	74

	Gross intake rate in grade 1		Cohort survival rate						Repeaters in primary school		Transition to secondary school	
	% of relevant age group		% of grade 1 students						% of enrollment		%	
			Reaching grade 5				Reaching last grade of primary education					
	Male	Female	Male		Female		Male	Female	Male	Female	Male	Female
	2008[a]	2008[a]	1991	2007[a]	1991	2007[a]	2007[a]	2007[a]	2008[a]	2008[a]	2007[a]	2007[a]
Hungary	99	98	..	..	..	..	98	98	2	2	100	95
India	132	124	..	66	..	65	66	65	3	3	86	84
Indonesia	131	125	34	92	78	94	78	81	4	3	99	98
Iran, Islamic Rep.	118	159	91	..	89	..	..	..	3	1	84	74
Iraq	..	..	..	..	..	..	..	..	..	..	..	..
Ireland	100	102	99	97	100	100	..	..	1	1	..	..
Israel	100	103	..	100	..	99	100	99	2	1	71	71
Italy	106	105	..	99	..	100	99	100	0[b]	0[b]	100	99
Jamaica	90	86	..	..	..	..	..	..	3	2	..	..
Japan	102	101	100	..	100	..	..	..	..	..	..	..
Jordan	94	96	..	..	..	..	..	..	1	1	98	97
Kazakhstan	108[c]	108[c]	..	..	..	..	99[d]	99[d]	0[b,c]	0[b,c]	100[d]	100[d]
Kenya	..	..	..	71	..	74	..	..	..	..	61[d]	59[d]
Korea, Dem. Rep.	..	..	..	..	..	..	..	..	..	..	..	..
Korea, Rep.	113	110	99	98	100	98	97	97	0[b]	0[b]	99	98
Kosovo	..	..	..	..	..	..	..	..	..	..	..	..
Kuwait	95	93	..	100	..	99	100	99	1	1	100	100
Kyrgyz Republic	97	96	..	..	..	..	98	98	0[b]	0[b]	100	100
Lao PDR	124	115	..	66	..	68	66	68	18	16	80	77
Latvia	100	101	..	..	..	..	97	97	4	2	97	97
Lebanon	97	95	..	91	..	95	86	93	10	7	83	89
Lesotho	101	94	58	55	73	69	37	56	24	18	68	66
Liberia	117	107	..	..	..	..	..	..	6	7	..	..
Libya	..	..	..	..	..	..	..	..	..	..	..	..
Lithuania	100	99	..	..	..	..	98	98	1	1	99	99
Macedonia, FYR	92	93	..	..	..	..	98	97	0[b]	0[b]	100	99
Madagascar	188	185	22	42	21	43	42	43	21	19	61	59
Malawi	137	144	71	44	57	43	37	35	21	20	79	75
Malaysia	96	96	97	92	97	92	89	90	..	..	100	98
Mali	104	91	71	87	67	81	79	72	14	14	68	64
Mauritania	117	125	76	48	75	51	40	42	2	2	45	39
Mauritius	100	102	97	100	98	98	100	97	5	3	63	74
Mexico	118	118	35	94	71	95	91	94	5	3	95	94
Moldova	95	91	..	..	..	..	94	97	0[b]	0[b]	99	98
Mongolia	134	133	..	94	..	95	94	95	0[b]	0[b]	96	98
Morocco	107	105	75	83	76	82	77	76	14	10	80	78
Mozambique	165	155	36	63	32	58	46	42	6	5	56	60
Myanmar	138	132	..	..	..	..	..	..	1	0[b]	75	70
Namibia	101	101	60	97	65	99	87	87	22	14	76	79
Nepal	..	..	51	60	51	64	60	64	17	17	81	81
Netherlands	103	102	..	..	..	..	..	..	..	..	..	..
New Zealand	..	..	..	..	..	..	..	..	..	..	..	..
Nicaragua	158	148	11	48	37	55	45	52	13	9	..	..
Niger	97[c]	83[c]	61	72[d]	65	66[d]	69[d]	64[d]	5[c]	5[c]	49[d]	44[d]
Nigeria	..	..	..	..	..	..	..	..	3	3	..	..
Norway	101	100	99	100	100	99	100	99	..	..	100	99
Oman	73	73	97	99	96	100	99	100	1	1	97	97
Pakistan	114	98	..	..	..	..	..	..	5	4	73	71
Panama	109	106	..	87	..	88	85	86	6	4	98	99
Papua New Guinea	33	29	70	..	68	..	..	..	..	..	..	..
Paraguay	107	103	73	82	75	82	75	78	3	4	..	..
Peru	108	111	..	93	..	93	90	90	8	8	99	96
Philippines	134	126	..	73	..	81	69	78	3	2	98	97
Poland	97	98	..	..	..	..	..	..	1	0[b]	..	..
Portugal	113	110	..	..	..	..	..	..	..	..	..	..
Puerto Rico	..	..	..	..	..	..	..	..	..	..	..	..
Qatar	106	107	63	93	65	100	94	100	1	1	97	100

2.13 Education efficiency

	Gross intake rate in grade 1		Cohort survival rate						Repeaters in primary school		Transition to secondary school	
					% of grade 1 students							
	% of relevant age group		Reaching grade 5				Reaching last grade of primary education		% of enrollment		%	
	Male	Female	Male		Female		Male	Female	Male	Female	Male	Female
	2008[a]	2008[a]	1991	2007[a]	1991	2007[a]	2007[a]	2007[a]	2008[a]	2008[a]	2007[a]	2007[a]
Romania	98	98	..	..	..	..	95	95	2	1	99	98
Russian Federation	102	101	..	..	..	..	..	..	1	1	..	..
Rwanda	213	207	61	..	59	..	..	..	18	18	..	..
Saudi Arabia	100	101	82	100	84	94	100	93	3	3	92	97
Senegal	97	102	..	70	..	72	57	60	8	8	65	58
Serbia	101	100	..	..	..	..	98	99	1	1	99	99
Sierra Leone	201	182	..	..	..	..	..	..	10	10	..	..
Singapore	..	..	..	..	..	..	..	..	0[b]	0[b]	88	95
Slovak Republic	102	102	..	..	..	..	98	98	3	2	97	98
Slovenia	100	100	..	..	..	..	..	..	1	0[b]	..	..
Somalia	..	..	..	..	..	..	..	..	..	..	..	..
South Africa	112	104	..	..	..	..	..	..	8	8	93	94
Spain	107	106	..	100	..	100	100	100	3	2	..	..
Sri Lanka	104	105	92	98	93	99	98	99	1	1	98	99
Sudan	86	76	90	89	99	100	88	100	4[c]	4[c]	90	98
Swaziland	105	101	74	76	80	88	71	76	21	15	90	87
Sweden	100	100	100	100	100	100	100	100	0	0	100	100
Switzerland	93	96	..	..	..	..	..	..	2	1	99	100
Syrian Arab Republic	118	116	97	..	95	..	96	97	8	6	95	96
Tajikistan	106	101	..	..	..	..	100	97	0[b]	0[b]	98	98
Tanzania	107	105	81	85	82	89	81	85	4	4	47	45
Thailand	..	..	..	..	..	..	..	..	12	6	85	89
Timor-Leste	144	134	..	..	..	..	..	..	13	12	100	100
Togo	106	99	52	58	42	50	49	39	23	24	56	49
Trinidad and Tobago	97	96	..	..	..	..	..	..	8	5	88	92
Tunisia	104	105	94	96	77	96	94	94	9	6	86	90
Turkey	100	96	98	100	97	94	..	..	3	3	..	..
Turkmenistan	..	..	..	..	..	..	..	..	..	..	..	..
Uganda	158	160	..	59	..	59	34	31	11	11	63	60
Ukraine	100	100	..	..	..	..	96	98	0[b]	0[b]	100	100
United Arab Emirates	110	109	80	100	80	100	100	100	2	2	98	99
United Kingdom	..	..	..	..	..	..	..	..	0	0	..	..
United States	100	106	..	96	..	98	..	..	0	0	..	..
Uruguay	104	103	96	93	98	96	92	95	8	6	71	83
Uzbekistan	94	91	..	..	..	..	99	99	0[b]	0[b]	100	100
Venezuela, RB	103	101	..	82	..	87	78	83	4	3	95	96
Vietnam	..	..	..	..	..	..	..	..	..	..	..	..
West Bank and Gaza	80	79	..	..	..	..	99	99	1	1	97	98
Yemen, Rep.	110	98	..	..	..	..	..	..	6	5	..	..
Zambia	122	127	..	92	..	88	82	75	6	6	69	72
Zimbabwe	..	..	72	..	81	..	..	..	..	..	..	..
World	**114** w	**110** w	.. w	.. w	.. w	.. w	.. w	.. w	**4** w	**4** w	.. w	.. w
Low income	120	113	..	..	..	..	..	..	..	..	..	..
Middle income	115	110	..	..	..	..	..	..	4	3	..	..
Lower middle income	115	111	..	..	..	..	..	..	3	3	..	..
Upper middle income	106	104	..	..	..	..	..	..	6	4	..	..
Low & middle income	116	111	..	..	..	..	..	..	5	4	..	..
East Asia & Pacific	103	104	55	..	78	..	..	..	2	1	..	..
Europe & Central Asia	99	98	..	..	..	..	..	..	1	1	..	..
Latin America & Carib.	..	..	..	..	..	..	..	..	..	..	..	..
Middle East & N. Africa	105	112	..	..	..	..	..	..	7	4	..	..
South Asia	126	117	..	65	..	65	65	65	4	4	85	83
Sub-Saharan Africa	121	113	..	..	..	..	..	..	10	10	..	..
High income	102	104	..	..	..	..	..	..	1	1	..	..
Euro area	105	104	..	..	..	..	98	99	1	1	..	..

a. Provisional data. b. Less than 0.5. c. Data are for 2009. d. Data are for 2008.

The United Nations Educational, Scientific, and Cultural Organization (UNESCO) Institute for Statistics estimates indicators of students' progress through school. These indicators measure an education system's success in reaching all students, efficiently moving students from one grade to the next, and imparting a particular level of education.

The gross intake rate indicates the level of access to primary education and the education system's capacity to provide access to primary education. Low gross intake rates in grade 1 reflect the fact that many children do not enter primary school even though school attendance, at least through the primary level, is mandatory in all countries. Because the gross intake rate includes all new entrants regardless of age, it can exceed 100 percent in some situations, such as immediately after fees have been abolished or when the number of reenrolled children is large. The quality of data is reduced when new entrants and repeaters are not correctly distinguished in grade 1.

The cohort survival rate is the estimated proportion of an entering cohort of grade 1 students that eventually reaches grade 5 or the last grade of primary education. It measures an education system's holding power and internal efficiency. Rates approaching 100 percent indicate high retention and low dropout levels. Cohort survival rates are typically estimated from data on enrollment and repetition by grade for two consecutive years. This procedure, called the reconstructed cohort method, makes three simplifying assumptions: dropouts never return to school; promotion, repetition, and dropout rates remain constant over the period in which the cohort is enrolled in school; and the same rates apply to all pupils enrolled in a grade, regardless of whether they previously repeated a grade (Fredricksen 1993). Cross-country comparisons should thus be made with caution, because other flows—caused by new entrants, reentrants, grade skipping, migration, or transfers during the school year—are not considered.

Data on repeaters are often used to indicate an education system's internal efficiency. Repeaters not only increase the cost of education for the family and the school system, but also use limited school resources. Country policies on repetition and promotion differ. In some cases the number of repeaters is controlled because of limited capacity. In other cases the number of repeaters is almost 0 because of automatic promotion—suggesting a system that is highly efficient but that may not be endowing students with enough cognitive skills. Care should be taken in interpreting this indicator.

The transition rate from primary to secondary school conveys the degree of access or transition between the two levels. As completing primary education is a prerequisite for participating in lower secondary school, growing numbers of primary completers will inevitably create pressure for more available places at the secondary level. A low transition rate can signal such problems as an inadequate examination and promotion system or insufficient secondary school capacity. The quality of data on the transition rate is affected when new entrants and repeaters are not correctly distinguished in the first grade of secondary school. Students who interrupt their studies after completing primary school could also affect data quality.

In 2006 the UNESCO Institute for Statistics changed its convention for citing the reference year. For more information, see *About the data* for table 2.11.

• **Gross intake rate in grade 1** is the number of new entrants in the first grade of primary education regardless of age as a percentage of the population of the official primary school entrance age. • **Cohort survival rate** is the percentage of children enrolled in the first grade of primary school who eventually reach grade 5 or the last grade of primary education. The estimate is based on the reconstructed cohort method (see *About the data*). • **Repeaters in primary school** are the number of students enrolled in the same grade as in the previous year as a percentage of all students enrolled in primary school. • **Transition to secondary school** is the number of new entrants to the first grade of secondary school in a given year as a percentage of the number of students enrolled in the final grade of primary school in the previous year.

Education completion and outcomes

	Primary completion rate						Youth literacy rate				Adult literacy rate	
	% of relevant age group						% ages 15–24				% ages 15 and older	
	Total		Male		Female		Male		Female		Male	Female
	1991	2008[a]	1991	2008[a]	1991	2008[a]	1990	2005–08[b]	1990	2005–08[b]	2005–08[b]	2005–08[b]
Afghanistan	..	..	..	..	..	..	..	..	..	..	..	..
Albania	..	..	..	..	..	..	..	99	..	100	99	99
Algeria	80	114	86	119	73	108	..	94	..	89	81	64
Angola	34	..	..	..	..	..	..	81	..	65	83	57
Argentina	..	100	..	98	..	102	98	99	99	99	98	98
Armenia	..	98	..	97	..	98	100	100	100	100	100	99
Australia	..	..	..	..	..	..	..	..	..	..	..	..
Austria	..	102	..	102	..	102	..	..	..	..	..	..
Azerbaijan	..	121	..	123	..	119	..	100	..	100	100	99
Bangladesh	..	58	..	56	..	60	52	73	38	76	60	50
Belarus	94	96	..	93	..	92	100	100	100	100	100	100
Belgium	79	86	76	84	82	88	..	..	..	..	..	..
Benin	22	65	30	75	14	55	55	64	27	42	54	28
Bolivia	71	98	78	98	64	98	96	100	92	99	96	86
Bosnia and Herzegovina	..	..	..	..	..	..	..	100	..	99	99	96
Botswana	90	99	83	96	98	102	86	94	92	96	83	84
Brazil	..	..	..	..	..	..	..	97	..	99	90	90
Bulgaria	101	98	101	99	101	98	..	97	..	97	99	98
Burkina Faso	20	38	25	42	15	34	27	47	14	33	37	22
Burundi	46	45	49	48	43	42	59	77	48	75	72	60
Cambodia	..	79	..	80	..	79	..	90	..	84	86	69
Cameroon	53	73	57	79	49	67	..	88	..	84	84	68
Canada	..	96	..	96	..	96	..	..	..	..	..	..
Central African Republic	28	33	37	41	20	25	63	72	35	56	69	41
Chad	18	31	29	40	7	22	..	54	..	37	44	22
Chile	..	96	..	94	..	96	98	99	99	99	99	99
China	107	99	..	98	..	102	97	99	91	99	97	91
Hong Kong SAR, China	102	..	..	..	..	..	..	..	..	..	..	..
Colombia	73	110	70	109	76	112	..	98	..	98	93	93
Congo, Dem. Rep.	48	53	61	63	36	44	..	69	..	62	78	56
Congo, Rep.	54	73	59	75	49	71	..	..	..	..	..	..
Costa Rica	79	93	77	91	81	95	..	98	..	99	96	96
Côte d'Ivoire	42	48	53	57	32	39	60	72	38	60	64	44
Croatia	..	102	..	102	..	101	100	100	100	100	100	98
Cuba	99	90	..	90	..	90	..	100	..	100	100	100
Czech Republic	..	94	..	95	..	94	..	..	..	..	..	..
Denmark	98	101	98	100	98	101	..	..	..	..	..	..
Dominican Republic	..	91	..	89	..	92	..	95	..	97	88	88
Ecuador	..	106	..	105	..	107	97	95	96	96	87	82
Egypt, Arab Rep.	..	95	..	97	..	93	..	88	..	82	75	58
El Salvador	65	89	64	88	66	91	85	95	85	96	87	81
Eritrea	..	47	..	52	..	42	..	91	..	84	77	55
Estonia	..	100	..	101	..	100	100	100	100	100	100	100
Ethiopia	..	52	..	56	..	48	..	..	..	..	..	..
Finland	97	98	98	98	97	98	..	..	..	..	..	..
France	106	..	..	..	..	..	..	..	..	..	..	..
Gabon	..	..	..	..	..	..	..	98	..	96	91	83
Gambia, The	..	79	..	76	..	83	..	70	..	58	57	34
Georgia	..	100	..	103	..	97	..	100	..	100	100	100
Germany	..	105	..	104	..	105	..	..	..	..	..	..
Ghana	64	79	71	81	56	77	..	81	..	78	72	59
Greece	..	101	..	102	..	101	99	99	99	99	98	96
Guatemala	..	80	..	83	..	77	..	89	..	84	80	69
Guinea	17	55	24	62	9	47	..	..	..	..	..	..
Guinea-Bissau	..	..	..	..	..	..	..	78	..	62	66	37
Haiti	27	..	29	..	26	..	..	..	..	..	..	..
Honduras	64	90	67	87	61	93	..	93	..	95	84	83

	Primary completion rate						Youth literacy rate				Adult literacy rate	
	% of relevant age group						% ages 15–24				% ages 15 and older	
	Total		Male		Female		Male		Female		Male	Female
	1991	2008[a]	1991	2008[a]	1991	2008[a]	1990	2005–08[b]	1990	2005–08[b]	2005–08[b]	2005–08[b]
Hungary	94	95	93	95	95	94	..	98	..	99	99	99
India	63	94	75	95	51	92	74[c]	88	49[c]	74	75	51
Indonesia	93	108	..	109	..	107	97	97	95	96	95	89
Iran, Islamic Rep.	88	117	93	108	82	126	92	97	81	96	87	77
Iraq	..	..	..	..	..	..	..	85	..	80	86	69
Ireland	..	97	..	96	..	98	..	..	..	..	..	..
Israel	..	102	..	101	..	104	..	..	..	..	..	..
Italy	98	101	98	101	97	100	..	100	..	100	99	99
Jamaica	94	89	90	88	98	90	..	92	..	98	81	91
Japan	102	..	102	..	102	..	..	..	..	..	..	..
Jordan	95	99	94	98	95	100	..	99	..	99	95	89
Kazakhstan	..	105[d]	..	105[d]	..	105[d]	100	100	100	100	100	100
Kenya	..	80	..	85	..	75	..	92	..	93	90	83
Korea, Dem. Rep.	..	..	..	..	..	..	..	..	..	..	..	..
Korea, Rep.	98	99	97	101	98	97	..	..	..	..	..	..
Kosovo	..	..	..	..	..	..	..	..	..	..	..	..
Kuwait	..	98	..	98	..	98	..	98	..	99	95	93
Kyrgyz Republic	..	92	..	93	..	92	..	100	..	100	100	99
Lao PDR	45	75	..	78	..	71	..	89	..	79	82	63
Latvia	..	95	..	97	..	94	100	100	100	100	100	100
Lebanon	..	87	..	84	..	89	..	98	..	99	93	86
Lesotho	59	73	42	62	76	84	..	86	..	98	83	95
Liberia	..	58	..	..	..	53	..	70	..	80	63	53
Libya	..	..	..	..	..	..	..	100	..	100	95	81
Lithuania	..	96	..	96	..	96	100	100	100	100	100	100
Macedonia, FYR	..	92	..	92	..	92	..	99	..	99	99	95
Madagascar	36	71	35	71	37	71	..	..	..	..	..	..
Malawi	28	54	36	54	21	54	..	87	..	85	80	66
Malaysia	91	96	91	97	91	96	96	98	95	99	94	90
Mali	12	57	15	65	9	48	..	47	..	31	35	18
Mauritania	33	64	39	63	26	66	..	71	..	63	64	50
Mauritius	115	90	115	90	115	91	91	95	92	97	90	85
Mexico	88	104	..	103	..	105	96	98	95	98	95	91
Moldova	..	84	..	85	..	84	100	99	100	100	99	98
Mongolia	..	93	..	94	..	92	..	93	..	97	97	98
Morocco	48	81	57	85	39	78	..	85	..	68	69	44
Mozambique	26	59	32	67	21	52	..	78	..	62	70	40
Myanmar	..	97	..	94	..	100	..	96	..	95	95	89
Namibia	..	81	..	76	..	86	86	91	90	95	89	88
Nepal	50	76	..	79	..	72	68	86	33	75	71	45
Netherlands	..	..	..	..	..	..	..	..	..	..	..	..
New Zealand	103	..	104	..	102	..	..	..	..	..	..	..
Nicaragua	42	75	..	71	..	78	..	85	..	89	78	78
Niger	17	40[d]	21	47[d]	13	34[d]	..	52	..	23	43	15
Nigeria	..	..	..	..	..	..	81	78	62	65	72	49
Norway	100	96	100	96	100	97	..	..	..	..	..	..
Oman	65	80	67	80	62	81	..	98	..	98	90	81
Pakistan	..	60	..	67	..	53	..	79	..	59	67	40
Panama	..	102	..	102	..	102	95	97	95	96	94	93
Papua New Guinea	46	..	51	..	42	..	..	65	..	69	64	56
Paraguay	68	95	68	95	69	95	96	99	95	99	96	93
Peru	..	103	..	103	..	102	..	98	..	97	95	85
Philippines	88	92	..	90	..	95	96	94	97	96	93	94
Poland	98	96	..	..	..	..	..	100	..	100	100	99
Portugal	95	..	94	..	95	..	99	100	99	100	97	93
Puerto Rico	..	..	..	..	..	..	92	86	94	85	90	90
Qatar	71	115	71	119	72	112	..	99	..	99	94	90

	Primary completion rate						Youth literacy rate				Adult literacy rate	
	% of relevant age group						% ages 15–24				% ages 15 and older	
	Total		Male		Female		Male		Female		Male	Female
	1991	2008[a]	1991	2008[a]	1991	2008[a]	1990	2005–08[b]	1990	2005–08[b]	2005–08[b]	2005–08[b]
Romania	100	120	100	120	100	121	99	97	99	98	98	97
Russian Federation	..	94	..	..	..	..	100	100	100	100	100	99
Rwanda	35	54	39	52	32	56	75	77	75	77	75	66
Saudi Arabia	55	95	60	99	51	92	94	98	81	96	90	80
Senegal	43	56	52	57	33	56	49	58	28	45	52	33
Serbia	..	104	..	104	..	105	99[e]	..	98[e]	..	..	..
Sierra Leone	..	88	..	101	..	75	..	66	..	46	52	29
Singapore	..	..	..	..	..	..	99	100	99	100	97	92
Slovak Republic	..	94	..	94	..	94	..	..	..	..	..	..
Slovenia	..	..	..	..	..	..	100	100	100	100	100	100
Somalia	..	..	..	..	..	..	..	..	..	..	..	..
South Africa	76	86	72	86	80	86	..	96	..	98	90	88
Spain	103	98	104	99	103	98	100	100	100	100	98	97
Sri Lanka	101	105	101	105	101	105	..	97	..	99	92	89
Sudan	40	57[d]	45	53	36	47	..	89	..	82	79	60
Swaziland	61	72	57	75	64	69	..	92	..	95	87	86
Sweden	96	95	96	94	96	95	..	..	..	..	..	..
Switzerland	53	93	53	92	54	94	..	..	..	..	..	..
Syrian Arab Republic	89	114	94	114	84	113	..	96	..	93	90	77
Tajikistan	..	98	..	97	..	93	100	100	100	100	100	100
Tanzania	63	83	62	85	64	81	86	79	78	76	79	66
Thailand	..	..	..	..	..	..	..	98	..	98	96	92
Timor-Leste	..	80	..	80	..	79	..	..	..	..	..	..
Togo	35	61	48	71	22	51	..	87	..	80	77	54
Trinidad and Tobago	102	92	99	92	105	92	99	100	99	100	99	98
Tunisia	74	102	79	103	70	102	..	97	..	95	86	70
Turkey	90	99	93	104	86	94	97	99	88	94	96	81
Turkmenistan	..	..	..	..	..	..	..	100	..	100	100	99
Uganda	..	56	..	57	..	55	77	89	63	86	82	67
Ukraine	94	99	..	98	..	99	..	100	..	100	100	100
United Arab Emirates	103	105	104	103	103	107	..	94	..	97	89	91
United Kingdom	..	..	..	..	..	..	..	..	..	..	..	..
United States	..	96	..	95	..	97	..	..	..	..	..	..
Uruguay	94	104	91	102	96	105	..	99	..	99	98	98
Uzbekistan	..	96	..	97	..	95	..	100	..	100	100	99
Venezuela, RB	79	95	..	94	..	97	95	98	96	99	95	95
Vietnam	..	..	..	..	..	..	94	97	93	96	95	90
West Bank and Gaza	..	83	..	83	..	83	..	99	..	99	97	91
Yemen, Rep.	..	61	..	72	..	49	..	95	..	70	79	43
Zambia	..	93	..	98	..	88	67	82	66	68	81	61
Zimbabwe	97	..	99	..	96	..	97	98	94	99	94	89
World	.. w	89 w	.. w	90 w	.. w	88 w	87 w	92 w	76 w	86 w	87 w	76 w
Low income	..	66	..	69	..	62	..	81	..	77	76	63
Middle income	..	94	..	95	..	93	89	93	79	88	88	77
Lower middle income	..	92	..	93	..	91	88	92	76	85	87	73
Upper middle income	..	100	..	..	..	..	96	98	94	98	95	92
Low & middle income	..	88	..	90	..	86	87	92	76	86	87	76
East Asia & Pacific	..	100	..	99	..	101	97	98	92	98	96	90
Europe & Central Asia	..	98	..	..	..	..	99	99	97	99	99	97
Latin America & Carib.	..	101	..	102	..	103	..	97	..	98	92	91
Middle East & N. Africa	..	94	..	95	..	92	82	92	62	86	82	65
South Asia	..	79	..	82	..	76	71	86	48	73	73	50
Sub-Saharan Africa	..	62	..	67	..	57	..	79	..	71	74	57
High income	..	..	..	..	..	..	..	..	..	..	..	..
Euro area	101	..	100	..	100	..	..	..	..	..	..	..

a. Provisional data. b. Data are for the most recent year available. c. Includes the Indian-held part of Jammu and Kashmir. d. Data are for 2009. e. Includes Montenegro.

About the data

Many governments publish statistics that indicate how their education systems are working and developing—statistics on enrollment and such efficiency indicators as repetition rates, pupil–teacher ratios, and cohort progression. The World Bank and the United Nations Educational, Scientific, and Cultural Organization (UNESCO) Institute for Statistics jointly developed the primary completion rate indicator. Increasingly used as a core indicator of an education system's performance, it reflects an education system's coverage and the educational attainment of students. The indicator is a key measure of education outcome at the primary level and of progress toward the Millennium Development Goals and the Education for All initiative. However, because curricula and standards for school completion vary across countries, a high primary completion rate does not necessarily mean high levels of student learning.

The primary completion rate reflects the primary cycle as defined by the International Standard Classification of Education, ranging from three or four years of primary education (in a very small number of countries) to five or six years (in most countries) and seven (in a small number of countries).

The table shows the proxy primary completion rate, calculated by subtracting the number of repeaters in the last grade of primary school from the total number of students in that grade and dividing by the total number of children of official graduation age. Data limitations preclude adjusting for students who drop out during the final year of primary school. Thus proxy rates should be taken as an upper estimate of the actual primary completion rate.

There are many reasons why the primary completion rate can exceed 100 percent. The numerator may include late entrants and overage children who have repeated one or more grades of primary school as well as children who entered school early, while the denominator is the number of children of official completing age. Other data limitations contribute to completion rates exceeding 100 percent, such as the use of population estimates of varying reliability, the conduct of school and population surveys at different times of year, and other discrepancies in the numbers used in the calculation.

Basic student outcomes include achievements in reading and mathematics judged against established standards. In many countries national assessments are enabling the ministry of education to monitor progress in these outcomes. Internationally comparable assessments are not yet available, except for a few, mostly industrialized, countries. The UNESCO Institute for Statistics has established literacy as an outcome indicator based on an internationally agreed definition.

The literacy rate is the percentage of people who can, with understanding, both read and write a short, simple statement about their everyday life. In practice, literacy is difficult to measure. To estimate literacy using such a definition requires census or survey measurements under controlled conditions. Many countries estimate the number of literate people from self-reported data. Some use educational attainment data as a proxy but apply different lengths of school attendance or levels of completion. Because definitions and methodologies of data collection differ across countries, data should be used cautiously.

The reported literacy data are compiled by the UNESCO Institute for Statistics based on national censuses and household surveys during 1985–2007. For countries that have not reported national estimates, the UNESCO Institute for Statistics derived the modeled estimates. For detailed information on sources, definitions, and methodology, consult the original source.

Literacy statistics for most countries cover the population ages 15 and older, but some include younger ages or are confined to age ranges that tend to inflate literacy rates. The literacy data in the narrower age range of 15–24 better captures the ability of participants in the formal education system and reflects recent progress in education. The youth literacy rate reported in the table measures the accumulated outcomes of primary education over the previous 10 years or so by indicating the proportion of people who have passed through the primary education system and acquired basic literacy and numeracy skills.

Definitions

• **Primary completion rate** is the percentage of students completing the last year of primary school. It is calculated by taking the total number of students in the last grade of primary school, minus the number of repeaters in that grade, divided by the total number of children of official completing age. • **Youth literacy rate** is the percentage of people ages 15–24 that can, with understanding, both read and write a short, simple statement about their everyday life. • **Adult literacy rate** is the literacy rate among people ages 15 and older.

Data sources

Data on primary completion rates and literacy rates are from the UNESCO Institute for Statistics.

Education gaps by income and gender

	Survey year	Gross intake rate in grade 1		Gross primary participation rate		Average years of schooling		Primary completion rate				Children out of school	
		% of relevant age group		% of relevant age group		Ages 15–19		% of relevant age group				% of relevant age group	
		Poorest quintile	Richest quintile	Poorest quintile	Richest quintile	Poorest quintile	Richest quintile	Poorest quintile	Richest quintile	Male	Female	Poorest quintile	Richest quintile
Armenia	2005	93	80	106	102	9	10	119	116	113	112	2	1
Azerbaijan	2006	92	118	100	108	9	11	94	109	103	105	20	11
Bangladesh	2006	144	147	96	105	8	13	65	97	83	86	12	6
Belize	2006	80	89	106	113	8	11	59	130	107	72	5	7
Benin	2006	67	107	61	114	6	8	31	95	67	52	57	12
Bolivia	2003	92	95	108	129	6	9	76	98	90	81	22	5
Burundi	2005	201	191	91	144	4	7	20	70	44	39	5	3
Cambodia	2005	208	151	113	134	5	8	42	121	88	85	37	13
Cameroon	2006	108	75	93	116	6	14	43	111	90	74	3	2
Colombia	2005	161	84	127	99	6	10	94	109	100	103	11	2
Côte d'Ivoire	2006	51	77	57	110	5	8	47	127	88	71	4	3
Dominican Republic	2007	130	112	113	107	7	11	69	109	88	106	12	4
Egypt, Arab Rep.	2005	107	97	95	99	9	12	84	92	92	88	12	1
Ethiopia	2005	86	124	47	112	3	6	14	90	46	33	74	30
Georgia	2006	90	104	101	103	15	14	102	102	106	104	2	1
Ghana	2006	107	121	81	117	5	8	62	88	93	86	22	12
Guatemala	2000	176	124	81	114	4	8	15	80	34	36	7	3
Guinea	2005	55	119	52	121	5	7	32	93	76	48	60	16
Guinea-Bissau	2006	135	184	94	166	4	7	34	125	80	54	12	11
Guyana	2006	74	76	105	101	10	10	109	118	91	112	2	1
Haiti	2005	177	188	87	159	4	7	31	136	73	82	69	24
Kazakhstan	2006	118	101	106	103	9	9	102	115	102	97	0ᵃ	1
Kenya	2003	134	125	92	106	6	9	40	76	71	72	38	11
Kosovo	2000	104	119	95	104	9	11	82	94	98	83	1	4
Lesotho	2004	169	111	116	124	5	8	36	122	69	85	18	3
Macedonia, FYR	2005	102	190	89	97	8	10	120	119	133	78	0ᵃ	0ᵃ
Madagascar	2003–04	250	153	118	145	3	8	42	141	77	77	33	3
Malawi	2006	234	207	133	169	5	7	30	80	49	52	0ᵃ	0ᵃ
Mali	2006	41	98	46	110	5	8	36	79	55	41	67	20
Mauritania	2007	67	96	62	116	5	9	17	89	48	52	2	2
Moldova	2005	96	84	99	95	9	12	97	100	96	98	2	1
Mozambique	2003	128	143	75	143	3	6	13	100	57	43	46	7
Namibia	2006	112	104	118	109	7	10	81	109	94	90	11	2
Nepal	2001	184	141	109	139	5	8	49	96	69	62	33	6
Nicaragua	2001	149	106	85	105	4	9	34	124	78	83	40	4
Niger	2006	50	90	35	89	4	7	31	71	60	30	74	28
Nigeria	2003	78	101	70	108	7	10	48	71	70	54	52	6
Panama	2003	125	116	108	102	7	11	100	94	105	88	1	1
Peru	2004	121	90	118	96	7	11	106	99	100	97	6	1
Rwanda	2005	274	195	131	151	3	5	31	88	48	42	13	8
Serbia	2005	90	98	98	100	9	10	86	96	94	89	1	0ᵃ
Somalia	2005	13	44	8	93	8	10	2	58	26	20	87	46
Swaziland	2006	147	117	117	114	6	9	69	110	85	98	17	4
Syrian Arab Republic	2006	110	149	102	107	7	8	92	93	93	92	0ᵃ	0ᵃ
Tanzania	2004	123	123	82	119	5	7	32	108	58	60	44	15
Togo	2006	115	148	99	128	6	7	40	82	67	56	1	1
Turkey	2003	108	111	97	97	6	7	95	85	100	81	20	5
Uganda	2006	180	144	107	124	5	8	27	68	50	42	25	7
Vietnam	2006	99	100	108	100	13	18	99	104	96	103	3	2
Yemen, Rep.	2006	66	109	50	101	7	10	25	103	84	31	2	2
Zambia	2007	135	123	105	112	5	9	50	101	88	73	22	3
Zimbabwe	1999	106	111	144	144	7	10	36	80	51	57	22	8

a. Less than 0.5.

About the data

The data in the table describe basic information on school participation and educational attainment by individuals in different socioeconomic groups within countries. The data are from Demographic and Health Surveys conducted by Macro International with the support of the U.S. Agency for International Development, Multiple Indicator Cluster Surveys conducted by the United Nations Children's Fund (UNICEF), and Living Standards Measurement Studies conducted by the World Bank's Development Economics Research Group. These large-scale household sample surveys, conducted periodically in developing countries, collect information on a large number of health, nutrition, and population measures as well as on respondents' social, demographic, and economic characteristics using a standard set of questionnaires. The data presented here draw on responses to individual and household questionnaires.

Typically, the surveys collect basic information on educational attainment and enrollment levels from every household member ages 5 or 6 and older as part of household socioeconomic characteristics. The surveys are not intended for the collection of detailed education data; thus the education section of the surveys is not as detailed as the Demographic and Health Surveys health section and the data obtained from them do not replace other data on education flows. Still, the education data provide micro-level information on education that cannot be obtained from administrative data, such as information on children not attending school.

Socioeconomic status as displayed in the table is based on a household's assets, including ownership of consumer items, features of the household's dwelling, and other characteristics related to wealth. Each household asset on which information was collected was assigned a weight generated through principal-component analysis, which is used to create break-points defining wealth quintiles, expressed as quintiles of individuals in the population.

The selection of the asset index for defining socioeconomic status was based on pragmatic rather than conceptual considerations: Demographic and Health Surveys do not collect income or consumption data but do have detailed information on households' ownership of consumer goods and access to a variety of goods and services. Like income or consumption, the asset index defines disparities primarily in economic terms. It therefore excludes other possibilities of disparities among groups, such as those based on gender, education, ethnic background, or other facets of social exclusion. To that extent the index provides only a partial view of the multidimensional concepts of poverty, inequality, and inequity.

Creating one index that includes all asset indicators limits the types of analysis that can be performed. In particular, the use of a unified index does not permit a disaggregated analysis to examine which asset indicators have a more or less important association with education status. In addition, some asset indicators may reflect household wealth better in some countries than in others—or reflect different degrees of wealth in different countries. Taking such information into account and creating country-specific asset indexes with country-specific choices of asset indicators might produce a more effective and accurate index for each country. The asset index used in the table does not have this flexibility.

The analysis was carried out for about 80 countries. The table shows the most recent estimates for the poorest and richest quintiles and by gender only; the full set of estimates for all other subgroups, including by urban and rural location and for other years, is available in the country reports (see *Data sources*). The data in the table differ from data for similar indicators in preceding tables either because the indicator refers to a period a few years preceding the survey date or because the indicator definition or methodology is different. Findings should be used with caution because of measurement error inherent in the use of survey data.

Definitions

• **Survey year** is the year in which the underlying data were collected. • **Gross intake rate in grade 1** is the number of students in the first grade of primary education regardless of age as a percentage of the population of the official primary school entrance age. These data may differ from those in table 2.13. • **Gross primary participation rate** is the ratio of total students attending primary school regardless of age to the population of the age group that officially corresponds to primary education. • **Average years of schooling** are the years of formal schooling received, on average, by youths and adults ages 15–19. • **Primary completion rate** is the number of students in the last year of primary school minus the number of repeaters in that grade, divided by the number of students of official graduation age. These data differ from those in table 2.14 because the definition and methodology are different. • **Children out of school** are the percentage of children of official primary school age who are not attending primary or secondary education. Children of official primary school age who are attending preprimary education are considered out of school. These data differ from those in table 2.12 because the definition and methodology are different.

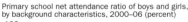

Gender disparities in net primary school attendance are largest in poor and rural households   **2.15a**

Primary school net attendance ratio of boys and girls, by background characteristics, 2000–06 (percent)

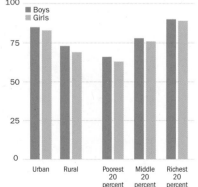

Source: UNICEF 2007.

Data sources

Data on education gaps by income and gender are from an analysis by the World Bank's Human Development Network Education Group of Demographic and Health Surveys conducted by Macro International, Multiple Indicator Cluster Surveys conducted by UNICEF, and Living Standards Measurement Studies conducted by the World Bank's Development Economics Research Group and the World Bank. Country reports are available at www.worldbank.org/education/edstats/.

2.16 Health services

	Health expenditure					Health workers		Hospital beds	Outpatient visits
				Per capita		per 1,000 people			
	Total % of GDP	Public % of total	Out of pocket % of private	$	PPP $	Physicians	Nurses and midwives	per 1,000 people	per capita
	2007	2007	2007	2007	2007	2003–08[a]	2003–08[a]	2003–08[a]	2000–08[a]
Afghanistan	7.6	23.6	98.9	42	126	2.0[b]	0.5	0.4	..
Albania	7.0	41.2	93.9	244	505	1.1	4.0	2.9	1.5
Algeria	4.4	81.6	94.7	173	338	1.2	1.9	1.7	..
Angola	2.5[c]	80.3[c]	100.0[c]	86[c]	131[c]	0.1	1.4	0.8	..
Argentina	10.0	50.8	42.9	663	1,322	3.2	0.5	4.0	..
Armenia	4.4	47.3	91.4	133	246	3.7	4.9	4.1	2.8
Australia	8.9	67.5	55.5	3,986	3,261	1.0	10.9	4.0	6.2
Austria	10.1	76.4	65.2	4,523	3,763	3.8	6.6	7.8	6.7
Azerbaijan	3.7	26.8	87.8	140	279	3.8	8.4	7.9	4.6
Bangladesh	3.4	33.6	97.4	15	42	0.3	0.3	0.4	..
Belarus	6.5	74.9	69.4[c]	302	704	4.9	12.6	11.2	13.2
Belgium	9.4	74.1	76.4	4,056	3,323	4.2	0.5	5.3	7.0
Benin	4.8	51.8	94.9	32	70	0.1	0.8	0.5	..
Bolivia	5.0	69.2	79.4	69	219	..	..	1.1	..
Bosnia and Herzegovina	9.8	56.8	100.0	397	766	1.4	4.7	3.0	3.3
Botswana	5.7	74.6	27.3	372	762	0.4	2.7	1.8	..
Brazil	8.4	41.6	58.8	606	799	1.7	2.9	2.4	..
Bulgaria	7.3	57.2	86.4	384	800	3.7	4.7	6.4	..
Burkina Faso	6.1	56.1	91.3	29	67	0.1	0.7	0.9	..
Burundi	13.9[c]	37.7[c]	60.5[c]	17[c]	51[c]	0.0[d]	0.2	0.7	..
Cambodia	5.9	29.0	84.7	36	108	..	..	0.1	..
Cameroon	4.9[c]	25.9[c]	94.5[c]	54[c]	104[c]	0.2	1.6	1.5	..
Canada	10.1	70.0	49.6	4,409	3,899	1.9	10.1	3.4	6.3
Central African Republic	4.1	34.7	95.0	16	30	0.1	0.4	1.2	..
Chad	4.8	56.3	96.2	32	72	0.0[d]	0.3	0.4	..
Chile	6.2	58.7	53.2	615	768	1.3	0.6	2.3	..
China	4.3	44.7	92.0	108	233	1.5	1.0	2.2	..
Hong Kong SAR, China	..	..	..	..	..	..	..	..	..
Colombia	6.1	84.2	48.7	284	516	1.4	..	1.0	..
Congo, Dem. Rep.	5.8	20.8	51.7	9	18	0.1	0.5	0.8	..
Congo, Rep.	2.4	70.4	100.0	52	90	0.1	0.8	1.6	..
Costa Rica	8.1	72.9	84.6	488	878	..	..	1.3	..
Côte d'Ivoire	4.2	24.0	88.7	41	67	0.1	0.5	0.4	..
Croatia	7.6	87.0	91.9	1,009	1,398	2.6	5.6	5.3	6.4
Cuba	10.4	95.5	91.3	585	1,001	6.4	8.6	6.0	..
Czech Republic	6.8	85.2	89.0	1,141	1,626	3.6	9.0	8.1	15.0
Denmark	9.8	84.5	89.0	5,551	3,558	3.2	9.8	3.5	4.1
Dominican Republic	5.4	35.9	65.3	224	411	..	..	1.0	..
Ecuador	5.8	39.1	75.2	200	434	..	..	0.6	..
Egypt, Arab Rep.	6.3	38.1	95.1	101	310	2.4	3.4	2.1	..
El Salvador	6.2	58.9	89.0	24	402	1.5	..	0.8	..
Eritrea	3.3[c]	45.3[c]	100.0[c]	9[c]	20[c]	0.1	0.6	1.2	..
Estonia	5.4	76.5	94.1	837	1,106	3.3	7.0	5.6	6.9
Ethiopia	3.8	58.1	80.6	9	30	0.0[d]	0.2	0.2	..
Finland	8.2	74.6	74.3	3,809	2,840	3.3	8.9	6.8	4.3
France	11.0	79.0	32.5	4,627	3,709	3.7	8.1	7.2	6.9
Gabon	4.6[c]	64.5[c]	100.0[c]	373[c]	650[c]	0.3	5.0	1.3	..
Gambia, The	5.5	47.9	48.4	22	90	0.0[d]	0.6	1.1[b]	..
Georgia	8.2	18.4	86.8	191	384	4.5	3.9	3.3	2.2
Germany	10.4	76.9	56.6	4,209	3,588	3.5	8.0	8.3	7.0
Ghana	8.3	51.6	79.3	54	113	0.1	1.0	0.9[b]	..
Greece	9.6	60.3	94.5	2,679	2,727	5.4	3.5	4.8	..
Guatemala	7.3	29.3	92.6	186	336	..	..	0.6	..
Guinea	5.6	11.0	99.5	26	62	0.1	0.0[d]	0.3	..
Guinea-Bissau	6.1[c]	25.9[c]	55.7[c]	16[c]	33[c]	0.0[d]	0.6	1.0[b]	..
Haiti	5.3	23.3	57.4	35	58	..	..	1.3	..
Honduras	6.2	65.7	96.0	107	260	..	..	0.7	..

	Health expenditure				Health workers		Hospital beds	Outpatient visits
					per 1,000 people			
	Total % of GDP	Public % of total	Out of pocket % of private	Per capita		Physicians	Nurses and midwives	per 1,000 people	per capita
				$	PPP $				
	2007	2007	2007	2007	2007	2003–08[a]	2003–08[a]	2003–08[a]	2000–08[a]
Hungary	7.4	70.6	84.7	1,019	1,388	2.8	9.2	7.1	12.9
India	4.1	26.2	89.9	40	109	0.6	1.3	0.9	..
Indonesia	2.2	54.5	66.2	42	81	0.1	0.8	..	..
Iran, Islamic Rep.	6.4	46.8	95.4	253	689	0.9	1.6	1.4	..
Iraq	2.5[e]	75.0[e]	100.0[e]	62[e]	121[e]	0.5	1.0	1.3	..
Ireland	7.6	80.7	51.2	4,556	3,424	3.1	15.8	5.3	..
Israel	8.0	55.9	74.4	1,893	2,181	3.6	6.1	5.8	7.1
Italy	8.7	76.5	85.9	3,136	2,686	3.7	6.9	3.9	6.1
Jamaica	4.7	50.3	71.0	224	357	0.9	1.7	1.7	..
Japan	8.0	81.3	80.8	2,751	2,696	2.1	9.5	14.0	14.4
Jordan	8.9[f]	60.6[f]	88.3[f]	248[f]	434[f]	2.6	3.2	1.8	..
Kazakhstan	3.7	66.1	98.4	253	405	3.9	7.8	7.7	6.6
Kenya	4.7	42.0	77.2	34	72	0.1	..	1.4	..
Korea, Dem. Rep.	3.6	83.7	100.0	22	..	3.3	4.1	..	..
Korea, Rep.	6.3	54.9	79.2	1,362	1,688	1.7	4.4	8.6	..
Kosovo	..	..	..	..	..	..	..	..	..
Kuwait	2.2	77.5	91.6	901	911	1.8	3.7	1.8	..
Kyrgyz Republic	6.5	54.0	91.9	46	111	2.3	5.7	5.1	3.6
Lao PDR	4.0	18.9	76.1	27	84	0.4	1.0	1.2	..
Latvia	6.2	57.9	97.1	784	1,071	3.0	5.7	7.6	5.5
Lebanon	8.8	44.7	77.6	525	921	3.3	1.3	3.4	..
Lesotho	6.2	58.3	68.9	51	92	0.1	0.6	1.3	..
Liberia	10.6[c]	26.2[c]	52.2[c]	22[c]	39[c]	0.0[d]	0.3	0.7[b]	..
Libya	2.7[c]	71.8[c]	100.0[c]	299[c]	453[c]	1.3	4.8	3.7	..
Lithuania	6.2	73.0	98.3	717	1,109	4.0	7.6	8.1	6.6
Macedonia, FYR	7.1	65.6	100.0	277	698	2.6	4.3	4.6	6.0
Madagascar	4.1	66.2	67.9	16	32	0.2	0.3	0.3	0.5
Malawi	9.9	59.7	28.4	17	50	0.0[d]	0.3	1.1	..
Malaysia	4.4	44.4	73.2	307	604	..	..	1.8	..
Mali	5.7	51.4	99.5	34	67	0.1	0.2	0.6	..
Mauritania	2.4[c]	65.3[c]	100.0[c]	22[c]	47[c]	0.1[b]	0.7[b]	0.4	..
Mauritius	4.2	49.0	81.5	247	502	1.1	3.7	3.3	..
Mexico	5.9	45.4	93.1	564	823	2.9	4.0	1.7	2.5
Moldova	10.3[g]	50.8[g]	97.6[g]	127[g]	281[g]	2.7	6.6	6.1	6.0
Mongolia	4.3	81.7	84.4	64	176	..	..	6.1	..
Morocco	5.0	33.8	86.3	120	215	0.6	0.8	1.1	..
Mozambique	4.9	71.8	42.1	18	38	0.0[d]	0.3	0.8	..
Myanmar	1.9	11.7	95.1	7	26	0.4	1.0	0.6	..
Namibia	7.6	42.1	5.8	319	467	0.3	3.1	2.7[b]	..
Nepal	5.1	39.7	90.8	20	55	0.2	0.5	5.0	..
Netherlands	8.9	82.0	33.5	4,243	3,621	3.9	15.1	4.8	5.4
New Zealand	9.0	78.9	71.7	2,790	2,497	2.2	8.9	..	4.4
Nicaragua	8.3	54.9	93.0	92	258	0.4	1.1	0.9	..
Niger	5.3	52.8	96.4	16	34	0.0[d]	0.1	0.3	..
Nigeria	6.6	25.3	95.9	74	131	0.4	1.6	0.5	..
Norway	8.9	84.1	95.1	7,354	4,774	3.9	16.3	3.9	..
Oman	2.4	78.7	61.3	375	513	1.8	3.9	2.0	..
Pakistan	2.7	30.0	82.1	23	64	0.8	0.4	0.6	..
Panama	6.7	64.6	82.7	396	773	..	..	2.2	..
Papua New Guinea	3.2	81.3	41.3	31	65	..	..	..	..
Paraguay	5.7	42.4	97.0	114	253	..	..	1.3	..
Peru	4.3	58.4	75.3	160	327	..	..	1.5	..
Philippines	3.9	34.7	83.7	63	130	..	..	1.1	..
Poland	6.4	70.9	83.2	716	1,035	2.0	5.2	5.2	6.1
Portugal	10.0	70.6	77.5	2,108	2,284	3.4	4.8	3.5	3.9
Puerto Rico	..	..	..	..	..	..	..	..	..
Qatar	3.8	75.6	88.2	2,403	2,571	2.8	7.4	2.5	..

	Health expenditure					Health workers		Hospital beds	Outpatient visits
	Total % of GDP	Public % of total	Out of pocket % of private	Per capita $	Per capita PPP $	per 1,000 people Physicians	Nurses and midwives	per 1,000 people	per capita
	2007	**2007**	**2007**	**2007**	**2007**	**2003–08ᵃ**	**2003–08ᵃ**	**2003–08ᵃ**	**2000–08ᵃ**
Romania	4.7	80.3	98.8	369	592	1.9	4.2	6.5	5.6
Russian Federation	5.4	64.2	83.0	493	797	4.3	8.5	9.7	9.0
Rwanda	10.3	47.0	44.4	37	90	0.0ᵈ	0.4	1.6	..
Saudi Arabia	3.4	79.5	32.2	531	768	1.6	3.6	2.2	..
Senegal	5.7	56.0	78.5	54	101	0.1	0.4	0.3	..
Serbia	9.9ʰ	61.8ʰ	91.7ʰ	408ʰ	784ʰ	2.0	4.4	5.4	..
Sierra Leone	4.4ᶜ	31.3ᶜ	58.8ᶜ	14ᶜ	32ᶜ	0.0ᵈ	0.2	0.4	..
Singapore	3.1	32.6	93.9	1,148	1,643	1.5	4.4	3.2	..
Slovak Republic	7.7	66.8	79.1	1,077	1,555	3.1	6.6	6.8	12.5
Slovenia	7.8	71.5	48.6	1,836	2,099	2.4	7.8	4.7	6.6
Somalia	..	..	..	..	..	0.0ᵈ	0.1	..	..
South Africa	8.6	41.4	29.7	497	819	0.8	4.1	2.8	..
Spain	8.5	71.8	74.6	2,712	2,671	3.8	7.6	3.4	9.5
Sri Lanka	4.2	47.5	86.7	68	179	0.6	1.7	3.1	..
Sudan	3.5ᶜ	36.8ᶜ	100.0ᶜ	40ᶜ	71ᶜ	0.3	0.9	0.7	..
Swaziland	6.0	62.5	42.3	151	287	0.2	6.3	2.1	..
Sweden	9.1	81.7	87.0	4,495	3,323	3.6	11.6	..	2.8
Switzerland	10.8	59.3	75.0	6,108	4,417	4.0	..	5.5	..
Syrian Arab Republic	3.6	45.9	100.0	68	154	0.5	1.4	1.5	..
Tajikistan	5.3	21.5	94.4	29	93	2.0	5.0	5.4	8.3
Tanzania	5.3	65.8	75.0	22	63	0.0ᵈ	0.2	1.1	..
Thailand	3.7	73.2	71.7	136	286	..	..	..	..
Timor-Leste	13.6	84.6	37.2	58	116	0.1	2.2	..	..
Togo	6.1	24.9	84.2	33	68	0.1	0.3	0.9	..
Trinidad and Tobago	4.8	56.1	89.7	785	1,178	1.2	3.6	2.7	..
Tunisia	6.0	50.5	84.3	211	463	1.3	2.9	2.0	..
Turkey	5.0	69.0	71.8	465	677	1.5	1.9	2.8	4.6
Turkmenistan	2.6ᶜ	52.1ᶜ	100.0ᶜ	139ᶜ	1ᶜ	2.4	4.5	4.1	3.7
Uganda	6.3	26.2	51.0	28	74	0.1	1.3	0.4ᵇ	..
Ukraine	6.9	57.6	92.4	210	470	3.1	8.5	8.7	10.8
United Arab Emirates	2.7	70.5	64.9	1,253	*1,414*	1.5	4.6	1.9	..
United Kingdom	8.4	81.7	62.7	3,867	2,992	2.2	0.6	3.9	4.9
United States	15.7	45.5	22.6	7,285	7,290	2.7	9.8	3.1	9.0
Uruguay	8.0	74.0	50.3	582	994	4.2	..	2.9	..
Uzbekistan	5.0	46.1	98.0	41	114	2.6	10.8	4.8	8.7
Venezuela, RB	5.8	46.5	88.1	477	641	..	..	1.3	..
Vietnam	7.1	39.3	90.2	58	183	..	0.7	2.7	..
West Bank and Gaza	..	..	..	..	..	..	..	..	..
Yemen, Rep.	3.9	39.6	97.8	43	104	0.3	0.7	0.7	..
Zambia	6.2	57.7	67.6	57	79	0.1	0.7	1.9	..
Zimbabwe	8.9ᶜ	46.3ᶜ	50.4ᶜ	79ᶜ	1ᶜ	0.2	0.7	3.0	..
World	**9.7 w**	**59.6 w**	**43.9 w**	**806 w**	**871 w**	**.. w**	**.. w**	**.. w**	**.. w**
Low income	5.4	42.7	83.2	27	69	..	..	..	..
Middle income	5.4	50.2	78.8	164	299	1.3	..	2.2	..
Lower middle income	4.3	42.4	90.5	80	182	1.1	..	1.7	..
Upper middle income	6.4	55.2	69.0	488	753	..	..	4.8	..
Low & middle income	5.4	49.9	78.9	140	261	..	..	..	..
East Asia & Pacific	4.1	46.3	89.1	95	208	1.5	1.0	2.1	..
Europe & Central Asia	5.6	65.7	83.8	396	647	3.1	6.6	7.1	7.6
Latin America & Carib.	7.1	48.5	68.2	473	715	..	..	..	..
Middle East & N. Africa	5.5	50.8	93.1	151	364	..	..	1.6	..
South Asia	4.0	27.5	89.8	36	98	0.6	1.3	0.9	..
Sub-Saharan Africa	6.4	41.1	60.2	69	124	..	..	..	..
High income	11.2	61.3	36.1	4,406	4,182	..	..	6.2	8.6
Euro area	9.7	76.4	60.8	3,695	3,189	3.6	7.9	6.0	6.8

a. Data are for the most recent year available. b. Data are for 2009. c. Derived from incomplete data. d. Less than 0.05. e. Excludes northern Iraq. f. Includes contributions from the United Nations Relief and Works Agency for Palestine Refugees. g. Excludes Transnistria. h. Excludes Metohija.

Health systems—the combined arrangements of institutions and actions whose primary purpose is to promote, restore, or maintain health (World Health Organization, *World Health Report 2000)*—are increasingly being recognized as key to combating disease and improving the health status of populations. The World Bank's (2007a) *Healthy Development: Strategy for Health, Nutrition, and Population Results* emphasizes the need to strengthen health systems, which are weak in many countries, in order to increase the effectiveness of programs aimed at reducing specific diseases and further reduce morbidity and mortality (World Bank 2007a). To evaluate health systems, the World Health Organization (WHO) has recommended that key components—such as financing, service delivery, workforce, governance, and information—be monitored using several key indicators (WHO 2008b). The data in the table are a subset of the first four indicators. Monitoring health systems allows the effectiveness, efficiency, and equity of different health system models to be compared. Health system data also help identify weaknesses and strengths and areas that need investment, such as additional health facilities, better health information systems, or better trained human resources.

Health expenditure data are broken down into public and private expenditures, with private expenditure further broken down into out-of-pocket expenditure (direct payments by households to providers), which make up the largest proportion of private expenditures. In general, low-income economies have a higher share of private health expenditure than do middle- and high-income countries. High out-of-pocket expenditures may discourage people from accessing preventive or curative care and can impoverish households that cannot afford needed care. Health financing data are collected through national health accounts, which systematically, comprehensively, and consistently monitoring health system resource flows. To establish a national health account, countries must define the boundaries of the health system and classify health expenditure information along several dimensions, including sources of financing, providers of health services, functional use of health expenditures, and beneficiaries of expenditures. The accounting system can then provide an accurate picture of resource envelopes and financial flows and allow analysis of the equity and efficiency of financing to inform policy.

Many low-income countries use Demographic and Health Surveys or Multiple Indicator Cluster Surveys funded by donors to obtain health system data. Data on health worker (physicians, nurses, and midwives) density shows the availability of medical personnel. The WHO estimates that at least 2.5 physicians, nurses, and midwives per 1,000 people are needed to provide adequate coverage with primary care interventions associated with achieving the Millennium Development Goals (WHO, *World Health Report 2006).* The WHO compiles data from household and labor force surveys, censuses, and administrative records. Data comparability is limited by differences in definitions and training of medical personnel varies. In addition, human resources tend to be concentrated in urban areas, so that average densities do not provide a full picture of health personnel available to the entire population.

Availability and use of health services, shown by hospital beds per 1,000 people and outpatient visits per capita, reflect both demand- and supply-side factors. In the absence of a consistent definition these are crude indicators of the extent of physical, financial, and other barriers to health care.

• **Total health expenditure** is the sum of public and private health expenditure. It covers the provision of health services (preventive and curative), family planning and nutrition activities, and emergency aid for health but excludes provision of water and sanitation. • **Public health expenditure** is recurrent and capital spending from central and local governments, external borrowing and grants (including donations from international agencies and nongovernmental organizations), and social (or compulsory) health insurance funds. • **Out-of-pocket health expenditure,** part of private health expenditure, is direct household outlays, including gratuities and in-kind payments, for health practitioners and pharmaceutical suppliers, therapeutic appliances, and other goods and services whose primary intent is to restore or enhance health. • **Health expenditure per capita** is total health expenditure divided by population in U.S. dollars and in international dollars converted using 2005 purchasing power parity (PPP) rates. • **Physicians** include generalist and specialist medical practitioners.• **Nurses and midwives** include professional nurses and midwives, auxiliary nurses and midwives, enrolled nurses and midwives, and other personnel, such as dental nurses and primary care nurses. • **Hospital beds** are inpatient beds for both acute and chronic care available in public, private, general, and specialized hospitals and rehabilitation centers. • **Outpatient visits per capita** are the number of visits to health care facilities per capita, including repeat visits.

	Year last national health account completed	Number of national health accounts completed	Year of last health survey	Year of last census	Completeness		
					%		
					Birth registration	Infant death reporting	Total death reporting
	1995–2008			2000–10	2000–08[a]	2003–08[a]	2003–08[a]
Afghanistan		0	2003		6	..	
Albania	2005	3	2005	2001	98	28	76
Algeria	2001	2	2006	2008	99	..	89
Angola		0	2001		29	..	..
Argentina	1999	5		2001	91	100	100
Armenia	2008	5	2005	2001	96	38	100
Australia	2007	13		2006	..	95	97
Austria	2007	13		2001	..	89	97
Azerbaijan		0	2006	2009	94	24	100
Bangladesh	2007	12	2007	2001	10	..	..
Belarus		0	2005	2009	..	55	94
Belgium	2007	5		2001	..	100	97
Benin	2006	3	2006	2002	60	..	..
Bolivia	2007	13	2008	2001	74	..	30
Bosnia and Herzegovina	2006	3	2006		100	54	92
Botswana	2003	3	2000	2001	58	..	..
Brazil	2006	7	1996	2000	89	47	86
Bulgaria	2006	5		2001	..	79	100
Burkina Faso	2006	4	2006	2006	64	29	61
Burundi	2007	1	2005	2008	60	..	..
Cambodia		0	2005	2008	66	0	100
Cameroon	1995	1	2006	2005	70	..	0
Canada	2008	14		2006	..	100	98
Central African Republic		0	2006	2003	49	..	..
Chad		0	2004		9	..	..
Chile	2007	13		2002	96	100	100
China	2006	12		2000	..	..	99
Hong Kong SAR, China		0		2006	..	66	97
Colombia	2003	9	2005	2005	90	57	76
Congo, Dem. Rep.		0	2007		31	..	..
Congo, Rep.	2005	1	2005	2007	81	..	..
Costa Rica	2003	2	1993	2000	..	91	97
Côte d'Ivoire		0	2006		55	..	..
Croatia		0		2001	..	75	100
Cuba		0	2006	2002	100	97	100
Czech Republic	2007	13	1993	2001	..	84	94
Denmark	2007	13		2001	..	97	97
Dominican Republic	2002	2	2007	2002	78	1	54
Ecuador	2005	5	2004	2001	85	59	85
Egypt, Arab Rep.	2002	2	2008	2006	99	49	96
El Salvador	2008	13	2008	2007	..	36	75
Eritrea		0	2002		..	..	0
Estonia	2007	5		2000	..	68	96
Ethiopia	2005	3	2005	2007	7	..	..
Finland	2007	13		2000	..	84	98
France	2007	13		2006	..	95	100
Gabon		0	2000	2003	89	..	..
Gambia, The	2004	3	2005/06	2003	55	..	..
Georgia	2008	8	2005	2002	92	54	83
Germany	2007	13		2001	..	96	99
Ghana	2002	1	2008	2000	51	..	..
Greece		0		2001	..	78	95
Guatemala	2007	13	2002	2002	..	62	93
Guinea		0	2005	2009	43	..	..
Guinea-Bissau		0	2006	2009	39	..	..
Haiti	2006	1	2005/06	2003	81	..	9
Honduras	2005	3	2005/06	2001	94	100	99

	Year last national health account completed	Number of national health accounts completed	Year of last health survey	Year of last census	Completeness		
					Birth registration 2000–08[a]	% Infant death reporting 2003–08[a]	Total death reporting 2003–08[a]
		1995–2008		2000–10			
Hungary	2007	13		2001	..	84	97
India	2004	2	2005/06	2001	41	..	..
Indonesia	2008	8	2007	2000	55	..	..
Iran, Islamic Rep.	2001	3	2000	2006	..	..	99
Iraq		0	2006		95	100	100
Ireland	2007	13		2006	..	75	99
Israel		0		2008	..	90	100
Italy		0		2001	..	99	98
Jamaica	2007	10	2005	2001	89	76	85
Japan	2006	12		2005	..	88	98
Jordan	2007	4	2007	2004	..	..	83
Kazakhstan	2007	1	2006		99	95	88
Kenya	2006	2	2004		48	37	39
Korea, Dem. Rep.		0	2000	2008	99	..	..
Korea, Rep.	2008	14		2005	..	85	94
Kosovo		0			..	..	..
Kuwait		0	1996	2005	..	97	100
Kyrgyz Republic	2008	4	2005/06	2009	94	86	97
Lao PDR		0	2006	2005	72	..	..
Latvia	2005	3		2000	..	79	99
Lebanon	2005	4	2000		..	..	72
Lesotho		0	2004	2006	26	..	..
Liberia	2008	1	2007	2008	4	..	..
Libya		0	2000	2006	..	..	..
Lithuania	2006	5		2001	..	64	100
Macedonia, FYR		0	2005	2002	94	94	100
Madagascar	2007	2	2003/04		75	..	..
Malawi	2006	5	2006	2008	..	..	100
Malaysia	2006	10		2000	..	62	100
Mali	2004	6	2006	2009	53	..	..
Mauritania		0	2007	2000	56	..	..
Mauritius	2004	2		2000	..	99	94
Mexico	2007	13	1995	2005	..	87	100
Moldova		0	2005	2004	98	43	88
Mongolia	2003	5	2005	2000	98	48	88
Morocco	2006	3	2006	2004	85	..	..
Mozambique	2006	4	2003	2007	31	..	..
Myanmar	2001	4	2000		65	49	50
Namibia	2006	9	2006/07	2001	67	..	100
Nepal	2005	5	2006	2001	35	..	..
Netherlands	2007	13		2001	..	84	97
New Zealand	2006	12		2006	..	100	97
Nicaragua	2004	9	2006/07	2005	81	64	65
Niger	2006	4	2006	2001	32	..	..
Nigeria	2005	8	2008	2006	30	..	..
Norway	2008	12		2001	..	82	100
Oman	1998	1	1995	2003	..	49	88
Pakistan	2006	1	2006/07		..	84	..
Panama	2003	1	2003	2000	..	77	88
Papua New Guinea	2000	3	1996	2000	..	19	14
Paraguay	2007	2	2004	2002	..	11	58
Peru	2005	11	2008	2007	93	80	54
Philippines	2007	13	2007/08	2007	83	39	100
Poland	2007	13		2002	..	95	100
Portugal	2007	8		2001	..	79	96
Puerto Rico		0	1996	2000	..	100	95
Qatar		0		2004	..	95	77

	Year last national health account completed	Number of national health accounts completed	Year of last health survey	Year of last census	Completeness		
					%		
					Birth registration	Infant death reporting	Total death reporting
		1995–2008		2000–10	2000–08[a]	2003–08[a]	2003–08[a]
Romania	2006	9	1999	2002	..	79	96
Russian Federation	2007	13	1996	2002	..	79	96
Rwanda	2006	5	2007/08	2002	82	..	..
Saudi Arabia		0	2007	2004	..	94	100
Senegal	2005	2	2005	2002	55	..	..
Serbia	2008	6	2005/06	2002	99	35	89
Sierra Leone		0	2008	2004	48	..	..
Singapore		0	2005	2000	..	84	75
Slovak Republic	2007	11		2001	..	90	99
Slovenia	2006	5		2002	..	72	95
Somalia		0	2006		3	..	..
South Africa	1998	3	1998	2001	78	81	87
Spain	2007	13		2001	..	99	100
Sri Lanka	2006	12	1987	2001	..	..	92
Sudan		0	2006	2008	33	..	..
Swaziland		0	2006/07	2007	30	..	..
Sweden	2007	7			..	83	99
Switzerland	2007	13		2000	..	100	98
Syrian Arab Republic		0	2006	2004	95	..	100
Tajikistan		0	2005	2000	88	19	69
Tanzania	2006	3	2004/05	2002	8	..	..
Thailand	2007	13	2005/06	2000	99	84	66
Timor-Leste		0	2003	2004	53	..	..
Togo	2002	1	2006		78	..	..
Trinidad and Tobago	2000	1	2006	2000	96	50	94
Tunisia	2005	5	2006	2004	..	..	93
Turkey	2005	8	2003	2000	84	56	..
Turkmenistan		0	2006		96	..	..
Uganda	2006	6	2006	2002	21	..	..
Ukraine	2004	2	2007	2001	100	90	100
United Arab Emirates		0		2005	..	75	100
United Kingdom	2007	11		2001	..	100	94
United States	2007	13	2009	2000	..	100	100
Uruguay	2008	13		2004	..	86	100
Uzbekistan		0	2006		100	..	..
Venezuela, RB		0	2000	2001	92	62	84
Vietnam	2007	10	2006	2009	88	72	83
West Bank and Gaza		0	2006	2007	96	..	..
Yemen, Rep.	2006	3	2006	2004	22	..	15
Zambia	2006	11	2007	2000	10	..	..
Zimbabwe	2001	3	2005/06	2002	74	..	..

a. Data are for the most recent year available.

According to the World Health Organization (WHO), health information systems are crucial for monitoring and evaluating health systems, which are increasingly recognized as important for combating disease and improving health status. Health information systems underpin decisionmaking through four data functions: generation, compilation, analysis and synthesis, and communication and use. The health information system collects data from the health sector and other relevant sectors; analyzes the data and ensures their overall quality, relevance, and timeliness; and converts data into information for health-related decisionmaking (WHO 2008b).

Numerous indicators have been proposed to assess a country's health information system. They can be grouped into two broad types: indicators related to data generation using core sources and methods (health surveys, civil registration, censuses, facility reporting, health system resource tracking) and indicators related to capacity for data synthesis, analysis, and validation. Indicators related to data generation reflect a country's capacity to collect relevant data at suitable intervals using the most appropriate data sources. Benchmarks include periodicity, timeliness, contents, and availability. Indicators related to capacity for synthesis, analysis, and validation measure the dimensions of the institutional frameworks needed to ensure data quality, including independence, transparency, and access. Benchmarks include the availability of independent coordination mechanisms and micro- and meta-data (WHO 2008a).

The indicators in the table are all related to data generation, including the years the last national health account, last health survey, and latest population census were completed. Frequency of data collection, a benchmark of data generation, is shown as the number of years for which a national health account was completed between 1995 and 2008. National health account data may be collected using different approaches such as Organisation for Economic Co-operation and Development (OECD) System of Health Accounts, WHO National Health Account producers guide approach, local national health accounting methods, or Pan American Health Organization/WHO satellite health accounts approach.

Indicators related to data generation include completeness of birth registration, infant death reporting, and total death reporting.

• **Year last national health account completed** is the latest year for which the health expenditure data are available using the national health account approach. • **Number of national health accounts completed** is the number of national health accounts completed between 1995 and 2008. • **Year of last health survey** is the latest year the national survey that collects health information was conducted. • **Year of last census** is the latest year a census was conducted in the last 10 years. • **Completeness of birth registration** is the percentage of children under age 5 whose births were registered at the time of the survey. The numerator of completeness of birth registration includes children whose birth certificate was seen by the interviewer or whose mother or caretaker says the birth has been registered. • **Completeness of infant death reporting** is the number of infant deaths reported by national statistical authorities to the United Nations Statistics Division's *Demographic Yearbook* divided by the number of infant deaths estimated by the United Nations Population Division. • **Completeness of total death reporting** is the number of total deaths reported by national statistical authorities to the United Nations Statistics Division's *Demographic Yearbook* divided by the number of total deaths estimated by the United Nations Population Division.

Data on year last national health account completed and number of national health accounts completed were compiled by staff in the World Bank's Health, Nutrition, and Population Unit using data on the health expenditures reported by the WHO and OECD and consultation with colleagues from countries and other international organizations. Data on year of last health survey are from Macro International and the United Nations Children's Fund (UNICEF). Data on year of last census are from United Nations Statistics Division's 2010 World Population and Housing Census Program (http://unstats.un.org/unsd/demographic/sources/census/2010_PHC/default.htm). Data on completeness of birth registration are compiled by UNICEF in *State of the World's Children 2010* based mostly on household surveys and ministry of health data. Data used to calculate completeness of infant death reporting and total death reporting are from the United Nations Statistics Division's *Population and Vital Statistics Report* and the United Nations Population Division's *World Population Prospects: The 2008 Revision*.

Disease prevention coverage and quality

	Access to an improved water source		Access to improved sanitation facilities		Child immunization rate		Children with acute respiratory infection taken to health provider	Children with diarrhea who received oral rehydration and continuous feeding	Children sleeping under treated nets[a]	Children with fever receiving antimalarial drugs	Tuberculosis	
											Treatment success rate	Case detection rate
	% of population		% of population		% of children ages 12–23 months[b]		% of children under age 5 with ARI	% of children under age 5 with diarrhea	% of children under age 5	% of children under age 5 with fever	% of new registered cases	% of new estimated cases
	1990	2006	1990	2006	Measles 2008	DTP3 2008	2003–08[c]	2003–08[c]	2003–08[c]	2003–08[c]	2007	2008
Afghanistan	..	22	..	30	75	85	28	48	..	..	87	55
Albania	..	97	..	97	98	99	45	50	..	..	85	87
Algeria	94	85	88	94	88	93	53	24	..	..	90	103
Angola	39	51	26	50	79	81	..	..	17.7	29.3	74	85
Argentina	94	96	81	91	99	96	..	..	..	..	62	78
Armenia	..	98	..	91	94	89	36	59	..	..	70	74
Australia	100	100	100	100	94	92	..	..	..	..	85	87
Austria	100	100	100	100	83	83	..	..	..	..	71	87
Azerbaijan	68	78	..	80	66	70	33	45	..	..	58	67
Bangladesh	78	80	26	36	89	95	28	68	..	..	92	42
Belarus	100	100	..	93	99	97	90	54	..	..	74	82
Belgium	..	..	..	..	93	99	..	..	..	..	73	87
Benin	63	65	12	30	61	67	36	42	20.1	54.0	87	49
Bolivia	72	86	33	43	86	83	51	54	..	..	85	65
Bosnia and Herzegovina	97	99	..	95	84	91	91	53	..	..	97	90
Botswana	93	96	38	47	94	96	..	..	..	..	73	63
Brazil	83	91	71	77	99	97	50	..	..	..	73	82
Bulgaria	99	99	99	99	96	95	..	..	..	..	80	91
Burkina Faso	34	72	5	13	75	79	39	42	9.6	48.0	72	13
Burundi	70	71	44	41	84	92	38	23	8.3	30.0	86	24
Cambodia	19	65	8	28	89	91	48	50	4.2	0.2	94	55
Cameroon	49	70	39	51	80	84	35	22	13.1	57.8	74	69
Canada	100	100	100	100	94	94	..	..	..	..	64	87
Central African Republic	58	66	11	31	62	54	32	47	15.1	57.0	67	47
Chad	..	48	5	9	23	20	12	27	..	44.0	54	22
Chile	91	95	84	94	92	96	..	..	..	..	85	126
China	67	88	48	65	94	97	..	..	..	..	94	75
Hong Kong SAR, China	..	..	..	..	..	..	..	..	..	..	66	87
Colombia	89	93	68	78	92	92	62	39	..	..	77	70
Congo, Dem. Rep.	43	46	15	31	67	69	42	42	5.8	29.8	87	43
Congo, Rep.	..	71	..	20	79	89	48	39	6.1	48.0	53	63
Costa Rica	..	98	94	96	91	90	..	..	..	..	88	104
Côte d'Ivoire	67	81	20	24	63	74	35	45	3.0	36.0	73	28
Croatia	99	99	99	99	96	96	..	..	..	..	30	87
Cuba	..	91	98	98	99	99	..	..	..	..	90	123
Czech Republic	100	100	100	99	97	99	..	..	..	..	69	87
Denmark	100	100	100	100	89	75	..	..	..	..	77	87
Dominican Republic	84	95	68	79	79	77	70	55	..	0.6	78	59
Ecuador	73	95	71	84	66	75	..	..	..	..	75	50
Egypt, Arab Rep.	94	98	50	66	92	97	73	19	..	..	89	57
El Salvador	69	84	73	86	95	94	62	..	..	..	91	88
Eritrea	43	60	3	5	95	97	..	..	..	..	88	62
Estonia	100	100	95	95	95	95	..	..	..	..	68	88
Ethiopia	13	42	4	11	74	81	19	15	33.1	9.5	84	47
Finland	100	100	100	100	97	99	..	..	..	..	..	87
France	..	100	..	..	87	98	..	..	..	..	..	87
Gabon	..	87	..	36	55	38	..	..	..	..	36	69
Gambia, The	..	86	..	52	91	96	69	38	49.0	62.6	84	48
Georgia	76	99	94	93	96	92	74	37	..	..	75	96
Germany	100	100	100	100	95	90	..	..	..	..	40	87
Ghana	56	80	6	10	86	87	51	29	28.2	43.0	84	30
Greece	96	100	97	98	99	99	..	..	..	..	..	87
Guatemala	79	96	70	84	96	93	..	..	..	..	47	38
Guinea	45	70	13	19	64	66	42	38	1.4	43.5	79	34
Guinea-Bissau	..	57	..	33	76	63	57	25	39.0	45.7	71	68
Haiti	52	58	29	19	58	53	31	43	..	5.1	82	60
Honduras	72	84	45	66	95	93	56	49	..	0.5	85	60

Disease prevention coverage and quality

	Access to an improved water source		Access to improved sanitation facilities		Child immunization rate		Children with acute respiratory infection taken to health provider	Children with diarrhea who received oral rehydration and continuous feeding	Children sleeping under treated nets[a]	Children with fever receiving antimalarial drugs	Tuberculosis	
	% of population		% of population		% of children ages 12–23 months[b]		% of children under age 5 with ARI	% of children under age 5 with diarrhea	% of children under age 5	% of children under age 5 with fever	Treatment success rate % of new registered cases	Case detection rate % of new estimated cases
	1990	2006	1990	2006	Measles 2008	DTP3 2008	2003–08[c]	2003–08[c]	2003–08[c]	2003–08[c]	2007	2008
Hungary	96	100	100	100	99	99	..	..	..	..	46	87
India	71	89	14	28	70	66	69	33	..	8.2	87	67
Indonesia	72	80	51	52	83	77	66	54	3.3	..	91	69
Iran, Islamic Rep.	92	..	83	..	98	99	..	..	..	..	83	65
Iraq	83	77	..	76	69	62	82	64	..	..	86	47
Ireland	..	..	..	..	89	93	..	..	..	..	66	87
Israel	100	100	..	..	84	93	..	..	..	..	74	87
Italy	..	..	..	..	91	96	..	..	..	..	0	87
Jamaica	92	93	83	83	88	87	75	39	..	..	56	59
Japan	100	100	100	100	97	98	..	..	..	..	46	87
Jordan	97	98	..	85	95	97	75	32	..	..	71	91
Kazakhstan	96	96	97	97	99	99	71	48	..	..	69	85
Kenya	41	57	39	42	90	85	49	33	4.6	26.5	85	79
Korea, Dem. Rep.	..	100	..	..	98	92	93	..	..	..	87	88
Korea, Rep.	..	..	..	..	92	94	..	..	..	..	81	87
Kosovo	..	..	..	..	..	..	..	..	..	..	..	..
Kuwait	..	..	..	..	99	99	..	..	..	..	79	87
Kyrgyz Republic	..	89	..	93	99	95	62	22	..	..	85	77
Lao PDR	..	60	..	48	52	61	32	49	40.5	..	92	44
Latvia	99	99	..	78	97	97	..	..	..	..	73	93
Lebanon	100	100	..	..	53	74	..	..	..	..	90	91
Lesotho	..	78	..	36	85	83	59	53	..	..	67	92
Liberia	57	64	40	32	64	64	62	47	..	58.8	71	46
Libya	71	..	97	97	98	98	..	..	..	..	67	192
Lithuania	..	..	..	..	97	96	..	..	..	..	74	89
Macedonia, FYR	..	100	..	89	98	95	93	45	..	..	87	91
Madagascar	39	47	8	12	81	82	42[d]	47	45.8[d]	19.7[d]	80	45
Malawi	41	76	46	60	88	91	52	27	24.7	24.9	85	50
Malaysia	98	99	..	94	95	90	..	..	..	..	72	62
Mali	33	60	35	45	68	68	38	38	27.1	31.7	78	15
Mauritania	37	60	20	24	65	74	45	32	2.1	20.7	66	26
Mauritius	100	100	94	94	98	99	..	..	..	..	85	38
Mexico	88	95	56	81	96	98	..	..	..	..	84	93
Moldova	..	90	..	79	94	95	60	48	..	..	62	70
Mongolia	64	72	..	50	97	96	63	47	..	..	89	83
Morocco	75	83	52	72	96	99	38	46	..	..	86	73
Mozambique	36	42	20	31	77	72	65	47	22.8	14.9	79	42
Myanmar	57	80	23	82	82	85	66	65	..	..	85	62
Namibia	57	93	26	35	73	83	72	48	10.5	9.8	82	84
Nepal	72	89	9	27	79	82	43	37	..	0.1	88	70
Netherlands	100	100	100	100	96	97	..	..	..	..	84	87
New Zealand	97	..	..	..	86	89	..	..	..	..	86	87
Nicaragua	70	79	42	48	99	96	..	..	..	..	86	89
Niger	41	42	3	7	80	66	47	34	7.4	33.0	79	35
Nigeria	50	47	26	30	62	54	32	28	5.5	33.9	82	19
Norway	100	100	..	..	93	94	..	..	..	..	93	87
Oman	81	..	85	..	99	92	..	..	..	..	91	87
Pakistan	86	90	33	58	85	73	69	37	..	3.3	91	60
Panama	..	92	..	74	85	82	..	..	..	..	79	95
Papua New Guinea	39	40	44	45	54	52	..	..	..	..	39	85
Paraguay	52	77	60	70	77	76	..	..	..	..	82	75
Peru	75	84	55	72	90	99	67	60	..	..	92	94
Philippines	83	93	58	78	92	91	50	76	..	0.2	89	54
Poland	..	..	..	..	98	99	..	..	..	..	75	79
Portugal	96	99	92	99	97	97	..	..	..	..	87	87
Puerto Rico	..	..	..	..	..	..	..	..	..	..	80	87
Qatar	100	100	100	100	92	94	..	..	..	..	69	81

2.18 Disease prevention coverage and quality

	Access to an improved water source		Access to improved sanitation facilities		Child immunization rate		Children with acute respiratory infection taken to health provider	Children with diarrhea who received oral rehydration and continuous feeding	Children sleeping under treated nets[a]	Children with fever receiving antimalarial drugs	Tuberculosis	
	% of population		% of population		% of children ages 12–23 months[b]		% of children under age 5 with ARI	% of children under age 5 with diarrhea	% of children under age 5	% of children under age 5 with fever	Treatment success rate % of new registered cases	Case detection rate % of new estimated cases
	1990	2006	1990	2006	Measles 2008	DTP3 2008	2003–08[c]	2003–08[c]	2003–08[c]	2003–08[c]	2007	2008
Romania	76	88	72	72	..	..	..	..	..	..	83	76
Russian Federation	94	97	87	87	99	98	..	..	..	..	58	85
Rwanda	65	65	29	23	92	97	28	24	55.7	12.3	86	20
Saudi Arabia	94	96	91	99	97	98	..	..	..	..	67	86
Senegal	67	77	26	28	77	88	47	43	29.2[d]	22.0	77	33
Serbia	..	99[e]	..	92[e]	92	95	93	71	..	..	84	95
Sierra Leone	..	53	..	11	60	60	46	31	25.9	51.9	89	32
Singapore	100	100	100	100	95	97	..	..	..	..	84	87
Slovak Republic	100	100	100	100	99	99	..	..	..	..	81	87
Slovenia	..	..	..	..	96	97	..	..	..	..	92	87
Somalia	..	29	..	23	24	31	13	7	11.4	7.9	86	36
South Africa	81	93	55	59	62	67	65	..	..	..	74	72
Spain	100	100	100	100	98	97	..	..	..	..	..	87
Sri Lanka	67	82	71	86	98	98	58	..	2.9	0.3	86	70
Sudan	64	70	33	35	79	86	90	56	27.6	54.2	78	49
Swaziland	..	60	..	50	95	95	73	22	0.6	0.6	58	61
Sweden	100	100	100	100	96	98	..	..	..	..	63	87
Switzerland	100	100	100	100	87	95	..	..	..	..	..	87
Syrian Arab Republic	83	89	81	92	81	82	77	34	..	..	88	79
Tajikistan	..	67	..	92	86	86	64	22	1.3	1.2	83	47
Tanzania	49	55	35	33	88	84	59	53	25.7	58.2	88	75
Thailand	95	98	78	96	98	99	84	46	..	..	83	60
Timor-Leste	..	62	..	41	..	..	24	..	..	..	84	60
Togo	49	59	13	12	77	89	23	22	38.4	47.7	76	10
Trinidad and Tobago	88	94	93	92	91	90	74	32	..	..	65	87
Tunisia	82	94	74	85	98	99	59	62	..	..	89	94
Turkey	85	97	85	88	97	96	41	..	..	..	91	79
Turkmenistan	..	..	..	..	99	96	83	25	..	..	84	110
Uganda	43	64	29	33	68	64	73	39	9.7	61.3	75	43
Ukraine	..	97	96	93	94	90	..	..	..	..	59	81
United Arab Emirates	100	100	97	97	92	92	..	..	..	..	64	37
United Kingdom	100	100	..	..	86	92	..	..	..	..	72	87
United States	99	99	100	100	92	96	..	..	..	..	85	87
Uruguay	100	100	100	100	95	94	..	..	..	..	87	93
Uzbekistan	90	88	93	96	98	98	68	28	..	..	79	49
Venezuela, RB	89	..	83	..	82	47	..	..	..	..	82	68
Vietnam	52	92	29	65	92	93	83	65	5.0	2.6	92	56
West Bank and Gaza	..	89	..	80	..	..	..	..	..	..	93	5
Yemen, Rep.	..	66	28	46	62	69	47	48	..	..	84	41
Zambia	50	58	42	52	85	80	68	56	41.1	38.4	85	74
Zimbabwe	78	81	44	46	66	62	25	47	2.9	4.7	78	39
World	76 w	86 w	51 w	60 w	83 w	82 w	.. w	.. w	.. w	.. w	85 w	61 w
Low income	54	67	25	38	78 w	80	45	..	..	28.3	85	48
Middle income	74	88	47	58	83	81	..	..	..	..	85	66
Lower middle income	71	86	39	52	81	79	..	..	..	..	87	64
Upper middle income	88	94	76	82	93	92	..	..	..	..	73	78
Low & middle income	72	84	43	55	82	81	..	..	..	..	85	61
East Asia & Pacific	68	87	48	66	91	92	..	..	..	..	91	69
Europe & Central Asia	90	95	88	89	96	96	..	..	..	..	70	78
Latin America & Carib.	84	91	68	78	93	91	..	..	..	..	76	77
Middle East & N. Africa	89	88	67	74	86	89	62	..	..	..	86	70
South Asia	73	87	18	33	75	71	..	..	..	7.2	87	63
Sub-Saharan Africa	49	58	26	31	72	72	44	..	15.9	34.4	76	46
High income	99	100	99	100	93	95	..	..	..	..	67	87
Euro area	..	100	..	..	93	95	..	..	..	..	..	87

a. For malaria prevention only. b. Refers to children who were immunized before age 12 months or in some cases at any time before the survey (12–23 months). c. Data are for the most recent year available. d. Data are for 2009. e. Includes Kosovo.

People's health is influenced by the environment in which they live. Lack of clean water and basic sanitation is the main reason diseases transmitted by feces are so common in developing countries. Access to drinking water from an improved source and access to improved sanitation do not ensure safety or adequacy, as these characteristics are not tested at the time of the surveys. But improved drinking water technologies and improved sanitation facilities are more likely than those characterized as unimproved to provide safe drinking water and to prevent contact with human excreta. The data are derived by the Joint Monitoring Programme (JMP) of the World Health Organization (WHO) and United Nations Children's Fund (UNICEF) based on national censuses and nationally representative household surveys. The coverage rates for water and sanitation are based on information from service users on the facilities their households actually use rather than on information from service providers, which may include nonfunctioning systems. While the estimates are based on use, the JMP reports use as access, because access is the term used in the Millennium Development Goal target for drinking water and sanitation.

Governments in developing countries usually finance immunization against measles and diphtheria, pertussis (whooping cough), and tetanus (DTP) as part of the basic public health package. In many developing countries lack of precise information on the size of the cohort of one-year-old children makes immunization coverage difficult to estimate from program statistics. The data shown here are based on an assessment of national immunization coverage rates by the WHO and UNICEF. The assessment considered both administrative data from service providers and household survey data on children's immunization histories. Based on the data available, consideration of potential biases, and contributions of local experts, the most likely true level of immunization coverage was determined for each year.

Acute respiratory infection continues to be a leading cause of death among young children, killing about 2 million children under age 5 in developing countries each year. Data are drawn mostly from household health surveys in which mothers report on number of episodes and treatment for acute respiratory infection.

Since 1990 diarrhea-related deaths among children have declined tremendously. Most diarrhea-related deaths are due to dehydration, and many of these deaths can be prevented with the use of oral rehydration salts at home. However, recommendations for the use of oral rehydration therapy have changed over time based on scientific progress, so it is difficult to accurately compare use rates across countries. Until the current recommended method for home management of diarrhea is adopted and applied in all countries, the data should be used with caution. Also, the prevalence of diarrhea may vary by season. Since country surveys are administered at different times, data comparability is further affected.

Malaria is endemic to the poorest countries in the world, mainly in tropical and subtropical regions of Africa, Asia, and the Americas. Insecticide-treated nets, properly used and maintained, are one of the most important malaria-preventive strategies to limit human-mosquito contact. Studies have emphasized that mortality rates could be reduced by about 25–30 percent if every child under age 5 in malaria-risk areas such as Africa slept under a treated net every night.

Prompt and effective treatment of malaria is a critical element of malaria control. It is vital that sufferers, especially children under age 5, start treatment within 24 hours of the onset of symptoms, to prevent progression—often rapid—to severe malaria and death.

Data on the success rate of tuberculosis treatment are provided for countries that have submitted data to the WHO. The treatment success rate for tuberculosis provides a useful indicator of the quality of health services. A low rate suggests that infectious patients may not be receiving adequate treatment. An important complement to the tuberculosis treatment success rate is the case detection rate, which indicates whether there is adequate coverage by the recommended case detection and treatment strategy.

Previous editions included the tuberculosis detection rates by DOTS, the internationally recommended strategy for tuberculosis control. This year's edition shows the tuberculosis detection rate for all detection methods, so data on the case detection rate cannot be compared with data in previous editions.

For indicators that are from household surveys, the year in the table refers to the survey year. For more information, consult the original sources.

• **Access to an improved water source** refers to people with access to at least 20 liters of water a person a day from an improved source, such as piped water into a dwelling, public tap, tubewell, protected dug well, and rainwater collection, within 1 kilometer of the dwelling. • **Access to improved sanitation facilities** refers to people with at least adequate access to excreta disposal facilities that can effectively prevent human, animal, and insect contact with excreta. Improved facilities range from protected pit latrines to flush toilets. • **Child immunization rate** refers to children ages 12–23 months who, before 12 months or at any time before the survey, had received one dose of measles vaccine and three doses of diphtheria, pertussis (whooping cough), and tetanus (DTP3) vaccine. • **Children with acute respiratory infection (ARI) taken to health provider** are children under age 5 with ARI in the two weeks before the survey who were taken to an appropriate health provider. • **Children with diarrhea who received oral rehydration and continuous feeding** are children under age 5 with diarrhea in the two weeks before the survey who received either oral rehydration therapy or increased fluids, with continuous feeding. • **Children sleeping under treated nets** are children under age 5 who slept under an insecticide-treated net to prevent malaria the night before the survey. • **Children with fever receiving antimalarial drugs** are children under age 5 who were ill with fever in the two weeks before the survey and received any appropriate (locally defined) antimalarial drugs. • **Tuberculosis treatment success rate** is new registered infectious tuberculosis cases that were cured or that completed a full course of treatment as a percentage of smear-positive cases registered for treatment outcome evaluation. • **Tuberculosis case detection rate** is newly identified tuberculosis cases (including relapses) as a percentage of estimated incident cases (case detection, all forms).

Data sources

Data on access to water and sanitation are from the WHO and UNICEF's *Progress on Drinking Water and Sanitation* (2008). Data on immunization are from WHO and UNICEF estimates (www.who.int/immunization_monitoring). Data on children with ARI, with diarrhea, sleeping under treated nets, and receiving antimalarial drugs are from UNICEF's *State of the World's Children 2009*, Childinfo, and Demographic and Health Surveys by Macro International. Data on tuberculosis are from the WHO's *Global Tuberculosis Control: A Short Update to the 2009 Report*.

	Total fertility rate		Wanted fertility rate	Adolescent fertility rate	Unmet need for contraception	Contraceptive prevalence rate	Pregnant women receiving prenatal care	Births attended by skilled health staff		Maternal mortality ratio	
	births per woman		births per woman	births per 1,000 women ages 15–19	% of married women ages 15–49	% of married women ages 15–49	%	% of total		per 100,000 live births National estimates	Modeled estimates
	1990	2008	2003–08[a]	2008	2003–08[a]	2003–08[a]	2003–08[a]	1990	2003–08[a]	2000–08[a]	2005
Afghanistan	8.0	6.6	..	120	..	15	36	..	24	1,600	1,800
Albania	2.9	1.9	..	14	..	60	97	..	100	20	92
Algeria	4.7	2.4	..	7	..	61	89	77	95	..	180
Angola	7.2	5.8	..	123	..	..	80	..	47	..	1,400
Argentina	3.0	2.2	..	57	..	..	99	96	99	44	77
Armenia	2.5	1.7	1.6	36	13	53	93	..	100	15	76
Australia	1.9	2.0	..	15	..	..	..	100	100	..	4
Austria	1.5	1.4	..	13	..	..	..	..	..	..	4
Azerbaijan	2.7	2.3	1.8	34	23	51	77	..	88	26	82
Bangladesh	4.4	2.3	1.9	70	17	56	51	..	18	351	570
Belarus	1.9	1.4	..	21	..	73	99	..	100	12	18
Belgium	1.6	1.8	..	8	..	..	..	..	..	..	8
Benin	6.7	5.4	4.8	111	30	17	84	..	74	397	840
Bolivia	4.9	3.5	2.1	78	23	61	77	43	66	229	290
Bosnia and Herzegovina	1.7	1.2	..	16	23	36	99	97	100	3	3
Botswana	4.7	2.9	..	51	..	..	..	77	..	..	380
Brazil	2.8	1.9	..	75	..	81	98	72	97	53	110
Bulgaria	1.8	1.5	..	42	..	..	..	..	99	7	11
Burkina Faso	6.8	5.9	5.1	129	29	17	85	..	54	..	700
Burundi	6.6	4.6	..	19	..	9	92	..	34	615	1,100
Cambodia	5.8	2.9	2.8	39	25	40	69	..	44	472	540
Cameroon	5.9	4.6	4.5	126	20	29	82	58	63	669	1,000
Canada	1.8	1.6	..	13	..	..	..	..	100	..	7
Central African Republic	5.8	4.8	..	104	..	19	69	..	53	543	980
Chad	6.7	6.2	6.1	162	21	3	39	..	14	1,099	1,500
Chile	2.6	1.9	..	59	..	58	..	..	100	20	16
China	2.3[b]	1.8[b]	..	10[b]	..	85	91	50	98	37	45
Hong Kong SAR, China	1.3	1.0	..	6	..	..	..	..	100	..	..
Colombia	3.1	2.4	1.7	74	6	78	94	82	96	75	130
Congo, Dem. Rep.	7.1	6.0	5.6	198	24	21	85	..	74	549	1,100
Congo, Rep.	5.4	4.4	4.4	111	16	44	86	..	83	781	740
Costa Rica	3.2	2.0	..	67	..	96	90	98	99	33	30
Côte d'Ivoire	6.3	4.6	..	128	29	13	85	..	57	543	810
Croatia	1.6	1.5	..	14	..	..	100	100	100	10	7
Cuba	1.8	1.5	..	45	8	77	100	..	100	29	45
Czech Republic	1.9	1.5	..	11	..	..	..	..	100	8	4
Denmark	1.7	1.9	..	6	..	..	..	..	..	..	3
Dominican Republic	3.5	2.6	1.9	108	11	73	99	93	98	159	150
Ecuador	3.7	2.6	..	83	..	73	84	..	75	60	210
Egypt, Arab Rep.	4.6	2.9	2.3	38	10	60	74	37	79	84	130
El Salvador	4.0	2.3	..	82	..	73	94	52	92	59	170
Eritrea	6.2	4.6	..	66	..	..	..	..	..	..	450
Estonia	2.0	1.7	..	21	..	..	..	..	100	7	25
Ethiopia	7.1	5.3	4.0	102	34	15	28	..	6	673	720
Finland	1.8	1.8	..	11	..	..	..	..	100	..	7
France	1.8	2.0	..	7	..	..	..	..	..	..	8
Gabon	5.2	3.3	..	89	..	..	..	..	..	519	520
Gambia, The	6.1	5.1	..	88	..	..	98	44	57	730	690
Georgia	2.2	1.6	..	44	..	47	94	..	98	23	66
Germany	1.5	1.4	..	8	..	..	..	..	100	..	4
Ghana	5.6	4.0	3.7	63	34	24	95	40	59	451	560
Greece	1.4	1.5	..	9	..	..	..	..	..	..	3
Guatemala	5.6	4.1	..	106	..	..	..	..	..	133	290
Guinea	6.7	5.4	5.1	151	21	9	88	31	46	980	910
Guinea-Bissau	5.9	5.7	..	128	..	10	78	..	39	405	1,100
Haiti	5.4	3.5	2.4	46	38	32	85	23	26	630	670
Honduras	5.1	3.3	2.3	92	17	65	92	45	67	..	280

Reproductive health | 2.19

	Total fertility rate		Wanted fertility rate	Adolescent fertility rate	Unmet need for contraception	Contraceptive prevalence rate	Pregnant women receiving prenatal care	Births attended by skilled health staff		Maternal mortality ratio	
	births per woman		births per woman	births per 1,000 women ages 15–19	% of married women ages 15–49	% of married women ages 15–49	%	% of total		per 100,000 live births	
										National estimates	Modeled estimates
	1990	2008	2003–08[a]	2008	2003–08[a]	2003–08[a]	2003–08[a]	1990	2003–08[a]	2000–08[a]	2005
Hungary	1.8	1.4	..	20	..	..	..	..	100	8	6
India	4.0	2.7	1.9	67	13	56	74	..	47	301	450
Indonesia	3.1	2.2	2.2	39	9	61	93	32	79	228	420
Iran, Islamic Rep.	4.8	1.8	..	18	..	79	98	..	97	25	140
Iraq	6.0	4.1	..	84	..	50	84	54	80	84	300
Ireland	2.1	2.1	..	16	..	..	..	..	100	..	1
Israel	2.8	3.0	..	14	..	..	..	..	..	..	4
Italy	1.3	1.4	..	5	..	..	..	..	99	..	3
Jamaica	2.9	2.4	..	77	..	..	91	79	95	95	170
Japan	1.5	1.3	..	5	..	..	..	100	100	..	6
Jordan	5.5	3.5	2.8	24	12	57	99	87	99	..	62
Kazakhstan	2.7	2.6	..	30	..	51	100	..	100	31	140
Kenya	6.0	4.9	3.6	103	25	39	88	50	42	414	560
Korea, Dem. Rep.	2.4	1.9	..	0	..	..	..	..	97	..	370
Korea, Rep.	1.6	1.2	..	6	..	..	..	98	100	..	14
Kosovo	3.9	2.4	..	..	..	..	..	..	..	..	..
Kuwait	3.5	2.2	..	13	..	..	..	..	..	..	4
Kyrgyz Republic	3.7	2.7	..	32	1	48	97	..	98	104	150
Lao PDR	6.0	3.5	..	37	..	38	35	..	20	405	660
Latvia	2.0	1.5	..	15	..	..	..	..	100	9	10
Lebanon	3.1	1.8	..	16	..	58	96	..	98	..	150
Lesotho	4.9	3.3	2.5	72	31	37	90	..	55	762	960
Liberia	6.5	5.9	4.6	140	36	11	79	..	46	994	1,200
Libya	4.8	2.7	..	3	..	..	..	..	..	..	97
Lithuania	2.0	1.5	..	21	..	..	..	..	100	13	11
Macedonia, FYR	2.1	1.4	..	21	34	14	94	..	99	4	10
Madagascar	6.3	4.7	4.6	131	24	40c	86c	57	44c	469	510
Malawi	7.0	5.5	4.9	133	28	41	92	55	54	807	1,100
Malaysia	3.7	2.6	..	13	..	..	79	..	98	30	62
Mali	6.7	6.5	6.0	161	31	8	70	..	49	464	970
Mauritania	5.9	4.5	..	88	..	9	75	40	61	686	820
Mauritius	2.3	1.6	..	40	..	..	..	91	99	22	15
Mexico	3.4	2.1	..	64	..	71	94	..	93	56	60
Moldova	2.4	1.5	..	33	7	68	98	..	100	16	22
Mongolia	4.2	2.0	..	16	14	66	89	..	100	49	46
Morocco	4.0	2.4	1.8	19	10	63	68	31	63	227	240
Mozambique	6.2	5.1	4.9	146	18	16	89	..	55	408	520
Myanmar	3.4	2.3	..	18	..	34	..	..	68	316	380
Namibia	5.2	3.4	2.7	72	7	55	95	68	81	449	210
Nepal	5.2	2.9	2.0	99	25	48	44	7	19	281	830
Netherlands	1.6	1.8	..	4	..	..	..	..	100	..	6
New Zealand	2.2	2.2	..	22	..	..	..	..	..	..	9
Nicaragua	4.8	2.7	..	112	8	72	90	..	74	87	170
Niger	7.9	7.1	6.8	156	16	11	46	15	33	648	1,800
Nigeria	6.6	5.7	5.3	124	17	15	58	33	39	..	1,100
Norway	1.9	2.0	..	8	..	..	..	100	..	..	7
Oman	6.6	3.0	..	10	..	..	..	..	99	23	64
Pakistan	6.1	4.0	3.1	45	25	30	61	19	39	276	320
Panama	3.0	2.5	..	82	..	..	..	..	92	60	130
Papua New Guinea	4.8	4.1	..	54	..	32	79	..	53	..	470
Paraguay	4.5	3.0	..	72	..	79	96	66	82	121	150
Peru	3.8	2.6	..	54	8	71	91	80	71	185	240
Philippines	4.3	3.1	2.5	44	22	51	91	..	62	162	230
Poland	2.0	1.4	..	14	..	..	..	..	100	3	8
Portugal	1.4	1.4	..	16	..	..	..	98	..	..	11
Puerto Rico	2.2	1.8	..	53	..	..	..	..	100	..	18
Qatar	4.4	2.4	..	16	..	..	..	..	..	..	12

	Total fertility rate (births per woman)		Wanted fertility rate (births per woman)	Adolescent fertility rate (births per 1,000 women ages 15–19)	Unmet need for contraception (% of married women ages 15–49)	Contraceptive prevalence rate (% of married women ages 15–49)	Pregnant women receiving prenatal care (%)	Births attended by skilled health staff (% of total)		Maternal mortality ratio (per 100,000 live births)	
	1990	2008	2003–08ᵃ	2008	2003–08ᵃ	2003–08ᵃ	2003–08ᵃ	1990	2003–08ᵃ	National estimates 2000–08ᵃ	Modeled estimates 2005
Romania	1.8	1.4	..	31	..	70	94	..	98	15	24
Russian Federation	1.9	1.5	..	25	..	..	..	..	100	22	28
Rwanda	6.8	5.4	4.6	36	38	36	96	26	52	750	1,300
Saudi Arabia	5.8	3.1	..	26	..	..	..	..	96	10	18
Senegal	6.7	4.8	4.5	102	32	12	87	..	52	401	980
Serbia	1.8	1.4	..	22	29	41	98	..	99	13	14ᵈ
Sierra Leone	5.5	5.2	..	125	..	8	81	..	43	857	2,100
Singapore	1.9	1.3	..	4	..	..	..	..	100	..	14
Slovak Republic	2.1	1.3	..	20	..	..	..	..	100	4	6
Slovenia	1.5	1.5	..	5	..	..	..	100	100	17	6
Somalia	6.6	6.4	..	70	..	15	26	..	33	1,044	1,400
South Africa	3.7	2.5	..	58	..	60	92	..	91	166	400
Spain	1.3	1.5	..	12	..	..	..	..	..	..	4
Sri Lanka	2.5	2.3	..	29	..	68	99	..	99	44	58
Sudan	6.0	4.2	..	56	6	8	64	69	49	1,107	450
Swaziland	5.7	3.5	2.1	82	24	51	85	..	69	589	390
Sweden	2.1	1.9	..	8	..	..	..	..	..	..	3
Switzerland	1.6	1.5	..	5	..	..	..	..	100	..	5
Syrian Arab Republic	5.5	3.2	..	59	..	58	84	..	93	65	130
Tajikistan	5.2	3.4	..	28	..	37	80	..	88	97	170
Tanzania	6.2	5.6	4.9	130	22	26	76	53	43	578	950
Thailand	2.1	1.8	..	37	..	77	98	..	97	12	110
Timor-Leste	5.3	6.5	..	53	..	20	61	..	18	..	380
Togo	6.3	4.3	..	64	..	17	84	31	62	..	510
Trinidad and Tobago	2.4	1.6	..	34	..	43	96	..	98	..	45
Tunisia	3.5	2.1	..	7	..	60	96	69	95	..	100
Turkey	3.1	2.1	..	38	..	73	54	..	91	29	44
Turkmenistan	4.3	2.5	..	19	..	48	99	..	100	14	130
Uganda	7.1	6.3	5.1	148	41	24	94	38	42	435	550
Ukraine	1.8	1.4	1.1	28	10	67	99	..	99	24	18
United Arab Emirates	4.4	1.9	..	16	..	..	..	..	100	..	37
United Kingdom	1.8	1.9	..	24	..	..	..	..	..	..	8
United States	2.1	2.1	..	35	..	..	..	99	99	..	11
Uruguay	2.5	2.0	..	61	..	..	97	..	99	18	20
Uzbekistan	4.1	2.6	..	13	8	65	99	..	100	28	24
Venezuela, RB	3.4	2.5	..	90	..	..	..	..	95	61	57
Vietnam	3.7	2.1	..	17	..	76	91	..	88	162	150
West Bank and Gaza	6.4	5.0	..	77	..	50	99	..	99	..	..
Yemen, Rep.	8.1	5.2	..	67	..	28	47	16	36	365	430
Zambia	6.5	5.8	5.2	139	27	41	94	51	47	591	830
Zimbabwe	5.2	3.4	3.3	64	13	60	94	70	69	555	880
World	**3.3 w**	**2.5 w**	**.. w**	**51 w**	**.. w**	**61 w**	**82 w**	**50 w**	**66 w**		**400 w**
Low income	5.4	4.0	..	90	..	38	69	..	44		790
Middle income	3.3	2.4	..	47	..	66	84	46	70		320
Lower middle income	3.4	2.5	..	46	..	65	83	41	65		370
Upper middle income	2.8	2.0	..	51	..	72	90	..	95		110
Low & middle income	3.6	2.7	..	55	..	61	82	46	63		440
East Asia & Pacific	2.6	1.9	..	17	..	77	91	48	89		150
Europe & Central Asia	2.3	1.8	..	27	..	..	..	..	97		45
Latin America & Carib.	3.2	2.2	..	72	..	75	95	72	90		130
Middle East & N. Africa	4.9	2.7	..	35	..	62	83	47	80		200
South Asia	4.3	2.9	1.9	66	13	53	69	32	42		500
Sub-Saharan Africa	6.3	5.1	..	116	..	23	72	..	46		900
High income	1.8	1.8	..	19	..	..	..	..	99		10
Euro area	1.5	1.6	..	8	..	..	..	..	..		5

a. Data are for most recent year available. b. Includes Taiwan, China. c. Data are for 2009. d. Includes Montenegro.

Reproductive health is a state of physical and mental well-being in relation to the reproductive system and its functions and processes. Means of achieving reproductive health include education and services during pregnancy and childbirth, safe and effective contraception, and prevention and treatment of sexually transmitted diseases. Complications of pregnancy and childbirth are the leading cause of death and disability among women of reproductive age in developing countries.

Total and adolescent fertility rates are based on data on registered live births from vital registration systems or, in the absence of such systems, from censuses or sample surveys. The estimated rates are generally considered reliable measures of fertility in the recent past. Where no empirical information on age-specific fertility rates is available, a model is used to estimate the share of births to adolescents. For countries without vital registration systems fertility rates are generally based on extrapolations from trends observed in censuses or surveys from earlier years.

Unwanted fertility—actual fertility minus desired fertility—can been avoided when couples use effective contraception. One approach to measuring unwanted fertility is to calculate what the total fertility rate would be if all unwanted births were avoided—the wanted fertility rate. It is calculated in the same manner as the total fertility rate (from a household survey), but unwanted births are excluded from the numerator. Unwanted births are defined as those that exceed the number considered ideal by the same respondent in the survey.

More couples in developing countries want to limit or postpone childbearing but are not using effective contraception. These couples have an unmet need for contraception. Common reasons are lack of knowledge about contraceptive methods and concerns about possible side effects. This indicator excludes women not exposed to the risk of unintended pregnancy because of menopause, infertility, or postpartum anovulation.

Contraceptive prevalence reflects all methods—ineffective traditional methods as well as highly effective modern methods. Contraceptive prevalence rates are obtained mainly from household surveys, including Demographic and Health Surveys, Multiple Indicator Cluster Surveys, and contraceptive prevalence surveys (see *Primary data documentation* for the most recent survey year). Unmarried women are often excluded from such surveys, which may bias the estimates.

Good prenatal and postnatal care improve maternal health and reduce maternal and infant mortality. But data may not reflect such improvements because health information systems are often weak, maternal deaths are underreported, and rates of maternal mortality are difficult to measure.

The share of births attended by skilled health staff is an indicator of a health system's ability to provide adequate care for pregnant women. Maternal mortality ratios are generally of unknown reliability, as are many other cause-specific mortality indicators. Household surveys such as Demographic and Health Surveys attempt to measure maternal mortality by asking respondents about survivorship of sisters. The main disadvantage of this method is that the estimates of maternal mortality that it produces pertain to 12 years or so before the survey, making them unsuitable for monitoring recent changes or observing the impact of interventions. In addition, measurement of maternal mortality is subject to many types of errors. Even in high-income countries with vital registration systems, misclassification of maternal deaths has been found to lead to serious underestimation.

The national estimates of maternal mortality ratios in the table are based on national surveys, vital registration records, and surveillance data or are derived from community and hospital records. The modeled estimates are based on an exercise by the World Health Organization (WHO), United Nations Children's Fund (UNICEF), United Nations Population Fund (UNFPA), and World Bank. For countries with complete vital registration systems with good attribution of cause of death, the data are used as reported. For countries with national data either from complete vital registration systems with uncertain or poor attribution of cause of death or from household surveys reported maternal mortality was adjusted, usually by a factor of underenumeration and misclassification. For countries with no empirical national data (about 35 percent of countries), maternal mortality was estimated with a regression model using socioeconomic information, including fertility, birth attendants, and GDP. Neither set of ratios can be assumed to provide an exact estimate of maternal mortality for any of the countries in the table.

For the indicators that are from household surveys, the year in the table refers to the survey year. For more information, consult the original sources.

• **Total fertility rate** is the number of children that would be born to a woman if she were to live to the end of her childbearing years and bear children in accordance with current age-specific fertility rates. • **Wanted fertility rate** is the estimated total fertility rate if all unwanted births were avoided. • **Adolescent fertility rate** is the number of births per 1,000 women ages 15–19. • **Unmet need for contraception** is the percentage of fertile, married women of reproductive age who do not want to become pregnant and are not using contraception. • **Contraceptive prevalence rate** is the percentage of women married or in union ages 15–49 who are practicing, or whose sexual partners are practicing, any form of contraception. • **Pregnant women receiving prenatal care** are the percentage of women attended at least once during pregnancy by skilled health personnel for reasons related to pregnancy. • **Births attended by skilled health staff** are the percentage of deliveries attended by personnel trained to give the necessary care to women during pregnancy, labor, and postpartum; to conduct deliveries on their own; and to care for newborns. • **Maternal mortality ratio** is the number of women who die from pregnancy-related causes during pregnancy and childbirth per 100,000 live births.

Data sources

Data on total fertility are compiled from the United Nations Population Division's *World Population Prospects: The 2008 Revision,* census reports and other statistical publications from national statistical offices, household surveys conducted by national agencies, Macro International, and the U.S. Centers for Disease Control and Prevention, Eurostat's *Demographic Statistics,* and the U.S. Bureau of the Census International Data Base. Data on wanted fertility are from Demographic and Health Surveys by Macro International. Data on adolescent fertility are from *World Population Prospects: The 2008 Revision,* with annual data linearly interpolated by the Development Data Group. Data on women with unmet need for contraception and contraceptive prevalence are from household surveys, including Demographic and Health Surveys by Macro International and Multiple Indicator Cluster Surveys by UNICEF. Data on pregnant women receiving prenatal care, births attended by skilled health staff, and national estimates of maternal mortality ratios are from UNICEF's *State of the World's Children 2010* and Childinfo and Demographic and Health Surveys by Macro International. Modeled estimates of maternal mortality ratios are from WHO, UNICEF, UNFPA and the World Bank's *Maternal Mortality in 2005* (2007).

Nutrition

	Prevalence of undernourishment		Prevalence of child malnutrition		Prevalence of overweight children	Low-birthweight babies	Exclusive breast-feeding	Consumption of iodized salt	Vitamin A supplementation	Prevalence of anemia	
	% of population		% of children under age 5		% of children under age 5	% of births	% of children under 6 months	% of households	% of children 6–59 months	% Children under age 5	Pregnant women
	1990–92	2004–06	Underweight 2000–08[a]	Stunting 2000–08[a]	2000–08[a]	2003–08[a]	2003–08[a]	2003–08[a]	2008	2000–06[a]	2000–06[a]
Afghanistan	..	..	32.9	59.3	4.6	..	83	28	96	38	61
Albania	<5	<5	6.6	27.0	25.2	7	40	60	..	31	34
Algeria	<5	<5	11.1	23.3	14.7	6	7	61	..	43	43
Angola	66	44	27.5	50.8	5.3	..	..	45	82	..	57
Argentina	<5	<5	2.3	8.2	6.5	7	..	..	..	18	25
Armenia	46	23	4.2	18.2	11.7	7	33	97	..	37	12
Australia	<5	<5	..	..	..	..	..	..	..	8	12
Austria	<5	<5	..	..	..	..	..	..	..	11	15
Azerbaijan	27	11	8.4	26.8	13.9	10	12	54	90[b]	32	38
Bangladesh	36	26	41.3	43.2	1.1	22	43	84	97	47	47
Belarus	<5	<5	1.3	4.5	9.7	4	9	55	..	27	26
Belgium	<5	<5	..	..	..	..	..	..	..	9	13
Benin	28	19	20.2	44.7	11.4	15	43	55	52	78	75
Bolivia	24	23	5.9	32.5	9.2	7	60	88	45	52	37
Bosnia and Herzegovina	<5	<5	1.6	11.8	25.6	5	18	62	..	27	35
Botswana	20	26	10.7	29.1	10.4	..	..	..	..	..	21
Brazil	10	6	2.2	7.1	7.3	8	40	96	..	55	29
Bulgaria	<5	<5	1.6	8.8	13.6	9	..	100	..	27	30
Burkina Faso	14	9	37.4	44.5	7.7	16	7	34	100	92	68
Burundi	44	63	38.9	63.1	1.4	11	45	98	80	56	47
Cambodia	38	25	28.8	39.5	2.0	14	60	73	88	62	66
Cameroon	34	23	16.6	36.4	9.6	11	21	49	..	68	51
Canada	<5	<5	..	..	..	..	..	..	..	8	12
Central African Republic	47	41	21.8	44.6	10.8	13	23	62	68	..	..
Chad	59	38	33.9	44.8	4.4	22	2	56	0	71	60
Chile	7	<5	0.5	2.0	9.5	6	85	..	..	24	28
China	15[c]	10[c]	6.8	21.8	9.2	2	51	95	..	20	29
Hong Kong SAR, China	..	..	..	..	..	..	..	..	..	..	..
Colombia	15	10	5.1	16.2	4.2	6	47	..	..	28	31
Congo, Dem. Rep.	29	75	28.2	45.8	6.8	8	36	79	85	71	67
Congo, Rep.	40	21	11.8	31.2	8.5	13	19	82	10	66	55
Costa Rica	<5	<5	..	..	..	7	15	..	..	..	..
Côte d'Ivoire	15	14	16.7	40.1	9.0	17	4	84	90	69	55
Croatia	<5	<5	..	..	..	5	..	..	..	23	28
Cuba	5	<5	..	..	..	5	26	88	..	27	39
Czech Republic	<5	<5	2.1	2.6	4.4	..	..	..	..	18	22
Denmark	<5	<5	..	..	..	..	..	..	..	9	12
Dominican Republic	27	21	3.4	10.1	8.3	11	9	19	..	35	40
Ecuador	24	13	6.2	29.0	5.1	10	40	..	..	38	38
Egypt, Arab Rep.	<5	<5	6.8	30.7	20.5	13	53	79	68[b]	49	34
El Salvador	9	10	6.1	24.6	5.8	7	31	..	20	18	..
Eritrea	67	66	34.5	43.7	1.6	..	..	..	49	70	55
Estonia	<5	<5	..	..	..	..	..	..	..	23	23
Ethiopia	71	44	34.6	50.7	5.1	20	49	20	88	75	63
Finland	<5	<5	..	..	..	..	..	..	..	11	15
France	<5	<5	..	..	..	..	..	..	..	8	11
Gabon	5	<5	8.8	26.3	5.6	..	..	..	0	44	46
Gambia, The	20	29	15.8	27.6	2.7	20	41	7	28	..	..
Georgia	47	12	2.3	14.7	21.0	5	11	87	..	41	42
Germany	<5	<5	1.1	1.3	3.5	..	..	..	..	8	12
Ghana	34	8	13.9	28.1	2.6	9	63	32	24	76	65
Greece	<5	<5	..	..	..	..	..	..	..	12	19
Guatemala	14	16	17.7	54.3	5.6	..	..	76	20	38	22
Guinea	19	16	22.5	39.3	5.1	12	48	41	94	76	63
Guinea-Bissau	20	31	17.4	47.7	17.0	24	16	1	66	75	58
Haiti	63	58	18.9	29.7	3.9	25	41	3	42	65	50
Honduras	19	12	8.6	29.9	5.8	10	30	..	40	30	21

	Prevalence of undernourishment		Prevalence of child malnutrition		Prevalence of overweight children	Low-birthweight babies	Exclusive breast-feeding	Consumption of iodized salt	Vitamin A supplemen-tation	Prevalence of anemia	
	% of population		% of children under age 5 Underweight	Stunting	% of children under age 5	% of births	% of children under 6 months	% of households	% of children 6-59 months	% Children under age 5	Pregnant women
	1990-92	2004-06	2000-08[a]	2000-08[a]	2000-08[a]	2003-08[a]	2003-08[a]	2003-08[a]	2008	2000-06[a]	2000-06[a]
Hungary	<5	<5	..	..	..	..	..	..	..	19	21
India	24	22	43.5	47.9	1.9	28	46	51	53	74	50
Indonesia	19	16	19.6	40.1	11.2	9	32	62	86	44	44
Iran, Islamic Rep.	<5	<5	..	..	..	7	23	99	..	35	21
Iraq	..	..	7.1	27.5	15.0	15	25	28	1	56	38
Ireland	<5	<5	..	..	..	..	..	..	..	10	15
Israel	<5	<5	..	..	..	..	..	..	..	12	17
Italy	<5	<5	..	..	..	..	..	..	..	11	15
Jamaica	11	5	2.2	3.7	7.5	14	15	..	..	..	..
Japan	<5	<5	..	..	..	..	..	..	..	11	15
Jordan	<5	<5	3.6	12.0	4.7	13	22	..	..	28	39
Kazakhstan	<5	<5	4.9	17.5	14.8	6	17	92	..	..	26
Kenya	33	30	16.5	35.8	5.8	10	13	..	27	..	..
Korea, Dem. Rep.	21	32	17.8	44.7	0.9	..	65	40	98	..	..
Korea, Rep.	<5	<5	..	..	..	..	..	..	..	..	23
Kosovo	..	..	..	..	..	..	..	..	..	..	..
Kuwait	20	<5	..	..	..	..	..	..	..	32	31
Kyrgyz Republic	17	<5	2.7	18.1	10.7	5	32	76	99	..	34
Lao PDR	27	19	31.6	47.6	1.3	11	26	84	83	48	56
Latvia	<5	<5	..	..	..	..	..	..	..	27	25
Lebanon	<5	<5	4.2	16.5	16.7	..	..	92	..	..	32
Lesotho	15	15	16.6	45.2	6.8	13	36	91	85	49	25
Liberia	30	38	20.4	39.4	4.2	14	29	..	85	..	..
Libya	<5	<5	5.6	21.0	22.4	..	..	..	..	34	34
Lithuania	<5	<5	..	..	..	..	..	..	..	24	24
Macedonia, FYR	<5	<5	1.8	11.5	16.2	6	16	94	..	..	32
Madagascar	32	35	36.8	52.8	6.2	17	67	75	97	68	50
Malawi	45	29	15.5	53.2	11.3	13	57	50	95	73	47
Malaysia	<5	<5	..	..	..	..	..	..	..	32	38
Mali	14	10	27.9	38.5	4.7	19	38	79	97	83	73
Mauritania	10	8	23.2	28.9	2.3	34	16	2	87	68	53
Mauritius	7	6	..	..	..	14	..	..	..	..	..
Mexico	<5	<5	3.4	15.5	7.6	8	..	91	68	24	21
Moldova	<5	<5	3.2	11.3	9.1	6	46	60	..	41	36
Mongolia	30	29	5.3	27.5	14.2	6	57	83	95	21	37
Morocco	5	<5	9.9	23.1	13.3	15	31	21	..	32	37
Mozambique	59	37	21.2	47.0	6.3	15	37	25	83	75	52
Myanmar	44	17	29.6	40.6	2.4	..	15	93	94	63	50
Namibia	29	19	17.5	29.6	4.6	16	24	..	68	41	31
Nepal	21	16	38.8	49.3	0.6	21	53	..	93	48	42
Netherlands	<5	<5	..	..	..	..	..	..	..	9	13
New Zealand	<5	<5	..	..	..	..	..	..	..	11	18
Nicaragua	52	21	4.3	18.8	5.2	8	31	97	95	17	33
Niger	38	28	39.9	54.8	3.5	27	4	46	92	81	61
Nigeria	15	8	27.2	43.0	6.2	14	13	97	74	..	..
Norway	<5	<5	..	..	..	..	..	..	..	6	9
Oman	..	..	..	..	..	9	..	..	..	42	43
Pakistan	22	23	31.3	41.5	4.8	32	37	..	97	51	39
Panama	18	17	..	..	..	10	..	..	4	..	..
Papua New Guinea	..	..	18.1	43.9	3.4	10	56	92	7	60	55
Paraguay	16	12	..	..	..	9	22	94	..	30	39
Peru	28	13	5.4	29.8	9.1	8	69	91	..	50	43
Philippines	21	15	26.2	27.9	2.0	20	34	81	86	36	44
Poland	<5	<5	..	..	..	..	..	..	..	23	25
Portugal	<5	<5	..	..	..	..	..	..	..	13	17
Puerto Rico	..	..	..	..	..	..	..	..	..	..	..
Qatar	..	..	..	..	..	..	..	..	..	..	29

	Prevalence of undernourishment		Prevalence of child malnutrition		Prevalence of overweight children	Low-birthweight babies	Exclusive breast-feeding	Consumption of iodized salt	Vitamin A supplementation	Prevalence of anemia %	
	% of population		% of children under age 5		% of children under age 5	% of births	% of children under 6 months	% of households	% of children 6–59 months	Children under age 5	Pregnant women
	1990–92	2004–06	Underweight 2000–08[a]	Stunting 2000–08[a]	2000–08[a]	2003–08[a]	2003–08[a]	2003–08[a]	2008	2000–06[a]	2000–06[a]
Romania	<5	<5	3.5	12.8	8.3	8	16	74	..	40	30
Russian Federation	<5	<5	..	..	..	6	..	..	..	27	21
Rwanda	45	40	18.0	51.7	6.7	6	88	88	89	56	..
Saudi Arabia	<5	<5	5.3	9.3	6.1	..	..	..	..	33	32
Senegal	28	25	14.5	20.1	2.4	19	34	41	90	70	58
Serbia	<5[d]	<5[d]	1.8	8.1	19.3	8	15	..	..	..	..
Sierra Leone	45	46	28.3	46.9	5.9	24	11	45	12	83	60
Singapore	..	..	3.3	4.4	2.6	..	..	..	..	19	24
Slovak Republic	<5	<5	..	..	..	..	..	..	..	23	25
Slovenia	<5	<5	..	..	..	..	..	..	..	14	19
Somalia	..	..	32.8	42.1	4.7	11	9	1	100	..	..
South Africa	<5	<5	..	..	..	..	8	..	39	..	22
Spain	<5	<5	..	..	..	..	..	..	..	13	18
Sri Lanka	27	21	21.1	17.3	1.6	18	76	94	64	30	29
Sudan	31	20	31.7	37.9	5.3	..	34	11	67	85	58
Swaziland	12	18	6.1	29.5	11.4	9	32	80	44	47	24
Sweden	<5	<5	..	..	..	..	..	..	..	9	13
Switzerland	<5	<5	..	..	..	..	..	..	..	6	..
Syrian Arab Republic	<5	<5	10.0	28.6	18.7	9	29	79	..	41	39
Tajikistan	34	26	14.9	33.1	6.7	10	25	49	87	38	45
Tanzania	28	35	16.7	44.4	4.9	10	41	43	93	72	58
Thailand	29	17	7.0	15.7	8.0	9	5	47	..	..	..
Timor-Leste	18	23	40.6	55.7	5.7	12	31	60	57	32	23
Togo	45	37	22.3	27.8	4.7	12	48	25	64	52	50
Trinidad and Tobago	11	10	4.4	5.3	4.9	19	13	28	..	30	30
Tunisia	<5	<5	3.3	9.0	8.8	5	6	..	..	..	..
Turkey	<5	<5	3.5	15.6	9.1	..	40	69	..	33	40
Turkmenistan	9	6	..	..	..	4	11	87	..	36	30
Uganda	19	15	16.4	38.7	4.9	14	60	96	67	73	64
Ukraine	<5	<5	4.1	22.9	26.5	4	18	18	..	22	27
United Arab Emirates	<5	<5	..	..	..	..	..	..	..	28	28
United Kingdom	<5	<5	..	..	..	..	..	..	..	..	15
United States	<5	<5	1.3	3.9	8.0	..	..	..	..	3	6
Uruguay	5	<5	6.0	13.9	9.4	9	57	..	..	19	27
Uzbekistan	5	13	4.4	19.6	12.8	5	26	53	38	38	..
Venezuela, RB	10	12	..	..	..	9	..	..	..	33	40
Vietnam	28	13	20.2	35.8	2.5	7	17	93	98[b]	34	32
West Bank and Gaza	8	15	2.2	11.8	11.4	7	27	86	..	..	..
Yemen, Rep.	30	32	43.1	57.7	5.0	..	12	30	47[b]	68	58
Zambia	40	45	14.9	45.8	8.4	11	61	..	96	53	..
Zimbabwe	40	39	14.0	35.8	9.1	11	22	91	20	58	47
World	**17 w**	**14 w**	**22.4 w**	**34.6 w**	**6.3 w**	**15 w**	**39 w**	**71 w**	**.. w**	**.. w**	**.. w**
Low income	35	30	27.5	43.6	4.7	15	37	62	81	..	..
Middle income	16	13	22.2	33.6	6.7	16	40	73	..	..	..
Lower middle income	19	15	25.1	36.8	6.4	17	40	72	..	..	..
Upper middle income	8	6	3.8	13.5	8.8	7	..	73	..	38	30
Low & middle income	19	16	23.5	36.1	6.2	15	39	71	..	..	..
East Asia & Pacific	18	12	11.9	27.4	8.1	6	42	86	..	20	29
Europe & Central Asia	7	6	..	..	..	6	..	50	..	30	30
Latin America & Carib.	12	9	4.5	15.9	7.2	9	..	89	..	..	..
Middle East & N. Africa	7	7	12.2	30.0	15.3	11	29	67	..	48	..
South Asia	25	22	41.1	46.6	2.2	27	45	55	65	74	50
Sub-Saharan Africa	31	28	25.3	43.3	6.0	14	31	60	73	..	..
High income	5	5	..	..	..	..	..	..	..	..	13
Euro area	5	5	..	..	..	..	..	..	..	10	14

a. Data are for the most recent year available. b. Country's vitamin A supplementation programs do not target children all the way up to 59 months of age. c. Includes Hong Kong SAR, China; Macau SAR, China; and Taiwan, China. d. Includes Montenegro.

Data on undernourishment are from the Food and Agriculture Organization (FAO) of the United Nations and measure food deprivation based on average food available for human consumption per person, the level of inequality in access to food, and the minimum calories required for an average person.

From a policy and program standpoint, however, this measure has its limits. First, food insecurity exists even where food availability is not a problem because of inadequate access of poor households to food. Second, food insecurity is an individual or household phenomenon, and the average food available to each person, even corrected for possible effects of low income, is not a good predictor of food insecurity among the population. And third, nutrition security is determined not only by food security but also by the quality of care of mothers and children and the quality of the household's health environment (Smith and Haddad 2000).

Estimates of child malnutrition, based on weight for age (underweight) and height for age (stunting), are from national survey data. The proportion of underweight children is the most common malnutrition indicator. Being even mildly underweight increases the risk of death and inhibits cognitive development in children. And it perpetuates the problem across generations, as malnourished women are more likely to have low-birthweight babies. Height for age reflects linear growth achieved pre- and postnatally; a deficit indicates long-term, cumulative effects of inadequate health, diet, or care. Stunting is often used as a proxy for multifaceted deprivation and as an indicator of long-term changes in malnutrition.

Estimates of overweight children are also from national survey data. Overweight children have become a growing concern in developing countries. Research shows an association between childhood obesity and a high prevalence of diabetes, respiratory disease, high blood pressure, and psychosocial and orthopedic disorders (de Onis and Blössner 2000).

New international growth reference standards for infants and young children were released in 2006 by the World Health Organization (WHO) to monitor children's nutritional status. They are also key in monitoring health targets for the Millennium Development Goals. Differences in growth to age 5 are influenced more by nutrition, feeding practices, environment, and healthcare than by genetics or ethnicity. The previously reported data were based on the U.S. National Center for Health Statistics–WHO growth reference. Because of the change in standards, the data in this edition should not be compared with data in editions prior to 2008.

Low birthweight, which is associated with maternal malnutrition, raises the risk of infant mortality and stunts growth in infancy and childhood. There is also emerging evidence that low-birthweight babies are more prone to noncommunicable diseases such as diabetes and cardiovascular diseases. Estimates of low-birthweight infants are drawn mostly from hospital records and household surveys. Many births in developing countries take place at home and are seldom recorded. A hospital birth may indicate higher income and therefore better nutrition, or it could indicate a higher risk birth, possibly skewing the data on birthweights downward. The data should therefore be used with caution.

Improved breastfeeding can save an estimated 1.3 million children a year. Breast milk alone contains all the nutrients, antibodies, hormones, and antioxidants an infant needs to thrive. It protects babies from diarrhea and acute respiratory infections, stimulates their immune systems and response to vaccination, and may confer cognitive benefits. The data on breastfeeding are derived from national surveys.

Iodine deficiency is the single most important cause of preventable mental retardation, and it contributes significantly to the risk of stillbirth and miscarriage. Widely used and inexpensive, iodized salt is the best source of iodine, and a global campaign to iodize edible salt is significantly reducing the risks (www.childinfo.org). The data on iodized salt are derived from household surveys.

Vitamin A is essential for immune system functioning. Vitamin A deficiency, a leading cause of blindness, also causes a 23 percent greater risk of dying from a range of childhood ailments such as measles, malaria, and diarrhea. Giving vitamin A to new breastfeeding mothers helps protect their children during the first months of life. Food fortification with vitamin A is being introduced in many developing countries.

Data on anemia are compiled by the WHO based mainly on nationally representative surveys between 1993 and 2005, which measured hemoglobin in the blood. WHO's hemoglobin thresholds were then used to determine anemia status based on age, sex, and physiological status. Children under age 5 and pregnant women have the highest risk for anemia. Data should be used with caution because surveys differ in quality, coverage, age group interviewed, and treatment of missing values across countries and over time.

For indicators from household surveys, the year in the table refers to the survey year. For more information, consult the original sources.

• **Prevalence of undernourishment** is the percentage of the population whose dietary energy consumption is continuously below a minimum requirement for maintaining a healthy life and carrying out light physical activity with an acceptable minimum weight for height. • **Prevalence of child malnutrition** is the percentage of children under age 5 whose weight for age (underweight) or height for age (stunting) is more than two standard deviations below the median for the international reference population ages 0–59 months. Height is measured by recumbent length for children up to two years old and by stature while standing for older children. Data are for the WHO child growth standards released in 2006. • **Prevalence of overweight children** is the percentage of children under age 5 whose weight for height is more than two standard deviations above the median for the international reference population of the corresponding age as established by the WHO child growth standards released in 2006. • **Low-birthweight babies** are the percentage of newborns weighing less than 2.5 kilograms within the first hours of life, before significant postnatal weight loss has occurred. • **Exclusive breastfeeding** is the percentage of children less than six months old who were fed breast milk alone (no other liquids) in the past 24 hours. • **Consumption of iodized salt** is the percentage of households that use edible salt fortified with iodine. • **Vitamin A supplementation** is the percentage of children ages 6–59 months old who received at least one dose of vitamin A in the previous six months, as reported by mothers. • **Prevalence of anemia, children under age 5,** is the percentage of children under age 5 whose hemoglobin level is less than 110 grams per liter at sea level. • **Prevalence of anemia, pregnant women,** is the percentage of pregnant women whose hemoglobin level is less than 110 grams per liter at sea level.

Data sources

Data on undernourishment are from www.fao.org/faostat/foodsecurity/index_en.htm. Data on malnutrition and overweight children are from the WHO's Global Database on Child Growth and Malnutrition (www.who.int/nutgrowthdb). Data on low-birthweight babies, breastfeeding, iodized salt consumption, and vitamin A supplementation are from the United Nations Children's Fund's *State of the World's Children 2010* and Childinfo. Data on anemia are from the WHO's *Worldwide Prevalence of Anemia 1993–2005* (2008) and Integrated WHO Nutrition Global Databases.

	Prevalence of smoking		Incidence of tuberculosis	Prevalence of diabetes	Prevalence of HIV						Condom use	
	% of adults		per 100,000 people	% of population ages 20–79	Total % of population ages 15–49		Female % of total population with HIV		Youth % of population ages 15–24		% of population ages 15–24	
	Male	Female							Male	Female	Male	Female
	2006	2006	2008	2010	1990	2007	2001	2007	2007	2007	2000–08[a]	2000–08[a]
Afghanistan	..	..	189	8.6	..	..	..	..	..	..	..	..
Albania	43	4	16	4.5	..	..	..	..	..	..	..	..
Algeria	26	0[b]	58	8.5	..	0.1	25.0	28.6	0.1	0.1	..	..
Angola	..	..	292	3.5	0.3	2.1	60.9	61.1	0.2	0.3	..	..
Argentina	34	24	30	5.7	0.2	0.5	25.0	26.7	0.6	0.3	..	..
Armenia	61	3	73	7.8	..	0.1	<27.8	<41.7	0.2	0.1	32	7
Australia	22	19	7	5.7	0.1	0.2	<7.1	6.7	0.2	<0.1	..	..
Austria	47	41	0	8.9	<0.1	0.2	27.3	29.6	0.2	0.1	..	..
Azerbaijan	..	..	110	7.5	..	0.2	..	16.7	0.3	0.1	25	1
Bangladesh	43	1	225	6.6	..	..	<1.3	16.7	..	..	..	..
Belarus	64	22	43	7.6	..	0.2	27.5	30.0	0.3	0.1	..	..
Belgium	30	24	9	5.3	0.1	0.2	26.2	27.3	0.2	0.1	..	..
Benin	13	1	92	4.6	0.1	1.2	63.3	62.7	0.3	0.9	39	10
Bolivia	34	26	144	6.0	0.1	0.2	24.6	27.8	0.2	0.1	29	10
Bosnia and Herzegovina	49	35	51	7.1	..	<0.1	..	..	..	..	..	..
Botswana	..	..	712	5.4	4.7	23.9	59.3	60.7	5.1	15.3	..	..
Brazil	19	12	46	6.4	0.4	0.6	34.4	33.8	1.0	0.6	..	..
Bulgaria	49	38	43	6.5	..	..	..	..	..	..	..	..
Burkina Faso	13	1	220	3.8	1.9	1.6	45.4	50.8	0.5	0.9	54	17
Burundi	..	..	357	1.8	1.7	2.0	59.2	58.9	0.4	1.3	..	..
Cambodia	46	6	490	5.2	0.7	0.8	25.8	28.6	0.8	0.3	31	3
Cameroon	9	1	187	3.9	0.8	5.1	61.2	60.0	1.2	4.3	52	24
Canada	21	18	5	9.2	0.2	0.4	26.5	27.4	0.4	0.2	..	..
Central African Republic	..	..	336	4.5	1.8	6.3	66.7	65.0	1.1	5.5	..	..
Chad	12	1	291	3.7	0.7	3.5	60.7	61.1	2.0	2.8	18	7
Chile	42	31	11	5.7	<0.1	0.3	26.0	28.1	0.3	0.2	..	..
China	59	4	97	4.2	..	0.1[c]	25.5[c]	29.0[c]	0.1[c]	0.1[c]	..	..
Hong Kong SAR, China	..	..	91	8.5	..	..	..	..	..	..	..	..
Colombia	..	..	36	5.2	0.1	0.6	26.9	29.4	0.7	0.3	..	23
Congo, Dem. Rep.	10	1	382	3.2	..	..	..	..	..	..	16	26
Congo, Rep.	9	0[b]	393	5.1	5.1	3.5	58.4	58.9	0.8	2.3	36	16
Costa Rica	26	7	11	9.3	0.1	0.4	27.5	28.1	0.4	0.2	..	..
Côte d'Ivoire	11	1	410	4.7	2.2	3.9	58.2	59.5	0.8	2.4	..	..
Croatia	39	29	25	6.9	..	<0.1	..	..	..	..	..	..
Cuba	36	28	6	9.5	..	0.1	<43.5	29.0	0.1	0.1	..	..
Czech Republic	35	27	9	6.4	..	..	<38.5	<33.3	<0.1	..	..	..
Denmark	35	30	7	5.6	0.1	0.2	..	22.9	0.2	0.1	..	..
Dominican Republic	15	11	73	11.2	0.6	1.1	54.0	50.8	0.3	0.6	58	19
Ecuador	23	5	72	5.9	0.1	0.3	25.8	28.4	0.4	0.2	..	..
Egypt, Arab Rep.	24	1	20	11.4	..	..	26.8	28.9	..	..	..	..
El Salvador	..	..	32	9.0	0.1	0.8	25.7	28.5	0.9	0.5	..	..
Eritrea	15	1	97	2.5	0.1	1.3	60.0	60.0	0.3	0.9	..	2
Estonia	48	25	34	7.6	..	1.3	<28.6	24.2	1.6	0.7	..	..
Ethiopia	8	1	368	2.5	0.7	2.1	59.5	59.6	0.5	1.5	18	2
Finland	33	23	7	5.7	..	0.1	<50.0	<41.7	0.1	<0.1	..	..
France	36	27	6	6.7	0.1	0.4	25.0	27.1	0.4	0.2	..	..
Gabon	..	..	452	5.0	0.9	5.9	58.3	58.7	1.3	3.9	..	..
Gambia, The	17	1	263	4.3	..	0.9	59.0	60.0	0.2	0.6	..	..
Georgia	57	6	107	7.5	..	0.1	20.0	37.0	0.1	0.1	..	..
Germany	37	26	5	8.9	<0.1	0.1	27.3	28.8	0.1	0.1	..	..
Ghana	7	1	202	4.3	0.1	1.9	58.3	60.0	0.4	1.3	45	19
Greece	63	39	6	6.0	0.1	0.2	26.5	27.3	0.2	0.1	..	..
Guatemala	24	4	63	8.6	<0.1	0.8	97.9	98.1	..	1.5	..	..
Guinea	..	..	302	4.3	0.2	1.6	59.6	59.3	0.4	1.2	35	10
Guinea-Bissau	..	..	224	3.9	0.2	1.8	59.2	58.0	0.4	1.2	..	..
Haiti	..	..	246	7.2	1.2	2.2	45.7	52.7	0.6	1.4	42	37
Honduras	..	..	64	9.1	1.3	0.7	25.7	28.5	0.7	0.4	..	7

Health risk factors and future challenges

	Prevalence of smoking		Incidence of tuberculosis	Prevalence of diabetes	Prevalence of HIV						Condom use	
					Total % of population ages 15–49		Female % of total population with HIV		Youth % of population ages 15–24		% of population ages 15–24	
	% of adults		per 100,000 people	% of population ages 20–79					Male	Female	Male	Female
	Male 2006	Female 2006	2008	2010	1990	2007	2001	2007	2007	2007	2000–08[a]	2000–08[a]
Hungary	45	35[b]	16	6.4	..	0.1	<35.7	<30.3	0.1	<0.1	..	..
India	28	1	168	7.8	0.1	0.3	38.5	38.3	0.3	0.3	37	18
Indonesia	58	4	189	4.8	..	0.2	10.8	20.0	0.3	0.1	..	1
Iran, Islamic Rep.	24	2	20	8.0	..	0.2	26.7	28.2	0.2	0.1	..	..
Iraq	29	3	64	10.2	..	..	..	..	..	..	..	..
Ireland	34	28	9	5.2	..	0.2	26.1	27.3	0.2	0.1	..	..
Israel	31	18	6	6.5	<0.1	0.1	60.0	59.2	<0.1	0.1	..	..
Italy	34	19	7	5.9	0.4	0.4	25.7	27.3	0.4	0.2	..	..
Jamaica	18	8	7	10.6	0.3	1.6	26.4	29.2	1.7	0.9	74	66
Japan	42	13	22	5.0	..	..	22.2	24.0	..	..	..	..
Jordan	59	10	6	10.1	..	..	..	..	..	..	..	4
Kazakhstan	43	9	175	5.8	..	0.1	<29.4	27.5	0.2	0.1	..	..
Kenya	23	1	328	3.5	..	..	..	..	..	..	39	9
Korea, Dem. Rep.	58	..	344	5.3	..	..	..	..	..	..	..	..
Korea, Rep.	53	6	88	7.9	..	<0.1	26.5	27.7	<0.1	<0.1	..	..
Kosovo	..	..	..	..	..	..	..	..	..	..	..	..
Kuwait	36	4	34	14.6	..	..	..	..	..	..	..	..
Kyrgyz Republic	46	2	159	5.2	..	0.1	<50	26.2	0.2	0.1	..	..
Lao PDR	60	13	150	5.6	..	0.2	<45.5	24.1	0.2	0.1	..	..
Latvia	53	24	50	7.6	..	0.8	<23.8	27.0	0.9	0.5	..	..
Lebanon	31	7	14	7.8	<0.1	0.1	<45.5	<33.3	0.1	0.1	..	..
Lesotho	..	..	635	3.9	0.8	23.2	58.3	57.7	5.9	14.9	44	26
Liberia	10	..	283	4.7	0.4	1.7	59.1	59.4	0.4	1.3	19	9
Libya	..	..	17	9.0	..	..	..	..	..	..	..	..
Lithuania	50	22	71	7.6	..	0.1	<35.7	<45.5	0.1	0.1	..	..
Macedonia, FYR	..	..	24	6.9	..	<0.1	..	..	..	..	..	..
Madagascar	..	..	256	3.2	..	0.1	23.8	26.2	0.2	0.1	8	2
Malawi	17	2	324	2.3	2.1	11.9	56.4	58.3	2.4	8.4	32	9
Malaysia	49	2	102	11.6	0.1	0.5	23.3	26.6	0.6	0.3	..	..
Mali	13	1	322	4.2	0.2	1.5	60.5	60.2	0.4	1.1	29	4
Mauritania	24	1	324	4.8	<0.1	0.8	25.8	27.9	0.9	0.5	..	..
Mauritius	34	1	22	16.2	<0.1	1.7	<27.8	29.2	1.8	1.0	..	..
Mexico	36	12	19	10.8	0.2	0.3	27.1	28.5	0.3	0.2	..	..
Moldova	45	5	175	7.6	..	0.4	<50.0	29.5	0.4	0.2	55	22
Mongolia	46	6	205	1.6	..	0.1	..	<20.0	0.1	..	..	..
Morocco	27	0[b]	116	8.3	..	0.1	27.5	28.1	0.1	0.1	..	..
Mozambique	19	1	420	4.0	1.4	12.5	59.4	57.9	2.9	8.5	27	12
Myanmar	40	13	404	3.2	0.4	0.7	33.4	41.7	0.7	0.6	..	..
Namibia	22	8	747	4.4	1.2	15.3	60.7	61.1	3.4	10.3	81	64
Nepal	30	28	163	3.9	<0.1	0.5	21.8	25.0	0.5	0.3	24	8
Netherlands	33	28	7	5.3	0.1	0.2	25.6	27.2	0.2	0.1	..	..
New Zealand	22	20	8	5.2	0.1	0.1	<16.7	<35.7	0.1	..	..	..
Nicaragua	..	..	46	10.0	<0.1	0.2	25.6	28.0	0.3	0.1	..	7
Niger	..	..	178	3.9	0.1	0.8	29.3	30.4	0.9	0.5	..	..
Nigeria	8	0[b]	303	4.7	0.7	3.1	60.0	58.3	0.8	2.3	38	8
Norway	30	30	6	3.6	<0.1	0.1	<41.7	<33.3	0.1	0.1	..	..
Oman	20	0[b]	14	13.4	..	..	..	..	..	..	..	..
Pakistan	30	3	231	9.1	..	0.1	26.0	28.7	0.1	0.1	..	..
Panama	..	..	47	9.6	0.4	1.0	26.9	28.9	1.1	0.6	..	..
Papua New Guinea	..	..	250	3.0	..	1.5	34.7	39.6	0.6	0.7	..	..
Paraguay	33	14	47	4.9	<0.1	0.6	26.4	29.0	0.7	0.3	..	..
Peru	..	..	119	6.2	0.1	0.5	26.8	28.4	0.5	0.3	..	9
Philippines	50	11	285	7.7	..	..	<50	26.8	..	..	13	3
Poland	30	38	25	7.6	..	0.1	26.0	28.9	0.1	0.1	..	..
Portugal	34	15	30	9.7	0.2	0.5	26.6	27.6	0.5	0.3	..	..
Puerto Rico	..	..	3	10.6	..	..	..	..	..	..	..	..
Qatar	..	..	55	15.4	..	..	..	..	..	..	..	..

2.21 Health risk factors and future challenges

	Prevalence of smoking % of adults		Incidence of tuberculosis per 100,000 people	Prevalence of diabetes % of population ages 20–79	Prevalence of HIV Total % of population ages 15–49		Female % of total population with HIV		Youth % of population ages 15–24		Condom use % of population ages 15–24	
	Male 2006	Female 2006	2008	2010	1990	2007	2001	2007	Male 2007	Female 2007	Male 2000–08ᵃ	Female 2000–08ᵃ
Romania	46	24	134	6.9	..	0.1	50.7	50.0	0.2	0.2	..	..
Russian Federation	70	28	107	7.6	..	1.1	22.1	25.5	1.3	0.6	..	..
Rwanda	..	..	387	1.6	9.2	2.8	60.6	60.0	0.5	1.4	19	5
Saudi Arabia	22	3	19	16.8	..	..	..	..	..	..	..	..
Senegal	13	1	277	4.7	0.1	1.0	60.9	59.4	0.3	0.8	48	5
Serbia	40	27	18	6.9ᵈ	<0.1	0.1	25.5	28.1	0.1	0.1	..	..
Sierra Leone	..	..	608	4.4	0.2	1.7	59.4	58.8	0.4	1.3	..	..
Singapore	34	5	39	10.2	..	0.2	<34.5	29.3	0.2	0.1	..	..
Slovak Republic	41	20	12	6.4	..	<0.1	..	..	..	..	..	..
Slovenia	32	21	12	7.7	..	<0.1	..	..	..	..	..	..
Somalia	..	..	388	3.0	<0.1	0.5	26.5	27.9	0.6	0.3	..	..
South Africa	27	8	960	4.5	0.8	18.1	58.7	59.3	4.0	12.7	57	46
Spain	37	27	17	6.6	0.4	0.5	20.8	20.0	0.6	0.2	..	..
Sri Lanka	27	0ᵇ	66	10.9	..	..	<33.3	37.8	<0.1	..	..	..
Sudan	25	2	119	4.2	0.8	1.4	56.0	58.6	0.3	1.0	..	..
Swaziland	21	2	1,227	4.2	0.9	26.1	60.7	58.8	5.8	22.6	66	44
Sweden	17	23	6	5.2	0.1	0.1	43.4	46.8	0.1	0.1	..	..
Switzerland	32	23	5	8.9	0.4	0.6	33.2	36.8	0.4	0.5	..	..
Syrian Arab Republic	40	..	22	10.8	..	..	..	..	..	..	..	..
Tajikistan	..	..	199	5.0	..	0.3	<20.8	21.0	0.4	0.1	..	..
Tanzania	20	2	190	3.2	4.8	6.2	61.7	58.5	0.5	0.9	36	13
Thailand	40	2	137	7.1	1.0	1.4	36.9	41.7	1.2	1.2	..	..
Timor-Leste	..	..	498	3.5	..	..	..	..	..	..	..	..
Togo	..	..	438	4.3	0.7	3.3	61.0	57.5	0.8	2.4	..	..
Trinidad and Tobago	..	..	24	11.7	0.2	1.5	57.5	59.2	0.3	1.0	..	..
Tunisia	53	6	24	9.3	..	0.1	<45.5	27.8	0.1	<0.1	..	..
Turkey	51	20	30	8.0	..	..	..	..	..	..	..	..
Turkmenistan	..	..	68	5.3	..	<0.1	..	..	..	..	..	1
Uganda	17	2	311	2.2	13.7	5.4	58.9	59.3	1.3	3.9	56	39
Ukraine	65	24	102	7.6	..	1.6	35.7	44.2	1.5	1.5	69	73
United Arab Emirates	24	2	6	18.7	..	..	..	..	..	..	..	..
United Kingdom	26	24	12	3.6	<0.1	0.2	..	..	..	..	..	..
United States	25	19	5	10.3	0.5	0.6	18.0	20.9	0.7	0.3	..	..
Uruguay	39	29	22	5.7	0.1	0.6	25.4	28.0	0.6	0.3	..	..
Uzbekistan	23	3	128	5.2	..	0.1	<35.7	28.8	0.1	0.1	18	2
Venezuela, RB	32	27	33	6.5	..	..	..	..	..	..	..	..
Vietnam	41	2	200	3.5	0.1	0.5	24.7	27.1	0.6	0.3	16	8
West Bank and Gaza	..	..	19	8.6	..	..	..	..	..	..	..	..
Yemen, Rep.	28	6	88	3.0	..	..	..	..	..	..	..	..
Zambia	17	2	468	4.0	8.9	15.2	54.7	57.1	3.6	11.3	47	39
Zimbabwe	28	2	762	4.1	14.2	15.3	58.8	56.7	2.9	7.7	52	9
World	**39 w**	**8 w**	**139 w**	**6.4 w**	**0.3 w**	**0.8 w**	**30.8 w**	**32.9 w**	**0.5 w**	**0.7 w**	..	..
Low income	29	3	282	4.3	2.1	2.3	35.0	39.2	..	..	..	..
Middle income	42	6	137	6.4	0.1	0.6	31.6	33.4	0.4	0.6	..	..
Lower middle income	43	3	145	6.2	0.1	0.4	31.8	33.7	0.3	0.4	..	..
Upper middle income	39	18	106	7.5	..	1.5	30.8	32.0	0.9	1.3	..	..
Low & middle income	40	6	162	6.1	0.4	0.9	32.1	34.2	0.5	0.7	..	..
East Asia & Pacific	56	4	138	4.6	0.1	0.2	25.5	28.5	0.2	0.2	..	..
Europe & Central Asia	55	24	87	7.3	..	0.6	28.6	30.5	0.8	0.5	..	..
Latin America & Carib.	27	15	47	7.4	0.3	0.5	32.1	32.8	0.7	0.4	..	..
Middle East & N. Africa	28	2	44	9.1	..	0.1	27.9	28.6	..	..	..	..
South Asia	30	2	180	7.8	0.1	0.3	32.8	34.6	0.3	0.3	36	17
Sub-Saharan Africa	14	2	352	3.8	2.1	5.0	57.1	56.9	1.1	3.3	36	15
High income	33	20	14	7.9	0.3	0.3	23.3	24.9	0.5	0.2	..	..
Euro area	37	25	8	7.1	0.2	0.3	25.8	26.9	0.3	0.2	..	..

a. Data are for the most recent year available. b. Less than 0.5. c. Includes Hong Kong SAR, China.

The limited availability of data on health status is a major constraint in assessing the health situation in developing countries. Surveillance data are lacking for many major public health concerns. Estimates of prevalence and incidence are available for some diseases but are often unreliable and incomplete. National health authorities differ widely in capacity and willingness to collect or report information. To compensate for this and improve reliability and international comparability, the World Health Organization (WHO) prepares estimates in accordance with epidemiological models and statistical standards.

Smoking is the most common form of tobacco use and the prevalence of smoking is therefore a good measure of the tobacco epidemic (Corrao and others 2000). Tobacco use causes heart and other vascular diseases and cancers of the lung and other organs. Given the long delay between starting to smoke and the onset of disease, the health impact of smoking in developing countries will increase rapidly only in the next few decades. Because the data present a one-time estimate, with no information on intensity or duration of smoking, and because the definition of adult varies, the data should be used with caution.

Tuberculosis is one of the main causes of adult deaths from a single infectious agent in developing countries. In developed countries tuberculosis has reemerged largely as a result of cases among immigrants. Since tuberculosis incidence cannot be directly measured, estimates are obtained by eliciting expert opinion or are derived from measurements of prevalence or mortality. These estimates include uncertainty intervals, which are not shown in the table.

Diabetes, an important cause of ill health and a risk factor for other diseases in developed countries, is spreading rapidly in developing countries. Highest among the elderly, prevalence rates are rising among younger and productive populations in developing countries. Economic development has led to the spread of Western lifestyles and diet to developing countries, resulting in a substantial increase in diabetes. Without effective prevention and control programs, diabetes will likely continue to increase. Data are estimated based on sample surveys.

Adult HIV prevalence rates reflect the rate of HIV infection in each country's population. Low national prevalence rates can be misleading, however. They often disguise epidemics that are initially concentrated in certain localities or population groups and threaten to spill over into the wider population. In many developing countries most new infections occur in young adults, with young women especially vulnerable.

The Joint United Nations Programme on HIV/AIDS (UNAIDS) and the WHO estimate HIV prevalence from sentinel surveillance, population-based surveys, and special studies. Since the 2009 edition the estimates in the table have been more reliable than previous estimates because of expanded sentinel surveillance and improved data quality. Findings from population-based HIV surveys, which are geographically more representative than sentinel surveillance and include both men and women, influenced a downward adjustment to prevalence rates based on sentinel surveillance. And assumptions about the average time people living with HIV survive without antiretroviral treatment were improved in the most recent model. Thus, estimates in this edition should not be compared with estimates in previous editions.

Estimates from recent Demographic and Health Surveys that have collected data on HIV/AIDS differ somewhat from those of UNAIDS and the WHO, which are based on surveillance systems that focus on pregnant women who attend sentinel antenatal clinics. Caution should be used in comparing the two sets of estimates. Demographic and Health Surveys are household surveys that use a representative sample from the whole population, whereas surveillance data from antenatal clinics are limited to pregnant women. Household surveys also frequently provide better coverage of rural populations. However, respondents who refuse to participate or are absent from the household add considerable uncertainty to survey-based HIV estimates, because the possible association of absence or refusal with higher HIV prevalence is unknown. UNAIDS and the WHO estimate HIV prevalence for the adult population (ages 15–49) by assuming that prevalence among pregnant women is a good approximation of prevalence among men and women. However, this assumption might not apply to all countries or over time. Other potential biases are associated with the use of antenatal clinic data, such as differences among women who attend antenatal clinics and those who do not.

Data on condom use are from household surveys and refer to condom use at last intercourse. However, condoms are not as effective at preventing transmission of HIV unless used consistently. Some surveys have asked directly about consistent use, but the question is subject to recall and other biases. Caution should be used in interpreting the data.

For indicators from household surveys, the year in the table refers to the survey year. For more information, consult the original sources.

• **Prevalence of smoking** is the adjusted and age-standardized prevalence estimate of smoking among adults. The age range varies but in most countries is 18 and older or 15 and older. • **Incidence of tuberculosis** is the estimated number of new tuberculosis cases (pulmonary, smear positive, extrapulmonary). • **Prevalence of diabetes** refers to the percentage of people ages 20–79 who have type 1 or type 2 diabetes. • **Prevalence of HIV** is the percentage of people who are infected with HIV. Total and youth rates are percentages of the relevant age group. Female rate is as a percentage of the total population with HIV. • **Condom use** is the percentage of the population ages 15–24 who used a condom at last intercourse in the last 12 months.

Data sources

Data on smoking are from the WHO's *Report on the Global Tobacco Epidemic 2009: Implementing Smoke-Free Environments*. Data on tuberculosis are from the WHO's *Global Tuberculosis Control Report 2009*. Data on diabetes are from the International Diabetes Federation's *Diabetes Atlas*, 3rd edition. Data on prevalence of HIV are from UNAIDS and the WHO's *2008 Report on the Global AIDS Epidemic*. Data on condom use are from Demographic and Health Surveys by Macro International.

Mortality

	Life expectancy at birth		Infant mortality rate		Under-five mortality rate		Child mortality rate		Adult mortality rate		Survival to age 65	
	years		per 1,000 live births		per 1,000		per 1,000 Male	Female	per 1,000 Male	Female	% of cohort Male	Female
	1990	2008	1990	2008	1990	2008	2003–08[a,b]	2003–08[a,b]	2005–08[a]	2005–08[a]	2008	2008
Afghanistan	41	44	168	165	260	257	..	..	439	412	34	36
Albania	72	77	37	13	46	14	3	1	100	52	82	90
Algeria	67	72	52	36	64	41	..	..	120	101	78	82
Angola	42	47	154	130	260	220	..	..	409	353	37	44
Argentina	72	75	25	15	29	16	..	..	165	77	74	87
Armenia	68	74	48	21	56	23	8	3	165	80	72	85
Australia	77	81	8	5	9	6	..	..	82	47	88	93
Austria	76	80	8	3	9	4	..	..	111	55	85	93
Azerbaijan	65	70	78	32	98	36	9	5	181	110	69	79
Bangladesh	54	66	103	43	149	54	16	20	209	176	65	70
Belarus	71	71	20	11	24	13	..	..	330	115	53	83
Belgium	76	80	9	4	10	5	..	..	111	61	85	92
Benin	54	61	111	76	184	121	64	65	211	174	61	67
Bolivia	59	66	88	46	122	54	18	20	235	175	63	71
Bosnia and Herzegovina	67	75	21	13	23	15	..	..	135	62	78	89
Botswana	64	54	39	26	50	31	..	..	487	497	42	44
Brazil	66	72	46	18	56	22	..	..	230	120	67	80
Bulgaria	72	73	15	9	18	11	..	..	213	91	71	87
Burkina Faso	47	53	110	92	201	169	110	113	335	280	45	51
Burundi	46	50	113	102	189	168	65	65	387	353	41	46
Cambodia	55	61	85	69	117	90	20	20	294	223	55	63
Cameroon	55	51	92	82	149	131	73	72	406	402	42	45
Canada	77	81	7	6	8	6	..	..	92	56	86	92
Central African Republic	49	47	116	115	178	173	74	82	456	428	35	40
Chad	51	49	120	124	201	209	96	101	361	319	41	47
Chile	74	79	18	7	22	9	..	..	129	64	80	90
China	68[c]	73[c]	37	18	46	21	..	..	149[c]	89[c]	76[c]	83[c]
Hong Kong SAR, China	77	82	..	..	..	..	..	..	76	33	87	94
Colombia	68	73	28	16	35	20	4	3	200	93	71	84
Congo, Dem. Rep.	48	48	126	126	199	199	70	64	400	350	38	44
Congo, Rep.	59	54	67	80	104	127	49	43	377	354	45	49
Costa Rica	76	79	19	10	22	11	..	..	113	59	82	90
Côte d'Ivoire	58	57	104	81	150	114	..	..	313	278	52	58
Croatia	72	76	11	5	13	6	..	..	147	58	77	90
Cuba	75	79	11	5	14	6	..	..	109	68	83	89
Czech Republic	71	77	10	3	12	4	..	..	143	65	79	90
Denmark	75	79	7	4	9	4	..	..	116	69	83	89
Dominican Republic	68	73	48	27	62	33	6	4	206	136	70	79
Ecuador	69	75	41	21	53	25	5	5	166	87	76	85
Egypt, Arab Rep.	63	70	66	20	90	23	5	5	163	107	72	80
El Salvador	66	71	48	16	62	18	..	..	288	123	63	80
Eritrea	48	59	92	41	150	58	..	..	381	286	46	57
Estonia	69	74	14	4	18	6	..	..	283	92	64	87
Ethiopia	47	55	124	69	210	109	56	56	339	297	48	54
Finland	75	80	6	3	7	3	..	..	133	57	83	93
France[d]	77	82	7	3	9	4	..	..	121	55	85	93
Gabon	61	60	67	57	92	77	..	..	323	278	55	61
Gambia, The	51	56	104	80	153	106	46	39	329	269	47	55
Georgia	70	72	41	26	47	30	5	4	198	78	69	84
Germany	75	80	7	4	9	4	..	..	107	56	85	92
Ghana	57	57	75	51	118	76	38	28	327	289	51	55
Greece	77	80	9	3	11	4	..	..	93	38	85	93
Guatemala	62	70	58	29	77	35	..	..	234	128	67	79
Guinea	48	58	137	90	231	146	89	86	256	198	54	63
Guinea-Bissau	44	48	142	117	240	195	110	88	403	350	38	44
Haiti	55	61	105	54	151	72	33	36	287	225	56	64
Honduras	66	72	43	26	55	31	8	9	172	120	73	80

	Life expectancy at birth		Infant mortality rate		Under-five mortality rate		Child mortality rate		Adult mortality rate		Survival to age 65	
	years		per 1,000 live births		per 1,000		per 1,000 Male	Female	per 1,000 Male	Female	% of cohort Male	Female
	1990	2008	1990	2008	1990	2008	2003–08[a,b]	2003–08[a,b]	2005–08[a]	2005–08[a]	2008	2008
Hungary	69	74	15	5	17	7	..	..	250	104	67	86
India	58	64	83	52	116	69	9	12	261	174	58	68
Indonesia	62	71	56	31	86	41	13	12	166	116	72	80
Iran, Islamic Rep.	65	71	55	27	73	32	..	..	144	99	75	81
Iraq	65	68	42	36	53	44	6	7	226	107	64	81
Ireland	75	80	8	3	9	4	..	..	88	56	87	92
Israel	77	81	10	4	11	5	..	..	86	48	87	93
Italy	77	82	9	3	10	4	..	..	82	43	86	94
Jamaica	71	72	28	26	33	31	5	6	225	117	69	81
Japan	79	83	5	3	6	4	..	..	87	43	87	94
Jordan	67	73	31	17	38	20	2	3	162	112	73	81
Kazakhstan	68	66	51	27	60	30	5	4	405	153	46	75
Kenya	60	54	68	81	105	128	42	39	402	412	46	47
Korea, Dem. Rep.	70	67	42	42	55	55	..	..	172	120	66	76
Korea, Rep.	71	80	8	5	9	5	..	..	106	42	83	93
Kosovo	68	69	..	..	..	..	..	..	..	..	..	..
Kuwait	75	78	13	9	15	11	..	..	85	52	85	90
Kyrgyz Republic	68	67	63	33	75	38	8	4	262	125	61	77
Lao PDR	54	65	108	48	157	61	..	..	226	184	63	69
Latvia	69	72	13	8	17	9	..	..	311	114	63	85
Lebanon	69	72	33	12	40	13	..	..	152	100	74	82
Lesotho	59	45	80	63	101	79	22	19	674	630	24	30
Liberia	49	58	146	100	219	145	62	64	255	209	56	62
Libya	68	74	33	15	38	17	..	..	147	91	75	84
Lithuania	71	72	12	6	16	7	..	..	346	116	59	86
Macedonia, FYR	71	74	32	10	36	11	2	1	134	80	77	85
Madagascar	51	60	101	68	167	106	45	45	270	220	57	63
Malawi	49	53	133	65	225	100	52	54	448	403	42	48
Malaysia	70	74	16	6	18	6	..	..	150	86	76	85
Mali	43	48	139	103	250	194	117	114	389	358	38	42
Mauritania	56	57	81	75	129	118	53	44	308	241	49	58
Mauritius	69	73	21	15	24	17	..	..	228	113	67	81
Mexico	71	75	36	15	45	17	..	..	139	77	78	86
Moldova	67	68	30	15	37	17	7	4	283	127	59	78
Mongolia	61	67	71	34	98	41	11	10	291	184	57	71
Morocco	64	71	68	32	88	36	9	11	147	97	74	82
Mozambique	43	48	166	90	249	130	61	64	489	462	36	40
Myanmar	59	62	85	71	120	98	..	..	257	195	57	65
Namibia	62	61	49	31	72	42	24	19	346	327	54	59
Nepal	54	67	99	41	142	51	21	18	199	175	67	71
Netherlands	77	80	7	4	8	5	..	..	81	59	87	92
New Zealand	75	80	9	5	11	6	..	..	92	59	87	91
Nicaragua	64	73	51	23	68	27	..	..	205	116	71	81
Niger	42	51	144	79	305	167	138	135	351	302	43	48
Nigeria	45	48	120	96	230	186	91	93	406	382	39	42
Norway	77	81	7	3	9	4	..	..	81	53	87	92
Oman	70	76	23	10	31	12	..	..	98	73	82	87
Pakistan	61	67	101	72	130	89	14	22	165	133	68	71
Panama	72	76	24	19	31	23	..	..	137	73	79	87
Papua New Guinea	55	61	67	53	91	69	..	..	348	255	49	60
Paraguay	68	72	34	24	42	28	..	..	172	125	73	79
Peru	66	73	64	22	81	24	13	4	164	101	73	83
Philippines	65	72	42	26	61	32	10	9	156	102	73	82
Poland	71	76	15	6	17	7	..	..	209	80	72	89
Portugal	74	79	11	3	15	4	..	..	128	53	82	92
Puerto Rico	75	79	..	..	..	..	..	..	133	53	80	91
Qatar	70	76	17	9	20	10	..	..	111	102	81	83

2.22 Mortality

	Life expectancy at birth		Infant mortality rate		Under-five mortality rate		Child mortality rate		Adult mortality rate		Survival to age 65	
	years		per 1,000 live births		per 1,000		per 1,000		per 1,000		% of cohort	
							Male	Female	Male	Female	Male	Female
	1990	**2008**	**1990**	**2008**	**1990**	**2008**	**2003–08[a,b]**	**2003–08[a,b]**	**2005–08[a]**	**2005–08[a]**	**2008**	**2008**
Romania	70	73	25	12	32	14	..	..	196	83	70	85
Russian Federation	69	68	23	12	27	13	..	..	429	158	46	78
Rwanda	33	50	106	72	174	112	69	55	403	357	40	46
Saudi Arabia	68	73	35	18	43	21	3	4	139	89	76	84
Senegal	52	56	72	57	149	108	43	39	329	271	47	54
Serbia	71	74	25	6	29	7	4	3	155[e]	83[e]	74[e]	85[e]
Sierra Leone	40	48	163	123	278	194	134	124	503	470	29	33
Singapore	74	81	6	2	7	3	..	..	81	41	86	93
Slovak Republic	71	75	13	7	15	8	..	..	196	76	72	88
Slovenia	73	79	9	3	10	4	..	..	149	57	81	92
Somalia	45	50	119	119	200	200	53	54	371	318	41	47
South Africa	61	51	44	48	56	67	13	9	577	511	31	41
Spain	77	81	8	4	9	4	..	..	106	44	85	94
Sri Lanka	70	74	23	13	29	15	..	..	196	77	71	86
Sudan	53	58	78	70	124	109	38	30	306	261	53	59
Swaziland	60	46	62	59	84	83	32	30	615	639	29	29
Sweden	78	81	6	2	7	3	..	..	78	48	88	93
Switzerland	77	82	7	4	8	5	..	..	78	46	88	93
Syrian Arab Republic	68	74	30	14	37	16	5	3	122	83	78	85
Tajikistan	63	67	91	54	117	64	18	13	210	139	63	73
Tanzania	51	56	97	67	157	104	56	52	377	362	48	51
Thailand	69	69	26	13	32	14	..	..	297	172	62	77
Timor-Leste	46	61	138	75	184	93	..	..	264	229	57	62
Togo	58	63	89	64	150	98	55	43	242	199	61	68
Trinidad and Tobago	69	69	30	31	34	35	5	8	239	141	63	77
Tunisia	70	74	40	18	50	21	..	..	123	72	78	86
Turkey	65	72	69	20	84	22	9	9	151	84	74	84
Turkmenistan	63	65	81	43	99	48	..	..	303	154	54	73
Uganda	48	53	114	85	186	135	75	62	412	411	43	45
Ukraine	70	68	18	14	21	16	4	1	385	142	53	80
United Arab Emirates	73	78	15	7	17	8	..	..	77	64	86	88
United Kingdom	76	80	8	5	9	6	..	..	100	61	85	91
United States	75	78	9	7	11	8	..	..	141	81	83	89
Uruguay	73	76	21	12	24	14	..	..	141	64	77	89
Uzbekistan	67	68	61	34	74	38	11	7	240	137	62	75
Venezuela, RB	71	74	27	16	32	18	..	..	177	93	74	84
Vietnam	65	74	39	12	56	14	5	4	136	90	78	85
West Bank and Gaza	68	73	33	24	38	27	3	3	128	92	78	84
Yemen, Rep.	54	63	90	53	127	69	10	11	251	202	59	66
Zambia	51	45	105	92	172	148	66	55	542	530	31	34
Zimbabwe	61	44	51	62	79	96	21	21	718	681	21	26
World	**65 w**	**69 w**	**64 w**	**46 w**	**92 w**	**67 w**			**216[f] w**	**153[f] w**	**68 w**	**77 w**
Low income	54	59	102	76	160	118			295	254	55	61
Middle income	64	69	60	41	85	57			205	136	67	76
Lower middle income	63	68	65	45	93	64			204	138	67	75
Upper middle income	68	71	38	19	47	23			210	127	66	81
Low & middle income	63	67	69	50	101	73			219	156	65	74
East Asia & Pacific	67	72	42	23	55	29			161	101	74	81
Europe & Central Asia	69	70	41	19	50	22			305[g]	126[g]	59	81
Latin America & Carib.	68	73	42	20	53	23			192	104	72	83
Middle East & N. Africa	64	71	58	29	76	34			158	106	73	81
South Asia	58	64	89	58	125	76			246	173	60	68
Sub-Saharan Africa	50	52	109	86	185	144			395	362	43	48
High income	76	80	10	6	12	7			116[g]	62[g]	84	91
Euro area	76	81	8	3	9	4			107[g]	52[g]	85	93

a. Data are for the most recent year available. b. Refers to a survey year. Values were estimated directly from surveys and cover the 5 or 10 years preceding the survey. c. Includes Taiwan, China. d. Excludes the French overseas departments of French Guiana, Guadeloupe, Martinique, and Réunion. e. Includes Kosovo. f. These world aggregates for 2008 do not include data for many lower mortality countries because recent estimates are unavailable. The world aggregates for 2006 are 213 for men and 143 for women. g. Data are for 2006.

Mortality rates for different age groups (infants, children, and adults) and overall mortality indicators (life expectancy at birth or survival to a given age) are important indicators of health status in a country. Because data on the incidence and prevalence of diseases are frequently unavailable, mortality rates are often used to identify vulnerable populations. And they are among the indicators most frequently used to compare socioeconomic development across countries.

The main sources of mortality data are vital registration systems and direct or indirect estimates based on sample surveys or censuses. A "complete" vital registration system—covering at least 90 percent of vital events in the population—is the best source of age-specific mortality data. Where reliable age-specific mortality data are available, life expectancy at birth is directly estimated from the life table constructed from age- specific mortality data.

But complete vital registration systems are fairly uncommon in developing countries. Thus estimates must be obtained from sample surveys or derived by applying indirect estimation techniques to registration, census, or survey data (see table 2.17 and *Primary data documentation*). Survey data are subject to recall error, and surveys estimating infant deaths require large samples because households in which a birth has occurred during a given year cannot ordinarily be preselected for sampling. Indirect estimates rely on model life tables that may be inappropriate for the population concerned. Because life expectancy at birth is estimated using infant mortality data and model life tables for many developing countries, similar reliability issues arise for this indicator. Extrapolations based on outdated surveys may not be reliable for monitoring changes in health status or for comparative analytical work.

Estimates of infant and under-five mortality tend to vary by source and method for a given time and place. Years for available estimates also vary by country, making comparison across countries and over time difficult. To make infant and under-five mortality estimates comparable and to ensure consistency across estimates by different agencies, the United Nations Children's Fund (UNICEF) and the World Bank (now working together with the World Health Organization (WHO), the United Nations Population Division, and other universities and research institutes as the Inter-agency Group for Child Mortality Estimation) developed and adopted a statistical method that uses all available information to reconcile differences. The method uses the weighted least squares method to fit a regression line to the relationship between mortality rates and their reference dates and then extrapolate the trend to the present. (For further discussion of childhood mortality estimates, see UNICEF, WHO, World Bank, and United Nations Population Division 2007; for a graphic presentation and detailed background data, see www.childmortality.org).

Infant and child mortality rates are higher for boys than for girls in countries in which parental gender preferences are insignificant. Child mortality captures the effect of gender discrimination better than infant mortality does, as malnutrition and medical interventions are more important in this age group. Where female child mortality is higher, as in some countries in South Asia, girls probably have unequal access to resources. Child mortality rates in the table are not compatible with infant mortality and under-five mortality rates because of differences in methodology and reference year. Child mortality data were estimated directly from surveys and cover the 10 years preceding the survey. In addition to estimates from Demographic Health Surveys, estimates derived from Multiple Indicator Cluster Surveys have been added to the table; they cover the 5 years preceding the survey.

Rates for adult mortality and survival to age 65 come from life tables. Adult mortality rates increased notably in a dozen countries in Sub-Saharan Africa between 1995–2000 and 2000–05 and in several countries in Europe and Central Asia during the first half of the 1990s. In Sub-Saharan Africa the increase stems from AIDS-related mortality and affects both sexes, though women are more affected. In Europe and Central Asia the causes are more diverse (high prevalence of smoking, high-fat diet, excessive alcohol use, stressful conditions related to the economic transition) and affect men more.

The percentage of a hypothetical cohort surviving to age 65 reflects both child and adult mortality rates. Like life expectancy, it is a synthetic measure based on current age-specific mortality rates. It shows that even in countries where mortality is high, a certain share of the current birth cohort will live well beyond the life expectancy at birth, while in low-mortality countries close to 90 percent will reach at least age 65.

Annual data series from the United Nations are interpolated based on five-year estimates and thus may not reflect actual events.

• **Life expectancy at birth** is the number of years a newborn infant would live if prevailing patterns of mortality at the time of its birth were to stay the same throughout its life. • **Infant mortality rate** is the number of infants dying before reaching one year of age, per 1,000 live births in a given year. • **Under-five mortality rate** is the probability per 1,000 that a newborn baby will die before reaching age 5, if subject to current age-specific mortality rates. • **Child mortality rate** is the probability per 1,000 of dying between ages 1 and 5—that is, the probability of a 1-year-old dying before reaching age 5—if subject to current age-specific mortality rates. • **Adult mortality rate** is the probability per 1,000 of dying between the ages of 15 and 60—that is, the probability of a 15-year-old dying before reaching age 60—if subject to current age-specific mortality rates between those ages. • **Survival to age 65** refers to the percentage of a hypothetical cohort of newborn infants that would survive to age 65, if subject to current age-specific mortality rates.

Data on infant and under-five mortality are estimates by the Inter-agency Group for Child Mortality Estimation based mainly on household surveys, censuses, and vital registration data, supplemented by the World Bank's Human Development Network estimates based on vital registration and sample registration data. Data on child mortality are from Demographic and Health Surveys by Macro International (Measure DHS) and World Bank calculations based on infant and under-five mortality from Multiple Indicator Cluster Surveys by UNICEF. Data on survival to age 65 and most data on adult mortality are linear interpolations of five-year data from *World Population Prospects: The 2008 Revision*. Remaining data on adult mortality are from the Human Mortality Database by the University of California, Berkeley, and the Max Planck Institute for Demographic Research (www.mortality.org). Data on life expectancy at birth are World Bank calculations based on male and female data from *World Population Prospects: The 2008 Revision* (for more than half of countries, most of them developing countries), census reports and other statistical publications from national statistical offices, Eurostat's *Demographic Statistics*, and the U.S. Bureau of the Census International Data Base.

ENVIRONMENT

Global climate change presents a significant challenge to achieving the Millennium Development Goals (MDGs). The expected extreme changes in weather—such as shifts in the intensity and pattern of rainfall and variations in temperature—may lower agricultural productivity and damage infrastructure, leading to slower economic growth, threatening food security, and increasing poverty. Projected floods and droughts could cause many people to lose their livelihoods, be displaced, or migrate, while rising temperatures could increase the incidence of vector-borne diseases and lead to heat-related deaths and water scarcity.

The poorest countries and regions face the greatest danger. Africa—with the most rainfed agricultural land of any continent, half its population without access to improved water sources, and about 70 percent without access to improved sanitation facilities—is particularly vulnerable to climate change.

International action on greenhouse gas emissions and developing countries

Economic growth—necessary for reducing poverty, improving people's lives, and achieving the MDGs—entails significant energy use. Generating this energy will affect greenhouse gas emissions. There is now consensus that greenhouse gas emissions need to peak by 2015 to curb emissions to about 50 percent of their 1990 levels by 2050, to keep global warming below 2°C, and to avoid more dangerous and catastrophic climate change (United Nations 2009b; World Bank 2009k). To meet this target and achieve the MDGs, sustainable energy systems need to be part of long-term economic planning for developed and developing countries.

The 2009 United Nations Climate Change Conference in Copenhagen did not reach a binding agreement on targets and timetables for reducing greenhouse gas emissions. The Copenhagen Accord recognized the critical importance of keeping global warming below 2°C and affirmed that the first priority of developing countries is to eradicate poverty and promote socioeconomic development—but that a low-emission development strategy is indispensable to sustainable development. On the principle of "differentiated responsibilities and respective capabilities," the accord urged developed countries to help developing countries in their mitigation efforts and their adaptation to the adverse effects of climate change (United Nations 2009c).

Greenhouse gas emissions have been rising at increasing rates

Carbon dioxide is the most common of the Kyoto Protocol greenhouse gases, which also include methane, nitrous oxide, and other artificial gases. It constitutes more than 75 percent of greenhouse gas emissions (figure 3a). About 80 percent of carbon dioxide is generated by the energy sector.

Carbon dioxide emissions, on the rise since the beginning of the industrial revolution 150 years ago, began to surge in the second half of the 20th century (figure 3b), reaching more than 30 petagrams (billion metric tons) a year in 2006 (see table 3.8).

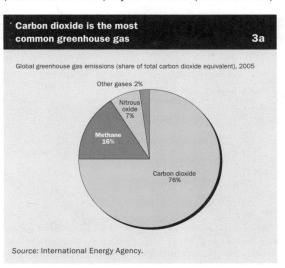

Carbon dioxide is the most common greenhouse gas **3a**

Global greenhouse gas emissions (share of total carbon dioxide equivalent), 2005

Other gases 2%
Nitrous oxide 7%
Methane 16%
Carbon dioxide 76%

Source: International Energy Agency.

High-income Organisation for Economic Co-operation and Development (OECD) countries, which have produced more than 55 percent of total cumulative emissions since the beginning of industrialization, stabilized their emissions growth at about 0.9 percent a year between 1990 and 2006.

Carbon dioxide emissions per capita from developing economies were less than a fourth those of developed economies in 2006, but their total emissions rate grew about twice as fast during 1990–2006 (table 3c). Over the same period carbon dioxide emissions grew 5.1 percent a year in China and 4.8 percent a year in India. China became the largest emitter of carbon dioxide in 2006 (see tables 3.8 and 3.9). During 1990–2006 developing economies' carbon energy intensity—the ratio of carbon dioxide emissions per unit of energy used—remained unchanged. But their carbon income intensity—the carbon dioxide emitted for each unit of gross domestic product—decreased 2 percent a year, indicating greater economic productivity and energy efficiency.

The world's top five carbon dioxide emitters —China, the United States, the Russian Federation, India, and Japan (figure 3d)—all decreased their carbon income intensity in 1990–2006. Only China and India increased their carbon energy intensity, because of a higher share of fossil fuel in their energy consumption. Energy use has been increasing in China and India, both as a share of the global total and per capita. Among the five economies with the highest energy consumption, India uses fossil fuels the least—but its dependence on fossil fuels is growing the most, at about 1.3 percent annually during 1990–2007 (table 3e).

World energy consumption has increased about 2 percent a year since 1970 but decreased in 2009 because of the economic crisis. According to the International Energy Agency (IEA), energy demand could increase 40 percent by 2030 under business as usual conditions. Fossil fuels would remain the main energy source, accounting for 77 percent of increased demand during 2007–30 (IEA 2009). The IEA estimates that using fossil fuels at this rate will increase carbon dioxide emissions to about 40 petagrams a year by 2030, resulting in a long-term atmospheric concentration of 1,000 parts per million. This increase will be environmentally, socially, and economically unsustainable.

In Copenhagen the IEA proposed an emission reduction scenario to limit the concentration

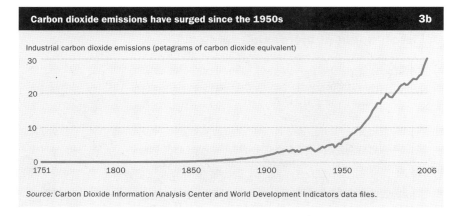

Carbon dioxide emissions have surged since the 1950s   **3b**

Industrial carbon dioxide emissions (petagrams of carbon dioxide equivalent)

Source: Carbon Dioxide Information Analysis Center and World Development Indicators data files.

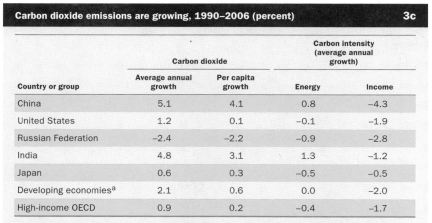

Carbon dioxide emissions are growing, 1990–2006 (percent)   **3c**

Country or group	Carbon dioxide		Carbon intensity (average annual growth)	
	Average annual growth	Per capita growth	Energy	Income
China	5.1	4.1	0.8	−4.3
United States	1.2	0.1	−0.1	−1.9
Russian Federation	−2.4	−2.2	−0.9	−2.8
India	4.8	3.1	1.3	−1.2
Japan	0.6	0.3	−0.5	−0.5
Developing economies[a]	2.1	0.6	0.0	−2.0
High-income OECD	0.9	0.2	−0.4	−1.7

a. Emissions from oil-producing economies constitute 8 percent (excluding the Russian Federation).
Source: World Development Indicators data files; International Energy Agency; Carbon Dioxide Information Analysis Center.

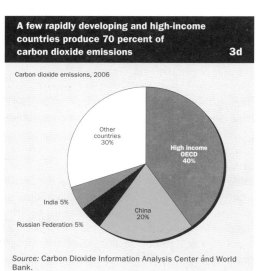

A few rapidly developing and high-income countries produce 70 percent of carbon dioxide emissions   **3d**

Carbon dioxide emissions, 2006

Source: Carbon Dioxide Information Analysis Center and World Bank.

of greenhouse gases in the atmosphere to 450 parts per million of carbon dioxide equivalent, which would reduce energy-related carbon dioxide emissions from 28.8 petagrams in 2007 to 26.4 petagrams in 2030. Under this scenario carbon dioxide emissions from the power sector are projected to be reduced the most (figure 3f). High-income OECD countries are projected to reduce their power generation emissions from 484 grams of carbon dioxide per kilowatt hour of energy produced to 145, a 70 percent reduction. According to this scenario, high-income OECD economies should also reduce their carbon energy intensity by about 38 percent, and other economies by less than half that (table 3g).

Trends in fossil fuel use and energy intensity (percent) — 3e

| Country or group | Energy use | | Fossil fuel | | Energy intensity of GDP | Net imports[a] |
	Share of world energy use, 2007	Average annual growth, 1990–2007	Share of total, 2007	Average annual growth, 1990–2007	Average annual growth, 1990–2007	Share of energy use, 2007
China	16.8	4.5	86.9	0.8	−4.9	7.2
United States	20.1	1.2	85.6	0.0	−1.8	28.8
Russian Federation	5.8	−1.3	89.3	−0.3	−2.1	−83.1
India	5.1	3.5	70.0	1.3	−2.6	24.2
Japan	4.4	0.9	83.2	−0.1	−0.2	82.4
Developing economies	52.1	2.2	79.8	0.2	−2.1	−20.1
High-income OECD	43.9	1.3	81.6	−0.1	−1.3	31.9

a. A negative value indicates that the economy is a net energy exporter.
Source: World Development Indicators data files and International Energy Agency.

Emission reductions by 2030 — 3f

Share of global energy-related carbon dioxide emissions (percent)

■ Power generation　■ Transport　■ Industry
■ Buildings　　　　■ Other

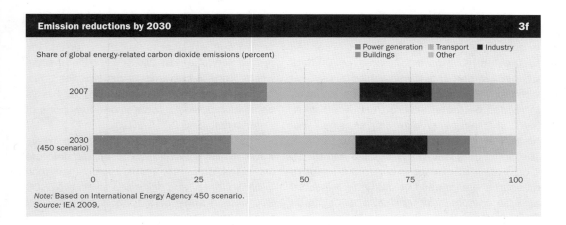

Note: Based on International Energy Agency 450 scenario.
Source: IEA 2009.

Future energy use under the IEA-450 scenario (percentage change, 2007–30) — 3g

| Group | Energy use | | Carbon dioxide emissions | | Carbon dioxide intensity | | Power intensity |
	Total	Per capita	Total	Per capita	Income	Energy	
World	17.6	−5.6	−8.3	−26.4	−55.0	−22.1	−53.1
European Union	−3.8	−5.7	−41.0	−42.2	−58.2	−38.7	−72.9
OECD[a]	−5.2	−13.3	−41.2	−46.3	−60.7	−38.0	−70.0
Other major economies[b]	36.3	21.1	14.4	1.7	−62.1	−16.0	−48.3
Other economies	55.9	14.3	28.0	−6.2	−51.5	−17.9	−49.9

a. OECD economies and European Union.
b. Other major economies are those in the Middle East and North Africa and Brazil, China, and South Africa.
Source: IEA 2009.

People affected by natural disasters and projected changes in rainfall and agricultural production (percent)					3h
Country	Average share of population affected by droughts, floods, and storms, 1971–2008	Projected change in precipitation outcome, 2000–50		Projected change in agricultural outcome, 2000–50	
		Total	Intensity	Output	Yield
Bangladesh	9.1	1.4	5.4	−21.7	8.9
China	5.2	4.5	5.4	−7.2	8.4
Ethiopia	6.6	2.4	5.0	−31.3	0.5
India	7.2	1.9	2.7	−38.1	−12.2
Malawi	12.3	−0.1	2.4	−31.3	−3.0
Mozambique	13.8	−2.7	1.4	−21.7	−10.7
Niger	13.2	5.6	2.5	−34.1	−1.7
Senegal	11.3	−1.9	3.1	−51.9	−19.3
Swaziland	18.3	..	..	..	..
Zimbabwe	10.7	−3.7	4.8	−37.9	−10.6

Source: World Bank 2009k.

Climate change will affect food and water security

During the last century rising atmospheric concentrations of carbon dioxide led to a 0.74°C increase in average global temperature. Even if greenhouse gas emissions stop growing, global warming is expected to continue because changes in temperature lag behind changes in concentrations, which lag behind changes in emissions (World Bank 2009k). According to the Intergovernmental Panel on Climate Change, during the coming decades global warming will cause droughts, floods, changes in rainfall patterns, severe freshwater shortages, and shifts in crop growing seasons—especially in developing countries (FAO 2008a). The agriculture and water sectors will be affected most by climate change, and adaptive measures are needed to mitigate expected adverse outcomes; otherwise, areas such as Southern Africa will suffer severe drops in agricultural yields by 2030 (World Bank 2009a) (table 3h). Developing countries already suffering from hunger and water supply problems, especially those in Southeast Asia and Sub-Saharan Africa, will be hardest hit without aid for adaptation.

Demand for water will increase, making better water management crucial

Properly using and managing water resources are important components of sustainable development—and essential for achieving the MDGs (World Bank and IMF 2008b; FAO 2010; Bates and others 2008) (table 3i). Some 1 billion people lack access to safe water, and more than 2.5 billion need access to improved sanitation facilities. The world's population is growing by about 80 million people a year, demanding an additional 64 billion cubic meters of freshwater a year (UNESCO 2009). And about 90 percent of population growth by 2050 is projected to occur in developing countries, where many people still lack access to safe water and improved sanitation. By 2025, 1.8 billion people will be living in countries or regions with absolute water scarcity, and two-thirds of the world's population could be living under conditions of water stress (FAO 2007, 2010).

The effects of climate change on freshwater availability will depend on temperature increases, droughts, floods, regional variation in precipitation, and rising sea levels (UNESCO 2009; Bates and others 2008; Kundzewicz and Mata 2007; FAO 2008b). Precipitation is the most important source of freshwater; 80 percent of the world's cultivated land and about 60 percent of crops depend on rainwater (UNESCO 2009). Climate change models predict more precipitation in high latitudes and the tropics but less precipitation in subtropical regions such as the northern Sahara (UNESCO 2009; Kundzewicz and Mata 2007; IPCC 2007). In addition, non-climate-related water stresses—such as industrial water pollution, extensive irrigation, construction of dams, and draining of wetlands—have already raised concerns about future freshwater shortages (Bates and others 2008).

Potential contributions of the water sector to attaining the Millennium Development Goals		3i
Goal	**Relation to water**	
1 Eradicate extreme poverty and hunger	Water is a factor in many production activities (agriculture, animal husbandry, cottage industries).	
3 Promote gender equity and empower women	More gender-sensitive water management programs can reduce time wasted and health burdens through improved water service, leading to more time for income earning and more-balanced gender roles.	
4 Reduce child mortality	Improved access to more and better quality drinking water and improved sanitation can reduce the main factors contributing to illness and death among young children.	
6 Combat HIV/AIDS, malaria, and other diseases	Improved access to water and sanitation supports HIV/AIDS-affected households and may improve the impact of health care programs. Better water management reduces mosquito habitats and the risk of malaria transmission.	
7 Ensure environmental sustainability	Improved water management reduces water consumption and allows recycling of nutrients and organics. Action could ensure improved water supply and sanitation services for poor communities, and reduced wastewater discharge and improved environmental health in slum areas.	

Source: Bates and others 2008.

In response to higher freshwater demand and geographic changes in water supply caused by climate change and other factors, countries must improve water storage, use water more efficiently, reuse freshwater (especially in agriculture), and use technology to anticipate regional, local, and seasonal variation in water availability and water use (UNESCO 2009; Bates and others 2008; Faurèsa, Hoogeveena, and Bruinsmab 2004; FAO 2009a).

Sustainable agriculture can help developing countries adapt to climate change

Sustainable agriculture is essential for development—and for achieving the MDG to eradicate poverty and hunger (World Bank and IFPRI 2006). Today's challenges for sustainable agricultural development are to respond to increasing demand for food, adjust to rapid climate changes caused by global warming, and reduce agricultural greenhouse gas emissions (FAO 2008a).

Adaptation strategies for agriculture will require balancing many environmental variables and socioeconomic factors—and their interactions. Countries may integrate climate change adaptation and MDG efforts into their sustainable development policies. Research and development in sustainable agriculture could significantly affect agricultural resource conservation, promoting synergy among human needs.

The agriculture sector also causes greenhouse gas emissions—primarily nitrous oxide and methane. Climate change mitigation in agriculture will require more efficient use of fertilizer, soil conservation, and better production management. Inefficient use of fertilizers has undesirable environmental impacts, such as increased nitrogen loss into the atmosphere. Under current fertilization practices, crop plant uptake of nitrogen as a nutrient is about 50 percent, with losses and emissions to the atmosphere through runoff and leaching from soil erosion (Takle and Hofstrand 2008; FAO 2001). Use of fossil fuels in agricultural production causes 7 percent of agricultural emissions, primarily from combustion of gasoline and diesel fuel (Takle and Hofstrand 2008). Capturing and using methane from livestock production as an energy source can reduce emissions and improve profitability by reducing the need to buy fossil fuel energy (Takle and Hofstrand 2008).

3.1 Rural population and land use

	Rural population			Land area	Land use							
	% of total		average annual % growth	thousand sq. km	Forest area		Permanent cropland		Arable land		Arable land hectares per 100 people	
					% of land area							
	1990	2008	1990–2008	2008	1990	2007	1990	2007	1990	2007	1990–92	2005–07
Afghanistan	..	..	..	652.2	2.0	1.2	0.2	0.2	12.1	13.1	..	..
Albania	64	53	−1.2	27.4	28.8	29.3	4.6	4.4	21.1	21.1	18.8	18.2
Algeria	48	35	−0.1	2,381.7	0.8	1.0	0.2	0.4	3.0	3.1	24.5	22.4
Angola	63	43	0.8	1,246.7	48.9	47.2	0.4	0.2	2.3	2.6	20.6	19.3
Argentina	13	8	−1.6	2,736.7	12.9	12.0	0.4	0.4	9.6	11.9	75.1	80.5
Armenia	33	36	−0.2	28.2	12.0	9.7	2.1	1.9	15.0	14.4	14.4[a]	13.4
Australia	15	11	−0.2	7,682.3	21.9	21.3	0.0	0.0	6.2	5.8	248.9	227.5
Austria	34	33	0.2	82.5	45.8	47.0	1.0	0.8	17.3	16.8	17.3	16.7
Azerbaijan	46	48	1.3	82.6	11.2	11.3	3.7	2.7	20.5	22.4	22.6[a]	21.8
Bangladesh	80	73	1.3	130.2	6.8	6.7	2.3	3.7	70.2	61.2	5.6	5.1
Belarus	34	27	−1.7	202.9	36.8	39.0	0.9	0.6	30.0	27.3	58.6[a]	56.9
Belgium	4	3	−1.3	30.3	22.3[b]	22.0	0.5[b]	0.8	0.6[b]	27.7	8.2	8.0
Benin	66	59	2.7	110.6	30.0	20.1	0.9	2.4	14.6	24.4	35.7	33.4
Bolivia	44	34	0.7	1,083.3	58.0	53.7	0.1	0.2	1.9	3.3	35.7	38.9
Bosnia and Herzegovina	61	53	−1.5	51.2	43.1	42.7	2.9	1.9	16.6	20.0	26.8[a]	27.1
Botswana	58	40	−0.1	566.7	24.2	20.7	0.0	0.0	0.7	0.4	15.2	13.0
Brazil	25	14	−1.7	8,459.4	61.5	55.7	0.8	0.8	6.0	7.0	33.2	31.6
Bulgaria	34	29	−1.6	108.6	30.1	34.3	2.7	1.8	34.9	28.4	43.4	40.5
Burkina Faso	86	80	2.7	273.6	26.1	24.7	0.2	0.2	12.9	19.0	36.5	35.3
Burundi	94	90	1.7	25.7	11.3	5.2	14.0	13.6	36.2	38.7	14.7	13.0
Cambodia	87	78	1.7	176.5	73.3	56.7	0.6	0.9	20.9	21.5	28.5	26.7
Cameroon	59	43	0.7	472.7	51.9	44.0	2.6	2.5	12.6	12.6	36.7	32.7
Canada	23	20	0.0	9,093.5	34.1	34.1	0.7	0.8	5.0	5.0	147.4	138.3
Central African Republic	63	61	2.0	623.0	37.2	36.4	0.1	0.1	3.1	3.1	50.6	46.0
Chad	79	73	2.8	1,259.2	10.4	9.3	0.0	0.0	2.6	3.4	41.0	41.3
Chile	17	12	−0.7	743.8	20.5	21.8	0.3	0.6	3.8	1.7	11.0	8.3
China	73	57	−0.5	9,327.5	16.8	22.0	0.8	1.3	13.3	15.1	10.4	10.5
Hong Kong SAR, China	1	0	..	1.0	..	..	..	..	..	..	..	..
Colombia	32	26	0.5	1,109.5	55.4	54.6	1.5	1.4	3.0	1.8	6.2	4.5
Congo, Dem. Rep.	72	66	2.6	2,267.1	62.0	58.7	0.5	0.4	2.9	3.0	12.8	11.0
Congo, Rep.	46	39	1.2	341.5	66.5	65.7	0.1	0.1	1.4	1.4	15.8	14.2
Costa Rica	49	37	0.5	51.1	50.2	46.9	4.9	5.9	5.1	3.9	5.1	4.6
Côte d'Ivoire	60	51	1.8	318.0	32.1	32.8	11.0	13.2	7.6	8.8	15.8	14.2
Croatia	46	43	−0.8	53.9	37.9	39.6	2.0	1.5	21.7	15.8	25.2[a]	19.4
Cuba	27	24	−0.2	109.8	18.7	25.7	4.1	3.8	30.9	32.5	32.5	32.4
Czech Republic	25	27	0.4	77.3	34.1	34.3	3.1	3.1	41.1	39.2	30.1	29.6
Denmark	15	13	−0.4	42.4	10.5	11.9	0.2	0.2	60.4	54.3	42.6	42.8
Dominican Republic	45	31	−0.4	48.3	28.5	28.5	9.3	10.3	18.6	17.0	9.1	8.5
Ecuador	45	34	0.0	276.8	49.9	37.8	4.8	4.4	5.8	4.3	12.0	9.4
Egypt, Arab Rep.	57	57	2.0	995.5	0.0	0.1	0.4	0.5	2.3	3.0	4.0	3.8
El Salvador	51	39	−0.6	20.7	18.1	13.9	12.5	11.4	26.5	32.9	11.2	11.6
Eritrea	84	79	2.1	101.0	15.9	15.3	0.0	0.0	4.9	6.3	14.8	13.8
Estonia	29	31	−0.6	42.4	51.4	54.3	0.3	0.2	26.3	14.1	52.1[a]	43.3
Ethiopia	87	83	2.6	1,000.0	14.7	12.7	0.5	1.0	10.0	14.0	15.2	17.5
Finland	39	37	0.1	304.1	72.9	74.0	0.0	0.0	7.4	7.4	42.2	42.7
France	26	23	−0.2	547.7	26.5	28.5	2.2	2.0	32.9	33.7	31.1	30.1
Gabon	31	15	−1.5	257.7	85.1	84.4	0.6	0.7	1.1	1.3	25.8	23.3
Gambia, The	62	44	1.5	10.0	44.2	47.5	0.5	0.6	18.2	34.8	22.4	21.7
Georgia	45	47	−1.0	69.5	39.7	39.7	4.8	1.6	11.4	6.7	17.0[a]	10.5
Germany	27	26	0.1	348.8	30.8	31.8	1.3	0.6	34.3	34.1	14.3	14.4
Ghana	64	50	1.1	227.5	32.7	23.2	6.6	10.5	11.9	18.0	20.3	18.2
Greece	41	39	0.3	128.9	25.6	29.6	8.3	8.8	22.5	19.8	24.9	23.1
Guatemala	59	51	1.6	107.2	44.3	35.7	4.5	8.8	12.1	14.7	12.2	11.5
Guinea	72	66	2.1	245.7	30.1	27.1	2.0	2.7	3.3	9.0	16.8	21.9
Guinea-Bissau	72	70	2.3	28.1	78.8	73.0	4.2	8.9	10.7	10.7	22.5	19.9
Haiti	72	53	0.2	27.6	4.2	3.8	11.6	10.9	28.3	32.7	10.2	9.4
Honduras	60	52	1.5	111.9	66.0	38.7	3.2	3.2	13.1	9.5	16.8	15.2

	Rural population			Land area	Land use							
	% of total		average ·annual % growth	thousand sq. km	Forest area		Permanent cropland		Arable land		Arable land hectares per 100 people	
											% of land area	
	1990	2008	1990–2008	2008	1990	2007	1990	2007	1990	2007	1990–92	2005–07
Hungary	34	33	−0.5	89.6	20.0	22.4	2.6	2.2	56.2	51.2	45.2	45.6
India	75	71	1.3	2,973.2	21.5	22.8	2.2	3.6	54.8	53.4	15.6	14.3
Indonesia	69	49	−0.6	1,811.6	64.3	46.8	6.5	8.6	11.2	12.1	9.7	9.9
Iran, Islamic Rep.	44	32	−0.3	1,628.6	6.8	6.8	0.8	1.0	9.3	10.4	24.0	23.8
Iraq	30	..	..	437.4	1.8	1.9	0.7	0.6	13.3	11.9	20.3	..
Ireland	43	39	0.7	68.9	6.4	10.1	0.0	0.0	15.1	15.4	29.7	26.6
Israel	10	8	1.7	21.6	7.1	8.0	4.1	3.2	15.9	14.2	5.3	4.4
Italy	33	32	0.1	294.1	28.5	34.6	10.1	8.6	30.6	24.4	14.7	12.6
Jamaica	51	47	0.2	10.8	31.9	31.2	9.2	10.2	11.0	16.1	6.7	6.5
Japan	37	34	−0.3	364.5	68.4	68.2	1.3	0.9	13.1	11.9	3.5	3.4
Jordan	28	22	2.0	88.2	0.9	0.9	0.8	0.9	2.0	1.6	3.9	3.1
Kazakhstan	44	42	−0.4	2,699.7	1.3	1.2	0.1	0.0	13.0	8.4	148.7[a]	148.1
Kenya	82	78	2.6	569.1	6.5	6.1	0.8	0.9	8.8	9.1	15.6	14.3
Korea, Dem. Rep.	42	37	0.3	120.4	68.1	49.3	1.5	1.7	19.0	23.3	11.4	11.8
Korea, Rep.	26	19	−1.2	96.9	64.5	64.5	1.6	1.9	19.8	16.5	3.6	3.4
Kosovo	..	..	..	10.9[c]	..	41.3[c]	..	..	..	27.6[c]	..	16.8[c]
Kuwait	2	2	0.3	17.8	0.2	0.3	0.1	0.2	0.2	0.8	0.6	0.6
Kyrgyz Republic	62	64	1.1	191.8	4.4	4.6	0.4	0.4	6.9	6.7	27.2[a]	24.7
Lao PDR	85	69	1.0	230.8	75.0	69.3	0.3	0.4	3.5	5.1	16.4	18.5
Latvia	31	32	−0.7	62.3	45.1	47.6	0.4	0.2	27.2	19.1	41.0[a]	50.8
Lebanon	17	13	0.5	10.2	11.8	13.6	11.9	14.0	17.9	14.1	3.3	3.5
Lesotho	86	75	0.6	30.4	0.2	0.3	0.1	0.1	10.4	9.9	16.7	15.4
Liberia	55	40	1.4	96.3	42.1	31.5	1.6	2.2	3.6	4.0	12.9	11.0
Libya	24	23	1.6	1,759.5	0.1	0.1	0.2	0.2	1.0	1.0	33.3	29.0
Lithuania	32	33	−0.4	62.7	31.3	34.0	0.7	0.5	46.0	29.3	58.8[a]	55.2
Macedonia, FYR	42	33	−1.0	25.4	35.6	35.6	2.2	1.4	23.8	16.9	26.8[a]	21.8
Madagascar	76	71	2.5	581.5	23.5	21.9	1.0	1.0	4.7	5.1	18.7	16.3
Malawi	88	81	2.0	94.1	41.4	35.5	1.4	1.3	23.9	31.9	23.1	21.4
Malaysia	50	30	−0.7	328.6	68.1	62.7	16.0	17.6	5.2	5.5	7.6	6.9
Mali	77	68	1.4	1,220.2	11.5	10.1	0.1	0.1	1.7	4.0	43.1	39.1
Mauritania	60	59	2.5	1,030.7	0.4	0.2	0.0	0.0	0.4	0.4	16.7	15.5
Mauritius	56	58	1.2	2.0	19.2	18.0	3.0	2.0	49.3	44.3	8.2	7.3
Mexico	29	23	0.1	1,944.0	35.5	32.8	1.0	1.2	12.5	12.6	25.4	23.7
Moldova	53	58	−0.5	32.9	9.7	10.0	14.2	9.2	52.8	55.3	45.7[a]	49.3
Mongolia	43	43	1.0	1,553.6	7.4	6.5	0.0	0.0	0.9	0.5	42.4	32.5
Morocco	52	44	0.5	446.3	9.6	9.8	1.6	2.0	19.5	18.1	29.7	26.5
Mozambique	79	63	1.6	786.4	25.4	24.4	0.3	0.4	4.4	5.7	21.9	21.2
Myanmar	75	67	0.5	653.5	60.0	47.9	0.8	1.7	14.6	16.2	21.1	21.2
Namibia	72	63	1.5	823.3	10.6	9.1	0.0	0.0	0.8	1.0	43.8	39.6
Nepal	91	83	1.7	143.4	33.7	24.6	0.5	0.8	16.0	16.4	9.4	8.5
Netherlands	31	18	−2.5	33.8	10.2	10.9	0.9	1.0	26.0	31.4	5.7	6.2
New Zealand	15	13	0.5	267.7	28.8	31.2	0.2	0.2	9.9	3.2	33.2	22.1
Nicaragua	48	43	1.2	120.0	54.5	41.5	1.6	2.0	10.8	16.3	37.6	36.0
Niger	85	84	3.4	1,266.7	1.5	1.0	0.0	0.0	8.7	11.6	122.6	106.2
Nigeria	65	52	1.2	910.8	18.9	11.3	2.8	3.3	32.4	40.1	24.0	24.8
Norway	28	23	−0.6	304.3	30.0	31.0	0.0	0.0	2.8	2.8	19.5	18.4
Oman	34	28	1.3	309.5	0.0	0.0	0.1	0.1	0.1	0.2	1.6	2.3
Pakistan	69	64	1.9	770.9	3.3	2.4	0.6	1.0	26.6	27.9	15.2	13.4
Panama	46	27	−1.1	74.3	58.9	57.7	2.1	2.0	6.7	7.4	18.2	16.7
Papua New Guinea	85	88	2.7	452.9	69.6	64.4	1.2	1.3	0.4	0.6	3.8	3.9
Paraguay	51	40	0.7	397.3	53.3	45.6	0.2	0.3	5.3	10.8	56.9	68.7
Peru	31	29	1.1	1,280.0	54.8	53.6	0.3	0.7	2.7	2.9	13.9	13.0
Philippines	51	35	0.0	298.2	35.5	23.0	14.8	16.4	18.4	17.1	6.3	5.8
Poland	39	39	0.0	304.3	29.2	30.4	1.1	1.3	47.3	41.1	35.3	32.3
Portugal	52	41	−1.0	91.5	33.9	42.2	8.5	6.4	25.6	11.8	15.4	11.0
Puerto Rico	28	2	−15.0	8.9	45.5	46.0	5.6	4.2	7.3	7.0	1.7	1.6
Qatar	8	4	2.4	11.6	..	..	0.1	0.3	0.9	1.6	2.8	1.8

3.1 | Rural population and land use

| | Rural population | | | Land area | Land use | | | | | | | |
| | % of total | | average annual % growth | thousand sq. km | Forest area (% of land area) | | Permanent cropland (% of land area) | | Arable land (% of land area) | | Arable land hectares per 100 people | |
	1990	2008	1990–2008	2008	1990	2007	1990	2007	1990	2007	1990–92	2005–07
Romania	47	46	−0.5	229.9	27.8	27.7	2.6	2.0	41.2	37.2	42.4	40.9
Russian Federation	27	27	−0.1	16,377.7	49.3	49.4	0.1	0.1	0.0	7.4	84.9a	85.3
Rwanda	95	82	0.9	24.7	12.9	21.7	12.4	11.1	35.7	48.6	12.1	12.7
Saudi Arabia	23	18	0.7	2,000.0d	1.4	1.4	0.0	0.1	1.7	1.7	17.0	14.6
Senegal	61	58	2.4	192.5	48.6	44.6	0.2	0.3	16.1	15.5	30.4	26.3
Serbia	50	48	−0.4	88.4	..	23.6	..	3.4	..	37.3	..	44.7
Sierra Leone	67	62	1.3	71.6	42.5	37.9	0.8	1.1	6.8	12.6	11.6	16.4
Singapore	0	0	..	0.7	3.4	3.3	1.5	0.3	1.5	0.9	0.0	0.0
Slovak Republic	44	43	0.1	48.1	40.0	40.2	0.5	0.5	32.5	28.6	27.1	25.6
Slovenia	50	51	0.3	20.1	59.5	63.3	1.8	1.3	9.9	8.8	8.6a	8.9
Somalia	70	64	1.1	627.3	13.2	11.1	0.0	0.0	1.6	1.6	14.4	13.7
South Africa	48	39	0.7	1,214.5	7.6	7.6	0.7	0.8	11.1	11.9	33.0	30.7
Spain	25	23	0.5	499.0	27.0	37.1	9.7	9.7	30.7	25.5	32.2	29.0
Sri Lanka	83	85	1.0	64.6	36.4	29.0	15.5	14.7	13.9	15.0	4.9	5.0
Sudan	73	57	0.9	2,376.0	32.1	27.9	0.0	0.1	5.4	8.1	45.9	48.9
Swaziland	77	75	1.5	17.2	27.4	32.0	0.7	0.8	10.5	10.3	16.3	15.6
Sweden	17	16	−0.1	410.3	66.7	67.1	0.0	0.0	6.9	6.4	30.2	29.3
Switzerland	27	27	0.7	40.0	28.9	30.7	0.5	0.6	9.8	10.2	5.7	5.4
Syrian Arab Republic	51	46	2.1	183.6	2.0	2.6	4.0	5.2	26.6	25.8	27.1	24.0
Tajikistan	68	74	1.8	140.0	2.9	2.9	0.9	0.7	6.1	5.1	12.5a	11.2
Tanzania	81	75	2.4	885.8	46.8	38.9	1.1	1.4	10.2	10.2	25.5	23.3
Thailand	71	67	0.6	510.9	31.2	28.2	6.1	7.3	34.2	29.8	24.7	22.9
Timor-Leste	79	73	1.7	14.9	65.0	52.2	3.9	4.6	7.4	11.4	16.3	16.5
Togo	70	58	1.7	54.4	12.6	6.4	1.7	3.1	38.6	45.2	46.5	40.2
Trinidad and Tobago	92	87	0.2	5.1	45.8	43.9	6.8	4.3	7.0	4.9	2.4	1.9
Tunisia	42	34	0.0	155.4	4.1	7.0	12.5	14.0	18.7	17.7	29.0	27.2
Turkey	41	31	0.1	769.6	12.6	13.3	3.9	3.8	32.0	28.5	35.4	31.8
Turkmenistan	55	51	1.4	469.9	8.8	8.8	0.1	0.1	2.9	3.9	37.8a	37.9
Uganda	89	87	3.1	197.1	25.0	17.5	9.4	11.2	25.4	27.9	20.2	18.3
Ukraine	33	32	−0.8	579.3	16.1	16.6	1.9	1.6	57.6	56.0	66.9a	69.3
United Arab Emirates	21	22	5.2	83.6	2.9	3.7	0.2	2.6	0.4	0.8	2.0	1.6
United Kingdom	11	10	−0.3	241.9	10.8	11.8	0.3	0.2	27.4	25.2	9.8	9.8
United States	25	18	−0.6	9,161.9	32.6	33.1	0.2	0.3	20.3	18.6	61.6	57.4
Uruguay	11	8	−1.6	175.0	5.2	8.8	0.3	0.2	7.2	7.7	40.8	40.1
Uzbekistan	60	63	1.9	425.4	7.2	7.8	0.9	0.8	10.5	10.1	18.0a	16.4
Venezuela, RB	16	7	−2.8	882.1	59.0	53.4	0.9	0.8	3.2	3.0	10.4	9.8
Vietnam	80	72	0.9	310.1	28.8	43.3	3.2	9.9	16.4	20.5	8.2	7.6
West Bank and Gaza	32	28	3.1	6.0	..	1.5	..	18.9	..	18.1	3.4	2.9
Yemen, Rep.	79	69	2.7	528.0	1.0	1.0	0.2	0.5	2.9	2.6	7.9	6.2
Zambia	61	65	2.9	743.4	66.1	55.9	0.0	0.0	7.1	7.1	49.1	43.8
Zimbabwe	71	63	0.3	386.9	57.5	43.7	0.3	0.3	7.5	8.3	25.9	25.9
World	**57 w**	**50 w**	**0.6 w**	**129,611.3 s**	**31.4 w**	**30.3 w**	**0.9 w**	**1.1 w**	**9.1 w**	**10.9 w**	**22.8 w**	**21.7 w**
Low income	77	71	1.8	18,731.9	27.9	24.7	0.7	1.0	6.8	8.7	18.1	17.3
Middle income	61	52	0.4	77,325.4	33.5	32.3	1.1	1.3	8.6	11.6	20.4	19.6
Lower middle income	69	59	0.5	31,182.2	25.7	24.8	1.7	2.3	14.8	17.0	15.0	14.5
Upper middle income	32	25	−0.3	46,143.3	38.7	37.3	0.6	0.7	4.3	7.9	40.9	39.0
Low & middle income	64	55	0.7	96,057.3	32.4	30.8	1.0	1.2	8.2	11.0	20.0	19.2
East Asia & Pacific	71	56	−0.3	15,853.6	28.9	28.5	2.2	3.0	12.1	13.3	11.0	10.9
Europe & Central Asia	37	36	0.0	23,054.0	38.2	38.4	0.4	0.4	2.7	10.8	58.5	57.1
Latin America & Carib.	29	21	−0.3	20,147.6	48.8	44.9	0.9	1.0	6.6	7.4	27.5	26.7
Middle East & N. Africa	48	43	1.3	8,643.6	2.3	2.5	0.8	1.0	5.9	6.0	17.9	16.4
South Asia	75	71	1.4	4,773.1	16.5	16.7	1.8	2.8	42.6	41.9	14.5	13.3
Sub-Saharan Africa	72	64	1.9	23,585.4	29.2	26.1	0.8	1.0	6.3	8.3	25.9	25.0
High income	27	22	−0.3	33,554.0	28.6	28.9	0.7	0.7	11.5	10.7	37.2	35.0
Euro area	29	27	−0.1	2,509.8	33.6	37.7	4.6	4.2	26.7	24.8	20.6	19.4

a. Data are not available for all three years. b. Includes Luxembourg. c. Data are from national sources. d. Provisional estimate.

With more than 3 billion people, including 70 percent of the world's poor people, living in rural areas, adequate indicators to monitor progress in rural areas are essential. However, few indicators are disaggregated between rural and urban areas (for some that are, see tables 2.7, 3.5, and 3.11). The table shows indicators of rural population and land use. Rural population is approximated as the midyear nonurban population. While a practical means of identifying the rural population, it is not precise (see box 3.1a for further discussion).

The data in the table show that land use patterns are changing. They also indicate major differences in resource endowments and uses among countries. True comparability of the data is limited, however, by variations in definitions, statistical methods, and quality of data. Countries use different definitions of rural and urban population and land use. The Food and Agriculture Organization of the United Nations (FAO), the primary compiler of the data, occasionally adjusts its definitions of land use categories and revises earlier data. Because the data reflect changes in reporting procedures as well as actual changes in land use, apparent trends should be interpreted cautiously.

Satellite images show land use that differs from that of ground-based measures in area under cultivation and type of land use. Moreover, land use data in some countries (India is an example) are based on reporting systems designed for collecting tax revenue. With land taxes no longer a major source of government revenue, the quality and coverage of land use data have declined. Data on forest area may be particularly unreliable because of irregular surveys and differences in definitions (see *About the data* for table 3.4). FAO's *Global Forest Resources Assessment 2005* is an important background document for the data. Conducted during 2003–05, it covers 229 countries and is the most comprehensive assessment of forests, forestry, and the benefits of forest resources in both scope and number of countries and people involved. It examines status and trends for about 40 variables on the extent, condition, uses, and values of forests and other wooded land.

• **Rural population** is calculated as the difference between the total population and the urban population (see *Definitions* for tables 2.1 and 3.11). • **Land area** is a country's total area, excluding area under inland water bodies and national claims to the continental shelf and to exclusive economic zones. In most cases the definition of inland water bodies includes major rivers and lakes. (See table 1.1 for the total surface area of countries.) Variations from year to year may be due to updated or revised data rather than to change in area. • **Land use** can be broken into several categories, three of which are presented in the table (not shown are land used as permanent pasture and land under urban developments). • **Forest area** is land under natural or planted stands of trees of at least 5 meters in height in situ, whether productive or not, and excludes tree stands in agricultural production systems (for example, in fruit plantations and agroforestry systems) and trees in urban parks and gardens. • **Permanent cropland** is land cultivated with crops that occupy the land for long periods and need not be replanted after each harvest, such as cocoa, coffee, and rubber. Land under flowering shrubs, fruit trees, nut trees, and vines is included, but land under trees grown for wood or timber is not. • **Arable land** is land defined by the FAO as under temporary crops (double-cropped areas are counted once), temporary meadows for mowing or pasture, land under market or kitchen gardens, and land temporarily fallow. Land abandoned as a result of shifting cultivation is excluded.

The rural population identified in table 3.1 is approximated as the difference between total population and urban population, calculated using the urban share reported by the United Nations Population Division. There is no universal standard for distinguishing rural from urban areas, and any urban-rural dichotomy is an oversimplification (see *About the data* for table 3.11). The two distinct images—isolated farm, thriving metropolis—represent poles on a continuum. Life changes along a variety of dimensions, moving from the most remote forest outpost through fields and pastures, past tiny hamlets, through small towns with weekly farm markets, into intensively cultivated areas near large towns and small cities, eventually reaching the center of a megacity. Along the way access to infrastructure, social services, and nonfarm employment increase, and with them population density and income. Because rurality has many dimensions, for policy purposes the rural-urban dichotomy presented in tables 3.1, 3.5, and 3.11 is inadequate.

A 2005 World Bank Policy Research Paper proposes an operational definition of rurality based on population density and distance to large cities (Chomitz, Buys, and Thomas 2005). The report argues that these criteria are important gradients along which economic behavior and appropriate development interventions vary substantially. Where population densities are low, markets of all kinds are thin, and the unit cost of delivering most social services and many types of infrastructure is high. Where large urban areas are distant, farm-gate or factory-gate prices of outputs will be low and input prices will be high, and it will be difficult to recruit skilled people to public service or private enterprises. Thus, low population density and remoteness together define a set of rural areas that face special development challenges.

Using these criteria and the Gridded Population of the World (CIESIN 2005), the authors' estimates of the rural population for Latin America and the Caribbean differ substantially from those in table 3.1. Their estimates range from 13 percent of the population, based on a population density of less than 20 people per square kilometer, to 64 percent, based on a population density of more than 500 people per square kilometer. Taking remoteness into account, the estimated rural population would be 13–52 percent. The estimate for Latin America and the Caribbean in table 3.1 is 21 percent.

Data on urban population shares used to estimate rural population are from the United Nations Population Division's *World Urbanization Prospects: The 2007 Revision,* and data on total population are World Bank estimates. Data on land area and land use are from the FAO's electronic files. The FAO gathers these data from national agencies through annual questionnaires and by analyzing the results of national agricultural censuses.

	Agricultural land[a]			Average annual precipitation	Land under cereal production		Fertilizer consumption		Agricultural employment		Agricultural machinery	
	% of land area		% irrigated	millimeters	thousand hectares		% of fertilizer production	kilograms per hectare of arable land	% of total employment		Tractors per 100 sq. km of arable land	
	1990–92	2005–07	2005–07	2008	1990–92	2006–08	2005–07	2005–07	1990–92	2005–07	1990–92	2005–07
Afghanistan	58	59	5.8	327	2,283.3	2,913.0	171.2	3.7	..	..	0.1	0.6
Albania	41	40	..	1,485	242.6	136.4		81.9		58.3	177.3	143.0
Algeria	16	17	2.0	89	3,104.9	2,831.5	86.1	12.7	..		128.5	136.9
Angola	46	46	..	1,010	892.6	1,487.5	..	2.9	5.1	..	30.5	27.3
Argentina	47	48	1.1	591	8,509.6	9,584.1	231.8	43.0	0.4	1.0	98.8	80.1
Armenia	41[b]	56	..	562	162.8[b]	178.4	523.6	27.5	..	46.2	345.5[b]	353.1
Australia	60	57	0.6	534	12,813.8	19,153.0	231.5	46.3	5.5	3.5	67.4	67.0
Austria	42	39	1.1	1,110	903.2	813.6	80.3	173.0	7.5	5.6	2,367.1	2,392.0
Azerbaijan	53[b]	58	30.0	447	627.0[b]	795.1	..	11.2	32.5[b]	39.0	194.8[b]	83.7
Bangladesh	73	70	55.7	2,666	10,985.4	11,616.4	149.1	185.6	66.4	48.1	2.4	3.2
Belarus	46[b]	44	1.3	618	2,603.0[b]	2,368.2	17.8	172.2	..	..	206.9[b]	94.3
Belgium	44[c]	46	1.6	847	354.3[c]	333.2	..	..	2.8	1.9	..	1,128.0
Benin	21	32	..	1,039	659.9	902.6	..	2.9	..	..	1.0	0.7
Bolivia	33	34	..	1,146	642.4	926.6	..	4.8	1.7	..	24.9	16.5
Bosnia and Herzegovina	43[b]	42	..	1,028	304.1[b]	308.0	..	44.9	..	..	235.3[b]	283.0
Botswana	46	46	0.0	416	140.1	81.7	..	..	..	29.9	142.9	117.4
Brazil	29	31	..	1,782	19,632.5	19,592.8	293.6	156.8	25.6	19.9	144.0	131.9
Bulgaria	56	48	1.3	608	2,179.3	1,598.5	71.4	97.0	19.7	8.2	127.8	132.2
Burkina Faso	35	40	..	748	2,724.5	3,529.1	..	8.5	..	..	2.9	16.9
Burundi	83	89	..	1,274	218.8	221.7	..	1.8	..	..	1.8	1.7
Cambodia	25	31	..	1,904	1,800.8	2,702.1	..	2.5	..	..	3.2	11.0
Cameroon	19	19	..	1,604	816.1	1,106.6	..	8.1	..	..	0.8	0.8
Canada	7	7	..	537	20,864.4	16,235.7	24.3	69.7	4.2	2.6	162.0	162.4
Central African Republic	8	8	..	1,343	104.0	204.7	..	..	..	..	0.2	0.2
Chad	38	39	..	322	1,241.9	2,541.1	..	..	..	..	0.5	0.4
Chile	21	21	6.1	1,522	741.6	542.3	101.6	428.2	18.8	12.8	143.7	396.6
China	57	59	..	..	93,430.3	86,057.9	103.4	327.9	53.5	..	64.4	124.3
Hong Kong, China	..	..	..	..	..	..	..	..	0.8	0.2	..	..
Colombia	41	38	..	2,612	1,598.1	997.6	827.6	344.1	1.4	20.1	97.8	106.3
Congo, Dem. Rep.	10	10	..	1,543	1,867.6	1,976.1	..	0.2	..	..	3.6	3.6
Congo, Rep.	31	31	..	1,646	9.1	27.4	..	0.5	..	..	14.7	14.1
Costa Rica	54	54	..	2,926	83.1	62.8	..	799.9	25.2	14.1	259.4	350.0
Côte d'Ivoire	60	63	..	1,348	1,434.0	808.6	..	25.7	..	..	19.7	33.4
Croatia	43[b]	22	0.6	1,113	592.7[b]	559.7	58.9	238.9	..	14.8	35.2[b]	2,203.3
Cuba	62	60	..	1,335	235.0	277.4	449.4	26.6	25.1	19.6	221.1	205.4
Czech Republic	..	55	1.5	677	..	1,561.9	137.6	146.4	..	3.8	..	281.0
Denmark	65	63	8.5	703	1,581.3	1,484.3	228.7	129.9	5.4	3.0	624.9	481.0
Dominican Republic	53	52	..	1,410	134.2	170.5	..	..	19.5	14.7	25.5	22.8
Ecuador	29	27	9.7	2,087	861.0	810.0	..	579.5	7.0	8.3	54.1	118.6
Egypt, Arab Rep.	3	4	..	51	2,410.2	2,956.4	86.2	570.5	36.2	31.1	250.7	333.1
El Salvador	69	76	1.9	1,724	452.6	361.9	..	84.9	23.1	19.5	60.3	48.6
Eritrea	..	75	..	384	345.6	419.2	..	2.3	..	..	..	7.3
Estonia	32[b]	19	..	626	453.6[b]	293.9	227.5	118.1	19.5[b]	5.0	455.3[b]	573.2
Ethiopia	..	34	0.4	848	..	8,589.5	..	8.3	..	44.4	..	2.2
Finland	8	8	2.8	536	1,050.5	1,158.6	88.0	138.2	8.8	4.6	899.9	779.8
France	56	54	5.8	867	9,211.6	9,260.9	219.8	205.2	5.6	3.6	784.1	624.7
Gabon	20	20	..	1,831	14.4	20.2	..	5.9	..	..	28.5	29.0
Gambia, The	63	81	..	836	89.5	212.7	..	4.9	..	..	1.9	2.6
Georgia	46[b]	36	4.0	1,026	248.5[b]	195.1	19.5	37.1	..	54.3	295.6[b]	468.4
Germany	50	49	..	700	6,673.0	6,770.8	54.2	212.8	3.9	2.2	1,253.3	673.0
Ghana	56	65	..	1,187	1,077.6	1,409.4	..	9.5	62.0	..	14.7	8.9
Greece	71	64	15.8	652	1,455.2	1,196.0	236.4	141.1	22.7	12.0	773.6	1,008.1
Guatemala	40	41	..	1,996	768.2	854.2	..	119.6	13.3	33.2	32.6	28.9
Guinea	49	55	..	1,651	774.2	1,822.9	..	1.6	..	..	43.4	27.0
Guinea-Bissau	53	58	..	1,577	112.4	142.6	..	..	..	..	0.6	0.7
Haiti	58	61	..	1,440	406.5	445.5	..	..	65.6	..	2.4	1.7
Honduras	30	28	..	1,976	502.3	409.3	..	117.8	42.1	39.2	31.1	49.6

	Agricultural land[a]			Average annual precipitation	Land under cereal production		Fertilizer consumption		Agricultural employment		Agricultural machinery	
	% of land area		% irrigated	millimeters	thousand hectares		% of fertilizer production	kilograms per hectare of arable land	% of total employment		Tractors per 100 sq. km of arable land	
	1990–92	2005–07	2005–07	2008	1990–92	2006–08	2005–07	2005–07	1990–92	2005–07	1990–92	2005–07
Hungary	71	65	2.2	589	2,803.5	2,899.4	215.4	118.0	15.2	4.9	157.8	264.2
India	61	61	30.4	1,083	100,759.8	99,791.3	133.0	121.3	..	..	65.4	186.9
Indonesia	24	27	15.4	2,702	13,861.2	15,740.9	117.3	158.8	54.9	42.4	2.7	2.3
Iran, Islamic Rep.	39	29	15.1	228	9,611.9	7,534.3	179.5	92.7	..	23.9	135.9	178.4
Iraq	23	22	..	216	3,506.1	3,334.8	132.7	22.0	..	..	64.9	139.3
Ireland	70	62	..	1,118	298.0	291.0	285.3	525.2	14.1	5.6	1,666.7	1,548.4
Israel	27	23	31.2	435	107.8	90.4	18.9	1,443.9	3.7	1.8	763.0	796.4
Italy	55	49	18.0	832	4,346.9	3,933.6	365.3	173.2	8.4	4.2	1,619.3	2,539.4
Jamaica	44	47	..	2,051	2.6	1.5	..	54.3	27.3	18.2	158.0	128.4
Japan	16	13	35.7	1,668	2,438.6	2,002.4	145.4	347.2	6.8	4.3	..	..
Jordan	12	11	7.6	111	111.9	56.4	10.7	911.4	..	..	351.9	323.9
Kazakhstan	82[b]	77	..	250	22,152.4[b]	14,857.6	119.0	5.9	..	..	62.0[b]	18.8
Kenya	47	47	0.1	630	1,765.9	2,149.1	..	35.0	..	..	20.0	26.2
Korea, Dem. Rep.	21	25	..	1,054	1,569.0	1,268.7	..	..	..	..	297.1	229.3
Korea, Rep.	22	19	52.7	1,274	1,367.8	1,030.5	150.8	453.6	16.7	7.7	274.6	1,458.2
Kosovo	..	52	..	..	..	..	..	..	..	..	..	..
Kuwait	8	9	..	121	0.4	1.4	4.4	1,022.2	..	..	215.0	70.0
Kyrgyz Republic	53[b]	56	9.4	533	578.0[b]	586.3	..	20.5	35.5[b]	37.4	189.4[b]	178.6
Lao PDR	7	9	..	1,834	625.3	951.8	..	..	..	..	11.4	9.8
Latvia	41[b]	29	..	641	696.7[b]	526.4	..	59.5	..	11.0	363.7[b]	498.3
Lebanon	59	66	19.9	661	41.5	70.4	31.8	273.5	..	..	187.6	576.6
Lesotho	77	76	..	788	177.6	222.9	..	..	..	..	57.1	64.6
Liberia	26	27	..	2,391	135.0	160.0	25.0	53.5	..	..	9.4	8.5
Libya	9	9	..	56	355.0	342.9	25.0	53.5	..	..	187.2	227.1
Lithuania	54[b]	44	..	656	1,134.0[b]	996.1	26.6	172.2	..	12.3	256.0[b]	650.6
Macedonia, FYR	51[b]	46	2.7	619	235.2[b]	179.2	..	50.2	..	19.3	730.2[b]	1,208.9
Madagascar	63	70	2.2	1,513	1,321.0	1,580.1	..	2.9	..	82.0	4.6	1.9
Malawi	45	53	..	1,181	1,442.6	1,701.1	..	36.4	..	..	6.1	4.8
Malaysia	23	24	..	2,875	699.3	683.2	229.6	821.3	24.4	14.7	..	..
Mali	26	32	..	282	2,392.7	3,424.1	..	0.0	..	..	10.5	2.3
Mauritania	38	39	..	92	132.9	235.0	..	..	..	..	8.2	8.2
Mauritius	56	51	20.4	2,041	0.5	0.1	507.5	278.7	15.5	9.6	36.2	60.0
Mexico	54	55	3.5	752	10,075.0	10,233.1	702.5	64.0	24.7	14.2	126.7	98.8
Moldova	78[b]	76	9.7	450	675.6[b]	923.1	..	12.9	38.5[b]	35.7	310.1[b]	208.5
Mongolia	81	75	..	241	620.0	134.0	..	6.0	..	38.8	73.2	46.1
Morocco	68	67	5.2	346	5,373.9	5,253.5	29.0	49.1	3.8	44.4	46.0	53.5
Mozambique	61	62	..	1,032	1,508.6	2,037.6	..	4.3	..	..	14.3	14.5
Myanmar	16	18	23.8	2,091	5,282.9	8,860.7	1,444.8	6.4	69.4	..	11.5	6.8
Namibia	47	47	..	285	206.4	289.1	..	2.6	48.2	..	30.3	24.7
Nepal	29	29	27.7	1,500	2,957.2	3,360.7	..	23.4	81.2	..	26.4	123.0
Netherlands	59	57	..	778	185.0	222.2	49.4	892.4	4.2	3.1	2,056.1	1,433.6
New Zealand	60	46	3.0	1,732	153.5	122.4	309.1	1,054.7	10.7	7.1	323.1	829.8
Nicaragua	34	44	..	2,391	299.3	458.9	..	29.9	38.7	29.0	20.3	20.1
Niger	27	34	..	151	7,010.6	9,313.6	..	0.4	..	..	0.1	0.1
Nigeria	79	85	..	1,150	16,416.7	19,152.0	974.8	5.0	..	..	4.9	6.7
Norway	3	3	4.2	1,414	361.4	336.8	28.0	237.0	5.9	3.2	1,731.8	1,544.2
Oman	3	6	..	125	2.4	4.8	3.6	285.7	..	..	42.0	35.2
Pakistan	34	35	64.9	494	11,776.8	13,145.5	132.6	160.8	48.9	43.3	133.3	207.8
Panama	29	30	..	2,692	182.4	149.0	..	39.9	26.2	15.4	103.3	147.8
Papua New Guinea	2	2	..	3,142	1.9	3.2	..	139.3	..	..	59.4	50.0
Paraguay	43	51	..	1,130	454.7	969.4	..	63.2	..	29.5	72.4	40.0
Peru	17	17	..	1,738	682.5	1,170.9	75,752.0	91.2	1.0	10.8	35.9	36.0
Philippines	37	38	..	2,348	6,957.4	6,924.3	265.1	150.6	45.3	36.6	72.1	124.4
Poland	62	53	0.5	600	8,522.7	8,444.3	102.8	170.8	25.2	16.0	820.7	1,211.8
Portugal	43	39	12.2	854	780.1	348.2	175.1	199.3	15.6	11.7	569.5	1,522.1
Puerto Rico	48	22	8.0	2,054	0.5	0.3	..	..	3.5	1.5	478.2	504.1
Qatar	64	61	..	74	5,842.3	5,006.4			30.6	30.7	146.1	197.1

	Agricultural land[a]			Average annual precipitation	Land under cereal production		Fertilizer consumption		Agricultural employment		Agricultural machinery	
	% of land area		% irrigated	millimeters	thousand hectares		% of fertilizer production	kilograms per hectare of arable land	% of total employment		Tractors per 100 sq. km of arable land	
	1990–92	2005–07	2005–07	2008	1990–92	2006–08	2005–07	2005–07	1990–92	2005–07	1990–92	2005–07
Romania	14	13	2.1	637	59,541.3	41,825.3	42.6	42.2	14.5	9.7	97.8	36.3
Russian Federation	76[b]	77	2.1	460	258.2[b]	328.0	12.1	12.4	..[b]	..	1.0[b]	0.5
Rwanda	5	6	..	1,212	1.2	2.0	..	2.6	..	3.0	75.9	41.3
Saudi Arabia	..	..	..	59	1,061.8	596.7	22.5	99.0	..	4.4	20.3	28.8
Senegal	46	45	0.7	686	1,153.8	1,230.8	78.3	9.0	..	33.7	1.7	3.0
Serbia	..	57	0.5	..	..	1,886.8	332.9	38.8	..	..	..	19.8
Sierra Leone	38	44	..	2,526	451.7	1,037.2	..	..	..	..	3.3	1.1
Singapore	2	1	..	2,497	..	..	..	13,528.1	0.3	1.2	636.7	1,083.3
Slovak Republic	..	40	2.7	824	..	772.2	50.9	84.3	..	4.4	..	158.6
Slovenia	28[b]	25	0.5	1,162	112.5[b]	101.5	38,791.4	354.9	..	9.5	..	..
Somalia	70	70	..	282	531.4	536.0	..	..	..	..	15.5	12.0
South Africa	80	82	..	495	5,735.9	3,408.5	170.2	48.7	..	8.3	101.1	43.3
Spain	61	58	12.1	636	7,588.5	6,381.8	117.0	155.5	10.5	4.9	494.2	782.0
Sri Lanka	36	37	..	1,712	834.3	955.1	2,497.4	289.5	44.3	31.3	175.0	213.2
Sudan	52	58	1.1	416	6,266.9	11,122.4	..	3.4	..	..	7.8	31.3
Swaziland	76	78	..	788	69.1	48.5	..	..	..	..	251.4	86.0
Sweden	8	8	..	624	1,184.3	1,009.4	316.9	100.3	3.3	2.1	604.4	596.7
Switzerland	47	39	..	1,537	207.3	159.8	..	214.0	4.2	3.8	2,870.2	2,624.7
Syrian Arab Republic	74	76	10.1	252	3,811.9	3,108.4	149.0	77.9	28.2	..	136.7	229.0
Tajikistan	32[b]	33	..	691	266.5[b]	403.3	369.3	22.0	45.8[b]	..	415.4[b]	299.0
Tanzania	38	39	..	1,071	3,003.3	5,013.0	..	6.0	..	74.6	8.2	23.1
Thailand	42	39	..	1,622	10,593.6	11,520.2	1,148.7	123.3	61.1	42.1	38.8	529.6
Timor-Leste	22	26	..	..	83.7	101.7	..	..	..	..	8.0	5.2
Togo	59	67	..	1,168	610.2	797.5	..	..	..	..	0.5	0.3
Trinidad and Tobago	16	11	12.7	2,200	6.4	2.0	3.5	406.8	11.8	4.3	..	..
Tunisia	58	63	3.6	207	1,524.7	1,311.0	9.1	39.3	..	..	88.3	142.5
Turkey	52	52	12.8	593	13,759.9	12,183.5	218.9	102.5	46.5	27.7	286.7	447.0
Turkmenistan	69[b]	69	..	161	331.3[b]	1,000.5	..	..	..	..	464.7[b]	268.8
Uganda	61	65	..	1,180	1,097.6	1,724.7	..	1.5	..	..	9.2	8.7
Ukraine	72[b]	71	5.3	565	12,542.3[b]	14,012.9	28.3	21.8	20.0[b]	17.9	153.3[b]	106.2
United Arab Emirates	4	7	..	78	1.4	0.0	14.4	615.8	..	4.9	49.8	56.0
United Kingdom	75	72	..	1,220	3,548.5	3,006.3	126.3	289.3	2.2	1.3	761.2	744.2
United States	47	45	..	715	64,547.3	58,581.6	134.1	149.9	2.9	1.5	235.8	258.9
Uruguay	85	84	1.2	1,265	509.4	711.4	1,040.8	133.4	1.5	8.9	259.5	274.4
Uzbekistan	65[b]	63	..	206	1,225.3[b]	1,562.9	..	..	..	..	402.3[b]	390.8
Venezuela, RB	25	24	..	1,875	798.7	1,138.7	61.7	167.1	12.6	8.9	176.1	184.9
Vietnam	21	32	..	1,821	6,726.1	8,390.6	441.2	374.3	..	..	60.4	256.6
West Bank and Gaza	..	62	4.3	402	..	32.8	..	..	..	15.4	..	694.2
Yemen, Rep.	45	45	2.8	167	738.2	879.7	..	10.0	52.6	..	40.4	48.4
Zambia	31	34	..	1,020	813.4	896.0	..	16.3	49.8	..	11.3	11.4
Zimbabwe	34	40	..	657	1,430.8	2,139.5	161.6	35.5	..	..	61.4	74.3
World	**38 w**	**38 w**	**1.8 w**		**707,271.9 s**	**697,843.7 s**	**99.5 w**	**117.7 w**	**.. w**	**.. w**	**189.6 w**	**198.7 w**
Low income	36	38	1.5		73,977.3	100,232.3	256.2	35.0	..	..	33.5	33.7
Middle income	38	38	2.3		483,693.9	456,809.5	101.5	120.2	..	..	131.7	152.1
Lower middle income	49	50	3.6		310,393.3	314,214.7	109.1	155.1	..	..	72.3	140.7
Upper middle income	30	30	1.0		173,300.6	142,594.7	83.1	70.5	20.9	15.7	252.6	175.2
Low & middle income	37	38	2.2		557,671.3	557,041.8	104.2	108.5	..	..	117.0	133.1
East Asia & Pacific	48	50	0.9		142,265.1	143,348.3	114.0	271.0	53.5	..	55.1	137.7
Europe & Central Asia	28	28	2.0		136,657.9	109,979.2	35.2	37.7	23.4	17.6	187.1	175.3
Latin America & Carib.	34	36	0.5		47,722.2	50,046.2	298.3	111.9	18.7	16.4	121.7	109.0
Middle East & N. Africa	24	23	5.9		30,590.3	27,701.1	58.0	89.9	..	..	114.2	161.4
South Asia	55	55	16.1		129,690.1	131,869.1	135.4	122.8	..	..	67.1	173.2
Sub-Saharan Africa	43	44	0.2		70,745.7	94,098.0	343.8	10.8	..	..	17.7	14.9
High income	38	38	0.8		149,600.7	140,801.9	90.8	143.8	5.6	3.2	360.2	380.7
Euro area	50	47	4.2		33,854.7	31,664.6	107.3	200.8	6.9	4.2	989.0	1,013.0

a. Includes permanent pastures, arable land, and land under permanent crops. b. Data are not available for all three years. c. Includes Luxembourg.

Agriculture is still a major sector in many economies, and agricultural activities provide developing countries with food and revenue. But agricultural activities also can degrade natural resources. Poor farming practices can cause soil erosion and loss of soil fertility. Efforts to increase productivity by using chemical fertilizers, pesticides, and intensive irrigation have environmental costs and health impacts. Excessive use of chemical fertilizers can alter the chemistry of soil. Pesticide poisoning is common in developing countries. And salinization of irrigated land diminishes soil fertility. Thus, inappropriate use of inputs for agricultural production has far-reaching effects.

The table provides indicators of major inputs to agricultural production: land, fertilizer, labor, and machinery. There is no single correct mix of inputs:

Nearly 40 percent of land globally is devoted to agriculture   **3.2a**

Total land area in 2007: 130 million sq. km

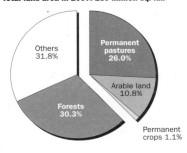

- Others 31.8%
- Permanent pastures 26.0%
- Arable land 10.8%
- Forests 30.3%
- Permanent crops 1.1%

Note: Agricultural land includes permanent pastures, arable land, and land under permanent crops.
Source: Tables 3.1 and 3.2.

Developing regions lag in agricultural machinery, which reduces their agricultural productivity   **3.2b**

Tractors per 100 square kilometers of arable land   ■ 1990–92   ■ 2005–07

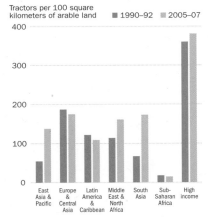

Source: Table 3.2.

appropriate levels and application rates vary by country and over time and depend on the type of crops, the climate and soils, and the production process used.

The agriculture sector is the most water-intensive sector, and water delivery in agriculture is increasingly important. The table shows irrigated agricultural land as share of total agricultural land area and data on average precipitation to illustrate how countries obtain water for agricultural use.

The data shown here and in table 3.3 are collected by the Food and Agriculture Organization of the United Nations (FAO) through annual questionnaires. The FAO tries to impose standard definitions and reporting methods, but complete consistency across countries and over time is not possible. Thus, data on agricultural land in different climates may not be comparable. For example, permanent pastures are quite different in nature and intensity in African countries and dry Middle Eastern countries. Data on agricultural employment, in particular, should be used with caution. In many countries much agricultural employment is informal and unrecorded, including substantial work performed by women and children. To address some of these concerns, this indicator is heavily footnoted in the database in sources, definition, and coverage.

Fertilizer consumption measures the quantity of plant nutrients. Consumption is calculated as production plus imports minus exports. Because some chemical compounds used for fertilizers have other industrial applications, the consumption data may overstate the quantity available for crops. Fertilizer consumption as a share of production shows the agriculture sector's vulnerability to import and energy price fluctuation. The FAO recently revised the time series for fertilizer consumption and irrigation for 2002 onward, but recent data are not available for all countries. FAO collects fertilizer statistics for production, imports, exports, and consumption through the new FAO fertilizer resources questionnaire. In the previous release, the data were based on total consumption of fertilizers, but the data in the recent release are based on the nutrients in fertilizers. Some countries compile fertilizer data on a calendar year basis, while others do so on a crop year basis (July–June). Previous editions of *World Development Indicators* reported data on a crop year basis, but this edition uses the calendar year, as adopted by the FAO. Caution should thus be used when comparing data over time.

To smooth annual fluctuations in agricultural activity, all the indicators in the table (except average annual precipitation) have been averaged over three years.

- **Agricultural land** is the share of land area that is permanent pastures, arable, or under permanent crops. Permanent pasture is land used for five or more years for forage, including natural and cultivated crops. Arable land includes land defined by the FAO as land under temporary crops (double-cropped areas are counted once), temporary meadows for mowing or for pasture, land under market or kitchen gardens, and land temporarily fallow. Land abandoned as a result of shifting cultivation is excluded. Land under permanent crops is land cultivated with crops that occupy the land for long periods and need not be replanted after each harvest, such as cocoa, coffee, and rubber. Land under flowering shrubs, fruit trees, nut trees, and vines is included, but land under trees grown for wood or timber is not. • **Irrigated land** refers to areas purposely provided with water, including land irrigated by controlled flooding. • **Average annual precipitation** is the long-term average in depth (over space and time) of annual precipitation in the country. Precipitation is defined as any kind of water that falls from clouds as a liquid or a solid. • **Land under cereal production** refers to harvested areas, although some countries report only sown or cultivated area. • **Fertilizer consumption** is the quantity of plant nutrients used per unit of arable land. Fertilizer products cover nitrogen, potash, and phosphate fertilizers (including ground rock phosphate). Traditional nutrients—animal and plant manures—are not included. • **Fertilizer production** is fertilizer consumption, exports, and nonfertilizer use of fertilizer products minus fertilizer imports. • **Agricultural employment** is employment in agriculture, forestry, hunting, and fishing (see table 2.3). • **Agricultural machinery** refers to wheel and crawler tractors (excluding garden tractors) in use in agriculture at the end of the calendar year specified or during the first quarter of the following year.

	Crop production index		Food production index		Livestock production index		Cereal yield		Agricultural productivity	
							kilograms per hectare		Agriculture value added per worker 2000 $	
	1999–2001 = 100		1999–2001 = 100		1999–2001 = 100					
	1990–92	2005–07	1990–92	2005–07	1990–92	2005–07	1990–92	2006–08	1990–92	2005–07
Afghanistan	148.0	124.0	119.7	94.3	100.0	71.0	1,153	1,603	..	..
Albania	81.0	112.3	69.7	112.0	62.0	110.3	2,372	3,717	837	1,663
Algeria	99.7	144.3	95.7	126.3	94.7	107.0	915	1,384	1,823	2,239
Angola	76.7	147.3	82.3	126.0	96.3	83.3	378	490	176	222
Argentina	74.3	120.0	81.7	113.3	99.0	102.0	2,652	3,991	6,919	11,191
Armenia	95.0[a]	180.3	101.0[a]	164.3	106.0[a]	131.7	1,843[a]	1,992	1,607[a]	4,508
Australia	66.7	73.3	104.0	77.3	155.0	84.3	1,739	1,292	20,676	30,830
Austria	96.3	99.3	93.3	91.7	95.7	91.0	5,400	6,128	12,060	21,440
Azerbaijan	147.0[a]	137.7	112.0[a]	132.0	103.0[a]	128.0	2,113[a]	2,669	1,067[a]	1,222
Bangladesh	90.7	103.0	88.7	104.3	87.3	114.3	2,567	3,896	255	387
Belarus	107.0[a]	146.3	132.0[a]	138.0	142.0[a]	129.0	2,741[a]	3,000	2,042[a]	4,266
Belgium	77.6[b]	103.0	87.8[b]	62.3	93.8[b]	50.7	6,122.0[b]	8,223	..	38,337
Benin	76.7	88.3	83.3	94.0	118.3	98.7	880	1,247	429	661
Bolivia	78.0	107.7	86.3	101.7	93.3	101.7	1,373	1,933	703	732
Bosnia and Herzegovina	101.0[a]	113.3	113.0[a]	119.0	114.0[a]	139.3	3,553[a]	3,977	..	10,352
Botswana	117.7	103.0	137.3	103.7	141.3	103.7	312	487	766	452
Brazil	87.3	122.0	79.7	118.0	74.3	113.3	1,916	3,531	1,611	3,315
Bulgaria	137.7	89.3	125.3	82.0	133.7	68.0	3,633	3,252	2,686	8,015
Burkina Faso	95.7	115.3	94.7	103.7	88.0	103.3	783	1,118	126	182
Burundi	128.7	86.7	128.3	86.0	153.0	74.7	1,370	1,307	117	70
Cambodia	82.7	145.3	82.7	139.0	82.3	104.0	1,356	2,672	..	376
Cameroon	89.0	98.3	93.0	98.7	106.0	90.0	1,166	1,343	409	703
Canada	95.3	101.0	91.0	103.0	83.7	104.7	2,559	3,133	28,541	46,138
Central African Republic	92.7	89.7	86.7	98.3	84.3	101.3	883	1,115	322	409
Chad	92.0	92.3	97.0	95.0	113.3	90.3	636	775	209	246
Chile	89.3	111.7	84.0	110.0	77.3	109.0	3,949	5,960	3,618	6,103
China	75.7	116.0	66.3	117.7	54.7	116.3	4,307	5,388	269	459
Hong Kong SAR, China	..	..	..	..	..	..	..	..	..	..
Colombia	106.3	92.7	93.3	95.3	94.0	101.3	2,492	4,046	3,342	3,001
Congo, Dem. Rep.	160.3	82.7	156.3	82.7	130.0	80.3	794	772	209	162
Congo, Rep.	102.0	98.3	100.7	103.7	96.7	128.3	688	776	..	..
Costa Rica	89.7	98.3	90.3	103.7	99.0	101.3	3,188	3,433	3,158	5,132
Côte d'Ivoire	92.7	95.3	95.3	101.0	117.3	100.0	863	1,713	652	875
Croatia	78.0[a]	84.0	98.0[a]	92.3	124.0[a]	113.0	3,975[a]	5,535	5,553[a]	14,823
Cuba	117.0	83.7	116.0	84.3	135.0	83.7	2,092	2,787	..	..
Czech Republic	..	94.3	..	96.0	..	89.7	..	4,679	..	5,871
Denmark	106.0	94.7	100.3	100.0	91.7	102.0	5,448	5,825	15,190	43,201
Dominican Republic	137.3	108.3	120.3	122.3	92.7	133.3	4,078	4,292	2,055	3,829
Ecuador	92.3	96.0	83.3	103.3	75.0	105.7	1,724	2,995	1,801	1,872
Egypt, Arab Rep.	81.3	104.7	79.3	105.3	77.0	104.7	5,738	7,537	1,826	2,758
El Salvador	120.7	88.7	106.3	100.0	92.3	113.7	1,871	2,957	1,774	2,404
Eritrea	..	83.7	..	81.3	..	78.7	..	456	..	118
Estonia	108.0[a]	113.3	162.0[a]	122.7	173.0[a]	108.7	1,304[a]	2,679	..	4,550
Ethiopia	..	115.7	..	116.0	..	113.3	..	1,489	..	187
Finland	100.0	107.0	106.7	101.7	109.7	100.0	3,246	3,497	19,011	35,653
France	97.0	90.0	100.7	91.7	100.7	92.7	6,370	6,880	22,254	47,418
Gabon	108.7	91.0	111.0	91.0	108.0	91.0	1,712	1,656	1,246	1,741
Gambia, The	77.3	68.3	83.0	69.3	136.0	87.3	1,114	935	262	269
Georgia	108.0[a]	87.3	93.0[a]	95.0	71.0[a]	96.0	1,998[a]	1,954	2,359[a]	1,871
Germany	86.0	90.3	101.0	94.0	110.0	99.7	5,578	6,596	13,863	26,745
Ghana	72.3	111.3	75.0	110.3	114.3	93.7	1,084	1,330	352	378
Greece	91.3	85.7	99.7	89.3	111.7	95.7	3,589	4,069	7,669	8,656
Guatemala	95.7	109.3	93.0	112.0	94.3	91.3	1,882	1,582	2,304	2,719
Guinea	98.7	107.3	99.0	107.7	78.3	121.0	1,423	1,501	156	208
Guinea-Bissau	92.3	95.0	95.0	95.0	105.3	95.0	1,529	1,464	236	315
Haiti	127.7	88.0	117.7	92.7	82.0	102.0	997	885	..	..
Honduras	113.7	128.0	107.0	125.3	84.7	117.0	1,371	1,662	1,227	1,858

	Crop production index		Food production index		Livestock production index		Cereal yield		Agricultural productivity	
	1999–2001 = 100		1999–2001 = 100		1999–2001 = 100		kilograms per hectare		Agriculture value added per worker 2000 $	
	1990–92	2005–07	1990–92	2005–07	1990–92	2005–07	1990–92	2006–08	1990–92	2005–07
Hungary	111.7	108.3	115.3	101.7	124.7	86.7	4,551	5,226	4,289	8,136
India	95.0	100.3	91.0	101.7	83.3	112.3	1,947	2,574	359	460
Indonesia	93.7	120.3	95.3	121.3	99.3	132.3	3,826	4,508	519	657
Iran, Islamic Rep.	85.7	117.3	83.3	118.7	77.7	119.7	1,523	2,574	2,042	2,931
Iraq	120.3	96.7	117.7	92.7	117.0	93.0	872	1,377	..	..
Ireland	99.3	80.0	102.0	84.7	101.0	85.7	6,653	7,417	..	14,217
Israel	127.0	100.7	108.0	93.3	94.7	93.7	3,132	2,741	..	..
Italy	98.7	94.3	98.0	94.0	96.3	95.0	4,340	5,282	11,714	26,784
Jamaica	91.0	88.0	82.0	92.7	70.7	104.0	1,298	1,227	2,366	2,400
Japan	115.0	93.3	110.7	96.7	109.0	98.7	5,713	5,977	20,350	39,368
Jordan	139.0	127.3	122.7	118.3	97.3	98.7	1,167	891	2,348	2,232
Kazakhstan	149.0[a]	121.7	149.0[a]	121.0	163.0[a]	124.7	1,338[a]	1,169	1,776[a]	1,730
Kenya	108.3	101.0	111.3	108.7	114.3	117.0	1,645	1,621	379	367
Korea, Dem. Rep.	140.7	106.0	129.0	109.7	131.7	128.7	5,073	3,607	..	..
Korea, Rep.	94.7	90.7	85.7	92.3	73.3	98.0	5,885	6,525	5,804	14,501
Kosovo	..	..	..	..	..	..	..	..	..	..
Kuwait	35.7	96.0	27.7	101.3	29.0	99.3	3,112	2,623	..	..
Kyrgyz Republic	76.0[a]	93.7	81.0[a]	96.7	118.0[a]	97.3	2,772[a]	2,481	684[a]	1,017
Lao PDR	77.0	117.7	73.0	115.7	74.3	109.3	2,355	3,612	382	495
Latvia	117.0[a]	139.3	203.0[a]	128.7	249.0[a]	114.3	1,641[a]	2,767	1,896[a]	3,260
Lebanon	136.3	88.0	124.3	96.7	80.3	115.0	2,001	2,351	..	30,573
Lesotho	77.3	68.0	91.3	78.3	110.3	87.0	703	569	259	193
Liberia	90.0	90.3	116.3	95.7	132.0	99.0	951	1,421	..	..
Libya	94.3	91.0	93.0	90.3	92.7	89.0	706	619	..	..
Lithuania	75.0[a]	99.3	149.0[a]	125.3	175.0[a]	125.0	1,938[a]	2,762	..	4,636
Macedonia, FYR	112.0[a]	101.0	116.0	105.7	119.0	118.0	2,652	3,135	2,413	4,395
Madagascar	122.3	103.7	121.0	100.7	130.7	89.7	1,935	2,418	210	182
Malawi	66.3	98.3	56.3	99.3	97.3	107.0	871	1,837	86	126
Malaysia	92.7	116.7	88.0	114.7	100.3	114.3	2,827	3,422	398	583
Mali	93.0	101.3	103.3	113.0	114.7	109.0	840	1,133	405	515
Mauritania	80.3	85.3	111.3	95.3	116.3	96.3	802	760	671	414
Mauritius	122.0	90.0	111.3	98.3	77.0	129.7	4,117	8,381	3,747	5,222
Mexico	94.0	105.7	89.0	110.0	83.3	110.0	2,520	3,341	2,274	3,022
Moldova	127.0[a]	102.7	146.0[a]	116.3	183.0[a]	116.7	2,928[a]	2,236	1,349[a]	1,278
Mongolia	270.0	115.0	110.0	72.7	104.3	70.7	967	1,141	1,150	1,511
Morocco	115.0	129.7	107.3	121.7	93.3	101.3	1,094	1,057	1,788	2,306
Mozambique	81.0	105.7	87.0	92.3	112.3	104.3	330	787	117	173
Myanmar	68.7	133.3	71.0	139.7	66.0	180.3	2,739	3,670	..	..
Namibia	90.3	117.0	133.3	93.0	141.7	86.3	388	434	1,307	1,917
Nepal	92.3	104.3	93.7	103.0	99.3	102.0	1,831	2,286	245	241
Netherlands	98.3	93.7	110.3	89.7	110.3	89.0	7,142	7,813	24,752	39,910
New Zealand	87.3	100.0	86.7	110.3	89.7	109.7	5,257	7,439	19,150	26,105
Nicaragua	91.7	112.3	76.0	119.3	68.7	125.0	1,543	1,866	..	2,334
Niger	96.7	116.3	90.0	112.3	81.3	106.0	323	460	242	..
Nigeria	86.7	108.0	86.7	106.3	90.3	99.0	1,135	1,502	..	..
Norway	125.0	99.0	108.7	94.3	103.0	91.7	3,744	3,690	19,077	39,206
Oman	78.0	87.7	74.7	104.0	81.7	139.3	2,206	3,265	1,012	..
Pakistan	99.7	102.7	87.3	106.0	83.3	108.7	1,818	2,656	765	888
Panama	130.7	100.3	107.0	97.0	82.7	95.0	1,862	2,195	2,341	4,011
Papua New Guinea	99.0	91.0	100.7	95.7	102.0	100.3	2,504	3,700	555	639
Paraguay	105.0	126.0	96.3	116.0	113.7	91.7	1,905	3,092	1,648	2,136
Peru	57.0	120.3	63.3	121.3	77.7	121.0	2,463	3,657	879	1,390
Philippines	103.7	109.7	95.3	108.0	74.7	105.3	2,070	3,278	905	1,148
Poland	109.3	88.0	110.0	104.0	115.0	106.0	2,958	3,022	1,605	2,901
Portugal	109.0	89.7	103.0	94.3	87.3	96.7	1,939	3,418	4,642	6,387
Puerto Rico	176.7	98.7	136.3	89.0	127.0	86.7	1,100	1,882	..	..
Qatar	83.3	73.0	98.0	51.7	109.7	34.3	2,941	3,585	..	..

	Crop production index		Food production index		Livestock production index		Cereal yield		Agricultural productivity	
							kilograms per hectare		Agriculture value added per worker 2000 $	
	1999–2001 = 100		1999–2001 = 100		1999–2001 = 100					
	1990–92	2005–07	1990–92	2005–07	1990–92	2005–07	1990–92	2006–08	1990–92	2005–07
Romania	87.3	97.3	94.7	104.3	116.3	112.7	2,777	2,664	2,129	6,179
Russian Federation	125.0[a]	134.7	130.0[a]	122.3	149.0[a]	111.0	1,743[a]	2,092	1,917[a]	2,914
Rwanda	129.0	102.3	125.0	103.3	93.3	105.3	1,088	1,110	193	226
Saudi Arabia	149.7	112.0	130.7	99.3	84.0	95.0	4,212	5,099	8,476	17,365
Senegal	90.0	67.3	92.3	72.7	110.3	96.7	803	892	251	224
Serbia	101.0[a,c]	123.0[a,c]	113.0[a,c]	109.0[a,c]	107.0[a,c]	97.0[a,c]	2,926[a,c]	4,087	..	1,890[a,c]
Sierra Leone	136.7	148.7	131.0	146.0	117.0	107.7	1,223	1,016	..	..
Singapore	204.3	343.7	467.3	122.0	526.0	100.7	..	..	22,695	50,828
Slovak Republic	..	99.0	..	93.7	..	79.3	..	4,244	..	4,995
Slovenia	84.0[a]	102.7	78.0[a]	100.7	78.0[a]	100.0	3,279[a]	5,310	13,217[a]	50,960
Somalia	110.3	87.0	90.7	87.0	88.0	87.0	622	408	..	..
South Africa	95.3	92.7	101.3	104.0	114.3	116.3	1,602	3,244	2,149	3,077
Spain	90.7	90.7	89.3	90.3	81.3	95.0	2,310	3,493	9,583	17,894
Sri Lanka	93.0	104.0	96.0	106.0	101.7	114.7	2,950	3,700	697	823
Sudan	83.3	100.3	78.0	107.3	77.0	113.7	596	600	526	844
Swaziland	126.3	101.0	128.7	106.7	152.3	110.7	1,299	845	993	1,108
Sweden	104.7	91.7	100.0	96.7	97.3	93.3	4,272	4,781	22,319	39,578
Switzerland	117.3	92.3	110.0	98.0	110.0	99.3	6,102	6,361	19,369	22,653
Syrian Arab Republic	92.0	103.0	94.0	107.3	95.0	116.7	947	1,749	2,778	4,479
Tajikistan	138.0[a]	141.7	151.0[a]	147.7	214.0[a]	168.0	1,020[a]	2,246	370[a]	517
Tanzania	118.0	122.3	111.0	109.7	100.3	92.3	1,276	1,209	261	324
Thailand	89.7	110.0	92.0	109.0	94.7	103.0	2,186	3,007	480	653
Timor-Leste	103.7	81.0	113.3	86.7	109.0	102.0	1,694	1,184	..	..
Togo	93.7	85.7	95.3	98.0	112.7	98.7	791	1,130	345	394
Trinidad and Tobago	122.7	65.0	93.0	106.3	77.0	140.3	3,159	2,656	1,818	1,317
Tunisia	119.7	118.3	103.7	109.3	68.7	95.0	1,401	1,278	2,975	3,424
Turkey	102.3	100.0	104.0	99.3	107.0	94.3	2,192	2,548	2,204	3,229
Turkmenistan	114.0[a]	119.0	69.0[a]	122.3	75.0[a]	118.3	2,210[a]	3,079	1,321[a]	..
Uganda	103.3	85.0	105.3	87.3	109.3	93.3	1,487	1,528	175	191
Ukraine	124.0[a]	133.3	139.0[a]	119.0	161.0[a]	108.3	2,834[a]	2,707	1,232[a]	2,010
United Arab Emirates	35.0	38.7	39.7	41.7	94.7	90.3	2,042	2,200	10,414	29,465
United Kingdom	105.7	91.7	109.3	93.0	108.3	95.0	6,321	7,110	21,817	28,065
United States	97.0	99.7	92.7	99.7	91.3	98.0	4,875	6,578	20,353	45,015
Uruguay	73.7	137.7	80.3	124.0	88.0	116.7	2,445	4,185	6,278	9,370
Uzbekistan	124.0[a]	124.7	107.0[a]	121.7	113.0[a]	112.3	1,777[a]	4,287	1,427[a]	2,231
Venezuela, RB	95.7	96.0	89.7	95.7	89.7	93.7	2,561	3,533	4,584	7,386
Vietnam	69.7	116.0	71.3	114.3	60.0	113.3	3,097	4,883	229	335
West Bank and Gaza	..	91.0	..	92.7	..	91.3	..	1,863	..	..
Yemen, Rep.	102.7	97.7	99.0	102.7	93.3	110.7	906	963	412	..
Zambia	95.3	116.3	105.3	103.7	106.3	96.0	1,251	1,803	189	232
Zimbabwe	81.0	56.3	90.7	81.0	105.0	94.7	1,125	592	271	239
World	**82.0 w**	**114.7 w**	**78.8 w**	**114.3 w**	**83.7 w**	**112.2 w**	**2,847 w**	**3,397 w**	**801 w**	**959 w**
Low income	77.3	122.8	76.0	123.2	82.5	122.9	1,710	2,190	249	307
Middle income	79.5	119.3	73.2	119.7	77.5	119.0	2,537	3,122	501	741
Lower middle income	76.0	119.3	69.6	120.3	64.9	121.2	2,672	3,324	383	570
Upper middle income	89.8	119.5	82.7	118.4	99.8	114.9	1,961	2,676	2,154	3,286
Low & middle income	79.3	119.7	73.4	120.1	77.9	119.2	2,419	2,954	465	663
East Asia & Pacific	71.6	122.6	65.0	124.0	53.9	122.2	3,816	4,767	307	491
Europe & Central Asia	114.2	115.8	116.7	113.9	150.7	109.0	1,935	2,335	2,009	2,842
Latin America & Carib.	77.2	124.0	73.5	121.7	73.0	117.9	2,234	3,487	2,213	3,273
Middle East & N. Africa	79.1	123.7	76.6	123.1	71.3	120.6	1,544	2,308	1,846	2,823
South Asia	80.0	112.1	75.8	114.0	69.9	122.8	1,977	2,678	372	480
Sub-Saharan Africa	74.9	118.0	76.4	119.5	82.6	120.1	987	1,205	305	318
High income	90.3	99.9	91.4	100.4	93.1	101.0	4,260	5,147	14,601	27,557
Euro area	91.8	95.1	96.0	94.8	97.8	96.0	4,631	5,597	12,696	22,921

a. Data are not available for all three years. b. Includes Luxembourg. c. Includes Montenegro.

About the data

The agricultural production indexes in the table are prepared by the Food and Agriculture Organization of the United Nations (FAO). The FAO obtains data from official and semiofficial reports of crop yields, area under production, and livestock numbers. If data are unavailable, the FAO makes estimates. The indexes are calculated using the Laspeyres formula: production quantities of each commodity are weighted by average international commodity prices in the base period and summed for each year. Because the FAO's indexes are based on the concept of agriculture as a single enterprise, estimates of the amounts retained for seed and feed are subtracted from the production data to avoid double counting. The resulting aggregate represents production available for any use except as seed and feed. The FAO's indexes may differ from those from other sources because of differences in coverage, weights, concepts, time periods, calculation methods, and use of international prices.

To facilitate cross-country comparisons, the FAO uses international commodity prices to value production. These prices, expressed in international dollars (equivalent in purchasing power to the U.S. dollar), are derived using a Geary-Khamis formula applied to agricultural outputs (see United Nations System of National Accounts 1993, sections 16.93–96). This method assigns a single price to each commodity so that, for example, one metric ton of wheat has the same price regardless of where it was produced. The use of international prices eliminates fluctuations in the value of output due to transitory movements of nominal exchange rates unrelated to the purchasing power of the domestic currency.

Data on cereal yield may be affected by a variety of reporting and timing differences. Millet and sorghum, which are grown as feed for livestock and poultry in Europe and North America, are used as food in Africa, Asia, and countries of the former Soviet Union. So some cereal crops are excluded from the data for some countries and included elsewhere, depending on their use. To smooth annual fluctuations in agricultural activity, the indicators in the table have been averaged over three years.

Definitions

- **Crop production index** is agricultural production for each period relative to the base period 1999–2001. It includes all crops except fodder crops. The regional and income group aggregates for the FAO's production indexes are calculated from the underlying values in international dollars, normalized to the base period 1999–2001. • **Food production index** covers food crops that are considered edible and that contain nutrients. Coffee and tea are excluded because, although edible, they have no nutritive value. • **Livestock production index** includes meat and milk from all sources, dairy products such as cheese, and eggs, honey, raw silk, wool, and hides and skins. • **Cereal yield,** measured in kilograms per hectare of harvested land, includes wheat, rice, maize, barley, oats, rye, millet, sorghum, buckwheat, and mixed grains. Production data on cereals refer to crops harvested for dry grain only. Cereal crops harvested for hay or harvested green for food, feed, or silage, and those used for grazing, are excluded. The FAO allocates production data to the calendar year in which the bulk of the harvest took place. But most of a crop harvested near the end of a year will be used in the following year. • **Agricultural productivity** is the ratio of agricultural value added, measured in 2000 U.S. dollars, to the number of workers in agriculture. Agricultural productivity is measured by value added per unit of input. (For further discussion of the calculation of value added in national accounts, see *About the data* for tables 4.1 and 4.2.) Agricultural value added includes that from forestry and fishing. Thus interpretations of land productivity should be made with caution.

Cereal yield in low-income economies is less than 40 percent of the yield in high-income countries
3.3a

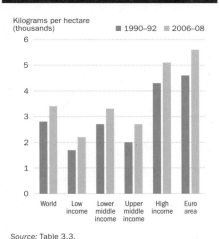

Kilograms per hectare (thousands)

■ 1990–92 ■ 2006–08

Source: Table 3.3.

Sub-Saharan Africa has the lowest yield, while East Asia and Pacific is closing the gap with high-income economies
3.3b

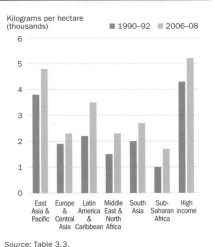

Kilograms per hectare (thousands)

■ 1990–92 ■ 2006–08

Source: Table 3.3.

Data sources

Data on agricultural production indexes, cereal yield, and agricultural employment are from electronic files that the FAO makes available to the World Bank. The files may contain more recent information than published versions. Data on agricultural value added are from the World Bank's national accounts files.

3.4 Deforestation and biodiversity

	Forest area		Average annual deforestation[a]		Threatened species				GEF benefits index for biodiversity	Nationally protected areas			
									0–100 (no biodiversity to maximum biodiversity)	Terrestrial		Marine	
	thousand sq. km		%		Mammals	Birds	Fish	Higher plants[b]		% of surface area	Number of areas	% of surface area	Number of areas
	1990	2007	1990–2000	2000–07	2008	2008	2008	2008	2008	2008	2008	2008	2008
Afghanistan	13	8	2.5	3.2	11	13	3	2	..	0.2	7	0.0	0
Albania	8	8	0.3	−0.6	3	6	33	0	0.2	8.0	80	1.1	7
Algeria	18	23	−1.8	−1.2	14	11	23	3	2.9	5.0	23	0.3	6
Angola	610	589	0.2	0.2	14	18	22	26	8.3	8.3	15	0.2	4
Argentina	353	327	0.4	0.4	35	49	31	44	17.7	6.5	307	0.6	36
Armenia	3	3	1.0	1.5	9	12	4	1	0.2	8.2	10	0.0	0
Australia	1,679	1,633	0.2	0.1	57	49	84	55	87.7	0.1	5,485	70.6	384
Austria	38	39	−0.2	−0.1	4	9	9	4	0.3	28.0	1,087	0.0	0
Azerbaijan	9	9	0.0	0.0	7	15	9	0	0.8	7.3	42	0.0	0
Bangladesh	9	9	0.0	0.3	34	28	12	12	1.4	2.2	20	0.5	7
Belarus	75	79	−0.5	−0.1	4	4	1	0	0.0	6.5	440	0.0	0
Belgium	..	7	..	0.0	3	2	9	1	0.0	3.2	502	0.1	2
Benin	33	22	2.1	2.6	10	4	15	14	0.2	23.2	49	0.0	0
Bolivia	628	582	0.4	0.5	19	29	0	71	12.5	21.2	53	0.0	0
Bosnia and Herzegovina	22	22	0.1	0.0	4	6	27	1	0.4	0.8	32	0.0	0
Botswana	137	117	0.9	1.0	6	7	2	0	1.4	30.1	60	0.0	0
Brazil	5,200	4,715	0.5	0.6	82	122	64	382	100.0	29.6	1,444	4.8	58
Bulgaria	33	37	−0.1	−1.4	7	12	17	0	0.8	10.1	905	0.0	1
Burkina Faso	72	67	0.3	0.4	8	5	0	2	0.3	14.4	72	0.0	0
Burundi	3	1	3.7	5.5	9	8	18	2	0.3	5.6	15	0.0	0
Cambodia	129	100	1.1	2.0	37	25	18	31	3.5	24.0	30	0.4	2
Cameroon	245	208	0.9	1.0	41	15	43	355	12.5	10.1	39	0.1	2
Canada	3,101	3,101	0.0	0.0	12	16	26	2	21.5	8.2	5,122	1.1	563
Central African Republic	232	227	0.1	0.1	7	5	0	15	1.5	18.2	32	0.0	0
Chad	131	118	0.6	0.7	12	7	0	2	2.2	9.0	9	0.0	0
Chile	153	162	−0.4	−0.4	21	32	18	40	15.3	18.8	102	0.3	9
China	1,571	2,054	−1.2	−2.1	74	85	70	446	66.6	15.1	1,981	0.3	36
Hong Kong SAR, China	..	..	..	..	2	16	13	6	..	44.1	98	0.0	22
Colombia	614	606	0.1	0.1	52	86	31	223	51.5	26.2	263	84.2	15
Congo, Dem. Rep.	1,405	1,330	0.4	0.2	29	31	25	65	19.9	12.2	66	1.8	1
Congo, Rep.	227	224	0.1	0.1	11	3	15	35	3.6	10.3	14	0.0	0
Costa Rica	26	24	0.8	−0.1	8	17	19	111	9.7	31.0	165	9.8	35
Côte d'Ivoire	102	104	−0.1	−0.1	24	14	19	105	3.4	21.1	240	0.0	3
Croatia	21	21	−0.1	−0.1	7	11	46	1	0.6	7.5	177	4.4	19
Cuba	21	28	−1.7	−2.1	14	17	28	163	12.5	18.8	71	12.6	42
Czech Republic	26	27	0.0	−0.1	2	6	5	4	0.1	15.8	1,765	0.0	0
Denmark	4	5	−0.9	−0.6	2	2	13	3	0.2	5.7	3,847	2.7	52
Dominican Republic	14	14	0.0	0.0	6	14	15	30	6.0	28.5	59	0.0	15
Ecuador	138	105	1.5	1.8	43	69	15	1,839	29.3	25.4	104	12.4	3
Egypt, Arab Rep.	0[c]	1	−3.0	−2.5	17	10	24	2	2.9	7.7	26	9.9	8
El Salvador	4	3	1.5	1.7	5	3	7	26	0.9	1.3	77	0.0	1
Eritrea	16	15	0.2	0.2	9	9	14	3	0.8	4.3	3	0.0	0
Estonia	22	23	−0.3	−0.4	1	3	4	0	0.1	46.8	9,617	2.5	3
Ethiopia	147	127	0.7	1.1	31	22	2	22	8.4	17.5	42	0.0	0
Finland	222	225	−0.1	0.0	1	4	5	1	0.2	9.3	6,046	3.4	15
France	145	156	−0.5	−0.3	9	6	31	8	5.3	15.4	1,541	3.2	64
Gabon	219	218	0.0	0.0	13	5	21	108	3.0	16.5	22	4.9	5
Gambia, The	4	5	−0.4	−0.4	9	5	16	4	0.1	2.0	6	1.5	6
Georgia	28	28	0.0	0.0	10	10	12	0	0.6	3.9	33	0.0	2
Germany	107	111	−0.3	0.0	6	6	20	12	0.6	56.2	14,388	26.7	21
Ghana	74	53	2.0	2.0	17	8	17	117	1.9	16.6	302	0.0	0
Greece	33	38	−0.9	−0.8	10	11	62	11	2.8	3.4	111	2.4	12
Guatemala	47	38	1.2	1.3	16	11	16	83	8.0	32.7	163	4.7	7
Guinea	74	67	0.7	0.5	22	12	19	22	2.3	6.6	102	0.0	0
Guinea-Bissau	22	21	0.4	0.5	11	2	18	4	0.6	18.2	9	54.4	4
Haiti	1	1	0.6	0.8	5	13	15	29	5.2	0.3	8	0.0	0
Honduras	74	43	3.0	3.2	6	7	19	110	7.2	21.0	77	2.8	22

Deforestation and biodiversity | 3.4

	Forest area		Average annual deforestation[a]		Threatened species				GEF benefits index for biodiversity	Nationally protected areas			
									0–100 (no biodiversity to maximum biodiversity)	Terrestrial		Marine	
	thousand sq. km		%		Mammals	Birds	Fish	Higher plants[b]		% of surface area	Number of areas	% of surface area	Number of areas
	1990	2007	1990–2000	2000–07	2008	2008	2008	2008	2008	2008	2008	2008	2008
Hungary	18	20	−0.6	−0.7	2	9	9	1	0.2	5.6	136	0.0	0
India	639	678	−0.6	0.0	96	76	40	246	39.9	4.8	556	1.5	117
Indonesia	1,166	848	1.7	2.0	183	115	111	386	81.0	15.7	469	1.8	139
Iran, Islamic Rep.	111	111	0.0	0.0	16	20	21	1	7.3	7.0	145	3.5	12
Iraq	8	8	−0.2	−0.1	13	18	6	0	1.6	0.0	8	0.0	0
Ireland	4	7	−3.3	−1.9	5	1	16	1	0.6	1.1	85	0.1	12
Israel	2	2	−0.6	−0.8	15	13	31	0	0.8	34.5	222	0.5	13
Italy	84	102	−1.2	−1.1	7	8	33	19	3.8	7.1	456	3.1	58
Jamaica	3	3	0.1	0.1	5	10	15	209	4.4	20.9	71	3.6	12
Japan	250	249	0.0	0.0	27	40	40	12	36.0	14.1	216	5.2	135
Jordan	1	1	0.0	0.0	13	8	14	0	0.4	10.5	12	21.6	1
Kazakhstan	34	33	0.1	0.2	16	21	13	16	5.1	2.8	77	0.0	0
Kenya	37	35	0.3	0.3	27	27	71	103	8.8	12.3	284	5.8	11
Korea, Dem. Rep.	82	59	1.8	2.0	9	20	8	3	0.7	2.6	31	0.0	0
Korea, Rep.	64	63	0.1	0.1	9	30	14	0	1.7	4.3	32	3.2	6
Kosovo	..	5[d]	..	..	0	0	..	0	..	..	..	..	..
Kuwait	0[c]	0[c]	−3.4	−2.4	6	8	10	0	0.1	0.8	5	1.8	5
Kyrgyz Republic	8	9	−0.2	−0.3	6	12	3	14	1.1	3.1	29	0.0	0
Lao PDR	173	160	0.5	0.5	46	23	6	21	5.0	15.9	25	0.0	0
Latvia	28	30	−0.3	−0.4	1	4	6	0	0.0	16.4	540	0.0	1
Lebanon	1	1	−0.8	−0.8	10	6	15	0	0.2	0.4	11	0.0	1
Lesotho	0[c]	0[c]	−3.4	−2.6	2	5	1	1	0.3	0.2	1	0.0	0
Liberia	41	30	1.6	1.8	20	11	19	46	2.6	15.0	16	0.0	1
Libya	2	2	0.0	0.0	12	4	14	1	1.6	0.1	8	1.0	4
Lithuania	20	21	−0.3	−0.8	3	4	6	0	0.0	6.0	250	7.9	3
Macedonia, FYR	9	9	0.0	0.0	5	10	14	0	0.2	6.0	61	0.0	0
Madagascar	137	128	0.5	0.3	62	35	75	281	29.2	3.1	53	0.1	8
Malawi	39	33	0.9	1.0	6	12	101	14	3.5	15.5	96	0.0	0
Malaysia	224	206	0.4	0.7	70	42	49	686	13.9	20.3	684	4.6	147
Mali	141	124	0.7	0.8	11	6	1	6	1.5	2.1	10	0.0	0
Mauritania	4	2	2.7	3.5	14	8	23	0	1.3	0.9	3	31.3	3
Mauritius	0[c]	0[c]	0.3	0.5	6	11	11	88	3.3	5.5	23	0.3	18
Mexico	690	637	0.5	0.4	100	54	114	261	68.7	8.0	182	14.0	38
Moldova	3	3	−0.2	−0.2	4	9	9	0	0.0	1.4	63	0.0	0
Mongolia	115	101	0.7	0.8	11	21	1	0	4.2	13.9	51	0.0	0
Morocco	43	44	−0.1	−0.2	18	10	31	2	3.5	1.2	31	1.6	11
Mozambique	200	192	0.3	0.3	11	21	45	46	7.2	15.7	46	4.0	3
Myanmar	392	313	1.3	1.4	45	41	17	38	10.0	6.7	49	0.5	6
Namibia	88	75	0.9	1.0	11	21	21	24	5.2	15.0	31	0.2	4
Nepal	48	35	2.1	1.4	32	32	0	7	2.1	16.6	19	0.0	0
Netherlands	3	4	−0.4	−0.3	4	2	11	0	0.2	19.8	1,948	3.1	6
New Zealand	77	83	−0.6	−0.2	8	69	14	21	20.2	29.5	3,878	7.1	87
Nicaragua	65	50	1.6	1.5	5	9	21	39	3.3	16.9	74	10.3	5
Niger	19	12	3.7	1.0	11	5	2	2	0.9	6.6	6	0.0	0
Nigeria	172	103	2.7	3.5	27	12	21	171	6.0	16.0	972	0.0	0
Norway	91	94	−0.2	−0.2	7	2	14	2	1.3	5.2	1,795	0.5	17
Oman	0[c]	0[c]	0.0	0.0	9	9	20	6	3.7	9.4	6	1.2	3
Pakistan	25	18	1.8	2.2	23	27	22	2	4.9	9.0	151	1.1	5
Panama	44	43	0.2	0.1	14	17	19	194	10.9	28.1	53	8.6	21
Papua New Guinea	315	292	0.5	0.5	41	36	38	142	25.4	9.7	67	0.5	24
Paraguay	212	181	0.9	0.9	8	27	0	10	2.8	6.0	33	0.0	0
Peru	702	686	0.1	0.1	53	93	10	275	33.4	13.8	61	2.9	2
Philippines	106	68	2.8	2.1	39	67	60	216	32.3	17.2	204	0.7	212
Poland	89	92	−0.2	−0.3	5	6	6	4	0.5	24.3	1,605	2.5	3
Portugal	31	39	−1.5	−1.1	11	8	38	16	5.5	6.6	59	1.1	27
Puerto Rico	4	4	−0.1	0.0	3	8	13	53	4.0	6.8	50	11.5	19
Qatar	..	..			2	4	7	0	0.1	0.0	0	..	..

	Forest area (thousand sq. km)		Average annual deforestation[a] (%)		Threatened species				GEF benefits index for biodiversity 0–100 (no biodiversity to maximum biodiversity)	Nationally protected areas			
										Terrestrial		Marine	
										% of surface area	Number of areas	% of surface area	Number of areas
					Mammals	Birds	Fish	Higher plants[b]					
	1990	2007	1990–2000	2000–07	2008	2008	2008	2008	2008	2008	2008	2008	2008
Romania	64	64	0.0	0.0	7	12	16	1	0.7	10.7	923	37.9	10
Russian Federation	8,090	8,086	0.0	0.0	33	51	32	7	34.1	9.0	11,181	6.3	27
Rwanda	3	5	−0.8	−6.5	19	10	9	3	0.9	7.6	5	0.0	0
Saudi Arabia	27	27	0.0	0.0	9	14	16	3	3.2	38.4	30	1.1	3
Senegal	93	86	0.5	0.5	15	8	28	7	1.0	25.0	109	13.0	11
Serbia	..	21	..	..	6	11	8	1	0.2	2.7	68	0.0	0
Sierra Leone	30	27	0.7	0.7	16	10	16	47	1.3	4.1	39	0.0	0
Singapore	0[c]	0[c]	0.0	0.0	12	14	22	54	0.1	5.2	7	0.8	3
Slovak Republic	19	19	0.0	−0.1	3	7	7	2	0.1	19.6	1,126	0.0	0
Slovenia	12	13	−0.4	−0.4	4	4	24	0	0.2	6.6	30	0.4	3
Somalia	83	70	1.0	1.1	14	12	26	17	6.1	0.6	7	0.2	2
South Africa	92	92	0.0	0.0	23	35	65	74	20.7	6.0	931	6.2	30
Spain	135	185	−2.0	−1.7	16	15	52	49	6.8	9.5	468	5.3	47
Sri Lanka	24	19	1.2	1.5	30	13	31	280	7.9	20.6	234	1.0	14
Sudan	764	664	0.8	0.9	14	13	13	17	5.1	4.6	20	0.0	1
Swaziland	5	6	−0.9	−0.9	4	7	3	11	0.1	3.1	7	0.0	0
Sweden	274	275	0.0	0.0	1	3	12	3	0.3	10.4	4,622	4.9	477
Switzerland	12	12	−0.4	−0.4	2	2	11	3	0.2	28.6	2,146	0.0	0
Syrian Arab Republic	4	5	−1.5	−1.3	16	13	27	0	0.9	0.7	9	1.3	4
Tajikistan	4	4	0.0	0.0	8	9	8	14	0.7	13.7	15	0.0	0
Tanzania	414	344	1.0	1.1	34	40	138	240	14.8	38.8	537	12.5	17
Thailand	160	144	0.7	0.4	57	44	50	86	8.0	20.4	206	3.9	19
Timor-Leste	10	8	1.2	1.4	4	5	5	0	0.6	14.6	6	0.0	0
Togo	7	3	3.4	4.7	10	2	16	10	0.3	11.1	90	0.2	1
Trinidad and Tobago	2	2	0.3	0.2	2	2	19	1	2.2	35.0	64	0.3	13
Tunisia	6	11	−4.1	−1.9	14	8	20	0	0.5	1.5	36	0.2	4
Turkey	97	102	−0.4	−0.2	17	15	60	3	6.2	1.9	236	2.8	13
Turkmenistan	41	41	0.0	0.0	9	15	12	3	1.8	2.6	18	0.0	0
Uganda	49	35	1.9	2.3	21	18	54	38	2.8	26.1	732	0.0	0
Ukraine	93	96	−0.2	−0.1	11	12	20	1	0.5	3.4	5,197	4.3	15
United Arab Emirates	2	3	−2.4	−0.1	7	8	9	0	0.2	0.3	10	0.1	3
United Kingdom	26	29	−0.7	−0.4	5	2	34	14	3.5	22.3	778	4.6	149
United States	2,986	3,034	−0.1	−0.1	37	74	164	244	94.2	27.1	6,770	67.6	787
Uruguay	9	15	−4.5	−1.3	10	24	28	1	1.2	0.4	20	0.1	4
Uzbekistan	31	33	−0.4	−0.5	11	15	8	15	1.1	1.9	13	0.0	0
Venezuela, RB	520	471	0.6	0.6	32	26	29	69	25.3	71.3	231	10.9	19
Vietnam	94	134	−2.3	−1.9	54	39	33	147	12.1	5.6	116	1.4	36
West Bank and Gaza	..	0[c]	..	0.0	3	7	1	0	..	0.0	0	0.0	0
Yemen, Rep.	5	5	0.0	0.0	9	13	18	159	3.2	0.3	3	2.7	1
Zambia	491	416	0.9	1.0	8	12	10	8	3.8	41.1	625	0.0	0
Zimbabwe	222	169	1.5	1.7	8	11	3	17	1.9	15.8	240	0.0	0
World	**40,678 s**	**39,280 s**	**0.2 w**	**0.2 w**	**1,141**	**1,222**	**1,275**	**8,457**		**14.4 w**	**112,355 s**	**1.7 w**	**4,949 s**
Low income	5,221	4,635	0.7	0.7						11.9	3,970	0.2	121
Middle income	25,888	24,955	0.2	0.2						12.9	33,010	0.9	1,484
Lower middle income	8,016	7,725	0.3	0.1						11.2	11,729	1.3	791
Upper middle income	17,872	17,230	0.2	0.2						14.0	21,281	0.6	693
Low & middle income	31,109	29,591	0.3	0.3						12.7	36,980	0.8	1,605
East Asia & Pacific	4,580	4,525	0.3	−0.2						14.7	4,044	1.8	754
Europe & Central Asia	8,812	8,837	0.0	0.0						7.8	21,825	0.4	84
Latin America & Carib.	9,834	9,052	0.5	0.5						22.8	3,801	1.6	422
Middle East & N. Africa	200	212	−0.4	−0.3						3.8	313	0.1	53
South Asia	789	799	−0.2	0.1						5.5	996	0.1	143
Sub-Saharan Africa	6,894	6,165	0.7	0.6						12.4	6,001	0.1	149
High income	9,569	9,689	−0.1	−0.1						19.1	75,375	4.3	3,344
Euro area	843	947	−0.7	−0.6						17.1	28,025	1.0	277

a. Negative values indicate an increase in forest area. b. Flowering plants only. c. Less than 0.5. d. Data are from national sources.

About the data

Biological diversity is defined in terms of variability in genes, species, and ecosystems. A 2008 comprehensive assessment of world species shows that at least 1,141 of 5,487 known mammals are threatened with extinction. As threats to biodiversity mount, the international community is increasingly focusing on conserving diversity. Deforestation is a major cause of loss of biodiversity, and habitat conservation is vital for stemming this loss. Conservation efforts have focused on protecting areas of high biodiversity.

The Food and Agriculture Organization of the United Nations (FAO) *Global Forest Resources Assessment 2005* provides detailed information on forest cover in 2005 and adjusted estimates of forest cover in 1990 and 2000. The current survey uses a uniform definition of forest. Because of space limitations, the table does not break down forest cover between natural forest and plantation, a breakdown the FAO provides for developing countries. Thus the deforestation data in the table may underestimate the rate at which natural forest is disappearing in some countries.

The number of threatened species is also an important measure of the immediate need for conservation in an area. Global analyses of the status of threatened species have been carried out for few groups of organisms. Only for mammals, birds, and amphibians has the status of virtually all known species been assessed. Threatened species are defined using the World Conservation Union's (IUCN) classification: *endangered* (in danger of extinction and unlikely to survive if causal factors continue operating) and *vulnerable* (likely to move into the endangered category in the near future if causal factors continue operating).

Unlike mammals, birds, and fish, it is difficult to accurately count plants. The number of plant species is highly debated. The *2008 IUCN Red List of Threatened Species*, the result of more than 20 years' work by botanists worldwide, is the most comprehensive list of threatened species on a global scale. Only 5 percent of plant species have been evaluated, and 70 percent of these are threatened with extinction. Plant species data may not be comparable across countries because of differences in taxonomic concepts and coverage and so should be used with caution. However, the data identify countries that are major sources of global biodiversity and that show national commitments to habitat protection.

The Global Environment Facility's (GEF) benefits index for biodiversity is a comprehensive indicator of national biodiversity status and is used to guide its biodiversity priorities. The indicator incorporates

information on individual species range maps available from the IUCN for virtually all mammals (5,487), amphibians (5,915), and endangered birds (1,098); country data from the World Resources Institute for reptiles and vascular plants; country data from FishBase for 31,190 fish species; and the ecological characteristics of 867 world terrestrial ecoregions from WWF International. For each country the biodiversity indicator incorporates the best available and comparable information in four relevant dimensions: represented species, threatened species, represented ecoregions, and threatened ecoregions. To combine these dimensions into one measure, the indicator uses dimensional weights that reflect the consensus of conservation scientists at the GEF, IUCN, WWF International, and other nongovernmental organizations.

The World Conservation Monitoring Centre (WCMC) compiles data on protected areas, numbers of certain species, and numbers of those species under threat from various sources. Because of differences in definitions, reporting practices, and reporting periods, cross-country comparability is limited.

Nationally protected areas are defined using the six IUCN management categories for areas of at least 1,000 hectares: scientific reserves and strict nature reserves with limited public access; national parks of national or international significance and not materially affected by human activity; natural monuments and natural landscapes with unique aspects; managed nature reserves and wildlife sanctuaries; protected landscapes (which may include cultural landscapes); and areas managed mainly for the sustainable use of natural systems to ensure long-term protection and maintenance of biological diversity. The data in the table cover these six categories as well as terrestrial protected areas that are not assigned to a category by the IUCN. Designating an area as protected does not mean that protection is in force. And for small countries that have only protected areas smaller than 1,000 hectares, the size limit in the definition leads to an underestimate of protected areas.

Due to variations in consistency and methods of collection, data quality is highly variable across countries. Some countries update their information more frequently than others, some have more accurate data on extent of coverage, and many underreport the number or extent of protected areas.

Definitions

• **Forest area** is land under natural or planted stands of trees, whether productive or not. • **Average annual deforestation** is the permanent conversion of natural forest area to other uses, including agriculture, ranching, settlements, and infrastructure. It does not include areas logged but intended for regeneration or areas degraded by fuelwood gathering, acid precipitation, or forest fires. • **Threatened species** are species classified by the IUCN as endangered, vulnerable, rare, indeterminate, out of danger, or insufficiently known. Mammals exclude whales and porpoises. Birds are listed for the country where their breeding or wintering ranges are located. Fish are cold-blooded aquatic vertebrates of the superclass *Pisces*. Higher plants are native vascular plant species. • **GEF benefits index for biodiversity** is a composite index of relative biodiversity potential based on the species in each country and their threat status and diversity of habitat types. The index is normalized from 0 (no biodiversity potential) to 100 (maximum biodiversity potential). • **Nationally protected areas** are totally or partially protected areas of at least 1,000 hectares that are designated as scientific reserves with limited public access, national parks, natural monuments, nature reserves or wildlife sanctuaries, and protected landscapes. Terrestrial protected areas exclude marine areas, unclassified areas, littoral (intertidal) areas, and sites protected under local or provincial law. Marine protected areas are areas of intertidal or subtidal terrain—and overlying water and associated flora and fauna and historical and cultural features—that have been reserved to protect part of or the entire enclosed environment.

Data sources

Data on forest area are from the FAO's electronic files. The FAO gathers these data from national agencies through annual questionnaires and country official publications and websites and by analyzing national agricultural censuses. Data on species are from the electronic files of the United Nations Environment Programme (UNEP) and WCMC, the *2008 IUCN Red List of Threatened Species,* and Froese and Pauly's (2008) FishBase database. The GEF benefits index for biodiversity is from Pandey and others' "Biodiversity Conservation Indicators: New Tools for Priority Setting at the Global Environment Facility" (2006a). Data on protected areas are from the UNEP and WCMC, as compiled by the World Resources Institute, based on data from national authorities and national legislation and international agreements.

	Internal renewable freshwater resources[a]		Annual freshwater withdrawals					Water productivity	Access to an improved water source	
	Flows billion cu. m	Per capita cu. m	billion cu. m	% of internal resources	% for agriculture	% for industry	% for domestic	GDP/water use 2000 $ per cu. m	% of urban population	% of rural population
	2007	2007	2007	2007	2007	2007	2007	2007	2006	2006
Afghanistan	55	..	23.3	42.3	98	0	2	..	..	..
Albania	27	8,588	1.7	6.4	62	11	27	36.2	97	97
Algeria	11	332	6.1	54.0	65	13	22	9.0	87	81
Angola	148	8,431	0.4	0.2	60	17	23	26.1	62	39
Argentina	276	6,989	29.2	10.6	74	9	17	9.7	98	80
Armenia	9	2,952	3.0	32.5	66	4	30	0.6	99	96
Australia	492	23,348	23.9	4.9	75	10	15	16.9	100	100
Austria	55	6,626	2.1	3.8	1	64	35	91.9	100	100
Azerbaijan	8	946	12.2	150.5	76	19	4	0.8	95	59
Bangladesh	105	666	79.4	75.6	96	1	3	0.6	85	78
Belarus	37	3,834	2.8	7.5	30	47	23	4.6	100	99
Belgium	12	1,129	..	..	..	..	..	..	100	..
Benin	10	1,227	0.1	1.3	45	23	32	18.2	78	57
Bolivia	304	31,868	1.4	0.5	81	7	13	5.8	96	69
Bosnia and Herzegovina	36	9,395	..	..	..	..	..	..	100	98
Botswana	2	1,268	0.2	8.1	41	18	41	31.8	100	90
Brazil	5,418	28,498	59.3	1.1	62	18	20	10.9	97	58
Bulgaria	21	2,742	10.5	50.0	19	78	3	1.2	100	97
Burkina Faso	13	849	0.8	6.4	86	1	13	3.3	97	66
Burundi	10	1,283	0.3	2.9	77	6	17	2.5	84	70
Cambodia	121	8,417	4.1	3.4	98	0	1	0.9	80	61
Cameroon	273	14,630	1.0	0.4	74	8	18	10.2	88	47
Canada	2,850	86,426	46.0	1.6	12	69	20	15.8	100	99
Central African Republic	141	33,119	0.0	0.0	4	16	80	38.4	90	51
Chad	15	1,412	0.2	1.5	83	0	17	6.0	71	40
Chile	884	53,137	12.6	1.4	64	25	11	6.0	98	72
China	2,812	2,134	630.3	22.4	68	26	7	1.9	98	81
Hong Kong SAR, China	..	..	..	..	..	..	..	..	..	..
Colombia	2,112	47,611	10.7	0.5	46	4	50	8.8	99	77
Congo, Dem. Rep.	900	14,395	0.4	0.0	31	17	53	12.0	82	29
Congo, Rep.	222	62,516	0.0	0.0	9	22	70	76.0	95	35
Costa Rica	112[b]	25,209[b]	2.7	2.4	53	17	29	6.0	99	96
Côte d'Ivoire	77	3,819	0.9	1.2	65	12	24	11.2	98	66
Croatia	38	8,493	..	..	..	..	..	..	100	98
Cuba	38	3,402	8.2	21.5	69	12	19	..	95	78
Czech Republic	13	1,272	2.6	19.6	2	57	41	22.0	100	100
Denmark	6	1,099	1.3	21.2	43	25	32	126.0	100	100
Dominican Republic	21	2,139	3.4	16.1	66	2	32	7.1	97	91
Ecuador	432	32,379	17.0	3.9	82	5	12	0.9	98	91
Egypt, Arab Rep.	2	22	68.3	3,794.4	86	6	8	1.5	99	98
El Salvador	18	2,907	1.3	7.2	59	16	25	10.3	94	68
Eritrea	3[b]	586[b]	0.6	20.8	95	0	5	1.2	74	57
Estonia	13	9,475	0.2	1.2	5	38	57	35.6	100	99
Ethiopia	122[b]	1,551[b]	5.6	4.6	94	0	6	1.6	96	31
Finland	107	20,232	2.5	2.3	3	84	14	49.2	100	100
France	179	2,882	40.0	22.4	10	74	16	33.2	100	100
Gabon	164	115,340	0.1	0.1	42	8	50	42.2	95	47
Gambia, The	3	1,857	0.0	1.0	65	12	23	13.8	91	81
Georgia	58	13,339	1.6	2.8	65	13	22	2.7	100	97
Germany	107	1,301	47.1	44.0	20	68	12	40.4	100	100
Ghana	30	1,325	1.0	3.2	66	10	24	5.1	90	71
Greece	58	5,182	7.8	13.4	80	3	16	16.2	100	99
Guatemala	109	8,177	2.0	1.8	80	13	6	9.6	99	94
Guinea	226	23,505	1.5	0.7	90	2	8	2.1	91	59
Guinea-Bissau	16	10,383	0.2	1.1	82	5	13	1.2	82	47
Haiti	13	1,338	1.0	7.6	94	1	5	3.7	70	51
Honduras	96	13,372	0.9	0.9	80	12	8	8.3	95	74

	Internal renewable freshwater resources[a]		Annual freshwater withdrawals					Water productivity	Access to an improved water source	
	Flows billion cu. m 2007	Per capita cu. m 2007	billion cu. m 2007	% of internal resources 2007	% for agriculture 2007	% for industry 2007	% for domestic 2007	GDP/water use 2000 $ per cu. m 2007	% of urban population 2006	% of rural population 2006
Hungary	6	597	7.6	127.3	32	59	9	6.3	100	100
India	1,261	1,121	645.8	51.2	86	5	8	0.7	96	86
Indonesia	2,838	12,578	82.8	2.9	91	1	8	2.0	89	71
Iran, Islamic Rep.	129	1,809	93.3	72.6	92	1	7	1.4	99	84
Iraq	35	..	66.0	187.5	79	15	7	0.4	..	..
Ireland	49	11,246	1.1	2.3	0	77	23	85.3	100	..
Israel	1	104	2.0	260.5	58	6	36	67.6	100	100
Italy	183	3,074	44.4	24.3	45	37	18	24.7	100	..
Jamaica	9	3,514	0.4	4.4	49	17	34	22.0	97	88
Japan	430	3,365	88.4	20.6	62	18	20	52.8	100	100
Jordan	1	119	0.9	138.0	65	4	31	12.2	99	91
Kazakhstan	75	4,871	35.0	46.4	82	17	2	0.5	99	91
Kenya	21	548	2.7	13.2	79	4	17	5.0	85	49
Korea, Dem. Rep.	67	2,824	9.0	13.5	55	25	20	..	100	100
Korea, Rep.	65	1,338	18.6	28.7	48	16	36	28.7	97	71
Kosovo	..	..	..	..	..	..	..	..	..	..
Kuwait	..	..	0.9	..	54	2	44	42.9	..	..
Kyrgyz Republic	46	8,873	10.1	21.7	94	3	3	0.1	99	83
Lao PDR	190	31,256	3.0	1.6	90	6	4	0.6	86	53
Latvia	17	7,355	0.3	1.8	13	33	53	26.1	100	96
Lebanon	5	1,153	1.3	27.3	60	11	29	15.9	100	100
Lesotho	5	2,574	0.1	1.0	20	40	40	15.7	93	74
Liberia	200[b]	55,138[b]	0.1	0.1	55	18	27	5.1	72	52
Libya	1	97	4.3	721.0	83	3	14	7.8	72	68
Lithuania	16	4,610	0.3	1.7	7	15	78	42.3	..	..
Macedonia, FYR	5	2,647	..	..	..	..	..	..	100	99
Madagascar	337	18,114	15.0	4.4	96	2	3	0.3	76	36
Malawi	16[b]	1,118[b]	1.0	6.3	80	5	15	1.7	96	72
Malaysia	580	21,841	9.0	1.6	62	21	17	10.4	100	96
Mali	60	4,835	6.5	10.9	90	1	9	0.4	86	48
Mauritania	0[c]	127	1.7	425.0	88	3	9	0.6	70	54
Mauritius	3	2,182	0.7	26.4	68	3	30	6.9	100	100
Mexico	409	3,885	78.2	19.1	77	5	17	7.4	98	85
Moldova	1	273	2.3	231.0	33	58	10	0.6	96	85
Mongolia	35	13,326	0.4	1.3	52	27	20	2.5	90	48
Morocco	29	940	12.6	43.4	87	3	10	2.9	100	58
Mozambique	100	4,586	0.6	0.6	87	2	11	6.7	71	26
Myanmar	881	17,924	33.2	3.8	98	1	1	..	80	80
Namibia	6	2,949	0.3	4.9	71	5	24	13.0	99	90
Nepal	198	7,007	10.2	5.1	96	1	3	0.5	94	88
Netherlands	11	671	7.9	72.2	34	60	6	48.5	100	100
New Zealand	327	77,336	2.1	0.6	42	9	48	24.1	100	..
Nicaragua	190	33,912	1.3	0.7	83	2	15	3.0	90	63
Niger	4	248	2.2	62.3	95	0	4	0.8	91	32
Nigeria	221	1,496	8.0	3.6	69	10	21	5.7	65	30
Norway	382	81,119	2.2	0.6	11	67	23	76.8	100	100
Oman	1	514	1.3	94.4	88	1	10	16.6	85	73
Pakistan	55[b]	338[b]	169.4	308.0	96	2	2	0.4	95	87
Panama	147	44,094	0.8	0.6	28	5	67	14.2	96	81
Papua New Guinea	801	124,716	0.1	0.0	1	42	56	49.6	88	32
Paraguay	94	15,343	0.5	0.5	71	8	20	14.4	94	52
Peru	1,616	56,685	20.1	1.2	82	10	8	2.6	92	63
Philippines	479	5,399	28.5	6.0	74	9	17	2.7	96	88
Poland	54	1,406	16.2	30.2	8	79	13	10.6	100	..
Portugal	38	3,582	11.3	29.6	78	12	10	10.0	99	100
Puerto Rico	7	1,802	..	..	..	..	..	..	..	..
Qatar	0.1	45	0.4	870.6	59	2	39	58.7	100	100

	Internal renewable freshwater resources[a]		Annual freshwater withdrawals					Water productivity	Access to an improved water source	
	Flows billion cu. m 2007	Per capita cu. m 2007	billion cu. m 2007	% of internal resources 2007	% for agriculture 2007	% for industry 2007	% for domestic 2007	GDP/water use 2000 $ per cu. m 2007	% of urban population 2006	% of rural population 2006
Romania	42	1,963	23.2	54.8	57	34	9	1.6	99	76
Russian Federation	4,313	30,350	76.7	1.8	18	63	19	3.4	100	88
Rwanda	10[b]	1,005[b]	0.2	1.6	68	8	24	11.6	82	61
Saudi Arabia	2	99	23.7	986.1	88	3	9	9.9	97	..
Senegal	26[b]	2,169[b]	2.2	8.6	93	3	4	2.2	93	65
Serbia	44[d]	5,419[d]	..	..	..	..	..	..	99[e]	..
Sierra Leone	160[b]	29,518[b]	0.4	0.2	92	3	5	1.7	83	32
Singapore	1	131	..	..	..	..	..	..	100	..
Slovak Republic	13	2,334	..	..	..	..	..	..	100	100
Slovenia	19	9,251	..	..	..	..	..	..	..	..
Somalia	6	687	3.3	55.0	99	0	0	..	63	10
South Africa	45	936	12.5	27.9	63	6	31	10.6	100	82
Spain	111	2,478	35.6	32.0	68	19	13	16.3	100	100
Sri Lanka	50	2,499	12.6	25.2	95	2	2	1.3	98	79
Sudan	30	742	37.3	124.4	97	1	3	0.3	78	64
Swaziland	3	2,293	1.0	39.5	97	1	2	1.4	87	51
Sweden	171	18,692	3.0	1.7	9	54	37	83.0	100	100
Switzerland	40	5,350	2.6	6.4	2	74	24	97.2	100	100
Syrian Arab Republic	7	349	16.7	238.4	88	4	9	1.3	95	83
Tajikistan	66	9,855	12.0	18.0	92	5	4	0.1	93	58
Tanzania	84	2,035	5.2	6.2	89	0	10	2.0	81	46
Thailand	210	3,135	87.1	41.5	95	2	2	1.4	99	97
Togo	12	1,825	0.2	1.5	45	2	53	8.2	86	40
Trinidad and Tobago	4	2,891	0.3	8.1	6	26	68	26.3	97	93
Tunisia	4	410	2.6	62.9	82	4	14	7.4	99	84
Turkey	227	3,109	40.1	17.7	74	11	15	7.0	98	95
Turkmenistan	1	273	24.7	1,812.5	98	1	2	0.1	..	..
Uganda	39	1,273	..	..	..	..	..	..	90	60
Ukraine	53	1,142	37.5	70.7	52	35	12	0.8	97	97
United Arab Emirates	0	34	4.0	2,665.3	83	2	15	24.5	100	100
United Kingdom	145	2,377	9.5	6.6	3	75	22	152.1	100	100
United States	2,800	9,293	479.3	17.1	41	46	13	20.4	100	94
Uruguay	59	17,750	3.2	5.3	96	1	3	7.2	100	100
Uzbekistan	16	608	58.3	357.0	93	2	5	0.2	98	82
Venezuela, RB	722	26,287	8.4	1.2	47	7	46	14.0	..	..
Vietnam	367	4,304	71.4	19.5	68	24	8	0.4	98	90
West Bank and Gaza	..	..	..	..	..	..	..	..	90	88
Yemen, Rep.	2	94	3.4	161.9	90	2	8	2.8	68	65
Zambia	80	6,513	1.7	2.2	76	7	17	1.9	90	41
Zimbabwe	12	985	4.2	34.3	79	7	14	1.6	98	72
World	**43,464 s**	**6,616 w**	**3,765.3 s**	**9.0 w**	**70 w**	**20 w**	**10 w**	**8.3 w**	**96 w**	**77 w**
Low income	4,784	5,004	357.3	7.9	88	6	5	1.2	86	60
Middle income	29,126	6,350	2,518.2	8.8	77	14	9	2.9	95	81
Lower middle income	11,525	3,154	2,039.5	18.1	81	12	7	1.7	94	81
Upper middle income	17,601	18,876	478.7	2.7	58	25	17	15.9	98	82
Low & middle income	33,910	6,118	2,875.5	8.7	78	13	8	2.9	94	76
East Asia & Pacific	9,454	4,938	959.0	10.2	74	20	7	1.9	96	81
Europe & Central Asia	5,129	11,867	356.5	7.2	60	30	10	1.0	99	88
Latin America & Carib.	13,425	24,004	264.9	2.0	71	10	19	7.8	97	73
Middle East & N. Africa	225	715	253.2	122.3	86	6	8	14.4	95	81
South Asia	1,819	1,194	941.1	51.7	90	4	6	0.7	94	84
Sub-Saharan Africa	3,858	4,829	100.8	3.2	87	3	10	1.2	81	46
High income	9,554	9,305	..	10.4	43	42	15	27.9	100	98
Euro area	942	2,905	200.0	22.3	38	48	15	29.8	100	100

a. Excludes river flows from other countries because of data unreliability. b. Food and Agriculture Organization estimates. c. Less than 0.5. d. Includes Montenegro. e. Includes Kosovo and Metohija.

About the data

The data on freshwater resources are based on estimates of runoff into rivers and recharge of groundwater. These estimates are based on different sources and refer to different years, so cross-country comparisons should be made with caution. Because the data are collected intermittently, they may hide significant variations in total renewable water resources from year to year. The data also fail to distinguish between seasonal and geographic variations in water availability within countries. Data for small countries and countries in arid and semiarid zones are less reliable than those for larger countries and countries with greater rainfall.

Caution should also be used in comparing data on annual freshwater withdrawals, which are subject to variations in collection and estimation methods. In addition, inflows and outflows are estimated at different times and at different levels of quality and precision, requiring caution in interpreting the data, particularly for water-short countries, notably in the Middle East and North Africa.

Water productivity is an indication only of the efficiency by which each country uses its water resources. Given the different economic structure of each country, these indicators should be used carefully, taking into account the countries' sectoral activities and natural resource endowments.

The data on access to an improved water source measure the percentage of the population with ready access to water for domestic purposes. The data are based on surveys and estimates provided by governments to the Joint Monitoring Programme of the World Health Organization (WHO) and the United Nations Children's Fund (UNICEF). The coverage rates are based on information from service users on actual household use rather than on information from service providers, which may include nonfunctioning systems. Access to drinking water from an improved source does not ensure that the water is safe or adequate, as these characteristics are not tested at the time of survey. While information on access to an improved water source is widely used, it is extremely subjective, and such terms as *safe, improved, adequate,* and *reasonable* may have different meaning in different countries despite official WHO definitions (see *Definitions*). Even in high-income countries treated water may not always be safe to drink. Access to an improved water source is equated with connection to a supply system; it does not take into account variations in the quality and cost (broadly defined) of the service.

Definitions

• **Internal renewable freshwater resources** are the average annual flows of rivers and groundwater from rainfall) in the country. Natural incoming flows originating outside a country's borders are excluded. Overlapping water resources between surface runoff and groundwater recharge are also deducted. • **Renewable internal freshwater resources per capita** are calculated using the World Bank's population estimates (see table 2.1). • **Annual freshwater withdrawals** are total water withdrawals, not counting evaporation losses from storage basins. Withdrawals also include water from desalination plants in countries where they are a significant source. Withdrawals can exceed 100 percent of total renewable resources where extraction from nonrenewable aquifers or desalination plants is considerable or where water reuse is significant. Withdrawals for agriculture and industry are total withdrawals for irrigation and livestock production and for direct industrial use (including for cooling thermoelectric plants). Withdrawals for domestic uses include drinking water, municipal use or supply, and use for public services, commercial establishments, and homes. • **Water productivity** is calculated as GDP in constant prices divided by annual total water withdrawal. • **Access to an improved water source** is the percentage of the population with reasonable access to an adequate amount of water from an improved source, such as piped water into a dwelling, plot, or yard; public tap or standpipe; tubewell or borehole; protected dug well or spring; and rainwater collection. Unimproved sources include unprotected dug wells or springs, carts with small tank or drum, bottled water, and tanker trucks. Reasonable access is defined as the availability of at least 20 liters a person a day from a source within 1 kilometer of the dwelling.

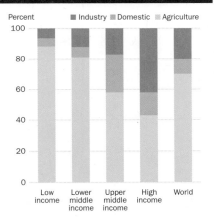

Agriculture is still the largest user of water, accounting for some 70 percent of global withdrawals in 2007 . . .   3.5a

Source: Table 3.5.

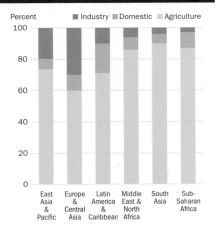

. . . and approaching 90 percent in some developing regions in 2007   3.5b

Source: Table 3.5.

Data sources

Data on freshwater resources and withdrawals are from the Food and Agriculture Organization of the United Nations AQUASTAT data. The GDP estimates used to calculate water productivity are from the World Bank national accounts database. Data on access to water are from WHO and UNICEF's *Progress on Drinking Water and Sanitation* (2008).

	Emissions of organic water pollutants				Industry shares of emissions of organic water pollutants							
	thousand kilograms per day		kilograms per day per worker						% of total			
					Primary metals	Paper and pulp	Chemicals	Food and beverages	Stone, ceramics, and glass	Textiles	Wood	Other
	1990	2006[a]	1990	2006[a]	2006[a]	2006[a]	2006[a]	2006[a]	2006[a]	2006[a]	2006[a]	2006[a]
Afghanistan	5.9	0.2	0.16	0.21	..	19.7	27.9	14.1	11.7	23.3	..	3.1
Albania	2.4	3.6	0.25	0.25	0.0	0.0	0.0	39.8	0.0	60.2	0.0	0.0
Algeria	107.0	..	0.25	..	..	..	..	..	..	..	..	..
Angola	4.5	..	0.19	..	..	..	..	..	..	..	..	..
Argentina	181.4	155.5	0.21	0.23	3.8	8.4	15.8	30.5	3.5	14.3	2.1	21.6
Armenia	37.9	7.1	0.11	0.28	..	..	..	77.6	..	22.4	..	..
Australia	186.1	111.7	0.18	0.18	12.4	22.8	6.7	43.5	0.2	5.3	2.8	6.3
Austria	90.5	84.8	0.15	0.14	5.7	7.1	9.2	12.5	5.9	4.5	5.9	49.0
Azerbaijan	41.3	18.8	0.15	0.18	9.7	2.5	18.7	19.0	6.5	13.6	1.4	28.5
Bangladesh	250.8	303.0	0.15	0.14	0.7	2.3	3.0	7.6	2.6	79.3	0.5	4.2
Belarus	..	..	..	..	..	..	..	..	..	..	..	..
Belgium	107.8	97.9	0.17	0.17	6.4	7.8	17.3	15.7	5.5	6.9	2.2	38.3
Benin	..	..	..	..	..	..	..	..	..	..	..	..
Bolivia	11.3	11.5	0.24	0.25	0.9	9.8	13.1	35.4	7.7	18.4	5.3	9.5
Bosnia and Herzegovina	50.7	..	0.14	..	..	..	..	..	..	..	..	..
Botswana	2.5	5.0	0.30	0.28	0.0	2.4	0.0	56.7	0.6	3.4	0.0	36.9
Brazil	780.4	..	0.19	..	..	..	..	..	..	..	..	..
Bulgaria	124.3	101.2	0.17	0.17	3.8	4.3	7.6	18.0	4.6	28.0	3.0	30.6
Burkina Faso	..	..	..	..	..	..	..	..	..	..	..	..
Burundi	1.6	..	0.24	..	..	..	..	..	..	..	..	..
Cambodia	3.6	..	0.21	..	..	..	..	..	..	..	..	..
Cameroon	14.0	10.0	0.28	0.19	0.4	5.2	36.1	48.8	0.0	3.8	5.0	0.8
Canada	300.9	310.3	0.17	0.16	4.4	9.1	10.6	13.9	2.8	7.9	6.7	44.6
Central African Republic	1.0	..	0.18	..	..	..	..	..	..	..	..	..
Chad	..	..	..	..	..	..	..	..	..	..	..	..
Chile	..	92.5	..	0.25	7.6	6.3	13.7	35.1	3.6	9.1	6.9	17.7
China	7,038.1	6,088.7	0.14	0.14	20.4	10.9	14.8	28.1	0.5	15.5	0.9	8.8
Hong Kong SAR, China	86.1	34.3	0.12	0.20	1.2	43.5	3.9	30.5	0.1	16.2	0.2	4.6
Colombia	..	87.0	..	0.20	2.3	8.9	17.3	21.3	5.3	24.1	0.9	19.9
Congo, Dem. Rep.	..	..	..	..	..	..	..	..	..	..	..	..
Congo, Rep.	2.5	..	0.32	..	..	..	..	..	..	..	..	..
Costa Rica	27.2	31.2	0.20	0.22	1.6	10.0	8.2	65.7	0.1	10.2	1.3	2.9
Côte d'Ivoire	7.9	..	0.22	..	..	..	..	..	..	..	..	..
Croatia	48.5	41.8	0.17	0.17	3.2	7.2	9.5	18.0	5.9	15.3	4.8	36.0
Cuba	173.0	..	0.25	..	..	..	..	..	..	..	..	..
Czech Republic	176.8	146.5	0.15	0.13	5.4	4.8	10.9	10.9	6.4	7.4	4.4	49.8
Denmark	84.5	60.5	0.18	0.16	1.4	11.3	12.4	16.2	4.4	2.2	4.0	48.1
Dominican Republic	88.6	88.6	0.18	0.18	0.1	1.3	2.3	18.6	1.4	73.1	0.1	3.1
Ecuador	28.6	44.7	0.24	0.28	1.8	7.8	12.8	46.4	4.4	12.3	2.2	12.3
Egypt, Arab Rep.	206.5	206.5	0.19	0.19	5.8	4.0	13.9	20.0	8.2	31.1	0.6	16.4
El Salvador	5.5	..	0.22	..	..	..	..	..	..	..	..	..
Eritrea	2.4	2.8	0.19	0.20	0.2	4.1	9.5	30.0	13.2	25.1	0.0	17.8
Estonia	21.7	16.4	0.15	0.15	0.4	7.3	8.4	15.1	5.1	8.8	17.0	37.9
Ethiopia	18.5	26.8	0.23	0.23	1.8	6.8	10.6	30.7	8.5	28.8	1.5	11.3
Finland	72.5	61.6	0.19	0.16	4.8	15.6	8.6	8.8	4.0	2.8	6.7	48.7
France	326.5	578.2	0.11	0.16	3.3	7.4	15.0	16.2	3.8	5.1	2.3	46.9
Gabon	2.0	..	0.25	..	..	..	..	..	..	..	..	..
Gambia, The	0.8	..	0.34	..	..	..	..	..	..	..	..	..
Georgia	..	..	..	..	..	..	..	..	..	..	..	..
Germany	1,020.9	954.2	0.14	0.14	3.8	7.2	12.0	11.8	3.4	2.5	2.0	57.4
Ghana	..	15.4	..	0.17	3.1	2.8	15.0	19.2	4.2	10.0	34.3	11.4
Greece	50.9	58.6	0.19	0.20	4.4	9.0	10.3	23.1	6.7	15.3	2.7	28.6
Guatemala	21.6	..	0.23	..	..	..	..	..	..	..	..	..
Guinea	..	..	..	..	..	..	..	..	..	..	..	..
Guinea-Bissau	..	..	..	..	..	..	..	..	..	..	..	..
Haiti	0.1	0.0	0.01	0.01	0.0	2.0	0.0	0.0	0.0	0.0	0.0	98.0
Honduras	17.8	..	0.23	..	..	..	..	..	..	..	..	..

	Emissions of organic water pollutants				Industry shares of emissions of organic water pollutants							
	thousand kilograms per day		kilograms per day per worker		% of total							
					Primary metals	Paper and pulp	Chemicals	Food and beverages	Stone, ceramics, and glass	Textiles	Wood	Other
	1990	2006[a]	1990	2006[a]	2006[a]	2006[a]	2006[a]	2006[a]	2006[a]	2006[a]	2006[a]	2006[a]
Hungary	122.1	115.1	0.18	0.15	2.7	6.4	10.5	15.8	3.8	10.5	3.4	46.9
India	1,410.6	1,519.8	0.20	0.20	12.2	7.6	9.2	53.7	0.3	12.7	0.3	3.9
Indonesia	721.8	764.0	0.18	0.18	1.3	4.0	13.0	21.5	3.9	29.0	7.4	19.8
Iran, Islamic Rep.	131.6	160.8	0.16	0.15	7.1	2.8	12.8	16.1	13.8	11.2	0.7	35.5
Iraq	7.7	7.7	0.27	0.27	13.1	25.6	29.9	16.9	5.4	9.1	..	..
Ireland	36.1	34.1	0.19	0.18	1.3	10.1	17.2	21.6	5.8	1.9	3.5	38.6
Israel	43.9	42.8	0.18	0.18	2.2	8.5	15.0	19.7	0.0	9.1	1.5	43.9
Italy	378.3	475.8	0.13	0.12	3.5	5.2	10.5	9.0	5.5	14.2	2.9	49.2
Jamaica	18.7	..	0.29	..	..	..	..	..	..	..	..	..
Japan	1,451.4	1,122.7	0.14	0.15	3.2	7.1	11.2	15.1	3.6	5.3	2.0	52.6
Jordan	15.0	27.2	0.18	0.18	2.5	6.1	14.7	21.6	11.6	16.8	2.6	24.2
Kazakhstan	1.3	1.7	0.40	0.41	0.0	50.0	0.0	47.6	0.0	0.0	0.0	2.4
Kenya	42.6	56.1	0.23	0.24	..	11.5	5.4	66.8	0.1	12.8	1.7	1.8
Korea, Dem. Rep.	..	..	..	..	..	..	..	..	..	..	..	..
Korea, Rep.	366.9	319.6	0.12	0.11	4.2	5.4	12.1	6.3	3.0	9.3	0.9	58.9
Kosovo	..	..	..	..	..	..	..	..	..	..	..	..
Kuwait	9.1	11.9	0.16	0.17	2.1	16.6	11.1	50.2	0.4	11.6	2.8	5.2
Kyrgyz Republic	28.9	11.8	0.14	0.20	8.6	6.0	8.4	24.8	14.9	11.8	1.8	23.7
Lao PDR	0.5	0.5	0.44	0.44	0.0	26.3	0.0	73.7	0.0	0.0	0.0	0.0
Latvia	39.8	29.3	0.12	0.18	2.6	6.8	5.6	21.9	3.7	12.6	19.7	27.2
Lebanon	14.7	14.7	0.19	0.19	0.5	7.5	6.0	25.5	12.9	16.7	4.5	26.3
Lesotho	..	15.3	..	0.13	0.9	0.5	1.2	3.6	1.2	90.7	..	1.9
Liberia	0.6	..	0.30	..	..	..	..	..	..	..	..	..
Libya	..	..	..	..	..	..	..	..	..	..	..	..
Lithuania	54.0	42.6	0.15	0.17	0.8	5.2	7.6	20.0	4.4	19.3	11.5	31.2
Macedonia, FYR	32.4	..	0.18	..	..	..	..	..	..	..	..	..
Madagascar	..	92.8	..	0.14	0.3	1.6	12.4	7.6	2.8	58.9	6.3	10.0
Malawi	37.2	32.7	0.40	0.39	..	1.4	3.7	82.1	0.6	7.5	1.1	3.6
Malaysia	..	208.4	..	0.13	2.9	5.2	16.2	9.5	3.9	6.8	7.9	47.5
Mali	..	..	..	..	..	..	..	..	..	..	..	..
Mauritania	..	..	..	..	..	..	..	..	..	..	..	..
Mauritius	0.3	0.4	0.05	0.06	0.0	13.7	0.0	0.0	..	0.0	0.0	86.3
Mexico	370.8	..	0.19	..	..	..	..	..	..	..	..	..
Moldova	29.2	21.1	0.44	0.45	0.0	3.3	0.0	95.7	0.0	0.0	..	1.0
Mongolia	10.2	..	0.18	..	..	..	..	..	..	..	..	..
Morocco	..	80.4	..	0.16	1.0	2.8	8.7	17.6	9.4	42.0	1.9	16.6
Mozambique	20.4	10.2	0.27	0.31	1.1	7.1	2.7	81.2	0.1	5.8	1.4	0.7
Myanmar	7.7	6.2	0.17	0.18	56.5	4.6	13.2	14.9	0.4	2.9	1.7	5.8
Namibia	7.4	..	0.35	..	..	..	..	..	..	..	..	..
Nepal	26.4	26.8	0.14	0.16	1.6	3.9	7.2	19.2	29.9	29.4	2.0	6.8
Netherlands	142.3	122.1	0.20	0.18	1.2	13.8	14.8	18.4	4.1	2.6	2.5	42.5
New Zealand	46.7	62.5	0.24	0.23	2.1	12.7	8.6	30.6	3.2	6.1	7.8	28.9
Nicaragua	10.5	..	0.27	..	..	..	..	..	..	..	..	..
Niger	..	0.4	..	0.32	..	17.0	4.4	76.9	0.3	..	0.8	0.6
Nigeria	70.8	..	0.22	..	..	..	..	..	..	..	..	..
Norway	51.8	50.5	0.20	0.20	5.1	14.3	7.5	20.9	4.0	2.1	5.6	40.5
Oman	3.8	6.6	0.15	0.17	4.3	5.1	16.3	21.6	23.7	5.2	2.1	21.6
Pakistan	104.1	..	0.18	..	..	..	..	..	..	..	..	..
Panama	10.3	13.7	0.30	0.32	0.9	11.7	7.0	55.7	4.0	4.8	1.7	14.2
Papua New Guinea	5.7	..	0.25	..	..	..	..	..	..	..	..	..
Paraguay	15.3	10.8	0.20	0.28	3.1	9.3	16.7	42.6	5.9	11.0	4.5	6.9
Peru	56.1	..	0.20	..	..	..	..	..	..	..	..	..
Philippines	118.4	97.9	0.26	0.23	5.8	6.3	13.2	33.1	6.2	3.1	0.0	32.4
Poland	446.7	364.5	0.16	0.16	3.1	5.2	11.1	18.8	5.4	11.0	4.8	40.6
Portugal	140.6	105.0	0.14	0.15	1.7	7.2	6.6	15.1	5.0	19.1	6.8	38.5
Puerto Rico	19.0	9.2	0.15	0.18	1.9	14.9	21.9	34.4	0.2	15.5	1.4	9.7
Qatar	..	3.7	..	0.12	5.6	1.3	17.2	10.7	29.7	2.2	20.4	12.8

3.6 Water pollution

	Emissions of organic water pollutants				Industry shares of emissions of organic water pollutants							
	thousand kilograms per day		kilograms per day per worker		Primary metals	Paper and pulp	Chemicals	Food and beverages	% of total Stone, ceramics, and glass	Textiles	Wood	Other
	1990	2006a	1990	2006a	2006a	2006a	2006a	2006a	2006a	2006a	2006a	2006a
Romania	411.2	228.1	0.12	0.15	4.6	3.4	6.7	13.4	3.9	27.4	5.1	35.4
Russian Federation	1,521.4	1,388.1	0.16	0.17	9.0	5.0	11.9	17.8	8.0	6.6	4.2	37.7
Rwanda	7.1	7.1	0.44	0.44	..	..	0.0	97.0	0.0	0.0	0.0	3.0
Saudi Arabia	..	6.8	..	0.39	0.0	96.9	0.0	0.5	0.0	0.0	0.0	2.6
Senegal	6.1	6.6	0.30	0.29	4.9	6.3	23.8	44.6	3.9	10.5	0.8	5.3
Serbia	..	..	..	..	..	..	..	..	..	..	..	..
Sierra Leone	4.2	..	0.32	..	..	..	..	..	..	..	..	..
Singapore	32.3	35.3	0.09	0.09	0.0	5.8	11.4	5.3	1.4	2.4	0.4	73.3
Slovak Republic	72.8	51.4	0.13	0.14	7.6	4.8	8.8	10.7	5.9	11.5	3.9	46.8
Slovenia	28.1	28.2	0.13	0.13	4.5	6.4	11.9	8.1	3.5	11.4	4.9	49.3
Somalia	6.2	..	0.38	..	..	..	..	..	..	..	..	..
South Africa	260.5	191.6	0.17	0.16	5.8	7.0	11.4	14.7	5.2	11.9	4.3	39.6
Spain	348.0	379.7	0.16	0.15	3.1	7.9	10.8	15.2	7.9	9.0	3.7	42.4
Sri Lanka	..	266.1	..	0.19	2.6	4.3	9.0	22.4	6.3	43.6	2.5	9.3
Sudan	..	38.6	..	0.29	0.6	1.9	7.0	57.5	14.2	8.0	1.7	9.1
Swaziland	146.0	..	0.16	..	..	..	..	..	..	..	..	..
Sweden	116.8	97.6	0.15	0.14	5.4	12.2	9.9	8.7	2.5	1.4	5.4	54.4
Switzerland	..	..	..	..	..	..	..	..	..	..	..	..
Syrian Arab Republic	6.6	4.5	0.45	0.45	0.0	6.2	0.0	93.8	0.0	0.0	0.0	0.0
Tajikistan	29.1	16.1	0.17	0.23	21.9	1.4	5.1	20.2	7.6	37.5	0.4	5.9
Tanzania	31.1	35.2	0.24	0.25	1.5	9.4	2.7	69.3	0.1	14.0	1.5	1.4
Thailand	369.4	333.8	0.15	0.16	1.8	4.1	13.2	16.5	3.4	22.5	2.4	36.1
Timor-Leste	..	..	..	..	..	..	..	..	..	..	..	..
Togo	..	..	..	..	..	..	..	..	..	..	..	..
Trinidad and Tobago	7.0	7.6	0.23	0.29	0.0	18.1	21.4	39.1	0.4	7.6	8.5	4.9
Tunisia	44.6	55.8	0.18	0.14	2.5	6.1	5.5	35.8	0.4	43.3	1.9	4.6
Turkey	174.9	177.7	0.18	0.16	5.2	3.0	9.8	15.2	6.2	35.7	1.0	24.0
Turkmenistan	..	..	..	..	..	..	..	..	..	..	..	..
Uganda	3.3	17.5	0.29	0.26	..	4.6	7.9	44.5	0.0	14.4	16.8	11.7
Ukraine	..	537.4	..	0.20	14.5	4.1	10.3	20.7	6.5	6.1	2.1	35.8
United Arab Emirates	5.6	..	0.14	..	..	..	..	..	..	..	..	..
United Kingdom	599.9	521.7	0.16	0.17	2.7	12.5	13.5	14.9	3.6	4.3	2.5	46.1
United States	2,307.0	1,889.4	0.14	0.14	3.4	8.3	13.1	12.0	3.7	4.7	4.1	50.6
Uruguay	38.7	15.8	0.23	0.28	1.2	3.7	6.6	79.2	0.1	7.4	0.6	1.2
Uzbekistan	..	..	..	..	..	..	..	..	..	..	..	..
Venezuela, RB	96.5	..	0.21	..	..	..	..	..	..	..	..	..
Vietnam	141.0	500.5	0.16	0.15	1.4	3.5	6.8	13.3	6.7	40.3	3.3	24.7
West Bank and Gaza	..	..	..	..	..	..	..	..	..	..	..	..
Yemen, Rep.	1.5	1.6	0.43	0.41	..	67.4	0.0	32.6	0.0	0.0	0.0	0.0
Zambia	15.9	..	0.23	..	..	..	..	..	..	..	..	..
Zimbabwe	29.3	29.3	0.20	0.20	8.0	4.7	11.0	21.5	6.3	25.2	1.7	21.5

a. Data are derived using the United Nations Industrial Development Organization's (UNIDO) industry database four-digit International Standard Industrial Classification (ISIC). Data in italics are for the most recent year available and are derived using UNIDO's industry database at the three-digit ISIC.

About the data

Emissions of organic pollutants from industrial activities are a major cause of degradation of water quality. Water quality and pollution levels are generally measured as concentration or load—the rate of occurrence of a substance in an aqueous solution. Polluting substances include organic matter, metals, minerals, sediment, bacteria, and toxic chemicals. The table focuses on organic water pollution resulting from industrial activities. Because water pollution tends to be sensitive to local conditions, the national-level data in the table may not reflect the quality of water in specific locations.

The data in the table come from an international study of industrial emissions that may have been the first to include data from developing countries (Hettige, Mani, and Wheeler 1998). These data were updated through 2006 by the World Bank's Development Research Group. Unlike estimates from earlier studies based on engineering or economic models, these estimates are based on actual measurements of plant-level water pollution. The focus is on organic water pollution caused by organic waste, measured in terms of biochemical oxygen demand (BOD), because the data for this indicator are the most plentiful and reliable for cross-country comparisons of emissions. BOD measures the strength of an organic waste by the amount of oxygen consumed in breaking it down. A sewage overload in natural waters exhausts the water's dissolved oxygen content. Wastewater treatment, by contrast, reduces BOD.

Data on water pollution are more readily available than are other emissions data because most industrial pollution control programs start by regulating emissions of organic water pollutants. Such data are fairly reliable because sampling techniques for measuring water pollution are more widely understood and much less expensive than those for air pollution.

Hettige, Mani, and Wheeler (1998) used plant- and sector-level information on emissions and employment from 13 national environmental protection agencies and sector-level information on output and employment from the United Nations Industrial Development Organization (UNIDO). Their econometric analysis found that the ratio of BOD to employment in each industrial sector is about the same across countries. This finding allowed the authors to estimate BOD loads across countries and over time. The estimated BOD intensities per unit of employment were multiplied by sectoral employment numbers from UNIDO's industry database for 1980–98. These estimates of sectoral emissions were then used to calculate kilograms of emissions of organic water pollutants per day for each country and year. The data in the table were derived by updating these estimates through 2006.

Definitions

• **Emissions of organic water pollutants** are measured as biochemical oxygen demand, or the amount of oxygen that bacteria in water will consume in breaking down waste, a standard water treatment test for the presence of organic pollutants. Emissions per worker are total emissions divided by the number of industrial workers. • **Industry shares of emissions of organic water pollutants** are emissions from manufacturing activities as defined by two-digit divisions of the International Standard Industrial Classification revision 3.

Emissions of organic water pollutants declined in most economies from 1990 to 2006, even in some of the top emitters

3.6a

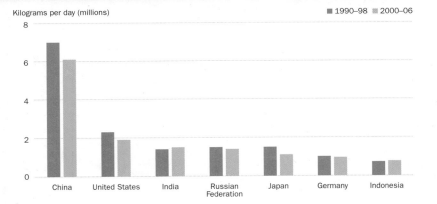

Note: Data are for the most recent year available during the period specified.

Source: Table 3.6.

Data sources

Data on water pollutants are from Hettige, Mani, and Wheeler, "Industrial Pollution in Economic Development: Kuznets Revisited" (1998). The data were updated through 2006 by the World Bank's Development Research Group using the same methodology as the initial study. Data on industrial sectoral employment are from UNIDO's industry database.

Energy production and use

	Energy production		Energy use									Alternative and nuclear energy production	
	Total million metric tons of oil equivalent		Total million metric tons of oil equivalent		average annual % growth	Per capita kilograms of oil equivalent		% of total				% of total energy use	
								Fossil fuel		Combustible renewables and waste			
	1990	2007	1990	2007	1990–2007	1990	2007	1990	2007	1990	2007	1990	2007
Afghanistan	..	..	..	..	..	..	..	..	..	..	..	..	..
Albania	2.4	1.1	2.7	2.2	2.0	809	694	76.5	67.8	13.6	9.9	9.2	11.1
Algeria	100.1	164.3	22.2	36.9	2.7	878	1,089	99.9	99.7	0.1	0.2	0.1	0.1
Angola	28.7	95.0	5.9	10.6	3.4	552	606	25.5	34.0	73.5	63.4	1.1	2.6
Argentina	48.4	81.9	46.1	73.1	2.1	1,418	1,850	88.7	89.5	3.7	3.5	7.5	6.2
Armenia	0.1	0.8	7.7	2.8	−3.7	2,171	926	97.2	70.7	0.1	0.0	1.7	29.0
Australia	157.5	289.2	86.2	124.1	2.3	5,053	5,888	93.9	94.4	4.6	4.3	1.5	1.3
Austria	8.1	10.9	24.8	33.2	2.0	3,214	3,997	79.2	72.6	10.0	15.4	11.0	10.3
Azerbaijan	21.3	52.1	25.8	11.9	−3.2	3,609	1,388	..	98.4	0.0	0.0	0.2	1.7
Bangladesh	10.8	21.3	12.7	25.8	4.5	110	163	45.5	66.2	53.9	33.3	0.6	0.5
Belarus	3.3	4.0	42.3	28.0	−1.9	4,155	2,891	95.4	91.5	0.5	5.2	0.0	0.0
Belgium	13.1	14.4	48.2	57.0	1.1	4,840	5,366	76.0	73.1	1.6	3.6	23.1	22.2
Benin	1.8	1.8	1.7	2.9	3.1	346	343	4.8	36.8	94.2	61.5	0.0	0.0
Bolivia	4.9	15.1	2.8	5.4	3.4	416	571	69.1	81.8	27.2	14.5	3.6	3.7
Bosnia and Herzegovina	4.6	3.9	7.0	5.6	2.2	1,627	1,483	93.9	91.5	2.3	3.3	3.8	6.1
Botswana	0.9	1.1	1.3	2.0	2.6	933	1,068	66.1	69.4	33.4	23.1	0.1	0.0
Brazil	103.7	215.6	139.5	235.6	3.1	933	1,239	51.1	52.6	34.1	30.7	13.2	15.1
Bulgaria	9.6	10.0	28.6	20.2	−1.3	3,277	2,641	84.3	77.8	0.6	3.7	13.9	20.4
Burkina Faso	..	..	..	..	..	..	..	..	..	..	..	..	..
Burundi	..	..	..	..	..	..	..	..	..	..	..	..	..
Cambodia	..	3.6	..	5.1	3.5	..	358	..	29.1	..	70.5	..	0.1
Cameroon	11.0	10.2	5.0	7.3	2.3	407	391	18.7	27.4	76.7	68.1	4.6	4.5
Canada	273.8	413.2	208.7	269.4	1.6	7,509	8,169	74.5	75.6	4.0	4.3	21.5	20.9
Central African Republic	..	..	..	..	..	..	..	..	..	..	..	..	..
Chad	..	..	..	..	..	..	..	..	..	..	..	..	..
Chile	7.4	8.5	13.8	30.8	5.0	1,048	1,851	75.1	77.7	19.4	15.4	5.5	6.5
China	886.3	1,814.0	863.1	1,955.8	4.5	760	1,484	75.5	86.9	23.2	9.9	1.3	3.2
Hong Kong SAR, China	0.0	0.0	8.8	13.7	2.4	1,539	1,985	99.4	95.3	0.6	0.4	0.0	0.0
Colombia	48.2	87.6	24.2	29.5	0.5	730	655	67.4	71.5	22.8	15.5	9.8	13.2
Congo, Dem. Rep.	12.0	18.4	11.8	18.1	2.5	319	289	11.2	4.2	84.7	92.7	4.1	3.9
Congo, Rep.	8.7	12.5	0.8	1.3	2.8	326	357	35.0	38.7	59.5	55.9	5.3	2.3
Costa Rica	1.0	2.5	2.0	4.8	5.1	643	1,070	47.2	47.1	37.4	17.7	14.7	35.0
Côte d'Ivoire	3.4	11.2	4.3	10.0	5.0	343	496	23.3	22.7	73.5	76.4	2.6	1.6
Croatia	5.1	4.1	9.0	9.3	1.4	1,884	2,099	86.5	86.7	3.5	3.5	3.6	4.0
Cuba	6.6	5.2	16.5	9.9	−1.7	1,558	884	64.3	86.8	35.6	13.1	0.1	0.1
Czech Republic	40.1	33.7	48.8	45.8	0.2	4,705	4,428	93.2	83.0	0.0	4.6	6.9	15.4
Denmark	10.1	27.0	17.3	19.6	0.2	3,374	3,598	89.6	82.3	6.6	14.8	0.3	3.3
Dominican Republic	1.0	1.5	4.1	7.9	4.0	556	804	74.8	80.5	24.4	18.0	0.7	1.5
Ecuador	16.5	28.9	6.0	11.8	3.9	583	885	79.1	86.6	13.8	6.2	7.2	6.6
Egypt, Arab Rep.	54.9	82.3	31.8	67.2	4.7	551	840	94.0	95.8	3.3	2.2	2.7	2.1
El Salvador	1.7	2.8	2.5	4.9	3.8	463	800	31.4	41.9	48.2	30.7	20.3	27.4
Eritrea	0.7	0.5	0.9	0.7	−2.2	276	151	19.3	26.5	80.7	73.5	0.0	0.0
Estonia	5.1	4.4	9.6	5.6	−2.2	6,099	4,198	99.8	91.3	2.0	10.5	0.0	0.2
Ethiopia	14.1	20.9	14.9	22.8	2.6	308	290	5.5	8.5	93.9	90.2	0.6	1.3
Finland	12.1	15.9	28.4	36.5	1.8	5,692	6,895	55.5	50.0	16.1	20.1	20.9	20.1
France	112.5	135.5	224.5	263.7	1.1	3,957	4,258	58.0	51.2	5.2	5.1	38.6	45.6
Gabon	14.6	12.0	1.2	1.8	2.3	1,275	1,300	32.0	39.6	62.9	56.6	5.2	3.7
Gambia, The	..	..	..	..	..	..	..	..	..	..	..	..	..
Georgia	1.8	1.1	12.1	3.3	−7.3	2,217	767	88.6	70.7	3.8	11.8	5.4	18.0
Germany	186.2	137.0	351.4	331.3	−0.1	4,424	4,027	86.8	80.8	1.4	6.8	11.8	12.8
Ghana	4.4	6.5	5.3	9.5	3.4	353	415	18.2	31.8	73.7	64.7	9.3	3.4
Greece	9.2	12.1	21.4	32.2	2.6	2,110	2,875	94.6	93.4	4.2	3.7	1.0	1.7
Guatemala	3.4	5.3	4.4	8.3	4.0	498	620	28.1	46.0	68.5	50.4	3.4	3.8
Guinea	..	..	..	..	..	..	..	..	..	..	..	..	..
Guinea-Bissau	..	..	..	..	..	..	..	..	..	..	..	..	..
Haiti	1.3	2.0	1.6	2.8	3.6	219	286	19.7	27.8	77.8	71.7	2.5	0.5
Honduras	1.7	2.1	2.4	4.7	3.6	486	661	30.0	55.3	62.9	40.7	8.2	4.0

Energy production and use

	Energy production		Energy use					% of total				Alternative and nuclear energy production	
	Total million metric tons of oil equivalent		Total million metric tons of oil equivalent		average annual % growth	Per capita kilograms of oil equivalent		Fossil fuel		Combustible renewables and waste		% of total energy use	
	1990	2007	1990	2007	1990–2007	1990	2007	1990	2007	1990	2007	1990	2007
Hungary	14.6	10.2	28.7	26.7	0.0	2,762	2,658	81.5	79.0	2.3	5.0	12.8	14.8
India	291.1	450.9	318.2	594.9	3.5	375	529	55.6	70.0	41.9	27.2	2.4	2.7
Indonesia	170.0	331.1	102.5	190.6	3.5	575	845	54.6	68.8	43.9	27.5	1.5	3.7
Iran, Islamic Rep.	179.8	323.1	68.3	184.9	5.7	1,256	2,604	98.2	98.7	1.0	0.5	0.8	0.8
Iraq	104.9	104.8	18.1	33.1	3.9	1,000	..	98.6	99.4	0.1	0.1	1.2	0.1
Ireland	3.5	1.4	10.0	15.1	2.9	2,843	3,457	84.8	90.9	1.1	1.6	0.6	1.5
Israel	0.4	2.7	11.6	22.0	3.6	2,486	3,059	97.2	97.4	0.0	0.0	3.1	3.4
Italy	25.3	26.4	146.7	178.2	1.4	2,586	3,001	93.4	90.5	0.6	2.6	3.9	4.6
Jamaica	0.5	0.5	2.8	5.0	2.8	1,167	1,852	82.6	89.9	17.1	9.8	0.3	0.4
Japan	75.1	90.5	438.1	513.5	0.9	3,546	4,019	84.5	83.2	1.1	1.4	14.4	15.3
Jordan	0.2	0.3	3.3	7.2	4.4	1,028	1,259	98.2	98.4	0.1	0.1	1.8	1.5
Kazakhstan	90.5	136.0	72.7	66.5	−1.5	4,450	4,292	96.9	98.9	0.2	0.1	0.9	1.1
Kenya	9.0	14.7	11.2	18.3	3.0	479	485	19.5	19.6	75.9	74.0	4.4	6.4
Korea, Dem. Rep.	28.9	19.7	33.2	18.4	−2.3	1,649	774	93.1	88.1	2.9	5.7	4.0	6.2
Korea, Rep.	22.6	42.5	93.1	222.2	5.0	2,171	4,586	83.8	81.9	0.8	1.2	15.4	16.9
Kosovo	..	..	..	..	..	..	..	..	..	..	..	..	..
Kuwait	50.4	146.6	7.8	25.2	7.5	3,681	9,463	99.9	100.0	0.1	0.0	0.0	0.0
Kyrgyz Republic	2.5	1.4	7.6	2.9	−4.3	1,713	556	93.6	65.7	0.1	0.1	11.3	41.2
Lao PDR	..	..	..	..	..	..	..	..	..	..	..	..	..
Latvia	1.1	1.8	7.8	4.7	−2.6	2,913	2,052	81.6	64.2	8.5	25.1	5.0	5.1
Lebanon	0.1	0.2	2.2	4.0	3.8	755	959	93.5	92.7	4.6	3.5	1.9	1.7
Lesotho	..	..	..	..	..	..	..	..	..	..	..	..	..
Liberia	..	..	..	..	..	..	..	..	..	..	..	..	..
Libya	73.2	101.6	11.3	17.8	2.3	2,596	2,889	98.9	99.1	1.1	0.9	0.0	0.0
Lithuania	4.9	3.8	16.1	9.3	−2.4	4,357	2,740	75.8	61.9	1.8	8.3	28.2	28.7
Macedonia, FYR	1.3	1.5	2.5	3.0	0.8	1,298	1,482	98.0	85.0	0.0	4.8	1.7	3.2
Madagascar	..	..	..	..	..	..	..	..	..	..	..	..	..
Malawi	..	..	..	..	..	..	..	..	..	..	..	..	..
Malaysia	50.3	94.4	22.7	72.6	6.2	1,252	2,733	89.1	95.5	9.4	4.0	1.5	0.8
Mali	..	..	..	..	..	..	..	..	..	..	..	..	..
Mauritania	..	..	..	..	..	..	..	..	..	..	..	..	..
Mauritius	..	..	..	..	..	..	..	..	..	..	..	..	..
Mexico	193.4	251.1	121.2	184.3	2.3	1,456	1,750	88.1	89.3	6.1	4.5	5.9	6.3
Moldova	0.1	0.1	9.9	3.3	−5.6	2,261	910	99.6	90.0	0.4	2.3	0.2	0.1
Mongolia	2.7	3.6	3.4	3.1	−1.3	1,541	1,182	97.0	96.1	2.5	3.3	0.0	0.0
Morocco	0.8	0.7	6.9	14.4	4.0	287	465	93.8	93.8	4.6	3.1	1.5	1.0
Mozambique	5.6	11.0	5.9	9.2	2.8	437	418	5.5	8.0	93.9	80.3	0.4	15.1
Myanmar	10.7	23.9	10.7	15.6	2.4	261	319	14.4	31.7	84.7	66.3	1.0	1.9
Namibia	0.2	0.3	0.7	1.6	5.1	446	745	62.0	68.0	16.0	12.3	17.5	8.7
Nepal	5.5	8.5	5.8	9.6	3.1	303	338	5.1	10.7	93.7	86.7	1.3	2.5
Netherlands	60.5	61.5	65.7	80.4	1.0	4,392	4,909	96.0	92.9	1.4	3.5	1.4	1.8
New Zealand	12.0	14.0	13.3	16.8	1.3	3,859	3,966	64.2	67.4	4.1	6.6	31.7	25.9
Nicaragua	1.5	2.1	2.1	3.5	3.2	506	621	28.3	40.6	53.9	52.4	17.5	6.8
Niger	..	..	..	..	..	..	..	..	..	..	..	..	..
Nigeria	150.5	231.7	70.6	106.7	2.4	725	722	19.3	19.3	80.2	80.2	0.5	0.5
Norway	119.1	213.9	21.0	26.9	1.7	4,951	5,704	51.9	54.8	4.9	5.1	49.6	43.2
Oman	38.3	59.3	4.2	15.5	7.0	2,304	5,678	100.0	100.0	0.0	0.0	0.0	0.0
Pakistan	34.2	63.6	42.9	83.3	3.7	397	512	52.7	62.1	43.8	33.9	3.6	3.9
Panama	0.6	0.7	1.5	2.8	3.5	618	845	58.4	75.7	28.3	13.5	12.7	11.2
Papua New Guinea	..	..	..	..	..	..	..	..	..	..	..	..	..
Paraguay	4.6	7.1	3.1	4.2	1.5	723	686	21.3	29.4	72.5	53.0	76.0	109.9
Peru	10.6	12.2	9.7	14.1	2.2	447	494	63.3	69.8	27.5	18.2	9.2	12.0
Philippines	15.7	22.4	27.5	40.0	2.3	440	451	45.8	57.0	35.2	19.2	19.0	23.8
Poland	103.9	72.6	103.1	97.1	−0.6	2,705	2,547	97.8	94.8	2.2	5.4	0.1	0.3
Portugal	3.4	4.6	16.7	25.1	2.9	1,691	2,363	80.4	79.1	14.8	12.6	4.8	5.7
Puerto Rico	..	..	..	..	..	..	..	..	..	..	..	..	..
Qatar	26.6	103.0	6.9	22.2	6.4	14,732	19,504	99.9	100.0	0.1	0.0	0.0	0.0

	Energy production		Energy use										Alternative and nuclear energy production	
	Total million metric tons of oil equivalent		Total million metric tons of oil equivalent		average annual % growth	Per capita kilograms of oil equivalent		% of total						% of total energy use	
								Fossil fuel		Combustible renewables and waste					
	1990	2007	1990	2007	1990–2007	1990	2007	1990	2007	1990	2007			1990	2007
Romania	40.8	27.6	62.3	38.9	−2.1	2,683	1,806	96.1	82.8	1.0	8.9			1.6	8.7
Russian Federation	1,280.3	1,230.6	870.0	672.1	−1.3	5,867	4,730	93.3	89.3	1.4	1.0			5.2	8.6
Rwanda	..	..	..	..	..	..	..	..	..	..	..			..	..
Saudi Arabia	370.8	551.3	59.3	150.3	4.8	3,618	6,223	100.0	100.0	0.0	0.0			0.0	0.0
Senegal	1.0	1.3	1.7	2.7	3.5	224	225	43.2	53.1	56.8	45.9			0.0	0.7
Serbia	13.4	9.8	19.3	15.8	..	2,550	2,141	90.6	89.2	6.0	5.1			4.2	5.7
Serbia	25.2	..	43.8	..	..	4,182	..	90.6	..	2.1	..			7.4	..
Sierra Leone	..	..	..	..	..	..	..	..	..	..	..			..	..
Singapore	0.0	0.0	11.5	26.8	3.8	3,760	5,831	100.0	100.0	0.0	0.0			0.0	0.0
Slovak Republic	5.3	6.0	21.3	17.8	−0.2	4,037	3,307	81.6	70.8	0.8	3.5			15.5	24.9
Slovenia	3.1	3.5	5.7	7.3	2.0	2,835	3,632	71.1	69.2	4.7	6.5			25.8	24.1
Somalia	..	..	..	..	..	..	..	..	..	..	..			..	..
South Africa	114.5	159.6	90.9	134.3	2.2	2,581	2,807	86.1	87.7	11.5	10.2			2.5	2.3
Spain	34.6	30.3	90.1	144.0	3.2	2,320	3,208	77.4	83.2	4.5	3.7			18.1	13.3
Sri Lanka	4.2	5.1	5.5	9.3	3.5	322	464	24.1	45.5	71.0	50.8			4.9	3.7
Sudan	8.8	34.6	10.6	14.7	2.6	392	363	17.5	26.3	81.8	72.8			0.8	0.9
Swaziland	..	..	..	..	..	..	..	..	..	..	..			..	..
Sweden	29.7	33.6	47.2	50.4	0.5	5,514	5,512	37.3	32.9	11.7	19.6			50.9	46.2
Switzerland	9.7	12.6	23.8	25.7	0.6	3,545	3,406	59.9	51.6	3.8	8.2			37.0	40.9
Syrian Arab Republic	22.3	24.4	11.4	19.6	2.9	895	958	97.9	98.4	0.0	0.0			2.1	1.5
Tajikistan	2.0	1.6	5.6	3.9	−1.9	1,051	580	72.7	62.0	0.0	0.0			25.5	37.7
Tanzania	9.1	16.9	9.7	18.3	4.1	382	443	6.9	10.3	91.7	88.6			1.4	1.2
Thailand	26.5	59.4	42.0	104.0	5.2	742	1,553	63.9	81.2	34.9	17.8			1.0	0.7
Timor-Leste	..	..	..	..	..	..	..	..	..	..	..			..	..
Togo	1.1	2.1	1.3	2.5	4.5	322	390	15.0	12.8	82.8	85.1			0.6	0.3
Trinidad and Tobago	12.6	37.0	6.0	15.3	6.1	4,899	11,506	99.2	99.9	0.8	0.1			0.0	0.0
Tunisia	5.7	7.9	4.9	8.8	3.7	607	864	87.0	86.3	12.9	13.6			0.1	0.1
Turkey	25.8	27.3	52.8	100.0	3.6	941	1,370	81.8	90.5	13.7	5.1			4.6	4.6
Turkmenistan	74.9	66.1	19.6	18.1	1.2	5,352	3,631	100.0	100.0	0.0	0.0			0.3	0.0
Uganda	..	..	..	..	..	..	..	..	..	..	..			..	..
Ukraine	135.8	81.6	251.8	137.3	−3.2	4,851	2,953	91.8	81.7	0.1	0.6			8.2	18.2
United Arab Emirates	110.2	178.4	19.9	51.6	5.2	10,645	11,833	100.0	100.0	0.0	0.0			0.0	0.0
United Kingdom	208.0	176.2	207.2	211.3	0.2	3,619	3,464	90.7	89.6	0.3	1.9			8.5	8.2
United States	1,649.4	1,665.2	1,913.2	2,339.9	1.2	7,664	7,766	86.4	85.6	3.3	3.5			10.3	10.8
Uruguay	1.1	1.2	2.3	3.2	1.3	725	953	58.7	62.3	24.3	16.4			26.8	21.9
Uzbekistan	38.6	60.1	46.4	48.7	0.6	2,261	1,812	99.2	98.9	0.0	0.0			1.2	1.1
Venezuela, RB	148.9	183.8	43.6	63.7	1.6	2,206	2,319	91.5	87.8	1.2	0.8			7.3	11.2
Vietnam	24.7	73.9	24.3	55.8	5.1	367	655	20.4	51.4	77.7	44.0			1.9	4.6
West Bank and Gaza	..	..	..	..	..	..	..	..	..	..	..			..	..
Yemen, Rep.	9.4	16.5	2.5	7.2	6.2	204	324	97.0	98.9	3.1	1.1			0.0	0.0
Zambia	4.9	6.8	5.4	7.4	1.8	683	604	15.6	10.7	74.3	78.3			12.7	11.3
Zimbabwe	8.6	8.7	9.3	9.4	−0.2	889	759	44.8	27.9	50.9	65.0			4.0	4.7
World		8,823.2 t 11,926.4 t	8,555.5 t 11,664.3 t		1.8 w	1,666 w	1,819 w	81.0 w	81.3 w	10.2 w	9.6 w			8.8 w	9.0 w
Low income	249.0	407.6	277.3	378.3	2.1	449	423	50.6	46.7	46.2	49.3			3.4	4.1
Middle income	4,811.7	6,906.3	3,884.6	5,715.4	2.2	1,054	1,242	79.5	81.6	16.4	13.2			4.1	5.1
Lower middle income	2,296.4	3,981.5	2,013.2	3,713.4	3.5	696	1,013	71.4	80.0	25.9	16.3			2.8	3.8
Upper middle income	2,515.6	2,926.8	1,871.9	2,004.7	0.5	2,354	2,130	88.1	84.7	6.2	7.3			5.4	7.4
Low & middle income	5,055.3	7,298.0	4,145.7	6,074.4	2.2	980	1,127	77.9	79.8	18.1	15.1			4.0	5.0
East Asia & Pacific	1,225.4	2,460.3	1,138.8	2,475.5	4.4	715	1,295	71.5	83.8	26.6	12.8			1.8	3.4
Europe & Central Asia	1,861.3	1,796.8	1,675.5	1,297.3	−1.3	3,885	2,948	93.2	89.2	1.6	2.1			5.1	8.1
Latin America & Carib.	608.4	919.8	453.0	711.2	2.5	1,042	1,273	71.2	72.8	19.7	16.3			9.2	10.8
Middle East & N. Africa	558.6	836.8	185.5	406.5	4.5	819	1,276	97.2	97.9	1.7	1.1			1.1	0.9
South Asia	348.7	554.1	388.3	728.9	3.6	347	484	53.7	67.9	43.7	29.3			2.5	2.8
Sub-Saharan Africa	475.6	779.9	310.8	474.1	2.5	676	662	41.3	41.8	56.5	55.8			2.2	2.5
High income	3,785.4	4,654.1	4,433.0	5,625.0	1.5	4,733	5,321	83.9	82.9	2.8	3.7			13.1	13.3
Euro area	477.1	459.9	1,060.4	1,229.2	1.1	3,516	3,789	79.8	75.7	3.2	5.6			16.7	18.2

About the data

In developing economies growth in energy use is closely related to growth in the modern sectors—industry, motorized transport, and urban areas—but energy use also reflects climatic, geographic, and economic factors (such as the relative price of energy). Energy use has been growing rapidly in low- and middle-income economies, but high-income economies still use almost five times as much energy on a per capita basis.

Energy data are compiled by the International Energy Agency (IEA). IEA data for economies that are not members of the Organisation for Economic Co-operation and Development (OECD) are based on national energy data adjusted to conform to annual questionnaires completed by OECD member governments.

Total energy use refers to the use of primary energy before transformation to other end-use fuels (such as electricity and refined petroleum products). It includes energy from combustible renewables and waste—solid biomass and animal products, gas and liquid from biomass, and industrial and municipal waste. Biomass is any plant matter used directly as fuel or converted into fuel, heat, or electricity. Data for combustible renewables and waste are often based on small surveys or other incomplete information and thus give only a broad impression of developments and are not strictly comparable across countries. The IEA reports include country notes that explain some of these differences (see Data sources). All forms of energy—primary energy and primary electricity—are converted into oil equivalents. A notional thermal efficiency of 33 percent is assumed for converting nuclear electricity into oil equivalents and 100 percent efficiency for converting hydroelectric power.

The IEA makes these estimates in consultation with national statistical offices, oil companies, electric utilities, and national energy experts. The IEA occasionally revises its time series to reflect political changes, and energy statistics undergo continual changes in coverage or methodology as more detailed energy accounts become available. Breaks in series are therefore unavoidable.

Definitions

• **Energy production** refers to forms of primary energy—petroleum (crude oil, natural gas liquids, and oil from nonconventional sources), natural gas, solid fuels (coal, lignite, and other derived fuels), and combustible renewables and waste—and primary electricity, all converted into oil equivalents (see About the data). • **Energy use** refers to the use of primary energy before transformation to other end-use fuels, which is equal to indigenous production plus imports and stock changes, minus exports and fuels supplied to ships and aircraft engaged in international transport (see About the data). • **Fossil fuel** comprises coal, oil, petroleum, and natural gas products. • **Combustible renewables and waste** comprise solid biomass, liquid biomass, biogas, industrial waste, and municipal waste. • **Alternative and nuclear energy production** is noncarbohydrate energy that does not produce carbon dioxide when generated. It includes hydropower and nuclear, geothermal, and solar power, among others.

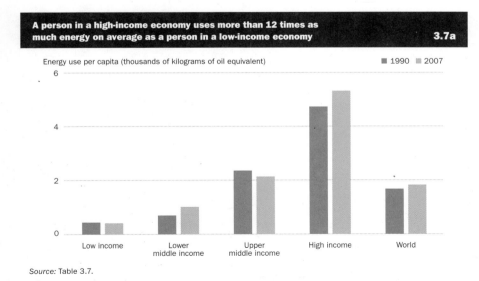

A person in a high-income economy uses more than 12 times as much energy on average as a person in a low-income economy — 3.7a

Energy use per capita (thousands of kilograms of oil equivalent) ■ 1990 ■ 2007

Low income | Lower middle income | Upper middle income | High income | World

Source: Table 3.7.

Data sources

Data on energy production and use are from IEA electronic files and are published in IEA's annual publications, *Energy Statistics and Balances of Non-OECD Countries*, *Energy Statistics of OECD Countries*, and *Energy Balances of OECD Countries*.

	Net energy importsa		GDP per unit of energy use		Carbon dioxide emissions							
			2005 PPP $ per kilogram of oil equivalent		Total million metric tons		Carbon intensity kilograms per kilogram of oil equivalent energy use		Per capita metric tons		kilograms per 2005 PPP $ of GDP	
	% of energy use											
	1990	2007	1990	2007	1990	2006	1990	2006	1990	2006	1990	2006
Afghanistan	..	..	..	..	2.7	0.7	..	..	0.2	0.0	..	0.0
Albania	8	51	4.5	9.2	7.5	4.3	2.8	2.0	2.3	1.4	0.6	0.2
Algeria	−351	−346	7.1	6.7	78.8	132.6	3.6	3.8	3.1	4.0	0.5	0.6
Angola	−387	−793	5.8	8.1	4.4	10.6	0.8	1.1	0.4	0.6	0.1	0.1
Argentina	−5	−12	5.3	6.8	112.5	173.4	2.4	2.5	3.5	4.4	0.5	0.4
Armenia	98	71	1.4	5.7	3.7	4.4	0.9	1.7	1.1	1.4	0.7	0.3
Australia	−83	−133	4.8	6.0	292.9	371.7	3.4	3.0	17.2	18.0	0.7	0.5
Austria	67	67	8.0	8.9	60.7	71.8	2.4	2.1	7.9	8.7	0.3	0.3
Azerbaijan	17	−337	1.3	5.3	44.1	35.0	2.7	2.6	6.0	4.1	1.7	0.7
Bangladesh	16	17	6.2	7.2	15.5	41.6	1.2	1.7	0.1	0.3	0.2	0.2
Belarus	92	86	1.5	3.6	98.5	68.8	2.6	2.4	9.6	7.1	1.7	0.7
Belgium	73	75	5.2	6.2	107.5	107.1	2.2	1.8	10.8	10.2	0.4	0.3
Benin	−7	39	3.2	3.9	0.7	3.1	0.4	1.1	0.1	0.4	0.1	0.3
Bolivia	−77	−177	7.0	6.6	5.5	11.4	2.0	2.4	0.8	1.2	0.3	0.3
Bosnia and Herzegovina	34	30	..	4.5	4.7	27.4	1.1	5.1	1.2	7.3	..	1.2
Botswana	28	45	7.5	11.6	2.2	4.8	1.7	2.4	1.6	2.6	0.2	0.2
Brazil	26	8	7.7	7.4	208.7	352.3	1.5	1.6	1.4	1.9	0.2	0.2
Bulgaria	66	51	2.2	3.8	76.6	48.0	2.7	2.4	8.8	6.2	1.2	0.7
Burkina Faso	..	..	..	..	0.6	0.8	..	..	0.1	0.1	0.1	0.1
Burundi	..	..	..	..	0.3	0.2	..	..	0.1	0.0	0.1	0.1
Cambodia	..	29	..	4.8	0.5	4.1	..	0.8	0.0	0.3	..	0.2
Cameroon	−120	−39	5.1	5.1	1.7	3.6	0.3	0.5	0.1	0.2	0.1	0.1
Canada	−31	−53	3.6	4.4	449.7	544.3	2.2	2.0	16.2	16.7	0.6	0.5
Central African Republic	..	..	..	..	0.2	0.2	..	..	0.1	0.1	0.1	0.1
Chad	..	..	..	..	0.1	0.4	..	..	0.0	0.0	0.0	0.0
Chile	46	73	6.3	7.1	35.5	60.1	2.6	2.0	2.7	3.6	0.4	0.3
China	−3	7	1.4	3.4	2,412.9	6,099.1	2.8	3.3	2.1	4.7	1.9	1.0
Hong Kong SAR, China	100	100	15.4	20.1	27.6	39.0	3.1	2.9	4.8	5.7	0.2	0.2
Colombia	−99	−202	8.2	12.3	57.3	63.4	2.4	2.1	1.7	1.5	0.3	0.2
Congo, Dem. Rep.	−2	−2	1.9	1.0	4.1	2.2	0.3	0.1	0.1	0.0	0.2	0.1
Congo, Rep.	−997	−891	10.7	9.9	1.2	1.5	1.5	1.2	0.5	0.4	0.1	0.1
Costa Rica	48	47	9.7	9.6	3.0	7.8	1.5	1.8	1.0	1.8	0.2	0.2
Côte d'Ivoire	22	−13	5.5	3.1	5.8	6.9	1.3	0.7	0.5	0.3	0.2	0.2
Croatia	43	57	6.6	7.5	16.9	23.7	2.5	2.6	3.8	5.3	0.4	0.4
Cuba	60	48	..	..	33.3	29.6	2.0	3.0	3.1	2.6	..	..
Czech Republic	18	26	3.5	5.2	131.0	114.8	3.0	2.5	12.7	11.2	0.9	0.5
Denmark	42	−38	7.5	9.6	50.4	53.9	2.9	2.7	9.8	9.9	0.4	0.3
Dominican Republic	75	80	6.7	9.0	9.6	20.3	2.3	2.6	1.3	2.1	0.3	0.3
Ecuador	−175	−145	9.4	7.9	16.8	31.3	2.8	2.9	1.6	2.4	0.3	0.3
Egypt, Arab Rep.	−72	−22	5.8	5.7	75.9	166.7	2.4	2.6	1.3	2.1	0.4	0.5
El Salvador	31	42	8.0	7.7	2.6	6.5	1.1	1.4	0.5	1.1	0.1	0.2
Eritrea	19	26	1.9	4.0	..	0.6	..	0.8	..	0.1	..	0.2
Estonia	47	22	1.7	4.7	25.0	17.5	4.0	3.5	16.3	13.0	2.2	0.7
Ethiopia	5	9	1.8	2.6	3.0	6.0	0.2	0.3	0.1	0.1	0.1	0.1
Finland	57	56	4.1	4.8	51.0	66.6	1.8	1.8	10.2	12.7	0.4	0.4
France	50	49	6.3	7.4	397.8	382.9	1.8	1.4	7.0	6.2	0.3	0.2
Gabon	−1,139	−549	11.8	10.3	6.1	2.1	5.2	1.2	6.6	1.5	0.4	0.1
Gambia, The	..	..	..	..	0.2	0.3	..	..	0.2	0.2	0.2	0.2
Georgia	85	68	2.4	5.8	15.3	5.5	1.8	1.8	2.9	1.3	1.2	0.3
Germany	47	59	5.8	8.2	962.7	804.5	2.8	2.4	12.0	9.8	0.4	0.3
Ghana	17	32	2.5	3.1	3.9	9.2	0.7	1.0	0.3	0.4	0.3	0.3
Greece	57	62	8.3	9.4	72.7	96.3	3.4	3.2	7.2	8.6	0.4	0.3
Guatemala	24	36	6.7	7.0	5.1	11.8	1.1	1.4	0.6	0.9	0.2	0.2
Guinea	..	..	..	..	1.1	1.4	..	..	0.2	0.1	0.2	0.2
Guinea-Bissau	..	..	..	..	0.3	0.3	..	..	0.2	0.2	0.4	0.4
Haiti	20	28	6.4	3.6	1.0	1.8	0.6	0.7	0.1	0.2	0.1	0.2
Honduras	29	55	5.5	5.4	2.6	7.2	1.1	1.8	0.5	1.0	0.2	0.3

| | Net energy imports[a] | | GDP per unit of energy use | | Carbon dioxide emissions | | | | | | | |
| | % of energy use | | 2005 PPP $ per kilogram of oil equivalent | | Total million metric tons | | Carbon intensity kilograms per kilogram of oil equivalent energy use | | Per capita metric tons | | kilograms per 2005 PPP $ of GDP | |
	1990	2007	1990	2007	1990	2006	1990	2006	1990	2006	1990	2006
Hungary	49	62	4.5	6.7	61.9	57.6	2.2	2.1	6.0	5.7	0.5	0.3
India	9	24	3.2	4.9	690.1	1,509.3	2.2	2.7	0.8	1.4	0.7	0.6
Indonesia	−66	−74	3.6	4.1	150.3	333.2	1.5	1.8	0.8	1.5	0.4	0.4
Iran, Islamic Rep.	−163	−75	5.0	4.0	227.0	466.6	3.3	2.7	4.2	6.7	0.7	0.7
Iraq	−480	−217	..	..	52.5	92.5	2.9	2.7	2.8	3.2	..	..
Ireland	65	91	6.2	11.9	30.9	43.8	3.1	3.0	8.8	10.3	0.5	0.3
Israel	96	88	7.2	8.2	33.5	70.4	2.9	3.3	7.2	10.0	0.4	0.4
Italy	83	85	9.2	9.6	424.7	473.8	2.9	2.6	7.5	8.0	0.3	0.3
Jamaica	83	90	5.1	3.9	8.0	12.1	2.9	2.8	3.3	4.6	0.6	0.6
Japan	83	82	7.3	7.9	1,171.4	1,292.5	2.7	2.5	9.5	10.1	0.4	0.3
Jordan	95	96	3.2	3.8	10.4	20.7	3.2	3.0	3.3	3.7	1.0	0.8
Kazakhstan	−24	−105	1.6	2.4	261.1	193.4	3.3	3.0	15.9	12.6	2.7	1.3
Kenya	20	20	3.0	3.0	5.8	12.1	0.5	0.7	0.3	0.3	0.2	0.2
Korea, Dem. Rep.	13	−7	..	..	244.6	84.7	7.4	3.9	12.1	3.6	..	..
Korea, Rep.	76	81	5.2	5.5	241.5	474.9	2.6	2.2	5.6	9.8	0.5	0.4
Kosovo	..	..	..	..	..	..	..	..	..	..	..	..
Kuwait	−544	−482	2.8	4.8	40.7	86.5	5.2	3.5	19.2	33.3	0.6	0.7
Kyrgyz Republic	67	51	1.5	3.4	11.0	5.6	2.2	2.0	2.4	1.1	1.3	0.6
Lao PDR	..	..	..	..	0.2	1.4	..	..	0.1	0.2	0.1	0.1
Latvia	86	61	3.2	7.4	13.3	7.5	2.2	1.6	5.1	3.3	0.9	0.2
Lebanon	94	95	7.5	10.5	9.1	15.3	4.0	3.3	3.1	3.7	0.5	0.4
Lesotho	..	..	..	..	..	..	..	..	..	..	..	..
Liberia	..	..	..	..	0.5	0.8	..	..	0.2	0.2	0.5	0.7
Libya	−546	−470	..	5.1	40.3	55.5	3.6	3.1	9.2	9.2	..	0.6
Lithuania	69	59	2.7	5.8	22.1	14.2	2.0	1.7	6.0	4.2	0.7	0.3
Macedonia, FYR	49	50	6.0	5.3	10.8	10.9	4.0	3.7	5.6	5.3	0.8	0.7
Madagascar	..	..	..	..	1.0	2.8	..	..	0.1	0.2	0.1	0.2
Malawi	..	..	..	..	0.6	1.0	..	..	0.1	0.1	0.1	0.1
Malaysia	−122	−30	5.3	4.7	56.5	187.7	2.5	2.8	3.1	7.2	0.5	0.6
Mali	..	..	..	..	0.4	0.6	..	..	0.0	0.0	0.1	0.0
Mauritania	..	..	..	..	2.7	1.7	..	..	1.3	0.5	0.9	0.3
Mauritius	..	..	..	..	1.5	3.8	..	..	1.4	3.1	0.2	0.3
Mexico	−60	−36	6.9	7.6	384.4	435.8	3.2	2.5	4.6	4.2	0.5	0.3
Moldova	99	97	1.7	2.7	21.0	7.8	3.1	2.3	4.8	2.1	2.1	0.9
Mongolia	20	−15	1.4	2.6	10.0	9.4	2.9	3.3	4.5	3.7	2.0	1.3
Morocco	89	95	9.7	8.3	23.5	45.3	3.4	3.4	0.9	1.5	0.4	0.4
Mozambique	5	−20	0.9	1.8	1.0	2.0	0.2	0.2	0.1	0.1	0.2	0.1
Myanmar	0	−53	..	..	4.3	10.0	0.4	0.6	0.1	0.2	..	..
Namibia	67	79	9.4	7.9	0.0	2.8	0.0	1.9	0.0	1.4	0.0	0.2
Nepal	5	11	2.3	2.9	0.6	3.2	0.1	0.3	0.0	0.1	0.0	0.1
Netherlands	8	24	6.0	7.6	167.3	168.4	2.5	2.2	11.2	10.3	0.4	0.3
New Zealand	10	16	4.8	6.4	22.7	30.5	1.7	1.8	6.6	7.3	0.4	0.3
Nicaragua	29	41	3.7	3.9	2.6	4.3	1.3	1.3	0.6	0.8	0.3	0.3
Niger	..	..	..	..	1.1	0.9	..	..	0.1	0.1	0.2	0.1
Nigeria	−113	−117	2.0	2.6	45.3	97.2	0.6	0.9	0.5	0.7	0.3	0.4
Norway	−467	−696	6.5	8.6	31.3	40.2	1.5	1.4	7.4	8.6	0.2	0.2
Oman	−802	−283	6.4	3.8	10.3	41.3	2.4	2.8	5.6	15.5	0.4	0.8
Pakistan	20	24	4.2	4.6	68.5	142.6	1.6	1.8	0.6	0.9	0.4	0.4
Panama	59	75	9.8	12.7	3.1	6.4	2.1	2.2	1.3	2.0	0.2	0.2
Papua New Guinea	..	..	..	..	2.1	4.6	..	..	0.5	0.7	0.3	0.4
Paraguay	−49	−70	5.5	6.1	2.3	4.0	0.7	1.0	0.5	0.7	0.1	0.2
Peru	−9	13	10.0	14.7	21.1	38.6	2.2	2.9	1.0	1.4	0.2	0.2
Philippines	43	44	5.4	7.1	44.5	68.3	1.6	1.7	0.7	0.8	0.3	0.3
Poland	−1	25	3.0	6.1	347.6	318.0	3.4	3.3	9.1	8.3	1.1	0.6
Portugal	80	82	9.4	9.0	44.3	60.0	2.6	2.4	4.5	5.7	0.3	0.3
Puerto Rico	..	..	..	..	..	..	..	..	..	..	..	..
Qatar	−286	−364	..	3.4	11.8	46.2	1.7	2.5	25.2	46.1	..	0.7

| | Net energy imports[a] | | GDP per unit of energy use | | Carbon dioxide emissions | | | | | | | |
| | % of energy use | | 2005 PPP $ per kilogram of oil equivalent | | Total million metric tons | | Carbon intensity kilograms per kilogram of oil equivalent energy use | | Per capita metric tons | | kilograms per 2005 PPP $ of GDP | |
	1990	2007	1990	2007	1990	2006	1990	2006	1990	2006	1990	2006
Romania	34	29	2.7	5.6	158.7	98.4	2.5	2.5	6.8	4.6	0.9	0.5
Russian Federation	−47	−83	2.2	2.9	2,073.5	1,563.5	2.7	2.3	13.9	11.0	1.4	0.9
Rwanda	..	..	..	..	0.7	0.8	..	..	0.1	0.1	0.1	0.1
Saudi Arabia	−526	−267	5.3	3.5	214.9	381.3	3.6	2.6	13.2	16.1	0.7	0.8
Senegal	43	53	6.3	7.3	3.2	4.3	1.9	1.5	0.4	0.4	0.3	0.2
Serbia	31	38	4.8	4.4	..	..	..	..	..	..	..	..
Sierra Leone	..	..	..	..	0.4	1.0	..	..	0.1	0.2	0.1	0.3
Singapore	100	100	6.3	8.1	46.9	56.2	4.1	2.1	15.4	12.8	0.6	0.3
Slovak Republic	75	67	3.1	5.9	44.3	37.4	2.4	2.0	8.4	6.9	0.8	0.4
Slovenia	46	53	5.8	7.2	12.3	15.2	2.4	2.1	6.2	7.6	0.4	0.3
Somalia	..	..	..	..	0.0	0.2	..	..	0.0	0.0	..	..
South Africa	−26	−19	3.0	3.3	333.3	414.3	3.7	3.2	9.5	8.7	1.2	1.0
Spain	62	79	8.5	8.9	229.0	352.0	2.5	2.5	5.9	8.0	0.3	0.3
Sri Lanka	24	45	6.3	8.6	3.8	11.9	0.7	1.3	0.2	0.6	0.1	0.2
Sudan	17	−136	2.5	5.2	5.6	10.8	0.5	0.7	0.2	0.3	0.2	0.2
Swaziland	..	..	..	..	0.4	1.0	..	..	0.5	0.9	0.1	0.2
Sweden	37	33	4.5	6.2	51.2	50.8	1.1	1.0	6.0	5.6	0.2	0.2
Switzerland	59	51	9.4	11.0	42.9	41.8	1.8	1.5	6.4	5.6	0.2	0.2
Syrian Arab Republic	−96	−24	3.3	4.2	37.4	68.4	3.3	3.7	2.9	3.5	1.0	0.9
Tajikistan	64	59	2.9	2.9	21.3	6.4	4.4	1.7	3.9	1.0	2.0	0.6
Tanzania	7	8	2.3	2.5	2.4	5.4	0.2	0.3	0.1	0.1	0.1	0.1
Thailand	37	43	5.3	4.7	95.8	272.3	2.3	2.7	1.7	4.1	0.4	0.6
Timor-Leste	..	..	..	..	..	0.2	..	..	..	0.2	..	0.3
Togo	17	15	2.7	2.0	0.8	1.2	0.6	0.5	0.2	0.2	0.2	0.3
Trinidad and Tobago	−111	−142	2.1	2.0	16.9	33.6	2.8	2.4	13.9	25.4	1.4	1.2
Tunisia	−16	11	6.6	8.2	13.3	23.1	2.7	2.7	1.6	2.3	0.4	0.3
Turkey	51	73	8.3	8.7	146.5	269.3	2.8	2.9	2.6	3.7	0.3	0.3
Turkmenistan	−281	−266	0.7	1.6	28.0	44.1	2.5	2.7	7.2	9.0	2.3	1.7
Uganda	..	..	..	..	0.8	2.7	..	..	0.0	0.1	0.1	0.1
Ukraine	46	41	1.7	2.2	611.0	318.9	2.8	2.3	11.7	6.8	1.8	1.1
United Arab Emirates	−454	−245	4.8	4.5	54.8	139.5	2.8	3.1	29.3	32.9	0.6	0.6
United Kingdom	0	17	6.6	9.9	573.3	568.1	2.8	2.6	10.0	9.4	0.4	0.3
United States	14	29	4.2	5.5	4,861.1	5,748.1	2.5	2.5	19.5	19.3	0.6	0.5
Uruguay	49	62	10.1	11.4	4.0	6.9	1.8	2.2	1.3	2.1	0.2	0.2
Uzbekistan	17	−23	0.9	1.3	113.9	115.6	2.5	2.4	5.3	4.4	3.1	2.1
Venezuela, RB	−242	−188	4.3	4.9	122.1	171.5	2.8	2.8	6.2	6.3	0.6	0.6
Vietnam	−2	−33	2.5	3.7	21.4	106.1	0.9	2.0	0.3	1.3	0.4	0.6
West Bank and Gaza	..	..	..	..	..	3.0	..	..	..	0.8	..	..
Yemen, Rep.	−273	−129	8.7	6.8	..	21.2	..	3.1	..	1.0	..	0.4
Zambia	9	8	1.8	2.0	2.4	2.5	0.5	0.3	0.3	0.2	0.2	0.2
Zimbabwe	8	8	0.3	0.2	16.6	11.1	1.8	1.2	1.6	0.9	6.0	5.0
World	**−3**[b] **w**	**−2**[b] **w**	**4.2 w**	**5.4 w**	**22,511.6**[c] **t**	**30,154.7**[c] **t**	**2.5**[c] **w**	**2.5**[c] **w**	**4.3**[c] **w**	**4.4**[c] **w**	**0.6**[c] **w**	**0.5**[c] **w**
Low income	10	−8	2.2	3.2	508.5	478.2	1.9	1.5	0.6	0.5	0.2	0.4
Middle income	−24	−21	3.0	4.4	9,936.6	14,821.4	2.6	2.7	1.8	3.3	0.7	0.6
Lower middle income	−14	−7	2.5	3.9	4,849.7	9,976.8	2.4	2.8	1.4	2.8	0.9	0.8
Upper middle income	−34	−46	3.6	5.2	5,086.1	4,837.2	2.8	2.5	3.8	5.2	0.5	0.5
Low & middle income	−22	−20	3.0	4.3	10,445.0	15,299.3	2.5	2.7	1.6	2.8	0.7	0.6
East Asia & Pacific	−8	1	2.0	3.6	3,046.8	7,188.2	2.7	3.1	1.9	3.8	1.3	0.9
Europe & Central Asia	−11	−39	2.3	3.7	4,566.0	3,195.3	3.2	2.5	9.4	7.3	1.3	0.7
Latin America & Carib.	−34	−29	6.9	7.5	1,044.8	1,462.3	2.3	2.2	2.4	2.6	0.3	0.3
Middle East & N. Africa	−201	−106	5.6	5.0	565.9	1,111.4	3.1	2.9	2.5	3.5	0.5	0.6
South Asia	10	24	3.5	5.0	781.5	1,710.4	2.0	2.5	0.7	1.1	0.6	0.5
Sub-Saharan Africa	−54	−64	2.6	3.2	466.4	640.8	1.7	1.5	0.9	0.8	0.6	0.5
High income	15	18	5.3	6.5	11,332.7	13,377.9	2.5	2.4	12.1	12.7	0.5	0.4
Euro area	55	63	6.7	8.2	2,602.0	2,701.4	2.5	2.2	7.5	8.4	0.3	0.3

a. Negative values indicate that a country is a net exporter. b. Deviation from zero is due to statistical errors and changes in stock. c. Includes emissions not allocated to specific countries.

About the data

Because commercial energy is widely traded, its production and use need to be distinguished. Net energy imports show the extent to which an economy's use exceeds its production. High-income economies are net energy importers; middle-income economies are their main suppliers.

The ratio of gross domestic product (GDP) to energy use indicates energy efficiency. To produce comparable and consistent estimates of real GDP across economies relative to physical inputs to GDP—that is, units of energy use—GDP is converted to 2005 international dollars using purchasing power parity (PPP) rates. Differences in this ratio over time and across economies reflect structural changes in an economy, changes in sectoral energy efficiency, and differences in fuel mixes.

Carbon dioxide emissions, largely by-products of energy production and use (see table 3.7), account for the largest share of greenhouse gases, which are associated with global warming. Anthropogenic carbon dioxide emissions result primarily from fossil fuel combustion and cement manufacturing. In combustion different fossil fuels release different amounts of carbon dioxide for the same level of energy use: oil releases about 50 percent more carbon dioxide than natural gas, and coal releases about twice as much. Cement manufacturing releases about half a metric ton of carbon dioxide for each metric ton of cement produced.

The U.S. Department of Energy's Carbon Dioxide Information Analysis Center (CDIAC) calculates annual anthropogenic emissions from data on fossil fuel consumption (from the United Nations Statistics Division's World Energy Data Set) and world cement manufacturing (from the U.S. Bureau of Mines's Cement Manufacturing Data Set). Carbon dioxide emissions, often calculated and reported as elemental carbon, were converted to actual carbon dioxide mass by multiplying them by 3.664 (the ratio of the mass of carbon to that of carbon dioxide). Although estimates of global carbon dioxide emissions are probably accurate within 10 percent (as calculated from global average fuel chemistry and use), country estimates may have larger error bounds. Trends estimated from a consistent time series tend to be more accurate than individual values. Each year the CDIAC recalculates the entire time series since 1949, incorporating recent findings and corrections. Estimates exclude fuels supplied to ships and aircraft in international transport because of the difficulty of apportioning the fuels among benefiting countries. The ratio of carbon dioxide per unit of energy shows carbon intensity, which is the amount of carbon dioxide emitted as a result of using one unit of energy in the process of production. The proportion of carbon dioxide per unit of GDP indicates how clean production processes are.

Definitions

• **Net energy imports** are estimated as energy use less production, both measured in oil equivalents. • **GDP per unit of energy use** is the ratio of gross domestic product (GDP) per kilogram of oil equivalent of energy use, with GDP converted to 2005 international dollars using purchasing power parity (PPP) rates. An international dollar has the same purchasing power over GDP that a U.S. dollar has in the United States. Energy use refers to the use of primary energy before transformation to other end-use fuel, which is equal to indigenous production plus imports and stock changes minus exports and fuel supplied to ships and aircraft engaged in international transport (see *About the data* for table 3.7). • **Carbon dioxide emissions** are emissions from the burning of fossil fuels and the manufacture of cement and include carbon dioxide produced during consumption of solid, liquid, and gas fuels and gas flaring.

High-income economies depend on imported energy . . . 3.8a

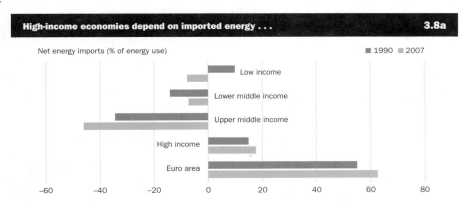

Note: Negative values indicate that the income group is a net energy exporter.
Source: Table 3.8.

. . . mostly from middle-income economies in the Middle East and North Africa and Latin America and the Caribbean 3.8b

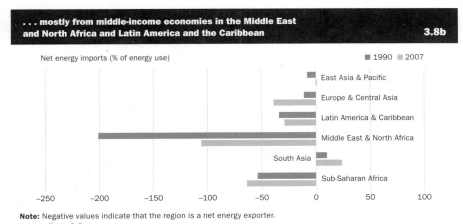

Note: Negative values indicate that the region is a net energy exporter.
Source: Table 3.8.

Data sources

Data on energy use are from the electronic files of the International Energy Agency. Data on carbon dioxide emissions are from the CDIAC, Environmental Sciences Division, Oak Ridge National Laboratory, Tennessee, United States.

3.9 Trends in greenhouse gas emissions

	Carbon dioxide emissions		Methane emissions				Nitrous oxide emissions				Other greenhouse gas emissions	
	average annual % growth[a] 1990–2006	% change[b] 1990–2006	Total thousand metric tons of carbon dioxide equivalent 2005	% change[b] 1990–2005	% of total From energy processes 2005	% of total Agricultural 2005	Total thousand metric tons of carbon dioxide equivalent 2005	% change[b] 1990–2005	% of total From energy processes 2005	% of total Agricultural 2005	Total thousand metric tons of carbon dioxide equivalent 2005	% change[b] 1990–2005
Afghanistan	−8.6	−74.0	..	..	..	..	..	..	..	..	..	..
Albania	2.3	−42.6	2,300	0.0	16.1	73.9	970	−21.1	5.2	82.5	60	..
Algeria	3.7	68.2	53,720	33.0	83.0	8.3	4,640	28.5	10.1	61.4	490	48.5
Angola	5.8	138.9	44,680	−9.6	14.3	28.4	68,590	4.9	0.2	21.7	20	..
Argentina	2.2	54.1	101,180	−8.7	18.4	71.0	35,890	5.8	1.8	89.8	790	−65.7
Armenia	0.6	5.2	2,960	10.9	50.7	36.8	570	−21.9	1.8	82.5	340	..
Australia	1.3	26.9	119,560	8.3	28.6	58.3	57,910	−0.7	5.3	84.5	6,510	33.4
Austria	1.1	18.3	8,210	−14.2	18.9	50.4	3,640	−19.8	14.3	63.2	2,330	45.6
Azerbaijan	−2.4	−29.7	36,600	111.3	82.0	13.6	2,460	−1.6	6.5	82.5	90	−50.0
Bangladesh	6.6	168.0	93,200	6.6	10.8	69.9	21,260	40.4	6.5	83.0	0	..
Belarus	−3	−38.1	11,110	−33.2	4.4	73.4	11,370	−26.4	3.3	74.4	460	..
Belgium	−0.1	−0.4	11,760	−18.0	8.6	48.5	5,940	−28.0	10.3	49.0	2,110	603.3
Benin	8.3	334.9	3,940	−17.4	12.7	49.5	4,320	−15.6	2.8	40.0	0	..
Bolivia	2.8	107.2	30,400	30.9	25.7	34.1	25,400	17.1	0.5	19.5	0	..
Bosnia and Herzegovina	14.7	292.5	2,550	−53.6	42.7	45.5	1,100	−42.7	27.3	61.8	570	−8.1
Botswana	4.1	119.8	4,460	−22.8	7.8	84.8	2,930	−43.0	1.4	96.6	0	..
Brazil	3.5	68.8	482,860	57.4	6.1	62.2	255,970	36.3	1.5	54.7	11,810	40.4
Bulgaria	−2.5	−37.3	7,160	−33.5	14.9	28.8	3,770	−56.7	6.9	53.8	380	..
Burkina Faso	1.9	34.4	..	..	..	..	..	..	..	..	..	..
Burundi	−4.6	−34.9	..	..	..	..	..	..	..	..	..	..
Cambodia	16.7	803.2	20,350	35.1	5.6	75.6	6,010	63.3	3.3	62.4	0	..
Cameroon	3.4	109.7	18,460	38.0	38.9	42.5	11,470	−10.4	2.1	59.5	420	−54.8
Canada	1.5	21.0	72,860	27.5	39.0	35.9	33,380	−12.5	16.3	64.4	21,940	69.7
Central African Republic	1	25.9	..	..	..	..	..	..	..	..	..	..
Chad	10.3	169.9	..	..	..	..	..	..	..	..	..	..
Chile	3.7	69.4	17,800	49.7	23.8	40.2	7,650	61.1	6.4	77.8	10	−50.0
China	5.1	152.8	1,287,860	32.6	44.1	40.2	414,800	43.3	8.7	82.0	137,120	1,085.1
Hong Kong SAR, China	2.3	41.1	2,610	97.7	28.7	0.0	200	25.0	95.0	0.0	120	−68.4
Colombia	−0.4	10.6	57,720	13.1	19.3	68.5	22,710	2.8	2.2	80.4	80	100.0
Congo, Dem. Rep.	−4.7	−45.9	56,230	−41.5	9.9	23.2	108,260	−20.9	1.1	15.7	0	..
Congo, Rep.	−1.4	23.1	5,460	−11.8	30.6	32.6	5,890	−8.7	0.7	31.2	0	..
Costa Rica	5.4	165.8	2,570	−31.3	9.3	67.3	1,250	−28.2	3.2	90.4	60	..
Côte d'Ivoire	1.9	18.7	10,420	−6.0	12.4	18.3	14,010	6.9	1.5	15.3	0	..
Croatia	1.7	−5.4	3,750	−61.0	55.7	34.4	2,550	−26.5	5.1	56.9	60	−93.3
Cuba	−1.3	−11.1	9,470	−23.1	11.4	62.3	6,010	−30.6	3.0	82.5	130	..
Czech Republic	−1.5	−29.4	9,250	−39.8	37.2	41.7	8,370	−4.1	41.0	38.8	1,130	..
Denmark	−1.1	7.0	11,990	−7.5	9.9	43.1	5,780	−21.3	5.9	79.8	1,420	468.0
Dominican Republic	5.1	112.7	5,940	2.4	5.6	65.3	1,980	3.7	8.1	86.9	60	..
Ecuador	3.3	86.1	17,120	31.8	31.3	57.8	4,280	44.6	4.0	89.7	60	..
Egypt, Arab Rep.	5.4	119.6	46,160	69.9	49.8	32.2	17,650	59.0	5.0	85.0	3,180	54.4
El Salvador	5	146.8	3,150	18.4	12.7	52.7	1,230	1.7	8.9	82.9	80	..
Eritrea	8.9	..	2,390	26.5	7.9	75.3	1,160	16.0	4.3	92.2	0	..
Estonia	−2.6	−37.9	1,990	−37.8	38.7	32.2	810	−51.8	19.8	69.1	30	..
Ethiopia	4.5	99.0	52,320	32.9	14.5	72.4	29,160	19.0	5.5	91.5	10	..
Finland	1.3	30.8	8,660	−2.3	6.5	23.3	5,050	−16.9	12.7	58.8	830	730.0
France	−0.3	−3.8	79,540	6.3	41.3	46.4	45,560	−30.7	4.8	71.0	15,540	57.1
Gabon	−7	−66.2	8,210	1.4	90.4	1.1	660	40.4	7.6	16.7	10	..
Gambia, The	4	75.0	..	..	..	..	..	..	..	..	..	..
Georgia	−7.4	−68.1	4,130	−14.0	31.7	54.2	1,970	−25.7	2.5	57.9	10	..
Germany	−1.1	−16.4	57,030	−46.0	26.8	51.9	52,590	−23.1	7.5	56.0	30,930	6.8
Ghana	4.8	135.1	8,520	22.6	19.1	41.7	5,060	−6.1	7.9	68.2	20	−96.7
Greece	2.3	32.5	5,770	−2.0	31.5	63.1	4,810	−21.7	10.6	71.9	1,840	−21.0
Guatemala	6	131.4	8,280	75.1	12.2	48.9	7,000	182.3	3.9	42.7	480	..
Guinea	1.6	28.8	..	..	..	..	..	..	..	..	..	..
Guinea-Bissau	0.1	10.2	..	..	..	..	..	..	..	..	..	..
Haiti	6.6	82.3	3,860	39.4	8.8	58.3	1,380	62.4	6.5	86.2	0	..
Honduras	7.4	177.5	5,180	31.5	6.9	78.6	2,620	21.3	4.2	92.4	0	..

Trends in greenhouse gas emissions

	Carbon dioxide emissions		Methane emissions				Nitrous oxide emissions				Other greenhouse gas emissions	
	average annual % growth[a] 1990–2006	% change[b] 1990–2006	Total thousand metric tons of carbon dioxide equivalent 2005	% change[b] 1990–2005	% of total From energy processes 2005	Agricultural 2005	Total thousand metric tons of carbon dioxide equivalent 2005	% change[b] 1990–2005	% of total From energy processes 2005	Agricultural 2005	Total thousand metric tons of carbon dioxide equivalent 2005	% change[b] 1990–2005
Hungary	−0.4	−6.9	7,510	−20.0	26.6	34.8	6,640	−29.8	4.4	62.5	1,550	121.4
India	4.8	118.7	589,630	10.5	16.8	63.8	196,110	30.1	12.3	77.1	8,430	−11.8
Indonesia	3.9	121.7	208,910	18.7	25.5	46.4	165,370	48.6	1.8	53.1	1,030	−40.5
Iran, Islamic Rep.	4.5	105.6	114,180	32.3	70.6	18.3	23,230	41.9	6.5	85.3	2,570	−2.7
Iraq	3.2	76.2	15,910	−45.8	58.3	18.6	2,540	−23.7	13.0	84.6	90	−64.0
Ireland	2.6	41.7	13,540	12.8	12.0	86.9	7,150	−9.3	2.7	94.7	1,150	3,733.3
Israel	4.4	110.1	3,510	84.7	18.2	31.3	1,410	43.9	20.6	66.7	1,980	90.4
Italy	0.7	11.5	40,190	−13.9	13.4	40.4	25,810	−1.5	9.1	47.5	13,580	213.6
Jamaica	2.1	52.6	1,230	12.8	6.5	53.7	440	10.0	11.4	79.5	50	..
Japan	0.6	10.3	39,300	−32.9	4.5	77.5	22,790	−24.0	28.8	36.0	52,740	105.6
Jordan	4.3	99.2	1,770	110.7	23.7	22.0	530	43.2	13.2	69.8	110	..
Kazakhstan	−3.1	−34.4	46,120	−28.5	65.4	25.8	15,950	−45.4	10.9	68.8	340	..
Kenya	4.8	108.7	20,100	19.5	8.6	72.1	10,200	15.4	5.5	90.2	0	..
Korea, Dem. Rep.	−9.6	−65.4	17,090	−14.8	55.9	25.0	2,730	−63.8	16.5	69.2	2,790	..
Korea, Rep.	4.2	96.7	146,330	296.3	3.8	8.5	10,960	41.8	24.5	43.8	10,220	66.2
Kosovo	..	..	..	..	..	..	..	..	..	..	..	..
Kuwait	9.6	112.5	14,350	119.1	93.4	1.0	390	129.4	59.0	28.2	940	261.5
Kyrgyz Republic	−4.8	−55.3	3,590	−37.9	6.7	72.4	1,460	−57.3	11.6	74.0	20	..
Lao PDR	14.5	507.8	..	..	..	..	..	..	..	..	..	..
Latvia	−5	−50.4	2,760	−45.8	49.3	31.2	1,180	−57.2	11.9	82.2	890	..
Lebanon	3.7	68.5	990	45.6	9.1	26.3	550	77.4	14.5	70.9	0	..
Lesotho	..	..	..	..	..	..	..	..	..	..	..	..
Liberia	5.2	62.1	..	..	..	..	..	..	..	..	..	..
Libya	2	37.7	14,630	−34.8	86.5	5.7	920	−6.1	17.4	71.7	280	0.0
Lithuania	−3.7	−43.2	5,330	−34.3	29.6	34.9	2,360	−44.1	5.1	88.6	660	..
Macedonia, FYR	−0.4	−31.8	1,350	−36.9	29.6	48.1	530	−32.9	17.0	71.7	120	..
Madagascar	7.7	187.4	..	..	..	..	..	..	..	..	..	..
Malawi	4	71.3	..	..	..	..	..	..	..	..	..	..
Malaysia	6.7	232.0	46,130	65.0	69.1	12.5	18,570	8.3	4.2	52.8	1,000	66.7
Mali	2	34.8	..	..	..	..	..	..	..	..	..	..
Mauritania	−5.5	−37.5	..	..	..	..	..	..	..	..	..	..
Mauritius	6.3	163.2	..	..	..	..	..	..	..	..	..	..
Mexico	0.6	13.4	127,490	25.8	40.0	42.5	41,030	12.8	6.8	76.5	4,560	53.0
Moldova	−7.3	−66.9	3,330	−14.4	44.4	29.7	780	−51.6	5.1	74.4	10	..
Mongolia	−1.2	−6.0	5,990	−25.0	1.3	93.2	3,410	−28.4	2.1	95.3	0	..
Morocco	3.9	92.5	10,490	15.4	7.3	52.1	5,460	10.8	3.1	86.4	0	..
Mozambique	5	103.7	12,570	17.5	21.0	45.2	10,020	−5.1	3.2	66.9	290	..
Myanmar	5.6	134.5	77,410	−7.0	12.9	68.8	64,000	−15.9	1.3	19.6	0	..
Namibia	47.2	38,647.9	5,070	47.4	0.4	94.7	3,620	48.4	0.6	98.9	0	..
Nepal	8.5	411.0	22,370	9.8	6.8	82.0	4,310	24.9	12.8	78.2	0	..
Netherlands	0	0.7	21,070	−30.5	22.9	43.8	13,840	−10.3	4.8	41.6	3,740	−41.1
New Zealand	2.1	34.1	27,570	3.6	3.4	90.4	12,700	24.0	3.0	95.8	970	3.2
Nicaragua	4.7	63.9	6,010	26.5	6.3	74.9	3,150	7.1	3.2	94.6	0	..
Niger	−1.2	−11.2	..	..	..	..	..	..	..	..	..	..
Nigeria	6.1	114.4	129,790	11.7	68.8	19.9	20,550	11.4	9.9	78.0	670	179.2
Norway	3.3	28.4	16,580	55.4	75.3	12.8	4,370	−0.5	5.0	42.3	5,200	−39.4
Oman	8.5	299.8	17,850	195.0	94.1	3.0	540	92.9	27.8	70.4	180	..
Pakistan	4.5	108.1	138,400	50.5	24.2	63.0	25,710	46.5	12.6	76.5	820	−18.8
Panama	4.3	105.0	3,230	16.6	4.3	78.9	1,100	12.2	4.5	90.9	0	..
Papua New Guinea	5.9	115.7	..	..	..	..	..	..	..	..	..	..
Paraguay	3.2	76.2	15,320	2.1	3.5	84.5	9,210	−6.9	1.6	68.9	0	..
Peru	3.6	82.6	17,010	22.8	13.2	62.0	8,000	27.6	2.8	76.6	330	..
Philippines	3.4	53.5	51,340	28.8	8.4	64.4	11,660	37.8	9.0	81.0	370	131.3
Poland	−1	−8.5	60,660	−41.6	56.8	25.3	27,770	5.5	10.6	62.5	2,450	362.3
Portugal	2.4	35.2	7,720	22.3	19.8	55.8	5,160	24.6	8.3	50.4	780	609.1
Puerto Rico	..	..	..	..	..	..	..	..	..	..	..	..
Qatar	4.7	292.3	15,700	387.6	96.4	0.4	200	122.2	75.0	25.0	0	..

	Carbon dioxide emissions			Methane emissions			Nitrous oxide emissions				Other greenhouse gas emissions	
	average annual % growth[a] 1990–2006	% change[b] 1990–2006	Total thousand metric tons of carbon dioxide equivalent 2005	% change[b] 1990–2005	% of total From energy processes 2005	Agricultural 2005	Total thousand metric tons of carbon dioxide equivalent 2005	% change[b] 1990–2005	% of total From energy processes 2005	Agricultural 2005	Total thousand metric tons of carbon dioxide equivalent 2005	% change[b] 1990–2005
Romania	–3.1	–38.0	23,270	–36.9	40.0	37.6	10,860	–44.3	5.7	58.7	740	–63.2
Russian Federation	–2.4	–33.2	557,200	–17.1	79.1	9.2	68,900	–48.6	10.4	48.4	58,600	130.4
Rwanda	1.2	16.7	..	..	..	..	..	..	..	..	..	..
Saudi Arabia	2.3	77.4	47,790	66.9	83.9	4.0	4,680	14.7	26.7	63.9	2,190	–10.6
Senegal	2.8	33.9	6,900	38.8	6.8	70.6	3,870	37.2	3.1	93.0	0	..
Serbia[c]	0.3	–20.6	6,720	–47.7	..	59.2	4,700	–48.2	..	81.5	840	147.1
Sierra Leone	5.4	155.6	..	..	..	..	..	..	..	..	..	..
Singapore	0.4	19.8	2,190	138.0	58.9	1.4	960	500.0	15.6	3.1	2,540	408.0
Slovak Republic	–1.8	–32.0	3,800	–39.2	15.8	40.3	3,140	–36.2	13.4	39.8	390	457.1
Slovenia	0.7	–16.9	3,380	0.3	28.4	33.1	1,010	–17.2	9.9	80.2	470	–39.0
Somalia	31	841.0	..	..	..	..	..	..	..	..	..	..
South Africa	1.2	24.3	61,610	23.8	43.7	32.5	20,530	10.6	10.8	69.5	2,170	45.6
Spain	3	53.7	37,510	16.5	9.1	55.1	23,170	4.3	8.4	71.3	9,080	47.6
Sri Lanka	7.9	214.8	10,220	–11.5	5.4	65.2	1,830	10.2	13.1	72.7	0	..
Sudan	6.2	94.5	65,270	55.2	4.0	88.1	46,880	36.4	1.3	97.5	0	..
Swaziland	10.9	138.8	..	..	..	..	..	..	..	..	..	..
Sweden	–0.3	–0.7	11,150	1.5	8.6	28.5	5,050	–13.2	13.5	69.7	2,080	136.4
Switzerland	–0.2	–2.7	4,780	–16.0	17.4	67.2	2,000	–14.2	10.0	71.5	2,110	97.2
Syrian Arab Republic	3.6	82.8	12,530	–10.4	54.1	27.9	5,010	35.4	4.2	84.0	0	..
Tajikistan	–8.2	–73.4	3,920	–5.3	13.3	68.1	1,350	–0.7	1.5	88.1	380	–86.5
Tanzania	4.4	126.4	30,240	19.1	7.4	67.0	23,420	5.7	2.6	72.2	0	..
Thailand	5.9	184.4	80,540	6.8	14.1	68.2	20,210	13.2	17.4	71.4	1,100	–23.1
Timor-Leste	..	..	..	..	..	..	..	..	..	..	..	..
Togo	3.9	57.8	2,660	2.3	16.9	43.2	1,980	–17.2	5.1	58.1	0	..
Trinidad and Tobago	3.6	98.1	9,940	30.3	84.9	0.7	210	23.5	23.8	66.7	0	..
Tunisia	3.3	74.3	8,000	107.3	54.8	26.0	2,150	16.8	5.6	71.6	0	..
Turkey	3.5	83.8	49,970	26.9	17.5	43.2	29,790	11.7	9.0	71.6	5,070	96.5
Turkmenistan	2.7	39.3	27,950	–4.7	75.2	21.6	4,280	98.1	3.0	78.0	70	..
Uganda	7.8	230.9	..	..	..	..	..	..	..	..	..	..
Ukraine	–4.8	–53.7	66,990	–42.4	60.2	24.5	24,160	–51.3	4.4	47.9	690	213.6
United Arab Emirates	6.6	154.6	23,250	57.9	93.1	2.6	1,080	151.2	43.5	47.2	1,080	27.1
United Kingdom	–0.3	–0.9	42,290	–43.2	34.6	59.4	27,750	–44.0	8.5	65.1	10,400	96.6
United States	1.2	18.2	610,910	–3.4	32.6	31.2	257,060	–2.4	24.9	59.1	238,510	158.7
Uruguay	2	71.9	19,570	24.0	1.5	94.4	6,750	13.4	0.6	98.4	60	..
Uzbekistan	0.1	–10.1	39,530	25.3	57.2	33.8	9,630	6.9	3.4	87.4	610	..
Venezuela, RB	2.4	40.5	61,170	5.8	47.4	40.1	16,760	25.6	4.7	66.9	2,470	–24.0
Vietnam	11.8	395.8	83,660	39.9	23.3	63.4	21,660	96.6	6.3	87.3	0	..
West Bank and Gaza	24.1	..	..	..	..	..	..	..	..	..	..	..
Yemen, Rep.	4.5	–806.8	6,650	73.6	16.7	55.0	2,710	39.0	4.1	86.3	0	..
Zambia	–0.7	1.0	18,600	–30.0	3.2	61.6	30,500	–22.9	0.7	58.9	0	..
Zimbabwe	–3.2	–33.5	9,500	–5.4	10.9	73.7	5,490	–14.5	3.6	93.8	0	..
World	**1.7 w**	**34.0 w**	**7,138,440 s**	**9.9 w**	**35.4 w**	**42.5 w**	**2,827,550 s**	**4.8 w**	**8.2 w**	**63.9 w**	**715,400 s**	**123.7 w**
Low income	–1.4	–6.0	595,600	2.6	17.0	60.0	369,940	–7.3	3.0	49.5	4,120	20.8
Middle income	2.2	49.2	4,962,640	12.9	38.7	42.8	1,786,860	15.7	6.2	67.7	256,890	206.4
Lower middle income	4.1	105.7	3,085,730	20.5	36.1	45.9	1,151,140	28.2	7.0	70.1	157,820	393.5
Upper middle income	–0.3	–4.9	1,876,910	2.2	42.8	37.7	635,720	–1.8	4.8	63.3	99,070	91.0
Low & middle income	2.1	46.5	5,558,240	11.7	36.4	44.7	2,156,800	11.0	5.7	64.6	261,010	199.2
East Asia & Pacific	4.5	135.9	1,879,280	27.2	37.7	44.7	728,420	33.1	6.5	68.9	..	..
Europe & Central Asia	–2.2	–30.0	966,150	–19.6	67.4	18.5	225,390	–35.3	8.5	60.9	77,050	117.8
Latin America & Carib.	2	40.0	996,560	30.3	16.5	59.3	459,810	24.8	2.4	62.4	20,970	23.4
Middle East & N. Africa	4.2	96.4	285,030	19.8	64.4	20.8	65,390	34.9	6.3	82.7	6,720	20.9
South Asia	4.8	118.9	853,820	14.7	16.9	64.8	249,220	32.2	11.8	77.5	9,250	–12.5
Sub-Saharan Africa	2	37.4	577,400	4.7	29.0	44.9	428,570	–3.2	2.6	51.1	..	..
High income	1.1	18.0	1,580,200	4.3	32.1	35.1	670,750	–11.0	16.2	61.7	454,390	95.4
Euro area	0.2	3.8	300,030	–16.1	23.8	49.3	197,530	–18.3	7.4	60.7	83,170	36.4

a. Calculated using the least squares method, which accounts for ups and downs of all data points in the period (see *Statistical methods*). b. Calculated as the change in emission since 1990, which is the baseline for Kyoto Protocol requirements. c. Includes Kosovo and Montenegro.

About the data

Greenhouse gases—which include carbon dioxide, methane, nitrous oxide, hydrofluorocarbons, perfluorocarbons, and sulfur hexafluoride—contribute to climate change.

Carbon dioxide emissions, largely a byproduct of energy production and use (see table 3.7), account for the largest share of greenhouse gases. Anthropogenic carbon dioxide emissions result primarily from fossil fuel combustion and cement manufacturing. Burning oil releases more carbon dioxide than burning natural gas, and burning coal releases even more for the same level of energy use. Cement manufacturing releases about half a metric ton of carbon dioxide for each metric ton of cement produced.

Methane emissions result largely from agricultural activities, industrial production landfills and wastewater treatment, and other sources such as tropical forest and other vegetation fires. The emissions are usually expressed in carbon dioxide equivalents using the global warming potential, which allows the effective contributions of different gases to be compared. A kilogram of methane is 21 times as effective at trapping heat in the earth's atmosphere as a kilogram of carbon dioxide within 100 years.

Nitrous oxide emissions are mainly from fossil fuel combustion, fertilizers, rainforest fires, and animal waste. Nitrous oxide is a powerful greenhouse gas, with an estimated atmospheric lifetime of 114 years, compared with 12 years for methane. The per kilogram global warming potential of nitrous oxide is nearly 310 times that of carbon dioxide within 100 years.

Other greenhouse gases covered under the Kyoto Protocol are hydrofluorocarbons, perfluorocarbons, and sulfur hexafluoride. Although emissions of these artificial gases are small, they are more powerful greenhouse gases than carbon dioxide, with much higher atmospheric lifetimes and high global warming potential.

For a discussion of carbon dioxide sources and the methodology behind emissions calculation, see *About the data* for table 3.8.

Definitions

• **Carbon dioxide emissions** are emissions from the burning of fossil fuels and the manufacture of cement and include carbon dioxide produced during consumption of solid, liquid, and gas fuels and gas flaring. • **Methane emissions** are emissions from human activities such as agriculture and from industrial methane production. • **Methane emissions from energy processes** are emissions from the production, handling, transmission, and combustion of fossil fuels and biofuels. • **Agricultural methane emissions** are emissions from animals, animal waste, rice production, agricultural waste burning (nonenergy, on-site), and savannah burning. • **Nitrous oxide emissions** are emissions from agricultural biomass burning, industrial activities, and livestock management. • **Nitrous oxide emissions from energy processes** are emissions produced by the combustion of fossil fuels and biofuels. • **Agricultural nitrous oxide emissions** are emissions produced through fertilizer use (synthetic and animal manure), animal waste management, agricultural waste burning (nonenergy, on-site), and savannah burning. • **Other greenhouse gas emissions** are byproduct emissions of hydrofluorocarbons (byproduct emissions of fluoroform from chlorodifluoromethane manufacture and use of hydrofluorocarbons), perfluoro carbons (byproduct emissions of tetrafluoromethane and hexafluoroethane from primary aluminum production and use of perfluoro carbons, in particular for semiconductor manufacturing), and sulfur hexafluoride (various sources, the largest being the use and manufacture of gas insulated switchgear used in electricity distribution networks).

The 10 largest contributors to methane emissions account for about 62 percent of emissions — 3.9a

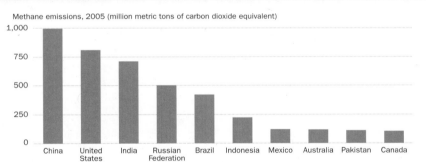

Methane emissions, 2005 (million metric tons of carbon dioxide equivalent)

Source: Table 3.9.

The 10 largest contributors to nitrous oxide emissions account for about 56 percent of emissions — 3.9b

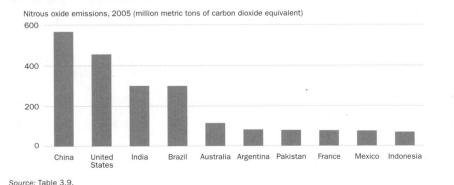

Nitrous oxide emissions, 2005 (million metric tons of carbon dioxide equivalent)

Source: Table 3.9.

Data sources

Data on carbon dioxide emissions are from the Carbon Dioxide Information Analysis Center, Environmental Sciences Division, Oak Ridge National Laboratory, Tennessee, United States. Data on methane, nitrous oxide, and other greenhouse gases emissions are compiled by the International Energy Agency.

	Electricity production		Sources of electricity[a]									
	billion kilowatt hours		Coal		Gas		Oil		Hydropower		Nuclear power	
							% of total					
	1990	2007	1990	2007	1990	2007	1990	2007	1990	2007	1990	2007
Afghanistan	..	..	..	..	..	..	..	..	..	..	..	..
Albania	3.2	2.9	0.0	0.0	0.0	0.0	10.9	2.5	89.1	97.5	0.0	0.0
Algeria	16.1	37.2	0.0	0.0	93.7	97.3	5.4	2.1	0.8	0.6	0.0	0.0
Angola	0.8	3.8	0.0	0.0	0.0	0.0	13.8	15.5	86.2	84.5	0.0	0.0
Argentina	50.7	115.1	1.3	2.2	39.2	54.3	9.8	9.4	35.2	26.5	14.3	6.3
Armenia	10.4	5.9	0.0	0.0	16.4	25.2	68.6	0.0	15.0	31.4	0.0	43.3
Australia	154.3	254.6	77.1	76.3	10.6	15.4	2.7	0.9	9.2	5.7	0.0	0.0
Austria	49.3	60.9	14.2	12.5	15.7	16.2	3.8	2.1	63.9	59.1	0.0	0.0
Azerbaijan	23.2	24.2	0.0	0.0	0.0	74.5	97.0	15.7	3.0	9.8	0.0	0.0
Bangladesh	7.7	24.4	0.0	0.0	84.3	87.6	4.3	6.7	11.4	5.7	0.0	0.0
Belarus	39.5	31.8	0.0	0.0	58.1	99.0	41.8	0.5	0.1	0.1	0.0	0.0
Belgium	70.3	87.5	28.2	9.5	7.7	29.0	1.9	0.9	0.4	0.4	60.8	55.1
Benin	0.0	0.1	0.0	0.0	0.0	0.0	100.0	99.2	0.0	0.8	0.0	0.0
Bolivia	2.1	5.7	0.0	0.0	37.6	42.3	5.3	14.3	55.3	40.4	0.0	0.0
Bosnia and Herzegovina	14.6	11.8	71.8	64.8	0.0	0.0	7.3	1.3	20.9	33.8	0.0	0.0
Botswana	0.9	1.1	88.1	99.5	0.0	0.0	11.9	0.5	0.0	0.0	0.0	0.0
Brazil	222.8	445.1	2.1	2.3	0.0	3.5	2.2	3.1	92.8	84.0	1.0	2.8
Bulgaria	42.1	42.9	50.3	52.3	7.6	5.4	2.9	1.3	4.5	6.7	34.8	34.1
Burkina Faso	..	..	..	..	..	..	..	..	..	..	..	..
Burundi	..	..	..	..	..	..	..	..	..	..	..	..
Cambodia	..	1.3	..	0.0	..	0.0	..	95.9	..	3.7	..	0.0
Cameroon	2.7	5.8	0.0	0.0	0.0	7.6	1.5	25.5	98.5	66.9	0.0	0.0
Canada	482.0	639.7	17.1	18.1	2.0	6.4	3.4	1.5	61.6	57.6	15.1	14.6
Central African Republic	..	..	..	..	..	..	..	..	..	..	..	..
Chad	..	..	..	..	..	..	..	..	..	..	..	..
Chile	18.4	58.5	38.3	22.7	2.1	7.9	9.2	24.6	48.5	39.5	0.0	0.0
China	621.2	3,279.2	71.3	81.0	0.4	0.9	7.9	1.0	20.4	14.8	0.0	1.9
Hong Kong SAR, China	28.9	39.0	98.3	73.3	0.0	26.5	1.7	0.2	0.0	0.0	0.0	0.0
Colombia	36.4	55.3	10.1	6.3	12.4	11.9	1.0	0.3	75.6	80.4	0.0	0.0
Congo, Dem. Rep.	5.7	8.3	0.0	0.0	0.0	0.0	0.4	0.3	99.6	99.7	0.0	0.0
Congo, Rep.	0.5	0.4	0.0	0.0	0.0	17.7	0.6	0.0	99.4	82.3	0.0	0.0
Costa Rica	3.5	9.1	0.0	0.0	0.0	0.0	2.5	8.0	97.5	74.8	0.0	0.0
Côte d'Ivoire	2.0	5.6	0.0	0.0	0.0	65.7	33.3	0.3	66.7	31.9	0.0	0.0
Croatia	9.2	12.1	6.8	20.1	20.2	25.4	31.6	19.2	41.3	35.1	0.0	0.0
Cuba	15.0	17.6	0.0	0.0	0.2	0.0	91.4	97.4	0.8	0.7	0.0	0.0
Czech Republic	62.3	87.8	76.4	62.5	0.6	3.6	0.9	0.1	1.9	2.4	20.2	29.8
Denmark	26.0	39.2	90.7	50.8	2.7	17.7	3.4	3.3	0.1	0.1	0.0	0.0
Dominican Republic	3.7	14.8	1.2	13.2	0.0	11.5	88.6	65.6	9.4	9.4	0.0	0.0
Ecuador	6.3	17.3	0.0	0.0	0.0	6.8	21.5	41.0	78.5	52.1	0.0	0.0
Egypt, Arab Rep.	42.3	125.1	0.0	0.0	39.6	68.4	36.9	18.6	23.5	12.4	0.0	0.0
El Salvador	2.2	5.8	0.0	0.0	0.0	0.0	6.9	45.7	73.5	30.0	0.0	0.0
Eritrea	0.1	0.3	0.0	0.0	0.0	0.0	100.0	99.3	0.0	0.0	0.0	0.0
Estonia	17.4	12.2	85.8	93.5	5.9	4.8	8.3	0.3	0.0	0.2	0.0	0.0
Ethiopia	1.2	3.5	0.0	0.0	0.0	0.0	11.6	3.8	88.4	96.2	0.0	0.0
Finland	54.4	81.2	18.5	17.9	8.6	13.0	3.1	0.6	20.0	17.4	35.3	28.8
France	417.2	564.4	8.5	5.0	0.7	3.9	2.1	1.1	12.9	10.3	75.3	77.9
Gabon	1.0	1.8	0.0	0.0	16.4	16.0	11.2	40.2	72.1	43.4	0.0	0.0
Gambia, The	..	..	..	..	..	..	..	..	..	..	..	..
Georgia	13.7	8.3	0.0	0.0	15.6	17.9	29.2	0.3	55.2	81.8	0.0	0.0
Germany	547.7	629.5	58.7	49.3	7.4	11.6	1.9	1.8	3.2	3.3	27.8	22.3
Ghana	5.7	7.0	0.0	0.0	0.0	0.0	0.0	46.6	100.0	53.4	0.0	0.0
Greece	34.8	62.7	72.4	55.3	0.3	22.0	22.3	15.4	5.1	4.1	0.0	0.0
Guatemala	2.3	8.8	0.0	12.8	0.0	0.0	9.0	30.1	76.0	41.5	0.0	0.0
Guinea	..	..	..	..	..	..	..	..	..	..	..	..
Guinea-Bissau	..	..	..	..	..	..	..	..	..	..	..	..
Haiti	0.6	0.5	0.0	0.0	0.0	0.0	20.6	67.2	76.5	32.8	0.0	0.0
Honduras	2.3	6.3	0.0	0.0	0.0	0.0	1.7	62.3	98.3	35.1	0.0	0.0

	Electricity production		Sources of electricity[a]									
							% of total					
	billion kilowatt hours		Coal		Gas		Oil		Hydropower		Nuclear power	
	1990	**2007**	**1990**	**2007**	**1990**	**2007**	**1990**	**2007**	**1990**	**2007**	**1990**	**2007**
Hungary	28.4	40.0	30.5	18.7	15.7	38.1	4.8	1.3	0.6	0.5	48.3	36.7
India	289.4	803.4	66.2	68.4	3.4	8.3	3.5	4.1	24.8	15.4	2.1	2.1
Indonesia	33.3	142.2	31.5	44.9	2.3	15.7	42.7	26.5	20.2	7.9	0.0	0.0
Iran, Islamic Rep.	59.1	204.0	0.0	0.0	52.5	78.6	37.3	12.5	10.3	8.8	0.0	0.0
Iraq	24.0	33.2	0.0	0.0	0.0	0.0	89.2	98.5	10.8	1.5	0.0	0.0
Ireland	14.2	27.9	41.6	19.7	27.7	55.5	10.0	7.1	4.9	2.4	0.0	0.0
Israel	20.9	53.8	50.1	69.5	0.0	19.7	49.9	10.8	0.0	0.0	0.0	0.0
Italy	213.1	308.2	16.8	16.1	18.6	56.0	48.2	11.5	14.8	10.6	0.0	0.0
Jamaica	2.5	7.8	0.0	0.0	0.0	0.0	92.4	95.9	3.6	2.1	0.0	0.0
Japan	835.5	1,123.5	14.0	27.7	20.0	25.8	18.5	9.8	10.7	6.6	24.2	23.5
Jordan	3.6	13.0	0.0	0.0	11.9	76.4	87.8	23.0	0.3	0.5	0.0	0.0
Kazakhstan	87.4	76.6	71.1	70.3	10.5	10.7	10.0	8.3	8.4	10.7	0.0	0.0
Kenya	3.2	6.8	0.0	0.0	0.0	0.0	7.1	28.8	76.6	51.4	0.0	0.0
Korea, Dem. Rep.	27.7	21.5	40.1	34.8	0.0	0.0	3.6	3.5	56.3	61.7	0.0	0.0
Korea, Rep.	105.4	425.9	16.8	40.1	9.1	19.3	17.9	5.9	6.0	0.9	50.2	33.6
Kosovo	..	..	..	..	..	..	..	..	..	..	..	..
Kuwait	18.5	48.8	0.0	0.0	45.7	27.7	54.3	72.3	0.0	0.0	0.0	0.0
Kyrgyz Republic	15.7	16.2	13.1	3.3	23.5	10.8	0.0	0.0	63.5	85.9	0.0	0.0
Lao PDR	..	..	..	..	..	..	..	..	..	..	..	..
Latvia	6.6	4.8	0.0	0.0	26.1	40.3	5.4	0.4	67.6	57.3	0.0	0.0
Lebanon	1.5	9.6	0.0	0.0	0.0	0.0	66.7	93.9	33.3	6.1	0.0	0.0
Lesotho	..	..	..	..	..	..	..	..	..	..	..	..
Liberia	..	..	..	..	..	..	..	..	..	..	..	..
Libya	10.2	25.7	0.0	0.0	0.0	44.9	100.0	55.1	0.0	0.0	0.0	0.0
Lithuania	28.4	13.5	0.0	0.0	23.8	17.9	14.6	2.1	1.5	3.1	60.0	73.0
Macedonia, FYR	5.8	6.7	89.7	77.9	0.0	0.0	1.8	7.1	8.5	15.0	0.0	0.0
Madagascar	..	..	..	..	..	..	..	..	..	..	..	..
Malawi	..	..	..	..	..	..	..	..	..	..	..	..
Malaysia	23.0	101.3	12.3	29.5	22.0	62.0	48.4	2.0	17.3	6.4	0.0	0.0
Mali	..	..	..	..	..	..	..	..	..	..	..	..
Mauritania	..	..	..	..	..	..	..	..	..	..	..	..
Mauritius	..	..	..	..	..	..	..	..	..	..	..	..
Mexico	124.1	257.5	6.3	12.3	11.6	48.8	56.7	20.3	18.9	10.6	2.4	4.0
Moldova	16.2	3.8	30.8	0.0	42.3	98.2	25.4	0.0	1.6	0.9	0.0	0.0
Mongolia	3.5	3.8	92.4	96.1	0.0	0.0	7.6	3.9	0.0	0.0	0.0	0.0
Morocco	9.6	22.9	23.0	57.1	0.0	13.6	64.4	22.3	12.7	5.8	0.0	0.0
Mozambique	0.5	16.1	13.9	0.0	0.0	0.1	23.6	0.0	62.6	99.9	0.0	0.0
Myanmar	2.5	6.5	1.6	0.0	39.3	41.6	10.9	4.5	48.1	53.9	.0.0	0.0
Namibia	1.4	1.7	1.5	7.1	0.0	0.0	3.3	0.5	95.2	92.3	0.0	0.0
Nepal	0.9	2.8	0.0	0.0	0.0	0.0	0.1	0.4	99.9	99.6	0.0	0.0
Netherlands	71.9	103.2	38.3	27.6	50.9	57.2	4.3	2.1	0.1	0.1	4.9	4.1
New Zealand	32.3	43.8	1.9	7.1	17.6	27.3	0.0	0.0	72.3	53.6	0.0	0.0
Nicaragua	1.4	3.2	0.0	0.0	0.0	0.0	39.8	71.1	28.8	9.5	0.0	0.0
Niger	..	..	..	..	..	..	..	..	..	..	..	..
Nigeria	13.5	23.0	0.1	0.0	53.7	67.2	13.7	4.9	32.6	27.9	0.0	0.0
Norway	121.6	136.4	0.1	0.1	0.0	0.5	0.0	0.0	99.6	98.2	0.0	0.0
Oman	4.5	14.4	0.0	0.0	81.6	82.0	18.4	18.0	0.0	0.0	0.0	0.0
Pakistan	37.7	95.7	0.1	0.1	33.6	34.4	20.6	32.2	44.9	30.0	0.8	3.2
Panama	2.7	6.5	0.0	0.0	0.0	0.0	14.7	43.1	83.2	56.6	0.0	0.0
Papua New Guinea	..	..	..	..	..	..	..	..	..	..	..	..
Paraguay	27.2	53.7	0.0	0.0	0.0	0.0	0.0	0.0	99.9	100.0	0.0	0.0
Peru	13.8	29.9	0.0	2.8	1.7	24.3	21.5	6.0	75.8	65.3	0.0	0.0
Philippines	27.4	59.6	7.0	28.2	0.0	32.6	45.3	7.5	22.1	14.4	0.0	0.0
Poland	134.4	158.8	97.5	93.0	0.1	1.9	1.2	1.5	1.1	1.5	0.0	0.0
Portugal	28.4	46.9	32.1	26.4	0.0	28.0	33.1	10.4	32.3	21.5	0.0	0.0
Puerto Rico	..	..	..	..	..	..	..	..	..	..	..	..
Qatar	4.8	16.1	0.0	0.0	100.0	100.0	0.0	0.0	0.0	0.0	0.0	0.0

	Electricity production		Sources of electricity[a]									
	billion kilowatt hours		Coal		Gas		Oil		Hydropower		Nuclear power	
							% of total					
	1990	2007	1990	2007	1990	2007	1990	2007	1990	2007	1990	2007
Romania	64.3	61.7	28.8	41.0	35.1	18.7	18.4	1.8	17.7	25.9	0.0	12.5
Russian Federation	1,082.2	1,013.4	14.3	16.7	47.3	48.0	11.9	1.7	15.3	17.5	10.9	15.8
Rwanda	..	..	..	..	..	..	..	..	..	..	..	..
Saudi Arabia	69.2	189.1	0.0	0.0	48.1	44.8	51.9	55.2	0.0	0.0	0.0	0.0
Senegal	0.9	2.0	0.0	0.0	2.3	2.0	93.0	83.1	0.0	10.8	0.0	0.0
Serbia	40.9[b]	36.5	69.1[b]	70.2	3.2[b]	1.1	4.6[b]	1.3	23.1[b]	27.5	0.0[b]	0.0
Sierra Leone	..	..	..	..	..	..	..	..	..	..	..	..
Singapore	15.7	41.1	0.0	0.0	0.0	78.7	100.0	21.3	0.0	0.0	0.0	0.0
Slovak Republic	25.5	27.9	31.9	18.7	7.1	5.8	6.4	2.5	7.4	16.0	47.2	55.0
Slovenia	12.4	15.0	31.3	36.5	0.0	3.0	7.9	0.2	23.7	21.7	37.1	37.9
Somalia	..	..	..	..	..	..	..	..	..	..	..	..
South Africa	165.4	260.5	94.3	94.7	0.0	0.0	0.0	0.4	0.6	0.4	5.1	4.3
Spain	151.2	300.2	40.1	24.8	1.0	30.8	5.7	6.2	16.8	9.2	35.9	18.4
Sri Lanka	3.2	9.9	0.0	0.0	0.0	0.0	0.2	59.9	99.8	39.9	0.0	0.0
Sudan	1.5	4.5	0.0	0.0	0.0	0.0	36.8	68.0	63.2	32.0	0.0	0.0
Swaziland	..	..	..	..	..	..	..	..	..	..	..	..
Sweden	146.0	148.8	1.1	0.9	0.3	0.6	0.9	0.7	49.7	44.5	46.7	45.0
Switzerland	55.0	66.5	0.1	0.0	0.6	1.1	0.7	0.3	54.2	53.0	43.0	42.0
Syrian Arab Republic	11.6	38.6	0.0	0.0	20.5	31.2	56.0	59.7	23.5	9.1	0.0	0.0
Tajikistan	18.1	17.5	0.0	0.0	9.1	2.2	0.0	0.0	90.9	97.8	0.0	0.0
Tanzania	1.6	4.2	0.0	2.7	0.0	36.2	4.9	0.9	95.1	60.1	0.0	0.0
Thailand	44.2	143.4	25.0	21.4	40.2	67.3	23.5	2.7	11.3	5.7	0.0	0.0
Timor-Leste	..	..	..	..	..	..	..	..	..	..	..	..
Togo	0.2	0.2	0.0	0.0	0.0	0.0	39.9	48.0	60.1	46.9	0.0	0.0
Trinidad and Tobago	3.6	7.7	0.0	0.0	99.0	99.6	0.1	0.2	0.0	0.0	0.0	0.0
Tunisia	5.8	14.7	0.0	0.0	63.7	83.1	35.5	16.2	0.8	0.3	0.0	0.0
Turkey	57.5	191.6	35.1	27.9	17.7	49.6	6.9	3.4	40.2	18.7	0.0	0.0
Turkmenistan	14.6	14.9	0.0	0.0	95.2	100.0	0.0	0.0	4.8	0.0	0.0	0.0
Uganda	..	..	..	..	..	..	..	..	..	..	..	..
Ukraine	298.6	196.1	38.2	34.2	16.7	13.0	16.1	0.4	3.5	5.2	25.5	47.2
United Arab Emirates	17.1	76.1	0.0	0.0	96.3	98.1	3.7	1.9	0.0	0.0	0.0	0.0
United Kingdom	317.8	392.3	65.0	35.3	1.6	41.9	10.9	1.2	1.6	1.3	20.7	16.1
United States	3,202.8	4,322.9	53.1	49.0	11.9	21.2	4.1	1.8	8.5	5.8	19.1	19.4
Uruguay	7.4	9.4	0.0	0.0	0.0	0.0	5.1	13.0	94.2	85.6	0.0	0.0
Uzbekistan	56.3	49.0	7.4	5.0	76.4	70.6	4.4	11.3	11.8	13.1	0.0	0.0
Venezuela, RB	59.3	114.9	0.0	0.0	26.2	16.3	11.5	11.4	62.3	72.3	0.0	0.0
Vietnam	8.7	69.5	23.1	21.4	0.1	32.1	15.0	3.5	61.8	43.0	0.0	0.0
West Bank and Gaza	..	..	..	..	..	..	..	..	..	..	..	..
Yemen, Rep.	1.7	6.0	0.0	0.0	0.0	0.0	100.0	100.0	0.0	0.0	0.0	0.0
Zambia	8.0	9.9	0.5	0.2	0.0	0.0	0.3	0.4	99.2	99.4	0.0	0.0
Zimbabwe	9.4	9.2	53.3	43.0	0.0	0.0	0.0	0.3	46.7	56.8	0.0	0.0
World	**11,847.9 t**	**19,818.9 t**	**37.3 w**	**41.5 w**	**14.6 w**	**20.8 w**	**10.3 w**	**5.3 w**	**18.0 w**	**15.5 w**	**17.0 w**	**13.7 w**
Low income	210.5	336.8	11.6	8.7	26.5	25.1	4.2	7.7	41.2	41.9	0.0	0.0
Middle income	4,066.0	8,665.5	34.9	49.1	20.8	18.9	14.5	5.8	22.5	19.8	6.2	4.7
Lower middle income	1,672.0	5,425.0	46.8	62.7	10.8	11.8	16.3	5.4	19.9	15.2	4.9	3.3
Upper middle income	2,393.6	3,244.0	26.5	26.3	27.8	30.7	13.2	6.4	24.3	27.5	7.1	7.2
Low & middle income	4,271.6	9,008.7	33.8	47.5	21.1	19.1	14.0	5.9	23.4	20.6	5.9	4.6
East Asia & Pacific	796.3	3,851.0	61.0	73.3	3.4	6.7	12.6	2.3	21.4	14.7	0.0	1.6
Europe & Central Asia	2,076.4	1,991.2	27.8	29.2	34.3	37.4	12.9	2.3	13.8	16.2	10.9	14.4
Latin America & Carib.	606.2	1,245.6	3.9	5.2	9.2	19.8	18.9	13.3	63.5	55.8	2.1	2.4
Middle East & N. Africa	187.9	536.9	1.2	2.4	36.9	61.6	48.3	27.0	12.4	7.4	0.0	0.0
South Asia	341.7	944.1	56.1	58.2	8.5	12.8	5.3	7.6	27.4	17.0	1.9	2.1
Sub-Saharan Africa	260.2	432.3	62.2	58.3	2.8	5.0	1.9	3.7	15.9	16.9	3.2	2.6
High income	7,595.3	10,858.4	39.2	36.2	10.9	22.2	8.3	4.7	14.9	11.1	23.2	21.3
Euro area	1,694.1	2,326.1	33.7	25.2	8.6	22.0	9.6	4.3	11.1	9.1	35.6	31.5

a. Shares may not sum to 100 percent because some sources of generated electricity (such as wind, solar, and geothermal) are not shown. b. Includes Kosovo and Montenegro.

About the data

Use of energy is important in improving people's standard of living. But electricity generation also can damage the environment. Whether such damage occurs depends largely on how electricity is generated. For example, burning coal releases twice as much carbon dioxide—a major contributor to global warming—as does burning an equivalent amount of natural gas (see *About the data* for table 3.8). Nuclear energy does not generate carbon dioxide emissions, but it produces other dangerous waste products. The table provides information on electricity production by source.

The International Energy Agency (IEA) compiles data on energy inputs used to generate electricity. IEA data for countries that are not members of the Organisation for Economic Co-operation and Development (OECD) are based on national energy data adjusted to conform to annual questionnaires completed by OECD member governments. In addition, estimates are sometimes made to complete major aggregates from which key data are missing, and adjustments are made to compensate for differences in definitions. The IEA makes these estimates in consultation with national statistical offices, oil companies, electric utilities, and national energy experts. It occasionally revises its time series to reflect political changes. For example, the IEA has constructed historical energy statistics for countries of the former Soviet Union. In addition, energy statistics for other countries have undergone continuous changes in coverage or methodology in recent years as more detailed energy accounts have become available. Breaks in series are therefore unavoidable.

Definitions

• **Electricity production** is measured at the terminals of all alternator sets in a station. In addition to hydropower, coal, oil, gas, and nuclear power generation, it covers generation by geothermal, solar, wind, and tide and wave energy as well as that from combustible renewables and waste. Production includes the output of electric plants designed to produce electricity only, as well as that of combined heat and power plants. • **Sources of electricity** are the inputs used to generate electricity: coal, gas, oil, hydropower, and nuclear power. • **Coal** is all coal and brown coal, both primary (including hard coal and lignite-brown coal) and derived fuels (including patent fuel, coke oven coke, gas coke, coke oven gas, and blast furnace gas). Peat is also included in this category. • **Gas** is natural gas but not natural gas liquids. • **Oil** is crude oil and petroleum products. • **Hydropower** is electricity produced by hydroelectric power plants. • **Nuclear power** is electricity produced by nuclear power plants.

Sources of electricity generation have shifted since 1990 . . .   3.10a

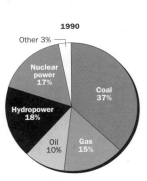
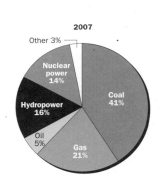

World

Source: Table 3.10.

. . . with developing economies relying more on coal   3.10b

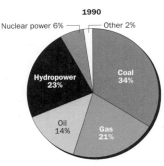
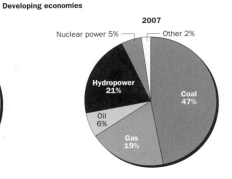

Developing economies

Source: Table 3.10.

Data sources

Data on electricity production are from the IEA's electronic files and its annual publications *Energy Statistics and Balances of Non-OECD Countries, Energy Statistics of OECD Countries,* and *Energy Balances of OECD Countries.*

	Urban population					Population in urban agglomerations of more than 1 million		Population in largest city		Access to improved sanitation facilities			
	millions		% of total population		average annual % growth	% of total population		% of urban population		% of urban population		% of rural population	
	1990	2008	1990	2008	1990–2008	1990	2007	1990	2007	1990	2006	1990	2006
Afghanistan	..	..	..	..	..	..	..	..	..	..	..	..	..
Albania	1.2	1.5	36	47	1.1	..	..	..	..	97	98	..	97
Algeria	13.2	22.4	52	65	3.0	8	10	14	15	99	98	77	87
Angola	4.0	10.2	37	57	5.3	15	23	40	41	55	79	9	16
Argentina	28.3	36.7	87	92	1.4	39	39	37	35	86	92	45	83
Armenia	2.4	2.0	68	64	−1.1	33	36	49	56	94	96	..	81
Australia	14.6	19.0	85	89	1.5	60	61	25	23	100	100	100	100
Austria	5.1	5.6	66	67	0.5	27	28	41	41	100	100	100	100
Azerbaijan	3.8	4.5	54	52	0.9	24	22	45	43	..	90	..	70
Bangladesh	22.9	43.4	20	27	3.6	8	12	29	32	56	48	18	32
Belarus	6.7	7.1	66	73	0.3	16	19	24	26	..	91	..	97
Belgium	9.6	10.4	96	97	0.5	10	17	10	17	..	..	..	..
Benin	1.7	3.6	35	41	4.3	..	..	..	..	32	59	2	11
Bolivia	3.7	6.4	56	66	3.0	25	32	29	26	47	54	15	22
Bosnia and Herzegovina	1.7	1.8	39	47	0.3	..	..	..	..	99	99	..	92
Botswana	0.6	1.1	42	60	3.9	..	..	..	..	60	60	22	30
Brazil	111.9	164.3	75	86	2.1	34	39	13	12	82	84	37	37
Bulgaria	5.8	5.4	66	71	−0.4	14	16	21	22	100	100	96	96
Burkina Faso	1.2	3.0	14	20	5.0	..	8	49	41	23	41	2	6
Burundi	0.4	0.8	6	10	4.7	..	..	..	..	41	44	44	41
Cambodia	1.2	3.1	13	22	5.2	6	10	49	49	..	62	2	19
Cameroon	5.0	10.8	41	57	4.3	14	19	19	18	47	58	34	42
Canada	21.3	26.8	77	80	1.3	40	44	18	20	100	100	99	99
Central African Republic	1.1	1.7	37	39	2.4	..	..	..	..	21	40	5	25
Chad	1.3	2.9	21	27	4.6	..	..	38	35	19	23	1	4
Chile	11.0	14.9	83	88	1.7	35	34	42	39	91	97	48	74
China	311.0	570.9	27	43	3.4	13	18	3	3	61	74	43	59
Hong Kong SAR, China	5.7	7.0	100	100	1.1	100	100	100	100	..	..	..	..
Colombia	22.7	33.5	68	75	2.2	32	35	22	23	81	85	39	58
Congo, Dem. Rep.	10.3	21.8	28	34	4.2	15	17	35	37	53	42	1	25
Congo, Rep.	1.3	2.2	54	61	2.8	29	38	53	63	..	19	..	21
Costa Rica	1.6	2.9	51	63	3.4	24	29	47	46	96	96	92	95
Côte d'Ivoire	5.0	10.0	40	49	3.9	17	19	42	39	39	38	8	12
Croatia	2.6	2.5	54	57	−0.1	..	..	..	..	99	99	98	98
Cuba	7.8	8.5	73	76	0.5	20	19	27	26	99	99	95	95
Czech Republic	7.8	7.7	75	74	−0.1	12	11	16	16	100	100	98	98
Denmark	4.4	4.8	85	87	0.5	26	20	31	23	100	100	100	100
Dominican Republic	4.1	6.9	55	69	2.9	21	22	37	32	77	81	57	74
Ecuador	5.7	8.8	55	66	2.5	26	32	28	29	88	91	50	72
Egypt, Arab Rep.	25.1	34.8	44	43	1.8	21	20	36	35	68	85	37	52
El Salvador	2.6	3.7	49	61	1.9	18	23	37	39	88	90	59	80
Eritrea	0.5	1.0	16	21	4.0	..	..	..	..	20	14	0	3
Estonia	1.1	0.9	71	69	−1.0	..	..	..	..	96	96	94	94
Ethiopia	6.1	13.7	13	17	4.5	4	4	29	22	19	27	2	8
Finland	3.1	3.4	61	63	0.5	17	21	28	34	100	100	100	100
France	42.0	48.2	74	77	0.8	23	22	22	21	..	..	..	..
Gabon	0.6	1.2	69	85	3.6	..	..	..	..	..	37	..	30
Gambia, The	0.3	0.9	38	56	5.6	..	..	..	..	..	50	..	55
Georgia	3.0	2.3	55	53	−1.6	22	25	41	48	96	94	91	92
Germany	58.1	60.5	73	74	0.2	8	9	6	6	100	100	100	100
Ghana	5.4	11.7	36	50	4.2	13	16	22	19	11	15	3	6
Greece	6.0	6.9	59	61	0.8	30	29	51	48	100	99	93	97
Guatemala	3.7	6.6	41	49	3.3	..	8	22	16	87	90	58	79
Guinea	1.7	3.4	28	34	3.8	15	16	52	46	19	33	10	12
Guinea-Bissau	0.3	0.5	28	30	2.7	..	..	..	..	..	48	..	26
Haiti	2.0	4.6	29	47	4.6	16	21	56	45	49	29	20	12
Honduras	2.0	3.5	40	48	3.2	..	..	29	29	68	78	29	55

	Urban population					Population in urban agglomerations of more than 1 million		Population in largest city		Access to improved sanitation facilities			
	millions		% of total population		average annual % growth	% of total population		% of urban population		% of urban population		% of rural population	
	1990	2008	1990	2008	1990–2008	1990	2007	1990	2007	1990	2006	1990	2006
Hungary	6.8	6.8	66	68	0.0	19	17	29	25	100	100	100	100
India	216.6	336.7	26	30	2.5	10	11	6	6	44	52	4	18
Indonesia	54.3	117.0	31	51	4.3	9	9	14	8	73	67	42	37
Iran, Islamic Rep.	30.6	49.3	56	68	2.6	23	23	21	16	86	..	78	..
Iraq	13.2	..	70	..	..	26	..	31	..	75	..	..	..
Ireland	2.0	2.7	57	61	1.7	26	25	46	40	..	..	..	..
Israel	4.2	6.7	90	92	2.6	43	60	48	49	100	100	..	..
Italy	37.8	40.7	67	68	0.4	19	17	9	8	..	..	..	..
Jamaica	1.2	1.4	49	53	1.1	..	..	..	..	82	82	83	84
Japan	78.0	84.9	63	66	0.5	46	48	42	42	100	100	100	100
Jordan	2.3	4.6	72	78	3.9	27	18	37	30	..	88	..	71
Kazakhstan	9.2	9.1	56	58	–0.1	7	8	12	14	97	97	96	98
Kenya	4.3	8.4	18	22	3.7	6	8	32	37	18	19	44	48
Korea, Dem. Rep.	11.8	14.9	58	63	1.3	15	19	21	22	..	..	..	..
Korea, Rep.	31.6	39.6	74	81	1.2	51	48	33	25	..	..	..	..
Kosovo	..	..	..	..	..	..	..	..	..	..	..	..	..
Kuwait	2.1	2.7	98	98	1.4	65	72	67	74	..	..	..	..
Kyrgyz Republic	1.7	1.9	38	36	0.8	..	..	38	43	..	94	..	93
Lao PDR	0.6	1.9	15	31	6.0	..	..	..	..	..	87	..	38
Latvia	1.9	1.5	69	68	–1.0	..	..	..	..	..	82	..	71
Lebanon	2.5	3.6	83	87	2.2	43	44	52	51	100	100	..	..
Lesotho	0.2	0.5	14	25	4.7	..	..	..	..	..	43	30	34
Liberia	1.0	2.3	45	60	4.7	..	29	54	48	59	49	24	7
Libya	3.3	4.9	76	78	2.2	48	55	45	46	97	97	96	96
Lithuania	2.5	2.2	68	67	–0.6	..	..	..	..	..	..	..	..
Macedonia, FYR	1.1	1.4	58	67	1.2	..	..	..	..	..	92	..	81
Madagascar	2.7	5.6	24	30	4.2	8	9	36	31	15	18	6	10
Malawi	1.1	2.8	12	19	5.2	..	..	..	..	50	51	46	62
Malaysia	9.0	19.0	50	70	4.1	6	5	12	8	95	95	..	93
Mali	2.0	4.1	23	32	3.9	9	12	37	38	53	59	30	39
Mauritania	0.8	1.3	40	41	2.9	..	..	..	..	33	44	11	10
Mauritius	0.5	0.5	44	42	0.8	..	..	..	..	95	95	94	94
Mexico	59.4	82.1	71	77	1.8	32	34	26	23	74	91	8	48
Moldova	2.0	1.5	47	42	–1.7	..	..	..	..	..	85	..	73
Mongolia	1.3	1.5	57	57	1.0	..	..	45	60	..	64	..	31
Morocco	12.0	17.7	48	56	2.2	16	19	22	18	80	85	25	54
Mozambique	2.9	8.2	21	37	5.9	6	7	27	18	..	53	12	19
Myanmar	10.2	16.1	25	33	2.6	7	8	28	26	47	85	15	81
Namibia	0.4	0.8	28	37	3.8	..	..	..	..	73	66	8	18
Nepal	1.7	5.0	9	17	6.0	..	..	23	19	36	45	6	24
Netherlands	10.3	13.5	69	82	1.5	14	12	10	8	100	100	100	100
New Zealand	2.9	3.7	85	87	1.3	25	30	30	34	..	..	88	..
Nicaragua	2.2	3.2	52	57	2.2	18	21	34	38	59	57	23	34
Niger	1.2	2.4	15	17	3.8	..	..	35	40	16	27	1	3
Nigeria	34.4	73.1	35	48	4.2	11	14	14	13	33	35	22	25
Norway	3.1	3.7	72	77	1.1	..	..	22	22	..	..	..	..
Oman	1.2	2.0	66	72	2.7	..	..	..	..	97	97	61	..
Pakistan	33.0	60.1	31	36	3.3	16	18	22	21	76	90	14	40
Panama	1.3	2.5	54	73	3.6	35	38	65	53	..	78	..	63
Papua New Guinea	0.6	0.8	15	13	1.6	..	..	..	..	67	67	41	41
Paraguay	2.1	3.8	49	60	3.3	22	30	45	51	88	89	34	42
Peru	15.0	20.6	69	71	1.8	27	28	39	39	73	85	15	36
Philippines	30.5	58.7	49	65	3.6	14	14	26	19	71	81	46	72
Poland	23.4	23.4	61	61	0.0	4	4	7	7	..	..	..	..
Portugal	4.7	6.3	48	59	1.6	37	39	54	45	97	99	88	98
Puerto Rico	2.6	3.9	72	98	2.3	44	67	60	69	..	..	..	..
Qatar	0.4	1.2	92	96	5.8	..	..	..	..	100	100	100	100

	Urban population					Population in urban agglomerations of more than 1 million		Population in largest city		Access to improved sanitation facilities			
	millions		% of total population		average annual % growth	% of total population		% of urban population		% of urban population		% of rural population	
	1990	2008	1990	2008	1990–2008	1990	2007	1990	2007	1990	2006	1990	2006
Romania	12.3	11.7	53	54	−0.3	8	9	14	17	88	88	52	54
Russian Federation	108.8	103.4	73	73	−0.3	18	18	8	10	93	93	70	70
Rwanda	0.4	1.8	5	18	8.5	..	..	57	49	31	34	29	20
Saudi Arabia	12.5	20.3	77	82	2.7	30	40	19	22	100	100	..	..
Senegal	2.9	5.2	39	42	3.1	18	22	47	52	52	54	9	9
Serbia	3.8	3.8	50	52	0.0	..	11	..	21	..	96[a]	..	88[a]
Sierra Leone	1.3	2.1	33	38	2.5	..	..	40	43	..	20	..	5
Singapore	3.0	4.8	100	100	2.6	99	100	99	100	100	100	..	..
Slovak Republic	3.0	3.1	57	57	0.1	..	..	..	..	100	100	99	99
Slovenia	1.0	1.0	50	49	−0.1	..	..	..	..	..	..	..	..
Somalia	2.0	3.3	30	37	2.8	14	13	48	35	..	51	..	7
South Africa	18.3	29.6	52	61	2.7	25	33	10	12	64	66	45	49
Spain	29.3	35.1	75	77	1.0	22	24	15	16	100	100	100	100
Sri Lanka	2.9	3.0	17	15	0.2	..	..	..	..	85	89	68	86
Sudan	7.2	18.0	27	43	5.1	9	12	33	28	53	50	26	24
Swaziland	0.2	0.3	23	25	2.1	..	..	..	..	..	64	..	46
Sweden	7.1	7.8	83	85	0.5	17	14	21	16	100	100	100	100
Switzerland	4.9	5.6	73	73	0.7	14	15	19	20	100	100	100	100
Syrian Arab Republic	6.2	11.2	49	54	3.2	26	31	25	25	94	96	69	88
Tajikistan	1.7	1.8	32	26	0.4	..	..	..	..	..	95	..	91
Tanzania	4.8	10.8	19	26	4.5	5	7	27	28	29	31	36	34
Thailand	16.7	22.5	29	33	1.7	10	10	35	30	92	95	72	96
Timor-Leste	0.2	0.3	21	27	3.7	..	..	..	..	..	64	..	32
Togo	1.2	2.7	30	42	4.6	16	23	53	56	25	24	8	3
Trinidad and Tobago	0.1	0.2	9	13	3.0	..	..	..	..	93	92	93	92
Tunisia	4.7	6.9	58	67	2.1	..	..	..	..	95	96	44	64
Turkey	33.2	50.8	59	69	2.4	22	27	20	20	96	96	69	72
Turkmenistan	1.7	2.5	45	49	2.2	..	..	..	..	..	..	..	..
Uganda	2.0	4.1	11	13	4.1	4	5	38	36	27	29	29	34
Ukraine	34.7	31.4	67	68	−0.5	12	11	7	9	98	97	93	83
United Arab Emirates	1.5	3.5	79	78	4.8	25	31	32	40	98	98	95	95
United Kingdom	50.8	55.2	89	90	0.5	26	26	15	16	..	..	..	..
United States	188.0	248.4	75	82	1.5	41	43	9	8	100	100	99	99
Uruguay	2.8	3.1	89	92	0.6	41	45	46	49	100	100	99	99
Uzbekistan	8.2	10.1	40	37	1.1	10	8	25	22	97	97	91	95
Venezuela, RB	16.6	26.1	84	93	2.5	34	32	17	12	90	..	47	..
Vietnam	13.4	24.0	20	28	3.2	13	13	30	22	62	88	21	56
West Bank and Gaza	1.3	2.8	68	72	4.1	..	..	..	..	..	84	..	69
Yemen, Rep.	2.6	7.0	21	31	5.6	5	9	25	30	79	88	14	30
Zambia	3.1	4.5	39	35	2.0	10	11	24	31	49	55	38	51
Zimbabwe	3.0	4.7	29	37	2.4	10	13	35	34	65	63	35	37
World	**2,257.4 s**	**3,330.6 s**	**43 w**	**50 w**	**2.2 w**	**18 w**	**20 w**	**17 w**	**16 w**	**76 w**	**78 w**	**34 w**	**44 w**
Low income	148.4	280.4	23	29	3.5	9	11	31	31	48	52	19	33
Middle income	1,435.2	2,238.0	39	48	2.5	15	18	14	12	71	75	32	43
Lower middle income	891.8	1,528.3	31	41	3.0	..	..	11	10	62	69	30	41
Upper middle income	543.4	709.7	68	75	1.5	24	27	18	18	86	89	52	63
Low & middle income	1,583.6	2,518.4	37	45	2.6	14	17	16	14	69	73	30	41
East Asia & Pacific	461.3	851.6	29	44	3.4	..	..	9	7	65	75	42	59
Europe & Central Asia	271.1	281.4	63	64	0.2	15	16	13	14	95	94	77	79
Latin America & Carib.	308.2	445.0	71	79	2.0	32	34	24	22	81	86	35	51
Middle East & N. Africa	117.5	186.4	52	57	2.6	20	20	27	24	83	89	50	59
South Asia	280.7	455.6	25	29	2.7	10	12	10	11	49	57	8	23
Sub-Saharan Africa	144.9	298.4	28	36	4.0	..	13	26	25	41	42	20	24
High income	673.7	812.1	73	78	1.0	..	..	20	19	100	100	99	99
Euro area	213.0	238.7	71	73	0.6	18	18	15	15	..	..	..	..

a. Includes Kosovo.

About the data

There is no consistent and universally accepted standard for distinguishing urban from rural areas, in part because of the wide variety of situations across countries (see *About the data* for table 3.1). Most countries use an urban classification related to the size or characteristics of settlements. Some define urban areas based on the presence of certain infrastructure and services. And other countries designate urban areas based on administrative arrangements.

The population of a city or metropolitan area depends on the boundaries chosen. For example, in 1990 Beijing, China, contained 2.3 million people in 87 square kilometers of "inner city" and 5.4 million in 158 square kilometers of "core city." The population of "inner city and inner suburban districts" was 6.3 million and that of "inner city, inner and outer suburban districts, and inner and outer counties" was 10.8 million. (Most countries use the last definition.) For further discussion of urban-rural issues see box 3.1a in *About the data* for table 3.1.

Estimates of the world's urban population would change significantly if China, India, and a few other populous nations were to change their definition of urban centers. According to China's State Statistical Bureau, by the end of 1996 urban residents accounted for about 43 percent of China's population, more than double the 20 percent considered urban in 1994. In addition to the continuous migration of people from rural to urban areas, one of the main reasons for this shift was the rapid growth in the hundreds of towns reclassified as cities in recent years.

Because the estimates in the table are based on national definitions of what constitutes a city or metropolitan area, cross-country comparisons should be made with caution. To estimate urban populations, UN ratios of urban to total population were applied to the World Bank's estimates of total population (see table 2.1).

The table shows access to improved sanitation facilities for both urban and rural populations to allow comparison of access. Definitions of access and urban areas vary, however, so comparisons between countries can be misleading.

Definitions

• **Urban population** is the midyear population of areas defined as urban in each country and reported to the United Nations (see *About the data*). • **Population in urban agglomerations of more than 1 million** is the percentage of a country's population living in metropolitan areas that in 2005 had a population of more than 1 million. • **Population in largest city** is the percentage of a country's urban population living in that country's largest metropolitan area. • **Access to improved sanitation facilities** is the percentage of the urban or rural population with access to at least adequate excreta disposal facilities (private or shared but not public) that can effectively prevent human, animal, and insect contact with excreta. Improved facilities range from simple but protected pit latrines to flush toilets with a sewerage connection. To be effective, facilities must be correctly constructed and properly maintained.

Urban population nearly doubled in low- and lower middle-income economies between 1990 and 2008 — 3.11a

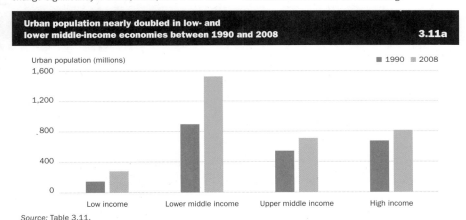

Source: Table 3.11.

Latin America and the Caribbean had the same share of urban population as high-income economies in 2008 — 3.11b

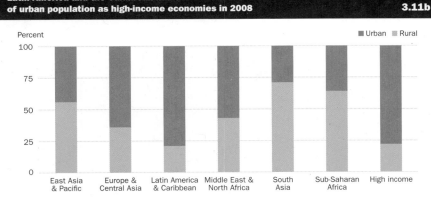

Source: Tables 3.1 and 3.11.

Data sources

Data on urban population and the population in urban agglomerations and in the largest city are from the United Nations Population Division's *World Urbanization Prospects: The 2007 Revision.* Data on total population are World Bank estimates. Data on access to sanitation are from the World Health Organization and United Nations Children's Fund's *Progress on Drinking Water and Sanitation* (2008).

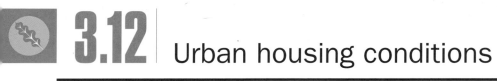

	Census year	Household size		Overcrowding		Durable dwelling units		Home ownership		Multiunit dwellings		Vacancy rate	
		number of people		Households living in overcrowded dwellings[a] % of total		Buildings with durable structure % of total		Privately owned dwellings % of total		% of total		Unoccupied dwellings % of total	
		National	Urban	National	Urban	National	Urban	National	Urban	National	Urban	National	Urban
Afghanistan		..	..	..	..	..	..	..	..	..	..	..	..
Albania	2001	4.2	3.9	..	..	..	..	65[b]	30[b]	..	..	12	13
Algeria	1998	4.9	..	..	..	..	..	67	..	..	..	19	..
Angola		..	..	..	..	..	..	..	..	..	..	..	..
Argentina	2001	3.6	..	19	..	97	..	..	..	4	..	16[b]	..
Armenia	2001	4.1	4.0	4	6	93	93	95	90	1	1	..	..
Australia	2001	3.8	..	1	..	..	..	..	..	..	..	..	..
Austria	2001	2.4	..	2	..	..	..	48	..	..	..	..	..
Azerbaijan	1999	4.7	4.4	..	..	..	..	74	62	4	5	..	..
Bangladesh	2001	4.8	4.8	..	..	21[b]	42[b]	88[b]	61[b]	..	..	..	..
Belarus	1999	..	..	..	..	..	..	..	..	..	..	..	..
Belgium	2001	2.6	..	0[b]	..	..	..	67	..	32[b]	..	..	..
Benin	1992	5.9	..	..	..	26	..	59	..	..	..	..	..
Bolivia	2001	4.2	4.3	40	..	43	58	70	59	3[b]	5[b]	6	4
Bosnia and Herzegovina		..	..	..	..	..	..	..	..	..	..	..	..
Botswana	2001	4.2	3.9	27	47	88	90[b]	61	47	1	..	..	..
Brazil	2000	3.8	3.7	..	..	..	..	74	75	..	..	..	..
Bulgaria	2001	2.7	2.7	..	..	79	89	98	98	..	..	23	17
Burkina Faso	1996	6.2	5.8	30	53	..	..	..	..	..	..	..	..
Burundi	1990	4.7	..	..	..	..	..	..	..	..	..	..	..
Cambodia	2005	5.0	4.9	35	32	79	88	58	57	27	32	..	..
Cameroon	1987	5.2	5.1	67	77	77	..	73	48	27	42	..	..
Canada	2001	2.6	..	..	..	..	..	64	..	32	..	8	..
Central African Republic	2003	5.2	5.8	32	36[b]	78	92	85	74	..	..	..	..
Chad	1993	5.1	5.1	..	..	..	..	..	..	..	..	..	..
Chile	2002	3.4	3.5	..	..	91	92	66	65	13	15	11	10
China	2000	3.4	3.2	..	..	82	..	88	74	..	..	1	..
Hong Kong SAR, China		..	..	..	..	..	..	..	..	..	..	..	..
Colombia	1993	4.8	..	27[b]	..	83[b]	..	68[b]	..	13	..	10[b]	..
Congo Dem Rep	1984	5.4	..	55	..	..	..	..	..	..	..	..	..
Congo Rep	1984	10.5	..	..	..	..	..	76	..	..	..	..	..
Costa Rica	2000	4.0	..	22	..	88	..	72	..	2	3	9	6
Côte D'Ivoire	1998	5.4	..	..	..	..	..	..	..	..	..	..	..
Croatia	2001	3.0	..	..	..	..	..	..	..	..	..	12	..
Cuba	1981	4.2	4.2	..	..	..	..	..	..	15	21	0	0
Czech Republic	2001	2.4	..	..	..	..	..	52	..	49	..	12	..
Denmark	2001	2.2	..	..	..	..	..	..	..	..	..	..	..
Dominican Republic	2002	3.9	..	..	..	97	..	..	..	8	..	11	..
Ecuador	2001	3.5	3.7	30	..	81	88	68[b]	58[b]	9	14	12	7
Egypt	1996	4.7	..	..	..	..	..	..	..	75	..	..	..
El Salvador	1992	..	..	63	..	67	83	70	68	3	6	11	11
Eritrea		..	..	..	..	..	..	..	..	..	..	..	..
Estonia	2000	2.4	2.3	3	..	..	..	..	..	72	..	13	..
Ethiopia	1994	4.8	4.7	..	..	..	23	..	54	..	..	..	..
Finland	2000	2.2	..	..	..	..	..	64	..	44	..	..	..
France	1999	2.5	..	..	..	..	..	55	..	..	..	7	..
Gabon	2003	5.2	..	..	..	..	..	..	..	..	..	..	..
Gambia	1993	8.9	..	..	..	18	..	68	..	..	..	..	..
Georgia	2002	3.5	3.5	..	..	..	..	..	..	..	..	..	..
Germany	2001	2.3	..	..	..	..	..	43	..	..	..	7	..
Ghana	2000	5.1	5.1	..	..	45	..	57	..	53	..	5	..
Greece	2001	3.0	..	1	..	..	..	..	..	..	..	..	..
Guatemala	2002	4.4	4.7	..	..	67	80	81	74	2	4	13	11
Guinea	1996	6.7	..	63	..	..	..	76	..	..	..	..	..
Guinea-Bissau		..	..	..	..	..	..	..	..	..	..	..	..
Haiti	1982	4.2	..	26	..	..	..	92	68	..	..	9	19
Honduras	2001	4.4	..	..	..	69	85	..	..	..	..	14	..

	Census year	Household size		Overcrowding		Durable dwelling units		Home ownership		Multiunit dwellings		Vacancy rate	
		number of people		Households living in overcrowded dwellings[a] % of total		Buildings with durable structure % of total		Privately owned dwellings % of total		% of total		Unoccupied dwellings % of total	
		National	Urban	National	Urban	National	Urban	National	Urban	National	Urban	National	Urban
Hungary	2001	2.6	..	2	..	..	..	..	..	..	..	4	..
India	2001	5.3	5.3	77	71	83	81	87	67	..	..	6	9
Indonesia	2000	4.0	..	..	..	..	..	..	..	..	..	..	..
Iran, Islamic Rep.	1996	4.8	4.6	33[b]	26[b]	72	76	73	67	..	..	..	..
Iraq	1997	7.7	7.2	..	..	88	96	70	66	4	5	13	15
Ireland	2002	3.0	..	..	..	..	..	..	..	8[b]	..	..	..
Israel	1995	3.5	..	..	..	..	..	..	..	..	..	..	..
Italy	2001	2.8	..	..	..	..	..	..	..	..	..	21	..
Jamaica	2001	3.5	..	..	..	98[b]	..	58[b]	..	2[b]	..	..	..
Japan	2000	2.7	..	..	..	..	..	61	..	37	..	..	..
Jordan	2004	5.3	5.1	35	34	..	..	64	60	72	80	..	..
Kazakhstan		..	..	..	..	..	..	..	..	..	..	..	..
Kenya	1999	4.6	3.4	..	..	35	72	72	25	..	..	39	17
Korea, Dem Rep	2000	3.8	..	23	..	..	..	50	..	15	..	..	..
Korea, Rep.	1993	4.4	..	..	..	..	..	..	..	..	..	..	..
Kosovo		..	..	..	..	..	..	..	..	..	..	..	..
Kuwait	1995	6.4	..	..	..	..	..	..	..	9[b]	..	11	..
Kyrgyz Republic	1999	4.4	3.6	..	..	..	..	..	..	..	..	..	..
Laos	1995	6.1	6.1	..	..	49	77	96	86	..	..	..	..
Latvia	2000	3.0	2.6	4	..	88	..	58	..	74	..	0	..
Lebanon		..	..	..	..	..	..	..	..	..	..	..	..
Lesotho	2001	5.0	..	10[b]	..	..	..	84	..	0	..	..	..
Liberia	1974	4.8	..	31	..	20	..	1	..	..	..	..	..
Libya		6.4	..	..	..	..	..	..	..	..	..	7	..
Lithuania	2001	2.6	..	7	..	..	..	..	..	..	..	..	..
Macedonia, FYR	2002	3.6	3.6[b]	8[b]	..	95[b]	95[b]	48[b]	..	..	..	7[b]	3[b]
Madagascar	1993	4.9	4.8	64	57	..	..	81	59	..	..	..	..
Malawi	1998	4.4	4.4	30	..	48	84	86	47	..	..	..	..
Malaysia	2000	4.5	4.4	..	..	..	..	..	..	10[b]	16[b]	..	..
Mali	1998	5.6	..	..	..	..	..	..	..	..	..	..	..
Mauritania	1988	..	..	..	..	..	..	..	..	..	..	..	..
Mauritius	2000	3.9	3.8	6	7	91	94	87	81	..	..	7	6
Mexico	2005	4.0	3.9	24	20	..	..	..	..	..	..	3	2
Moldova	2003	..	..	..	..	..	..	..	..	..	..	..	..
Mongolia	2000	4.4	4.5	..	..	..	..	..	..	48	56	..	..
Morocco	1982	5.9	5.3	..	..	..	..	..	..	..	..	..	..
Mozambique	1997	4.4	4.9	37	28	7	20	92	83	1	1	0	..
Myanmar		..	..	..	..	..	..	..	..	..	..	..	..
Namibia	2001	5.3	..	..	..	..	..	..	..	..	..	..	..
Nepal	2001	5.4	4.9	..	..	..	..	88	..	..	..	0	..
Netherlands		..	..	..	..	..	..	..	..	..	..	..	..
New Zealand	2001	2.8	..	1[b]	..	..	..	65	..	17	..	10	..
Nicaragua	1995	5.3	..	..	..	79	87	84	86	0	0	8	..
Niger	2001	6.4	6.0	..	..	..	..	77	40	..	..	..	..
Nigeria	1991	5.0	4.7	..	..	..	..	..	..	..	..	..	..
Norway	1980	2.7	..	1	..	..	..	67	..	38	..	..	..
Oman	2003	7.1	..	..	..	..	..	..	..	..	..	..	..
Pakistan	1998	6.8	6.8	..	..	58	86	81	..	..	..	..	..
Panama	2000	4.1	..	28[b]	..	88	98[b]	80	66[b]	10[b]	10[b]	14	..
Papua New Guinea	1990	4.5[b]	6.5	..	..	..	..	..	44	..	8	..	..
Paraguay	2002	4.6	4.5	38[b]	..[b]	95[b]	98[b]	79	75	1[b]	2[b]	6[b]	6[b]
Peru	1993	..	..	..	..	49	64	..	..	..	..	7	3
Philippines	2000	4.9	..	..	..	..	..	71	..	12	..	..	..
Poland	1988	3.2	..	..	..	..	..	..	..	..	..	1	..
Portugal	2001	2.8	..	..	..	..	..	76	..	86	..	..	..
Puerto Rico	1990	3.3	..	..	..	..	..	72	..	..	..	11	..
Qatar		..	..	..	..	..	..	..	..	..	..	..	..

3.12 | Urban housing conditions

	Census year	Household size		Overcrowding		Durable dwelling units		Home ownership		Multiunit dwellings		Vacancy rate	
		number of people		Households living in overcrowded dwellings[a] % of total		Buildings with durable structure % of total		Privately owned dwellings % of total		% of total		Unoccupied dwellings % of total	
		National	Urban	National	Urban	National	Urban	National	Urban	National	Urban	National	Urban
Romania	2002	2.9	2.8	20	20	..	..	84	72	..	..	..	..
Russia	2002	2.8	2.7	7	5	..	..	..	..	73	86	..	..
Rwanda	2002	4.4	3.7	43	36	13	31	79	41	36	60	..	..
Saudi Arabia	2004	5.5	..	..	..	92[b]		43	..	..	..	..	..
Senegal		..	..	..	..	..	..	..	..	..	..	..	..
Serbia	2001	2.9	2.2	..	..	..	..	..	..	..	..	..	..
Sierra Leone	1985	6.8	..	..	..	34	..	68	..	..	..	..	..
Singapore	2000	4.4	..	..	..	..	..	..	..	..	..	..	..
Slovak Republic		..	..	..	..	..	..	..	..	..	..	..	..
Slovenia	2002	2.8	2.7	14	17	..	..	91	87	33	56	..	..
Somalia	1975	..	..	..	..	..	..	..	..	..	..	..	..
South Africa	2007	3.0	2.8	16	15	..	..	43	40	..	..	..	..
Spain	2001	2.9	..	1	..	..	..	82	..	..	..	..	..
Sri Lanka	2001	3.8	..	..	..	93[b]	92[b]	70[b]	58[b]	1	14[b]	13	1[b]
Sudan	1993	5.8	6.0	..	..	..	..	86[b]	58[b]	0[b]	1[b]	..	..
Swaziland	1997	5.4	3.7	..	..	..	..	..	..	..	..	..	..
Sweden	1990	2.0	..	..	..	..	..	..	..	54	..	1	..
Switzerland	1990	2.4	2.1	..	..	..	..	31	24	28	32	11	7
Syrian Arab Republic	1981	6.3	6.0	..	..	..	..	..	..	..	..	..	..
Tajikistan	2000	..	..	..	..	..	..	..	..	..	..	..	..
Tanzania	2002	4.9	4.5[b]	33[b]	7[b]	..	..	82[b]	43[b]	..	..	..	..
Thailand	2000	3.8	..	..	..	93	93	81	62	3	..	3	..
Timor-Leste		..	..	..	..	..	..	..	..	..	..	..	..
Togo		..	..	..	..	..	..	..	..	..	..	..	..
Trinidad and Tobago	2000	3.7	..	9[b]	..	98[b]	..	74[b]	..	17[b]	..	..	..
Tunisia	1994	8.0	..	..	..	99	..	71	89[b]	6	10[b]	15	12[b]
Turkey	1990	5.0	..	..	..	..	..	70	..	..	..	..	..
Turkmenistan		..	..	..	..	..	..	..	..	..	..	..	..
Uganda	2002	4.7	3.9	..	..	19	61	76	28	37	71	..	..
Ukraine	2003	..	..	..	..	..	..	..	..	..	..	..	..
United Arab Emirates		..	..	..	..	..	..	..	..	..	..	..	..
United Kingdom	2001	..	2.4	..	..	..	..	..	69	..	19	..	..
United States	2005	2.5	..	0	..	..	..	74	..	26	..	..	..
Uruguay	1996	3.3	3.4[b]	22[b]	..	..	..	57[b]	57[b]	..	..	13[b]	13[b]
Uzbekistan		..	..	..	..	..	..	..	..	..	..	..	..
Venezuela. RB	2001	4.4	..	..	..	..	..	78	..	14	..	16	..
Vietnam	1999	4.6	4.5	..	..	77	89	95	86	..	..	..	..
West Bank and Gaza	1997	7.1	..	..	..	..	..	78	..	45	..	..	..
Yemen	1994	6.7	6.8	54[b]	6[b]	..	..	88[b]	68[b]	3[b]	11[b]	..	..
Zambia	2000	5.3	5.9	..	..	..	..	94	30	..	..	..	..
Zimbabwe	1992	4.8	4.2	..	..	..	..	94	30	6	..	..	..

a. More than two people per room. b. Data are from a previous census.

About the data

Urbanization can yield important social benefits, improving access to public services and the job market. It also leads to significant demands for services. Inadequate living quarters and demand for housing and shelter are major concerns for policymakers.

The unmet demand for affordable housing, along with urban poverty, has led to the emergence of slums in many poor countries. Improving the shelter situation requires a better understanding of the mechanisms governing housing markets and the processes governing housing availability. That requires good data and adequate policy-oriented analysis so that housing policy can be formulated in a global comparative perspective and drawn from lessons learned in other countries. Housing policies and outcomes affect such broad socioeconomic conditions as the infant mortality rate, performance in school, household saving, productivity levels, capital formation, and government budget deficits. A good understanding of housing conditions thus requires an extensive set of indicators within a reasonable framework.

There is a strong demand for quantitative indicators that can measure housing conditions on a regular basis to monitor progress. However, data deficiencies and lack of rigorous quantitative analysis hamper informed decisionmaking on desirable policies to improve housing conditions. The data in the table are from housing and population censuses, collected using similar definitions. The table will incorporate household survey data in future editions. The table focuses attention on urban areas, where housing conditions are typically most severe. Not all the compiled indicators are presented in the table because of space limitations.

Definitions

• **Census year** is the year in which the underlying data were collected. • **Household size** is the average number of people within a household, calculated by dividing total population by the number of households in the country and in urban areas. • **Overcrowding** refers to the number of households living in dwellings with two or more people per room as a percentage of total households in the country and in urban areas. • **Durable dwelling units** are the number of housing units in structures made of durable building materials (concrete, stone, cement, brick, asbestos, zinc, and stucco) expected to maintain their stability for 20 years or longer under local conditions with normal maintenance and repair, taking into account location and environmental hazards such as floods, mudslides, and earthquakes, as a percentage of total dwellings. • **Home ownership** refers to the number of privately owned dwellings as a percentage of total dwellings. When the number of private dwellings is not available from the census data, the share of households that own their housing unit is used. Privately owned and owner-occupied units are included, depending on the definition used in the census data. State- and community-owned units and rented, squatted, and rent-free units are excluded. • **Multiunit dwellings** are the number of multiunit dwellings, such as apartments, flats, condominiums, barracks, boardinghouses, orphanages, retirement houses, hostels, hotels, and collective dwellings, as a percentage of total dwellings. • **Vacancy rate** is the percentage of completed dwelling units that are currently unoccupied. It includes all vacant units, whether on the market or not (such as second homes).

Selected housing indicators for smaller economies 3.12a

	Census year	Household size	Overcrowding	Durable dwelling units	Home ownership	Multiunit dwellings	Vacancy rate
			Households living in overcrowded dwellings[a]	Buildings with durable structure	Privately owned dwellings		Unoccupied dwellings
		number of people	% of total	% of total	% of total	% of total	% of total
Antigua and Barbuda	2001	3.0	..	99[b]	65[b]	3[b]	22
Bahamas	1990	3.8	12	99	55	13	14
Bahrain	2001	5.9	..	94[b]	51	28	6
Barbados	1990	3.5	3	100	76	9	9
Belize	2000	4.6	..	93	63	4	..
Cape Verde	1990	5.1	28	78	72	2	..
Cayman Islands	1999	3.1	..	100	53	38	19
Equatorial Guinea	1993	7.5	14	56[b]	75	14	..
Fiji	1996	5.4	..	60	65	7	..
Guam	2000	4.0	2[b]	93	48	29	19
Isle of Man	2001	2.4	0	..	68	16	..
Maldives	2000	6.6	..	93	..	1	15
Marshall Islands	1999	7.8	..	95	72	12	8
Netherlands Antilles	2001	2.9	24[b]	99	60	16	12
New Caledonia	1989	4.1	..	77	53	9	13
Northern Mariana Islands	1995	4.9	9[b]	99	33	27	17
Palau	2000	5.7	8	76	79	11	3
Seychelles	1997	4.2	15[b]	97	78	..	0
Solomon Islands	1999	6.3	51	23	85	1	..
St. Vincent & Grenadines	1991	3.9	..	98	71	7	..
Turks and Caicos	1990	3.3	4	96	66	11	..
Virgin Islands (UK)	1991	3.0	2	99	40	46	..
Western Samoa	1991	7.3	..	42	90	47	30

a. More than two people per room. b. Data are from a previous census.
Source: National population and housing censuses.

Data sources

Data on urban housing conditions are from national population and housing censuses.

	Motor vehicles		Passenger cars	Road density	Road sector energy consumption				Fuel price		Particulate matter concentration	
				km. of road per 100 sq. km. of land area			kilograms of oil equivalent		$ per liter		Urban-population-weighted PM10 micrograms per cubic meter	
	per 1,000 people	per kilometer of road	per 1,000 people		% of total consumption	Per capita	Diesel fuel	Gasoline fuel	Super grade gasoline	Diesel		
	2007	2007	2007	2007	2007	2007	2007	2007	2008	2008	1990	2006
Afghanistan	23	9	15	6	..	..	..	..	1.05	0.96	78	41
Albania	102	15	75	63	29	198	151	42	1.36	1.31	92	44
Algeria	91	27	58	5	16	170	91	61	0.34	0.20	115	71
Angola	40	..	8	..	11	68	41	24	0.53	0.39	142	66
Argentina	314	..	..	8	19	343	172	102	0.78	0.58	105	73
Armenia	105	42	96	25	6	58	0	55	1.08	1.11	453	59
Australia	653	17	545	11	19	1,103	315	664	0.74	0.94	23	15
Austria	556	43	511	128	23	933	646	233	1.37	1.43	38	33
Azerbaijan	61	10	57	68	10	134	30	92	0.74	0.56	226	60
Bangladesh	2	..	1	166	5	8	5	2	1.17	0.70	231	135
Belarus	282	..	240	46	5	147	86	50	1.33	1.06	23	6
Belgium	539	37	471	499	14	762	599	131	1.50	1.34	30	22
Benin	21	..	17	17	22	77	27	46	1.03	1.03	75	46
Bolivia	68	7	18	6	26	149	67	53	0.68	0.53	120	94
Bosnia and Herzegovina	170	..	152	43	15	230	143	80	1.13	1.18	36	19
Botswana	113	7	56	4	26	283	96	172	0.88	1.02	95	67
Brazil	198	18	158	20	23	281	143	72	1.26	1.03	40	23
Bulgaria	295	63	257	37	12	315	175	78	1.28	1.37	111	57
Burkina Faso	11	..	7	34	..	..	..	..	1.38	1.33	151	84
Burundi	6	..	2	48	..	..	..	..	1.39	1.23	56	29
Cambodia	..	..	..	22	8	27	15	11	0.94	0.89	86	46
Cameroon	..	..	11	11	9	37	14	20	1.14	1.04	116	62
Canada	597	14	372	14	16	1,341	328	914	0.76	0.90	25	17
Central African Republic	0	..	0	..	..	..	..	..	1.44	1.44	62	44
Chad	6	2	..	3	..	..	..	..	1.30	1.32	217	109
Chile	164	..	103	..	18	338	187	134	0.95	0.95	88	48
China	32	12	22	36	5	72	29	40	0.99	1.01	114	73
Hong Kong SAR, China	72	247	54	184	11	209	152	48	1.95	1.16	..	..
Colombia	66	16	38	15	24	159	79	65	1.04	0.73	39	22
Congo, Dem. Rep.	5	..	..	..	1	3	0	3	1.23	1.21	73	47
Congo, Rep.	26	..	15	5	23	80	51	26	0.81	0.57	135	64
Costa Rica	152	18	118	72	30	322	160	145	1.24	1.10	45	36
Côte d'Ivoire	..	..	7	25	4	18	11	6	1.33	1.20	94	36
Croatia	377	58	336	51	21	445	260	160	1.27	1.37	44	30
Cuba	38	..	21	..	3	26	19	5	1.67	1.51	44	17
Czech Republic	470	38	414	163	13	576	344	203	1.37	1.45	67	21
Denmark	466	35	370	168	22	799	446	326	1.54	1.54	30	19
Dominican Republic	123	..	62	..	20	161	57	96	1.04	0.94	44	20
Ecuador	63	19	38	15	33	288	134	139	0.51	0.27	38	25
Egypt, Arab Rep.	..	..	29	9	16	138	80	48	0.49	0.20	223	119
El Salvador	84	..	41	..	19	151	76	67	0.78	0.81	46	33
Eritrea	11	..	6	..	5	8	8	1	2.53	1.07	118	56
Estonia	444	10	390	128	13	559	302	240	1.18	1.30	45	13
Ethiopia	3	4	1	3	5	15	12	2	0.92	0.89	112	68
Finland	559	37	483	23	11	782	417	340	1.57	1.39	23	18
France	600	39	498	172	16	691	501	147	1.52	1.45	18	13
Gabon	..	..	..	3	9	117	87	25	1.14	0.90	10	8
Gambia, The	7	3	5	33	..	..	..	..	0.79	0.75	144	86
Georgia	116	16	95	29	20	150	48	93	1.09	1.16	208	47
Germany	623	80	566	181	15	623	304	250	1.56	1.56	27	19
Ghana	33	9	21	25	13	52	23	27	0.90	0.90	39	34
Greece	112	47	429	89	21	597	198	367	1.23	1.41	67	36
Guatemala	117	..	..	..	24	150	76	66	0.86	0.82	63	62
Guinea	..	..	..	10	..	..	..	..	1.02	1.02	108	70
Guinea-Bissau	33	1	27	12	..	..	..	..	0.00	0.00	119	72
Haiti	..	..	..	..	9	25	0	23	1.16	0.89	70	37
Honduras	97	..	69	..	22	149	85	57	0.80	0.80	45	43

	Motor vehicles		Passenger cars	Road density	Road sector energy consumption				Fuel price		Particulate matter concentration	
	per 1,000 people	per kilometer of road	per 1,000 people	km. of road per 100 sq. km. of land area	% of total consumption	kilograms of oil equivalent Per capita	Diesel fuel	Gasoline fuel	$ per liter Super grade gasoline	Diesel	Urban-population-weighted PM10 micrograms per cubic meter	
	2007	2007	2007	2007	2007	2007	2007	2007	2008	2008	1990	2006
Hungary	384	20	300	210	16	423	252	152	1.27	1.38	36	19
India	12	3	8	1,001	6	33	21	9	1.09	0.70	112	65
Indonesia	76	62	42	20	12	99	32	62	0.60	0.46	137	83
Iran, Islamic Rep.	16	..	13	10	19	497	214	242	0.53[a]	0.03	86	51
Iraq	..	..	..	..	30	332	186	131	0.03	0.01	146	115
Ireland	537	20	437	132	31	1,064	610	417	1.56	1.64	25	16
Israel	305	122	251	81	16	504	163	314	1.47	1.27	71	31
Italy	677	81	601	162	22	659	415	199	1.57	1.63	42	27
Jamaica	188	24	138	201	11	198	0	185	0.74	0.84	59	43
Japan	595	64	325	316	14	572	195	340	1.74	1.54	43	30
Jordan	137	101	94	9	23	295	125	162	0.61	0.61	110	45
Kazakhstan	170	28	141	3	5	234	22	200	0.83	0.72	43	19
Kenya	21	10	15	11	6	29	16	11	1.20	1.14	67	36
Korea, Dem. Rep.	..	..	..	21	2	17	9	7	0.76	0.95	165	68
Korea, Rep.	338	161	248	103	13	573	297	151	1.65	1.33	51	35
Kosovo	..	..	..	..								
Kuwait	502	181	282	32	13	1,232	302	860	0.24	0.20	75	97
Kyrgyz Republic	59	9	44	..	9	51	0	49	0.80	0.88	75	22
Lao PDR	21	10	2	13	..	..	..	..	0.92	0.76	91	49
Latvia	459	15	398	108	25	511	305	178	1.12	1.23	38	16
Lebanon	..	..	..	67	26	252	2	234	0.76	0.76	43	36
Lesotho	..	..	..	..	..	..	..	..	0.79	0.93	86	41
Liberia	3	..	2	..	..	..	..	..	0.74	1.03	61	40
Libya	291	..	225	..	19	536	313	198	0.14	0.12	106	88
Lithuania	479	0	470	124	18	485	267	123	1.13	1.22	53	19
Macedonia, FYR	136	20	122	54	13	190	106	56	1.15	1.12	46	21
Madagascar	..	..	..	..	..	..	..	..	1.55	1.43	78	34
Malawi	9	..	4	16	..	..	..	..	1.78	1.67	75	33
Malaysia	272	72	225	28	18	505	180	306	0.53	0.53	37	23
Mali	9	..	7	1	..	..	..	..	1.30	1.10	274	152
Mauritania	..	..	..	1	..	..	..	..	1.49	1.06	147	86
Mauritius	150	93	115	99	..	..	..	..	0.74	0.56	23	18
Mexico	244	71	167	18	26	455	119	299	0.74	0.54	69	36
Moldova	120	36	89	38	9	78	50	22	1.20	1.04	97	36
Mongolia	61	2	42	3	13	150	7	133	1.38	1.42	198	110
Morocco	71	38	53	13	23	105	88	13	1.29	0.83	34	21
Mozambique	10	..	7	..	5	20	14	5	1.71	1.37	111	28
Myanmar	7	..	6	4	8	26	17	8	0.43	0.52	107	58
Namibia	109	4	52	5	37	278	78	173	0.78	0.88	74	47
Nepal	5	..	3	12	3	10	7	2	1.13	0.82	67	34
Netherlands	503	62	441	372	14	711	394	255	1.68	1.45	46	34
New Zealand	729	33	615	35	27	1,062	450	558	1.09	0.85	16	14
Nicaragua	48	13	18	14	15	92	53	36	0.87	0.82	48	28
Niger	5	4	4	1	..	..	..	..	0.99	0.97	220	132
Nigeria	31	..	31	21	7	50	5	41	0.59	1.13	175	45
Norway	572	29	458	29	14	773	449	293	1.63	1.63	24	15
Oman	225	12	174	16	10	582	53	492	0.31	0.38	148	108
Pakistan	11	8	9	34	13	66	45	9	0.84	0.77	224	120
Panama	188	..	131	..	16	136	0	127	0.67	0.68	58	35
Papua New Guinea	9	..	6	..	..	..	..	..	0.94	0.90	34	21
Paraguay	82	..	39	..	27	185	147	29	1.17	0.96	106	77
Peru	52	16	33	6	25	124	87	26	1.42	0.99	98	54
Philippines	32	14	11	67	20	90	56	29	0.91	0.81	55	37
Poland	451	66	383	83	14	365	197	106	1.43	1.40	59	37
Portugal	507	67	471	90	24	578	398	150	1.61	1.47	51	23
Puerto Rico	642	..	614	289	..	..	..	..	0.65	0.78	27	21
Qatar	724	..	335	68	9	2	1	1	0.22	0.19	57	51

3.13 Traffic and congestion

	Motor vehicles		Passenger cars	Road density	Road sector energy consumption				Fuel price		Particulate matter concentration	
	per 1,000 people	per kilometer of road	per 1,000 people	km. of road per 100 sq. km. of land area	% of total consumption	Per capita	Diesel fuel	Gasoline fuel	Super grade gasoline	Diesel	Urban-population-weighted PM10 micrograms per cubic meter	
						kilograms of oil equivalent			$ per liter			
	2007	2007	2007	2007	2007	2007	2007	2007	2008	2008	1990	2006
Romania	180	20	156	..	10	188	111	67	1.11	1.22	36	14
Russian Federation	245	35	206	5	6	291	69	202	0.89	0.86	41	18
Rwanda	4	..	2	57	..	..	..	..	1.37	1.37	49	26
Saudi Arabia	..	20	415	10	20	1,230	553	615	0.16	0.09	161	113
Senegal	20	..	15	7	19	42	35	6	1.35	1.26	97	95
Serbia	244	46	204	44	..	..	..	..	1.11	1.29	33[b]	15[b]
Sierra Leone	5	2	3	16	..	..	..	..	0.91	0.91	92	50
Singapore	149	207	113	472	9	527	325	179	1.07	0.90	106	41
Slovak Republic	282	35	272	89	11	354	214	114	1.57	1.68	41	15
Slovenia	547	29	505	191	23	838	502	305	1.18	1.26	40	30
Somalia	..	..	..	..	..	..	..	..	1.12	1.15	78	31
South Africa	159	..	108	..	11	303	119	172	0.87	0.95	34	21
Spain	601	35	485	132	23	749	573	149	1.23	1.28	42	32
Sri Lanka	58	11	18	148	21	96	65	25	1.43	0.75	94	82
Sudan	28	..	20	..	14	51	33	16	0.65	0.45	296	165
Swaziland	89	25	46	21	..	..	..	..	0.86	0.93	56	33
Sweden	523	11	465	95	15	807	354	394	1.38	1.52	15	12
Switzerland	569	60	524	173	22	746	259	457	1.30	1.52	37	26
Syrian Arab Republic	52	26	22	21	21	198	115	74	0.85	0.53	159	75
Tajikistan	38	..	29	..	39	224	0	214	1.03	1.00	103	50
Tanzania	12	..	2	8	5	24	18	6	1.11	1.30	57	25
Thailand	..	..	54	35	17	269	172	78	0.87	0.64	88	71
Timor-Leste	..	..	..	..	..	..	..	..	1.22	1.35	..	..
Togo	2	..	2	..	9	34	15	17	0.89	0.88	57	35
Trinidad and Tobago	351	..	..	..	5	546	203	314	0.36	0.24	142	101
Tunisia	103	49	73	12	17	151	101	41	0.96	0.84	74	30
Turkey	131	20	88	55	14	193	125	33	1.87	1.63	68	40
Turkmenistan	106	..	81	..	5	179	0	170	0.22	0.20	177	55
Uganda	7	..	3	17	..	..	..	..	1.30	1.22	28	12
Ukraine	140	39	128	28	6	173	52	112	0.88	0.96	72	21
United Arab Emirates	313	..	293	5	16	1,867	958	819	0.37	0.52	266	127
United Kingdom	527	76	463	172	19	662	345	288	1.44	1.65	25	15
United States	814[c]	31	461[c,d]	68	23	1,785	422	1,218	0.56	0.78	30	21
Uruguay	176	..	151	102	26	250	164	71	1.18	1.17	237	175
Uzbekistan	..	..	..	..	3	58	9	43	1.35	0.75	85	55
Venezuela, RB	147	..	107	..	24	553	81	416	0.02	0.01	22	11
Vietnam	13	7	13	49	13	86	48	35	0.80	0.77	123	55
West Bank and Gaza	16	18	16	..	..	..	..	..	1.34	1.25	..	..
Yemen, Rep.	35	..	..	14	26	83	15	59	0.30	0.17	..	..
Zambia	18	..	11	..	4	25	11	14	1.70	1.61	96	40
Zimbabwe	106	..	91	25	4	29	17	11	1.30	1.05	35	27
World	**183 w**	**.. w**	**132 w**	**.. w**	**14 w**	**262 w**	**103 w**	**138 w**	**1.11 m**	**1.03 m**	**80 w**	**50 w**
Low income	12	..	8	..	7	31	15	15	1.13	1.03	120	65
Middle income	85	..	61	89	10	125	55	59	0.91	0.90	96	57
Lower middle income	18	10	14	240	8	81	39	37	0.87	0.82	121	69
Upper middle income	206	..	155	..	14	296	118	142	1.11	1.01	55	32
Low & middle income	70	..	51	..	10	112	49	52	1.03	0.95	98	58
East Asia & Pacific	36	12	23	36	7	87	38	45	0.92	0.85	112	69
Europe & Central Asia	219	30	182	9	8	232	88	121	1.13	1.12	63	27
Latin America & Carib.	175	..	119	18	23	292	117	133	0.87	0.83	59	35
Middle East & N. Africa	..	..	32	..	20	250	125	107	0.61	0.53	125	73
South Asia	12	3	8	1,001	7	34	22	8	1.09	0.76	134	78
Sub-Saharan Africa	30	..	24	..	8	56	23	31	1.14	1.06	114	53
High income	621	41	434	76	19	1,019	372	568	1.28	1.37	37	26
Euro area	588	66	418[e]	123	18	686	432	207	1.54	1.44	33	23

a. $1.12 for consumption below 120 liters a month. b. Includes Montenegro. c. Data are from the U.S. Federal Highway Administration. d. Excludes personal passenger vans, passenger minivans, and utility-type vehicles, which are all treated as trucks. e. Data are from the European Commission and the European Road Federation.

About the data

Traffic congestion in urban areas constrains economic productivity, damages people's health, and degrades the quality of life. In recent years ownership of passenger cars has increased, and the expansion of economic activity has led to more goods and services being transported by road over greater distances (see table 5.10). These developments have increased demand for roads and vehicles, adding to urban congestion, air pollution, health hazards, and traffic accidents and injuries. Congestion, the most visible cost of expanding vehicle ownership, is reflected in the indicators in the table. Other relevant indicators—such as average vehicle speed and the economic cost of traffic congestion—are not included because data are incomplete or difficult to compare.

The data in the table—except those on fuel prices and particulate matter—are compiled by the International Road Federation (IRF) through questionnaires sent to national organizations. Primary sources are national road associations. If they lack data or do not respond, other agencies are contacted, including road directorates, ministries of transport or public works, and central statistical offices. As a result, data quality is uneven. Coverage of each indicator may differ across countries because of different definitions. The IRF is taking steps to improve the quality of the data in its *World Road Statistics 2009*. Because this effort covers only 2002–07, time series data may not be comparable. Another reason is coverage. For example, the 2005 estimate for U.S. passenger cars from the U.S. Federal Highway Administration excludes personal passenger vans, passenger minivans, and utility-type vehicles. Road density is a rough indicator of accessibility and does not capture road width, type, or condition. Thus comparisons over time and across countries require caution.

Road sector energy consumption includes energy from petroleum products, natural gas, renewable and combustible waste, and electricity. Biodiesel and biogasoline, forms of renewable energy, are biodegradable and emit less sulfur and carbon monoxide than petroleum-derived fuels. They can be produced from vegetable oils, such as soybean, corn, palm, peanut, or sunflower oil, and can be used directly only in a modified internal combustion engine.

Data on fuel prices are compiled by the German Agency for Technical Cooperation (GTZ), from its global network and other sources, including the Allgemeiner Deutscher Automobile Club (for Europe) and the Latin American Energy Organization (for Latin America). Local prices are converted to U.S. dollars using the exchange rate in the *Financial Times* international monetary table on the survey date. When multiple exchange rates exist, the market, parallel, or black market rate is used. Prices were compiled in mid-November 2008, when crude oil prices had dropped to $48 a barrel Brent (from a high of $148 in July).

Considerable uncertainty surrounds estimates of particulate matter concentrations, and caution should be used in interpreting them. They allow for cross-country comparisons of the relative risk of particulate matter pollution facing urban residents. Major sources of urban outdoor particulate matter pollution are traffic and industrial emissions, but nonanthropogenic sources such as dust storms may be a substantial contributor for some cities. Country technology and pollution controls are important determinants of particulate matter. Data on particulate matter for selected cities are in table 3.14. Estimates of economic damages from death and illness due to particulate matter pollution are in table 3.16.

Definitions

• **Motor vehicles** include cars, buses, and freight vehicles but not two-wheelers. Population figures are midyear population in the year for which data are available. Roads refer to motorways (a road designed and built for motor traffic that separates the traffic flowing in opposite directions), highways, main or national roads, and secondary or regional roads. • **Passenger cars** are road motor vehicles, other than two-wheelers, intended for the carriage of passengers and designed to seat no more than nine people (including the driver). • **Road density** is the ratio of the length of the country's total road network to the country's land area. It includes all roads in the country—motorways, highways, main or national roads, secondary or regional roads, and other urban and rural roads. • **Road sector energy consumption** is the total energy used in the road sector from all sources, including energy from petroleum products, natural gas, combustible and renewable waste, and electricity (see table 3.7). • **Gasoline** is light hydrocarbon oil use in internal combustion engines such as motor vehicles, excluding aircraft. • **Diesel** is heavy oils used as a fuel for internal combustion in diesel engines and heating installations. • **Fuel price** is the pump price of super grade gasoline (usually 95 octane) and diesel fuel, converted from the local currency to U.S. dollars (see *About the data*). • **Particulate matter concentration** is fine suspended particulates of less than 10 microns in diameter (PM10) that are capable of penetrating deep into the respiratory tract and causing severe health damage. Data are urban-population-weighted PM10 levels in residential areas of cities with more than 100,000 residents. The estimates represent the average annual exposure level of the average urban resident to outdoor particulate matter.

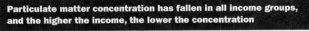

Particulate matter concentration has fallen in all income groups, and the higher the income, the lower the concentration 3.13a

Urban-population-weighted particulate matter (PM10, micrograms per cubic meter) ■ 1990 ■ 2006

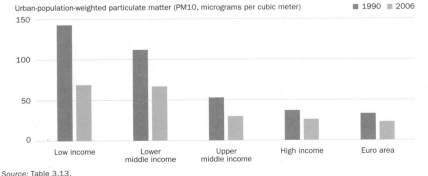

Source: Table 3.13.

Data sources

Data on vehicles and road density are from the IRF's electronic files and its annual *World Road Statistics*, except where noted. Data on road sector energy consumption are from the IRF and the International Energy Agency. Data on fuel prices are from the GTZ's electronic files. Data on particulate matter concentrations are from Pandey and others' "Ambient Particulate Matter Concentrations in Residential and Pollution Hotspot Areas of World Cities: New Estimates Based on the Global Model of Ambient Particulates (GMAPS)" (2006b).

	City	City population	Particulate matter concentration	Sulfur dioxide	Nitrogen dioxide
			Urban-population-weighted PM10 micrograms per cubic meter	micrograms per cubic meter	micrograms per cubic meter
		thousands 2007	2006	2001[a]	2001[a]
Argentina	Córdoba	1,452	55	..	97
Australia	Melbourne	3,728	12	..	30
	Perth	1,532	12	5	19
	Sydney	4,327	19	28	81
Austria	Vienna	2,315	39	14	42
Belgium	Brussels	1,743	25	20	48
Brazil	Rio de Janeiro	11,748	29	129	..
	São Paulo	18,845	34	43	83
Bulgaria	Sofia	1,185	63	39	122
Canada	Montréal	3,678	17	10	42
	Toronto	5,213	20	17	43
	Vancouver	2,146	12	14	37
Chile	Santiago	5,720	54	29	81
China	Anshan	1,639	83	115	88
	Beijing	11,106	90	90	122
	Changchun	3,183	75	21	64
	Chengdu	4,123	87	77	74
	Chongqing	6,461	124	340	70
	Dalian	3,167	50	61	100
	Guangzhou	8,829	64	57	136
	Guiyang	3,662	71	424	53
	Harbin	3,621	77	23	30
	Jinan	2,798	95	132	45
	Kunming	2,931	71	19	33
	Lanzhou	2,561	92	102	104
	Liupanshui	1,221	60	102	..
	Nanchang	2,350	79	69	29
	Pingxiang	905	67	75	..
	Quingdao	2,817	62	190	64
	Shanghai	14,987	74	53	73
	Shenyang	4,787	102	99	73
	Taiyuan	2,794	89	211	55
	Tianjin	7,180	126	82	50
	Wulumqi	2,025	57	60	70
	Wuhan	7,243	80	40	43
	Zhengzhou	2,636	98	63	95
	Zibo	3,061	75	198	43
Colombia	Bogotá	7,772	30	..	..
Croatia	Zagreb	908	32	31	..
Cuba	Havana	2,174	20	1	5
Czech Republic	Prague	1,162	21	14	33
Denmark	Copenhagen	1,085	19	7	54
Ecuador	Guayaquil	2,514	23	15	..
	Quito	1,701	30	22	..
Egypt, Arab Rep.	Cairo	11,893	149	69	..
Finland	Helsinki	1,115	19	4	35
France	Paris	9,904	11	14	57
Germany	Berlin	3,406	21	18	26
	Frankfurt	668	18	11	45
	Munich	1,275	19	8	53
Ghana	Accra	2,121	33	..	..
Greece	Athens	3,242	38	34	64
Hungary	Budapest	1,679	20	39	51
Iceland	Reykjavik	164	18	5	42
India	Ahmadabad	5,375	76	30	21
	Bengaluru	6,787	41	..	..

About the data

Indoor and outdoor air pollution place a major burden on world health. More than half the world's people rely on dung, wood, crop waste, or coal to meet basic energy needs. Cooking and heating with these fuels on open fires or stoves without chimneys lead to indoor air pollution, which is responsible for 1.6 million deaths a year—one every 20 seconds. In many urban areas air pollution exposure is the main environmental threat to health. Long-term exposure to high levels of soot and small particles contributes to a range of health effects, including respiratory diseases, lung cancer, and heart disease. Particulate pollution, alone or with sulfur dioxide, creates an enormous burden of ill health.

Sulfur dioxide and nitrogen dioxide emissions lead to deposition of acid rain and other acidic compounds over long distances, which can lead to the leaching of trace minerals and nutrients critical to trees and plants. Sulfur dioxide emissions can damage human health, particularly that of the young and old. Nitrogen dioxide is emitted by bacteria, motor vehicles, industrial activities, nitrogen fertilizers, fuel and biomass combustion, and aerobic decomposition of organic matter in soils and oceans.

Where coal is the primary fuel for power plants without effective dust controls, steel mills, industrial boilers, and domestic heating, high levels of urban air pollution are common—especially particulates and sulfur dioxide. Elsewhere the worst emissions are from petroleum product combustion.

Sulfur dioxide and nitrogen dioxide concentration data are based on average observed concentrations at urban monitoring sites, which not all cities have.

The data on particulate matter are estimated average annual concentrations in residential areas away from air pollution "hotspots," such as industrial districts and transport corridors. The data are from the World Bank's Development Research Group and Environment Department estimates of annual ambient concentrations of particulate matter in cities with populations exceeding 100,000 (Pandey and others 2006b). A country's technology and pollution controls are important determinants of particulate matter concentrations.

Pollutant concentrations are sensitive to local conditions, and even monitoring sites in the same city may register different levels. Thus these data should be considered only a general indication of air quality, and comparisons should be made with caution. Current World Health Organization (WHO) air quality guidelines are annual mean concentrations of 20 micrograms per cubic meter for particulate matter less than 10 microns in diameter and 40 micrograms for nitrogen dioxide and daily mean concentrations of 20 micrograms per cubic meter for sulfur dioxide.

Air pollution | 3.14

City		City population	Particulate matter concentration	Sulfur dioxide	Nitrogen dioxide
			Urban-population-weighted PM10 micrograms per cubic meter	micrograms per cubic meter	micrograms per cubic meter
		thousands 2007	2006	2001[a]	2001[a]
India	Chennai	7,163	34	15	17
	Delhi	15,926	136	24	41
	Hyderabad	6,376	37	12	17
	Kanpur	3,162	99	15	14
	Kolkata	14,787	116	49	34
	Lucknow	2,695	99	26	25
	Mumbai	18,978	57	33	39
	Nagpur	2,454	50	6	13
	Pune	4,672	42	..	..
Indonesia	Jakarta	9,125	84	..	..
Iran, Islamic Rep.	Tehran	7,873	50	209	..
Ireland	Dublin	1,059	16	20	..
Italy	Milan	2,945	30	31	248
	Rome	3,339	29	..	..
	Turin	1,652	43	..	..
Japan	Osaka-Kobe	11,294	33	19	63
	Tokyo	35,676	38	18	68
	Yokohama	3,366	29	100	13
Kenya	Nairobi	3,010	40	..	..
Korea, Rep.	Pusan	3,480	35	60	51
	Seoul	9,796	37	44	60
	Taegu	2,460	40	81	62
Malaysia	Kuala Lumpur	1,448	23	24	..
Mexico	Mexico City	19,028	48	74	130
Netherlands	Amsterdam	1,031	34	10	58
New Zealand	Auckland	1,245	13	3	20
Norway	Oslo	802	18	8	43
Philippines	Manila	11,100	28	33	..
Poland	Katowice	2,914	39	83	79
	Lódz	776	38	21	43
	Warsaw	1,707	42	16	32
Portugal	Lisbon	2,812	21	8	52
Romania	Bucharest	1,942	16	10	71
Russian Federation	Moscow	10,452	19	109	..
	Omsk	1,135	19	20	34
Singapore	Singapore	4,436	41	20	30
Slovak Republic	Bratislava	456	15	21	27
South Africa	Cape Town	3,215	13	21	72
	Durban	2,729	25	31	..
	Johannesburg	3,435	26	19	31
Spain	Barcelona	4,920	33	11	43
	Madrid	5,567	29	24	66
Sweden	Stockholm	1,264	11	3	20
Switzerland	Zurich	1,108	24	11	39
Thailand	Bangkok	6,704	76	11	23
Turkey	Ankara	3,716	39	55	46
	Istanbul	10,061	46	120	..
Ukraine	Kiev	2,709	26	14	51
United Kingdom	Birmingham	2,285	14	9	45
	London	8,567	19	25	77
	Manchester	2,230	15	26	49
United States	Chicago	8,990	23	14	57
	Los Angeles	12,500	32	9	74
	New York-Newark	19,040	20	26	79
Venezuela, RB	Caracas	2,985	16	33	57

a. Data are for the most recent year available.

Definitions

• **City population** is the number of residents of the city or metropolitan area as defined by national authorities and reported to the United Nations. • **Particulate matter concentration** is fine suspended particulates of less than 10 microns in diameter (PM10) that are capable of penetrating deep into the respiratory tract and causing significant health damage. Data are urban-population-weighted PM10 levels in residential areas of cities with more than 100,000 residents. The estimates represent the average annual exposure level of the average urban resident to outdoor particulate matter. • **Sulfur dioxide** is an air pollutant produced when fossil fuels containing sulfur are burned. • **Nitrogen dioxide** is a poisonous, pungent gas formed when nitric oxide combines with hydrocarbons and sunlight, producing a photochemical reaction. These conditions occur in both natural and anthropogenic activities.

Data sources

Data on city population are from the United Nations Population Division. Data on particulate matter concentrations are from Pandey and others' "Ambient Particulate Matter Concentration in Residential and Pollution Hotspot Areas of World Cities: New Estimates Based on the Global Model of Ambient Particulates (GMAPS)" (2006b). Data on sulfur dioxide and nitrogen dioxide concentrations are from the WHO's Healthy Cities Air Management Information System and the World Resources Institute.

	Environmental strategies or action plans	Biodiversity assessments, strategies, or action plans	Participation in treaties[a]								
			Climate change[b] 1992	Ozone layer 1985	CFC control 1987	Law of the Sea[c] 1982	Biological diversity[b] 1992	Kyoto Protocol 1997	CITES 1973	CCD 1994	Stockholm Convention 2001
Afghanistan			2002	2004[d]	2004[d]		2002		1985[d]	1995[d]	
Albania	1993		1995	1999[d]	1999[d]	2003[d]	1994[d]	2005[d]	2003[d]	2000[d]	2004
Algeria	2001		1994	1992[d]	1992[d]	1996	1995	2005[d]	1983[d]	1996	2006
Angola			2000	2000[d]	2000[d]	1994	1998	2007		1997	2006
Argentina	1992		1994	1990	1990	1995	1994	2001	1981	1997	2005
Armenia			1994	1999[d]	1999[d]	2002[d]	1993[e]	2008[e]		1997	2003
Australia	1992	1994	1994	1987[d]	1989	1994	1993		1976	2000	2004
Austria			1994	1987	1989	1995	1994	2002	1982[d]	1997[d]	2002
Azerbaijan	1998		1995	1996[d]	1996[d]		2000[f]	2000[d]	1998[d]	1998[d]	2004[d]
Bangladesh	1991	1990	1994	1990[d]	1990[d]	2001	1994	2001[d]	1981	1996	2007
Belarus			2000	1986[e]	1988[e]	2006[d]	1993	2007[e]	1995[d]	2001[d]	2004[d]
Belgium			1996	1988	1988	1998	1996	2002	1983	1997[d]	2006
Benin	1993		1994	1993[d]	1993[d]	1997	1994	2002[d]	1984[d]	1996	2004
Bolivia	1994	1988	1995	1994[d]	1994[d]	1995	1994	1999	1979	1996	2003
Bosnia and Herzegovina			2000	1992[g]	1992[g]	1994[g]	2002[d]	2007	2002	2002[d]	
Botswana	1990	1991	1994	1991[d]	1991[d]	1994	1995	2003[d]	1977[d]	1996	2002[d]
Brazil		1988	1994	1990[d]	1990[d]	1994	1994	2002	1975	1997	2004
Bulgaria		1994	1995	1990[d]	1990[d]	1996	1996	2002	1991[d]	2001[d]	2004
Burkina Faso	1993		1994	1989	1989	2005	1993	2005[d]	1989[d]	1996	2004
Burundi	1994	1989	1997	1997[d]	1997[d]		1997	2001[d]	1988[d]	1997	2005
Cambodia	1999		1996	2001[d]	2001[d]		1995[d]	2002[d]	1997	1997	2006
Cameroon		1989	1995	1989[d]	1989[d]	1994	1994	2002[d]	1981[d]	1997	
Canada	1990	1994	1994	1986	1988	2003	1992	2002	1975	1995	2001
Central African Republic			1995	1993[d]	1993[d]		1995	2008	1980[d]	1996	
Chad	1990		1994	1989[d]	1994		1994		1989[d]	1996	2004
Chile		1993	1995	1990	1990	1997	1994	2002	1975	1997	2005
China	1994	1994	1994	1989[d]	1991[d]	1996	1993	2002[f]	1981[d]	1997	2004
Hong Kong SAR, China											
Colombia	1998	1988	1995	1990[d]	1993[d]		1994	2001[d]	1981	1999	
Congo, Dem. Rep.		1990	1995	1994[d]	1994[d]	1995	1996	2005[d]	1976[d]	1997	2005[d]
Congo, Rep.		1990	1997	1994[d]	1994[d]	2008	1994	2007	1983[d]	1999	2007
Costa Rica	1990	1992	1994	1991[d]	1991[d]	1994	1994	2002	1975	1998	2007
Côte d'Ivoire	1994	1991	1995	1993[d]	1993[d]	1994	1994	2007	1994[d]	1997	2004
Croatia	2001	2000	1996	1991[e]	1991[e]	1994[g]	1996		2000[d]	2000[e]	2007
Cuba			1994	1992[d]	1992[d]	1994	1994	2002	1990[d]	1997	2007
Czech Republic	1994		1994	1993[e]	1993[e]	1996	1993[f]	2007[e]	993[g]	2000[d]	2002
Denmark	1994		1994	1988	1988	2004	1993	2002	1977	1995[d]	2003
Dominican Republic		1995	1999	1993[d]	1993[d]		1996	2002[d]	1986[d]	1997[d]	2007
Ecuador	1993	1995	1994	1990[d]	1990[d]		1993	2000	1975	1995	2004
Egypt, Arab Rep.	1992	1988	1995	1988	1988	1994	1994	2005[d]	1978	1995	2003
El Salvador	1994	1988	1996	1992	1992		1994	1998	1987[d]	1997[d]	
Eritrea	1995		1995	2005[d]	2005[d]		1996[d]	2005[d]	1994[d]	1996	2005[d]
Estonia	1998		1994	1996[d]	1996[d]	2005[d]	1994	2002	1992[d]		
Ethiopia	1994	1991	1994	1994[d]	1994[d]		1994	2005[d]	1989[d]	1997	2003
Finland	1995		1994	1986	1988	1996	1994[e]	2002	1976[d]	1995[e]	2002[e]
France	1990		1994	1987[f]	1988[f]	1996	1994	2002[f]	978	1997	2004[f]
Gabon		1990	1998	1994[d]	1994[d]	1998	1997		1989[d]	1996[d]	2007
Gambia, The	1992	1989	1994	1990[d]	1990[d]	1994	1994	2001[d]	1977[d]	1996	2006
Georgia	1998		1994	1996[d]	1996[d]	1996[d]	1994[d]	1999[d]	1996[d]	1999	2006
Germany			1994	1988	1988	1994[d]	1993	2002	1976	1996	2002
Ghana	1992	1988	1995	1989[d]	1989	1994	1994	2003[d]	1975	1996	2003
Greece			1994	1988	1988	1995	1994	2002	1992[d]	1997	2006
Guatemala	1994	1988	1996	1987[d]	1989[d]	1997	1995	1999	1979	1998[d]	
Guinea	1994	1988	1994	1992[d]	1992[d]	1994	1993	2000[d]	1981[d]	1997	
Guinea-Bissau	1993	1991	1996	2002[d]	2002[d]	1994	1995		1990[d]	1995	2008
Haiti	1999		1996	2000[d]	2000[d]	1996	1996	2005[d]		1996	
Honduras	1993		1996	1993[d]	1993[d]	1994	1995	2000	1985[d]	1997	2005

Government commitment

	Environ-mental strategies or action plans	Biodiversity assessments, strategies, or action plans	Participation in treaties[a]								
			Climate change[b] 1992	Ozone layer 1985	CFC control 1987	Law of the Sea[c] 1982	Biological diversity[b] 1992	Kyoto Protocol 1997	CITES 1973	CCD 1994	Stockholm Convention 2001
Hungary	1995		1994	1988[d]	1989[d]	2002	1994	2002[d]	1985[d]	1999[d]	2008
India	1993	1994	1994	1991[d]	1992[d]	1995	1994	2008[e]	1976	1996	2006
Indonesia	1993	1993	1994	1992[d]	1992	1994	1994	2004	1978[d]	1998	
Iran, Islamic Rep.			1996	1990[d]	1990[d]		1996	2005[d]	1976	1997	2006
Iraq						1994					
Ireland			1994	1988[d]	1988	1996	1996	2002	2002	1997	
Israel			1996	1992[d]	1992		1995	2004	1979	1996	
Italy			1994	1988	1988	1995	1994	2002	1979	1997	
Jamaica	1994		1995	1993[d]	1993[d]	1994	1995	1999[d]	1997[d]	1997[d]	2007
Japan			1994	1988[d]	1988	1996	1993[e]	2002[e]	1980	1998[e]	2002[d]
Jordan	1991		1994	1989[d]	1989[d]	1995[d]	1993	2003[d]	1978[d]	1996	2004
Kazakhstan			1995	1998[d]	1998[d]		1994		2000[d]	1997	
Kenya	1994	1992	1994	1988[d]	1988	1994	1994	2005[d]	1978	1997	2004
Korea, Dem. Rep.			1995	1995[d]	1995[d]		1994[f]	2005[d]		2003[d]	2002[d]
Korea, Rep.			1994	1992	1992	1996	1994	2002	1993[d]	1999	2007
Kosovo											
Kuwait			1995	1992[d]	1992[d]	1994	2002	2005[d]	2002	1997	2006
Kyrgyz Republic	1995		2000	2000[d]	2000[d]		1996[f]	2003[d]		1997[d]	2006
Lao PDR	1995		1995	1998[d]	1998[d]	1998	1996[f]	2003[d]	2004[d]	1996[e]	2006
Latvia			1995	1995[d]	1995[d]	2004[d]	1995	2002	1997[d]	2002[d]	2004
Lebanon			1995	1993[d]	1993[d]	1995	1994	2006		1996	2003
Lesotho	1989		1995	1994[d]	1994[d]	2007	1995	2000[d]	2003	1995	2002
Liberia			2003	1996[d]	1996[d]	2008	2000	2002[d]	2005[d]	1998[d]	2002[d]
Libya			1999	1990[d]	1990[d]		2001	2006	2003[d]	1996	2005[d]
Lithuania			1995	1995[d]	1995[d]	2003[d]	1996	2003	2001[d]	2003[d]	2006
Macedonia, FYR			1998	1994[g]	1994[g]	1994[g]	1997[d]	2004[d]	2000[d]	2002[d]	2004
Madagascar	1988	1991	1999	1996[d]	1996[d]	2001	1996	2003[d]	1975	1997	
Malawi	1994		1994	1991[d]	1991[d]		1994	2001[d]	1982[d]	1996	
Malaysia	1991	1988	1994	1989[d]	1989[d]	1996	1994	2002	1977[d]	1997	
Mali		1989	1995	1994[d]	1994[d]	1994	1995	2002	1994[d]	1995	2003
Mauritania	1988		1994	1994[d]	1994[d]	1996	1996	2005[d]	1998[d]	1996	2005
Mauritius	1990		1994	1992[d]	1992[d]	1994	1992	2001[d]	1975	1996	2004
Mexico		1988	1994	1987	1988	1994	1993	2000	1991[d]	1995	2003
Moldova	2002		1995	1996[d]	1996[d]	2007	1995	2008[e]	2001[d]	1999[d]	2004
Mongolia	1995		1994	1996[d]	1996[d]	1996	1993	1999[d]	1996[d]	1996	2004
Morocco		1988	1996	1995	1995	2007	1995	2002[d]	1981[d]	1995	2004
Mozambique	1994		1995	1994[d]	1994[d]	1997	1995	2005[d]	1981[d]	1997	2005
Myanmar		1989	1995	1993[d]	1993[d]	1996	1995	2003[d]	1997[d]	1997[d]	2004[d]
Namibia	1992		1995	1993[d]	1993[d]	1994	1997	2003[d]	1990[d]	1997	2005[d]
Nepal	1993		1994	1994[d]	1994[d]	1998	1993	2005[d]	1975[d]	1996	2007
Netherlands	1994		1994	1988[d]	1988[e]	1996	1994[e]	2002[d]	1984	1995[e]	2002[e]
New Zealand	1994		1994	1987	1988	1996	1993	2002	1989[d]	2000[d]	2004
Nicaragua	1994		1996	1993[d]	1993[d]	2000	1995	1999	1977[d]	1998	
Niger		1991	1995	1992[d]	1992[d]		1995	2004	1975	1996	2006
Nigeria	1990	1992	1994	1988[d]	1988[d]	1994	1994	2004[d]	1974	1997	2004
Norway		1994	1994	1986	1988	1996	1993	2008[e]	1976	1996	2002
Oman			1995	1999[d]	1999[d]	1994	1995	2005[d]		1996[d]	2005
Pakistan	1994	1991	1994	1992[d]	1992[d]	1997	1994	2005[d]	1976[d]	1997	
Panama	1990		1995	1989[d]	1989	1996	1995	1999	1978	1996	2003
Papua New Guinea	1992	1993	1994	1992[d]	1992[d]	1997	1993	2002	1975[d]	2000[d]	2003
Paraguay			1994	1992[d]	1992[d]	1994	1994	1999	1976	1997	2004
Peru		1988	1994	1989	1993[d]		1993	2002	1975	1995	2005
Philippines	1989	1989	1994	1991[d]	1991	1994	1993	2003	1981	2000	2004
Poland	1993	1991	1994	1990[d]	1990[d]	1998	1996	2002	1989	2001[d]	2008
Portugal	1995		1994	1988[d]	1988	1997	1993	2002[f]	1980	1996	2004[e]
Puerto Rico											
Qatar											

	Environmental strategies or action plans	Biodiversity assessments, strategies, or action plans	Participation in treaties[a]								
			Climate change[b] 1992	Ozone layer 1985	CFC control 1987	Law of the Sea[c] 1982	Biological diversity[b] 1992	Kyoto Protocol 1997	CITES 1973	CCD 1994	Stockholm Convention 2001
Romania	1995		1994	1993[d]	1993[d]	1996	1994	2001	1994[d]	1998[d]	2004
Russian Federation	1999	1994	1995	1986[e]	1988[e]	1997	1995	2008[e]	1992	2003[d]	
Rwanda	1991		1998	2001[d]	2001[d]		1996	2004[d]	1980[d]	1998	2002[d]
Saudi Arabia			1995	1993[d]	1993[d]	1996	2001[f]	2005[d]	1996[d]	1997[d]	
Senegal	1984	1991	1995	1993[d]	1993	1994	1994	2001[d]	1977[d]	1995	2003
Serbia			2001[h]	2001[g,h]	2001[g,h]	2001[g,h]	2002[h]	2007	2002[h]		2002[h]
Sierra Leone	1994		1995	2001[d]	2001[d]	1994	1994[f]	2006[d]	1994[d]	1997	2003[d]
Singapore	1993	1995	1997	1989[d]	1989[d]	1994	1995	2006[d]	1986[d]	1999[d]	2005
Slovak Republic			1994	1993[g]	1993[g]	1996	1994[f]	2002	1993	2002[d]	2002
Slovenia	1994		1996	1992[g]	1992[g]	1995[g]	1996	2002	2000[d]	2001[d]	2004
Somalia				2001[d]	2001[d]	1994			1985[d]	2002[d]	
South Africa	1993		1997	1990[d]	1990[d]	1997	1995	2002[d]	1975	1997	2002
Spain			1994	1988[d]	1988	1997	1995	2002	1986[d]	1996	2004
Sri Lanka	1994	1991	1994	1989[d]	1989[d]	1994	1994	2002[d]	1979[d]	1998[d]	
Sudan			1994	1993[d]	1993[d]	1994	1995	2004[d]	1982	1995	2006
Swaziland			1997	1992[d]	1992[d]		1994		1997[d]	1996	2006
Sweden			1994	1986	1988	1996	1993	2002	1974	1995	2002
Switzerland			1994	1987	1988		1994	2006[d]	1974	1996	2003
Syrian Arab Republic	1999		1996	1989[d]	1989[d]		1996	2006[d]	2003[d]	1997	2005
Tajikistan			1998	1996[d]	1998[d]		1997[f]			1997[d]	2007
Tanzania	1994	1988	1996	1993[d]	1993[d]	1994	1996	2002[d]	1979	1997	2004
Thailand			1995	1989[d]	1989		2004	2002	1983	2001[d]	2005
Togo	1991		1995	1991[d]	1991	1994	1995[e]	2004[d]	1978	1995[e]	2004
Trinidad and Tobago			1994	1989[d]	1989[d]	1994	1996	1999	1984[d]	2000[d]	2002[d]
Tunisia	1994	1988	1994	1989[d]	1989[d]	1994	1993	2003[d]	1974	1995	2004
Turkey	1998		2004	1991[d]	1991[d]		1997		1996[d]	1998	
Turkmenistan			1995	1993[d]	1993[d]		1996[f]	2008[e]		1996	
Uganda	1994	1988	1994	1988[d]	1988	1994	1993	2002[d]	1991[d]	1997	2004[d]
Ukraine	1999		1997	1986[e]	1988[e]	1999	1995	2004	1999[d]	2002[d]	
United Arab Emirates			1996	1989[d]	1989[d]		2000	2005[d]	1990[d]	1998[d]	2002
United Kingdom	1995	1994	1994	1987	1988	1997[d]	1994	2002	1976	1996	2005
United States	1995	1995	1994	1986	1988				1974	2000	
Uruguay			1994	1989[d]	1991[d]	1994	1993	2001	1975	1999[d]	2004
Uzbekistan			1994	1993[d]	1993[d]		1995[f]	2007[e]	1997[d]	1995	
Venezuela			1995	1988[d]	1989		1994		1977	1998[d]	2005
Vietnam		1993	1995	1994[d]	1994[d]	2006[d]	1994	2008[e]	1994[d]	1998[d]	2002
West Bank and Gaza											
Yemen, Rep.	1996	1992	1996	1996[d]	1996[d]	1994	1996	2004[d]	1997[d]	1997[d]	2004
Zambia	1994		1994	1990[d]	1990[d]	1994	1993	2006[d]	1980[d]	1996	2006
Zimbabwe	1987		1994	1992[d]	1992[d]	1994	1994		1981[d]	1997	

a. Ratification of the treaty. b. Year the treaty entered into force in the country. c. Convention became effective November 16, 1994. d. Accession. e. Acceptance. f. Approval. g. Succession. h. Signed by Serbia and Montenegro as a unified country before Montenegro declared its independence.

National environmental strategies and participation in international treaties on environmental issues provide some evidence of government commitment to sound environmental management. But the signing of these treaties does not always imply ratification, nor does it guarantee that governments will comply with treaty obligations.

In many countries efforts to halt environmental degradation have failed, primarily because governments have neglected to make this issue a priority, a reflection of competing claims on scarce resources. To address this problem, many countries are preparing national environmental strategies—some focusing narrowly on environmental issues, and others integrating environmental, economic, and social concerns. Among such initiatives are conservation strategies and environmental action plans. Some countries have also prepared country environmental profiles and biodiversity strategies and profiles.

National conservation strategies—promoted by the World Conservation Union (IUCN)—provide a comprehensive, cross-sectoral analysis of conservation and resource management issues to help integrate environmental concerns with the development process. Such strategies discuss current and future needs, institutional capabilities, prevailing technical conditions, and the status of natural resources in a country.

National environmental action plans, supported by the World Bank and other development agencies, describe a country's main environmental concerns, identify the principal causes of environmental problems, and formulate policies and actions to deal with them. These plans are a continuing process in which governments develop comprehensive environmental policies, recommend specific actions, and outline the investment strategies, legislation, and institutional arrangements required to implement them.

Biodiversity profiles—prepared by the World Conservation Monitoring Centre and the IUCN—provide basic background on species diversity, protected areas, major ecosystems and habitat types, and legislative and administrative support. In an effort to establish a scientific baseline for measuring progress in biodiversity conservation, the United Nations Environment Programme (UNEP) coordinates global biodiversity assessments.

To address global issues, many governments have also signed international treaties and agreements launched in the wake of the 1972 United Nations Conference on the Human Environment in Stockholm and the 1992 United Nations Conference on Environment and Development (the Earth Summit) in Rio de Janeiro, which produced Agenda 21—an array of actions to address environmental challenges:

· The Framework Convention on Climate Change aims to stabilize atmospheric concentrations of greenhouse gases at levels that will prevent human activities from interfering dangerously with the global climate.

· The Vienna Convention for the Protection of the Ozone Layer aims to protect human health and the environment by promoting research on the effects of changes in the ozone layer and on alternative substances (such as substitutes for chlorofluorocarbon) and technologies, monitoring the ozone layer, and taking measures to control the activities that produce adverse effects.

· The Montreal Protocol for Chlorofluorocarbon Control requires that countries help protect the earth from excessive ultraviolet radiation by cutting chlorofluorocarbon consumption by 20 percent over their 1986 level by 1994 and by 50 percent over their 1986 level by 1999, with allowances for increases in consumption by developing countries.

· The United Nations Convention on the Law of the Sea, which became effective in November 1994, establishes a comprehensive legal regime for seas and oceans, establishes rules for environmental standards and enforcement provisions, and develops international rules and national legislation to prevent and control marine pollution.

· The Convention on Biological Diversity promotes conservation of biodiversity through scientific and technological cooperation among countries, access to financial and genetic resources, and transfer of ecologically sound technologies.

But 10 years after the Earth Summit in Rio de Janeiro the World Summit on Sustainable Development in Johannesburg recognized that many of the proposed actions had yet to materialize. To help developing countries comply with their obligations under these agreements, the Global Environment Facility (GEF) was created to focus on global improvement in biodiversity, climate change, international waters, and ozone layer depletion. The UNEP, United Nations Development Programme, and World Bank manage the GEF according to the policies of its governing body of country representatives. The World Bank is responsible for the GEF Trust Fund and chairs the GEF.

· **Environmental strategies or action plans** provide a comprehensive analysis of conservation and resource management issues that integrate environmental concerns with development. They include national conservation strategies, environmental action plans, environmental management strategies, and sustainable development strategies. The date is the year a country adopted a strategy or action plan. • **Biodiversity assessments, strategies, or action plans** include biodiversity profiles (see *About the data*). • **Participation in treaties** covers nine international treaties (see *About the data*). • **Climate change** refers to the Framework Convention on Climate Change (signed in 1992). • **Ozone layer** refers to the Vienna Convention for the Protection of the Ozone Layer (signed in 1985). • **CFC control** refers to the Protocol on Substances That Deplete the Ozone Layer (the Montreal Protocol for Chlorofluorocarbon Control) (signed in 1987). • **Law of the Sea** refers to the United Nations Convention on the Law of the Sea (signed in 1982). • **Biological diversity** refers to the Convention on Biological Diversity (signed at the Earth Summit in 1992). • **Kyoto Protocol** refers to the protocol on climate change adopted at the third conference of the parties to the United Nations Framework Convention on Climate Change in December 1997. • **CITES** is the Convention on International Trade in Endangered Species of Wild Fauna and Flora, an agreement among governments to ensure that the survival of wild animals and plants is not threatened by uncontrolled exploitation. Adopted in 1973, it entered into force in 1975. • **CCD** is the United Nations Convention to Combat Desertification, an international convention addressing the problems of land degradation in the world's drylands. Adopted in 1994, it entered into force in 1996. • **Stockholm Convention** is an international legally binding instrument to protect human health and the environment from persistent organic pollutants. Adopted in 2001, it entered into force in 2004.

Data sources

Data on environmental strategies and participation in international environmental treaties are from the Secretariat of the United Nations Framework Convention on Climate Change, the Ozone Secretariat of the UNEP, the World Resources Institute, the UNEP, the Center for International Earth Science Information Network, and the United Nations Treaty Series.

	Gross savings	Consumption of fixed capital	Net national savings	Education expenditure	Energy depletion	Mineral depletion	Net forest depletion	Carbon dioxide damage	Particulate emission damage	Adjusted net savings
	% of GNI 2008	% of GNI 2008	% of GNI 2008	% of GNI 2008	% of GNI 2008	% of GNI 2008	% of GNI 2008	% of GNI 2008	% of GNI 2008	% of GNI 2008
Afghanistan	..	7.0	−7.0	..	0.0	0.0	3.4	0.1	0.2	..
Albania	18.0	10.1	7.9	2.8	1.7	0.0	0.0	0.3	0.2	8.5
Algeria	58.8	10.9	47.9	4.5	29.9	0.2	0.1	0.6	0.2	21.4
Angola	24.1	12.9	11.2	2.3	54.6	0.0	0.0	0.2	1.3	−42.6
Argentina	25.5	11.8	13.8	4.5	8.6	0.4	0.0	0.5	1.1	7.7
Armenia	28.1	10.0	18.1	2.2	0.0	0.8	0.0	0.3	1.2	18.1
Australia	32.9	14.7	18.1	5.1	4.1	3.8	0.0	0.3	0.0	15.0
Austria	27.2	14.3	12.9	5.3	0.2	0.0	0.0	0.1	0.1	17.6[a]
Azerbaijan	63.0	12.3	50.7	2.0	51.4	0.0	0.0	1.2	0.3	−0.1
Bangladesh	33.9	6.8	27.1	2.0	4.0	0.0	0.6	0.4	0.4	23.7
Belarus	28.4	11.2	17.2	4.9	1.3	0.0	0.0	1.1	0.0	19.8
Belgium	..	13.9	..	5.8	0.0	0.0	0.0	0.2	0.1	..
Benin	..	8.1	..	3.3	0.0	0.0	1.0	0.3	0.3	..
Bolivia	29.9	9.5	20.4	4.7	27.6	0.8	0.0	0.5	0.9	−4.7
Bosnia and Herzegovina	41.0	10.4	30.6	..	2.0	0.0	..	1.2	0.1	..
Botswana	46.3	11.5	34.8	6.6	0.5	3.2	0.0	0.3	0.2	37.2[b]
Brazil	17.5	11.8	5.8	4.8	2.7	2.3	0.0	0.2	0.1	5.2
Bulgaria	14.1	11.6	2.5	4.1	1.1	0.8	0.0	0.9	0.9	2.9
Burkina Faso	..	7.5	..	3.3	0.0	0.0	1.2	0.1	0.6	..
Burundi	..	5.6	..	5.1	0.0	0.6	10.9	0.1	0.1	..
Cambodia	..	8.3	..	1.7	0.0	0.0	0.2	0.4	0.3	..
Cameroon	..	8.8	..	2.6	7.8	0.0	0.0	0.1	0.4	..
Canada	23.4	14.0	9.4	4.8	5.5	0.6	0.0	0.3	0.1	7.6
Central African Republic	1.8	7.4	−5.6	1.3	0.0	0.0	0.0	0.1	0.2	−4.6
Chad	3.7	10.0	−6.4	1.2	43.7	0.0	0.0	0.0	1.0	−49.9
Chile	24.2	12.9	11.4	3.6	0.3	14.3	0.0	0.3	0.4	−0.4
China	53.9	10.1	43.8	1.8	6.7	1.7	0.0	1.3	0.8	35.1
Hong Kong SAR, China	29.7	13.4	16.3	3.0	0.0	0.0	0.0	0.2	..	19.1[c]
Colombia	20.2	11.4	8.8	3.6	10.0	0.6	0.0	0.2	0.1	1.5
Congo, Dem. Rep.	9.4	6.7	2.7	0.9	3.1	2.3	0.0	0.2	0.6	−2.5
Congo, Rep.	26.7	14.1	12.6	2.3	71.2	0.0	0.0	0.2	0.6	−57.1
Costa Rica	15.9	11.5	4.5	5.0	0.0	0.0	0.1	0.2	0.1	9.1
Côte d'Ivoire	12.7	9.0	3.8	4.7	6.2	0.0	0.0	0.2	0.3	1.7
Croatia	21.8	12.9	8.9	4.3	1.3	0.0	0.2	0.3	0.2	11.3
Cuba	..	..	..	13.2	..	..	..	..	0.1	..
Czech Republic	24.2	13.8	10.4	4.4	0.7	0.0	0.0	0.5	0.0	13.4
Denmark	23.6	14.2	9.4	7.4	3.0	0.0	0.0	0.1	0.0	13.7
Dominican Republic	9.0	11.1	−2.1	3.5	0.0	1.3	0.0	0.4	0.4	−0.3
Ecuador	31.8	10.8	21.0	1.4	21.1	0.4	0.0	0.5	0.1	0.4
Egypt, Arab Rep.	23.5	9.3	14.2	4.4	14.5	0.5	0.2	0.9	0.5	2.1
El Salvador	7.9	10.5	−2.6	3.3	0.0	0.0	0.4	0.2	0.1	−0.1
Eritrea	..	6.9	..	1.9	0.0	0.0	0.8	0.3	0.3	..
Estonia	20.1	13.5	6.6	4.6	1.5	0.0	0.0	0.7	0.0	9.0
Ethiopia	17.3	6.7	10.6	3.7	0.0	0.3	4.7	0.2	0.2	8.9
Finland	24.8	14.1	10.7	5.6	0.0	0.1	0.0	0.2	0.0	16.0[a]
France	18.7	13.9	4.9	5.1	0.0	0.0	0.0	0.1	0.0	9.8
Gabon	48.8	13.9	34.9	3.1	34.3	0.0	0.0	0.1	0.0	3.6
Gambia, The	11.1	7.9	3.2	2.0	0.0	0.0	0.6	0.4	0.4	3.9
Georgia	8.3	10.1	−1.8	2.8	0.2	0.0	0.0	0.3	0.7	−0.3
Germany	..	13.8	..	4.3	0.3	0.0	0.0	0.2	0.0	..
Ghana	7.3	8.8	−1.5	4.7	0.0	6.5	2.8	0.5	0.1	−6.5
Greece	7.4	13.9	−6.5	2.8	0.3	0.1	0.0	0.2	0.3	−4.8
Guatemala	14.4	10.1	4.3	2.9	0.8	0.0	0.7	0.3	0.1	5.3
Guinea	2.9	7.7	−4.8	2.0	0.0	5.2	2.6	0.3	0.5	−11.3
Guinea-Bissau	22.4	6.7	15.7	2.3	0.0	0.0	0.0	0.5	0.8	16.6
Haiti	..	..	..	1.5	..	..	..	..	0.4	..
Honduras	21.2	9.5	11.7	3.5	0.0	1.4	0.0	0.5	0.2	13.1

Toward a broader measure of savings

	Gross savings	Consumption of fixed capital	Net national savings	Education expenditure	Energy depletion	Mineral depletion	Net forest depletion	Carbon dioxide damage	Particulate emission damage	Adjusted net savings
	% of GNI	% of GNI	% of GNI	% of GNI	% of GNI	% of GNI	% of GNI	% of GNI	% of GNI	% of GNI
	2008	2008	2008	2008	2008	2008	2008	2008	2008	2008
Hungary	15.9	15.1	0.8	5.3	0.8	0.0	0.0	0.3	0.0	5.0
India	38.2	8.5	29.7	3.2	4.9	1.4	0.8	1.2	0.5	24.2
Indonesia	22.2	10.7	11.6	1.1	12.6	1.4	0.0	0.6	0.5	−2.4
Iran, Islamic Rep.	..	..	..	4.2	..	..	..	..	0.4	..
Iraq	..	..	..	..	..	..	..	..	2.7	..
Ireland	19.7	17.1	2.5	5.2	0.0	0.0	0.0	0.1	0.0	7.5[a]
Israel	19.8	13.5	6.3	5.9	0.2	0.3	0.0	0.3	0.1	11.3
Italy	18.5	14.0	4.5	4.5	0.2	0.0	0.0	0.2	0.1	8.5
Jamaica	..	11.4	..	5.3	0.0	1.3	0.0	0.6	0.2	..
Japan	25.9	13.3	12.6	3.2	0.0	0.0	0.0	0.2	0.3	15.3[a]
Jordan	13.7	9.8	3.8	5.6	0.2	4.5	0.0	0.8	0.2	3.6
Kazakhstan	46.2	13.5	32.8	4.4	31.3	1.8	0.0	1.4	0.1	2.5
Kenya	13.1	8.0	5.0	6.6	0.0	0.1	1.0	0.3	0.1	10.2
Korea, Dem. Rep.	..	..	..	..	..	..	..	..	0.8	..
Korea, Rep.	30.5	12.6	17.9	3.9	0.0	0.0	0.0	0.4	0.3	21.1
Kosovo	..	..	..	..	..	..	..	..	..	..
Kuwait	58.7	13.3	45.3	3.0	38.0	0.0	0.0	0.4	0.3	9.7
Kyrgyz Republic	14.9	8.5	6.4	5.8	0.7	0.0	0.0	1.0	0.2	10.4
Lao PDR	25.2	8.6	16.6	1.2	0.0	0.0	0.0	0.2	0.5	17.1
Latvia	22.3	12.6	9.6	5.6	0.0	0.0	0.2	0.2	0.0	14.8
Lebanon	10.2	11.3	−1.1	1.8	0.0	0.0	0.0	0.5	0.1	0.1
Lesotho	17.8	6.4	11.4	9.4	0.0	0.0	1.3	0.0	0.1	19.4
Liberia	−2.7	7.8	−10.5	..	0.0	0.0	7.7	0.9	0.3	..
Libya	66.8	12.3	54.5	..	38.8	0.0	0.0	0.5	1.0	..
Lithuania	15.2	12.7	2.5	4.6	0.1	0.0	0.1	0.3	0.1	6.6
Macedonia, FYR	16.1	10.8	5.3	4.9	0.0	0.0	0.1	1.0	0.1	9.0
Madagascar	14.7	7.4	7.2	2.6	0.0	0.0	2.5	0.3	0.1	7.0
Malawi	29.3	6.5	22.8	3.5	0.0	0.0	0.9	0.2	0.1	25.1
Malaysia	..	11.9	..	4.0	13.1	0.1	0.0	0.7	0.0	..
Mali	..	8.1	..	3.6	0.0	0.0	0.0	0.1	1.1	..
Mauritania	..	..	..	2.8	..	..	..	..	0.5	..
Mauritius	16.5	11.1	5.4	3.4	0.0	0.0	0.0	0.3	0.0	8.5
Mexico	25.3	12.0	13.3	4.8	8.2	0.3	0.0	0.3	0.3	9.0
Moldova	20.8	8.3	12.5	6.5	0.0	0.0	0.1	1.0	0.5	17.3
Mongolia	26.5	9.7	16.8	4.6	5.9	9.2	0.0	1.7	1.6	3.0
Morocco	31.4	10.1	21.3	5.2	0.0	6.1	0.0	0.4	0.1	19.8
Mozambique	7.4	7.9	−0.5	3.8	7.0	0.0	0.5	0.2	0.1	−4.6
Myanmar	..	..	..	0.8	..	..	..	..	0.4	..
Namibia	17.1	12.1	5.0	7.3	0.0	2.1	0.0	0.3	0.0	9.9
Nepal	37.5	7.1	30.4	3.4	0.0	0.0	3.1	0.2	0.0	30.5
Netherlands	10.3	13.9	−3.6	4.8	2.0	0.0	0.0	0.2	0.2	−1.2
New Zealand	..	14.5	..	6.6	2.3	0.2	0.0	0.2	0.0	..
Nicaragua	..	8.9	..	3.0	0.0	0.6	0.0	0.6	0.0	..
Niger	..	2.6	..	2.6	0.0	0.0	2.3	0.2	1.1	..
Nigeria	..	1.2	..	0.9	23.8	0.0	0.2	0.5	0.5	..
Norway	41.2	15.0	26.2	6.0	15.9	0.0	0.0	0.1	0.0	16.2
Oman	..	..	..	3.9	..	..	0.0	..	0.0	..
Pakistan	19.3	8.2	11.1	2.1	4.9	0.0	0.7	0.7	0.8	6.1
Panama	25.9	11.1	14.8	4.4	0.0	0.0	0.0	0.3	0.1	18.8
Papua New Guinea	30.8	9.4	21.4	6.3	0.0	24.1	0.0	0.5	0.0	3.1
Paraguay	16.1	9.9	6.2	3.9	0.0	0.0	0.0	0.2	0.8	9.0
Peru	24.1	11.4	12.7	2.5	1.4	6.2	0.0	0.3	0.3	7.0
Philippines	30.3	8.4	21.9	2.2	0.5	0.8	0.1	0.3	0.1	22.3
Poland	19.1	12.7	6.4	5.4	1.5	0.3	0.1	0.5	0.2	9.2
Portugal	12.6	13.6	−1.0	5.3	0.0	0.1	0.0	0.2	0.0	4.1
Puerto Rico	..	..	..	..	..	..	..	..	..	..
Qatar	..	..	..	..	..	..	..	..	0.1	..

3.16 Toward a broader measure of savings

	Gross savings	Consumption of fixed capital	Net national savings	Education expenditure	Energy depletion	Mineral depletion	Net forest depletion	Carbon dioxide damage	Particulate emission damage	Adjusted net savings
	% of GNI 2008	% of GNI 2008	% of GNI 2008	% of GNI 2008	% of GNI 2008	% of GNI 2008	% of GNI 2008	% of GNI 2008	% of GNI 2008	% of GNI 2008
Romania	25.0	11.7	13.3	3.4	2.4	0.1	0.0	0.4	0.0	13.7
Russian Federation	32.8	12.4	20.4	3.5	20.5	1.0	0.0	0.9	0.1	1.5
Rwanda	25.4	6.7	18.7	4.6	0.0	0.0	3.0	0.2	0.1	20.1
Saudi Arabia	48.3	12.5	35.9	7.2	43.5	0.0	0.0	0.6	0.7	–1.8
Senegal	18.0	8.6	9.4	4.5	0.0	0.9	0.0	0.3	0.5	12.2
Serbia	..	..	..	..	..	..	..	..	..	..
Sierra Leone	5.5	7.0	–1.6	3.9	0.0	0.5	1.5	0.4	0.8	–1.0
Singapore	47.0	14.1	32.9	2.7	0.0	0.0	0.0	0.3	0.6	34.7
Slovak Republic	–70.9	13.1	–83.9	3.7	0.1	0.0	0.4	0.4	0.0	–81.1
Slovenia	27.0	13.6	13.4	5.3	0.1	0.0	0.2	0.2	0.1	18.1
Somalia	..	..	..	..	..	..	..	..	0.5	..
South Africa	16.1	13.9	2.2	5.1	6.4	2.6	0.5	1.3	0.1	–3.4
Spain	20.6	14.0	6.6	3.9	0.0	0.0	0.0	0.2	0.2	10.1
Sri Lanka	18.4	9.7	8.8	2.6	0.0	0.0	0.4	0.3	0.2	10.4
Sudan	15.9	9.9	6.0	0.9	19.1	0.1	0.0	0.2	0.5	–13.1
Swaziland	10.7	9.6	1.1	6.4	0.0	0.0	0.0	0.3	0.0	7.1
Sweden	27.1	12.5	14.6	6.4	0.0	0.4	0.0	0.1	0.0	20.5
Switzerland	..	13.3	..	4.7	0.0	0.0	0.0	0.1	0.1	..
Syrian Arab Republic	12.6	10.1	2.6	2.6	17.6	1.1	0.0	1.1	0.7	–15.2
Tajikistan	25.5	8.2	17.3	3.2	0.4	0.0	0.0	1.1	0.3	18.8
Tanzania	..	7.6	..	2.4	0.7	5.0	0.0	0.2	0.1	..
Thailand	30.7	10.9	19.8	4.8	5.3	0.0	0.2	0.8	0.2	18.0
Timor-Leste	..	1.2	..	0.9	0.0	0.0	..	0.1	..	..
Togo	..	7.3	..	3.7	0.0	5.2	2.5	0.4	0.1	..
Trinidad and Tobago	41.8	13.1	28.7	4.0	50.5	0.0	0.0	1.2	0.2	–19.2
Tunisia	22.6	11.1	11.5	6.7	5.8	4.7	0.1	0.5	0.1	7.0
Turkey	17.7	11.8	5.9	3.7	0.3	0.1	0.0	0.3	0.6	8.3
Turkmenistan	32.1	10.9	21.2	..	133.3	0.0	..	3.1	0.6	..
Uganda	12.6	7.4	5.2	3.3	0.0	0.0	5.1	0.1	0.0	3.3
Ukraine	20.2	10.5	9.7	5.9	5.3	0.0	0.0	1.6	0.2	8.5
United Arab Emirates	..	..	..	..	..	..	..	..	0.6	..
United Kingdom	14.8	13.7	1.2	5.1	2.1	0.0	0.0	0.2	0.0	3.9
United States	12.6	14.0	–1.4	4.8	1.9	0.1	0.0	0.3	0.1	0.9
Uruguay	18.2	11.9	6.3	2.6	0.0	0.0	0.4	0.2	1.1	7.2
Uzbekistan	40.5	8.5	32.0	9.4	51.1	0.0	0.0	4.0	0.4	–14.1
Venezuela, RB	34.6	11.9	22.7	3.5	18.6	0.6	0.0	0.5	0.0	6.5
Vietnam	30.4	8.8	21.6	2.8	12.9	0.3	0.2	1.0	0.3	9.7
West Bank and Gaza	..	..	..	..	..	..	..	..	..	..
Yemen, Rep.	..	9.4	..	..	22.3	0.0	0.0	0.7	..	..
Zambia	21.4	9.5	11.9	1.3	0.1	13.4	0.0	0.2	0.3	–0.7
Zimbabwe	..	..	..	6.9	..	..	..	..	0.1	..
World	**20.9 w**	**13.0 w**	**7.9 w**	**4.2 w**	**3.9 w**	**0.5 w**	**0.0 w**	**0.4 w**	**0.2 w**	**7.2 w**
Low income	25.3	7.9	17.4	3.4	7.8	1.0	1.0	0.7	0.3	10.1
Middle income	31.6	10.9	20.7	3.3	8.8	1.3	0.1	0.8	0.4	12.6
Lower middle income	41.1	9.6	31.4	2.3	8.1	1.4	0.2	1.1	0.6	22.4
Upper middle income	23.8	12.1	11.8	4.2	9.4	1.3	0.0	0.5	0.2	4.6
Low & middle income	31.4	10.8	20.6	3.3	8.7	1.3	0.1	0.8	0.4	12.5
East Asia & Pacific	47.3	10.1	37.1	2.0	7.2	1.5	0.0	1.1	0.7	28.6
Europe & Central Asia	24.8	12.1	12.7	4.1	12.1	0.6	0.0	0.8	0.2	3.2
Latin America & Carib.	22.4	11.8	10.6	4.4	6.3	1.8	0.0	0.3	0.3	6.3
Middle East & N. Africa	..	10.5	..	4.4	18.6	1.5	0.1	0.7	0.4	..
South Asia	35.0	8.4	26.6	3.0	4.6	1.1	0.8	1.0	0.5	21.6
Sub-Saharan Africa	16.5	9.0	7.6	3.3	14.2	1.3	0.6	0.6	0.4	–6.2
High income	18.5	13.8	4.7	4.6	2.0	0.2	0.0	0.2	0.1	6.7
Euro area	..	14.0	..	4.6	0.3	0.0	0.0	0.2	0.1	..

a. World Bank staff estimate. b. Likely to be overestimated because mineral depletion excludes diamonds. c. Excludes particulate emissions damage.

About the data

Adjusted net savings measure the change in value of a specified set of assets, excluding capital gains. If a country's net savings are positive and the accounting includes a sufficiently broad range of assets, economic theory suggests that the present value of social welfare is increasing. Conversely, persistently negative adjusted net savings indicate that an economy is on an unsustainable path.

The table provides a check on the extent to which today's rents from a number of natural resources and changes in human capital are balanced by net savings, or this generation's bequest to future generations.

Adjusted net savings are derived from standard national accounting measures of gross savings by making four adjustments. First, estimates of capital consumption of produced assets are deducted to obtain net savings. Second, current public expenditures on education are added to net savings (in standard national accounting these expenditures are treated as consumption). Third, estimates of the depletion of a variety of natural resources are deducted to reflect the decline in asset values associated with their extraction and harvest. And fourth, deductions are made for damages from carbon dioxide and particulate emissions.

The exercise treats public education expenditures as an addition to savings. However, because of the wide variability in the effectiveness of public education expenditures, these figures cannot be construed as the value of investments in human capital. A current expenditure of $1 on education does not necessarily yield $1 of human capital. The calculation should also consider private education expenditure, but data are not available for a large number of countries.

While extensive, the accounting of natural resource depletion and pollution costs still has some gaps. Key estimates missing on the resource side include the value of fossil water extracted from aquifers, net depletion of fish stocks, and depletion and degradation of soils. Important pollutants affecting human health and economic assets are excluded because no internationally comparable data are widely available on damage from ground-level ozone or sulfur oxides.

Estimates of resource depletion are based on the "change in real wealth" method described in Hamilton and Ruta (2008), which estimates depletion as the ratio between the total value of the resource and the remaining reserve lifetime. The total value of the resource is the present value of current and future rents from resource extractions. An economic rent represents an excess return to a given factor of production. Natural resources give rise to rents because they are not produced; in contrast, for produced goods and services competitive forces will expand supply until economic profits are driven to zero. For each type of resource and each country, unit resource rents are derived by taking the difference between world prices (to reflect the social opportunity cost of resource extraction) and the average unit extraction or harvest costs (including a "normal" return on capital). Unit rents are then multiplied by the physical quantity extracted or harvested to arrive at total rent. To estimate the value of the resource, rents are assumed to be constant over the life of the resource (the El Serafy approach), and the present value of the rent flow is calculated using a 4 percent social discount rate. For details on the estimation of natural wealth see World Bank (2006).

A positive net depletion figure for forest resources implies that the harvest rate exceeds the rate of natural growth; this is not the same as deforestation, which represents a change in land use (see *Definitions* for table 3.4). In principle, there should be an addition to savings in countries where growth exceeds harvest, but empirical estimates suggest that most of this net growth is in forested areas that cannot currently be exploited economically. Because the depletion estimates reflect only timber values, they ignore all the external and nontimber benefits associated with standing forests.

Pollution damage from emissions of carbon dioxide is calculated as the marginal social cost per unit multiplied by the increase in the stock of carbon dioxide. The unit damage figure represents the present value of global damage to economic assets and to human welfare over the time the unit of pollution remains in the atmosphere.

Pollution damage from particulate emissions is estimated by valuing the human health effects from exposure to particulate matter pollution in urban areas. The estimates are calculated as willingness to pay to avoid illness and death from cardiopulmonary disease and lung cancer in adults and acute respiratory infections in children that is attributable to particulate emissions.

For a detailed note on methodology, see www.worldbank.org/data.

Definitions

• **Gross savings** are the difference between gross national income and public and private consumption, plus net current transfers. • **Consumption of fixed capital** is the replacement value of capital used up in production. • **Net national savings** are gross savings minus consumption of fixed capital. • **Education expenditure** is public current operating expenditures in education, including wages and salaries and excluding capital investments in buildings and equipment. • **Energy depletion** is the ratio of the value of the stock of energy resources to the remaining reserve lifetime (capped at 25 years). It covers coal, crude oil, and natural gas. • **Mineral depletion** is the ratio of the value of the stock of mineral resources to the remaining reserve lifetime (capped at 25 years). It covers tin, gold, lead, zinc, iron, copper, nickel, silver, bauxite, and phosphate. • **Net forest depletion** is unit resource rents times the excess of roundwood harvest over natural growth. • **Carbon dioxide damage** is estimated at $20 per ton of carbon (the unit damage in 1995 U.S. dollars) times tons of carbon emitted. • **Particulate emission damage** is the willingness to pay to avoid illness and death attributable to particulate emissions.• **Adjusted net savings** are net savings plus education expenditure minus energy depletion, mineral depletion, net forest depletion, and carbon dioxide and particulate emissions damage.

Data sources

Data on gross savings are from World Bank national accounts data files (see table 4.8). Data on consumption of fixed capital are from the United Nations Statistics Division's *National Accounts Statistics: Main Aggregates and Detailed Tables, 1997,* extrapolated to 2008. Data on education expenditure are from the United Nations Statistics Division's *Statistical Yearbook 1997* and from the United Nations Educational, Scientific, and Cultural Organization Institute for Statistics online database. Missing data are estimated by World Bank staff. Data on energy, mineral, and forest depletion are estimates based on sources and methods in Kunte and others' "Estimating National Wealth: Methodology and Results" (1998). Data on carbon dioxide damage are from Fankhauser's *Valuing Climate Change: The Economics of the Greenhouse* (1995). Data on particulate emission damage are from Pandey and others' "The Human Costs of Air Pollution: New Estimates for Developing Countries" (2006). The conceptual underpinnings of the savings measure appear in Hamilton and Clemens' "Genuine Savings Rates in Developing Countries" (1999).

ECONOMY

conomic growth is not explicitly targeted in the Millennium Development Goals (MDGs), yet income per capita measures are highly correlated with widely used indicators of poverty, health, and education. As countries become richer, poverty rates generally fall (figure 4a). During 2000–08 low- and middle-income countries averaged economic growth of 6.2 percent a year, and during 1999–2005 the number of people living on less than $1.25 a day fell by 325 million. Economic growth is clearly necessary for achieving the MDG targets.

The 2008 financial crisis and ensuing global recession have substantially increased the challenge of meeting the MDG targets. In contrast to the record growth in 2000–07, the global economy grew only 1.9 percent in 2008 and declined an estimated 2.2 percent in 2009. Some 64 million more people will be living in extreme poverty by 2010 because of the crisis. The effects on human welfare may be costly and long-lasting.

Relationship between economic growth and development outcomes

Income per capita is highly correlated with many development indicators, such as secondary school enrollment, access to water and sanitation, births attended by skilled staff, total fertility rate, children immunized against measles, malnutrition prevalence, and infant mortality. The correlation coefficients—measuring the degree of relationship—between gross national income (GNI) per capita and selected nonmonetary measures of welfare are generally high using either the World Bank Atlas method for calculating GNI or purchasing power parity–converted GNI (figure 4b). The highest correlation is between GNI per capita and the poverty headcount ratio ($2 a day).

The global economy in 2009

The 2008 financial crisis led to a global economic recession in 2009, the most severe in 50 years. GDP fell 3.2 percent in high-income economies and grew only 1.2 percent in developing economies (figure 4c). The effects of the crisis were transmitted from high-income economies to developing economies as exports, private capital flows, commodity prices, and workers' remittances declined.

Global trade, whose growth had slowed to 3 percent in 2008, declined an estimated 12 percent in 2009 (figure 4d). Developing economies' trade shrank an estimated 9 percent in 2009. Private capital flows to developing economies—after peaking at

nearly $1 trillion in 2007—dropped to $765 billion in 2008 and are estimated to have been much lower in 2009 (figure 4e). Workers' remittances were more

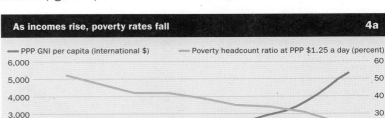

As incomes rise, poverty rates fall   **4a**

PPP GNI per capita (international $)   Poverty headcount ratio at PPP $1.25 a day (percent)

Note: PPP is purchasing power parity.
Source: World Development Indicators data files.

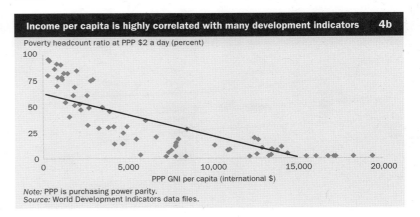

Income per capita is highly correlated with many development indicators   **4b**

Poverty headcount ratio at PPP $2 a day (percent)

PPP GNI per capita (international $)

Note: PPP is purchasing power parity.
Source: World Development Indicators data files.

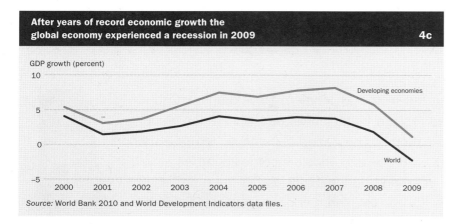

After years of record economic growth the global economy experienced a recession in 2009   **4c**

GDP growth (percent)

Developing economies

World

Source: World Bank 2010 and World Development Indicators data files.

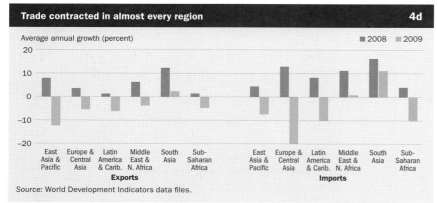

Trade contracted in almost every region   **4d**

Average annual growth (percent)   ■ 2008   ■ 2009

East Asia & Pacific | Europe & Central Asia | Latin America & Carib. | Middle East & N. Africa | South Asia | Sub-Saharan Africa

Exports

East Asia & Pacific | Europe & Central Asia | Latin America & Carib. | Middle East & N. Africa | South Asia | Sub-Saharan Africa

Imports

Source: World Development Indicators data files.

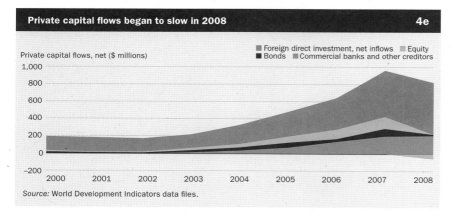

Private capital flows began to slow in 2008   **4e**

Private capital flows, net ($ millions)   ■ Foreign direct investment, net inflows   ■ Equity   ■ Bonds   ■ Commercial banks and other creditors

Source: World Development Indicators data files.

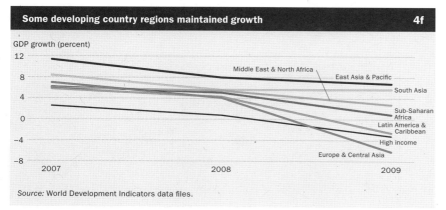

Some developing country regions maintained growth   **4f**

GDP growth (percent)

Middle East & North Africa

East Asia & Pacific

South Asia

Sub-Saharan Africa

Latin America & Caribbean

High income

Europe & Central Asia

Source: World Development Indicators data files.

resilient—falling 6.1 percent to $317 billion in 2009—but varied by country.

Among developing country regions Europe and Central Asia fared the worst, as GDP fell 6.2 percent (figure 4f). Severe economic adjustments were necessary as private capital flows, which had financed large current account deficits, were cut from $97 billion in 2007 to $50 billion in 2008. Latin America and the Caribbean economies contracted 2.6 percent, with Mexico—relying almost solely on the U.S. market for its exports—the worst off. China and India managed to continue growing at nearly the same rate as before the crisis, but other economies in Asia did not do as well. Growth in the Middle East and North Africa dropped to 2.3 percent on lower oil prices and exports to Europe.

Sub-Saharan Africa barely grew, hurt by falling export commodity prices, falling remittances, lower tourism revenues, and declining private capital flows. Home to 30 of the 43 low-income economies, Sub-Saharan Africa has been subject to the most severe consequences of the crisis. Low-income households, at risk of being pushed into poverty, have suffered from deteriorating health and lost education opportunities.

Global imbalances are easing

The structural imbalances in the global economy predating the crisis eased as the current account balances of the largest surplus and deficit economies moderated (figure 4g). The crisis has given impetus to rebalancing the economies of China and the United States. China focused on domestic sources of growth in its 11th five-year plan, and in the United States the *2010 Economic Report of the President* proposed a transition from consumption-driven growth to an emphasis on investment and exports.

Consumers in high-income economies have reduced spending, and imports have declined faster than exports. In 2008 and 2009 private consumption expenditures declined in the United States.

In China imports outpaced exports, driven by domestic demand as the government increased spending on infrastructure, social programs, and environmental protection. The result: China's current account surplus dropped from its peak of 11.0 percent of GDP in 2007 to 6.6 percent in the first half of 2009. And the U.S. current account deficit was more than halved, from −6.0 percent in 2006 to −2.8 percent in the second quarter of 2009.

New risks have emerged

If household consumption in high-income economies continues to decline, new drivers of global economic growth will be crucial. China and India might become new drivers, but large differences between the scale and structure of their economies and of the U.S. economy will delay their replacing the U.S. role in the global economy. For example, U.S. household consumption was more than $10 trillion in 2008, four times that of China and India combined. Developing economies have growth potential because they have room for productivity gains from increased investment. High-income economies face overcapacity that could limit recovery, but they are investing in transforming their economies through technological innovations to protect the environment and combat global warming.

Although the world avoided the most catastrophic potential effects of the crisis, the resulting conditions require careful navigation and eventual resolution. Fiscal deficits and public debt have increased substantially in many high-income economies (figures 4h and 4i). In some cases high deficits and debt levels raised perceptions of sovereign default risk, indicated by the mounting cost of credit default swaps (figure 4j).

Rising public deficits and debt are accompanied by increased uncertainty in measuring risk when debt includes derivatives. Private corporations took on high levels of debt in the run-up to the financial crisis. They believed—as did creditors, rating agencies, and regulators—that complex financial instruments, or derivatives, provided a hedge against default. Derivatives also play a role in public debt. For example, governments can use interest and currency swaps to raise capital in return for increased future payments. But such derivatives are not included in traditional measures of indebtedness.

Governments must maintain reasonable budget balances and debt levels to keep the confidence of taxpayers and creditors. Without fiscal credibility, creditors will refuse to continue lending. To reduce deficits, governments must raise revenues or reduce spending. Economic expansion can boost revenues through higher tax receipts, but if expansion is too slow, governments must resort to the unpopular alternatives of increasing tax rates and cutting spending—as in the United Kingdom and the United States, where buoyant revenues created by structural imbalances cannot be restored by returning to the unsustainable conditions of 2007.

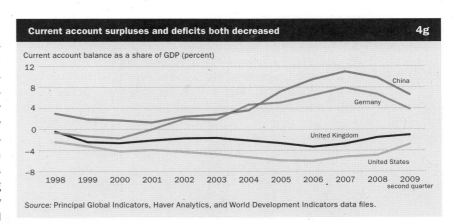

Current account surpluses and deficits both decreased   **4g**

Current account balance as a share of GDP (percent)

Source: Principal Global Indicators, Haver Analytics, and World Development Indicators data files.

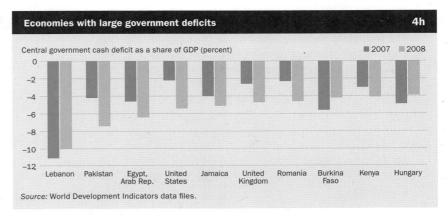

Economies with large government deficits   **4h**

Central government cash deficit as a share of GDP (percent)   ■ 2007 ■ 2008

Source: World Development Indicators data files.

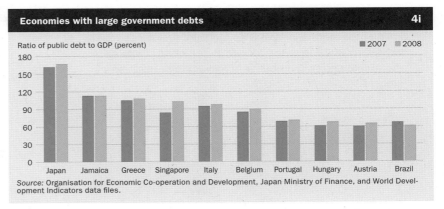

Economies with large government debts   **4i**

Ratio of public debt to GDP (percent)   ■ 2007 ■ 2008

Source: Organisation for Economic Co-operation and Development, Japan Ministry of Finance, and World Development Indicators data files.

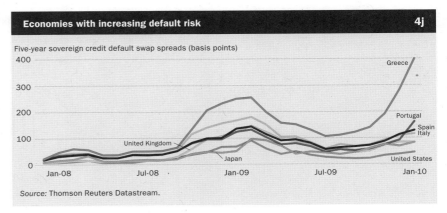

Economies with increasing default risk   **4j**

Five-year sovereign credit default swap spreads (basis points)

Source: Thomson Reuters Datastream.

Growth in GDP

Quarterly data for selected major economies in each developing country region show economic contraction in Brazil, the Russian Federation, and South Africa and slowing output in China, Egypt, and India. The contractions and slowdowns bottom out around the first quarter of 2009.

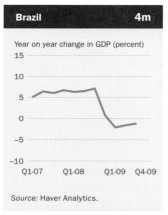

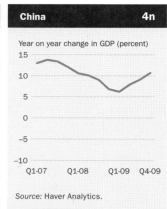

Growth in industrial production

The industrial sector shrank in all the large developing countries shown here except China. The low point at the end of 2008 was followed by improvements throughout 2009.

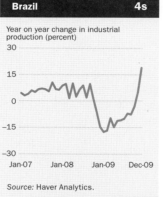

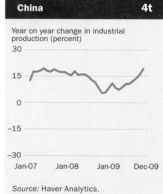

Lending and inflation rates

Inflation accelerated in 2008 as food and fuel prices rose but fell in 2009 with the slowdown in output. India was the exception, as food prices remained high because of drought.

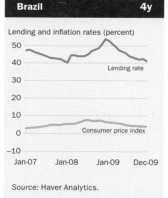

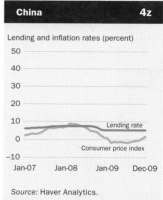

Central government debt

These countries have increased public spending without substantially increasing debt levels.

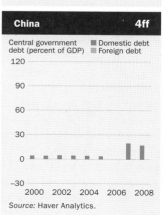

Arab Republic of Egypt 4o

Year on year change in GDP (percent)

15
10
5
0
−5
−10

Q1-07 Q1-08 Q1-09 Q4-09

Source: Haver Analytics.

India 4p

Year on year change in GDP (percent)

15
10
5
0
−5
−10

Q1-07 Q1-08 Q1-09 Q4-09

Source: Haver Analytics.

Russian Federation 4q

Year on year change in GDP (percent)

15
10
5
0
−5
−10

Q1-07 Q1-08 Q1-09 Q4-09

Source: Haver Analytics.

South Africa 4r

Year on year change in GDP (percent)

15
10
5
0
−5
−10

Q1-07 Q1-08 Q1-09 Q4-09

Source: Haver Analytics.

Arab Republic of Egypt 4u

Year on year change in industrial production (percent)

30
15
0
−15
−30

Jan-07 Jan-08 Jan-09 Dec-09

Source: Haver Analytics.

India 4v

Year on year change in industrial production (percent)

30
15
0
−15
−30

Jan-07 Jan-08 Jan-09 Dec-09

Source: Haver Analytics.

Russian Federation 4w

Year on year change in industrial production (percent)

30
15
0
−15
−30

Jan-07 Jan-08 Jan-09 Dec-09

Source: Haver Analytics.

South Africa 4x

Year on year change in industrial production (percent)

30
15
0
−15
−30

Jan-07 Jan-08 Jan-09 Dec-09

Source: Haver Analytics.

Arab Republic of Egypt 4aa

Lending and inflation rates (percent)

50
40
30
20
10
0
−10

Consumer price index
Lending rate

Jan-07 Jan-08 Jan-09 Dec-09

Source: Haver Analytics.

India 4bb

Lending and inflation rates (percent)

50
40
30
20
10
0
−10

Lending rate
Consumer price index

Jan-07 Jan-08 Jan-09 Dec-09

Source: Haver Analytics.

Russian Federation 4cc

Lending and inflation rates (percent)

50
40
30
20
10
0
−10

Lending rate
Consumer price index

Jan-07 Jan-08 Jan-09 Dec-09

Source: Haver Analytics.

South Africa 4dd

Lending and inflation rates (percent)

50
40
30
20
10
0
−10

Lending rate
Consumer price index

Jan-07 Jan-08 Jan-09 Dec-09

Source: Haver Analytics.

Arab Republic of Egypt 4gg

Central government debt (percent of GDP)   ■ Domestic debt ■ Foreign debt

120
90
60
30
0
−30

Q1-07 Q1-08 Q1-09 Q4-09

Source: Haver Analytics.

India 4hh

Central government debt (percent of GDP)   ■ Domestic debt ■ Foreign debt

120
90
60
30
0
−30

Q1-07 Q1-08 Q1-09 Q4-09

Source: Haver Analytics.

Russian Federation 4ii

Central government debt (percent of GDP)   ■ Domestic debt ■ Foreign debt

120
90
60
30
0
−30

Q1-07 Q1-08 Q1-09 Q4-09

Source: Haver Analytics.

South Africa 4jj

Central government debt (percent of GDP)   ■ Domestic debt ■ Foreign debt

120
90
60
30
0
−30

Q1-07 Q1-08 Q1-09 Q4-09

Source: Haver Analytics.

Merchandise trade

China's imports have declined less than exports, resulting in a smaller trade surplus. For most countries trade has declined in absolute terms as well as relative to GDP.

Brazil 4kk

Percent of GDP

Merchandise exports

Merchandise imports

Source: Haver Analytics.

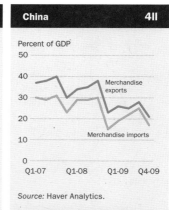

China 4ll

Percent of GDP

Merchandise exports

Merchandise imports

Source: Haver Analytics.

Equity price indexes

Equity prices in large developing countries have rebounded from their lows in late 2008 as investors regained confidence on growing signs of economic recovery.

Brazil 4qq

MSCI equity price index
(January 1, 2008 = 100)

Source: MSCI Barra and Thomson Reuters Datastream.

China 4rr

MSCI equity price index
(January 1, 2008 = 100)

Source: MSCI Barra and Thomson Reuters Datastream.

Bond spreads

The cost of borrowing for large developing countries has declined after rising in reaction to the financial crisis but remains above precrisis levels.

Brazil 4ww

Spreads over U.S. Treasury notes
(basis points)

Corporate—CEMBI

Sovereign EMBI-Global

Source: JP Morgan Chase, Bloomberg, and Thomson Reuters Datastream.

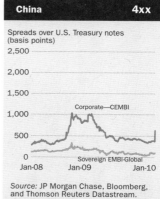

China 4xx

Spreads over U.S. Treasury notes
(basis points)

Corporate—CEMBI

Sovereign EMBI-Global

Source: JP Morgan Chase, Bloomberg, and Thomson Reuters Datastream.

Financing through international capital markets

Capital flows to large developing countries rebounded somewhat in 2008 but remain below their peak levels of 2007.

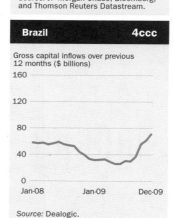

Brazil 4ccc

Gross capital inflows over previous
12 months ($ billions)

Source: Dealogic.

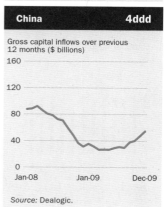

China 4ddd

Gross capital inflows over previous
12 months ($ billions)

Source: Dealogic.

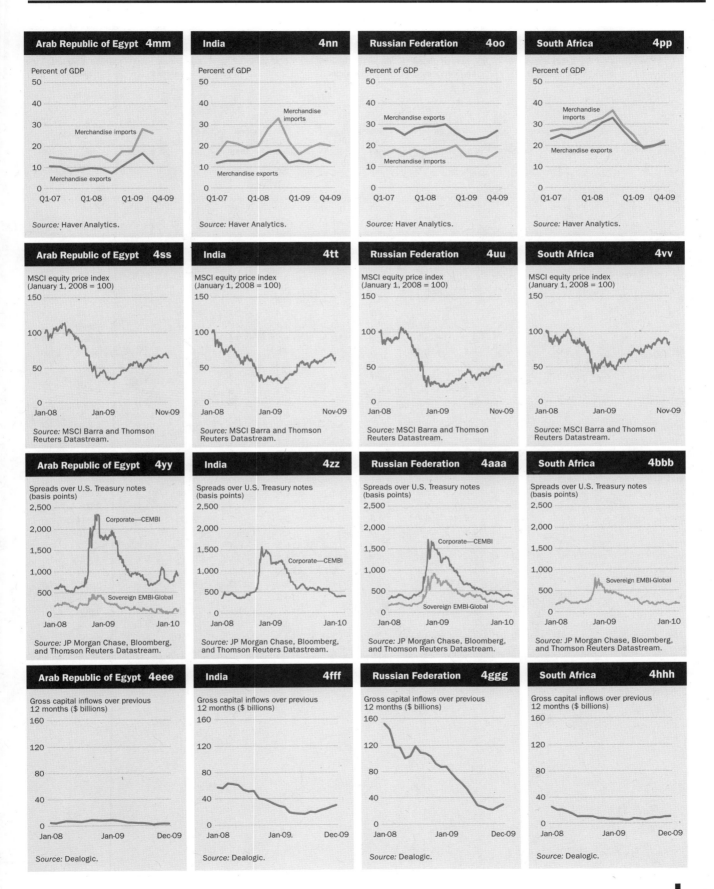

Arab Republic of Egypt   4mm

Percent of GDP

Merchandise imports

Merchandise exports

Q1-07   Q1-08   Q1-09   Q4-09

Source: Haver Analytics.

India   4nn

Percent of GDP

Merchandise imports

Merchandise exports

Q1-07   Q1-08   Q1-09   Q4-09

Source: Haver Analytics.

Russian Federation   4oo

Percent of GDP

Merchandise exports

Merchandise imports

Q1-07   Q1-08   Q1-09   Q4-09

Source: Haver Analytics.

South Africa   4pp

Percent of GDP

Merchandise imports

Merchandise exports

Q1-07   Q1-08   Q1-09   Q4-09

Source: Haver Analytics.

Arab Republic of Egypt   4ss

MSCI equity price index
(January 1, 2008 = 100)

Jan-08   Jan-09   Nov-09

Source: MSCI Barra and Thomson
Reuters Datastream.

India   4tt

MSCI equity price index
(January 1, 2008 = 100)

Jan-08   Jan-09   Nov-09

Source: MSCI Barra and Thomson
Reuters Datastream.

Russian Federation   4uu

MSCI equity price index
(January 1, 2008 = 100)

Jan-08   Jan-09   Nov-09

Source: MSCI Barra and Thomson
Reuters Datastream.

South Africa   4vv

MSCI equity price index
(January 1, 2008 = 100)

Jan-08   Jan-09   Nov-09

Source: MSCI Barra and Thomson
Reuters Datastream.

Arab Republic of Egypt   4yy

Spreads over U.S. Treasury notes
(basis points)

Corporate—CEMBI

Sovereign EMBI-Global

Jan-08   Jan-09   Jan-10

Source: JP Morgan Chase, Bloomberg,
and Thomson Reuters Datastream.

India   4zz

Spreads over U.S. Treasury notes
(basis points)

Corporate—CEMBI

Jan-08   Jan-09   Jan-10

Source: JP Morgan Chase, Bloomberg,
and Thomson Reuters Datastream.

Russian Federation   4aaa

Spreads over U.S. Treasury notes
(basis points)

Corporate—CEMBI

Sovereign EMBI-Global

Jan-08   Jan-09   Jan-10

Source: JP Morgan Chase, Bloomberg,
and Thomson Reuters Datastream.

South Africa   4bbb

Spreads over U.S. Treasury notes
(basis points)

Sovereign EMBI-Global

Jan-08   Jan-09   Jan-10

Source: JP Morgan Chase, Bloomberg,
and Thomson Reuters Datastream.

Arab Republic of Egypt   4eee

Gross capital inflows over previous
12 months ($ billions)

Jan-08   Jan-09   Dec-09

Source: Dealogic.

India   4fff

Gross capital inflows over previous
12 months ($ billions)

Jan-08   Jan-09   Dec-09

Source: Dealogic.

Russian Federation   4ggg

Gross capital inflows over previous
12 months ($ billions)

Jan-08   Jan-09   Dec-09

Source: Dealogic.

South Africa   4hhh

Gross capital inflows over previous
12 months ($ billions)

Jan-08   Jan-09   Dec-09

Source: Dealogic.

4.a

Recent economic performance of selected developing countries

	Gross domestic product		Exports of goods and services		Imports of goods and services		GDP deflator		Current account balance		Gross international reserves	
	average annual % growth		average annual % growth		average annual % growth		average annual % growth		% of GDP		$ millions	months of import coverage
	2008	2009[a]	2008	2009[a]	2008	2009[a]	2008	2009[a]	2008	2009[a]	2009[a]	2009[a]
Algeria	3.0	2.1	1.6	−3.0	6.6	..	10.8	..	..	..	149,347	34.4
Angola	13.2	0.2	..	..	..	..	23.9	..	7.5	..	13,349	5.6
Argentina[b]	6.8	−1.5	1.2	..	14.1	..	19.1	13.1	2.2	..	46,190	..
Armenia	6.8	−15.6	−13.1	−32.8	7.3	−21.0	8.4	1.5	−11.6	−12.5	2,003	7.6
Azerbaijan	10.8	2.1	10.4	2.8	13.2	−5.3	20.9	−17.8	35.7	22.9	5,364	6.2
Bangladesh	6.2	5.9	7.0	12.2	−2.1	15.2	8.8	6.4	1.3	2.8	10,225	5.2
Belarus	10.0	−1.0	1.7	−6.1	14.6	−8.7	20.5	9.8	−8.6	1.8	4,872	1.2
Bolivia	6.1	0.9	2.2	−5.9	9.4	3.1	10.4	−5.6	12.1	−0.1	7,634	15.6
Bosnia and Herzegovina	5.4	−4.0	4.2	−3.5	−1.9	−4.5	7.8	1.6	−14.9	−9.4	6,269	5.6
Botswana	2.9	−1.8	2.5	0.4	11.8	6.5	17.0	−10.6	3.7	−7.6	12,438	19.5
Brazil	5.1	−0.5	−0.6	11.4	18.5	8.1	5.9	4.2	−1.8	−1.0	237,424	13.4
Bulgaria	6.0	−6.3	2.9	−9.2	4.9	−12.8	11.4	2.7	−25.2	−11.6	17,198	7.1
Cameroon	3.9	4.1	4.7	6.1	5.1	3.4	1.7	−2.6	−2.2	−4.0	4,590	7.2
Chile	3.2	−1.6	3.1	−4.7	12.9	−13.8	0.2	−0.8	−2.0	1.5	25,282	5.6
China	9.0	8.7	−9.6	−12.1	−13.4	−5.7	7.2	0.3	9.8	7.4	2,544,706	21.6
Colombia	2.5	−0.2	7.0	6.6	9.8	9.5	8.3	3.5	−2.8	−2.9	24,760	7.3
Congo, Dem. Rep.	6.2	2.7	−3.9	−32.9	15.7	−17.4	19.4	32.7	..	−21.0	..	..
Costa Rica	2.6	−1.5	−1.8	0.6	4.3	−12.4	12.1	8.9	−9.2	−3.6	4,066	3.6
Côte d'Ivoire	2.2	3.6	−8.1	9.3	−5.4	11.0	8.1	1.3	2.1	1.6	..	..
Croatia	2.4	−5.8	1.7	−4.0	3.6	−5.9	6.4	3.5	−9.0	−7.4	14,895	5.4
Dominican Republic	5.3	0.5	−1.8	−21.8	0.0	−35.9	9.8	3.9	−9.7	−6.1	2,886	2.9
Ecuador	6.5	−1.0	3.3	−3.8	10.2	3.3	12.1	2.7	2.0	−1.5	2,920	2.0
Egypt, Arab Rep.	7.2	4.7	28.8	−12.8	26.3	−17.9	11.8	10.8	−0.9	−2.3	45,757	6.3
El Salvador	2.5	−2.5	6.8	−14.6	4.8	−14.8	5.9	2.8	−7.2	−1.8	2,882	4.1
Gabon	2.3	−1.0	0.3	−4.9	3.1	−2.8	14.7	−19.0	..	2.8	..	..
Ghana	7.3	4.5	2.0	4.4	13.3	1.7	16.9	17.2	−21.3	−6.9	3,050	2.8
Guatemala	4.0	0.6	3.0	−4.2	−3.4	..	8.5	2.4	−4.8	−1.7	4,976	4.8
Honduras	4.0	−2.0	2.6	−6.7	8.8	−7.5	9.8	5.3	−14.8	−9.2	3,004	2.9
India	6.1	6.8	12.8	−15.8	17.9	−17.2	6.2	3.6	−3.1	−2.7	266,166	9.0
Indonesia	6.1	4.5	9.5	−9.7	10.0	−15.0	18.3	8.4	0.0	2.0	63,692	8.7
Jordan	7.9	3.2	−11.3	−8.0	3.3	−14.1	15.7	4.1	−11.3	−10.1	11,132	8.6
Kazakhstan	3.2	1.2	1.0	6.9	8.9	9.1	21.1	−4.0	4.9	−3.1	20,844	6.1
Kenya	1.7	3.0	3.6	1.6	5.3	4.5	13.1	17.0	−6.5	−6.6	3,127	3.0
Latvia	−4.6	−18.4	−1.3	..	−13.6	..	15.2	..	−13.3	..	6,645	..
Lebanon	8.5	6.0	14.8	10.0	28.4	3.8	7.7	4.0	−10.4	−13.9	29,609	14.8
Lesotho	3.9	2.1	−22.0	−17.1	7.5	−5.9	9.6	8.7	15.1	−8.5	1,323	8.0
Lithuania	3.0	−15.0	..	−29.3	..	−15.5	10.3	..	−11.9	..	6,463	..
Macedonia, FYR	5.0	−1.3	−9.2	−12.8	−1.0	−10.6	7.2	1.1	−12.7	−9.4	2,063	3.9

	Gross domestic product		Exports of goods and services		Imports of goods and services		GDP deflator		Current account balance		Gross international reserves	
	average annual % growth		average annual % growth		average annual % growth		average annual % growth		% of GDP		$ millions	months of import coverage
	2008	2009[a]	2008	2009[a]	2008	2009[a]	2008	2009[a]	2008	2009[a]	2009[a]	2009[a]
Malawi	9.7	6.9	−5.4	−5.4	−4.6	−4.6	8.9	10.0	..	..	..	..
Malaysia	4.6	−1.7	..	−10.1	..	−12.5	10.3	−7.1	17.5	15.3	95,496	6.4
Mauritius	4.5	2.0	2.6	−12.6	2.0	−5.4	7.6	3.7	−10.5	−8.8	2,186	5.0
Mexico	1.8	−6.5	1.0	−15.9	4.1	−21.0	6.5	5.4	−1.5	−0.6	99,604	4.8
Moldova	7.2	−9.0	−11.4	−22.5	−6.1	−36.4	9.7	5.4	−16.3	−21.2	1,480	2.5
Morocco	5.6	5.0	−1.1	−9.4	10.9	−3.2	5.9	2.5	−5.1	−6.0	22,836	7.3
Montenegro	7.7	5.1	7.7	5.1	7.7	5.1	10.4	−5.1	−33.1	−20.3	573	2.9
Nicaragua	3.5	4.0	..	..	..	..	16.8	11.2	−22.9	−22.7	1,573	3.2
Nigeria	6.0	2.9	..	..	..	..	11.0	−2.0	19.0	7.1	102,614	12.1
Pakistan	2.0	3.7	−5.3	9.0	3.6	−9.2	16.3	22.7	−9.4	−5.1	11,434	3.6
Panama	9.2	1.5	9.2	−3.1	9.2	11.9	8.5	5.3	−11.6	−9.4	2,492	1.3
Papua New Guinea	6.6	3.9	..	..	..	..	11.6	−3.3	..	−6.7	2,620	4.9
Paraguay	5.8	−3.8	11.6	−14.9	18.0	−11.5	7.1	3.0	−2.2	−0.6	3,840	6.5
Peru	9.8	1.0	8.2	0.2	19.9	−8.9	2.3	3.0	−3.2	−3.0	32,074	14.3
Philippines	3.8	0.9	−1.9	−14.2	2.4	−5.8	7.5	2.3	2.3	3.4	38,152	5.1
Poland	4.9	1.7	7.2	−10.5	8.2	−13.9	3.0	3.5	−5.1	−2.0	76,105	4.5
Romania	9.4	−8.5	19.4	−11.8	17.5	−24.6	11.6	7.0	−11.9	−5.3	42,353	5.9
Russian Federation	5.6	−7.9	0.2	−4.9	17.7	−26.6	19.2	10.0	6.1	3.8	417,773	19.8
Senegal	3.3	1.5	6.2	−11.2	6.9	−10.5	6.0	2.2	..	..	2,227	3.8
Serbia	1.2	−3.4	11.6	−25.3	11.4	−33.1	12.7	−1.1	−17.7	−27.4	14,792	5.6
Slovak Republic	6.2	−4.7	3.2	..	3.3	..	2.9	0.0	−6.5	−0.9	..	..
South Africa	3.1	−1.8	1.7	−9.2	2.2	..	10.8	8.0	−7.3	−5.3	35,458	4.8
Sri Lanka	6.0	3.5	..	..	..	..	16.3	4.0	−9.3	−1.4	5,578	4.2
Sudan	8.3	9.7	23.0	..	0.3	..	15.8	4.2	−2.3	−7.5	..	..
Swaziland	2.4	0.4	−12.3	2.9	1.4	3.5	10.1	8.0	..	−6.9	660	2.7
Syrian Arab Republic	5.2	5.7	−2.4	5.6	2.5	6.4	20.5	−14.4	..	−1.1	6,512	3.7
Thailand	2.5	−2.3	5.1	−12.7	8.5	−21.8	3.8	2.0	0.0	7.7	135,631	6.4
Tunisia	4.5	3.3	3.5	−1.6	8.3	6.7	5.9	3.5	−4.2	−3.5	11,069	5.5
Turkey	0.9	−6.0	2.3	..	−3.8	..	11.7	6.0	−5.6	−1.8	71,078	6.2
Uganda	9.5	2.1	7.3	9.3	28.1	12.3	6.3	2.5	−5.9	..	2,664	5.5
Ukraine	2.1	−15.0	2.5	−16.0	12.5	−32.8	29.1	13.0	−7.1	−1.7	25,605	3.2
Uruguay	8.9	1.5	10.5	3.8	19.9	1.1	8.8	8.5	−3.8	0.1	8,029	11.2
Uzbekistan	9.0	7.0	15.8	13.6	20.0	13.4	19.9	19.9	..	12.8	2,747	3.1
Venezuela, RB	4.8	−3.5	−2.8	−4.4	3.8	−19.1	31.3	24.0	11.9	3.0	22,339	5.8
Vietnam	6.2	5.3	5.0	−11.6	7.6	−10.9	21.7	5.8	−11.8	−5.1	..	..
Zambia	6.0	4.0	20.7	21.5	15.3	15.6	10.8	7.9	−7.3	..	2,562	2.4

a. Data are preliminary estimates. b. Private analysts estimate that consumer price index inflation was considerably higher for 2007–09 and believe that GDP volume growth has been significantly lower than official reports indicate since the last quarter of 2008.
Source: World Development Indicators data files.

	Gross domestic product		Agriculture		Industry		Manufacturing		Services	
	average annual % growth		average annual % growth		average annual % growth		average annual % growth		average annual % growth	
	1990–2000	2000–08	1990–2000	2000–08	1990–2000	2000–08	1990–2000	2000–08	1990–2000	2000–08
Afghanistan	..	11.8	..	4.4	..	17.5	..	..	..	15.4
Albania	3.8	5.4	4.3	1.4	−0.5	4.0	..	−0.2	6.9	8.3
Algeria	1.9	4.3	3.6	5.3	1.8	3.5	−2.1	2.4	1.8	5.3
Angola[a]	1.6	13.5	−1.4	13.6	4.4	13.9	−0.3	20.7	−2.2	12.4
Argentina	4.3	5.3[b]	3.5	3.7	3.8	6.4	2.7	6.0	4.5	4.4
Armenia	−1.9	12.4	0.5	7.3	−7.8	15.1	−4.3	5.7	6.4	13.4
Australia	3.6	3.3	3.1	0.0	2.7	2.6	1.8	1.3	4.2	3.7
Austria	2.4	2.2	−0.1	0.9	2.5	3.1	2.5	3.3	2.5	2.1
Azerbaijan	−6.3	18.1	−1.7	5.4	−2.1	24.2	−15.7	10.8	−2.7	10.6
Bangladesh	4.8	5.8	2.9	3.2	7.3	7.9	7.2	7.9	4.5	6.0
Belarus	−1.6	8.6	−4.0	5.5	−1.8	12.6	−0.7	11.6	−0.4	6.0
Belgium	2.1	2.0	2.7	−2.7	1.8	1.4	3.1	1.1	1.9	2.2
Benin[a]	4.8	3.9	5.8	4.6	4.1	3.8	5.8	2.7	4.2	3.2
Bolivia	4.0	4.1	2.9	3.2	4.1	5.1	3.8	4.3	4.3	3.2
Bosnia and Herzegovina	..	5.4	..	5.2	..	7.4	..	8.3	..	4.6
Botswana	6.0	4.5	−1.2	−1.0	5.8	4.2	4.4	3.5	7.8	5.2
Brazil	2.7	3.6	3.6	4.2	2.4	3.2	2.0	3.1	3.8	3.8
Bulgaria	−1.8	5.8	3.0	−3.8	−5.0	6.1	..	6.7	−5.2	6.4
Burkina Faso	5.5	5.6	5.9	6.2	5.9	7.3	5.9	6.3	3.9	5.5
Burundi	−2.9	2.9	−1.9	−1.5	−4.3	−6.2	−8.7	..	−2.8	10.4
Cambodia	7.0	9.8	3.7	5.6	14.3	13.3	18.6	12.9	7.1	10.2
Cameroon	1.7	3.5	5.4	3.4	−0.9	−0.4	1.4	5.8	0.2	6.2
Canada	3.1	2.5	1.1	2.3	3.2	1.5	..	0.1	..	..
Central African Republic	2.0	0.5	3.8	0.3	0.7	−0.4	−0.2	−0.1	0.2	−2.5
Chad	2.2	11.9	4.9	2.2	0.6	50.7	..	..	0.8	9.1
Chile	6.6	4.4	2.2	5.6	5.6	3.2	4.4	3.8	6.9	4.9
China[a]	10.6	10.4	4.1	4.4	13.7	11.7	12.9	11.6	11.0	10.7
Hong Kong SAR, China	3.6	5.2	..	−3.3	..	−2.6	..	−3.1	..	5.3
Colombia	2.8	4.9	−2.6	3.0	1.5	4.9	−2.5	5.3	4.1	4.8
Congo, Dem. Rep.	−4.9	5.2	1.4	1.5	−8.0	9.5	−8.7	6.3	−13.0	11.5
Congo, Rep.[a]	1.0	3.9	0.7	..	1.7	..	−2.4	..	−0.7	..
Costa Rica	5.3	5.4	4.1	4.0	6.2	5.8	6.8	5.5	4.7	5.7
Côte d'Ivoire[a]	3.2	0.5	3.5	1.3	6.3	−0.7	5.5	−2.3	2.0	0.7
Croatia	0.5	4.5	−2.1	1.7	−2.3	5.1	−3.5	3.7	1.9	4.7
Cuba[a]	4.2	..	..	..	..	..	..	..	..	..
Czech Republic	1.1	4.6	0.0	0.1	0.2	6.6	4.3	8.3	1.2	4.3
Denmark	2.7	1.6	4.6	−3.5	2.5	0.4	2.2	0.4	2.7	1.7
Dominican Republic[a]	6.3	5.4	1.9	2.9	7.1	2.6	7.0	3.0	5.9	7.0
Ecuador	1.9	5.0	−1.7	4.9	2.6	4.9	1.5	5.5	2.4	3.1
Egypt, Arab Rep.	4.4	4.7	3.1	3.3	5.1	5.3	6.3	4.5	4.1	5.2
El Salvador	4.8	2.9	1.2	3.9	5.1	2.3	5.2	2.4	4.0	3.0
Eritrea	5.7	1.3	1.5	9.3	15.0	0.8	10.6	−4.9	5.7	0.1
Estonia	0.5	7.4	..	−2.9	−14.6	8.6	7.7	8.9	..	7.0
Ethiopia	3.8	8.2	2.6	6.8	4.1	9.2	3.9	6.7	5.2	9.5
Finland	2.7	3.0	−1.1	1.2	4.1	4.7	6.4	5.4	2.5	1.8
France	1.9	1.8	2.0	−0.1	1.1	1.0	..	0.8	2.2	2.1
Gabon[a]	2.3	2.2	2.0	1.5	1.6	1.1	3.0	3.3	3.1	3.1
Gambia, The	3.0	5.1	3.3	2.8	1.0	7.4	0.9	4.2	3.7	6.1
Georgia	−7.1	8.1	−11.0	2.3	−8.1	11.3	..	10.8	−0.3	9.7
Germany	1.8	1.2	0.1	0.2	−0.1	1.9	0.2	2.8	2.9	1.2
Ghana[a]	4.3	5.6	3.4	3.5	2.7	7.4	..	..	5.6	6.7
Greece	2.2	4.2	0.5	−4.3	1.0	4.5	..	5.2	2.6	4.8
Guatemala[a]	4.2	3.9	2.8	3.1	4.3	3.0	2.8	2.9	4.7	4.4
Guinea	4.4	3.2	4.3	9.9	4.9	4.0	4.0	3.1	3.6	−4.2
Guinea-Bissau	1.2	0.6	3.9	4.5	−3.1	3.7	−2.0	3.7	−0.6	1.0
Haiti	0.5	0.5	..	−0.6	..	0.9	..	0.6	..	0.8
Honduras	3.2	5.3	2.2	3.8	3.6	4.6	4.0	5.4	3.8	6.4

Growth of output

ECONOMY

	Gross domestic product		Agriculture		Industry		Manufacturing		Services	
	average annual % growth		average annual % growth		average annual % growth		average annual % growth		average annual % growth	
	1990–2000	2000–08	1990–2000	2000–08	1990–2000	2000–08	1990–2000	2000–08	1990–2000	2000–08
Hungary	1.5	3.6	–2.4	5.3	3.6	3.5	8.0	5.0	1.3	3.4
India	5.9	7.9	3.2	3.2	6.1	8.4	6.7	7.8	7.7	9.5
Indonesia[a]	4.2	5.2	2.0	3.3	5.2	4.2	6.7	4.9	4.0	7.1
Iran, Islamic Rep.	3.1	5.9	3.2	5.9	2.6	6.9	5.1	9.9	3.8	5.3
Iraq	..	–11.4	..	..	..	..	..	..	..	..
Ireland	7.4	5.0	1.1	–3.4	12.7	5.2	..	..	7.9	6.0
Israel[a]	5.5	3.5	..	..	..	..	..	..	..	..
Italy	1.5	1.0	2.1	0.0	1.0	0.4	1.6	–0.4	1.6	1.3
Jamaica	1.6	1.8	–0.6	–1.1	–0.8	1.4	–1.8	–1.3	3.8	2.2
Japan	1.1	1.6	–1.3	–1.1	–0.3	1.9	..	1.9	2.0	1.6
Jordan	5.0	7.2	–3.0	8.5	5.2	8.8	5.6	10.1	5.0	6.4
Kazakhstan	–4.1	9.5	–8.0	5.3	0.6	10.6	2.7	8.2	0.3	10.6
Kenya	2.2	4.5	1.9	2.7	1.2	4.9	1.3	4.4	3.2	4.4
Korea, Dem. Rep.	..	..	..	..	..	..	..	..	..	..
Korea, Rep.	5.8	4.5	1.6	1.7	6.0	5.9	7.3	6.9	5.6	3.9
Kosovo	..	..	..	..	..	..	..	..	..	..
Kuwait[a]	4.9	8.4	1.0	..	0.3	..	–0.1	..	3.5	..
Kyrgyz Republic	–4.1	4.4	1.5	1.8	–10.3	0.8	–7.5	–1.2	–5.2	7.9
Lao PDR	6.4	6.9	4.8	3.3	11.1	11.9	11.7	–1.9	6.6	7.6
Latvia	–1.5	8.2	–5.2	2.7	–8.3	7.6	–7.3	5.2	2.7	8.7
Lebanon	5.3	4.0	2.9	0.7	–0.2	3.6	1.9	2.5	1.5	3.6
Lesotho	3.8	3.9	0.9	–3.6	4.0	5.8	7.7	9.5	5.0	3.0
Liberia	4.1	–1.1	..	..	..	..	..	..	..	..
Libya	..	5.6	..	..	..	..	..	..	..	..
Lithuania	–2.7	7.7	–3.3	1.7	3.3	0.3	7.0	10.0	5.8	6.0
Macedonia, FYR	–0.8	3.2	0.2	1.7	–2.3	2.9	–5.3	2.3	0.5	3.4
Madagascar	2.0	3.8	1.8	2.0	2.4	3.5	2.0	4.3	2.3	4.4
Malawi	3.7	4.2	8.6	1.1	2.0	5.1	0.5	3.6	1.6	4.3
Malaysia[a]	7.0	5.5	0.3	3.8	8.6	4.6	9.5	5.8	7.3	6.6
Mali	4.1	5.2	2.6	4.8	6.4	4.5	–1.4	5.1	3.0	6.5
Mauritania	2.9	5.1	–0.2	0.6	3.4	4.2	5.8	–1.4	4.9	6.9
Mauritius	5.2	3.7	0.0	–1.2	5.4	1.4	5.3	0.2	6.3	5.9
Mexico	3.1	2.7	1.5	2.1	3.8	1.8	4.3	1.8	2.9	3.1
Moldova	–9.6	6.3	–11.2	–1.6	–13.6	0.6	–7.1	4.1	0.7	11.3
Mongolia	1.0	7.8	2.5	5.6	–2.5	7.4	–9.7	8.2	0.7	8.8
Morocco	2.4	5.0	–0.4	4.9	3.2	4.4	2.6	3.2	3.1	5.2
Mozambique	6.1	8.0	5.2	7.8	12.3	10.1	10.2	9.4	5.0	7.2
Myanmar[a]	7.0	..	5.7	..	..	..	7.9	..	7.2	..
Namibia	4.0	5.6	3.8	1.3	2.4	7.4	7.4	5.4	4.2	5.4
Nepal	4.9	3.5	2.5	3.2	7.1	2.8	8.9	1.0	6.2	3.8
Netherlands	3.2	1.9	1.8	1.0	1.7	1.1	2.6	1.4	3.6	2.3
New Zealand	3.3	3.1	2.9	2.0	2.5	2.7	2.2	2.6	..	..
Nicaragua	3.7	3.5	4.7	3.0	5.5	4.4	5.3	5.5	5.0	3.5
Niger[a]	2.4	4.4	3.0	..	2.0	..	2.6	..	1.9	..
Nigeria	2.5	6.6	..	7.0	..	3.8	..	..	..	14.4
Norway	3.9	2.4	2.6	3.4	3.8	0.1	1.5	3.3	3.8	3.2
Oman[a]	4.5	4.0	5.0	2.2	3.9	–0.5	6.0	9.3	5.0	5.9
Pakistan	3.8	5.4	4.4	3.4	4.1	7.6	3.8	9.6	4.4	6.2
Panama	4.7	6.6	3.1	4.1	6.0	5.2	2.7	1.2	4.5	7.1
Papua New Guinea	3.8	2.9	4.5	1.9	5.4	3.8	4.6	3.7	–0.6	3.5
Paraguay[a]	2.2	3.7	3.3	5.8	0.6	1.8	1.4	1.3	2.5	3.4
Peru	4.7	6.0	5.5	4.0	5.4	6.8	3.8	6.7	4.0	5.9
Philippines[a]	3.3	5.1	1.7	3.8	3.5	4.2	3.0	4.4	4.0	6.4
Poland	4.7	4.4	0.5	1.3	7.1	5.7	9.9	8.5	5.1	3.7
Portugal	2.8	0.9	–0.4	–0.2	3.2	–0.3	2.6	–0.2	2.4	1.7
Puerto Rico[a]	4.2	..	..	..	..	..	..	..	..	..
Qatar	..	9.0	..	..	..	..	..	..	..	..

	Gross domestic product		Agriculture		Industry		Manufacturing		Services	
	average annual % growth		average annual % growth		average annual % growth		average annual % growth		average annual % growth	
	1990–2000	2000–08	1990–2000	2000–08	1990–2000	2000–08	1990–2000	2000–08	1990–2000	2000–08
Romania	−0.6	6.4	−1.9	7.5	−1.2	6.2	..	5.7	0.9	5.0
Russian Federation	−4.7	6.7	−4.9	4.0	−7.1	5.6	..	..	−1.7	7.4
Rwanda[a]	−0.2	6.7	2.5	3.5	−3.8	8.7	−5.8	5.4	−0.9	8.9
Saudi Arabia[a]	2.1	4.1	1.6	1.5	2.2	4.4	5.6	6.0	2.2	4.2
Senegal	3.0	4.5	2.4	1.3	3.8	3.5	3.1	1.4	3.0	6.5
Serbia	−4.7	5.4	..	..	..	..	..	..	..	..
Sierra Leone	−5.0	10.3	−13.0	..	−4.5	..	6.1	..	−2.9	..
Singapore	7.6	5.8	−2.4	2.3	7.8	5.4	7.0	6.5	7.8	6.2
Slovak Republic	2.2	6.3	0.4	0.6	3.8	7.7	9.3	10.7	5.3	5.6
Slovenia	2.7	4.4	0.4	−1.8	1.6	5.3	1.8	5.3	3.3	4.2
Somalia	..	..	..	..	..	..	..	..	..	..
South Africa	2.1	4.3	1.0	1.7	1.1	3.3	1.6	3.2	2.7	4.9
Spain	2.7	3.3	3.1	−1.3	2.3	2.3	5.2	1.2	2.7	3.8
Sri Lanka[a]	5.3	5.5	1.8	2.4	6.9	5.4	8.1	4.3	5.7	6.4
Sudan	5.5	7.4	7.4	2.1	8.5	10.6	7.5	3.8	1.9	10.5
Swaziland	3.4	2.6	0.9	1.3	3.2	1.7	2.8	1.8	3.9	4.1
Sweden	2.1	2.8	−0.8	3.9	4.3	3.9	8.7	5.4	1.8	2.4
Switzerland	1.0	1.9	−0.9	−0.8	0.3	2.1	..	2.1	1.2	1.7
Syrian Arab Republic	5.1	4.4	6.0	3.6	9.2	2.7	..	15.5	1.5	7.9
Tajikistan	−10.4	8.6	−6.8	8.3	−11.4	8.8	−12.6	9.0	−10.8	8.3
Tanzania[c]	2.9	6.8	3.2	4.9	3.1	9.6	2.7	8.0	2.7	6.2
Thailand[a]	4.2	5.2	1.0	2.5	5.7	6.3	6.9	6.6	3.7	4.5
Timor-Leste[a]	..	1.9	..	..	..	..	..	..	..	..
Togo[a]	3.5	2.4	4.0	2.8	1.8	8.1	1.8	7.5	3.9	−0.7
Trinidad and Tobago	3.2	8.4	2.7	−9.2	3.2	11.4	4.9	10.4	3.2	6.2
Tunisia[a]	4.7	4.9	2.3	2.7	2.3	2.7	4.6	3.5	5.5	3.4
Turkey	3.9	5.7	1.3	1.4	4.7	6.5	4.7	6.3	4.0	5.9
Turkmenistan	−4.9	14.5	4.9	−13.3	−2.7	27.3	..	..	−4.7	17.1
Uganda	7.1	7.5	3.7	1.8	12.1	10.2	14.1	6.7	8.2	10.0
Ukraine	−9.3	7.2	−5.6	3.1	−12.6	6.6	−11.2	10.5	−8.1	7.0
United Arab Emirates	4.8	7.8	13.2	3.6	3.0	6.0	11.9	8.1	7.2	9.6
United Kingdom	2.8	2.5	−0.2	1.1	1.5	0.2	1.3	−0.4	3.4	3.2
United States	3.5	2.4	3.7	2.8	3.7	1.2	..	2.5	3.4	2.9
Uruguay	3.4	3.8	2.8	4.4	1.1	4.4	−0.1	6.3	1.3	2.9
Uzbekistan	−0.2	6.6	0.5	6.6	−3.4	4.6	0.7	2.1	0.4	7.8
Venezuela, RB	1.6	5.2	1.2	3.9	1.2	3.2	4.5	3.4	−0.1	6.5
Vietnam[a]	7.9	7.7	4.3	3.9	11.9	10.0	11.2	11.9	7.5	7.5
West Bank and Gaza	7.3	−0.9	..	..	..	..	..	..	..	..
Yemen, Rep.[a]	6.0	3.9	5.6	..	8.2	..	5.7	..	5.0	..
Zambia	0.5	5.3	4.2	1.3	−4.2	9.0	0.8	5.3	2.5	7.3
Zimbabwe	2.1	−5.7	4.3	−8.5	0.4	−10.0	0.4	−12.0	2.9	−10.0
World	**2.9 w**	**3.2 w**	**2.0 w**	**2.5 w**	**2.4 w**	**3.0 w**	**.. w**	**3.2 w**	**3.1 w**	**3.2 w**
Low income	3.5	5.8	2.9	3.8	4.6	7.5	5.0	7.6	3.4	6.3
Middle income	3.9	6.4	2.4	3.6	4.7	7.3	6.3	7.7	4.3	6.4
Lower middle income	6.3	8.3	3.1	3.8	8.4	9.5	9.0	9.8	6.7	8.8
Upper middle income	2.3	4.6	0.8	3.2	1.7	4.3	3.5	4.4	3.1	4.7
Low & middle income	3.9	6.4	2.5	3.7	4.7	7.3	6.3	7.7	4.3	6.4
East Asia & Pacific	8.5	9.1	3.5	4.1	11.0	10.2	10.9	10.3	8.5	9.4
Europe & Central Asia	−0.8	6.2	−1.7	3.0	−2.6	6.7	..	..	0.9	6.2
Latin America & Carib.	3.2	3.9	2.1	3.6	3.1	3.5	2.9	3.4	3.5	4.0
Middle East & N. Africa	3.8	4.8	2.9	4.2	4.2	3.6	4.3	5.4	3.3	5.6
South Asia	5.5	7.3	3.3	3.2	6.0	8.1	6.4	7.9	6.9	8.7
Sub-Saharan Africa	2.5	5.2	3.2	3.2	2.0	5.1	2.2	3.3	2.5	5.3
High income	2.7	2.3	1.3	0.7	1.9	1.7	..	2.1	2.9	2.6
Euro area	2.1	1.8	1.6	−0.6	1.1	1.6	2.2	1.1	2.5	2.0

a. Components are at producer prices. b. Private analysts estimate that consumer price index inflation was considerably higher for 2007–09 and believe that GDP volume growth has been significantly lower than official reports indicate since the last quarter of 2008. c. Covers mainland Tanzania only.

About the data

An economy's growth is measured by the change in the volume of its output or in the real incomes of its residents. The 1993 United Nations System of National Accounts (1993 SNA) offers three plausible indicators for calculating growth: the volume of gross domestic product (GDP), real gross domestic income, and real gross national income. The volume of GDP is the sum of value added, measured at constant prices, by households, government, and industries operating in the economy.

Each industry's contribution to growth in the economy's output is measured by growth in the industry's value added. In principle, value added in constant prices can be estimated by measuring the quantity of goods and services produced in a period, valuing them at an agreed set of base year prices, and subtracting the cost of intermediate inputs, also in constant prices. This double-deflation method, recommended by the 1993 SNA and its predecessors, requires detailed information on the structure of prices of inputs and outputs.

In many industries, however, value added is extrapolated from the base year using single volume indexes of outputs or, less commonly, inputs. Particularly in the services industries, including most of government, value added in constant prices is often imputed from labor inputs, such as real wages or number of employees. In the absence of well defined measures of output, measuring the growth of services remains difficult.

Moreover, technical progress can lead to improvements in production processes and in the quality of goods and services that, if not properly accounted for, can distort measures of value added and thus of growth. When inputs are used to estimate output, as for nonmarket services, unmeasured technical progress leads to underestimates of the volume of output. Similarly, unmeasured improvements in quality lead to underestimates of the value of output and value added. The result can be underestimates of growth and productivity improvement and overestimates of inflation.

Informal economic activities pose a particular measurement problem, especially in developing countries, where much economic activity is unrecorded. A complete picture of the economy requires estimating household outputs produced for home use, sales in informal markets, barter exchanges, and illicit or deliberately unreported activities. The consistency and completeness of such estimates depend on the skill and methods of the compiling statisticians.

Rebasing national accounts

When countries rebase their national accounts, they update the weights assigned to various components to better reflect current patterns of production or uses of output. The new base year should represent normal operation of the economy—it should be a year without major shocks or distortions. Some developing countries have not rebased their national accounts for many years. Using an old base year can be misleading because implicit price and volume weights become progressively less relevant and useful.

To obtain comparable series of constant price data, the World Bank rescales GDP and value added by industrial origin to a common reference year. This year's *World Development Indicators* continues to use 2000 as the reference year. Because rescaling changes the implicit weights used in forming regional and income group aggregates, aggregate growth rates in this year's edition are not comparable with those from earlier editions with different base years.

Rescaling may result in a discrepancy between the rescaled GDP and the sum of the rescaled components. Because allocating the discrepancy would cause distortions in the growth rates, the discrepancy is left unallocated. As a result, the weighted average of the growth rates of the components generally will not equal the GDP growth rate.

Computing growth rates

Growth rates of GDP and its components are calculated using the least squares method and constant price data in the local currency. Constant price U.S. dollar series are used to calculate regional and income group growth rates. Local currency series are converted to constant U.S. dollars using an exchange rate in the common reference year. The growth rates in the table are average annual compound growth rates. Methods of computing growth are described in *Statistical methods*.

Changes in the System of National Accounts

World Development Indicators adopted the terminology of the 1993 SNA in 2001. Although many countries continue to compile their national accounts according to the SNA version 3 (referred to as the 1968 SNA), more and more are adopting the 1993 SNA. Some low-income countries still use concepts from the even older 1953 SNA guidelines, including valuations such as factor cost, in describing major economic aggregates. Countries that use the 1993 SNA are identified in *Primary data documentation*.

Definitions

• **Gross domestic product (GDP)** at purchaser prices is the sum of gross value added by all resident producers in the economy plus any product taxes (less subsidies) not included in the valuation of output. It is calculated without deducting for depreciation of fabricated capital assets or for depletion and degradation of natural resources. Value added is the net output of an industry after adding up all outputs and subtracting intermediate inputs. The industrial origin of value added is determined by the International Standard Industrial Classification (ISIC) revision 3. • **Agriculture** is the sum of gross output less the value of intermediate input used in production for industries classified in ISIC divisions 1–5 and includes forestry and fishing. • **Industry** is the sum of gross output less the value of intermediate input used in production for industries classified in ISIC divisions 10–45, which cover mining, manufacturing (also reported separately), construction, electricity, water, and gas. • **Manufacturing** is the sum of gross output less the value of intermediate input used in production for industries classified in ISIC divisions 15–37. • **Services** correspond to ISIC divisions 50–99. This sector is derived as a residual (from GDP less agriculture and industry) and may not properly reflect the sum of services output, including banking and financial services. For some countries it includes product taxes (minus subsidies) and may also include statistical discrepancies.

Data sources

Data on national accounts for most developing countries are collected from national statistical organizations and central banks by visiting and resident World Bank missions. Data for high-income economies are from Organisation for Economic Co-operation and Development (OECD) data files. The World Bank rescales constant price data to a common reference year. The complete national accounts time series is available on the *World Development Indicators 2010* CD-ROM. The United Nations Statistics Division publishes detailed national accounts for UN member countries in *National Accounts Statistics: Main Aggregates and Detailed Tables* and publishes updates in the *Monthly Bulletin of Statistics*.

	Gross domestic product		Agriculture		Industry		Manufacturing		Services	
	$ millions		% of GDP		% of GDP		% of GDP		% of GDP	
	1995	2008	1995	2008	1995	2008	1995	2008	1995	2008
Afghanistan	..	10,624	..	32	..	26	..	16	..	42
Albania	2,424	12,295	56	21	22	20	14	20	22	60
Algeria	41,764	166,545	10	7	50	62	11	5	39	31
Angola[a]	5,040	84,945	7	7	66	68	4	5	26	26
Argentina	258,032	328,465	6	10	28	32	18	21	66	58
Armenia	1,468	11,917	42	18	32	45	25	15	26	37
Australia	361,306	1,015,217	3	3	29	29	15	10	68	68
Austria	238,314	413,503	3	2	31	31	20	20	67	67
Azerbaijan	3,052	46,135	27	6	34	70	13	4	39	24
Bangladesh	37,940	79,554	26	19	25	29	15	18	49	52
Belarus	13,973	60,313	17	10	37	44	31	33	46	46
Belgium	284,321	504,206	2	1	28	23	20	16	70	76
Benin[a]	2,009	6,680	34	..	15	..	9	..	51	..
Bolivia	6,715	16,674	17	13	33	38	19	14	50	48
Bosnia and Herzegovina	1,867	18,512	..	..	..	..	..	..	..	..
Botswana	4,774	13,414	4	2	51	53	5	4	45	45
Brazil	768,951	1,575,151	6	7	28	28	19	16	67	65
Bulgaria	13,107	49,900	14	7	35	31	24	15	50	62
Burkina Faso	2,380	7,948	35	33	21	22	15	14	43	44
Burundi	1,000	1,163	48	..	19	..	9	..	33	..
Cambodia	3,441	10,354	50	35	15	24	10	16	36	41
Cameroon	8,733	23,396	24	19	31	31	22	17	45	50
Canada	590,517	1,501,329	3	..	31	..	18	..	66	..
Central African Republic	1,122	1,988	46	53	21	14	10	8	33	33
Chad	1,446	8,400	36	14	14	49	11	7	51	38
Chile	71,349	169,458	9	4	35	44	18	13	55	52
China[a]	728,007	4,326,996	20	11	47	49	34	34	33	40
Hong Kong SAR, China	144,230	215,355	0	0	15	8	8	3	85	92
Colombia	92,503	243,765	15	9	32	36	16	16	53	55
Congo, Dem. Rep.	5,643	11,668	57	40	17	28	9	6	26	32
Congo, Rep.[a]	2,116	10,723	10	4	45	75	8	4	45	21
Costa Rica	11,722	29,664	14	7	30	29	22	21	57	64
Côte d'Ivoire[a]	11,000	23,414	25	25	21	26	15	18	55	49
Croatia	22,122	69,332	10	6	31	28	22	17	59	65
Cuba[a]	..	..	6	..	45	..	38	..	49	..
Czech Republic	55,257	215,500	5	3	38	38	24	25	57	60
Denmark	181,984	341,255	3	1	25	26	17	15	71	73
Dominican Republic[a]	16,358	45,541	10	7	36	33	26	24	54	60
Ecuador	20,206	54,686	..	7	..	41	..	10	..	53
Egypt, Arab Rep.	60,159	162,283	17	13	32	38	17	16	51	49
El Salvador	9,500	22,115	14	13	30	28	23	22	56	58
Eritrea	578	1,654	21	24	17	19	9	5	62	56
Estonia	4,353	23,401	6	3	33	29	21	17	61	68
Ethiopia	7,606	25,585	57	44	10	13	5	5	33	42
Finland	130,599	272,700	4	3	33	32	25	24	63	65
France	1,569,983	2,856,556	3	2	25	20	..	12	72	78
Gabon[a]	4,959	14,535	8	4	52	64	5	3	40	32
Gambia, The	382	811	30	29	13	15	6	5	57	56
Georgia	2,694	12,791	52	10	16	21	17	12	32	69
Germany	2,522,792	3,649,494	1	1	32	30	23	24	67	69
Ghana[a]	6,457	16,653	39	33	24	25	9	6	37	41
Greece	131,718	355,876	9	3	21	20	..	10	70	77
Guatemala[a]	14,657	38,983	24	12	20	30	14	20	56	58
Guinea	3,694	3,799	19	25	29	46	4	4	52	29
Guinea-Bissau	254	430	55	55	12	13	8	10	33	32
Haiti	2,696	7,205	..	..	..	..	..	..	..	..
Honduras	3,911	13,343	22	14	31	31	18	22	48	55

	Gross domestic product		Agriculture		Industry		Manufacturing		Services	
	$ millions		% of GDP		% of GDP		% of GDP		% of GDP	
	1995	2008	1995	2008	1995	2008	1995	2008	1995	2008
Hungary	44,656	154,668	7	4	32	29	24	22	61	66
India	356,299	1,159,171	26	17	28	29	18	16	46	54
Indonesia[a]	202,132	510,730	17	14	42	48	24	28	41	37
Iran, Islamic Rep.	90,829	286,058	18	10	34	44	12	11	47	45
Iraq	10,114	..	9	..	75	..	1	..	16	..
Ireland	67,036	267,576	7	2	38	34	30	22	55	64
Israel[a]	96,065	202,101	..	..	..	..	..	..	..	..
Italy	1,126,041	2,303,079	3	2	30	27	22	18	66	71
Jamaica	5,813	14,614	9	5	37	25	16	9	54	69
Japan	5,247,610	4,910,840	2	1	34	29	23	21	64	69
Jordan	6,727	21,238	4	3	29	34	15	20	67	63
Kazakhstan	20,374	133,442	13	6	31	43	15	13	56	51
Kenya	9,046	30,355	31	27	16	19	10	12	53	54
Korea, Dem. Rep.	..	..	..	..	..	..	..	..	..	..
Korea, Rep.	517,118	929,121	6	3	42	37	28	28	52	60
Kosovo	..	5,448	..	12	..	20	..	16	..	68
Kuwait[a]	27,192	148,024	0	..	55	..	4	..	45	..
Kyrgyz Republic	1,661	5,059	44	30	20	20	9	13	37	51
Lao PDR	1,764	5,543	56	35	19	28	14	9	25	37
Latvia	5,236	33,784	9	3	30	23	21	11	61	74
Lebanon	11,719	29,264	8	5	25	21	14	10	68	73
Lesotho	890	1,622	17	7	39	35	16	16	44	58
Liberia	135	843	82	61	5	17	3	13	13	22
Libya	25,541	93,168	..	2	..	78	..	4	..	20
Lithuania	7,621	47,341	11	4	33	33	20	19	56	63
Macedonia, FYR	4,449	9,521	13	11	30	34	23	22	57	55
Madagascar	3,160	9,463	27	25	9	17	8	15	64	57
Malawi	1,397	4,269	30	34	20	21	16	14	50	45
Malaysia[a]	88,832	221,773	13	10	41	48	26	28	46	42
Mali	2,466	8,740	50	37	19	24	8	3	32	39
Mauritania	1,415	2,858	37	13	25	47	8	..	37	41
Mauritius	4,040	9,320	10	4	32	29	23	20	58	67
Mexico	286,698	1,088,128	6	4	28	37	21	19	66	59
Moldova	1,753	6,047	33	11	32	15	26	14	35	74
Mongolia	1,227	5,258	41	21	29	40	12	4	30	39
Morocco	32,986	88,883	15	15	34	30	19	14	51	55
Mozambique	2,247	9,846	35	29	15	24	8	14	51	47
Myanmar[a]	..	..	60	..	10	..	7	..	30	..
Namibia	3,503	8,837	12	9	28	37	13	14	60	53
Nepal	4,401	12,615	42	34	23	17	10	7	35	50
Netherlands	418,969	871,004	3	2	27	25	17	14	69	73
New Zealand	62,049	129,940	7	..	27	..	19	..	66	..
Nicaragua	3,191	6,592	23	19	27	30	19	19	49	51
Niger[a]	1,881	5,354	40	..	17	..	6	..	43	..
Nigeria	28,109	207,118	..	33	..	41	..	3	..	27
Norway	148,920	451,830	3	1	34	46	13	9	63	53
Oman[a]	13,803	41,638	3	..	46	..	5	..	51	..
Pakistan	60,636	164,539	26	20	24	27	16	20	50	53
Panama	7,906	23,088	8	6	18	17	9	7	74	76
Papua New Guinea	4,636	8,239	35	34	34	48	8	6	31	18
Paraguay[a]	8,066	15,977	21	20	23	18	16	13	56	61
Peru	53,674	129,109	9	7	31	36	17	16	60	57
Philippines[a]	74,120	166,909	22	15	32	32	23	22	46	53
Poland	139,062	527,866	8	5	35	31	21	17	57	65
Portugal	112,960	243,497	6	2	28	24	18	14	66	74
Puerto Rico[a]	42,647	..	1	..	44	..	42	..	55	..
Qatar	8,138	71,041	..	..	..	..	..	..	..	..

	Gross domestic product		Agriculture		Industry		Manufacturing		Services	
	$ millions		% of GDP		% of GDP		% of GDP		% of GDP	
	1995	**2008**	**1995**	**2008**	**1995**	**2008**	**1995**	**2008**	**1995**	**2008**
Romania	35,477	200,071	21	7	43	25	29	21	36	68
Russian Federation	395,528	1,679,484	7	5	37	37	..	18	56	58
Rwanda[a]	1,293	4,457	44	37	16	14	10	4	40	48
Saudi Arabia[a]	142,458	468,800	6	2	49	70	10	8	45	27
Senegal	4,879	13,273	21	16	24	22	17	13	55	63
Serbia	19,681	50,061	..	..	..	..	..	..	..	..
Sierra Leone	871	1,954	43	50	39	23	9	..	18	26
Singapore	84,291	181,948	0	0	35	28	27	21	65	72
Slovak Republic	19,579	94,957	6	4	38	41	27	22	56	55
Slovenia	20,814	54,613	4	2	35	34	26	23	60	63
Somalia	..	..	..	..	..	..	..	..	..	..
South Africa	151,113	276,445	4	3	35	34	21	19	61	63
Spain	596,751	1,604,235	5	3	29	29	18	15	66	68
Sri Lanka[a]	13,030	40,565	23	13	27	29	16	18	50	57
Sudan	13,830	55,927	39	26	11	34	5	6	51	40
Swaziland	1,699	2,837	12	7	45	49	39	44	43	43
Sweden	253,705	478,961	3	2	31	28	23	20	67	70
Switzerland	315,940	491,950	2	1	30	28	20	20	68	71
Syrian Arab Republic	11,397	55,204	32	20	20	35	15	13	48	45
Tajikistan	1,232	5,134	38	18	39	23	28	16	22	59
Tanzania[b]	5,255	20,490	47	45	14	17	7	7	38	37
Thailand[a]	168,019	272,429	10	12	41	44	30	35	50	44
Timor-Leste[a]	..	498	..	..	..	..	..	..	..	..
Togo[a]	1,309	2,898	38	..	22	..	10	..	40	..
Trinidad and Tobago	5,329	24,145	2	0	47	62	9	5	51	37
Tunisia[a]	18,031	40,309	11	10	29	33	19	18	59	58
Turkey	169,708	734,853	16	9	33	28	23	18	50	64
Turkmenistan	2,482	15,327	17	12	63	54	40	50	20	34
Uganda	5,756	14,326	49	23	14	26	7	8	36	52
Ukraine	48,214	180,355	15	8	43	37	35	23	42	55
United Arab Emirates	42,807	198,693	3	2	52	61	10	12	45	38
United Kingdom	1,157,119	2,674,057	2	1	31	24	21	..	67	76
United States	7,342,300	14,591,381	2	1	26	22	19	14	72	77
Uruguay	19,298	32,186	9	11	29	27	20	18	62	63
Uzbekistan	13,350	27,934	32	21	28	31	12	12	40	48
Venezuela, RB	74,889	314,150	6	..	41	..	15	..	53	..
Vietnam[a]	20,736	90,645	27	22	29	40	15	21	44	38
West Bank and Gaza	3,220	..	..	..	..	..	..	..	..	..
Yemen, Rep.[a]	4,236	26,576	20	..	32	..	14	..	48	..
Zambia	3,478	14,314	18	21	36	46	11	12	46	33
Zimbabwe	7,111	..	15	..	29	..	22	..	56	..
World	**29,604,170 t**	**60,521,123 t**	**4 w**	**3 w**	**31 w**	**28 w**	**20 w**	**18 w**	**65 w**	**69 w**
Low income	195,611	564,572	35	25	22	28	12	14	43	47
Middle income	4,894,312	16,722,126	14	9	35	37	23	22	51	53
Lower middle income	2,044,366	8,277,781	21	13	39	41	26	27	41	46
Upper middle income	2,851,464	8,442,445	8	6	32	34	20	17	60	60
Low & middle income	5,091,618	17,299,923	15	10	34	37	22	21	51	53
East Asia & Pacific	1,312,702	5,695,585	19	12	44	47	31	33	36	41
Europe & Central Asia	904,254	3,872,528	13	7	36	32	22	18	52	61
Latin America & Carib.	1,755,662	4,216,075	7	7	29	33	19	18	64	61
Middle East & N. Africa	315,651	1,074,015	16	11	34	43	15	12	50	46
South Asia	476,175	1,469,613	26	18	27	28	17	16	46	53
Sub-Saharan Africa	327,684	978,062	18	12	29	33	16	15	53	55
High income	24,508,224	43,273,506	2	1	30	26	20	17	68	73
Euro area	7,274,360	13,566,882	3	2	29	27	22	18	68	72

a. Components are at producer prices. b. Covers mainland Tanzania only.

An economy's gross domestic product (GDP) represents the sum of value added by all its producers. Value added is the value of the gross output of producers less the value of intermediate goods and services consumed in production, before accounting for consumption of fixed capital in production. The United Nations System of National Accounts calls for value added to be valued at either basic prices (excluding net taxes on products) or producer prices (including net taxes on products paid by producers but excluding sales or value added taxes). Both valuations exclude transport charges that are invoiced separately by producers. Total GDP shown in the table and elsewhere in this volume is measured at purchaser prices. Value added by industry is normally measured at basic prices. When value added is measured at producer prices, this is noted in *Primary data documentation* and footnoted in the table.

While GDP estimates based on the production approach are generally more reliable than estimates compiled from the income or expenditure side, different countries use different definitions, methods, and reporting standards. World Bank staff review the quality of national accounts data and sometimes make adjustments to improve consistency with international guidelines. Nevertheless, significant discrepancies remain between international standards and actual practice. Many statistical offices, especially those in developing countries, face severe limitations in the resources, time, training, and budgets required to produce reliable and comprehensive series of national accounts statistics.

Data problems in measuring output

Among the difficulties faced by compilers of national accounts is the extent of unreported economic activity in the informal or secondary economy. In developing countries a large share of agricultural output is either not exchanged (because it is consumed within the household) or not exchanged for money.

Agricultural production often must be estimated indirectly, using a combination of methods involving estimates of inputs, yields, and area under cultivation. This approach sometimes leads to crude approximations that can differ from the true values over time and across crops for reasons other than climate conditions or farming techniques. Similarly, agricultural inputs that cannot easily be allocated to specific outputs are frequently "netted out" using equally crude and ad hoc approximations. For further discussion of the measurement of agricultural production, see *About the data* for table 3.3.

Ideally, industrial output should be measured through regular censuses and surveys of firms. But in most developing countries such surveys are infrequent, so earlier survey results must be extrapolated using an appropriate indicator. The choice of sampling unit, which may be the enterprise (where responses may be based on financial records) or the establishment (where production units may be recorded separately), also affects the quality of the data. Moreover, much industrial production is organized in unincorporated or owner-operated ventures that are not captured by surveys aimed at the formal sector. Even in large industries, where regular surveys are more likely, evasion of excise and other taxes and nondisclosure of income lower the estimates of value added. Such problems become more acute as countries move from state control of industry to private enterprise, because new firms and growing numbers of established firms fail to report. In accordance with the System of National Accounts, output should include all such unreported activity as well as the value of illegal activities and other unrecorded, informal, or small-scale operations. Data on these activities need to be collected using techniques other than conventional surveys of firms.

In industries dominated by large organizations and enterprises, such as public utilities, data on output, employment, and wages are usually readily available and reasonably reliable. But in the services industry the many self-employed workers and one-person businesses are sometimes difficult to locate, and they have little incentive to respond to surveys, let alone to report their full earnings. Compounding these problems are the many forms of economic activity that go unrecorded, including the work that women and children do for little or no pay. For further discussion of the problems of using national accounts data, see Srinivasan (1994) and Heston (1994).

Dollar conversion

To produce national accounts aggregates that are measured in the same standard monetary units, the value of output must be converted to a single common currency. The World Bank conventionally uses the U.S. dollar and applies the average official exchange rate reported by the International Monetary Fund for the year shown. An alternative conversion factor is applied if the official exchange rate is judged to diverge by an exceptionally large margin from the rate effectively applied to transactions in foreign currencies and traded products.

• **Gross domestic product (GDP)** at purchaser prices is the sum of gross value added by all resident producers in the economy plus any product taxes (less subsidies) not included in the valuation of output. It is calculated without deducting for depreciation of fabricated assets or for depletion and degradation of natural resources. Value added is the net output of an industry after adding up all outputs and subtracting intermediate inputs. The industrial origin of value added is determined by the International Standard Industrial Classification (ISIC) revision 3. • **Agriculture** is the sum of gross output less the value of intermediate input used in production for industries classified in ISIC divisions 1–5 and includes forestry and fishing. • **Industry** is the sum of gross output less the value of intermediate input used in production for industries classified in ISIC divisions 10–45, which cover mining, manufacturing (also reported separately), construction, electricity, water, and gas. • **Manufacturing** is the sum of gross output less the value of intermediate input used in production for industries classified in ISIC divisions 15–37. • **Services** correspond to ISIC divisions 50–99. This sector is derived as a residual (from GDP less agriculture and industry) and may not properly reflect the sum of services output, including banking and financial services. For some countries it includes product taxes (minus subsidies) and may also include statistical discrepancies.

Data on national accounts for most developing countries are collected from national statistical organizations and central banks by visiting and resident World Bank missions. Data for high-income economies are from Organisation for Economic Co-operation and Development (OECD) data files. The complete national accounts time series is available on the *World Development Indicators 2010* CD-ROM. The United Nations Statistics Division publishes detailed national accounts for UN member countries in *National Accounts Statistics: Main Aggregates and Detailed Tables* and publishes updates in the *Monthly Bulletin of Statistics*.

	Manufacturing value added		Food, beverages, and tobacco		Textiles and clothing		Machinery and transport equipment		Chemicals		Other manufacturing[a]	
	$ millions		% of total		% of total		% of total		% of total		% of total	
	1995	2008	1995	2005	1995	2005	1995	2005	1995	2005	1995	2005
Afghanistan	..	1,663	..	..	..	..	..	..	..	..	..	..
Albania	405	2,047	..	17	..	22	..	3	..	17	..	41
Algeria	4,366	7,471	..	..	..	..	..	..	..	..	..	..
Angola	202	4,040	..	..	..	..	..	..	..	..	..	..
Argentina	44,502	63,983	29	..	7	..	13	..	4	..	46	..
Armenia	356	1,558	..	..	..	..	..	..	..	..	..	..
Australia	50,044	97,613	..	17	..	1	..	5	..	7	..	69
Austria	42,134	67,615	10	9	5	3	27	31	2	6	56	51
Azerbaijan	352	1,922	..	15	..	1	..	13	..	4	..	67
Bangladesh	5,586	13,672	28	..	44	..	4	..	11	..	13	..
Belarus	3,909	16,966	..	..	..	..	..	..	..	..	..	..
Belgium	51,721	66,902	13	13	6	4	23	21	8	22	50	41
Benin	174	..	..	..	..	..	..	..	..	..	..	..
Bolivia	1,123	1,862	31	..	4	..	1	..	4	..	60	..
Bosnia and Herzegovina	213	2,130	..	..	..	..	..	..	..	..	..	..
Botswana	242	458	25	22	8	5	15	..	5	..	66	73
Brazil	124,976	212,923	21	19	8	6	23	21	13	11	35	43
Bulgaria	2,015	6,199	23	16	12	13	20	18	15	7	30	45
Burkina Faso	336	775	..	..	..	..	..	..	..	..	..	..
Burundi	83	..	..	..	..	..	..	..	..	..	..	..
Cambodia	315	1,589	20	..	22	..	0	..	0	..	57	..
Cameroon	1,758	3,328	..	..	..	..	..	..	..	..	..	..
Canada	100,393	..	14	..	4	..	23	..	10	..	49	..
Central African Republic	108	106	..	..	..	..	..	..	..	..	..	..
Chad	159	383	..	..	..	..	..	..	..	..	..	..
Chile	10,594	21,660	..	14	..	2	..	2	..	14	..	68
China	245,002	1,487,812	4	4	2	2	2	3	..	..	93	93
Hong Kong SAR, China	10,524	5,040	..	..	..	..	..	..	..	..	..	..
Colombia	13,506	35,885	..	27	..	9	..	7	..	13	..	44
Congo, Dem. Rep.	510	630	..	..	..	..	..	..	..	..	..	..
Congo, Rep.	172	411	..	..	..	..	..	..	..	..	..	..
Costa Rica	2,339	5,505	..	..	..	..	..	..	..	..	..	..
Côte d'Ivoire	1,655	4,219	..	..	..	..	..	..	..	..	..	..
Croatia	4,121	10,137	..	..	..	..	..	..	..	..	..	..
Cuba	..	..	..	..	..	..	..	..	..	..	..	..
Czech Republic	12,124	47,842	12	9	7	3	23	37	4	3	54	48
Denmark	26,925	39,213	20	14	2	2	23	17	1	2	53	65
Dominican Republic	3,824	9,785	..	..	..	..	..	..	..	..	..	..
Ecuador	2,830	5,004	26	30	6	4	4	3	7	5	56	58
Egypt, Arab Rep.	9,829	24,461	19	..	13	..	12	..	18	..	38	..
El Salvador	2,026	4,452	..	..	..	..	..	..	..	..	..	..
Eritrea	47	72	63	35	9	16	1	4	13	10	15	34
Estonia	804	3,472	..	12	..	5	..	10	..	4	..	69
Ethiopia	344	1,149	52	47	18	9	2	2	4	4	23	38
Finland	28,814	50,717	10	7	3	2	30	36	6	3	51	51
France	..	306,281	13	13	5	4	28	29	12	12	41	42
Gabon	224	503	..	..	..	..	..	..	..	..	..	..
Gambia, The	20	35	65	..	8	..	1	..	9	..	17	..
Georgia	523	1,362	..	36	..	2	..	5	..	15	..	42
Germany	516,542	711,089	8	8	3	2	43	42	10	10	37	38
Ghana	602	1,055	..	..	..	..	..	..	..	..	..	..
Greece	..	28,544	25	23	14	9	13	13	10	6	38	50
Guatemala	2,069	7,312	..	..	..	..	..	..	..	..	..	..
Guinea	142	155	..	..	..	..	..	..	..	..	..	..
Guinea-Bissau	19	41	..	..	..	..	..	..	..	..	..	..
Haiti	..	..	..	..	..	..	..	..	..	..	..	..
Honduras	607	2,593	..	..	..	..	..	..	..	..	..	..

Structure of manufacturing | 4.3

	Manufacturing value added		Food, beverages, and tobacco		Textiles and clothing		Machinery and transport equipment		Chemicals		Other manufacturing[a]	
	$ millions		% of total		% of total		% of total		% of total		% of total	
	1995	2008	1995	2005	1995	2005	1995	2005	1995	2005	1995	2005
Hungary	8,839	28,619	18	12	3	3	14	42	11	10	54	33
India	57,917	169,986	13	9	12	9	20	20	22	16	34	46
Indonesia	48,781	142,345	21	25	18	12	16	23	10	11	35	30
Iran, Islamic Rep.	10,918	29,832	13	10	10	4	18	27	16	13	44	46
Iraq	67	..	23	..	26	..	4	..	8	..	39	..
Ireland	18,096	50,926	15	14	1	0	21	10	18	26	45	50
Israel	..	..	13	11	6	4	25	23	6	10	50	53
Italy	225,513	344,676	9	9	14	10	27	27	8	7	43	46
Jamaica	865	983	..	..	..	..	..	..	..	..	..	..
Japan	1,077,348	923,108	10	11	4	2	38	41	10	11	38	35
Jordan	866	3,834	31	24	6	11	4	6	15	15	43	44
Kazakhstan	2,976	15,711	..	..	..	..	..	..	..	..	..	..
Kenya	757	3,229	..	30	..	6	..	4	..	5	..	55
Korea, Dem. Rep.	..	..	..	..	..	..	..	..	..	..	..	..
Korea, Rep.	128,839	234,688	9	6	10	5	40	50	8	8	33	31
Kosovo	..	732	..	..	..	..	..	..	..	..	..	..
Kuwait	1,032	..	..	..	..	..	..	..	..	..	..	..
Kyrgyz Republic	142	570	..	14	..	5	..	1	..	1	..	78
Lao PDR	245	484	..	..	..	..	..	..	..	..	..	..
Latvia	965	3,200	39	20	11	7	15	11	4	4	31	58
Lebanon	1,465	2,448	26	..	10	..	5	..	6	..	53	..
Lesotho	129	234	..	..	..	..	..	..	..	..	..	..
Liberia	4	105	..	..	..	..	..	..	..	..	..	..
Libya	..	3,879	..	..	..	..	..	..	..	..	..	..
Lithuania	1,351	6,615	..	22	..	11	..	13	..	6	..	49
Macedonia, FYR	873	1,780	35	..	17	..	9	..	8	..	31	..
Madagascar	233	1,345	..	46	..	31	..	1	..	2	..	20
Malawi	195	504	..	..	..	..	..	..	..	..	..	..
Malaysia	23,432	52,224	..	9	..	3	..	34	..	13	..	42
Mali	174	195	..	..	..	..	..	..	..	..	..	..
Mauritania	107	..	..	..	..	..	..	..	..	..	..	..
Mauritius	822	1,648	25	30	52	42	2	3	..	..	21	25
Mexico	54,546	199,410	26	..	4	..	24	..	14	..	31	..
Moldova	400	702	..	50	..	13	..	5	..	..	..	31
Mongolia	143	210	46	..	36	..	3	..	2	..	12	..
Morocco	6,056	11,225	..	37	..	14	..	8	..	13	..	28
Mozambique	166	1,298	..	..	..	..	..	..	..	..	..	..
Myanmar	..	..	..	..	..	..	..	..	..	..	..	..
Namibia	403	1,108	..	..	..	..	..	..	..	..	..	..
Nepal	393	862	35	..	34	..	2	..	..	..	29	..
Netherlands	65,999	94,324	19	15	3	1	16	19	14	18	48	47
New Zealand	10,645	..	29	25	..	..	..	..	..	..	71	75
Nicaragua	533	946	..	..	..	..	..	..	..	..	..	..
Niger	120	..	..	..	..	..	..	..	..	..	..	..
Nigeria	..	3,760	..	..	..	..	..	..	..	..	..	..
Norway	17,018	38,595	17	23	2	1	25	23	9	9	48	43
Oman	643	..	15	6	6	0	4	2	8	11	66	80
Pakistan	8,864	31,196	..	..	..	..	..	..	..	..	..	..
Panama	694	1,454	54	..	7	..	..	..	7	..	32	..
Papua New Guinea	372	446	..	..	..	..	..	..	..	..	..	..
Paraguay	1,280	2,022	..	..	..	..	..	..	..	..	..	..
Peru	8,105	18,770	26	30	10	13	6	3	9	11	49	44
Philippines	17,043	37,247	29	24	7	6	20	30	11	8	34	33
Poland	25,885	80,227	23	23	8	4	22	20	3	7	44	46
Portugal	18,249	23,939	13	14	22	9	18	15	6	2	41	61
Puerto Rico	17,867	..	..	..	..	..	..	..	..	..	..	..
Qatar	..	..	..	1	..	2	..	0	..	17	..	80

	Manufacturing value added		Food, beverages, and tobacco		Textiles and clothing		Machinery and transport equipment		Chemicals		Other manufacturing[a]	
	$ millions		% of total		% of total		% of total		% of total		% of total	
	1995	2008	1995	2005	1995	2005	1995	2005	1995	2005	1995	2005
Romania	9,387	37,959	31	15	12	14	18	18	6	5	33	47
Russian Federation	..	256,618	..	15	..	2	..	12	..	8	..	63
Rwanda	132	200	..	..	..	..	..	..	..	..	..	..
Saudi Arabia	13,714	38,737	..	19	..	5	..	13	..	27	..	35
Senegal	730	1,548	44	..	3	..	1	..	29	..	23	..
Serbia	..	..	..	..	..	..	..	..	..	..	..	..
Sierra Leone	75	..	..	..	..	..	..	..	..	..	..	..
Singapore	20,799	35,535	4	2	1	1	60	49	9	29	26	19
Slovak Republic	6,064	21,332	13	7	2	4	19	24	8	3	57	62
Slovenia	4,573	9,677	10	7	12	6	21	26	2	2	56	60
Somalia	..	..	..	..	..	..	..	..	..	..	..	..
South Africa	29,274	46,692	15	18	8	4	19	17	10	7	47	55
Spain	101,524	195,804	16	15	7	5	25	21	9	8	42	51
Sri Lanka	1,836	7,283	..	29	..	29	..	4	..	14	..	24
Sudan	640	3,028	..	..	..	..	..	..	..	..	..	..
Swaziland	557	1,054	..	..	..	..	..	..	..	..	..	..
Sweden	49,767	79,279	8	7	1	1	35	29	2	12	53	51
Switzerland	50,562	72,675	..	..	..	..	..	..	..	..	..	..
Syrian Arab Republic	1,574	6,092	..	..	..	..	..	..	..	..	..	..
Tajikistan	331	745	..	..	..	..	..	..	..	..	..	..
Tanzania[b]	349	819	..	..	..	..	..	..	..	..	..	..
Thailand	50,231	95,146	21	..	9	..	29	..	6	..	35	..
Timor-Leste	..	..	..	..	..	..	..	..	..	..	..	..
Togo	130	..	..	..	..	..	..	..	..	..	..	..
Trinidad and Tobago	439	1,263	30	12	1	1	2	1	26	38	41	48
Tunisia	3,419	7,209	..	..	..	..	..	..	..	..	..	..
Turkey	38,296	118,702	16	..	17	..	16	..	10	..	41	..
Turkmenistan	948	9,158	..	..	..	..	..	..	..	..	..	..
Uganda	359	1,000	50	..	3	..	6	..	..	..	41	..
Ukraine	14,922	37,161	..	..	..	..	..	..	..	..	..	..
United Arab Emirates	4,452	24,643	..	..	..	..	..	..	..	..	..	..
United Kingdom	219,282	..	14	15	5	3	29	26	11	11	41	45
United States	1,289,100	1,755,600	12	14	4	2	34	28	12	15	38	40
Uruguay	3,801	4,996	36	42	9	9	4	2	8	9	43	38
Uzbekistan	1,376	3,061	..	..	..	..	..	..	..	..	..	..
Venezuela, RB	10,668	..	..	..	..	..	..	..	..	..	..	..
Vietnam	3,109	19,129	30	..	22	..	12	..	7	..	29	..
West Bank and Gaza	..	..	..	..	..	..	..	..	..	..	..	..
Yemen, Rep.	599	..	45	60	5	9	0	0	2	4	48	27
Zambia	344	1,421	..	..	..	..	..	..	..	..	..	..
Zimbabwe	1,370	..	30	..	7	..	29	..	6	..	29	..
World	**5,484,300 t**	**9,054,590 t**	..	..	..	..	..	..	..	..	..	..
Low income	22,364	68,035	..	..	..	..	..	..	..	..	..	..
Middle income	990,706	3,514,162	..	..	..	..	..	..	..	..	..	..
Lower middle income	496,790	2,159,122	..	..	..	..	..	..	..	..	..	..
Upper middle income	503,477	1,319,723	..	..	..	..	..	..	..	..	..	..
Low & middle income	1,013,160	3,584,044	..	..	..	..	..	..	..	..	..	..
East Asia & Pacific	390,767	1,859,969	..	..	..	..	..	..	..	..	..	..
Europe & Central Asia	..	..	..	..	..	..	..	..	..	..	..	..
Latin America & Carib.	292,587	640,171	..	..	..	..	..	..	..	..	..	..
Middle East & N. Africa	39,269	106,905	..	..	..	..	..	..	..	..	..	..
South Asia	75,041	224,444	..	..	..	..	..	..	..	..	..	..
Sub-Saharan Africa	46,018	89,446	..	..	..	..	..	..	..	..	..	..
High income	4,490,475	6,039,774	..	..	..	..	..	..	..	..	..	..
Euro area	1,325,850	1,958,265	..	..	..	..	..	..	..	..	..	..

a. Includes unallocated data. b. Covers mainland Tanzania only.

About the data

The data on the distribution of manufacturing value added by industry are provided by the United Nations Industrial Development Organization (UNIDO). UNIDO obtains the data from a variety of national and international sources, including the United Nations Statistics Division, the World Bank, the Organisation for Economic Co-operation and Development, and the International Monetary Fund. To improve comparability over time and across countries, UNIDO supplements these data with information from industrial censuses, statistics from national and international organizations, unpublished data that it collects in the field, and estimates by the UNIDO Secretariat. Nevertheless, coverage may be incomplete, particularly for the informal sector. When direct information on inputs and outputs is not available, estimates may be used, which may result in errors in industry totals. Moreover, countries use different reference periods (calendar or fiscal year) and valuation methods (basic or producer prices) to estimate value added. (See *About the data* for table 4.2.)

The data on manufacturing value added in U.S. dollars are from the World Bank's national accounts files and may differ from those UNIDO uses to calculate shares of value added by industry, in part because of differences in exchange rates. Thus value added in a particular industry estimated by applying the shares to total manufacturing value added will not match those from UNIDO sources. Classification of manufacturing industries in the table accords with the United Nations International Standard Industrial Classification (ISIC) revision 3. Editions of *World Development Indicators* prior to 2008 used revision 2, first published in 1948. Revision 3 was completed in 1989, and many countries now use it. But revision 2 is still widely used for compiling cross-country data. UNIDO has converted these data to accord with revision 3. Concordances matching ISIC categories to national classification systems and to related systems such as the Standard International Trade Classification are available.

In establishing classifications systems compilers must define both the types of activities to be described and the units whose activities are to be reported. There are many possibilities, and the choices affect how the statistics can be interpreted and how useful they are in analyzing economic behavior. The ISIC emphasizes commonalities in the production process and is explicitly not intended to measure outputs (for which there is a newly developed Central Product Classification). Nevertheless, the ISIC views an activity as defined by "a process resulting in a homogeneous set of products" (United Nations 1990 [ISIC, series M, no. 4, rev. 3], p. 9).

Firms typically use multiple processes to produce a product. For example, an automobile manufacturer engages in forging, welding, and painting as well as advertising, accounting, and other service activities. Collecting data at such a detailed level is not practical, nor is it useful to record production data at the highest level of a large, multiplant, multiproduct firm. The ISIC has therefore adopted as the definition of an establishment "an enterprise or part of an enterprise which independently engages in one, or predominantly one, kind of economic activity at or from one location . . . for which data are available . . ." (United Nations 1990, p. 25). By design, this definition matches the reporting unit required for the production accounts of the United Nations System of National Accounts. The ISIC system is described in the United Nations' *International Standard Industrial Classification of All Economic Activities, Third Revision* (1990). The discussion of the ISIC draws on Ryten (1998).

Definitions

• **Manufacturing value added** is the sum of gross output less the value of intermediate inputs used in production for industries classified in ISIC major division 3. • **Food, beverages, and tobacco** correspond to ISIC divisions 15 and 16. • **Textiles and clothing** correspond to ISIC divisions 17–19. • **Machinery and transport equipment** correspond to ISIC divisions 29, 30, 32, 34, and 35. • **Chemicals** correspond to ISIC division 24. • **Other manufacturing,** a residual, covers wood and related products (ISIC division 20), paper and related products (ISIC divisions 21 and 22), petroleum and related products (ISIC division 23), basic metals and mineral products (ISIC division 27), fabricated metal products and professional goods (ISIC division 28), and other industries (ISIC divisions 25, 26, 31, 33, 36, and 37).

Manufacturing continues to show strong growth in East Asia through 2008   **4.3a**

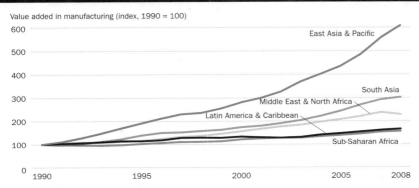

Value added in manufacturing (index, 1990 = 100)

East Asia & Pacific

South Asia

Middle East & North Africa

Latin America & Caribbean

Sub-Saharan Africa

Manufacturing continues to be the dominant sector in East Asia and Pacific, growing an average of about 10.5 percent a year between 1990 and 2008.

Source: World Development Indicators data files.

Data sources

Data on manufacturing value added are from the World Bank's national accounts files. Data used to calculate shares of industry value added are provided to the World Bank in electronic files by UNIDO. The most recent published source is UNIDO's *International Yearbook of Industrial Statistics 2010.*

	Merchandise exports		Food		Agricultural raw materials		Fuels		Ores and metals		Manufactures	
	$ millions		% of total		% of total		% of total		% of total		% of total	
	1995	2008	1995	2008	1995	2008	1995	2008	1995	2008	1995	2008
Afghanistan	166	680	..	5	..	0	..	..	..	..	..	41
Albania	202	1,353	11	4	9	8	3	22	12	33	65	33
Algeria	10,258	78,233	1	0	0	0	95	98	1	1	4	2
Angola	3,642	66,300	..	..	..	..	..	..	..	..	..	..
Argentina	20,967	70,588	50	53	4	1	10	10	2	3	34	31
Armenia	271	1,069	11	19	5	2	1	0	26	29	54	51
Australia	53,111	187,428	22	12	8	2	19	34	18	27	30	20
Austria	57,738	182,158	4	7	3	2	1	3	3	3	88	81
Azerbaijan	635	31,500	4	1	8	0	66	97	1	0	20	1
Bangladesh	3,501	15,369	10	7	3	3	0	2	0	0	85	88
Belarus	4,803	32,902	..	7	..	1	..	37	..	1	..	52
Belgium	178,265[a]	476,953	10[a]	9	1[a]	1	3[a]	9	3[a]	3	78[a]	75
Benin	420	1,050	14	41	75	44	5	0	0	1	6	14
Bolivia	1,100	6,370	21	14	10	1	15	52	35	27	19	6
Bosnia and Herzegovina	152	5,064	..	6	..	7	..	10	..	13	..	64
Botswana	2,142	5,040	..	3	..	0	..	0	..	20	..	77
Brazil	46,506	197,942	29	28	5	4	1	9	10	12	54	45
Bulgaria	5,355	23,124	18	12	3	1	7	16	10	17	60	51
Burkina Faso	276	620	25	..	69	..	0	..	0	..	6	..
Burundi	105	56	91	65	4	6	0	1	1	9	3	18
Cambodia	855	4,290	..	..	..	..	..	..	..	..	..	..
Cameroon	1,651	4,350	27	12	28	16	29	62	8	5	8	3
Canada	192,197	456,420	8	9	9	5	9	29	7	8	63	47
Central African Republic	171	185	4	..	20	..	1	..	30	..	45	..
Chad	243	4,800	..	..	..	..	..	..	..	..	..	..
Chile	16,024	67,788	24	16	12	6	0	1	48	61	13	12
China†	148,780	1,428,488	8	3	2	0	4	2	2	2	84	93
Hong Kong SAR, China[b]	173,871	370,242	3	4	0	2	0	3	1	8	94	83
Colombia	10,056	37,626	31	15	5	4	28	47	1	2	35	32
Congo, Dem. Rep.	1,563	3,950	..	..	..	..	..	..	..	..	..	..
Congo, Rep.	1,172	9,050	1	..	8	..	88	..	0	..	3	..
Costa Rica	3,453	9,675	63	32	5	3	1	1	1	1	25	63
Côte d'Ivoire	3,806	10,100	63	41	20	9	10	37	0	1	7	12
Croatia	4,517	14,112	11	10	5	3	9	13	2	4	74	70
Cuba	1,600	3,500	..	10	..	0	..	0	..	2	..	24
Czech Republic	21,335	146,934	6	4	4	1	4	3	3	2	82	87
Denmark	50,906	117,174	24	17	3	2	3	11	1	2	60	66
Dominican Republic	3,780	6,910	19	21	0	1	0	0	0	3	78	75
Ecuador	4,307	18,511	53	25	3	4	36	62	0	1	8	9
Egypt, Arab Rep.	3,450	25,483	10	10	6	2	37	44	6	7	40	37
El Salvador	1,652	4,549	57	20	1	1	0	3	3	2	39	74
Eritrea	86	20	..	..	..	..	..	..	..	..	..	..
Estonia	1,840	12,343	16	9	10	4	6	12	3	4	65	66
Ethiopia	422	1,500	73	75	13	14	3	0	0	1	11	9
Finland	40,490	96,714	2	2	8	4	2	7	3	4	83	81
France	301,162	608,684	14	12	1	1	2	5	3	3	79	78
Gabon	2,713	8,350	0	1	13	7	83	86	2	3	2	4
Gambia, The	16	14	60	60	1	4	0	0	1	15	36	21
Georgia	151	1,498	29	18	3	2	19	3	8	22	41	55
Germany	523,461	1,465,215	5	5	1	1	1	3	3	3	87	82
Ghana	1,724	5,650	58	63	15	9	5	2	9	6	13	19
Greece	11,054	25,311	30	21	4	2	7	11	7	9	50	54
Guatemala	2,155	7,765	65	38	4	4	2	7	0	4	28	47
Guinea	702	1,300	8	2	1	5	0	2	67	59	24	32
Guinea-Bissau	24	98	89	..	11	..	0	..	0	..	0	..
Haiti	110	490	37	..	0	..	0	..	0	..	62	..
Honduras	1,769	6,130	87	53	3	2	0	6	0	8	9	29
†Data for Taiwan, China	113,047	255,629	3	1	2	1	1	7	1	2	93	88

	Merchandise exports		Food		Agricultural raw materials		Fuels		Ores and metals		Manufactures	
	$ millions		% of total		% of total		% of total		% of total		% of total	
	1995	2008	1995	2008	1995	2008	1995	2008	1995	2008	1995	2008
Hungary	12,865	107,904	21	7	2	1	3	3	5	2	68	80
India	30,630	179,073	19	10	1	2	2	18	3	6	74	63
Indonesia	45,417	139,281	11	18	7	6	25	29	6	8	51	39
Iran, Islamic Rep.	18,360	116,350	4	4	1	0	86	83	1	2	9	10
Iraq	496	59,800	..	0	..	0	..	34	..	0	..	0
Ireland	44,705	124,158	19	10	1	0	0	1	1	1	72	85
Israel	19,046	60,825	5	3	2	1	0	1	1	1	89	92
Italy	233,766	539,727	7	7	1	1	1	5	1	2	89	83
Jamaica	1,427	2,400	22	15	0	0	1	18	6	6	71	61
Japan	443,116	782,337	0	1	1	1	1	2	1	3	95	89
Jordan	1,769	7,790	25	14	2	0	0	0	24	11	49	75
Kazakhstan	5,250	71,184	10	4	3	0	25	69	24	12	38	15
Kenya	1,878	4,972	56	44	7	14	6	2	3	3	28	37
Korea, Dem. Rep.	959	1,950	..	..	..	..	..	..	..	..	..	..
Korea, Rep.	125,058	422,007	2	1	1	1	2	7	1	3	93	89
Kosovo	..	..	..	..	..	..	..	..	..	..	..	..
Kuwait	12,785	93,180	0	0	0	0	95	96	0	0	5	3
Kyrgyz Republic	409	1,642	23	23	13	7	11	16	13	5	40	47
Lao PDR	311	1,080	..	..	..	..	..	..	..	..	..	..
Latvia	1,305	10,081	14	16	23	9	2	3	1	4	58	63
Lebanon	816	4,454	20	11	2	1	0	0	8	11	70	34
Lesotho	160	900	..	..	..	..	..	..	..	..	..	..
Liberia	820	262	..	..	..	..	..	..	..	..	..	..
Libya	8,975	63,050	0	..	0	..	95	..	0	..	5	..
Lithuania	2,705	23,728	18	15	8	2	11	25	5	2	58	55
Macedonia, FYR	1,204	3,978	18	14	5	1	0	5	18	5	58	76
Madagascar	507	1,345	69	21	6	3	1	6	7	3	14	67
Malawi	405	790	90	86	2	4	0	0	0	0	7	10
Malaysia	73,914	199,516	10	12	6	2	7	18	1	2	75	54
Mali	441	1,650	23	28	75	42	0	6	0	1	2	22
Mauritania	488	1,750	57	12	0	0	1	22	42	60	0	0
Mauritius	1,538	2,351	29	27	1	1	0	0	0	1	70	57
Mexico	79,542	291,807	8	6	1	0	10	17	3	3	78	74
Moldova	745	1,597	72	59	2	1	1	0	3	8	23	32
Mongolia	473	2,539	2	2	28	12	0	10	60	70	10	6
Morocco	6,881	20,065	31	19	3	2	2	2	12	10	51	67
Mozambique	168	2,600	66	15	16	4	2	11	2	57	13	6
Myanmar	860	6,900	..	..	..	..	..	..	..	..	..	..
Namibia	1,409	2,960	..	23	..	0	..	0	..	31	..	45
Nepal	345	1,100	8	..	1	..	0	..	0	..	84	..
Netherlands	203,171	633,974	20	13	4	3	7	11	3	2	63	55
New Zealand	13,645	30,586	45	53	19	9	2	7	5	5	29	23
Nicaragua	466	1,489	75	85	3	1	1	1	1	2	21	10
Niger	288	820	17	18	1	4	0	2	80	69	1	7
Nigeria	12,342	81,900	2	1	2	1	96	92	0	0	1	5
Norway	41,992	167,941	8	5	2	0	47	68	9	6	27	17
Oman	6,068	37,670	5	2	0	0	79	86	2	1	14	7
Pakistan	8,029	20,375	12	18	4	1	1	6	0	1	83	73
Panama	625	1,180	75	84	0	1	3	1	1	5	20	9
Papua New Guinea	2,654	5,700	13	..	20	..	38	..	25	..	4	..
Paraguay	919	4,434	44	88	36	3	0	0	0	1	19	8
Peru	5,575	31,529	31	19	3	1	5	11	46	52	15	16
Philippines	17,502	49,025	13	7	1	1	2	3	4	5	42	83
Poland	22,895	167,944	10	9	3	1	8	4	7	4	71	80
Portugal	22,783	55,861	7	10	5	2	3	6	2	3	83	72
Puerto Rico	..	..	..	..	..	..	..	..	..	..	..	..
Qatar	3,651	63,830	0	0	0	0	82	94	0	0	17	5

4.4 Structure of merchandise exports

	Merchandise exports		Food		Agricultural raw materials		Fuels		Ores and metals		Manufactures	
	$ millions		% of total		% of total		% of total		% of total		% of total	
	1995	2008	1995	2008	1995	2008	1995	2008	1995	2008	1995	2008
Romania	7,910	49,546	7	6	3	2	8	9	3	5	78	77
Russian Federation	81,095	471,763	2	2	3	2	43	66	10	6	26	17
Rwanda	54	250	57	66	16	1	0	0	12	28	14	4
Saudi Arabia	50,040	328,930	1	1	0	0	88	90	1	0	10	9
Senegal	993	2,390	9	21	7	2	22	34	12	4	48	39
Serbia	..	10,973	28	19	4	2	2	3	15	10	49	66
Sierra Leone	42	220	..	..	..	..	..	..	..	..	..	..
Singapore[b]	118,268	338,176	4	2	1	0	7	18	2	1	84	70
Slovak Republic	8,580	70,967	6	4	4	1	4	5	4	2	82	86
Slovenia	8,316	34,199	4	4	2	2	1	3	3	4	90	87
Somalia	..	..	..	..	..	..	..	..	..	..	..	..
South Africa	27,853[c]	80,781	8[c]	7	4[c]	2	9[c]	9	8[c]	29	44[c]	52
Spain	97,849	268,108	15	13	2	1	2	5	2	3	78	76
Sri Lanka	3,798	8,370	21	25	4	3	0	0	1	2	73	67
Sudan	555	12,450	44	3	47	1	0	94	0	1	6	0
Swaziland	866	1,790	..	21	..	7	..	1	..	1	..	70
Sweden	80,440	183,975	2	4	6	4	2	7	3	4	79	75
Switzerland	81,641	200,387	3	3	1	0	0	3	3	4	94	89
Syrian Arab Republic	3,563	14,300	12	21	7	1	63	41	1	1	17	35
Tajikistan	750	1,406	..	..	..	..	..	..	..	..	..	..
Tanzania	682	2,870	65	49	23	9	0	1	0	18	10	23
Thailand	56,439	177,844	19	13	5	5	1	6	1	1	73	74
Timor-Leste	..	..	..	..	..	..	..	..	..	..	..	..
Togo	378	790	19	16	42	9	0	0	32	13	7	62
Trinidad and Tobago	2,455	17,800	8	2	0	0	48	70	0	3	43	25
Tunisia	5,475	19,319	10	9	1	0	8	17	2	2	79	72
Turkey	21,637	131,975	20	8	1	0	1	6	3	3	74	81
Turkmenistan	1,880	10,780	1	..	13	..	77	..	1	..	8	..
Uganda	460	2,180	90	63	5	6	0	1	1	2	4	27
Ukraine	13,128	67,049	19	16	1	1	4	6	7	6	68	70
United Arab Emirates	28,364	231,550	8	1	0	0	9	65	55	1	28	4
United Kingdom	237,953	457,983	8	6	1	1	6	13	3	5	81	70
United States	584,743	1,300,532	11	10	4	2	2	7	3	4	77	74
Uruguay	2,106	5,949	44	59	15	8	1	3	1	0	39	29
Uzbekistan	3,430	10,360	..	..	..	..	..	..	..	..	..	..
Venezuela, RB	18,457	93,542	3	0	0	0	77	94	6	2	14	4
Vietnam	5,449	62,906	30	20	3	3	18	21	0	1	44	55
West Bank and Gaza	..	..	..	..	..	..	..	..	..	..	..	..
Yemen, Rep.	1,945	9,270	3	5	1	0	95	92	1	0	1	2
Zambia	1,040	5,093	3	6	1	1	3	1	87	85	7	7
Zimbabwe	2,118	2,150	43	17	7	12	1	1	12	20	37	50
World	5,172,492 t	16,129,607 t	9 w	8 w	3 w	2 w	7 w	12 w	3 w	4 w	76 w	70 w
Low income	35,717	167,308	27	21	7	5	19	20	6	7	40	46
Middle income	906,854	4,905,095	14	10	3	2	11	21	5	6	64	59
Lower middle income	408,391	2,627,173	14	8	3	2	7	13	3	3	70	71
Upper middle income	498,548	2,276,454	15	11	4	2	15	27	6	8	59	49
Low & middle income	942,571	5,072,412	15	10	4	2	11	21	5	6	63	59
East Asia & Pacific	354,784	2,081,208	11	8	4	2	6	9	2	3	74	76
Europe & Central Asia	179,048	1,141,248	9	6	3	2	25	39	8	5	47	43
Latin America & Carib.	223,927	873,299	20	16	3	2	15	22	7	8	55	51
Middle East & N. Africa	62,002	418,183	6	5	1	0	73	75	3	2	17	16
South Asia	46,657	225,882	17	13	2	2	1	14	3	5	76	65
Sub-Saharan Africa	76,554	336,637	18	12	7	3	36	36	8	16	28	32
High income	4,229,538	11,060,159	8	7	3	2	6	10	3	4	79	73
Euro area	1,742,200	4,612,227	11	8	2	1	2	5	2	3	81	77

Note: Components may not sum to 100 percent because of unclassified trade. Exports of gold are excluded.
a. Includes Luxembourg. b. Includes re-exports. c. Refers to the South African Customs Union (Botswana, Lesotho, Namibia, South Africa, and Swaziland).

About the data

Data on merchandise trade are from customs reports of goods moving into or out of an economy or from reports of financial transactions related to merchandise trade recorded in the balance of payments. Because of differences in timing and definitions, trade flow estimates from customs reports and balance of payments may differ. Several international agencies process trade data, each correcting unreported or misreported data, leading to other differences.

The most detailed source of data on international trade in goods is the United Nations Statistics Division's Commodity Trade (Comtrade) database. The International Monetary Fund (IMF) also collects customs-based data on trade in goods. Exports are recorded as the cost of the goods delivered to the frontier of the exporting country for shipment—the free on board (f.o.b.) value. Many countries report trade data in U.S. dollars. When countries report in local currency, the United Nations Statistics Division applies the average official exchange rate to the U.S. dollar for the period shown.

Countries may report trade according to the general or special system of trade. Under the general system exports comprise outward-moving goods that are (a) goods wholly or partly produced in the country; (b) foreign goods, neither transformed nor declared for domestic consumption in the country, that move outward from customs storage; and (c) goods previously included as imports for domestic consumption but subsequently exported without transformation. Under the special system exports comprise categories a and c. In some compilations categories b and c

are classified as re-exports. Because of differences in reporting practices, data on exports may not be fully comparable across economies.

The data on total exports of goods (merchandise) are from the World Trade Organization (WTO), which obtains data from national statistical offices and the IMF's *International Financial Statistics,* supplemented by the Comtrade database and publications or databases of regional organizations, specialized agencies, economic groups, and private sources (such as Eurostat, the Food and Agriculture Organization, and country reports of the Economist Intelligence Unit). Country websites and email contact have improved collection of up-to-date statistics, reducing the proportion of estimates. The WTO database now covers most major traders in Africa, Asia, and Latin America, which together with high-income countries account for nearly 95 percent of world trade. Reliability of data for countries in Europe and Central Asia has also improved.

Export shares by major commodity group are from Comtrade. The values of total exports reported here have not been fully reconciled with the estimates from the national accounts or the balance of payments.

The classification of commodity groups is based on the Standard International Trade Classification (SITC) revision 3. Previous editions contained data based on the SITC revision 1. Data for earlier years in previous editions may differ because of this change in methodology. Concordance tables are available to convert data reported in one system to another.

Definitions

• **Merchandise exports** are the f.o.b. value of goods provided to the rest of the world. • **Food** corresponds to the commodities in SITC sections 0 (food and live animals), 1 (beverages and tobacco), and 4 (animal and vegetable oils and fats) and SITC division 22 (oil seeds, oil nuts, and oil kernels). • **Agricultural raw materials** correspond to SITC section 2 (crude materials except fuels), excluding divisions 22, 27 (crude fertilizers and minerals excluding coal, petroleum, and precious stones), and 28 (metalliferous ores and scrap). • **Fuels** correspond to SITC section 3 (mineral fuels). • **Ores and metals** correspond to the commodities in SITC divisions 27, 28, and 68 (nonferrous metals). • **Manufactures** correspond to the commodities in SITC sections 5 (chemicals), 6 (basic manufactures), 7 (machinery and transport equipment), and 8 (miscellaneous manufactured goods), excluding division 68.

Developing economies' share of world merchandise exports continues to expand   4.4a

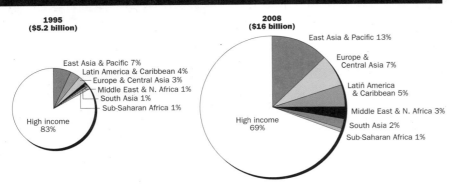

1995
($5.2 billion)

- East Asia & Pacific 7%
- Latin America & Caribbean 4%
- Europe & Central Asia 3%
- Middle East & N. Africa 1%
- South Asia 1%
- Sub-Saharan Africa 1%
- High income 83%

2008
($16 billion)

- East Asia & Pacific 13%
- Europe & Central Asia 7%
- Latin America & Caribbean 5%
- Middle East & N. Africa 3%
- South Asia 2%
- Sub-Saharan Africa 1%
- High income 69%

Developing economies' share of world merchandise exports increased 13 percentage points from 1995 to 2008. East Asia and Pacific was the biggest gainer, capturing an additional 6 percentage points. Every region increased its share in world trade.

Source: World Development Indicators data files and World Trade Organization.

Data sources

Data on merchandise exports are from the WTO. Data on shares of exports by major commodity group are from Comtrade. The WTO publishes data on world trade in its *Annual Report.* The IMF publishes estimates of total exports of goods in its *International Financial Statistics* and *Direction of Trade Statistics,* as does the United Nations Statistics Division in its *Monthly Bulletin of Statistics.* And the United Nations Conference on Trade and Development publishes data on the structure of exports in its *Handbook of Statistics.* Tariff line records of exports are compiled in the United Nations Statistics Division's Comtrade database.

4.5 Structure of merchandise imports

	Merchandise imports ($ millions)		Food (% of total)		Agricultural raw materials (% of total)		Fuels (% of total)		Ores and metals (% of total)		Manufactures (% of total)	
	1995	2008	1995	2008	1995	2008	1995	2008	1995	2008	1995	2008
Afghanistan	387	3,350	..	7	..	..	..	8	..	..	..	12
Albania	714	5,230	34	16	1	1	2	16	1	3	61	63
Algeria	10,100	39,156	29	20	3	2	1	1	2	2	65	75
Angola	1,468	21,100	..	..	..	..	..	..	..	..	..	..
Argentina	20,122	57,413	5	5	2	1	4	7	2	3	86	83
Armenia	674	4,412	31	19	0	2	27	16	0	3	39	61
Australia	61,283	200,272	5	5	2	1	5	16	1	2	86	75
Austria	66,237	184,247	6	7	3	2	4	12	4	5	82	73
Azerbaijan	668	7,200	39	16	1	1	4	2	2	2	53	79
Bangladesh	6,694	23,860	17	22	3	8	8	11	2	3	69	54
Belarus	5,564	39,483	..	7	..	1	..	35	..	4	..	49
Belgium	164,934[a]	469,889	11[a]	8	2[a]	1	7[a]	15	5[a]	4	70[a]	70
Benin	746	1,990	27	31	3	5	9	22	1	1	59	42
Bolivia	1,424	4,987	10	9	2	1	5	11	3	1	82	77
Bosnia and Herzegovina	1,082	12,282	..	16	..	1	..	16	..	3	..	63
Botswana	1,911	5,180	..	12	..	1	..	17	..	2	..	67
Brazil	54,137	182,810	11	4	3	1	12	20	3	4	71	70
Bulgaria	5,660	38,256	8	7	3	1	34	14	4	8	48	66
Burkina Faso	455	1,800	21	..	2	..	14	..	1	..	62	..
Burundi	234	403	21	11	2	2	11	3	1	1	64	83
Cambodia	1,187	6,510	..	..	..	..	..	..	..	..	..	..
Cameroon	1,199	4,360	17	18	3	2	3	31	2	1	76	48
Canada	168,426	418,336	6	6	2	1	4	12	3	3	83	76
Central African Republic	175	310	16	..	10	..	9	..	2	..	64	..
Chad	365	1,700	24	..	1	..	18	..	1	..	56	..
Chile	15,900	61,901	7	7	2	1	9	29	2	3	79	60
China[†]	132,084	1,133,040	7	5	5	4	4	16	4	13	79	62
Hong Kong SAR, China	196,072	392,962	5	4	2	1	2	4	2	2	88	90
Colombia	13,853	39,669	9	10	3	1	3	5	2	3	78	80
Congo, Dem. Rep.	871	4,100	..	..	..	..	..	..	..	..	..	..
Congo, Rep.	670	2,850	21	..	1	..	20	..	1	..	58	..
Costa Rica	4,036	15,374	10	9	1	1	9	14	2	2	78	74
Côte d'Ivoire	2,931	7,150	21	20	1	1	19	36	1	1	57	42
Croatia	7,352	30,728	12	8	2	1	12	18	3	3	67	70
Cuba	2,825	14,500	..	12	..	0	..	0	..	1	..	50
Czech Republic	25,085	141,882	7	5	3	1	8	10	4	4	77	78
Denmark	45,939	112,296	12	12	3	2	3	8	2	2	73	75
Dominican Republic	5,170	16,400	..	12	..	1	..	26	..	1	..	60
Ecuador	4,152	18,686	8	9	3	1	6	14	2	1	82	75
Egypt, Arab Rep.	11,760	48,382	28	17	7	3	1	12	3	9	61	59
El Salvador	3,329	9,755	15	15	2	2	9	19	2	1	72	63
Eritrea	454	530	..	..	..	..	..	..	..	..	..	..
Estonia	2,546	15,990	14	10	3	2	11	16	1	2	71	66
Ethiopia	1,145	7,600	14	14	2	1	11	23	1	1	72	60
Finland	29,470	91,045	6	5	4	3	9	18	6	7	74	64
France	289,391	707,720	11	8	3	1	7	17	4	3	76	70
Gabon	882	2,550	19	17	1	0	4	4	1	1	75	77
Gambia, The	182	329	36	30	1	2	14	20	0	1	46	47
Georgia	392	6,058	36	15	0	1	39	18	0	2	24	64
Germany	463,872	1,206,213	10	7	3	1	6	14	4	5	73	65
Ghana	1,906	10,400	8	15	1	1	6	14	0	1	77	69
Greece	25,898	77,970	16	11	2	1	7	20	3	4	71	64
Guatemala	3,292	14,545	12	13	2	1	12	20	1	1	73	65
Guinea	819	1,600	31	13	1	0	19	33	1	0	47	53
Guinea-Bissau	133	160	44	..	0	..	16	..	0	..	40	..
Haiti	653	2,148	..	..	..	..	..	..	..	..	..	..
Honduras	1,879	9,990	13	15	1	1	12	20	1	1	74	64
[†]Data for Taiwan, China	103,558	240,448	6	4	4	1	7	26	6	8	75	60

	Merchandise imports		Food		Agricultural raw materials		Fuels		Ores and metals		Manufactures	
	$ millions		% of total		% of total		% of total		% of total		% of total	
	1995	2008	1995	2008	1995	2008	1995	2008	1995	2008	1995	2008
Hungary	15,465	107,864	6	4	3	1	12	9	4	2	75	73
India	34,707	291,598	4	2	4	2	24	39	7	6	54	47
Indonesia	40,630	126,177	9	7	6	3	8	24	4	4	73	62
Iran, Islamic Rep.	13,882	57,230	21	2	2	1	2	4	3	0	71	16
Iraq	665	31,200	..	..	..	..	..	..	..	..	..	..
Ireland	32,340	82,774	8	10	1	1	3	12	2	2	76	70
Israel	29,578	67,410	7	7	2	1	6	20	2	2	82	70
Italy	205,990	556,311	12	8	6	2	7	14	5	5	68	62
Jamaica	2,818	7,880	14	12	2	1	13	41	1	0	68	45
Japan	335,882	761,984	16	9	6	2	16	35	7	8	54	45
Jordan	3,697	16,888	21	17	2	1	13	22	3	3	61	56
Kazakhstan	3,807	37,889	10	8	2	1	25	14	5	2	59	74
Kenya	2,991	11,074	10	12	2	1	15	27	2	2	71	58
Korea, Dem. Rep.	1,380	3,950	..	..	..	..	..	..	..	..	..	..
Korea, Rep.	135,119	435,275	6	4	6	2	14	27	6	9	68	58
Kosovo	..	..	..	..	..	..	..	..	..	..	..	..
Kuwait	7,790	25,125	16	13	1	1	1	1	2	3	81	83
Kyrgyz Republic	522	4,058	18	15	3	2	36	31	3	2	40	50
Lao PDR	589	1,390	..	..	..	..	..	..	..	..	..	..
Latvia	1,815	16,007	10	13	2	2	21	15	1	2	66	65
Lebanon	7,278	16,754	21	16	2	1	9	22	2	2	66	35
Lesotho	1,107	2,030	..	..	..	..	..	..	..	..	..	..
Liberia	510	865	..	..	..	..	..	..	..	..	..	..
Libya	5,392	11,500	23	..	1	..	0	..	1	..	75	..
Lithuania	3,650	30,811	13	11	4	1	19	28	4	2	58	56
Macedonia, FYR	1,719	6,852	17	11	3	1	12	21	3	5	64	62
Madagascar	628	4,040	16	11	2	1	14	13	1	0	65	75
Malawi	475	1,700	14	12	1	1	11	10	1	1	73	77
Malaysia	77,691	156,896	5	7	1	2	2	11	3	5	86	66
Mali	772	2,550	20	12	1	0	16	21	1	1	62	65
Mauritania	431	1,750	24	28	1	1	22	35	0	0	53	36
Mauritius	1,976	4,646	17	21	3	3	7	21	1	1	72	54
Mexico	75,858	323,151	6	7	2	1	2	10	2	3	80	78
Moldova	840	4,899	8	12	3	1	46	23	2	1	42	61
Mongolia	415	3,616	14	12	1	0	19	27	1	1	65	60
Morocco	10,023	41,699	20	12	6	3	14	20	4	4	56	61
Mozambique	704	4,100	22	14	3	1	10	20	1	0	62	47
Myanmar	1,348	4,290	..	..	..	..	..	..	..	..	..	..
Namibia	1,616	4,520	..	14	..	1	..	14	..	1	..	70
Nepal	1,333	3,570	12	..	3	..	12	..	3	..	46	..
Netherlands	185,232	573,924	14	10	2	1	8	15	3	3	72	58
New Zealand	13,957	34,366	7	9	1	1	5	18	3	3	83	69
Nicaragua	975	4,287	18	16	1	0	18	23	1	0	63	60
Niger	374	1,450	32	25	1	5	13	17	3	2	51	52
Nigeria	8,222	41,700	18	10	1	1	1	2	2	2	77	85
Norway	32,968	89,070	7	7	3	1	3	5	6	7	81	79
Oman	4,379	23,095	20	11	1	1	2	3	2	4	70	80
Pakistan	11,515	42,326	18	12	6	5	16	33	3	3	57	47
Panama	2,510	9,050	11	11	1	0	14	21	1	1	73	67
Papua New Guinea	1,452	3,550	..	..	..	..	..	..	..	..	..	..
Paraguay	3,144	10,180	19	7	0	0	7	16	1	1	74	77
Peru	7,584	29,981	14	4	2	5	9	0	1	0	75	77
Philippines	28,341	59,170	8	11	2	1	9	21	3	2	58	65
Poland	29,050	203,924	10	7	3	2	9	11	3	3	74	73
Portugal	32,610	89,753	14	12	4	1	8	17	2	3	72	61
Puerto Rico	..	..	..	..	..	..	..	..	..	..	..	..
Qatar	3,398	26,850	9	6	1	0	1	1	2	3	87	90

	Merchandise imports		Food		Agricultural raw materials		Fuels		Ores and metals		Manufactures	
	$ millions		% of total		% of total		% of total		% of total		% of total	
	1995	2008	1995	2008	1995	2008	1995	2008	1995	2008	1995	2008
Romania	10,278	82,707	8	7	2	1	21	13	4	3	63	74
Russian Federation	60,945	291,971	18	12	1	1	3	2	2	2	45	79
Rwanda	236	1,110	19	10	3	2	12	7	3	3	64	78
Saudi Arabia	28,091	111,870	17	13	1	1	0	0	4	5	76	81
Senegal	1,412	5,702	25	26	2	1	30	28	1	2	42	42
Serbia	..	22,999	14	6	4	2	14	17	7	6	60	69
Sierra Leone	133	560	..	..	..	..	..	..	..	..	..	..
Singapore	124,507	319,780	5	3	1	0	8	27	2	2	83	64
Slovak Republic	8,770	73,321	9	6	3	1	13	13	6	3	70	77
Slovenia	9,492	36,993	8	7	5	3	7	13	4	5	74	72
Somalia	..	..	..	..	..	..	..	..	..	..	..	..
South Africa	30,546[b]	99,480	7[b]	5	2[b]	1	8[b]	22	2[b]	3	78[b]	62
Spain	113,537	402,302	14	9	3	1	8	15	4	4	71	70
Sri Lanka	5,306	14,008	16	14	2	1	6	23	1	2	75	60
Sudan	1,218	9,200	24	7	2	0	14	0	0	0	59	68
Swaziland	1,008	2,200	..	21	..	1	..	14	..	1	..	63
Sweden	65,036	166,971	7	8	2	1	6	15	4	4	80	69
Switzerland	80,152	183,491	6	6	2	1	3	9	3	5	85	80
Syrian Arab Republic	4,709	18,320	17	13	3	2	1	33	1	4	76	48
Tajikistan	810	3,270	..	..	..	..	..	..	..	..	..	..
Tanzania	1,675	6,954	10	12	1	1	1	30	4	1	84	55
Thailand	70,786	178,655	4	5	4	2	7	21	3	5	81	66
Timor-Leste	..	..	..	..	..	..	..	..	..	..	..	..
Togo	594	1,540	18	15	2	1	30	27	1	2	49	55
Trinidad and Tobago	1,714	9,900	16	8	1	0	1	35	6	6	77	50
Tunisia	7,902	24,612	13	10	4	2	7	17	3	6	73	65
Turkey	35,709	201,960	7	4	6	2	13	17	6	9	68	60
Turkmenistan	1,365	4,680	24	..	0		3	..	2	..	71	
Uganda	1,056	4,800	16	13	3	1	2	19	2	1	78	66
Ukraine	15,484	84,032	8	7	2	1	48	27	3	4	38	60
United Arab Emirates	23,778	158,900	15	7	0	0	4	1	6	5	75	73
United Kingdom	267,250	631,913	10	9	2	1	4	13	3	4	80	68
United States	770,852	2,165,982	5	4	2	1	8	23	3	3	79	66
Uruguay	2,867	8,933	10	8	4	2	10	30	1	1	74	59
Uzbekistan	2,750	5,260	..	..	..	..	..	..	..	..	..	..
Venezuela, RB	12,649	49,635	14	16	4	1	1	1	4	2	77	79
Vietnam	8,155	80,416	5	6	2	3	10	14	2	4	76	72
West Bank and Gaza	..	..	..	..	..	..	..	..	..	..	..	..
Yemen, Rep.	1,582	9,300	29	25	2	1	8	29	1	1	59	45
Zambia	700	5,070	10	6	2	0	13	16	2	13	72	64
Zimbabwe	2,660	2,900	6	11	2	1	9	17	2	6	78	57
World	5,228,953 t	16,300,527 w	9 w	7 w	3 w	1 w	7 w	18 w	4 w	4 w	75 w	67 w
Low income	50,461	239,464	13	13	3	3	13	16	2	3	67	63
Middle income	965,308	4,547,215	8	7	4	2	7	16	3	6	75	67
Lower middle income	436,271	2,376,905	8	7	5	3	8	21	4	8	72	61
Upper middle income	528,947	2,164,216	8	7	3	1	7	13	3	4	77	71
Low & middle income	1,015,776	4,786,667	8	7	3	2	7	16	3	6	75	67
East Asia & Pacific	366,057	1,762,013	6	6	4	3	5	17	4	9	78	64
Europe & Central Asia	193,383	1,146,612	11	8	3	1	14	14	3	4	61	68
Latin America & Carib.	241,363	896,683	8	8	2	1	5	13	2	3	78	74
Middle East & N. Africa	77,167	315,621	22	12	4	2	6	14	3	2	66	50
South Asia	60,322	380,660	8	5	4	1	21	36	6	5	56	48
Sub-Saharan Africa	78,377	296,944	12	10	2	1	10	19	2	2	73	64
High income	4,212,901	11,522,679	9	7	3	1	7	18	4	4	76	67
Euro area	1,644,739	4,599,680	11	8	3	1	7	15	4	4	73	66

Note: Components may not sum to 100 percent because of unclassified trade.

a. Includes Luxembourg. b. Refers to the South African Customs Union (Botswana, Lesotho, Namibia, South Africa, and Swaziland).

Structure of merchandise imports | 4.5

Data on imports of goods are derived from the same sources as data on exports. In principle, world exports and imports should be identical. Similarly, exports from an economy should equal the sum of imports by the rest of the world from that economy. But differences in timing and definitions result in discrepancies in reported values at all levels. For further discussion of indicators of merchandise trade, see *About the data* for tables 4.4 and 6.2.

The value of imports is generally recorded as the cost of the goods when purchased by the importer plus the cost of transport and insurance to the frontier of the importing country—the cost, insurance, and freight (c.i.f.) value, corresponding to the landed cost at the point of entry of foreign goods into the country. A few countries, including Australia, Canada, and the United States, collect import data on a free on board (f.o.b.) basis and adjust them for freight and insurance costs. Many countries report trade data in U.S. dollars. When countries report in local currency, the United Nations Statistics Division applies the average official exchange rate to the U.S. dollar for the period shown.

Countries may report trade according to the general or special system of trade. Under the general system imports include goods imported for domestic consumption and imports into bonded warehouses and free trade zones. Under the special system imports comprise goods imported for domestic consumption (including transformation and repair) and withdrawals for domestic consumption from bonded warehouses

and free trade zones. Goods transported through a country en route to another are excluded.

The data on total imports of goods (merchandise) in the table come from the World Trade Organization (WTO). For further discussion of the WTO's sources and methodology, see *About the data* for table 4.4. The import shares by major commodity group are from the United Nations Statistics Division's Commodity Trade (Comtrade) database. The values of total imports reported here have not been fully reconciled with the estimates of imports of goods and services from the national accounts (shown in table 4.8) or those from the balance of payments (table 4.15).

The classification of commodity groups is based on the Standard International Trade Classification (SITC) revision 3. Previous editions contained data based on the SITC revision 1. Data for earlier years in previous editions may differ because of this change in methodology. Concordance tables are available to convert data reported in one system to another.

• **Merchandise imports** are the c.i.f. value of goods purchased from the rest of the world valued in U.S. dollars. • **Food** corresponds to the commodities in SITC sections 0 (food and live animals), 1 (beverages and tobacco), and 4 (animal and vegetable oils and fats) and SITC division 22 (oil seeds, oil nuts, and oil kernels). • **Agricultural raw materials** correspond to SITC section 2 (crude materials except fuels), excluding divisions 22, 27 (crude fertilizers and minerals excluding coal, petroleum, and precious stones), and 28 (metalliferous ores and scrap). • **Fuels** correspond to SITC section 3 (mineral fuels). • **Ores and metals** correspond to the commodities in SITC divisions 27, 28, and 68 (nonferrous metals). • **Manufactures** correspond to the commodities in SITC sections 5 (chemicals), 6 (basic manufactures), 7 (machinery and transport equipment), and 8 (miscellaneous manufactured goods), excluding division 68.

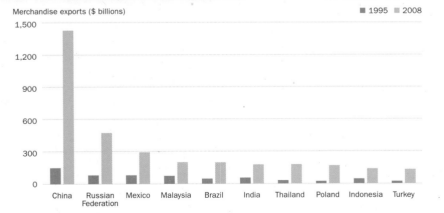

Merchandise exports ($ billions)   ■ 1995 ■ 2008

China continues to dominate merchandise exports among developing economies. Even when developed economies are included, China ranks as the second leading merchandise exporter.

Source: World Development Indicators data files and World Trade Organization.

Data on merchandise imports are from the WTO. Data on shares of imports by major commodity group are from Comtrade. The WTO publishes data on world trade in its *Annual Report.* The International Monetary Fund publishes estimates of total imports of goods in its *International Financial Statistics* and *Direction of Trade Statistics,* as does the United Nations Statistics Division in its *Monthly Bulletin of Statistics.* And the United Nations Conference on Trade and Development publishes data on the structure of imports in its *Handbook of Statistics.* Tariff line records of imports are compiled in the United Nations Statistics Division's Comtrade database.

	Commercial service exports		Transport		Travel		Insurance and financial services		Computer, information, communications, and other commercial services	
	$ millions		% of total		% of total		% of total		% of total	
	1995	2008	1995	2008	1995	2008	1995	2008	1995	2008
Afghanistan	..	..	..	..	..	..	..	..	..	..
Albania	94	2,419	19.1	8.8	69.3	70.8	1.4	3.1	10.2	17.3
Algeria	..	..	..	..	..	..	..	..	..	..
Angola	113	329	31.8	4.4	0.7	86.5	9.2	..	59.0	9.1
Argentina	3,676	11,929	27.4	15.6	60.5	39.0	0.2	0.1	11.9	45.3
Armenia	27	636	53.4	21.7	5.2	52.0	6.7	3.0	41.3	23.3
Australia	16,076	44,513	29.3	17.8	50.6	56.3	5.4	3.4	14.8	22.5
Austria	31,692	61,447	11.8	21.9	42.4	35.2	3.9	4.6	41.9	38.2
Azerbaijan	166	1,454	45.9	54.6	42.3	13.1	0.1	0.3	11.7	32.0
Bangladesh	469	891	15.0	12.5	5.3	10.2	0.1	4.6	79.6	72.6
Belarus	466	4,221	64.8	70.9	5.0	8.6	0.5	0.4	29.7	20.1
Belgium	33,619[a]	84,065	29.4[a]	32.9	17.4[a]	14.0	14.8[a]	6.3	38.4[a]	46.7
Benin	159	281	25.8	4.5	53.2	73.5	6.9	2.2	14.1	19.8
Bolivia	174	482	44.8	13.1	31.5	57.0	9.8	12.9	13.9	17.1
Bosnia and Herzegovina	457	1,658	3.8	19.9	54.1	49.8	2.6	0.9	39.5	29.4
Botswana	236	878	16.2	9.5	68.5	58.4	7.8	3.8	7.5	28.3
Brazil	6,005	28,822	43.3	18.8	16.2	20.1	16.9	7.2	23.6	54.0
Bulgaria	1,431	8,000	34.5	28.9	33.0	47.5	7.6	1.2	32.5	22.4
Burkina Faso	38	..	17.3	..	47.8	..	..	..	34.8	..
Burundi	4	3	46.2	27.3	32.4	40.8	0.5	7.6	21.0	24.4
Cambodia	103	1,615	30.5	14.8	51.7	75.6	..	0.4	17.7	9.2
Cameroon	242	1,384	48.3	46.4	14.8	11.1	7.2	3.6	29.7	38.8
Canada	25,425	64,795	20.7	18.4	31.1	23.6	11.4	10.4	36.8	47.7
Central African Republic	0	..	34.1	..	33.9	..	19.6	..	12.5	..
Chad	23	..	4.5	..	49.8	..	1.7	..	43.9	..
Chile	3,249	10,645	36.8	59.9	28.0	16.5	7.4	2.9	27.8	20.6
China	18,430	146,446	18.2	26.2	47.4	27.9	10.1	1.2	24.4	44.7
Hong Kong SAR, China	33,790	92,318	32.5	30.2	16.8	16.3	9.2	15.2	41.5	38.3
Colombia	1,641	3,967	34.4	31.2	40.0	46.5	6.5	1.8	19.1	20.5
Congo, Dem. Rep.	..	..	..	..	..	..	..	..	..	..
Congo, Rep.	61	303	52.2	4.0	22.4	18.0	0.0	31.4	25.4	46.6
Costa Rica	957	4,055	14.0	9.1	71.2	56.1	−0.2	0.3	14.9	34.4
Côte d'Ivoire	426	845	28.9	28.2	20.9	13.5	12.3	12.8	37.9	58.3
Croatia	2,223	15,160	31.8	11.8	60.7	74.4	1.3	0.5	6.2	13.3
Cuba	..	..	..	..	..	..	..	..	..	..
Czech Republic	6,638	22,179	22.0	28.1	43.4	34.8	1.1	1.3	33.5	35.8
Denmark	15,171	72,468	44.6	..	24.3	..	..	..	31.0	..
Dominican Republic	1,894	4,866	2.2	7.8	82.9	85.8	0.1	0.9	14.9	5.5
Ecuador	687	1,223	46.8	29.9	37.1	60.7	0.0	0.0	16.0	9.4
Egypt, Arab Rep.	8,262	24,668	38.8	33.1	32.5	44.5	1.0	2.0	27.8	20.4
El Salvador	342	1,483	28.3	23.7	25.0	60.2	7.8	2.1	39.0	14.0
Eritrea	49	..	70.4	..	3.1	..	1.0	..	26.5	..
Estonia	868	5,129	43.0	39.3	41.1	23.6	0.4	2.1	15.5	35.0
Ethiopia	310	1,775	76.9	59.0	5.3	21.2	1.5	1.3	16.4	18.4
Finland	7,334	31,784	28.1	11.5	22.4	10.1	2.0	2.6	47.5	75.8
France	83,108	163,573	24.6	25.1	33.2	34.4	5.3	1.6	36.9	38.9
Gabon	191	120	46.4	22.0	9.0	7.7	3.3	24.1	41.3	46.2
Gambia, The	38	123	21.7	16.8	73.4	67.6	0.3	0.4	4.7	15.1
Georgia	188	1,157	48.2	53.1	25.0	38.6	..	2.1	26.9	6.2
Germany	73,576	241,590	27.0	24.4	24.5	16.6	5.0	7.3	43.5	51.8
Ghana	139	1,559	58.7	15.4	7.9	58.9	3.0	0.9	30.3	24.8
Greece	9,528	50,377	3.9	56.2	43.4	34.6	0.3	1.2	52.4	8.0
Guatemala	628	1,649	8.6	11.4	33.9	64.8	4.0	1.7	53.6	22.2
Guinea	17	99	75.3	11.7	5.1	1.5	1.4	4.9	18.2	81.9
Guinea-Bissau	2	..	18.2	..	14.0	..	..	..	81.8	..
Haiti	98	288	5.1	..	91.9	96.7	0.6	..	2.4	3.3
Honduras	221	903	25.6	5.8	36.3	68.8	2.0	7.7	36.1	17.8

Structure of service exports

	Commercial service exports		Transport		Travel		Insurance and financial services		Computer, information, communications, and other commercial services	
	$ millions		% of total		% of total		% of total		% of total	
	1995	2008	1995	2008	1995	2008	1995	2008	1995	2008
Hungary	5,086	19,910	8.0	20.0	57.6	30.3	3.2	1.5	31.3	48.2
India	6,763	102,562	28.0	11.0	38.2	11.5	2.5	5.5	31.4	72.0
Indonesia	5,342	14,731	1.1	19.0	97.9	50.1	..	2.2	2.1	28.7
Iran, Islamic Rep.	533	..	25.9	..	12.6	..	8.8	..	52.7	..
Iraq	..	839	..	30.7	..	61.5	..	2.3	..	5.6
Ireland	4,799	101,580	22.2	4.4	46.1	6.2	17.9	22.3	31.7	67.0
Israel	7,906	24,061	25.5	21.5	37.9	16.9	0.2	0.1	36.5	61.6
Italy	61,173	118,398	17.7	15.5	47.0	39.0	6.6	5.2	28.8	40.3
Jamaica	1,568	2,762	16.0	17.0	68.2	71.5	1.1	1.9	14.7	9.6
Japan	63,966	146,440	35.2	32.0	5.0	7.4	0.9	4.4	58.8	56.3
Jordan	1,689	4,291	24.8	19.5	39.1	68.6	0.2	..	36.1	12.0
Kazakhstan	535	3,936	65.7	56.9	22.7	25.7	0.0	5.0	11.6	12.4
Kenya	1,183	2,520	59.4	51.0	35.7	29.9	1.4	0.4	3.4	18.7
Korea, Dem. Rep.	..	..	..	..	..	..	..	..	..	..
Korea, Rep.	22,133	74,107	41.9	58.8	23.3	12.2	0.4	5.6	34.5	23.4
Kosovo	..	..	..	..	..	..	..	..	..	..
Kuwait	1,124	10,301	83.6	37.4	10.7	2.5	5.7	1.2	0.0	58.9
Kyrgyz Republic	39	884	39.6	16.6	11.9	58.2	0.6	2.5	48.4	22.8
Lao PDR	68	278	22.8	..	76.0	..	0.6	..	0.6	..
Latvia	718	4,496	91.9	51.2	2.8	17.9	2.4	6.8	3.0	24.1
Lebanon	..	18,928	..	2.6	..	38.0	..	2.0	..	57.4
Lesotho	30	60	7.0	1.1	90.9	56.4	1.4	0.5	0.7	42.0
Liberia	..	182	..	10.6	..	86.9	..	..	..	2.5
Libya	20	208	62.7	56.7	12.0	35.7	..	2.2	25.3	5.3
Lithuania	482	4,767	59.6	59.6	16.0	28.2	0.9	1.2	23.5	11.0
Macedonia, FYR	151	992	32.0	33.0	13.6	23.0	3.6	1.3	50.7	42.6
Madagascar	219	420	29.8	28.2	26.3	43.7	2.2	0.1	41.6	28.1
Malawi	24	..	27.6	..	72.4	..	0.3	..	0.0	..
Malaysia	11,438	30,283	21.6	22.3	34.7	50.5	0.1	1.5	43.7	25.6
Mali	68	359	32.5	7.2	37.3	61.5	5.1	1.3	25.2	30.0
Mauritania	19	..	9.1	..	57.9	..	..	..	33.0	..
Mauritius	773	2,530	25.8	17.6	55.6	57.5	0.0	2.5	18.5	22.4
Mexico	9,585	18,474	12.1	12.5	64.5	71.9	6.7	10.9	16.7	4.7
Moldova	143	817	29.5	43.7	39.8	25.9	11.6	0.8	19.1	29.6
Mongolia	47	483	31.7	44.4	43.6	46.6	5.3	2.0	19.5	7.0
Morocco	2,020	12,840	20.3	19.5	64.2	56.2	1.4	1.2	14.2	23.1
Mozambique	242	488	24.8	32.3	..	38.9	..	0.9	75.2	27.9
Myanmar	353	256	6.5	50.8	42.7	18.1	0.0	..	50.9	31.2
Namibia	301	538	..	21.4	92.4	71.1	1.5	3.5	6.2	4.0
Nepal	592	494	9.3	5.5	30.0	67.7	..	0.1	60.7	26.6
Netherlands	44,646	102,710	40.4	30.2	14.7	13.0	1.2	2.1	43.7	54.7
New Zealand	4,401	8,997	34.7	21.9	52.7	57.0	0.1	1.3	12.6	19.8
Nicaragua	94	357	17.7	12.6	52.5	77.3	2.5	1.2	27.4	8.9
Niger	12	79	3.3	14.8	57.8	52.0	0.0	6.9	38.9	26.2
Nigeria	608	1,421	16.4	80.7	2.8	15.5	0.6	1.1	80.2	2.7
Norway	13,458	45,595	63.3	47.4	16.6	10.2	3.7	3.3	16.4	39.1
Oman	13	1,974	..	23.7	..	40.7	..	0.8	..	34.8
Pakistan	1,432	2,393	58.0	49.6	7.7	10.2	1.0	5.3	33.4	34.9
Panama	1,298	5,756	60.4	53.8	23.8	24.5	6.1	10.0	9.6	11.7
Papua New Guinea	321	285	10.8	10.9	7.8	1.3	1.2	5.4	80.2	82.4
Paraguay	566	999	13.3	20.4	24.3	11.0	5.0	2.3	57.4	66.4
Peru	1,042	3,502	32.5	23.4	41.1	56.8	7.2	7.8	19.3	11.9
Philippines	9,323	10,195	2.9	13.4	12.2	43.0	0.7	0.8	84.2	42.8
Poland	10,637	35,428	28.6	30.9	21.7	33.2	8.3	2.0	41.4	33.8
Portugal	8,161	26,135	18.6	26.9	59.2	42.0	4.5	1.9	17.7	29.2
Puerto Rico	..	..	..	..	..	..	..	..	..	..
Qatar	..	..	..	..	..	..	..	..	..	..

	Commercial service exports		Transport		Travel		Insurance and financial services		Computer, information, communications, and other commercial services	
	$ millions		% of total		% of total		% of total		% of total	
	1995	2008	1995	2008	1995	2008	1995	2008	1995	2008
Romania	1,476	12,818	31.9	30.8	40.0	15.5	5.4	4.1	22.7	49.6
Russian Federation	10,567	50,694	35.8	29.6	40.8	23.6	0.6	3.6	22.8	43.2
Rwanda	11	326	60.6	17.2	21.9	62.0	1.1	1.8	17.6	19.0
Saudi Arabia	3,475	9,383	..	26.3	..	63.0	..	6.1	..	4.6
Senegal	364	1,097	15.4	12.3	46.1	48.4	0.6	1.9	37.9	37.4
Serbia	..	3,985	..	24.0	..	23.6	..	1.7	..	50.7
Sierra Leone	71	60	13.7	33.5	80.5	56.2	0.3	1.7	5.6	8.6
Singapore	25,404	83,049	32.7	34.8	30.0	12.7	8.5	10.2	28.9	42.3
Slovak Republic	2,378	8,435	25.9	34.5	26.2	30.7	4.9	2.9	43.0	31.8
Slovenia	2,016	7,417	25.1	28.5	53.8	38.5	0.6	2.1	20.6	30.9
Somalia	..	..	..	..	..	..	..	..	..	..
South Africa	4,414	12,394	24.2	12.6	48.2	64.2	9.9	8.5	17.7	14.7
Spain	40,019	142,612	15.8	17.0	63.4	43.5	3.9	5.1	16.9	34.5
Sri Lanka	800	1,982	41.9	50.4	28.2	17.3	3.4	3.5	26.5	28.9
Sudan	82	457	0.9	3.8	9.7	72.4	3.7	15.4	85.8	8.4
Swaziland	150	447	18.2	2.0	32.2	7.1	0.0	6.9	49.6	84.0
Sweden	15,336	71,592	32.2	17.7	22.6	17.6	2.4	3.9	42.7	60.8
Switzerland	25,179	76,349	15.1	8.5	37.6	18.9	27.8	32.7	19.5	39.8
Syrian Arab Republic	1,632	3,562	14.5	6.3	77.1	81.0	..	2.9	8.4	9.8
Tajikistan	..	134	..	35.4	..	3.1	..	12.9	..	48.5
Tanzania	566	2,136	0.3	17.1	88.6	63.4	0.0	1.1	11.1	18.4
Thailand	14,652	33,392	16.8	21.8	54.8	52.8	0.7	1.3	27.7	24.1
Timor-Leste	..	..	..	..	..	..	..	..	..	..
Togo	64	197	33.9	53.5	19.9	17.3	1.8	4.8	44.3	24.4
Trinidad and Tobago	331	910	58.6	25.2	23.4	50.9	9.2	15.4	8.8	8.5
Tunisia	2,401	5,831	24.9	32.5	63.7	50.7	1.5	2.2	9.8	14.6
Turkey	14,475	34,519	11.8	22.5	34.2	63.6	1.5	4.6	52.4	9.3
Turkmenistan	79	..	79.9	..	9.3	..	0.9	..	10.0	..
Uganda	104	696	17.9	7.4	75.1	71.6	..	3.8	7.0	17.1
Ukraine	2,846	17,302	75.6	44.1	6.7	33.3	2.7	3.2	15.0	19.4
United Arab Emirates	..	..	..	..	..	..	..	..	..	..
United Kingdom	77,549	285,123	20.7	14.0	26.4	12.8	17.5	28.8	35.4	44.5
United States	198,501	518,319	22.7	17.5	37.7	26.0	4.2	13.7	35.5	42.8
Uruguay	1,309	2,192	30.5	29.7	46.7	48.1	1.5	4.0	21.3	18.3
Uzbekistan	..	..	..	..	..	..	..	..	..	..
Venezuela, RB	1,529	2,003	38.2	36.8	55.5	45.8	0.1	0.1	6.1	17.3
Vietnam	2,243	7,096	..	..	..	..	..	..	..	..
West Bank and Gaza	265	261	0.3	2.1	96.2	81.3	..	..	3.5	16.5
Yemen, Rep.	141	1,049	21.9	4.3	35.3	84.5	0.0	0.0	42.8	11.2
Zambia	112	297	64.3	35.3	25.9	49.2	..	6.4	9.8	9.1
Zimbabwe	353	..	26.4	..	50.6	..	0.3	..	22.7	..
World	**1,211,384 t**	**3,799,197 t**	**26.9 w**	**24.3 w**	**32.5 w**	**26.3 w**	**6.0 w**	**7.8 w**	**35.3 w**	**41.7 w**
Low income	9,383	32,263	..	..	..	..	..	..	..	..
Middle income	183,323	753,498	24.8	24.8	44.1	41.2	5.8	3.7	27.7	30.3
Lower middle income	85,495	424,953	21.6	25.6	44.9	35.0	6.1	1.9	30.9	37.6
Upper middle income	97,818	330,409	27.4	24.2	43.3	46.3	5.6	5.1	24.8	24.4
Low & middle income	192,169	785,087	24.9	24.7	43.8	41.3	5.7	3.7	28.0	30.4
East Asia & Pacific	62,745	247,458	17.4	23.1	49.2	39.4	7.1	1.3	30.6	36.2
Europe & Central Asia	46,721	195,032	37.3	33.1	32.0	30.4	2.4	3.3	28.5	33.2
Latin America & Carib.	37,663	108,606	24.0	19.8	51.3	53.8	6.9	7.0	17.9	19.5
Middle East & N. Africa	..	..	..	..	..	..	..	..	..	..
South Asia	10,333	109,513	31.8	19.9	29.7	12.5	2.1	5.1	36.4	62.5
Sub-Saharan Africa	12,142	37,475	26.2	32.7	31.3	48.0	5.8	5.2	40.1	14.9
High income	1,016,999	3,012,629	27.5	24.1	29.3	22.1	6.1	8.9	37.5	44.9
Euro area	422,580	1,225,741	25.6	23.6	31.5	24.1	5.6	5.4	37.6	46.9

a. Includes Luxembourg.

Structure of service exports | 4.6

Balance of payments statistics, the main source of information on international trade in services, have many weaknesses. Disaggregation of important components may be limited and varies considerably across countries. There are inconsistencies in the methods used to report items. And the recording of major flows as net items is common (for example, insurance transactions are often recorded as premiums less claims). These factors contribute to a downward bias in the value of the service trade reported in the balance of payments.

Efforts are being made to improve the coverage, quality, and consistency of these data. Eurostat and the Organisation for Economic Co-operation and Development, for example, are working together to improve the collection of statistics on trade in services in member countries. In addition, the International Monetary Fund (IMF) has implemented the new classification of trade in services introduced in the fifth edition of its *Balance of Payments Manual* (1993).

Still, difficulties in capturing all the dimensions of international trade in services mean that the record is likely to remain incomplete. Cross-border intrafirm service transactions, which are usually not captured in the balance of payments, have increased in recent years. An example is transnational corporations' use of mainframe computers around the clock for data processing, exploiting time zone differences between their home country and the host countries of their affiliates. Another important dimension of service trade not captured by conventional balance of

payments statistics is establishment trade—sales in the host country by foreign affiliates. By contrast, cross-border intrafirm transactions in merchandise may be reported as exports or imports in the balance of payments.

The data on exports of services in the table and on imports of services in table 4.7, unlike those in editions before 2000, include only commercial services and exclude the category "government services not included elsewhere." The data are compiled by the IMF based on returns from national sources. Data on total trade in goods and services from the IMF's Balance of Payments database are shown in table 4.15.

International transactions in services are defined by the IMF's *Balance of Payments Manual* (1993) as the economic output of intangible commodities that may be produced, transferred, and consumed at the same time. Definitions may vary among reporting economies. Travel services include the goods and services consumed by travelers, such as meals, lodging, and transport (within the economy visited), including car rental.

• **Commercial service exports** are total service exports minus exports of government services not included elsewhere. • **Transport** covers all transport services (sea, air, land, internal waterway, space, and pipeline) performed by residents of one economy for those of another and involving the carriage of passengers, movement of goods (freight), rental of carriers with crew, and related support and auxiliary services. Excluded are freight insurance, which is included in insurance services; goods procured in ports by nonresident carriers and repairs of transport equipment, which are included in goods; repairs of harbors, railway facilities, and airfield facilities, which are included in construction services; and rental of carriers without crew, which is included in other services. • **Travel** covers goods and services acquired from an economy by travelers in that economy for their own use during visits of less than one year for business or personal purposes. • **Insurance and financial services** cover freight insurance on goods exported and other direct insurance such as life insurance; financial intermediation services such as commissions, foreign exchange transactions, and brokerage services; and auxiliary services such as financial market operational and regulatory services. • **Computer, information, communications, and other commercial services** cover such activities as international telecommunications and postal and courier services; computer data; news-related service transactions between residents and nonresidents; construction services; royalties and license fees; miscellaneous business, professional, and technical services; and personal, cultural, and recreational services.

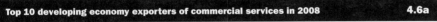

Top 10 developing economy exporters of commercial services in 2008   **4.6a**

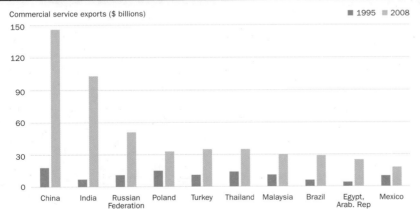

Commercial service exports ($ billions)   ■ 1995   ■ 2008

The top 10 developing economy exporters of commercial services accounted for almost 64 percent of developing economy commercial service exports and 13 percent of world commercial service exports.

Source: International Monetary Fund balance of payments data files.

Data on exports of commercial services are from the IMF, which publishes balance of payments data in its *International Financial Statistics* and *Balance of Payments Statistics Yearbook*.

Structure of service imports

	Commercial service imports		Transport		Travel		Insurance and financial services		Computer, information, communications, and other commercial services	
	$ millions		% of total		% of total		% of total		% of total	
	1995	2008	1995	2008	1995	2008	1995	2008	1995	2008
Afghanistan	..	..	..	..	..	..	..	..	..	..
Albania	98	2,361	61	15	7	66	22	6	10	13
Algeria	..	..	..	..	..	..	..	..	..	..
Angola	1,665	20,020	18	19	5	1	3	10	75	70
Argentina	6,992	12,664	30	31	47	36	7	4	16	29
Armenia	52	952	83	49	6	34	10	8	1	8
Australia	16,979	47,613	37	31	30	39	7	3	26	27
Austria	27,552	42,738	12	32	40	27	6	4	43	37
Azerbaijan	297	3,826	31	18	49	9	1	2	19	72
Bangladesh	1,192	3,684	65	87	20	5	6	1	10	6
Belarus	276	2,614	36	50	32	26	4	3	29	22
Belgium	32,511[a]	81,978	24[a]	28	28[a]	24	10[a]	6	38[a]	42
Benin	235	491	59	60	15	15	10	10	16	15
Bolivia	321	1,018	66	42	15	28	9	13	10	18
Bosnia and Herzegovina	262	632	51	43	31	33	10	7	8	17
Botswana	440	1,348	43	34	33	36	8	4	16	26
Brazil	13,161	44,396	44	23	26	25	10	6	21	46
Bulgaria	1,278	6,696	42	33	15	36	9	4	43	28
Burkina Faso	116	..	56	..	20	..	5	..	20	..
Burundi	62	173	49	39	41	52	6	4	4	5
Cambodia	181	959	46	64	5	11	4	5	45	20
Cameroon	485	2,859	35	31	22	12	7	6	36	51
Canada	32,985	86,644	24	23	31	32	11	11	34	34
Central African Republic	114	..	44	..	38	..	8	..	10	..
Chad	174	..	55	..	15	..	2	..	29	..
Chile	3,524	11,143	54	60	20	12	4	9	22	19
China	24,635	158,004	39	32	15	23	17	8	29	37
Hong Kong SAR, China	24,962	45,849	22	33	54	35	6	8	18	23
Colombia	2,813	7,108	42	42	31	24	12	8	15	25
Congo, Dem. Rep.	..	..	..	..	..	..	..	..	..	..
Congo, Rep.	690	3,523	19	15	8	5	7	5	67	75
Costa Rica	895	1,878	41	36	36	32	5	9	18	23
Côte d'Ivoire	1,235	2,444	50	59	15	16	11	10	23	25
Croatia	1,373	4,517	28	23	31	25	3	4	38	49
Cuba	..	..	..	..	..	..	..	..	..	..
Czech Republic	4,860	17,256	16	26	34	27	5	6	45	42
Denmark	13,945	62,432	45	..	31	..	..	..	24	..
Dominican Republic	957	1,757	61	67	18	18	10	8	11	7
Ecuador	1,141	2,885	42	57	21	19	6	6	31	18
Egypt, Arab Rep.	4,511	16,335	35	45	28	18	5	10	32	27
El Salvador	488	1,972	55	48	15	32	11	10	19	10
Eritrea	45	..	2	..	7	..	0	..	93	..
Estonia	420	3,374	53	39	22	24	5	2	21	35
Ethiopia	337	2,379	63	68	8	7	7	4	22	22
Finland	9,418	29,257	23	23	24	15	5	1	48	61
France	64,523	141,704	33	30	25	31	6	3	36	37
Gabon	832	1,020	18	31	17	27	9	7	57	35
Gambia, The	47	88	60	46	30	9	6	8	4	36
Georgia	249	1,154	27	56	63	18	8	14	2	12
Germany	128,865	283,196	18	23	47	32	2	4	33	41
Ghana	331	2,038	61	54	6	27	6	5	26	14
Greece	4,003	24,392	30	56	33	16	5	7	33	20
Guatemala	672	2,125	41	54	21	29	9	10	29	7
Guinea	252	398	58	67	8	2	7	4	26	27
Guinea-Bissau	27	..	53	..	14	..	5	..	28	..
Haiti	236	753	78	63	15	8	2	1	6	27
Honduras	326	1,204	60	60	18	29	2	4	20	7

	Commercial service imports		Transport		Travel		Insurance and financial services		Computer, information, communications, and other commercial services	
	$ millions		% of total		% of total		% of total		% of total	
	1995	2008	1995	2008	1995	2008	1995	2008	1995	2008
Hungary	3,765	18,491	13	20	40	22	5	3	43	56
India	10,062	56,053	57	24	10	17	6	8	28	50
Indonesia	13,230	27,994	37	50	16	20	3	4	43	27
Iran, Islamic Rep.	2,192	..	43	..	11	..	10	..	36	..
Iraq	..	4,741	..	48	..	13	..	24	..	14
Ireland	11,252	109,290	16	3	18	10	1	15	65	73
Israel	8,131	19,629	45	34	26	18	3	2	26	46
Italy	54,613	127,861	24	23	27	24	10	4	39	49
Jamaica	1,073	2,304	46	48	14	12	9	10	31	30
Japan	121,547	167,443	30	32	30	17	2	5	38	46
Jordan	1,385	3,926	52	57	31	26	6	9	11	9
Kazakhstan	776	10,794	38	22	36	9	2	5	25	63
Kenya	900	1,663	46	52	21	16	10	7	22	25
Korea, Dem. Rep.	..	..	..	..	..	..	..	..	..	..
Korea, Rep.	25,394	91,768	38	40	25	19	2	2	36	39
Kosovo	..	..	..	..	..	..	..	..	..	..
Kuwait	3,826	12,149	39	35	59	62	2	2	0	1
Kyrgyz Republic	193	988	27	49	3	31	4	2	65	18
Lao PDR	119	76	43	..	25	..	4	..	28	..
Latvia	225	3,163	68	26	11	36	7	5	14	33
Lebanon	..	13,392	..	14	..	27	..	2	..	57
Lesotho	58	85	75	79	23	16	0	..	2	5
Liberia	..	323	..	65	..	9	..	3	..	23
Libya	510	3,572	60	42	15	36	..	7	25	16
Lithuania	457	4,133	64	48	23	36	1	2	12	13
Macedonia, FYR	300	970	50	42	9	14	21	3	21	41
Madagascar	277	462	56	48	21	16	4	1	20	35
Malawi	151	..	67	..	26	..	0	..	7	..
Malaysia	14,821	30,060	38	38	16	22	..	3	47	36
Mali	412	774	60	59	12	18	1	4	27	19
Mauritania	197	..	62	..	12	..	1	..	25	..
Mauritius	630	1,911	40	34	25	24	5	6	30	37
Mexico	9,021	24,701	38	14	35	35	12	50	14	1
Moldova	193	779	52	42	29	35	9	3	10	20
Mongolia	87	514	70	50	22	37	2	4	8	10
Morocco	1,350	5,628	48	47	22	19	4	3	26	31
Mozambique	350	901	33	40	..	23	2	1	65	35
Myanmar	233	547	11	46	8	7	1	..	81	47
Namibia	538	559	37	43	17	16	9	4	37	37
Nepal	305	840	36	40	45	45	3	4	16	12
Netherlands	43,618	91,918	29	25	27	24	3	3	41	48
New Zealand	4,571	9,553	41	33	28	31	5	3	26	32
Nicaragua	207	572	39	54	19	25	3	10	38	11
Niger	120	369	74	74	11	8	3	3	12	15
Nigeria	4,398	12,320	22	30	21	29	3	2	54	39
Norway	13,052	43,928	38	33	32	36	6	2	24	28
Oman	985	6,122	42	42	5	14	5	7	49	37
Pakistan	2,431	9,079	67	44	18	17	4	4	10	35
Panama	1,049	2,550	71	61	12	14	9	16	9	9
Papua New Guinea	642	1,151	25	24	9	5	3	10	63	61
Paraguay	676	563	66	66	20	22	12	9	1	3
Peru	1,781	5,425	51	46	17	20	10	9	22	25
Philippines	6,906	8,570	30	50	6	26	2	4	63	20
Poland	7,008	30,035	25	24	6	33	14	5	55	39
Portugal	6,339	16,497	27	31	33	26	9	4	31	39
Puerto Rico	..	..	..	..	..	..	..	..	..	..
Qatar	..	..	..	..	..	..	..	..	..	..

	Commercial service imports		Transport		Travel		Insurance and financial services		Computer, information, communications, and other commercial services	
	$ millions		% of total		% of total		% of total		% of total	
	1995	2008	1995	2008	1995	2008	1995	2008	1995	2008
Romania	1,801	11,776	34	34	39	18	5	4	22	43
Russian Federation	20,205	74,572	16	17	57	33	0	4	26	45
Rwanda	58	504	73	56	17	14	1	0	10	29
Saudi Arabia	8,670	48,926	25	32	..	31	3	7	72	30
Senegal	405	1,205	57	50	18	21	7	9	18	21
Serbia	..	4,223	..	30	..	30	..	3	..	37
Sierra Leone	79	117	17	47	63	21	4	10	16	22
Singapore	20,728	78,967	45	38	22	18	10	6	23	39
Slovak Republic	1,800	9,084	17	27	18	24	5	11	60	38
Slovenia	1,429	4,944	31	25	40	27	2	3	27	45
Somalia	..	..	..	..	..	..	..	..	..	..
South Africa	5,756	16,515	40	46	32	27	14	4	14	23
Spain	22,354	104,263	31	25	20	20	7	7	41	49
Sri Lanka	1,169	2,967	58	66	16	14	5	6	21	13
Sudan	150	2,552	27	51	29	47	0	1	44	2
Swaziland	206	494	16	12	21	10	4	12	59	66
Sweden	17,112	54,280	28	17	32	28	1	2	38	52
Switzerland	14,899	36,277	35	23	50	30	1	8	14	38
Syrian Arab Republic	1,358	2,917	57	58	37	22	6	9	6	11
Tajikistan	..	453	..	40	..	2	..	11	..	47
Tanzania	729	1,576	30	42	49	46	3	4	18	8
Thailand	18,629	46,314	42	50	23	11	5	5	30	34
Timor-Leste	..	..	..	..	..	..	..	..	..	..
Togo	148	303	71	71	12	6	4	11	12	12
Trinidad and Tobago	223	320	42	54	31	29	8	0	19	17
Tunisia	1,245	3,226	45	58	20	14	6	8	28	20
Turkey	4,654	16,228	30	46	20	22	8	15	42	17
Turkmenistan	403	..	40	..	18	..	7	..	35	..
Uganda	563	1,219	38	72	14	13	4	8	43	8
Ukraine	1,334	15,777	34	42	16	25	7	10	43	22
United Arab Emirates	..	..	..	..	..	..	..	..	..	..
United Kingdom	62,524	196,896	27	18	40	35	4	8	29	38
United States	129,227	364,928	32	29	36	23	6	17	26	31
Uruguay	814	1,365	46	51	29	26	5	4	20	19
Uzbekistan	..	..	..	..	..	..	..	..	..	..
Venezuela, RB	4,654	10,073	31	48	37	18	3	6	30	28
Vietnam	2,304	7,931	..	..	..	..	..	..	..	..
West Bank and Gaza	349	638	28	12	46	57	3	2	25	29
Yemen, Rep.	604	2,289	36	48	12	8	7	9	45	34
Zambia	282	881	79	58	9	7	0	11	12	24
Zimbabwe	645	..	56	..	19	..	3	..	23	..
World	**1,219,124 t**	**3,440,367 t**	**31 w**	**29 w**	**31 w**	**25 w**	**6 w**	**9 w**	**32 w**	**37 w**
Low income	13,458	43,441	..	..	..	..	..	..	..	..
Middle income	222,345	807,544	39	34	23	25	10	13	29	28
Lower middle income	108,492	441,066	42	39	16	21	10	7	32	33
Upper middle income	113,681	366,143	37	30	28	28	9	18	27	24
Low & middle income	235,415	850,688	39	35	23	25	10	13	29	28
East Asia & Pacific	82,593	285,803	38	38	16	21	12	6	37	34
Europe & Central Asia	42,554	202,447	29	33	26	28	7	7	38	32
Latin America & Carib.	52,171	139,670	41	27	31	29	10	28	17	15
Middle East & N. Africa	19,565	65,951	45	47	21	20	..	11	28	22
South Asia	15,377	73,655	59	38	13	16	5	7	23	39
Sub-Saharan Africa	24,584	91,672	40	45	24	24	9	5	28	27
High income	983,235	2,596,070	29	27	33	26	5	8	33	39
Euro area	421,722	1,114,691	25	26	32	26	5	4	38	43

a. Includes Luxembourg.

Structure of service imports | 4.7

About the data

Trade in services differs from trade in goods because services are produced and consumed at the same time. Thus services to a traveler may be consumed in the producing country (for example, use of a hotel room) but are classified as imports of the traveler's country. In other cases services may be supplied from a remote location; for example, insurance services may be supplied from one location and consumed in another. For further discussion of the problems of measuring trade in services, see *About the data* for table 4.6.

The data on imports of services in the table and on exports of services in table 4.6, unlike those in editions before 2000, include only commercial services and exclude the category "government services not included elsewhere." The data are compiled by the International Monetary Fund (IMF) based on returns from national sources.

International transactions in services are defined by the IMF's *Balance of Payments Manual* (1993) as the economic output of intangible commodities that may be produced, transferred, and consumed at the same time. Definitions may vary among reporting economies.

Travel services include the goods and services consumed by travelers, such as meals, lodging, and transport (within the economy visited), including car rental.

Definitions

• **Commercial service imports** are total service imports minus imports of government services not included elsewhere. • **Transport** covers all transport services (sea, air, land, internal waterway, space, and pipeline) performed by residents of one economy for those of another and involving the carriage of passengers, movement of goods (freight), rental of carriers with crew, and related support and auxiliary services. Excluded are freight insurance, which is included in insurance services; goods procured in ports by nonresident carriers and repairs of transport equipment, which are included in goods; repairs of harbors, railway facilities, and airfield facilities, which are included in construction services; and rental of carriers without crew, which is included in other services. • **Travel** covers goods and services acquired from an economy by travelers in that economy for their own use during visits of less than one year for business or personal purposes. • **Insurance and financial services** cover freight insurance on goods imported and other direct insurance such as life insurance; financial intermediation services such as commissions, foreign exchange transactions, and brokerage services; and auxiliary services such as financial market operational and regulatory services. • **Computer, information, communications, and other commercial services** cover such activities as international telecommunications, and postal and courier services; computer data; news-related service transactions between residents and nonresidents; construction services; royalties and license fees; miscellaneous business, professional, and technical services; and personal, cultural, and recreational services.

The mix of commercial service imports by developing economies is changing | 4.7a

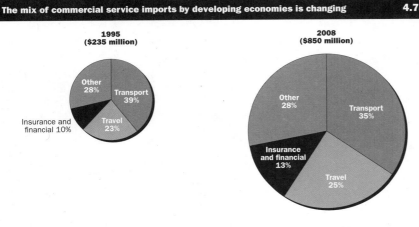

1995
($235 million)

2008
($850 million)

Between 1995 and 2008 developing economies' commercial service imports more than tripled. Insurance and financial services and travel services are displacing transport and other services as the most important services imported.

Source: International Monetary Fund balance of payments data files.

Data sources

Data on imports of commercial services are from the IMF, which publishes balance of payments data in its *International Financial Statistics* and *Balance of Payments Statistics Yearbook*.

4.8 Structure of demand

	Household final consumption expenditure		General government final consumption expenditure		Gross capital formation		Exports of goods and services		Imports of goods and services		Gross savings	
	% of GDP		% of GDP		% of GDP		% of GDP		% of GDP		% of GDP	
	1995	2008	1995	2008	1995	2008	1995	2008	1995	2008	1995	2008
Afghanistan	..	98	..	10	..	28	..	17	..	53	..	..
Albania	87	86	14	9	21	32	12	31	35	59	20	19
Algeria	55	29	17	13	31	34	26	48	29	24	..	..
Angola	..	..	..	..	35	12	82	76	68	51	78	20
Argentina	69	59	13	13	18	23	10	24	10	21	16	25
Armenia	109	73	11	12	18	41	24	15	62	40	−9	29
Australia	59	55	18	18	24	29	18	21	20	23	23	29
Austria	56	53	20	18	25	23	35	59	36	54	22	27
Azerbaijan	77	24	13	11	24	20	28	69	42	25	13	56
Bangladesh	83	79	5	5	19	24	11	20	17	29	22	37
Belarus	59	54	21	17	25	36	50	62	54	69	21	28
Belgium	54	54	22	23	20	24	68	92	63	93	24	22
Benin	82	..	11	..	20	21	20	15	33	29	11	9
Bolivia	76	62	14	13	15	18	23	45	27	38	11	29
Bosnia and Herzegovina	..	87	..	21	20	24	20	37	71	69	..	42
Botswana	34	40	29	20	25	32	51	46	38	39	36	45
Brazil	62	61	21	20	18	19	7	14	9	14	16	17
Bulgaria	71	68	15	16	16	38	45	60	46	83	12	14
Burkina Faso	63	75	25	22	24	18	14	12	27	27	29	..
Burundi	89	91	19	29	6	16	13	11	27	47	6	4
Cambodia	95	83	6	3	15	21	31	65	47	73	5	16
Cameroon	72	72	9	9	13	18	24	30	18	29	14	20
Canada	57	55	21	19	19	23	37	35	34	33	18	24
Central African Republic	79	94	15	7	14	12	20	11	28	23	11	..
Chad	91	68	7	12	13	15	22	54	34	50	12	..
Chile	61	59	10	12	26	25	29	45	27	41	25	22
China	42	34	14	14	42	44	23	37	21	28	43	54
Hong Kong SAR, China	62	60	8	8	34	20	143	212	148	202	..	30
Colombia	65	63	15	16	26	25	15	18	21	22	19	19
Congo, Dem. Rep.	81	80	5	11	9	24	28	23	24	39	..	..
Congo, Rep.	49	39	13	13	37	21	65	79	64	51	−2	14
Costa Rica	71	70	14	14	18	26	38	46	40	55	15	16
Côte d'Ivoire	66	74	11	9	16	10	42	47	34	39	12	12
Croatia	66	59	25	19	16	31	33	42	41	50	11	21
Cuba	71	..	24	..	7	..	13	..	16	..	..	..
Czech Republic	51	50	21	20	33	25	51	77	55	73	29	22
Denmark	51	49	25	27	20	22	38	55	33	52	22	25
Dominican Republic	81	87	5	8	18	18	36	26	39	39	16	9
Ecuador	68	61	13	11	22	28	26	38	28	38	17	31
Egypt, Arab Rep.	74	72	11	11	20	22	23	33	28	39	21	24
El Salvador	87	98	9	9	20	15	22	28	38	50	18	8
Eritrea	94	86	44	31	23	11	22	6	83	34	19	..
Estonia	54	55	26	19	28	30	68	76	76	80	24	20
Ethiopia	80	90	8	10	18	20	10	12	16	31	21	17
Finland	52	53	23	22	18	21	36	44	29	40	22	24
France	57	57	24	23	19	22	23	26	22	29	19	19
Gabon	41	33	12	8	23	24	59	67	36	32	33	..
Gambia, The	90	78	14	16	20	25	49	30	73	49	8	10
Georgia	102	85	11	14	4	30	26	29	42	58	1	8
Germany	58	56	20	18	22	19	24	47	23	41	20	26
Ghana	76	77	12	20	20	36	24	42	33	75	18	7
Greece	75	71	15	17	19	21	17	23	27	32	18	10
Guatemala	86	88	6	9	15	18	19	25	25	40	11	14
Guinea	74	81	8	9	21	15	21	33	25	38	21	3
Guinea-Bissau	95	81	6	14	22	25	12	30	35	50	10	..
Haiti	..	..	..	..	26	26	9	11	29	37	..	..
Honduras	64	83	9	16	32	34	44	49	48	82	27	21

Structure of demand | 4.8

	Household final consumption expenditure		General government final consumption expenditure		Gross capital formation		Exports of goods and services		Imports of goods and services		Gross savings	
	% of GDP		% of GDP		% of GDP		% of GDP		% of GDP		% of GDP	
	1995	2008	1995	2008	1995	2008	1995	2008	1995	2008	1995	2008
Hungary	66	67	11	9	23	22	45	81	45	80	19	15
India	64	54	11	12	27	40	11	23	12	28	27	38
Indonesia	62	63	8	8	32	28	26	30	28	29	28	20
Iran, Islamic Rep.	46	45	16	11	29	33	22	32	13	22	37	..
Iraq	..	..	..	..	..	..	..	..	..	..	..	..
Ireland	54	47	16	16	18	26	76	79	65	69	23	22
Israel	56	58	28	25	25	18	29	40	37	42	13	19
Italy	58	59	18	20	20	21	26	29	22	29	22	18
Jamaica	70	82	11	14	29	..	51	..	61	..	25	14
Japan	55	56	15	18	28	24	9	18	8	16	30	29
Jordan	65	81	24	25	33	26	52	58	73	91	29	14
Kazakhstan	68	35	14	10	23	34	39	57	44	37	18	40
Kenya	70	78	15	17	22	19	33	27	39	41	23	13
Korea, Dem. Rep.	..	..	..	..	..	..	..	..	..	..	..	..
Korea, Rep.	52	55	11	15	38	31	29	53	30	54	36	31
Kosovo	..	97	..	18	..	27	..	14	..	57	..	..
Kuwait	43	28	32	13	15	19	52	66	42	26	38	63
Kyrgyz Republic	75	104	20	9	18	24	29	57	42	94	8	15
Lao PDR	..	66	..	8	..	37	23	33	37	44	..	22
Latvia	63	58	24	20	14	35	43	42	45	55	14	22
Lebanon	103	84	12	14	36	31	11	27	62	57	..	10
Lesotho	105	108	27	27	63	28	22	47	117	111	30	22
Liberia	..	202	..	19	..	20	9	31	72	173	..	−2
Libya	59	23	22	9	12	28	29	67	22	27	..	67
Lithuania	67	66	22	18	22	27	49	59	60	71	12	15
Macedonia, FYR	70	79	19	19	21	28	33	53	43	79	13	16
Madagascar	90	85	7	5	11	36	24	27	32	52	2	..
Malawi	79	63	21	13	17	27	30	23	48	26	8	..
Malaysia	48	46	12	12	44	22	94	110	98	90	34	38
Mali	83	76	10	11	23	23	21	27	36	37	15	28
Mauritania	77	61	11	20	20	26	37	58	45	65	14	..
Mauritius	63	74	14	13	26	27	59	53	61	68	25	17
Mexico	67	66	10	10	20	26	30	28	28	30	19	25
Moldova	57	93	27	21	25	37	49	41	58	92	18	23
Mongolia	56	61	13	15	32	39	48	57	49	72	35	46
Morocco	68	60	17	17	21	36	27	37	34	50	17	31
Mozambique	90	82	8	12	27	19	16	33	41	46	9	7
Myanmar	..	..	..	..	14	..	1	..	2	..	..	..
Namibia	54	74	30	20	22	26	49	42	56	61	32	17
Nepal	75	79	9	10	25	32	25	12	35	33	21	38
Netherlands	49	46	24	25	21	21	59	77	54	69	27	26
New Zealand	58	58	17	19	23	24	29	29	28	30	18	16
Nicaragua	83	90	11	12	22	32	19	33	35	67	−1	14
Niger	86	..	14	..	7	..	17	..	24	..	−1	..
Nigeria	..	..	..	..	..	..	44	42	42	25	..	..
Norway	50	39	22	19	22	23	38	48	32	29	26	42
Oman	51	35	25	18	15	31	44	56	36	40	10	36
Pakistan	72	77	12	12	19	22	17	13	19	24	21	20
Panama	52	65	15	11	30	23	101	75	98	74	30	26
Papua New Guinea	44	58	17	10	22	19	61	72	44	60	35	..
Paraguay	76	75	10	11	26	20	59	53	71	59	18	16
Peru	71	64	10	9	25	26	13	27	18	26	16	22
Philippines	74	77	11	10	22	15	36	37	44	39	19	34
Poland	60	60	20	19	19	24	23	40	21	43	20	18
Portugal	65	67	18	21	23	22	29	33	35	42	23	10
Puerto Rico	..	..	..	..	..	..	72	..	97	..	..	..
Qatar	32	21	32	21	35	32	44	64	43	38	..	..

	Household final consumption expenditure		General government final consumption expenditure		Gross capital formation		Exports of goods and services		Imports of goods and services		Gross savings	
	% of GDP		% of GDP		% of GDP		% of GDP		% of GDP		% of GDP	
	1995	2008	1995	2008	1995	2008	1995	2008	1995	2008	1995	2008
Romania	68	64	14	16	24	31	28	30	33	40	19	25
Russian Federation	52	48	19	17	25	26	29	31	26	22	28	32
Rwanda	97	82	10	10	13	24	5	15	26	31	20	27
Saudi Arabia	47	27	24	20	20	21	38	69	28	38	20	49
Senegal	80	82	13	10	14	30	31	25	37	47	8	19
Serbia	73	78	23	21	12	23	17	30	24	52	..	7
Sierra Leone	88	86	14	12	6	15	19	16	26	29	–3	5
Singapore	41	39	8	11	34	31	..	234	..	215	52	46
Slovak Republic	52	56	22	17	24	29	58	83	56	85	41	–16
Slovenia	60	52	19	18	24	31	50	70	52	71	23	27
Somalia	..	..	..	..	..	..	..	..	..	..	..	..
South Africa	63	60	18	20	18	23	23	35	22	38	17	16
Spain	60	57	18	19	22	30	22	26	22	32	22	20
Sri Lanka	73	70	11	16	26	27	36	25	46	38	20	18
Sudan	85	59	5	16	14	24	5	24	10	23	3	14
Swaziland	82	74	15	21	16	17	60	69	74	81	16	19
Sweden	50	46	27	26	17	20	40	54	33	47	20	28
Switzerland	60	58	12	11	23	22	36	56	31	47	30	36
Syrian Arab Republic	66	75	13	12	27	14	31	31	38	32	27	20
Tajikistan	62	114	16	8	29	20	66	17	72	58	..	25
Tanzania[a]	86	73	12	16	20	17	24	22	42	27	7	13
Thailand	55	56	10	12	42	29	42	77	49	74	34	29
Timor-Leste	..	..	..	..	..	..	..	..	..	..	..	..
Togo	77	..	12	9	16	..	32	42	37	62	17	..
Trinidad and Tobago	53	45	12	11	21	13	54	73	39	42	27	38
Tunisia	63	63	16	15	25	27	45	61	49	65	20	21
Turkey	68	70	11	13	25	22	20	24	24	28	22	18
Turkmenistan	44	55	12	8	49	6	84	81	84	51	50	..
Uganda	85	82	11	12	12	24	12	16	21	33	13	12
Ukraine	55	64	21	17	27	25	47	42	50	48	23	20
United Arab Emirates	48	44	16	10	30	21	69	91	63	67	..	..
United Kingdom	63	64	20	22	17	17	28	29	28	32	15	15
United States	68	71	15	16	18	18	11	12	12	17	15	14
Uruguay	73	69	12	12	15	23	19	28	19	32	14	18
Uzbekistan	51	49	22	18	27	23	28	42	28	32	..	..
Venezuela, RB	69	54	7	11	18	25	27	30	22	20	21	35
Vietnam	74	69	8	6	27	41	33	78	42	95	20	29
West Bank and Gaza	98	..	18	..	35	..	16	..	68	..	12	..
Yemen, Rep.	71	..	14	..	22	..	51	..	58	..	26	..
Zambia	72	66	15	9	16	22	36	37	40	34	9	19
Zimbabwe	65	..	18	..	20	..	38	..	41	..	18	..
World	**61 w**	**61 w**	**17 w**	**17 w**	**22 w**	**22 w**	**21 w**	**28 w**	**21 w**	**28 w**	**20 w**	**21 w**
Low income	77	76	11	10	20	27	22	34	30	47	17	..
Middle income	60	55	14	14	27	30	23	31	24	30	26	31
Lower middle income	54	49	13	13	34	37	24	35	24	34	33	41
Upper middle income	64	60	15	15	21	24	23	28	24	27	20	23
Low & middle income	60	56	14	14	27	30	23	31	24	31	26	31
East Asia & Pacific	47	42	13	13	40	40	29	40	29	35	39	48
Europe & Central Asia	61	59	17	16	23	25	28	34	29	35	23	24
Latin America & Carib.	66	63	15	15	19	23	18	24	19	24	18	22
Middle East & N. Africa	63	55	15	13	25	28	26	38	29	33	..	..
South Asia	67	60	10	11	25	36	12	21	15	28	25	35
Sub-Saharan Africa	69	66	15	17	18	23	28	36	30	39	16	16
High income	61	62	17	18	21	21	21	27	20	28	19	19
Euro area	57	57	20	20	21	22	29	41	28	39	15	16

a. Covers mainland Tanzania only.

Gross domestic product (GDP) from the expenditure side is made up of household final consumption expenditure, general government final consumption expenditure, gross capital formation (private and public investment in fixed assets, changes in inventories, and net acquisitions of valuables), and net exports (exports minus imports) of goods and services. Such expenditures are recorded in purchaser prices and include net taxes on products.

Because policymakers have tended to focus on fostering the growth of output, and because data on production are easier to collect than data on spending, many countries generate their primary estimate of GDP using the production approach. Moreover, many countries do not estimate all the components of national expenditures but instead derive some of the main aggregates indirectly using GDP (based on the production approach) as the control total. Household final consumption expenditure (private consumption in the 1968 United Nations System of National Accounts, or SNA) is often estimated as a residual, by subtracting all other known expenditures from GDP. The resulting aggregate may incorporate fairly large discrepancies. When household consumption is calculated separately, many of the estimates are based on household surveys, which tend to be one-year studies with limited coverage. Thus the estimates quickly become outdated and must be supplemented by estimates using price- and quantity-based statistical procedures. Complicating the issue, in many developing countries the distinction between cash outlays for personal business and those for household use may be blurred. *World Development Indicators* includes in household consumption the expenditures of nonprofit institutions serving households.

General government final consumption expenditure (general government consumption in the 1968 SNA) includes expenditures on goods and services for individual consumption as well as those on services for collective consumption. Defense expenditures, including those on capital outlays (with certain exceptions), are treated as current spending.

Gross capital formation (gross domestic investment in the 1968 SNA) consists of outlays on additions to the economy's fixed assets plus net changes in the level of inventories. It is generally obtained from industry reports of acquisitions and distinguishes only the broad categories of capital formation. The 1993 SNA recognizes a third category of capital formation: net acquisitions of valuables. Included in gross capital formation under the 1993 SNA guidelines are

capital outlays on defense establishments that may be used by the general public, such as schools, airfields, and hospitals, and intangibles such as computer software and mineral exploration outlays. Data on capital formation may be estimated from direct surveys of enterprises and administrative records or based on the commodity flow method using data from production, trade, and construction activities. The quality of data on government fixed capital formation depends on the quality of government accounting systems (which tend to be weak in developing countries). Measures of fixed capital formation by households and corporations—particularly capital outlays by small, unincorporated enterprises—are usually unreliable.

Estimates of changes in inventories are rarely complete but usually include the most important activities or commodities. In some countries these estimates are derived as a composite residual along with household final consumption expenditure. According to national accounts conventions, adjustments should be made for appreciation of the value of inventory holdings due to price changes, but this is not always done. In highly inflationary economies this element can be substantial.

Data on exports and imports are compiled from customs reports and balance of payments data. Although the data from the payments side provide reasonably reliable records of cross-border transactions, they may not adhere strictly to the appropriate definitions of valuation and timing used in the balance of payments or correspond to the change-of-ownership criterion. This issue has assumed greater significance with the increasing globalization of international business. Neither customs nor balance of payments data usually capture the illegal transactions that occur in many countries. Goods carried by travelers across borders in legal but unreported shuttle trade may further distort trade statistics.

Gross savings represent the difference between disposable income and consumption and replace gross domestic savings, a concept used by the World Bank and included in *World Development Indicators* editions before 2006. The change was made to conform to SNA concepts and definitions. For further discussion of the problems in compiling national accounts, see Srinivasan (1994), Heston (1994), and Ruggles (1994). For an analysis of the reliability of foreign trade and national income statistics, see Morgenstern (1963).

• **Household final consumption expenditure** is the market value of all goods and services, including durable products (such as cars and computers), purchased by households. It excludes purchases of dwellings but includes imputed rent for owner-occupied dwellings. It also includes government fees for permits and licenses. Expenditures of nonprofit institutions serving households are included, even when reported separately. Household consumption expenditure may include any statistical discrepancy in the use of resources relative to the supply of resources. • **General government final consumption expenditure** is all government current expenditures for purchases of goods and services (including compensation of employees). It also includes most expenditures on national defense and security but excludes military expenditures with potentially wider public use that are part of government capital formation. • **Gross capital formation** is outlays on additions to fixed assets of the economy, net changes in inventories, and net acquisitions of valuables. Fixed assets include land improvements (fences, ditches, drains); plant, machinery, and equipment purchases; and construction (roads, railways, schools, buildings, and so on). Inventories are goods held to meet temporary or unexpected fluctuations in production or sales, and "work in progress." • **Exports** and **imports of goods and services** are the value of all goods and other market services provided to or received from the rest of the world. They include the value of merchandise, freight, insurance, transport, travel, royalties, license fees, and other services (communication, construction, financial, information, business, personal, government services, and so on). They exclude compensation of employees and investment income (factor services in the 1968 SNA) and transfer payments. • **Gross savings** are gross national income less total consumption, plus net transfers.

Data on national accounts indicators for most developing countries are collected from national statistical organizations and central banks by visiting and resident World Bank missions. Data for high-income economies are from Organisation for Economic Co-operation and Development (OECD) data files.

Growth of consumption and investment

	Household final consumption expenditure				General government final consumption expenditure		Gross capital formation		Goods and services			
	average annual % growth				average annual % growth		average annual % growth		average annual % growth			
	Total		Per capita						Exports		Imports	
	1990–2000	2000–08	1990–2000	2000–08	1990–2000	2000–08	1990–2000	2000–08	1990–2000	2000–08	1990–2000	2000–08
Afghanistan	..	..	..	..	..	..	..	..	..	..	..	..
Albania	1.3	5.3	2.2	4.9	14.5	8.0	25.8	6.4	18.9	10.4	15.7	15.1
Algeria	−0.1	5.2	−1.9	3.7	3.6	5.3	−0.6	8.4	3.2	2.9	−1.0	7.5
Angola	..	..	..	..	..	..	..	..	..	..	..	..
Argentina	2.8	4.6	1.5	3.6	2.2	3.0	7.4	12.0	8.7	7.2	15.6	10.0
Armenia	−0.5	8.8	1.1	8.7	−1.5	11.3	−1.9	23.4	−18.4	9.6	−12.7	10.8
Australia	3.2	3.9	2.0	2.4	2.9	3.2	5.1	7.6	7.7	2.2	7.6	9.2
Austria	1.7	1.7	1.3	1.1	2.7	1.3	2.3	1.8	5.8	6.1	4.8	5.4
Azerbaijan	2.0	14.5	1.0	13.4	−4.8	24.2	41.6	23.6	5.7	23.8	14.1	22.2
Bangladesh	2.6	4.3	0.6	2.6	4.7	9.4	9.2	8.2	13.1	12.0	9.7	9.5
Belarus	−0.5	11.5	−0.3	12.0	−1.9	0.1	−7.5	19.2	−4.8	6.9	−8.7	11.9
Belgium	1.8	1.3	1.5	0.8	1.4	1.6	2.3	4.4	4.7	3.3	4.5	3.4
Benin	2.6	2.3	−0.7	−1.1	4.4	8.3	12.2	7.7	1.8	2.7	2.1	1.8
Bolivia	3.6	3.4	1.4	1.5	3.6	3.4	8.5	2.6	4.5	9.3	6.0	6.5
Bosnia and Herzegovina	..	1.9	..	..	..	7.0	..	8.9	..	9.8	..	8.0
Botswana	2.5	7.7	0.1	6.3	6.5	3.6	6.7	−2.6	4.7	4.0	3.8	4.6
Brazil	3.7	3.3	2.2	2.0	1.0	3.3	4.2	4.0	5.9	8.6	11.6	8.0
Bulgaria	−3.7	6.3	−3.0	7.0	−8.4	3.1	−5.0	17.2	3.9	8.8	2.7	12.1
Burkina Faso	5.7	4.5	2.8	1.1	2.9	8.7	3.1	9.0	4.4	10.9	1.9	7.2
Burundi	−4.9	..	..	..	−2.6	..	−0.5	..	−1.2	..	−1.6	..
Cambodia	6.0	8.9	3.4	7.1	7.2	1.9	10.3	13.5	21.7	16.9	14.8	15.4
Cameroon	3.1	4.5	0.5	2.1	0.7	2.8	0.4	3.9	3.2	0.4	5.1	4.2
Canada	2.6	3.5	1.6	2.5	0.3	2.7	4.6	6.6	8.7	0.9	7.1	4.4
Central African Republic	..	−0.9	..	−2.7	..	−1.3	..	−0.1	..	−3.6	..	−3.9
Chad	1.5	9.2	−1.7	5.4	−8.3	5.8	4.0	19.7	2.3	52.0	−1.8	27.0
Chile	7.3	5.7	5.6	4.5	3.7	5.1	9.3	9.6	9.4	6.4	11.7	12.0
China	8.9	7.1	7.8	6.5	9.7	8.2	11.7	12.1	12.9	18.9	14.3	13.7
Hong Kong SAR, China	3.8	3.4	2.0	2.9	3.7	1.0	4.8	2.2	7.8	9.7	8.4	8.6
Colombia	2.2	4.5	0.4	2.9	10.5	4.3	2.0	13.4	5.3	5.8	9.0	11.2
Congo, Dem. Rep.	−4.5	..	−3.8	..	−17.4	..	−0.7	..	−0.5	7.0	−2.4	18.9
Congo, Rep.	−1.8	..	..	..	−4.4	..	10.4	..	3.0	..	2.0	..
Costa Rica	5.1	4.1	2.5	2.3	2.0	1.6	5.1	8.6	10.9	7.5	9.2	6.6
Côte d'Ivoire	4.1	..	0.9	..	0.8	3.1	8.1	1.0	1.9	3.0	8.2	3.9
Croatia	2.3	4.8	3.0	4.8	1.5	1.7	4.9	10.7	6.3	5.5	4.9	7.5
Cuba	..	..	..	..	..	..	..	..	..	..	..	..
Czech Republic	3.0	3.8	3.0	3.6	−0.9	2.2	4.6	4.5	8.7	11.8	12.0	10.4
Denmark	2.2	2.7	1.8	2.3	2.4	1.5	5.7	3.2	5.0	4.1	6.0	6.4
Dominican Republic	6.1	6.6	4.2	5.0	7.0	5.0	11.7	1.7	8.3	2.0	9.9	2.9
Ecuador	2.1	5.7	0.3	4.5	−1.5	3.9	−0.6	8.1	5.3	7.1	2.8	9.8
Egypt, Arab Rep.	3.7	4.2	1.7	2.2	4.4	2.6	5.8	7.4	3.5	18.1	3.0	15.5
El Salvador	5.3	3.8	4.1	3.4	2.8	1.4	7.1	2.3	13.4	5.1	11.6	5.3
Eritrea	−5.0	1.6	−6.6	−2.2	22.6	1.2	19.1	−1.0	−2.5	−6.3	7.5	−3.7
Estonia	0.7	8.8	2.2	9.1	5.6	2.1	0.5	12.0	11.0	8.3	12.0	10.9
Ethiopia	3.6	9.7	0.4	6.9	9.0	2.2	6.5	10.0	7.1	11.2	5.8	16.1
Finland	1.7	3.3	1.4	3.0	0.6	1.6	2.2	4.2	10.3	5.3	6.5	5.9
France[a]	1.6	2.3	1.2	1.6	1.4	1.6	1.8	2.8	6.9	2.3	5.7	4.2
Gabon	−0.3	5.1	−3.1	3.0	3.7	0.7	3.0	5.9	2.1	−2.0	0.1	3.9
Gambia, The	3.6	1.8	−0.2	−1.5	−2.2	4.2	1.9	..	0.1	0.6	0.1	1.1
Georgia	6.1	9.5	7.6	10.9	12.0	8.8	−12.5	17.2	12.2	6.9	11.2	9.4
Germany	1.9	0.2	1.6	0.2	1.9	0.7	1.1	0.6	6.0	7.2	5.8	5.6
Ghana	4.7	..	..	..	4.8	−6.0	4.3	19.3	10.1	5.9	10.4	8.5
Greece	2.1	3.9	1.4	3.6	2.1	2.5	4.1	4.1	7.6	4.5	7.4	3.1
Guatemala	4.2	3.9	1.8	1.4	5.1	1.6	6.1	3.2	6.1	2.5	9.2	3.1
Guinea	5.2	4.0	2.0	1.9	−0.5	−0.3	0.1	−3.7	0.3	1.9	−1.1	−0.8
Guinea-Bissau	2.6	3.9	0.2	1.4	1.9	−1.9	−6.5	−0.1	15.4	2.6	−0.4	−0.6
Haiti	..	..	..	..	..	..	9.0	1.1	10.1	3.7	19.4	1.5
Honduras	3.0	6.1	0.6	4.0	2.0	6.1	6.9	7.2	1.6	6.5	3.8	7.9

	Household final consumption expenditure				General government final consumption expenditure		Gross capital formation		Goods and services			
	average annual % growth				average annual % growth		average annual % growth		average annual % growth			
	Total		Per capita						Exports		Imports	
	1990–2000	2000–08	1990–2000	2000–08	1990–2000	2000–08	1990–2000	2000–08	1990–2000	2000–08	1990–2000	2000–08
Hungary	−0.1	3.8	0.1	4.1	0.9	1.3	9.6	1.3	9.9	11.2	11.4	10.0
India	4.8	5.9	2.9	4.4	6.6	5.0	6.9	15.0	12.3	15.2	14.4	19.5
Indonesia	6.6	4.2	5.0	2.8	0.1	7.8	−0.6	6.0	5.9	8.7	5.7	10.0
Iran, Islamic Rep.	3.2	7.4	1.6	5.8	1.6	3.6	−0.1	8.3	1.2	5.0	−6.8	13.2
Iraq	..	..	..	..	..	..	..	..	..	..	..	..
Ireland	5.5	5.0	4.7	3.0	4.0	4.5	10.0	6.2	15.7	5.2	14.5	4.9
Israel	5.0	3.4	2.5	1.5	2.7	1.4	2.0	2.3	10.9	5.9	7.6	3.8
Italy	1.5	0.8	1.5	0.1	−0.2	1.7	1.6	1.4	5.9	1.7	4.4	2.4
Jamaica	..	..	..	..	..	..	..	..	..	..	..	..
Japan	1.5	1.2	1.3	1.1	2.9	1.9	−0.8	0.4	4.1	8.0	4.2	4.2
Jordan	4.9	6.8	1.1	4.1	4.7	6.6	0.3	11.0	2.6	7.0	1.5	8.0
Kazakhstan	−8.1	10.4	−7.0	9.6	−7.1	8.1	−18.3	21.0	−2.6	6.9	−11.2	8.6
Kenya	3.6	4.2	0.6	1.5	6.9	2.6	6.1	8.5	1.0	7.0	9.4	8.4
Korea, Dem. Rep.	..	..	..	..	..	..	..	..	..	..	..	..
Korea, Rep.	4.9	3.5	3.9	3.1	4.7	4.8	3.4	3.4	16.0	11.4	10.0	9.4
Kosovo	..	..	..	..	..	..	..	..	..	..	..	..
Kuwait	4.5	5.9	0.6	2.9	−2.4	6.6	1.0	13.7	−1.6	5.4	0.8	9.4
Kyrgyz Republic	−5.0	11.8	−5.9	10.8	−7.2	3.4	−1.1	2.9	−0.3	14.2	−2.0	20.6
Lao PDR	..	−7.8	..	−9.4	..	9.7	..	15.2	..	−7.6	..	−7.2
Latvia	−3.9	10.0	−2.7	10.6	1.8	2.8	−3.7	16.4	4.3	8.8	7.6	12.1
Lebanon	−0.2	2.5	−1.9	1.1	10.9	2.4	−5.8	8.5	18.6	11.1	−1.1	6.3
Lesotho	1.8	13.7	0.2	12.6	7.2	1.4	−1.5	−2.1	9.7	11.5	2.1	13.7
Liberia	..	..	..	..	..	..	..	..	..	..	..	..
Libya	..	..	..	..	..	..	..	..	..	..	..	..
Lithuania	5.2	10.0	5.9	10.6	1.9	4.1	11.1	14.2	4.9	11.7	7.5	14.5
Macedonia, FYR	2.2	5.1	1.7	4.9	−0.4	−0.2	3.6	4.8	4.2	3.3	7.5	4.6
Madagascar	2.2	3.8	−0.8	1.0	0.0	8.3	3.3	19.3	3.8	5.3	4.1	8.3
Malawi	5.4	3.6	3.2	0.7	−4.4	5.6	−8.4	24.5	4.0	−9.6	−1.1	1.0
Malaysia	5.3	7.5	2.6	5.6	4.8	8.4	5.3	2.7	12.0	6.8	10.3	7.8
Mali	3.0	0.9	1.0	−1.5	3.2	..	0.4	6.2	9.9	6.3	3.5	3.9
Mauritania	..	7.4	..	4.5	..	3.1	..	23.8	−1.3	11.5	0.6	14.1
Mauritius	5.1	5.7	3.9	4.8	3.6	3.9	4.8	6.1	5.6	2.2	5.1	2.6
Mexico	3.9	3.7	2.2	2.7	1.8	0.4	4.7	1.4	14.6	5.7	12.3	6.3
Moldova[b]	9.9	9.4	11.7	9.7	−12.4	6.7	−15.5	11.9	1.0	11.2	5.9	13.8
Mongolia	..	..	..	..	..	..	..	..	..	..	..	..
Morocco[c]	1.8	4.9	0.3	3.7	3.9	3.3	2.5	9.1	5.9	7.1	5.1	8.8
Mozambique	5.8	7.6	2.6	4.9	3.2	−7.0	8.6	3.3	13.1	16.5	7.6	6.7
Myanmar	..	..	..	..	..	..	..	..	..	..	..	..
Namibia	4.8	5.8	2.3	3.8	3.3	3.3	7.3	8.8	3.8	7.6	5.4	8.6
Nepal	..	..	..	..	..	..	..	..	..	..	..	..
Netherlands	3.1	0.9	2.4	0.5	2.0	3.0	4.4	1.5	7.3	4.8	7.6	4.5
New Zealand	3.3	4.5	2.0	3.1	2.4	4.0	6.1	6.5	5.2	3.1	6.2	7.2
Nicaragua	6.1	3.6	3.9	2.3	−1.5	2.7	11.3	2.2	9.3	8.8	12.2	5.5
Niger	1.8	..	..	..	0.8	..	4.0	..	3.1	..	−2.1	..
Nigeria	..	..	..	..	..	..	..	..	..	..	..	..
Norway	3.5	4.0	2.9	3.3	2.7	2.2	6.0	6.7	5.5	1.0	5.8	5.7
Oman	5.4	1.3	2.6	−0.4	2.4	6.1	4.0	17.0	6.2	7.0	5.9	12.8
Pakistan	4.9	4.6	2.3	2.2	0.7	10.2	1.8	6.7	1.7	8.6	2.5	9.0
Panama	6.4	7.1	4.2	5.2	1.7	4.4	10.4	8.3	−0.4	6.8	1.2	7.2
Papua New Guinea	2.5	0.4	−0.2	−2.2	2.5	1.1	1.9	−1.1	5.1	6.3	3.4	6.3
Paraguay	2.6	3.0	0.3	1.0	2.5	3.0	0.7	3.5	3.1	8.0	2.9	6.6
Peru	4.0	5.1	2.2	3.7	5.2	4.6	7.4	10.9	8.5	8.6	9.0	10.1
Philippines	3.7	5.1	1.5	3.1	3.8	2.6	4.1	1.3	7.8	6.6	7.8	3.7
Poland	5.2	3.7	5.1	3.8	3.7	4.2	10.6	6.4	11.3	10.2	16.7	9.4
Portugal	3.0	1.6	2.7	1.1	2.9	1.3	5.8	−1.3	5.3	4.0	7.3	3.2
Puerto Rico	..	..	..	..	..	..	..	..	1.6	..	4.5	..
Qatar	..	..	..	..	..	..	..	..	..	..	..	..

	Household final consumption expenditure				General government final consumption expenditure		Gross capital formation		Goods and services			
	Total average annual % growth		Per capita		average annual % growth		average annual % growth		Exports average annual % growth		Imports	
	1990–2000	2000–08	1990–2000	2000–08	1990–2000	2000–08	1990–2000	2000–08	1990–2000	2000–08	1990–2000	2000–08
Romania	1.3	6.7	1.7	7.2	0.8	5.0	–5.1	12.3	8.1	10.8	6.0	15.8
Russian Federation	–0.9	10.5	–0.7	11.0	–2.2	2.1	–19.1	12.3	0.8	8.2	–6.1	19.7
Rwanda	0.4	..	..	..	–2.6	..	0.4	..	–6.4	..	6.1	..
Saudi Arabia	..	5.5	..	3.1	..	7.6	..	11.4	..	6.9	..	16.9
Senegal	2.6	5.3	–0.2	2.6	0.9	0.5	3.5	9.9	4.1	4.0	2.0	7.9
Serbia	..	5.4	..	5.7	..	2.7	..	15.8	..	12.1	..	12.8
Sierra Leone	–4.4	..	..	..	10.4	..	–5.6	..	–11.2	..	–0.2	..
Singapore	..	..	..	..	..	..	..	..	..	..	..	..
Slovak Republic	6.0	5.2	5.8	5.1	1.8	3.2	7.7	7.5	9.6	11.2	12.4	9.8
Slovenia	3.9	3.0	4.0	2.8	2.2	3.2	10.4	7.2	1.7	9.2	5.2	8.8
Somalia	..	..	..	..	..	..	..	..	..	..	..	..
South Africa	2.9	5.5	0.6	4.3	0.3	5.2	5.0	9.3	5.6	4.0	7.1	10.0
Spain	2.4	3.4	2.0	1.8	2.7	5.1	3.2	4.9	10.5	3.8	9.4	6.6
Sri Lanka	..	..	..	..	10.5	..	6.9	..	7.5	..	8.6	..
Sudan	3.7	5.9	1.1	3.7	5.5	8.4	22.0	12.5	11.6	14.3	8.4	12.0
Swaziland	7.3	2.2	4.9	1.3	7.1	3.2	–4.7	–1.1	6.4	7.0	6.2	5.7
Sweden	1.4	2.2	1.0	1.7	0.6	0.8	1.8	4.8	8.5	5.8	6.3	5.1
Switzerland	1.1	1.4	0.5	0.7	0.5	1.0	0.7	1.1	4.1	4.9	4.3	4.2
Syrian Arab Republic	3.0	7.6	0.3	4.7	2.0	8.0	3.3	0.4	12.0	6.6	4.4	12.1
Tajikistan	–11.8	11.9	–13.1	10.5	–15.7	1.5	–17.6	8.6	–5.3	8.8	–6.0	10.0
Tanzania[d]	4.9	2.8	1.9	0.1	–7.0	16.9	–1.6	7.3	9.3	12.0	3.9	5.7
Thailand	3.7	4.5	2.7	3.5	5.1	5.2	–4.0	7.0	9.5	7.0	4.5	7.7
Timor-Leste	..	..	..	..	..	..	..	..	..	..	..	..
Togo	5.0	0.5	2.0	–2.1	0.0	1.3	–0.1	5.9	1.2	6.0	1.1	3.1
Trinidad and Tobago	0.7	13.3	0.1	12.9	0.3	4.3	12.5	4.2	6.9	5.8	9.9	9.5
Tunisia	4.3	5.0	2.6	4.1	4.1	4.3	3.6	2.1	5.1	4.3	3.8	3.0
Turkey	3.8	6.0	2.1	4.6	4.6	3.7	4.7	10.1	11.1	7.2	10.8	11.1
Turkmenistan	..	..	..	..	..	..	..	–16.9	–2.4	21.5	7.2	13.3
Uganda	6.7	7.9	3.3	4.5	7.1	3.9	8.9	12.1	14.7	12.4	10.0	11.4
Ukraine	–6.9	13.8	–6.4	14.7	–4.1	2.9	–18.5	9.6	–3.6	3.2	–6.6	8.0
United Arab Emirates	7.1	12.9	1.2	7.5	6.8	0.8	5.5	5.5	5.5	12.2	6.4	13.6
United Kingdom	3.0	2.6	2.7	2.1	1.0	2.6	4.7	3.3	6.5	3.8	6.8	4.7
United States	3.7	3.0	2.4	2.0	0.7	2.3	7.5	2.1	7.3	4.4	9.8	5.2
Uruguay	5.0	2.7	4.3	2.6	2.3	0.3	6.1	5.6	6.0	7.9	9.9	6.3
Uzbekistan	..	..	..	..	..	..	–2.5	8.3	2.5	8.2	–0.4	10.4
Venezuela, RB	0.6	9.0	–1.5	7.1	3.7	7.0	11.0	12.4	1.0	–1.1	8.2	15.3
Vietnam	5.4	7.9	3.9	6.5	3.2	7.6	19.8	12.7	19.2	12.1	19.5	14.4
West Bank and Gaza	5.3	–1.5	1.1	–4.9	12.7	1.3	9.2	–3.0	8.7	–3.1	7.5	–2.3
Yemen, Rep.	3.2	..	–0.7	..	1.7	..	11.4	..	16.6	..	8.3	..
Zambia	2.4	0.2	–0.5	–2.1	–8.1	25.2	3.9	6.8	6.7	21.7	15.5	15.6
Zimbabwe	0.0	–3.8	–1.7	–3.8	–2.2	–3.0	–2.5	–10.6	10.5	–7.5	9.4	–3.3
World	3.0 w	3.0 w	1.6 w	1.8 w	1.7 w	2.6 w	3.3 w	4.1 w	6.9 w	6.8 w	7.0 w	6.6 w
Low income	3.7	4.7	1.3	2.5	0.2	5.8	6.5	9.9	9.4	10.3	8.2	10.9
Middle income	4.1	5.6	2.6	4.4	3.5	5.0	2.9	9.7	7.3	10.4	6.6	11.0
Lower middle income	5.6	6.2	4.0	4.9	6.4	6.9	6.1	11.3	8.1	14.0	6.9	12.2
Upper middle income	3.0	5.1	1.9	4.3	1.7	3.4	–0.1	7.4	6.8	6.8	6.4	10.1
Low & middle income	4.0	5.6	2.4	4.2	3.4	5.0	3.0	9.7	7.4	10.4	6.6	11.0
East Asia & Pacific	7.4	6.5	6.1	5.7	8.1	7.8	8.3	11.0	10.9	13.8	10.2	11.0
Europe & Central Asia	1.3	7.5	1.1	7.4	0.2	3.5	–8.5	10.9	2.7	8.6	0.1	13.6
Latin America & Carib.	3.6	4.2	2.0	2.9	2.1	3.0	5.4	5.7	8.5	6.0	10.8	7.9
Middle East & N. Africa	2.8	5.3	0.7	3.4	3.5	3.6	1.2	7.5	4.0	7.7	0.0	10.6
South Asia	4.6	5.5	2.6	3.9	5.9	5.7	6.5	13.8	10.0	14.0	11.2	17.5
Sub-Saharan Africa	3.1	5.3	0.4	2.7	0.5	5.0	4.5	8.5	5.0	4.3	6.0	8.7
High income	2.8	2.4	2.0	1.7	1.5	2.2	3.3	2.3	6.8	5.1	7.1	5.3
Euro area	1.9	1.5	1.6	0.9	1.5	1.8	2.1	2.3	6.8	4.7	6.2	4.7

a. Includes the French overseas departments of French Guiana, Guadeloupe, Martinique, and Réunion. b. Excludes Transnistria. c. Includes Former Spanish Sahara. d. Covers mainland Tanzania only.

Growth of consumption and investment

Measures of growth in consumption and capital formation are subject to two kinds of inaccuracy. The first stems from the difficulty of measuring expenditures at current price levels, as described in *About the data* for table 4.8. The second arises in deflating current price data to measure volume growth, where results depend on the relevance and reliability of the price indexes and weights used. Measuring price changes is more difficult for investment goods than for consumption goods because of the one-time nature of many investments and because the rate of technological progress in capital goods makes capturing change in quality difficult. (An example is computers—prices have fallen as quality has improved.) Several countries estimate capital formation from the supply side, identifying capital goods entering an economy directly from detailed production and international trade statistics. This means that the price indexes used in deflating production and international trade, reflecting delivered or offered prices, will determine the deflator for capital formation expenditures on the demand side.

Growth rates of household final consumption expenditure, household final consumption expenditure per capita, general government final consumption expenditure, gross capital formation, and exports and imports of goods and services are estimated using constant price data. (Consumption, capital formation, and exports and imports of goods and services as shares of GDP are shown in table 4.8.)

To obtain government consumption in constant prices, countries may deflate current values by applying a wage (price) index or extrapolate from the change in government employment. Neither technique captures improvements in productivity or changes in the quality of government services. Deflators for household consumption are usually calculated on the basis of the consumer price index. Many countries estimate household consumption as a residual that includes statistical discrepancies associated with the estimation of other expenditure items, including changes in inventories; thus these estimates lack detailed breakdowns of household consumption expenditures.

• **Household final consumption expenditure** is the market value of all goods and services, including durable products (such as cars and computers), purchased by households. It excludes purchases of dwellings but includes imputed rent for owner-occupied dwellings. It also includes government fees for permits and licenses. Expenditures of nonprofit institutions serving households are included, even when reported separately. Household consumption expenditure may include any statistical discrepancy in the use of resources relative to the supply of resources. • **Household final consumption expenditure per capita** is household final consumption expenditure divided by midyear population. • **General government final consumption expenditure** is all government current expenditures for goods and services (including compensation of employees). It also includes most expenditures on national defense and security but excludes military expenditures with potentially wider public use that are part of government capital formation. • **Gross capital formation** is outlays on additions to fixed assets of the economy, net changes in inventories, and net acquisitions of valuables. Fixed assets include land improvements (fences, ditches, drains); plant, machinery, and equipment purchases; and construction (roads, railways, schools, buildings, and so on). Inventories are goods held to meet temporary or unexpected fluctuations in production or sales, and "work in progress." • **Exports** and **imports of goods and services** are the value of all goods and other market services provided to or received from the rest of the world. They include the value of merchandise, freight, insurance, transport, travel, royalties, license fees, and other services (communication, construction, financial, information, business, personal, government services, and so on). They exclude compensation of employees and investment income (factor services in the 1968 System of National Accounts) and transfer payments.

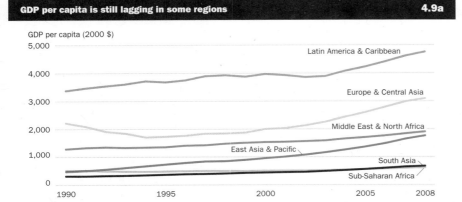

GDP per capita is still lagging in some regions 4.9a

GDP per capita (2000 $)

Although GDP per capita more than tripled in East Asia and Pacific between 1990 and 2008, it is still less than GDP per capita in Latin America and Caribbean, Europe and Central Asia, and Middle East and North Africa.

Source: World Development Indicators data files.

Data on national accounts indicators for most developing countries are collected from national statistical organizations and central banks by visiting and resident World Bank missions. Data for high-income economies are from Organisation for Economic Co-operation and Development (OECD) data files.

	Revenue[a]		Expense		Cash surplus or deficit		Net incurrence of liabilities				Debt and interest payments	
	% of GDP		% of GDP		% of GDP		% of GDP				Total debt % of GDP	Interest % of revenue
							Domestic		Foreign			
	1995	2008	1995	2008	1995	2008	1995	2008	1995	2008	2008	2008
Afghanistan[b]	..	7.6	..	23.0	..	−2.2	..	0.2	..	1.9	9.6	0.1
Albania[b]	21.2	..	25.6	..	−8.9	..	7.4	..	2.1	..	..	..
Algeria[b]	..	48.5	..	23.9	..	9.5	..	1.2	..	0.0	..	1.2
Angola	..	..	..	..	..	..	..	..	..	..	..	..
Argentina	..	..	..	..	..	..	..	..	..	..	..	..
Armenia[b]	..	22.4	..	20.7	..	−0.5	..	0.7	..	1.2	..	1.3
Australia	..	25.4	..	23.6	..	1.5	..	..	..	..	19.4	3.5
Austria	36.6	37.4	42.5	38.4	−5.5	−0.7	..	..	..	..	64.5	6.5
Azerbaijan[b]	18.0	27.3	19.8	15.5	−3.1	0.4	..	0.0	..	0.2	..	0.3
Bangladesh[b]	..	11.0	..	10.9	..	−1.0	..	4.1	..	1.1	..	21.8
Belarus[b]	30.0	39.2	28.7	34.2	−2.7	2.4	2.2	1.3	0.4	2.3	10.7	1.4
Belgium	41.5	41.2	45.6	42.5	−3.9	−1.1	2.5	1.0	−0.5	6.5	88.0	8.5
Benin[b]	..	18.6	..	14.9	..	−0.3	..	−2.6	..	2.4	..	1.7
Bolivia	..	23.3	..	21.8	..	1.2	..	−0.2	..	−0.1	..	8.0
Bosnia and Herzegovina	..	39.1	..	38.9	..	−1.5	..	1.0	..	0.6	..	1.2
Botswana[b]	40.5	..	30.3	..	4.9	..	0.2	..	−0.4	..	..	..
Brazil[b]	..	24.7	..	25.0	..	−1.3	..	4.6	..	−0.2	60.9	15.2
Bulgaria[b]	35.5	36.4	39.4	30.9	−5.1	3.2	7.4	−0.5	−0.8	−1.4	..	2.3
Burkina Faso	..	13.6	..	12.8	..	−4.2	..	0.5	..	2.8	..	2.0
Burundi[b]	19.3	..	23.6	..	−4.7	..	3.1	..	4.0	..	..	..
Cambodia	..	9.8	..	8.6	..	−1.7	..	−0.3	..	2.1	..	1.5
Cameroon[b]	11.8	..	10.6	..	0.2	..	−0.3	..	0.3	..	..	..
Canada[b]	20.3	19.6	24.2	17.8	−4.3	1.6	4.9	−0.9	0.0	0.2	45.2	6.1
Central African Republic[b]	..	..	..	..	..	..	..	..	..	..	..	..
Chad	..	..	..	..	..	..	..	..	..	..	..	..
Chile	..	26.0	..	19.7	..	4.8	..	−0.3	..	−0.4	..	1.9
China[b]	5.4	10.3	..	11.4	..	−1.4	1.6	1.2	..	−0.1	..	4.3
Hong Kong SAR, China	..	..	..	..	..	..	..	..	..	..	..	..
Colombia	..	23.5	..	23.7	..	−2.1	..	−2.0	..	1.5	54.3	29.4
Congo, Dem. Rep.[b]	5.3	..	8.2	..	0.0	..	0.0	..	0.2	..	..	..
Congo, Rep.	..	39.9	..	24.8	..	9.6	..	..	..	..	..	6.5
Costa Rica[b]	..	25.3	..	22.5	..	−0.8	..	..	−0.8	..	..	8.6
Côte d'Ivoire[b]	..	18.9	..	17.9	..	−0.3	..	−0.1	..	..	..	8.4
Croatia[b]	36.7	35.9	36.1	34.7	−1.1	−1.1	−2.3	0.6	0.7	−0.5	..	4.8
Cuba	..	..	..	..	..	..	..	..	..	..	..	..
Czech Republic[b]	33.2	31.4	32.6	34.1	−0.9	−1.5	−0.5	1.5	−0.4	0.8	26.6	3.6
Denmark	39.1	40.6	38.2	36.5	1.5	4.8	..	..	..	..	24.1	4.5
Dominican Republic[b]	..	17.6	..	14.8	..	0.3	..	−0.4	..	0.6	..	6.8
Ecuador[b]	30.9	..	26.3	..	0.1	..	..	..	..	..	..	..
Egypt, Arab Rep.[b]	34.8	27.7	28.1	30.4	3.4	−6.4	..	8.5	..	1.3	..	16.5
El Salvador	..	19.9	..	18.5	..	0.3	..	−0.7	..	−0.8	39.4	9.8
Eritrea	..	..	..	..	..	..	..	..	..	..	..	..
Estonia	..	31.9	..	26.8	..	3.1	..	..	..	..	4.1	0.2
Ethiopia[b]	..	..	..	..	..	..	..	..	..	..	..	..
Finland	40.6	38.7	49.9	33.8	−7.5	5.5	8.9	−0.4	0.2	−0.8	37.3	3.2
France	43.3	41.8	47.6	44.4	−4.1	−2.3	..	..	..	..	66.6	5.9
Gabon	..	..	..	..	..	..	..	..	..	..	..	..
Gambia, The[b]	23.7	..	..	..	..	..	..	..	..	..	..	..
Georgia[b]	12.2	25.7	15.4	29.1	−4.3	−1.9	2.2	−0.3	2.4	5.3	27.0	2.2
Germany	29.9	28.5	38.6	29.0	−8.3	−0.4	..	0.2	..	0.1	40.8	6.0
Ghana[b]	17.0	25.8	..	29.5	..	−7.7	..	5.1	..	2.3	..	9.6
Greece	35.1	39.0	42.6	41.8	−9.1	−3.7	..	..	..	..	114.1	11.1
Guatemala[b]	8.4	11.9	7.6	11.7	−0.5	−1.6	..	0.6	0.4	0.3	20.1	11.2
Guinea[b]	11.2	..	12.1	..	−4.3	..	−0.1	..	4.5	..	..	..
Guinea-Bissau	..	..	..	..	..	..	..	..	..	..	..	..
Haiti	..	..	..	..	..	..	..	..	..	..	..	..
Honduras	..	22.3	..	21.6	..	−0.2	..	−1.2	..	2.6	..	2.5

Central government finances

	Revenue[a]		Expense		Cash surplus or deficit		Net incurrence of liabilities				Debt and interest payments	
	% of GDP		% of GDP		% of GDP		Domestic	% of GDP	Foreign		Total debt % of GDP	Interest % of revenue
	1995	2008	1995	2008	1995	2008	1995	2008	1995	2008	2008	2008
Hungary	43.0	40.7	53.2	45.0	−9.1	−3.9	17.0	2.3	0.2	6.1	73.8	9.7
India[b]	12.3	15.0	14.4	16.2	−2.2	−1.6	5.1	2.1	0.0	0.1	57.6	23.3
Indonesia[b]	17.7	..	9.7	..	3.0	..	−0.6	..	−0.4	..	..	..
Iran, Islamic Rep.[b]	24.2	34.8	15.8	20.6	1.1	7.9	..	1.4	0.1	0.0	..	0.8
Iraq	..	..	..	..	..	..	..	..	..	..	..	..
Ireland	33.6	33.1	37.5	32.0	−2.2	0.4	..	..	..	..	27.2	2.8
Israel	..	36.8	..	40.7	..	−1.9	..	..	..	..	..	9.0
Italy	40.4	37.5	48.0	40.1	−7.5	−2.5	..	..	..	..	106.3	12.8
Jamaica[b]	..	29.1	..	33.2	..	−5.1	..	−0.8	..	6.3	112.9	39.1
Japan	20.7	..	..	..	..	..	1.5	..	..	..	..	..
Jordan[b]	..	32.9	..	36.6	..	−1.1	..	13.5	..	−11.6	115.1	6.7
Kazakhstan[b]	14.0	13.4	18.7	14.8	−1.8	4.3	0.8	1.9	2.8	0.0	6.3	1.9
Kenya[b]	21.6	19.5	25.8	21.5	−5.1	−4.1	3.9	−0.7	−1.3	0.1	..	11.3
Korea, Dem. Rep.	..	..	..	..	..	..	..	..	..	..	..	..
Korea, Rep.[b]	17.8	24.6	14.3	18.6	2.4	4.3	−0.3	−2.4	−0.1	−0.1	..	5.6
Kosovo	..	..	..	..	..	..	..	..	..	..	..	..
Kuwait	36.8	47.4	46.4	24.0	−13.6	23.4	..	..	..	..	..	0.0
Kyrgyz Republic[b]	16.7	20.5	25.6	17.0	−10.8	0.0	..	0.1	..	0.3	..	3.3
Lao PDR	..	13.0	..	10.3	..	−2.9	..	0.1	..	3.6	..	3.1
Latvia[b]	25.8	26.0	28.3	29.4	−2.7	−2.6	2.4	5.0	1.5	4.7	22.8	1.3
Lebanon	..	21.5	..	30.4	..	−10.0	..	17.1	..	−0.1	..	50.1
Lesotho[b]	52.2	65.3	36.0	51.2	5.3	5.7	0.0	−0.4	6.5	1.5	..	1.3
Liberia	..	..	..	..	..	..	..	..	..	..	..	..
Libya	..	..	..	..	..	..	..	..	..	..	..	..
Lithuania	..	28.7	..	31.4	..	−3.1	..	1.1	..	−0.1	18.4	2.0
Macedonia, FYR	..	34.0	..	31.3	..	−0.8	..	−0.6	..	0.2	..	1.9
Madagascar	..	11.9	..	11.2	..	−2.7	..	0.7	..	2.2	..	7.0
Malawi	..	..	..	..	..	..	..	..	..	..	..	..
Malaysia[b]	24.4	..	17.2	..	2.4	..	..	..	−0.8	..	..	..
Mali	..	16.2	..	15.2	..	−5.6	..	−1.0	..	3.5	..	1.7
Mauritania	..	..	..	..	..	..	..	..	..	..	..	..
Mauritius[b]	20.5	21.7	18.9	19.3	−1.2	0.6	2.9	2.0	−0.5	−0.1	36.1	13.7
Mexico[b]	15.3	..	15.0	..	−0.6	..	..	..	5.5	..	..	..
Moldova[b]	28.4	34.4	38.4	32.8	−6.3	−0.4	3.0	−0.5	2.7	0.0	18.5	3.2
Mongolia	19.0	32.1	13.8	26.3	2.9	−3.5	1.6	−0.4	1.3	0.7	46.9	1.0
Morocco[b]	..	36.0	..	30.1	..	2.9	..	−0.7	..	0.3	..	3.6
Mozambique	..	..	..	..	..	..	..	..	..	..	..	..
Myanmar	6.4	..	..	..	..	..	..	..	..	..	..	..
Namibia[b]	31.7	29.1	35.7	24.0	−5.0	2.0	..	−0.8	..	−0.1	..	6.3
Nepal[b]	10.5	12.3	..	15.1	..	−1.0	0.6	1.5	2.5	0.1	43.7	5.3
Netherlands	41.5	40.8	50.8	40.3	−9.2	0.3	..	..	..	..	43.4	4.4
New Zealand	..	37.1	..	32.9	..	3.2	..	−1.7	..	2.8	38.9	3.4
Nicaragua[b]	12.8	18.4	14.2	19.6	0.6	−1.1	..	..	..	3.4	..	5.4
Niger	..	13.6	..	11.8	..	−0.9	..	−1.9	..	2.4	..	1.8
Nigeria	..	..	..	..	..	..	..	..	..	..	..	..
Norway	..	51.2	..	30.7	..	19.9	..	1.9	..	−10.7	44.9	1.6
Oman[b]	27.8	..	32.4	..	−8.9	..	−0.1	..	0.0	..	..	..
Pakistan[b]	17.2	13.4	19.1	18.6	−5.3	−7.4	..	..	..	..	..	34.8
Panama[b]	26.1	..	22.0	..	1.5	..	..	..	..	..	..	..
Papua New Guinea[b]	22.7	..	24.5	..	−0.5	..	1.5	..	−0.7	..	..	..
Paraguay[b]	..	21.3	..	16.7	..	3.4	..	−0.6	..	−0.5	..	2.9
Peru[b]	17.4	19.6	17.4	16.5	−1.3	2.0	..	0.1	3.9	−1.0	24.3	7.7
Philippines[b]	17.7	15.8	15.9	17.0	−0.8	−1.3	−0.5	1.5	−0.7	0.2	..	24.1
Poland	..	32.0	..	35.3	..	−3.7	..	5.0	..	−0.9	44.8	7.0
Portugal	33.3	39.2	38.9	42.9	−5.1	−2.7	−1.4	−0.9	4.3	4.6	76.0	7.2
Puerto Rico	..	..	..	..	..	..	..	..	..	..	..	..
Qatar	..	45.5	..	17.8	..	12.5	..	..	..	..	..	1.5

4.10 | Central government finances

	Revenue[a]		Expense		Cash surplus or deficit		Net incurrence of liabilities				Debt and interest payments	
	% of GDP		% of GDP		% of GDP		% of GDP				Total debt % of GDP	Interest % of revenue
							Domestic		Foreign			
	1995	2008	1995	2008	1995	2008	1995	2008	1995	2008	2008	2008
Romania	..	30.9	..	33.8	..	−4.6	..	2.4	..	0.9	..	2.0
Russian Federation	..	33.4	..	21.3	..	5.6	..	0.2	..	0.2	6.4	1.1
Rwanda[b]	10.6	..	15.0	..	−5.6	..	2.9	..	..	..	..	..
Saudi Arabia	..	..	..	..	..	..	..	..	..	..	..	..
Senegal[b]	15.2	..	..	..	..	..	..	..	..	..	..	..
Serbia[b]	..	37.6	..	37.4	..	−1.6	..	−0.8	..	−0.1	..	1.4
Sierra Leone[b]	9.4	..	..	..	..	..	0.3	..	..	..	..	..
Singapore[b]	26.7	21.7	12.4	15.4	19.8	8.1	10.3	7.9	0.0	..	102.6	0.1
Slovak Republic	..	28.9	..	30.8	..	−2.2	..	1.2	..	0.0	36.5	4.1
Slovenia[b]	35.8	38.1	34.3	37.4	−0.1	−0.2	−0.4	−0.5	0.3	−0.1	..	2.8
Somalia	..	..	..	..	..	..	..	..	..	..	..	..
South Africa	..	30.7	..	30.9	..	−0.4	..	1.6	..	−0.1	..	7.8
Spain	32.0	24.5	37.1	26.3	−5.8	−2.0	..	..	..	..	33.8	4.8
Sri Lanka[b]	20.4	15.8	26.0	20.0	−7.6	−6.5	5.2	4.2	3.2	2.8	85.0	30.7
Sudan[b]	7.2	..	6.8	..	−0.4	..	0.3	..	..	..	..	..
Swaziland[b]	..	..	..	..	..	..	..	..	..	..	..	..
Sweden	35.0	..	44.1	..	−9.3	..	..	..	−1.2	..	47.3	..
Switzerland[b]	22.6	18.3	25.7	17.6	−0.6	1.1	−0.5	−1.1	..	..	23.6	4.4
Syrian Arab Republic[b]	22.9	..	..	..	..	..	..	..	..	..	..	..
Tajikistan[b]	9.3	..	11.4	..	−3.3	..	0.1	..	2.3	..	..	..
Tanzania	..	..	..	..	..	..	..	..	..	..	..	..
Thailand	..	20.1	..	18.2	..	0.5	..	1.1	..	−0.5	24.0	4.9
Timor-Leste	..	..	..	..	..	..	..	..	..	..	..	..
Togo[b]	..	17.0	..	15.1	..	0.3	..	1.8	..	−0.2	..	4.3
Trinidad and Tobago[b]	27.2	30.3	25.3	24.4	−0.1	0.7	2.8	−0.8	2.6	0.5	..	6.5
Tunisia[b]	30.0	32.5	28.4	30.4	−2.4	−0.7	0.9	−1.3	2.9	0.3	48.2	7.0
Turkey[b]	..	22.6	..	22.8	..	−1.9	..	1.7	..	0.4	44.5	24.2
Turkmenistan	..	..	..	..	..	..	..	..	..	..	..	..
Uganda[b]	10.6	13.2	..	15.2	..	−1.5	..	2.1	..	1.7	28.9	7.9
Ukraine[b]	..	35.7	..	37.2	..	−1.5	..	3.1	..	0.4	..	1.3
United Arab Emirates[b]	10.1	..	9.3	..	0.5	..	..	..	..	..	..	..
United Kingdom	35.2	38.4	40.4	42.8	−5.5	−4.7	−0.3	..	0.0	..	57.5	5.8
United States	..	17.3	..	22.7	..	−5.4	..	4.1	..	5.0	53.8	11.6
Uruguay[b]	27.6	25.0	27.1	24.2	−1.2	−0.9	7.9	1.4	1.1	−1.3	54.0	10.9
Uzbekistan	..	..	..	..	..	..	..	..	..	..	..	..
Venezuela, RB[b]	16.9	28.3	18.5	25.1	−2.3	2.2	1.1	1.2	0.1	3.3	..	10.4
Vietnam	..	..	..	..	..	..	..	..	..	..	..	..
West Bank and Gaza	..	..	..	..	..	..	..	..	..	..	..	..
Yemen, Rep.[b]	17.3	..	19.1	..	−3.9	..	..	..	..	..	..	..
Zambia[b]	20.0	17.6	21.4	22.9	−3.1	−0.8	28.0	..	16.2	..	..	7.2
Zimbabwe[b]	26.7	..	32.1	..	−5.4	..	−1.4	..	1.6	..	..	..
World	.. w	**27.4 w**	.. w	**28.1 w**	.. w	**−0.9 w**	.. m	.. m	.. m	.. m	.. m	**5.6 m**
Low income	..	..	..	..	..	..	..	..	..	..	..	..
Middle income	..	20.2	..	19.7	..	−0.6	..	0.9	..	0.2	..	3.6
Lower middle income	11.4	15.2	..	15.6	..	−1.5	..	..	..	..	..	4.3
Upper middle income	..	..	..	..	..	..	..	1.2	..	0.0	..	2.3
Low & middle income	..	20.0	..	19.6	..	−0.6	..	..	..	..	..	5.8
East Asia & Pacific	8.4	11.6	..	12.2	..	−1.1	..	..	..	..	..	..
Europe & Central Asia	..	29.6	..	26.7	..	0.3	..	0.9	..	0.3	..	1.9
Latin America & Carib.	..	..	..	..	..	..	..	0.9	..	−0.2	..	9.2
Middle East & N. Africa	..	32.2	..	24.9	..	1.7	..	4.8	..	0.1	..	6.7
South Asia	13.1	14.4	15.3	16.1	−2.7	−2.2	3.8	1.8	1.1	0.6	61.3	21.8
Sub-Saharan Africa	..	..	..	..	..	..	..	..	..	..	..	..
High income	..	27.9	..	28.9	..	−1.0	..	..	..	..	43.4	4.8
Euro area	34.8	38.1	42.3	39.0	−7.4	−0.9	..	..	..	..	51.7	6.5

a. Excludes grants. b. Data were reported on a cash basis and have been adjusted to the accrual framework.

About the data

Tables 4.10–4.12 present an overview of the size and role of central governments relative to national economies. The tables are based on the concepts and recommendations of the second edition of the International Monetary Fund's (IMF) *Government Finance Statistics Manual 2001*. Before 2005 *World Development Indicators* reported data derived on the basis of the 1986 manual's cash-based method. The 2001 manual, harmonized with the 1993 United Nations System of National Accounts, recommends an accrual accounting method, focusing on all economic events affecting assets, liabilities, revenues, and expenses, not only those represented by cash transactions. It takes all stocks into account, so that stock data at the end of an accounting period equal stock data at the beginning of the period plus flows over the period. The 1986 manual considered only the debt stock data. Further, the new manual no longer distinguishes between current and capital revenue or expenditures, and it introduces the concepts of nonfinancial and financial assets. Most countries still follow the 1986 manual, however. The IMF has reclassified historical *Government Finance Statistics Yearbook* data to conform to the 2001 manual's format. Because of reporting differences, the reclassified data understate both revenue and expense.

The 2001 manual describes government's economic functions as the provision of goods and services on a nonmarket basis for collective or individual consumption, and the redistribution of income and wealth through transfer payments. Government activities are financed mainly by taxation and other income transfers, though other financing such as

borrowing for temporary periods can also be used. *Government* excludes public corporations and quasi corporations (such as the central bank).

Units of government at many levels meet this definition, from local administrative units to the national government, but inadequate statistical coverage precludes presenting subnational data. Although data for general government under the 2001 manual are available for a few countries, only data for the central government are shown to minimize disparities. Still, different accounting concepts of central government make cross-country comparisons potentially misleading.

Central government can refer to consolidated or budgetary accounting. For most countries central government finance data have been consolidated into one account, but for others only budgetary central government accounts are available. Countries reporting budgetary data are noted in *Primary data documentation*. Because budgetary accounts may not include all central government units (such as social security funds), they usually provide an incomplete picture.

Data on government revenue and expense are collected by the IMF through questionnaires to member countries and by the Organisation for Economic Cooperation and Development. Despite IMF efforts to standardize data collection, statistics are often incomplete, untimely, and not comparable across countries.

Government finance statistics are reported in local currency. The indicators here are shown as percentages of GDP. Many countries report government finance data by fiscal year; see *Primary data documentation* for information on fiscal year end by country.

Definitions

• **Revenue** is cash receipts from taxes, social contributions, and other revenues such as fines, fees, rent, and income from property or sales. Grants, usually considered revenue, are excluded. • **Expense** is cash payments for government operating activities in providing goods and services. It includes compensation of employees, interest and subsidies, grants, social benefits, and other expenses such as rent and dividends. • **Cash surplus or deficit** is revenue (including grants) minus expense, minus net acquisition of nonfinancial assets. In editions before 2005 nonfinancial assets were included under revenue and expenditure in gross terms. This cash surplus or deficit is close to the earlier overall budget balance (still missing is lending minus repayments, which are included as a financing item under net acquisition of financial assets). • **Net incurrence of liabilities** is domestic financing (obtained from residents) and foreign financing (obtained from nonresidents), or the means by which a government provides financial resources to cover a budget deficit or allocates financial resources arising from a budget surplus. The net incurrence of liabilities should be offset by the net acquisition of financial assets (a third financing item). The difference between the cash surplus or deficit and the three financing items is the net change in the stock of cash. • **Total debt** is the entire stock of direct government fixed-term contractual obligations to others outstanding on a particular date. It includes domestic and foreign liabilities such as currency and money deposits, securities other than shares, and loans. It is the gross amount of government liabilities reduced by the amount of equity and financial derivatives held by the government. Because debt is a stock rather than a flow, it is measured as of a given date, usually the last day of the fiscal year. • **Interest payments** are interest payments on government debt—including long-term bonds, long-term loans, and other debt instruments —to domestic and foreign residents.

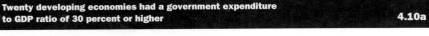

Twenty developing economies had a government expenditure to GDP ratio of 30 percent or higher   4.10a

Central government expense, 2008 (percent of GDP)

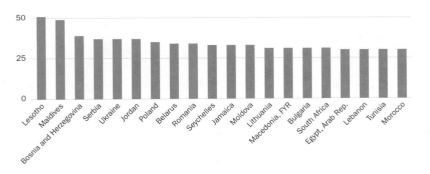

Source: International Monetary Fund, Government Finance Statistics data files, and World Development Indicators data files.

Data sources

Data on central government finances are from the IMF's *Government Finance Statistics Yearbook 2008* and data files. Each country's accounts are reported using the system of common definitions and classifications in the IMF's *Government Finance Statistics Manual 2001*. See these sources for complete and authoritative explanations of concepts, definitions, and data sources.

	Goods and services		Compensation of employees		Interest payments		Subsidies and other transfers		Other expense	
	% of expense		% of expense		% of expense		% of expense		% of expense	
	1995	**2008**	**1995**	**2008**	**1995**	**2008**	**1995**	**2008**	**1995**	**2008**
Afghanistan[a]	..	42	..	39	..	0	..	16	..	4
Albania[a]	18	..	14	..	9	..	59	..	0	..
Algeria[a]	..	12	..	31	..	3	..	49	..	6
Angola	..	..	..	..	..	..	..	..	..	..
Argentina	..	..	..	..	..	..	..	..	..	..
Armenia[a]	..	12	..	21	..	2	..	43	..	22
Australia	..	*11*	..	*11*	..	4	..	70	..	6
Austria	5	6	14	13	9	6	68	70	6	6
Azerbaijan[a]	..	9	..	12	..	1	..	18	..	61
Bangladesh[a]	..	12	..	21	..	23	..	32	..	13
Belarus[a]	39	12	5	10	1	2	55	69	0	7
Belgium	3	3	7	7	18	8	71	81	2	2
Benin[a]	..	23	..	40	..	2	..	33	..	2
Bolivia	..	14	..	22	..	10	..	47	..	7
Bosnia and Herzegovina	..	23	..	28	..	1	..	45	..	3
Botswana[a]	32	..	31	..	2	..	36	..	2	..
Brazil[a]	..	13	..	18	..	15	..	52	..	2
Bulgaria[a]	18	13	7	18	37	3	38	60	2	6
Burkina Faso	..	21	..	44	..	3	..	10	..	23
Burundi[a]	20	..	30	..	6	..	14	..	10	..
Cambodia	..	*41*	..	*33*	..	2	..	19	..	5
Cameroon[a]	17	..	40	..	26	..	14	..	..	..
Canada[a]	8	*8*	10	*12*	18	7	64	67	..	6
Central African Republic[a]	..	..	..	..	..	..	..	..	..	..
Chad	..	..	..	..	..	..	..	..	..	..
Chile	..	10	..	20	..	3	..	59	..	13
China[a]	..	*27*	..	*5*	..	*4*	..	60	..	*4*
Hong Kong SAR, China	..	..	..	..	..	..	..	..	..	..
Colombia	..	8	..	15	..	29	..	41	..	7
Congo, Dem. Rep.[a]	37	..	58	..	1	..	2	..	..	..
Congo, Rep.	..	*18*	..	*18*	..	*11*	..	53	..	*0*
Costa Rica[a]	..	12	..	44	..	10	..	14	..	20
Côte d'Ivoire[a]	..	32	..	38	..	10	..	13	..	7
Croatia[a]	35	*10*	27	*26*	3	*5*	32	53	3	*6*
Cuba	..	..	..	..	..	..	..	..	..	..
Czech Republic[a]	7	6	9	8	3	4	75	70	5	12
Denmark	8	9	*13*	*13*	*13*	5	64	70	5	4
Dominican Republic[a]	..	19	..	34	..	8	..	29	..	8
Ecuador[a]	6	..	49	..	26	..	..	..	..	..
Egypt, Arab Rep.[a]	18	7	22	23	26	15	6	46	..	9
El Salvador	..	17	..	37	..	11	..	22	..	15
Eritrea	..	..	..	..	..	..	..	..	..	..
Estonia	..	14	..	22	..	0	..	43	..	4
Ethiopia[a]	..	..	..	..	..	..	..	..	..	..
Finland	8	*10*	9	*10*	8	4	68	72	11	8
France	8	6	23	22	7	6	59	62	6	6
Gabon	..	..	..	..	..	..	..	..	..	..
Gambia, The[a]	..	..	..	..	..	..	..	..	..	..
Georgia[a]	*52*	27	*11*	16	*10*	2	*26*	45	..	9
Germany	4	5	5	*5*	6	6	67	82	20	3
Ghana[a]	..	15	..	38	..	11	..	37	..	0
Greece	10	*11*	22	24	27	10	36	45	5	4
Guatemala[a]	15	15	50	27	12	12	18	37	6	10
Guinea[a]	*17*	..	*34*	..	*28*	..	9	..	*1*	..
Guinea-Bissau	..	..	..	..	..	..	..	..	..	..
Haiti	..	..	..	..	..	..	..	..	..	..
Honduras	..	16	..	50	..	3	..	13	..	18

	Goods and services % of expense		Compensation of employees % of expense		Interest payments % of expense		Subsidies and other transfers % of expense		Other expense % of expense	
	1995	2008	1995	2008	1995	2008	1995	2008	1995	2008
Hungary	8	9	10	13	17	9	56	63	13	9
India[a]	15	11	10	7	27	22	33	54	0	7
Indonesia[a]	21	..	20	..	16	..	41	..	2	..
Iran, Islamic Rep.[a]	21	10	56	38	0	1	..	37	..	13
Iraq	..	..	..	..	..	..	..	..	..	..
Ireland	5	12	15	24	14	3	33	37	1	1
Israel	..	28	..	25	..	9	..	31	..	9
Italy	4	4	14	15	24	12	54	65	6	5
Jamaica[a]	..	8	..	17	..	35	..	6	..	33
Japan	..	..	..	..	..	..	..	..	..	..
Jordan[a]	..	8	..	45	..	7	..	36	..	5
Kazakhstan[a]	..	20	..	7	3	3	58	68	..	2
Kenya[a]	15	20	28	38	46	11	..	31	2	0
Korea, Dem. Rep.	..	..	..	..	..	..	..	..	..	..
Korea, Rep.[a]	16	7	15	12	3	7	63	58	3	15
Kosovo	..	..	..	..	..	..	..	..	..	..
Kuwait	33	19	31	29	5	0	24	29	7	23
Kyrgyz Republic[a]	32	29	37	28	5	4	27	36	..	3
Lao PDR	..	37	..	38	..	5	..	18	..	3
Latvia[a]	20	11	20	19	3	1	56	65	0	4
Lebanon	..	3	..	27	..	37	..	29	..	3
Lesotho[a]	32	42	45	35	5	2	8	14	3	7
Liberia	..	..	..	..	..	..	..	..	..	..
Libya	..	..	..	..	..	..	..	..	..	..
Lithuania	..	13	..	18	..	2	..	65	..	6
Macedonia, FYR	..	28	..	17	..	2	..	49	..	4
Madagascar	..	14	..	46	..	10	..	14	..	16
Malawi	..	..	..	..	..	..	..	..	..	..
Malaysia[a]	23	..	34	..	17	..	27	..	1	..
Mali	..	38	..	33	..	2	..	16	..	11
Mauritania	..	..	..	..	..	..	..	..	..	..
Mauritius[a]	12	11	45	34	13	16	28	34	2	6
Mexico[a]	9	..	19	..	19	..	..	..	..	..
Moldova[a]	10	20	8	14	11	4	71	57	1	6
Mongolia	30	27	12	34	2	1	56	38	0	1
Morocco[a]	..	9	..	43	..	5	..	36	..	9
Mozambique	..	..	..	..	..	..	..	..	..	..
Myanmar	..	..	..	..	..	..	..	..	..	..
Namibia[a]	29	20	53	45	1	8	..	13	4	14
Nepal[a]	..	..	..	..	..	7	..	..	..	..
Netherlands	5	8	8	8	9	5	77	79	3	3
New Zealand	..	30	..	25	..	4	..	38	..	7
Nicaragua[a]	14	16	25	36	17	6	29	36	14	7
Niger	..	30	..	30	..	3	..	9	..	28
Nigeria	..	..	..	..	..	..	..	..	..	..
Norway	..	11	..	17	..	3	..	67	..	6
Oman[a]	55	..	30	..	7	..	8	..	0	..
Pakistan[a]	..	21	..	4	28	26	2	27	..	23
Panama[a]	16	..	45	..	8	..	30	..	1	..
Papua New Guinea[a]	19	..	36	..	20	..	26	..	1	..
Paraguay[a]	..	10	..	55	..	4	..	23	..	8
Peru[a]	20	18	19	18	19	9	33	49	8	7
Philippines[a]	15	25	34	30	33	22	15	19	..	4
Poland	..	8	..	12	..	6	..	69	..	7
Portugal	8	7	29	26	14	7	42	50	9	2
Puerto Rico	..	..	..	..	..	..	..	..	..	..
Qatar	..	29	..	33	..	4	..	17	..	18

	Goods and services		Compensation of employees		Interest payments		Subsidies and other transfers		Other expense	
	% of expense		% of expense		% of expense		% of expense		% of expense	
	1995	2008	1995	2008	1995	2008	1995	2008	1995	2008
Romania	..	13	..	19	..	2	..	60	..	8
Russian Federation	..	14	..	18	..	2	..	64	..	7
Rwanda[a]	52	..	36	..	12	..	5	..	..	..
Saudi Arabia	..	..	..	..	..	..	..	..	..	..
Senegal[a]	..	..	..	..	..	..	..	..	..	..
Serbia	..	13	..	27	..	2	..	57	..	1
Sierra Leone[a]	..	..	..	..	..	..	..	..	..	..
Singapore[a]	38	40	39	27	8	0	15	0	..	..
Slovak Republic	..	11	..	14	..	4	..	67	..	5
Slovenia[a]	19	13	21	19	3	3	55	62	3	3
Somalia	..	..	..	..	..	..	..	..	..	..
South Africa	..	12	..	13	..	8	..	61	..	6
Spain	5	4	14	9	12	5	42	79	2	6
Sri Lanka[a]	23	11	20	30	22	26	24	23	10	10
Sudan[a]	44	..	38	..	8	..	10	..	..	..
Swaziland[a]	..	..	..	..	..	..	..	..	..	..
Sweden	10	..	5	..	13	..	71	..	1	..
Switzerland[a]	24	8	6	7	4	5	66	76	1	4
Syrian Arab Republic[a]	..	..	..	..	..	..	..	..	..	..
Tajikistan[a]	47	..	8	..	12	..	33	..	..	..
Tanzania	..	..	..	..	..	..	..	..	..	..
Thailand	..	27	..	35	..	5	..	31	..	4
Timor-Leste	..	..	..	..	..	..	..	..	..	..
Togo[a]	..	21	..	35	..	6	..	19	..	19
Trinidad and Tobago[a]	20	17	36	26	20	8	24	40	1	8
Tunisia[a]	7	6	37	35	13	8	36	41	7	11
Turkey[a]	..	8	..	26	..	24	..	41	..	4
Turkmenistan	..	..	..	..	..	..	..	..	..	..
Uganda[a]	..	28	..	13	..	8	..	51	..	0
Ukraine[a]	..	12	..	13	..	1	..	71	..	4
United Arab Emirates[a]	50	..	37	..	..	..	..	..	..	..
United Kingdom	14	18	15	14	9	5	57	51	8	13
United States	..	16	..	12	..	9	..	60	..	5
Uruguay[a]	13	15	17	24	6	11	64	50	0	..
Uzbekistan	..	..	..	..	..	..	..	..	..	..
Venezuela, RB[a]	6	6	22	16	27	12	61	64	2	3
Vietnam	..	..	..	..	..	..	..	..	..	..
West Bank and Gaza	..	..	..	..	..	..	..	..	..	..
Yemen, Rep.[a]	8	..	67	..	16	..	8	..	0	..
Zambia[a]	32	32	35	30	16	7	19	24	0	7
Zimbabwe[a]	16	..	34	..	31	..	19	..	..	..
World	.. m	**14 m**	.. m	**24 m**	.. m	**6 m**	.. m	**43 m**	.. m	**7 m**
Low income	..	..	..	..	..	..	..	..	..	..
Middle income	..	13	..	23	..	5	..	43	..	7
Lower middle income	..	16	..	34	..	5	..	36	..	9
Upper middle income	..	12	..	18	..	3	..	52	..	6
Low & middle income	..	15	..	26	..	6	..	36	..	..
East Asia & Pacific	..	..	..	..	..	..	..	..	..	..
Europe & Central Asia	..	13	..	18	..	2	..	59	..	6
Latin America & Carib.	..	14	..	25	..	10	..	36	..	10
Middle East & N. Africa	..	8	..	35	..	7	..	37	..	9
South Asia	..	17	..	14	27	22	24	29	..	10
Sub-Saharan Africa	..	..	..	..	..	..	..	..	..	..
High income	8	10	14	15	9	5	56	62	4	6
Euro area	5	6	14	14	12	6	55	67	5	5

Note: Components may not sum to 100 percent because of rounding or missing data.
a. Data were reported on a cash basis and have been adjusted to the accrual framework.

Central government expenses | 4.11

The term *expense* has replaced *expenditure* in the table since the 2005 edition of *World Development Indicators* in accordance with use in the International Monetary Fund's (IMF) *Government Finance Statistics Manual 2001*. Government expenses include all nonrepayable payments, whether current or capital, requited or unrequited. The concept of total central government expense as presented in the IMF's *Government Finance Statistics Yearbook* is comparable to the concept used in the 1993 United Nations System of National Accounts.

Expenses can be measured either by function (health, defense, education) or by economic type (interest payments, wages and salaries, purchases of goods and services). Functional data are often incomplete, and coverage varies by country because functional responsibilities stretch across levels of government for which no data are available. Defense expenses, usually the central government's responsibility, are shown in table 5.7. For more information on education expenses, see table 2.11; for more on health expenses, see table 2.16.

The classification of expenses by economic type in the table shows whether the government produces goods and services and distributes them, purchases the goods and services from a third party and distributes them, or transfers cash to households to make the purchases directly. When the government produces and provides goods and services, the cost is reflected in compensation of employees, use of goods and services, and consumption of fixed capital. Purchases from a third party and cash transfers to households are shown as subsidies and other

transfers, and other expenses. The economic classification can be problematic. For example, the distinction between current and capital expense may be arbitrary, and subsidies to public corporations or banks may be disguised as capital financing. Subsidies may also be hidden in special contractual pricing for goods and services. For further discussion of government finance statistics, see *About the data* for tables 4.10 and 4.12.

• **Goods and services** are all government payments in exchange for goods and services used for the production of market and nonmarket goods and services. Own-account capital formation is excluded. • **Compensation of employees** is all payments in cash, as well as in kind (such as food and housing), to employees in return for services rendered, and government contributions to social insurance schemes such as social security and pensions that provide benefits to employees. • **Interest payments** are payments made to nonresidents, to residents, and to other general government units for the use of borrowed money. (Repayment of principal is shown as a financing item, and commission charges are shown as purchases of services.) • **Subsidies and other transfers** include all unrequited, nonrepayable transfers on current account to private and public enterprises; grants to foreign governments, international organizations, and other government units; and social security, social assistance benefits, and employer social benefits in cash and in kind. • **Other expense** is spending on dividends, rent, and other miscellaneous expenses, including provision for consumption of fixed capital.

Central government interest payments as a share of total expense, 2008 (percent)

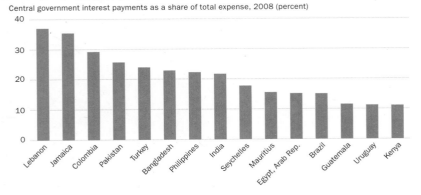

Interest payments accounted for more than 11 percent of total expenses in 2008 for 15 countries.

Source: International Monetary Fund, Government Finance Statistics data files.

Data on central government expenses are from the IMF's *Government Finance Statistics Yearbook 2008* and data files. Each country's accounts are reported using the system of common definitions and classifications in the IMF's *Government Finance Statistics Manual 2001*. See these sources for complete and authoritative explanations of concepts, definitions, and data sources.

	Taxes on income, profits, and capital gains		Taxes on goods and services		Taxes on international trade		Other taxes		Social contributions		Grants and other revenue	
	% of revenue		% of revenue		% of revenue		% of revenue		% of revenue		% of revenue	
	1995	2008	1995	2008	1995	2008	1995	2008	1995	2008	1995	2008
Afghanistan[a]	..	5	..	5	..	9	..	0	..	1	..	80
Albania[a]	8	..	39	..	14	..	1	..	15	..	23	..
Algeria[a]	..	58	..	34	..	3	..	1	..	..	..	4
Angola	..	..	..	..	..	..	..	..	..	..	..	..
Argentina	..	..	..	..	..	..	..	..	..	..	..	..
Armenia[a]	..	17	..	43	..	5	..	10	..	13	..	13
Australia	..	66	..	23	..	2	..	0	..	..	..	9
Austria	21	26	22	23	0	0	5	5	43	40	9	6
Azerbaijan[a]	..	33	..	23	..	4	..	1	..	..	..	39
Bangladesh[a]	..	19	..	28	..	27	..	4	..	..	..	23
Belarus[a]	16	7	33	30	6	21	11	7	31	29	3	6
Belgium	36	37	23	24	..	..	2	1	36	35	3	3
Benin[a]	..	18	..	38	..	20	..	10	..	2	..	13
Bolivia	..	10	..	43	..	3	..	9	..	7	..	28
Bosnia and Herzegovina	..	3	..	46	..	0	..	4	..	37	..	10
Botswana[a]	21	..	4	..	15	..	0	..	..	..	59	..
Brazil[a]	..	31	..	23	..	2	..	10	..	23	..	11
Bulgaria[a]	17	17	28	47	8	1	4	0	21	22	23	14
Burkina Faso	..	12	..	39	..	13	..	7	..	..	..	30
Burundi[a]	14	..	30	..	20	..	1	..	5	..	31	..
Cambodia	..	10	..	40	..	22	..	0	..	..	..	28
Cameroon[a]	17	..	25	..	28	..	3	..	2	..	25	..
Canada[a]	50	55	17	16	2	1	..	..	22	21	10	7
Central African Republic[a]	..	..	..	..	..	..	..	..	..	..	..	..
Chad	..	..	..	..	..	..	..	..	..	..	..	..
Chile	..	29	..	39	..	1	..	7	..	6	..	18
China[a]	9	25	61	57	8	5	0	1	..	..	22	12
Hong Kong SAR, China	..	..	..	..	..	..	..	..	..	..	..	..
Colombia	..	16	..	25	..	5	..	8	..	4	..	42
Congo, Dem. Rep.[a]	21	..	12	..	21	..	5	..	1	..	41	..
Congo, Rep.	..	5	..	6	..	3	..	1	..	1	..	84
Costa Rica[a]	..	17	..	37	..	5	..	3	..	31	..	7
Côte d'Ivoire[a]	..	23	..	15	..	35	..	3	..	7	..	18
Croatia[a]	11	9	42	45	9	1	1	1	33	33	4	11
Cuba	..	..	..	..	..	..	..	..	..	..	..	..
Czech Republic[a]	15	18	32	26	4	0	1	1	40	45	8	10
Denmark	34	44	40	40	..	..	7	2	5	3	14	10
Dominican Republic[a]	..	22	..	52	..	10	..	4	..	1	..	11
Ecuador[a]	50	..	26	..	11	..	1	..	..	..	12	..
Egypt, Arab Rep.[a]	17	27	13	20	10	6	10	3	10	..	41	45
El Salvador	..	24	..	41	..	4	..	1	..	10	..	21
Eritrea	..	..	..	..	..	..	..	..	..	..	..	..
Estonia	..	11	..	41	..	..	..	..	..	34	..	..
Ethiopia[a]	..	..	..	..	..	..	..	..	..	..	..	..
Finland	16	21	31	32	0	0	1	2	34	31	17	14
France	17	25	26	23	0	0	3	4	47	43	8	6
Gabon	..	..	..	..	..	..	..	..	..	..	..	..
Gambia, The[a]	14	..	32	..	42	..	0	..	0	..	7	..
Georgia[a]	7	33	48	47	10	1	..	2	13	17	22	18
Germany	16	18	20	23	..	..	0	..	58	55	6	4
Ghana[a]	15	19	31	34	24	18	..	..	..	..	9	30
Greece	18	19	32	29	0	0	3	3	31	36	16	14
Guatemala[a]	19	27	46	58	23	8	3	1	2	2	6	4
Guinea[a]	8	..	5	..	62	..	2	..	1	..	23	..
Guinea-Bissau	..	..	..	..	..	..	..	..	..	..	..	..
Haiti	..	..	..	..	..	..	..	..	..	..	..	..
Honduras	..	20	..	39	..	5	..	1	..	11	..	24

Central government revenues

	Taxes on income, profits, and capital gains		Taxes on goods and services		Taxes on international trade		Other taxes		Social contributions		Grants and other revenue	
	% of revenue		% of revenue		% of revenue		% of revenue		% of revenue		% of revenue	
	1995	2008	1995	2008	1995	2008	1995	2008	1995	2008	1995	2008
Hungary	16	25	28	31	10	0	1	2	35	34	9	9
India[a]	23	44	28	27	24	15	0	0	0	0	25	14
Indonesia[a]	46	..	33	..	4	..	1	..	6	..	9	..
Iran, Islamic Rep.[a]	12	16	6	2	9	6	1	1	7	14	66	62
Iraq	..	..	..	..	..	..	..	..	..	..	..	..
Ireland	37	*37*	..	*34*	0	*0*	2	6	17	*18*	9	*4*
Israel	..	29	..	30	..	1	..	5	..	17	..	18
Italy	32	35	21	20	..	..	6	5	35	36	6	4
Jamaica[a]	..	37	..	31	..	7	..	10	..	2	..	13
Japan	35	..	*14*	..	*1*	..	6	..	26	..	18	..
Jordan[a]	..	11	..	30	..	5	..	3	..	0	..	51
Kazakhstan[a]	*11*	28	*28*	21	3	13	5	0	*48*	..	6	38
Kenya	35	37	40	41	14	11	1	1	0	0	10	10
Korea, Dem. Rep.	..	..	..	..	..	..	..	..	..	..	..	..
Korea, Rep.[a]	32	*31*	32	25	7	3	10	8	8	*15*	12	*18*
Kosovo	..	..	..	..	..	..	..	..	..	..	..	..
Kuwait	1	1	0	..	2	1	0	0	..	..	97	98
Kyrgyz Republic[a]	26	11	56	53	5	11	1	..	..	..	11	25
Lao PDR	..	19	..	36	..	9	..	1	..	..	..	36
Latvia[a]	7	15	41	36	3	1	0	0	35	30	14	18
Lebanon	..	13	..	39	..	7	..	14	..	1	..	26
Lesotho[a]	15	17	12	12	49	57	1	3	..	..	24	11
Liberia	..	..	..	..	..	..	..	..	..	..	..	..
Libya	..	..	..	..	..	..	..	..	..	..	..	..
Lithuania	..	21	..	37	..	..	..	0	..	32	..	10
Macedonia, FYR	..	13	..	40	..	5	..	0	..	29	..	14
Madagascar	..	9	..	*18*	..	35	..	9	..	..	..	29
Malawi	..	..	..	..	..	..	..	..	..	..	..	..
Malaysia[a]	37	..	26	..	12	..	5	..	1	..	19	..
Mali	..	18	..	38	..	9	..	8	..	..	..	27
Mauritania	..	..	..	..	..	..	..	..	..	..	..	..
Mauritius[a]	12	18	25	46	34	11	6	8	6	4	17	13
Mexico[a]	27	..	54	..	4	..	2	..	14	..	16	..
Moldova[a]	6	1	38	50	5	5	*1*	0	38	29	2	14
Mongolia	31	38	18	26	9	8	0	1	15	11	27	17
Morocco[a]	..	31	..	32	..	6	..	5	..	10	..	16
Mozambique	..	..	..	..	..	..	..	..	..	..	42	42
Myanmar	20	25	26	*31*	12	2	..	..	..	..	42	42
Namibia[a]	27	28	32	19	28	44	2	2	..	0	11	7
Nepal[a]	10	14	33	35	26	18	4	5	..	..	27	29
Netherlands	26	27	24	28	..	1	2	3	40	34	8	8
New Zealand	..	57	..	26	..	3	..	0	..	0	..	15
Nicaragua[a]	9	26	52	50	7	4	0	0	11	19	31	20
Niger	..	12	..	18	..	26	..	3	..	..	..	41
Nigeria	..	..	..	..	..	..	..	..	..	..	..	..
Norway	..	33	..	21	..	0	..	1	..	17	..	28
Oman[a]	21	..	1	..	3	..	2	..	..	..	74	..
Pakistan[a]	18	27	27	33	24	11	7	1	..	..	24	28
Panama[a]	20	..	*17*	..	*11*	..	3	..	16	..	34	..
Papua New Guinea[a]	40	..	8	..	27	..	2	..	1	..	23	..
Paraguay[a]	..	10	..	39	..	7	..	1	..	17	..	26
Peru[a]	15	33	46	37	10	3	8	6	11	8	11	13
Philippines[a]	33	41	26	26	29	22	4	6	..	..	8	11
Poland	..	16	..	39	..	0	..	1	..	35	..	9
Portugal	22	23	32	32	0	0	2	2	30	33	14	..
Puerto Rico	..	..	..	..	..	..	..	..	..	..	..	..
Qatar	..	45	..	..	..	3	..	..	..	..	..	53

	Taxes on income, profits, and capital gains		Taxes on goods and services		Taxes on international trade		Other taxes		Social contributions		Grants and other revenue	
	% of revenue		% of revenue		% of revenue		% of revenue		% of revenue		% of revenue	
	1995	2008	1995	2008	1995	2008	1995	2008	1995	2008	1995	2008
Romania	..	22	..	35	..	0	..	0	..	33	..	10
Russian Federation	..	5	..	16	..	25	..	0	..	16	..	38
Rwanda[a]	11	..	25	..	23	..	3	..	2	..	36	..
Saudi Arabia	..	..	..	..	..	..	..	..	..	..	..	..
Senegal[a]	17	..	19	..	36	..	2	..	..	..	26	..
Serbia[a]	..	10	..	42	..	6	..	0	..	35	..	7
Sierra Leone[a]	15	..	34	..	39	..	0	..	..	..	12	..
Singapore[a]	26	34	20	22	1	0	15	11	..	..	38	33
Slovak Republic	..	13	..	33	..	0	..	0	..	41	..	14
Slovenia[a]	13	17	33	32	9	0	0	2	42	38	3	11
Somalia	..	..	..	..	..	..	..	..	..	..	..	..
South Africa	..	54	..	30	..	3	..	3	..	2	..	8
Spain	28	28	21	15	0	..	0	0	40	52	..	5
Sri Lanka[a]	12	18	50	48	17	14	4	5	1	2	18	13
Sudan[a]	17	..	41	..	27	..	1	..	..	..	14	..
Swaziland[a]	..	..	..	..	..	..	..	..	..	..	..	..
Sweden	12	..	31	..	1	..	7	..	37	..	13	..
Switzerland[a]	11	19	21	32	1	1	2	2	49	36	17	10
Syrian Arab Republic[a]	23	..	37	..	13	..	8	..	0	..	19	..
Tajikistan[a]	6	..	63	..	12	..	0	..	14	..	5	..
Tanzania	..	..	..	..	..	..	..	..	..	..	..	..
Thailand	..	39	..	37	..	5	..	1	..	5	..	14
Timor-Leste	..	..	..	..	..	..	..	..	..	..	..	..
Togo[a]	..	17	..	43	..	21	..	3	..	..	..	16
Trinidad and Tobago[a]	50	57	26	15	6	5	1	9	2	4	15	11
Tunisia[a]	16	28	20	31	28	6	4	4	15	17	17	13
Turkey[a]	..	26	..	49	..	1	..	6	..	..	..	18
Turkmenistan	..	..	..	..	..	..	..	..	..	..	..	..
Uganda[a]	10	22	45	49	7	9	2	0	..	..	37	19
Ukraine[a]	..	14	..	31	..	4	..	0	..	36	..	16
United Arab Emirates[a]	..	..	15	..	..	..	..	..	1	..	84	..
United Kingdom	37	37	32	27	..	..	6	10	20	21	6	5
United States	..	53	..	3	..	1	..	1	..	39	..	4
Uruguay[a]	10	20	32	48	4	4	10	−3	31	22	8	9
Uzbekistan	..	..	..	..	..	..	..	..	..	..	..	..
Venezuela, RB[a]	38	22	33	25	9	5	0	4	4	2	20	43
Vietnam	..	..	..	..	..	..	..	..	..	..	..	..
West Bank and Gaza	..	..	..	..	..	..	..	..	..	..	..	..
Yemen, Rep.[a]	17	..	10	..	18	..	3	..	..	..	51	..
Zambia[a]	27	33	22	36	36	8	0	0	0	..	15	23
Zimbabwe[a]	36	..	23	..	17	..	3	..	3	..	19	..
World	.. m	21 m	.. m	33 m	.. m	5 m	.. m	2 m	.. m	.. m	.. m	14 m
Low income	..	..	..	..	..	..	..	..	..	..	..	..
Middle income	..	22	..	36	..	5	..	1	..	13	..	14
Lower middle income	..	26	..	32	..	6	..	1	..	..	..	17
Upper middle income	..	18	..	37	..	4	..	3	..	22	..	13
Low & middle income	..	18	..	36	..	7	..	2	..	..	..	16
East Asia & Pacific	33	..	26	..	12	..	2	..	..	..	22	..
Europe & Central Asia	..	16	..	40	..	4	..	0	..	30	..	14
Latin America & Carib.	..	25	..	39	..	4	..	2	..	10	..	16
Middle East & N. Africa	..	27	..	31	..	6	..	3	..	..	..	26
South Asia	15	19	31	28	24	15	4	1	..	0	25	28
Sub-Saharan Africa	..	..	..	..	..	..	..	..	..	..	..	..
High income	21	29	25	27	..	1	2	2	35	34	10	10
Euro area	22	26	24	24	0	0	2	2	36	38	8	6

Note: Components may not sum to 100 percent because of missing data or adjustment to tax revenue.
a. Data were reported on a cash basis and have been adjusted to the accrual framework.

The International Monetary Fund (IMF) classifies government revenues as taxes, grants, and property income. Taxes are classified by the base on which the tax is levied, grants by the source, and property income by type (for example, interest, dividends, or rent). The most important source of revenue is taxes. Grants are unrequited, nonrepayable, noncompulsory receipts from other government units and foreign governments or from international organizations. Transactions are generally recorded on an accrual basis.

The IMF's *Government Finance Statistics Manual 2001* describes taxes as compulsory, unrequited payments made to governments by individuals, businesses, or institutions. Taxes are classified in six major groups by the base on which the tax is levied: income, profits, and capital gains; payroll and workforce; property; goods and services; international trade and transactions; and other. However, the distinctions are not always clear. Taxes levied on the income and profits of individuals and corporations are classified as direct taxes, and taxes and duties levied on goods and services are classified as indirect taxes. This distinction may be a useful simplification, but it has no particular analytical significance except with respect to the capacity to fix tax rates.

Direct taxes tend to be progressive, whereas indirect taxes are proportional.

Social security taxes do not reflect compulsory payments made by employers to provident funds or other agencies with a like purpose. Similarly, expenditures from such funds are not reflected in government expenses (see table 4.11). For further discussion of taxes and tax policies, see *About the data* for table 5.6. For further discussion of government revenues and expenditures, see *About the data* for tables 4.10 and 4.11.

• **Taxes on income, profits, and capital gains** are levied on the actual or presumptive net income of individuals, on the profits of corporations and enterprises, and on capital gains, whether realized or not, on land, securities, and other assets. Intragovernmental payments are eliminated in consolidation. • **Taxes on goods and services** include general sales and turnover or value added taxes, selective excises on goods, selective taxes on services, taxes on the use of goods or property, taxes on extraction and production of minerals, and profits of fiscal monopolies. • **Taxes on international trade** include import duties, export duties, profits of export or import monopolies, exchange profits, and exchange taxes. • **Other taxes** include employer payroll or labor taxes, taxes on property, and taxes not allocable to other categories, such as penalties for late payment or nonpayment of taxes. • **Social contributions** include social security contributions by employees, employers, and self-employed individuals, and other contributions whose source cannot be determined. They also include actual or imputed contributions to social insurance schemes operated by governments. • **Grants and other revenue** include grants from other foreign governments, international organizations, and other government units; interest; dividends; rent; requited, nonrepayable receipts for public purposes (such as fines, administrative fees, and entrepreneurial income from government ownership of property); and voluntary, unrequited, nonrepayable receipts other than grants.

Taxes on income and capital gains as a share of central government revenue, 2008 (percent)

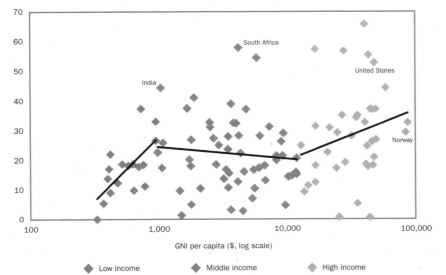

GNI per capita ($, log scale)

◆ Low income ◆ Middle income ◆ High income

High-income economies tend to tax income and property, whereas low-income economies tend to rely on indirect taxes on international trade and goods and services. But there are exceptions in all groups.

Note: Data are for the most recent year for 2005–08.
Source: International Monetary Fund, Government Finance Statistics data files, and World Development Indicators data files.

4.13 Monetary indicators

	Money and quasi money		Claims on private sector		Claims on governments and other public entities		Interest rate					
	annual % growth		Annual growth % of M2		Annual growth % of M2		Deposit		% Lending		Real	
	1995	2008	1995	2008	1995	2008	1995	2008	1995	2008	1995	2008
Afghanistan	..	27.8	..	12.8	..	1.2	..	..	..	14.9	..	9.6
Albania	51.8	7.7	1.8	12.3	−8.3	2.1	15.3	6.8	19.7	13.0	13.3	10.3
Algeria	9.6	15.7	1.0	3.6	−10.0	−26.9	16.6	1.8	18.4	8.0	−7.9	−2.5
Angola	4,105.6	66.2	471.4	36.9	119.5	18.0	125.9	6.2	206.3	12.5	−84.7	−9.2
Argentina	−2.8	8.1	−1.1	9.1	7.8	−1.2	11.9	11.0	17.9	19.5	14.2	0.3
Armenia	64.3	2.4	70.3	29.9	7.2	2.2	63.2	6.6	111.9	17.1	−18.9	8.0
Australia	8.5	14.2	12.5	15.0	0.4	3.3	6.1	5.2	10.7	8.9	9.1	4.3
Austriaa	..	..	..	..	..	..	2.2	..	6.4	..	6.1	..
Azerbaijan	25.4	44.3	6.1	37.2	−32.7	−15.2	..	12.2	..	19.8	..	−1.0
Bangladesh	12.1	16.3	25.0	13.5	4.8	3.4	6.0	9.7	14.0	16.4	6.2	7.0
Belarus	158.4	28.3	61.4	55.8	44.7	−12.5	100.8	8.5	175.0	8.6	−63.9	−9.9
Belgiuma	..	..	..	..	..	..	4.0	..	8.4	8.6	7.1	6.8
Benin	−1.8	26.6	2.2	12.0	6.0	12.2	3.5	3.5	16.8	..	13.0	..
Bolivia	7.7	22.7	13.7	4.5	1.1	−2.1	18.9	4.7	51.0	13.9	35.5	3.2
Bosnia and Herzegovina	22.0	−0.1	23.9	17.3	−0.4	0.6	51.9	3.5	73.5	7.0	76.3	−0.7
Botswana	12.3	21.1	−1.7	12.6	10.0	−5.9	9.8	8.7	14.4	16.5	5.2	−0.4
Brazil	44.3	17.3	40.5	20.6	14.6	7.6	52.2	11.7	78.2	47.3	65.5	39.1
Bulgaria	40.5	8.8	22.1	27.5	−7.2	−2.0	35.9	4.4	79.4	10.9	10.1	−0.5
Burkina Faso	22.3	12.3	2.9	15.3	−7.3	4.1	3.5	3.5	16.8	..	16.5	..
Burundi	−8.0	42.4	−7.1	11.3	0.2	4.0	..	..	15.3	16.5	−0.7	−6.4
Cambodia	43.6	5.4	12.5	30.7	1.2	−10.5	8.7	1.9	18.7	16.4	6.4	11.2
Cameroon	−6.2	13.7	0.3	9.3	−2.2	−9.1	5.5	3.8	16.0	15.0	6.0	12.7
Canada	4.8	15.1	3.8	6.1	0.2	5.0	5.3	1.5	8.7	4.7	6.2	0.5
Central African Republic	4.3	16.5	3.9	6.0	−7.9	10.2	5.5	3.8	16.0	15.0	5.2	12.2
Chad	48.8	13.6	6.4	10.1	−18.6	−46.5	5.5	3.8	16.0	15.0	6.6	9.4
Chile	24.3	15.6	34.9	24.6	−2.0	−3.6	13.7	7.5	18.2	13.3	7.0	13.0
China	29.5	17.8	22.5	9.9	0.8	0.3	11.0	2.3	12.1	5.3	−1.5	−1.8
Hong Kong SAR, China	10.6	4.2	9.8	2.8	−2.4	−1.5	5.6	0.4	8.8	5.0	4.4	3.5
Colombia	28.2	8.5	34.3	23.1	2.9	2.5	32.3	9.7	42.7	17.2	20.1	8.2
Congo, Dem. Rep.	357.6	55.7	59.6	42.7	−7.9	5.3	60.0	..	293.9	..	−30.5	..
Congo, Rep.	−0.1	37.1	6.3	10.6	2.0	−83.4	5.5	3.8	16.0	15.0	12.2	24.9
Costa Rica	4.7	11.2	−1.4	51.7	5.6	0.4	23.9	4.2	36.7	15.8	11.9	3.3
Côte d'Ivoire	18.1	5.7	13.3	6.1	0.3	−1.1	3.5	3.5	16.8	..	16.8	..
Croatia	40.4	4.4	30.5	11.0	−2.4	2.9	5.5	2.8	20.2	10.1	−2.9	3.5
Cuba	..	..	..	..	..	..	..	..	..	..	..	..
Czech Republic	29.3	8.6	15.8	9.7	2.1	0.4	7.0	1.6	12.8	6.3	−3.6	4.3
Denmark	6.2	7.8	2.6	30.7	−1.5	−14.0	3.9	..	10.3	..	9.0	..
Dominican Republic	16.6	1.3	14.4	10.5	−1.7	12.3	14.9	10.3	30.7	20.0	19.4	9.2
Ecuador	6.8	23.6	15.1	21.6	−74.8	−12.8	43.3	4.9	55.7	12.1	45.7	4.8
Egypt, Arab Rep.	9.9	10.5	12.1	6.2	0.6	4.6	10.9	6.6	16.5	12.3	4.6	0.4
El Salvador	13.5	−0.4	22.6	4.5	−0.9	0.7	14.4	..	19.1	..	7.8	..
Eritrea	21.0	15.9	27.8	1.9	20.5	14.0	..	..	..	..	..	..
Estonia	27.5	6.0	28.9	12.5	−9.3	1.8	8.7	5.7	19.0	8.6	−11.4	1.8
Ethiopia	9.0	23.4	13.4	17.7	−3.5	2.5	11.5	3.6	15.1	8.0	2.1	−15.9
Finlanda	..	..	..	..	..	..	3.2	..	7.8	..	2.9	..
Francea	..	..	..	..	..	..	4.5	3.7	8.1	..	6.7	..
Gabon	10.1	9.1	11.9	−10.6	5.8	30.3	5.5	3.8	16.0	15.0	14.5	9.3
Gambia, The	14.2	18.4	−5.0	6.8	15.2	21.4	12.5	12.9	25.0	27.0	20.3	21.0
Georgia	40.2	6.9	−11.1	37.9	73.8	−13.6	31.0	10.4	58.2	21.2	10.6	10.2
Germanya	..	..	..	..	..	..	3.9	..	10.9	..	8.9	..
Ghana	43.2	42.8	10.2	20.1	28.1	10.9	28.7	8.9	..	..	..	..
Greecea	..	..	..	..	..	..	15.8	2.2	23.1	..	12.1	..
Guatemala	15.6	8.9	36.1	6.2	−7.1	0.1	7.9	5.1	21.2	13.4	11.5	4.5
Guinea	11.3	33.4	12.1	19.8	8.4	18.1	17.5	14.4	21.5	..	14.7	..
Guinea-Bissau	43.0	29.5	−6.7	11.8	−20.4	−1.6	3.5	3.5	32.9	..	−8.2	..
Haiti	27.1	11.1	15.7	2.7	0.1	−3.6	32.5	2.1	15.1	17.8	−0.8	−2.8
Honduras	28.9	5.4	18.0	10.8	−7.5	2.9	12.0	9.5	27.0	17.9	1.7	7.4

Monetary indicators

	Money and quasi money		Claims on private sector		Claims on governments and other public entities		Interest rate					
	annual % growth		Annual growth % of M2		Annual growth % of M2		%					
							Deposit		Lending		Real	
	1995	2008	1995	2008	1995	2008	1995	2008	1995	2008	1995	2008
Hungary	20.9	9.4	4.9	21.0	20.2	−2.3	24.4	9.9	32.6	10.2	4.6	6.1
India	11.0	20.5	6.0	14.1	3.4	7.9	..	..	15.5	13.3	5.9	6.7
Indonesia	27.5	15.0	25.9	18.7	−2.3	−7.0	16.7	8.5	18.9	13.6	8.3	−4.0
Iran, Islamic Rep.	30.1	7.9	9.8	8.4	17.3	−4.7	..	11.6	..	12.0	..	−7.0
Iraq	..	35.2	..	5.3	..	−54.7	..	11.4	..	19.7	..	..
Ireland[a]	..	..	..	..	..	..	0.4	0.0	6.6	2.7	3.4	0.1
Israel	21.7	−3.4	18.3	6.9	−0.5	3.6	14.1	3.3	20.2	6.1	−0.3	4.4
Italy[a]	..	..	..	..	..	..	6.4	..	13.2	6.8	7.9	3.8
Jamaica	28.0	5.7	18.0	14.2	6.1	11.3	23.2	7.6	43.6	16.8	17.5	−3.6
Japan	4.1	0.8	1.3	0.5	2.5	2.7	0.9	0.6	3.5	1.9	4.0	3.0
Jordan	5.7	21.1	9.6	9.5	−3.8	12.0	7.7	5.5	10.7	9.0	8.6	−5.8
Kazakhstan	108.2	35.4	−72.5	8.6	24.7	−9.6	..	..	..	..	..	..
Kenya	29.0	15.6	26.7	17.3	6.6	3.3	13.6	5.3	28.8	14.0	15.8	0.8
Korea, Dem. Rep.	..	..	..	..	..	..	..	..	..	..	..	..
Korea, Rep.	15.6	15.9	21.6	24.5	−1.2	2.5	8.8	5.9	9.0	7.2	1.5	4.3
Kosovo	..	23.6	..	25.8	..	−1.6	..	..	..	13.8	..	..
Kuwait	9.4	15.6	10.9	20.3	−2.0	−0.8	6.5	4.8	8.4	7.6	3.4	2.5
Kyrgyz Republic	14.8	33.2	0.1	29.2	62.6	−8.8	36.7	4.0	65.0	19.9	21.9	−1.1
Lao PDR	16.4	18.3	18.1	19.4	−9.7	−3.4	14.0	5.0	25.7	24.0	5.0	14.6
Latvia	−21.4	−4.0	−23.8	24.2	6.5	−4.7	14.8	6.3	34.6	11.9	5.5	−2.9
Lebanon	16.4	14.8	13.1	6.4	5.1	2.1	16.3	7.7	24.7	10.0	12.8	2.1
Lesotho	9.8	19.7	−2.3	6.8	−18.7	−15.9	13.3	7.6	16.4	16.2	6.0	6.0
Liberia	29.5	42.6	−6.0	17.5	37.2	21.6	6.4	3.8	15.6	14.4	8.5	3.6
Libya	9.6	49.2	3.1	9.5	3.6	−37.4	5.5	2.5	7.0	6.0	..	−15.5
Lithuania	28.9	−0.7	12.7	24.3	−2.4	3.9	20.1	7.7	27.1	8.4	−14.5	−1.7
Macedonia, FYR	1.8	10.9	−138.9	24.7	−229.7	2.2	24.1	5.9	46.0	9.7	24.6	2.4
Madagascar	16.2	12.8	9.4	12.8	−10.3	−8.5	18.5	11.5	37.5	45.0	−5.3	32.5
Malawi	56.2	62.6	2.8	39.8	−10.4	74.3	37.3	6.0	47.3	25.3	−16.9	15.0
Malaysia	18.5	11.3	29.2	8.8	−0.7	4.1	5.9	3.1	8.7	6.1	4.9	−3.8
Mali	7.3	−1.5	18.9	5.1	−11.6	−2.5	3.5	3.5	16.8	..	14.5	..
Mauritania	−5.1	..	−42.5	..	−28.9	..	9.0	8.0	20.3	23.5	17.0	26.7
Mauritius	18.6	14.7	8.7	20.8	3.0	0.6	12.2	10.1	20.8	21.5	14.6	12.9
Mexico	31.9	9.9	−2.9	1.3	27.6	2.1	39.8	3.0	59.4	8.7	15.6	2.1
Moldova	65.3	15.9	34.6	11.9	19.1	−2.5	25.4	17.9	36.7	21.1	7.7	10.3
Mongolia	32.6	−6.7	14.4	24.4	−31.8	5.8	74.6	11.2	134.4	20.6	46.9	−1.5
Morocco	7.0	10.8	6.9	16.0	5.1	−0.1	7.3	3.9	11.3	..	3.1	..
Mozambique	47.7	23.9	21.8	24.5	−12.5	−1.8	38.8	11.0	24.4	18.3	18.0	9.8
Myanmar	36.5	14.8	13.4	2.6	19.7	13.2	9.8	12.0	16.5	17.0	−2.6	..
Namibia	22.6	17.9	30.5	9.2	1.7	−10.0	10.8	8.4	18.5	13.7	12.1	0.0
Nepal	15.4	23.3	18.1	15.9	3.3	0.5	9.6	2.3	12.9	8.0	4.7	0.3
Netherlands[a]	..	..	..	..	..	..	4.4	4.4	7.2	4.6	5.0	1.7
New Zealand	9.4	10.3	16.2	14.0	−4.1	4.5	8.5	7.6	11.3	12.2	9.1	7.9
Nicaragua	35.1	7.3	30.3	11.9	−21.5	4.4	11.1	6.6	19.9	13.2	5.7	−3.1
Niger	3.8	11.9	−22.8	19.9	10.2	−18.3	3.5	3.5	16.8	..	15.5	..
Nigeria	19.4	52.5	22.3	51.9	−9.1	−23.5	13.5	12.0	20.2	15.5	−22.9	4.1
Norway	3.8	..	9.5	..	−1.9	..	5.0	5.5	7.6	7.3	4.4	−1.8
Oman	7.7	23.3	9.3	40.5	−2.3	−20.4	6.5	4.5	9.4	7.1	7.5	2.1
Pakistan	13.8	19.5	10.8	10.0	8.7	7.1	..	6.9	..	12.9	..	−2.9
Panama	8.4	14.6	14.5	16.4	−4.3	−3.1	7.2	3.5	11.1	8.2	10.6	−0.3
Papua New Guinea	13.7	11.2	0.2	17.4	5.0	−2.8	7.3	1.3	13.1	9.3	−2.3	−2.1
Paraguay	0.5	12.2	4.9	29.4	0.1	−8.8	21.2	3.1	33.9	25.8	17.9	17.4
Peru	29.3	23.2	31.1	22.0	−8.1	−7.2	9.6	3.5	36.2	23.7	20.5	20.9
Philippines	23.9	5.4	27.9	2.1	3.0	0.1	8.4	4.5	14.7	8.8	6.6	1.1
Poland	35.6	19.1	19.1	29.9	3.1	9.0	26.8	2.2	33.5	5.5	−5.2	3.9
Portugal[a]	..	..	..	..	..	..	8.4	..	13.8	..	10.0	..
Puerto Rico	..	..	..	..	..	..	..	..	..	..	..	..
Qatar	1.1	19.7	3.9	32.9	−3.8	−1.3	6.2	3.0	8.9	6.8	..	−10.0

4.13 Monetary indicators

	Money and quasi money		Claims on private sector		Claims on governments and other public entities		Interest rate					
	annual % growth		Annual growth % of M2		Annual growth % of M2		Deposit		Lending		Real	
	1995	2008	1995	2008	1995	2008	1995	2008	1995	2008	1995	2008
Romania	69.6	17.5	23.1	33.2	11.6	7.9	44.7	9.5	50.7	15.0	11.4	3.1
Russian Federation	112.6	14.6	46.2	31.2	73.6	−17.2	102.0	5.8	320.3	12.2	72.3	−5.8
Rwanda	69.5	18.0	32.7	14.5	−41.0	−13.8	11.1	6.8	18.5	16.5	6.9	−0.8
Saudi Arabia	3.4	18.0	3.4	19.7	1.4	−59.6	6.2	2.9	..	..	..	..
Senegal	7.4	1.8	1.2	10.6	1.0	−3.3	3.5	3.5	16.8	..	17.8	..
Serbia	33.0	9.8	88.5	29.8	34.1	6.8	19.1	7.3	78.0	18.1	23.0	0.5
Sierra Leone	19.6	22.5	1.6	13.9	−101.6	19.9	7.0	9.7	28.8	24.5	−3.6	12.0
Singapore	8.5	12.0	19.7	11.9	−8.1	−4.9	3.5	0.4	6.4	5.4	4.0	4.2
Slovak Republic[a]	..	..	..	..	..	..	9.0	3.7	16.9	8.0	7.1	6.8
Slovenia[a]	..	..	..	..	..	..	15.4	4.1	23.4	6.7	−4.0	2.5
Somalia	..	..	..	..	..	..	..	..	..	..	..	..
South Africa	16.0	15.2	18.9	12.1	−4.1	0.4	13.5	11.6	17.9	15.1	6.9	3.9
Spain[a]	..	..	..	..	..	..	7.7	..	10.1	..	4.9	..
Sri Lanka	35.8	8.4	75.4	6.2	5.4	13.3	12.1	10.9	18.0	18.9	8.0	2.2
Sudan	72.7	16.3	10.6	4.8	389.1	0.7	..	..	..	..	..	..
Swaziland	3.9	15.4	1.3	6.5	−14.8	−26.2	9.4	8.2	17.1	14.8	−1.5	4.3
Sweden	..	10.1	..	17.2	..	−2.8	6.2	0.8	11.1	3.3	7.2	2.4
Switzerland	4.6	3.0	4.0	−1.2	0.2	2.7	1.3	0.2	5.5	3.3	4.7	1.1
Syrian Arab Republic	9.2	25.2	3.9	7.3	6.1	−2.9	4.0	8.3	9.0	10.2	2.2	−3.2
Tajikistan	..	−3.6	..	145.1	..	−9.8	23.9	8.4	75.5	23.7	6.2	−3.1
Tanzania	33.0	19.8	−3.9	13.9	16.3	−0.2	24.6	8.0	42.8	15.0	12.6	5.6
Thailand	17.7	8.7	40.3	8.0	−4.2	0.9	11.6	2.5	13.3	7.0	7.3	3.1
Timor-Leste	..	34.1	..	1.4	..	−7.6	..	0.8	..	13.1	..	2.2
Togo	22.3	18.2	17.6	−2.6	14.9	15.7	3.5	3.5	17.5	..	13.8	..
Trinidad and Tobago	4.0	17.1	9.0	7.9	0.6	−17.4	6.9	7.4	15.2	12.4	10.7	5.1
Tunisia	6.6	14.8	10.4	14.7	−1.2	−0.3	..	..	..	..	..	..
Turkey	104.2	24.9	66.9	16.5	30.1	5.8	76.0	22.9	..	..	..	..
Turkmenistan	449.5	..	76.3	..	−573.1	..	..	..	..	..	..	..
Uganda	13.9	30.8	9.6	28.2	−41.2	12.0	7.6	9.3	20.2	20.5	9.9	13.3
Ukraine	115.5	31.0	7.7	71.9	95.4	7.0	70.3	9.9	122.7	17.5	−56.8	−9.0
United Arab Emirates	10.2	19.2	10.7	43.6	−4.3	−1.3	..	..	..	..	..	..
United Kingdom	..	..	..	..	..	..	4.1	..	6.7	4.6	3.9	2.2
United States	6.9	8.0	6.0	1.7	0.2	−3.1	..	..	8.8	5.1	6.7	2.9
Uruguay	36.9	31.2	35.2	22.4	1.0	16.4	57.7	3.2	93.1	12.5	36.9	3.4
Uzbekistan	..	..	..	..	..	..	..	..	..	..	..	..
Venezuela, RB	36.6	26.1	15.3	18.6	32.8	−1.9	24.7	16.2	39.7	22.4	−7.9	−6.8
Vietnam	25.8	20.7	18.9	21.7	0.7	2.6	8.5	12.7	20.1	15.8	10.5	−4.9
West Bank and Gaza	..	5.6	..	2.9	..	2.4	..	3.0	..	7.7	..	2.3
Yemen, Rep.	50.7	13.2	6.0	4.1	13.3	1.6	23.8	13.0	31.5	18.0	−3.2	−0.5
Zambia	55.5	23.2	34.2	26.5	185.8	2.0	30.2	6.6	45.5	19.1	5.4	7.5
Zimbabwe	25.5	60,376.3	25.5	67,582.1	−0.3	11,566.1	25.9	121.5	34.7	579.0	23.0	−0.7

a. As members of the European Monetary Union, these countries share a single currency, the euro.

About the data

Money and the financial accounts that record the supply of money lie at the heart of a country's financial system. There are several commonly used definitions of the money supply. The narrowest, M1, encompasses currency held by the public and demand deposits with banks. M2 includes M1 plus time and savings deposits with banks that require prior notice for withdrawal. M3 includes M2 as well as various money market instruments, such as certificates of deposit issued by banks, bank deposits denominated in foreign currency, and deposits with financial institutions other than banks. However defined, money is a liability of the banking system, distinguished from other bank liabilities by the special role it plays as a medium of exchange, a unit of account, and a store of value.

The banking system's assets include its net foreign assets and net domestic credit. Net domestic credit includes credit extended to the private sector and general government and credit extended to the nonfinancial public sector in the form of investments in short- and long-term government securities and loans to state enterprises; liabilities to the public and private sectors in the form of deposits with the banking system are netted out. Net domestic credit also includes credit to banking and nonbank financial institutions.

Domestic credit is the main vehicle through which changes in the money supply are regulated, with central bank lending to the government often playing the most important role. The central bank can regulate lending to the private sector in several ways—for example, by adjusting the cost of the refinancing facilities it provides to banks, by changing market interest rates through open market operations, or by controlling the availability of credit through changes in the reserve requirements imposed on banks and ceilings on the credit provided by banks to the private sector.

Monetary accounts are derived from the balance sheets of financial institutions—the central bank, commercial banks, and nonbank financial intermediaries. Although these balance sheets are usually reliable, they are subject to errors of classification, valuation, and timing and to differences in accounting practices. For example, whether interest income is recorded on an accrual or a cash basis can make a substantial difference, as can the treatment of non-performing assets. Valuation errors typically arise for foreign exchange transactions, particularly in countries with flexible exchange rates or in countries that have undergone currency devaluation during the reporting period. The valuation of financial derivatives and the net liabilities of the banking system can also be difficult. The quality of commercial bank reporting also may be adversely affected by delays in reports from bank branches, especially in countries where branch accounts are not computerized. Thus the data in the balance sheets of commercial banks may be based on preliminary estimates subject to constant revision. This problem is likely to be even more serious for nonbank financial intermediaries.

Many interest rates coexist in an economy, reflecting competitive conditions, the terms governing loans and deposits, and differences in the position and status of creditors and debtors. In some economies interest rates are set by regulation or administrative fiat. In economies with imperfect markets, or where reported nominal rates are not indicative of effective rates, it may be difficult to obtain data on interest rates that reflect actual market transactions. Deposit and lending rates are collected by the International Monetary Fund (IMF) as representative interest rates offered by banks to resident customers. The terms and conditions attached to these rates differ by country, however, limiting their comparability. Real interest rates are calculated by adjusting nominal rates by an estimate of the inflation rate in the economy. A negative real interest rate indicates a loss in the purchasing power of the principal. The real interest rates in the table are calculated as $(i - P) / (1 + P)$, where i is the nominal lending interest rate and P is the inflation rate (as measured by the GDP deflator).

Definitions

- **Money and quasi money** are the sum of currency outside banks, demand deposits other than those of the central government, and the time, savings, and foreign currency deposits of resident sectors other than the central government. This definition of the money supply, often called M2, corresponds to lines 34 and 35 in the IMF's *International Financial Statistics* (IFS). The change in money supply is measured as the difference in end-of-year totals relative to M2 in the preceding year. • **Claims on private sector** (IFS line 32 d) include gross credit from the financial system to individuals, enterprises, nonfinancial public entities not included under net domestic credit, and financial institutions not included elsewhere. • **Claims on governments and other public entities** (IFS line 32 an + 32 b + 32 bx + 32 c) usually comprise direct credit for specific purposes, such as financing the government budget deficit; loans to state enterprises; advances against future credit authorizations; and purchases of treasury bills and bonds, net of deposits by the public sector. Public sector deposits with the banking system also include sinking funds for the service of debt and temporary deposits of government revenues. • **Deposit interest rate** is the rate paid by commercial or similar banks for demand, time, or savings deposits. • **Lending interest rate** is the rate charged by banks on loans to prime customers. • **Real interest rate** is the lending interest rate adjusted for inflation as measured by the GDP deflator.

Data sources

Data on monetary and financial statistics are published by the IMF in its monthly *International Financial Statistics* and annual *International Financial Statistics Yearbook*. The IMF collects data on the financial systems of its member countries. The World Bank receives data from the IMF in electronic files that may contain more recent revisions than the published sources. The discussion of monetary indicators draws from an IMF publication by Marcello Caiola, *A Manual for Country Economists* (1995). Also see the IMF's *Monetary and Financial Statistics Manual* (2000) for guidelines for the presentation of monetary and financial statistics. Data on real interest rates are derived from World Bank data on the GDP deflator.

4.14 Exchange rates and prices

	Official exchange rate		Purchasing power parity (PPP) conversion factor		Ratio of PPP conversion factor to market exchange rate	Real effective exchange rate	GDP implicit deflator		Consumer price index		Wholesale price index	
	local currency units to $		local currency units to international $			Index 2000 = 100	average annual % growth		average annual % growth		average annual % growth	
	2008	2009[a]	1995	2008	2008	2008	1990–2000	2000–08	1990–2000	2000–08	1990–2000	2000–08
Afghanistan	50.25	49.04	..	17.0	0.3	..	..	6.9	..	12.9	..	..
Albania	83.89	93.98	26.0	46.4	0.5	..	37.7	3.5	27.8	2.9	..	4.8
Algeria	64.58	72.93	15.4	39.0	0.6	101.9	18.5	9.2	17.3	2.8	..	3.5
Angola	75.03	88.75	0.0	60.8	0.8	..	739.4	48.4	711.0	47.0	..	..
Argentina	3.14	3.79	1.0	1.8	0.6	..	5.2	12.8[b]	8.9	10.4[b]	0.1	16.9
Armenia	305.97	380.47	116.6	195.2	0.6	140.4	212.5	4.6	70.5	3.8	..	1.0
Australia	1.19	1.11	1.3	1.5	1.3	105.6	1.5	3.8	2.1	3.0	1.1	3.9
Austria[c]	0.68	0.68	0.9	0.9	1.3	101.8	1.6	1.8	2.2	2.0	0.3	2.8
Azerbaijan	0.82	0.80	0.2	0.5	0.6	..	203.0	10.9	170.9	10.0	..	..
Bangladesh	68.60	69.16	19.2	25.6	0.4	..	4.1	4.9	5.5	6.7	..	..
Belarus	2,136.40	2,838.98	3.5	1,084.7	0.5	..	355.1	25.5	271.3	20.2	267.8	24.3
Belgium[c]	0.68	0.68	0.9	0.9	1.3	104.9	1.8	2.1	1.9	2.2	1.2	2.8
Benin	447.81	449.31	187.5	234.6	0.5	..	8.7	3.4	8.7	3.1	..	..
Bolivia	7.24	7.02	1.7	2.9	0.4	117.6	8.6	7.0	8.7	4.9	..	..
Bosnia and Herzegovina	1.34	1.34	0.6	0.8	0.6	..	3.7	4.2	..	..	..	..
Botswana	6.83	6.54	1.4	3.5	0.5	..	9.7	9.2	10.4	8.7	..	..
Brazil	1.83	1.75	0.7	1.5	0.8	..	211.8	8.1	199.5	7.3	204.9	11.0
Bulgaria	1.34	1.34	0.0	0.7	0.6	121.6	103.3	5.6	117.5	6.3	85.7	6.7
Burkina Faso	447.81	449.31	189.6	201.5	0.5	..	3.7	2.4	5.5	2.9	..	..
Burundi	1,185.73	1,230.50	126.6	446.2	0.4	99.5	13.4	9.6	16.1	8.5	..	..
Cambodia	4,054.17	4,160.00	1,142.8	1,478.8	0.4	94.3	4.4	4.6	6.3	5.6	..	..
Cameroon	447.81	449.31	241.2	250.3	0.6	108.7	6.3	2.2	6.5	2.3	..	..
Canada	1.07	1.05	1.2	1.2	1.2	108.8	1.5	2.8	1.7	2.2	2.7	1.5
Central African Republic	447.81	449.31	272.0	277.1	0.6	113.6	4.5	2.4	5.3	3.0	6.0	4.4
Chad	447.81	449.31	163.2	256.9	0.6	126.7	7.1	6.5	6.9	2.2	..	..
Chile	522.46	501.45	263.8	365.3	0.7	106.0	7.9	6.6	8.9	3.2	7.0	6.5
China	6.95	6.83	3.4	3.8	0.6	116.2	7.9	4.3	8.6	2.2	..	..
Hong Kong SAR, China	7.79	7.75	7.9	5.5	0.7	..	4.5	–1.7	5.9	0.0	0.6	1.1
Colombia	1,967.71	2,016.70	423.8	1,212.2	0.6	114.3	22.3	7.0	20.2	5.9	16.4	5.2
Congo, Dem. Rep.	559.29	904.31	0.0	323.8	0.6	107.4	964.9	28.5	930.2	26.9	..	..
Congo, Rep.	447.81	449.31	149.1	336.6	0.8	..	9.0	7.2	9.3	3.1	..	..
Costa Rica	526.24	567.99	103.1	307.8	0.6	109.2	15.9	10.2	15.6	11.3	14.1	13.0
Côte d'Ivoire	447.81	449.31	261.9	308.4	0.7	106.0	9.2	3.4	7.2	3.0	..	..
Croatia	4.94	4.98	3.1	4.4	0.9	107.1	90.1	3.8	86.3	2.8	69.8	2.9
Cuba	..	..	..	..	..	..	3.0	2.6	..	..	..	..
Czech Republic	17.07	17.84	11.1	14.4	0.8	125.9	12.8	2.2	7.8	2.5	8.2	2.5
Denmark	5.10	5.09	8.5	8.6	1.7	103.6	1.6	2.4	2.1	2.0	1.1	2.7
Dominican Republic	34.62	36.21	7.3	19.5	0.6	97.3	9.8	15.1	8.7	16.0	..	..
Ecuador	1.00	1.00	0.4	0.5	0.5	93.1	4.4	9.8	37.1	7.0	..	9.3
Egypt, Arab Rep.	5.43	5.60	1.2	2.0	0.4	..	8.7	7.8	8.8	7.2	6.1	10.2
El Salvador	1.00	1.00	0.4	0.5	0.5	..	6.2	3.7	8.5	3.9	..	5.2
Eritrea	15.38	15.38	1.9	8.1	0.5	..	7.9	18.0	..	..	..	..
Estonia	10.69	10.70	4.8	9.1	0.9	..	53.6	5.6	21.6	4.3	8.1	3.3
Ethiopia	9.60	12.58	2.1	3.5	0.4	99.6	6.5	8.7	5.5	11.1	..	..
Finland[c]	0.68	0.68	1.0	1.0	1.4	104.2	2.0	1.2	1.5	1.5	1.0	2.4
France[c]	0.68	0.68	1.0	0.9	1.4	103.0	1.3	2.1	1.6	1.9	..	2.1
Gabon	447.81	449.31	188.0	308.6	0.7	105.9	7.0	6.0	4.6	1.5	..	..
Gambia, The	22.19	26.90	3.9	8.0	0.4	125.6	4.2	10.8	4.0	8.1	..	..
Georgia	1.49	1.68	0.4	0.9	0.6	127.4	356.7	7.3	24.7	7.1	..	7.4
Germany[c]	0.68	0.68	1.0	0.9	1.3	103.0	1.7	1.1	2.1	1.7	0.4	2.7
Ghana	1.06	1.43	0.1	0.5	0.5	101.7	26.7	18.6	28.4	16.4	..	..
Greece[c]	0.68	0.68	0.6	0.7	1.1	105.6	9.2	3.3	9.0	3.4	3.6	4.7
Guatemala	7.56	8.33	2.9	4.5	0.6	..	10.4	5.2	10.1	7.5	..	..
Guinea	5,500.00	..	747.7	2,013.9	0.4	..	5.5	16.5	..	..	..	..
Guinea-Bissau	447.81	449.31	114.6	243.1	0.5	..	32.5	3.3	34.0	2.3	..	..
Haiti	39.11	41.88	5.8	25.4	0.7	..	18.1	17.5	21.9	18.0	..	..
Honduras	18.90	18.90	3.0	9.3	0.5	..	19.9	6.5	18.8	7.9	..	..

Exchange rates and prices | 4.14

	Official exchange rate		Purchasing power parity (PPP) conversion factor		Ratio of PPP conversion factor to market exchange rate	Real effective exchange rate	GDP implicit deflator		Consumer price index		Wholesale price index	
	local currency units to $		local currency units to international $			Index 2000 = 100	average annual % growth		average annual % growth		average annual % growth	
	2008	2009[a]	1995	2008	2008	2008	1990–2000	2000–08	1990–2000	2000–08	1990–2000	2000–08
Hungary	172.11	186.76	61.7	134.0	0.8	112.9	19.6	5.0	20.3	5.5	16.8	3.3
India	43.51	46.63	11.1	15.9	0.4	..	8.1	4.5	9.1	4.8	7.4	5.2
Indonesia	9,698.96	9,457.75	1,031.8	5,460.4	0.6	..	15.8	10.9	13.7	9.3	15.4	11.0
Iran, Islamic Rep.	9,428.53	9,969.95	567.5	3,412.4	0.4	126.7	27.7	17.4	26.0	15.1	28.4	10.8
Iraq	1,193.08	1,170.00	..	..	..	..	..	..	..	..	..	..
Ireland[c]	0.68	0.68	0.8	1.0	1.4	113.8	3.6	2.6	2.6	3.6	1.6	–1.9
Israel	3.59	3.79	3.1	3.6	1.0	114.3	11.0	1.2	9.7	1.7	8.1	4.9
Italy[c]	0.68	0.68	0.8	0.8	1.2	103.5	3.8	2.6	3.7	2.3	2.9	3.0
Jamaica	72.76	88.92	14.6	51.3	0.7	..	24.8	11.5	23.5	11.4	..	..
Japan	103.36	89.56	174.6	116.5	1.1	91.5	0.1	–1.2	0.8	–0.1	–1.0	0.8
Jordan	0.71	0.71	0.4	0.5	0.7	..	3.2	4.3	3.5	4.2	..	13.6
Kazakhstan	120.30	148.69	17.5	90.5	0.8	..	204.7	15.1	67.8	8.3	16.3	14.9
Kenya	69.18	74.74	15.8	35.0	0.5	..	16.6	5.7	15.6	10.7	..	..
Korea, Dem. Rep.	..	..	..	..	..	..	..	..	..	..	..	..
Korea, Rep.	1,102.05	1,166.13	691.1	761.7	0.7	..	5.9	2.2	5.1	3.1	3.7	2.5
Kosovo	..	..	..	..	..	..	..	..	..	1.3	..	..
Kuwait	0.27	0.29	0.2	0.3	0.9	..	1.5	9.8	2.0	3.0	1.4	2.5
Kyrgyz Republic	36.57	43.99	3.5	16.0	0.4	..	110.6	7.8	23.3	6.1	35.6	9.4
Lao PDR	8,744.06	8,486.32	327.7	3,634.2	0.4	..	27.2	9.6	28.3	9.0	..	..
Latvia	0.48	0.48	0.2	0.4	0.9	..	48.0	8.7	29.2	6.1	12.0	7.6
Lebanon	1,507.50	1,507.50	775.4	893.9	0.6	..	19.0	2.0	..	..	..	..
Lesotho	8.26	7.48	2.1	4.2	0.5	87.7	9.5	7.2	5.9	7.8	..	..
Liberia	63.21	67.81	0.6	36.2	0.6	..	51.8	10.3	..	..	..	..
Libya	1.22	1.21	..	1.1	0.9	..	..	21.9	5.6	–0.5	..	..
Lithuania	2.36	2.36	1.2	1.9	0.8	..	75.2	4.0	32.6	2.5	24.8	5.5
Macedonia, FYR	41.87	41.81	17.7	20.9	0.5	104.7	79.3	3.5	10.6	2.3	8.5	0.7
Madagascar	1,708.37	1,951.98	287.6	803.1	0.5	..	19.1	11.5	18.7	10.8	..	..
Malawi	140.52	142.73	3.9	50.2	0.4	102.7	33.6	19.3	33.8	12.7	..	..
Malaysia	3.34	3.41	1.4	1.9	0.6	108.4	4.1	4.4	3.6	2.3	3.4	5.0
Mali	447.81	449.31	226.8	273.1	0.6	..	7.0	4.2	5.2	2.2	..	..
Mauritania	258.59	..	62.4	118.1	0.4	..	8.7	11.3	6.1	7.5	..	..
Mauritius	28.45	29.29	10.5	16.9	0.6	..	6.3	6.3	6.9	6.3	..	..
Mexico	11.13	12.85	2.9	7.8	0.7	..	19.0	8.2	19.5	4.5	18.4	6.1
Moldova	10.39	11.93	1.2	5.9	0.6	134.8	119.6	11.6	21.4	11.3	..	..
Mongolia	1,165.74	1,446.52	158.7	653.0	0.6	..	57.8	15.0	35.7	8.1	..	..
Morocco	7.75	7.76	4.9	5.0	0.7	102.0	4.0	1.8	3.9	1.9	2.9	..
Mozambique	24.30	27.15	4.0	12.8	0.5	..	34.1	8.2	31.8	11.5	..	..
Myanmar	5.39	5.38	..	..	..	..	25.3	23.5	25.9	23.7	..	..
Namibia	8.26	7.48	2.2	5.4	0.7	..	11.1	6.7	..	5.4	..	..
Nepal	69.76	74.54	15.4	25.7	0.4	..	8.0	6.2	8.7	5.6	..	..
Netherlands[c]	0.68	0.68	0.9	0.9	1.3	102.5	2.1	2.3	2.4	2.0	1.3	3.0
New Zealand	1.42	1.40	1.5	1.6	1.1	93.7	1.7	2.7	1.8	2.7	1.4	3.2
Nicaragua	19.37	20.80	3.5	8.4	0.4	107.8	42.4	8.5	..	8.6	..	..
Niger	447.81	449.31	209.8	239.0	0.5	..	6.0	2.6	6.1	2.4	..	..
Nigeria	118.55	149.36	15.5	77.4	0.7	116.6	29.5	16.8	32.5	12.9	..	..
Norway	5.64	5.75	9.2	9.1	1.6	102.0	2.7	4.8	2.2	1.7	1.6	7.8
Oman	0.38	0.38	0.2	0.3	0.7	..	0.1	7.9	..	2.3	..	..
Pakistan	70.41	84.12	10.1	24.4	0.4	100.1	11.1	7.4	9.7	7.1	10.4	8.3
Panama	1.00	1.00	0.5	0.5	0.5	..	3.6	2.2	1.1	2.1	1.0	3.8
Papua New Guinea	2.70	2.70	0.7	1.6	0.6	108.7	7.6	7.4	9.3	5.9	..	..
Paraguay	4,363.24	4,654.00	949.3	2,377.3	0.5	146.0	11.5	10.5	13.1	8.7	..	11.2
Peru	2.92	2.88	1.2	1.5	0.5	..	26.7	3.6	27.3	2.3	23.7	2.8
Philippines	44.32	46.42	14.1	23.4	0.5	128.6	8.4	5.2	7.7	5.5	5.6	7.7
Poland	2.41	2.84	1.2	1.9	0.8	116.8	24.7	2.6	25.3	2.4	19.8	2.7
Portugal[c]	0.68	0.68	0.7	0.7	1.0	103.7	5.2	2.9	4.5	2.9	..	2.9
Puerto Rico	1.00	1.00	..	..	..	..	3.0	..	..	..	..	..
Qatar	3.64	3.64	..	3.2	0.9	..	..	12.6	2.8	7.3	..	..

	Official exchange rate		Purchasing power parity (PPP) conversion factor		Ratio of PPP conversion factor to market exchange rate	Real effective exchange rate	GDP implicit deflator		Consumer price index		Wholesale price index	
	local currency units to $		local currency units to international $			Index 2000 = 100	average annual % growth		average annual % growth		average annual % growth	
	2008	2009ᵃ	1995	2008	2008	2008	1990–2000	2000–08	1990–2000	2000–08	1990–2000	2000–08
Romania	2.52	2.90	0.1	1.7	0.7	112.4	98.0	17.1	100.5	12.5	93.8	16.6
Russian Federation	24.85	29.94	1.5	18.5	0.7	123.4	161.5	16.8	99.1	12.7	99.8	17.1
Rwanda	546.85	568.80	128.7	244.3	0.5	..	14.3	10.0	16.2	8.5	..	..
Saudi Arabia	3.75	3.75	1.8	3.0	0.8	97.8	1.6	8.9	1.0	1.7	1.3	2.5
Senegal	447.81	449.31	252.0	271.6	0.6	..	6.0	2.8	5.4	2.2	..	..
Serbia	55.72	65.73	2.8	36.0	0.7	..	..	17.6	50.2	16.6	..	..
Sierra Leone	2,981.51	3,280.15	379.6	1,340.7	0.5	109.5	31.9	9.4	..	..	..	..
Singapore	1.41	1.40	1.3	1.1	0.8	110.1	1.3	1.5	1.7	1.3	–1.0	3.7
Slovak Republicᶜ	0.68	0.68	0.4	0.6	0.0	127.8	11.1	3.7	8.4	5.2	9.5	5.2
Sloveniaᶜ	0.68	0.68	0.4	0.7	1.0	..	29.3	4.2	12.0	4.4	9.1	4.1
Somalia	..	..	..	..	..	..	..	..	..	..	..	..
South Africa	8.26	7.48	2.3	4.6	0.6	81.8	9.9	7.1	8.7	4.3	7.7	6.7
Spainᶜ	0.68	0.68	0.7	0.8	1.1	106.9	3.9	4.0	3.8	3.3	2.4	3.4
Sri Lanka	108.33	114.35	18.3	48.0	0.4	..	9.1	10.6	9.9	11.0	8.1	12.6
Sudan	2.09	2.20	0.3	1.3	0.6	..	65.5	9.9	72.0	8.2	..	..
Swaziland	8.26	7.48	2.2	4.1	0.5	..	10.5	7.8	9.5	6.9	..	..
Sweden	6.59	7.13	9.4	9.3	1.4	100.6	2.2	1.6	1.9	1.5	2.0	2.9
Switzerland	1.08	1.03	2.0	1.6	1.5	99.2	1.1	1.0	1.6	1.0	–0.4	1.1
Syrian Arab Republic	11.23	..	12.8	27.2	0.6	..	7.9	8.4	6.4	5.9	4.7	2.2
Tajikistan	3.43	4.37	0.0	1.4	0.4	..	235.0	21.0	..	13.0	..	..
Tanzania	1,196.31	1,327.00	154.8	456.9	0.4	..	21.6	9.4	20.9	6.0	..	..
Thailand	33.31	33.18	15.1	16.7	0.5	..	4.2	3.2	4.9	3.0	3.8	5.8
Timor-Leste	1.00	1.00	..	0.6	0.6	..	..	3.6	..	5.2	..	..
Togo	447.81	449.31	238.6	242.3	0.5	107.1	7.0	1.3	8.5	2.7	..	..
Trinidad and Tobago	6.29	6.35	2.9	4.5	0.7	113.9	5.4	6.9	5.7	6.1	2.8	2.0
Tunisia	1.23	1.29	0.5	0.6	0.5	95.8	4.4	3.0	4.4	3.2	3.6	4.3
Turkey	1.30	1.45	0.0	1.0	0.7	..	81.7	16.8	79.9	18.6	75.2	19.0
Turkmenistan	..	..	0.0	1.3	0.5	..	408.2	11.5	..	..	..	..
Uganda	1,720.44	1,873.78	472.1	668.5	0.4	104.0	12.0	5.1	8.3	6.0	..	..
Ukraine	5.27	7.98	0.3	2.8	0.5	115.8	271.0	15.7	155.7	9.8	161.6	14.1
United Arab Emirates	3.67	3.67	1.7	3.0	0.8	..	2.2	8.9	..	..	..	..
United Kingdom	0.54	0.62	0.6	0.7	1.2	93.8	2.8	2.6	2.9	3.0	2.4	1.8
United States	1.00	1.00	1.0	1.0	1.0	92.5	2.0	2.9	2.7	2.8	1.2	4.7
Uruguay	20.95	19.70	5.5	15.9	0.8	116.2	33.2	8.2	33.9	9.5	27.2	14.6
Uzbekistan	..	..	11.2	507.8	0.4	..	245.8	25.5	..	..	..	..
Venezuela, RB	2.14	2.14	0.1	1.9	0.9	144.9	45.3	26.3	49.0	20.6	44.1	26.4
Vietnam	16,302.25	16,968.00	3,170.2	6,154.4	0.4	..	15.2	7.7	4.1	7.1	..	..
West Bank and Gaza	..	..	..	..	..	..	5.7	3.4	..	3.8	..	..
Yemen, Rep.	199.76	205.04	22.0	95.9	0.5	..	22.4	13.6	26.3	11.7	..	..
Zambia	3,745.66	4,682.22	404.2	3,133.5	0.8	145.2	52.1	17.1	57.0	16.6	101.4	..
Zimbabwe	6,715,424,238.75	..	25.7	..	..	..	26.7	232.0	29.0	497.7	25.9	..

Note: The differences in the growth rates of the GDP deflator and consumer and wholesale price indexes are due mainly to differences in data availability for each of the indexes during the period.

a. Average for December or latest monthly data available. b. Private analysts estimate that consumer price index inflation was considerably higher for 2007–09 and believe that GDP volume growth has been significantly lower than official reports indicate since the last quarter of 2008. c. As members of the euro area, these countries share a single currency, the euro.

Exchange rates and prices | 4.14

In a market-based economy, household, producer, and government choices about resource allocation are influenced by relative prices, including the real exchange rate, real wages, real interest rates, and other prices in the economy. Relative prices also largely reflect these agents' choices. Thus relative prices convey vital information about the interaction of economic agents in an economy and with the rest of the world.

The exchange rate is the price of one currency in terms of another. Official exchange rates and exchange rate arrangements are established by governments. Other exchange rates recognized by governments include market rates, which are determined largely by legal market forces, and for countries with multiple exchange arrangements, principal rates, secondary rates, and tertiary rates. (Also see *Statistical methods* for alternative conversion factors in the *World Bank Atlas* method of calculating gross national income [GNI] per capita in U.S. dollars.)

Official or market exchange rates are often used to convert economic statistics in local currencies to a common currency in order to make comparisons across countries. Since market rates reflect at best the relative prices of tradable goods, the volume of goods and services that a U.S. dollar buys in the United States may not correspond to what a U.S. dollar converted to another country's currency at the official exchange rate would buy in that country, particularly when nontradable goods and services account for a significant share of a country's output. An alternative exchange rate—the purchasing power parity (PPP) conversion factor—is preferred because it reflects differences in price levels for both tradable and nontradable goods and services and therefore provides a more meaningful comparison of real output. See table 1.1 for further discussion.

The ratio of the PPP conversion factor to the official exchange rate—the national price level or comparative price level—measures differences in the price level at the gross domestic product (GDP) level. The price level index tends to be lower in poorer countries and to rise with income. The market exchange rate (or alternative conversion factor) is the official exchange rate adjusted for some countries by World Bank staff to reflect actual price changes. National price levels vary systematically, rising with GNI per capita. The real effective exchange rate is a nominal effective exchange rate index adjusted for relative movements in national price or cost indicators of the home country, selected countries, and the euro area. A nominal effective exchange rate index is the ratio (expressed on the base 2000 = 100) of an index of a currency's period-average exchange rate to a weighted geometric average of exchange rates

for currencies of selected countries and the euro area. For most high-income countries weights are derived from industrial country trade in manufactured goods. Data are compiled from the nominal effective exchange rate index and a cost indicator of relative normalized unit labor costs in manufacturing. For selected other countries the nominal effective exchange rate index is based on manufactured goods and primary products trade with partner or competitor countries. For these countries the real effective exchange rate index is the nominal index adjusted for relative changes in consumer prices; an increase represents an appreciation of the local currency. Because of conceptual and data limitations, changes in real effective exchange rates should be interpreted with caution.

Inflation is measured by the rate of increase in a price index, but actual price change can be negative. The index used depends on the prices being examined. The GDP deflator reflects price changes for total GDP. The most general measure of the overall price level, it accounts for changes in government consumption, capital formation (including inventory appreciation), international trade, and the main component, household final consumption expenditure. The GDP deflator is usually derived implicitly as the ratio of current to constant price GDP—or a Paasche index. It is defective as a general measure of inflation for policy use because of long lags in deriving estimates and because it is often an annual measure.

Consumer price indexes are produced more frequently and so are more current. They are also constructed explicitly, based on surveys of the cost of a defined basket of consumer goods and services. Nevertheless, consumer price indexes should be interpreted with caution. The definition of a household, the basket of goods, and the geographic (urban or rural) and income group coverage of consumer price surveys can vary widely by country. In addition, weights are derived from household expenditure surveys, which, for budgetary reasons, tend to be conducted infrequently in developing countries, impairing comparability over time. Although useful for measuring consumer price inflation within a country, consumer price indexes are of less value in comparing countries.

Wholesale price indexes are based on the prices at the first commercial transaction of commodities that are important in a country's output or consumption. Prices are farm-gate for agricultural commodities and ex-factory for industrial goods. Preference is given to indexes with the broadest coverage of the economy.

The least squares method is used to calculate growth rates of the GDP implicit deflator, consumer price index, and wholesale price index.

• **Official exchange rate** is the exchange rate determined by national authorities or the rate determined in the legally sanctioned exchange market. It is calculated as an annual average based on monthly averages (local currency units relative to the U.S. dollar). • **Purchasing power parity (PPP) conversion factor** is the number of units of a country's currency required to buy the same amount of goods and services in the domestic market that a U.S. dollar would buy in the United States. • **Ratio of PPP conversion factor to market exchange rate** is the result obtained by dividing the PPP conversion factor by the market exchange rate. • **Real effective exchange rate** is the nominal effective exchange rate (a measure of the value of a currency against a weighted average of several foreign currencies) divided by a price deflator or index of costs. • **GDP implicit deflator** measures the average annual rate of price change in the economy as a whole for the periods shown. • **Consumer price index** reflects changes in the cost to the average consumer of acquiring a basket of goods and services that may be fixed or may change at specified intervals, such as yearly. The Laspeyres formula is generally used. • **Wholesale price index** refers to a mix of agricultural and industrial goods at various stages of production and distribution, including import duties. The Laspeyres formula is generally used.

Data on official and real effective exchange rates and consumer and wholesale price indexes are from the International Monetary Fund's *International Financial Statistics*. PPP conversion factors and GDP deflators are from the World Bank's data files.

	Goods and services				Net income		Net current transfers		Current account balance		Total reserves[a]	
	$ millions				$ millions		$ millions		$ millions		$ millions	
	Exports		Imports									
	1995	2008	1995	2008	1995	2008	1995	2008	1995	2008	1995	2008
Afghanistan	..	..	..	..	..	..	..	..	..	..	..	..
Albania	304	3,833	836	7,287	44	150	477	1,379	−12	−1,924	265	2,364
Algeria	..	..	..	..	..	..	..	..	..	..	4,164	148,099
Angola	3,836	64,243	3,519	43,122	−767	−14,504	156	−210	−295	6,408	213	17,869
Argentina	24,987	82,101	26,066	67,588	−4,636	−7,550	597	115	−5,118	7,078	15,979	46,385
Armenia	300	1,757	726	4,749	40	471	168	1,138	−218	−1,383	111	1,407
Australia	69,710	234,298	74,841	242,311	−14,036	−39,399	−109	−374	−19,277	−47,786	14,952	32,924
Austria	89,906	241,307	92,055	222,639	−1,597	−2,867	−1,702	−2,647	−5,448	13,154	23,369	16,741
Azerbaijan	785	32,133	1,290	11,464	−6	−5,266	111	1,050	−401	16,454	121	6,467
Bangladesh	4,431	17,372	7,589	25,344	68	−771	2,265	9,774	−824	1,032	2,376	5,787
Belarus	5,269	37,063	5,752	41,676	−51	−788	76	192	−458	−5,209	377	3,063
Belgium	190,686[b]	459,890	178,798[b]	470,702	6,808[b]	6,966	−4,463[b]	−8,255	14,232[b]	−12,101	24,120	15,681
Benin	614	1,348	895	2,102	−8	−50	121	268	−167	−535	198	1,263
Bolivia	1,234	6,947	1,574	5,680	−207	−536	244	1,284	−303	2,015	1,005	7,720
Bosnia and Herzegovina	..	6,856	..	12,935	..	603	..	2,712	..	−2,764	80	3,516
Botswana	2,421	5,585	2,050	5,837	−32	−256	−39	1,010	300	502	4,695	9,119
Brazil	52,641	228,393	63,293	220,247	−11,105	−40,562	3,621	4,224	−18,136	−28,192	51,477	193,783
Bulgaria	6,776	30,589	6,502	42,158	−432	−1,798	132	791	−26	−12,577	1,635	17,930
Burkina Faso	272	..	483	..	−29	..	255	..	15	..	347	928
Burundi	129	136	259	529	−13	−4	153	186	10	−212	216	267
Cambodia	969	6,356	1,375	7,594	−57	−409	277	594	−186	−1,053	192	2,639
Cameroon	2,040	7,454	1,608	8,349	−412	−205	69	590	90	−510	15	3,112
Canada	219,501	529,160	200,991	486,728	−22,721	−14,065	−117	−1,085	−4,328	27,281	16,369	43,872
Central African Republic	179	..	244	..	−23	..	63	..	−25	..	238	131
Chad	190	..	411	..	−7	..	191	..	−38	..	147	1,355
Chile	19,358	77,210	18,301	69,010	−2,714	−14,563	307	2,924	−1,350	−3,440	14,860	23,079
China[†]	147,240	1,581,713	135,282	1,232,843	−11,774	31,438	1,435	45,799	1,618	426,107	80,288	1,966,037
Hong Kong SAR, China	..	457,554	..	434,202	..	10,457	..	−3,277	..	30,532	55,424	182,527
Colombia	12,294	42,579	16,012	44,743	−1,596	−10,063	799	5,514	−4,516	−6,713	8,452	23,671
Congo, Dem. Rep.	..	..	..	..	..	..	..	..	..	..	157	78
Congo, Rep.	1,374	6,127	1,346	6,386	−695	−1,885	42	−38	−625	−2,181	64	3,881
Costa Rica	4,451	13,651	4,717	16,433	−226	−389	134	442	−358	−2,729	1,060	3,801
Côte d'Ivoire	4,337	11,103	3,806	9,377	−787	−894	−237	−345	−492	488	529	2,253
Croatia	6,972	29,623	9,152	35,007	−53	−2,406	802	1,524	−1,431	−6,267	1,896	12,957
Cuba	..	..	..	..	..	..	..	..	..	..	..	..
Czech Republic	28,202	167,927	30,044	156,708	−104	−17,276	572	−575	−1,374	−6,631	14,613	37,009
Denmark	65,655	187,208	57,860	177,818	−4,549	3,892	−1,391	−5,734	1,855	7,549	11,652	42,327
Dominican Republic	5,731	11,888	6,137	17,941	−769	−1,815	992	3,432	−183	−4,437	373	2,288
Ecuador	5,196	20,460	5,708	20,730	−930	−1,598	442	2,989	−1,000	1,120	1,788	4,473
Egypt, Arab Rep.	13,260	54,761	17,140	67,223	−405	1,289	4,031	9,758	−254	−1,415	17,122	34,331
El Salvador	2,040	6,121	3,623	11,012	−67	−536	1,389	3,832	−262	−1,596	940	2,646
Eritrea	135	..	498	..	8	..	324	..	−31	..	40	58
Estonia	2,573	17,750	2,860	18,757	3	−1,512	126	273	−158	−2,245	583	3,972
Ethiopia	768	3,514	1,446	9,617	−19	2	736	4,295	39	−1,806	815	871
Finland	47,973	128,904	37,705	117,521	−4,440	−1,093	−597	−2,335	5,231	7,955	10,657	8,354
France	362,717	770,104	333,746	835,249	−8,964	36,057	−9,167	−35,141	10,840	−64,229	58,510	103,306
Gabon	2,945	..	1,723	..	−665	..	−42	..	515	..	153	1,935
Gambia, The	177	271	232	371	−5	−27	52	84	−8	−43	106	117
Georgia	575	3,688	1,413	7,499	127	−166	197	1,061	−514	−2,915	199	1,480
Germany	600,347	1,744,963	586,662	1,516,863	−2,814	64,513	−38,768	−48,738	−27,897	243,875	121,816	138,564
Ghana	1,582	7,071	2,120	12,567	−129	−259	523	2,212	−144	−3,543	804	2,269
Greece	15,523	79,635	24,711	119,112	−1,684	−16,015	8,008	4,180	−2,864	−51,313	16,119	3,490
Guatemala	2,823	9,637	3,728	15,581	−159	−930	491	5,011	−572	−1,863	783	4,654
Guinea	700	1,449	1,011	1,810	−85	−91	179	18	−216	−434	87	..
Guinea-Bissau	30	..	89	..	−21	..	46	..	−35	..	20	124
Haiti	192	833	802	2,871	−31	6	553	1,876	−87	−156	199	543
Honduras	1,635	6,956	1,852	11,603	−226	−350	243	3,021	−201	−1,977	270	2,492
[†]Data for Taiwan, China	128,369	288,756	124,171	271,117	4,188	9,978	−2,912	−2,979	5,474	24,638	95,559	303,553

Balance of payments current account | 4.15

	Goods and services (Exports) $ millions		Goods and services (Imports) $ millions		Net income $ millions		Net current transfers $ millions		Current account balance $ millions		Total reserves[a] $ millions	
	1995	2008	1995	2008	1995	2008	1995	2008	1995	2008	1995	2008
Hungary	19,765	127,274	19,916	126,041	−1,701	−11,190	203	−982	−1,650	−10,939	12,017	33,874
India	38,013	290,861	48,225	371,616	−3,734	−3,539	8,382	48,206	−5,563	−36,088	22,865	257,423
Indonesia	52,923	154,852	54,461	144,935	−5,874	−15,155	981	5,364	−6,431	125	14,908	51,641
Iran, Islamic Rep.	18,953	..	15,113	..	−478	..	−4	..	3,358	..	..	..
Iraq	..	40,455	..	21,488	..	−3,067	..	−381	..	15,519	8,347	50,207
Ireland	49,439	221,383	42,169	194,363	−7,325	−39,430	1,776	−1,812	1,721	−14,222	8,770	1,024
Israel	27,478	81,245	35,287	84,309	−2,654	−3,298	5,673	8,482	−4,790	2,120	8,123	42,513
Italy	295,618	666,484	250,319	677,886	−15,644	−43,548	−4,579	−23,194	25,076	−78,144	60,690	105,649
Jamaica	3,394	5,294	3,729	9,914	−371	−568	607	2,150	−99	−3,038	681	1,773
Japan	493,991	895,228	419,556	877,887	44,285	152,336	−7,676	−13,043	111,044	156,634	192,620	1,030,763
Jordan	3,479	12,353	4,903	19,228	−279	951	1,444	3,532	−259	−2,393	2,279	8,918
Kazakhstan	5,975	76,354	6,102	49,451	−146	−19,323	59	−985	−213	6,596	1,660	19,883
Kenya	3,526	8,291	5,922	12,559	−219	−45	1,037	2,336	−1,578	−1,978	384	2,879
Korea, Dem. Rep.	..	..	..	..	..	..	..	..	..	..	..	..
Korea, Rep.	147,761	509,417	155,104	520,157	−1,303	5,107	−19	−773	−8,665	−6,406	32,804	201,545
Kosovo	..	..	..	..	..	..	..	..	..	..	..	892
Kuwait	14,215	98,335	12,615	37,948	4,881	10,119	−1,465	−5,765	5,016	64,742	4,543	19,321
Kyrgyz Republic	448	2,743	726	4,747	−35	−103	79	1,477	−235	−631	134	1,225
Lao PDR	408	1,201	748	1,141	−6	−50	110	98	−237	107	99	875
Latvia	2,088	14,172	2,193	18,838	19	−596	71	769	−16	−4,492	602	5,244
Lebanon	..	24,041	..	29,718	..	−77	..	2,698	..	−3,056	8,100	28,265
Lesotho	199	950	1,046	1,728	314	507	210	515	−323	244	457	658
Liberia	..	635	..	2,344	..	−653	..	1,175	..	−1,187	28	161
Libya	7,513	62,158	5,755	26,003	133	586	−220	−1,040	1,672	35,702	7,415	96,335
Lithuania	3,191	28,594	3,902	33,759	−13	−1,539	109	1,077	−614	−5,627	829	6,442
Macedonia, FYR	1,302	4,982	1,773	7,532	−30	−108	213	1,448	−288	−1,210	275	2,110
Madagascar	749	..	987	..	−167	..	129	..	−276	..	109	982
Malawi	470	..	660	..	−44	..	157	..	−78	..	115	254
Malaysia	83,369	230,054	86,851	178,741	−4,144	−7,137	−1,017	−5,262	−8,644	38,914	24,699	92,166
Mali	529	1,933	991	2,623	−41	−291	219	400	−284	−581	323	1,072
Mauritania	504	..	510	..	−48	..	76	..	22	..	90	207
Mauritius	2,349	4,944	2,454	6,320	−19	178	101	224	−22	−974	887	1,796
Mexico	89,321	309,822	82,168	333,838	−12,689	−17,250	3,960	25,461	−1,576	−15,805	17,046	95,300
Moldova	884	2,483	1,006	5,691	−18	598	56	1,623	−85	−987	257	1,672
Mongolia	508	2,031	521	1,880	−25	−145	77	215	39	222	158	1,396
Morocco	9,044	33,746	11,243	46,521	−1,318	−522	2,330	8,768	−1,186	−4,528	3,874	22,720
Mozambique	411	3,208	1,055	4,406	−140	−631	339	854	−445	−975	195	1,661
Myanmar	1,307	4,834	2,020	2,906	−110	−1,248	562	122	−261	802	651	1,383
Namibia	1,734	3,671	2,100	4,400	139	−40	403	1,127	176	358	221	1,293
Nepal	1,029	1,710	1,624	4,371	9	151	230	3,243	−356	733	646	..
Netherlands	241,517	638,348	216,558	568,373	7,247	−14,582	−6,434	−12,822	25,773	42,571	47,162	28,603
New Zealand	17,883	40,320	17,248	42,482	−3,955	−9,831	255	756	−3,065	−11,237	4,410	11,052
Nicaragua	662	2,937	1,150	5,357	−372	−161	138	1,068	−722	−1,513	142	1,141
Niger	321	748	457	1,284	−47	0	31	185	−152	−351	95	705
Nigeria	12,342	80,160	12,841	47,592	−2,878	−11,180	799	17,969	−2,578	39,357	1,709	53,599
Norway	56,058	219,417	46,848	130,667	−1,919	2,915	−2,059	−3,323	5,233	88,341	22,976	50,950
Oman	6,078	39,693	5,035	26,830	−374	−2,214	−1,469	−5,181	−801	5,469	1,943	11,582
Pakistan	10,214	25,454	14,185	47,586	−1,939	−4,294	2,562	11,024	−3,349	−15,402	2,528	9,024
Panama	7,610	16,149	7,768	17,490	−466	−1,574	153	238	−471	−2,677	781	1,935
Papua New Guinea	2,992	..	1,905	..	−488	..	75	..	674	..	267	2,008
Paraguay	4,802	8,831	5,200	9,393	110	−151	195	369	−92	−345	1,106	2,863
Peru	6,622	35,166	9,597	34,005	−2,482	−8,144	832	2,803	−4,625	−4,180	8,653	31,241
Philippines	26,795	58,448	33,317	69,917	3,662	140	880	15,226	−1,980	3,897	7,781	37,498
Poland	35,716	214,004	33,825	234,960	−1,995	−14,210	958	8,257	854	−26,909	14,957	62,184
Portugal	32,260	82,807	39,545	104,560	21	−11,495	7,132	3,649	−132	−29,599	22,063	12,006
Puerto Rico	..	..	..	..	..	..	..	..	..	..	..	..
Qatar	..	..	..	..	..	..	..	..	..	..	848	9,997

| | Goods and services ($ millions) | | | | Net income | | Net current transfers | | Current account balance | | Total reserves[a] | |
| | Exports | | Imports | | $ millions | | $ millions | | $ millions | | $ millions | |
	1995	2008	1995	2008	1995	2008	1995	2008	1995	2008	1995	2008
Romania	9,404	62,616	11,306	89,847	−241	−5,372	369	8,884	−1,774	−23,719	2,624	39,768
Russian Federation	92,987	522,909	82,809	368,217	−3,372	−49,196	157	−3,096	6,963	102,401	18,024	427,077
Rwanda	75	665	374	1,401	7	−34	350	518	57	−252	99	596
Saudi Arabia	53,450	323,071	44,874	176,040	2,800	10,027	−16,694	−23,012	−5,318	134,046	10,399	34,340
Senegal	1,506	2,875	1,821	5,402	−124	−74	195	1,290	−244	−1,311	272	1,602
Serbia	..	14,986	..	26,631	..	−1,348	..	4,138	..	−8,855	..	11,478
Sierra Leone	128	334	260	597	−30	−75	43	111	−118	−227	35	220
Singapore	157,658	427,595	144,520	392,690	2,133	−4,969	−894	−2,756	14,377	27,181	68,816	174,193
Slovak Republic	10,969	78,765	10,658	80,348	−14	−3,344	93	−1,257	390	−6,185	3,863	18,836
Slovenia	10,377	37,008	10,749	38,505	201	−1,533	95	−299	−75	−3,329	1,821	957
Somalia	..	..	..	..	..	..	..	..	..	..	..	..
South Africa	34,402	98,923	33,375	107,542	−2,875	−9,132	−645	−2,333	−2,493	−20,084	4,464	34,070
Spain	133,910	429,488	135,000	520,200	−5,402	−49,585	4,525	−13,832	−1,967	−154,129	40,531	20,288
Sri Lanka	4,617	10,140	5,982	15,609	−137	−972	732	2,666	−770	−3,775	2,112	2,617
Sudan	681	12,163	1,238	10,849	−3	−3,013	60	385	−500	−1,314	163	1,399
Swaziland	1,020	2,199	1,274	2,523	81	64	144	194	−30	−66	298	752
Sweden	95,525	258,075	81,142	222,243	−6,473	10,814	−2,970	−6,330	4,940	40,317	25,870	29,727
Switzerland	123,320	319,253	108,916	264,149	10,708	−37,311	−4,409	−12,699	20,703	5,094	68,620	74,146
Syrian Arab Republic	5,757	15,617	5,541	15,289	−560	−689	607	821	263	459	..	..
Tajikistan	..	1,756	..	4,155	..	−52	..	2,498	..	48	39	204
Tanzania	1,265	5,206	2,139	8,038	−110	−92	395	617	−590	−2,307	270	2,863
Thailand	70,292	208,998	82,246	203,874	−2,114	−10,003	487	4,766	−13,582	−113	36,939	111,009
Timor-Leste												210
Togo	465	913	671	1,377	−34	−30	118	279	−122	−216	130	582
Trinidad and Tobago	2,799	14,315	2,110	8,047	−390	−964	−4	60	294	5,364	379	9,496
Tunisia	7,979	25,197	8,811	26,564	−716	−2,267	774	1,922	−774	−1,711	1,689	9,039
Turkey	36,581	175,978	40,113	211,309	−3,204	−7,964	4,398	2,006	−2,338	−41,289	13,891	73,675
Turkmenistan	1,774	..	1,796	..	17	..	5	..	0	..	1,168	..
Uganda	664	3,426	1,490	5,224	−96	−288	639	1,240	−281	−845	459	2,301
Ukraine	17,090	85,612	18,280	99,962	−434	−1,540	472	3,127	−1,152	−12,763	1,069	31,543
United Arab Emirates	..	..	..	..	..	..	..	..	..	..	7,778	31,694
United Kingdom	322,114	756,476	327,000	845,303	3,393	75,372	−11,943	−26,449	−13,436	−39,904	49,144	53,024
United States	794,397	1,826,595	890,784	2,522,531	20,899	118,233	−38,073	−128,363	−113,561	−706,066	175,996	294,046
Uruguay	3,507	9,334	3,568	10,083	−227	−627	76	150	−213	−1,225	1,813	6,360
Uzbekistan	..	..	..	..	..	..	..	..	..	..	..	..
Venezuela, RB	20,753	97,300	16,905	59,998	−1,943	698	109	−608	2,014	37,392	10,715	43,065
Vietnam	9,498	69,781	12,334	83,398	−384	−4,400	1,200	7,311	−2,020	−10,706	1,324	23,890
West Bank and Gaza	764	926	2,789	4,430	607	734	435	2,361	−984	−408	..	..
Yemen, Rep.	2,160	10,182	2,471	11,681	−561	−1,915	1,056	2,163	184	−1,251	638	8,155
Zambia	1,222	5,254	1,338	5,466	−249	−1,398	182	565	−182	−1,046	223	1,096
Zimbabwe	2,344	..	2,515	..	−294	..	40	..	−425	..	888	..
World	**6,393,697 t**	**19,557,280 t**	**6,247,179 t**	**19,164,685 t**								
Low income	45,519	207,241	64,928	282,482								
Middle income	1,110,795	5,731,256	1,154,326	5,223,924								
Lower middle income	497,910	3,110,947	531,746	2,758,700								
Upper middle income	612,966	2,636,805	622,049	2,469,508								
Low & middle income	1,152,982	5,938,347	1,217,464	5,502,978								
East Asia & Pacific	397,583	2,334,814	413,802	1,947,840								
Europe & Central Asia	231,676	1,366,736	239,492	1,352,255								
Latin America & Carib.	272,861	1,001,523	288,143	1,002,903								
Middle East & N. Africa	..	..	106,333	374,714								
South Asia	58,893	348,172	78,652	470,488								
Sub-Saharan Africa	89,262	378,970	99,763	371,927								
High income	5,235,576	13,709,918	5,028,511	13,740,945								
Euro area	2,097,732	5,619,649	1,974,159	5,491,628								

a. International reserves including gold valued at London gold price. b. Includes Luxembourg.

About the data

The balance of payments records an economy's transactions with the rest of the world. Balance of payments accounts are divided into two groups: the current account, which records transactions in goods, services, income, and current transfers, and the capital and financial account, which records capital transfers, acquisition or disposal of nonproduced, nonfinancial assets, and transactions in financial assets and liabilities. The table presents data from the current account plus gross international reserves.

The balance of payments is a double-entry accounting system that shows all flows of goods and services into and out of an economy; all transfers that are the counterpart of real resources or financial claims provided to or by the rest of the world without a quid pro quo, such as donations and grants; and all changes in residents' claims on and liabilities to nonresidents that arise from economic transactions. All transactions are recorded twice—once as a credit and once as a debit. In principle the net balance should be zero, but in practice the accounts often do not balance, requiring inclusion of a balancing item, net errors and omissions.

Discrepancies may arise in the balance of payments because there is no single source for balance of payments data and therefore no way to ensure that the data are fully consistent. Sources include customs data, monetary accounts of the banking system, external debt records, information provided by enterprises, surveys to estimate service transactions, and foreign exchange records. Differences in collection methods—such as in timing, definitions of residence and ownership, and the exchange rate used to value transactions—contribute to net errors and omissions. In addition, smuggling and other illegal or quasi-legal transactions may be unrecorded or misrecorded. For further discussion of issues relating to the recording of data on trade in goods and services, see *About the data* for tables 4.4–4.7.

The concepts and definitions underlying the data in the table are based on the fifth edition of the International Monetary Fund's (IMF) *Balance of Payments Manual* (1993). That edition redefined as capital transfers some transactions previously included in the current account, such as debt forgiveness, migrants' capital transfers, and foreign aid to acquire capital goods. Thus the current account balance now reflects more accurately net current transfer receipts in addition to transactions in goods, services (previously nonfactor services), and income (previously factor income). Many countries maintain their data collection systems according to the fourth edition of the *Balance of Payments Manual* (1977). Where necessary, the IMF converts such reported data to conform to the fifth edition (see *Primary data documentation*). Values are in U.S. dollars converted at market exchange rates.

Definitions

• **Exports** and **imports of goods and services** are all transactions between residents of an economy and the rest of the world involving a change in ownership of general merchandise, goods sent for processing and repairs, nonmonetary gold, and services. • **Net income** is receipts and payments of employee compensation for nonresident workers, and investment income (receipts and payments on direct investment, portfolio investment, and other investments and receipts on reserve assets). Income derived from the use of intangible assets is recorded under business services. • **Net current transfers** are recorded in the balance of payments whenever an economy provides or receives goods, services, income, or financial items without a quid pro quo. All transfers not considered to be capital are current. • **Current account balance** is the sum of net exports of goods and services, net income, and net current transfers.
• **Total reserves** are holdings of monetary gold, special drawing rights, reserves of IMF members held by the IMF, and holdings of foreign exchange under the control of monetary authorities. The gold component of these reserves is valued at year-end (December 31) London prices ($386.75 an ounce in 1995 and $871.70 an ounce in 2008).

Top 15 economies with the largest reserves in 2008 | 4.15a

	Total reserves ($ billions)		Share of world total (%) 2008	Annual change (%) 2007–08	Months of imports 2008
	2007	2008			
China	1,546	1,966	25.8	27.1	18.2
Japan	973	1,031	13.5	5.9	13.2
Russian Federation	479	427	5.6	–10.8	10.8
United States	278	294	3.9	5.9	1.1
India	277	257	3.4	–6.9	7.9
Korea, Rep.	263	202	2.6	–23.2	4.5
Brazil	180	194	2.5	7.5	8.5
Hong Kong, China	153	183	2.4	19.5	4.0
Singapore	163	174	2.3	6.9	4.6
Algeria	115	148	1.9	28.8	..
Germany	136	139	1.8	1.9	0.9
Thailand	87	111	1.5	26.9	6.0
Italy	94	106	1.4	12.3	1.5
France	115	103	1.4	–10.5	1.2
Libya	83	96	1.3	15.7	38.7

Source: International Monetary Fund, International Financial Statistics data files.

Data sources

Data on the balance of payments are published in the IMF's *Balance of Payments Statistics Yearbook* and *International Financial Statistics*. The World Bank exchanges data with the IMF through electronic files that in most cases are more timely and cover a longer period than the published sources. More information about the design and compilation of the balance of payments can be found in the IMF's *Balance of Payments Manual*, fifth edition (1993), *Balance of Payments Textbook* (1996), and *Balance of Payments Compilation Guide* (1995). The IMF's International Financial Statistics and Balance of Payments databases are available on CD-ROM.

STATES AND MARKETS

nfrastructure is the missing link of the Millennium Development Goals (MDGs). Infrastructure—the basic framework for delivering energy, transport, water and sanitation, and information and communication technology services to people—directly or indirectly affects people's lives everywhere. That relationship is reflected in the MDGs. Yet only two MDG targets touch on infrastructure services: water and sanitation (target 7.C) and telephones and the Internet (target 8.F); energy and transport are missing entirely. And no goal or target addresses the comprehensive role of infrastructure in achieving the MDGs.

Although income influences performance on the MDGs, it has long been recognized that growth in productivity and incomes and improvements in health and education outcomes require investment in infrastructure. The MDGs are designed to make economic growth more inclusive. Since a large share of people live in rural areas, often far from employment opportunities, policies to reduce poverty require investment in infrastructure and transport. By improving productivity, investments in infrastructure reduce poverty. Access to clean water and sanitation reduces infant mortality. Electricity powers hospitals and refrigerators for vaccines. Roads in rural areas boost school attendance and use of medical clinics. And information and communication technologies can improve teacher training and promote better health practices.

How infrastructure affects the Millennium Development Goals

The results of infrastructure investments are reflected in progress toward the MDGs. Infrastructure that reaches poor people raises their income and welfare by increasing the value of their assets or lowering the costs of inputs and providing better access to markets for their products.

Access to energy improves health and raises household and business productivity. Modern, clean, efficient fuels and electricity power lights that extend livelihood activities beyond daylight hours and power manufacturing equipment that lowers unit costs and increases labor productivity. Modern energy also reduces the cost of home cooking, heating, and lighting, freeing resources for other essential needs, and relieves girls of the need to collect water and wood

for fuel, enabling them to attend school. A household energy and universal access project in Mali is extending electricity to semi-urban and rural areas, improving the quality and efficiency of health and education services and helping sustainably manage forest resources and biomass energy. The project has connected 40,000 homes, 1,080 enterprises, 1,025 rural schools, and 107 health clinics.

Clean cooking fuels and efficient, ventilated stoves improve indoor air quality by reducing particulate matter, a risk factor for acute respiratory infections and other health problems. The World Health Organization estimates that the indoor air pollution created by the more than 3 billion people who use wood, dung, coal, and other traditional fuels inside their homes for cooking and heating is responsible for 1.5 million deaths a year. A rural energy project in Vietnam connected 976 communes with 555,327 households and 2.7 million people to the national power grid, providing some of the poorest rural areas with reliable electricity. However, some energy production, transformation, and transportation has detrimental effects on people and the environment; these can be mitigated by using cleaner, more efficient fuels.

Improved transport can boost income and improve health and education outcomes. Transport infrastructure and services—the roads, bridges, rails,

> Improved infrastructure not only improves the living conditions of the poor, but also reduces the costs of business and further encourages business to invest in productive assets. It enlarges markets. It is not surprising that the poor of Africa perceive the isolation associated with the lack of infrastructure to be the cause of their poverty and marginalization. Too far from markets, too far from arable land, too far from hospitals and clinics.
>
> —Trevor Manuel, Finance Minister, South Africa

waterways, ports, and equipment and services they provide—can eliminate growth-constraining bottlenecks and shortages, increase agricultural productivity, improve poor rural farmers' incomes and nutrition, and expand nonfarm employment. Lower transportation costs enable farmers to use fertilizers, mechanized equipment, and new seed varieties, boosting yields and lowering costs. A rural road project in Bangladesh reduced transport costs by 36–38 percent, lowered fertilizer prices, and increased output. Extreme poverty fell 5 percent. In Vietnam rehabilitating rural roads increased the availability of food, boosted wages for agricultural workers, raised completion rates of primary school students, and lifted more than 200,000 people out of poverty (Calderon and Servin 2008).

Timely and affordable delivery of basic services for health, education, water, and sanitation depends on transportation systems. There is a clear association between infant, child, and maternal mortality rates and distance to health care services. Some 40–60 percent of people in developing countries live more than 8 kilometers from a health care facility. In Morocco the number of visits to primary health care facilities doubled in areas with an expanded rural road network compared with a control area. In Pakistan women in villages without an all-weather road have less access to health services (figure 5a).

Improved and affordable transportation systems and safer roads raise school attendance by reducing travel time from home to school. Better accessibility also makes it easier to hire teachers who commute between rural and urban areas. In the Philippines school enrollment rose 10 percent and dropout rates fell 55 percent after rural roads were built. A similar project in Morocco raised girls' enrollments from 28 percent to 68 percent in less than 10 years.

Transportation services contribute strongly to growth and poverty reduction, but emissions from the transport sector have a deleterious impact on the health and environmental MDG targets. The transport sector generates about 13 percent of global greenhouse gas emissions. Transport policy measures can reduce emissions through greater use of railways and inland waterways for freight, better urban public transport services, management of urban road traffic demand to reduce congestion, support of nonmotorized transport, and management of vehicle emissions. Improving energy efficiency in

transport has added benefits for development—more energy savings, less local air pollution, greater energy security, more employment in local industry, and greater competitiveness from higher productivity. Many countries are setting targets and policies for clean energy technologies. China has achieved a vehicle fuel economy standard of 35 miles per gallon of gas and plans to be the world leader in electric vehicles.

Water and sanitation services promote health, increase productivity, and raise school enrollment. Water and sanitation are crucial for promoting health, enabling people to work productively, and contributing to human dignity and social development. Worldwide, more than 1.1 billion people lack clean water, and about 2.6 billion lack access to basic sanitation. About 90 percent of diarrhea cases are attributable to inadequate sanitation, hygiene, and water supply, causing 1.7 million deaths a year, mostly in children under age 5.

Water and sanitation services at home and in schools increase learning capacity because students are healthier. School attendance also rises for girls if they can spend less time fetching water and if separate sanitation facilities are provided in schools. In a village in Morocco girls' primary school attendance more than doubled a year after a new water supply system began operating, with separate sanitation facilities for girls. An improved water quality project for Uganda's small towns reduced water-borne diseases and benefited women and children by saving time associated with collecting water (World Bank 2007b).

The number of countries that are off track to meet the sanitation MDG target is second only to the number off track in reducing child mortality. Investment in water and sanitation with private participation remains low compared with other infrastructure sectors, accounting for about 2–3 percent of investment in infrastructure (figure 5b).

Information and communication technologies reach into all sectors to improve living conditions. Information and communication technologies (ICTs) are enabling tools used in all sectors, ranging from telecommunication infrastructure (voice, data, and media services) to information applications in banking and finance, land management, education, health, and electronic government services. ICT use has grown

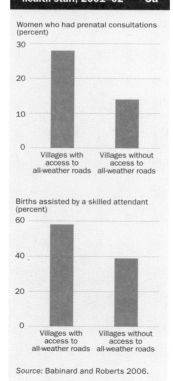

Pakistani women without access to an all-weather road have fewer prenatal consultations and fewer births attended by skilled health staff, 2001–02   5a

Women who had prenatal consultations (percent)

Births assisted by a skilled attendant (percent)

Source: Babinard and Roberts 2006.

dramatically since 2000—mobile cellular subscriptions in developing countries increased from 220 million to about 2.9 billion by the end of 2008. Worldwide, more than 1.5 billion people have access to the Internet. But even within the same region, access is uneven. In 2008 mobile phone penetration was about 60 percent in Equatorial Guinea, the Gambia, and Mauritania but just 4 percent in Eritrea and Ethiopia.

There is a strong association between ICT adoption (such as mobile phones and Internet access) and GDP growth. Mobile communications have a particularly important impact in rural areas, home to half the world's population and 75 percent of poor people. The mobility, ease of use, and relatively low and declining rollout costs of wireless technologies enable them to reach rural populations with low incomes and literacy rates. Farmers with mobile phones are more likely to have better information on market prices and therefore to get better prices from traders. For farmers in rural areas of the Philippines, having a mobile phone increased income 11–17 percent during 2003–06. India's e-Choupal program, which expanded broadband to millions of small farmers through centers set up by a large agricultural exporter, enabled farmers to access information on local weather, crop prices, and farming techniques, increasing productivity and incomes (World Bank 2009l).

Information and communication technologies also contribute to women's economic opportunities. In the Philippines 65 percent of professional and technical workers in ICT-enabled services are women. Information and communication technologies can improve health outcomes and combat diseases. In rural Niger the number of emergency evacuations from outlying health centers to the district hospital increased from 10 to 197 following the introduction of a radio-ambulance system. Good communications and information sharing help to deliver diagnostic information and drugs and to spread information on reproductive health and communicable diseases. Through the Global Media AIDS Initiative more than 50 broadcast networks are promoting AIDS prevention messages. In the fight against malaria satellite monitoring identifies and targets mosquito breeding areas for control.

Information and communication technologies are also used for early disaster warning and for mitigation and relief following natural disasters. Remote sensing is used in managing resources

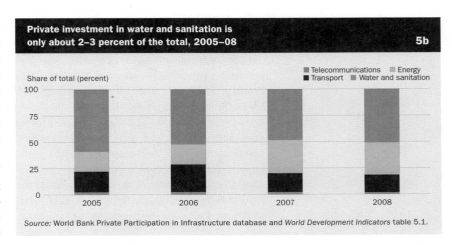

Private investment in water and sanitation is only about 2–3 percent of the total, 2005–08 5b

Share of total (percent)

■ Telecommunications ■ Energy
■ Transport ■ Water and sanitation

Source: World Bank Private Participation in Infrastructure database and *World Development Indicators* table 5.1.

and monitoring environmental risks. Telecommuting and attending virtual meetings through video conferencing can reduce travel and energy use, helping lower greenhouse gases. Smart grids and building construction using information and communication technologies lower energy consumption and greenhouse gases, leading to a more sustainable environment and way of life.

Bridging the infrastructure gap through public and private financing and better management of infrastructure services

Meeting the world's infrastructure needs involves enormous challenges. More than 1.1 billion people do not have safe water to drink and 2.6 billion lack access to adequate sanitation services. Some 1.6 billion have no electricity in their homes. And 1 billion rural residents live more than 2 kilometers from an all-weather road. World Bank Enterprise Surveys, completed in more than 100 countries, find that the three main deterrents to private investment are the regulatory environment, access to finance, and infrastructure. In many developing countries inadequate infrastructure constrains businesses as much as crime, red tape, corruption, and underdeveloped financial markets. In South Asia and Sub-Saharan Africa more than half of firms report that lack of reliable electricity is a major constraint to doing business (figure 5c).

Job creation and economic growth in the private sector require a supportive investment climate. Developing countries need about $900 billion (7–9 percent of GDP) to maintain existing infrastructure and to build new infrastructure, but only half that amount is available. The global financial and economic crisis is expected to severely curtail infrastructure services as governments face shrinking budgets and declining private financial flows. Capital market financing for developing country infrastructure has contracted from $200 billion in 2007 to $135 billion in 2008, with a further decline expected for 2009 (World Bank 2009j).

As budgets shrink, priorities are to protect poor and vulnerable groups by strengthening social safety nets and supporting economic growth. But there is also a need to invest in infrastructure, which can create jobs and lay the groundwork for productivity and growth. Infrastructure spending can provide an important

countercyclical stimulus by increasing demand and employment while supporting longer term growth. Over time, inadequate infrastructure slows economic development and poverty reduction. During a crisis countries under financial stress often cut infrastructure more than other government spending. In Latin America and the Caribbean during the fiscal austerity of the 1980s and 1990s, half the fiscal adjustment came from cuts in public infrastructure, reducing long-term growth by 1–3 percent (Schwartz, Andres, and Dragoiu 2009).

The World Bank has focused its response to the crisis on protecting the most vulnerable groups, maintaining long-term infrastructure investment, and supporting private sector–led economic growth, microfinance, and employment creation, especially among small and medium-size enterprises. The World Bank Infrastructure Recovery and Assets platform mobilizes finance to support infrastructure spending critical for growth. The International Finance Corporation's Infrastructure Crisis Facility supports and refinances public-private partnerships at risk; it is investing about $300 million to mobilize $1.5–$10 billion from other sources.

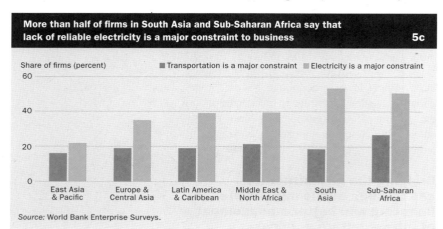

More than half of firms in South Asia and Sub-Saharan Africa say that lack of reliable electricity is a major constraint to business **5c**

Share of firms (percent) — ■ Transportation is a major constraint ■ Electricity is a major constraint

Source: World Bank Enterprise Surveys.

Regional collaboration in infrastructure— the Greater Mekong Subregion program **5d**

In East Asia and Pacific, where countries are increasingly interconnected through land, sea, and air transportation networks, national economic development plans are often supplemented by regional and subregional programs. With support from the Asian Development Bank since 1992 and the World Bank since 2007, Greater Mekong Subregion countries (Cambodia, China, Lao PDR, Myanmar, Thailand, and Vietnam) have established priority transport corridors, laid the groundwork for power interconnection and trade, and developed an information superhighway network. These projects have improved market access, increased trade and investment, and enabled businesses to take advantage of regional and global production chains.

Governments can leverage the benefits of private investment in infrastructure by introducing competition. Regional collaboration on infrastructure projects, by sharing scarce resources such as energy, capital, knowledge, and services, can lower unit costs, improve international competitiveness, and increase connectivity (box 5d). Private companies can better manage infrastructure services by operating efficiently (improving bill collection, reducing corruption and red tape, improving labor productivity, reducing transmission losses) and getting infrastructure prices right (prices should also cover basic operations and maintenance). If countries in Sub-Saharan Africa addressed these inefficiencies, the funding required to close the infrastructure gap might be halved.

Despite the financial crisis, private sector investment in infrastructure remains strong. Commitments to infrastructure projects with private participation fell in 2008, but they were still at the second highest level since 1990. In 48 low- and middle-income economies, 216 projects reached financial or contractual closure. Infrastructure investments, including new commitments for projects implemented in previous years, totaled $154.4 billion in 2008. Investment grew in all developing country regions

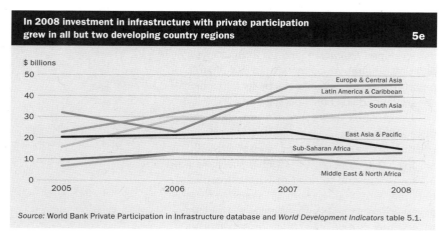

In 2008 investment in infrastructure with private participation grew in all but two developing country regions **5e**

$ billions

Europe & Central Asia
Latin America & Caribbean
South Asia
East Asia & Pacific
Sub-Saharan Africa
Middle East & North Africa

Source: World Bank Private Participation in Infrastructure database and *World Development Indicators* table 5.1.

except East Asia and Pacific and the Middle East and North Africa. But there were large disparities. Five countries accounted for almost half the investment in infrastructure with private participation over 1990–2008—Brazil, India, China, Mexico, and the Russian Federation (figures 5e and 5f).

Telecommunications was the only infrastructure sector with increasing investment in 2008, up 1 percent over 2007. Investment was down 7 percent in energy, 10 percent in transport, and 27 percent in water and sanitation. Over 1990–2008 water and sanitation had the lowest share of infrastructure investment with private participation, attracting only 4.4 percent (World Bank Private Participation in Infrastructure Project Database 2008) (figures 5g and 5h).

Special focus on Africa's infrastructure

With 15 landlocked countries, transport costs in Sub-Saharan Africa are high, hampering trade and slowing growth. Sub-Saharan Africa also has the lowest population density and the second lowest urbanization rate of all developing country regions, raising the cost of infrastructure investments. Not surprisingly, Africa has a major infrastructure deficit—unreliable power supplies, only about 12 percent of roads paved, and the lowest rates of access to water and sanitation among developing country regions. Sub-Saharan Africa is farthest behind in achieving the MDGs and is expected to fall short of meeting most targets related to poverty, health, education, and water and sanitation—which all depend on infrastructure services.

Inadequate infrastructure in Sub-Saharan Africa also contributes to the region's poor economic performance and competitiveness. Business managers report that the main infrastructure deficiencies hampering business activity are electricity (48 percent), transportation (25 percent), and telecommunications (22 percent). Improvements in infrastructure sectors, such as rural roads in Guinea, have raised incomes and increased food supplies for farming families, reducing poverty and hunger.

Expanding information and communications services in Sub-Saharan Africa is connecting the region to the rest of the world and is a key factor in fostering long-term growth. Many governments are beginning to provide affordable ICT services more broadly. Mobile phones, used in all walks of

life (by farmers to receive crop price information and health workers to increase the effectiveness and reach of health programs), increased almost 20-fold on a per capita subscription basis over 2000–08. In 2008 almost a third of Sub-Saharan Africa's people had mobile phone subscriptions. Despite this impressive expansion, a "digital divide" remains: Eritrea has 2 subscriptions per 100 people while South Africa has more than 90.

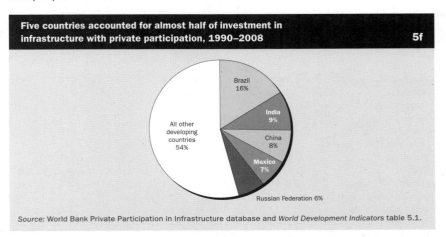

Five countries accounted for almost half of investment in infrastructure with private participation, 1990–2008   **5f**

Source: World Bank Private Participation in Infrastructure database and *World Development Indicators* table 5.1.

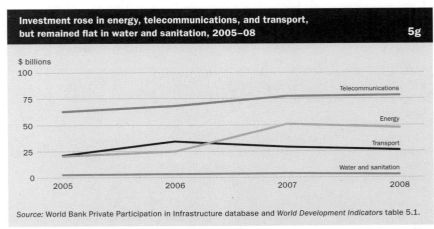

Investment rose in energy, telecommunications, and transport, but remained flat in water and sanitation, 2005–08   **5g**

Source: World Bank Private Participation in Infrastructure database and *World Development Indicators* table 5.1.

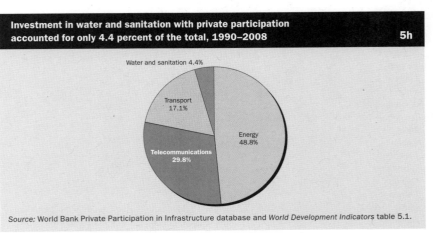

Investment in water and sanitation with private participation accounted for only 4.4 percent of the total, 1990–2008   **5h**

Source: World Bank Private Participation in Infrastructure database and *World Development Indicators* table 5.1.

	Investment commitments in infrastructure projects with private participation[a] $ millions								Domestic credit to private sector	Businesses registered	
	Telecommunications		Energy		Transport		Water and sanitation		% of GDP	New	Total
	2000–05	2006–08	2000–05	2006–08	2000–05	2006–08	2000–05	2006–08	2008	2007	2007
Afghanistan	466.1	980.4	1.6	..	..	..	..	..	8.9	..	..
Albania	569.2	331.0	790.6	..	308.0	..	8.0	0.0	36.0	2,176	16,110
Algeria	3,422.5	1,527.0	962.0	2,320.0	120.9	161.0	510.0	1,104.0	13.5	10,662	105,128
Angola	278.7	775.0	45.0	9.4	..	53.0	..	..	12.5	..	..
Argentina	5,836.8	3,714.2	3,826.9	3,126.5	203.6	1,396.7	791.6	..	13.7	16,400	218,700
Armenia	317.1	214.6	74.0	57.0	63.0	585.0	0.0	0.0	17.4	3,822	56,461
Australia	..	..	..	..	..	..	..	..	121.5	89,960	641,538
Austria	..	..	..	..	..	..	..	..	119.1	3,484	76,374
Azerbaijan	355.6	1,075.6	375.2	..	..	..	0.0	..	16.5	4,945	69,309
Bangladesh	1,294.3	3,357.8	501.5	48.8	0.0	0.0	..	..	39.2	5,328	67,459
Belarus	735.4	2,011.3	..	..	..	4.0	..	..	28.8	..	..
Belgium	..	..	..	..	..	..	..	..	94.5	28,016	354,489
Benin	116.9	272.7	590.0	..	..	..	..	..	20.9	..	..
Bolivia	520.5	247.3	884.4	137.3	16.6	..	..	..	34.7	1,625	24,649
Bosnia and Herzegovina	0.0	916.0	..	800.0	..	..	..	..	57.8	314	23,634
Botswana	104.0	97.9	..	..	..	..	..	..	21.1	7,301	..
Brazil	41,053.8	21,365.2	25,625.6	17,490.8	4,469.3	10,625.9	1,215.3	1,507.5	55.7	490,542	5,668,003
Bulgaria	2,179.1	1,526.8	3,062.1	1,547.8	2.1	531.6	152.0	..	74.5	49,328	315,037
Burkina Faso	41.9	487.6	..	..	..	..	..	..	18.6	639	..
Burundi	53.6	0.0	..	..	..	..	..	..	21.5	..	..
Cambodia	136.1	205.9	82.1	695.8	125.3	200.0	..	..	23.5	..	..
Cameroon	394.4	423.4	91.8	440.0	0.0	..	..	0.0	10.4	..	..
Canada	..	..	..	..	..	..	..	..	128.4	207,000	2,500,000
Central African Republic	0.0	14.8	..	..	..	..	..	..	7.0	..	..
Chad	11.0	178.4	0.0	..	..	..	..	..	3.7	..	..
Chile	3,561.6	3,060.2	1,590.5	1,370.8	4,821.2	830.1	1,495.2	3.1	97.7	25,124	223,345
China	8,548.0	0.0	10,970.9	4,075.5	15,350.1	13,320.1	3,505.2	3,904.8	108.3	..	..
Hong Kong SAR, China	..	..	..	..	..	..	..	..	142.8	80,935	524,445
Colombia	1,570.9	4,395.0	351.6	709.7	1,005.4	2,344.4	314.3	305.0	34.2	28,801	497,778
Congo, Dem. Rep.	473.4	729.0	..	..	..	..	..	..	7.1	..	..
Congo, Rep.	61.8	220.7	..	..	..	735.0	0.0	..	3.5	237	..
Costa Rica	..	..	80.0	80.0	465.2	373.0	..	..	50.8	10,567	102,311
Côte d'Ivoire	134.9	567.4	0.0	0.0	176.4	..	..	0.0	16.3	..	..
Croatia	1,205.7	3,035.0	7.1	85.0	451.0	492.0	298.7	..	64.9	11,055	200,955
Cuba	60.0	0.0	116.0	60.0	0.0	..	600.0	..	..	..	..
Czech Republic	..	..	..	..	..	..	..	..	52.8	16,395	244,417
Denmark	..	..	..	..	..	..	..	..	218.0	28,811	200,060
Dominican Republic	393.0	110.1	1,306.6	0.0	898.9	250.0	..	..	20.9	..	20,808
Ecuador	357.8	1,505.6	302.0	129.0	685.0	1,166.0	500.0	..	26.1	3,196	37,434
Egypt, Arab Rep.	3,471.9	7,073.0	678.0	469.0	821.5	1,370.0	..	..	42.9	9,595	367,559
El Salvador	1,110.6	822.1	85.0	0.0	..	..	..	..	41.3	1,802	..
Eritrea	40.0	0.0	..	..	..	..	..	..	18.4	..	..
Estonia	..	..	..	..	..	..	..	..	97.4	..	..
Ethiopia	..	..	..	..	..	..	..	..	18.0	..	..
Finland	..	..	..	..	..	..	..	..	85.8	10,424	120,294
France	..	..	..	..	..	..	..	..	107.8	137,481	1,267,419
Gabon	26.6	187.8	0.0	0.0	177.4	3.9	..	..	8.5	..	..
Gambia, The	6.6	35.0	..	0.0	..	..	..	..	17.6	..	..
Georgia	173.8	564.7	40.0	607.3	..	573.0	..	435.0	33.3	5,260	59,641
Germany	..	..	..	..	..	..	..	..	107.8	66,747	573,985
Ghana	156.5	2,069.0	590.0	100.0	10.0	..	0.0	..	17.8	..	..
Greece	..	..	..	..	..	..	..	..	93.5	..	..
Guatemala	560.1	1,305.1	110.0	263.8	..	..	..	6.7	27.2	4,251	..
Guinea	50.6	155.2	..	..	..	..	..	..	9.1	..	..
Guinea-Bissau	21.9	68.4	..	..	..	..	..	..		..	..
Haiti	18.0	306.0	5.5	..	..	..	..	..	12.1	9	300
Honduras	135.0	653.9	358.8	..	120.0	..	207.9	..	51.4	..	..

	Investment commitments in infrastructure projects with private participation[a]								Domestic credit to private sector	Businesses registered	
	$ millions										
	Telecommunications		Energy		Transport		Water and sanitation		% of GDP	New	Total
	2000–05	2006–08	2000–05	2006–08	2000–05	2006–08	2000–05	2006–08	2008	2007	2007
Hungary	5,172.8	1,523.3	851.6	1,707.0	3,297.5	1,588.0	0.0	0.0	69.6	28,153	273,549
India	20,642.0	24,702.2	8,369.2	28,507.7	4,281.3	19,009.2	112.9	218.2	51.4	20,000	732,000
Indonesia	6,557.2	8,068.7	1,828.5	3,779.3	159.2	1,433.9	44.8	20.2	26.5	18,960	271,255
Iran, Islamic Rep.	695.0	1,023.0	650.0	..	..	..	..	..	49.2	..	..
Iraq	984.0	4,074.0	..	590.0	..	..	..	..	..	..	..
Ireland	..	..	..	..	..	..	..	..	217.0	18,704	180,891
Israel	..	..	..	..	..	..	..	..	90.1	18,814	162,910
Italy	..	..	..	..	..	..	..	..	105.1	77,587	638,987
Jamaica	700.3	241.2	201.0	78.0	565.0	..	..	..	28.3	2,023	54,116
Japan	..	..	..	..	..	..	..	..	163.5	145,151	2,572,088
Jordan	1,589.0	484.6	..	524.0	0.0	1,380.0	169.0	..	83.8	2,361	..
Kazakhstan	1,153.7	2,619.8	300.0	0.0	231.0	31.0	..	..	49.6	..	..
Kenya	1,434.0	2,695.8	..	306.7	..	404.0	..	..	30.0	7,371	125,102
Korea, Dem. Rep.	..	400.0	..	..	..	..	..	..	..	..	..
Korea, Rep.	..	..	..	..	..	..	..	..	109.1	..	..
Kosovo	..	..	..	..	..	..	..	..	34.3	..	..
Kuwait	..	..	..	..	..	..	..	..	66.4	..	..
Kyrgyz Republic	11.5	115.9	..	..	..	..	0.0	..	15.1	3,987	..
Lao PDR	87.7	10.0	1,250.0	1,465.0	0.0	..	..	..	9.5	..	..
Latvia	700.0	428.1	71.1	..	..	135.0	..	..	90.2	12,017	..
Lebanon	138.1	0.0	..	..	153.0	..	0.0	..	75.9	1,030	..
Lesotho	88.4	19.6	0.0	..	..	..	..	..	10.9	..	..
Liberia	70.3	49.8	..	..	..	..	..	..	12.5	..	..
Libya	..	..	..	..	..	..	..	..	6.8	..	..
Lithuania	993.0	489.2	514.3	350.6	..	..	..	..	62.7	6,578	67,095
Macedonia, FYR	706.6	256.6	..	391.0	..	295.0	..	..	43.8	..	..
Madagascar	12.6	221.8	0.0	..	61.0	17.5	..	..	11.1	1,234	19,305
Malawi	36.3	124.7	0.0	..	..	..	..	..	11.4	420	5,595
Malaysia	3,777.0	1,494.0	6,637.6	203.0	4,263.0	1,379.0	6,502.2	0.0	100.6	43,279	..
Mali	82.6	154.0	365.9	..	55.4	..	..	..	17.1	..	..
Mauritania	92.1	90.1	..	..	..	..	..	..	..	..	..
Mauritius	413.0	67.1	0.0	..	..	..	..	0.0	87.7	..	..
Mexico	18,191.4	9,278.7	6,749.3	1,883.0	2,970.4	10,113.5	523.7	303.8	21.1	306,400	4,290,000
Moldova	46.1	278.3	127.2	434.0	0.0	60.0	..	..	36.5	6,806	73,532
Mongolia	22.1	0.0	..	..	..	..	..	..	43.6	..	..
Morocco	6,139.5	2,309.6	1,049.0	..	200.0	200.0	..	..	77.4	24,811	..
Mozambique	123.0	104.2	1,205.8	..	334.6	0.0	..	..	18.4	..	..
Myanmar	..	..	..	556.1	..	..	..	..	..	..	..
Namibia	35.0	8.5	1.0	..	..	..	0.0	..	45.6	..	..
Nepal	109.3	26.0	15.1	..	..	..	..	..	40.8	..	..
Netherlands	..	..	..	..	..	..	..	..	193.2	116,000	1,030,000
New Zealand	..	..	..	..	..	..	..	..	150.4	74,247	474,212
Nicaragua	218.5	327.2	126.3	95.0	104.0	..	..	..	36.4	2,070	..
Niger	85.5	164.7	..	..	..	..	3.4	..	11.0	..	..
Nigeria	6,949.7	8,291.1	1,920.0	280.0	2,355.4	644.1	..	..	33.9	..	..
Norway	..	..	..	..	..	..	..	..	..	18,082	132,788
Oman	..	..	..	..	..	..	..	..	35.9	6,362	38,864
Pakistan	6,595.1	7,868.4	375.4	2,578.7	153.8	923.7	..	..	29.5	4,840	..
Panama	211.4	1,141.5	429.8	495.7	51.4	..	..	..	89.7	..	..
Papua New Guinea	..	150.0	..	..	..	..	..	..	24.8	..	..
Paraguay	199.0	498.5	..	..	..	..	..	..	24.5	..	..
Peru	2,241.4	1,959.4	2,498.9	743.8	522.5	2,329.8	152.0	..	24.8	..	..
Philippines	4,616.4	3,353.0	3,428.4	5,076.8	943.5	515.3	0.0	503.9	28.8	18,189	..
Poland	16,800.1	6,158.7	2,555.5	1,410.4	1,672.0	1,439.3	64.3	0.8	49.8	26,388	523,584
Portugal	..	..	..	..	..	..	..	..	179.7	30,934	423,719
Puerto Rico	..	..	..	..	..	..	..	..	..	..	..
Qatar	..	..	..	..	..	..	..	..	46.7	..	..

	Investment commitments in infrastructure projects with private participation[a]								Domestic credit to private sector	Businesses registered	
	$ millions										
	Telecommunications		Energy		Transport		Water and sanitation		% of GDP	New	Total
	2000–05	2006–08	2000–05	2006–08	2000–05	2006–08	2000–05	2006–08	2008	2007	2007
Romania	3,793.9	4,921.5	1,240.8	4,090.5	..	116.8	116.0	41.0	38.5	103,733	870,195
Russian Federation	22,049.4	20,675.1	1,726.0	25,376.2	109.4	191.0	904.7	1,212.3	41.0	489,955	3,267,325
Rwanda	72.3	168.0	1.6	..	..	..	..	..	..	..	455
Saudi Arabia	..	..	..	..	..	..	..	..	55.4	..	..
Senegal	593.1	1,077.0	93.3	..	55.4	134.0	0.0	0.0	24.2	23	1,000
Serbia	563.5	3,107.4	..	..	..	..	0.0	..	38.4	10,876	83,499
Sierra Leone	48.8	88.2	..	1.2	..	..	..	..	7.1	..	..
Singapore	..	..	..	..	..	..	..	..	107.9	25,904	133,235
Slovak Republic	..	..	..	..	..	..	..	..	44.7	16,025	135,330
Slovenia	..	..	..	..	..	..	..	..	85.6	4,957	47,312
Somalia	13.4	0.0	..	..	..	..	..	..	..	..	..
South Africa	10,519.5	5,327.0	1,251.3	9.9	504.7	3,483.0	31.3	0.0	145.2	41,356	553,425
Spain	..	..	..	..	..	..	..	..	201.4	145,593	2,435,689
Sri Lanka	766.1	1,024.4	270.8	..	..	..	..	..	28.9	4,529	..
Sudan	747.7	1,391.3	..	..	..	30.0	..	120.7	10.9	..	..
Swaziland	27.7	23.3	..	..	..	..	..	..	23.6	..	..
Sweden	..	..	..	..	..	..	..	..	129.6	27,994	326,052
Switzerland	..	..	..	..	..	..	..	..	168.2	18,284	162,326
Syrian Arab Republic	583.0	199.7	..	..	..	37.0	..	..	15.6	216	2,268
Tajikistan	8.5	64.0	16.0	..	..	..	..	..	29.0	794	..
Tanzania	515.3	962.5	348.0	28.4	27.7	134.0	8.5	..	16.3	3,933	59,163
Thailand	5,602.7	2,567.0	4,693.3	2,341.0	939.0	..	522.7	18.8	113.1	25,184	297,084
Timor-Leste	0.0	0.0	..	..	..	..	..	..	20.6	..	..
Togo	0.0	0.0	657.7	190.0	..	..	..	..	18.7	..	..
Trinidad and Tobago	..	..	..	..	..	..	..	..	28.9	..	..
Tunisia	751.0	2,518.0	30.0	..	..	840.0	..	..	66.6	6,675	63,584
Turkey	12,788.6	8,160.7	6,754.8	3,762.7	3,118.6	4,441.0	..	..	32.6	93,634	764,240
Turkmenistan	20.0	106.1	..	..	..	..	..	..	..	..	..
Uganda	387.6	1,180.0	113.9	964.6	..	404.0	0.0	..	13.9	8,906	89,503
Ukraine	3,162.9	3,574.8	160.0	..	..	..	100.0	..	73.7	41,809	528,864
United Arab Emirates	..	..	..	..	..	..	..	..	72.7	..	..
United Kingdom	..	..	..	..	..	..	..	..	211.1	449,700	2,546,200
United States	..	..	..	..	..	..	..	..	187.1	676,830	5,156,000
Uruguay	114.2	113.8	330.0	..	251.1	..	368.0	..	26.3	..	..
Uzbekistan	285.6	680.9	..	..	..	25.0	0.0	..	..	10,264	56,465
Venezuela, RB	3,337.0	2,074.0	39.5	..	34.0	..	15.0	..	21.5	..	..
Vietnam	430.0	1,326.7	2,360.6	287.0	20.0	765.0	174.0	..	90.6	..	52,506
West Bank and Gaza	279.8	0.0	150.0	..	..	..	..	..	..	..	..
Yemen, Rep.	376.8	342.2	..	15.8	..	220.0	..	..	7.8	50	..
Zambia	208.3	510.0	3.0	..	15.6	..	0.0	..	15.3	5,300	..
Zimbabwe	72.0	143.0	..	..	..	..	..	..	..	..	..
World	.. s	.. s	.. s	.. s	.. s	.. s	.. s	.. s	**129.7 w**		
Low income	8,043.3	19,559.7	8,201.6	4,659.3	705.4	2,303.5	185.9	0.0	36.5		
Middle income	243,326.2	196,510.7	106,361.7	116,921.3	53,504.4	83,650.3	18,975.5	9,705.6	62.6		
Lower middle income	84,659.7	88,720.8	38,070.8	50,571.3	26,894.4	43,175.4	5,220.1	5,228.2	82.6		
Upper middle income	158,666.6	107,789.9	68,290.9	66,350.1	26,610.0	40,474.9	13,755.5	4,477.4	44.6		
Low & middle income	251,369.6	216,070.4	114,563.3	121,580.7	54,209.9	85,953.8	19,161.4	9,705.6	61.9		
East Asia & Pacific	29,862.2	17,755.8	31,258.4	18,479.5	21,800.1	17,613.3	10,748.9	4,447.7	99.8		
Europe & Central Asia	67,661.7	58,420.5	17,807.6	38,827.4	5,504.1	8,427.7	1,345.0	1,689.1	43.0		
Latin America & Carib.	80,834.5	53,217.6	45,116.5	26,889.7	17,221.2	29,429.3	6,232.5	2,126.1	38.8		
Middle East & N. Africa	18,430.6	19,551.1	3,519.0	3,918.8	1,475.4	4,508.0	679.0	1,104.0	35.8		
South Asia	29,926.2	37,976.7	9,533.6	31,135.2	4,435.1	19,932.9	112.9	218.2	49.5		
Sub-Saharan Africa	24,654.4	29,148.6	7,328.3	2,330.2	3,774.1	6,042.5	43.2	120.7	58.5		
High income	..	..	..	..	..	..	..	..	155.9		
Euro area	..	..	..	..	..	..	..	..	126.4		

a. Data refer to total for the period shown. Includes infrastructure projects with private sector participation that reached financial closure in 1990–2008.

About the data

Private sector development and investment—tapping private sector initiative and investment for socially useful purposes—are critical for poverty reduction. In parallel with public sector efforts, private investment, especially in competitive markets, has tremendous potential to contribute to growth. Private markets are the engine of productivity growth, creating productive jobs and higher incomes. And with government playing a complementary role of regulation, funding, and service provision, private initiative and investment can help provide the basic services and conditions that empower poor people—by improving health, education, and infrastructure.

Investment in infrastructure projects with private participation has made important contributions to easing fiscal constraints, improving the efficiency of infrastructure services, and extending delivery to poor people. Developing countries have been in the forefront, pioneering better approaches to infrastructure services and reaping the benefits of greater competition and customer focus.

The data on investment in infrastructure projects with private participation refer to all investment (public and private) in projects in which a private company assumes operating risk during the operating period or development and operating risk during the contract period. Investment refers to commitments not disbursements. Foreign state-owned companies are considered private entities for the purposes of this measure.

Investments are classified into two types: investments in physical assets—the resources a company commits to invest in expanding and modernizing facilities—and payments to the government to acquire state-owned enterprises or rights to provide services in a specific area or to use part of the radio spectrum.

The data are from the World Bank's Private Participation in Infrastructure (PPI) Project database, which tracks infrastructure projects with private participation in developing countries. It provides information on more than 4,300 infrastructure projects in 137 developing economies from 1984 to 2008. The database contains more than 30 fields per project record, including country, financial closure year, infrastructure services provided, type of private participation, investment, technology, capacity, project location, contract duration, private sponsors, bidding process, and development bank support. Data on the projects are compiled from publicly available information. The database aims to be as comprehensive as possible, but some projects—particularly those involving local

and small-scale operators—may be omitted because they are not publicly reported. The database is a joint product of the World Bank's Finance, Economics, and Urban Development Department and the Public-Private Infrastructure Advisory Facility. Geographic and income aggregates are calculated by the World Bank's Development Data Group. For more information, see http://ppi.worldbank.org/.

Credit is an important link in money transmission; it finances production, consumption, and capital formation, which in turn affect economic activity. The data on domestic credit to the private sector are taken from the banking survey of the International Monetary Fund's (IMF) *International Financial Statistics* or, when unavailable, from its monetary survey. The monetary survey includes monetary authorities (the central bank), deposit money banks, and other banking institutions, such as finance companies, development banks, and savings and loan institutions. Credit to the private sector may sometimes include credit to state-owned or partially state-owned enterprises.

Entrepreneurship is essential to the dynamism of the modern market economy, and a greater entry rate of new businesses can foster competition and economic growth. The table includes data on business registrations from the 2008 World Bank Group Entrepreneurship Survey, which includes entrepreneurial activity in more than 100 countries for 2000–08. Survey data are used to analyze firm creation, its relationship to economic growth and poverty reduction, and the impact of regulatory and institutional reforms. The 2008 survey improves on earlier surveys' methodology and country coverage for better cross-country comparability. Data on total and newly registered businesses were collected directly from national registrars of companies. For cross-country comparability, only limited liability corporations that operate in the formal sector are included. For additional information on sources, methodology, calculation of entrepreneurship rates, and data limitations see http://econ.worldbank.org/research/entrepreneurship.

Definitions

• **Investment commitments in infrastructure projects with private participation** refers to infrastructure projects in telecommunications, energy (electricity and natural gas transmission and distribution), transport, and water and sanitation that have reached financial closure and directly or indirectly serve the public. Incinerators, movable assets, standalone solid waste projects, and small projects such as windmills are excluded. Included are operation and management contracts, operation and management contracts with major capital expenditure, greenfield projects (new facilities built and operated by a private entity or a public-private joint venture), and divestitures. Investment commitments are the sum of investments in facilities and investments in government assets. Investments in facilities are resources the project company commits to invest during the contract period in new facilities or in expansion and modernization of existing facilities. Investments in government assets are the resources the project company spends on acquiring government assets such as state-owned enterprises, rights to provide services in a specific area, or use of specific radio spectrums. • **Domestic credit to private sector** is financial resources provided to the private sector—such as through loans, purchases of nonequity securities, and trade credits and other accounts receivable—that establish a claim for repayment. For some countries these claims include credit to public enterprises. • **New businesses registered** are the number of limited liability firms registered in the calendar year. • **Total businesses registered** are the year-end stock of total registered limited liability firms.

Data sources

Data on investment commitments in infrastructure projects with private participation are from the World Bank's PPI Project database (http://ppi.worldbank.org). Data on domestic credit are from the IMF's *International Financial Statistics*. Data on business registration and are from the World Bank's Entrepreneurship Survey and database (http://econ.worldbank.org/research/entrepreneurship).

5.2 Business environment: enterprise surveys

	Survey year	Regulations and tax		Permits and licenses	Corruption	Crime	Informality	Gender	Finance	Infrastructure	Innovation	Trade	Workforce
		Time dealing with officials % of management time	Average number of times meeting with tax officials	Time required to obtain operating license days	Informal payments to public officials % of firms	Losses due to theft, robbery, vandalism, and arson % of sales	Firms formally registered when operations started % of firms	Firms with female participation in ownership % of firms	Firms using banks to finance investment % of firms	Value lost due to electrical outages % of sales	Internationally recognized quality certification ownership % of firms	Average time to clear direct exports through customs days	Firms offering formal training % of firms
Afghanistan	2008	6.8	1.2	13.8	41.5	1.5	88.0	2.8	1.4	6.5	8.5	14.6	14.6
Albania	2007	18.7	3.9	21.2	57.7	0.5	89.4	10.8	12.4	13.7	24.6	1.9	19.9
Algeria	2007	25.1	2.3	19.3	64.7	0.9	98.3	15.0	8.9	4.0	5.0	14.1	17.3
Angola	2006	7.1	3.3	24.1	46.8	0.4	..	23.4	2.1	3.7	5.1	16.5	19.4
Argentina	2006	13.8	2.5	116.0	18.7	1.3	93.8	30.3	6.9	1.4	26.9	5.5	52.2
Armenia	2009	10.3	2.1	20.0	11.6	0.6	96.2	31.8	31.9	1.8	26.9	3.3	30.4
Australia		..	..	..	..	..	..	..	..	..	..	..	..
Austria		..	..	..	..	..	..	..	..	..	..	..	..
Azerbaijan	2009	3.0	2.1	15.8	32.0	0.3	85.1	10.8	19.0	1.8	18.2	1.9	10.5
Bangladesh	2007	3.2	1.3	6.0	85.1	0.1	..	16.1	24.7	10.6	7.8	8.4	16.2
Belarus	2008	13.6	1.1	38.2	13.5	0.4	98.5	52.9	35.8	0.8	13.9	2.6	44.4
Belgium		..	..	..	..	..	..	..	..	..	..	..	..
Benin	2009	20.7	1.2	64.3	54.5	1.9	87.9	43.9	4.2	7.5	7.3	9.6	32.4
Bolivia	2006	13.5	1.7	26.0	32.4	0.9	90.5	41.1	22.2	4.4	13.8	15.3	53.9
Bosnia and Herzegovina	2009	11.2	1.0	21.4	8.1	0.2	98.6	32.8	59.7	1.9	30.1	1.4	66.5
Botswana	2006	5.0	0.9	13.7	27.6	1.3	..	40.9	11.3	1.4	12.7	1.4	37.7
Brazil	2009	18.7	1.2	83.5	9.7	1.7	95.8	59.3	48.4	3.0	25.7	15.9	52.9
Bulgaria	2009	10.6	2.2	20.8	8.5	0.5	98.5	33.9	34.7	1.6	19.9	4.2	30.7
Burkina Faso	2009	22.2	1.5	35.8	8.5	0.3	77.7	19.2	25.6	5.8	14.4	7.4	24.8
Burundi	2006	5.7	1.8	27.3	56.5	1.1	..	34.8	12.3	10.7	7.1	..	22.1
Cambodia	2007	5.6	1.0	..	61.2	1.6	87.5	..	11.3	2.4	2.8	1.5	48.4
Cameroon	2009	7.0	4.4	30.0	50.8	1.7	82.1	15.7	31.4	4.9	20.4	15.1	25.5
Canada		..	..	..	..	..	..	..	..	..	..	..	..
Central African Republic		..	..	..	..	..	..	..	..	..	..	..	..
Chad	2009	20.8	3.4	24.3	41.8	2.5	77.1	40.1	4.2	3.3	43.3	11.9	43.4
Chile	2006	9.0	3.0	67.7	8.2	0.6	97.8	27.8	29.1	1.8	22.0	5.8	46.9
China	2003	18.3	14.4	11.6	72.6	0.1	..	..	28.8	1.3	35.9	6.6	84.8
Hong Kong SAR, China		..	..	..	..	..	..	..	..	..	..	..	..
Colombia	2006	14.3	0.6	28.2	8.2	0.7	85.6	43.0	30.6	2.3	5.9	7.0	39.5
Congo, Dem. Rep.	2006	6.3	8.4	17.8	83.8	2.0	..	21.2	3.3	5.6	4.3	3.6	11.4
Congo, Rep.	2009	6.0	2.7	..	49.2	3.3	84.3	31.8	7.7	16.4	19.6	..	37.5
Costa Rica[a]	2005	9.6	0.5	..	33.8	0.4	..	65.3	14.9	1.9	10.5	3.5	46.4
Côte d'Ivoire	2009	1.8	3.6	14.5	30.6	3.4	56.4	61.9	13.9	5.0	4.3	16.6	19.1
Croatia	2007	10.9	0.7	26.5	14.5	0.2	98.1	33.5	60.0	0.8	16.5	1.3	28.0
Cuba		..	..	..	..	..	..	..	..	..	..	..	..
Czech Republic	2009	10.4	1.5	19.9	8.7	0.4	98.0	25.0	33.4	0.6	43.5	5.7	70.7
Denmark		..	..	..	..	..	..	..	..	..	..	..	..
Dominican Republic[a]	2005	8.8	0.5	..	26.3	0.7	..	..	12.5	15.2	9.6	11.4	53.3
Ecuador	2006	17.3	0.6	19.9	21.5	0.9	91.1	32.7	24.0	2.7	18.2	7.0	61.6
Egypt, Arab Rep.	2008	8.8	3.4	90.6	98.3	3.0	14.3	34.0	5.6	3.4	21.1	6.2	21.7
El Salvador	2006	9.2	2.7	35.4	34.3	2.6	79.5	39.6	17.3	2.9	11.0	2.5	49.6
Eritrea	2009	0.5	0.2	..	0.0	..	100.0	4.2	11.9	0.2	15.1	9.6	26.1
Estonia	2009	5.5	0.4	8.3	1.6	0.9	97.4	36.3	41.5	0.5	21.2	1.8	69.3
Ethiopia	2006	3.8	1.1	11.4	12.4	1.4	..	30.9	11.0	0.9	4.2	4.3	38.2
Finland		..	..	..	..	..	..	..	..	..	..	..	..
France		..	..	..	..	..	..	..	..	..	..	..	..
Gabon	2009	2.8	15.2	12.1	26.1	0.4	63.7	33.1	6.3	1.7	18.6	3.8	30.9
Gambia, The	2006	7.3	2.5	8.4	52.4	2.7	..	21.3	7.6	11.8	22.2	5.0	25.6
Georgia	2008	2.1	0.6	11.8	4.1	0.7	99.6	40.8	38.2	1.4	16.0	3.8	14.5
Germany	2005	1.2	1.3	..	..	0.5	..	20.3	45.0		..	4.7	35.4
Ghana	2007	4.0	4.1	6.4	38.8	0.9	66.4	44.0	16.0	6.0	6.8	7.8	33.0
Greece	2005	1.8	1.7	..	21.6	0.0	..	24.4	25.9	..	11.7	5.5	20.0
Guatemala	2006	9.2	2.1	75.4	15.7	1.5	91.3	28.4	12.8	4.5	8.0	4.5	28.1
Guinea	2006	2.7	2.8	13.0	84.8	2.0	..	25.4	0.9	14.0	5.2	4.3	21.1
Guinea-Bissau	2006	2.9	3.4	30.4	62.7	1.1	..	19.9	0.7	5.3	8.4	5.6	12.4
Haiti		..	..	..	..	..	..	..	..	..	..	..	..
Honduras	2006	4.6	1.5	31.6	16.7	2.2	89.4	39.9	8.5	3.8	16.5	6.0	33.3

Business environment: enterprise surveys

	Survey year	Regulations and tax		Permits and licenses	Corruption	Crime	Informality	Gender	Finance	Infrastructure	Innovation	Trade	Workforce
		Time dealing with officials % of management time	Average number of times meeting with tax officials	Time required to obtain operating license days	Informal payments to public officials % of firms	Losses due to theft, robbery, vandalism, and arson % of sales	Firms formally registered when operations started % of firms	Firms with female participation in ownership % of firms	Firms using banks to finance investment % of firms	Value lost due to electrical outages % of sales	Internationally recognized quality certification ownership % of firms	Average time to clear direct exports through customs days	Firms offering formal training % of firms
Hungary	2009	13.5	0.8	35.6	4.0	0.1	100.0	42.4	48.7	0.9	39.4	4.3	14.8
India	2006	6.7	2.6	..	47.5	0.1	..	9.1	46.7	6.6	22.5	15.1	15.9
Indonesia[a]	2003	4.0	1.0	..	44.2	0.2	..	..	34.0	3.3	22.1	3.7	23.8
Iran, Islamic Rep.		..	..	..	..	..	..	..	..	..	..	..	..
Iraq		..	..	..	..	..	..	..	..	..	..	..	..
Ireland	2005	2.3	1.3	..	8.3	0.3	..	41.6	37.4	1.5	17.2	2.6	73.2
Israel		..	..	..	..	..	..	..	..	..	..	..	..
Italy		..	..	..	..	..	..	..	..	..	..	..	..
Jamaica[a]	2005	6.3	1.8	..	17.7	1.1	..	32.2	37.0	11.8	16.4	4.3	53.5
Japan		..	..	..	..	..	..	..	..	..	..	..	..
Jordan	2006	6.7	1.7	6.4	18.1	0.1	..	13.1	8.6	1.7	15.5	3.8	23.9
Kazakhstan	2009	4.7	2.6	30.8	23.3	1.0	97.4	34.4	31.0	3.7	10.8	8.5	40.9
Kenya	2007	5.1	6.7	23.4	79.2	3.9	..	37.1	22.9	6.4	9.8	5.6	40.7
Korea, Dem. Rep.		..	..	..	..	..	..	..	..	..	..	..	..
Korea, Rep.[a]	2005	0.1	2.2	..	14.1	0.0	..	19.1	39.9	..	17.6	7.2	39.5
Kosovo	2009	9.8	4.5	18.8	2.2	0.3	89.2	10.9	25.3	17.1	7.9	1.7	24.6
Kuwait		..	..	..	..	..	..	..	..	..	..	..	..
Kyrgyz Republic	2009	4.9	2.1	18.0	37.5	0.3	95.9	60.4	17.9	10.5	16.2	15.8	29.7
Lao PDR	2009	1.6	4.4	13.6	39.8	0.1	93.5	39.4	0.0	0.0	7.2	7.5	11.1
Latvia	2009	9.7	1.5	11.5	11.3	0.3	98.5	46.3	37.3	1.1	18.2	1.9	43.4
Lebanon	2006	12.0	3.2	..	51.2	0.5	..	27.9	53.5	6.0	20.9	6.7	67.8
Lesotho	2009	5.6	1.8	16.4	14.0	2.9	86.8	18.4	32.7	6.7	24.7	5.4	42.5
Liberia	2009	7.5	6.5	16.0	55.2	2.8	73.8	53.0	10.1	2.9	2.4	0.0	17.0
Libya		..	..	..	..	..	..	..	..	..	..	..	..
Lithuania	2009	9.3	0.8	65.5	8.5	0.4	97.1	38.7	47.4	0.7	15.6	2.4	46.0
Macedonia, FYR	2009	14.5	3.0	33.8	11.5	0.7	99.2	36.4	47.0	5.9	21.5	2.5	19.0
Madagascar	2009	17.1	0.9	41.3	19.2	1.2	97.5	50.0	12.2	7.7	8.7	14.2	27.0
Malawi	2009	3.5	2.7	15.0	10.8	5.7	78.6	23.9	20.6	17.0	17.9	4.9	48.4
Malaysia[a]	2007	7.8	2.6	22.4	..	1.0	53.0	13.1	48.6	3.0	54.1	2.7	50.1
Mali	2007	2.4	1.6	41.0	28.9	0.6	85.4	18.4	7.0	1.8	8.6	4.8	22.5
Mauritania	2006	5.8	1.8	10.7	82.1	0.6	..	17.3	3.2	1.6	5.9	3.9	25.5
Mauritius	2009	9.4	0.5	19.1	1.6	1.4	84.2	16.9	37.5	2.2	11.1	10.3	25.6
Mexico	2006	20.5	0.6	11.2	22.6	0.7	94.1	24.8	2.6	2.4	20.3	5.2	24.6
Moldova	2009	7.0	1.9	13.9	25.4	0.4	97.9	53.1	30.8	2.0	9.1	2.4	33.1
Mongolia	2009	12.1	2.0	43.5	30.4	0.6	90.1	52.0	26.5	0.8	16.7	18.6	61.2
Morocco	2007	11.4	0.9	3.4	13.4	0.0	86.0	13.1	12.3	1.3	17.3	1.8	24.7
Mozambique	2007	3.3	1.9	35.2	14.8	1.8	85.9	24.4	10.5	2.4	18.7	10.1	22.1
Myanmar		..	..	..	..	..	..	..	..	..	..	..	..
Namibia	2006	2.9	0.3	9.6	11.4	1.3	..	33.4	8.1	0.7	17.6	1.4	44.5
Nepal	2009	6.5	1.3	14.5	15.2	0.9	94.0	27.4	17.5	27.0	3.1	5.6	8.8
Netherlands		..	..	..	..	..	..	..	..	..	..	..	..
New Zealand		..	..	..	..	..	..	..	..	..	..	..	..
Nicaragua	2006	9.3	1.3	19.7	17.2	0.9	85.4	41.4	13.0	8.7	18.7	5.0	28.9
Niger	2009	21.1	1.6	39.7	35.2	0.9	90.5	17.6	9.3	1.9	4.6	2.6	32.1
Nigeria	2007	6.1	3.0	12.1	40.9	4.1	..	20.0	2.7	8.9	8.5	7.5	25.7
Norway		..	..	..	..	..	..	..	..	..	..	..	..
Oman		..	4.4	11.8	33.2	..	..	..	31.0	4.2	10.8	3.4	20.9
Pakistan[a]	2007	2.2	1.6	16.4	27.2	0.5	..	6.7	9.7	9.9	9.6	4.8	6.7
Panama	2006	10.3	1.4	41.2	25.4	0.5	98.0	37.1	19.2	2.4	14.7	5.7	43.9
Papua New Guinea		..	..	..	..	..	..	..	..	..	..	..	..
Paraguay	2006	7.9	0.7	37.8	84.8	0.9	94.0	44.8	8.2	2.5	7.1	5.5	46.9
Peru	2006	13.5	1.4	81.1	11.3	0.4	99.2	32.8	30.9	3.2	14.6	5.4	57.7
Philippines[a]	2003	6.9	3.2	18.8	44.7	0.9	..	..	21.8	5.9	15.8	6.6	21.7
Poland	2009	12.8	0.6	14.6	5.0	0.5	99.3	47.9	40.7	1.9	17.3	6.0	60.9
Portugal	2005	1.1	1.6	..	14.5	0.2	..	50.8	24.4	..	12.7	7.2	31.9
Puerto Rico		..	..	..	..	..	..	..	..	..	..	..	..
Qatar		..	..	..	..	..	..	..	..	..	..	..	..

5.2 Business environment: enterprise surveys

	Survey year	Regulations and tax		Permits and licenses	Corruption	Crime	Informality	Gender	Finance	Infrastructure	Innovation	Trade	Workforce
		Time dealing with officials %of management time	Average number of times meeting with tax officials	Time required to obtain operating license days	Informal payments to public officials % of firms	Losses due to theft, robbery, vandalism, and arson % of sales	Firms formally registered when operations started % of firms	Firms with female participation in ownership % of firms	Firms using banks to finance investment % of firms	Value lost due to electrical outages % of sales	Inter-nationally recognized quality certification ownership % of firms	Average time to clear direct exports through customs days	Firms offering formal training % of firms
Romania	2009	9.2	2.3	23.7	9.8	0.3	98.7	47.9	37.3	2.2	26.1	2.0	24.9
Russian Federation	2009	19.9	1.6	57.4	29.4	0.8	94.7	33.1	30.6	1.2	11.7	4.6	52.2
Rwanda	2006	5.9	3.3	6.5	20.0	1.3	..	41.0	15.9	8.7	10.8	6.7	27.6
Saudi Arabia		..	..	..	..	..	..	..	..	..	..	..	..
Senegal	2007	2.9	1.3	21.4	18.1	0.5	78.9	26.3	19.8	5.0	6.1	7.4	16.3
Serbia	2009	12.2	1.4	28.0	18.0	0.6	95.0	28.8	42.8	1.3	21.8	1.6	36.5
Sierra Leone	2009	7.4	1.9	12.6	18.8	0.8	89.2	7.9	6.9	6.6	13.8	0.0	18.6
Singapore		..	..	..	..	..	..	..	..	..	..	..	..
Slovak Republic	2009	6.7	0.9	36.2	11.6	0.6	100.0	30.9	31.5	0.5	27.0	2.3	31.3
Slovenia	2009	7.3	0.3	56.1	5.4	0.4	99.9	42.2	52.2	0.5	28.0	2.2	47.5
Somalia		..	..	..	..	..	..	..	..	..	..	..	..
South Africa	2007	6.0	0.8	36.2	15.1	1.0	91.0	22.6	34.8	1.6	26.4	4.5	36.8
Spain	2005	0.8	1.5	..	4.4	0.2	..	34.1	32.6	3.0	21.3	4.9	51.3
Sri Lanka[a]	2004	3.5	4.9	49.5	16.3	0.5	..	..	26.2	..	..	7.6	32.6
Sudan		..	..	..	..	..	..	..	..	..	..	..	..
Swaziland	2006	4.4	1.4	24.0	40.6	1.3	..	28.6	7.7	2.5	22.1	2.1	51.0
Sweden		..	..	..	..	..	..	..	..	..	..	..	..
Switzerland		..	..	..	..	..	..	..	..	..	..	..	..
Syrian Arab Republic[a]	2003	10.3	4.4	..	..	..	..	..	7.6	8.6	7.4	5.9	21.0
Tajikistan	2008	11.7	1.4	22.6	40.5	0.3	92.7	34.4	21.4	15.1	16.7	20.4	21.1
Tanzania	2006	4.0	2.7	15.9	49.5	1.2	..	30.9	6.8	9.6	14.7	5.7	36.5
Thailand[a]	2006	0.4	1.0	32.1	..	0.1	..	..	74.4	1.5	39.0	1.3	75.3
Timor-Leste		..	..	..	..	..	..	..	..	..	..	..	..
Togo	2009	2.7	1.2	56.4	16.7	2.4	75.8	31.8	16.9	10.5	6.6	6.7	31.0
Trinidad and Tobago		..	..	..	..	..	..	..	..	..	..	..	..
Tunisia		..	..	..	..	..	..	..	..	..	..	..	..
Turkey	2008	27.1	1.3	36.0	17.7	0.4	94.1	40.7	51.9	2.8	30.0	5.2	28.8
Turkmenistan		..	..	..	..	..	..	..	..	..	..	..	..
Uganda	2006	5.2	2.4	9.3	51.7	1.0	..	34.7	7.7	10.2	15.5	3.2	35.0
Ukraine	2008	11.3	2.1	31.0	22.9	0.6	95.8	47.1	32.1	4.4	13.0	3.4	24.8
United Arab Emirates		..	..	..	..	..	..	..	..	..	..	..	..
United Kingdom		..	..	..	..	..	..	..	..	..	..	..	..
United States		..	..	..	..	..	..	..	..	..	..	..	..
Uruguay	2006	7.0	0.7	133.8	7.3	0.7	97.8	41.6	6.9	0.9	6.8	2.5	24.6
Uzbekistan	2008	11.1	0.7	9.1	56.2	0.7	100.0	39.8	8.2	5.4	1.3	5.1	9.6
Venezuela, RB	2006	33.6	2.9	41.6	..	1.4	97.3	..	35.7	4.4	12.5	14.1	42.3
Vietnam[a]	2005	0.8	1.9	..	67.2	0.1	..	27.4	29.4	..	11.4	4.9	44.0
West Bank and Gaza	2006	5.7	1.7	21.3	13.3	1.2	..	18.0	4.2	4.6	18.2	6.0	26.5
Yemen, Rep.		..	..	..	..	..	..	..	..	..	..	..	..
Zambia	2007	4.6	1.9	48.3	14.3	1.0	96.2	37.2	10.2	3.7	17.2	2.3	26.0
Zimbabwe		..	..	..	..	..	..	..	..	..	..	..	..

Note: Enterprise surveys are updated several times a year; see www.enterprisesurveys.org for the most recent updates.
a. The sample was drawn from the manufacturing sector only.

About the data

The World Bank Group's Enterprise Survey gathers firm-level data on the business environment to assess constraints to private sector growth and enterprise performance. Standardized surveys are conducted all over the world, and data are available on more than 100,000 firms in 118 countries. The survey covers 11 dimensions of the business environment, including regulation, corruption, crime, informality, finance, infrastructure, and trade. For some countries, firm-level panel data are available, making it possible to track changes in the business environment over time.

Firms evaluating investment options, governments interested in improving business conditions, and economists seeking to explain economic performance have all grappled with defining and measuring the business environment. The firm-level data from Enterprise Surveys provide a useful tool for benchmarking economies across a large number of indicators measured at the firm level.

Most countries can improve regulation and taxation without compromising broader social interests. Excessive regulation may harm business performance and growth. For example, time spent with tax officials is a burden firms may face in paying taxes. The business environment suffers when governments increase uncertainty and risks or impose unnecessary costs and unsound regulation and taxation. Time to obtain licenses and permits and the associated red tape constrain firm operations.

In some countries doing business requires informal payments to "get things done" in customs, taxes, licenses, regulations, services, and the like. Such corruption harms the business environment by distorting policymaking, undermining government credibility, and diverting public resources. Crime, theft, and disorder also impose costs on businesses and society.

In many developing countries informal businesses operate without formal registration. These firms have less access to financial and public services and can engage in fewer types of contracts and investments, constraining growth.

Equal opportunities for men and women contribute to development. Female participation in firm ownership is a measure of women's integration as decisionmakers.

Financial markets connect firms to lenders and investors, allowing firms to grow their businesses: creditworthy firms can obtain credit from financial intermediaries at competitive prices. But too often market imperfections and government-induced distortions limit access to credit and thus restrain growth.

The reliability and availability of infrastructure benefit households and support development. Firms with access to modern and efficient infrastructure—telecommunications, electricity, and transport—can be more productive. Firm-level innovation and use of modern technology may help firms compete.

Delays in clearing customs can be costly, deterring firms from engaging in trade or making them uncompetitive globally. Ill-considered labor regulations discourage firms from creating jobs, and while employed workers may benefit, unemployed, low-skilled, and informally employed workers will not. A trained labor force enables firms to thrive, compete, innovate, and adopt new technology.

The data in the table are from Enterprise Surveys implemented by the World Bank's Financial and Private Sector Development Enterprise Analysis Unit. All economies in East Asia and Pacific, Europe and Central Asia, Latin America and the Caribbean, Middle East and North Africa, and Sub-Saharan Africa (for 2009) and Afghanistan, Bangladesh, and India draw a sample of registered nonagricultural businesses, excluding those in the financial and public sectors. Samples for other economies are drawn only from the manufacturing sector and are footnoted in the table. Typical Enterprise Survey sample sizes range from 150 to 1,800, depending on the size of the economy. In each country samples are selected by stratified random sampling, unless otherwise noted. Stratified random sampling allows indicators to be computed by sector, firm size, and region and increases the precision of economywide indicators compared with alternative simple random sampling. Stratification by sector of activity divides the economy into manufacturing and retail and other services sectors. For medium-size and large economies the manufacturing sector is further stratified by industry. Firm size is stratified into small (5–19 employees), medium-size (20–100 employees), and large (more than 100 employees). Geographic stratification divides the national economy into the main centers of economic activity.

Definitions

• **Survey year** is the year in which the underlying data were collected. • **Time dealing with officials** is the average percentage of senior management's time that is spent in a typical week dealing with requirements imposed by government regulations. • **Average number of times meeting with tax officials** is the average number of visits or required meetings with tax officials. • **Time required to obtain operating license** is the average wait to obtain an operating license from the day applied for to the day granted. • **Informal payments to public officials** are the percentage of firms that answered positively to the question "Was a gift or informal payment expected or requested during a meeting with tax officials?" • **Losses due to theft, robbery, vandalism, and arson** are the estimated losses from those causes that occurred on establishments' premises as a percentage of annual sales. • **Firms formally registered when operations started** are the percentage of firms formally registered when they started operations in the country. Firms not formally registered (the residual) are in the informal sector of the economy. • **Firms with female participation in ownership** are the percentage of firms with a woman among the owners. • **Firms using banks to finance investment** are the percentage of firms that invested in fixed assets during the last fiscal year that used banks to finance fixed assets. • **Value lost due to electrical outages** is losses that resulted from power outages as a percentage of annual sales. • **Internationally recognized quality certification ownership** is the percentage of firms that have an internationally recognized quality certification, such as International Organization for Standardization 9000, 9002, or 14000. • **Average time to clear direct exports through customs** is the average number of days to clear direct exports through customs. • **Firms offering formal training** are the percentage of firms offering formal training programs for their permanent, full-time employees.

Data sources

Data on the business environment are from the World Bank Group's Enterprise Surveys website (www.enterprisesurveys.org).

	Starting a business			Registering property		Dealing with construction permits		Employing workers	Enforcing contracts		Protecting investors	Closing a business
	Number of procedures	Time required days	Cost % of per capita income	Number of procedures	Time required days	Number of procedures to build a warehouse	Time required to build a warehouse days	Rigidity of employment index 0–100 (least to most rigid)	Number of procedures	Time required days	Disclosure index 0–10 (least to most disclosure)	Time to resolve insolvency years
	June 2009	June 2009	June 2009	June 2009	June 2009	June 2009	June 2009	June 2009	June 2009	June 2009	June 2009	June 2009
Afghanistan	4	7	30.2	9	250	13	340	20	47	1,642	0	..
Albania	5	5	17.0	6	42	24	331	25	39	390	8	..
Algeria	14	24	12.1	11	47	22	240	41	46	630	6	2.5
Angola	8	68	151.1	7	184	12	328	66	46	1,011	5	6.2
Argentina	15	27	11.0	6	52	28	338	21	36	590	6	2.8
Armenia	6	15	2.6	3	4	20	137	21	48	285	5	1.9
Australia	2	2	0.8	5	5	16	221	0	28	395	8	1.0
Austria	8	28	5.1	3	32	14	194	24	25	397	3	1.1
Azerbaijan	6	10	2.9	4	11	31	207	10	39	237	7	2.7
Bangladesh	7	44	36.2	8	245	14	231	28	41	1,442	6	4.0
Belarus	5	6	1.7	3	18	15	161	11	28	225	5	5.8
Belgium	3	4	5.3	7	79	14	169	17	25	505	8	0.9
Benin	7	31	155.5	4	120	15	410	40	42	825	6	4.0
Bolivia	15	50	99.2	7	92	17	249	77	40	591	1	1.8
Bosnia and Herzegovina	12	60	15.8	7	84	16	255	33	38	595	3	3.3
Botswana	10	61	2.1	5	16	24	167	13	29	687	7	1.7
Brazil	16	120	6.9	14	42	18	411	46	45	616	6	4.0
Bulgaria	4	18	1.7	8	15	24	139	19	39	564	10	3.3
Burkina Faso	4	14	50.3	4	59	15	132	21	37	446	6	4.0
Burundi	11	32	151.6	5	94	22	212	28	44	832	4	..
Cambodia	9	85	138.4	7	56	23	709	36	44	401	5	..
Cameroon	12	34	121.1	5	93	15	426	39	43	800	6	3.2
Canada	1	5	0.4	6	17	14	75	4	36	570	8	0.8
Central African Republic	8	22	244.9	5	75	21	239	50	43	660	6	4.8
Chad	19	75	176.7	6	44	9	181	33	41	743	6	..
Chile	9	27	6.9	6	31	18	155	18	36	480	7	4.5
China	14	37	4.9	4	29	37	336	31	34	406	10	1.7
Hong Kong SAR, China	3	6	1.8	5	45	7	67	0	24	280	10	1.1
Colombia	9	20	12.8	7	20	11	51	10	34	1,346	8	3.0
Congo, Dem. Rep.	13	149	391.0	8	57	14	322	63	43	625	3	5.2
Congo, Rep.	10	37	86.5	7	116	14	169	63	44	560	6	3.0
Costa Rica	12	60	20.0	6	21	23	191	39	40	852	2	3.5
Côte d'Ivoire	10	40	133.3	6	62	22	629	33	33	770	6	2.2
Croatia	7	22	8.4	5	104	14	420	50	38	561	1	3.1
Cuba	..	..	..	..	..	..	..	..	..	..	..	..
Czech Republic	8	15	9.2	4	78	36	150	11	27	611	2	6.5
Denmark	4	6	0.0	6	42	6	69	7	34	380	7	1.1
Dominican Republic	8	19	17.3	7	60	17	214	21	34	460	5	3.5
Ecuador	13	64	37.7	9	16	19	155	38	39	588	1	5.3
Egypt, Arab Rep.	6	7	16.1	7	72	25	218	27	41	1,010	8	4.2
El Salvador	8	17	38.7	5	31	34	155	24	30	786	5	4.0
Eritrea	13	84	76.5	12	101	..	..	20	39	405	4	..
Estonia	5	7	1.7	3	18	14	118	51	36	425	8	3.0
Ethiopia	5	9	18.9	10	41	12	128	28	37	620	4	3.0
Finland	3	14	0.9	3	14	18	38	41	32	375	6	0.9
France	5	7	0.9	8	98	13	137	52	29	331	10	1.9
Gabon	9	58	17.8	7	39	16	210	52	38	1,070	6	5.0
Gambia, The	8	27	215.1	5	371	17	146	27	32	434	2	3.0
Georgia	3	3	3.7	2	3	10	98	7	36	285	8	3.3
Germany	9	18	4.7	4	40	12	100	42	30	394	5	1.2
Ghana	8	33	26.4	5	34	18	220	27	36	487	7	1.9
Greece	15	19	10.9	11	22	15	169	50	39	819	1	2.0
Guatemala	11	29	45.4	4	27	22	178	28	31	1,459	3	3.0
Guinea	13	41	139.2	6	104	32	255	24	50	276	6	3.8
Guinea-Bissau	16	213	323.0	9	211	15	167	54	41	1,140	6	..
Haiti	13	195	227.9	5	405	11	1,179	10	35	508	2	5.7
Honduras	13	14	47.3	7	23	17	106	57	45	900	0	3.8

Business environment: Doing Business indicators

5.3

	Starting a business			Registering property		Dealing with construction permits		Employing workers	Enforcing contracts		Protecting investors	Closing a business
	Number of procedures	Time required days	Cost % of per capita income	Number of procedures	Time required days	Number of procedures to build a warehouse	Time required to build a warehouse days	Rigidity of employment index 0–100 (least to most rigid)	Number of procedures	Time required days	Disclosure index 0–10 (least to most disclosure)	Time to resolve insolvency years
	June 2009	June 2009	June 2009	June 2009	June 2009	June 2009	June 2009	June 2009	June 2009	June 2009	June 2009	June 2009
Hungary	4	4	8.0	4	17	31	204	22	33	395	2	2.0
India	13	30	66.1	5	44	37	195	30	46	1,420	7	7.0
Indonesia	9	60	26.0	6	22	14	160	40	39	570	10	5.5
Iran, Islamic Rep.	7	9	3.9	9	36	17	322	29	39	520	5	4.5
Iraq	11	77	75.9	5	8	14	215	24	51	520	4	..
Ireland	4	13	0.3	5	38	11	185	10	20	515	10	0.4
Israel	5	34	4.2	7	144	20	235	17	35	890	7	4.0
Italy	6	10	17.9	8	27	14	257	38	40	1,210	7	1.8
Jamaica	6	8	5.3	6	55	10	156	4	35	655	4	1.1
Japan	8	23	7.5	6	14	15	187	16	30	360	7	0.6
Jordan	8	13	49.5	7	21	19	87	24	38	689	5	4.3
Kazakhstan	7	20	4.8	5	40	37	211	17	38	390	7	1.5
Kenya	12	34	36.5	8	64	11	120	17	40	465	3	4.5
Korea, Dem. Rep.	..	..	..	..	..	..	..	..	..	..	..	..
Korea, Rep.	8	14	14.7	7	11	13	34	38	35	230	7	1.5
Kosovo	..	..	..	..	..	..	..	..	..	..	..	..
Kuwait	13	35	1.0	8	55	25	104	0	50	566	7	4.2
Kyrgyz Republic	3	11	5.2	4	5	12	137	18	39	260	8	4.0
Lao PDR	7	100	12.3	9	135	24	172	20	42	443	0	..
Latvia	5	16	2.1	6	45	25	187	43	27	309	5	3.0
Lebanon	5	9	78.2	8	25	20	211	25	37	721	9	4.0
Lesotho	7	40	27.0	6	101	15	601	14	41	695	2	2.6
Liberia	5	20	52.9	10	50	24	77	27	41	1,280	4	3.0
Libya	..	..	..	..	..	..	..	..	..	..	..	..
Lithuania	7	26	2.4	2	3	17	162	38	30	275	5	1.5
Macedonia, FYR	4	4	2.5	5	58	21	146	14	37	370	9	2.9
Madagascar	2	7	7.1	7	74	16	178	56	38	871	5	..
Malawi	10	39	108.0	6	88	21	213	21	42	432	4	2.6
Malaysia	9	11	11.9	5	144	25	261	10	30	585	10	2.3
Mali	7	15	89.2	5	29	14	185	31	36	626	6	3.6
Mauritania	9	19	34.7	4	49	25	201	39	46	370	5	8.0
Mauritius	5	6	4.1	4	26	18	107	18	36	720	6	1.7
Mexico	8	13	11.7	5	74	12	138	41	38	415	8	1.8
Moldova	8	10	7.0	5	5	30	292	41	31	365	7	2.8
Mongolia	7	13	3.0	5	11	21	215	17	32	314	5	4.0
Morocco	6	12	16.1	8	47	19	163	60	40	615	6	1.8
Mozambique	10	26	19.3	8	42	17	381	40	30	730	5	5.0
Myanmar	..	..	..	..	..	..	..	..	..	..	..	..
Namibia	10	66	20.4	9	23	12	139	13	33	270	5	1.5
Nepal	7	31	53.6	3	5	15	424	46	39	735	6	5.0
Netherlands	6	10	5.6	2	5	18	230	42	25	514	4	1.1
New Zealand	1	1	0.4	2	2	7	65	7	30	216	10	1.3
Nicaragua	6	39	111.7	8	124	17	219	27	35	540	4	2.2
Niger	9	17	118.7	4	35	17	265	68	39	545	6	5.0
Nigeria	8	31	76.7	13	82	18	350	7	39	457	5	2.0
Norway	5	7	1.9	1	3	14	252	44	33	280	7	0.9
Oman	5	12	2.2	2	16	16	242	13	51	598	8	4.0
Pakistan	10	20	5.8	6	50	12	223	43	47	976	6	2.8
Panama	6	12	10.3	7	32	20	116	66	31	686	1	2.5
Papua New Guinea	8	56	20.5	4	72	24	217	4	42	591	5	3.0
Paraguay	7	35	56.7	6	46	13	291	56	38	591	6	3.9
Peru	9	41	24.5	4	14	21	205	39	41	428	8	3.1
Philippines	15	52	28.2	8	33	24	203	29	37	842	2	5.7
Poland	6	32	17.9	6	197	30	308	25	38	830	7	3.0
Portugal	6	6	6.4	5	12	19	287	43	31	547	6	2.0
Puerto Rico	7	7	0.7	8	194	22	209	14	39	620	7	3.8
Qatar	19	76	0.6	10	16	19	76	13	43	570	5	2.8

	Starting a business			Registering property		Dealing with construction permits		Employing workers	Enforcing contracts		Protecting investors	Closing a business
	Number of procedures	Time required days	Cost % of per capita income	Number of procedures	Time required days	Number of procedures to build a warehouse	Time required to build a warehouse days	Rigidity of employment index 0–100 (least to most rigid)	Number of procedures	Time required days	Disclosure index 0–10 (least to most disclosure)	Time to resolve insolvency years
	June 2009	June 2009	June 2009	June 2009	June 2009	June 2009	June 2009	June 2009	June 2009	June 2009	June 2009	June 2009
Romania	6	10	2.9	8	48	17	243	46	31	512	9	3.3
Russian Federation	9	30	2.7	6	43	54	704	38	37	281	6	3.8
Rwanda	2	3	10.1	4	60	14	210	7	24	260	7	..
Saudi Arabia	4	5	7.7	2	2	17	94	13	43	635	9	1.5
Senegal	4	8	63.7	6	124	16	220	59	44	780	6	3.0
Serbia	7	13	7.1	6	111	20	279	35	36	635	7	2.7
Sierra Leone	6	12	118.8	7	236	25	283	41	40	515	6	2.6
Singapore	3	3	0.7	3	5	11	25	0	21	150	10	0.8
Slovak Republic	6	16	2.0	3	17	13	287	22	30	565	3	4.0
Slovenia	3	6	0.0	6	391	14	197	54	32	1,290	3	2.0
Somalia	..	..	..	..	..	..	..	..	..	..	..	..
South Africa	6	22	5.9	6	24	17	174	35	30	600	8	2.0
Spain	10	47	15.0	4	18	11	233	49	39	515	5	1.0
Sri Lanka	4	38	5.9	8	83	22	214	20	40	1,318	4	1.7
Sudan	10	36	36.0	6	9	19	271	36	53	810	0	..
Swaziland	13	61	33.9	11	46	13	93	10	40	972	0	2.0
Sweden	3	15	0.6	2	15	8	116	38	30	508	6	2.0
Switzerland	6	20	2.0	4	16	14	154	7	31	417	0	3.0
Syrian Arab Republic	7	17	27.8	4	19	26	128	20	55	872	6	4.1
Tajikistan	12	25	24.3	6	37	32	250	49	34	430	6	3.0
Tanzania	12	29	36.8	9	73	22	328	54	38	462	3	3.0
Thailand	7	32	6.3	2	2	11	156	11	35	479	10	2.7
Timor-Leste	10	83	4.1	..	..	22	208	32	51	1,435	3	..
Togo	7	75	205.0	5	295	15	277	54	41	588	6	3.0
Trinidad and Tobago	9	43	0.7	8	162	20	261	7	42	1,340	4	..
Tunisia	10	11	5.7	4	39	20	84	40	39	565	5	1.3
Turkey	6	6	14.2	6	6	25	188	35	35	420	9	3.3
Turkmenistan	..	..	..	..	..	..	..	..	..	..	..	..
Uganda	18	25	84.4	13	77	16	143	0	38	510	2	2.2
Ukraine	10	27	5.8	10	93	30	476	31	30	345	5	2.9
United Arab Emirates	8	15	6.2	1	2	17	64	7	49	537	4	5.1
United Kingdom	6	13	0.7	2	8	11	95	10	30	399	10	1.0
United States	6	6	0.7	4	12	19	40	0	32	300	7	1.5
Uruguay	11	65	40.0	9	66	30	234	18	40	720	3	2.1
Uzbekistan	7	15	11.2	12	78	26	260	32	42	195	4	4.0
Venezuela, RB	16	141	24.0	8	47	11	395	69	29	510	3	4.0
Vietnam	11	50	13.3	4	57	13	194	21	34	295	6	5.0
West Bank and Gaza	11	49	55.0	7	47	21	199	31	44	600	6	..
Yemen, Rep.	6	12	83.0	6	19	15	107	24	36	520	6	3.0
Zambia	6	18	28.4	6	39	17	254	21	35	471	3	2.7
Zimbabwe	10	96	499.5	5	31	19	1,426	33	38	410	8	3.3
World	**8 u**	**36 u**	**41.5 u**	**6 u**	**65 u**	**18 u**	**216 u**	**27 u**	**38 u**	**607 u**	**5 u**	**3.0 u**
Low income	9	44	107.5	7	100	18	291	33	39	605	5	3.8
Middle income	8	40	31.0	6	61	19	209	27	39	649	5	3.1
Lower middle income	9	34	42.7	6	69	19	209	28	40	678	5	3.3
Upper middle income	8	47	16.0	6	52	20	209	26	37	612	6	2.9
Low & middle income	9	41	53.5	6	73	19	232	29	39	636	5	3.3
East Asia & Pacific	8	42	30.1	5	112	18	182	17	37	572	5	3.1
Europe & Central Asia	7	19	8.8	6	46	24	249	27	37	398	6	3.0
Latin America & Carib.	10	67	41.2	7	65	17	228	29	39	710	4	3.2
Middle East & N. Africa	9	23	51.5	7	35	19	181	33	42	707	6	3.5
South Asia	7	28	27.0	6	106	18	241	27	44	1,053	4	4.5
Sub-Saharan Africa	9	44	99.7	7	82	17	262	35	39	646	5	3.4
High income	6	19	6.7	5	43	16	169	24	35	526	6	2.1
Euro area	6	15	6.0	5	57	14	225	38	31	602	5	1.6

About the data

The economic health of a country is measured not only in macroeconomic terms but also by other factors that shape daily economic activity such as laws, regulations, and institutional arrangements. The Doing Business indicators measure business regulation, gauge regulatory outcomes, and measure the extent of legal protection of property, the flexibility of employment regulation, and the tax burden on businesses.

The table presents a subset of Doing Business indicators covering 7 of the 10 sets of indicators: starting a business, registering property, dealing with construction permits, employing workers, enforcing contracts, protecting investors, and closing a business. Table 5.5 includes Doing Business measures of getting credit, and table 5.6 presents data on paying taxes.

The fundamental premise of the Doing Business project is that economic activity requires good rules and regulations that are efficient, accessible to all who need to use them, and simple to implement. Thus some Doing Business indicators give a higher score for more regulation, such as stricter disclosure requirements in related-party transactions, and others give a higher score for simplified regulations, such as a one-stop shop for completing business startup formalities.

In constructing the indicators, it is assumed that entrepreneurs know about all regulations and comply with them; in practice, entrepreneurs may not be aware of all required procedures or may avoid legally required procedures altogether. But where regulation is particularly onerous, levels of informality are higher, which comes at a cost: firms in the informal sector usually grow more slowly, have less access to credit, and employ fewer workers—and those workers remain outside the protections of labor law. The indicators in the table can help policymakers understand the business environment in a country and—along with information from other sources such as the World Bank's Enterprise Surveys—provide insights into potential areas of reform.

Doing Business data are collected with a standardized survey that uses a simple business case to ensure comparability across economies and over time—with assumptions about the legal form of the business, its size, its location, and nature of its operation. Surveys in 183 countries are administered through more than 8,000 local experts, including lawyers, business consultants, accountants, freight forwarders, government officials, and other professionals who routinely administer or advise on legal and regulatory requirements.

The Doing Business project encompasses two types of data: data from readings of laws and regulations and data on time and motion indicators that measure efficiency in achieving a regulatory goal. Within the time and motion indicators cost estimates are recorded from official fee schedules where applicable. The data from surveys are subjected to numerous tests for robustness, which lead to revision or expansion of the information collected.

The Doing Business methodology has limitations that should be considered when interpreting the data. First, the data collected refer to businesses in the economy's largest city and may not represent regulations in other locations of the economy. To address this limitation, subnational indicators are being collected for selected economies. These subnational studies point to significant differences in the speed of reform and the ease of doing business across cities in the same economy. Second, the data often focus on a specific business form—generally a limited liability company of a specified size—and may not represent regulation for other types of businesses such as sole proprietorships. Third, transactions described in a standardized business case refer to a specific set of issues and may not represent the full set of issues a business encounters. Fourth, the time measures involve an element of judgment by the expert respondents. When sources indicate different estimates, the Doing Business time indicators represent the median values of several responses given under the assumptions of the standardized case. Fifth, the methodology assumes that a business has full information on what is required and does not waste time when completing procedures.

Definitions

• **Number of procedures for starting a business** is the number of procedures required to start a business, including interactions to obtain necessary permits and licenses and to complete all inscriptions, verifications, and notifications to start operations for businesses with specific characteristics of ownership, size, and type of production. • **Time required for starting a business** is the number of calendar days to complete the procedures for legally operating a business using the fastest procedure, independent of cost. • **Cost for starting a business** is normalized as a percentage of gross national income (GNI) per capita. It includes all official fees for professional or legal services if they are required by law. • **Number of procedures for registering property** is the number of procedures required for a business to legally transfer property. • **Time required for registering property** is the number of calendar days for a business to legally transfer property. • **Number of procedures for dealing with licenses to build a warehouse** is the number of interactions of a company's employees or managers with external parties, including government staff, public inspectors, notaries, land registry and cadastre staff, and technical experts apart from architects and engineers. • **Time required for dealing with construction permits to build a warehouse** is the number of calendar days to complete the required procedures for building a warehouse using the fastest procedure, independent of cost. • **Rigidity of employment index**, a measure of employment regulation, is the average of three subindexes: a difficulty of hiring index, a rigidity of hours index, and a difficulty of firing index. Higher values indicate more rigid regulations. • **Number of procedures for enforcing contracts** is the number of independent actions, mandated by law or court regulation, that demand interaction between the parties to a contract or between them and the judge or court officer. • **Time required for enforcing contracts** is the number of calendar days from the time of the filing of a lawsuit in court to the final determination and payment. • **Extent of disclosure index** measures the degree to which investors are protected through disclosure of ownership and financial information. Higher values indicate more disclosure. • **Time to resolve insolvency** is the number of years from time of filing for insolvency in court until resolution of distressed assets and payment of creditors.

Data sources

Data on the business environment are from the World Bank's Doing Business project (www.doingbusiness.org).

5.4 Stock markets

	Market capitalization				Market liquidity		Turnover ratio		Listed domestic companies		S&P/Global Equity Indices	
	$ millions		% of GDP		Value of shares traded % of GDP		Value of shares traded % of market capitalization		number		% change	
	2000	2009	2000	2008	2000	2008	2000	2009	2000	2009	2008	2009
Afghanistan	..	..	..	..	..	..	..	..	..	..	..	..
Albania	..	..	..	..	..	..	..	..	..	..	..	..
Algeria	..	..	..	..	..	..	..	..	..	..	..	..
Angola	..	..	..	..	..	..	..	..	..	..	..	..
Argentina	166,068	48,033	58.4	15.9	2.1	4.1	4.8	5.4	127	107	−56.2[a]	97.8[a]
Armenia	2	176	0.1	1.5	0.0	0.0	4.6	0.6	105	26	..	..
Australia	372,794	675,619	92.0	66.5	55.9	99.9	56.5	103.1	1,330	1,924	..	..
Austria	29,935	72,300	15.7	17.5	4.9	25.3	29.8	69.0	97	85	..	..
Azerbaijan	3	..	0.1	..	..	..	..	..	2	..	..	..
Bangladesh	1,186	7,068	2.5	8.4	1.6	11.6	74.4	212.6	221	295	4.3[a]	38.6[a]
Belarus	..	..	..	..	..	..	..	..	..	..	..	..
Belgium	182,481	167,447	78.7	33.2	16.4	41.9	20.7	76.1	174	167	..	..
Benin	..	..	..	..	..	..	..	..	..	..	..	..
Bolivia	1,742	2,672	20.7	16.0	0.8	0.0	0.1	..	26	37	..	..
Bosnia and Herzegovina	..	..	..	..	..	..	..	..	..	..	..	..
Botswana	978	4,283	15.8	26.5	0.8	1.1	4.8	2.6	16	20	−38.4[a]	24.3[a]
Brazil	226,152	1,337,723	35.1	37.4	15.7	46.2	43.5	67.4	459	425	−57.2	125.1
Bulgaria	617	7,330	4.9	17.8	0.5	3.3	9.2	4.9	503	337	−70.2[a]	17.2[a]
Burkina Faso	..	..	..	..	..	..	..	..	..	..	..	..
Burundi	..	..	..	..	..	..	..	..	..	..	..	..
Cambodia	..	..	..	..	..	..	..	..	..	..	..	..
Cameroon	..	..	..	..	..	..	..	..	..	..	..	..
Canada	841,385	1,002,215	116.1	66.8	87.6	117.3	77.3	123.7	1,418	3,755	..	..
Central African Republic	..	..	..	..	..	..	..	..	..	..	..	..
Chad	..	..	..	..	..	..	..	..	..	..	..	..
Chile	60,401	230,732	80.3	78.1	8.1	21.6	9.4	20.7	258	232	−41.2	84.0
China	580,991	5,010,656	48.5	64.6	60.2	126.4	158.3	229.5	1,086	1,700	−52.7	66.3
Hong Kong SAR, China	623,398	468,595	368.6	217.6	223.4	288.7	61.3	81.8	779	1,017	..	..
Colombia	9,560	140,520	10.2	35.7	0.4	5.1	3.8	11.4	126	96	..	75.7[a]
Congo, Dem. Rep.	..	..	..	..	..	..	..	..	..	..	..	..
Congo, Rep.	..	..	..	..	..	..	..	..	..	..	..	..
Costa Rica	2,924	1,887	18.3	6.4	0.7	0.2	12.0	3.0	21	11	..	..
Côte d'Ivoire	1,185	6,141	11.4	30.2	0.3	1.3	2.6	2.0	41	38	−16.9[a]	−10.7[a]
Croatia	2,742	26,619	12.8	38.6	0.9	5.0	7.4	5.3	64	368	−59.3[a]	31.1[a]
Cuba	..	..	..	..	..	..	..	..	..	..	..	..
Czech Republic	11,002	54,477	19.4	22.7	11.6	20.0	60.3	39.9	131	25	−45.9	23.0
Denmark	107,666	131,526	67.3	38.5	57.2	62.1	86.0	104.8	225	216	..	..
Dominican Republic	..	..	..	..	..	..	..	..	..	..	..	..
Ecuador	704	4,248	4.4	8.3	0.1	0.3	5.5	30.7	30	39	−8.8[a]	−13.1[a]
Egypt, Arab Rep.	28,741	91,091	28.8	52.9	11.1	42.9	34.7	59.7	1,076	306	−55.8	35.6
El Salvador	2,041	4,656	15.5	21.1	0.2	0.9	1.3	..	40	51	..	..
Eritrea	..	..	..	..	..	..	..	..	..	..	..	..
Estonia	1,846	170	32.5	8.3	5.7	3.3	18.9	0.8	23	16	−65.5[a]	32.9[a]
Ethiopia	..	..	..	..	..	..	..	..	..	..	..	..
Finland	293,635	154,367	241.1	56.6	169.7	143.2	64.3	155.1	154	126	..	..
France	1,446,634	1,492,327	108.9	52.2	81.6	114.0	74.1	152.4	808	966	..	22.0[b]
Gabon	..	..	..	..	..	..	..	..	..	..	..	..
Gambia, The	..	..	..	..	..	..	..	..	..	..	..	..
Georgia	24	327	0.8	2.6	0.1	0.1	..	4.4	269	161	..	..
Germany	1,270,243	1,107,957	66.8	30.4	56.3	84.8	79.1	191.5	1,022	638	..	18.0[c]
Ghana	502	2,507	10.1	20.4	0.2	0.9	1.5	2.0	22	35	−10.4[a]	−42.7[a]
Greece	110,839	90,396	88.3	25.4	75.7	29.7	63.7	59.2	329	280	..	..
Guatemala	172	..	0.9	..	0.1	..	0.0	..	7	..	..	..
Guinea	..	..	..	..	..	..	..	..	..	..	..	..
Guinea-Bissau	..	..	..	..	..	..	..	..	..	..	..	..
Haiti	..	..	..	..	..	..	..	..	..	..	..	..
Honduras	458	..	8.8	..	..	..	..	..	94	..	..	..

	Market capitalization				Market liquidity		Turnover ratio		Listed domestic companies		S&P/Global Equity Indices	
					Value of shares traded % of GDP		Value of shares traded % of market capitalization		number		% change	
	$ millions		% of GDP									
	2000	2009	2000	2008	2000	2008	2000	2009	2000	2009	2008	2009
Hungary	12,021	30,332	25.1	12.0	25.4	19.9	90.7	106.1	60	45	−62.5	73.0
India	148,064	1,226,676	32.2	55.7	110.8	90.6	133.6	116.3	5,937	4,946	−64.1	94.1
Indonesia	26,834	196,661	16.3	19.3	8.7	21.7	32.9	78.1	290	401	−61.1	130.1
Iran, Islamic Rep.	7,350	49,040	7.3	15.9	1.1	2.9	12.7	33.6	304	356	..	..
Iraq	..	..	..	..	..	..	..	..	..	..	..	..
Ireland	81,882	49,401	84.8	18.5	14.9	30.8	19.2	85.0	76	58	..	..
Israel	64,081	188,734	51.4	66.5	18.8	54.0	36.3	54.6	654	622	−33.1	56.8
Italy	768,364	520,855	70.0	22.6	70.9	64.2	104.0	284.2	291	294	..	..
Jamaica	3,582	6,127	39.8	51.4	0.8	2.5	2.5	1.8	46	38	−38.2[a]	−15.8[a]
Japan	3,157,222	3,220,485	67.6	65.6	57.7	119.5	69.9	153.2	2,561	3,299	−40.0[d]	6.0[d]
Jordan	4,943	31,891	58.4	168.8	4.9	131.9	7.7	40.3	163	272	..	−13.9
Kazakhstan	1,342	57,273	7.3	23.3	0.5	2.6	25.1	9.1	23	72	−47.0[a]	1.5[a]
Kenya	1,283	10,967	10.1	36.0	0.4	4.7	3.6	4.5	57	53	−40.3[a]	0.6[a]
Korea, Dem. Rep.	..	..	..	..	..	..	..	..	..	..	..	..
Korea, Rep.	171,587	836,462	32.2	53.2	200.2	157.8	233.2	238.2	1,308	1,798	−55.6	67.2
Kosovo	..	..	..	..	..	..	..	..	..	..	..	..
Kuwait	20,772	96,317	55.1	72.4	11.2	82.9	21.3	23.7	77	207	..	−10.4[a]
Kyrgyz Republic	4	94	0.3	1.9	1.7	2.2	..	131.2	80	8	..	..
Lao PDR	..	..	..	..	..	..	..	..	..	..	..	..
Latvia	563	1,872	7.2	4.8	2.9	0.1	48.6	0.0	64	34	−58.7[a]	2.2[a]
Lebanon	1,583	12,885	9.2	32.9	0.7	2.4	6.7	14.4	12	11	−25.3[a]	43.4[a]
Lesotho	..	..	..	..	..	..	..	..	..	..	..	..
Liberia	..	..	..	..	..	..	..	..	..	..	..	..
Libya	..	..	..	..	..	..	..	..	..	..	..	..
Lithuania	1,588	4,619	13.9	7.7	1.8	1.0	14.8	4.3	54	40	−73.0[a]	36.7[a]
Macedonia, FYR	7	823	0.2	8.6	3.3	1.6	6.6	8.9	1	38	..	..
Madagascar	..	..	..	..	..	..	..	..	..	..	..	..
Malawi	..	1,771	..	41.5	..	1.4	13.8	3.9	..	14	..	..
Malaysia	116,935	263,362	124.7	84.4	62.4	38.4	44.6	54.7	795	957	−43.7	46.7
Mali	..	..	..	..	..	..	..	..	..	..	..	..
Mauritania	..	..	..	..	..	..	..	..	..	..	..	..
Mauritius	1,331	4,982	29.0	36.9	1.6	4.3	5.0	0.3	40	40	−49.2[a]	44.2[a]
Mexico	125,204	352,045	21.5	21.4	7.8	9.9	32.3	43.4	179	125	−45.1	55.8
Moldova	392	..	30.4	..	1.9	2.6	5.8	..	36	..	..	..
Mongolia	37	407	3.4	7.7	0.7	1.0	7.3	14.7	410	420	..	..
Morocco	10,899	64,479	29.4	74.0	3.0	24.7	9.2	12.0	53	78	−17.0	−1.7
Mozambique	..	..	..	..	..	..	..	..	..	..	..	..
Myanmar	..	..	..	..	..	..	..	..	..	..	..	..
Namibia	311	968	8.0	7.0	0.6	0.2	4.5	0.1	13	7	−9.9[a]	22.6[a]
Nepal	790	4,894	14.4	38.8	0.6	2.9	6.9	7.5	110	149	..	..
Netherlands	640,456	387,906	166.3	44.5	175.9	130.9	101.4	169.2	234	110	..	..
New Zealand	18,866	24,166	37.1	18.6	21.2	12.7	45.9	46.1	142	149	..	..
Nicaragua	..	..	..	..	..	..	..	..	..	..	..	..
Niger	..	..	..	..	..	..	..	..	..	..	..	..
Nigeria	4,237	33,374	9.2	24.0	0.6	9.6	7.3	26.9	195	216	..	−35.4
Norway	65,034	125,920	38.6	27.9	35.7	81.4	93.4	152.2	191	209	..	..
Oman	3,463	17,304	17.4	55.4	2.8	13.0	14.2	17.4	131	125	..	22.0[a]
Pakistan	6,581	32,206	8.9	14.3	44.6	33.0	475.5	99.9	762	650	..	56.7
Panama	2,794	8,048	24.0	28.4	1.3	1.1	1.7	0.3	29	30	−15.7[a]	15.4[a]
Papua New Guinea	1,520	..	49.3	118.3	0.0	0.4	..	..	7	15	..	..
Paraguay	224	..	3.5	4.4	0.1	0.0	3.5	..	56	50	..	..
Peru	10,562	69,753	19.8	43.1	2.9	4.0	12.6	8.2	230	201	−41.1	79.3
Philippines	25,957	82,546	34.2	31.2	10.8	10.3	15.8	24.9	228	245	−53.7	71.5
Poland	31,279	147,178	18.3	17.1	8.5	12.9	49.9	56.0	225	354	−57.8	41.9
Portugal	60,681	68,713	53.9	28.2	48.3	33.9	85.5	81.8	109	49	..	..
Puerto Rico	..	..	..	..	..	..	..	..	..	..	..	..
Qatar	5,152	87,843	29.0	134.4	1.3	42.1	4.5	28.7	22	44	..	5.1[a]

	Market capitalization				Market liquidity		Turnover ratio		Listed domestic companies		S&P/Global Equity Indices	
	$ millions		% of GDP		Value of shares traded % of GDP		Value of shares traded % of market capitalization		number		% change	
	2000	2009	2000	2008	2000	2008	2000	2009	2000	2009	2008	2009
Romania	1,069	31,318	2.9	10.0	0.6	1.8	23.1	3.5	5,555	1,571	−72.2[a]	26.1[a]
Russian Federation	38,922	861,424	15.0	78.7	7.8	33.5	36.9	154.9	249	333	−73.4	106.6
Rwanda	..	..	..	..	..	..	..	..	..	..	..	..
Saudi Arabia	67,171	318,737	35.6	52.5	9.2	111.9	27.1	41.1	75	135	..	28.5
Senegal	..	..	..	..	..	..	..	..	..	..	..	..
Serbia	734	12,165	4.6	24.3	0.1	2.5	0.0	14.6	6	1,771	..	..
Sierra Leone	..	..	..	..	..	..	..	..	..	..	..	..
Singapore	152,827	180,021	164.8	98.9	98.7	148.9	52.1	101.3	418	455	..	..
Slovak Republic	1,217	4,672	4.2	5.2	3.1	0.0	129.8	0.1	493	111	−36.0[a]	−23.1[a]
Slovenia	2,547	12,141	12.8	21.6	2.3	2.6	20.7	11.9	38	80	−66.9[a]	16.1[a]
Somalia	..	..	..	..	..	..	..	..	..	..	..	..
South Africa	204,952	805,169	154.2	177.7	58.3	145.2	33.9	83.8	616	411	−41.7	53.7
Spain	504,219	946,113	86.8	59.0	169.8	152.1	210.7	177.6	1,019	3,536	..	..
Sri Lanka	1,074	8,172	6.6	10.7	0.9	2.5	11.0	14.2	239	232	..	118.0[a]
Sudan	..	..	..	..	..	..	..	..	..	..	..	..
Swaziland	73	203	4.9	6.9	0.0	0.0	9.8	..	6	7	..	..
Sweden	328,339	252,542	133.7	52.7	158.8	133.4	111.2	157.0	292	341	..	..
Switzerland	792,316	862,663	317.0	175.4	243.7	307.1	82.0	145.6	252	253	..	..
Syrian Arab Republic	..	..	..	..	..	..	..	..	..	..	..	..
Tajikistan	..	..	..	..	..	..	..	..	..	..	..	..
Tanzania	233	1,293	2.6	6.3	0.4	0.1	2.4	..	4	7	..	..
Thailand	29,489	142,247	24.0	37.7	19.0	42.9	53.2	110.2	381	497	−50.5	72.8
Timor-Leste	..	..	..	..	..	..	..	..	..	..	..	..
Togo	..	..	..	..	..	..	..	..	..	..	..	..
Trinidad and Tobago	4,330	11,145	53.1	50.4	1.7	1.5	3.1	2.0	27	37	−9.9[a]	−10.2[a]
Tunisia	2,828	9,309	14.5	15.8	3.2	3.7	23.3	16.0	44	50	−3.1[a]	40.6[a]
Turkey	69,659	234,004	26.1	16.0	67.1	32.6	206.2	138.4	315	315	−62.4	99.6
Turkmenistan	..	..	..	..	..	..	..	..	..	..	..	..
Uganda	35	..	0.6	1.2	0.0	0.1	..	..	2	6	..	..
Ukraine	1,881	16,859	6.0	13.5	0.9	1.4	19.6	2.9	139	149	−82.2[a]	31.1[a]
United Arab Emirates	5,727	109,613	8.1	113.1	0.2	75.7	3.9	63.3	54	101	..	24.6[a]
United Kingdom	2,576,992	1,851,954	174.4	69.3	124.2	242.5	66.6	226.9	1,904	2,415	−40.0[e]	22.0[e]
United States	15,104,037	11,737,646	154.7	80.4	326.3	249.9	200.8	232.3	7,524	5,603	−39.0[f]	23.0[f]
Uruguay	161	159	0.7	0.7	0.0	0.1	0.5	12.0	16	8	..	..
Uzbekistan	32	..	0.2	4.2	0.1	0.3	..	..	5	114	..	..
Venezuela, RB	8,128	..	6.9	4.5	0.6	0.4	8.9	1.3	85	60	..	..
Vietnam	..	21,529	..	10.6	..	4.6	..	42.7	..	162	−68.2[a]	46.9[a]
West Bank and Gaza	765	2,123	18.6	..	4.6	..	10.0	31.3	24	35	..	..
Yemen, Rep.	..	..	..	..	..	..	..	..	..	..	..	..
Zambia	236	2,346	7.3	20.6	0.2	0.6	20.8	4.1	9	15	..	16.7[a]
Zimbabwe	2,432	5,333	32.9	..	3.8	..	10.8	5.1	69	81	..	..
World	**32,187,516 s**	..[g] s	**102.2 w**	59.2 w	152.2 w	136.9 w	122.3 w	..[g] w	**47,787 s**	..[g] s		
Low income	..	..	..	..	..	..	..	..	..	..		
Middle income	1,973,751	11,586,208	36.1	49.5	33.8	61.3	83.5	213.8	21,842	15,575		
Lower middle income	886,833	6,956,558	35.3	53.5	52.7	93.4	128.1	228.5	11,779	9,819		
Upper middle income	1,086,918	4,629,650	36.7	45.5	17.5	29.9	46.7	59.3	10,063	5,756		
Low & middle income	1,980,449	11,628,278	35.5	48.9	33.2	60.4	83.1	213.8	22,419	16,120		
East Asia & Pacific	780,487	5,717,001	47.1	58.0	49.8	103.7	125.0	229.5	3,190	3,962		
Europe & Central Asia	147,380	1,635,890	17.6	44.4	25.4	23.8	94.4	68.0	7,524	3,610		
Latin America & Carib.	620,023	1,178,104	31.8	31.9	8.5	24.9	27.2	46.1	1,672	1,471		
Middle East & N. Africa	57,110	209,656	19.9	55.9	5.1	18.8	12.4	28.7	1,676	717		
South Asia	157,695	1,274,122	26.1	47.0	90.2	76.5	167.9	88.9	7,269	6,123		
Sub-Saharan Africa	217,754	868,391	89.7	148.5	32.3	101.3	22.1	76.5	1,088	820		
High income	30,207,068	27,380,501	116.6	62.9	177.7	164.0	130.4	187.1	25,368	31,198		
Euro area	5,433,547	5,152,619	86.9	37.9	80.3	91.3	90.7	176.8	5,028	6,700		

a. Refers to the S&P Frontier BMI index. b. Refers to the CAC 40 index. c. Refers to the DAX index. d. Refers to the Nikkei 225 index. e. Refers to the FT 100 index. f. Refers to the S&P 500 index. g. Aggregates not preserved because data for high-income economies are not available for 2008.

About the data

The development of an economy's financial markets is closely related to its overall development. Well functioning financial systems provide good and easily accessible information. That lowers transaction costs, which in turn improves resource allocation and boosts economic growth. Both banking systems and stock markets enhance growth, the main factor in poverty reduction. At low levels of economic development commercial banks tend to dominate the financial system, while at higher levels domestic stock markets tend to become more active and efficient relative to domestic banks.

Open economies with sound macroeconomic policies, good legal systems, and shareholder protection attract capital and therefore have larger financial markets. Recent research on stock market development shows that modern communications technology and increased financial integration have resulted in more cross-border capital flows, a stronger presence of financial firms around the world, and the migration of stock exchange activities to international exchanges. Many firms in emerging markets now cross-list on international exchanges, which provides them with lower cost capital and more liquidity-traded shares. However, this also means that exchanges in emerging markets may not have enough financial activity to sustain them, putting pressure on them to rethink their operations.

The indicators in the table are from Standard & Poor's Emerging Markets Data Base. They include measures of size (market capitalization, number of listed domestic companies) and liquidity (value of shares traded as a percentage of gross domestic product, value of shares traded as a percentage of market capitalization). The comparability of such indicators across countries may be limited by conceptual and statistical weaknesses, such as inaccurate reporting and differences in accounting standards. The percentage change in stock market prices in U.S. dollars for developing economies is from Standard & Poor's Global Equity Indices (S&P IFCI) and Standard & Poor's Frontier Broad Market Index (BMI). The percentage change for France, Germany, Japan, the United Kingdom, and the United States is from local stock market prices. The indicator is an important measure of overall performance. Regulatory and institutional factors that can affect investor confidence, such as entry and exit restrictions, the existence of a securities and exchange commission, and the quality of laws to protect investors, may influence the functioning of stock markets but are not included in the table.

Stock market size can be measured in various ways, and each may produce a different ranking of countries. Market capitalization shows the overall size of the stock market in U.S. dollars and as a percentage of GDP. The number of listed domestic companies is another measure of market size. Market size is positively correlated with the ability to mobilize capital and diversify risk.

Market liquidity, the ability to easily buy and sell securities, is measured by dividing the total value of shares traded by GDP. The turnover ratio—the value of shares traded as a percentage of market capitalization—is also a measure of liquidity as well as of transaction costs. (High turnover indicates low transaction costs.) The turnover ratio complements the ratio of value traded to GDP, because the turnover ratio is related to the size of the market and the value traded ratio to the size of the economy. A small, liquid market will have a high turnover ratio but a low value of shares traded ratio. Liquidity is an important attribute of stock markets because, in theory, liquid markets improve the allocation of capital and enhance prospects for long-term economic growth. A more comprehensive measure of liquidity would include trading costs and the time and uncertainty in finding a counterpart in settling trades.

Standard & Poor's Index Services, the source for all the data in the table, provides regular updates on 22 emerging stock markets and 36 frontier markets. Standard & Poor's maintains a series of indexes for investors interested in investing in stock markets in developing countries. The S&P/IFCI index, Standard & Poor's leading emerging markets index, is designed to be sufficiently investable to support index tracking portfolios in emerging market stocks that are legally and practically open to foreign portfolio investment. The S&P/Frontier BMI measures the performance of 36 smaller and less liquid markets. The individual country indexes include all publicly listed equities representing an aggregate of at least 80 percent or more of market capitalization in each market. These indexes are widely used benchmarks for international portfolio management. See www.standardandpoors.com for further information on the indexes.

Because markets included in Standard & Poor's emerging markets category vary widely in level of development, it is best to look at the entire category to identify the most significant market trends. And it is useful to remember that stock market trends may be distorted by currency conversions, especially when a currency has registered a significant devaluation.

About the data is based on Demirgüç-Kunt and Levine (1996), Beck and Levine (2001), and Claessens, Klingebiel, and Schmukler (2002).

Definitions

• **Market capitalization** (also known as market value) is the share price times the number of shares outstanding. • **Market liquidity** is the total value of shares traded during the period divided by gross domestic product (GDP). This indicator complements the market capitalization ratio by showing whether market size is matched by trading. • **Turnover ratio** is the total value of shares traded during the period divided by the average market capitalization for the period. Average market capitalization is calculated as the average of the end-of-period values for the current period and the previous period. • **Listed domestic companies** are the domestically incorporated companies listed on the country's stock exchanges at the end of the year. This indicator does not include investment companies, mutual funds, or other collective investment vehicles. • **S&P/Global Equity Indices** measure the U.S. dollar price change in the stock markets.

Data sources

Data on stock markets are from Standard & Poor's *Global Stock Markets Factbook 2009,* which draws on the Emerging Markets Data Base, supplemented by other data from Standard & Poor's. The firm collects data through an annual survey of the world's stock exchanges, supplemented by information provided by its network of correspondents and by Reuters. Data on GDP are from the World Bank's national accounts data files.

Financial access, stability, and efficiency

	Getting credit				Bank capital to asset ratio	Ratio of bank nonperforming loans to total gross loans	Domestic credit provided by banking sector	Interest rate spread	Risk premium on lending
	Strength of legal rights index 0–10 (weak to strong)	Depth of credit information index 0–6 (low to high)	% of adult population Public credit registry coverage	Private credit bureau coverage				Lending rate minus deposit rate percentage points	Prime lending rate minus treasury bill rate percentage points
					%	%	% of GDP		
	June 2009	**June 2009**	**June 2009**	**June 2009**	**2008**	**2008**	**2008**	**2008**	**2008**
Afghanistan	6	0	0.0	0.0	..	..	3.5	..	..
Albania	9	4	9.9	0.0	6.7	6.6	67.6	6.2	6.8
Algeria	3	2	0.2	0.0	..	..	–13.0	6.3	7.7
Angola	4	4	2.5	0.0	..	..	9.3	6.3	..
Argentina	4	6	34.3	100.0	12.9	2.7	24.4	8.4	..
Armenia	6	5	4.4	34.5	23.0	4.4	16.7	10.4	9.4
Australia	9	5	0.0	100.0	4.2	0.5	137.8	3.7	..
Austria	7	6	1.4	39.2	6.3	2.0	129.7	..	..
Azerbaijan	8	5	6.9	0.0	..	..	17.1	7.5	8.5
Bangladesh	7	2	0.9	0.0	6.5	11.2	59.4	6.7	..
Belarus	2	5	23.4	0.0	17.4	0.6	31.5	0.0	..
Belgium	7	4	56.5	0.0	3.3	1.7	113.8	..	4.8
Benin	3	1	10.9	0.0	..	..	14.8	..	..
Bolivia	1	6	11.6	33.9	9.3	4.3	48.4	9.2	5.6
Bosnia and Herzegovina	5	5	23.2	64.3	*13.1*	3.1	58.5	3.5	..
Botswana	7	4	0.0	51.9	..	..	–11.2	7.9	..
Brazil	3	5	23.7	59.2	9.1	3.1	101.7	35.6	33.6
Bulgaria	8	6	34.8	6.2	8.5	2.4	66.7	6.4	6.2
Burkina Faso	3	1	1.9	0.0	..	..	15.5	..	..
Burundi	2	1	0.2	0.0	..	..	34.9	..	8.2
Cambodia	8	0	0.0	0.0	..	..	16.2	*14.6*	..
Cameroon	3	2	1.8	0.0	..	..	5.8	*10.8*	..
Canada	6	6	0.0	100.0	5.1	1.1	177.8	3.2	2.3
Central African Republic	3	2	2.1	0.0	..	..	18.0	*10.8*	..
Chad	3	1	0.2	0.0	..	..	–2.7	*10.8*	..
Chile	4	5	32.9	33.9	6.9	1.0	98.3	5.8	..
China	6	4	62.1	0.0	6.1	2.4	126.2	3.1	..
Hong Kong SAR, China	10	4	0.0	71.9	*12.0*	0.9	124.6	4.6	5.0
Colombia	5	5	0.0	60.5	12.2	4.0	43.1	7.4	..
Congo, Dem. Rep.	3	0	0.0	0.0	..	..	9.1	..	..
Congo, Rep.	3	2	3.0	0.0	..	..	–18.5	*10.8*	..
Costa Rica	5	5	24.3	56.0	13.3	1.5	53.9	11.7	..
Côte d'Ivoire	3	1	2.7	0.0	..	..	20.1	..	..
Croatia	6	4	0.0	77.0	13.5	4.9	75.1	7.2	..
Cuba	..	..	..	..	..	..	..	..	..
Czech Republic	6	5	4.9	73.1	5.7	3.3	58.0	4.6	2.6
Denmark	9	4	0.0	5.2	*5.7*	*0.3*	211.2	..	..
Dominican Republic	3	6	29.7	46.1	9.7	3.5	39.1	9.6	..
Ecuador	3	5	37.2	46.0	8.8	2.5	17.3	*7.1*	..
Egypt, Arab Rep.	3	6	2.5	8.2	5.3	14.8	78.0	5.7	1.0
El Salvador	5	6	21.0	94.6	12.7	2.8	44.9	..	..
Eritrea	2	0	0.0	0.0	..	..	112.7	..	..
Estonia	6	5	0.0	20.6	9.3	1.9	97.3	2.8	..
Ethiopia	4	2	0.1	0.0	..	..	37.6	3.4	7.3
Finland	7	5	0.0	14.7	7.4	0.4	87.7	..	..
France	7	4	32.5	0.0	4.2	2.8	126.1	..	..
Gabon	3	2	3.9	0.0	10.7	8.5	6.1	*10.8*	..
Gambia, The	5	0	0.0	0.0	..	..	34.3	*15.0*	..
Georgia	6	6	0.0	12.2	17.1	4.1	32.9	10.9	..
Germany	7	6	0.8	98.3	4.5	*2.7*	125.7	..	..
Ghana	7	0	0.0	0.0	12.8	7.7	*32.9*	..	..
Greece	3	5	0.0	46.9	4.5	5.0	109.0	..	..
Guatemala	8	6	16.9	28.4	10.3	2.4	36.8	8.3	..
Guinea	3	0	0.0	0.0	..	..	..	..	..
Guinea-Bissau	3	1	1.1	0.0	..	..	13.5	..	..
Haiti	3	2	0.7	0.0	..	..	*24.6*	15.7	..
Honduras	6	6	21.7	58.7	..	..	50.4	8.4	..

	Getting credit				Bank capital to asset ratio	Ratio of bank nonperforming loans to total gross loans	Domestic credit provided by banking sector	Interest rate spread	Risk premium on lending
	Strength of legal rights index 0–10 (weak to strong)	Depth of credit information index 0–6 (low to high)	% of adult population Public credit registry coverage	Private credit bureau coverage				Lending rate minus deposit rate percentage points	Prime lending rate minus treasury bill rate percentage points
	June 2009	June 2009	June 2009	June 2009	% 2008	% 2008	% of GDP 2008	2008	2008
Hungary	7	5	0.0	10.3	8.0	3.0	80.7	0.3	1.3
India	8	4	0.0	10.2	6.4	2.3	71.6	..	..
Indonesia	3	4	22.0	0.0	9.2	3.2	36.7	5.1	..
Iran, Islamic Rep.	4	3	31.3	0.0	..	..	50.5	0.4	..
Iraq	3	0	0.0	0.0	..	..	..	8.4	–1.3
Ireland	8	5	0.0	100.0	4.7	2.6	204.3	..	..
Israel	9	5	0.0	89.8	5.7	1.5	79.9	2.8	2.2
Italy	3	5	12.2	77.5	6.6	4.9	132.4	..	3.1
Jamaica	8	0	0.0	0.0	..	..	54.1	9.3	0.9
Japan	7	6	0.0	76.2	3.6	1.7	293.0	1.3	1.6
Jordan	4	2	1.0	0.0	10.4	4.2	114.9	3.6	..
Kazakhstan	5	6	0.0	29.5	12.2	5.1	33.5	..	..
Kenya	10	4	0.0	2.3	11.4	9.0	40.1	8.7	6.3
Korea, Dem. Rep.	..	..	..	..	..	..	..	..	..
Korea, Rep.	7	6	0.0	93.8	8.8	1.1	112.6	1.3	..
Kosovo	8	3	18.9	0.0	..	3.7	10.9	..	..
Kuwait	4	4	0.0	30.4	11.6	3.1	68.1	2.8	..
Kyrgyz Republic	10	3	0.0	5.9	..	..	14.0	15.9	6.7
Lao PDR	4	0	0.0	0.0	..	..	10.5	23.5	11.5
Latvia	9	5	46.5	0.0	7.3	3.6	89.1	5.5	4.9
Lebanon	3	5	8.3	0.0	7.8	7.5	172.9	2.3	4.8
Lesotho	7	0	0.0	0.0	7.9	3.5	–18.4	8.5	6.4
Liberia	4	1	0.3	0.0	..	..	144.5	11.3	..
Libya	..	..	..	..	..	..	–50.0	3.5	..
Lithuania	5	6	12.1	18.4	7.6	4.6	64.2	0.8	2.6
Macedonia, FYR	7	4	28.1	0.0	..	6.8	42.7	3.8	..
Madagascar	2	1	0.1	0.0	..	..	9.3	33.5	36.2
Malawi	8	0	0.0	0.0	..	..	26.2	21.7	14.0
Malaysia	10	6	48.5	82.0	8.0	4.8	115.2	3.0	2.7
Mali	3	1	4.0	0.0	..	..	13.2	..	..
Mauritania	3	1	0.2	0.0	..	..	..	15.5	13.1
Mauritius	5	3	36.8	0.0	..	..	111.7	11.4	..
Mexico	4	6	0.0	77.5	9.6	3.2	37.5	5.7	1.0
Moldova	8	0	0.0	0.0	17.0	5.2	39.8	3.1	3.0
Mongolia	6	3	22.2	0.0	..	..	34.4	9.4	20.4
Morocco	3	5	0.0	14.0	7.3	6.0	95.5	..	..
Mozambique	2	4	2.3	0.0	6.7	2.8	14.2	7.3	4.6
Myanmar	..	..	..	..	..	..	..	5.0	..
Namibia	8	5	0.0	57.7	8.0	3.1	43.8	5.4	4.1
Nepal	5	2	0.0	0.3	..	..	52.7	5.8	4.4
Netherlands	6	5	0.0	83.5	3.2	0.8	196.0	0.2	..
New Zealand	9	5	0.0	100.0	..	..	156.3	4.7	5.2
Nicaragua	3	5	16.0	28.4	..	..	66.2	6.6	..
Niger	3	1	0.9	0.0	..	..	6.2	..	..
Nigeria	8	0	0.0	0.0	18.0	6.3	26.7	3.5	7.3
Norway	7	4	0.0	100.0	4.2	0.8	..	1.8	..
Oman	4	2	17.0	0.0	15.5	2.4	32.9	2.6	..
Pakistan	6	4	5.6	1.5	10.4	9.1	45.9	6.0	1.6
Panama	6	6	0.0	45.9	13.4	1.7	85.8	4.6	..
Papua New Guinea	5	0	0.0	0.0	..	..	24.9	8.0	3.1
Paraguay	3	6	10.9	47.4	11.2	1.2	22.0	22.7	..
Peru	7	6	23.0	31.8	8.3	2.2	18.5	20.2	..
Philippines	3	3	0.0	6.1	11.1	4.5	46.0	4.3	5.3
Poland	9	4	0.0	68.3	7.9	4.4	60.1	3.3	1.3
Portugal	3	5	81.3	16.4	6.1	2.0	183.8	..	..
Puerto Rico	7	5	0.0	73.8	..	..	..	..	..
Qatar	3	2	0.0	0.0	..	..	56.9	3.9	..

	Getting credit				Bank capital to asset ratio	Ratio of bank nonperforming loans to total gross loans	Domestic credit provided by banking sector	Interest rate spread	Risk premium on lending
	Strength of legal rights index 0–10 (weak to strong)	Depth of credit information index 0–6 (low to high)	% of adult population Public credit registry coverage	Private credit bureau coverage	%	%	% of GDP	Lending rate minus deposit rate percentage points	Prime lending rate minus treasury bill rate percentage points
	June 2009	June 2009	June 2009	June 2009	2008	2008	2008	2008	2008
Romania	8	5	5.7	30.2	7.0	13.8	40.9	5.5	4.6
Russian Federation	3	5	0.0	14.3	13.6	3.8	25.9	6.5	..
Rwanda	8	2	0.4	0.0	12.3	12.6	..	9.3	8.9
Saudi Arabia	4	6	0.0	17.9	10.0	1.4	9.5	..	..
Senegal	3	1	4.4	0.0	9.1	19.1	24.7	..	..
Serbia	8	6	0.0	94.2	20.5	5.3	38.4	10.8	8.5
Sierra Leone	6	0	0.0	0.0	18.7	23.3	7.4	14.8	9.0
Singapore	10	4	0.0	40.3	8.5	1.4	84.1	5.0	4.5
Slovak Republic	9	4	1.4	44.0	9.8	3.2	53.8	4.3	..
Slovenia	6	2	2.7	0.0	8.4	1.6	87.5	2.6	2.8
Somalia	..	..	..	..	..	..	..	..	..
South Africa	9	6	0.0	54.7	7.9	3.9	172.2	3.5	4.3
Spain	6	5	45.3	7.6	6.4	3.4	212.9	..	..
Sri Lanka	4	5	0.0	14.3	..	..	42.8	8.0	0.0
Sudan	5	0	0.0	0.0	..	..	17.1	..	..
Swaziland	6	5	0.0	42.3	20.7	8.4	2.0	6.7	4.1
Sweden	5	4	0.0	100.0	4.7	1.0	135.8	..	..
Switzerland	8	5	0.0	22.5	4.6	0.5	183.6	3.2	2.0
Syrian Arab Republic	1	0	0.0	0.0	..	..	36.9	1.8	..
Tajikistan	3	0	0.0	0.0	..	..	27.5	14.4	..
Tanzania	8	0	0.0	0.0	..	..	17.2	6.9	6.9
Thailand	4	5	0.0	32.9	9.5	5.7	130.6	4.6	3.9
Timor-Leste	1	0	0.0	0.0	..	..	−25.5	12.3	..
Togo	3	1	2.7	0.0	..	..	24.8	..	..
Trinidad and Tobago	8	4	0.0	41.7	..	..	12.8	5.1	5.4
Tunisia	3	5	19.9	0.0	..	15.5	73.0	..	..
Turkey	4	5	15.9	42.9	11.7	3.6	52.6	..	..
Turkmenistan	..	..	..	..	..	..	..	..	..
Uganda	7	0	0.0	0.0	13.8	2.2	11.4	9.8	11.9
Ukraine	9	3	0.0	3.0	14.0	17.4	81.9	7.5	..
United Arab Emirates	4	5	7.3	12.6	10.6	2.5	78.1	..	..
United Kingdom	9	6	0.0	100.0	4.4	1.6	212.3	..	0.3
United States	8	6	0.0	100.0	9.3	3.0	216.1	..	3.6
Uruguay	5	6	17.8	97.2	8.9	1.0	32.5	9.2	1.8
Uzbekistan	2	3	2.6	2.1	..	..	..	..	..
Venezuela, RB	2	0	0.0	0.0	9.4	1.9	20.3	6.2	..
Vietnam	8	4	19.0	0.0	..	..	95.0	3.1	7.0
West Bank and Gaza	0	3	6.5	0.0	..	..	..	4.8	..
Yemen, Rep.	2	2	0.2	0.0	..	..	11.4	5.0	2.8
Zambia	9	3	0.0	0.4	..	..	19.3	12.5	5.6
Zimbabwe	7	0	0.0	0.0	..	..	..	457.5	330.2
World	**5.4 u**	**2.9 u**	**6.6 u**	**21.8 u**	**9.0 m**	**3.2 m**	**156.8 w**	**6.0 m**	
Low income	4.7	1.2	1.4	0.3	..	..	43.7	10.8	
Middle income	5.2	3.1	9.2	18.6	9.7	3.9	76.1	6.4	
Lower middle income	4.7	2.6	7.1	9.6	10.2	4.4	98.7	6.6	
Upper middle income	5.8	3.7	11.9	30.3	9.4	3.6	55.7	6.2	
Low & middle income	5.0	2.5	6.9	13.2	..	4.1	75.2	6.5	
East Asia & Pacific	5.3	1.7	8.7	8.5	..	..	116.4	5.1	
Europe & Central Asia	6.6	4.2	11.3	18.5	12.2	4.4	41.5	6.2	
Latin America & Carib.	5.2	3.5	11.5	33.8	9.7	2.5	62.0	7.9	
Middle East & N. Africa	2.5	2.8	5.8	1.9	..	..	39.7	4.3	
South Asia	5.3	2.1	0.8	3.3	6.4	9.1	69.3	6.6	
Sub-Saharan Africa	4.7	1.4	2.3	4.7	..	..	65.5	10.0	
High income	6.6	4.1	5.7	46.5	6.3	1.9	188.4	..	
Euro area	6.3	4.1	15.6	35.2	6.1	2.6	142.7	..	

About the data

Financial sector development has positive impacts on economic growth and poverty. The size of the sector determines the resources mobilized for investment. Access to finance can expand opportunities for all with higher levels of access and use of banking services associated with lower financing obstacles for people and businesses. A stable financial system that promotes efficient savings and investment is also crucial for a thriving democracy and market economy. The banking system is the largest sector in the financial system in most countries, so most indicators in the table cover the banking system.

There are several aspects of access to financial services: availability, cost, and quality of services. The development and growth of credit markets depend on access to timely, reliable, and accurate data on borrowers' credit experiences. For secured transactions, such as mortgages or vehicle loans, rapid access to information in property registries is also vital, and for small business loans corporate registry data are needed. Access to credit can be improved by increasing information about potential borrowers' creditworthiness and making it easy to create and enforce collateral agreements. Lenders look at a borrower's credit history and collateral. Where credit registries and effective collateral laws are absent—as in many developing countries—banks make fewer loans. Indicators that cover financial access, or getting credit, include the strength of legal rights index (ranges from 0, weak, to 10, strong), depth of credit information index (ranges from 0, low, to 6, high), public registry coverage, and private bureau coverage.

The strength of legal rights index is based on eight aspects related to legal rights in collateral law and two aspects in bankruptcy law. It is based on a standardized case scenario and measures the degree to which collateral and bankruptcy laws protect the rights of borrowers and lenders and thus facilitate lending. The indicator focuses on revolving movable collateral, such as accounts receivable and inventory, rather than tangible movable collateral, such as equipment. The depth of credit information index assesses six features of the public registry or the private credit bureau (or both). For more information on these indexes, see www.doingbusiness.org/MethodologySurveys/.

The size and mobility of international capital flows make it increasingly important to monitor the strength of financial systems. Robust financial systems can increase economic activity and welfare, but instability in the financial system can disrupt financial activity and impose widespread costs on the economy. The ratio of bank capital to assets, a measure of bank solvency and resiliency, shows the extent to which banks can deal with unexpected losses. Capital includes tier 1 capital (paid-up shares and common stock), a common feature in all countries' banking systems, and total regulatory capital, which includes several types of subordinated debt instruments that need not be repaid if the funds are required to maintain minimum capital levels (tier 2 and tier 3 capital). Total assets include all nonfinancial and financial assets. Data are from internally consistent financial statements.

The ratio of bank nonperforming loans to total gross loans, a measure of bank health and efficiency, helps to identify problems with asset quality in the loan portfolio. A high ratio may signal deterioration of the credit portfolio. International guidelines recommend that loans be classified as nonperforming when payments of principal and interest are 90 days or more past due or when future payments are not expected to be received in full. See the International Monetary Fund's (IMF) *Global Financial Stability Report* for details.

Domestic credit by the banking sector as a share of GDP is a measure of banking sector depth and financial sector development in terms of size. In a few countries governments may hold international reserves as deposits in the banking system rather than in the central bank. Since the claims on the central government are a net item (claims on the central government minus central government deposits), this net figure may be negative, resulting in a negative figure of domestic credit provided by the banking sector.

The interest rate spread—the margin between the cost of mobilizing liabilities and the earnings on assets—is a measure of financial sector efficiency in intermediation. A narrow interest rate spread means low transaction costs, which lowers the cost of funds for investment, crucial to economic growth.

The risk premium on lending is the spread between the lending rate to the private sector and the "risk-free" government rate. Spreads are expressed as annual averages. A small spread indicates that the market considers its best corporate customers to be low risk. A negative rate indicates that the market considers its best corporate clients to be lower risk than the government.

Definitions

• **Strength of legal rights index** measures the degree to which collateral and bankruptcy laws protect the rights of borrowers and lenders and thus facilitate lending. Higher values indicate that the laws are better designed to expand access to credit. • **Depth of credit information index** measures rules affecting the scope, accessibility, and quality of information available through public or private credit registries. Higher values indicate the availability of more credit information. • **Public credit registry coverage** is the number of individuals and firms listed in a public credit registry with current information on repayment history, unpaid debts, or credit outstanding as a percentage of the adult population. • **Private credit bureau coverage** is the number of individuals or firms listed by a private credit bureau with current information on repayment history, unpaid debts, or credit outstanding as a percentage of the adult population. • **Bank capital to asset ratio** is the ratio of bank capital and reserves to total assets. Capital and reserves include funds contributed by owners, retained earnings, general and special reserves, provisions, and valuation adjustments. • **Ratio of bank nonperforming loans to total gross loans** is the value of nonperforming loans divided by the total value of the loan portfolio (including nonperforming loans before the deduction of loan loss provisions). The amount recorded as nonperforming should be the gross value of the loan as recorded on the balance sheet, not just the amount overdue. • **Domestic credit provided by banking sector** is all credit to various sectors on a gross basis, except to the central government, which is net. The banking sector includes monetary authorities, deposit money banks, and other banking institutions for which data are available. • **Interest rate spread** is the interest rate charged by banks on loans to prime customers minus the interest rate paid by commercial or similar banks for demand, time, or savings deposits. • **Risk premium on lending** is the interest rate charged by banks on loans to prime private sector customers minus the "risk-free" treasury bill interest rate at which short-term government securities are issued or traded in the market.

Data sources

Data on getting credit are from the World Bank's Doing Business project (www.doingbusiness.org). Data on bank capital and nonperforming loans are from the IMF's *Global Financial Stability Report*. Data on credit and interest rates are from the IMF's *International Financial Statistics*.

5.6 Tax policies

	Tax revenue collected by central government		Taxes payable by businesses			Highest marginal tax rate[a]		
	% of GDP		Number of payments	Time to prepare, file, and pay taxes hours	Total tax rate % of profit	Individual		Corporate %
						%	On income over $	
	2000	2008	June 2009	June 2009	June 2009	2009	2009	2009
Afghanistan[b]	..	5.8	8	275	36.4	..	..	20
Albania[b]	16.1	..	44	244	44.9	..	..	10
Algeria[b]	..	46.5	34	451	72.0	..	..	..
Angola	..	..	31	272	53.2	..	..	35
Argentina	9.8	..	9	453	108.1	35	32,434	35
Armenia[b]	..	17.0	50	958	36.2	20	2,577	20
Australia	22.1	23.1	12	107	48.0	45	133,560	30
Austria	19.9	20.1	22	170	55.5	50	80,268	25
Azerbaijan[b]	..	0.0	22	376	40.9	..	..	..
Bangladesh[b]	7.6	8.8	21	302	35.0	..	..	28
Belarus[b]	16.6	25.5	107	900	99.7	..	..	24
Belgium	27.4	25.6	11	156	57.3	50	45,926	34
Benin[b]	15.5	17.3	55	270	73.3	..	..	..
Bolivia	13.2	17.0	42	1,080	80.0	..	..	25
Bosnia and Herzegovina	..	21.0	51	422	27.1	..	..	10
Botswana[b]	..	..	19	140	17.1	25[c]	17,647[c]	25[c]
Brazil[b]	..	16.4	10	2,600	69.2	28	20,218	34
Bulgaria[b]	18.3	24.2	17	616	31.4	10	..	10
Burkina Faso	..	12.5	46	270	44.9	..	..	..
Burundi[b]	13.6	..	32	140	278.6	..	..	..
Cambodia	8.2	8.2	39	173	22.7	..	..	..
Cameroon[b]	11.2	..	41	1,400	50.5	..	..	..
Canada[b]	15.0	14.2	9	119	43.6	29	107,542	33
Central African Republic[b]	..	..	54	504	203.8	..	..	..
Chad	..	..	54	122	60.9	..	..	..
Chile	16.7	19.8	10	316	25.3	40	109,484	17
China[b]	6.8	9.4	7	504	78.5	45	175,716	25
Hong Kong SAR, China	..	..	4	80	24.2	15	..	17
Colombia	11.7	12.6	20	208	78.7	33	43,467	33
Congo, Dem. Rep.[b]	3.5	..	32	308	322.0	50[c]	14,304[c]	38[c]
Congo, Rep.	9.2	..	61	606	65.5	..	..	..
Costa Rica[b]	..	15.8	42	282	54.8	15	1,526	30
Côte d'Ivoire[b]	..	15.6	66	270	44.7	10[c]	5,360[c]	25[c]
Croatia[b]	22.6	20.4	17	196	32.5	45	54,696	20
Cuba	..	..	..	..	..	..	..	..
Czech Republic[b]	15.4	14.8	12	613	47.2	15	..	20
Denmark	31.0	35.6	9	135	29.2	62	62,286	25
Dominican Republic[b]	..	15.9	9	324	39.0	..	..	25
Ecuador[b]	..	..	8	600	34.9	35	62,000	25
Egypt, Arab Rep.[b]	13.4	15.4	29	480	43.0	20	7,146	20
El Salvador	10.7	13.9	53	320	35.0	..	..	..
Eritrea	..	..	18	216	84.5	..	..	..
Estonia	15.8	16.8	10	81	49.1	21	..	21
Ethiopia[b]	10.2	..	19	198	31.1	35	..	30
Finland	24.6	21.7	8	243	47.7	31	86,288	26
France	23.2	21.8	7	132	65.8	40	92,983	33
Gabon	..	..	26	272	44.7	..	..	..
Gambia, The[b]	..	..	50	376	292.4	..	..	..
Georgia[b]	7.7	23.8	18	387	15.3	..	..	..
Germany	11.9	11.8	16	196	44.9	45	334,448	29
Ghana[b]	17.2	22.9	33	224	32.7	25[c]	10,213[c]	25[c]
Greece	23.3	19.9	10	224	47.4	40	100,334	25
Guatemala[b]	10.1	11.3	24	344	40.9	31	37,389	31
Guinea[b]	11.1	..	56	416	49.9	..	..	..
Guinea-Bissau	..	..	46	208	45.9	..	..	..
Haiti	..	..	42	160	40.1	..	..	..
Honduras	..	15.8	47	224	48.3	..	..	30

	Tax revenue collected by central government		Taxes payable by businesses			Highest marginal tax rate[a]		
	% of GDP		Number of payments	Time to prepare, file, and pay taxes hours	Total tax rate % of profit	Individual		Corporate %
	2000	2008	June 2009	June 2009	June 2009	% 2009	On income over $ 2009	2009
Hungary	21.9	23.6	14	330	57.5	36	8,014	16
India[b]	9.0	12.9	59	271	64.7	30	10,115	34
Indonesia[b]	11.6	..	51	266	37.6	30	47,500	28
Iran, Islamic Rep.[b]	6.3	7.3	22	344	44.2	..	..	25
Iraq	..	..	13	312	28.4	..	..	..
Ireland	26.0	25.4	9	76	26.5	46	48,697	13
Israel	28.7	25.3	33	230	32.6	46	110,230	26
Italy	23.2	22.6	15	334	68.4	43	100,334	31
Jamaica[b]	..	25.4	72	414	51.3	25	..	33
Japan	..	..	13	355	55.7	50	182,062	41
Jordan[b]	..	18.3	26	101	31.1	..	..	25
Kazakhstan[b]	10.2	12.7	9	271	35.9	10	..	20
Kenya[b]	16.8	18.9	41	417	49.7	..	..	..
Korea, Dem. Rep.	..	..	..	..	..	..	..	..
Korea, Rep.[b]	15.4	16.6	14	250	31.9	35	69,379	24
Kosovo	..	25.5	33	163	28.3	..	..	..
Kuwait	1.3	0.9	15	118	15.5	0	..	15
Kyrgyz Republic[b]	11.7	16.8	75	202	59.4	..	..	..
Lao PDR	..	10.1	34	362	33.7	..	..	..
Latvia[b]	14.2	15.0	7	279	33.0	23	..	15
Lebanon	11.9	16.3	19	180	30.2	..	..	..
Lesotho[b]	35.6	58.9	21	324	18.5	..	..	..
Liberia	..	..	32	158	43.7	..	..	..
Libya	..	..	..	..	..	..	..	40
Lithuania	14.6	17.4	12	166	42.7	15	..	20
Macedonia, FYR[b]	..	19.7	40	75	16.4	..	..	10
Madagascar	11.3	11.4	23	201	39.2	..	..	..
Malawi	..	..	19	157	25.8	..	..	..
Malaysia[b]	13.8	..	12	145	34.2	27	28,470	25
Mali	13.2	15.6	58	270	52.1	..	..	..
Mauritania	..	..	38	696	86.1	..	..	..
Mauritius[b]	17.3	18.2	7	161	22.9	15[c]	..	15[c]
Mexico[b]	11.7	..	6	517	51.0	28	29,591	28
Moldova[b]	14.7	20.5	48	228	31.1	..	..	..
Mongolia	14.5	23.2	43	192	22.8	..	..	..
Morocco[b]	19.9	27.5	28	358	41.7	..	..	..
Mozambique	..	..	37	230	34.3	32[c]	58,514[c]	32[c]
Myanmar	3.0	..	..	..	..	..	..	..
Namibia[b]	27.5	27.2	37	375	9.6	37[c]	90,361[c]	35[c]
Nepal[b]	8.7	10.4	34	338	38.8	..	..	..
Netherlands	22.3	23.6	9	164	39.3	52	73,279	26
New Zealand	29.5	31.7	8	70	32.8	38	40,498	30
Nicaragua[b]	13.8	17.0	64	240	63.2	..	..	..
Niger	..	11.5	41	270	46.5	..	..	..
Nigeria	..	..	35	938	32.2	..	..	30
Norway	27.4	28.1	4	87	41.6	40	110,229	28
Oman[b]	7.2	..	14	62	21.6	0	..	12
Pakistan[b]	10.1	9.8	47	560	31.6	20	107,838	35
Panama[b]	10.2	..	59	482	50.1	27	29,294	30
Papua New Guinea[b]	19.0	..	33	194	42.3	42	92,996	30
Paraguay[b]	..	12.5	35	328	35.0	10	31,600	10
Peru[b]	12.2	15.4	9	380	40.3	30	63,033	30
Philippines[b]	13.7	14.1	47	195	49.4	32	10,474	30
Poland	16.0	18.4	40	395	42.5	32	26,116	19
Portugal	21.3	22.2	8	328	42.9	42	85,766	25
Puerto Rico	..	..	16	218	64.7	..	..	..
Qatar	..	23.1	1	36	11.3	0	..	35

	Tax revenue collected by central government		Taxes payable by businesses			Highest marginal tax rate[a]		
	% of GDP		Number of payments	Time to prepare, file, and pay taxes hours	Total tax rate % of profit	Individual		Corporate %
						%	On income over $	
	2000	2008	June 2009	June 2009	June 2009	2009	2009	2009
Romania	11.7	17.9	113	202	44.6	16	..	16
Russian Federation	13.6	15.7	11	320	48.3	13	..	20
Rwanda[b]	..	..	34	160	31.3	..	..	..
Saudi Arabia	..	..	14	79	14.5	0	..	20
Senegal[b]	16.1	..	59	666	46.0	..	..	..
Serbia[b]	..	22.0	66	279	34.0	15	46,146	10
Sierra Leone[b]	10.2	..	29	357	235.6	..	..	..
Singapore[b]	15.4	14.6	5	84	27.8	20	217,317	18
Slovak Republic	..	13.4	31	257	48.6	19	..	19
Slovenia[b]	20.6	83.5	22	260	37.5	41	19,827	21
Somalia	..	..	..	..	..	..	..	..
South Africa	24.0	27.7	9	200	30.2	40[c]	63,253[c]	35[c]
Spain	16.2	10.6	8	213	56.9	43	71,447	30
Sri Lanka[b]	14.5	14.2	62	256	63.7	35	13,346	35
Sudan[b]	6.4	..	42	180	36.1	..	..	35
Swaziland[b]	..	..	33	104	36.6	33[c]	12,048[c]	30[c]
Sweden	20.6	..	2	122	54.6	57	66,419	26
Switzerland[b]	11.1	10.2	24	63	29.7	40	630,312	21
Syrian Arab Republic[b]	17.4	..	20	336	42.9	..	..	28
Tajikistan[b]	7.7	..	54	224	85.9	..	..	..
Tanzania	..	..	48	172	45.2	30[c]	7,222[c]	30[c]
Thailand	..	16.5	23	264	37.2	37	113,147	30
Timor-Leste	..	..	6	276	0.2	..	..	..
Togo[b]	..	16.3	53	270	52.7	..	..	..
Trinidad and Tobago[b]	22.1	25.9	40	114	33.1	..	..	..
Tunisia[b]	21.3	22.8	22	228	62.8	..	..	30
Turkey[b]	..	18.6	15	223	44.5	35	28,564	20
Turkmenistan	..	..	..	..	..	..	..	..
Uganda[b]	10.4	12.8	32	161	35.7	30[c]	2,855[c]	45[c]
Ukraine[b]	14.1	17.8	147	736	57.2	15	..	25
United Arab Emirates[b]	1.7	..	14	12	14.1	0	..	55
United Kingdom	28.4	28.6	8	110	35.9	40	66,047	28
United States	12.7	9.9	10	187	46.3	35	372,950	40
Uruguay[b]	14.7	17.2	53	336	46.7	25	96,076	25
Uzbekistan	..	..	106	356	94.9	..	..	..
Venezuela, RB[b]	13.3	..	71	864	61.1	34	156,000	34
Vietnam	..	..	32	1,050	40.1	35	4,447	25
West Bank and Gaza	..	..	27	154	16.8	..	..	16
Yemen, Rep.[b]	9.4	..	44	248	47.8	..	..	35
Zambia[b]	18.6	17.1	37	132	16.1	..	..	35
Zimbabwe[b]	..	..	51	270	39.4	..	..	31
World	**15.6 w**	**17.5 w**	**31 u**	**286 u**	**48.3 u**	**..**	**..**	**..**
Low income	..	..	41	291	74.4			
Middle income	11.2	14.2	34	341	42.0			
Lower middle income	8.1	10.9	36	332	40.1			
Upper middle income	..	18.1	32	352	44.3			
Low & middle income	11.2	14.1	36	326	51.5			
East Asia & Pacific	7.7	10.1	27	243	38.0			
Europe & Central Asia	14.5	17.0	51	365	44.5			
Latin America & Carib.	..	..	33	419	48.5			
Middle East & N. Africa	11.8	28.4	27	276	41.6			
South Asia	9.3	12.3	31	285	40.0			
Sub-Saharan Africa	..	..	38	306	67.6			
High income	16.4	17.8	16	170	39.2			
Euro area	19.1	21.4	15	197	45.9			

a. Data are from KPMG's *Individual Income and Corporate Tax Rate Surveys 2009*, unless otherwise noted. b. Data on central government taxes were reported on a cash basis and have been adjusted to the accrual framework of the International Monetary Fund's *Government Finance Statistics Manual 2001*. c. Data are from PriceWaterhouseCooper's *Worldwide Tax Summaries* online.

About the data

Taxes are the main source of revenue for most governments. The sources of tax revenue and their relative contributions are determined by government policy choices about where and how to impose taxes and by changes in the structure of the economy. Tax policy may reflect concerns about distributional effects, economic efficiency (including corrections for externalities), and the practical problems of administering a tax system. There is no ideal level of taxation. But taxes influence incentives and thus the behavior of economic actors and the economy's competitiveness.

The level of taxation is typically measured by tax revenue as a share of gross domestic product (GDP). Comparing levels of taxation across countries provides a quick overview of the fiscal obligations and incentives facing the private sector. The table shows only central government data, which may significantly understate the total tax burden, particularly in countries where provincial and municipal governments are large or have considerable tax authority.

Low ratios of tax revenue to GDP may reflect weak administration and large-scale tax avoidance or evasion. Low ratios may also reflect a sizable parallel economy with unrecorded and undisclosed incomes. Tax revenue ratios tend to rise with income, with higher income countries relying on taxes to finance a much broader range of social services and social security than lower income countries are able to.

The indicators covering taxes payable by businesses measure all taxes and contributions that are government mandated (at any level—federal, state, or local), apply to standardized businesses, and have an impact in their income statements. The taxes covered go beyond the definition of a tax for government national accounts (compulsory, unrequited payments to general government) and also measure any imposts that affect business accounts. The main differences are in labor contributions and value added taxes. The indicators account for government-mandated contributions paid by the employer to a requited private pension fund or workers insurance fund but exclude value added taxes because they do not affect the accounting profits of the business—that is, they are not reflected in the income statement.

To make the data comparable across countries, several assumptions are made about businesses. The main assumptions are that they are limited liability companies, they operate in the country's most populous city, they are domestically owned, they perform general industrial or commercial activities, and

they have certain levels of start-up capital, employees, and turnover. For details about the assumptions, see the World Bank's *Doing Business 2010*.

A potentially important influence on both domestic and international investors is a tax system's progressivity, as reflected in the highest marginal tax rate levied at the national level on individual and corporate income. Data for individual marginal tax rates generally refer to employment income. In some countries the highest marginal tax rate is also the basic or flat rate, and other surtaxes, deductions, and the like may apply. And in many countries several different corporate tax rates may be levied, depending on the type of business (mining, banking, insurance, agriculture, manufacturing), ownership (domestic or foreign), volume of sales, and whether surtaxes or exemptions are included. The corporate tax rates in the table are general headline rates applied to domestic companies. For more detailed information, see the country's laws, regulations, and tax treaties; KPMG's *Corporate and Indirect Tax Rate Survey 2009* and *Individual Income Tax and Social Security Rate Survey 2009* (www.kpmg.com); and Pricewaterhouse-Coopers's *Worldwide Tax Summaries Online* (www.pwc.com).

Definitions

• **Tax revenue collected by central government** is compulsory transfers to the central government for public purposes. Certain compulsory transfers such as fines, penalties, and most social security contributions are excluded. Refunds and corrections of erroneously collected tax revenue are treated as negative revenue. The analytic framework of the International Monetary Fund's (IMF) *Government Finance Statistics Manual 2001* (GFSM 2001) is based on accrual accounting and balance sheets. For countries still reporting government finance data on a cash basis, the IMF adjusts reported data to the GFSM 2001 accrual framework. These countries are footnoted in the table. • **Number of tax payments by businesses** is the total number of taxes paid by businesses during one year. When electronic filing is available, the tax is counted as paid once a year even if payments are more frequent. • **Time to prepare, file, and pay taxes** is the time, in hours per year, it takes to prepare, file, and pay (or withhold) three major types of taxes: the corporate income tax, the value-added or sales tax, and labor taxes, including payroll taxes and social security contributions. • **Total tax rate** is the total amount of taxes payable by a standard business in the second year of operation after accounting for deductions and exemptions as a percentage of profit. Taxes withheld (such as personal income tax) or collected by the company and remitted to tax authorities but not borne by the company (such as value added tax, sales tax on goods, and taxes on services) are excluded. For further details on the method used for assessing the total tax payable, see the World Bank's *Doing Business 2010*. • **Highest marginal tax rate** is the highest rate shown on the national schedule of tax rates applied to the annual taxable income of individuals and corporations. Also presented are the income levels for individuals above which the highest marginal tax rates levied at the national level apply.

Data sources

Data on central government tax revenue are from print and electronic editions of the IMF's *Government Finance Statistics Yearbook*. Data on taxes payable by businesses are from *Doing Business 2010* (www.doingbusiness.org). Data on individual and corporate tax rates are from KPMG's *Corporate and Indirect Tax Rate Survey 2009* and *Individual Income Tax and Social Security Rate Survey 2009* (www.kpmg.com), and PricewaterhouseCoopers's *Worldwide Tax Summaries Online* (www.pwc.com).

	Military expenditures				Armed forces personnel				Arms transfers			
	% of GDP		% of central government expenditure		thousands		% of labor force		1990 $ millions Exports		Imports	
	2000	2008	2000	2008	2000	2008	2000	2008	2000	2008	2000	2008
Afghanistan	..	2.2	..	9.7	400	53	5.4	0.6	..	..	33	134
Albania	1.2	2.0	5.4	..	68	15	5.2	1.0	..	..	..	13
Algeria	3.4	3.1	..	13.0	305	334	2.7	2.3	..	..	418	1,590
Angola	6.4	2.9	..	..	118	117	1.9	1.5	1	..	180	37
Argentina	1.3	0.8	6.2	..	102	107	0.6	0.6	2	..	228	32
Armenia	3.6	3.2	..	15.4	42	42	2.9	2.6	..	..	2	1
Australia	1.8	1.8	7.8	7.7	52	55	0.5	0.5	43	6	364	344
Austria	1.0	0.9	2.5	2.2	41	35	1.0	0.8	21	30	25	434
Azerbaijan	2.3	2.7	..	17.4	87	82	2.5	2.0	..	..	3	1
Bangladesh	1.4	1.1	14.9	10.4	137	221	0.2	0.3	..	..	205	10
Belarus	1.3	1.4	5.3	4.0	91	183	1.9	3.7	295	72	41	254
Belgium	1.4	1.1	3.2	2.6	39	39	0.9	0.8	24	408	39	171
Benin	0.6	1.0	4.7	6.8	7	8	0.3	0.2	..	..	6	2
Bolivia	1.9	1.5	7.6	8.0	70	83	2.0	1.9	..	..	19	5
Bosnia and Herzegovina	3.6	1.4	..	3.6	76	9	4.1	0.5	4	..	25	..
Botswana	3.0	3.4	..	..	10	11	1.3	1.1	..	..	52	..
Brazil	1.8	1.5	..	5.9	673	721	0.8	0.7	26	48	124	156
Bulgaria	2.8	2.2	8.6	7.1	114	75	3.2	2.0	2	5	7	127
Burkina Faso	1.2	1.8	..	14.0	11	11	0.2	0.2	..	..	..	4
Burundi	6.0	3.8	30.3	..	46	51	1.4	1.2	..	..	1	..
Cambodia	2.2	1.1	16.8	12.8	360	191	6.1	2.5	..	..	..	40
Cameroon	1.3	1.5	12.0	..	22	23	0.4	0.3	..	..	1	0
Canada	1.1	1.3	6.0	6.9	69	64	0.4	0.3	110	215	557	434
Central African Republic	1.0	1.6	..	..	5	3	0.3	0.1	..	..	..	9
Chad	1.9	1.0	..	..	35	35	1.1	0.8	..	..	15	36
Chile	3.7	3.5	17.7	17.9	117	103	1.9	1.3	1	133	176	543
China	1.8[a]	2.0[a]	19.8[a]	18.0[a]	3,910	2,885	0.5	0.4	268	428	1,960	1,241
Hong Kong SAR, China	..	..	..	..	..	..	..	..	..	..	..	..
Colombia	3.0	3.7	15.6	15.7	247	411	1.6	2.2	..	..	62	131
Congo, Dem. Rep.	1.0	1.4	11.4	..	93	151	0.5	0.6	..	..	41	17
Congo, Rep.	1.4	1.3	5.9	..	15	12	1.2	0.8	..	..	0	0
Costa Rica	..	..	..	..	15	10	1.0	0.5	..	0	..	..
Côte d'Ivoire	..	1.5	..	8.2	15	19	0.2	0.2	..	..	32	..
Croatia	3.1	1.8	7.8	4.7	101	22	5.1	1.1	2	..	70	99
Cuba	..	..	..	..	85	76	1.8	1.5	..	..	..	..
Czech Republic	2.0	1.5	6.1	4.3	63	27	1.2	0.5	78	20	16	17
Denmark	1.5	1.3	4.2	3.7	22	30	0.8	1.0	20	12	64	90
Dominican Republic	0.7	0.6	..	3.8	40	65	1.1	1.5	..	..	13	..
Ecuador	1.7	2.8	..	..	58	58	1.2	1.0	..	..	12	133
Egypt, Arab Rep.	3.2	2.3	12.3	7.6	679	866	3.1	3.3	38	..	810	119
El Salvador	0.9	0.5	4.3	2.9	29	33	1.3	1.3	..	..	16	4
Eritrea	36.4	..	..	..	200	202	14.5	9.8	0	..	4	10
Estonia	1.4	2.2	4.7	8.0	8	7	1.2	1.0	..	..	27	50
Ethiopia	7.6	1.5	18.0	..	353	138	1.2	0.4	..	..	125	..
Finland	1.3	1.3	3.7	3.6	35	32	1.3	1.2	9	76	516	142
France	2.5	2.3	5.7	5.3	389	353	1.5	1.2	1,052	1,585	106	68
Gabon	1.8	1.1	..	..	7	7	1.2	1.0	..	..	..	21
Gambia, The	0.8	0.7	..	..	1	1	0.1	0.1	..	..	..	..
Georgia	0.6	8.1	5.3	27.9	33	33	1.4	1.5	22	..	6	63
Germany	1.5	1.3	4.7	4.4	221	244	0.5	0.6	..	..	135	104
Ghana	1.0	0.7	3.3	2.9	8	14	0.1	0.1	..	..	1	13
Greece	4.3	3.5	9.8	7.9	163	161	3.3	3.1	2	23	710	518
Guatemala	0.8	0.5	7.5	4.1	53	35	1.3	0.7	..	..	1	12
Guinea	1.5	..	11.8	..	19	19	0.5	0.4	..	..	19	..
Guinea-Bissau	4.4	..	..	..	9	6	1.7	0.9	..	..	..	..
Haiti	..	..	..	..	5	0	0.1	0.0	..	..	..	1
Honduras	0.5	0.7	..	3.1	14	20	0.6	0.7	..	..	..	0

	Military expenditures				Armed forces personnel				Arms transfers			
	% of GDP		% of central government expenditure		thousands		% of labor force		1990 $ millions			
									Exports		Imports	
	2000	2008	2000	2008	2000	2008	2000	2008	2000	2008	2000	2008
Hungary	1.7	1.2	4.1	2.7	58	37	1.4	0.9	34	6	14	5
India	3.1	2.5	19.5	15.2	2,372	2,582	0.6	0.6	16	21	822	1,847
Indonesia	1.0	1.0	5.7	..	492	582	0.5	0.5	16	8	171	290
Iran, Islamic Rep.	3.8	2.9	22.5	12.6	753	563	3.4	2.0	0	2	411	87
Iraq	..	..	..	..	479	577	8.0	7.7	..	..	..	351
Ireland	0.7	0.6	2.6	1.6	12	10	0.7	0.5	..	..	0	16
Israel	7.8	8.0	17.6	19.7	181	185	7.2	5.9	354	410	350	524
Italy	2.0	1.8	5.2	4.4	503	436	2.2	1.7	176	484	241	270
Jamaica	0.5	0.5	..	1.7	3	3	0.3	0.2	..	..	5	2
Japan	1.0	0.9	..	..	249	242	0.4	0.4	..	..	431	578
Jordan	6.2	5.9	..	16.1	149	111	10.4	5.8	..	20	130	336
Kazakhstan	0.8	1.0	5.7	6.7	99	81	1.3	1.0	16	12	147	3
Kenya	1.3	2.0	7.8	9.1	27	29	0.2	0.2	..	..	9	8
Korea, Dem. Rep.	..	..	..	..	1,244	1,295	11.2	10.6	13	..	19	5
Korea, Rep.	2.4	2.6	14.4	13.1	688	692	3.0	2.8	8	141	1,262	1,898
Kosovo												
Kuwait	7.1	3.2	18.9	13.2	20	23	1.8	1.6	99	..	238	276
Kyrgyz Republic	2.9	2.4	18.0	14.2	14	21	0.7	0.8	..	16	..	2
Lao PDR	0.8	0.3	..	3.3	129	129	5.2	4.3	..	..	7	..
Latvia	0.9	1.9	3.2	6.4	9	16	0.8	1.3	..	..	3	44
Lebanon	5.4	4.4	17.7	14.6	77	76	6.5	5.4	45	..	4	3
Lesotho	3.9	2.6	7.8	5.0	2	2	0.2	0.2	..	..	6	1
Liberia	..	0.5	..	..	15	2	1.3	0.1	..	..	8	..
Libya	3.2	1.2	..	..	77	76	4.2	3.3	11	9	145	3
Lithuania	1.7	1.6	6.5	5.0	17	24	1.0	1.5	3	..	5	26
Macedonia, FYR	1.9	2.0	..	6.5	24	19	2.8	2.1	..	..	11	0
Madagascar	1.2	1.1	11.5	10.0	29	22	0.4	0.2	..	..	..	..
Malawi	0.7	1.2	..	..	6	7	0.1	0.1	1	..	..	..
Malaysia	1.6	2.0	10.5	..	116	134	1.2	1.1	8	..	30	529
Mali	2.4	2.0	20.7	15.1	15	12	0.5	0.3	..	..	7	8
Mauritania	3.5	3.8	..	..	21	21	2.0	1.6	..	..	31	..
Mauritius	0.2	0.2	1.0	0.8	2	2	0.3	0.3	..	..	..	4
Mexico	0.5	0.4	3.4	..	208	286	0.5	0.6	..	..	227	11
Moldova	0.4	0.4	1.4	1.4	13	8	0.7	0.5	6	37	..	..
Mongolia	2.2	1.4	9.5	5.8	16	17	1.4	1.2	..	..	..	14
Morocco	2.3	3.3	12.0	11.0	241	246	2.4	2.1	..	..	123	32
Mozambique	1.3	0.9	..	..	6	11	0.1	0.1	..	..	0	..
Myanmar	2.3	..	..	..	429	513	1.7	1.9	..	..	3	1
Namibia	2.4	3.0	8.3	10.7	9	15	1.5	2.0	..	..	18	66
Nepal	1.0	1.5	..	..	90	131	0.9	1.0	..	..	11	..
Netherlands	1.6	1.4	4.0	3.7	57	47	0.7	0.5	258	554	141	152
New Zealand	1.2	1.1	3.5	3.1	9	9	0.5	0.4	1	..	45	4
Nicaragua	0.8	0.6	4.7	3.2	16	12	0.9	0.5	..	..	..	..
Niger	0.0	..	..	..	11	10	0.3	0.2	..	..	..	7
Nigeria	0.0	0.0	..	..	107	162	0.3	0.3	..	..	39	17
Norway	1.7	1.3	5.3	4.2	27	19	1.1	0.7	3	14	263	590
Oman	10.6	10.4	40.4	..	48	47	5.4	4.5	..	..	120	66
Pakistan	4.0	3.3	23.4	17.6	900	921	2.2	1.6	3	..	158	1,094
Panama	1.0	..	4.6	..	12	12	0.9	0.8	..	..	0	..
Papua New Guinea	0.9	0.4	2.9	..	4	3	0.2	0.1	..	..	..	..
Paraguay	1.1	0.8	..	5.0	35	26	1.5	0.9	..	..	6	..
Peru	1.7	1.2	9.7	7.5	193	191	1.7	1.4	10	..	24	172
Philippines	1.1	0.8	6.2	4.8	149	147	0.5	0.4	..	4	9	11
Poland	1.8	2.0	5.4	5.8	239	143	1.4	0.8	45	96	159	611
Portugal	2.0	2.0	5.1	4.6	91	91	1.7	1.6	..	87	2	183
Puerto Rico	..	..	..	..	..	..	..	..	..	..	..	..
Qatar	..	..	..	..	12	12	3.6	1.3	9	6	11	..

5.7 | Military expenditures and arms transfers

	Military expenditures				Armed forces personnel				Arms transfers			
	% of GDP		% of central government expenditure		thousands		% of labor force		1990 $ millions			
									Exports		Imports	
	2000	2008	2000	2008	2000	2008	2000	2008	2000	2008	2000	2008
Romania	2.5	1.5	8.9	4.4	283	153	2.4	1.5	3	32	23	37
Russian Federation	3.7	3.5	19.3	16.4	1,427	1,476	2.0	1.9	4,302	5,953	..	100
Rwanda	3.5	1.5	..	..	76	35	2.0	0.7	..	..	14	15
Saudi Arabia	10.6	8.2	..	..	217	238	3.1	2.6	..	..	80	56
Senegal	1.3	1.6	10.4	..	15	19	0.4	0.4	..	..	..	19
Serbia	5.4	2.3	..	6.1	136	24	..	..	..	6	..	..
Sierra Leone	3.7	2.3	12.8	..	4	11	0.2	0.5	..	..	13	10
Singapore	4.7	4.1	28.7	26.7	169	167	8.2	6.4	10	1	612	1,014
Slovak Republic	1.7	1.6	..	5.0	41	17	1.6	0.6	92	3	2	1
Slovenia	1.1	1.6	2.9	4.4	14	12	1.4	1.2	..	..	1	8
Somalia	..	..	..	..	50	..	1.7	..	..	..	1	..
South Africa	1.6	1.4	5.6	4.4	72	62	0.5	0.3	18	95	16	312
Spain	1.2	1.2	3.9	4.6	242	223	1.3	1.0	46	623	334	363
Sri Lanka	4.5	3.0	19.7	14.2	204	213	2.6	2.6	..	..	274	75
Sudan	4.7	4.2	53.0	..	120	127	1.1	1.0	..	..	146	94
Swaziland	1.6	2.1	..	..	3	..	0.8	..	..	..	1	..
Sweden	2.0	1.3	5.5	..	88	18	2.0	0.4	306	380	210	21
Switzerland	1.1	0.8	4.2	4.6	28	23	0.7	0.5	111	378	14	32
Syrian Arab Republic	5.3	3.4	..	..	425	401	8.6	6.0	..	3	439	81
Tajikistan	1.2	..	13.4	..	7	17	0.4	0.6	..	..	..	13
Tanzania	1.5	0.9	..	..	35	28	0.2	0.1	..	..	..	0
Thailand	1.4	1.5	..	8.3	417	421	1.2	1.1	..	..	90	12
Timor-Leste	..	..	..	..	..	1	..	0.2	..	..	..	..
Togo	..	2.0	..	13.0	8	10	0.4	0.3	..	..	..	..
Trinidad and Tobago	..	..	..	..	8	4	1.3	0.6	..	..	10	..
Tunisia	1.7	1.3	6.2	4.3	47	48	1.5	1.3	..	..	11	7
Turkey	-3.7	2.2	..	9.5	828	613	3.6	2.4	15	29	1,148	723
Turkmenistan	2.9	..	..	..	15	22	0.8	0.9	..	..	..	..
Uganda	2.5	2.3	16.0	13.7	51	47	0.5	0.3	..	..	6	3
Ukraine	3.6	2.7	13.5	7.2	420	215	1.8	0.9	288	233	..	..
United Arab Emirates	3.4	..	45.7	..	66	51	3.5	1.8	..	3	310	671
United Kingdom	2.4	2.4	6.6	5.7	213	160	0.7	0.5	1,474	1,075	824	590
United States	3.1	4.2	15.6	18.4	1,455	1,540	1.0	1.0	7,526	6,159	301	904
Uruguay	1.3	1.2	5.0	5.1	25	26	1.6	1.6	1	..	4	63
Uzbekistan	0.8	..	..	..	79	87	0.9	0.7	..	..	6	..
Venezuela, RB	1.5	1.1	7.1	..	79	115	0.8	0.9	..	1	85	733
Vietnam	..	2.0	..	..	524	495	1.4	1.1	..	14	5	250
West Bank and Gaza	..	..	..	..	..	56	..	5.9	..	..	..	2
Yemen, Rep.	5.0	4.5	23.9	..	136	138	3.2	2.3	..	..	158	44
Zambia	1.8	1.8	10.3	5.7	23	16	0.6	0.3	..	..	27	3
Zimbabwe	4.7	..	..	..	62	51	1.2	1.0	3	..	2	20
World	**2.3 w**	**2.4 w**	**10.2 w**	**10.2 w**	**29,353 s**	**27,469 s**	**1.1 w**	**0.9 w**	**.. s**	**.. s**	**18,556 s**	**22,681 s**
Low income	2.3	1.7	..	..	4,795	4,261	1.3	1.0	..	..	691	480
Middle income	2.1	2.0	15.6	12.9	18,417	17,484	1.0	0.8	..	..	8,598	11,720
Lower middle income	2.2	2.0	17.8	16.1	12,599	11,804	0.8	0.7	1,282	1,231	5,639	5,971
Upper middle income	2.0	2.0	..	9.7	5,817	5,680	1.5	1.3	..	..	2,959	6,157
Low & middle income	2.1	2.0	..	12.9	23,212	21,745	1.0	0.8	..	..	9,289	12,224
East Asia & Pacific	1.7	1.8	18.6	17.0	7,794	6,817	0.8	0.6	367	428	2,285	2,352
Europe & Central Asia	3.1	2.7	12.8	11.4	4,119	3,373	2.0	1.6	4,994	6,441	..	2,565
Latin America & Carib.	1.4	1.3	..	..	2,084	2,399	0.9	0.9	..	..	963	2,067
Middle East & N. Africa	3.5	2.8	12.3	10.8	3,379	3,505	3.8	3.2	..	..	2,494	2,647
South Asia	3.1	2.5	19.9	15.3	4,114	4,121	0.8	0.7	19	21	1,459	3,160
Sub-Saharan Africa	1.9	1.3	..	..	1,724	1,530	0.7	0.5	..	..	583	608
High income	2.3	2.6	10.1	10.2	6,141	5,724	1.2	1.0	11,681	..	9,267	10,457
Euro area	1.8	1.6	4.8	4.5	1,862	1,714	1.3	1.1	..	..	2,254	2,429

Note: For some countries data are partial or uncertain or based on rough estimates; see SIPRI (2009).

a. Estimates differ from official statistics of the government of China, which has published the following estimates: military expenditure as 1.2 percent of GDP in 2000 and 1.4 percent in 2007 and 7.6 percent of central government expenditure in 2000 and 7.1 percent in 2007 (see National Bureau of Statistics of China, www.stats.gov.cn).

Although national defense is an important function of government and security from external threats that contributes to economic development, high levels of military expenditures for defense or civil conflicts burden the economy and may impede growth. Data on military expenditures as a share of gross domestic product (GDP) are a rough indicator of the portion of national resources used for military activities and of the burden on the national economy. As an "input" measure military expenditures are not directly related to the "output" of military activities, capabilities, or security. Comparisons of military spending between countries should take into account the many factors that influence perceptions of vulnerability and risk, including historical and cultural traditions, the length of borders that need defending, the quality of relations with neighbors, and the role of the armed forces in the body politic.

Data on military spending reported by governments are not compiled using standard definitions. They are often incomplete and unreliable. Even in countries where the parliament vigilantly reviews budgets and spending, military expenditures and arms transfers rarely receive close scrutiny or full, public disclosure (see Ball 1984 and Happe and Wakeman-Linn 1994). Therefore, SIPRI has adopted a definition of military expenditure derived from the North Atlantic Treaty Organization (NATO) definition (see *Definitions*). The data on military expenditures as a share of GDP and as a share of central government expenditure are estimated by the Stockholm International Peace Research Institute (SIPRI). Central government expenditures are from the International Monetary Fund (IMF). Therefore the data in the table may differ from comparable data published by national governments.

SIPRI's primary source of military expenditure data is official data provided by national governments. These data are derived from national budget documents, defense white papers, and other public documents from official government agencies, including governments' responses to questionnaires sent by SIPRI, the United Nations, or the Organization for Security and Co-operation in Europe. Secondary sources include international statistics, such as those of NATO and the IMF's *Government Finance Statistics Yearbook*. Other secondary sources include country reports of the Economist Intelligence Unit, country reports by IMF staff, and specialist journals and newspapers.

In the many cases where SIPRI cannot make independent estimates, it uses the national data provided. Because of the differences in definitions and the difficulty in verifying the accuracy and completeness of data, data on military expenditures are not strictly comparable across countries. More information on SIPRI's military expenditure project can be found at www.sipri.org/contents/milap/.

Data on armed forces refer to military personnel on active duty, including paramilitary forces. Because data exclude personnel not on active duty, they underestimate the share of the labor force working for the defense establishment. Governments rarely report the size of their armed forces, so such data typically come from intelligence sources.

SIPRI's Arms Transfers Project collects data on arms transfers from open sources. Since publicly available information is inadequate for tracking all weapons and other military equipment, SIPRI covers only what it terms *major conventional weapons*. Data cover the supply of weapons through sales, aid, gifts, and manufacturing licenses; therefore the term *arms transfers* rather than *arms trade* is used. SIPRI data also cover weapons supplied to or from rebel forces in an armed conflict as well as arms deliveries for which neither the supplier nor the recipient can be identified with acceptable certainty; these data are available in SIPRI's database.

SIPRI's estimates of arms transfers are designed as a trend-measuring device in which similar weapons have similar values, reflecting both the value and quality of weapons transferred. SIPRI cautions that the estimated values do not reflect financial value (payments for weapons transferred) because reliable data on the value of the transfer are not available, and even when values are known, the transfer usually includes more than the actual conventional weapons, such as spares, support systems, and training, and details of the financial arrangements (such as credit and loan conditions and discounts) are usually not known.

Given these measurement issues, SIPRI's method of estimating the transfer of military resources includes an evaluation of the technical parameters of the weapons. Weapons for which a price is not known are compared with the same weapons for which actual acquisition prices are available (core weapons) or for the closest match. These weapons are assigned a value in an index that reflects their military resource value in relation to the core weapons. These matches are based on such characteristics as size, performance, and type of electronics, and adjustments are made for secondhand weapons. More information on SIPRI's Arms Transfers Project is available at www.sipri.org/contents/armstrad/.

• **Military expenditures** are SIPRI data derived from the NATO definition, which includes all current and capital expenditures on the armed forces, including peacekeeping forces; defense ministries and other government agencies engaged in defense projects; paramilitary forces, if judged to be trained and equipped for military operations; and military space activities. Such expenditures include military and civil personnel, including retirement pensions and social services for military personnel; operation and maintenance; procurement; military research and development; and military aid (in the military expenditures of the donor country). Excluded are civil defense and current expenditures for previous military activities, such as for veterans benefits, demobilization, and weapons conversion and destruction. This definition cannot be applied for all countries, however, since that would require more detailed information than is available about military budgets and off-budget military expenditures (for example, whether military budgets cover civil defense, reserves and auxiliary forces, police and paramilitary forces, and military pensions).
• **Armed forces personnel** are active duty military personnel, including paramilitary forces if the training, organization, equipment, and control suggest they may be used to support or replace regular military forces. Reserve forces, which are not fully staffed or operational in peace time, are not included. The data also exclude civilians in the defense establishment and so are not consistent with the data on military expenditures on personnel. • **Arms transfers** cover the supply of military weapons through sales, aid, gifts, and manufacturing licenses. Weapons must be transferred voluntarily by the supplier, have a military purpose, and be destined for the armed forces, paramilitary forces, or intelligence agencies of another country. The trends shown in the table are based on actual deliveries only. Data cover major conventional weapons such as aircraft, armored vehicles, artillery, radar systems, missiles, and ships designed for military use. Excluded are transfers of other military equipment such as small arms and light weapons, trucks, small artillery, ammunition, support equipment, technology transfers, and other services.

Data on military expenditures are from SIPRI's *Yearbook 2009: Armaments, Disarmament, and International Security*. Data on armed forces personnel are from the International Institute for Strategic Studies' *The Military Balance 2010*. Data on arms transfers are from SIPRI's Arms Transfer Project (www.sipri.org/contents/armstrad/).

	International Development Association Resource Allocation Index 1–6 (low to high) 2008	Peacebuilding and peacekeeping Operation name[a] December 2009	Peacebuilding and peacekeeping Troops, police, and military observers number December 2009	Battle-related deaths number 2000–08[b]	Intentional homicides per 100,000 people WHO 2004	Intentional homicides per 100,000 people CTS and national sources 2004	Military expenditures % of GDP 2008	Business environment Survey year	Business environment Losses due to theft, robbery, vandalism, and arson % of sales	Business environment Firms formally registered when operations started % of firms
Afghanistan	2.6	UNAMA	20	26,589	3.4	..	2.2	2008	1.5	88.0
Angola	2.7		..	3,534	36.0	5.2e	2.9	2006	0.4	..
Bosnia and Herzegovina	3.7		..	0	1.9	1.8f	1.4	2009	0.2	98.6
Burundi	3.0	BINUB	15	4,937	35.4	..	3.8	2006	1.1	..
Cameroon	3.2		..	0	16.1	5.8g	1.5	2009	1.3	82.1
Central African Republic	2.5	MINURCAT[h]	2,777	350	29.1	..	1.6		..	..
Chad	2.5	MINURCAT	..	4,328	19.0	..	1.0	2009	2.5	77.1
Comoros	2.3		..	0	9.3	..	..		..	..
Congo, Rep.	2.7		..	116	18.8	..	1.3	2009	3.3	84.3
Côte d'Ivoire	2.7	UNOCI	8,536	1,265	45.7	..	1.5	2009	3.4	56.4
Congo, Dem. Rep.	2.7	MONUC	20,509	75,118	35.2	..	1.4	2006	2.0	..
Djibouti	3.1		..	0	3.5	..	4.1		..	..
Eritrea	2.3		..	57	15.9	..	..	2009		100.0
Gambia, The	3.2		..	0	13.5	..	0.7	2006	2.7	..
Georgia	4.4		..	648	3.7	6.2i	8.1	2008	0.7	99.6
Guinea	3.0		..	1,174	17.3	..	..	2006	2.0	..
Guinea-Bissau	2.6		..	0	16.3	..	..	2006	1.1	..
Haiti	2.9	MINUSTAH	9,057	244	5.3	33.9j	..		..	..
Kiribati	3.0		..	0	6.5	..	..		..	..
Kosovo	..	UNMIK	17	0	..	..	..	2009	0.3	89.2
Liberia	..	UNMIL	10,947	2,487	16.8	..	0.5	2009	2.8	73.8
Myanmar	..		..	2,833	15.7	..	..		..	..
Nepal	3.3	UNMIN	72	11,520	8.0	2.1f	1.5	2009	0.9	94.0
Papua New Guinea	3.3		..	0	15.2	..	0.4		..	..
São Tomé and Príncipe	3.0		..	0	5.4	..	..		..	..
Sierra Leone	3.1		..	212	34.0	2.1k	2.3	2009	0.8	89.2
Solomon Islands	2.8	RAMSI[l]	572	0	1.5	..	..		..	..
Somalia	..		..	3,983	3.3	..	..		..	..
Sudan	2.5	UNMIS[m]	10,262	12,363	28.6	..	4.2		..	..
Tajikistan	3.2		..	0	2.2	2.4i	..	2008	0.3	92.7
Timor-Leste	2.8	UNMIT	1,552	0	11.7	..	..		..	..
Togo	2.7		..	0	13.7	..	2.0	2009	2.4	75.8
Tonga	3.2		..	0	1.0	..	1.5		..	..
West Bank and Gaza	..		..	0	..	4.0	..	2006	1.2	..
Western Sahara[n]	..	MINURSO	232	..	..	..	..		..	..
Yemen, Rep.	3.2		..	0	2.5	3.2o	4.5		..	..
Zimbabwe	1.4		..	0	32.9	8.4i	..		..	..
Fragile situations	..			151,759 s	..	..	3.0 w			
Low income				147,275	..	..	1.7			

Note: The countries with fragile situations in the table are International Development Association–eligible countries with a 3.2 or lower harmonized average of the World Bank's Country Policy and Institutional Assessment (CPIA) rating and the corresponding rating by a regional development bank or that have had a UN or regional peacebuilding mission (for example, by the African Union, European Union, or Organization of American States) or peacekeeping mission (for example, by the African Union, European Union, North Atlantic Treaty Organization, or Organization of American States) during the last three years. Because fragility is an evolving concept, this definition will be updated as understanding changes.

a. UNAMA is United Nations Assistance Mission in Afghanistan, BINUB is Bureau Intégré des Nations Unies au Burundi (United Nations Integrated Office in Burundi), MINURCAT is United Nations Mission in the Central African Republic and Chad, UNOCI is United Nations Operation in Côte d'Ivoire, MONUC is United Nations Organization Mission in DR Congo, MINUSTAH is United Nations Stabilization Mission in Haiti, UNMIK is Interim Administration Mission in Kosovo, UNMIL is United Nations Mission in Liberia, UNMIN is United Nations Mission in Nepal, RAMSI is Regional Assistance Mission to Solomon Islands, UNMIS is United Nations Missions in Sudan, UNMIT is United Nations Integrated Mission in Timor-Leste, and MINURSO is United Nations Mission for the Referendum in Western Sahara. b. Total over the period. c. Data are for the most recent year available. d. Average over the period. e. Data are from Interpol. f. Data are from UNODC's *10th UN Survey of Crime Trends* and are for 2005. g. National Statistical Office of Cameroon. h. Includes peacekeepers in Chad. i. Data are from UNODC's *9th UN Survey of Crime Trends*. j. Data are for 2001. k. National Statistical Office of Sierra Leone. l. Data are for 2007. m. Does not include 19,949 troops, police, and military observers from the African Union-UN Hybrid Operation in Darfur. n. The designation Western Sahara is used instead of Former Spanish Sahara (the designation used on the maps on the front and back cover flaps) because it is the designation used by the UN operation established there by Security Council resolution 690/1991. Neither designation expresses any World Bank view on the status of the territory so-identified. o. National Statistical Office of Yemen.

	Children in employment		Refugees		Internally displaced persons	Access to an improved water source	Access to improved sanitation facilities	Maternal mortality ratio		Under-five mortality rate	Depth of hunger	Primary gross enrollment ratio
			By country of origin	By country of asylum	number	% of population	% of population	per 100,000 live births National estimates	Modeled estimates	per 1,000	kilocalories per person per day	% of relevant age group
	Survey year	% of children ages 7–14	2008	2008	2008	2006	2006	2000–08c	2005	2008	2004–06d	2008
Afghanistan	..	..	37	2,833,128	230,670	22	30	1,600	1,800	257	..	106
Angola	2001	30.1	12,710	171,393	..	51	50	..	1,400	220	290	..
Bosnia and Herzegovina	2005	10.6	7,257	74,366	124,529	99	95	23	3	15	140	111
Burundi	2000	37.0	21,093	281,592	100,000	71	41	615	1,100	168	360	136
Cameroon	2001	15.9	81,037	13,870	..	70	51	669	1,000	131	160	111
Central African Republic	2000	67.0	7,429	125,106	197,000	66	31	543	980	173	280	77
Chad	2004	60.4	330,510	55,105	166,718	48	9	1,099	1,500	209	290	83
Comoros	..	..	1	378	..	85	35	380	400	105	340	..
Congo, Rep.	2005	30.1	24,779	19,925	3,492	71	20	781	740	127	250	114
Côte d'Ivoire	2006	45.7	24,811	22,227	683,956	81	24	543	810	114	190	74
Congo, Dem. Rep.	2000	39.8	155,162	367,995	1,460,102	46	31	1,838	1,100	199	430	90
Djibouti			9,228	650	..	92	67	546	650	95	220	55
Eritrea			4,862	186,398	..	60	5	..	450	58	350	52
Gambia, The	2005	43.5	14,836	1,352	..	86	52	730	690	106	240	86
Georgia			996	12,598	293,048	99	93	98	66	30	180	107
Guinea			21,488	9,495	..	70	19	980	910	146	130	90
Guinea-Bissau	2000	67.5	7,884	1,065	..	57	33	405	1,100	195	240	120
Haiti	2005	33.4	3	23,066	..	58	19	1,150	670	72	430	..
Kiribati	..	..	..	38	..	65	33	56	..	48	140	..
Kosovo	..	..	..	..	..	..	..	..	..	..	..	..
Liberia	2007	37.4	10,224	75,213	..	64	32	994	1,200	145	310	91
Myanmar	..	..	..	184,413	67,290	80	82	316	380	98	300	115
Nepal	1999	47.2	124,832	4,189	50,000	89	27	281	830	51	190	124
Papua New Guinea	..	..	..	10,006	46	40	45	..	470	69	..	55
São Tomé and Príncipe	..	..	..	35	..	86	24	248	..	98	110	130
Sierra Leone	2005	62.7	7,826	32,536	..	53	11	2,657	2,100	194	390	158
Solomon Islands	..	..	..	52	..	70	32	..	220	36	130	107
Somalia	2006	43.5	1,842	561,155	1,277,200	29	23	1,044	1,400	200	..	..
Sudan	..	..	181,605	419,248	1,201,040	70	35	1,107	450	109	240	69
Tajikistan	2005	8.9	1,799	544	..	67	92	179	170	64	190	102
Timor-Leste	..	..	1	7	15,860	62	41	..	380	93	230	107
Togo	2006	39.6	9,377	16,750	..	59	12	..	510	98	280	105
Tonga	..	..	..	7	..	100	96	214	..	19	..	112
West Bank and Gaza	..	..	1,836,123	340,026	..	89	80	..	..	27	180	80
Western Sahara[n]	..	..	..	..	..	..	..	..	..	..	..	..
Yemen, Rep.	..	..	140,169	1,777	100,000	66	46	365	430	69	270	85
Zimbabwe	..	..	3,468	16,841	..	81	46	1,655	880	96	310	104
Fragile situations			**3,051,394 s**	**5,852,585 s**	**..**	**63 w**	**41 w**		**958 w**	**148 w**	**285 w**	**.. w**
Low income			2,024,889	5,386,084	..	67	38	..	790	118	277	101

About the data

The table focuses on countries with fragile situations and highlights the links among weak institutions, poor development outcomes, fragility, and risk of conflict. These countries often have weak institutions that are ill-equipped to handle economic shocks, natural disasters, and illegal trade or to resist conflict, which increasingly spills across borders. Organized violence, including violent crime, interrupts economic and social development through lost human and social capital, disrupted services, displaced populations and reduced confidence for future investment. As a result, countries with fragile situations achieve lower development outcomes and make slower progress toward the Millennium Development Goals.

According to the Geneva Declaration on Armed Violence and Development, more than 740,000 people die each year because of the violence associated with armed conflict and large- and small-scale criminality. Recovery and rebuilding can take years, and the challenges are numerous: infrastructure to be rebuilt, persistently high crime, widespread health problems, education systems in disrepair, and landmines to be cleared. Most countries emerging from conflict lack the capacity to rebuild the economy. Thus, capacity building is one of the first tasks for restoring growth and is linked to building peace and creating the conditions that lead to sustained poverty reduction. The World Bank and other international development agencies can help, but countries with fragile situations have to build their own institutions tailored to their own needs. Peacekeeping operations in post-conflict situations have been effective in reducing the risks of reversion to conflict.

The countries with fragile situations in the table are International Development Association–eligible countries with a 3.2 or lower harmonized average of the World Bank's Country Policy and Institutional Assessment (CPIA) rating and the corresponding rating by a regional development bank or that have had a UN or regional peacebuilding mission (for example, by the African Union, European Union, or Organization of American States) or peacekeeping mission (for example, by the African Union, European Union, North Atlantic Treaty Organization, or Organization of American States) during the last three years. Peacebuilding and peacekeeping involve many elements—military, police, and civilian—working together to lay the foundations for sustainable peace. Because fragility is an evolving concept, this definition will be updated as understanding changes.

An armed conflict is a contested incompatibility that concerns a government or territory where the use of armed force between two parties (one of them the government) results in at least 25 battle-related deaths in a calendar year. There were 36 active armed conflicts in 26 locations in 2008. Separate measures are presented for intentional homicides—unlawful deaths purposefully inflicted on a person by another person—which exclude deaths arising from armed conflict. One measure draws from public health data sources, while the other draws from estimates by the United Nations Office on Drugs and Crime, which obtains data from criminal justice sources. Data from these two sources measure different phenomena and are therefore unlikely to provide identical numbers.

Data on military expenditures reported by governments are not compiled using standard definitions and are often incomplete and unreliable. Even in countries where the parliament vigilantly reviews budgets and spending, military expenditures and arms transfers rarely receive close scrutiny or full public disclosure. Data in the table are from the Stockholm International Peace Research Institute (SIPRI), which has adopted a definition of military expenditure derived from the North Atlantic Treaty Organization (NATO) definition (see *Definitions*). Therefore, the data in the table may differ from comparable data published by national governments. For a more detailed discussion of military expenditures, see *About the data* for table 5.7.

Along with public sector efforts, private sector development and investment, especially in competitive markets, has tremendous potential to contribute to growth and poverty reduction. The World Bank's Enterprise Surveys review the business environment, assessing constraints to private sector growth and enterprise performance. In some countries doing business requires informal payments to "get things done" in customs, taxes, licenses, regulations, services, and the like. Crime, theft, and disorder also

impose costs on businesses and society. And in many developing countries informal businesses operate without licenses. These firms have less access to financial and public services and can engage in fewer types of contracts and investments, constraining growth. The table presents data on the loss of sales due to theft, robbery, vandalism, and arson and on the percentage of firms operating informally. For further information on enterprise surveys, see *About the data* for table 5.2.

As the table shows, the human toll of armed violence across various contexts is severe. Additionally, in countries with fragile situations weak institutional capacity often results in poor performance and failure to meet expectations of effective service delivery. Failure to deliver water, health, and education services can weaken struggling governments. The table includes several indicators related to living conditions in fragile situations: children in employment, refugees, internally displaced persons, access to water and sanitation, maternal and under-five mortality, depth of hunger, and primary school enrollment. For more detailed information on these indicators, see *About the data* for table 2.6 (children in employment), table 6.18 (refugees), table 2.18 (access to improved water and sanitation), table 2.19 (maternal mortality), table 2.22 (under-five mortality), and table 2.12 (primary school enrollment).

Definitions

• **International Development Association Resource Allocation Index** is from the Country Policy and Institutional Assessment rating, which is the average score of four clusters of indicators designed to measure macroeconomic, governance, social, and structural dimensions of development: economic management, structural policies, policies for social inclusion and equity, and public sector management and institutions (see table 5.9). Countries are rated on a scale of 1 (low) to 6 (high). • **Peacebuilding and peacekeeping** refer to operations that engage in peacebuilding (reducing the risk of lapsing or relapsing into conflict by strengthening national capacities for conflict management and laying the foundation for sustainable peace and development) or peacekeeping (providing essential security to preserve the peace where fighting has been halted and to assist in implementing agreements achieved by the peacemakers). UN peacekeeping operations are authorized by the UN Secretary-General and planned, managed, directed, and supported by the United Nations Department of Peacekeeping Operations and the

Department of Field Support. The UN Charter gives the Security Council primary responsibility for maintaining international peace and security, including the establishment of a UN peacekeeping operation. • **Troops, police, and military observers in peacebuilding and peacekeeping** refer to people active in peacebuilding and peacekeeping as part of an official operation. Peacekeepers deploy to war-torn regions where no one else is willing or able to go to prevent conflict from returning or escalating. • **Battle-related deaths** are deaths of members of warring parties in battle-related conflicts. Typically, battle-related deaths occur in warfare involving the armed forces of the warring parties (battlefield fighting, guerrilla activities, and all kinds of bombardments of military units, cities, and villages). The targets are usually the military and its installations or state institutions and state representatives, but there is often substantial collateral damage of civilians killed in crossfire, indiscriminate bombings, and other military activities. All deaths—civilian as well as military—incurred in such situations are counted as battle-related deaths. • **Intentional homicides** are estimates of unlawful homicides purposely inflicted as a result of domestic disputes, interpersonal violence, violent conflicts over land resources, intergang violence over turf or control, and predatory violence and killing by armed groups. Intentional homicide does not include all intentional killing; the difference is usually in the organization of the killing. Individuals or small groups usually commit homicide, whereas killing in armed conflict is usually committed by fairly cohesive groups of up to several hundred members and is thus usually excluded. Data from the World Health Organization (WHO) are from public health sources; data from the United Nations Survey of Crime Trends and Operations of Criminal Justice Systems (CTS) and national sources are based on criminal justice sources. • **Military expenditures** are SIPRI data derived from the NATO definition, which includes all current and capital expenditures on the armed forces, including peacekeeping forces; defense ministries and other government agencies engaged in defense projects; paramilitary forces, if judged to be trained and equipped for military operations; and military space activities. Such expenditures include military and civil personnel, including retirement pensions and social services for military personnel; operation and maintenance; procurement; military research and development; and military aid (in the military expenditures of the donor country). Excluded are civil defense and current expenditures for previous military activities, such as for veterans benefits, demobilization, and weapons conversion and destruction. This definition cannot be applied to all countries, however, since the necessary detailed information is missing in some cases for military budgets and off-budget military expenditures (for example, whether military budgets cover civil defense, reserves and auxiliary forces, police and paramilitary forces, and military pensions). • **Survey year** is the year in which the underlying data were collected. • **Losses due to theft, robbery, vandalism, and arson** are the estimated losses from those causes that occurred on business establishment premises calculated as a percentage of annual sales. • **Firms formally registered when operations started** are the percentage of firms formally registered when they started operations in the country. • **Children in employment** are children involved in any economic activity for at least one hour in the reference week of the survey. • **Refugees** are people who are recognized as refugees under the 1951 Convention Relating to the Status of Refugees or its 1967 Protocol, the 1969 Organization of African Unity Convention Governing the Specific Aspects of Refugee Problems in Africa, people recognized as refugees in accordance with the UN Refugee Agency (UNHCR) statute, people granted refugee-like humanitarian status, and people provided temporary protection. Asylum seekers—people who have applied for asylum or refugee status and who have not yet received a decision, or who are registered as asylum seekers—are excluded. Palestinian refugees are people (and their descendants) whose residence was Palestine between June 1946 and May 1948 and who lost their homes and means of livelihood as a result of the 1948 Arab-Israeli conflict. • **Country of origin** refers to the nationality or country of citizenship of a claimant. • **Country of asylum** is the country where an asylum claim was filed and granted. • **Internally displaced persons** are people or groups of people who have been forced to leave their homes or places of habitual residence, in particular as a result of armed conflict, or to avoid the effects of armed conflict, situations of generalized violence, violations of human rights, or natural or human-made disasters and who have not crossed an international border. UNHCR statistics for this population include conflict-generated internally displaced persons to whom UNHCR extends protection or assistance and people in an internally displaced person–like situation. • **Access to an improved water source** refers to people with reasonable access to water from an

improved source, such as piped water into a dwelling, public tap, tubewell, protected dug well, and rainwater collection. Reasonable access is the availability of at least 20 liters a person a day from a source within 1 kilometer of the dwelling. • **Access to improved sanitation facilities** refers to people with at least adequate access to excreta disposal facilities that can effectively prevent human, animal, and insect contact with excreta. Improved facilities range from protected pit latrines to flush toilets. • **Maternal mortality ratio** is the number of women who die from pregnancy-related causes during pregnancy and childbirth per 100,000 live births. National estimates are based on national surveys, vital registration records, and surveillance data or are derived from community and hospital records. Modeled estimates are based on an exercise by the WHO, United Nations Children's Fund (UNICEF), United Nations Population Fund (UNFPA), and the World Bank. See *About the data* for table 2.19 for further details. • **Under-five mortality rate** is the probability per 1,000 that a newborn baby will die before reaching age 5, if subject to current age-specific mortality rates • **Depth of hunger,** or the intensity of food deprivation, indicates how much people who are food-deprived fall short of minimum food needs in terms of dietary energy. It is measured by comparing the average amount of dietary energy that undernourished people get from the foods they eat with the minimum amount of dietary energy they need to maintain body weight and undertake light activity. Depth of hunger is low when it is less than 200 kilocalories per person per day and high when it is above 300. • **Primary gross enrollment ratio** is the ratio of total enrollment, regardless of age, to the population of the age group that officially corresponds to the primary level of education. Primary education provides children with basic reading, writing, and mathematics skills along with an elementary understanding of such subjects as history, geography, natural science, social science, art, and music.

Data sources

Data on the International Development Association Resource Allocation Index are from the World Bank Group's International Development Association database (www.worldbank.org/ida). Data on peacebuilding and peacekeeping operations are from the UN Department of Peacekeeping Operations. Data on battle-related deaths are

from the Uppsala Conflict Data Program (www.pcr.uu.se/research/UCDP/index.htm). Data on intentional homicides are from the UN Office on Drugs and Crime's International Homicide Statistics database. Data on military expenditures are from SIPRI's *Yearbook 2009: Armaments, Disarmament, and International Security* and database (www.sipri.org/databases/milex). Data on the business environment are from the World Bank's Enterprise Surveys (www.enterprisesurveys.org). Data on children in employment are estimates produced by the Understanding Children's Work project based on household survey data sets made available by the International Labour Organization's International Programme on the Elimination of Child Labour under its Statistical Monitoring Programme on Child Labour, UNICEF under its Multiple Indicator Cluster Survey program, the World Bank under its Living Standards Measurement Study program, and national statistical offices (see table 2.6). Data on refugees and internally displaced persons are from the UNHCR's *Statistical Yearbook 2008,* complemented by statistics on Palestinian refugees under the mandate of the United Nations Relief and Works Agency for Palestine Refugees in the Near East as published on its website (www.unrwa.org). Data on access to water and sanitation are from the WHO and UNICEF's *Progress on Drinking Water and Sanitation* (2008). National estimates of maternal mortality are from UNICEF's *The State of the World's Children 2009* and Childinfo and Demographic and Health Surveys by Macro International. Modeled estimates for maternal mortality are from WHO, UNICEF, UNFPA, and the World Bank's *Maternal Mortality in 2005* (2007). Data on under-five mortality estimates by the Inter-agency Group for Child Mortality Estimation (which comprises UNICEF, WHO, the World Bank, United Nations Population Division, and other universities and research institutes) and are based mainly on household surveys, censuses, and vital registration data, supplemented by the World Bank's Human Development Network estimates based on vital registration and sample registration data (see table 2.22). Data on depth of hunger are from the Food and Agriculture Organization's Food Security Statistics (www.fao.org/economic/ess/food-security-statistics/en/). Data on primary gross enrollment are from the United Nations Educational, Scientific, and Cultural Organization's Institute for Statistics.

5.9 | Public policies and institutions

	International Development Association Resource Allocation Index 1–6 (low to high)	Economic management 1–6 (low to high)				Structural policies 1–6 (low to high)			
		Macroeconomic management	Fiscal policy	Debt policy	Average	Trade	Financial sector	Business regulatory environment	Average
	2008	**2008**	**2008**	**2008**	**2008**	**2008**	**2008**	**2008**	**2008**
Afghanistan	2.6	3.5	3.0	3.0	3.2	2.5	2.5	2.5	2.5
Angola	2.7	3.0	3.0	3.0	3.0	4.0	2.5	2.0	2.8
Armenia	4.4	5.5	5.0	6.0	5.5	4.5	4.0	4.0	4.2
Azerbaijan	3.8	4.0	4.5	5.0	4.5	4.0	3.5	4.0	3.8
Bangladesh	3.5	4.0	4.0	4.5	4.2	3.5	3.0	3.5	3.3
Benin	3.6	4.5	4.0	3.5	4.0	4.0	3.5	3.5	3.7
Bhutan	3.9	4.5	4.5	4.5	4.5	3.0	3.0	3.5	3.2
Bolivia	3.8	4.0	4.0	4.5	4.2	5.0	4.0	2.5	3.8
Bosnia and Herzegovina	3.7	4.0	3.5	4.0	3.8	4.0	4.0	4.0	4.0
Burkina Faso	3.7	4.5	4.5	4.0	4.3	4.0	3.0	3.5	3.5
Burundi	3.0	3.5	3.5	3.0	3.3	3.5	2.5	2.5	2.8
Cambodia	3.3	4.5	3.5	3.5	3.8	4.0	2.5	3.5	3.3
Cameroon	3.2	4.0	4.0	3.0	3.7	3.5	3.0	3.0	3.2
Cape Verde	4.2	4.5	4.5	4.5	4.5	4.0	4.0	3.5	3.8
Central African Republic	2.5	3.5	3.0	2.0	2.8	3.5	2.5	2.0	2.7
Chad	2.5	2.5	2.5	3.0	2.7	3.0	3.0	2.5	2.8
Comoros	2.3	2.5	1.5	2.0	2.0	3.0	2.5	2.5	2.7
Congo, Dem. Rep.	2.7	3.5	3.5	2.5	3.2	4.0	2.0	2.0	2.7
Congo, Rep.	2.7	3.5	2.5	2.5	2.8	3.5	2.5	2.5	2.8
Côte d'Ivoire	2.7	3.0	2.5	2.0	2.5	4.0	3.0	3.0	3.3
Djibouti	3.1	3.5	3.0	2.5	3.0	4.0	3.5	3.5	3.7
Dominica	3.9	4.0	4.5	3.0	3.8	4.0	4.0	4.5	4.2
Eritrea	2.3	2.0	2.0	2.5	2.2	1.5	1.0	2.0	1.5
Ethiopia	3.4	2.5	4.0	3.5	3.3	3.0	3.0	3.5	3.2
Gambia, The	3.2	4.0	3.5	3.0	3.5	3.5	3.0	3.5	3.3
Georgia	4.4	4.5	4.5	5.0	4.7	6.0	3.5	5.5	5.0
Ghana	3.9	3.5	3.5	4.0	3.7	4.0	4.0	4.0	4.0
Grenada	3.7	3.5	2.5	3.0	3.0	4.5	4.0	4.0	4.2
Guinea	3.0	3.0	3.5	2.5	3.0	4.0	3.0	3.0	3.3
Guinea-Bissau	2.6	2.0	2.5	1.0	1.8	4.0	3.0	2.5	3.2
Guyana	3.4	3.5	3.5	4.0	3.7	4.0	3.5	3.0	3.5
Haiti	2.9	3.5	3.5	2.5	3.2	4.0	3.0	2.5	3.2
Honduras	3.7	3.5	3.5	4.0	3.7	4.5	3.0	4.0	3.8
India	3.8	4.5	3.5	4.5	4.2	3.5	4.0	3.5	3.7
Kenya	3.6	4.0	4.0	4.0	4.0	4.0	3.5	4.0	3.8
Kiribati	3.0	2.5	2.0	5.0	3.2	3.0	3.0	3.0	3.0
Kyrgyz Republic	3.7	4.5	4.0	4.0	4.2	5.0	3.5	4.0	4.2
Lao PDR	3.3	4.5	4.0	3.5	4.0	3.5	2.0	3.0	2.8

About the data

The International Development Association (IDA) is the part of the World Bank Group that helps the poorest countries reduce poverty by providing concessional loans and grants for programs aimed at boosting economic growth and improving living conditions. IDA funding helps these countries deal with the complex challenges they face in meeting the Millennium Development Goals.

The World Bank's IDA Resource Allocation Index (IRAI), presented in the table, is based on the results of the annual Country Policy and Institutional Assessment (CPIA) exercise, which covers the IDA-eligible countries. The table does not include Kosovo, Liberia, Myanmar, and Somalia because they were not rated in the 2008 exercise even though they are

IDA eligible. Country assessments have been carried out annually since the mid-1970s by World Bank staff. Over time the criteria have been revised from a largely macroeconomic focus to include governance aspects and a broader coverage of social and structural dimensions. Country performance is assessed against a set of 16 criteria grouped into four clusters: economic management, structural policies, policies for social inclusion and equity, and public sector management and institutions. IDA resources are allocated to a country on per capita terms based on its IDA country performance rating and, to a limited extent, based on its per capita gross national income. This ensures that good performers receive a

higher IDA allocation in per capita terms. The IRAI is a key element in the country performance rating.

The CPIA exercise is intended to capture the quality of a country's policies and institutional arrangements, focusing on key elements that are within the country's control, rather than on outcomes (such as economic growth rates) that are influenced by events beyond the country's control. More specifically, the CPIA measures the extent to which a country's policy and institutional framework supports sustainable growth and poverty reduction and, consequently, the effective use of development assistance.

All criteria within each cluster receive equal weight, and each cluster has a 25 percent weight in the over-

	International Development Association Resource Allocation Index 1–6 (low to high)	Economic management 1–6 (low to high)				Structural policies 1–6 (low to high)			
		Macroeconomic management	Fiscal policy	Debt policy	Average	Trade	Financial sector	Business regulatory environment	Average
	2008	2008	2008	2008	2008	2008	2008	2008	2008
Lesotho	3.5	4.0	4.0	4.0	4.0	3.5	3.5	3.0	3.3
Madagascar	3.7	4.0	3.5	4.0	3.8	4.0	3.0	3.5	3.5
Malawi	3.4	3.5	3.5	3.0	3.3	4.0	3.0	3.5	3.5
Maldives	3.4	2.5	2.0	3.0	2.5	4.0	3.5	4.0	3.8
Mali	3.7	4.5	4.0	4.5	4.3	4.0	3.0	3.5	3.5
Mauritania	3.3	3.5	3.0	4.0	3.5	4.0	2.5	3.5	3.3
Moldova	3.8	4.0	4.0	4.0	4.0	4.5	3.5	3.5	3.8
Mongolia	3.3	3.0	2.5	3.0	2.8	4.5	2.5	3.5	3.5
Mozambique	3.7	4.5	4.0	4.5	4.3	4.5	3.5	3.0	3.7
Nepal	3.3	4.0	3.5	3.5	3.7	3.5	3.0	3.0	3.2
Nicaragua	3.8	4.0	4.0	4.5	4.2	4.5	3.5	3.5	3.8
Niger	3.3	4.0	3.5	3.5	3.7	4.0	3.0	3.0	3.3
Nigeria	3.4	4.0	4.5	4.5	4.3	3.5	3.5	3.0	3.3
Pakistan	3.3	2.5	2.5	4.0	3.0	4.0	4.0	4.0	4.0
Papua New Guinea	3.3	4.0	3.5	4.5	4.0	4.5	3.0	3.0	3.5
Rwanda	3.7	4.0	4.0	3.5	3.8	3.5	3.5	3.5	3.5
Samoa	4.0	4.0	4.0	4.5	4.2	4.5	4.0	3.5	4.0
São Tomé and Príncipe	3.0	3.0	3.0	2.5	2.8	4.0	2.5	3.0	3.2
Senegal	3.6	4.0	3.5	4.0	3.8	4.0	3.5	4.0	3.8
Sierra Leone	3.1	4.0	3.5	3.5	3.7	3.5	3.0	3.0	3.2
Solomon Islands	2.8	3.5	2.5	2.5	2.8	3.0	3.0	3.0	3.0
Sri Lanka	3.4	2.5	3.0	3.5	3.0	3.5	3.5	4.0	3.7
St. Lucia	3.9	4.0	3.5	3.5	3.7	4.0	4.0	4.5	4.2
St. Vincent & Grenadines	3.8	4.0	3.5	3.5	3.7	4.0	4.0	4.5	4.2
Sudan	2.5	3.5	3.0	1.5	2.7	2.5	2.5	3.0	2.7
Tajikistan	3.2	3.5	3.5	3.5	3.5	4.0	2.5	3.0	3.2
Tanzania	3.8	4.5	4.5	4.0	4.3	4.0	4.0	3.5	3.8
Timor-Leste	2.8	2.5	3.0	3.5	3.0	4.5	2.5	1.5	2.8
Togo	2.7	3.0	3.0	2.0	2.7	4.0	2.5	3.0	3.2
Tonga	3.2	3.0	3.0	3.0	3.0	3.5	3.0	3.0	3.2
Uganda	3.9	4.5	4.5	4.5	4.5	4.0	3.5	4.0	3.8
Uzbekistan	3.3	4.0	4.0	4.0	4.0	2.5	3.0	3.0	2.8
Vanuatu	3.3	4.0	3.5	4.0	3.8	3.5	3.0	3.0	3.2
Vietnam	3.8	4.5	4.5	4.0	4.3	3.5	3.0	3.5	3.3
Yemen, Rep.	3.2	3.5	3.0	4.0	3.5	4.0	2.0	3.5	3.2
Zambia	3.5	4.0	3.5	3.5	3.7	4.0	3.5	3.5	3.7
Zimbabwe	1.4	1.0	1.0	1.0	1.0	2.0	1.0	1.5	1.5

all score, which is obtained by averaging the average scores of the four clusters. For each of the 16 criteria countries are rated on a scale of 1 (low) to 6 (high). The scores depend on the level of performance in a given year assessed against the criteria, rather than on changes in performance compared with the previous year. All 16 CPIA criteria contain a detailed description of each rating level. In assessing country performance, World Bank staff evaluate the country's performance on each of the criteria and assign a rating. The ratings reflect a variety of indicators, observations, and judgments based on country knowledge and on relevant publicly available indicators. In interpreting the assessment scores, it

should be noted that the criteria are designed in a developmentally neutral manner. Accordingly, higher scores can be attained by a country that, given its stage of development, has a policy and institutional framework that more strongly fosters growth and poverty reduction.

The country teams that prepare the ratings are very familiar with the country, and their assessments are based on country diagnostic studies prepared by the World Bank or other development organizations and on their own professional judgment. An early consultation is conducted with country authorities to make sure that the assessments are informed by up-to-date information. To ensure that scores are

consistent across countries, the process involves two key phases. In the benchmarking phase a small representative sample of countries drawn from all regions is rated. Country teams prepare proposals that are reviewed first at the regional level and then in a Bankwide review process. A similar process is followed to assess the performance of the remaining countries, using the benchmark countries' scores as guideposts. The final ratings are determined following a Bankwide review. The overall numerical IRAI score and the separate criteria scores were first publicly disclosed in June 2006.

See IDA's website at www.worldbank.org/ida for more information.

	Policies for social inclusion and equity 1–6 (low to high)						Public sector management and institutions 1–6 (low to high)					
	Gender equality 2008	Equity of public resource use 2008	Building human resources 2008	Social protection and labor 2008	Policies and institutions for environmental sustainability 2008	Average 2008	Property rights and rule-based governance 2008	Quality of budgetary and financial management 2008	Efficiency of revenue mobilization 2008	Quality of public administration 2008	Transparency, accountability, and corruption in the public sector 2008	Average 2008
Afghanistan	2.0	2.5	3.0	2.5	2.5	2.5	1.5	3.0	2.5	2.0	2.0	2.2
Angola	3.0	2.5	2.5	2.5	3.0	2.7	2.0	2.5	2.5	2.5	2.5	2.4
Armenia	4.5	4.5	4.0	4.5	3.0	4.1	3.5	4.5	3.5	4.0	3.0	3.7
Azerbaijan	4.0	4.0	4.0	4.0	3.0	3.8	3.0	4.0	3.5	3.0	2.5	3.2
Bangladesh	4.0	3.5	4.0	3.5	3.0	3.6	3.0	3.0	3.0	3.0	3.0	3.0
Benin	3.5	3.0	3.5	3.0	3.5	3.3	3.0	3.5	3.5	3.0	3.5	3.3
Bhutan	4.0	4.0	4.0	3.5	4.5	4.0	3.5	3.5	4.0	4.0	4.0	3.8
Bolivia	4.0	4.0	4.0	3.5	3.5	3.8	2.5	3.5	4.0	3.0	3.5	3.3
Bosnia and Herzegovina	4.5	3.0	3.5	3.5	3.5	3.6	3.0	3.5	4.0	3.0	3.0	3.3
Burkina Faso	3.5	4.0	3.5	3.5	3.5	3.6	3.5	4.0	3.5	3.5	3.0	3.5
Burundi	4.0	3.5	3.0	3.0	3.0	3.3	2.5	3.0	3.0	2.5	2.0	2.6
Cambodia	4.0	3.0	3.5	3.0	3.0	3.3	2.5	3.0	3.0	2.5	2.5	2.7
Cameroon	3.0	3.0	3.5	3.0	3.0	3.1	2.5	3.0	3.5	3.0	2.5	2.9
Cape Verde	4.5	4.5	4.5	4.5	3.5	4.3	4.0	4.0	3.5	4.0	4.5	4.0
Central African Republic	2.5	2.0	2.0	2.0	2.5	2.2	2.0	2.0	2.5	2.5	2.5	2.3
Chad	2.5	2.5	2.5	2.5	2.0	2.4	2.0	2.0	2.5	2.5	2.0	2.2
Comoros	3.0	2.5	2.5	2.5	2.0	2.5	2.5	1.5	2.5	2.0	2.5	2.2
Congo, Dem. Rep.	3.0	3.0	3.0	3.0	2.5	2.9	2.0	2.5	2.5	2.0	2.0	2.2
Congo, Rep.	3.0	2.5	3.0	2.5	2.5	2.7	2.5	2.5	3.0	2.5	2.5	2.6
Côte d'Ivoire	2.5	1.5	2.5	2.5	2.5	2.3	2.0	2.0	4.0	2.0	2.5	2.5
Djibouti	2.5	3.0	3.5	3.0	3.0	3.0	2.5	3.0	3.5	2.5	2.5	2.8
Dominica	3.5	3.5	4.0	3.5	3.5	3.6	4.0	3.5	4.0	3.5	4.0	3.8
Eritrea	3.5	3.0	3.5	3.0	2.0	3.0	2.5	2.5	3.5	3.0	2.0	2.7
Ethiopia	3.0	4.5	4.0	3.5	3.0	3.6	3.0	4.0	4.0	3.0	2.5	3.3
Gambia, The	3.5	3.0	3.5	2.5	3.5	3.2	3.0	3.0	3.5	3.0	2.0	2.9
Georgia	4.5	4.5	4.5	4.5	3.0	4.2	3.5	4.0	4.5	4.0	3.0	3.8
Ghana	4.0	4.0	4.5	4.0	3.5	4.0	3.5	4.0	4.5	3.5	4.0	3.9
Grenada	5.0	3.5	4.0	3.5	4.0	4.0	3.5	4.0	3.5	3.5	4.0	3.7
Guinea	3.5	3.0	3.0	3.0	2.5	3.0	2.0	3.0	3.0	3.0	2.0	2.6
Guinea-Bissau	2.5	3.0	2.5	2.5	2.5	2.6	2.5	2.5	3.0	2.5	2.5	2.6
Guyana	4.0	3.5	4.0	3.0	3.0	3.5	3.0	3.5	3.5	2.5	3.0	3.1
Haiti	3.0	3.0	2.5	2.5	2.5	2.7	2.0	3.0	2.5	2.5	2.0	2.4
Honduras	4.0	4.0	4.0	3.5	3.5	3.8	3.0	4.0	4.0	3.0	3.0	3.4
India	3.5	4.0	4.0	3.5	3.5	3.7	3.5	4.0	4.0	3.5	3.5	3.7
Kenya	3.0	3.0	3.5	3.0	3.5	3.2	2.5	3.5	4.0	3.5	3.0	3.3
Kiribati	2.5	3.0	2.5	3.0	3.0	2.8	3.5	3.0	3.0	3.0	3.0	3.1
Kyrgyz Republic	4.5	3.5	3.5	3.5	3.0	3.6	2.5	3.5	3.5	3.0	2.5	3.0
Lao PDR	3.5	4.0	3.0	2.5	4.0	3.4	3.0	3.5	3.0	3.0	2.0	2.9

Definitions

• **International Development Association Resource Allocation Index** is obtained by calculating the average score for each cluster and then by averaging those scores. For each of 16 criteria countries are rated on a scale of 1 (low) to 6 (high) • **Economic management** cluster: **Macroeconomic management** assesses the monetary, exchange rate, and aggregate demand policy framework. • **Fiscal policy** assesses the short- and medium-term sustainability of fiscal policy (taking into account monetary and exchange rate policy and the sustainability of the public debt) and its impact on growth. • **Debt policy** assesses whether the debt management strategy is conducive to minimizing budgetary risks and ensuring

long-term debt sustainability. • **Structural policies** cluster: **Trade** assesses how the policy framework fosters trade in goods. • **Financial sector** assesses the structure of the financial sector and the policies and regulations that affect it. • **Business regulatory environment** assesses the extent to which the legal, regulatory, and policy environments help or hinder private businesses in investing, creating jobs, and becoming more productive. • **Policies for social inclusion and equity** cluster: **Gender equality** assesses the extent to which the country has installed institutions and programs to enforce laws and policies that promote equal access for men and women in education, health, the economy, and

protection under law. • **Equity of public resource use** assesses the extent to which the pattern of public expenditures and revenue collection affects the poor and is consistent with national poverty reduction priorities. • **Building human resources** assesses the national policies and public and private sector service delivery that affect the access to and quality of health and education services, including prevention and treatment of HIV/AIDS, tuberculosis, and malaria. • **Social protection and labor** assess government policies in social protection and labor market regulations that reduce the risk of becoming poor, assist those who are poor to better manage further risks, and ensure a minimal level of welfare

	Policies for social inclusion and equity 1–6 (low to high)						Public sector management and institutions 1–6 (low to high)					
	Gender equality 2008	Equity of public resource use 2008	Building human resources 2008	Social protection and labor 2008	Policies and institutions for environmental sustainability 2008	Average 2008	Property rights and rule-based governance 2008	Quality of budgetary and financial management 2008	Efficiency of revenue mobilization 2008	Quality of public administration 2008	Transparency, accountability, and corruption in the public sector 2008	Average 2008
Lesotho	4.0	3.0	3.5	3.0	3.0	3.3	3.5	3.0	4.0	3.0	3.5	3.4
Madagascar	3.5	4.0	3.5	3.5	4.0	3.7	3.5	3.5	4.0	3.5	3.5	3.6
Malawi	3.5	3.5	3.0	3.5	3.5	3.4	3.5	3.0	4.0	3.5	3.0	3.4
Maldives	4.0	4.0	4.0	3.5	4.0	3.9	4.0	3.0	4.0	4.0	2.5	3.5
Mali	3.5	3.5	3.5	3.5	3.0	3.4	3.5	3.5	3.5	3.0	3.5	3.4
Mauritania	4.0	3.5	3.5	3.0	3.5	3.5	3.0	3.0	3.5	3.0	2.5	3.0
Moldova	5.0	3.5	4.0	3.5	3.5	3.9	3.5	4.0	3.5	3.5	3.0	3.5
Mongolia	3.5	3.5	4.0	3.5	3.0	3.5	3.0	4.0	3.0	3.5	3.0	3.3
Mozambique	3.5	3.5	4.0	3.0	3.0	3.4	3.0	3.5	4.0	3.0	3.0	3.3
Nepal	3.5	3.5	4.0	3.0	3.0	3.4	2.5	3.0	3.5	3.0	3.0	3.0
Nicaragua	3.5	4.0	3.5	3.5	3.5	3.6	3.0	4.0	4.0	3.0	3.0	3.4
Niger	2.5	3.5	3.0	3.0	3.0	3.0	3.0	3.5	3.5	3.0	3.0	3.2
Nigeria	3.0	3.5	3.0	3.5	3.0	3.2	2.5	3.0	3.0	3.0	3.0	2.9
Pakistan	2.0	3.5	3.5	3.0	3.0	3.0	2.5	3.5	3.0	3.5	2.5	3.0
Papua New Guinea	2.5	3.0	2.5	3.0	2.0	2.6	2.0	3.5	3.5	2.5	3.0	2.9
Rwanda	3.5	4.5	4.5	3.5	3.5	3.9	3.0	4.0	3.5	3.5	3.5	3.5
Samoa	3.5	4.0	4.0	4.0	4.0	3.9	4.0	3.5	4.0	4.0	4.0	3.9
São Tomé and Príncipe	3.0	3.0	3.0	2.5	2.5	2.8	2.5	3.0	3.5	3.0	3.5	3.1
Senegal	3.5	3.5	3.5	3.0	3.5	3.4	3.5	3.0	4.0	3.5	3.0	3.4
Sierra Leone	3.0	3.0	3.5	3.0	2.0	2.9	2.5	3.5	2.5	2.5	2.5	2.7
Solomon Islands	3.0	2.5	3.0	2.5	2.0	2.6	3.0	2.5	2.5	2.0	3.0	2.6
Sri Lanka	4.0	3.5	4.5	3.5	3.5	3.8	3.0	4.0	3.5	3.0	3.0	3.3
St. Lucia	3.5	4.0	4.0	4.0	3.5	3.8	4.0	3.5	4.0	3.5	4.5	3.9
St. Vincent & Grenadines	4.0	3.5	4.0	3.5	3.5	3.7	4.0	3.5	4.0	3.5	4.0	3.8
Sudan	2.0	2.5	2.5	2.5	2.0	2.3	2.0	2.0	3.0	2.5	2.0	2.3
Tajikistan	4.0	3.5	3.0	3.5	3.0	3.4	2.5	3.0	3.0	2.5	2.0	2.6
Tanzania	3.5	4.0	4.0	3.5	3.5	3.7	3.5	3.5	4.0	3.5	3.0	3.5
Timor-Leste	3.5	3.0	2.5	2.0	2.5	2.7	2.0	3.0	3.0	2.5	3.0	2.7
Togo	3.0	2.0	3.0	3.0	2.5	2.7	2.5	2.0	2.5	2.0	2.0	2.2
Tonga	3.0	3.5	4.0	3.0	3.0	3.3	3.5	3.0	3.0	3.5	3.5	3.3
Uganda	3.5	4.0	4.0	3.5	4.0	3.8	3.5	4.0	3.5	3.0	3.0	3.4
Uzbekistan	4.0	3.5	4.0	3.5	3.5	3.7	2.5	3.0	3.5	3.0	1.5	2.7
Vanuatu	3.5	3.5	2.5	2.0	3.0	2.9	3.5	3.5	3.5	3.0	3.0	3.3
Vietnam	4.5	4.5	4.0	3.5	3.5	4.0	3.5	4.0	4.0	3.5	3.0	3.6
Yemen, Rep.	2.0	3.5	3.0	3.5	3.5	3.1	2.5	3.5	3.0	3.0	3.0	3.0
Zambia	3.5	3.5	4.0	3.0	3.5	3.5	3.0	3.5	3.5	3.0	3.0	3.2
Zimbabwe	2.5	1.0	1.0	1.0	2.0	1.5	1.0	1.5	3.5	1.0	1.0	1.6

to all people. • **Policies and institutions for environmental sustainability** assess the extent to which environmental policies foster the protection and sustainable use of natural resources and the management of pollution. • **Public sector management and institutions** cluster: **Property rights and rule-based governance** assess the extent to which private economic activity is facilitated by an effective legal system and rule-based governance structure in which property and contract rights are reliably respected and enforced. • **Quality of budgetary and financial management** assesses the extent to which there is a comprehensive and credible budget linked to policy priorities, effective financial management systems,

and timely and accurate accounting and fiscal reporting, including timely and audited public accounts. • **Efficiency of revenue mobilization** assesses the overall pattern of revenue mobilization—not only the de facto tax structure, but also revenue from all sources as actually collected. • **Quality of public administration** assesses the extent to which civilian central government staff is structured to design and implement government policy and deliver services effectively. • **Transparency, accountability, and corruption in the public sector** assess the extent to which the executive can be held accountable for its use of funds and for the results of its actions by the electorate, the legislature, and the judiciary and the

extent to which public employees within the executive are required to account for administrative decisions, use of resources, and results obtained. The three main dimensions assessed are the accountability of the executive to oversight institutions and of public employees for their performance, access of civil society to information on public affairs, and state capture by narrow vested interests.

Data sources

Data on public policies and institutions are from the World Bank Group's CPIA database available at www.worldbank.org/ida.

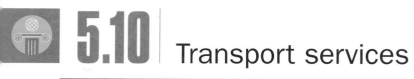

	Roads				Railways			Ports	Air		
	Total road network km 2000–07[a]	Paved roads % 2000–07[a]	Passengers carried million passenger-km 2000–07[a]	Goods hauled million ton-km 2000–07[a]	Rail lines total route-km 2000–08[a]	Passengers carried million passenger-km 2000–08[a]	Goods hauled million ton-km 2000–08[a]	Port container traffic thousand TEU 2008	Registered carrier departures worldwide thousands 2008	Passengers carried thousands 2008	Air freight million ton-km 2008
Afghanistan	42,150	29.3	..	..	..	..	..	..	..	..	..
Albania	18,000	39.0	197	2,200	423	51	53	..	..	..	0
Algeria	108,302	70.2	..	..	3,572	937	1,562	311	31	2,885	17
Angola	51,429	10.4	166,045	4,709	..	..	..	..	3	284	71
Argentina	231,374	30.0	..	..	35,753	..	12,871	1,997	75	6,147	132
Armenia	7,515	89.8	2,693	434	845	27	354	..	..	..	7
Australia	815,074	..	301,550	173,000	9,661	1,526	61,019	6,143	393	51,488	2,212
Austria	107,206	100.0	69,000	26,411	5,755	10,275	18,710	..	151	9,141	421
Azerbaijan	59,141	49.4	11,786	8,222	2,099	1,047	10,021	12	..	756	12
Bangladesh	239,226	9.5	..	..	2,835	5,609	870	1,070	11	1,224	84
Belarus	94,797	88.6	9,353	15,779	5,491	8,188	47,933	..	6	500	66
Belgium	153,070	78.2	130,868	51,572	3,513	10,403	7,882	10,938	179	5,879	982
Benin	19,000	9.5	..	..	758	..	36	..	..	..	..
Bolivia	62,479	7.0	..	..	2,866	313	1,060	..	21	1,718	9
Bosnia and Herzegovina	21,846	52.3	..	300	1,016	78	1,237	..	..	..	..
Botswana	25,798	32.6	..	..	888	94	674	..	6	236	0
Brazil	1,751,868	5.5	..	..	29,817	..	267,700	6,879	648	58,763	1,807
Bulgaria	40,231	98.4	13,688	11,843	4,159	2,335	4,673	..	16	1,073	2
Burkina Faso	92,495	4.2	..	..	622	..	..	..	1	81	0
Burundi	12,322	10.4	..	..	..	..	..	..	..	..	..
Cambodia	38,257	6.3	201	3	..	..	..	..	4	211	1
Cameroon	51,346	8.4	..	..	977	379	978	..	9	471	26
Canada	1,409,000	39.9	493,814	184,774	57,216	3,056	358,154	4,721	1,200	53,719	1,389
Central African Republic	24,307	..	..	..	..	..	..	..	..	..	..
Chad	40,000	0.8	..	..	..	..	..	..	..	..	..
Chile	79,814	20.2	..	..	5,898	759	4,296	3,123	109	8,022	1,308
China	3,583,715	70.7	1,150,677	975,420	60,809	772,834	2,511,804	115,061	1,853	191,001	11,386
Hong Kong SAR, China	2,009	100.0	..	..	..	..	..	24,494	..	..	8,326
Colombia	164,278	..	157	39,726	1,663	..	9,049	1,955	187	12,339	1,100
Congo, Dem. Rep.	153,497	1.8	..	..	4,007	95	352	..	..	..	..
Congo, Rep.	17,289	5.0	..	..	795	211	234	..	..	..	..
Costa Rica	36,654	25.5	27	..	..	..	..	1,005	37	1,024	11
Côte d'Ivoire	80,000	8.1	..	..	639	..	675	710	..	..	..
Croatia	29,038	89.1	3,277	10,175	2,722	1,810	3,312	113	25	1,753	2
Cuba	60,856	49.0	5,266	2,133	5,076	1,285	1,351	..	12	861	32
Czech Republic	128,511	100.0	90,055	46,600	9,487	6,759	15,961	..	78	4,975	27
Denmark	72,412	100.0	70,635	11,495	2,133	5,843	..	680	..	..	1
Dominican Republic	12,600	49.4	..	..	..	..	..	1,092	..	..	..
Ecuador	43,670	14.8	11,819	5,453	..	..	• ..	671	49	2,927	5
Egypt, Arab Rep.	92,370	81.0	..	..	5,063	40,830	4,188	6,115	58	6,689	195
El Salvador	10,029	19.8	..	..	..	..	..	..	21	2,280	18
Eritrea	4,010	21.8	..	..	..	..	..	..	..	..	..
Estonia	58,034	28.8	3,190	7,641	816	274	5,683	..	11	686	1
Ethiopia	42,429	12.8	219,113	2,456	..	..	..	..	40	2,715	228
Finland	78,889	65.4	71,300	26,400	5,919	4,052	10,777	1,605	114	7,916	543
France	951,125	100.0	775,000	313,000	29,901	88,283	41,530	4,619	828	61,215	6,188
Gabon	9,170	10.2	..	..	810	99	2,502	..	6	546	68
Gambia, The	3,742	19.3	16	..	..	..	..	..	..	..	..
Georgia	20,329	38.6	5,269	586	1,513	774	6,928	..	..	..	3
Germany	644,471	100.0	966,692	461,900	33,862	76,997	91,178	17,177	1,154	107,942	8,353
Ghana	57,614	14.9	..	..	953	85	181	..	..	..	..
Greece	117,533	91.8	..	18,360	2,552	2,003	786	1,769	128	9,443	78
Guatemala	14,095	34.5	..	..	..	..	..	910	..	..	..
Guinea	44,348	9.8	..	..	..	..	..	..	..	..	..
Guinea-Bissau	3,455	27.9	..	..	..	..	..	..	..	..	..
Haiti	4,160	24.3	..	..	..	..	..	..	..	..	..
Honduras	13,600	20.4	..	..	..	..	..	553	..	..	..

	Roads				Railways			Ports	Air		
	Total road network km	Paved roads %	Passengers carried million passenger-km	Goods hauled million ton-km	Rail lines total route-km	Passengers carried million passenger-km	Goods hauled million ton-km	Port container traffic thousand TEU	Registered carrier departures worldwide thousands	Passengers carried thousands	Air freight million ton-km
	2000–07[a]	2000–07[a]	2000–07[a]	2000–07[a]	2000–08[a]	2000–08[a]	2000–08[a]	2008	2008	2008	2008
Hungary	195,719	37.7	11,784	30,495	7,942	5,927	7,786	..	..	..	20
India	3,316,452	47.4	..	..	63,327	769,956	521,371	6,623	592	49,878	1,234
Indonesia	391,009	55.4	..	..	3,370	14,344	4,390	6,788	345	29,766	395
Iran, Islamic Rep.	172,927	72.8	..	..	7,335	13,900	21,829	2,000	122	12,029	97
Iraq	45,550	84.3	..	..	2,032	61	640	..	..	..	..
Ireland	96,602	100.0	..	15,900	1,919	1,976	103	1,044	..	..	131
Israel	17,870	100.0	..	..	1,005	1,968	1,055	2,090	45	4,563	902
Italy	487,700	100.0	97,560	192,700	16,862	46,998	19,918	10,520	383	30,672	1,279
Jamaica	22,121	73.3	..	..	..	..	..	1,916	..	..	15
Japan	1,196,999	79.3	947,562	327,632	20,048	255,865	23,032	18,795	655	97,022	8,173
Jordan	7,768	100.0	..	..	251	..	789	..	31	2,355	141
Kazakhstan	93,123	90.3	103,381	53,816	14,205	14,450	214,907	..	19	1,276	16
Kenya	63,265	14.1	..	22	1,917	250	1,399	..	32	2,881	295
Korea, Dem. Rep.	25,554	2.8	..	..	..	..	..	..	..	..	2
Korea, Rep.	102,061	77.6	97,854	12,545	3,381	32,025	11,566	17,774	250	36,078	8,727
Kosovo	..	..	..	..	..	..	..	..	..	..	..
Kuwait	5,749	85.0	..	..	..	..	..	750	..	..	239
Kyrgyz Republic	34,000	91.1	6,468	819	417	60	849	..	4	205	2
Lao PDR	29,811	13.4	..	..	..	..	..	..	10	323	3
Latvia	69,687	100.0	2,664	2,729	2,263	951	17,704	..	..	..	13
Lebanon	6,970	..	..	..	..	..	..	945	..	..	74
Lesotho	5,940	18.3	..	..	..	..	..	..	..	..	..
Liberia	10,600	6.2	..	..	..	..	..	..	..	..	..
Libya	83,200	57.2	..	..	..	..	..	..	10	1,214	0
Lithuania	80,715	28.6	42,739	18,134	1,765	398	14,748	..	12	610	1
Macedonia, FYR	13,840	..	1,027	8,299	699	148	743	..	..	..	0
Madagascar	49,827	11.6	..	..	854	10	1	..	12	559	12
Malawi	15,451	45.0	..	..	797	44	33	..	4	160	2
Malaysia	93,109	79.8	..	..	1,665	2,268	1,350	15,742	177	22,421	2,444
Mali	18,709	18.0	..	..	..	..	..	..	..	..	..
Mauritania	11,066	26.8	..	..	728	47	7,622	..	1	154	0
Mauritius	2,028	98.0	..	..	..	..	..	381	12	1,257	191
Mexico	360,075	38.2	449,917	209,392	26,677	84	71,136	3,161	266	18,826	483
Moldova	12,755	85.7	1,640	1,577	1,156	485	3,092	..	..	..	1
Mongolia	49,250	3.5	557	242	1,810	1,400	8,261	..	6	364	6
Morocco	57,799	62.0	..	1,212	1,989	3,836	4,959	561	61	4,927	55
Mozambique	30,400	18.7	..	..	3,116	114	695	..	11	461	7
Myanmar	27,000	11.9	..	..	..	4,163	885	..	30	1,638	3
Namibia	42,237	12.8	47	591	..	..	..	..	5	452	0
Nepal	17,280	56.9	..	..	..	..	..	..	7	520	7
Netherlands	126,100	90.0	..	77,100	2,896	15,313	..	11,362	263	29,601	4,903
New Zealand	93,748	65.4	..	..	..	..	..	2,296	220	12,951	921
Nicaragua	18,669	11.4	..	..	..	..	..	..	..	..	..
Niger	18,951	20.7	..	..	..	..	..	..	..	..	..
Nigeria	193,200	15.0	..	..	3,528	174	77	513	18	1,461	10
Norway	92,920	79.6	60,597	14,966	4,114	2,705	..	..	..	..	..
Oman	48,874	41.3	..	..	..	..	..	3,428	..	..	..
Pakistan	260,420	65.4	263,788	129,249	7,791	24,731	6,187	1,938	52	5,606	320
Panama	11,643	34.6	..	..	..	..	..	5,127	..	..	36
Papua New Guinea	19,600	3.5	..	..	..	..	..	..	22	905	22
Paraguay	29,500	50.8	..	..	..	..	..	..	11	466	0
Peru	78,986	13.9	..	..	2,020	55	627	1,396	68	6,184	230
Philippines	200,037	9.9	..	..	479	83	..	4,466	72	9,508	277
Poland	258,910	90.3	27,359	136,490	19,627	17,958	39,200	859	90	4,635	79
Portugal	82,900	86.0	..	45,032	2,842	3,814	2,550	1,238	159	11,171	347
Puerto Rico	25,645	95.0	..	10	..	..	..	1,685	..	..	..
Qatar	7,790	90.0	..	..	..	..	..	..	..	..	888

	Roads				Railways			Ports	Air		
	Total road network km	Paved roads %	Passengers carried million passenger-km	Goods hauled million ton-km	Rail lines total route-km	Passengers carried million passenger-km	Goods hauled million ton-km	Port container traffic thousand TEU	Registered carrier departures worldwide thousands	Passengers carried thousands	Air freight million ton-km
	2000–07[a]	2000–07[a]	2000–07[a]	2000–07[a]	2000–08[a]	2000–08[a]	2000–08[a]	2008	2008	2008	2008
Romania	198,817	30.2	7,985	51,531	10,784	6,880	12,861	1,381	55	3,253	6
Russian Federation	933,000	80.9	78,000	199,000	84,158	175,800	2,400,000	3,303	523	37,940	2,400
Rwanda	14,008	19.0	..	..	..	..	..	..	..	..	..
Saudi Arabia	221,372	21.5	..	..	2,758	337	1,748	4,652	148	16,708	1,383
Senegal	13,576	29.3	..	..	..	129	384	..	0	567	0
Serbia	39,184	62.7	3,865	452	4,058	749	4,214	..	..	..	4
Sierra Leone	11,300	8.0	..	..	..	..	..	..	..	..	10
Singapore	3,297	100.0	..	..	..	..	..	29,918	..	..	7,981
Slovak Republic	43,761	87.0	7,816	22,114	3,592	2,279	9,004	..	24	2,690	46
Slovenia	38,708	100.0	817	12,112	1,228	834	3,520	..	..	..	2
Somalia	22,100	11.8	..	..	..	..	..	..	..	..	..
South Africa	362,099	17.3	..	434	24,487	13,865	106,014	3,797	157	13,135	761
Spain	666,292	99.0	397,117	132,868	15,046	23,344	10,224	13,248	617	55,214	1,306
Sri Lanka	97,286	81.0	21,067	..	1,463	4,767	135	3,687	..	..	325
Sudan	11,900	36.3	..	..	4,578	34	766	..	7	618	47
Swaziland	3,594	30.0	..	..	300	0	2	..	..	..	..
Sweden	427,045	31.7	109,300	40,123	9,830	7,156	11,500	1,312	..	..	..
Switzerland	71,354	100.0	94,250	16,337	3,499	18,367	16,227	..	159	14,353	1,182
Syrian Arab Republic	40,032	100.0	589	..	2,139	1,120	2,370	..	19	1,358	14
Tajikistan	27,767	..	150	14,572	616	53	1,274	..	8	683	5
Tanzania	78,891	8.6	..	..	2,600[b]	475[b]	728[b]	..	5	203	1
Thailand	180,053	98.5	..	..	4,429	8,037	3,161	6,586	126	19,993	2,289
Timor-Leste	..	..	..	..	..	..	..	..	..	..	..
Togo	7,520	31.6	..	..	..	..	..	..	..	..	..
Trinidad and Tobago	8,320	51.1	..	..	..	..	..	440	15	1,103	49
Tunisia	19,232	65.8	..	16,611	2,218	1,487	2,197	..	..	..	19
Turkey	426,951	..	209,115	177,399	8,699	5,097	10,104	5,218	215	25,505	481
Turkmenistan	24,000	81.2	..	..	3,181	1,570	10,973	..	16	1,823	11
Uganda	70,746	23.0	..	..	..	..	..	..	..	..	34
Ukraine	169,422	97.8	55,446	26,625	21,676	53,056	257,006	1,112	53	3,456	63
United Arab Emirates	4,030	100.0	..	..	..	..	..	12,254	..	..	..
United Kingdom	420,009	100.0	736,000	166,728	16,321	51,759	12,512	7,081	1,056	104,714	6,284
United States	6,544,257	65.3	7,940,003	1,889,923	227,058	9,935	2,788,230[c]	40,345	9,054[d]	701,780[d]	39,314[d]
Uruguay	77,732	10.0	2,032	..	2,993	15	284	302	..	..	4
Uzbekistan	81,600	87.3	..	1,200	4,230	2,264	21,594	..	22	2,034	72
Venezuela, RB	96,155	33.6	..	..	336	..	81	1,325	138	5,767	2
Vietnam	160,089	47.6	49,372	20,537	3,147	4,659	3,910	4,394	75	9,991	296
West Bank and Gaza	5,147	100.0	..	..	..	..	..	..	..	..	..
Yemen, Rep.	71,300	8.7	..	..	..	..	..	377	14	1,065	33
Zambia	66,781	22.0	..	..	..	..	..	..	4	62	0
Zimbabwe	97,267	19.0	..	..	2,583	..	1,580	..	6	264	7
World	**37.6 m**	**.. m**	**.. m**	**.. s**	**2,003 m**	**4,343 m**	**486,792 s**	**24,225 s**	**2,049,275 s**	**124,557 s**	
Low income	12.1	..	..	..	..	..	..	..	302	26,002	1,057
Middle income	37.6	..	..	..	1,120	4,296	215,508	6,565	588,155	28,431	
Lower middle income	37.6	..	..	..	1,400	3,127	155,286	3,622	351,921	16,708	
Upper middle income	41.8	..	..	..	944	9,049	60,222	2,942	236,233	11,723	
Low & middle income	24.3	..	..	..	937	3,127	220,972	6,867	614,156	29,488	
East Asia & Pacific	34.3	..	..	..	4,248	3,447	153,036	2,795	287,490	17,220	
Europe & Central Asia	..	11,786	15,779	193,080	999	10,063	11,874	1,051	83,250	3,151	
Latin America & Carib.	22.0	..	..	..	..	..	29,887	1,646	125,654	5,163	
Middle East & N. Africa	75.6	..	..	..	1,487	2,284	..	346	32,523	554	
South Asia	56.9	..	..	..	15,170	3,529	13,319	663	57,228	1,645	
Sub-Saharan Africa	11.9	..	..	..	..	..	..	366	28,012	1,754	
High income	87.0	..	41,824	..	6,343	10,777	265,820	17,358	1,435,119	95,069	
Euro area	100.0	97,840	45,032	126,162	10,275	9,614	74,159	4,000	330,883	24,446	

a. Data are for the latest year available in the period shown. b. Includes Tazara railway. c. Refers to class 1 railways only. d. Covers only carriers designated by the U.S. Department of Transportation as major and national air carriers.

About the data

Transport infrastructure—highways, railways, ports and waterways, and airports and air traffic control systems—and the services that flow from it are crucial to the activities of households, producers, and governments. Because performance indicators vary widely by transport mode and focus (whether physical infrastructure or the services flowing from that infrastructure), highly specialized and carefully specified indicators are required. The table provides selected indicators of the size, extent, and productivity of roads, railways, and air transport systems and of the volume of traffic in these modes as well as in ports.

Data for transport sectors are not always internationally comparable. Unlike for demographic statistics, national income accounts, and international trade data, the collection of infrastructure data has not been "internationalized." But data on roads are collected by the International Road Federation (IRF), and data on air transport by the International Civil Aviation Organization (ICAO).

National road associations are the primary source of IRF data. In countries where a national road association is lacking or does not respond, other agencies are contacted, such as road directorates, ministries of transport or public works, or central statistical offices. As a result, definitions and data collection methods and quality differ, and the compiled data are of uneven quality. Moreover, the quality of transport service (reliability, transit time, and condition of goods delivered) is rarely measured, though it may be as important as quantity in assessing an economy's transport system.

Unlike the road sector, where numerous qualified motor vehicle operators can operate anywhere on the road network, railways are a restricted transport system with vehicles confined to a fixed guideway. Considering the cost and service characteristics, railways generally are best suited to carry—and can effectively compete for—bulk commodities and containerized freight for distances of 500–5,000 kilometers, and passengers for distances of 50–1,000 kilometers. Below these limits road transport tends to be more competitive, while above these limits air transport for passengers and freight and sea transport for freight tend to be more competitive. The railways indicators in the table focus on scale and output measures: total route-kilometers, passenger-kilometers, and goods (freight) hauled in ton-kilometers.

Measures of port container traffic, much of it commodities of medium to high value added, give some indication of economic growth in a country. But when traffic is merely transshipment, much of the economic benefit goes to the terminal operator and ancillary services for ships and containers rather than to the country more broadly. In transshipment centers empty containers may account for as much as 40 percent of traffic.

The air transport data represent the total (international and domestic) scheduled traffic carried by the air carriers registered in a country. Countries submit air transport data to ICAO on the basis of standard instructions and definitions issued by ICAO. In many cases, however, the data include estimates by ICAO for nonreporting carriers. Where possible, these estimates are based on previous submissions supplemented by information published by the air carriers, such as flight schedules.

The data cover the air traffic carried on scheduled services, but changes in air transport regulations in Europe have made it more difficult to classify traffic as scheduled or nonscheduled. Thus recent increases shown for some European countries may be due to changes in the classification of air traffic rather than actual growth. For countries with few air carriers or only one, the addition or discontinuation of a home-based air carrier may cause significant changes in air traffic.

Definitions

• **Total road network** covers motorways, highways, main or national roads, secondary or regional roads, and all other roads in a country. • **Paved roads** are roads surfaced with crushed stone (macadam) and hydrocarbon binder or bituminized agents, with concrete, or with cobblestones. • **Passengers carried by road** are the number of passengers transported by road times kilometers traveled. • **Goods hauled by road** are the volume of goods transported by road vehicles, measured in millions of metric tons times kilometers traveled. • **Rail lines** are the length of railway route available for train service, irrespective of the number of parallel tracks. • **Passengers carried by railway** are the number of passengers transported by rail times kilometers traveled. • **Goods hauled by railway** are the volume of goods transported by railway, measured in metric tons times kilometers traveled. • **Port container traffic** measures the flow of containers from land to sea transport modes and vice versa in twenty-foot-equivalent units (TEUs), a standard-size container. Data cover coastal shipping as well as international journeys. Transshipment traffic is counted as two lifts at the intermediate port (once to off-load and again as an outbound lift) and includes empty units. • **Registered carrier departures worldwide** are domestic takeoffs and takeoffs abroad of air carriers registered in the country. • **Passengers carried by air** include both domestic and international passengers of air carriers registered in the country. • **Air freight** is the volume of freight, express, and diplomatic bags carried on each flight stage (operation of an aircraft from takeoff to its next landing), measured in metric tons times kilometers traveled.

Data sources

Data on roads are from the IRF's *World Road Statistics,* supplemented by World Bank staff estimates. Data on railways are from a database maintained by the World Bank's Transport and Urban Development Department, Transport Division, based on data from the International Union of Railways. Data on port container traffic are from Containerisation International's *Containerisation International Yearbook.* Data on air transport are from the ICAO's *Civil Aviation Statistics of the World* and ICAO staff estimates.

5.11 Power and communications

	Electric power		Telephones				Affordability and efficiency			
			Access and use			Quality				
	Consumption per capita kWh	Transmission and distribution losses % of output	per 100 people		International voice traffic[a] minutes per person	Population covered by mobile cellular network[a] %	$ per month		Telecommunications revenue[a] % of GDP	Mobile cellular and fixed-line subscribers per employee[a]
			Fixed lines[a]	Mobile cellular subscriptions[a]			Residential fixed-line tariff[a]	Mobile cellular prepaid tariff[a]		
	2007	2007	2008	2008	2008	2008	2008	2008	2008	2008
Afghanistan	..	..	0	27	1	75	..	..	..	58
Albania	1,186	69	11	100	127	99	4.3	22.7	6.0	871
Algeria	902	18	10	93	18	82	4.6	8.2	2.7	285
Angola	185	14	1	38	..	40	20.2	11.8	..	..
Argentina	2,659	16	24	117	42	94	4.8	12.5	3.1	1,929
Armenia	1,692	13	20	100	..	88	5.1	8.4	..	..
Australia	11,249	7	44	103	..	99	27.5	26.5	3.3	346
Austria	8,033	6	39	130	..	99	28.7	24.3	1.7	843
Azerbaijan	2,394	14	15	75	..	99	2.4	15.2	2.4	484
Bangladesh	144	7	1	28	6	90	1.3	1.3	..	..
Belarus	3,345	12	38	84	..	99	..	..	2.1	..
Belgium	8,614	5	42	110	..	100	36.4	21.9	2.8	732
Benin	72	87	2	40	12	80	7.5	15.5	1.0	1,539
Bolivia	515	14	7	50	80	46	22.7	5.9	6.8	376
Bosnia and Herzegovina	2,381	19	27	84	109	99	9.5	9.9	5.5	567
Botswana	1,435	15	7	77	115	99	16.9	8.3	3.0	1,018
Brazil	2,171	16	21	78	..	91	29.1	37.0	4.6	358
Bulgaria	4,456	11	29	138	27	100	9.2	18.6	5.3	565
Burkina Faso	..	..	1	17	11	61	10.3	16.9	4.0	..
Burundi	..	..	0	6	..	80	..	..	3.1	492
Cambodia	94	12	0	29	..	87	8.0	5.0	..	1,712
Cameroon	265	14	1	32	4	58	14.8	17.8	3.1	1,050
Canada	16,995	8	55	66	..	98	32.8	19.2	2.5	..
Central African Republic	..	..	0	4	..	19	10.6	12.6	..	293
Chad	..	..	0	17	..	24	..	..	..	..
Chile	3,318	8	21	88	35	100	27.0	13.7	..	592
China	2,332	6	26	48	9	97	3.7	3.6	2.9	1,310
Hong Kong SAR, China	5,899	13	59	166	1,435	100	11.3	2.6	3.6	980
Colombia	977	20	18	92	142	83	7.6	9.6	3.7	..
Congo, Dem. Rep.	97	4	..	..	..	..	..	..	..	..
Congo, Rep.	135	93	1	50	..	53	..	..	..	..
Costa Rica	1,863	10	32	42	120	69	4.6	4.5	1.8	497
Côte d'Ivoire	178	23	2	51	..	59	22.8	14.8	5.5	1,445
Croatia	3,738	17	42	133	229	100	16.4	18.7	4.6	892
Cuba	1,309	17	10	3	..	77	13.2	22.7	..	..
Czech Republic	6,496	6	22	132	136	100	30.9	18.6	3.8	812
Denmark	6,670	5	45	125	210	114	28.5	5.8	2.4	543
Dominican Republic	1,378	9	10	72	..	..	14.4	9.1	..	..
Ecuador	788	44	14	86	3	84	1.1	9.0	4.1	513
Egypt, Arab Rep.	1,384	11	15	51	27	95	3.0	4.7	3.7	856
El Salvador	939	2	18	113	578	95	10.4	10.5	4.8	2,275
Eritrea	..	..	1	2	17	80	..	..	3.0	117
Estonia	6,273	11	37	188	..	100	13.7	13.6	4.5	742
Ethiopia	40	9	1	2	2	10	1.5	3.1	1.3	233
Finland	17,162	4	31	129	..	100	19.3	14.1	2.3	708
France	7,772	6	56	93	242	99	30.9	35.7	2.0	695
Gabon	1,066	18	2	90	..	79	..	..	2.0	..
Gambia, The	..	..	3	70	..	85	4.0	6.0	..	466
Georgia	1,620	13	14	64	44	98	7.3	8.5	6.9	355
Germany	7,184	5	63	129	..	99	28.8	10.1	2.5	789
Ghana	259	18	1	50	6	73	4.7	5.9	..	1,780
Greece	5,628	8	53	123	..	100	26.7	25.1	3.7	813
Guatemala	558	14	11	109	..	76	8.7	4.5	..	..
Guinea	..	..	0	39	..	80	3.4	3.5	..	..
Guinea-Bissau	..	..	0	32	..	65	..	..	..	..
Haiti	30	37	1	32	..	..	..	..	..	..
Honduras	692	22	11	85	39	90	..	..	7.1	391

	Electric power		Telephones							
			Access and use			Quality	Affordability and efficiency			
	Consumption per capita kWh	Transmission and distribution losses % of output	per 100 people		International voice traffic[a] minutes per person	Population covered by mobile cellular network[a] %	$ per month		Telecommunications revenue[a] % of GDP	Mobile cellular and fixed-line subscribers per employee[a]
			Fixed lines[a]	Mobile cellular subscriptions[a]			Residential fixed-line tariff[a]	Mobile cellular prepaid tariff[a]		
	2007	2007	2008	2008	2008	2008	2008	2008	2008	2008
Hungary	3,977	10	31	122	120	99	30.2	16.1	3.8	1,127
India	542	25	3	30	..	61	3.5	1.6	2.0	..
Indonesia	566	11	13	62	..	90	4.5	5.3	..	..
Iran, Islamic Rep.	2,325	19	34	60	..	95	0.2	3.8	..	913
Iraq	1,080	7	4	57	0	72	..	..	..	1,098
Ireland	6,263	8	50	121	..	99	42.2	18.7	2.5	..
Israel	7,002	3	44	123	413	100	..	..	1.1	..
Italy	5,713	7	36	151	..	100	27.4	17.1	2.9	1,657
Jamaica	2,542	13	12	101	39	101	10.8	7.0	1.4	..
Japan	8,474	5	38	86	..	100	18.3	32.2	3.0	12
Jordan	1,956	14	9	90	66	99	8.3	4.5	6.7	1,105
Kazakhstan	4,448	10	22	95	47	94	..	..	2.9	253
Kenya	151	15	1	42	3	83	11.6	13.4	6.3	2,298
Korea, Dem. Rep.	764	16	5	0	..	0	..	..	..	..
Korea, Rep.	8,502	4	44	94	33	94	6.4	14.6	4.7	657
Kosovo	..	..	..	..	..	..	..	..	..	..
Kuwait	16,198	12	20	107	..	100	9.3	7.9	..	..
Kyrgyz Republic	1,772	28	9	64	..	24	..	..	4.8	311
Lao PDR	..	..	2	33	..	..	3.9	3.0	..	748
Latvia	3,064	17	28	99	..	99	11.9	7.3	4.0	697
Lebanon	2,154	17	18	34	..	100	10.9	22.2	..	..
Lesotho	..	..	3	28	..	55	12.5	12.6	..	..
Liberia	..	..	0	19	..	..	..	..	8.2	..
Libya	3,871	7	16	77	65	71	..	..	..	1,717
Lithuania	3,414	8	23	150	57	100	15.0	8.7	2.8	402
Macedonia, FYR	3,780	22	22	123	159	100	8.7	13.2	6.3	1,065
Madagascar	..	..	1	25	1	23	18.3	12.4	3.9	2,427
Malawi	..	..	1	12	..	93	3.3	12.0	3.4	..
Malaysia	3,667	2	16	103	..	92	5.1	5.9	..	..
Mali	..	..	1	27	2	22	9.9	10.0	4.3	2,059
Mauritania	..	..	2	65	4	62	12.9	9.9	7.7	2,842
Mauritius	..	..	29	81	100	99	5.5	4.4	3.6	..
Mexico	2,036	16	19	71	174	100	22.3	15.0	2.7	840
Moldova	1,319	50	31	67	155	98	3.1	8.9	10.1	294
Mongolia	1,369	12	8	67	5	66	..	..	6.0	393
Morocco	707	19	9	72	21	98	27.4	22.2	5.1	..
Mozambique	472	14	0	20	..	44	17.7	10.1	1.2	..
Myanmar	94	29	2	1	..	10	..	..	..	90
Namibia	1,541	28	7	49	..	95	14.5	11.5	..	..
Nepal	80	22	3	15	..	10	3.4	2.9	1.0	565
Netherlands	7,097	4	44	125	..	98	31.2	17.7	0.7	..
New Zealand	9,622	7	41	108	310	97	34.4	23.1	2.9	605
Nicaragua	446	24	6	55	39	..	5.1	13.8	..	..
Niger	..	..	0	13	..	45	13.6	13.8	..	..
Nigeria	137	12	1	42	1	83	10.3	12.1	3.4	..
Norway	24,980	7	40	110	..	..	37.6	9.7	1.2	..
Oman	4,484	15	10	116	30	96	32.6	5.5	3.4	967
Pakistan	474	19	3	53	..	90	3.6	1.9	2.7	50
Panama	1,592	16	15	115	61	83	9.1	5.1	3.2	380
Papua New Guinea	..	..	1	9	..	..	4.0	12.8	..	..
Paraguay	958	5	8	95	35	..	7.2	5.7	4.8	799
Peru	961	8	10	73	..	95	15.4	8.0	3.1	624
Philippines	586	13	5	75	..	99	14.2	5.7	..	..
Poland	3,662	9	25	115	..	99	28.0	12.5	3.9	396
Portugal	4,860	7	39	140	..	99	25.7	26.4	4.6	1,534
Puerto Rico	..	..	26	..	..	..	..	..	..	..
Qatar	12,915	9	21	131	..	100	..	..	1.8	597

| | Electric power | | Telephones | | | | | | | |
	Consumption per capita kWh	Transmission and distribution losses % of output	Access and use per 100 people Fixed lines[a]	Access and use per 100 people Mobile cellular subscriptions[a]	International voice traffic[a] minutes per person	Quality Population covered by mobile cellular network[a] %	Affordability and efficiency $ per month Residential fixed-line tariff[a]	Affordability and efficiency $ per month Mobile cellular prepaid tariff[a]	Telecommunications revenue[a] % of GDP	Mobile cellular and fixed-line subscribers per employee[a]
	2007	2007	2008	2008	2008	2008	2008	2008	2008	2008
Romania	2,452	11	23	114	*41*	98	12.2	11.9	3.4	*561*
Russian Federation	6,317	10	32	141	..	95	11.7	8.6	2.6	..
Rwanda	..	..	0	14	*11*	92	7.3	10.0	3.1	1,952
Saudi Arabia	7,247	7	17	146	..	98	9.2	8.8	2.7	1,618
Senegal	128	25	2	44	*27*	85	17.4	8.4	9.8	*1,859*
Serbia	4,155	16	42	131	142	93	4.9	4.9	5.3	872
Sierra Leone	..	..	1	18	..	70	..	..	..	..
Singapore	8,514	5	38	132	*1,531*	*100*	7.1	4.0	2.8	..
Slovak Republic	5,250	5	20	102	123	100	24.5	16.1	3.3	665
Slovenia	7,138	6	50	102	96	100	20.5	12.4	3.3	644
Somalia	..	..	1	7	..	..	..	..	..	..
South Africa	4,986	8	9	92	..	*100*	22.4	12.3	7.4	..
Spain	6,296	5	44	109	..	99	30.8	33.3	4.0	855
Sri Lanka	417	16	17	55	*34*	95	4.8	2.4	..	919
Sudan	90	20	1	29	6	66	4.4	4.8	3.3	2,168
Swaziland	..	..	4	46	..	91	4.8	12.1	4.5	1,118
Sweden	15,238	7	58	118	..	98	22.8	7.5	2.7	894
Switzerland	8,164	6	63	116	..	100	29.0	35.5	3.3	601
Syrian Arab Republic	1,469	24	18	34	78	96	1.2	9.1	3.0	*409*
Tajikistan	2,176	17	4	54	..	..	..	..	..	..
Tanzania	82	19	0	31	*0*	65	10.9	11.1	..	..
Thailand	2,055	6	10	92	..	*38*	5.8	3.9	4.0	*1,957*
Timor-Leste	..	..	..	..	..	..	..	..	7.9	..
Togo	96	53	2	24	6	85	13.1	18.0	7.4	*1,059*
Trinidad and Tobago	5,642	2	23	113	..	*100*	19.7	7.9	2.5	..
Tunisia	1,248	13	12	83	79	100	3.0	7.2	4.3	1,004
Turkey	2,238	14	24	89	39	100	..	..	2.3	2,145
Turkmenistan	2,279	14	9	23	..	*14*	..	..	..	..
Uganda	..	..	1	27	*7*	100	12.6	10.4	..	..
Ukraine	3,529	12	28	120	*0*	100	4.2	8.2	5.7	..
United Arab Emirates	16,165	7	34	209	..	100	5.0	4.1	*3.1*	924
United Kingdom	6,120	7	54	126	..	100	27.3	20.5	4.3	..
United States	13,652	6	51	89	..	*100*	17.2	15.3	..	..
Uruguay	2,197	20	29	105	*0*	100	13.0	13.8	3.1	692
Uzbekistan	1,658	9	7	47	..	93	..	..	2.5	758
Venezuela, RB	3,077	27	23	97	..	90	7.0	24.7	3.5	*914*
Vietnam	728	11	34	81	..	70	2.3	4.2	..	..
West Bank and Gaza	..	..	9	29	..	95	..	..	..	*880*
Yemen, Rep.	202	25	5	16	..	68	0.8	4.9	..	..
Zambia	720	7	1	28	..	50	27.7	12.3	2.6	..
Zimbabwe	898	7	3	13	*22*	75	..	..	..	711
World	**2,846 w**	**8 w**	**19 w**	**61 w**	**.. w**	**80 w**	**10.9 m**	**10.1 m**	**.. w**	**651 m**
Low income	324	13	5	28	..	56	9.0	10.0	..	..
Middle income	1,666	11	15	57	..	80	8.5	9.0	3.2	595
Lower middle income	1,310	11	14	47	..	77	4.8	8.4	3.0	685
Upper middle income	3,052	13	22	95	..	94	11.7	9.9	3.3	559
Low & middle income	1,478	11	13	52	..	76	8.5	9.1	3.2	559
East Asia & Pacific	1,883	6	22	53	9	93	4.5	5.0	3.0	..
Europe & Central Asia	3,958	11	26	110	..	92	8.7	8.9	2.8	462
Latin America & Carib.	1,866	17	19	80	..	92	10.4	9.6	3.8	550
Middle East & N. Africa	1,435	16	16	58	27	93	3.0	7.2	..	880
South Asia	482	24	3	33	..	61	3.5	1.9	2.1	565
Sub-Saharan Africa	550	10	2	33	..	56	11.6	11.8	..	..
High income	9,753	6	47	106	..	99	27.0	16.1	..	801
Euro area	6,963	5	49	122	..	99	28.7	18.7	2.6	789

a. Data are from the International Telecommunication Union's (ITU) World Telecommunication Development Report database. Please cite the ITU for third-party use of these data.

The quality of an economy's infrastructure, including power and communications, is an important element in investment decisions for both domestic and foreign investors. Government effort alone is not enough to meet the need for investments in modern infrastructure; public-private partnerships, especially those involving local providers and financiers, are critical for lowering costs and delivering value for money. In telecommunications, competition in the marketplace, along with sound regulation, is lowering costs, improving quality, and easing access to services around the globe.

An economy's production and consumption of electricity are basic indicators of its size and level of development. Although a few countries export electric power, most production is for domestic consumption. Expanding the supply of electricity to meet the growing demand of increasingly urbanized and industrialized economies without incurring unacceptable social, economic, and environmental costs is one of the great challenges facing developing countries.

Data on electric power production and consumption are collected from national energy agencies by the International Energy Agency (IEA) and adjusted by the IEA to meet international definitions (for data on electricity production, see table 3.10). Electricity consumption is equivalent to production less power plants' own use and transmission, distribution, and transformation losses less exports plus imports. It includes consumption by auxiliary stations, losses in transformers that are considered integral parts of those stations, and electricity produced by pumping installations. Where data are available, it covers electricity generated by primary sources of energy—coal, oil, gas, nuclear, hydro, geothermal, wind, tide and wave, and combustible renewables. Neither production nor consumption data capture the reliability of supplies, including breakdowns, load factors, and frequency of outages.

Over the past decade new financing and technology, along with privatization and liberalization, have spurred dramatic growth in telecommunications in many countries. With the rapid development of mobile telephony and the global expansion of the Internet, information and communication technologies are increasingly recognized as essential tools of development, contributing to global integration and enhancing public sector effectiveness, efficiency, and transparency. The table presents telecommunications indicators covering access and use, quality, and affordability and efficiency.

Access to telephone services rose on an unprecedented scale over the past 15 years. This growth was driven primarily by wireless technologies and liberalization of telecommunications markets, which have enabled faster and less costly network rollout. In 2002 the number of mobile phones in the world surpassed the number of fixed telephones; by the end of 2008 there were an estimated 4 billion mobile phones globally. No technology has ever spread faster around the world. Mobile communications have had a particularly important impact in rural areas. The mobility, ease of use, flexible deployment, and relatively low and declining rollout costs of wireless technologies enable them to reach rural populations with low levels of income and literacy. The next billion mobile subscribers will consist mainly of the rural poor.

Access is the key to delivering telecommunications services to people. If the service is not affordable to most people, goals of universal usage will not be met. Two indicators of telecommunications affordability are presented in the table: fixed-line telephone service tariff and prepaid mobile cellular service tariff. Telecommunications efficiency is measured by total telecommunications revenue divided by GDP and by mobile cellular and fixed-line telephone subscribers per employee.

Operators have traditionally been the main source of telecommunications data, so information on subscribers has been widely available for most countries. This gives a general idea of access, but a more precise measure is the penetration rate—the share of households with access to telecommunications. During the past few years more information on information and communication technology use has become available from household and business surveys. Also important are data on actual use of telecommunications equipment. Ideally, statistics on telecommunications (and other information and communications technologies) should be compiled for all three measures: subscription and possession, access, and use. The quality of data varies among reporting countries as a result of differences in regulations covering data provision and availability.

- **Electric power consumption per capita** measures the production of power plants and combined heat and power plants less transmission, distribution, and transformation losses and own use by heat and power plants divided by midyear population. • **Electric power transmission and distribution losses** are losses in transmission between sources of supply and points of distribution and in distribution to consumers, including pilferage. • **Fixed telephone lines** are telephone lines connecting a subscriber to the telephone exchange equipment. • **Mobile cellular telephone subscriptions** are subscriptions to a public mobile telephone service using cellular technology, which provide access to the public switched telephone network. Post-paid and prepaid subscriptions are included. • **International voice traffic** is the sum of international incoming and outgoing telephone traffic (in minutes) divided by total population.
- **Population covered by mobile cellular network** is the percentage of people that live in areas served by a mobile cellular signal regardless of whether they use it. • **Residential fixed-line tariff** is the monthly subscription charge plus the cost of 30 three-minute local calls (15 peak and 15 off-peak). • **Mobile cellular prepaid tariff** is based on the Organisation for Economic Co-operation and Development's low-user definition, which includes the cost of monthly mobile use for 25 outgoing calls per month spread over the same mobile network, other mobile networks, and mobile to fixed-line calls and during peak, off-peak, and weekend times as well as 30 text messages per month. • **Telecommunications revenue** is the revenue from the provision of telecommunications services such as fixed-line, mobile, and data divided by GDP. • **Mobile cellular and fixed-line subscribers per employee** are telephone subscribers (fixed-line plus mobile) divided by the total number of telecommunications employees.

Data sources

Data on electricity consumption and losses are from the IEA's *Energy Statistics and Balances of Non-OECD Countries 2009*, the IEA's *Energy Statistics of OECD Countries 2009*, and the United Nations Statistics Division's *Energy Statistics Yearbook*. Data on telecommunications are from the International Telecommunication Union's *World Telecommunication Development Report* database and World Bank estimates.

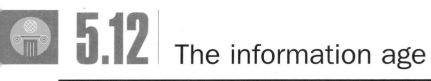

	Daily newspapers	Households with television[a]	Personal computers and the Internet							Information and communications technology trade		
			Access and use		Quality		Affordability	Application		Goods		Services
					Fixed broadband Internet subscribers[a] per 100 people	International Internet bandwidth[a] bits per second per capita	Fixed broadband Internet access tariff[a] $ per month	Secure Internet servers per million people	Information and communications technology expenditures % of GDP	Exports % of total goods exports	Imports % of total goods imports	Exports % of total service exports
	per 1,000 people	%	Personal computers[a]	Internet users[a]								
	2000–07[b]	2007	2008	2008	2008	2008	2008	December 2009	2008	2008	2008	2008
Afghanistan	..	..	0.4	1.7	0.00	1	..	0	..	..	0.4	..
Albania	24	..	4.6	23.9	2.04	220	31	7	..	0.8	4.0	6.8
Algeria	..	..	..	11.9	1.41	..	17	1	2.3	0.0	5.8	..
Angola	2	34	0.6	3.1	0.09	17	164	2	..	..	..	..
Argentina	36	..	..	28.1	7.99	2,320	38	20	4.8	0.5	9.4	9.1
Armenia	8	85	..	6.2	0.16	..	39	7	..	1.3	5.9	17.4
Australia	155	..	..	70.8	23.98	5,457	28	1,212	4.9	1.5	10.0	4.9
Austria	311	97	..	71.2	20.74	20,323	61	553	5.5	5.8	6.9	6.3
Azerbaijan	16	99	8.0	28.2	0.69	1,180	85	2	..	0.0	5.0	3.6
Bangladesh	..	..	2.3	0.3	0.03	4	54	0	9.0	0.6	5.7	6.2
Belarus	81	93	..	32.1	4.94	748	..	3	..	0.6	2.7	7.2
Belgium	165	99	..	68.1	27.66	24,945	31	310	5.2	2.9	4.0	8.7
Benin	0	23	0.7	1.8	0.03	18	105	0	..	0.1	3.5	0.8
Bolivia	..	63	..	10.8	0.68	225	34	4	4.9	0.0	4.2	12.4
Bosnia and Herzegovina	..	..	6.4	34.7	4.99	529	15	8	..	0.5	4.1	..
Botswana	41	..	6.2	6.2	0.46	220	30	4	..	0.2	4.3	3.1
Brazil	36	97	..	37.5	5.26	2,108	47	26	5.3	1.8	10.9	2.2
Bulgaria	79	98	11.0	34.7	11.07	37,657	16	35	6.3	2.6	6.1	5.5
Burkina Faso	..	..	0.6	0.9	0.03	15	1,861	0	..	..	..	..
Burundi	..	..	0.9	0.8	0.00	2	..	0	..	0.8	8.3	0.0
Cambodia	..	63	0.4	0.5	0.11	19	91	1	..	..	..	2.8
Cameroon	..	..	..	3.8	0.00	8	184	1	4.6	0.0	3.2	6.4
Canada	175	99	94.3	75.3	29.55	16,193	20	984	6.6	3.8	8.8	10.4
Central African Republic	..	..	..	0.4	0.00	..	1,396	0	..	..	..	..
Chad	..	..	..	1.2	0.00	1	..	..	..	..	..	..
Chile	51	100	..	32.5	8.49	4,076	53	39	5.1	0.2	6.4	2.5
China	74	..	5.7	22.5	6.29	483	19	1	6.0	27.5	23.2	5.3
Hong Kong SAR, China	222	99	69.3	67.0	28.13	548,318	25	350	9.2	42.6	40.8	1.3
Colombia	23	85	11.2	38.5	4.23	2,233	36	12	4.7	0.2	11.2	7.3
Congo, Dem. Rep.	..	..	..	..	..	..	..	0	..	..	..	..
Congo, Rep.	..	25	..	4.3	0.00	0	..	1	..	..	..	..
Costa Rica	65	94	..	32.3	2.38	857	17	98	6.2	23.8	19.0	17.9
Côte d'Ivoire	..	38	..	3.2	0.05	40	47	1	..	0.3	3.9	11.0
Croatia	..	..	..	50.5	11.83	15,892	21	117	..	5.0	6.1	3.1
Cuba	65	88	5.6	12.9	0.02	27	1,630	0	..	1.9	2.9	..
Czech Republic	183	..	..	57.8	16.88	7,075	29	185	7.6	15.2	15.2	8.6
Denmark	353	98	54.9	83.3	36.88	34,506	30	1,167	5.0	5.0	8.1	..
Dominican Republic	39	77	..	21.6	2.27	1,407	28	14	..	6.0	5.2	3.5
Ecuador	99	90	13.0	28.8	0.26	443	40	12	5.3	0.2	8.2	8.1
Egypt, Arab Rep.	..	97	3.9	16.6	0.94	332	8	1	5.7	1.8	4.4	7.3
El Salvador	38	..	..	10.6	2.01	33	18	12	..	2.5	5.3	10.2
Eritrea	..	..	1.0	4.1	0.00	5	..	..	..	..	..	..
Estonia	191	98	25.5	66.2	23.71	126,802	39	315	..	6.5	7.2	7.1
Ethiopia	5	5	0.7	0.4	0.00	3	644	0	..	0.5	7.9	3.9
Finland	431	93	..	82.5	30.45	17,221	38	802	6.5	16.5	12.0	27.4
France	164	97	65.2	67.9	28.41	29,356	38	210	5.2	5.4	7.2	3.7
Gabon	..	..	3.4	6.2	0.15	141	..	7	..	0.1	6.6	..
Gambia, The	..	..	3.5	6.9	0.02	38	384	3	..	2.9	3.8	10.4
Georgia	4	..	27.2	23.8	2.23	752	48	9	..	0.4	7.8	2.2
Germany	267	95	65.6	75.5	27.52	25,654	38	641	5.4	6.9	8.8	8.3
Ghana	..	..	1.1	4.3	0.10	86	64	1	..	0.1	7.3	0.0
Greece		100	9.4	43.1	13.41	4,537	25	79	4.5	3.2	5.6	1.7
Guatemala	..	..	..	14.3	0.58	186	34	9	..	0.5	6.3	16.1
Guinea	..	11	..	0.9	0.00	0	800	0	..	0.0	5.8	11.2
Guinea-Bissau	..	..	..	2.4	0.00	1	..	..	..	..	..	..
Haiti	..	25	5.1	10.1	0.00	16	..	1	..	..	..	5.1
Honduras	..	64	2.5	13.1	0.00	241	..	7	8.6	0.2	6.4	14.4

	Daily newspapers	Households with television[a]	Personal computers and the Internet							Information and communications technology trade		
			Access and use		Quality		Affordability	Application		Goods		Services
					Fixed broadband Internet subscribers[a] per 100 people	International Internet bandwidth[a] bits per second per capita	Fixed broadband Internet access tariff[a] $ per month	Secure Internet servers per million people	Information and communications technology expenditures % of GDP	Exports % of total goods exports	Imports % of total goods imports	Exports % of total service exports
	per 1,000 people	%	Personal computers[a]	Internet users[a]								
	2000–07[b]	2007	2008	2008	2008	2008	2008	December 2009	2008	2008	2008	2008
Hungary	217	99	25.6	58.5	17.43	5,977	25	113	8.9	24.6	18.8	8.3
India	71	46	3.3	4.5	0.46	32	6	2	4.5	1.3	5.0	50.3
Indonesia	..	..	2.0	7.9	0.18	120	22	1	3.3	4.6	9.8	8.4
Iran, Islamic Rep.	..	..	10.6	32.0	0.42	151	43	0	3.5	0.1	1.9	..
Iraq	..	..	..	1.0	0.00	1	..	0	..	..	..	3.3
Ireland	182	98	58.2	62.7	20.14	15,261	38	737	4.6	16.3	17.5	34.4
Israel	..	..	..	47.9	23.04	2,003	..	291	5.4	13.5	9.1	29.6
Italy	137	94	..	41.8	18.86	12,989	26	109	4.9	2.8	5.7	3.0
Jamaica	..	..	..	57.3	3.62	744	30	36	3.3	0.3	3.9	5.9
Japan	551	..	..	75.2	23.58	5,770	32	519	6.7	14.3	10.3	1.1
Jordan	..	..	7.5	27.0	2.32	781	31	12	7.3	5.5	7.2	0.0
Kazakhstan	..	..	..	10.9	4.22	702	..	3	..	0.1	3.3	2.4
Kenya	..	..	..	8.7	0.01	21	168	1	5.8	1.3	6.2	13.5
Korea, Dem. Rep.	..	..	..	0.0	0.00	0	..	0	..	..	..	..
Korea, Rep.	..	..	57.6	75.8	31.84	4,528	20	927	9.1	26.2	15.2	1.3
Kosovo	..	..	..	..	..	..	..	..	..	..	..	..
Kuwait	..	..	..	36.7	1.47	871	46	85	3.2	0.3	6.0	45.9
Kyrgyz Republic	1	..	..	16.1	0.09	113	..	1	..	0.8	5.1	2.0
Lao PDR	3	..	..	8.5	0.10	129	268	0	..	..	..	..
Latvia	154	99	32.7	60.4	8.83	3,537	26	114	..	5.1	6.6	5.2
Lebanon	54	..	10.2	22.5	5.03	223	23	15	..	..	..	1.9
Lesotho	..	..	..	3.6	0.01	5	49	0	..	..	..	..
Liberia	..	7	..	0.5	..	..	..	0	..	..	..	2.5
Libya	..	..	..	5.1	0.16	50	..	1	..	..	..	..
Lithuania	108	98	24.2	54.4	17.57	9,751	16	121	..	3.2	5.1	3.1
Macedonia, FYR	89	99	36.8	41.5	8.87	17	15	17	..	0.4	5.0	12.9
Madagascar	..	..	..	1.7	0.02	8	120	0	..	0.3	4.2	..
Malawi	..	..	..	2.1	0.02	5	900	0	..	0.2	3.4	..
Malaysia	109	..	23.1	55.8	4.93	2,374	20	34	9.7	26.2	25.3	5.4
Mali	..	22	0.8	1.6	0.04	51	58	1	..	0.2	3.6	..
Mauritania	..	..	4.5	1.9	0.18	76	62	2	..	..	1.6	..
Mauritius	77	96	17.6	22.2	7.23	364	51	62	..	4.0	5.9	3.6
Mexico	93	93	14.4	22.2	7.14	285	37	17	4.6	20.9	17.2	2.3
Moldova	..	..	11.4	23.4	3.17	966	23	10	..	6.8	3.4	16.8
Mongolia	20	86	24.6	12.5	1.37	947	..	8	..	0.1	5.1	3.7
Morocco	12	77	5.7	33.0	1.53	795	20	2	12.5	5.7	6.7	5.9
Mozambique	3	..	..	1.6	0.05	3	100	0	..	0.2	3.9	6.1
Myanmar	..	..	0.9	0.2	0.02	20	..	0	..	..	..	..
Namibia	28	..	23.9	5.3	0.02	27	46	9	..	0.6	4.9	2.3
Nepal	..	28	..	1.7	0.03	5	23	1	..	..	..	..
Netherlands	307	98	91.2	87.0	35.31	78,156	38	1,416	6.3	11.8	12.6	10.6
New Zealand	182	99	52.6	71.4	21.43	4,544	31	1,059	5.5	1.8	8.4	4.9
Nicaragua	..	..	..	3.3	0.64	144	30	6	..	0.2	6.2	8.2
Niger	0	6	..	0.5	0.00	11	58	0	..	0.7	3.6	32.8
Nigeria	..	..	..	15.9	0.04	5	690	1	3.1	0.0	10.2	..
Norway	516	95	62.9	82.5	33.26	26,904	57	1,011	3.7	2.0	8.2	5.7
Oman	..	..	16.9	20.0	1.15	894	31	11	..	1.6	3.2	..
Pakistan	50	56	..	11.1	0.10	43	18	1	4.4	0.5	5.7	6.7
Panama	65	83	2.8	27.5	5.76	15,964	15	86	5.5	0.0	6.9	4.5
Papua New Guinea	9	..	..	1.8	0.00	2	144	1	..	..	..	..
Paraguay	..	79	..	14.3	1.43	481	35	6	..	0.2	21.3	1.3
Peru	..	69	..	24.7	2.52	2,646	36	10	3.4	0.1	5.3	3.9
Philippines	79	..	7.2	6.2	1.16	113	23	5	6.1	54.1	34.7	7.9
Poland	114	98	16.9	49.0	12.57	2,748	27	123	5.5	7.5	8.9	4.5
Portugal	..	99	18.2	42.1	15.39	4,790	30	136	6.0	7.4	7.9	5.0
Puerto Rico	..	..	..	25.3	5.42	..	..	61	..	..	..	..
Qatar	..	..	15.7	34.0	8.07	2,044	..	64	..	0.0	8.2	..

	Daily newspapers	Households with television[a]	Personal computers and the Internet							Information and communications technology trade		
			Access and use		Quality		Affordability	Application		Goods		Services
					Fixed broadband Internet subscribers[a]	International Internet bandwidth[a]	Fixed broadband Internet access	Secure Internet servers	Information and communications technology expenditures	Exports % of total goods exports	Imports % of total goods imports	Exports % of total service exports
	per 1,000 people	%	Personal computers[a]	Internet users[a]	per 100 people	bits per second per capita	tariff[a] $ per month	per million people	% of GDP			
	2000–07[b]	2007	2008	2008	2008	2008	2008	December 2009	2008	2008	2008	2008
Romania	70	97	19.2	28.8	11.65	9,111	23	21	4.9	5.3	7.5	15.8
Russian Federation	92	..	13.3	31.9	6.54	573	14	11	3.5	0.4	8.9	6.1
Rwanda	..	2	0.3	3.1	0.04	27	92	1	..	0.5	12.5	1.9
Saudi Arabia	..	..	69.8	31.5	4.25	1,224	40	11	5.2	0.4	8.0	..
Senegal	9	43	..	8.4	0.39	237	29	1	10.8	0.6	3.4	15.5
Serbia	..	..	25.8	44.9	6.14	4,506	9	2	..	2.2	5.4	6.7
Sierra Leone	..	..	..	0.3	..	..	..	0	..	..	..	0.2
Singapore	361	..	74.3	69.6	20.73	22,783	22	421	7.1	35.9	28.2	3.5
Slovak Republic	126	99	58.1	66.0	11.18	5,555	28	79	6.4	17.5	14.7	7.2
Slovenia	173	99	42.5	55.7	21.11	6,720	27	210	4.7	3.5	5.1	6.7
Somalia	..	..	..	1.1	0.00	..	..	0	..	..	..	..
South Africa	30	..	..	8.6	0.87	71	26	40	10.1	1.6	8.8	3.2
Spain	144	100	39.3	55.4	19.75	11,008	29	192	4.8	3.2	7.9	5.8
Sri Lanka	26	..	..	5.8	0.51	190	21	4	4.3	1.8	4.6	15.5
Sudan	..	16	10.7	10.2	0.11	322	29	0	..	0.0	2.3	1.2
Swaziland	24	35	3.7	6.9	0.07	31	1,877	4	..	0.1	3.6	1.4
Sweden	481	94	88.1	87.7	41.12	49,828	32	858	5.7	9.5	10.1	13.6
Switzerland	420	..	96.2	75.9	33.68	29,413	32	1,118	7.2	3.5	6.6	..
Syrian Arab Republic	..	..	9.0	17.3	0.05	102	51	0	..	0.6	2.0	4.5
Tajikistan	..	..	..	8.8	0.05	37	..	0	..	..	..	21.6
Tanzania	2	6	..	1.2	0.02	2	68	0	..	0.4	6.2	2.0
Thailand	..	..	..	23.9	1.41	818	18	10	6.2	19.4	15.4	..
Timor-Leste	..	..	..	..	..	..	..	..	..	..	..	..
Togo	2	..	..	5.4	0.03	8	106	2	..	0.1	4.2	..
Trinidad and Tobago	149	..	13.2	17.0	4.58	678	13	46	..	0.1	3.4	..
Tunisia	23	..	9.7	27.1	2.20	1,115	13	12	5.4	5.0	5.6	2.4
Turkey	..	98	6.1	34.4	7.78	2,794	..	66	4.1	2.1	4.7	2.1
Turkmenistan	9	..	..	1.5	0.05	48	..	0	..	..	..	..
Uganda	..	6	1.7	7.9	0.02	12	170	0	..	4.9	9.3	7.2
Ukraine	131	..	4.5	10.5	3.46	206	21	6	5.9	1.3	2.6	3.3
United Arab Emirates	..	..	33.1	65.2	12.43	8,686	22	165	4.9	2.0	5.3	..
United Kingdom	290	99	80.2	76.0	28.13	39,648	29	905	6.3	7.7	10.1	8.0
United States	193	98	80.6	75.9	24.05	11,289	15	1,234	7.1	12.8	12.5	4.0
Uruguay	..	91	..	40.2	7.33	903	24	36	4.3	0.1	6.2	9.0
Uzbekistan	..	..	3.1	9.0	0.24	30	..	0	..	..	..	..
Venezuela, RB	93	92	..	25.7	4.76	628	31	7	3.5	0.0	11.6	7.4
Vietnam	..	..	9.6	24.2	2.38	581	17	2	4.9	5.6	8.2	..
West Bank and Gaza	10	95	..	9.0	2.54	313	..	2	..	..	..	7.6
Yemen, Rep.	4	..	2.8	1.6	0.00	28	226	0	..	0.3	1.8	18.9
Zambia	5	..	..	5.5	0.04	8	91	1	..	0.1	3.4	8.1
Zimbabwe	..	31	7.6	11.4	0.14	10	..	1	..	0.3	2.1	..
World	**105 w**	**.. m**	**15.3 w**	**23.9 w**	**6.21 w**	**3,546 w**	**31.4 m**	**114 w**	**6.0 w**	**12.2 w**	**12.5 w**	**8.3 w**
Low income	..	..	..	4.6	0.26	24	102.4	1	..	2.5	6.3	..
Middle income	70	..	5.6	17.3	3.26	377	29.4	7	5.1	14.4	14.6	12.6
Lower middle income	72	..	4.5	13.9	2.59	153	31.4	2	5.5	19.7	17.0	18.6
Upper middle income	61	..	..	30.6	5.88	1,281	26.3	28	4.8	10.1	12.7	5.2
Low & middle income	59	..	5.2	15.3	2.78	320	36.4	6	5.2	14.3	14.4	12.4
East Asia & Pacific	74	..	5.6	19.4	4.63	470	21.7	2	5.9	25.5	22.4	5.6
Europe & Central Asia	94	..	10.7	28.6	6.34	1,244	22.7	30	4.2	2.1	6.5	5.4
Latin America & Carib.	64	88	..	28.9	4.88	1,391	34.0	20	4.8	10.9	13.5	4.8
Middle East & N. Africa	..	..	5.7	18.9	0.84	323	23.0	2	5.8	..	..	..
South Asia	68	46	3.3	4.7	0.36	31	21.0	1	4.7	1.2	5.1	47.3
Sub-Saharan Africa	..	..	..	6.5	0.11	34	100.1	3	8.5	0.9	7.5	..
High income	261	98	67.8	69.1	24.05	20,143	29.8	715	6.3	11.7	12.0	7.3
Euro area	201	98	56.1	62.6	23.96	32,540	30.5	380	5.3	7.0	8.2	9.1

a. Data are from the International Telecommunication Union's (ITU) World Telecommunication Development Report database. Please cite the ITU for third-party use of these data. b. Data are for the most recent year available.

The digital and information revolution has changed the way the world learns, communicates, does business, and treats illnesses. New information and communications technologies (ICT) offer vast opportunities for progress in all walks of life in all countries—opportunities for economic growth, improved health, better service delivery, learning through distance education, and social and cultural advances.

Comparable statistics on access, use, quality, and affordability of ICT are needed to formulate growth-enabling policies for the sector and to monitor and evaluate the sector's impact on development. Although basic access data are available for many countries, in most developing countries little is known about who uses ICT; what they are used for (school, work, business, research, government); and how they affect people and businesses. The global Partnership on Measuring ICT for Development is helping to set standards, harmonize information and communications technology statistics, and build statistical capacity in developing countries. For more information see www.itu.int/ITU-D/ict/partnership/.

Data on daily newspapers in circulation are from United Nations Educational, Scientific, and Cultural Organization (UNESCO) Institute for Statistics surveys on circulation, online newspapers, journalists, community newspapers, and news agencies.

Estimates of households with television are derived from household surveys. Some countries report only the number of households with a color television set, and so the true number may be higher than reported.

Estimates of personal computers are from an annual International Telecommunication Union (ITU) questionnaire sent to member states, supplemented by other sources. Many governments lack the capacity to survey all places where personal computers are used (homes, schools, businesses, government offices, libraries, Internet cafes) so most estimates are derived from the number of personal computers sold each year. Annual shipment data can also be multiplied by an estimated average useful lifespan before replacement to approximate the number of personal computers. There is no precise method for determining replacement rates, but in general personal computers are replaced every three to five years.

Data on Internet users and related indicators (broadband and bandwidth) are based on nationally reported data to the ITU. Some countries derive these data from surveys, but since survey questions and definitions differ, the estimates may not be strictly comparable. Countries without surveys generally derive their estimates by multiplying subscriber counts reported by Internet service providers by a multiplier. This method may undercount actual users,

particularly in developing countries, where many commercial subscribers rent out computers connected to the Internet or prepaid cards are used to access the Internet.

Broadband refers to technologies that provide Internet speeds of at least 256 kilobits a second of upstream and downstream capacity and includes digital subscriber lines, cable modems, satellite broadband Internet, fiber-to-home Internet access, ethernet local access networks, and wireless area networks. Bandwidth refers to the range of frequencies available for signals. The higher the bandwidth, the more information that can be transmitted at one time. Reporting countries may have different definitions of broadband, so data are not strictly comparable.

The number of secure Internet servers, from the Netcraft Secure Server Survey, indicates how many companies conduct encrypted transactions over the Internet. The survey examines the use of encrypted transactions through extensive automated exploration, tallying the number of Web sites using a secure socket layer (SSL). The country of origin of about a third of the 1.2 million distinct valid third-party certificates is unknown. Some countries, such as the Republic of Korea, use application layers to establish the encryption channel, which is SSL equivalent.

According to the World Information Technology and Services Alliance's (WITSA) *Digital Planet 2009,* the global marketplace for information and communications technologies was estimated to be about $3.4 trillion in 2009 and to rise to about $3.6 trillion in 2010. The data on information and communications technology expenditures cover the world's 75 largest buyers among countries and regions.

Information and communication technology goods exports and imports are defined by the Working Party on Indicators for the Information Society and are reported in the Organisation for Economic Co-operation and Development's *Guide to Measuring the Information Society* (2005). Information and communication technology service exports data are based on the International Monetary Fund's (IMF) *Balance of Payments Statistics Yearbook* classification.

Definitions

• **Daily newspapers** are newspapers issued at least four times a week that report mainly on events in the 24-hour period before going to press. The indicator is average circulation (or copies printed) per 1,000 people. • **Households with television** are the percentage of households with a television set. • **Personal computers** are self-contained computers designed for use by a single individual, including laptops and notebooks and excluding terminals connected to mainframe and

minicomputers intended primarily for shared use and devices such as smart phones and personal digital assistants. • **Internet users** are people with access to the worldwide network. • **Fixed broadband Internet subscribers** are the number of broadband subscribers with a digital subscriber line, cable modem, or other high-speed technology. • **International Internet bandwidth** is the contracted capacity of international connections between countries for transmitting Internet traffic. • **Fixed broadband Internet access tariff** is the lowest sampled cost per 100 kilobits a second per month and are calculated from low- and high-speed monthly service charges. Monthly charges do not include installation fees or modem rentals. • **Secure Internet servers** are servers using encryption technology in Internet transactions. • **Information and communications technology expenditures** include computer hardware (computers, storage devices, printers, and other peripherals); computer software (operating systems, programming tools, utilities, applications, and internal software development); computer services (information technology consulting, computer and network systems integration, Web hosting, data processing services, and other services); and communications services (voice and data communications services) and wired and wireless communications equipment. • **Information and communication technology goods exports** and **imports** include telecommunications, audio and video, computer and related equipment; electronic components; and other information and communication technology goods. Software is excluded. • **Information and communication technology service exports** include computer and communications services (telecommunications and postal and courier services) and information services (computer data and news-related service transactions).

Data sources

Data on newspapers are compiled by the UNESCO Institute for Statistics. Data on televisions, personal computers, Internet users, Internet broadband users and cost, and Internet bandwidth are from the ITU's World Telecommunication Development Report database. Data on secure Internet servers are from Netcraft (www.netcraft.com/) and official government sources. Data on information and communication technology goods trade are from the United Nations Statistics Division's Commodity Trade (Comtrade) database. Data on information and communication technology expenditures are from WITSA's *Digital Planet 2009* and Global Insight, Inc. Data on information and communication technology service exports are from the IMF's Balance of Payments Statistics database.

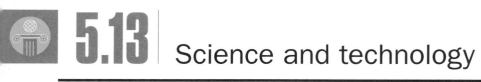

5.13 Science and technology

	Researchers in R&D	Technicians in R&D	Scientific and technical journal articles	Expenditures for R&D	High-technology exports		Royalty and license fees		Patent applications filed[a,b]		Trademark applications filed[a,c]
	per million people	per million people		% of GDP	$ millions	% of manufactured exports	$ millions			Non-residents	Total
							Receipts	Payments	Residents		
	2000–07[d]	2000–07[d]	2005	2000–07[d]	2008	2008	2008	2008	2008	2008	2008
Afghanistan	..	..	..	..	..	..	..	..	..	..	..
Albania	..	..	..	..	7	4	39	12	..	..	4,596
Algeria	170	35	350	0.07	7	1	..	..	84	765	2,489
Angola	..	..	..	..	..	..	12	0	..	..	..
Argentina	980	196	3,058	0.51	1,949	9	94	1,274	..	..	73,717
Armenia	..	..	180	0.21	11	2	..	..	226	4	4,735
Australia	4,231	993	15,957	2.17	4,154	12	703	3,026	2,718	24,122	59,370
Austria	3,774	1,792	4,566	2.52	15,230	11	905	1,598	2,298	329	5,216
Azerbaijan	..	..	116	0.18	6	1	0	5	222	5	5,609
Bangladesh	..	..	193	..	97	1	0	19	29	270	8,232
Belarus	..	..	490	0.97	405	2	5	75	1,188	337	11,454
Belgium	3,413	1,445	6,841	1.91	29,163	8	1,188	2,133	575	133	28,897[e]
Benin	..	..	..	..	0	0	0	2	..	..	..
Bolivia	120	..	..	0.28	17	4	2	18	..	..	6,081
Bosnia and Herzegovina	197	71	..	0.03	125	4	5	11	59	12	5,538
Botswana	..	..	..	0.38	21	1	1	13	..	..	920
Brazil	629	..	9,889	1.02	10,572	12	465	2,697	3,810	20,264	119,841
Bulgaria	1,466	500	764	0.48	755	7	11	95	249	22	10,853
Burkina Faso	..	..	..	0.11	..	..	..	..	..	..	..
Burundi	..	..	..	..	1	8	0	..	..	..	..
Cambodia	17	13	..	0.05	..	..	1	6	..	..	2,866
Cameroon	..	..	131	..	3	3	0	17	..	..	..
Canada	4,157	1,595	25,836	2.03	29,388	14	3,432	8,766	5,061	37,028	45,619
Central African Republic	..	..	..	..	..	..	..	..	..	..	..
Chad	..	..	..	..	..	..	..	..	..	..	..
Chile	833	302	1,559	0.67	515	6	64	526	291	2,924	44,320
China	1,071	..	41,596	1.49	381,345	29	571	10,319	194,579	95,259	669,088
Hong Kong SAR, China	2,650	459	..	0.81	2,164	22	358	1,504	173	13,489	24,230
Colombia	151	..	400	0.18	445	4	30	263	121	1,860	23,994
Congo, Dem. Rep.	..	..	..	0.48	..	..	..	..	..	..	..
Congo, Rep.	34	37	..	..	..	..	..	..	..	..	..
Costa Rica	122	..	105	0.37	2,378	39	1	62	..	..	11,754
Côte d'Ivoire	66	..	..	..	180	16	0	22	..	..	..
Croatia	1,384	643	953	0.93	898	9	44	257	330	71	10,324
Cuba	..	..	261	0.44	248	35	..	..	69	189	3,041
Czech Republic	2,715	1,503	3,169	1.59	18,200	14	55	726	712	142	13,106
Denmark	5,431	2,006	5,040	2.57	11,850	16	..	..	1,634	195	8,015
Dominican Republic	..	..	..	..	315	8	0	33	..	..	5,208
Ecuador	69	20	..	0.15	71	5	0	47	..	794	12,605
Egypt, Arab Rep.	617	378	1,658	0.23	85	1	122	322	516	1,589	3,340
El Salvador	49	..	..	..	146	4	1	34	..	..	..
Eritrea	..	..	..	..	..	..	..	..	..	..	..
Estonia	2,748	599	439	1.12	950	10	27	50	62	10	4,652
Ethiopia	21	12	88	0.17	8	6	0	2	12	25	719
Finland	7,382	..	4,811	3.47	16,664	21	1,495	2,047	1,799	147	7,328
France	3,440	1,768	30,309	2.10	93,209	20	10,269	4,916	14,743	1,962	79,206
Gabon	..	..	..	..	71	32	..	..	..	..	..
Gambia, The	..	..	..	..	0	14	..	..	0	0	327
Georgia	..	..	145	0.18	21	3	6	8	221	26	5,441
Germany	3,453	1,200	44,145	2.55	162,421	14	8,792	11,958	49,240	13,177	80,865
Ghana	..	..	81	..	6	1	0	..	..	..	61
Greece	1,873	764	4,291	0.50	1,380	10	44	713	803	3,675	10,598
Guatemala	25	12	..	0.05	150	4	12	80	5	306	11,003
Guinea	..	..	..	..	0	0	0	0	..	..	..
Guinea-Bissau	..	..	..	..	..	..	..	..	..	..	6
Haiti	..	..	..	..	..	..	..	0	..	..	..
Honduras	..	..	..	0.04	8	1	..	18	..	..	7,403

Science and technology

	Researchers in R&D	Technicians in R&D	Scientific and technical journal articles	Expenditures for R&D	High-technology exports		Royalty and license fees		Patent applications filed[a,b]		Trademark applications filed[a,c]
	per million people	per million people		% of GDP	$ millions	% of manufactured exports	$ millions Receipts	Payments	Residents	Non-residents	Total
	2000–07[d]	2000–07[d]	2005	2000–07[d]	2008	2008	2008	2008	2008	2008	2008
Hungary	1,733	512	2,614	0.97	20,990	24	803	2,007	683	89	7,903
India	137	86	14,608	0.80	6,497	6	148	1,578	5,314	23,626	103,419
Indonesia	205	..	205	0.05	5,625	11	27	1,328	282	4,324	52,649
Iran, Islamic Rep.	706	..	2,635	0.67	375	6	..	..	..	..	3,468
Iraq	..	..	..	..	0	0	0	204	..	..	..
Ireland	2,849	734	2,120	1.34	28,606	26	1,321	30,082	931	76	5,183
Israel	..	..	6,309	4.74	9,239	16	804	1,107	1,528	6,214	13,801
Italy	1,499	..	24,645	1.14	29,814	7	864	1,811	9,255	870	6,181
Jamaica	..	..	..	0.07	6	0	17	48	21	132	1,708
Japan	5,573	589	55,471	3.45	123,733	18	25,701	18,312	330,110	60,892	119,448
Jordan	..	..	275	0.34	41	1	0	0	59	507	..
Kazakhstan	..	..	96	0.21	2,250	22	..	87	11	162	8,407
Kenya	..	..	226	..	78	5	33	28	38	33	1,729
Korea, Dem. Rep.	..	..	..	..	..	..	..	..	6,846	76	2,007
Korea, Rep.	4,627	720	16,396	3.47	110,633	33	2,403	5,543	127,114	43,518	137,461
Kosovo	..	..	..	..	..	..	..	..	..	..	..
Kuwait	166	33	233	0.09	9	0	0	0	..	..	..
Kyrgyz Republic	..	..	..	0.25	8	2	3	15	135	3	3,966
Lao PDR	16	..	..	0.04	..	..	..	..	..	..	..
Latvia	1,861	496	134	0.63	419	7	13	36	114	37	5,101
Lebanon	..	..	234	..	4	0	..	..	..	..	..
Lesotho	10	11	..	0.06	..	..	20	..	..	..	910
Liberia	..	..	..	..	..	..	..	..	..	..	781
Libya	..	..	..	..	..	..	..	0	..	..	..
Lithuania	2,529	530	406	0.83	1,493	11	1	34	87	18	6,332
Macedonia, FYR	521	75	..	0.21	21	1	6	25	34	406	4,890
Madagascar	50	15	..	0.14	7	1	..	..	14	63	1,318
Malawi	..	..	..	..	2	2	..	..	..	..	804
Malaysia	372	44	615	0.64	42,764	40	199	1,268	818	4,485	26,027
Mali	42	13	..	..	3	3	0	1	..	..	..
Mauritania	..	..	..	..	..	..	..	..	..	..	..
Mauritius	..	..	..	0.38	99	7	0	6	..	..	..
Mexico	460	257	3,902	0.50	41,201	19	440	503	685	15,896	84,287
Moldova	724	116	89	0.55	13	4	4	15	273	22	6,643
Mongolia	..	..	..	0.23	7	8	..	..	103	110	1,936
Morocco	647	48	443	0.64	858	9	0	15	177	834	4,367
Mozambique	..	..	..	0.50	6	4	0	2	18	22	1,240
Myanmar	18	137	..	0.16	..	..	..	..	..	..	..
Namibia	..	..	..	..	21	1	..	15	..	..	1,139
Nepal	59	137	..	..	..	..	..	..	..	..	1,132
Netherlands	2,680	1,677	13,885	1.75	67,056	22	4,870	3,529	2,421	311	..
New Zealand	4,365	894	2,983	1.26	616	9	178	573	1,256	4,468	17,582
Nicaragua	..	..	..	0.05	5	4	0	..	..	..	5,975
Niger	8	10	..	..	2	8	0	0	..	..	..
Nigeria	..	..	362	..	15	0	..	178	..	..	..
Norway	5,247	..	3,644	1.67	5,729	20	642	712	1,223	5,431	16,324
Oman	..	..	111	..	18	1	..	..	..	..	1,847
Pakistan	152	64	492	0.67	275	2	38	117	91	1,647	14,872
Panama	62	20	..	0.25	0	0	0	38	..	371	10,716
Papua New Guinea	..	..	..	..	..	..	..	..	1	45	612
Paraguay	71	..	..	0.09	32	9	282	2	..	..	..
Peru	..	..	133	0.15	92	2	3	140	31	1,504	24,825
Philippines	81	10	178	0.12	26,875	66	5	382	216	3,095	15,834
Poland	1,610	226	6,844	0.57	7,172	5	204	1,770	2,488	290	20,609
Portugal	2,630	389	2,910	1.19	3,355	8	80	496	381	24	20,325
Puerto Rico	..	..	..	..	..	..	..	..	..	..	..
Qatar	..	..	..	..	0	0	..	..	..	..	..

	Researchers in R&D	Technicians in R&D	Scientific and technical journal articles	Expenditures for R&D	High-technology exports		Royalty and license fees		Patent applications filed[a,b]		Trademark applications filed[a,c]
	per million people	per million people		% of GDP	$ millions	% of manufactured exports	$ millions Receipts	Payments	Residents	Non-residents	Total
	2000–07[d]	2000–07[d]	2005	2000–07[d]	2008	2008	2008	2008	2008	2008	2008
Romania	877	203	887	0.54	2,744	7	240	346	995	36	15,578
Russian Federation	3,305	516	14,412	1.12	5,107	7	453	4,595	27,712	14,137	57,165
Rwanda	..	..	..	..	1	7	62	1	..	..	238
Saudi Arabia	..	..	575	0.05	121	1	0	0	128	642	..
Senegal	276	..	83	0.09	46	5	1	8	..	..	..
Serbia	1,190	298	849	0.34	..	..	27	192	386	237	9,479
Sierra Leone	..	..	..	..	..	..	..	1	..	..	1,017
Singapore	6,088	529	3,609	2.61	120,345	51	839	9,148	793	8,899	18,263
Slovak Republic	2,290	415	919	0.46	3,171	5	164	182	167	75	7,267
Slovenia	3,109	1,537	1,035	1.48	1,558	6	41	250	301	6	5,192
Somalia	..	..	..	..	..	..	..	..	..	..	..
South Africa	382	130	2,392	0.96	2,011	5	54	1,676	..	5,781	29,833
Spain	2,784	1,029	18,336	1.28	9,916	5	801	3,251	3,632	252	55,586
Sri Lanka	93	65	136	0.17	101	2	0	0	201	264	5,916
Sudan	..	..	..	0.29	0	0	..	0	3	13	1,075
Swaziland	..	..	..	..	0	0	0	121	..	..	1,004
Sweden	5,215	..	10,012	3.68	21,778	16	4,938	2,005	2,527	398	14,998
Switzerland	3,436	2,317	8,749	2.93	41,111	23	..	..	1,594	439	31,514
Syrian Arab Republic	..	..	77	..	51	1	0	25	124	133	2,757
Tajikistan	..	..	..	0.06	..	..	1	0	26	..	2,284
Tanzania	..	..	107	..	5	1	0	0	..	..	556
Thailand	311	160	1,249	0.25	32,370	25	101	2,559	802	5,939	35,422
Timor-Leste	..	..	..	..	..	..	..	..	..	..	..
Togo	34	17	..	..	0	0	0	5	..	..	..
Trinidad and Tobago	..	..	..	0.10	36	1	..	..	..	551	..
Tunisia	1,588	43	571	1.02	674	5	32	12	..	..	..
Turkey	680	102	7,815	0.71	1,807	2	..	729	2,221	176	76,333
Turkmenistan	..	..	..	..	..	..	..	..	..	..	2,819
Uganda	..	..	93	0.41	5	1	3	2	6	1	..
Ukraine	1,458	325	2,105	0.87	1,519	3	72	754	2,825	2,872	33,019
United Arab Emirates	..	..	229	..	207	3	..	..	..	..	..
United Kingdom	2,881	879	45,572	1.84	61,767	19	13,904	10,615	16,523	6,856	35,705
United States	4,663	..	205,320	2.67	231,126	27	91,600	26,615	231,588	224,733	294,070
Uruguay	373	..	204	0.36	72	4	0	8	33	706	11,501
Uzbekistan	..	..	157	..	..	..	..	..	262	186	5,007
Venezuela, RB	..	..	534	..	122	4	0	349	..	..	..
Vietnam	115	..	221	0.19	2,376	9	..	..	..	..	4,971
West Bank and Gaza	..	..	..	..	..	..	0	1	..	..	..
Yemen, Rep.	..	..	..	..	0	0	9	−5	11	24	4,375
Zambia	..	..	..	0.03	8	2	0	1	..	..	1,159
Zimbabwe	..	..	..	..	48	3	..	..	..	..	..
World	**1,270 w**	**.. w**	**708,086 s**	**2.21 w**	**1,856,930 s**	**17 w**	**181,285 s**	**187,563 s**	**988,514 s**	**633,066 s**	**2,963,306 s**
Low income	..	..	..	..	..	6	111	73	..	..	..
Middle income	613	..	123,584	0.96	540,759	16	3,751	34,266	175,013	192,993	1,750,931
Lower middle income	479	..	67,251	1.23	339,779	22	1,420	17,845	134,138	130,987	1,096,947
Upper middle income	1,252	..	56,333	0.81	124,869	9	2,331	16,421	40,875	62,006	558,047
Low & middle income	595	..	124,833	0.96	467,925	16	3,862	34,339	181,806	193,656	1,815,399
East Asia & Pacific	1,071	..	44,064	1.49	..	28	898	15,864	196,416	108,823	755,285
Europe & Central Asia	2,013	336	35,489	0.83	23,854	6	1,090	8,805	38,406	18,614	317,547
Latin America & Carib.	495	..	20,045	0.66	58,093	12	1,453	5,669	..	..	440,687
Middle East & N. Africa	..	..	6,243	0.48	1,528	4	41	345	..	..	16,421
South Asia	129	86	15,429	0.79	..	5	196	1,714	5,580	25,831	132,894
Sub-Saharan Africa	..	..	..	..	3,260	3	184	1,942	..	..	..
High income	3,948	..	583,253	2.47	1,313,457	18	177,423	153,224	796,585	427,519	1,223,790
Euro area	2,872	1,313	158,985	2.04	454,048	14	31,349	63,603	77,364	20,234	316,397

a. Original information was provided by the World Intellectual Property Organization (WIPO). The International Bureau of WIPO assumes no responsibility with respect to the transformation of these data. b. Excludes applications filed under the auspices of the African Regional Intellectual Property Organization (11 by residents, 424 by nonresidents), the European Patent Office (146,150 by nonresidents), and the Eurasian Patent Organization (3,066 by nonresidents). c. Excludes applications filed under the auspices of the Office for Harmonization in the Internal Market (87,640). d. Data are for the most recent year available. e. Includes Luxembourg and the Netherlands.

About the data

Science and technology is too broad and complex to quantify with a single set of indicators, but those in the table shed light on countries' technology base. Technological innovation, often fueled by government-led research and development (R&D), has been the driving force for industrial growth. The best opportunities to improve living standards come from science and technology. Countries able to access, generate, and apply scientific knowledge have a competitive edge. And high-quality scientific input improves public policy.

The United Nations Educational, Scientific, and Cultural Organization (UNESCO) Institute for Statistics collects data on researchers, technicians, and expenditure on R&D through surveys and from other international sources. R&D covers basic research, applied research, and experimental development. Data on researchers and technicians are calculated as full-time equivalents.

Scientific and technical article counts are from journals classified by the Institute for Scientific Information's Science Citation Index (SCI) and Social Sciences Citation Index (SSCI). Counts are based on fractional assignments; articles with authors from different countries are allocated proportionally to each country (see *Definitions* for fields covered). The SCI and SSCI databases cover the core set of scientific journals but may exclude some of local importance and may reflect some bias toward English-language journals.

R&D expenditures include all expenditures for R&D performed within a country, including capital costs and current costs (wages and associated costs of researchers, technicians, and supporting staff and other current costs, including noncapital purchases of materials, supplies, and R&D equipment such as utilities, reference materials, subscriptions to libraries and scientific societies, and lab materials).

The method for determining high-technology exports was developed by the Organisation for Economic Cooperation and Development in collaboration with Eurostat. It takes a "product approach" (as distinguished from a "sectoral approach") based on R&D intensity (R&D expenditure divided by total sales) for groups of products from Germany, Italy, Japan, the Netherlands, Sweden, and the United States. Because industrial sectors specializing in a few high-technology products may also produce low-technology products, the product approach is more appropriate for analyzing international trade. This method takes only R&D intensity into account, but other characteristics of high technology are also important, such as know-how, scientific personnel, and technology embodied in patents. Considering these characteristics would yield a different list (see Hatzichronoglou 1997).

A patent is an exclusive right granted for a specified period (generally 20 years) for a new way of doing something or a new technical solution to a problem—an invention. The invention must be of practical use and display a characteristic unknown in the existing body of knowledge in its field.

Most countries have systems to protect patentable inventions. The Patent Cooperation Treaty provides a two-phase system for filing patent applications. An applicant files an international application and designates the countries in which protection is sought (all eligible countries are automatically designated in every application under the treaty). The application is searched and published, and, optionally, an international preliminary examination is conducted. In the national (or regional) phase the applicant requests national processing of the application and initiates the national search and granting procedure. International applications under the treaty provide for a national patent grant only—there is no international patent. The national filing represents the applicant's seeking of patent protection for a given territory, whereas international filings, while representing a legal right, do not accurately reflect where patent protection is sought. Resident filings are those from residents of the country or region concerned. Nonresident filings are from outside applicants. For regional offices such as the European Patent Office, applications from residents of any member state of the regional patent convention are considered a resident filing. Some offices (notably the U.S. Patent and Trademark Office) use the residence of the inventor rather than the applicant to classify filings.

A trademark is a distinctive sign identifying goods or services as produced or provided by a specific person or enterprise. A trademark protects the owner of the mark by ensuring exclusive right to use it to identify goods or services or to authorize another to use it. The period of protection varies, but a trademark can be renewed indefinitely for an additional fee. Detailed components of trademark filings, available on the *World Development Indicators* CD-ROM and *WDI Online,* include applications filed by direct residents (domestic applicants filing directly at a given national intellectual property [IP] office); direct nonresident (foreign applicants filing directly at a given national IP office); aggregate direct (applicants not identified as direct resident or direct nonresident by the national office); and Madrid (international applications filed via the World Intellectual Property Organization (WIPO)–administered Madrid System to the national or regional IP office). Data are based on information supplied to WIPO by IP offices in annual surveys, supplemented by data in national IP office reports. Data may be missing for some offices or periods.

Definitions

• **Researchers in R&D** are professionals engaged in conceiving of or creating new knowledge, products, processes, methods, and systems and in managing the projects concerned. Postgraduate doctoral students (ISCED97 level 6) engaged in R&D are considered researchers. • **Technicians in R&D** and equivalent staff are people whose main tasks require technical knowledge and experience in engineering, physical and life sciences (technicians), and social sciences and humanities (equivalent staff). They engage in R&D by performing scientific and technical tasks involving the application of concepts and operational methods, normally under researcher supervision. • **Scientific and technical journal articles** are published articles in physics, biology, chemistry, mathematics, clinical medicine, biomedical research, engineering and technology, and earth and space sciences. • **Expenditures for R&D** are current and capital expenditures on creative work undertaken to increase the stock of knowledge, including on humanity, culture, and society, and the use of knowledge to devise new applications. • **High-technology exports** are products with high R&D intensity, such as in aerospace, computers, pharmaceuticals, scientific instruments, and electrical machinery. • **Royalty and license fees** are payments and receipts between residents and nonresidents for authorized use of intangible, nonproduced, nonfinancial assets and proprietary rights (such as patents, copyrights, trademarks, and industrial processes) and for the use, through licensing, of produced originals of prototypes (such as films and manuscripts). • **Patent applications filed** are worldwide patent applications filed through the Patent Cooperation Treaty procedure or with a national patent office. • **Trademark applications filed** are annual applications to register a trademark with a national or regional IP office.

Data sources

Data on R&D are provided by the UNESCO Institute for Statistics. Data on scientific and technical journal articles are from the U.S. National Science Board's *Science and Engineering Indicators 2008.* Data on high-technology exports are from the United Nations Statistics Division's Commodity Trade (Comtrade) database. Data on royalty and license fees are from the International Monetary Fund's *Balance of Payments Statistics Yearbook.* Data on patents and trademarks are from the World Intellectual Property Organization's *WIPO Patent Report: Statistics on Worldwide Patent Activity* (2009) and www.wipo.int.

GLOBAL
LINKS

T he Millennium Development Goals (MDGs) recognize that expanding international trade can help developing economies achieve the MDGs by fostering economic growth and increasing job opportunities. At the 2000 Millennium Summit developed countries agreed to increase market access for developing countries by lowering tariffs and granting tariff-free access to all goods (except weapons). They also agreed to increase aid for promoting trade and to decrease domestic agricultural subsidies that harm imports from developing economies.

The world today is a more integrated place than in 1990—the MDGs benchmark year. World exports of goods and services nearly tripled between 1990 and 2007—a 7 percent annual average growth rate—and foreign direct investment increased ninefold between 1990 and 2008. More people are moving abroad (temporarily or permanently), more investors are buying foreign stocks, and more companies are expanding to overseas markets. And developing economies' trade has expanded from 17.3 percent of world exports and 17.0 percent of world imports in 1990 to 28.1 percent of exports and 25.9 percent of imports in 2007.

Though all economies may benefit from international integration, the benefits may not be shared equally among them. Successful integration depends partly on geography and natural resources: economies with substantial coastal areas or located near large economic centers may increase their share of the global market much faster than landlocked or isolated economies. And economies with abundant natural resources and cheap labor may attract foreign investors and grow faster than economies with fewer resources.

The question remains: can trade expansion and economic integration promote human development? Trade expansion provides developing economies with a larger market in which to sell goods and services, boosting production. But trade liberalization can also harm domestic industries by exposing them to fierce international competition. Trade expansion can promote rapid economic growth, potentially furthering human development. But greater engagement with international markets is sometimes accompanied by increased income inequality. Developing economies must consider how integration affects the most vulnerable segments of the population. Increased trade can accelerate progress toward the MDGs only if it both fosters economic growth and improves living standards for the poorest and most vulnerable.

Four MDG indicators track developed economies' commitments to increase market access for developing economies and support their programs to promote trade: the proportion of total developed country imports (by value and excluding arms) admitted free of duty from developing economies and least developed countries; average tariffs imposed by developed economies on agricultural products, textiles, and clothing from developing economies; agricultural support in Organisation for Economic Co-operation and Development (OECD) economies as a percentage of their gross domestic product (GDP); and the share of official development assistance provided to build trade capacity.

But these indicators are not enough to describe the many instruments of trade policy, the changing patterns of trade, and their impact on human development. This introduction looks beyond the MDG indicators to the characteristics of economies and their trade policies that may ultimately affect their success in achieving the MDGs.

Trade expansion and development

How does trade expansion affect human development and poverty? In theory, trade expansion should contribute directly to poverty reduction by increasing the returns on the most abundant factor of production, which in developing economies tends to be low-skilled labor. But empirical studies disagree on the causal relationship between trade expansion and poverty reduction. Some studies find an increase in inequality after trade liberalization (World Bank and others 2005; UNDP 2005; Kremer and Maskin 2006). Others find that trade has a beneficial effect on poverty reduction—but may not be the most important factor (Billmeier and Nannicini 2007).

Despite the lack of agreement on the effects of trade expansion on poverty, economic theory and empirical evidence offer no reason to restrict trade. An increase in trade, especially exports, is associated with economic growth (figure 6a). This simple association between GDP growth and export growth overlooks differences between countries and other factors that affect economic growth. For example, small island economies may have to be more open in order to generate economic growth, while economies with sufficient domestic markets may require less export expansion to achieve economic growth. Analysis in *World Development Indicators 2007* showed that for countries starting from similar positions, countries that opened their economy (as measured by the ratio of imports and exports of goods and services to GDP) less rapidly recorded much lower per capita GDP growth.

In recent years many economies, especially in East Asia, experienced rapid growth in GDP and exports. But did export expansion trigger this economic growth or are increasing exports an outcome of growth? Although economists do not agree on causality, most empirical evidence indicates that greater openness to trade is an important element explaining growth performance—and has been a central feature of successful economic development (OECD 2009b; Commission on Growth and Development 2008).

Economies benefit from increased international trade because it allows them to produce commodities for which they have a comparative advantage, sell those goods in a larger world market, and import goods and services that are more costly to produce domestically. Export expansion increases output, generates jobs, and raises household income, which may in turn improve health and other living conditions. Trade expansion can also raise education standards by giving people greater incentives to improve their skills. Foreign direct investors that are initially attracted by developing economies' cheap and abundant labor supply may also introduce new technology and know-how, and foreign competition may spur productivity and efficiency gains. Exports generate the foreign exchange needed to finance critical imports and may increase government revenue through taxes that can be used to finance social protection programs. Economies with small domestic markets likely have lower welfare and growth rates if they isolate themselves from the international movement of goods, factors, people, and ideas.

But trade liberalization brings additional challenges for developing economies in managing their external accounts. Economies that import more than they export are vulnerable to trade imbalance. Eighty of 111 developing economies for which data are available had a negative trade balance in 2008. For 67 of them the trade balance to GDP ratio has deteriorated since 1990. The ratio has worsened by more than 5 percentage points for 44 economies and by more than 10 percentage points for 26 economies. Dependence on imports may put poor countries at risk for currency crises, especially if they have limited access to foreign capital. Many developing economies are sensitive to opening their economies to trade because they worry that liberalization might merely increase cheap imports and harm local businesses instead of creating new export enterprises.

Developing economies have increased their share of world trade

Developing economies have become more open, as measured by the ratio of trade (imports plus exports) to GDP, which rose from 34 percent in 1990 to 62 percent in 2008. Export revenues, constituting 30 percent of

Growth of exports and growth of GDP go hand in hand   **6a**

Average annual growth of GDP, 2000–08 (percent)

Average annual growth of exports of goods and services, 2000–08 (percent)

Source: World Development Indicators data files.

developing economies' outputs in 2008 (up from 18 percent in 1990), are especially important for low-income economies (figure 6b). Developing economies increased their share of world trade from 16 percent of merchandise exports in 1990 to 33 percent in 2008 and from 12 percent of services exports in 1990 to 21 percent in 2008 (figure 6c). But the benefits were not shared equally. Low-income economies accounted for only 1 percent of world merchandise exports and less than 1 percent of world service exports in 2008.

Low-income exporters specialize in labor-intensive goods

Export-led growth can improve human development outcomes and reduce poverty if it fosters employment in labor-intensive sectors where the poor have a stake. As the share of agriculture and labor-intensive manufacturing —such as textiles, clothing, and footwear—in world exports has fallen, both developing and high-income economies have adjusted by moving to capital-intensive manufacturing. But low-income economies, following their comparative advantage, still specialize in labor-intensive exports (figure 6d), which face higher tariffs than do other products (figure 6e).

Transitioning from labor-intensive exports to capital-intensive exports may be difficult. Ideally, increased trade should mean more jobs, lower unemployment, and higher wages. But trade liberalization has often failed to improve employment because new export industries have been capital-intensive manufactures, unable to create sufficient employment to absorb all of the workers transitioning from the agriculture sector.

The poorest of the world's population live in rural areas and work in agriculture or fisheries. Boosting agricultural exports could increase agricultural employment and wages, thereby reducing poverty.

Most world trade in agriculture occurs between high-income economies, with low-income economies providing only about 2 percent of global agricultural exports (figure 6f). Developing economies have limited representation in global agricultural markets partly because their exports face higher tariffs from both high-income and developing economy partners. High-income economies also provide subsidies to their farmers, enabling them to sell agricultural products at very low prices that developing

economies cannot match. Under the MDG framework, OECD members promised to lower subsidies to agricultural producers, exporters, and consumers. Total agricultural supports as a share of GDP have fallen for most OECD members, but in nominal dollar terms support actually increased 3.2 percent between 2007 and 2008, to $376 billion.

In the last decade some developing economies, especially the least developed countries, became net food importers. In the mid-1970s

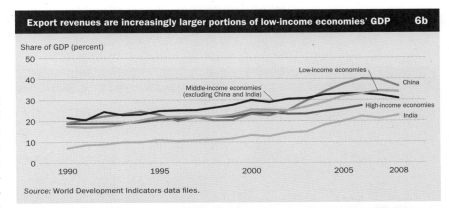

Export revenues are increasingly larger portions of low-income economies' GDP 6b

Source: World Development Indicators data files.

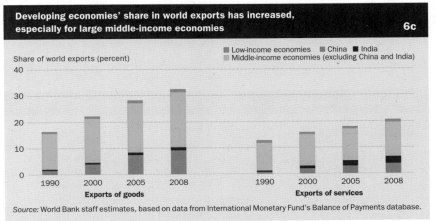

Developing economies' share in world exports has increased, especially for large middle-income economies 6c

Source: World Bank staff estimates, based on data from International Monetary Fund's Balance of Payments database.

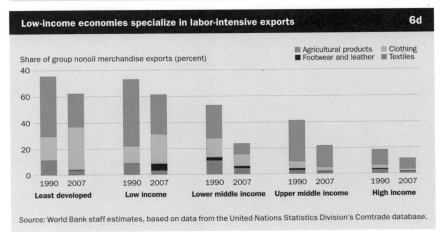

Low-income economies specialize in labor-intensive exports 6d

Source: World Bank staff estimates, based on data from the United Nations Statistics Division's Comtrade database.

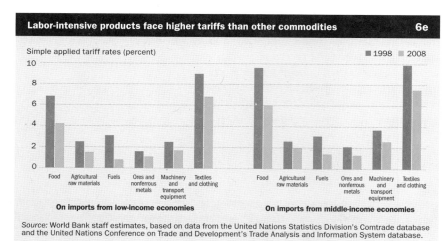

Labor-intensive products face higher tariffs than other commodities | 6e

Simple applied tariff rates (percent) ■ 1998 ■ 2008

On imports from low-income economies

On imports from middle-income economies

Source: World Bank staff estimates, based on data from the United Nations Statistics Division's Comtrade database and the United Nations Conference on Trade and Development's Trade Analysis and Information System database.

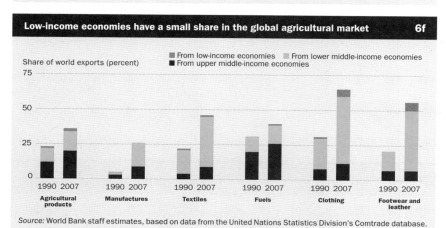

Low-income economies have a small share in the global agricultural market | 6f

Share of world exports (percent)

■ From low-income economies ■ From lower middle-income economies
■ From upper middle-income economies

Agricultural products · Manufactures · Textiles · Fuels · Clothing · Footwear and leather

Source: World Bank staff estimates, based on data from the United Nations Statistics Division's Comtrade database.

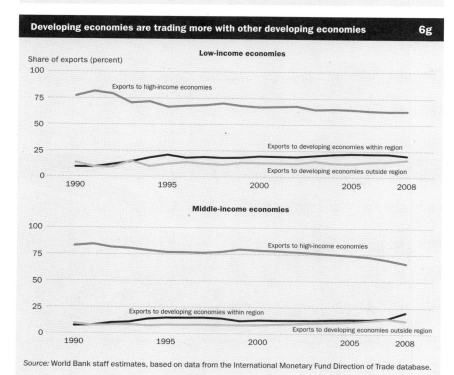

Developing economies are trading more with other developing economies | 6g

Share of exports (percent)

Low-income economies

Exports to high-income economies

Exports to developing economies within region

Exports to developing economies outside region

Middle-income economies

Exports to high-income economies

Exports to developing economies within region

Exports to developing economies outside region

Source: World Bank staff estimates, based on data from the International Monetary Fund Direction of Trade database.

18 of 28 least developed countries were net food exporters; by the mid-1990s 7 of them had become net food importers; and by the mid-2000s 10 of them had become net food importers. Vulnerable to increasing food prices, net food importers can suffer food insecurity and malnutrition.

Trade diversification has improved—but unevenly

Trade diversification—in both partners and products—affects developing economies' ability to cope with external shocks such as commodity price changes and demand fluctuations.

Compared with two decades ago, developing economies are trading more with other developing economies, especially with economies in the same region (figure 6g). Developing economies' exports to other developing economies increased from 16 percent of merchandise exports in 1990 to 31 percent in 2008. Expansion of East Asia and Pacific and Sub-Saharan African economies' trade with other developing economies has been remarkable. East Asia and Pacific's exports to other developing economies rose from 13 percent of the region's total merchandise exports in 1990 to 29 percent in 2008. Sub-Saharan Africa's exports to other developing economies rose from 12 percent in 1990 to 37 percent in 2008. Still, more than 60 percent of developing economies' merchandise exports in 2008 were directed to high-income economies. The economic crisis that began in 2008 lowered developed economies' demand for imports, hurting the export revenues of developing economies that depended on high-income markets. Some economies, especially the poorest, depend on just a few partner economies. For example, more than 95 percent of the merchandise exports from Chad, Guinea-Bissau, and Niger in 2008 were directed to their five largest trading partners.

Many developing economies have improved their product diversification, but some remain dependent on only a few products. The top-five export commodities (which differ by country) made up around 75 percent of Sub-Saharan African economies' merchandise exports. And for some developing economies the top-five share exceeds 90 percent of total merchandise exports (figure 6h). On average, the share of the top-five export commodities in total exports tends to be higher for low-income economies

(71 percent) than for middle-income (59 percent) and high-income (50 percent) economies.

Developed economies have lowered trade barriers, but not enough

Trade barriers encompass tariffs, quotas, anti-dumping duties, export subsidies, monopolistic measures, and technical regulations. Measuring overall trade restrictiveness involves aggregating these different forms of trade barriers across goods with different economic importance. The World Bank's Tariff Trade Restrictiveness Index (TTRI) and Overall Trade Restrictiveness Index (OTRI) measure the impact of a country's trade policy on its imports. The TTRI is the estimated uniform tariff equivalent to the effectively applied tariffs currently imposed on various import products. The OTRI is the uniform tariff equivalent to current tariff and nontariff barriers to imports. A comparison of the TTRI and the OTRI implies that nontariff barriers are much higher than tariffs (figure 6i). On average, low-income economies impose higher tariffs and nontariff barriers than do other income groups to protect domestic production and raise revenue through taxes on imports. Although the average tariff and nontariff barriers imposed by high-income economies are low, their restrictions on agricultural products tend to be high. Because most of the world's poor earn their living through agriculture and other labor-intensive activities, substantial trade restrictions on these commodities block market access by the poor. Because high-income economies have the largest consumer markets, their trade policies have the most impact on developing economies' exports.

Exports from most economies face tariff and nontariff barriers in other economies. But low-income economies tend to face higher overall restrictions, especially for agricultural products (figure 6j). Market access by developing economies may also be affected by strict rules of origin that restrict preferential treatment of commodities not wholly produced in the exporting country.

As tariffs are the most widely known trade barrier, the MDG framework monitors the average tariffs imposed by OECD members on imports from developing economies. When examined in isolation, this indicator appears to show that developed economies have significantly lowered tariff barriers. But the actual situation is more complex. Averaging tariff rates

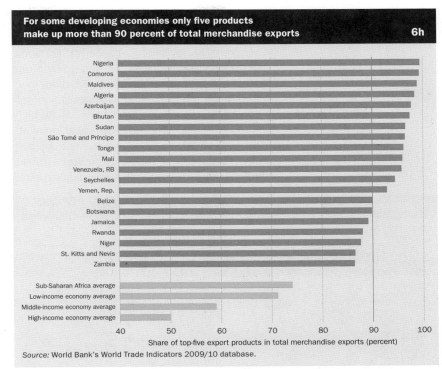

For some developing economies only five products make up more than 90 percent of total merchandise exports 6h

Source: World Bank's World Trade Indicators 2009/10 database.

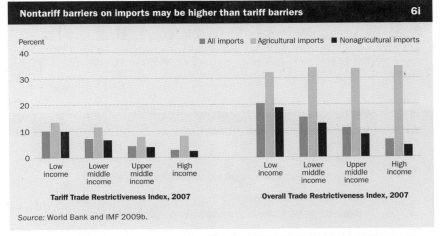

Nontariff barriers on imports may be higher than tariff barriers 6i

Source: World Bank and IMF 2009b.

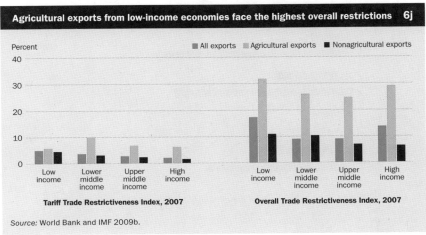

Agricultural exports from low-income economies face the highest overall restrictions 6j

Source: World Bank and IMF 2009b.

across thousands of products can mask high tariffs on certain commodities that are particularly important to developing economies. For some OECD members the maximum applied tariff rate can be as high as 887 percent (table 6k).

Among the most commonly used nontariff barriers are antidumping actions. Many high-income economies—and recently developing economies as well—initiate antidumping investigations. Whether for shiitake mushrooms entering Japan, steel entering the United States, or shoes entering the European Union, antidumping initiations have a chilling effect on imports—even when they do not result in imposition of antidumping duties. Only about half of antidumping initiations are later imposed.

Trade in services has grown rapidly, but total value remains small

Growth in developing economies' trade in services averaged 21 percent a year between 2005 and 2008, surpassing their previous performances and those of high-income economies (figure 6l). Europe and Central Asia experienced the highest growth, while Sub-Saharan Africa lagged behind. But trade in services still made up less than 20 percent of world trade in 2008.

The World Trade Organization recognizes four modes of trade in services: cross-border exchange of services (such as the purchase of services from a foreign supplier and outsourcing), consumption abroad (such as tourism, education, and health services), commercial presence of foreign companies in a country (involving foreign direct investments), and movement of people. Trade in services usually faces tighter regulation and higher barriers than trade in merchandise.

Large middle-income economies recently increased their market shares in the outsourcing of services. For example, China is a key product development center for General Electric, Intel, Microsoft, Philips, and other large electronic firms focused on hardware and software design. India is the largest offshore provider of information technology services, technical help desks, and web support. But few developing economies have benefited from the recent expansion of outsourcing. Poorer countries tend to lack the necessary infrastructure—such as robust telecommunication networks and a reliable power supply—and skilled and educated workers. Outsourcing companies also require strong legal systems that ensure data security and privacy, which many developing economies lack.

Tourism is one of the largest segments of trade in services, generating employment, providing valuable foreign currency exchange, and increasing government revenues through taxation. The tourism industry employs people with various skill sets, including cleaners, drivers, beauticians, managers, and chefs. Developing economies' receipts from tourism

Some OECD members apply very high tariffs selectively (percent)   6k

	Year	Simple average tariff rate	Weighted average tariff rate	Maximum tariff rate	Share of tariff lines with rate of 15 percent or more
Australia	2008	4	2	18	5
Canada	2008	4	1	95	7
Iceland	2008	2	1	76	6
Japan	2008	3	1	50	7
Korea, Rep.	2007	8	7	887	5
New Zealand	2008	3	2	13	0
Norway	2008	1	0	555	1
United States	2008	3	1	350	4
European Union	2008	2	1	75	2

Note: Based on effectively applied tariffs across all imports.
Source: World Bank staff estimates, based on data from the United Nations Conference on Trade and Development's Trade Analysis and Information System database.

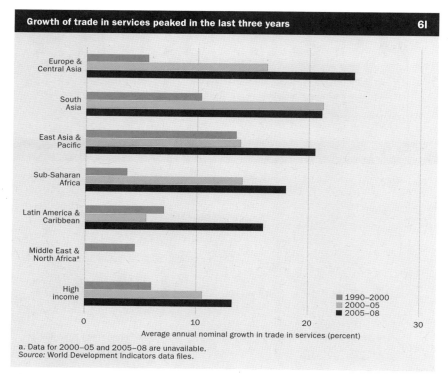

Growth of trade in services peaked in the last three years   6l

a. Data for 2000–05 and 2005–08 are unavailable.
Source: World Development Indicators data files.

have increased considerably, from $92 billion (19 percent of the world total) in 1995 to $324 billion (28 percent) in 2008 (figure 6m). East Asia and Pacific and Europe and Central Asia are the biggest benefiters. Residents of developing economies are also increasing their spending on tourism to other countries.

Human migration brings many benefits, such as remittances, improved skills and experience, and the transfer of technology during return migration. Workers' remittances—including employee compensation and migrant transfers—have become a large source of foreign exchange for many developing economies, increasing consumption and investment as well as the income of recipient families (figure 6n). For low-income economies with a negative trade balance, remittances provide an important source of external financing. Yet migration may have negative effects, siphoning off skilled workers and increasing inequality between remittance recipients and other families. Some economies have increased restrictions on labor services, including restrictions on the temporary cross-border movement of construction workers.

Trade facilitation is improving slowly—but lower income economies lag behind

Trade facilitation may boost trade as effectively as tariff reduction (Hertel, Walmsley, and Itakura 2001; Wilson, Mann, and Otsuki 2004). The MDG framework recognizes the importance of trade facilitation by including an indicator to monitor aid for building trade capacity.

Aid for trade aims to help developing economies—especially low-income ones—overcome structural and capacity limitations that undermine their ability to produce, compete, and fully benefit from global integration. One of many ways aid for trade can help developing economies is by identifying infrastructure bottlenecks, improving logistics efficiency, and smoothing the supply chain. But how should the impact of aid for trade on the performance of developing economies be measured? Outcome indicators such as value and growth of exports and imports are important; so are indicators that measure trade logistics performance and trade-related infrastructure. Better logistics performance is associated with trade expansion, export diversification, and the ability to attract foreign direct investment.

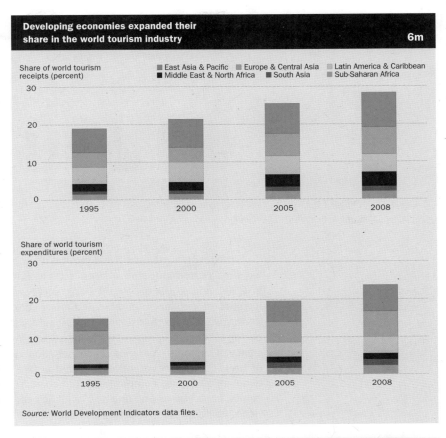

Developing economies expanded their share in the world tourism industry 6m

Source: World Development Indicators data files.

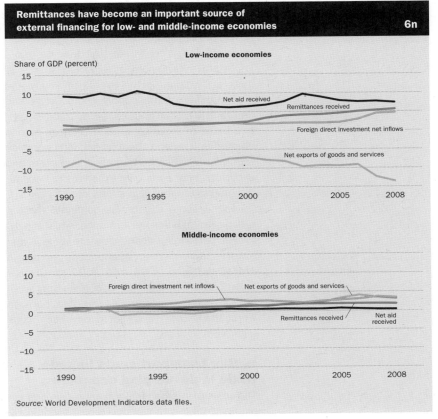

Remittances have become an important source of external financing for low- and middle-income economies 6n

Source: World Development Indicators data files.

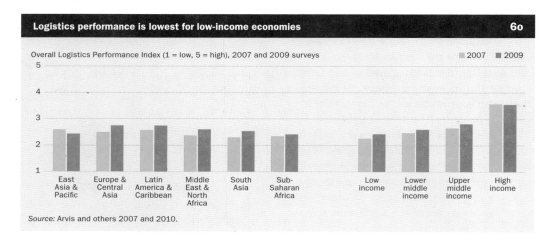

Logistics performance is lowest for low-income economies 6o

Overall Logistics Performance Index (1 = low, 5 = high), 2007 and 2009 surveys   ■ 2007   ■ 2009

Source: Arvis and others 2007 and 2010.

Until recently, data on trade facilitation and logistics performance have been scarce. But in 2007 and 2009 the World Bank surveyed logistics professionals and created a Logistics Performance Index that summarizes a country's performance in six areas of trade logistics: efficiency of customs clearance processes, quality of trade- and transport-related infrastructure, ease of arranging competitively priced shipments, competence and quality of logistics services, ability to track and trace consignments, and frequency with which shipments reach the consignee within the scheduled or expected time. The surveys suggest that transportation costs, the time to import and export, and customs efficiency are all key but that the most important determinant of export competitiveness and volume is the overall reliability and predictability of the supply chain (Arvis and others 2007, 2010). In essence, traders need to be able to move goods and services across borders quickly and cheaply. And in economies with poor logistics performance, importers and exporters incur additional expenses to mitigate the effects of unreliable supply chains.

High-income economies dominate the top ratings for logistics performance, while the 10 lowest performing economies are all low- and lower middle-income economies, mostly in Africa. Between 2006 and 2009 the overall logistics performance of economies improved, but low-income economies tend to perform worse than middle- and high-income economies (figure 6o).

Higher transport costs impede trade in developing economies

The costs of international transport services are a crucial determinant of developing economies'

export competitiveness. For example, a 2001 study found that a 1 percent reduction in the cost of maritime and air transport services could increase Asian GDP by $3.3 billion (UNCTAD 2001). Transport costs are asymmetric worldwide and are especially high for landlocked developing economies. In Central Asia the cost of transporting a 40 ton container by road between Central Asia and Europe varies depending on the direction traveled: moving goods west to east costs $6,000 but moving them east to west costs only $4,000 (Arvis, Raballand, and Marteau 2007).

Comprehensive data on transport costs for all developing economies are not available. One proxy indicator for transport costs is the shipping rates of companies that operate globally in the international freight moving business. For example, the median DHL rate for sending a 1 kilogram package to the United States was 1.6 times higher from low-income economies than from high-income economies.

Transport costs depend on a mixture of geographic and economic circumstances. Freight costs tend to be higher for low-income economies. Landlocked countries or countries without access to large economic centers face much higher transportation costs than do coastal countries and countries located near business centers (box 6p). These economies tend to have poor infrastructure and thin traffic densities, further impeding their export competitiveness.

Improving trade infrastructure to facilitate trade

Infrastructure, especially transport services infrastructure, is vital for trade facilitation. Port quality and accessibility, road quality, and access to global shipping and air freight networks influence the overall logistics performance of international traders. For example, a 2006 study concluded that investment in upgrading and maintaining a trans-African highway network linking 83 major African cities could increase intra-African trade from $10 billion a year to $30 billion (Buys, Deichmann, and Wheeler 2006). Similarly, improving road networks in 27 European and Central Asian economies could increase their trade by as much as 50 percent (Shepherd and Wilson 2007).

Infrastructure quality may be just as important as its availability. According to a survey of logistics professionals, poor infrastructure quality is a widespread constraint on the logistics performance of developing economies. Moreover, satisfaction with infrastructure quality was much higher for economies ranked highest in overall logistics performance (Arvis and others 2010). Port infrastructure is important for economies that rely heavily on sea transport. According to a survey of business executives, 62 of 69 economies ranked below average in port quality were developing economies, 22 of them low-income (World Economic Forum 2009).

Time delays add to trading costs

Traders also face indirect transport costs: the time required to import and export goods, border inefficiency, and the risk of freight loss or damage. Indirect costs can be higher than direct costs. For example, World Bank research suggests that one additional day of shipping delays cuts trade by at least 1 percent (Djankov, Freund, and Pham 2010). In Europe and Central Asia and Sub-Saharan Africa tariff equivalents of time to export were more than twice the average applied tariff (USAID 2007). According to the 2009 Logistics Performance

Challenges for landlocked economies	6p

Millennium Development Goal 8 focuses on landlocked countries. Like other small, low-income economies, landlocked developing economies have unpredictable supply chains, reflecting uncertainty in shipment delivery time, low demand levels, greater inventory costs, and low private sector capacities. Rent-seeking activities are higher when shipments transit through other economies and international corridors, contributing to higher trading costs (Arvis, Raballand, and Marteau 2007). On average, landlocked economies trade 30 percent less than coastal economies (Limao and Venables 2001).

Access to global shipping and freight networks is an important determinant of a country's export competitiveness. Because landlocked economies lack direct access to liner shipping networks, access to air cargo networks is especially important to them. Though faster and more reliable than road transport, air freight typically costs 4–5 times more than road transport and 12–16 times more than sea transport (World Bank 2009a). Consequently, demand for air freight is limited in landlocked developing economies that ship small volumes of low-value-per-unit goods. Establishing and improving the efficiency of international trade corridors could significantly benefit landlocked economies.

Source: World Bank staff.

Lead time to import and export is longest for low-income economies	6q

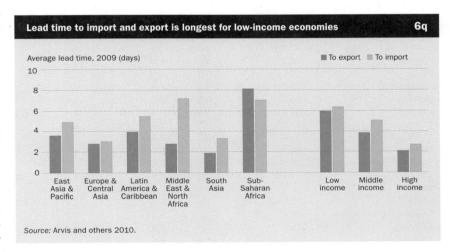

Source: Arvis and others 2010.

Survey, for 50 percent of shipments, import and export lead times are three times longer for low-income economies than for high-income economies (figure 6q). And lead time to export from or import to Sub-Saharan African economies averages 7–8 days—much longer than for other developing regions such as Europe and Central Asia and South Asia.

	Trade		International finance				Movement of people			Communication	
	% of GDP		Financing through international capital markets Gross inflows	Foreign direct investment Net inflows	Net outflows	Workers' remittances and compensation of employees received	Net migration thousands	International migrant stock % of total population	Emigration of people with tertiary education to OECD countries % of population age 25 and older with tertiary education	International voice traffic minutes per person	International Internet bandwidth bits per second per capita
	Merchandise	Services									
	2008	2008	2008	2008	2008	2008	2000–05	2005	2000	2008	2008
Afghanistan	37.9	..	0.0	2.8	..	..	805	0.3	22.6	1	1
Albania	53.5	39.5	0.0	7.6	0.8	12.2	–100	2.7	17.4	127	220
Algeria	70.5	..	1.0	1.6	..	1.3[b]	–140	0.7	9.4	18	..
Angola	102.9	26.5	4.6	2.0	3.0	0.1	175	0.3	3.6	..	17
Argentina	39.0	7.6	0.5	3.0	0.4	0.2	–100	3.9	2.8	42	2,320
Armenia	46.0	13.6	0.0	7.8	0.1	8.9	–100	16.1	8.9	..	..
Australia	38.2	9.2	..	4.7	3.8	0.5	641	21.3	2.7	..	5,457
Austria	88.0	25.2	..	3.5	7.4	0.8	220	14.0	13.5	..	20,323
Azerbaijan	83.9	11.8	2.8	0.0	1.2	3.4	–100	3.0	1.8	..	1,180
Bangladesh	49.3	7.2	0.1	1.2	..	11.3	–700	0.7	4.4	6	4
Belarus	120.0	11.4	0.5	3.6	0.0	0.7	20	11.3	3.2	..	748
Belgium	190.3	33.9	..	19.8	23.6	2.1	196	8.4	5.5	..	24,945
Benin	45.5	14.5	0.0	1.8	–0.1	4.1[b]	99	2.4	8.6	12	18
Bolivia	68.1	9.2	0.0	3.1	0.0	6.9	–100	1.2	5.8	80	225
Bosnia and Herzegovina	93.7	12.5	0.0	5.7	0.1	14.8	62	0.9	20.3	109	529
Botswana	76.2	16.6	0.0	0.8	0.0	0.9	20	4.4	5.1	115	220
Brazil	24.2	4.9	2.1	2.9	1.3	0.3	–229	0.4	2.0	..	2,108
Bulgaria	123.0	29.5	2.5	18.4	1.5	5.3	–41	1.3	9.6	27	37,657
Burkina Faso	30.4	..	0.0	1.7	..	0.6[b]	100	5.6	2.5	11	15
Burundi	39.5	22.1	0.0	0.3	0.0	0.3	192	1.1	7.3	..	2
Cambodia	104.3	26.2	0.3	7.9	0.2	3.1	10	2.2	21.4	..	19
Cameroon	37.2	19.1	0.0	0.2	–0.2	0.6	–12	1.2	17.1	4	8
Canada	62.5	11.0	..	3.0	5.3	..	1,089	19.5	4.7	..	16,193
Central African Republic	24.9	..	0.1	6.1	..	..	–45	1.8	7.2	..	..
Chad	77.4	..	0.0	9.9	..	..	219	3.6	9.0	..	1
Chile	76.5	13.1	4.0	9.9	4.1	0.0	30	1.4	6.0	35	4,076
China	59.2	7.1	0.7	3.4	1.2	1.1[b]	–2,058[c]	0.0	3.8	9	483
Hong Kong SAR, China	354.4	64.2	..	29.3	27.8	0.2	113	39.9	29.6	1,435	548,318
Colombia	31.7	4.6	0.6	4.3	0.9	2.0	–120	0.3	10.4	142	2,233
Congo, Dem. Rep.	69.0	..	0.0	8.6	..	..	–237	0.8	9.0	..	..
Congo, Rep.	111.0	50.3	0.0	24.5	..	0.1[b]	4	3.8	22.9	..	0
Costa Rica	84.4	20.1	1.7	6.8	0.0	2.0	84	10.2	7.1	120	857
Côte d'Ivoire	73.7	15.5	0.2	1.7	..	0.8	–339	12.3	6.1	..	40
Croatia	64.7	28.5	..	6.9	0.3	2.3	–13	14.9	24.6	229	15,892
Cuba	..	..	..	..	..	..	–163	0.1	28.8	..	27
Czech Republic	134.0	18.4	..	5.0	0.9	0.7	67	4.4	8.5	136	7,075
Denmark	67.0	39.4	..	0.9	4.4	0.3	46	7.8	7.8	210	34,506
Dominican Republic	51.2	14.9	1.3	6.3	0.0	7.8	–148	4.1	22.4	..	1,407
Ecuador	68.0	7.8	0.0	1.8	0.0	5.2	–400	0.9	9.5	3	443
Egypt, Arab Rep.	45.5	26.2	5.1	5.9	1.2	5.4	–291	0.3	4.7	27	332
El Salvador	64.7	15.9	0.0	3.5	0.3	17.2	–340	0.6	31.7	578	33
Eritrea	33.3	..	0.0	2.2	..	..	229	0.3	35.2	17	5
Estonia	121.1	36.8	..	8.3	4.6	1.7	1	15.0	9.9	..	126,802
Ethiopia	35.6	17.1	0.0	0.4	0.0	1.5	–340	0.7	9.8	2	3
Finland	69.2	22.6	..	–2.8	1.1	0.3	33	3.3	7.2	..	17,221
France	46.1	10.8	..	3.5	7.2	0.6	761	10.6	3.4	242	29,356
Gabon	75.0	..	4.1	0.1	..	0.1[b]	10	17.9	14.4	..	141
Gambia, The	42.3	26.0	0.0	8.9	..	8.2	31	15.2	67.8	..	38
Georgia	59.1	19.5	4.7	12.2	0.3	5.7	–309	4.3	2.8	44	752
Germany	73.1	14.6	..	0.6	4.3	0.3	930	12.9	5.7	..	25,654
Ghana	96.4	24.6	8.0	12.7	0.0	0.8	12	7.6	44.6	6	86
Greece	28.9	21.1	..	1.5	0.8	0.8	154	8.8	12.1	..	4,537
Guatemala	57.2	10.1	0.0	2.1	0.0	11.4	–300	0.4	23.9	..	186
Guinea	76.3	14.5	3.3	10.1	3.3	1.9	–425	4.4	4.6	..	0
Guinea-Bissau	60.1	..	0.0	3.5	..	7.0[b]	1	1.3	27.7	..	1
Haiti	36.6	15.4	0.0	0.4	..	19.6	–140	0.3	83.4	..	16
Honduras	120.8	15.9	1.6	6.6	0.0	21.5	–150	0.4	24.8	39	241

Integration with the global economy

	Trade		International finance				Movement of people			Communication	
	% of GDP		% of GDP								
			Financing through international capital markets Gross inflows	Foreign direct investment		Workers' remittances and compensation of employees received	Net migration thousands	International migrant stock % of total population	Emigration of people with tertiary education to OECD countries % of population age 25 and older with tertiary education	International voice traffic[a] minutes per person	International Internet bandwidth[a] bits per second per capita
	Merchandise	Services		Net inflows	Net outflows						
	2008	2008	2008	2008	2008	2008	2000–05	2005	2000	2008	2008
Hungary	139.5	25.1	..	40.6	39.5	1.7	70	3.3	12.8	120	5,977
India	40.6	13.8	2.7	3.6	1.6	4.3	–1,540	0.5	4.3	..	32
Indonesia	52.0	8.5	4.1	1.8	1.2	1.3	–1,000	0.1	2.9	..	120
Iran, Islamic Rep.	46.7	..	0.0	0.6	..	0.4[b]	–993	3.0	14.3	..	151
Iraq	..	..	..	..	..	..	–224	0.4	10.9	0	1
Ireland	73.4	74.9	..	–7.4	5.0	0.2	230	14.8	33.7	..	15,261
Israel	63.5	21.8	..	4.8	3.9	0.7	115	38.4	7.8	413	2,003
Italy	47.8	10.9	..	0.7	1.9	0.1	1,750	5.2	9.6	..	12,989
Jamaica	70.3	35.3	3.1	9.8	0.5	14.9	–76	1.0	84.7	39	744
Japan	31.5	6.5	..	0.5	2.7	0.0	82	1.6	1.2	..	5,770
Jordan	116.2	40.2	8.2	9.3	0.1	17.9	104	43.3	7.4	66	781
Kazakhstan	81.7	11.5	15.3	11.0	2.9	0.1	–200	19.6	1.2	47	702
Kenya	52.9	16.9	0.8	0.3	0.1	5.6[b]	25	2.2	38.5	3	21
Korea, Dem. Rep.	..	..	..	..	..	..	0	0.2	..	..	0
Korea, Rep.	92.3	18.2	..	0.2	1.4	0.3	–65	1.1	7.5	33	4,528
Kosovo	..	..	0.0	..	..	..	..	..	..	..	..
Kuwait	79.9	17.8	..	0.0	5.9	..	264	73.7	7.1	..	871
Kyrgyz Republic	112.7	37.4	0.0	4.6	0.0	24.4	–75	5.6	0.9	..	113
Lao PDR	44.6	8.2	10.9	4.1	..	0.0[b]	–115	0.3	37.2	..	129
Latvia	77.2	22.9	4.2	4.0	0.8	1.8	–20	16.5	8.5	..	3,537
Lebanon	72.5	110.6	5.2	12.3	3.4	24.5	100	17.7	43.8	..	223
Lesotho	180.6	10.9	0.0	13.4	..	27.0	–36	0.3	4.1	..	5
Liberia	133.8	209.9	117.5	17.1	0.0	6.9	62	2.9	44.3	..	..
Libya	80.0	4.9	0.0	4.4	6.3	0.0[b]	14	10.4	4.3	65	50
Lithuania	115.2	19.2	0.0	3.7	0.8	3.1	–36	4.8	8.3	57	9,751
Macedonia, FYR	113.7	21.2	0.0	6.3	–0.1	4.3	–10	5.9	29.4	159	17
Madagascar	56.9	..	0.0	15.6	..	0.1[b]	–5	0.2	7.7	1	8
Malawi	58.3	..	0.0	0.9	..	0.0[b]	–30	2.0	20.9	..	5
Malaysia	160.7	27.3	3.2	3.3	6.9	0.9[b]	150	7.9	10.5	..	2,374
Mali	48.1	16.8	1.3	1.5	0.1	3.9[b]	–134	1.4	14.7	2	51
Mauritania	122.5	..	0.0	3.6	..	0.1[b]	30	2.2	8.5	4	76
Mauritius	75.1	47.9	0.1	4.1	0.6	2.3	0	3.3	55.8	100	364
Mexico	56.5	4.0	1.7	2.1	0.1	2.4	–2,702	0.6	15.5	174	285
Moldova	107.4	27.5	0.0	11.7	0.3	31.4	–320	11.7	4.1	155	966
Mongolia	117.1	32.2	0.0	13.0	..	3.8[b]	17	0.4	7.4	5	947
Morocco	69.5	22.6	1.7	2.8	0.4	7.8	–550	0.2	18.0	21	795
Mozambique	68.1	15.3	0.8	6.0	0.0	1.2	–20	1.9	22.5	..	3
Myanmar	..	..	..	..	..	..	–1,000	0.2	3.9	..	20
Namibia	84.6	12.7	0.0	6.1	0.1	0.2	–1	6.6	3.4	..	27
Nepal	37.0	12.5	0.0	0.0	..	21.6	–100	3.0	4.0	..	5
Netherlands	140.4	23.0	..	–0.3	2.2	0.4	110	10.6	9.5	..	78,156
New Zealand	49.7	14.4	..	4.2	0.2	0.5	103	20.7	21.8	310	4,544
Nicaragua	87.6	15.3	0.0	9.5	0.0	12.4	–206	0.6	30.2	39	144
Niger	42.4	10.7	0.0	2.7	0.2	1.5[b]	–28	1.4	5.4	..	11
Nigeria	59.7	7.3	1.1	1.8	0.2	4.8[b]	–170	0.7	10.5	1	5
Norway	57.1	20.1	..	–0.3	5.9	0.2	84	8.0	6.2	..	26,904
Oman	97.8	15.6	..	7.5	0.6	0.1	–50	25.5	0.4	30	894
Pakistan	38.1	8.3	0.4	3.3	0.0	4.3	–1,239	2.3	12.7	..	43
Panama	44.3	36.6	11.0	10.4	0.0	0.9	8	3.2	16.7	61	15,964
Papua New Guinea	112.3	..	5.3	–0.4	..	0.2[b]	0	0.4	27.8	..	2
Paraguay	91.5	10.3	0.0	2.0	0.1	3.1	–45	2.8	3.8	35	481
Peru	47.6	7.1	2.2	3.2	..	1:9	–525	0.1	5.8	..	2,646
Philippines	64.8	11.4	1.7	0.8	0.2	11.2	–900	0.4	13.5	..	113
Poland	70.4	12.5	1.7	2.8	0.6	2.0	–200	2.2	14.2	..	2,748
Portugal	60.0	17.8	..	1.5	0.9	1.7	291	7.2	18.9	..	4,790
Puerto Rico	..	..	..	..	..	..	–27	9.0	..	..	..
Qatar	90.1	..	..	..	..	..	219	80.5	2.1	..	2,044

6.1 Integration with the global economy

	Trade		International finance % of GDP				Movement of people			Communication	
	% of GDP		Financing through international capital markets Gross inflows	Foreign direct investment		Workers' remittances and compensation of employees received	International migrant stock	International migrant stock % of total population	Emigration of people with tertiary education to OECD countries % of population age 25 and older with tertiary education	International voice traffic[a] minutes per person	International Internet bandwidth[a] bits per second per capita
	Merchandise	Services		Net inflows	Net outflows		Net migration thousands				
	2008	2008	2008	2008	2008	2008	2000–05	2005	2000	2008	2008
Romania	66.1	12.4	1.2	6.9	0.1	4.7	−270	0.6	11.2	41	9,111
Russian Federation	45.5	7.6	5.2	4.3	3.1	0.4	964	8.4	1.4	..	573
Rwanda	30.5	20.9	0.0	2.3	−0.4	1.5	6	4.8	26.3	11	27
Saudi Arabia	94.0	18.0	..	4.8	0.7	0.0	285	27.4	0.9	..	1,224
Senegal	61.0	21.6	0.0	5.3	0.2	9.7[b]	−100	2.0	17.1	27	237
Serbia	67.9	16.6	0.8	6.0	0.6	11.1[b,d]	−339	9.1	..	142	4,506
Sierra Leone	39.9	9.5	0.0	−0.2	..	7.7[b]	336	3.0	49.2	..	..
Singapore	361.6	89.3	..	12.5	4.9	..	139	35.0	14.5	1,531	22,783
Slovak Republic	152.0	18.6	..	3.3	0.3	2.0	10	2.3	14.3	123	5,555
Slovenia	130.4	22.8	..	3.5	2.6	0.6	23	8.4	10.9	96	6,720
Somalia	..	..	..	..	..	..	−200	0.3	34.5	..	..
South Africa	65.2	10.8	2.5	3.5	−0.8	0.3	700	2.7	7.4	..	71
Spain	41.8	15.5	..	4.4	5.0	0.7	2,504	10.6	4.2	..	11,008
Sri Lanka	55.2	12.3	1.0	1.9	0.2	7.3	−442	1.9	28.2	34	190
Sudan	38.7	5.6	0.0	4.6	0.2	5.5	−532	1.7	6.8	6	322
Swaziland	140.6	32.6	0.0	0.4	0.8	3.5[b]	−46	3.4	5.3	..	31
Sweden	73.1	26.4	..	8.7	8.4	0.2	186	12.3	4.5	..	49,828
Switzerland	78.6	23.5	..	1.3	10.2	0.4	200	22.3	9.5	..	29,413
Syrian Arab Republic	59.1	17.0	0.7	3.1	0.0	1.5[b]	300	6.9	6.1	78	102
Tajikistan	91.1	12.4	0.0	7.3	0.0	49.6	−345	4.7	0.6	..	37
Tanzania	47.9	18.4	4.1	3.6	..	0.1	−345	2.0	12.1	0	2
Thailand	130.9	29.5	1.5	3.6	1.0	0.7	1,411	1.5	2.2	..	818
Timor-Leste	..	..	0.0	..	..	..	41	1.2	16.5	..	..
Togo	80.4	21.7	0.0	2.3	0.0	9.8[b]	−4	3.1	16.3	6	8
Trinidad and Tobago	114.7	6.0	..	3.8	2.0	0.5[b]	−20	2.9	78.9	..	678
Tunisia	109.0	23.3	0.4	6.5	0.1	4.9	−81	0.3	12.4	79	1,115
Turkey	45.4	7.1	2.9	2.5	0.3	0.2	−71	1.9	5.8	39	2,794
Turkmenistan	100.9	..	0.0	5.3	..	..	−25	4.6	0.4	..	48
Uganda	48.7	13.7	0.0	5.5	0.0	5.1	−5	2.3	36.0	7	12
Ukraine	83.8	18.9	2.9	6.1	0.6	3.2	−173	11.4	4.3	0	206
United Arab Emirates	157.7	..	..	..	..	..	577	70.0	0.7	..	8,686
United Kingdom	41.2	18.6	..	3.5	6.1	0.3	948	9.7	17.1	..	39,648
United States	24.4	6.7	..	2.2	2.3	0.0	5,676	13.3	0.5	..	11,289
Uruguay	46.2	11.3	10.9	6.9	0.0	0.3	−104	2.5	9.0	0	903
Uzbekistan	55.9	..	0.0	3.3	..	0.0	−400	4.8	0.8	..	30
Venezuela, RB	45.6	4.0	1.9	0.1	0.4	0.0	40	3.8	3.8	..	628
Vietnam	158.1	16.6	3.1	10.6	0.3	7.9[b]	−200	0.1	26.9	..	581
West Bank and Gaza	..	..	..	..	..	..	11	46.5	12.0	..	313
Yemen, Rep.	69.9	13.4	10.5	5.8	0.0	5.3	−100	2.2	6.0	..	28
Zambia	71.0	8.4	1.9	6.6	0.0	0.5	−82	2.4	16.4	..	8
Zimbabwe	..	..	..	..	..	..	−700	3.1	13.1	22	10
World	**53.0 w**	**12.3 w**	**.. w**	**3.0 w**	**3.5 w**	**0.8 s**	**..[e] s**	**3.0 w**	**5.4 w**	**..**	**3,546 w**
Low income	74.9	15.2	2.0	5.1	..	7.1	−3,728	1.6	13.2	..	24
Middle income	56.2	9.6	2.2	3.5	1.3	1.9	−14,512	1.4	6.7	..	377
Lower middle income	60.0	10.6	1.5	3.4	1.1	2.6	−11,119	0.9	6.4	..	153
Upper middle income	52.5	8.6	2.9	3.6	1.5	1.2	−3,393	3.3	7.1	..	1,281
Low & middle income	56.7	9.7	2.2	3.6	1.3	2.0	−18,240	1.4	7.2	..	320
East Asia & Pacific	68.0	9.4	1.2	3.3	1.4	1.5	−3,722	0.3	7.0	9	470
Europe & Central Asia	58.1	10.2	3.9	4.4	1.7	1.5	−2,138	6.6	4.2	..	1,244
Latin America & Carib.	41.9	6.1	1.9	3.0	0.8	1.5	−5,738	1.1	10.6	..	1,391
Middle East & N. Africa	68.6	26.3	2.7	4.6	..	4.8	−1,850	3.2	10.4	27	323
South Asia	41.3	12.8	2.2	3.3	1.4	4.9	−3,181	0.8	5.3	..	31
Sub-Saharan Africa	64.9	13.3	1.8	3.5	0.1	2.3	−1,611	2.1	12.3	..	34
High income	51.5	13.3	..	2.8	4.4	0.3	18,091	11.4	4.0	..	20,143
Euro area	67.9	17.4	..	3.1	6.1	0.5	7,269	9.9	7.0	..	32,540

a. Data are from the International Telecommunication Union's (ITU) World Telecommunication Development Report database. Please cite the ITU for third-party use of these data. b. World Bank estimates. c. Includes Taiwan, China. d. Includes Montenegro. e. World totals computed by the United Nations sum to zero, but because the aggregates shown here refer to World Bank definitions, regional and income group totals do not equal zero.

About the data

Globalization—the integration of the world economy—has been a persistent theme of the past 25 years. Growth of cross-border economic activity has changed countries' economic structure and political and social organization. Not all effects of globalization can be measured directly. But the scope and pace of change can be monitored along four key dimensions: trade in goods and services, financial flows, movement of people, and communication.

Trade data are based on gross flows that capture the two-way flow of goods and services. In conventional balance of payments accounting, exports are recorded as a credit and imports as a debit. See tables 4.4 and 4.5 for data on the main trade components of merchandise trade and tables 4.6 and 4.7 for the same data on services trade.

Financing through international capital markets includes gross bond issuance, bank lending, and new equity placement as reported by Dealogic, a company specializing in the investment banking industry. In financial accounting inward investment is a credit and outward investment a debit. Gross flow is a better measure of integration than net flow because gross flow shows the total value of financial transactions over a period, while net flow is the sum of credits and debits and represents a balance in which many transactions are canceled out. Components of financing through international capital markets are reported in U.S. dollars by market sources.

Foreign direct investment (FDI) includes equity investment, reinvested earnings, and short- and long-term loans between parent firms and foreign affiliates. Distinguished from other kinds of international investment, FDI establishes a lasting interest in or effective management control over an enterprise in another country. FDI may be understated in developing countries because some fail to report reinvested earnings and because the definition of long-term loans differs by country. However, data quality and coverage are improving as a result of continuous efforts by international and national statistics agencies (see *About the data* for table 6.12).

Workers' remittances are current private transfers from migrant workers resident in the host country for more than a year, irrespective of their immigration status, to recipients in their country of origin. Compensation of employees is the income of migrants resident in the host country for less than a year. Migration has increased in importance, accounting for a substantial part of global integration. The estimates of the international migrant stock are derived from data on people who reside in one country but were born in another, mainly from population censuses (see *About the data* and *Definitions* for table 6.18). One negative effect of migration is "brain drain"—emigration of highly educated people. The table shows data on emigration of people with tertiary education, drawn from Docquier, Marfouk, and Lowell (2007), who analyzed skilled migration using data from censuses and registers of Organisation for Economic Development and Co-operation (OECD) countries and provide data disaggregated by gender for 1990 and 2000.

Well developed communications infrastructure attracts investments and allows investors to capitalize on benefits of the digital age. See *About the data* for tables 5.11 and 5.12 for more information.

Definitions

• **Trade in merchandise** is the sum of merchandise exports and imports. • **Trade in services** is the sum of services exports and imports. • **Financing through international capital markets** is the sum of the absolute values of new bond issuance, syndicated bank lending, and new equity placements. • **Foreign direct investment net inflows and outflows** are net inflows and outflows of FDI (equity capital, reinvestment of earnings, and other short- and long-term capital). • **Workers' remittances and compensation of employees received** are current transfers by migrant workers and wages and salaries of nonresident workers. • **Net migration** is the number of immigrants minus the number of emigrants, including citizens and noncitizens, for the five-year period. • **International migrant stock** is the number of people born in a country other than that in which they live, including refugees. • **Emigration of people with tertiary education to OECD countries** is adults ages 25 and older, residing in an OECD country other than that in which they were born, with at least one year of tertiary education. • **International voice traffic** is the sum of international incoming and outgoing telephone traffic divided by total population. • **International Internet bandwidth** is the contracted capacity of international connections between countries for transmitting Internet traffic.

Data sources

Data on merchandise trade are from the World Trade Organization's *Annual Report*. Data on trade in services are from the International Monetary Fund's (IMF) Balance of Payments database. Data on international capital market financing are based on data from Dealogic. Data on FDI are based on balance of payments data from the IMF, supplemented by staff estimates using data from the United Nations Conference on Trade and Development and official national sources. Data on workers' remittances are World Bank staff estimates based on IMF balance of payments data. Data on net migration are from the United Nations Population Division's *World Population Prospects: The 2008 Revision*. Data on international migrant stock are from the United Nations Population Division's *Trends in Total Migrant Stock: The 2008 Revision*. Data on emigration of people with tertiary education are from Docquier, Marfouk, and Lowell's "A Gendered Assessment of the Brain Drain" (2007). Data on international voice traffic and international Internet bandwidth are from the International Telecommunication Union's International Development Report database.

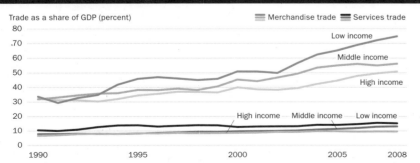

Services trade has not grown as rapidly as merchandise trade 6.1a

Trade as a share of GDP (percent)

☰ Merchandise trade ☰ Services trade

Merchandise trade in low-income economies grew from 34 percent of GDP in 1990 to 75 percent in 2008 and in middle-income economies from 32 percent to 56 percent. The shares of services trade in GDP also rose but not as much.

Source: World Development Indicators data files.

	Export volume		Import volume		Export value		Import value		Net barter terms of trade index	
	average annual % growth		average annual % growth		average annual % growth		average annual % growth		2000 = 100	
	1990–2000	2000–08	1990–2000	2000–08	1990–2000	2000–08	1990–2000	2000–08	1995	2008
Afghanistan	..	..	..	..	..	..	..	..	..	..
Albania	..	..	..	..	..	..	..	..	..	..
Algeria	2.8	1.8	−0.8	12.2	2.1	21.8	−1.3	18.6	57.9	238.8
Angola	6.2	13.4	7.1	20.4	6.1	34.9	7.8	25.0	80.8	253.9
Argentina	8.4	6.6	17.7	12.6	10.1	13.6	17.0	16.3	91.6	132.7
Armenia	..	..	..	..	..	..	..	..	..	..
Australia[a]	7.3	7.7	9.2	8.1	5.7	21.1	8.7	13.4	99.4	174.6
Austria[a]	6.2	6.6	5.6	5.6	..	..	..	..	..	..
Azerbaijan	..	..	..	..	..	..	..	..	..	..
Bangladesh	12.9	11.8	5.9	5.0	15.7	12.8	10.4	13.6	111.8	57.7
Belarus	..	..	..	..	..	..	..	..	..	..
Belgium[a]	6.0	4.1	5.7	4.7	4.8	13.3	5.3	14.1	104.3	98.3
Benin	1.0	9.8	8.2	5.2	3.3	15.2	9.7	14.8	106.6	68.6
Bolivia	2.8	11.3	9.1	7.2	4.3	24.4	9.7	13.2	89.4	144.0
Bosnia and Herzegovina	..	..	..	..	..	..	..	..	..	..
Botswana	4.8	4.6	4.0	5.0	4.7	10.2	2.7	11.5	89.3	90.0
Brazil	5.1	9.5	16.7	7.7	5.9	18.7	12.5	15.3	110.4	110.4
Bulgaria	..	..	..	..	..	..	..	..	..	..
Burkina Faso	13.2	12.7	3.6	6.6	12.9	17.4	3.6	15.6	131.0	71.5
Burundi	8.6	−5.9	4.0	10.8	−4.3	5.2	−6.9	17.0	163.6	140.3
Cambodia	..	14.1	..	10.5	26.8	16.6	25.2	17.0	..	78.5
Cameroon	0.3	−1.9	5.0	3.8	−3.6	13.0	2.1	13.7	90.4	138.2
Canada[a]	9.1	0.6	9.0	4.6	9.4	7.8	8.9	9.5	103.2	120.7
Central African Republic	20.0	0.5	4.3	5.3	3.5	4.1	0.2	13.2	193.0	72.9
Chad	..	..	..	..	..	..	..	..	..	..
Chile	11.1	6.2	10.7	13.1	9.4	21.9	10.3	18.1	135.6	164.9
China[†]	13.8	25.0	12.8	17.4	14.5	26.9	13.0	24.2	101.9	73.8
Hong Kong SAR, China	8.4	8.9	8.9	8.3	8.3	9.3	8.8	9.5	99.1	96.4
Colombia	4.5	6.1	8.5	12.6	7.3	15.8	9.7	17.4	86.8	138.1
Congo, Dem. Rep.	−1.8	8.4	4.6	17.1	−7.2	20.8	−0.5	24.6	79.8	147.2
Congo, Rep.	6.6	1.4	4.9	19.2	7.5	20.1	8.7	26.1	52.0	212.3
Costa Rica	14.0	8.5	14.9	9.0	17.0	8.5	13.9	11.9	104.6	81.7
Côte d'Ivoire	5.0	0.7	−0.3	7.6	6.0	13.1	2.4	17.2	122.0	138.8
Croatia	..	..	..	..	..	..	..	..	..	..
Cuba	..	1.9	..	6.6	−1.7	13.2	2.5	15.6	..	111.1
Czech Republic	..	..	..	..	..	..	..	..	..	..
Denmark[a]	5.4	3.3	5.8	4.8	4.1	11.6	4.9	13.1	102.1	100.2
Dominican Republic	3.9	0.5	11.6	3.1	4.2	3.9	12.0	7.5	98.1	93.6
Ecuador	6.3	9.3	5.9	13.7	6.8	19.9	7.9	20.0	80.6	124.0
Egypt, Arab Rep.	−0.2	9.7	1.8	7.2	0.7	25.6	4.7	15.9	116.3	144.4
El Salvador	2.9	3.2	7.6	5.5	8.9	5.6	10.9	9.2	121.1	91.0
Eritrea	−28.3	−11.3	−3.2	−4.9	−31.1	−5.7	−0.2	1.7	101.7	90.1
Estonia	..	..	..	..	..	..	..	..	..	..
Ethiopia	10.5	7.7	7.3	18.0	10.7	18.2	7.3	26.4	151.0	111.5
Finland	..	..	..	..	..	..	..	..	110.6	81.0
France[a]	8.3	4.9	6.6	6.4	4.9	10.5	3.7	12.2	106.4	99.8
Gabon	5.2	−0.6	2.5	8.5	0.8	16.8	2.2	14.0	125.4	215.3
Gambia, The	−11.6	−4.6	0.1	2.6	−12.3	0.7	0.2	10.7	100.0	83.4
Georgia	..	..	..	..	..	..	..	..	..	..
Germany[a]	..	..	..	..	..	..	..	..	107.5	100.1
Ghana	7.7	4.7	8.6	11.4	9.0	15.7	8.3	18.3	106.7	151.3
Greece[a]	8.9	..	9.3	..	8.2	..	8.2	..	89.6	94.9
Guatemala	8.5	10.3	10.0	8.0	10.1	14.7	10.4	14.1	117.9	87.1
Guinea	5.0	−8.2	−1.4	4.3	0.6	8.2	−2.6	11.9	89.6	168.9
Guinea-Bissau	..	..	..	..	..	..	..	..	..	..
Haiti	12.6	5.8	13.3	2.5	12.2	8.6	14.4	9.9	113.2	62.4
Honduras	2.5	8.0	12.7	9.6	7.2	10.8	13.8	15.2	96.3	80.9
[†]Data for Taiwan, China	3.1	7.4	4.8	3.6	7.2	9.9	8.5	10.3	89.9	73.8

	Export volume		Import volume		Export value		Import value		Net barter terms of trade index	
	average annual % growth		average annual % growth		average annual % growth		average annual % growth		2000 = 100	
	1990–2000	2000–08	1990–2000	2000–08	1990–2000	2000–08	1990–2000	2000–08	1995	2008
Hungary[a]	10.1	12.3	11.6	9.7	10.1	19.1	11.8	17.4	104.3	93.8
India	6.9	11.6	9.0	18.5	5.3	21.4	7.9	26.8	108.0	91.5
Indonesia	10.0	..	2.9	..	7.8	..	0.1	..	90.4	..
Iran, Islamic Rep.	..	3.2	..	12.1	1.2	21.5	–4.8	20.9	..	175.3
Iraq	..	..	..	..	..	..	..	..	..	..
Ireland[a]	15.2	2.5	11.4	2.5	14.3	6.1	10.9	7.8	98.9	87.9
Israel[a]	9.7	4.9	8.9	2.7	10.0	10.1	8.2	8.9	92.1	92.9
Italy[a]	4.8	1.6	4.2	1.6	4.6	11.6	3.2	12.6	96.6	94.8
Jamaica	2.2	2.2	..	2.1	2.2	9.7	6.9	11.2	..	83.7
Japan[a]	2.6	4.5	5.3	3.0	2.1	5.2	5.2	10.2	114.9	61.7
Jordan	4.7	6.3	3.8	7.6	6.6	18.1	5.1	19.1	115.6	118.0
Kazakhstan	..	..	..	..	..	..	..	..	..	..
Kenya	3.9	6.1	7.4	8.9	6.3	13.7	6.0	18.8	103.9	83.2
Korea, Dem. Rep.	..	..	..	..	..	..	..	..	..	..
Korea, Rep.	15.8	13.2	10.0	7.9	10.1	14.4	7.1	15.4	138.5	62.3
Kosovo	..	..	..	..	..	..	..	..	..	..
Kuwait	..	10.6	..	13.0	16.5	25.0	5.5	18.1	..	165.7
Kyrgyz Republic	..	..	..	..	..	..	..	..	..	..
Lao PDR	..	9.5	..	7.6	15.4	19.3	12.7	15.0	..	112.9
Latvia[a]	7.2	..	..	..	11.8	..	..	..	..	..
Lebanon	..	14.8	..	1.8	4.1	23.7	8.7	10.9	..	91.8
Lesotho	13.3	18.7	3.1	8.6	12.8	18.8	1.9	13.5	100.0	71.9
Liberia	..	..	..	..	..	..	..	..	..	..
Libya	..	5.8	0.0	19.9	–2.6	26.0	–1.4	27.4	..	205.3
Lithuania	..	..	..	..	..	..	..	..	..	..
Macedonia, FYR	..	..	..	..	..	..	..	..	..	..
Madagascar	4.1	5.7	4.5	10.5	9.0	8.9	6.3	18.1	79.6	71.2
Malawi	2.7	6.8	–2.4	9.9	0.9	11.0	–0.6	17.7	105.7	76.2
Malaysia	13.6	7.4	10.6	7.2	12.2	11.5	9.5	10.8	108.5	104.4
Mali	10.3	2.5	6.4	8.3	6.3	15.7	4.7	17.4	109.6	140.1
Mauritania	1.9	7.8	4.2	13.3	–1.9	25.5	–1.6	20.6	102.2	190.9
Mauritius	2.7	4.3	3.4	8.2	2.2	4.6	3.3	11.1	88.5	81.8
Mexico	15.5	3.7	13.2	4.4	16.1	8.7	14.2	8.3	92.5	105.9
Moldova	..	..	..	..	..	..	..	..	..	..
Mongolia	..	5.3	..	13.9	0.7	23.8	0.5	23.4	..	180.5
Morocco	7.5	3.6	7.2	8.8	7.2	12.1	5.5	17.8	89.1	98.4
Mozambique	15.2	15.9	1.0	9.6	10.2	27.6	1.1	17.4	151.1	107.7
Myanmar	15.5	5.6	13.8	–2.0	14.4	18.0	22.6	4.8	214.3	144.4
Namibia	2.4	6.7	7.7	10.0	0.9	15.4	3.9	14.8	82.6	120.6
Nepal	..	–1.4	..	–6.0	10.7	4.9	9.3	3.4	..	78.5
Netherlands[a]	8.0	5.4	8.4	5.4	5.7	13.5	5.5	13.1	97.6	103.1
New Zealand[a]	4.6	3.0	5.9	7.6	3.9	11.2	5.7	13.5	102.0	126.2
Nicaragua	10.4	9.3	9.3	6.1	10.3	12.4	11.6	12.3	128.9	75.2
Niger	3.1	–7.1	–2.1	9.1	0.0	15.7	0.8	18.3	121.4	232.9
Nigeria	3.3	0.8	2.5	13.6	1.1	19.9	3.1	21.1	55.6	209.8
Norway[a]	6.6	0.4	7.8	6.8	5.7	15.4	4.4	14.8	60.3	156.7
Oman	4.0	–3.2	..	8.5	5.7	16.1	6.1	19.3	..	155.6
Pakistan	2.5	8.5	2.4	9.8	4.3	11.6	3.1	21.2	119.2	57.6
Panama	6.0	2.5	7.8	9.5	9.4	4.4	8.7	13.8	100.0	85.9
Papua New Guinea	–7.7	–2.5	..	6.9	3.7	16.4	–0.8	16.1	..	177.1
Paraguay	–0.2	15.7	5.4	18.9	1.7	20.8	7.0	23.7	118.3	107.3
Peru	9.4	9.1	10.6	9.6	9.0	24.3	10.8	17.3	123.4	136.9
Philippines	16.0	4.1	11.3	1.9	18.8	4.7	12.5	7.6	80.2	66.5
Poland[a]	9.8	13.4	19.0	10.9	9.5	24.9	17.0	21.0	102.4	106.9
Portugal[a]	0.3	..	0.5	..	–3.0	..	–2.6	..	104.7	..
Puerto Rico	..	..	..	..	..	..	..	..	..	..
Qatar	..	5.5	..	26.7	10.1	25.0	7.4	32.2	..	249.4

	Export volume		Import volume		Export value		Import value		Net barter terms of trade index	
	average annual % growth		average annual % growth		average annual % growth		average annual % growth		2000 = 100	
	1990–2000	2000–08	1990–2000	2000–08	1990–2000	2000–08	1990–2000	2000–08	1995	2008
Romania	..	..	..	..	..	..	..	..	..	..
Russian Federation	..	..	..	..	..	..	..	..	..	..
Rwanda	–8.0	4.7	0.8	14.0	–4.0	19.4	–1.7	21.6	110.1	169.5
Saudi Arabia	2.9	2.2	..	13.7	3.1	22.1	0.8	19.4	..	236.2
Senegal	10.6	0.7	4.9	6.7	4.0	9.7	3.6	16.8	156.3	94.0
Serbia	..	..	..	..	..	..	..	..	..	..
Sierra Leone	..	..	..	..	..	..	..	..	..	..
Singapore	11.7	12.7	8.3	9.2	9.9	14.8	7.8	13.9	104.3	83.0
Slovak Republic	..	..	..	..	..	..	..	..	..	..
Slovenia	..	..	..	..	..	..	..	..	..	..
Somalia	..	..	..	..	..	..	..	..	..	..
South Africa	4.5	1.7	7.6	8.8	2.5	15.0	5.8	19.3	106.0	130.0
Spain[a]	11.4	4.0	9.3	6.5	8.6	12.8	6.2	15.1	104.3	102.8
Sri Lanka	7.4	3.9	8.0	2.7	11.3	7.2	8.9	11.1	99.0	68.6
Sudan	12.6	9.1	8.4	21.5	14.0	28.8	9.8	27.2	100.0	232.2
Swaziland	4.0	10.1	3.1	7.5	5.9	16.0	5.0	14.4	100.0	92.5
Sweden[a]	8.9	3.9	6.4	2.1	7.4	10.2	5.4	10.3	110.2	86.6
Switzerland[a]	3.7	4.9	4.2	3.2	4.4	6.6	3.6	5.5	96.4	99.4
Syrian Arab Republic	2.2	0.3	..	13.8	0.9	15.0	3.6	22.7	..	145.3
Tajikistan	..	..	..	..	..	..	..	..	..	..
Tanzania	6.0	5.9	–2.0	12.3	6.4	16.8	0.1	21.9	98.0	108.9
Thailand	9.6	8.8	2.6	10.0	10.5	14.0	5.0	15.3	116.0	94.3
Timor-Leste	..	..	..	..	..	..	..	..	..	..
Togo	9.1	16.8	6.0	–7.3	6.6	10.1	5.5	16.6	99.1	21.4
Trinidad and Tobago	..	5.8	..	3.8	6.8	23.8	12.1	14.3	..	157.5
Tunisia	5.7	9.3	4.3	5.8	6.0	15.3	5.2	13.1	95.8	95.0
Turkey	10.7	13.1	11.1	11.9	9.2	22.3	10.3	22.1	105.7	91.2
Turkmenistan	..	..	..	..	..	..	..	..	..	..
Uganda	17.8	15.3	22.4	8.6	15.4	25.4	21.0	16.6	197.2	106.2
Ukraine	..	..	..	..	..	..	..	..	..	..
United Arab Emirates	..	8.5	..	16.6	6.5	22.8	10.7	23.0	..	148.1
United Kingdom[a]	6.2	2.1	6.5	4.5	6.2	8.5	6.5	10.4	100.1	105.0
United States[a]	6.6	4.9	9.1	4.5	7.2	7.7	9.5	8.7	103.3	91.8
Uruguay	6.1	9.1	10.5	6.3	5.2	15.0	10.1	14.3	116.2	92.3
Uzbekistan	..	..	..	..	..	..	..	..	..	..
Venezuela, RB	5.2	–2.4	4.8	14.2	5.4	16.2	5.3	18.3	63.4	249.5
Vietnam	..	13.2	..	14.3	22.7	21.3	22.7	23.4	..	92.8
West Bank and Gaza	..	..	..	..	..	..	..	..	..	..
Yemen, Rep.	..	–4.5	4.4	11.1	20.6	12.8	0.6	21.0	..	165.4
Zambia	6.1	8.4	2.9	17.1	–4.6	28.0	1.3	24.8	189.7	170.6
Zimbabwe ·	8.8	–5.8	8.0	–5.6	3.4	3.5	1.9	4.7	96.8	91.5

a. Data are from the International Monetary Fund's International Financial Statistics database.

About the data

Data on international trade in goods are available from each country's balance of payments and customs records. While the balance of payments focuses on the financial transactions that accompany trade, customs data record the direction of trade and the physical quantities and value of goods entering or leaving the customs area. Customs data may differ from data recorded in the balance of payments because of differences in valuation and time of recording. The 1993 United Nations System of National Accounts and the fifth edition of the International Monetary Fund's (IMF) *Balance of Payments Manual* (1993) attempted to reconcile definitions and reporting standards for international trade statistics, but differences in sources, timing, and national practices limit comparability. Real growth rates derived from trade volume indexes and terms of trade based on unit price indexes may therefore differ from those derived from national accounts aggregates.

Trade in goods, or merchandise trade, includes all goods that add to or subtract from an economy's material resources. Trade data are collected on the basis of a country's customs area, which in most cases is the same as its geographic area. Goods provided as part of foreign aid are included, but goods destined for extraterritorial agencies (such as embassies) are not.

Collecting and tabulating trade statistics are difficult. Some developing countries lack the capacity to report timely data, especially landlocked countries and countries whose territorial boundaries are porous. Their trade has to be estimated from the data reported by their partners. (For further discussion of the use of partner country reports, see *About the data* for table 6.3.) Countries that belong to common customs unions may need to collect data through direct inquiry of companies. Economic or political concerns may lead some national authorities to suppress or misrepresent data on certain trade flows, such as oil, military equipment, or the exports of a dominant producer. In other cases reported trade data may be distorted by deliberate under- or over-invoicing to affect capital transfers or avoid taxes. And in some regions smuggling and black market trading result in unreported trade flows.

By international agreement customs data are reported to the United Nations Statistics Division, which maintains the Commodity Trade (Comtrade) and Monthly Bulletin of Statistics databases. The United Nations Conference on Trade and Development (UNCTAD) compiles international trade statistics, including price, value, and volume indexes, from national and international sources such as the IMF's International Financial Statistics database, the United Nations Economic Commission for Latin America and the Caribbean, the United Nations Statistics Division's Monthly Bulletin of Statistics database, the World Bank Africa Database, the U.S. Bureau of Labor Statistics, Japan Customs, and UNCTAD's Commodity Price Statistics. The IMF also compiles data on trade prices and volumes in its International Financial Statistics (IFS) database.

Unless otherwise noted, the growth rates and terms of trade in the table were calculated from index numbers compiled by UNCTAD. The growth rates and terms of trade for selected economies were calculated from index numbers compiled in the IMF's *International Financial Statistics*. In some cases price and volume indexes from different sources vary significantly as a result of differences in estimation procedures. Because the IMF does not publish trade value indexes, for selected economies the trade value indexes were derived from the volume and price indexes. All indexes are rescaled to a 2000 base year.

The terms of trade measures the relative prices of a country's exports and imports. There are several ways to calculate it. The most common is the net barter (or commodity) terms of trade index, or the ratio of the export price index to the import price index. When a country's net barter terms of trade index increases, its exports become more valuable or its imports cheaper.

Definitions

• **Export** and **import volumes** are indexes of the quantity of goods traded. They are derived from UNCTAD's volume index series and are the ratio of the export or import value indexes to the corresponding unit value indexes. Unit value indexes are based on data reported by countries that demonstrate consistency under UNCTAD quality controls, supplemented by UNCTAD's estimates using the previous year's trade values at the Standard International Trade Classification three-digit level as weights. For economies for which UNCTAD does not publish data, the export and import volume indexes (lines 72 and 73) in the IMF's *International Financial Statistics* are used to calculate the average annual growth rates.
• **Export** and **import values** are the current value of exports (free on board, f.o.b.) or imports (cost, insurance, and freight, c.i.f.), converted to U.S. dollars and expressed as a percentage of the average for the base period (2000). UNCTAD's export or import value indexes are reported for most economies. For selected economies for which UNCTAD does not publish data, the value indexes are derived from export or import volume indexes (lines 72 and 73) and corresponding unit value indexes of exports or imports (lines 74 and 75) in the IMF's *International Financial Statistics*. • **Net barter terms of trade index** is calculated as the percentage ratio of the export unit value indexes to the import unit value indexes, measured relative to the base year 2000.

Data sources

Data on trade indexes are from UNCTAD's annual *Handbook of Statistics* for most economies and from the IMF's *International Financial Statistics* for selected economies.

6.3 Direction and growth of merchandise trade

High-income importers

% of world trade, 2008

Source of exports	European Union	Japan	United States	Other high-income	Total
High-income economies	27.9	2.5	7.1	11.6	49.2
European Union	22.1	0.4	2.3	3.4	28.2
Japan	0.7	..	0.9	1.5	3.0
United States	1.7	0.4	..	3.0	5.1
Other high-income economies	3.5	1.7	4.0	3.6	12.9
Low- and middle-income economies	8.2	1.7	5.6	5.5	21.0
East Asia & Pacific	2.2	1.3	2.1	3.8	9.3
China	1.7	0.7	1.6	2.7	6.7
Europe & Central Asia	3.4	0.1	0.2	0.5	4.2
Russian Federation	1.4	0.1	0.1	0.2	1.7
Latin America & Caribbean	0.8	0.1	2.3	0.5	3.7
Brazil	0.3	0.0	0.2	0.1	0.6
Middle East & N. Africa	1.0	0.1	0.3	0.3	1.7
Algeria	0.3	0.0	0.1	0.0	0.4
South Asia	0.3	0.0	0.2	0.4	0.9
India	0.2	0.0	0.1	0.3	0.7
Sub-Saharan Africa	0.5	0.1	0.5	0.1	1.2
South Africa	0.1	0.1	0.1	0.1	0.3
World	36.2	4.3	12.7	17.1	70.2

Low- and middle-income importers

% of world trade, 2008

Source of exports	East Asia & Pacific	Europe & Central Asia	Latin America & Caribbean	Middle East & N. Africa	South Asia	Sub-Saharan Africa	Total
High-income economies	7.3	4.1	3.3	1.2	1.3	1.0	18.4
European Union	1.0	3.3	0.7	0.7	0.3	0.5	6.6
Japan	1.3	0.2	0.2	0.0	0.1	0.1	1.8
United States	0.7	0.2	1.7	0.1	0.1	0.1	3.0
Other high-income economies	4.3	0.4	0.6	0.4	0.8	0.3	6.9
Low- and middle-income economies	2.3	2.9	1.9	0.8	0.9	0.7	9.8
East Asia & Pacific	1.4	0.6	0.5	0.2	0.4	0.3	3.5
China	0.5	0.6	0.4	0.2	0.3	0.2	2.2
Europe & Central Asia	0.2	2.0	0.1	0.2	0.1	0.0	2.7
Russian Federation	0.2	0.8	0.0	0.1	0.0	0.0	1.1
Latin America & Caribbean	0.3	0.1	1.1	0.1	0.1	0.1	1.7
Brazil	0.1	0.0	0.3	0.0	0.0	0.0	0.6
Middle East & N. Africa	0.2	0.1	0.1	0.2	0.2	0.1	0.8
Algeria	0.0	0.0	0.0	0.0	0.0	0.0	0.1
South Asia	0.1	0.0	0.0	0.1	0.1	0.1	0.4
India	0.1	0.0	0.0	0.0	0.1	0.1	0.4
Sub-Saharan Africa	0.1	0.0	0.1	0.0	0.1	0.2	0.7
South Africa	0.0	0.0	0.0	0.0	0.0	0.1	0.2
World	10.2	6.9	5.1	2.0	2.3	1.7	28.2

Direction and growth of merchandise trade

Nominal growth of trade

High-income importers

average annual % growth, 1998–2008

Source of exports	European Union	Japan	United States	Other high-income	Total
High-income economies	9.7	7.9	5.8	9.0	8.8
European Union	10.1	5.9	7.6	9.7	9.8
Japan	4.1	..	1.4	8.1	4.8
United States	5.4	0.7	..	6.0	5.3
Other high-income economies	10.8	11.7	6.1	12.3	9.5
Low- and middle-income economies	18.4	13.1	12.9	18.2	16.1
East Asia & Pacific	19.4	12.4	16.3	18.0	17.0
China	27.7	15.1	23.5	23.7	23.2
Europe & Central Asia	22.0	16.5	10.1	20.8	20.9
Russian Federation	23.9	15.8	5.9	20.0	21.5
Latin America & Caribbean	13.2	11.8	9.3	17.1	10.8
Brazil	12.7	10.1	11.1	20.7	13.3
Middle East & N. Africa	16.6	19.0	26.7	20.5	18.7
Algeria	18.1	16.8	30.7	29.8	22.0
South Asia	14.1	6.1	9.7	20.0	14.5
India	15.9	7.5	12.1	22.4	17.0
Sub-Saharan Africa	12.3	23.2	21.4	14.1	16.1
South Africa[a]	12.6	25.0	17.4	14.6	15.2
World	11.1	9.7	8.4	11.2	10.5

Low- and middle-income importers

average annual % growth, 1998–2008

Source of exports	East Asia & Pacific	Europe & Central Asia	Latin America & Caribbean	Middle East & N. Africa	South Asia	Sub-Saharan Africa	Total
High-income economies	16.4	18.8	7.6	12.9	18.2	12.6	14.4
European Union	15.9	18.8	8.0	11.2	16.1	11.5	14.9
Japan	14.2	28.0	7.4	10.5	11.2	10.7	13.3
United States	12.1	12.6	6.5	10.6	18.5	11.6	8.6
Other high-income economies	18.2	20.1	11.9	19.0	20.3	15.9	17.8
Low- and middle-income economies	23.9	23.9	17.1	23.0	24.3	21.3	22.3
East Asia & Pacific	22.4	37.6	25.7	24.6	26.1	26.1	25.5
China	28.4	41.1	30.8	30.1	35.0	30.7	32.5
Europe & Central Asia	20.8	21.9	20.2	22.3	23.2	20.6	21.9
Russian Federation	21.2	21.9	21.8	23.7	21.7	14.7	21.8
Latin America & Caribbean	31.8	20.8	13.9	16.3	22.7	25.1	17.1
Brazil	31.2	22.2	15.9	19.3	18.0	27.0	19.4
Middle East & N. Africa	31.2	22.1	18.8	27.3	31.8	27.5	26.9
Algeria	64.2	14.1	12.1	27.7	86.5	8.3	19.9
South Asia	27.5	15.5	23.0	24.1	20.8	24.0	23.1
India	29.8	14.7	26.0	27.9	21.1	25.1	24.9
Sub-Saharan Africa	22.8	23.2	25.0	13.6	14.0	15.2	21.5
South Africa[a]	28.5	20.0	10.9	19.5	17.9	12.4	16.0
World	18.1	20.6	10.1	15.8	20.3	15.5	16.5

a. Data for 1998 are based on imports from South Africa reported by other economies because data on exports for South Africa were not available.

The table provides estimates of the flow of trade in goods between groups of economies. The data are from the International Monetary Fund's (IMF) Direction of Trade database. All high-income economies and major developing economies report trade on a timely basis, covering about 85 percent of trade for recent years. Trade by less timely reporters and by countries that do not report is estimated using reports of trading partner countries. Because the largest exporting and importing countries are reliable reporters, a large portion of the missing trade flows can be estimated from partner reports. Partner country data may introduce discrepancies due to smuggling, confidentiality, different exchange rates, overreporting of transit trade, inclusion or exclusion of freight rates, and different points of valuation and times of recording.

In addition, estimates of trade within the European Union (EU) have been significantly affected by changes in reporting methods following the creation of a customs union. The current system for collecting data on trade between EU members—Intrastat, introduced in 1993—has less exhaustive coverage than the previous customs-based system and has resulted in some problems of asymmetry (estimated imports are about 5 percent less than exports). Despite these issues, only a small portion of world trade is estimated to be omitted from the IMF's *Direction of Trade Statistics Yearbook* and Direction of Trade database.

Most countries report their trade data in national currencies, which are converted into U.S. dollars using the IMF's published period average exchange rate (series rf or rh, monthly averages of the market or official rates) for the reporting country or, if unavailable, monthly average rates in New York. Because imports are reported at cost, insurance, and freight (c.i.f.) valuations, and exports at free on board (f.o.b.) valuations, the IMF adjusts country reports of import values by dividing them by 1.10 to estimate equivalent export values. The accuracy of this approximation depends on the set of partners and the items traded. Other factors affecting the accuracy of trade data include lags in reporting, recording differences across countries, and whether the country reports trade according to the general or special system of trade. (For further discussion of the measurement of exports and imports, see *About the data* for tables 4.4 and 4.5.)

The regional trade flows in the table are calculated from current price values. The growth rates are in nominal terms; that is, they include the effects of changes in both volumes and prices.

• **Merchandise trade** includes all trade in goods; trade in services is excluded. • **High-income economies** are those classified as such by the World Bank (see inside front cover). • **European Union** is defined as all high-income EU members: Austria, Belgium, Cyprus, Czech Republic, Denmark, Estonia, Finland, France, Germany, Greece, Hungary, Ireland, Italy, Luxembourg, Malta, the Netherlands, Portugal, Slovak Republic, Slovenia, Spain, Sweden, and the United Kingdom. • **Other high-income economies** include all high-income economies (both Organisation for Economic Co-operation and Development members and others) except the high-income European Union, Japan, and the United States. • **Low- and middle-income regional groupings** are based on World Bank classifications (see inside back cover for regional groupings) and may differ from those used by other organizations.

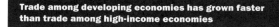

Trade among developing economies has grown faster than trade among high-income economies   **6.3a**

Annual average growth of merchandise trade, 1998–2008 (percent)

 High-income importers   Low- and middle-income importers

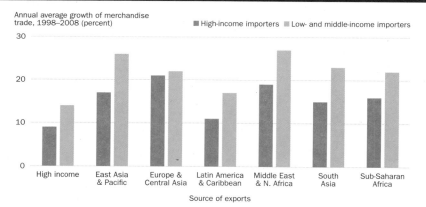

Low- and middle-income economies increased their imports from other low- and middle-income economies. High-income economies are also increasingly importing from low- and middle-income economies.

Source: World Bank staff calculations based on data from the International Monetary Fund's Direction of Trade database.

Exports to low-income economies

	High-income economies		European Union		Japan		United States	
	1998	2008	1998	2008	1998	2008	1998	2008
Total ($ billions)	47.0	146.3	21.7	56.2	5.2	15.4	4.5	15.9
% of total exports								
Food	12.2	8.9	14.4	10.2	1.0	0.9	23.9	21.4
Cereals	4.3	3.0	3.6	2.3	0.5	0.1	17.0	12.9
Agricultural raw materials	2.1	2.1	1.5	1.5	1.2	1.6	5.1	6.2
Ores and nonferrous metals	1.1	1.9	0.9	1.3	0.6	1.4	0.6	1.9
Fuels	3.7	15.9	2.2	14.8	1.1	2.4	1.0	6.7
Crude petroleum	0.0	0.5	0.0	0.0	0.0	0.0	0.0	0.0
Petroleum products	3.5	15.0	2.0	14.5	1.0	2.3	0.8	6.3
Manufactured goods	78.9	65.9	79.0	69.2	92.6	90.2	65.2	59.4
Chemical products	12.3	10.3	14.2	11.1	5.1	5.3	11.6	6.3
Iron and steel	3.0	3.8	2.4	2.3	7.7	11.4	1.7	1.4
Machinery and transport equipment	45.4	38.6	46.2	42.0	66.4	61.3	40.1	43.6
Furniture	0.3	0.2	0.5	0.4	0.1	0.1	0.3	0.2
Textiles	6.2	3.7	2.3	1.8	5.0	3.3	4.0	0.7
Footwear	0.4	0.2	0.3	0.2	0.0	0.0	0.5	0.3
Other	11.2	9.0	13.2	11.4	8.3	8.7	7.1	6.9
Miscellaneous goods	1.7	4.8	1.2	2.9	3.6	3.5	4.2	4.4

Imports from low-income economies

	High-income economies		European Union		Japan		United States	
Total ($ billions)	49.6	188.4	25.4	73.7	4.0	14.8	11.7	71.4
% of total imports								
Food	23.5	11.9	30.4	18.5	32.1	11.8	10.6	4.3
Cereals	0.3	0.6	0.2	0.4	0.1	0.2	0.1	0.1
Agricultural raw materials	6.6	2.3	8.5	3.7	6.1	2.4	1.0	0.6
Ores and nonferrous metals	4.6	4.0	4.9	5.9	9.8	7.0	2.4	0.4
Fuels	21.0	43.7	10.9	31.2	14.3	37.8	41.1	62.1
Crude petroleum	19.6	36.9	10.4	23.1	11.7	22.5	37.6	58.3
Petroleum products	1.1	1.9	0.3	0.4	0.6	2.2	3.1	3.2
Manufactured goods	42.7	35.9	43.8	40.0	35.5	38.2	44.2	32.2
Chemical products	0.9	1.1	1.1	1.0	0.4	1.5	0.3	0.7
Iron and steel	0.5	0.3	0.4	0.3	1.4	0.5	0.3	0.2
Machinery and transport equipment	3.5	3.6	2.6	2.3	3.7	16.4	0.2	1.4
Furniture	0.6	2.0	0.6	1.7	1.9	2.1	0.2	2.6
Textiles	26.1	20.4	23.1	23.3	21.8	9.2	38.0	22.9
Footwear	3.4	3.8	5.2	6.5	1.5	2.7	1.1	1.8
Other	7.8	4.5	10.8	5.1	4.8	5.8	4.2	2.6
Miscellaneous goods	1.6	2.3	1.2	0.7	2.3	2.8	0.7	0.5

Simple applied tariff rates on imports from low-income economies (%)[a]

	High-income economies		European Union		Japan		United States	
Average	5.5	3.9	1.7	0.9	3.3	1.9	5.3	4.2
Food	6.8	4.2	5.3	1.0	9.6	3.8	3.4	1.5
Cereals	8.9	2.2	30.0	0.0	4.4	7.4	1.7	1.0
Agricultural raw materials	2.5	1.5	0.2	0.1	1.5	0.2	0.3	0.2
Ores and nonferrous metals	1.6	1.1	0.3	0.3	0.8	0.0	0.2	0.6
Fuels	3.1	1.1	0.0	0.0	2.6	0.2	0.5	0.7
Crude petroleum	1.3	0.7	0.0	0.0	1.2	0.0	0.9	1.2
Petroleum products	5.1	1.5	0.0	0.0	6.0	0.6	6.2	4.8
Manufactured goods	5.6	4.1	1.2	1.0	2.3	1.8	5.6	
Chemical products	3.8	2.6	1.2	0.4	3.3	0.3	0.7	1.1
Iron and steel	5.1	2.1	0.3	0.2	0.6	0.0	1.3	0.8
Machinery and transport equipment	2.5	1.7	0.3	0.2	0.1	0.0	0.5	0.6
Furniture	4.3	3.5	0.2	0.1	0.0	0.0	0.9	1.2
Textiles	9.0	6.8	3.1	2.8	4.3	3.4	11.2	9.5
Footwear	8.6	6.4	3.1	2.0	7.7	7.1	13.4	8.4
Other	3.3	2.4	0.5	0.2	0.6	0.7	1.6	1.2
Miscellaneous goods	0.9	0.8	0.0	0.0	0.0	0.0	0.0	0.0

Exports to middle-income economies

	High-income economies		European Union		Japan		United States	
	1998	2008	1998	2008	1998	2008	1998	2008
Total ($ billions)	691.6	2,371.8	280.7	1,004.8	81.8	280.1	191.8	425.5
% of total exports								
Food	7.3	5.9	8.1	5.7	0.6	0.3	8.8	12.0
Cereals	1.6	1.3	1.1	0.9	0.2	0.0	2.8	3.8
Agricultural raw materials	1.8	1.8	1.2	1.4	1.1	0.9	2.5	3.5
Ores and nonferrous metals	1.8	4.1	1.5	2.6	1.7	3.4	1.6	4.3
Fuels	2.4	7.0	1.4	3.3	0.5	2.6	2.0	7.7
Crude petroleum	0.4	1.0	0.1	0.1	0.0	0.0	0.0	0.0
Petroleum products	1.4	4.9	1.1	2.8	0.4	2.5	1.3	6.0
Manufactured goods	84.2	77.2	85.7	83.4	94.0	88.5	81.4	69.2
Chemical products	11.6	13.0	12.9	13.3	7.6	8.8	10.5	14.1
Iron and steel	2.7	3.8	2.8	4.0	6.1	7.5	1.0	1.7
Machinery and transport equipment	49.3	44.5	46.7	46.9	66.6	60.6	50.5	39.8
Furniture	0.6	0.4	0.8	0.7	0.1	0.2	0.7	0.3
Textiles	6.0	2.5	5.7	3.4	3.1	1.4	5.3	2.0
Footwear	0.4	0.2	0.6	0.5	0.0	0.0	0.2	0.1
Other	13.7	12.7	16.0	14.5	10.6	10.0	13.1	11.2
Miscellaneous goods	2.2	3.5	1.6	3.1	2.1	4.2	3.8	3.3

Imports from middle-income economies

	High-income economies		European Union		Japan		United States	
Total ($ billions)	914.3	3,595.8	285.2	1,364.7	90.5	315.7	320.0	1,023.2
% of total imports								
Food	10.8	6.5	14.8	8.4	17.2	7.3	7.2	4.7
Cereals	0.5	0.4	0.3	0.6	0.6	0.2	0.2	0.2
Agricultural raw materials	2.6	1.3	3.7	1.6	4.6	2.2	1.3	0.9
Ores and nonferrous metals	5.3	4.8	7.0	4.9	9.5	11.0	2.9	2.4
Fuels	11.2	24.0	15.3	27.7	13.1	23.4	9.8	26.1
Crude petroleum	7.2	16.2	9.8	19.1	5.5	10.7	7.5	21.8
Petroleum products	1.5	4.1	1.9	4.1	0.8	3.1	1.9	3.7
Manufactured goods	68.1	61.3	56.9	55.2	54.2	54.5	76.1	63.8
Chemical products	3.2	3.9	4.1	3.9	3.0	4.4	2.1	3.2
Iron and steel	2.5	3.7	2.7	3.7	1.3	2.1	2.2	2.5
Machinery and transport equipment	27.9	29.4	17.7	23.9	20.2	25.1	35.9	32.1
Furniture	1.6	1.8	1.7	1.8	1.3	1.3	2.0	2.4
Textiles	14.5	7.9	15.7	8.8	14.4	8.7	13.5	7.6
Footwear	2.8	1.4	1.9	1.4	1.7	1.1	3.6	1.7
Other	15.6	13.4	13.1	11.9	12.3	11.8	16.8	14.3
Miscellaneous goods	2.0	1.8	1.9	1.3	1.4	1.5	2.6	2.1

Simple applied tariff rates on imports from middle-income economies (%)[a]

	High-income economies		European Union		Japan		United States	
Average	5.9	4.2	3.5	1.1	2.7	2.5	3.8	2.6
Food	9.6	6.0	13.0	2.8	12.2	7.0	3.9	2.9
Cereals	11.3	6.4	32.3	0.5	15.7	11.2	1.2	0.7
Agricultural raw materials	2.6	2.0	0.9	0.4	1.3	0.6	0.6	0.4
Ores and nonferrous metals	2.1	1.3	1.3	0.5	0.1	0.1	0.6	0.4
Fuels	3.1	1.4	0.1	0.0	1.4	0.3	0.5	1.1
Crude petroleum	5.5	0.6	0.0	0.0	1.2	0.0	0.5	0.0
Petroleum products	6.1	2.4	0.3	0.1	6.0	1.0	1.5	2.9
Manufactured goods	5.6	4.1	2.7	0.9	1.5	2.1	4.0	2.7
Chemical products	3.7	2.5	2.0	0.6	0.7	0.3	1.7	1.1
Iron and steel	3.4	2.0	1.2	0.1	0.1	0.2	2.8	0.3
Machinery and transport equipment	3.7	2.6	1.1	0.2	0.0	0.0	0.6	0.5
Furniture	5.8	4.6	0.6	0.0	0.0	0.1	0.6	0.4
Textiles	9.9	7.5	6.8	3.1	4.4	5.7	11.1	7.6
Footwear	9.6	7.2	6.5	2.8	12.8	16.7	11.6	6.9
Other	5.3	5.1	1.4	0.3	0.4	0.8	1.2	0.8
Miscellaneous goods	0.8	0.4	0.0	0.0	0.0	0.0	0.9	0.2

a. Includes ad valorem equivalents of specific rates.

Developing economies are becoming increasingly important in the global trading system. Since the early 1990s trade between high-income economies and low- and middle-income economies has grown faster than trade among high-income economies. The increased trade benefits consumers and producers. But as was apparent at the World Trade Organization's (WTO) Ministerial Conferences in Doha, Qatar, in October 2001; Cancun, Mexico, in September 2003; and Hong Kong SAR, China, in December 2005, achieving a more pro-development outcome from trade remains a challenge. Doing so will require strengthening international consultation. After the Doha meetings negotiations were launched on services, agriculture, manufactures, WTO rules, the environment, dispute settlement, intellectual property rights protection, and disciplines on regional integration. At the most recent negotiations in Hong Kong SAR, China, trade ministers agreed to eliminate subsidies of agricultural exports by 2013; to abolish cotton export subsidies and grant unlimited export access to selected cotton-growing countries in Sub-Saharan Africa; to cut more domestic farm supports in the European Union, Japan, and the United States; and to offer more aid to developing countries to help them compete in global trade.

Trade flows between high-income and low- and middle-income economies reflect the changing mix of exports to and imports from developing economies. While food and primary commodities have continued to fall as a share of high-income economies' imports,

manufactures as a share of goods imports from both low- and middle-income economies have grown. And trade between developing economies has grown substantially over the past decade, a result of their increasing share of world output and liberalization of trade, among other influences.

Yet trade barriers remain high. The table includes information about tariff rates by selected product groups. Applied tariff rates are the tariffs in effect for partners in preferential trade agreements such as the North American Free Trade Agreement. When these rates are unavailable, most favored nation rates are used. The difference between most favored nation and applied rates can be substantial. Simple averages of applied rates are shown because they are generally a better indicator of tariff protection than weighted average rates are.

The data are from the United Nations Conference on Trade and Development (UNCTAD). Partner country reports by high-income economies were used for both exports and imports. Because of differences in sources of data, timing, and treatment of missing data, the numbers in the table may not be fully comparable with those used to calculate the direction of trade statistics in table 6.3 or the aggregate flows in tables 4.4, 4.5, and 6.2. Tariff line data were matched to Standard International Trade Classification (SITC) revision 3 codes to define commodity groups. For further discussion of merchandise trade statistics, see *About the data* for tables 4.4, 4.5, 6.2, 6.3, and 6.5, and for information about tariff barriers, see table 6.8.

The product groups in the table are defined in accordance with SITC revision 3: **food** (0, 1, 22, and 4) and **cereals** (04); **agricultural raw materials** (2 excluding 22, 27, and 28); **ores and nonferrous metals** (27, 28, and 68); **fuels** (3), **crude petroleum** (crude petroleum oils and oils obtained from bituminous minerals; 333), and **petroleum products** (noncrude petroleum and preparations; 334); **manufactured goods** (5–8 excluding 68), **chemical products** (5), **iron and steel** (67), **machinery and transport equipment** (7), **furniture** (82), **textiles** (65 and 84), **footwear** (85), and **other manufactured goods** (6 and 8 excluding 65, 67, 68, 82, 84, and 85); and **miscellaneous goods** (9). • **Exports** are all merchandise exports by high-income economies to low-income and middle-income economies as recorded in the United Nations Statistics Division's Comtrade database. Exports are recorded free on board (f.o.b.). • **Imports** are all merchandise imports by high-income economies from low-income and middle-income economies as recorded in the United Nations Statistics Division's Commodity Trade (Comtrade) database. Imports include insurance and freight charges (c.i.f.). • **High-, middle-, and low-income economies** are those classified as such by the World Bank (see inside front cover). • **European Union** is defined as all high-income EU members: Austria, Belgium, Cyprus, Czech Republic, Denmark, Estonia, Finland, France, Germany, Greece, Hungary, Ireland, Italy, Luxembourg, Malta, the Netherlands, Portugal, Slovak Republic, Slovenia, Spain, Sweden, and the United Kingdom.

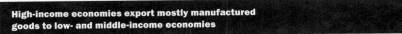

High-income economies export mostly manufactured goods to low- and middle-income economies   **6.4a**

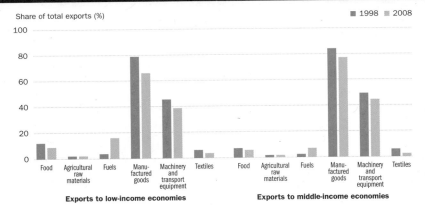

Some 65–75 percent of high-income economy exports to low-income and middle-income economies in 2008 were manufactured goods. Machinery and equipment accounted for nearly 60 percent of manufactured goods exports from high-income economies.

Source: World Bank staff calculations based on data from the United Nations Statistics Division's Comtrade database.

Data on trade values are from United Nations Statistics Division's Comtrade database. Data on tariffs are from UNCTAD's Trade Analysis and Information System database and are calculated by World Bank staff using the World Integrated Trade Solution system.

	Exports — % of total merchandise exports						Imports — % of total merchandise imports					
	To developing economies				To high-income economies		From developing economies				From high-income economies	
	Within region		Outside region				Within region		Outside region			
	1998	2008	1998	2008	1998	2008	1998	2008	1998	2008	1998	2008
East Asia & Pacific	**7.7 w**	**10.8 w**	**7.9 w**	**16.3 w**	**83.1 w**	**72.0 w**	**7.6 w**	**12.6 w**	**7.9 w**	**16.3 w**	**81.3 w**	**63.9 w**
Cambodia	..	..	0.8	1.8	66.1	90.4	..	65.6	1.8	1.4	60.4	32.9
China	4.1	6.0	9.4	18.9	86.4	75.0	6.2	8.8	8.1	18.4	83.6	64.6
Indonesia	11.2	19.1	8.0	13.7	80.7	67.3	10.8	24.8	6.8	9.4	81.9	65.7
Kiribati	..	..	..	..	67.5	50.9	..	..	..	..	..	..
Korea, Dem. Rep.	..	..	43.6	52.3	48.6	11.1	..	..	17.7	55.1	46.5	7.8
Lao PDR	..	..	0.5	1.0	39.4	19.0	..	..	..	1.2	16.1	12.2
Malaysia	9.9	20.5	8.1	11.5	82.0	67.9	12.4	26.1	3.0	6.1	83.3	66.7
Mongolia	..	..	12.3	4.2	58.4	31.2	..	..	..	43.6	52.5	26.7
Myanmar	11.6	65.5	18.0	15.6	55.4	13.6	..	..	2.0	4.2	50.9	33.0
Papua New Guinea	8.8	9.0	0.9	2.3	58.6	51.0	8.3	21.8	1.3	1.2	89.5	75.3
Philippines	7.9	20.4	1.9	2.4	90.0	76.8	13.4	22.7	3.7	4.2	82.3	73.1
Thailand	11.8	26.2	5.5	12.2	76.5	61.0	13.3	24.6	5.7	8.5	75.2	65.5
Tonga	6.1	18.0	..	..	74.3	79.9	7.4	47.6	..	..	84.6	48.5
Vietnam	18.6	19.3	6.5	4.1	74.9	68.9	17.1	32.0	3.9	5.6	78.9	49.0
Europe & Central Asia	**28.6 w**	**28.1 w**	**8.8 w**	**10.3 w**	**60.5 w**	**60.2 w**	**28.8 w**	**28.3 w**	**8.8 w**	**10.3 w**	**65.1 w**	**55.8 w**
Albania	3.1	11.1	0.3	7.8	96.5	81.1	9.9	22.6	1.1	7.4	88.8	70.0
Armenia	37.5	37.5	..	4.5	43.1	57.3	34.5	41.6	..	19.3	..	39.0
Azerbaijan	63.7	5.7	..	13.2	28.1	81.2	60.0	45.6	..	13.4	33.1	41.0
Belarus	81.3	59.3	6.6	10.1	12.0	30.6	72.2	70.7	2.9	5.9	24.8	21.8
Bosnia and Herzegovina	4.8	5.9	..	..	89.9	92.0	5.2	13.6	..	..	..	..
Bulgaria	29.4	31.3	6.5	7.8	62.5	58.1	31.7	38.9	8.9	7.7	58.9	52.9
Georgia	69.5	63.3	5.8	6.5	25.8	30.1	50.3	51.5	3.4	9.4	45.2	39.0
Kazakhstan	42.4	31.7	10.9	15.4	45.2	45.3	54.1	47.0	4.6	26.3	40.7	26.7
Kyrgyz Republic	49.6	53.1	..	..	45.1	40.4	58.1	56.8	..	19.5	29.7	23.8
Latvia	28.1	39.3	2.3	4.3	69.5	56.2	26.5	40.2	1.5	3.2	72.0	56.6
Lithuania	50.8	44.2	1.1	3.8	47.9	51.7	34.2	49.9	3.2	4.1	61.3	46.0
Macedonia, FYR	28.1	37.9	1.2	0.8	70.6	61.2	34.1	35.5	5.3	3.5	60.6	61.0
Moldova	79.5	35.7	1.7	49.8	18.4	14.4	57.9	69.1	1.7	3.3	35.8	27.4
Poland	14.6	16.2	3.0	3.1	82.1	80.1	7.6	14.5	7.0	6.9	85.3	77.8
Romania	11.7	21.8	9.3	6.6	78.5	71.2	16.1	23.2	6.1	7.2	76.7	69.6
Russian Federation	29.1	29.2	9.6	10.8	58.9	59.9	31.7	20.1	10.5	20.3	57.7	59.5
Serbia	..	40.9	..	1.6	..	56.2	..	25.3	..	4.3	..	62.8
Tajikistan	34.5	46.2	..	..	61.9	39.6	65.2	66.4	..	..	32.5	13.8
Turkey	14.3	17.9	12.0	16.8	69.5	60.7	9.3	24.9	11.2	22.9	77.9	51.5
Turkmenistan	45.3	73.3	..	..	24.6	19.8	63.5	45.0	..	..	28.4	29.3
Ukraine	46.3	51.1	19.3	17.0	34.0	30.5	61.2	49.3	4.1	12.3	34.7	38.4
Uzbekistan	52.1	66.1	..	..	36.9	20.3	44.0	49.7	..	..	51.5	33.5
Latin America & Carib.	**18.3 w**	**18.9 w**	**4.6 w**	**11.4 w**	**73.1 w**	**64.5 w**	**19.9 w**	**21.4 w**	**4.6 w**	**11.4 w**	**76.0 w**	**59.7 w**
Argentina	48.3	39.3	14.3	26.6	33.4	32.1	30.4	40.9	7.6	19.1	58.6	34.5
Bolivia	44.3	72.9	0.4	3.1	54.1	23.6	35.2	68.8	1.5	6.5	63.3	24.5
Brazil	27.2	24.3	11.4	21.1	60.0	49.8	21.6	16.3	8.6	29.8	69.7	53.7
Chile	21.9	18.5	5.7	20.3	62.1	56.1	24.2	32.6	7.9	19.7	54.1	45.8
Colombia	28.6	34.0	1.2	2.5	68.7	60.2	24.2	26.2	4.4	16.4	68.9	53.9
Costa Rica	14.6	20.6	1.7	17.3	39.9	62.1	19.1	29.5	3.4	6.9	46.1	63.0
Cuba	5.9	15.3	40.6	34.8	53.5	49.9	23.4	41.1	14.5	18.3	62.1	40.5
Dominican Republic	2.5	15.2	0.5	3.1	96.7	73.3	16.5	27.4	2.3	6.0	81.0	63.5
Ecuador	26.2	35.8	5.2	6.2	67.9	57.5	34.2	44.7	4.5	15.4	60.6	38.9
El Salvador	55.4	42.6	2.8	0.6	41.7	56.7	37.9	42.1	3.8	7.6	57.0	48.7
Guatemala	22.6	45.7	2.9	1.9	72.6	51.3	29.2	33.5	3.7	9.3	66.2	56.1
Haiti	0.7	10.7	..	..	98.6	83.4	12.9	33.7	5.0	10.7	81.7	55.6
Honduras	15.4	20.8	0.0	2.0	65.2	77.1	21.0	29.6	0.0	6.5	62.5	63.6
Jamaica	2.5	2.6	8.4	8.3	88.7	88.5	10.2	21.8	3.6	5.9	83.2	71.5
Mexico	4.3	6.9	0.3	1.7	94.8	90.4	2.3	4.6	3.5	15.7	93.8	78.8
Nicaragua	26.0	43.4	..	0.9	67.9	55.0	49.5	53.3	0.5	13.1	45.2	32.9
Panama	22.2	15.6	1.0	5.5	74.7	77.0	21.2	21.5	1.2	7.0	64.2	46.7
Paraguay	60.1	68.4	0.8	9.8	35.2	17.5	52.5	53.1	3.4	11.7	44.0	32.6
Peru	17.8	21.9	8.1	18.5	74.0	59.6	28.0	36.2	3.1	18.5	68.8	45.3
Uruguay	62.8	42.7	6.1	19.6	30.6	34.9	48.9	47.8	7.7	21.9	42.9	30.2
Venezuela, RB	22.2	10.7	0.9	7.8	59.0	58.8	18.9	37.9	1.7	11.6	67.7	47.1

	Exports						Imports					
	% of total merchandise exports						% of total merchandise imports					
	To developing economies				To high-income economies		From developing economies				From high-income economies	
	Within region		Outside region				Within region		Outside region			
	1998	2008	1998	2008	1998	2008	1998	2008	1998	2008	1998	2008
Middle East & N. Africa	**4.9 w**	**6.1 w**	**14.3 w**	**22.7 w**	**76.6 w**	**66.1 w**	**5.2 w**	**6.7 w**	**14.3 w**	**22.7 w**	**71.4 w**	**60.0 w**
Algeria	1.2	2.9	14.3	12.6	84.5	84.5	2.2	2.1	15.7	29.5	82.1	68.4
Djibouti	22.4	4.1	..	..	17.5	13.6	2.9	0.9	..	..	67.6	45.8
Egypt, Arab Rep.	8.7	11.8	10.6	19.3	70.5	59.8	1.1	3.6	23.4	32.0	65.8	58.4
Iran, Islamic Rep.	0.0	2.0	14.4	38.0	78.1	45.7	0.0	0.5	21.8	36.4	67.4	61.9
Iraq	5.9	2.0	17.1	19.4	77.0	78.6	13.9	35.3	31.5	36.4	54.6	28.4
Jordan	26.1	27.2	26.3	25.0	43.6	38.5	12.8	8.3	20.8	29.6	63.8	61.9
Lebanon	17.3	37.2	11.6	14.2	69.2	47.9	5.7	14.2	18.0	23.5	75.7	60.4
Libya	7.3	2.8	9.9	10.2	82.9	87.0	8.2	9.9	9.4	25.6	82.4	64.4
Morocco	3.9	2.3	14.1	25.2	71.2	71.5	2.4	6.3	12.4	24.1	71.4	69.6
Syrian Arab Republic	15.6	50.6	14.2	6.8	65.2	42.6	4.9	20.1	25.5	33.5	47.9	46.5
Tunisia	6.3	9.7	7.2	10.2	83.3	77.6	4.2	9.7	9.7	19.3	85.2	70.3
Yemen, Rep.	3.4	1.4	51.6	81.5	44.3	16.5	3.6	3.2	23.1	37.6	70.7	58.3
South Asia	**5.0 w**	**5.9 w**	**15.8 w**	**25.5 w**	**78.2 w**	**65.9 w**	**6.2 w**	**6.8 w**	**15.8 w**	**25.5 w**	**69.6 w**	**58.0 w**
Afghanistan	31.6	41.5	14.4	25.9	54.0	32.6	15.0	43.4	40.3	25.3	44.7	31.4
Bangladesh	2.9	3.1	6.4	7.1	90.2	75.9	17.3	16.4	18.7	29.5	48.4	47.6
India	5.0	4.9	18.0	28.1	76.5	65.0	1.0	0.7	24.1	39.0	74.8	59.8
Nepal	36.2	64.4	..	..	61.7	29.0	31.7	55.6	..	..	56.2	15.1
Pakistan	5.3	12.2	13.6	20.6	78.9	66.1	2.7	4.3	24.9	30.8	70.5	61.5
Sri Lanka	2.4	6.1	13.1	15.3	81.0	73.6	10.4	20.6	17.5	31.2	63.0	47.6
Sub-Saharan Africa	**12.6 w**	**11.1 w**	**10.0 w**	**26.1 w**	**64.7 w**	**61.1 w**	**12.6 w**	**11.9 w**	**10.0 w**	**26.1 w**	**71.8 w**	**53.7 w**
Angola	0.3	4.6	6.4	42.1	93.3	53.3	11.8	5.3	12.2	32.3	76.0	62.3
Benin	14.5	26.0	58.0	45.4	27.4	28.6	14.6	7.0	17.2	57.2	67.9	35.7
Burkina Faso	8.7	17.2	..	..	52.1	45.7	26.6	38.5	25.6	15.7	44.7	38.8
Burundi	3.0	11.9	0.3	18.2	61.5	53.7	21.2	25.0	..	10.6	63.3	56.7
Cameroon	8.2	9.8	6.2	11.8	84.9	76.3	14.5	19.8	9.9	27.0	71.3	52.7
Central African Republic	1.8	8.6	8.3	43.9	90.0	47.4	17.4	12.7	10.6	8.2	57.5	56.0
Chad	4.5	0.3	..	..	83.4	98.1	33.2	20.7	..	..	63.2	54.9
Congo, Dem. Rep.	1.3	7.5	2.0	52.5	96.4	39.8	42.4	55.4	10.4	10.6	45.8	33.8
Congo, Rep.	1.5	1.0	6.4	37.5	89.5	61.3	9.8	5.5	12.0	35.3	68.9	57.6
Côte d'Ivoire	25.1	28.3	8.9	13.6	58.9	57.1	13.3	32.5	15.7	24.8	61.8	41.9
Ethiopia	0.9	5.9	13.3	19.2	81.1	74.1	1.6	2.4	16.3	38.4	74.6	41.2
Gabon	1.5	2.3	7.6	28.5	83.3	58.6	15.3	10.0	4.0	14.7	79.7	73.7
Gambia, The	10.8	7.9	6.6	58.4	82.6	33.7	11.4	21.3	31.8	49.5	56.7	29.2
Ghana	7.6	9.0	9.4	28.3	77.2	51.3	26.0	23.2	12.7	35.5	60.7	40.5
Guinea	4.8	1.9	0.9	37.7	90.9	44.0	11.6	5.8	15.2	20.9	73.0	36.5
Guinea-Bissau	3.4	31.1	..	..	25.9	2.5	11.5	20.8	..	..	59.6	39.3
Kenya	39.0	33.5	18.8	16.7	40.9	41.8	8.5	9.1	17.7	33.4	73.3	56.6
Liberia	1.2	5.5	3.3	39.9	95.5	54.6	0.7	1.3	1.9	16.2	97.4	82.6
Madagascar	9.8	4.9	6.2	5.9	75.7	81.2	8.1	9.0	25.3	35.2	58.1	40.6
Malawi	21.8	28.8	12.6	28.0	65.2	42.6	68.0	57.1	3.9	19.0	27.1	23.2
Mali	8.2	7.9	34.7	56.5	55.5	25.8	24.7	30.7	5.4	11.4	39.8	28.2
Mauritania	9.6	10.3	6.9	44.4	82.5	44.2	5.2	5.2	17.1	29.6	69.7	55.2
Mauritius	6.3	10.7	0.9	4.2	92.7	85.0	14.5	12.6	24.3	43.7	61.1	43.4
Mozambique	44.4	13.8	11.6	3.4	44.0	61.7	43.7	30.0	11.2	16.6	36.9	37.0
Niger	31.6	55.0	0.4	1.9	68.0	43.0	26.8	17.9	16.6	32.8	54.2	49.3
Nigeria	10.4	8.1	17.9	21.1	71.1	69.8	4.2	4.6	23.1	26.4	72.5	54.9
Rwanda	2.5	4.2	14.7	26.2	63.7	24.5	32.4	35.3	6.2	11.1	44.7	33.6
Senegal	26.2	43.5	20.2	12.9	45.5	27.3	11.0	8.8	17.9	25.4	69.1	65.7
Sierra Leone	0.0	3.3	0.0	12.9	72.1	80.3	13.1	11.9	9.6	40.5	72.8	42.5
Somalia	0.5	4.5	29.9	26.3	69.6	69.2	13.3	10.7	60.8	53.6	14.3	23.2
South Africa	13.1	16.5	7.1	16.8	51.7	66.7	2.1	7.4	15.3	32.0	81.2	60.6
Sudan	0.8	1.1	24.9	59.2	74.2	39.6	4.1	5.9	37.9	43.3	58.0	47.5
Tanzania	12.7	19.7	26.8	24.0	59.2	43.9	18.6	17.0	22.6	36.5	57.9	42.6
Togo	17.8	47.0	29.0	26.6	52.4	25.4	45.1	20.5	9.3	56.8	70.0	35.2
Uganda	1.7	46.0	8.5	3.7	89.8	47.4	45.1	20.5	..	28.9	43.5	50.6
Zambia	22.7	26.9	13.3	32.8	59.3	40.2	52.6	64.0	4.0	11.7	43.3	24.2
Zimbabwe	34.7	57.5	9.1	13.4	55.9	29.0	42.4	72.9	6.4	8.2	46.0	14.6

Note: Bilateral trade data are not available for Timor-Leste, Kosovo, West Bank and Gaza, Botswana, Eritrea, Lesotho, Namibia, and Swaziland. Components may not sum to 100 percent because of trade with unspecified partners or with economies not covered by World Bank classification.

About the data

Developing economies are an increasingly important part of the global trading system. Their share of world merchandise exports rose from 15 percent in 1990 to 31 percent in 2008. And trade between high-income economies and low- and middle-income economies has grown faster than trade between high-income economies. This increased trade benefits both producers and consumers in developing and high-income economies.

The table shows trade in goods between developing economies in the same region and other regions and between developing economies and high-income economies. Data on exports and imports are from the International Monetary Fund's (IMF) Direction of Trade database and should be broadly consistent with data from other sources, such as the United Nations Statistics Division's Commodity Trade (Comtrade) database. Generally, data on trade between developing and high-income economies are complete. But trade flows between many developing economies—particularly those in Sub-Saharan Africa—are not well recorded, and the value of trade among developing economies may be understated. The table does not include some developing economies because data on their bilateral trade flows are not available. Data on the direction of trade between selected high-income economies are presented and discussed in tables 6.3 and 6.4.

At the regional level most exports from developing economies are to high-income economies, but the share of intraregional trade is increasing. Geographic patterns of trade vary widely by country

and commodity. Larger shares of exports from oil- and resource-rich economies are to high-income economies.

The relative importance of intraregional trade is higher for both landlocked countries and small countries with close trade links to the largest regional economy. For most developing economies—especially smaller ones—there is a "geographic bias" favoring intraregional trade. Despite the broad trend toward globalization and the reduction of trade barriers, the relative share of intraregional trade increased for most economies between 1998 and 2008. This is due partly to trade-related advantages, such as proximity, lower transport costs, increased knowledge from repeated interaction, and cultural and historical affinity. The direction of trade is also influenced by preferential trade agreements that a country has made with other economies. Though formal agreements on trade liberalization do not automatically increase trade, they nevertheless affect the direction of trade between the participating economies. Table 6.7 illustrates the size of existing regional trade blocs that have formal preferential trade agreements.

Although global integration has increased, developing economies still face trade barriers when accessing other markets (see table 6.8).

Developing economies are increasingly trading with other developing economies in the same region 6.5a

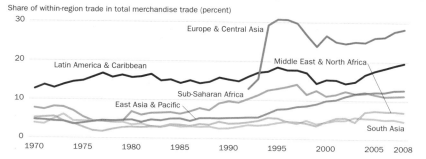

Share of within-region trade in total merchandise trade (percent)

Within-region trade (merchandise exports plus merchandise imports) has increased in all regions. In 2008 nearly 30 percent of merchandise trade in Europe and Central Asia and 20 percent in East Asia and Pacific was with other economies in the region.

Source: World Bank staff calculations based on data from International Monetary Fund's Direction of Trade database.

Data sources

Data on merchandise trade flows are published in the IMF's *Direction of Trade Statistics Yearbook* and *Direction of Trade Statistics Quarterly;* the data in the table were calculated using the IMF's Direction of Trade database. Regional and income group classifications are according to the World Bank classification of economies as of July 1, 2009, and are as shown on the cover flaps.

	1970	1980	1990	1995	2000	2003	2004	2005	2006	2007	2008	2009
World Bank commodity price index (2000 = 100)												
Energy	19	153	79	53	100	101	123	171	197	207	273	180
Nonenergy commodities	183	177	115	117	100	108	121	135	172	190	217	179
Agriculture	188	195	113	122	100	114	118	121	134	153	183	166
Beverages	230	273	117	136	100	117	109	125	130	144	168	185
Food	201	199	116	117	100	117	123	121	131	156	198	172
Fats and oils	237	196	105	126	100	129	134	120	123	177	222	182
Grains	204	199	121	124	100	112	115	115	134	160	225	181
Other food	151	205	124	101	100	105	117	129	140	126	142	153
Raw materials	136	143	105	125	100	107	109	119	143	148	156	142
Timber	97	92	88	105	100	91	90	100	113	116	120	117
Other raw materials	179	198	124	146	100	124	129	140	177	184	196	169
Fertilizers	82	177	98	110	100	110	125	148	151	203	453	246
Metals and minerals	185	141	122	106	100	96	126	162	251	266	260	198
Steel products[a]	0	134	131	118	100	100	153	170	162	154	231	191
Commodity prices (2000 prices)												
Energy												
Coal, Australian ($/mt)	..	49	39	33	26	25	48	43	44	56	102	60
Natural gas, Europe ($/mmBtu)	..	5	2	2	4	4	4	6	8	7	11	7
Natural gas, U.S. ($/mmBtu)	1	2	2	1	4	5	5	8	6	6	7	3
Natural gas, liquefied, Japan ($/mmBtu)	..	7	4	3	5	5	5	5	6	7	10	7
Petroleum, avg, spot ($/bbl)	4	45	22	14	28	28	34	48	57	60	78	52
Beverages (cents/kg)												
Cocoa	233	321	123	119	91	170	141	140	142	165	206	243
Coffee, Arabica	397	427	192	277	192	137	161	230	225	231	246	267
Coffee, robusta	321	400	115	230	91	79	72	101	133	162	186	138
Tea, avg., 3 auctions	289	205	200	124	188	147	153	150	168	172	193	229
Tea, Colombo auctions	217	137	182	118	179	150	162	167	171	214	223	264
Tea, Kolkata auctions	343	253	273	145	181	142	156	147	157	163	180	211
Tea, Mombasa auctions	307	224	144	108	203	150	141	134	175	141	177	212
Food												
Fats and oils ($/mt)												
Coconut oil	1,376	831	327	556	450	454	600	560	542	778	978	610
Copra[a]	779	558	224	364	305	291	409	376	360	514	652	403
Groundnut oil	1,312	1,059	937	823	714	1,207	1,054	963	867	1,145	1,704	995
Palm oil	901	719	282	521	310	430	428	383	427	661	758	574
Palm kernel oil[a]	..	..	..	..	444	445	588	569	519	753	903	589
Soybeans	405	365	240	215	212	256	278	249	240	325	418	367
Soybean meal	357	323	195	164	189	205	219	195	187	261	339	343
Soybean oil	992	737	435	519	338	538	559	495	535	747	1,006	714
Grains ($/mt)												
Barley	..	96	78	86	77	102	90	86	104	146	160	108
Maize	202	154	106	103	89	102	102	90	109	139	178	139
Rice, Thailand, 5%	438	506	263	266	202	192	216	260	272	277	520	467
Sorghum[a]	179	159	101	99	88	103	100	87	110	138	166	127
Wheat, Canada[a]	218	235	152	172	147	172	169	179	194	254	363	253
Wheat, U.S., hard red winter	190	213	132	147	114	142	142	138	172	216	261	188
Wheat, U.S., soft red winter[a]	197	208	125	139	99	134	131	123	142	202	217	156

6.6 Primary commodity prices

	1970	1980	1990	1995	2000	2003	2004	2005	2006	2007	2008	2009
Commodity prices (continued)												
(2000 prices)												
Food (continued)												
Other food												
Bananas, U.S. ($/mt)	573	467	526	369	424	364	476	547	605	572	675	712
Beef (cents/kg)	452	340	249	158	193	192	228	238	228	220	251	222
Chicken meat (cents/kg)	..	85	96	92	119	129	138	135	124	133	136	144
Fishmeal ($/mt)[a]	682	621	401	411	413	593	589	664	1,040	997	906	1,034
Oranges ($/mt)	582	482	516	441	363	661	780	794	741	810	885	764
Shrimp, Mexico (cents/kg)	..	1,420	1,039	1,253	1,515	1,110	928	939	915	855	854	795
Sugar, EU domestic (cents/kg)	39	60	57	57	56	58	61	60	58	58	56	44
Sugar, U.S. domestic (cents/kg)	57	82	50	42	43	46	41	43	44	39	37	46
Sugar, world (cents/kg)	29	78	27	24	18	15	14	20	29	19	23	34
Agricultural raw materials												
Cotton A index (cents/kg)	219	252	177	177	130	136	124	110	113	118	126	116
Logs, Cameroon ($/cu. m)[a]	149	310	334	282	275	271	301	304	285	323	421	354
Logs, Malaysian ($/cu. m)	149	241	172	212	190	182	179	184	214	227	234	241
Rubber, Singapore (cents/kg)	141	176	84	131	67	105	116	135	186	192	207	161
Plywood (cents/sheet)[a]	357	338	345	485	448	419	422	462	532	543	516	475
Sawnwood, Malaysian ($/cu. m)	608	489	518	614	595	535	528	599	670	683	711	677
Tobacco ($/mt)[a]	3,727	2,806	3,297	2,194	2,976	2,568	2,488	2,533	2,653	2,808	2,869	3,523
Woodpulp ($/mt)[a]	615	661	792	708	664	510	582	577	624	650	656	517
Fertilizers ($/mt)												
Diammonium phosphate	187	274	167	180	154	174	201	224	233	366	773	272
Phosphate rock	38	58	39	29	44	37	37	38	40	60	276	102
Potassium chloride	109	143	95	98	123	110	113	144	156	170	456	530
Triple superphosphate	147	222	128	124	138	145	169	183	180	287	703	216
Urea	..	..	116	155	101	135	159	199	199	262	394	210
Metals and minerals												
Aluminum ($/mt)	1,926	1,795	1,593	1,499	1,549	1,389	1,558	1,724	2,297	2,235	2,057	1,400
Copper ($/mt)	4,895	2,690	2,586	2,437	1,813	1,727	2,602	3,340	6,007	6,030	5,560	4,330
Gold ($/toz)[a]	125	750	373	319	279	353	372	404	540	590	697	818
Iron ore (cents/dmtu)	34	35	32	24	29	31	34	59	69	72	112	85
Lead (cents/kg)	105	112	79	52	45	50	80	89	115	219	167	145
Nickel ($/mt)	9,860	8,037	8,614	6,830	8,638	9,346	12,551	13,387	21,675	31,537	16,875	12,322
Silver (cents/toz)[a]	614	2,544	475	431	500	477	607	666	1,034	1,136	1,199	1,235
Tin (cents/kg)	1,273	2,068	591	516	544	475	773	670	785	1,231	1,480	1,141
Zinc (cents/kg)	102	94	147	86	113	80	95	125	293	275	150	139
MUV G-5 index (2000 = 100)	29	81	103	120	100	103	110	110	112	118	125	119

Note: bbl = barrel, cu. m = cubic meter, dmtu = dry metric ton unit, kg = kilogram, mmBtu = million British thermal units, mt = metric ton, toz = troy ounce.
a. Series not included in the nonenergy index.

About the data

Primary commodities—raw or partially processed materials that will be transformed into finished goods—are often developing countries' most important exports, and commodity revenues can affect living standards. Price data are collected from various sources, including international commodity study groups, government agencies, industry trade journals, and Bloomberg and Datastream. Prices are compiled in U.S. dollars or converted to U.S. dollars when quoted in local currencies.

The table is based on frequently updated price reports. Prices are those received by exporters when available, or the prices paid by importers or trade unit values. Annual price series are generally simple averages based on higher frequency data. The constant price series in the table are deflated by the manufactures unit value (MUV) index for the Group of Five (G-5) countries (see below).

Commodity price indexes are calculated as Laspeyres index numbers; the fixed weights are the 2002–04 average export values for low- and middle-income economies (based on 2001 gross national income) rebased to 2000. Data for exports are from the United Nations Statistics Division's Commodity Trade Statistics (Comtrade) database Standard International Trade Classification (SITC) revision 3, the Food Agriculture Organization's FAOSTAT database, the International Energy Agency database, BP's *Statistical Review of World Energy,* the World Bureau of Metal Statistics, World Bank staff estimates, and other sources.

Each index in the table represents a fixed basket of primary commodity exports over time. The nonenergy commodity price index contains 41 price series for 34 nonenergy commodities.

Separate indexes are compiled for energy and steel products, which are not included in the nonenergy commodity price index.

The MUV index is a composite index of prices for manufactured exports from the five major (G-5) industrial economies (France, Germany, Japan, the United Kingdom, and the United States) to low- and middle-income economies, valued in U.S. dollars. The index covers products in groups 5–8 of SITC revision 1. For the MUV G-5 index, unit value indexes in local currency for each country are converted to U.S. dollars using market exchange rates and are combined using weights determined by each country's export share in the base year (1995). The export shares were 8.2 percent for France, 17.4 percent for Germany, 35.6 percent for Japan, 6.6 percent for the United Kingdom, and 32.2 percent for the United States.

Definitions

• **Energy price index** is the composite price index for coal, petroleum, and natural gas, weighted by exports of each commodity from low- and middle-income countries. • **Nonenergy commodity price index** covers the 34 nonenergy primary commodities that make up the agriculture, fertilizer, and metals and minerals indexes. • **Agriculture** includes beverages, food, and agricultural raw materials. • **Beverages** include cocoa, coffee, and tea. • **Food** includes fats and oils, grains, and other food items. Fats and oils include coconut oil, groundnut oil, palm oil, soybeans, soybean oil, and soybean meal. Grains include barley, maize, rice, and wheat. Other food items include bananas, beef, chicken meat, oranges, shrimp, and sugar. • **Agricultural raw materials** include timber and other raw materials. Timber includes tropical hard logs and sawnwood. Other raw materials include cotton, natural rubber, and tobacco. • **Fertilizers** include phosphate, phosphate rock, potassium, and nitrogenous products. • **Metals and minerals** include aluminum, copper, iron ore, lead, nickel, tin, and zinc. • **Steel products price index** is the composite price index for eight steel products based on quotations free on board (f.o.b.) Japan excluding shipments to the United States for all years and to China prior to 2001, weighted by product shares of apparent combined consumption (volume of deliveries) for Germany, Japan, and the United States. • **Commodity prices**—for definitions and sources, see "Commodity price data" (also known as the "Pink Sheet") at the World Bank Prospects for Development website (www.worldbank.org/prospects, click on Products). • **MUV G-5 index** is the manufactures unit value index for G-5 country exports to low- and middle-income economies.

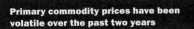

Primary commodity prices have been volatile over the past two years   6.6a

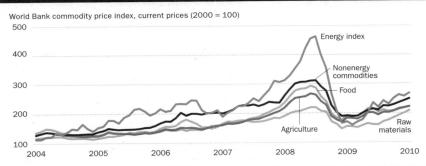

World Bank commodity price index, current prices (2000 = 100)

Commodity prices rose rapidly in early 2008 before collapsing in the second half of the year. But prices rose again in 2009. Between January 2009 and January 2010 the average price of energy commodities increased 57 percent and the average price of nonenergy commodities increased 30 percent.

Source: World Bank commodity price data.

Data sources

Data on commodity prices and the MUV G-5 index are compiled by the World Bank's Development Prospects Group. Monthly updates of commodity prices are available at www.worldbank.org/prospects.

Merchandise exports within bloc

	Year of creation	Year of entry into force of the most recent agreement	Type of most recent agreement[a]	$ millions						
				1990	1995	2000	2005	2006	2007	2008
High-income and low- and middle-income economies										
APEC[b]	1989		None	901,560	1,688,708	2,261,791	3,310,523	3,775,795	4,193,036	4,607,766
EEA	1994	1994	EIA	1,079,711	1,463,232	1,714,018	2,863,903	3,237,586	3,805,786	4,190,268
EFTA	1960	2002	EIA	782	925	831	1,252	1,524	2,196	2,910
European Union	1957	1958	EIA, CU	1,032,397	1,404,255	1,641,609	2,732,159	3,089,257	3,627,406	3,977,321
NAFTA	1994	1994	FTA	226,273	394,472	676,141	824,658	902,193	951,551	1,013,245
SPARTECA	1981	1981	PTA	5,299	9,135	8,579	15,201	15,562	18,617	20,263
Trans-Pacific SEP	2006	2006	EIA, FTA	1,110	2,614	1,438	2,345	2,927	3,290	4,278
East Asia and Pacific and South Asia										
APTA	1975	1976	PTA	2,429	21,728	37,895	127,340	154,380	193,951	233,606
ASEAN	1967	1992	FTA	27,365	79,544	98,060	165,458	191,392	216,727	251,367
MSG	1993	1994	PTA	5	18	22	51	63	78	89
PICTA	2001	2003	FTA	6	53	81	158	195	242	277
SAARC	1985	2006	FTA	863	2,024	2,680	7,301	8,053	10,720	10,665
Europe, Central Asia, and Middle East										
CEFTA	1992	1994	FTA	..	619	1,047	2,452	4,801	7,029	8,266
CIS	1991	1994	FTA	..	31,529	28,753	59,441	67,926	100,540	126,005
EAEC	1997	2000	CU	..	10,919	13,936	24,818	24,711	45,714	51,186
ECO	1985	2003	PTA	1,243	4,746	4,518	12,579	17,365	22,064	26,739
GCC	1981	2003[c]	CU	6,906	6,832	8,029	15,408	19,257	23,988	32,699
PAFTA (GAFTA)	1997	1998	FTA	13,204	12,948	16,188	43,393	52,733	63,563	83,484
UMA	1989	1994[c]	NNA	958	1,109	1,041	1,885	2,402	2,695	4,570
Latin America and the Caribbean										
Andean Community	1969	1988	CU	544	1,788	2,046	4,572	5,011	5,875	6,757
CACM	1961	1961	CU	667	1,594	2,586	4,342	4,808	5,677	6,708
CARICOM	1973	1997	EIA	456	877	1,078	2,090	2,429	3,112	3,808
LAIA (ALADI)	1980	1981	PTA	13,350	35,986	44,253	71,720	90,358	110,421	136,896
MERCOSUR	1991	2005	EIA	4,127	14,199	17,829	21,128	25,775	33,038	42,733
OECS	1981	1981[c]	NNA	29	39	38	68	84	104	118
Sub-Saharan Africa										
CEMAC	1994	1999	CU	139	120	96	201	247	305	355
COMESA	1994	1994	FTA	1,146	1,367	1,443	2,962	3,363	4,501	5,296
EAC	1996	2000	CU	335	628	689	1,075	1,062	1,385	1,616
ECCAS	1983	2004[c]	NNA	160	157	182	255	313	385	449
ECOWAS	1975	1993	PTA	1,532	1,875	2,715	5,497	5,956	6,676	8,251
Indian Ocean Commission	1984	2005[c]	NNA	63	113	106	162	182	214	190
SADC	1992	2000	FTA	1,655	3,615	4,427	7,799	8,701	11,912	15,468
UEMOA	1994	2000	CU	621	560	741	1,390	1,544	1,835	2,096

Note: Regional bloc memberships are as follows: **Andean Community**, Bolivia, Colombia, Ecuador, and Peru; **Arab Maghreb Union (UMA)**, Algeria, Libyan Arab Republic, Mauritania, Morocco, and Tunisia; **Asia Pacific Economic Cooperation (APEC)**, Australia, Brunei Darussalam, Canada, Chile, China, Hong Kong SAR, China, Indonesia, Japan, the Republic of Korea, Malaysia, Mexico, New Zealand, Papua New Guinea, Peru, the Philippines, the Russian Federation, Singapore, Taiwan (China), Thailand, the United States, and Vietnam; **Asia-Pacific Trade Agreement (APTA; formerly Bangkok Agreement),** Bangladesh, China, India, the Republic of Korea, the Lao People's Democratic Republic, and Sri Lanka; **Association of South East Asian Nations (ASEAN)**, Brunei Darussalam, Cambodia, Indonesia, the Lao People's Democratic Republic, Malaysia, Myanmar, the Philippines, Singapore, Thailand, and Vietnam; **Caribbean Community and Common Market (CARICOM)**, Antigua and Barbuda, the Bahamas, Barbados, Belize, Dominica, Grenada, Guyana, Haiti, Jamaica, Montserrat, St. Kitts and Nevis, St. Lucia, St. Vincent and the Grenadines, Suriname, and Trinidad and Tobago; **Central American Common Market (CACM)**, Costa Rica, El Salvador, Guatemala, Honduras, and Nicaragua; **Central European Free Trade Area (CEFTA)**, Albania, Bosnia and Herzegovina, Croatia, Kosovo, Macedonia, Moldova, Montenegro, and Serbia; **Common Market for Eastern and Southern Africa (COMESA)**, Burundi, Comoros, the Democratic Republic of Congo, Djibouti, the Arab Republic of Egypt, Eritrea, Ethiopia, Kenya, Libyan Arab Republic, Madagascar, Malawi, Mauritius, Rwanda, Seychelles, Sudan, Swaziland, Uganda, Zambia, and Zimbabwe; **Commonwealth of Independent States (CIS)**, Armenia, Azerbaijan, Belarus, Georgia, Kazakhstan, Kyrgyz Republic, Moldova, the Russian Federation, Tajikistan, Turkmenistan, Ukraine, and Uzbekistan; **East African Community (EAC)**, Burundi, Kenya, Rwanda, Tanzania, and Uganda; **Economic and Monetary Community of Central Africa (CEMAC; formerly Central African Customs and Economic Union [UDEAC])**, Cameroon, the Central African Republic, Chad, the Republic of Congo, Equatorial Guinea, and Gabon; **Economic Community of Central African States (ECCAS)**, Angola, Burundi, Cameroon, the Central African Republic, Chad, the Democratic Republic of Congo, the Republic of Congo, Equatorial Guinea, Gabon, and São Tomé and Principe; **Economic Community of West African States (ECOWAS)**, Benin, Burkina Faso, Cape Verde, Côte d'Ivoire, the Gambia, Ghana, Guinea, Guinea-Bissau, Liberia, Mali, Niger, Nigeria, Senegal, Sierra Leone, and Togo; **Economic Cooperation Organization (ECO)**, Afghanistan, Azerbaijan, the Islamic Republic of Iran, Kazakhstan, the Kyrgyz Republic, Pakistan, Tajikistan, Turkey, Turkmenistan, and Uzbekistan; **Eurasian Economic Community (EAEC)**, Belarus, Kazakhstan, Kyrgyz Republic, the Russian Federation, Tajikistan, and Uzbekistan; **European Economic Area (EEA)**, European Union plus Iceland, Liechten-

Merchandise exports within bloc

	Year of creation	Year of entry into force of the most recent agreement	Type of most recent agreement[a]	% of total bloc exports						
				1990	1995	2000	2005	2006	2007	2008
High-income and low-and middle-income economies										
APEC[b]	1989		None	68.3	71.7	73.0	70.8	69.4	67.4	65.3
EEA	1994	1994	EIA	68.8	67.9	69.0	68.8	69.0	69.4	68.8
EFTA	1960	2002	EIA	0.8	0.7	0.6	0.5	0.6	0.7	0.8
European Union	1957	1958	EIA, CU	67.3	66.5	67.7	67.4	67.6	67.9	67.3
NAFTA	1994	1994	FTA	41.4	46.2	55.7	55.7	53.9	51.3	49.5
SPARTECA	1981	1981	PTA	10.5	12.9	10.7	11.4	10.2	10.5	8.9
Trans-Pacific SEP	2006	2006	EIA, FTA	1.5	1.7	0.8	0.8	0.8	0.8	1.0
East Asia and Pacific and South Asia										
APTA	1975	1976	PTA	1.6	6.8	8.0	11.0	10.7	11.0	11.4
ASEAN	1967	1992	FTA	18.9	24.4	23.0	25.3	24.9	25.2	25.6
MSG	1993	1994	PTA	0.3	0.4	0.6	0.8	0.8	0.8	0.8
PICTA	2001	2003	FTA	0.3	1.3	2.1	2.3	2.4	2.6	2.4
SAARC	1985	2006	FTA	3.2	4.4	4.2	5.6	5.1	5.5	4.8
Europe, Central Asia, and Middle East										
CEFTA	1992	1994	FTA	..	9.0	13.4	14.1	19.8	21.9	22.6
CIS	1991	1994	FTA	..	28.6	20.0	18.0	16.9	20.5	18.4
EAEC	1997	2000	CU	..	12.3	11.5	8.9	7.2	10.9	9.3
ECO	1985	2003	PTA	3.2	7.9	5.6	6.9	7.6	8.0	6.8
GCC	1981	2003[c]	CU	8.0	6.8	4.9	4.5	4.5	4.9	4.7
PAFTA (GAFTA)	1997	1998	FTA	10.2	9.8	7.2	9.6	9.2	9.7	9.0
UMA	1989	1994[c]	NNA	2.9	3.8	2.2	1.9	2.0	2.0	2.5
Latin America and the Caribbean										
Andean Community	1969	1988	CU	4.0	8.6	7.7	9.0	7.8	7.9	7.5
CACM	1961	1961	CU	15.3	21.8	19.1	20.1	16.3	17.4	18.7
CARICOM	1973	1997	EIA	8.0	12.0	14.4	11.5	11.2	13.1	12.9
LAIA (ALADI)	1980	1981	PTA	11.6	17.3	13.2	13.6	14.3	15.2	16.0
MERCOSUR	1991	2005	EIA	8.9	20.3	20.0	12.9	13.5	14.9	15.0
OECS	1981	1981[c]	NNA	8.1	12.6	10.0	11.4	8.0	12.0	12.0
Sub-Saharan Africa										
CEMAC	1994	1999	CU	2.3	2.1	1.0	0.9	0.9	1.0	0.8
COMESA	1994	1994	FTA	4.7	6.1	4.6	4.7	4.0	4.5	4.1
EAC	1996	2000	CU	17.7	19.5	22.6	17.7	15.9	17.5	17.6
ECCAS	1983	2004[c]	NNA	1.4	1.5	1.0	0.6	0.5	0.6	0.4
ECOWAS	1975	1993	PTA	8.0	9.0	7.6	9.3	7.9	7.7	7.6
Indian Ocean Commission	1984	2005[c]	NNA	3.9	5.9	4.4	4.9	5.0	5.8	5.1
SADC	1992	2000	FTA	6.6	10.2	9.5	9.3	9.1	10.0	10.1
UEMOA	1994	2000	CU	13.0	10.3	13.1	13.4	13.1	14.8	14.5

stein, and Norway; **European Free Trade Association (EFTA)**, Iceland, Liechtenstein, Norway, and Switzerland; **European Union (EU; formerly European Economic Community and European Community)**, Austria, Belgium, Bulgaria, Cyprus, Czech Republic, Denmark, Estonia, Finland, France, Germany, Greece, Hungary, Ireland, Italy, Latvia, Lithuania, Luxembourg, Malta, the Netherlands, Poland, Portugal, Romania, Slovak Republic, Slovenia, Spain, Sweden, and the United Kingdom; **Gulf Cooperation Council (GCC)**, Bahrain, Kuwait, Oman, Qatar, Saudi Arabia, and the United Arab Emirates; **Indian Ocean Commission**, Comoros, Madagascar, Mauritius, Réunion, and Seychelles; **Latin American Integration Association (LAIA; formerly Latin American Free Trade Area)**, Argentina, Bolivia, Brazil, Chile, Colombia, Cuba, Ecuador, Mexico, Paraguay, Peru, Uruguay, and Bolivarian Republic of Venezuela; **Melanesian Spearhead Group (MSG)**, Fiji, Papua New Guinea, Solomon Islands, and Vanuatu; **North American Free Trade Agreement (NAFTA)**, Canada, Mexico, and the United States; **Organization of Eastern Caribbean States (OECS)**, Anguilla, Antigua and Barbuda, British Virgin Islands, Dominica, Grenada, Montserrat, St. Kitts and Nevis, St. Lucia, and St. Vincent and the Grenadines; **Pacific Island Countries Trade Agreement (PICTA)**, Cook Islands, Fiji, Kiribati, Nauru, Niue, Papua New Guinea, Samoa, Solomon Islands, Tonga, Tuvalu, and Vanuatu; **Pan-Arab Free Trade Area (PAFTA; also known as Greater Arab Trade Area [GAFTA])**, Bahrain, Egypt, Iraq, Jordan, Kuwait, Lebanon, Libya, Morocco, Oman, Qatar, Saudi Arabia, Sudan, Syrian Arab Republic, Tunisia, the United Arab Emirates, and Yemen; **South Asian Association for Regional Cooperation (SAARC)**, Bangladesh, Bhutan, India, Maldives, Nepal, Pakistan, and Sri Lanka; **South Pacific Regional Trade and Economic Cooperation Agreement (SPARTECA)**, Australia, Cook Islands, Fiji, Kiribati, Marshall Islands, Federated States of Micronesia, Nauru, New Zealand, Niue, Papua New Guinea, Solomon Islands, Tonga, Tuvalu, Vanuatu, and Western Samoa; **Southern African Development Community (SADC)**, Angola, Botswana, the Democratic Republic of Congo, Lesotho, Madagascar, Malawi, Mauritius, Mozambique, Namibia, Seychelles, South Africa, Swaziland, Tanzania, Zambia, and Zimbabwe; **Southern Common Market (MERCOSUR)**, Argentina, Brazil, Paraguay, Uruguay, and Bolivarian Republic of Venezuela; **Trans-Pacific Strategic Economic Partnership (Trans-Pacific SEP)**, Brunei Darussalam, Chile, New Zealand, and Singapore; **West African Economic and Monetary Union (UEMOA)**, Benin, Burkina Faso, Côte d'Ivoire, Guinea-Bissau, Mali, Niger, Senegal, and Togo.

6.7 | Regional trade blocs

Merchandise exports by bloc

	Year of creation	Year of entry into force of the most recent agreement	Type of most recent agreement[a]	% of world exports						
				1990	1995	2000	2005	2006	2007	2008
High-income and low- and middle-income economies										
APEC[b]	1989		None	39.0	46.4	48.5	45.1	45.3	44.7	44.0
EEA	1994	1994	EIA	46.4	42.4	38.9	40.1	39.1	39.4	38.0
EFTA	1960	2002	EIA	2.9	2.4	2.2	2.3	2.3	2.3	2.3
European Union	1957	1958	EIA, CU	45.3	41.5	38.0	39.1	38.1	38.4	36.9
NAFTA	1994	1994	FTA	16.2	16.8	19.0	14.3	14.0	13.3	12.8
SPARTECA	1981	1981	PTA	1.5	1.4	1.3	1.3	1.3	1.3	1.4
Trans-Pacific SEP	2006	2006	EIA, FTA	2.2	3.0	2.7	2.9	3.0	2.9	2.8
East Asia and Pacific and South Asia										
APTA	1975	1976	PTA	4.5	6.3	7.5	11.2	12.0	12.7	12.8
ASEAN	1967	1992	FTA	4.3	6.4	6.7	6.3	6.4	6.2	6.1
MSG	1993	1994	PTA	0.1	0.1	0.1	0.1	0.1	0.1	0.1
PICTA	2001	2003	FTA	0.1	0.1	0.1	0.1	0.1	0.1	0.1
SAARC	1985	2006	FTA	0.8	0.9	1.0	1.3	1.3	1.4	1.4
Europe, Central Asia, and Middle East										
CEFTA	1992	1994	FTA	..	0.1	0.1	0.2	0.2	0.2	0.2
CIS	1991	1994	FTA	..	2.2	2.2	3.2	3.4	3.5	4.3
EAEC	1997	2000	CU	..	1.7	1.9	2.7	2.9	3.0	3.4
ECO	1985	2003	PTA	1.1	1.2	1.3	1.8	1.9	2.0	2.4
GCC	1981	2003[c]	CU	2.6	2.0	2.6	3.3	3.6	3.5	4.3
PAFTA (GAFTA)	1997	1998	FTA	3.8	2.6	3.5	4.3	4.8	4.7	5.8
UMA	1989	1994[c]	NNA	1.0	0.6	0.8	0.9	1.0	1.0	1.1
Latin America and the Caribbean										
Andean Community	1969	1988	CU	0.4	0.4	0.4	0.5	0.5	0.5	0.6
CACM	1961	1961	CU	0.1	0.1	0.2	0.2	0.2	0.2	0.2
CARICOM	1973	1997	EIA	0.2	0.1	0.1	0.2	0.2	0.2	0.2
LAIA (ALADI)	1980	1981	PTA	3.4	4.1	5.3	5.1	5.2	5.2	5.4
MERCOSUR	1991	2005	EIA	1.4	1.4	1.4	1.6	1.6	1.6	1.8
OECS	1981	1981[c]	NNA	0.0	0.0	0.0	0.0	0.0	0.0	0.0
Sub-Saharan Africa										
CEMAC	1994	1999	CU	0.2	0.1	0.1	0.2	0.2	0.2	0.3
COMESA	1994	1994	FTA	0.7	0.4	0.5	0.6	0.7	0.7	0.8
EAC	1996	2000	CU	0.1	0.1	0.0	0.1	0.1	0.1	0.1
ECCAS	1983	2004[c]	NNA	0.3	0.2	0.3	0.4	0.5	0.5	0.7
ECOWAS	1975	1993	PTA	0.6	0.4	0.6	0.6	0.6	0.6	0.7
Indian Ocean Commission	1984	2005[c]	NNA	0.0	0.0	0.0	0.0	0.0	0.0	0.0
SADC	1992	2000	FTA	0.7	0.7	0.7	0.8	0.8	0.9	1.0
UEMOA	1994	2000	CU	0.1	0.1	0.1	0.1	0.1	0.1	0.1

a. CU is customs union; EIA is economic integration agreement; FTA is free trade agreement; PTA is preferential trade agreement; and NNA is not notified agreement, which refers to preferential trade arrangements established among member countries that are not notified to the World Trade Organization (these agreements may be functionally equivalent to any of the other agreements). b. No preferential trade agreement c. Years of the most recent agreement are collected from the official website of the trade bloc.

About the data

Trade blocs are groups of countries with preferential arrangements governing trade between members. Although the preferences—such as lower tariff duties or exemptions from quantitative restrictions—may be no greater than those available to other trading partners, such arrangements are intended to encourage exports by bloc members to one another—sometimes called intratrade.

Most countries are members of a regional trade bloc, and more than a third of world trade takes place within such arrangements. While trade blocs vary in structure, they have the same objective: to reduce trade barriers between members. But effective integration requires more than reducing tariffs and quotas. Economic gains from competition and scale may not be achieved unless other barriers that divide markets and impede the free flow of goods, services, and investments are lifted. For example, many regional trade blocs retain contingent protections on intratrade, including antidumping, countervailing duties, and "emergency protection" to address balance of payments problems or protect an industry from import surges. Other barriers include differing product standards, discrimination in public procurement, and cumbersome border formalities.

Trade bloc membership may reduce the frictional costs of trade, increase the credibility of reform initiatives, and strengthen security among partners. But making it work effectively is challenging. All economic sectors may be affected, and some may expand while others contract, so it is important to weigh the potential costs and benefits of membership.

The table shows the value of merchandise intratrade (service exports are excluded) for important regional trade blocs and the size of intratrade relative to each bloc's exports of goods and the share of the bloc's exports in world exports. Although the Asia Pacific Economic Cooperation (APEC) has no preferential arrangements, it is included because of the volume of trade between its members.

The data on country exports are from the International Monetary Fund's (IMF) Direction of Trade database and should be broadly consistent with those from sources such as the United Nations Statistics Division's Commodity Trade (Comtrade) database. However, trade flows between many developing countries, particularly in Sub-Saharan Africa, are not well recorded, so the value of intratrade for certain groups may be understated. Data on trade between developing and high-income countries are generally complete.

Unless otherwise noted, the type of agreement and date of enforcement are based on the World Trade Organization's (WTO) list of regional trade agreements. Other types of preferential trade agreements may have entered into force earlier than those shown in the table and may still be effective.

Although bloc exports have been calculated back to 1990 based on current membership, several blocs came into existence after that and membership may have changed over time. For this reason, and because systems of preferences also change over time, intratrade in earlier years may not have been affected by the same preferences as in recent years. In addition, some countries belong to more than one trade bloc, so shares of world exports exceed 100 percent. Exports include all commodity trade, which may include items not specified in trade bloc agreements. Differences from previously published estimates may be due to changes in membership or revisions in underlying data.

Definitions

• **Merchandise exports within bloc** are the sum of merchandise exports by members of a trade bloc to other members of the bloc. They are shown both in U.S. dollars and as a percentage of total merchandise exports by the bloc. • **Merchandise exports by bloc** as a share of world exports are the bloc's total merchandise exports (within the bloc and to the rest of the world) as a share of total merchandise exports by all economies in the world. • **Type of most recent agreement** includes customs union, under which members substantially eliminate all tariff and nontariff barriers among themselves and establish a common external tariff for nonmembers; economic integration agreement, which liberalizes trade in services among members and covers a substantial number of sectors, affects a sufficient volume of trade, includes substantial modes of supply, and is nondiscriminatory (in the sense that similarly situated service suppliers are treated the same); free trade agreement, under which members substantially eliminate all tariff and nontariff barriers but set tariffs on imports from nonmembers; preferential trade agreement, which is an agreement notified to the WTO that is not a free trade agreement, a customs union, or an economic integration agreement; and not notified agreement, which is a preferential trade arrangement established among member countries that is not notified to the World Trade Organization (the agreement may be functionally equivalent to any of the other agreements).

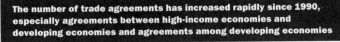

The number of trade agreements has increased rapidly since 1990, especially agreements between high-income economies and developing economies and agreements among developing economies — 6.7a

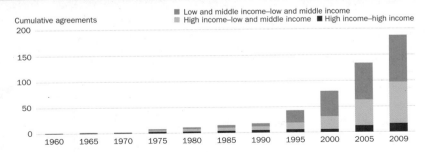

Cumulative agreements

■ Low and middle income–low and middle income
■ High income–low and middle income ■ High income–high income

Note: Data are cumulative number of trade agreements notified to the General Agreement on Tariffs and Trade/World Trade Organization (GATT/WTO) at the time they entered into force. Includes only agreements that are currently in force. Excludes agreements on services and accessions of new members to an existing agreement.
Source: World Bank staff calculations based on the World Trade Organization's Regional Trade Agreements Information System.

Data sources

Data on merchandise trade flows are published in the IMF's *Direction of Trade Statistics Yearbook* and *Direction of Trade Statistics Quarterly;* the data in the table were calculated using the IMF's Direction of Trade database. Data on trade bloc membership are from the World Bank Policy Research Report *Trade Blocs* (2000b), UNCTAD's *Trade and Development Report 2007,* WTO's Regional Trade Agreements Information System, and the World Bank's International Trade Unit.

	Most recent year	Binding coverage	Simple mean bound rate	All products %				Primary products %		Manufactured products %	
				Simple mean tariff	Weighted mean tariff	Share of tariff lines with international peaks	Share of tariff lines with specific rates	Simple mean tariff	Weighted mean tariff	Simple mean tariff	Weighted mean tariff
Afghanistan	2008	..	..	6.2	6.5	4.2	0.0	7.0	6.7	6.1	6.3
Albania	2008	100.0	7.0	2.4	2.1	10.4	0.0	4.8	3.2	2.1	1.4
Algeria	2008	..	..	16.3	9.7	60.6	0.0	17.0	8.8	16.2	9.8
Angola	2008	100.0	59.2	7.5	7.7	23.0	0.0	11.6	14.0	6.8	6.2
Antigua and Barbuda	2008	97.9	58.7	11.6	13.6	48.3	0.0	13.8	13.1	11.2	13.7
Argentina	2008	100.0	31.9	9.8	5.3	21.9	0.0	7.8	1.3	10.1	5.9
Armenia	2008	100.0	8.5	3.7	2.3	0.0	0.0	5.5	2.2	3.5	2.4
Australia	2008	97.1	9.9	3.9	2.5	5.2	0.0	1.4	0.4	4.4	3.3
Azerbaijan	2008	..	..	8.4	3.9	47.4	0.0	9.8	3.4	8.2	4.1
Bahamas, The	2006	..	..	28.5	23.9	77.4	0.0	24.4	15.1	29.3	29.7
Bahrain	2008	73.4	34.4	4.3	3.6	0.2	0.0	6.8	6.9	4.0	3.1
Bangladesh	2007	15.5	169.3	14.5	11.0	41.1	0.0	15.1	7.3	14.5	13.1
Barbados	2007	97.9	78.1	15.1	14.8	44.9	0.6	26.3	21.9	13.4	12.3
Belarus	2008	..	..	8.0	2.3	27.3	0.0	7.0	0.6	8.1	3.9
Belize	2008	97.9	58.2	11.6	9.3	43.3	0.0	15.5	6.5	11.1	11.0
Benin	2008	39.0	28.6	13.3	15.5	50.6	0.0	15.1	11.3	13.0	17.5
Bermuda	2008	..	..	18.1	29.5	66.7	0.0	10.0	16.1	19.6	31.3
Bhutan	2007	..	..	17.7	16.5	49.3	0.0	43.5	44.9	15.5	16.0
Bolivia	2008	100.0	40.0	6.2	4.1	0.0	0.0	6.1	3.3	6.2	4.1
Bosnia and Herzegovina	2008	..	..	6.6	4.7	10.9	0.0	3.2	1.9	7.0	6.2
Botswana	2008	96.3	18.9	8.0	8.7	30.8	0.0	4.5	1.1	8.5	9.9
Brazil	2008	100.0	31.4	13.1	6.7	26.4	0.0	7.9	1.1	13.7	9.3
Brunei Darussalam	2007	95.4	24.3	3.1	6.1	21.6	0.1	0.9	13.2	3.4	4.6
Burkina Faso	2008	39.2	41.9	11.5	6.9	40.9	0.0	11.0	6.8	11.5	6.6
Burundi	2008	21.8	68.3	12.8	10.7	34.1	0.0	11.7	7.9	12.9	11.3
Cambodia	2007	..	..	12.5	10.0	49.2	0.0	14.7	10.5	12.1	9.9
Cameroon	2007	13.3	79.9	18.6	12.7	52.4	0.0	21.9	10.8	18.2	14.4
Canada	2008	99.7	5.1	3.6	1.0	6.7	0.0	1.9	0.3	4.1	1.2
Cape Verde	2008	..	..	15.3	12.2	46.8	0.0	15.9	12.6	15.0	11.8
Central African Republic	2007	..	..	17.5	13.5	46.8	0.0	18.9	13.9	17.3	13.2
Chad	2007	..	..	16.9	13.3	44.3	0.0	20.6	18.3	16.5	12.7
Chile	2008	100.0	25.1	1.4	1.0	0.0	0.0	1.4	1.4	1.4	0.8
China†	2008	100.0	10.0	8.6	3.9	13.3	0.0	8.8	2.4	8.7	5.8
Hong Kong SAR, China	2008	46.5	0.0	0.0	0.0	0.0	0.0	0.0	0.0	0.0	0.0
Macau SAR, China	2008	28.7	0.0	0.0	0.0	0.0	0.0	0.0	0.0	0.0	0.0
Colombia	2008	100.0	42.8	10.7	8.7	41.0	0.0	9.7	7.7	10.8	9.4
Congo, Dem. Rep.	2008	..	..	12.8	11.0	42.1	0.0	14.1	10.8	12.6	11.1
Congo, Rep.	2007	16.1	27.3	18.6	14.5	52.3	0.0	21.9	18.6	18.2	14.1
Costa Rica	2007	100.0	42.9	6.0	3.8	0.3	0.0	8.5	5.1	5.8	3.8
Côte d'Ivoire	2008	33.1	11.2	13.2	6.6	48.6	0.0	15.3	4.1	12.9	9.8
Croatia	2008	100.0	6.0	2.5	1.1	3.9	0.0	4.4	1.9	2.3	0.9
Cuba	2008	31.6	21.0	11.0	9.1	33.6	0.0	10.6	8.1	11.1	9.4
Djibouti	2006	100.0	41.0	30.2	29.1	87.9	0.0	23.1	23.2	31.3	31.0
Dominica	2007	94.8	58.7	11.9	7.9	43.3	0.0	19.3	5.7	10.6	9.3
Dominican Republic	2008	100.0	34.9	9.0	5.1	29.2	0.0	11.6	4.5	8.7	5.2
Ecuador	2008	100.0	21.8	9.7	5.4	32.1	0.0	7.7	4.2	9.9	5.5
Egypt, Arab Rep.	2008	99.3	36.8	12.3	8.0	18.1	0.0	36.2	6.3	9.5	9.8
El Salvador	2008	100.0	36.6	3.9	3.1	15.7	0.0	5.2	2.4	3.8	3.9
Eritrea	2006	..	..	9.6	5.4	22.4	0.0	9.2	3.5	9.6	7.2
Ethiopia	2008	..	..	18.2	10.1	56.0	0.0	19.4	6.6	18.0	12.8
European Union	2008	100.0	4.2	1.6	1.7	1.4	0.0	2.3	0.4	1.5	1.2
Fiji	2008	51.3	40.1	11.0	8.9	38.2	0.0	11.9	7.3	10.8	10.5
Gabon	2008	100.0	21.2	18.6	14.4	52.1	0.0	21.0	15.2	18.3	14.2
Gambia, The	2008	13.7	101.8	18.7	14.7	90.9	0.0	17.0	12.2	19.2	17.4
Georgia	2008	100.0	7.2	0.6	0.5	0.0	0.0	4.3	1.2	0.1	0.1
Ghana	2008	14.3	92.5	13.0	9.8	40.8	0.0	16.8	14.4	12.5	8.8
Grenada	2008	100.0	56.8	10.6	8.8	43.3	0.0	14.1	9.9	10.0	8.4
Guatemala	2008	100.0	42.2	4.4	3.0	18.9	0.0	5.1	2.4	4.3	3.5
Guinea	2008	38.6	20.3	13.9	12.5	57.7	0.0	15.4	14.0	13.7	11.2
†Data for Taiwan, China	2008	100.0	5.9	5.3	1.9	6.8	0.0	8.0	2.0	4.8	1.9

	Most recent year	Binding coverage	Simple mean bound rate	All products %				Primary products %		Manufactured products %	
				Simple mean tariff	Weighted mean tariff	Share of tariff lines with international peaks	Share of tariff lines with specific rates	Simple mean tariff	Weighted mean tariff	Simple mean tariff	Weighted mean tariff
Guinea-Bissau	2008	..	..	12.9	10.7	50.3	0.0	14.9	10.9	12.6	10.4
Guyana	2008	100.0	56.7	10.8	6.9	41.9	0.0	17.7	5.9	9.7	7.3
Haiti	2008	..	..	3.0	4.8	5.0	0.0	5.6	3.9	2.4	5.6
Honduras	2008	100.0	32.4	4.6	3.2	20.6	0.0	5.6	3.5	4.4	3.1
Iceland	2008	95.0	13.5	2.4	1.1	6.5	0.0	2.7	1.7	2.4	0.9
India	2008	73.8	49.6	9.7	6.1	7.3	0.0	19.5	7.3	8.4	5.9
Indonesia	2007	96.6	37.1	5.8	3.6	12.6	0.0	6.6	2.6	5.8	4.4
Iran, Islamic Rep.	2008	..	..	24.8	20.1	56.6	0.0	21.5	12.5	25.1	21.2
Iraq	..	..	..	..	..	..	..	..	..	..	..
Israel	2008	75.0	21.5	2.2	1.1	0.9	0.0	3.5	1.2	2.1	1.1
Jamaica	2006	100.0	49.6	9.2	8.9	35.8	0.0	15.8	9.4	8.3	8.5
Japan	2008	99.7	2.9	2.6	1.3	6.9	0.0	4.9	1.2	2.3	1.6
Jordan	2008	99.9	16.2	10.7	5.6	33.2	0.0	14.4	3.8	10.1	7.3
Kazakhstan	2008	..	..	3.9	2.1	6.7	0.0	5.8	0.8	3.7	2.6
Kenya	2008	14.8	95.4	12.1	6.3	36.5	0.0	15.2	5.6	11.7	6.9
Kosovo	..	..	..	..	..	..	..	..	..	..	..
Korea, Dem. Rep.	..	..	..	..	..	..	..	..	..	..	..
Korea, Rep.	2008	94.6	15.8	8.3	7.1	4.6	0.0	20.7	11.6	6.6	4.8
Kuwait	2008	99.9	100.0	4.1	4.0	0.0	0.0	3.3	3.1	4.3	4.4
Kyrgyz Republic	2008	99.9	7.4	3.5	8.5	0.9	0.0	4.3	1.2	3.4	9.4
Lao PDR	2007	..	..	5.8	8.3	15.1	0.0	9.9	8.3	5.3	8.3
Lebanon	2007	..	..	5.7	4.8	11.6	0.0	8.2	5.0	5.2	5.1
Lesotho	2008	..	..	9.2	14.4	37.8	0.0	7.7	1.1	9.6	17.2
Liberia	..	..	..	..	..	..	..	..	..	..	..
Libya	2006	..	..	0.0	0.0	0.0	0.0	0.0	0.0	0.0	0.0
Macedonia, FYR	2008	100.0	6.9	4.9	3.3	15.7	0.0	7.9	4.8	4.7	2.6
Madagascar	2008	30.0	27.3	12.1	8.4	41.6	0.0	13.9	4.2	11.9	10.4
Malawi	2008	31.6	75.4	12.1	6.0	43.8	0.0	12.8	5.7	11.8	6.0
Malaysia	2007	83.7	14.5	5.9	3.1	24.8	0.0	2.9	2.3	6.5	3.4
Maldives	2008	97.1	36.9	21.5	20.3	87.0	0.0	17.5	18.4	22.8	22.6
Mali	2008	40.2	28.5	12.9	8.4	48.4	0.0	12.8	7.9	12.8	8.7
Mauritania	2007	39.3	19.6	12.6	10.1	49.0	0.0	11.2	9.2	12.8	11.0
Mauritius	2008	17.8	94.4	4.2	2.1	16.8	0.0	6.2	1.5	4.0	2.6
Mayotte	2008	..	..	5.3	1.9	2.3	0.0	3.8	1.3	5.6	2.1
Mexico	2008	100.0	35.0	6.4	1.9	11.5	0.0	7.3	0.9	6.4	2.2
Moldova	2008	..	..	4.1	2.4	6.7	0.0	6.5	2.1	3.8	2.7
Mongolia	2008	100.0	17.5	4.9	5.1	0.4	0.0	5.2	5.4	4.9	4.9
Morocco	2008	100.0	41.3	11.7	9.4	41.1	0.0	19.3	11.4	10.9	8.2
Mozambique	2007	..	..	11.0	7.7	36.7	0.0	13.9	8.0	10.5	7.5
Myanmar	2007	17.4	83.6	4.1	3.9	8.1	0.0	5.8	4.5	3.9	3.6
Namibia	2008	96.3	19.2	6.3	1.1	25.3	0.0	3.6	0.6	6.9	1.3
Nepal	2007	..	..	12.4	13.1	40.9	0.0	12.5	9.7	12.6	15.8
New Zealand	2008	99.9	10.0	2.8	2.0	0.0	0.0	1.5	0.4	3.0	2.7
Nicaragua	2007	100.0	41.7	5.4	3.6	0.4	0.0	7.7	3.9	5.1	3.4
Niger	2008	96.7	44.7	13.0	9.2	49.3	0.0	14.0	10.7	12.8	7.6
Nigeria	2008	19.3	118.4	10.7	8.9	33.5	0.0	12.3	9.6	10.5	8.1
Norway	2008	100.0	3.0	0.6	0.4	0.6	0.0	1.9	1.1	0.4	0.2
Oman	2008	100.0	13.8	3.8	3.3	0.2	0.0	4.6	3.0	3.7	3.4
Pakistan	2008	98.7	60.0	14.0	9.0	51.1	0.0	12.8	6.3	14.3	12.3
Panama	2008	99.9	23.4	7.2	7.1	33.6	0.0	11.1	7.9	6.8	6.8
Papua New Guinea	2008	100.0	31.7	4.5	2.3	23.3	0.0	12.6	2.7	3.4	2.2
Paraguay	2008	100.0	33.5	8.3	3.3	18.0	0.0	6.4	1.1	8.6	3.9
Peru	2008	100.0	30.1	3.8	2.1	6.3	0.0	5.3	1.7	3.8	2.3
Philippines	2007	67.0	25.7	5.0	3.6	15.8	0.0	6.0	5.2	4.8	2.7
Puerto Rico	..	..	..	..	..	..	..	..	..	..	..
Qatar	2008	100.0	15.9	4.3	3.7	0.2	0.0	5.4	4.0	4.2	3.8
Russian Federation	2008	..	..	8.2	5.8	25.1	0.0	7.7	4.8	8.2	5.9
Rwanda	2008	100.0	89.5	18.6	12.0	52.9	0.0	15.8	9.1	19.0	13.7
Saudi Arabia	2008	..	..	4.0	3.8	0.0	0.0	3.3	2.7	4.1	4.2

6.8 | Tariff barriers

	Most recent year	Binding coverage	Simple mean bound rate	All products % Simple mean tariff	Weighted mean tariff	Share of tariff lines with international peaks	Share of tariff lines with specific rates	Primary products % Simple mean tariff	Weighted mean tariff	Manufactured products % Simple mean tariff	Weighted mean tariff
Senegal	2008	100.0	30.0	13.4	8.5	50.6	0.0	14.1	7.0	13.3	10.4
Serbia[a]	2005	..	..	8.1	6.0	17.8	0.0	10.9	4.5	7.3	6.8
Seychelles	2007	..	..	6.5	28.3	12.8	0.0	14.0	50.5	4.8	6.4
Sierra Leone	2004	100.0	47.4	..	..	..	..	..	..	..	..
Singapore	2008	69.7	7.0	0.0	0.0	0.0	0.0	0.0	0.0	0.0	0.0
Solomon Islands	2008	100.0	78.7	9.2	13.8	1.9	0.0	10.3	17.5	9.1	8.6
Somalia		..	..	..	..	..	..	..	..	..	..
South Africa	2008	96.0	19.2	7.7	4.5	25.4	0.0	5.2	1.7	8.2	6.1
Sri Lanka	2006	38.1	29.8	11.3	7.1	23.5	0.8	17.6	9.0	10.6	6.4
St. Kitts and Nevis	2008	97.9	75.9	12.3	12.3	44.3	0.0	12.7	11.5	12.1	12.6
St. Lucia	2007	99.6	61.9	9.6	9.0	39.9	0.0	12.6	4.9	9.1	12.2
St. Vincent & Grenadines	2007	..	..	11.3	8.4	44.4	0.2	15.1	7.8	10.6	8.6
Sudan	2008	..	..	14.3	11.4	34.9	0.0	18.0	11.6	13.7	11.3
Suriname	2007	..	..	11.5	11.8	39.4	0.0	17.8	15.9	10.6	10.9
Swaziland	2008	96.3	19.2	9.5	5.2	34.2	0.0	9.2	1.5	10.0	7.3
Switzerland	2008	99.8	0.0	0.0	0.0	0.0	0.0	0.0	0.0	0.0	0.0
Syrian Arab Republic	2002	..	..	14.7	15.5	23.3	0.0	14.4	11.7	14.7	17.1
Tajikistan	2006	..	..	4.9	3.8	0.1	0.7	5.4	2.6	4.8	4.4
Tanzania	2008	13.4	120.0	11.7	10.2	35.4	0.0	15.8	12.8	11.2	10.1
Thailand	2006	75.0	25.7	10.8	4.6	22.9	0.9	13.5	2.1	10.4	5.8
Timor-Leste		..	..	..	..	..	..	..	..	..	..
Togo	2008	14.0	80.0	13.1	13.9	48.9	0.0	14.7	10.4	12.9	15.9
Trinidad and Tobago	2008	100.0	55.7	8.2	4.2	43.6	0.0	13.1	2.7	7.5	5.6
Tunisia	2006	57.9	57.9	23.0	18.3	55.5	0.0	32.2	13.9	22.2	20.0
Turkey	2008	50.6	28.5	2.4	1.8	4.4	0.0	12.4	2.8	1.4	1.5
Turkmenistan	2002	..	..	5.4	2.9	14.8	2.8	14.8	12.6	3.8	1.1
Uganda	2008	15.7	73.4	12.0	7.4	37.3	0.0	14.4	7.4	11.7	8.0
Ukraine	2008	..	..	4.9	3.7	4.7	0.0	4.8	0.8	5.0	5.6
United Arab Emirates	2008	100.0	14.7	4.2	3.6	0.2	0.0	4.5	2.6	4.2	4.4
United States	2008	100.0	3.6	3.0	1.5	3.6	0.0	2.5	1.0	3.1	1.9
Uruguay	2008	100.0	31.6	9.5	3.6	26.6	0.0	5.7	1.1	9.9	4.9
Uzbekistan	2008	..	..	12.1	7.3	21.6	0.0	12.4	3.6	11.9	7.1
Vanuatu	2008	..	..	16.8	15.0	65.0	0.0	19.5	16.9	16.2	14.3
Venezuela, RB	2008	100.0	36.5	11.9	11.4	44.0	0.0	11.4	10.0	12.0	11.6
Vietnam	2007	..	..	11.7	10.6	32.2	0.0	14.5	10.2	11.3	11.0
West Bank and Gaza		..	..	..	..	..	..	..	..	..	..
Yemen, Rep.	2006	..	..	6.7	6.9	1.8	0.0	9.6	8.6	6.3	5.6
Zambia	2008	16.8	106.0	10.8	5.0	49.7	0.0	8.0	5.7	10.8	4.4
Zimbabwe	2007	22.4	89.8	16.7	17.3	38.8	0.0	19.5	19.8	16.3	15.3
World		**79.6 w**	**31.9 w**	**7.1 w**	**2.8 w**	**16.6 w**	**0.1 w**	**8.7 w**	**2.2 w**	**6.9 w**	**3.3 w**
Low income		40.7	52.4	12.1	9.2	35.3	0.0	13.5	8.0	11.8	9.9
Middle income		87.4	34.0	8.2	4.6	21.8	0.3	10.5	3.3	7.9	5.5
Lower middle income		84.2	35.7	9.7	5.2	25.6	0.1	12.7	3.7	9.3	6.6
Upper middle income		90.4	32.3	7.2	4.0	19.5	0.1	8.8	2.8	7.0	4.5
Low & middle income		75.4	36.5	8.8	4.8	23.4	0.1	11.0	3.6	8.6	5.7
East Asia & Pacific		79.1	32.5	8.4	4.1	21.7	0.1	9.2	2.8	8.3	5.5
Europe & Central Asia		94.7	11.6	4.8	3.6	12.6	0.2	8.2	3.0	4.4	3.8
Latin America & Carib.		97.0	40.9	8.0	4.3	21.7	0.0	8.9	2.1	8.0	5.2
Middle East & N. Africa		92.9	32.8	12.8	10.8	37.7	0.0	17.8	8.3	12.3	11.9
South Asia		64.7	52.5	13.3	7.0	37.8	0.0	15.8	7.0	13.0	7.1
Sub-Saharan Africa		47.9	43.2	11.7	7.5	37.9	0.0	13.1	6.4	11.5	8.1
High income		92.2	21.5	4.2	1.8	6.0	0.2	5.4	1.6	4.1	2.1
OECD		98.6	7.2	4.0	1.8	4.9	0.0	4.5	1.6	4.1	2.1
Non-OECD		87.8	31.7	4.4	1.5	7.7	0.4	6.7	1.6	4.1	1.9

a. Includes Montenegro.

About the data

Poor people in developing countries work primarily in agriculture and labor-intensive manufactures, sectors that confront the greatest trade barriers. Removing barriers to merchandise trade could increase growth in these countries—even more if trade in services (retailing, business, financial, and telecommunications services) were also liberalized.

In general, tariffs in high-income countries on imports from developing countries, though low, are twice those collected from other high-income countries. But protection is also an issue for developing countries, which maintain high tariffs on agricultural commodities, labor-intensive manufactures, and other products and services. In some developing country regions new trade policies could make the difference between achieving important Millennium Development Goals—reducing poverty, lowering maternal and child mortality rates, improving educational attainment—and falling far short.

Countries use a combination of tariff and nontariff measures to regulate imports. The most common form of tariff is an ad valorem duty, based on the value of the import, but tariffs may also be levied on a specific, or per unit, basis or may combine ad valorem and specific rates. Tariffs may be used to raise fiscal revenues or to protect domestic industries from foreign competition—or both. Nontariff barriers, which limit the quantity of imports of a particular good, include quotas, prohibitions, licensing schemes, export restraint arrangements, and health and quarantine measures. Because of the difficulty of combining nontariff barriers into an aggregate indicator, they are not included in the table.

Unless specified as most favored nation rates, the tariff rates used in calculating the indicators in the table are effectively applied rates. Effectively applied rates are those in effect for partners in preferential trade arrangements such as the North American Free Trade Agreement. The difference between most favored nation and applied rates can be substantial. As more countries report their free trade agreements, suspensions of tariffs, or other special preferences, *World Development Indicators* will include their effectively applied rates. All estimates are calculated using the most recent information, which is not necessarily revised every year. As a result, data for the same year may differ from data in last year's edition.

Three measures of average tariffs are shown: simple bound rates and the simple and the weighted tariffs. Bound rates are based on all products in a country's tariff schedule, while the most favored nation or applied rates are calculated using all traded items. Weighted mean tariffs are weighted by the value of the country's trade with each trading partner. Simple averages are often a better indicator of tariff protection than weighted averages, which are biased downward because higher tariffs discourage trade and reduce the weights applied to these tariffs. Bound rates result from trade negotiations incorporated into a country's schedule of concessions and are thus enforceable.

Some countries set fairly uniform tariff rates across all imports. Others are selective, setting high tariffs to protect favored domestic industries. The share of tariff lines with international peaks provides an indication of how selectively tariffs are applied. The effective rate of protection—the degree to which the value added in an industry is protected—may exceed the nominal rate if the tariff system systematically differentiates among imports of raw materials, intermediate products, and finished goods.

The share of tariff lines with specific rates shows the extent to which countries use tariffs based on physical quantities or other, non–ad valorem measures. Some countries such as Switzerland apply mainly specific duties. To the extent possible, these specific rates have been converted to their ad valorem equivalent rates and have been included in the calculation of simple and weighted tariffs.

Data are classified using the Harmonized System of trade at the six- or eight-digit level. Tariff line data were matched to Standard International Trade Classification (SITC) revision 3 codes to define commodity groups and import weights. Import weights were calculated using the United Nations Statistics Division's Commodity Trade (Comtrade) database. The table shows tariff rates for three commodity groups: all products, primary products, and manufactured products. Effectively applied tariff rates at the six- and eight-digit product level are averaged for products in each commodity group. When the effectively applied rate is unavailable, the most favored nation rate is used instead.

Data are shown only for the last year for which complete data are available and for all economies with populations of 1 million or more and for countries with populations of less than 1 million when available. EU member countries apply a common tariff schedule that is listed under European Union and are thus not listed separately.

Definitions

• **Binding coverage** is the percentage of product lines with an agreed bound rate. • **Simple mean bound rate** is the unweighted average of all the lines in the tariff schedule in which bound rates have been set. • **Simple mean tariff** is the unweighted average of effectively applied rates or most favored nation rates for all products subject to tariffs calculated for all traded goods. • **Weighted mean tariff** is the average of effectively applied rates or most favored nation rates weighted by the product import shares corresponding to each partner country. • **Share of tariff lines with international peaks** is the share of lines in the tariff schedule with tariff rates that exceed 15 percent. • **Share of tariff lines with specific rates** is the share of lines in the tariff schedule that are set on a per unit basis or that combine ad valorem and per unit rates. • **Primary products** are commodities classified in SITC revision 3 sections 0–4 plus division 68 (nonferrous metals). • **Manufactured products** are commodities classified in SITC revision 3 sections 5–8 excluding division 68.

Data sources

All indicators in the table were calculated by World Bank staff using the World Integrated Trade Solution system. Data on tariffs were provided by the United Nations Conference on Trade and Development and the World Trade Organization. Data on global imports are from the United Nations Statistics Division's Comtrade database.

Trade facilitation

	Logistics Performance Index	Burden of customs procedures	Lead time		Documents		Liner Shipping Connectivity Index	Quality of port infrastructure	Freight costs to the United States
			days		number				1 kilogram DHL air package $
	1–5 (worst to best) 2009	1–7 (worst to best) 2008–09[a]	To export 2009	To import 2009	To export June 2009	To import June 2009	0–100 (low to high) 2009	1–7 (worst to best) 2008–09	2010
Afghanistan	2.24	..	2.0	4.0	12	11	..	..	143.10
Albania	2.46	3.6	1.7	2.0	7	9	2.3	3.2	150.40
Algeria	2.36	2.7	4.6	7.1	8	9	8.4	2.9	154.40
Angola	2.25	..	6.0	8.0	11	8	11.3	..	154.40
Argentina	3.10	2.8	3.7	3.8	9	7	26.0	3.6	88.55
Armenia	2.52	2.7	..	..	5	7	..	2.9[b]	143.10
Australia	3.84	4.9	2.6	2.8	6	5	28.8	4.6	90.75
Austria	3.76	5.3	2.0	3.7	4	5	..	5.0[b]	113.80
Azerbaijan	2.64	3.9	7.0	3.0	9	14	..	4.2[b]	150.40
Bangladesh	2.74	2.8	1.4	1.4	6	8	7.9	3.0	90.75
Belarus	2.53	..	..	..	8	8	..	..	150.40
Belgium	3.94	4.6	1.7	1.6	4	5	82.8	6.3	103.00
Benin	2.79	3.4	3.0	7.0	7	7	13.5	3.3	154.40
Bolivia	2.51	2.8	15.0	28.3	8	7	..	3.0[b]	88.55
Bosnia and Herzegovina	2.66	3.5	2.0	2.0	6	7	..	1.5	150.40
Botswana	2.32	4.4	..	..	6	9	..	3.7[b]	154.40
Brazil	3.20	2.9	2.8	3.9	8	7	31.1	2.6	88.55
Bulgaria	2.83	3.6	2.0	3.9	5	7	5.8	3.6	150.40
Burkina Faso	2.23	3.8	4.0	14.0	11	11	..	4.0[b]	154.40
Burundi	2.29	3.0	..	..	9	10	..	3.1[b]	154.40
Cambodia	2.37	3.3	1.3	4.0	11	11	4.7	3.5	88.50
Cameroon	2.55	3.2	3.4	8.9	10	11	11.6	2.7	154.40
Canada	3.87	4.7	2.8	3.7	3	4	41.3	5.6	68.20
Central African Republic	..	..	..	..	9	17	..	..	154.40
Chad	2.49	2.3	74.0	35.0	6	10	..	2.7[b]	154.40
Chile	3.09	5.8	3.5	3.0	6	7	18.8	5.4	88.55
China	3.49	4.6	2.8	2.6	7	5	132.5	4.3	78.25
Hong Kong SAR, China	3.88	6.1	1.7	1.6	4	4	104.5	6.8	82.10
Colombia	2.77	3.8	7.0	7.0	6	8	23.2	3.2	88.55
Congo, Dem. Rep.	2.68	..	2.0	3.0	8	9	3.8	..	154.40
Congo, Rep.	2.48	..	..	..	11	12	11.4	..	154.40
Costa Rica	2.91	3.9	2.0	2.0	6	7	14.6	2.6	88.55
Côte d'Ivoire	2.53	3.3	1.0	1.0	10	9	19.4	5.0	154.40
Croatia	2.77	3.8	1.0	1.0	7	8	8.5	3.8	150.40
Cuba	2.07	..	..	..	..	..	5.9	..	72.85
Czech Republic	3.51	4.6	2.5	3.5	4	7	0.4	4.2[b]	150.40
Denmark	3.85	5.8	1.0	1.0	4	3	27.7	6.2	113.80
Dominican Republic	2.82	4.5	2.2	3.5	6	7	21.6	4.3	72.85
Ecuador	2.77	3.1	2.1	3.4	9	7	17.1	3.3	88.55
Egypt, Arab Rep.	2.61	4.0	1.3	3.1	6	6	52.0	4.3	143.10
El Salvador	2.67	4.1	2.0	2.0	8	8	10.3	4.2	88.55
Eritrea	1.70	..	3.0	3.0	9	13	3.3	..	154.40
Estonia	3.16	5.5	4.0	4.0	3	4	5.7	5.6	150.40
Ethiopia	2.41	3.3	5.0	6.0	8	8	..	3.8[b]	154.40
Finland	3.89	5.7	1.6	1.8	4	5	10.2	6.5	113.80
France	3.84	4.8	3.2	4.5	2	2	67.0	5.9	103.00
Gabon	2.41	..	4.3	13.0	7	8	9.2	..	154.40
Gambia, The	2.49	5.1	4.6	3.5	6	8	7.5	4.7	154.40
Georgia	2.61	4.6	..	..	4	4	3.8	4.0	150.40
Germany	4.11	5.1	3.6	2.4	4	5	84.3	6.4	103.00
Ghana	2.47	3.4	2.9	6.8	6	7	19.3	4.0	154.40
Greece	2.96	4.1	3.0	3.5	5	6	41.9	4.1	113.80
Guatemala	2.63	4.2	2.6	3.4	10	10	14.7	4.3	88.55
Guinea	2.60	..	3.5	3.9	7	9	8.3	..	154.40
Guinea-Bissau	2.10	..	..	..	6	6	3.5	..	154.40
Haiti	2.59	..	4.2	5.3	8	10	4.4	..	72.85
Honduras	2.78	4.0	2.4	3.2	7	10	10.7	5.1	88.55

	Logistics Performance Index	Burden of customs procedures	Lead time		Documents		Liner Shipping Connectivity Index	Quality of port infrastructure	Freight costs to the United States
			days		number				1 kilogram DHL air package $
	1–5 (worst to best) 2009	1–7 (worst to best) 2008–09[a]	To export 2009	To import 2009	To export June 2009	To import June 2009	0–100 (low to high) 2009	1–7 (worst to best) 2008–09	2010
Hungary	2.99	4.3	3.5	5.0	5	7	..	3.9[b]	150.40
India	3.12	3.9	2.3	5.3	8	9	41.0	3.5	90.75
Indonesia	2.76	3.7	2.1	5.4	5	6	25.7	3.4	90.75
Iran, Islamic Rep.	2.57	..	2.6	28.3	7	8	28.9	..	143.10
Iraq	2.11	..	..	..	10	10	5.1	..	143.10
Ireland	3.89	5.1	1.0	1.0	4	4	7.6	4.4	103.00
Israel	3.41	4.0	2.0	2.0	5	4	18.7	4.6	143.10
Italy	3.64	4.0	2.6	3.0	4	4	70.0	3.7	103.00
Jamaica	2.53	3.4	10.0	10.0	6	6	19.6	5.3	72.85
Japan	3.97	4.4	1.0	1.0	4	5	66.3	5.2	113.80
Jordan	2.74	4.6	3.2	4.6	7	7	23.7	4.5	143.10
Kazakhstan	2.83	3.3	2.8	11.5	11	13	..	3.0[b]	150.40
Kenya	2.59	3.3	3.0	5.9	9	8	12.8	3.6	154.40
Korea, Dem. Rep.	..	..	..	..	..	..	..	..	88.50
Korea, Rep.	3.64	4.6	1.6	2.0	3	3	86.7	5.1	90.75
Kosovo	..	..	..	..	8	8	..	..	..
Kuwait	3.28	3.5	2.0	3.0	8	10	6.5	4.1	143.10
Kyrgyz Republic	2.62	2.8	2.0	..	7	7	..	1.6[b]	150.40
Lao PDR	2.46	..	..	..	9	10	..	..	88.50
Latvia	3.25	4.1	1.3	1.6	6	6	5.2	4.4	150.40
Lebanon	3.34	..	3.4	2.2	5	7	29.6	..	143.10
Lesotho	2.30	3.8	..	..	6	8	..	3.0[b]	154.40
Liberia	2.38	..	4.0	5.0	10	9	5.5	..	154.40
Libya	2.33	3.5	3.2	10.0	..	..	9.4	3.3	154.40
Lithuania	3.13	4.8	2.0	2.3	6	6	8.1	4.7	150.40
Macedonia, FYR	2.77	4.0	..	..	6	6	..	3.4[b]	150.40
Madagascar	2.66	3.6	..	..	4	9	8.6	3.0	154.40
Malawi	2.42	3.7	4.2	3.7	11	10	..	3.5[b]	154.40
Malaysia	3.44	4.8	2.6	2.8	7	7	81.2	5.5	90.75
Mali	2.27	3.7	5.0	4.0	7	10	..	3.8[b]	154.40
Mauritania	2.63	4.0	2.0	3.0	11	11	7.5	3.5	154.40
Mauritius	2.72	4.6	3.0	2.4	5	6	14.8	4.3	154.40
Mexico	3.05	3.7	2.1	2.5	5	5	31.9	3.7	58.80
Moldova	2.57	..	..	..	6	7	..	..	150.40
Mongolia	2.25	3.1	14.0	12.0	8	8	..	2.9[b]	88.50
Morocco	2.38	4.1	2.0	3.2	7	10	38.4	4.2	154.40
Mozambique	2.29	3.1	..	..	7	10	9.4	3.2	154.40
Myanmar	2.33	..	4.6	8.4	..	..	3.8	..	88.50
Namibia	2.02	4.2	3.0	3.0	11	9	13.6	5.4	154.40
Nepal	2.20	3.1	1.8	6.3	9	10	..	2.8[b]	88.50
Netherlands	4.07	5.2	1.8	1.9	4	5	88.7	6.6	103.00
New Zealand	3.65	5.9	1.3	1.6	7	5	10.6	5.5	90.75
Nicaragua	2.54	3.8	3.2	3.2	5	5	10.6	2.7	88.55
Niger	2.54	..	..	..	8	10	..	..	154.40
Nigeria	2.59	3.1	2.5	4.1	10	9	19.9	2.8	154.40
Norway	3.93	5.2	1.0	2.0	4	4	7.9	5.8	113.80
Oman	2.84	5.1	..	..	10	10	45.3	5.2	143.10
Pakistan	2.53	3.6	2.3	1.6	9	8	26.6	4.0	143.10
Panama	3.02	4.3	1.4	1.4	3	4	32.7	5.5	88.55
Papua New Guinea	2.41	..	..	..	7	9	6.6	..	88.50
Paraguay	2.75	3.6	1.0	4.0	8	10	0.0	3.5[b]	88.55
Peru	2.80	3.8	2.0	3.8	7	8	17.0	2.7	88.55
Philippines	3.14	3.0	1.8	5.0	8	8	15.9	3.0	90.75
Poland	3.44	3.9	3.0	3.6	5	5	9.2	2.8	150.40
Portugal	3.34	4.9	2.5	5.0	4	5	33.0	4.7	113.80
Puerto Rico	..	4.7	..	..	7	10	10.9	5.4	..
Qatar	2.95	4.5	3.8	2.3	5	7	2.1	5.0	143.10

6.9 Trade facilitation

	Logistics Performance Index	Burden of customs procedures	Lead time		Documents		Liner Shipping Connectivity Index	Quality of port infrastructure	Freight costs to the United States
			days		number				1 kilogram DHL air package $
	1–5 (worst to best) 2009	1–7 (worst to best) 2008–09[a]	To export 2009	To import 2009	To export June 2009	To import June 2009	0–100 (low to high) 2009	1–7 (worst to best) 2008–09	2010
Romania	2.84	4.1	2.0	2.0	5	6	23.3	3.3	150.40
Russian Federation	2.61	2.7	4.0	2.9	8	13	20.6	3.5	150.40
Rwanda	2.04	..	..	..	9	9	..	..	154.40
Saudi Arabia	3.22	4.8	2.3	6.3	5	5	47.3	4.7	143.10
Senegal	2.86	4.4	1.4	2.7	6	5	15.0	4.4	154.40
Serbia	2.69[c]	3.3	2.0[c]	3.0[c]	6	6	..	3.3[c]	150.40
Sierra Leone	1.97	..	2.0	32.0	7	7	5.6	..	154.40
Singapore	4.09	6.4	2.2	1.8	4	4	99.5	6.8	82.10
Slovak Republic	3.24	4.7	3.0	5.0	6	8	..	4.1[b]	150.40
Slovenia	2.87	5.4	1.0	2.0	6	8	19.8	5.2	150.40
Somalia	1.34	..	..	..	..	..	2.8	..	154.40
South Africa	3.46	4.3	2.3	3.3	8	9	32.1	4.7	154.40
Spain	3.63	4.4	4.0	7.1	6	8	70.2	5.2	113.80
Sri Lanka	2.29	3.7	1.3	2.5	8	6	34.7	4.8	90.75
Sudan	2.21	..	39.0	5.0	6	6	9.3	..	154.40
Swaziland	..	..	..	..	9	11	..	..	154.40
Sweden	4.08	5.8	1.0	2.6	4	3	31.3	5.9	113.80
Switzerland	3.97	5.1	2.6	2.6	4	5	2.7	5.4[b]	113.80
Syrian Arab Republic	2.74	2.9	2.5	3.2	8	9	11.0	3.3	143.10
Tajikistan	2.35	3.2	7.0	..	10	10	..	1.9[b]	150.40
Tanzania	2.60	3.0	3.2	7.1	5	7	9.5	2.8	154.40
Thailand	3.29	4.1	1.6	2.6	4	3	36.8	4.7	90.75
Timor-Leste	1.71	3.0	..	..	6	7	..	2.3	88.50
Togo	2.60	..	..	..	6	8	14.4	..	154.40
Trinidad and Tobago	..	2.8	..	..	5	6	15.9	4.0	72.85
Tunisia	2.84	4.2	1.7	7.0	5	7	6.5	4.9	154.40
Turkey	3.22	3.4	2.2	3.8	7	8	32.0	3.7	143.10
Turkmenistan	2.49	..	3.0	..	..	..	..	..	150.40
Uganda	2.82	3.4	5.5	14.0	6	7	..	3.4[b]	154.40
Ukraine	2.57	3.0	1.7	7.0	6	10	22.8	3.7	150.40
United Arab Emirates	3.63	5.9	2.5	2.0	4	5	60.5	6.2	143.10
United Kingdom	3.95	4.6	3.3	1.9	4	4	84.8	5.2	103.00
United States	3.86	4.6	2.8	4.0	4	5	82.4	5.7	..
Uruguay	2.75	3.8	3.0	3.0	10	10	22.3	4.9	88.55
Uzbekistan	2.79	..	1.4	2.0	7	11	..	..	150.40
Venezuela, RB	2.68	1.8	9.4	12.1	8	9	20.4	2.4	88.55
Vietnam	2.96	3.6	1.4	1.7	6	8	26.4	3.3	90.75
West Bank and Gaza	..	..	..	..	6	6	..	..	..
Yemen, Rep.	2.58	..	3.1	3.6	6	9	14.6	..	143.10
Zambia	2.28	3.8	9.2	4.0	6	9	..	3.7[b]	154.40
Zimbabwe	2.29	3.0	25.0	18.0	7	9	..	4.4[b]	154.40
World	**2.87[d] u**	**4.1[d] u**	**3.8[d] u**	**4.6[d] u**	**7 u**	**7 u**	..	**4.2 u**	..
Low income	2.43[d]	3.4[d]	6.0[d]	6.4[d]	8	9	..	3.4	..
Middle income	2.69[d]	3.7[d]	3.8[d]	5.1[d]	7	8	..	3.7	..
Lower middle income	2.59[d]	3.6[d]	4.7[d]	6.1[d]	7	8	..	3.7	..
Upper middle income	2.80[d]	3.8[d]	2.9[d]	4.0[d]	7	8	..	3.7	..
Low & middle income	2.61[d]	3.6[d]	4.5[d]	5.5[d]	7	8	..	3.6	..
East Asia & Pacific	2.73[d]	3.7[d]	3.6[d]	4.9[d]	7	7	..	3.7	..
Europe & Central Asia	2.74[d]	3.6[d]	2.8[d]	3.0[d]	7	8	..	3.3	..
Latin America & Carib.	2.74[d]	3.6[d]	3.9[d]	5.5[d]	7	7	..	3.8	..
Middle East & N. Africa	2.60[d]	3.7[d]	2.7[d]	7.2[d]	7	8	..	3.9	..
South Asia	2.49[d]	3.4[d]	1.9[d]	3.3[d]	9	9	..	3.6	..
Sub-Saharan Africa	2.42[d]	3.6[d]	8.1[d]	7.0[d]	8	9	..	3.7	..
High income	3.55[d]	4.9[d]	2.1[d]	2.7[d]	5	5	..	5.3	..
Euro area	3.57[d]	4.9[d]	2.2[d]	2.9[d]	4	5	..	5.3	..

a. Average of the 2008 and 2009 survey ratings. b. Landlocked country. c. Includes Montenegro. d. Aggregates are computed according to the World Bank classification of economies as of July 1, 2009, and may differ from data published in the original source.

About the data

Broadly defined, trade facilitation encompasses customs efficiency and other physical and regulatory environments where trade takes place, harmonization of standards and conformance to international regulations, and the logistics of moving goods and associated documentation through countries and ports. Though collection of trade facilitation data has improved over the last decade, data that allow meaningful evaluation, especially for developing economies, are lacking. Data on trade facilitation are drawn from research by private and international agencies. Most data are perception-based evaluations by business executives and professionals. Because of different backgrounds, values, and personalities, those surveyed may evaluate the same situation quite differently. Perception-based indicators are thus subject to bias and require caution when interpreting the results. Nevertheless, they convey much needed information on trade facilitation.

The table presents data from Logistics Performance Surveys conducted by the World Bank in partnership with academic and international institutions and private companies and individuals engaged in international logistics. The Logistics Performance Index assesses logistics performance across six aspects of the logistics environment (see *Definitions*), based on more than 5,000 country assessments by nearly 1,000 international freight forwarders. Respondents evaluate eight markets on six core dimensions on a scale from 1 (worst) to 5 (best). The markets are chosen based on the most important export and import markets of the respondent's country, random selection, and, for landlocked countries, neighboring countries that connect them with international markets. Scores for the six areas are averaged across all respondents and aggregated to a single score. Details of the survey methodology and index construction methodology are in Arvis and others (2010).

Data on the burden of customs procedures are from the World Economic Forum's Executive Opinion Survey. The 2009 round included more than 13,000 respondents from 133 countries. Sampling follows a dual stratification based on company size and the sector of activity. Data are collected online or through in-person interviews. Responses are aggregated using sector-weighted averaging. The data for the latest year are combined with the data for the previous year to create a two-year moving average. Respondents evaluated the efficiency of customs procedures in their country. The lowest value (1) rates the customs procedure as extremely inefficient, and the highest score (7) as extremely efficient.

The direct costs of cross-border trade include freight, customs, and storage fees. Indirect costs include the value of time to import or export and the risk of delay or loss of shipments. Long lead times and burdensome regulatory procedures may lower competitiveness. Data on lead time are from the LPI survey. Respondents provided separate values for the best case (10 percent of shipments) and the median case (50 percent of shipments). The data are exponentiated averages of the logarithm of single value responses and of midpoint values of range responses for the median case.

Data on the number of documents needed to export or import are from the World Bank's Doing Business surveys, which compile procedural requirements for exporting and importing a standardized cargo of goods by ocean transport from local freight forwarders, shipping lines, customs brokers, port officials, and banks. To make the data comparable across economies, several assumptions about the business and the traded goods are used (see www.doingbusiness.org).

Access to global shipping and air freight networks and the quality and accessibility of ports and roads affect logistics performance. The table shows two indicators related to trade and transport service infrastructure: the Liner Shipping Connectivity Index and the quality of port infrastructure rating. The Liner Shipping Connectivity Index captures how well countries are connected to global shipping networks. It is computed by the United Nations Conference on Trade and Development (UNCTAD) based on five components of the maritime transport sector: number of ships, their container-carrying capacity, maximum vessel size, number of services, and number of companies that deploy container ships in a country's ports. For each component a country's value is divided by the maximum value of each component in 2004, the five components are averaged for each country, and the average is divided by the maximum average for 2004 and multiplied by 100. The index generates a value of 100 for the country with the highest average index in 2004.

The quality of port infrastructure measures business executives' perception of their country's port facilities. Values range from 1 (port infrastructure considered extremely underdeveloped) to 7 (port infrastructure considered efficient by international standards). Respondents in landlocked countries were asked: "How accessible are port facilities (1 = extremely inaccessible; 7 = extremely accessible.)"

The costs of transport services are a crucial determinant of export competitiveness. The proxy indicator in the table is the shipping rates to the United States of an international freight moving business.

Definitions

• **Logistics Performance Index** reflects perceptions of a country's logistics based on efficiency of customs clearance process, quality of trade- and transport-related infrastructure, ease of arranging competitively priced shipments, quality of logistics services, ability to track and trace consignments, and frequency with which shipments reach the consignee within the scheduled time. The index ranges from 1 to 5, with a higher score representing better performance.
• **Burden of customs procedure** measures business executives' perceptions of their country's efficiency of customs procedures. Values range from 1 to 7, with a higher rating indicating greater efficiency. • **Lead time to export** is the median time (the value for 50 percent of shipments) from shipment point to port of loading.
• **Lead time to import** is the median time (the value for 50 percent of shipments) from port of discharge to arrival at the consignee. • **Documents to export** and **documents to import** are all documents required per shipment by government ministries, customs authorities, port and container terminals, health and technical control agencies, and banks to export or import goods. Documents renewed annually and not requiring renewal per shipment are excluded. • **Liner Shipping Connectivity Index** indicates how well countries are connected to global shipping networks based on the status of their maritime transport sector. The highest value in 2004 is 100. • **Quality of port infrastructure** measures business executives' perceptions of their country's port facilities. Values range from 1 to 7, with a higher rating indicating better development of port infrastructure. • **Freight costs to the United States** is the DHL international U.S. inbound worldwide priority express rate for a 1 kilogram air package. Any surcharges are excluded.

Data sources

Data on the Logistics Performance Index and lead time to export and import are from Arvis and others' *Connecting to Compete: Trade Logistics in the Global Economy 2010*. Data on the burden of customs procedure and quality of port infrastructure ratings are from the World Economic Forum's *Global Competitiveness Report 2009–2010*. Data on number of documents to export and import are from the World Bank's Doing Business project (www.doingbusiness.org). Data on the Liner Shipping Connectivity Index are from UNCTAD's *Transport Newsletter*, No. 43 (2009). Freight costs to the United States are based on DHL's "DHL Express Standard Rate Guideline 2010" (2010).

	Total external debt		Long-term debt						Short-term debt		Use of IMF credit	
					$ millions Public and publicly guaranteed							
						IBRD loans and IDA credits		Private nonguaranteed				
	$ millions		Total						$ millions		$ millions	
	1995	2008	1995	2008	1995	2008	1995	2008	1995	2008	1995	2008
Afghanistan	..	2,200	..	2,096	..	444	..	0	..	17	..	87
Albania	456	3,188	330	2,222	109	835	0	106	62	779	65	80
Algeria	33,042	5,476	31,303	3,011	2,049	11	0	1,161	261	1,304	1,478	0
Angola	11,500	15,130	9,543	12,711	81	369	0	0	1,958	2,419	0	0
Argentina	98,465	128,285	54,913	66,410	4,913	5,069	16,066	24,352	21,355	37,523	6,131	0
Armenia	371	3,418	298	1,446	96	1,030	0	1,373	2	465	70	135
Australia	..	..	..	..	..	..	..	..	..	..	..	..
Austria	..	..	..	..	..	..	..	..	..	..	..	..
Azerbaijan	321	4,309	206	2,734	30	775	0	327	14	1,169	101	79
Bangladesh	15,941	23,644	15,121	20,973	5,692	10,613	0	0	199	1,986	622	686
Belarus	1,694	12,299	1,301	3,752	116	42	0	1,589	110	6,959	283	0
Belgium	..	..	..	..	..	..	..	..	..	..	..	..
Benin	1,614	986	1,483	926	498	255	0	0	47	38	84	22
Bolivia	5,272	5,537	4,459	2,403	865	282	239	2,969	307	166	268	0
Bosnia and Herzegovina	..	8,316	..	3,006	472	1,520	..	4,398	..	912	48	0
Botswana	717	438	707	395	108	5	0	0	10	43	0	0
Brazil	160,469	255,614	98,260	73,623	6,038	10,671	30,830	145,339	31,238	36,652	142	0
Bulgaria	10,379	38,045	8,808	4,663	444	1,207	342	14,889	512	18,493	717	0
Burkina Faso	1,271	1,681	1,140	1,517	608	626	0	0	56	110	75	54
Burundi	1,162	1,445	1,099	1,308	591	819	0	0	15	19	48	117
Cambodia	2,284	4,215	2,110	3,892	65	545	0	0	102	323	72	0
Cameroon	10,942	2,794	9,612	2,129	1,082	260	288	636	991	5	51	24
Canada	..	..	..	..	..	..	..	..	..	..	..	..
Central African Republic	946	949	854	815	414	390	0	0	57	71	35	63
Chad	843	1,749	777	1,705	379	905	0	0	17	4	49	41
Chile	22,038	64,277	7,178	8,818	1,383	202	11,429	40,549	3,431	14,910	0	0
China	118,090	378,245	94,674	89,283	14,248	22,250	1,090	101,774	22,325	187,188	0	0
Hong Kong SAR, China	..	..	..	..	..	..	..	..	..	..	..	..
Colombia	25,044	46,887	13,946	29,390	2,559	5,439	5,553	11,812	5,545	5,684	0	0
Congo, Dem. Rep.	13,239	12,199	9,636	10,872	1,413	2,437	0	0	3,118	673	485	654
Congo, Rep.	5,893	5,485	4,872	5,084	279	299	0	0	1,002	363	19	38
Costa Rica	3,774	8,812	3,106	3,043	303	41	214	1,904	430	3,864	24	0
Côte d'Ivoire	18,899	12,561	11,902	10,615	2,386	1,914	2,660	414	3,910	1,344	427	188
Croatia	..	..	..	..	..	..	..	..	..	..	..	..
Cuba	..	..	..	..	..	..	..	..	..	..	..	..
Czech Republic	..	..	..	..	..	..	..	..	..	..	..	..
Denmark	..	..	..	..	..	..	..	..	..	..	..	..
Dominican Republic	4,447	10,484	3,653	7,146	300	458	19	843	616	2,003	160	492
Ecuador	13,877	16,851	11,951	9,595	1,108	624	440	5,592	1,312	1,664	173	0
Egypt, Arab Rep.	33,475	32,616	30,687	28,518	2,356	2,700	313	1,579	2,372	2,519	103	0
El Salvador	2,509	10,110	1,979	5,742	327	409	5	3,316	525	1,052	0	0
Eritrea	37	962	37	957	24	473	0	0	0	5	0	0
Estonia	..	..	..	..	..	..	..	..	..	..	..	..
Ethiopia	10,322	2,882	9,788	2,826	1,470	859	0	0	460	56	73	0
Finland	..	..	..	..	..	..	..	..	..	..	..	..
France	..	..	..	..	..	..	..	..	..	..	..	..
Gabon	4,361	2,367	3,977	2,247	110	20	0	0	287	120	97	0
Gambia, The	426	453	385	420	162	62	0	0	15	20	26	12
Georgia	1,240	3,380	1,039	2,222	84	989	0	341	85	357	116	460
Germany	..	..	..	..	..	..	..	..	..	..	..	..
Ghana	5,495	4,970	4,200	3,412	2,434	1,330	27	39	620	1,356	648	162
Greece	..	..	..	..	..	..	..	..	..	..	..	..
Guatemala	3,282	15,889	2,328	4,374	158	806	142	9,364	811	2,151	0	0
Guinea	3,248	3,092	2,991	2,830	847	1,288	0	0	164	192	94	71
Guinea-Bissau	895	1,157	794	1,004	210	309	0	0	95	144	6	9
Haiti	821	1,935	766	1,830	389	507	0	0	27	0	29	105
Honduras	4,851	3,430	4,247	2,291	828	449	123	590	382	518	99	31

	Total external debt $ millions		Long-term debt — $ millions — Public and publicly guaranteed — Total		IBRD loans and IDA credits		Private nonguaranteed		Short-term debt $ millions		Use of IMF credit $ millions	
	1995	2008	1995	2008	1995	2008	1995	2008	1995	2008	1995	2008
Hungary	..	..	..	..	..	..	..	..	..	..	..	..
India	95,174	230,611	81,091	78,733	27,348	32,848	6,618	106,632	5,049	45,246	2,416	0
Indonesia	124,413	150,851	65,323	76,904	13,259	8,974	33,123	47,383	25,966	26,565	0	0
Iran, Islamic Rep.	21,565	13,937	15,116	8,902	316	761	0	0	6,449	5,035	0	0
Iraq	..	..	..	..	..	..	..	..	..	..	..	..
Ireland	..	..	..	..	..	..	..	..	..	..	..	..
Israel	..	..	..	..	..	..	..	..	..	..	..	..
Italy	..	..	..	..	..	..	..	..	..	..	..	..
Jamaica	4,581	10,034	3,721	6,598	595	327	128	2,164	492	1,271	240	0
Japan	..	..	..	..	..	..	..	..	..	..	..	..
Jordan	7,661	6,577	6,624	5,123	806	872	0	0	785	1,426	251	28
Kazakhstan	3,750	107,595	2,834	1,915	295	463	103	95,043	381	10,637	432	0
Kenya	7,309	7,441	5,857	6,268	2,412	3,050	445	0	634	921	374	252
Korea, Dem. Rep.	..	..	..	..	..	..	..	..	..	..	..	..
Korea, Rep.	..	..	..	..	..	..	..	..	..	..	..	..
Kosovo	..	..	..	..	..	..	..	..	..	..	..	..
Kuwait	..	..	..	..	..	..	..	..	..	..	..	..
Kyrgyz Republic	609	2,464	472	1,963	141	655	0	307	13	30	124	165
Lao PDR	2,155	4,944	2,091	2,710	285	685	0	2,213	0	0	64	21
Latvia	463	42,108	271	2,258	55	61	0	24,934	31	14,091	160	825
Lebanon	2,966	24,395	1,550	20,561	113	368	50	470	1,365	3,246	0	117
Lesotho	684	682	642	653	207	306	0	0	4	0	38	30
Liberia	2,478	3,484	1,164	1,237	269	72	0	0	978	1,389	336	858
Libya	..	..	..	..	..	..	..	..	..	..	..	..
Lithuania	769	31,719	430	5,329	62	27	29	18,222	49	8,169	262	0
Macedonia, FYR	1,277	4,678	788	1,538	181	591	289	1,412	143	1,729	57	0
Madagascar	4,302	2,086	3,687	1,722	1,121	1,066	0	6	542	258	73	99
Malawi	2,238	963	2,078	838	1,306	188	0	0	44	0	116	125
Malaysia	34,343	66,182	16,023	21,464	1,059	85	11,046	21,918	7,274	22,800	0	0
Mali	2,958	2,190	2,739	2,150	863	534	0	0	72	0	147	40
Mauritania	2,396	1,960	2,127	1,643	347	243	0	0	169	301	100	16
Mauritius	1,416	626	1,148	577	157	111	267	49	1	0	0	0
Mexico	165,379	203,984	93,902	113,955	13,823	5,867	18,348	65,602	37,300	24,427	15,828	0
Moldova	695	3,787	450	792	152	440	9	1,516	6	1,314	230	166
Mongolia	520	1,721	472	1,653	59	338	0	48	0	0	47	20
Morocco	23,771	20,825	23,190	16,538	3,999	2,555	331	2,656	198	1,631	52	0
Mozambique	7,458	3,432	5,209	2,788	890	1,149	1,769	0	279	629	202	15
Myanmar	5,771	7,210	5,378	5,413	777	770	0	0	393	1,797	0	0
Namibia	..	..	..	..	..	..	..	..	..	..	..	..
Nepal	2,410	3,685	2,339	3,551	1,023	1,507	0	0	23	57	48	77
Netherlands	..	..	..	..	..	..	..	..	..	..	..	..
New Zealand	..	..	..	..	..	..	..	..	..	..	..	..
Nicaragua	10,396	3,558	8,572	2,259	341	347	0	468	1,785	720	39	111
Niger	1,608	966	1,351	883	598	248	133	13	72	19	52	51
Nigeria	34,092	11,221	28,140	3,590	3,489	2,455	301	175	5,651	7,456	0	0
Norway	..	..	..	..	..	..	..	..	..	..	..	..
Oman	..	..	..	..	..	..	..	..	..	..	..	..
Pakistan	30,229	49,337	23,788	39,359	6,403	10,999	1,593	4,232	3,235	1,395	1,613	4,352
Panama	6,098	10,722	3,781	9,661	175	271	0	1,061	2,207	0	111	0
Papua New Guinea	2,506	1,418	1,668	1,064	407	229	711	345	78	9	50	0
Paraguay	2,574	4,163	1,453	2,265	189	230	338	751	784	1,146	0	0
Peru	30,833	28,555	18,931	19,330	1,729	2,712	1,288	3,078	9,659	6,147	955	0
Philippines	39,379	64,856	28,525	39,058	5,185	2,720	4,847	18,797	5,279	7,001	728	0
Poland	44,080	218,022	40,890	43,426	2,067	1,776	1,012	109,692	2,178	64,904	0	0
Portugal	..	..	..	..	..	..	..	..	..	..	..	..
Puerto Rico	..	..	..	..	..	..	..	..	..	..	..	..
Qatar	..	..	..	..	..	..	..	..	..	..	..	..

	Total external debt ($ millions)		Long-term debt						Short-term debt ($ millions)		Use of IMF credit ($ millions)	
			Public and publicly guaranteed ($ millions)				Private nonguaranteed					
			Total		IBRD loans and IDA credits							
	1995	2008	1995	2008	1995	2008	1995	2008	1995	2008	1995	2008
Romania	6,832	104,943	3,957	14,988	844	2,572	534	58,839	1,303	31,116	1,038	0
Russian Federation	121,401	402,453	101,582	103,246	1,524	3,851	0	244,552	10,201	54,655	9,617	0
Rwanda	1,029	679	971	645	512	242	0	0	32	23	26	11
Saudi Arabia	..	..	..	..	..	..	..	..	..	..	..	..
Senegal	3,916	2,861	3,266	2,419	1,160	791	44	180	260	197	347	64
Serbia	10,785[a]	30,918	6,788[a]	8,475	1,252[a]	2,931	1,773[a]	18,320	2,139[a]	4,123	84[a]	0
Sierra Leone	1,220	389	1,028	327	234	108	0	0	27	9	165	53
Singapore	..	..	..	..	..	..	..	..	..	..	..	..
Slovak Republic	..	..	..	..	..	..	..	..	..	..	..	..
Slovenia	..	..	..	..	..	..	..	..	..	..	..	..
Somalia	2,678	2,949	1,961	1,983	432	446	0	0	551	793	166	173
South Africa	25,358	41,943	9,837	13,173	0	26	4,935	10,833	9,673	17,937	913	0
Spain	..	..	..	..	..	..	..	..	..	..	..	..
Sri Lanka	8,395	15,154	7,175	12,624	1,512	2,381	90	275	535	2,087	595	169
Sudan	17,603	19,633	9,779	12,599	1,279	1,300	496	0	6,368	6,628	960	406
Swaziland	249	362	238	348	25	17	0	0	11	15	0	0
Sweden	..	..	..	..	..	..	..	..	..	..	..	..
Switzerland	..	..	..	..	..	..	..	..	..	..	..	..
Syrian Arab Republic	..	..	..	..	..	..	..	..	..	..	..	..
Tajikistan	634	1,466	590	1,357	0	365	0	53	43	41	0	15
Tanzania	7,364	5,938	6,203	3,710	2,269	1,971	0	889	963	1,322	197	17
Thailand	100,039	64,798	16,826	12,167	1,906	128	39,117	28,421	44,095	24,210	0	0
Timor-Leste	..	..	..	..	..	..	..	..	..	..	..	..
Togo	1,476	1,573	1,286	1,433	541	604	0	0	85	92	105	48
Trinidad and Tobago	..	..	..	..	..	..	..	..	..	..	..	..
Tunisia	10,818	20,776	9,215	16,449	1,766	1,375	0	0	1,310	4,327	293	0
Turkey	73,781	277,277	50,317	77,945	5,069	8,100	7,079	140,094	15,701	50,714	685	8,524
Turkmenistan	402	638	385	587	1	14	0	1	17	51	0	0
Uganda	3,609	2,249	3,089	1,781	1,792	1,004	0	0	103	458	417	9
Ukraine	8,429	92,479	6,581	10,726	491	3,022	84	56,648	223	20,397	1,542	4,709
United Arab Emirates	..	..	..	..	..	..	..	..	..	..	..	..
United Kingdom	..	..	..	..	..	..	..	..	..	..	..	..
United States	..	..	..	..	..	..	..	..	..	..	..	..
Uruguay	5,318	11,049	3,833	10,044	513	713	127	187	1,336	817	21	0
Uzbekistan	1,799	3,995	1,415	3,156	157	368	15	629	212	211	157	0
Venezuela, RB	35,744	50,229	28,428	29,925	1,639	0	2,013	3,310	3,063	16,994	2,239	0
Vietnam	25,428	26,158	21,778	21,618	231	5,074	0	0	3,272	4,419	377	121
West Bank and Gaza	..	..	..	..	..	..	..	..	..	..	..	..
Yemen, Rep.	6,251	6,258	5,562	5,679	827	2,113	0	0	689	483	0	95
Zambia	6,958	2,986	5,291	1,167	1,434	371	13	1,049	415	676	1,239	96
Zimbabwe	4,989	..[b]	3,462	..	896	..	381	..	685	..	461	..
World	..s	..s	..s	..s	..s	..s	..s	..s	..s	..s	..s	..s
Low income	167,801	168,325	141,776	137,779	35,778	46,592	2,827	5,390	15,555	20,533	7,642	4,623
Middle income	1,704,407	3,550,214	1,133,675	1,241,882	143,754	163,171	206,482	1,463,386	312,058	823,829	52,239	21,117
Lower middle income	805,205	1,324,547	545,642	547,976	95,455	109,824	94,294	399,839	153,797	365,611	11,472	11,122
Upper middle income	899,202	2,225,666	588,033	693,906	48,299	53,347	112,188	1,063,547	158,262	458,218	40,767	9,996
Low & middle income	1,872,207	3,718,539	1,275,451	1,379,661	179,531	209,763	209,310	1,468,776	327,614	844,362	59,881	25,740
East Asia & Pacific	455,541	771,628	255,407	276,172	37,604	41,959	89,982	220,924	108,814	274,370	1,337	162
Europe & Central Asia	290,169	1,398,989	229,733	298,622	13,644	31,975	11,268	793,291	33,428	291,917	15,788	15,158
Latin America & Carib.	598,197	894,367	361,873	411,812	38,485	35,635	87,303	323,261	122,389	158,470	26,632	824
Middle East & N. Africa	139,821	131,545	123,516	105,449	12,279	10,907	694	5,866	13,434	19,972	2,177	258
South Asia	152,409	326,311	129,770	158,527	42,036	58,965	8,301	111,139	9,045	51,271	5,293	5,374
Sub-Saharan Africa	236,070	195,699	175,152	129,079	35,483	30,324	11,760	14,295	40,504	48,361	8,654	3,963
High income												
Euro area												

a. Includes Montenegro. b. Data are likely to be revised after being reconciled with creditor data. Total external debt for 2008 was $5.199 billion, according to debtor reports published in *Global Development Finance*.

About the data

External indebtedness affects a country's creditworthiness and investor perceptions. Data on external debt are gathered through the World Bank's Debtor Reporting System. Indebtedness is calculated using loan-by-loan reports submitted by countries on long-term public and publicly guaranteed borrowing and information on short-term debt collected by the countries or from creditors through the reporting systems of the Bank for International Settlements. These data are supplemented by information from major multilateral banks and official lending agencies in major creditor countries and by estimates by World Bank and International Monetary Fund (IMF) staff. The table includes data on long-term private nonguaranteed debt reported to the World Bank or estimated by its staff.

Data coverage, quality, and timeliness vary by country. Coverage varies for debt instruments and borrowers. The widening spectrum of debt instruments and investors alongside the expansion of private nonguaranteed borrowing makes comprehensive coverage of external debt more complex. Reporting countries differ in their capacity to monitor debt, especially private nonguaranteed debt. Even data on public and publicly guaranteed debt are affected by coverage and reporting accuracy—because of monitoring capacity and sometimes because of unwillingness to provide information. A key part often underreported is military debt. Currently, 128 developing countries report to the Debtor Reporting System. Nonreporting countries might have outstanding debt with the World Bank, other international financial institutions, and private creditors.

Debt data, normally reported in the currency of repayment, are converted into U.S. dollars to produce summary tables. Stock figures (amount of debt outstanding) are converted using end-of-period exchange rates, as published in the IMF's *International Financial Statistics* (line ae). Flow figures are converted at annual average exchange rates (line rf). Projected debt service is converted using end-of-period exchange rates. Debt repayable in multiple currencies, goods, or services and debt with a provision for maintenance of the value of the currency of repayment are shown at book value.

Because flow data are converted at annual average exchange rates and stock data at end-of-period exchange rates, year-to-year changes in debt outstanding and disbursed are sometimes not equal to net flows (disbursements less principal repayments); similarly, changes in debt outstanding, including undisbursed debt, differ from commitments less repayments. Discrepancies are particularly notable when exchange rates have moved sharply during the year. Cancellations and reschedulings of other liabilities into long-term public debt also contribute to the differences.

Variations in reporting rescheduled debt also affect cross-country comparability. For example, rescheduling of official Paris Club creditors may be subject to lags between completion of the general rescheduling agreement and completion of the specific bilateral agreements that define the terms of the rescheduled debt. Other areas of inconsistency include country treatment of arrears and of nonresident national deposits denominated in foreign currency.

Definitions

• **Total external debt** is debt owed to nonresidents repayable in foreign currency, goods, or services. It is the sum of public, publicly guaranteed, and private nonguaranteed long-term debt, short-term debt, and use of IMF credit. • **Long-term debt** is debt that has an original or extended maturity of more than one year. It has three components: public, publicly guaranteed, and private nonguaranteed debt. • **Public and publicly guaranteed debt** comprises the long-term external obligations of public debtors, including the national government and political subdivisions (or an agency of either) and autonomous public bodies, and the external obligations of private debtors that are guaranteed for repayment by a public entity. • **IBRD loans and IDA credits** are extended by the World Bank. The International Bank for Reconstruction and Development (IBRD) lends at market rates. The International Development Association (IDA) provides credits at concessional rates. • **Private nonguaranteed debt** consists of the long-term external obligations of private debtors that are not guaranteed for repayment by a public entity. • **Short-term debt** is debt owed to nonresidents having an original maturity of one year or less and interest in arrears on long-term debt. • **Use of IMF credit** denotes members' drawings on the IMF other than those drawn against the country's reserve tranche position and includes purchases and drawings under Stand-By, Extended, Structural Adjustment, Enhanced Structural Adjustment, and Systemic Transformation Facility Arrangements, together with Trust Fund loans.

Debt flows from private creditors to low- and middle-income economies fell sharply in 2008　　6.10a

Low-income economies

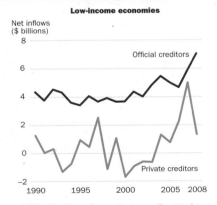

Middle-income economies

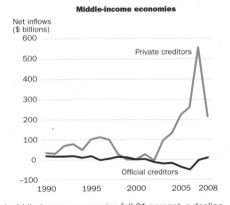

In 2008 debt flows from private creditors to low- and middle-income economies fell 61 percent, a decline only partially offset by an increase in net flows from official creditors.

Source: Global Development Finance data files.

Data sources

Data on external debt are mainly from reports to the World Bank through its Debtor Reporting System from member countries that have received IBRD loans or IDA credits, with additional information from the files of the World Bank, the IMF, the African Development Bank and African Development Fund, the Asian Development Bank and Asian Development Fund, and the Inter-American Development Bank. Summary tables of the external debt of developing countries are published annually in the World Bank's *Global Development Finance,* on its *Global Development Finance* CD-ROM, and on *GDF Online.*

	Total external debt		Total debt service		Multilateral debt service		Short-term debt				Present value of debt	
	% of GNI		% of exports of goods and services and income[a]		% of public and publicly guaranteed debt service		% of total debt		% of total reserves		% of GNI	% of exports of goods, services, and income[a]
	1995	2008	1995	2008	1995	2008	1995	2008	1995	2008	2008[b]	2008[b]
Afghanistan	..	..	..	..	..	96.7	..	0.8	..	..	4	21
Albania	18.4	25.2	1.4	3.0	11.4	50.2	13.7	24.4	23.5	33.0	21	51
Algeria	83.5	3.2	17.7	..	17.7	13.6	0.8	23.8	6.3	0.9	3	6
Angola	311.9	21.3	12.0	2.5	0.6	0.7	17.0	16.0	919.7	13.5	24	27
Argentina	38.9	39.9	30.1	10.7	21.6	74.6	21.7	29.2	133.6	80.9	48	171
Armenia	25.3	27.6	3.1	12.7	69.8	83.6	0.6	13.6	1.9	33.1	27	97
Australia	..	..	..	..	..	..	..	..	..	..	..	..
Austria	..	..	..	..	..	..	..	..	..	..	..	..
Azerbaijan	10.6	10.5	1.3	0.9	21.8	23.8	4.4	27.1	11.6	18.1	12	14
Bangladesh	40.8	27.7	13.2	3.9	27.1	61.3	1.2	8.4	8.4	34.3	20	67
Belarus	12.2	20.6	3.4	3.1	55.4	6.8	6.5	56.6	29.2	227.2	24	38
Belgium	..	..	..	..	..	..	..	..	..	..	..	..
Benin	82.1	14.8	6.8	..	54.8	38.1	2.9	3.8	23.7	3.0	10[c]	35[c]
Bolivia	81.2	34.3	29.4	11.3	75.5	92.6	5.8	3.0	30.5	2.2	14[c]	29[c]
Bosnia and Herzegovina	..	43.9	..	4.4	..	73.3	..	11.0	..	25.9	44	81
Botswana	15.1	3.4	3.1	..	76.0	47.3	1.4	9.8	0.2	0.5	3	5
Brazil	21.2	16.2	36.6	22.7	18.5	8.9	19.5	14.3	60.7	18.9	19	121
Bulgaria	81.8	79.0	16.5	14.7	10.5	76.8	4.9	48.6	31.3	103.1	91	128
Burkina Faso	53.6	21.2	..	..	76.7	52.6	4.4	6.5	16.1	11.9	14[c]	110[c]
Burundi	117.6	124.7	27.6	28.1	70.6	94.1	1.3	1.3	6.9	7.2	80[c]	705[c]
Cambodia	71.8	46.0	0.7	0.6	11.9	75.5	4.5	7.7	53.1	12.2	42	57
Cameroon	133.3	12.1	20.9	..	61.0	39.8	9.1	0.2	6,444.5	0.2	4[c]	15[c]
Canada	..	..	..	..	..	..	..	..	..	..	..	..
Central African Republic	85.9	48.7	..	..	100.0	85.1	6.0	7.5	24.0	54.2	41[c]	267[c]
Chad	58.5	26.1	..	..	86.1	92.5	2.0	0.2	11.6	0.3	19[c]	32[c]
Chile	32.1	41.3	24.5	18.2	76.2	13.5	15.6	23.2	23.1	64.6	41	74
China	16.5	8.7	9.9	2.0	7.6	24.1	18.9	49.5	27.8	9.5	10	25
Hong Kong SAR, China	..	..	..	..	..	..	..	..	..	..	..	..
Colombia	27.5	20.2	31.5	16.2	32.7	32.3	22.1	12.1	65.6	24.0	23	108
Congo, Dem. Rep.	271.4	118.2	..	..	..	45.9	23.6	5.5	1,980.9	865.3	100[c]	316[c]
Congo, Rep.	479.7	65.6	13.2	..	21.8	24.5	17.0	6.6	1,575.1	9.3	74[c]	70[c]
Costa Rica	32.8	30.3	13.8	10.5	50.5	44.0	11.4	43.9	40.5	101.7	33	61
Côte d'Ivoire	188.7	56.0	23.1	9.2	59.3	99.8	20.7	10.7	739.1	59.7	76[c]	144[c]
Croatia	..	..	..	..	..	..	..	..	..	..	..	..
Cuba	..	..	..	..	..	..	..	..	..	..	..	..
Czech Republic	..	..	..	..	..	..	..	..	..	..	..	..
Denmark	..	..	..	..	..	..	..	..	..	..	..	..
Dominican Republic	28.5	23.8	6.1	..	39.8	28.5	13.8	19.1	165.3	87.6	24	61
Ecuador	72.0	33.1	24.8	..	32.0	62.3	9.5	9.9	73.4	37.2	34	75
Egypt, Arab Rep.	55.8	19.9	13.2	4.7	26.3	23.7	7.1	7.7	13.9	7.3	20	49
El Salvador	26.7	46.6	8.9	9.9	55.1	59.3	20.9	10.4	55.9	39.8	47	98
Eritrea	6.3	58.6	0.1	..	100.0	66.8	0.0	0.5	0.0	8.0	38[c]	697[c]
Estonia	..	..	..	..	..	..	..	..	..	..	..	..
Ethiopia	136.8	10.9	18.5	2.8	41.9	45.0	4.5	1.9	56.5	6.4	8[c]	49[c]
Finland	..	..	..	..	..	..	..	..	..	..	..	..
France	..	..	..	..	..	..	..	..	..	..	..	..
Gabon	101.6	19.4	15.3	..	17.9	13.1	6.6	5.1	187.8	6.2	23	27
Gambia, The	113.0	61.5	15.5	..	49.1	56.0	3.5	4.5	14.0	17.5	29[c]	63[c]
Georgia	48.2	26.6	..	4.2	0.4	37.4	6.9	10.6	43.0	24.1	24	65
Germany	..	..	..	..	..	..	..	..	..	..	..	..
Ghana	86.9	31.3	24.0	3.2	48.4	20.7	11.3	27.3	77.1	..	20[c]	46[c]
Greece	..	..	..	..	..	..	..	..	..	..	..	..
Guatemala	22.6	41.3	11.1	12.2	47.5	74.3	24.7	13.5	103.6	46.2	42	109
Guinea	90.0	73.2	24.8	9.6	30.5	66.7	5.0	6.2	188.9	..	49[c]	149[c]
Guinea-Bissau	379.4	274.1	52.4	..	86.3	100.0	10.6	12.5	469.2	116.0	214[c]	496[c]
Haiti	28.1	27.8	51.0	1.9	92.2	79.2	3.2	0.0	13.4	0.0	17[c]	51[c]
Honduras	132.9	25.0	32.3	..	55.9	66.7	7.9	15.1	141.7	20.8	12[c]	15[c]

	Total external debt		Total debt service		Multilateral debt service		Short-term debt				Present value of debt	
	% of GNI		% of exports of goods and services and income[a]		% of public and publicly guaranteed debt service		% of total debt		% of total reserves		% of GNI	% of exports of goods, services, and income[a]
	1995	2008	1995	2008	1995	2008	1995	2008	1995	2008	2008[b]	2008[b]
Hungary	..	..	..	..	..	..	..	..	..	..	..	..
India	27.0	19.0	29.8	8.7	24.2	14.3	5.3	19.6	22.1	17.6	18	70
Indonesia	63.4	30.4	29.9	13.4	28.4	30.6	20.9	17.6	174.2	51.4	35	102
Iran, Islamic Rep.	23.9	..	29.7	..	1.3	3.4	29.9	36.1	..	..	4	12
Iraq	..	..	..	..	..	..	..	..	..	..	..	..
Ireland	..	..	..	..	..	..	..	..	..	..	..	..
Israel	..	..	..	..	..	..	..	..	..	..	..	..
Italy	..	..	..	..	..	..	..	..	..	..	..	..
Jamaica	82.3	69.7	16.2	14.2	40.6	23.8	10.7	12.7	72.2	71.7	87	148
Japan	..	..	..	..	..	..	..	..	..	..	..	..
Jordan	118.8	31.4	12.4	16.0	33.5	10.4	10.2	21.7	34.4	16.0	32	41
Kazakhstan	18.5	95.0	3.9	41.8	7.8	47.3	10.2	9.9	23.0	53.5	106	164
Kenya	83.8	21.7	24.7	4.5	32.5	36.9	8.7	12.4	164.9	32.0	19	68
Korea, Dem. Rep.	..	..	..	..	..	..	..	..	..	..	..	..
Korea, Rep.	..	..	..	..	..	..	..	..	..	..	..	..
Kosovo	..	..	..	..	..	..	..	..	..	..	..	..
Kuwait	..	..	..	..	..	..	..	..	..	..	..	..
Kyrgyz Republic	37.5	56.9	13.2	8.2	59.0	79.7	2.1	1.2	9.7	2.4	42[c]	53[c]
Lao PDR	122.6	99.5	6.1	..	37.4	87.6	0.0	0.0	0.0	0.0	83	261
Latvia	8.8	127.3	1.6	37.7	60.3	16.8	6.7	33.5	5.2	268.7	147	301
Lebanon	24.3	90.6	..	14.0	13.2	5.1	46.0	13.3	16.9	11.5	95	89
Lesotho	55.8	33.4	6.1	2.5	60.3	71.3	0.6	0.0	0.9	..	18	27
Liberia	..	515.4	..	131.3	..	100.0	39.5	39.9	3,481.0	863.2	340[c]	306[c]
Libya	..	..	..	..	..	..	..	..	..	..	..	..
Lithuania	10.1	69.3	1.3	30.6	31.8	6.0	6.4	25.8	6.0	126.8	78	120
Macedonia, FYR	29.0	49.6	..	8.7	99.9	64.1	11.2	37.0	51.9	81.9	55	96
Madagascar	143.3	23.4	7.6	..	74.3	74.8	12.6	12.4	497.1	26.3	20[c]	68[c]
Malawi	165.8	22.7	24.9	..	51.4	35.2	1.9	0.0	37.8	0.0	9[c]	39[c]
Malaysia	40.6	35.1	7.0	..	15.5	4.8	21.2	34.5	29.5	24.7	35	30
Mali	122.3	25.8	13.4	..	45.5	54.2	2.4	0.0	22.2	0.0	11[c]	33[c]
Mauritania	175.3	..	22.9	..	49.6	65.5	7.1	15.4	187.9	..	41[c]	65[c]
Mauritius	37.3	7.0	8.7	2.8	34.5	27.6	0.1	0.0	0.1	0.0	7	10
Mexico	60.5	19.1	27.0	12.1	19.5	7.7	22.6	12.0	218.8	25.6	20	62
Moldova	40.3	57.0	7.9	11.3	79.1	56.9	0.9	34.7	2.3	78.5	67	96
Mongolia	43.3	33.6	10.1	..	2.8	37.6	0.1	0.0	0.3	..	28	42
Morocco	75.1	24.4	33.4	10.3	30.3	39.0	0.8	7.8	5.1	7.2	24	51
Mozambique	360.6	39.4	34.5	1.2	17.4	59.0	3.7	18.3	142.8	37.9	15[c]	36[c]
Myanmar	..	..	17.8	..	15.0	0.6	6.8	24.9	60.4	..	35	84
Namibia	..	..	..	..	..	..	..	..	..	..	..	..
Nepal	54.7	28.9	7.5	3.6	54.2	76.3	0.9	1.5	3.5	..	21	63
Netherlands	..	..	..	..	..	..	..	..	..	..	..	..
New Zealand	..	..	..	..	..	..	..	..	..	..	..	..
Nicaragua	368.6	55.3	38.7	7.3	30.3	51.3	17.2	20.2	1,256.8	63.1	32[c]	53[c]
Niger	87.9	18.1	16.7	..	95.5	89.7	4.5	2.0	75.6	2.7	13[c]	63[c]
Nigeria	131.7	5.7	13.8	..	45.4	80.0	16.6	66.4	330.7	13.9	6	12
Norway	..	..	..	..	..	..	..	..	..	..	..	..
Oman	..	..	..	..	..	..	..	..	..	..	..	..
Pakistan	49.5	28.7	26.5	8.7	43.2	66.3	10.7	2.8	128.0	15.5	24	120
Panama	80.9	49.8	3.4	9.2	52.7	13.0	36.2	0.0	282.4	..	54	62
Papua New Guinea	57.3	19.2	20.8	..	31.7	41.1	3.1	0.6	29.1	0.4	21	22
Paraguay	31.5	25.5	5.6	4.8	48.0	59.0	30.4	27.5	70.8	40.0	29	50
Peru	60.3	23.9	15.9	12.5	49.9	35.9	31.3	21.5	111.6	19.7	28	81
Philippines	51.7	35.0	16.1	15.5	29.2	19.9	13.4	10.8	67.8	18.7	37	77
Poland	32.2	42.1	11.0	25.0	13.5	4.9	4.9	29.8	14.6	104.4	46	103
Portugal	..	..	..	..	..	..	..	..	..	..	..	..
Puerto Rico	..	..	..	..	..	..	..	..	..	..	..	..
Qatar	..	..	..	..	..	..	..	..	..	..	..	..

	Total external debt		Total debt service		Multilateral debt service		Short-term debt				Present value of debt	
			% of exports of goods and services and income[a]		% of public and publicly guaranteed debt service		% of total debt		% of total reserves		% of GNI	% of exports of goods, services, and income[a]
	% of GNI											
	1995	2008	1995	2008	1995	2008	1995	2008	1995	2008	2008[b]	2008[b]
Romania	19.4	54.7	10.5	25.3	21.3	28.3	19.1	29.7	49.7	78.2	57	149
Russian Federation	31.0	25.8	6.3	11.5	9.7	4.0	8.4	13.6	56.6	12.8	30	81
Rwanda	79.2	15.4	20.5	..	99.0	69.7	3.1	3.3	32.3	3.8	8[c]	74[c]
Saudi Arabia	..	..	..	..	..	..	..	..	..	..	..	..
Senegal	..	21.8	16.8	..	62.2	55.7	6.6	6.9	95.6	12.3	16[c]	50[c]
Serbia	..	63.5	..	13.9	100.0[d]	60.4	19.8[d]	13.3	..	35.9	70	111
Sierra Leone	149.0	20.3	53.7	..	8.4	63.5	2.2	2.3	77.8	4.1	10[c]	36[c]
Singapore	..	..	..	..	..	..	..	..	..	..	..	..
Slovak Republic	..	..	..	..	..	..	..	..	..	..	..	..
Slovenia	..	..	..	..	..	..	..	..	..	..	..	..
Somalia	..	..	..	..	..	..	20.6	26.9	..	..	..	..
South Africa	17.1	15.7	9.5	4.4	0.0	1.8	38.1	42.8	216.7	52.6	16	46
Spain	..	..	..	..	..	..	..	..	..	..	..	..
Sri Lanka	65.3	38.1	8.0	9.3	14.0	21.0	6.4	13.8	25.3	79.7	35	96
Sudan	136.3	37.5	6.7	2.5	100.0	20.6	36.2	33.8	3,898.2	473.7	78[c]	296[c]
Swaziland	14.0	13.6	1.5	..	64.0	73.4	4.5	4.1	3.7	2.0	12	14
Sweden	..	..	..	..	..	..	..	..	..	..	..	..
Switzerland	..	..	..	..	..	..	..	..	..	..	..	..
Syrian Arab Republic	..	..	..	..	..	..	..	..	..	..	..	..
Tajikistan	53.6	29.2	..	3.1	..	27.0	6.8	2.8	..	..	23	26
Tanzania	143.5	29.9	17.4	1.2	66.7	99.9	13.1	22.3	356.6	46.2	14[c]	54[c]
Thailand	60.6	32.0	11.6	7.7	20.9	1.4	44.1	37.4	119.4	21.8	31	32
Timor-Leste	..	..	..	..	..	..	..	..	..	..	..	..
Togo	116.7	56.1	6.0	..	75.5	99.3	5.8	5.9	65.1	15.9	51[c]	106[c]
Trinidad and Tobago	..	..	..	..	..	..	..	..	..	..	..	..
Tunisia	63.0	58.5	16.9	..	43.8	48.2	12.1	20.8	77.6	47.9	58	85
Turkey	44.3	35.3	27.7	29.5	20.7	10.6	21.3	18.3	113.0	68.8	40	170
Turkmenistan	16.1	3.7	..	..	1.9	2.4	4.3	8.0	1.5	..	5	6
Uganda	63.3	15.8	19.8	1.7	69.7	56.7	2.8	20.4	22.4	19.9	10[c]	37[c]
Ukraine	17.8	51.7	6.6	19.4	13.6	29.7	2.6	22.1	20.9	64.7	63	124
United Arab Emirates	..	..	..	..	..	..	..	..	..	..	..	..
United Kingdom	..	..	..	..	..	..	..	..	..	..	..	..
United States	..	..	..	..	..	..	..	..	..	..	..	..
Uruguay	28.0	34.9	22.1	14.6	27.3	26.7	25.1	7.4	73.7	12.8	40	122
Uzbekistan	13.5	14.3	..	..	1.9	19.2	11.8	5.3	..	..	15	31
Venezuela, RB	49.0	16.0	22.9	5.6	11.6	11.2	8.6	33.8	28.6	39.5	21	58
Vietnam	124.0	29.7	..	1.9	2.9	13.2	12.9	16.9	247.2	18.5	29	36
West Bank and Gaza	..	..	..	..	..	..	..	..	..	..	..	..
Yemen, Rep.	169.9	25.6	3.1	2.4	78.3	57.1	11.0	7.7	107.9	5.9	18	39
Zambia	215.1	23.0	..	3.2	50.6	50.4	6.0	22.6	186.2	61.7	6[c]	14[c]
Zimbabwe	73.5	..	..	..	33.6	..	13.7	..	77.2	..	..	..
World	.. w	.. w	.. w	.. w	.. w	.. w	.. w	.. w	.. w	.. w	.. w	
Low income	89.2	30.8	18.0	3.5	37.8	45.0	9.3	12.2	111.8	22.0	..	..
Middle income	36.0	21.9	17.0	9.7	21.5	17.7	18.3	23.2	69.0	19.8	..	..
Lower middle income	39.5	16.0	16.7	5.2	23.5	26.6	19.1	27.6	66.8	13.3	..	..
Upper middle income	33.4	28.0	17.3	15.2	19.6	12.7	17.6	20.6	70.9	31.8	..	..
Low & middle income	38.1	22.1	17.1	9.5	22.1	18.5	17.5	22.7	70.2	19.9	..	..
East Asia & Pacific	35.5	13.7	12.7	3.9	18.2	21.7	23.9	35.6	64.8	11.9	..	..
Europe & Central Asia	32.5	37.3	10.6	18.6	16.3	10.7	11.5	20.9	53.3	40.6	..	..
Latin America & Carib.	35.2	21.8	25.4	14.0	24.2	20.2	20.5	17.7	88.6	31.8	..	..
Middle East & N. Africa	53.5	15.1	19.7	5.3	19.3	18.9	9.6	15.2	18.4	..	..	..
South Asia	32.2	21.3	25.6	8.4	27.4	23.1	5.9	15.7	29.5	18.6	..	..
Sub-Saharan Africa	76.2	21.2	15.9	3.3	35.0	32.8	17.2	24.7	193.5	29.1	..	..
High income												
Euro area												

a. Includes workers' remittances. b. The numerator refers to 2008, whereas the denominator is a three year average of 2006–08 data. c. Data are from debt sustainability analyses for low-income countries. Present value estimates for these countries are for public and publicly guaranteed debt only. d. Includes Montenegro.

About the data

A country's external debt burden, both debt outstanding and debt service, affects its creditworthiness and vulnerability. The table shows total external debt relative to a country's size—gross national income (GNI). Total debt service is contrasted with countries' ability to obtain foreign exchange through exports of goods, services, income, and workers' remittances.

Multilateral debt service (shown as a share of the country's total public and publicly guaranteed debt service) are obligations to international financial institutions, such as the World Bank, the International Monetary Fund (IMF), and regional development banks. Multilateral debt service takes priority over private and bilateral debt service, and borrowers must stay current with multilateral debts to remain creditworthy. While bilateral and private creditors often write off debts, international financial institution bylaws prohibit granting debt relief or canceling debts directly. However, the recent decrease in multilateral debt service ratios for some countries reflects debt relief from special programs, such as the Heavily Indebted Poor Countries (HIPC) Debt Initiative and the Multilateral Debt Relief Initiative (MDRI) (see table 1.4.) Other countries have accelerated repayment of debt outstanding. Indebted countries may also apply to the Paris and London Clubs to renegotiate obligations to public and private creditors.

Because short-term debt poses an immediate burden and is particularly important for monitoring vulnerability, it is compared with the total debt and foreign exchange reserves that are instrumental in providing coverage for such obligations. The present value of external debt provides a measure of future debt service obligations.

The present value of external debt is calculated by discounting the debt service (interest plus amortization) due on long-term external debt over the life of existing loans. Short-term debt is included at face value. The data on debt are in U.S. dollars converted at official exchange rates (see *About the data* for table 6.10). The discount rate on long-term debt depends on the currency of repayment and is based on commercial interest reference rates established by the Organisation for Economic Co-operation and Development. Loans from the International Bank for Reconstruction and Development (IBRD), credits from the International Development Association (IDA), and obligations to the IMF are discounted using a special drawing rights reference rate. When the discount rate is greater than the loan interest rate, the present value is less than the nominal sum of future debt service obligations.

Debt ratios are used to assess the sustainability of a country's debt service obligations, but no absolute rules determine what values are too high. Empirical analysis of developing countries' experience and debt service performance shows that debt service difficulties become increasingly likely when the present value of debt reaches 200 percent of exports. Still, what constitutes a sustainable debt burden varies by country. Countries with fast-growing economies and exports are likely to be able to sustain higher debt levels.

Definitions

- **Total external debt** is debt owed to nonresidents and comprises public, publicly guaranteed, and private nonguaranteed long-term debt, short-term debt, and use of IMF credit. It is presented as a share of GNI. • **Total debt service** is the sum of principal repayments and interest actually paid in foreign currency, goods, or services on long-term debt; interest paid on short-term debt; and repayments (repurchases and charges) to the IMF. • **Exports of goods, services, and income** refer to international transactions involving a change in ownership of general merchandise, goods sent for processing and repairs, nonmonetary gold, services, receipts of employee compensation for nonresident workers, investment income, and workers' remittances. • **Multilateral debt service** is the repayment of principal and interest to the World Bank, regional development banks, and other multilateral and intergovernmental agencies. • **Short-term debt** includes all debt having an original maturity of one year or less and interest in arrears on long-term debt. • **Total reserves** comprise holdings of monetary gold, special drawing rights, reserves of IMF members held by the IMF, and holdings of foreign exchange under the control of monetary authorities. • **Present value of debt** is the sum of short-term external debt plus the discounted sum of total debt service payments due on public, publicly guaranteed, and private nonguaranteed long-term external debt over the life of existing loans.

The burden of external debt service declined over 2000–08 — 6.11a

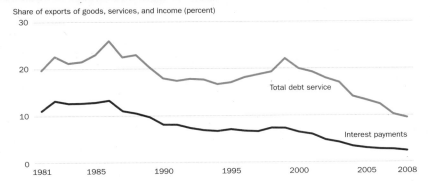

Share of exports of goods, services, and income (percent)

The total external debt service of low- and middle-income economies fell from 20 percent of export revenues in 2000 to under 10 percent in 2008. About 26 percent of the total debt service in 2008 was interest payments on outstanding debt compared with 32 percent in 2000.

Source: Global Development Finance data files.

Data sources

Data on external debt are mainly from reports to the World Bank through its Debtor Reporting System from member countries that have received IBRD loans or IDA credits, with additional information from the files of the World Bank, the IMF, the African Development Bank and African Development Fund, the Asian Development Bank and Asian Development Fund, and the Inter-American Development Bank. Data on GNI, exports of goods and services, and total reserves are from the World Bank's national accounts files and the IMF's Balance of Payments and International Financial Statistics databases. Summary tables of the external debt of developing countries are published annually in the World Bank's *Global Development Finance,* on its *Global Development Finance* CD-ROM, and on *GDF Online.*

	Equity flows				Debt flows			
	$ millions				$ millions			
	Foreign direct investment		Portfolio equity		Bonds		Commercial bank and other lending	
	1995	**2008**	**1995**	**2008**	**1995**	**2008**	**1995**	**2008**
Afghanistan	..	300	..	..	..	0	..	0
Albania	70	937	0	..	0	0	0	396
Algeria	0	2,646	..	..	−278	0	788	−474
Angola	472	1,679	0	..	0	0	123	2,667
Argentina	5,609	9,753	1,552	−531	3,705	14	754	1,889
Armenia	25	935	..	−1	0	0	0	374
Australia	12,026	47,281	2,585	19,408	..	..	..	..
Austria	1,901	14,440	1,262	−6,945	..	..	..	..
Azerbaijan	330	15	..	0	0	0	0	350
Bangladesh	2	973	−15	10	0	0	−21	112
Belarus	15	2,158	..	1	0	0	103	385
Belgium	10,689[a]	99,732	6,505[a]	8,818	..	..	..	..
Benin	13	120	0	..	0	0	0	0
Bolivia	393	512	0	0	0	0	41	343
Bosnia and Herzegovina	0	1,056	..	..	..	0	..	254
Botswana	70	109	6	−37	0	0	−6	−1
Brazil	4,859	45,058	2,775	−7,565	2,636	1,637	8,283	25,551
Bulgaria	90	9,205	0	−106	−6	−287	−93	4,379
Burkina Faso	10	137	..	..	0	0	0	−3
Burundi	2	4	0	..	0	0	−1	0
Cambodia	151	815	..	0	0	0	13	0
Cameroon	7	38	0	−1	0	0	−65	−106
Canada	9,319	45,364	−3,077	3,109	..	..	..	..
Central African Republic	6	121	..	..	0	0	0	0
Chad	33	834	..	..	0	0	0	0
Chile	2,957	16,787	−249	1,823	489	−1,688	1,773	5,053
China	35,849	147,791	0	8,721	317	−2,096	4,696	14,238
Hong Kong SAR, China	..	63,005	..	19,477	..	..	..	..
Colombia	968	10,583	165	−86	1,008	47	1,250	486
Congo, Dem. Rep.	122	1,000	..	..	0	0	0	−7
Congo, Rep.	125	2,622	0	..	0	0	−50	−6
Costa Rica	337	2,021	0	0	−4	−240	−20	258
Côte d'Ivoire	211	402	1	79	0	0	14	−177
Croatia	108	4,798	4	−115	..	..	..	..
Cuba	..	..	..	..	..	..	..	..
Czech Republic	2,568	10,864	1,236	−1,124	..	..	..	..
Denmark	4,139	3,111	..	2,792	..	..	..	..
Dominican Republic	414	2,885	..	0	0	−20	−31	−89
Ecuador	452	993	13	1	0	0	59	592
Egypt, Arab Rep.	598	9,495	0	−674	0	0	−311	−235
El Salvador	38	784	0	0	0	0	−31	298
Eritrea	..	36	..	..	0	0	0	1
Estonia	201	1,947	10	−308	..	..	..	..
Ethiopia	14	109	..	0	0	0	−48	−33
Finland	1,044	−7,765	2,027	−1,782	..	..	..	..
France	23,736	100,372	6,823	−16,145	..	..	..	..
Gabon	−315	20	..	..	0	−50	−75	−3
Gambia, The	8	72	..	..	0	0	0	11
Georgia	6	1,564	..	118	0	500	0	123
Germany	11,985	21,248	−1,513	−85,366	..	..	..	..
Ghana	107	2,112	0	0	..	..	38	68
Greece	1,053	5,304	0	−5,260	..	..	..	..
Guatemala	75	838	..	0	44	5	−34	1,007
Guinea	1	382	..	..	0	0	−15	4
Guinea-Bissau	0	15	..	..	0	0	0	0
Haiti	7	30	..	0	0	0	0	50
Honduras	50	877	0	0	−13	0	38	−5

	Equity flows				Debt flows			
	\$ millions				\$ millions			
	Foreign direct investment		Portfolio equity		Bonds		Commercial bank and other lending	
	1995	**2008**	**1995**	**2008**	**1995**	**2008**	**1995**	**2008**
Hungary	4,804	62,786	−62	−197	..	..	..	..
India	2,144	41,169	1,590	−15,030	285	1,754	955	10,028
Indonesia	4,346	9,318	1,493	322	2,248	3,519	60	3,573
Iran, Islamic Rep.	17	1,492	0	..	0	0	−37	−1,197
Iraq	..	..	..	..	..	..	..	..
Ireland	1,447	−19,886	0	931	..	..	..	..
Israel	1,350	9,638	991	994	..	..	..	..
Italy	4,842	15,442	5,358	−29,022	..	..	..	..
Jamaica	147	1,437	0	0	13	250	15	12
Japan	39	24,552	50,597	−69,692	..	..	..	..
Jordan	13	1,966	0	500	0	−2	−201	−65
Kazakhstan	964	14,648	..	−1,280	0	−310	240	12,174
Kenya	32	96	5	5	0	0	−163	−8
Korea, Dem. Rep.	..	..	..	..	..	..	..	..
Korea, Rep.	1,776	2,200	4,219	−41,247	..	..	..	..
Kosovo	..	..	..	..	..	..	..	..
Kuwait	7	57	0	0	..	..	..	..
Kyrgyz Republic	96	233	..	6	0	0	0	−74
Lao PDR	95	228	0	..	0	0	0	366
Latvia	180	1,357	0	−50	43	154	3	5,020
Lebanon	35	3,606	..	466	350	−233	333	−80
Lesotho	275	218	..	..	0	0	12	−3
Liberia	5	144	..	0	0	0	0	0
Libya	−88	4,111	..	0	0	0	..	..
Lithuania	73	1,770	6	113	0	−184	55	2,942
Macedonia, FYR	9	598	..	−49	0	0	0	460
Madagascar	10	1,477	..	..	0	0	−4	3
Malawi	6	37	..	..	0	0	−23	0
Malaysia	4,178	7,376	0	−10,716	2,440	−250	1,231	−106
Mali	111	127	..	..	0	0	0	−1
Mauritania	7	103	0	..	0	0	0	−6
Mauritius	19	378	22	34	150	0	126	−29
Mexico	9,526	22,481	519	−3,503	3,758	−4,540	1,401	16,603
Moldova	26	708	−1	11	0	−6	24	386
Mongolia	10	683	0	..	0	0	−14	44
Morocco	92	2,466	20	148	0	−589	158	−67
Mozambique	45	587	0	0	0	0	24	−1
Myanmar	280	283	..	..	0	0	36	0
Namibia	153	535	46	4	..	..	..	..
Nepal	..	1	0	..	0	0	−5	−1
Netherlands	12,206	−2,389	−743	−12,565	..	..	..	..
New Zealand	3,316	5,466	..	170	..	..	..	..
Nicaragua	89	626	0	0	0	0	−81	77
Niger	7	147	..	..	0	0	−24	−7
Nigeria	1,079	3,636	0	−4,684	0	0	−448	−37
Norway	2,393	−1,543	636	−11,888	..	..	..	..
Oman	46	2,928	0	−809	..	..	317	652
Pakistan	723	5,438	10	−270	0	0	−12	157
Panama	223	2,402	0	0	0	−507	−311	149
Papua New Guinea	455	−30	..	..	−32	0	−16	91
Paraguay	103	320	0	0	0	0	43	−83
Peru	2,557	4,079	171	180	0	−1,488	−215	−1,351
Philippines	1,478	1,403	0	−1,289	1,110	−839	228	26,111
Poland	3,659	14,849	219	564	250	2,811	..	..
Portugal	685	3,575	−179	6,776	..	..	..	..
Puerto Rico	..	..	..	..	..	..	..	..
Qatar	..	..	..	..	..	..	..	..

	Equity flows				Debt flows			
	$ millions				$ millions			
	Foreign direct investment		Portfolio equity		Bonds		Commercial bank and other lending	
	1995	**2008**	**1995**	**2008**	**1995**	**2008**	**1995**	**2008**
Romania	419	13,883	0	23	0	221	413	17,036
Russian Federation	2,065	72,885	47	−15,005	−810	15,402	444	23,060
Rwanda	2	103	0	0	0	0	0	0
Saudi Arabia	−1,875	22,486	0	..	..	..	..	..
Senegal	32	706	4	..	0	0	−25	−37
Serbia	45[b]	2,992	..	−57	0[b]	0	0[b]	3,400
Sierra Leone	7	−3	0	0	0	0	−28	0
Singapore	11,535	22,724	−159	−2,209	..	..	..	..
Slovak Republic	236	3,231	−16	103	..	..	..	..
Slovenia	150	1,917	..	−291	..	..	..	..
Somalia	1	87	..	..	0	0	0	0
South Africa	1,248	9,645	2,914	−4,707	731	−698	748	−805
Spain	8,086	71,207	4,216	−446	..	..	..	..
Sri Lanka	56	752	..	−488	0	−65	103	155
Sudan	12	2,601	0	0	0	0	0	0
Swaziland	52	10	1	..	0	0	0	0
Sweden	14,939	41,908	1,853	−1,494	..	..	..	..
Switzerland	4,158	6,549	5,851	24,352	..	..	..	..
Syrian Arab Republic	100	..	0	..	..	..	..	..
Tajikistan	10	376	..	0	0	0	0	17
Tanzania	120	744	0	3	0	0	18	−9
Thailand	2,068	9,835	2,253	−4,594	2,123	−778	3,702	−554
Timor-Leste	..	..	..	..	..	..	..	..
Togo	26	68	0	..	0	0	0	0
Trinidad and Tobago	299	..	17	..	..	..	..	..
Tunisia	264	2,638	12	−39	588	0	−96	29
Turkey	885	18,299	195	716	627	248	174	21,760
Turkmenistan	233	820	..	..	0	0	20	−36
Uganda	121	788	0	−32	0	0	−9	−1
Ukraine	267	10,913	..	388	−200	780	−19	16,521
United Arab Emirates	..	..	..	..	..	..	..	..
United Kingdom	21,731	93,506	8,070	72,710	..	..	..	..
United States	57,800	319,737	16,523	110,447	..	..	..	..
Uruguay	157	2,205	0	2	144	−534	39	32
Uzbekistan	−24	918	..	..	0	0	201	−146
Venezuela, RB	985	349	270	3	−468	3,051	−216	−434
Vietnam	1,780	9,579	..	−578	0	−26	356	−51
West Bank and Gaza	123	..	0	..	..	..	..	..
Yemen, Rep.	−218	1,555	..	0	0	0	−2	−1
Zambia	97	939	..	−6	0	0	−37	71
Zimbabwe	118	52	..	..	−30	0	140	11
World	**328,496 s**	**1,823,282 s**	**127,074 s**	**−207,952 s**	**.. s**	**.. s**	**.. s**	**.. s**
Low income	3,243	26,440	−6	−591	−30	−26	420	329
Middle income	95,596	571,567	14,050	−56,548	21,247	14,984	26,959	213,213
Lower middle income	52,899	267,487	5,393	−16,777	6,470	692	8,429	48,183
Upper middle income	42,698	304,080	8,657	−39,771	14,777	14,291	18,529	165,030
Low & middle income	98,839	598,007	14,043	−57,139	21,216	14,958	27,379	213,542
East Asia & Pacific	50,798	187,724	3,746	−8,139	8,206	−470	9,554	16,310
Europe & Central Asia	9,443	172,056	467	−14,608	−96	19,329	1,794	134,897
Latin America & Carib.	30,181	125,669	5,216	−9,674	11,311	−4,015	13,833	51,851
Middle East & N. Africa	940	30,229	32	402	660	−824	633	−2,090
South Asia	2,931	48,678	1,585	−15,778	285	1,689	1,349	10,978
Sub-Saharan Africa	4,546	33,651	2,998	−9,342	851	−750	217	1,597
High income	229,657	1,225,275	113,030	−150,812	..	..	..	..
Euro area	78,432	426,921	23,737	−273,433	..	..	..	..

a. Includes Luxembourg. b. Includes Montenegro.

About the data

Private financial flows—equity and debt—account for the bulk of development finance. Equity flows comprise foreign direct investment (FDI) and portfolio equity. Debt flows are financing raised through bond issuance, bank lending, and supplier credits. Data on equity flows are based on balance of payments data reported by the International Monetary Fund (IMF). FDI data are supplemented by staff estimates using data from the United Nations Conference on Trade and Development and official national sources.

The internationally accepted definition of FDI (from the fifth edition of the IMF's *Balance of Payments Manual* [1993]), includes three components: equity investment, reinvested earnings, and short- and long-term loans between parent firms and foreign affiliates. Distinguished from other kinds of international investment, FDI is made to establish a lasting interest in or effective management control over an enterprise in another country. The IMF suggests that investments should account for at least 10 percent of voting stock to be counted as FDI. In practice many countries set a higher threshold. Many countries fail to report reinvested earnings, and the definition of long-term loans differs among countries.

FDI data do not give a complete picture of international investment in an economy. Balance of payments data on FDI do not include capital raised locally, an important source of investment financing in some developing countries. In addition, FDI data omit nonequity cross-border transactions such as intrafirm flows of goods and services. For a detailed discussion of the data issues, see the World Bank's *World Debt Tables 1993–94* (vol. 1, chap. 3).

Statistics on bonds, bank lending, and supplier credits are produced by aggregating transactions of public and publicly guaranteed debt and private nonguaranteed debt. Data on public and publicly guaranteed debt are reported through the Debtor Reporting System by World Bank member economies that have received loans from the International Bank for Reconstruction and Development or credits from the International Development Association. The reports are cross-checked with data from market sources that include transactions data. Information on private nonguaranteed bonds and bank lending is collected from market sources, because official national sources reporting to the Debtor Reporting System are not asked for a breakdown of private nonguaranteed bonds and loans.

Data on equity flows are shown for all countries for which data are available. Debt flows are shown only for 128 developing countries that report to the Debtor Reporting System; nonreporting countries may also receive debt flows.

The volume of global private financial flows reported by the World Bank generally differs from that reported by other sources because of differences in sources, classification of economies, and method used to adjust and disaggregate reported information. In addition, particularly for debt financing, differences may also reflect how some installments of the transactions and certain offshore issuances are treated.

Definitions

• **Foreign direct investment** is net inflows of investment to acquire a lasting interest in or management control over an enterprise operating in an economy other than that of the investor. It is the sum of equity capital, reinvested earnings, other long-term capital, and short-term capital, as shown in the balance of payments. • **Portfolio equity** includes net inflows from equity securities other than those recorded as direct investment and including shares, stocks, depository receipts, and direct purchases of shares in local stock markets by foreign investors • **Bonds** are securities issued with a fixed rate of interest for a period of more than one year. They include net flows through cross-border public and publicly guaranteed and private nonguaranteed bond issues. • **Commercial bank and other lending** includes net commercial bank lending (public and publicly guaranteed and private nonguaranteed) and other private credits.

Most global foreign direct investment is directed to high-income economies and a few large middle-income economies   6.12a

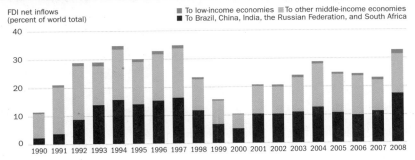

FDI net inflows
(percent of world total)

■ To low-income economies ■ To other middle-income economies
■ To Brazil, China, India, the Russian Federation, and South Africa

The share of FDI net inflows to developing economies increased 10 percentage points between 2007 and 2008 because of decreasing inflows to high-income economies. Brazil, China, India, the Russian Federation, and South Africa received more than half the FDI net inflows to all developing economies.

Source: World Development Indicators data files.

Data sources

Data on equity and debt flows are compiled from a variety of public and private sources, including the World Bank's Debtor Reporting System, the IMF's International Financial Statistics and Balance of Payments databases, and Dealogic. These data are also published annually in the World Bank's *Global Development Finance,* on its *Global Development Finance* CD-ROM, and on *GDF Online.*

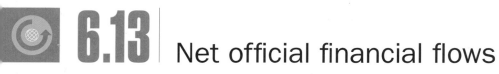
	Total		International financial institutions							United Nations[b,c]			
	$ millions		World Bank[a]		IMF		Regional development banks[b]			$ millions			
	From bilateral sources	From multilateral sources[a,b,c]	IDA	IBRD	Concessional	Non-concessional	Concessional	Non-concessional	Other institutions	UNICEF	UNRWA	UNTA	Others
	2008	2008	2008	2008	2008	2008	2008	2008	2008	2008	2008	2008	2008
Afghanistan	8.5	190.5	41.3	0.0	35.7	0.0	50.9	0.0	3.2	35.7	0.0	1.0	22.7
Albania	7.8	140.9	19.9	11.7	−11.4	3.8	0.0	26.5	85.4	0.8	0.0	0.4	3.8
Algeria	−162.9	−106.2	0.0	−102.2	0.0	0.0	0.0	0.0	−13.9	1.1	0.0	0.9	7.9
Angola	816.6	34.8	6.1	0.0	0.0	0.0	2.1	−0.4	0.1	16.3	0.0	0.8	9.8
Argentina	−70.4	−401.3	0.0	−604.6	0.0	0.0	0.0	−60.6	260.5	0.7	0.0	1.0	1.7
Armenia	69.7	69.6	68.8	−0.9	−19.6	0.0	8.0	0.0	3.6	0.6	0.0	1.6	7.5
Australia													
Austria													
Azerbaijan	29.1	174.0	42.2	56.3	−15.4	−6.2	8.8	48.8	28.1	1.0	0.0	0.6	9.8
Bangladesh	57.5	1,274.0	607.0	0.0	198.7	0.0	298.5	121.7	−2.0	20.8	0.0	0.8	28.5
Belarus	1,501.4	0.9	0.0	−0.9	0.0	0.0	0.0	−2.1	0.0	0.6	0.0	0.5	2.8
Belgium													
Benin	−31.9	154.8	84.1	0.0	18.9	0.0	29.5	0.0	3.6	5.4	0.0	0.8	12.5
Bolivia	46.4	119.6	24.3	0.0	0.0	0.0	36.9	−43.4	92.0	1.1	0.0	0.6	8.1
Bosnia and Herzegovina	24.1	63.6	16.5	−24.6	0.0	−2.4	0.0	56.9	8.9	0.8	0.0	0.8	6.7
Botswana	−19.4	23.0	−0.5	0.0	0.0	0.0	−2.3	−4.7	25.5	0.7	0.0	0.4	3.9
Brazil	581.5	943.4	0.0	914.2	0.0	0.0	3.0	−592.7	603.9	1.8	0.0	1.5	11.7
Bulgaria	71.9	−432.1	0.0	−406.5	0.0	0.0	0.0	−2.6	−23.0	..	..	..	..
Burkina Faso	40.5	299.1	159.2	0.0	18.2	0.0	38.8	0.0	46.0	15.8	0.0	1.1	20.0
Burundi	−0.8	43.7	−6.2	0.0	21.7	0.0	2.2	0.0	−1.7	9.2	0.0	0.6	17.9
Cambodia	235.8	156.8	14.1	0.0	0.0	0.0	97.3	0.0	16.7	6.4	0.0	0.8	21.5
Cameroon	60.5	94.7	28.7	−5.4	8.4	0.0	45.3	−20.9	18.5	6.1	0.0	1.0	13.0
Canada													
Central African Republic	−2.3	17.9	−10.5	0.0	15.3	0.0	−3.7	0.0	−2.1	5.6	0.0	0.5	12.8
Chad	53.4	−46.5	−57.0	−25.7	−14.0	0.0	5.2	0.0	15.9	11.1	0.0	0.5	17.5
Chile	138.1	−101.8	−0.7	−154.3	0.0	0.0	0.0	50.9	0.0	0.4	0.0	0.9	1.0
China	−447.0	1,394.2	−299.8	632.9	0.0	0.0	0.0	1,001.7	15.7	12.0	0.0	2.2	29.5
Hong Kong SAR, China	..	..	..	..	..	..	..	..	..	..	..	..	..
Colombia	−102.6	1,946.8	−0.7	689.0	0.0	0.0	−5.5	1,349.8	−97.4	2.0	0.0	0.8	8.8
Congo, Dem. Rep.	−108.4	−16.7	50.7	0.0	−137.0	0.0	1.2	−33.7	−15.4	57.9	0.0	1.3	58.3
Congo, Rep.	−18.1	10.1	−2.4	0.0	1.9	0.0	−0.4	−8.7	−0.6	2.8	0.0	0.2	17.3
Costa Rica	22.2	−228.8	−0.2	−4.2	0.0	0.0	−9.7	−261.5	42.6	0.6	0.0	0.7	2.9
Côte d'Ivoire	1.7	−503.4	−103.6	−377.4	−44.5	64.3	−0.6	−59.6	−13.1	7.7	0.0	1.1	22.3
Croatia	..	..	..	143.0	..	..	..	..	..	0.4	0.0	0.6	3.7
Cuba	..	..	..	..	..	..	..	..	..	0.6	0.0	1.4	2.0
Czech Republic	..	..	0.0	0.0	..	..	..	..	..	..	..	..	..
Denmark													
Dominican Republic	696.7	−41.0	−0.7	−22.9	0.0	−42.6	−21.3	−9.3	52.4	0.6	0.0	0.8	2.0
Ecuador	−121.8	−434.7	−1.1	−71.3	0.0	0.0	−26.4	−17.8	−323.3	1.1	0.0	0.8	3.3
Egypt, Arab Rep.	−960.1	118.6	−39.2	65.4	0.0	0.0	8.5	125.5	−60.2	3.0	0.0	1.4	14.2
El Salvador	−2.2	264.6	−0.8	−1.0	0.0	0.0	−14.1	201.0	74.9	0.6	0.0	0.7	3.3
Eritrea	71.9	40.0	19.5	0.0	0.0	0.0	4.8	0.0	1.7	2.6	0.0	1.1	10.3
Estonia	..	..	0.0	−7.2	..	..	..	..	..	..	..	..	..
Ethiopia	86.6	354.7	156.5	0.0	0.0	0.0	72.2	−6.4	31.8	45.9	0.0	1.1	53.6
Finland													
France													
Gabon	−194.9	−56.9	0.0	9.2	0.0	−24.7	−0.2	−25.1	−19.8	0.7	0.0	0.4	2.6
Gambia, The	5.3	54.0	2.3	0.0	6.3	0.0	13.5	0.0	22.6	1.2	0.0	0.3	7.8
Georgia	1.8	417.8	110.2	0.0	−35.0	255.6	69.9	0.3	2.8	1.3	0.0	0.8	11.9
Germany													
Ghana	25.9	371.4	256.5	0.0	0.0	0.0	85.9	−4.1	1.5	9.4	0.0	0.9	21.3
Greece	..	..	0.0	0.0	..	..	..	..	..	..	..	..	..
Guatemala	−24.5	167.6	0.0	66.1	0.0	0.0	−6.4	58.5	40.6	1.6	0.0	0.6	6.6
Guinea	−7.1	15.5	−8.4	0.0	7.9	0.0	11.6	−5.6	−16.8	6.0	0.0	0.5	20.3
Guinea-Bissau	0.0	8.3	−3.9	0.0	−2.0	5.6	−1.2	0.0	0.0	2.2	0.0	0.2	7.4
Haiti	162.3	183.5	−3.9	0.0	50.5	0.0	100.5	0.0	6.7	4.7	0.0	0.8	24.2
Honduras	219.1	175.0	51.1	0.0	0.0	0.0	100.7	−18.4	28.7	0.9	0.0	1.1	10.9

	Total ($ millions)		International financial institutions ($ millions)							United Nations[b,c] ($ millions)			
	From bilateral sources	From multilateral sources[a,b,c]	World Bank[a]		IMF		Regional development banks[b]		Other institutions	UNICEF	UNRWA	UNTA	Others
			IDA	IBRD	Concessional	Non-concessional	Concessional	Non-concessional					
	2008	2008	2008	2008	2008	2008	2008	2008	2008	2008	2008	2008	2008
Hungary	..	..	0.0	−29.8	..	..	..	..	..	..	..	..	..
India	551.1	2,359.6	192.2	731.6	0.0	0.0	0.0	1,306.4	57.6	36.6	0.0	0.3	34.9
Indonesia	−2,040.2	942.5	466.6	146.7	0.0	0.0	24.6	283.7	0.0	5.2	0.0	1.1	14.6
Iran, Islamic Rep.	−89.6	84.7	0.0	77.2	0.0	0.0	0.0	0.0	0.0	1.4	0.0	0.6	5.5
Iraq	..	..	..	..	..	..	..	..	..	2.1	0.0	0.4	7.3
Ireland													
Israel	..	..	..	..	..	..	..	..	..	..	..	..	..
Italy													
Jamaica	−82.3	62.2	0.0	−34.0	0.0	0.0	−5.3	73.8	25.5	0.6	0.0	0.3	1.3
Japan													
Jordan	−2,086.4	51.8	−2.5	−44.4	0.0	−59.3	0.0	0.0	19.9	0.6	130.8	0.9	5.8
Kazakhstan	−11.0	40.9	0.0	36.4	0.0	0.0	−0.2	−1.1	1.5	1.1	0.0	0.3	2.9
Kenya	−83.9	182.4	103.6	0.0	−10.6	0.0	28.9	−3.6	−4.4	15.1	0.0	1.9	51.5
Korea, Dem. Rep.	..	..	..	..	..	..	..	..	..	2.3	0.0	1.4	5.5
Korea, Rep.	..	..	−3.5	−458.0	..	..	..	..	..	..	..	..	..
Kosovo	..	..	..	..	..	..	..	..	..	..	..	..	..
Kuwait	..	..	..	..	..	..	..	..	..	..	..	..	..
Kyrgyz Republic	−5.2	58.3	9.3	0.0	19.0	0.0	17.3	−5.0	−0.7	1.0	0.0	1.3	16.1
Lao PDR	86.5	74.7	3.8	0.0	−4.3	0.0	24.8	0.7	15.0	2.5	0.0	0.7	31.5
Latvia	−0.4	1,066.0	0.0	−23.8	0.0	846.2	0.0	−2.0	245.6	..	..	..	..
Lebanon	115.2	128.3	0.0	−75.7	0.0	40.1	0.0	0.0	38.0	0.6	122.5	1.0	1.8
Lesotho	5.1	13.8	10.9	−1.0	−5.0	0.0	2.2	0.0	−0.8	1.1	0.0	0.6	5.8
Liberia	0.0	527.7	−4.3	0.0	302.5	226.0	−26.8	−6.4	0.0	5.6	0.0	0.4	30.7
Libya	..	..	..	..	..	..	..	..	..	0.0	0.0	0.4	1.1
Lithuania	−2.4	−19.7	0.0	3.0	0.0	0.0	0.0	−7.7	−15.0	..	..	..	..
Macedonia, FYR	30.5	32.7	−5.9	37.0	0.0	0.0	0.0	6.1	−8.9	0.7	0.0	1.0	2.7
Madagascar	27.8	390.3	210.2	0.0	59.0	0.0	75.5	0.0	8.2	17.1	0.0	1.3	19.0
Malawi	−6.5	185.5	11.7	0.0	97.0	0.0	43.5	−2.2	1.9	9.2	0.0	1.0	23.4
Malaysia	−634.9	−82.1	0.0	−49.8	0.0	0.0	0.0	−34.5	−2.5	0.4	0.0	0.6	3.7
Mali	−5.3	263.5	87.1	0.0	28.4	0.0	56.8	0.0	65.6	11.2	0.0	0.7	13.7
Mauritania	128.3	157.7	42.6	0.0	3.1	0.0	19.2	−7.6	80.1	2.6	0.0	0.7	17.0
Mauritius	−16.4	23.9	−0.6	20.5	0.0	0.0	−0.1	10.5	−7.9	0.0	0.0	0.6	0.9
Mexico	−192.0	1,503.0	0.0	1,343.3	0.0	0.0	0.0	153.1	0.0	0.8	0.0	1.0	4.8
Moldova	−12.9	50.2	22.2	−16.8	10.9	0.0	0.0	−3.3	18.9	0.7	0.0	1.5	16.1
Mongolia	6.2	33.0	9.9	0.0	−5.0	0.0	15.2	0.0	3.6	1.2	0.0	1.2	6.9
Morocco	816.9	952.5	−1.3	−20.0	0.0	0.0	−1.1	398.9	564.5	1.3	0.0	0.9	9.3
Mozambique	−4.3	403.3	254.4	0.0	0.0	0.0	65.3	0.0	36.1	15.7	0.0	0.8	31.0
Myanmar	−150.4	38.0	0.0	0.0	0.0	0.0	0.0	0.0	−0.7	13.9	0.0	1.1	23.7
Namibia	..	..	..	..	..	..	..	..	..	1.3	0.0	0.7	5.2
Nepal	−31.1	42.9	−7.9	0.0	0.0	0.0	13.7	0.0	2.6	6.0	0.0	1.1	27.4
Netherlands													
New Zealand													
Nicaragua	21.5	154.4	28.3	0.0	29.1	0.0	79.9	−4.5	9.6	0.7	0.0	1.4	9.9
Niger	17.3	123.4	15.0	0.0	11.9	0.0	19.7	0.0	30.9	19.5	0.0	0.7	25.7
Nigeria	−27.3	167.4	333.0	−188.8	0.0	0.0	27.9	−81.9	0.0	43.3	0.0	1.0	32.9
Norway													
Oman	..	..	0.0	0.0	..	..	..	..	..	0.2	0.0	0.1	0.4
Pakistan	195.5	4,210.7	37.9	−243.2	−162.7	3,183.5	435.6	1,065.8	−163.5	21.0	0.0	1.9	34.4
Panama	−4.2	147.1	0.0	53.8	0.0	−5.3	−6.9	94.3	7.2	0.4	0.0	0.5	3.1
Papua New Guinea	−97.0	−27.6	−1.7	−25.7	0.0	0.0	−7.6	4.0	−3.5	1.3	0.0	0.0	5.6
Paraguay	3.3	−22.1	−1.5	−20.7	0.0	0.0	−6.9	−0.2	2.4	1.2	0.0	0.5	3.1
Peru	−122.0	21.8	0.0	63.2	0.0	0.0	−7.0	103.6	−147.7	0.9	0.0	0.8	8.0
Philippines	−761.0	−94.1	−7.1	−279.6	0.0	0.0	−33.0	205.7	1.0	3.0	0.0	0.8	15.1
Poland	−3,201.7	−73.6	0.0	−73.6	0.0	0.0	0.0	0.0	0.0	..	..	..	..
Portugal													
Puerto Rico	..	..	..	..	..	..	..	..	..	..	..	..	..
Qatar	..	..	..	..	..	..	..	..	..	..	..	..	..

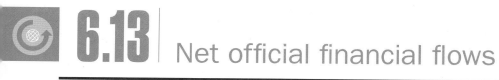

	Total ($ millions)		International financial institutions ($ millions)							United Nations[b,c] ($ millions)			
			World Bank[a]		IMF		Regional development banks[b]						
	From bilateral sources	From multilateral sources[a,b,c]	IDA	IBRD	Concessional	Non-concessional	Concessional	Non-concessional	Other institutions	UNICEF	UNRWA	UNTA	Others
	2008	2008	2008	2008	2008	2008	2008	2008	2008	2008	2008	2008	2008
Romania	17.8	811.6	0.0	−48.5	0.0	0.0	0.7	64.5	794.9	..	..	..	..
Russian Federation	−539.3	−679.2	0.0	−485.2	0.0	0.0	0.0	−193.8	−0.2	..	..	..	..
Rwanda	3.4	156.7	40.5	0.0	3.6	0.0	31.3	0.0	25.2	8.3	0.0	0.8	47.0
Saudi Arabia	..	..	..	..	..	..	..	..	..	0.0	0.0	0.7	..
Senegal	233.6	261.3	133.9	0.0	38.4	0.0	68.5	−10.9	6.7	5.4	0.0	1.3	18.0
Serbia	−48.7	439.0	34.5	−22.1	0.0	0.0	0.0	301.8	107.4	2.3	0.0	1.0	14.1
Sierra Leone	12.2	92.4	25.6	0.0	18.0	0.0	15.5	0.0	6.6	8.3	0.0	1.1	17.3
Singapore	..	..	..	..	..	..	..	..	..	..	..	..	..
Slovak Republic	..	..	0.0	−50.2	..	..	..	..	..	..	..	..	..
Slovenia	..	..	0.0	−14.3	..	..	..	..	..	..	..	..	..
Somalia	0.0	31.8	0.0	0.0	0.0	0.0	0.0	0.0	0.0	12.2	0.0	0.0	19.6
South Africa	0.0	−14.2	0.0	−0.3	0.0	0.0	0.0	−22.4	0.0	2.8	0.0	0.5	5.2
Spain													
Sri Lanka	34.0	167.0	40.0	0.0	−6.1	−72.2	74.1	84.8	28.9	1.1	0.0	1.2	15.2
Sudan	274.2	157.2	−1.2	0.0	0.0	−65.5	0.0	0.0	149.5	17.7	0.0	0.8	55.9
Swaziland	10.1	22.8	−0.2	−5.9	0.0	0.0	1.9	−8.2	30.3	1.4	0.0	0.6	2.9
Sweden													
Switzerland													
Syrian Arab Republic	..	..	−1.5	0.0	..	..	..	..	..	0.8	57.1	1.3	6.2
Tajikistan	234.5	54.0	7.4	0.0	−31.0	0.0	48.9	−1.3	2.7	2.2	0.0	0.8	24.3
Tanzania	0.0	567.9	392.9	0.0	0.0	0.0	98.8	−1.0	19.8	17.9	0.0	1.1	38.4
Thailand	−219.7	−12.9	−3.4	1.6	0.0	0.0	−4.2	−4.0	−12.7	1.0	0.0	1.2	7.6
Timor-Leste	..	..	..	..	..	..	..	..	..	1.1	0.0	0.5	6.1
Togo	−0.7	−76.3	−117.0	0.0	47.7	0.0	−14.9	0.0	−6.3	4.3	0.0	0.5	9.4
Trinidad and Tobago	..	..	0.0	−11.1	..	..	..	..	..	0.0	0.0	0.1	0.6
Tunisia	−30.6	−76.1	−2.1	−203.1	0.0	0.0	0.0	−19.2	139.8	0.7	0.0	0.8	7.0
Turkey	434.9	3,424.6	−5.9	570.0	0.0	1,587.7	0.0	0.0	1,259.3	1.6	0.0	0.6	11.3
Turkmenistan	−76.0	0.8	0.0	−1.2	0.0	0.0	0.0	0.0	−1.5	0.9	0.0	0.0	2.6
Uganda	−16.1	295.2	171.8	0.0	0.0	0.0	67.6	−0.9	0.9	22.4	0.0	1.1	32.3
Ukraine	−220.7	5,070.5	0.0	686.6	0.0	4,401.4	0.0	−34.5	9.1	1.2	0.0	1.8	4.9
United Arab Emirates	..	..	..	..	..	..	..	..	..	..	..	..	..
United Kingdom													
United States													
Uruguay	−19.8	408.6	0.0	61.4	0.0	0.0	−2.4	200.2	146.4	0.5	0.0	0.6	1.9
Uzbekistan	−1.1	52.6	12.7	−13.8	0.0	0.0	2.7	12.2	29.6	3.0	0.0	0.4	5.8
Venezuela, RB	−56.9	251.7	0.0	0.0	0.0	0.0	0.0	159.1	87.2	1.0	0.0	0.5	3.9
Vietnam	410.7	770.3	555.1	0.0	−39.3	0.0	194.5	17.8	16.6	4.1	0.0	1.5	20.0
West Bank and Gaza	..	..	..	..	..	..	..	..	..	3.7	496.6	0.1	9.3
Yemen, Rep.	−9.7	118.9	69.9	0.0	−61.6	−9.9	0.0	0.0	93.2	10.3	0.0	0.9	16.1
Zambia	−16.3	125.6	50.7	0.0	11.0	0.0	45.6	−5.0	−15.8	8.8	0.0	1.6	28.7
Zimbabwe	13.0	10.6	0.0	0.0	−1.7	0.0	−0.3	−0.1	−2.2	4.6	0.0	0.5	9.8
World	.. s	.. s	.. s	.. s	.. s	.. s	.. s	.. s	.. s	984.1 s	807.1 s	645.3 s	1,941.2 s
Low income	1,433.9	8,021.8	3,369.2	−39.4	716.6	221.8	1,697.9	58.8	523.4	473.9	0.0	37.3	962.3
Middle income	−5,743.3	26,241.4	1,121.8	2,619.3	−243.5	10,112.2	828.3	5,893.3	4,262.5	238.0	807.1	107.4	495.0
Lower middle income	−4,014.2	17,133.6	1,062.3	964.7	−252.0	7,703.0	879.5	4,589.2	738.4	212.0	684.5	36.8	515.2
Upper middle income	−1,729.1	9,213.7	59.5	1,654.6	8.5	2,409.2	−51.2	1,304.2	3,524.1	26.0	122.5	23.1	133.2
Low & middle income	−4,309.4	35,140.6	4,491.0	2,579.9	473.1	10,334.0	2,526.2	5,952.1	4,785.9	982.9	807.1	644.0	1,564.4
East Asia & Pacific	−3,563.6	3,304.2	738.5	424.8	−48.6	0.0	306.7	1,480.7	48.0	59.8	0.0	98.3	196.0
Europe & Central Asia	−1,682.4	10,789.2	347.3	272.6	−82.5	7,086.2	156.2	263.2	2,566.1	20.1	0.0	13.7	146.3
Latin America & Carib.	1,151.3	5,245.4	102.2	2,271.8	88.1	−47.5	251.0	1,434.9	916.4	27.9	0.0	67.5	133.1
Middle East & N. Africa	−2,391.2	1,945.5	30.3	−302.8	−59.8	−29.1	13.6	505.2	784.9	27.2	807.1	71.9	97.0
South Asia	823.5	8,284.8	921.1	488.3	65.7	3,108.9	876.1	2,578.8	−52.9	122.5	0.0	6.4	169.9
Sub-Saharan Africa	1,353.0	5,140.7	2,351.5	−574.9	510.2	215.4	922.6	−310.7	523.4	466.6	0.0	156.0	880.6
High income	..	..	..	..	..	..	..	..	..	1.2	0.0	1.3	7.2
Euro area	..	..	..	..	..	..	..	..	..	..	..	..	..

a. Aggregates include amounts for economies that do not report to the World Bank's Debtor Reporting System and may differ from aggregates published in *Global Development Finance 2010*.
b. Aggregates include amounts for economies not specified elsewhere. c. World and income group aggregates include flows not allocated by country or region.

About the data

The table shows concessional and nonconcessional financial flows from official bilateral sources, the major international financial institutions, and UN agencies. The international financial institutions fund nonconcessional lending operations primarily by selling low-interest, highly rated bonds backed by prudent lending and financial policies and the strong financial support of their members. Funds are then on-lent to developing countries at slightly higher interest rates with 15- to 20-year maturities. Lending terms vary with market conditions and institutional policies.

Concessional flows from international financial institutions are credits provided through concessional lending facilities. Subsidies from donors or other resources reduce the cost of these loans. Grants are not included in net flows. The Organisation for Economic Co-operation and Development's (OECD) Development Assistance Committee (DAC) defines concessional flows from bilateral donors as flows with a grant element of at least 25 percent, evaluated assuming a 10 percent nominal discount rate.

World Bank concessional lending is done by the International Development Association (IDA) based on gross national income (GNI) per capita and performance standards assessed by World Bank staff. Cut-off for IDA eligibility, set at the beginning of the World Bank's fiscal year, has been $1,135 since July 1, 2009, measured in 2008 U.S. dollars using the *Atlas* method (see *Users guide*). In exceptional circumstances IDA extends temporary eligibility to countries above the cut-off that are undertaking major adjustments but are not

creditworthy for International Bank for Reconstruction and Development (IBRD) lending. Exceptions are also made for small island economies. The IBRD lends to creditworthy countries at a variable base rate of six-month LIBOR plus a spread, either variable or fixed, for the life of the loan. The rate is reset every six months and applies to the interest period beginning on that date. Although some outstanding IBRD loans have a low enough interest rate to be classified as concessional under the DAC definition, all IBRD loans in the table are classified as nonconcessional. Lending by the International Finance Corporation is not included.

The International Monetary Fund makes concessional funds available through its Poverty Reduction and Growth Facility and the IMF Trust Fund. Eligibility is based principally on a country's per capita income and eligibility under IDA.

Regional development banks also maintain concessional windows. Their loans are recorded in the table according to each institution's classification and not according to the DAC definition.

Data for flows from international financial institutions are available for 128 countries that report to the World Bank's Debtor Reporting System. World Bank flows for nonreporting countries were collected from its operational records. Nonreporting countries may have net flows from other international financial institutions.

Official flows from the United Nations are mainly concessional flows classified as official development assistance but may include nonconcessional flows classified as other official flows in OECD-DAC databases.

Definitions

• **Total net official financial flows** are disbursements of public or publicly guaranteed loans and credits, less repayments of principal. • **IDA** is the International Development Association, the concessional loan window of the World Bank Group. • **IBRD** is the International Bank for Reconstruction and Development, the founding and largest member of the World Bank Group. • **IMF** is the International Monetary Fund, which provides concessional lending through the Poverty Reduction and Growth Facility and the IMF Trust Fund and nonconcessional lending through credit to its members, mainly for balance of payments needs. • **Regional development banks** are the African Development Bank, which serves all of Africa, including North Africa; the Asian Development Bank, which serves South and Central Asia and East Asia and Pacific; the European Bank for Reconstruction and Development, which serves Europe and Central Asia; and the Inter-American Development Bank, which serves the Americas. • **Concessional** financial flows are disbursements made through concessional lending facilities. • **Nonconcessional** financial flows are all disbursements that are not concessional. • **Other institutions,** a residual category in the World Bank's Debtor Reporting System, includes other multilateral institutions such as the Caribbean Development Fund, Council of Europe, European Development Fund, Islamic Development Bank, and Nordic Development Fund. • **United Nations** includes the United Nations Children's Fund (UNICEF), United Nations Relief and Works Agency for Palestine Refugees in the Near East (UNRWA), United Nations Regular Programme for Technical Assistance (UNTA), and other UN agencies, such as the International Fund for Agricultural Development, Joint United Nations Programme on HIV/AIDS, United Nations Development Programme, United Nations Population Fund, United Nations Refugee Agency, and World Food Programme.

Data sources

Data on net financial flows from international financial institutions are from the World Bank's Debtor Reporting System and published annually in the World Bank's *Global Development Finance,* on its *Global Development Finance* CD-ROM, and on *GDF Online.* Data on official flows from UN agencies are from the OECD DAC annual *Development Co-operation Report* and are available electronically on the OECD DAC's *International Development Statistics* CD-ROM and at www.oecd.org/dac/stats/idsonline.

Net lending from the International Bank for Reconstruction and Development declined as countries paid off loans, and concessional lending from the International Development Association increased
6.13a

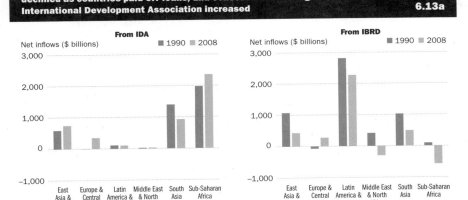

All regions except Middle East and North Africa and Sub-Saharan Africa received positive net disbursements from the IBRD. The world's poorest countries in Sub-Saharan Africa continue to receive concessional lending from the International Development Association.

Source: Global Development Finance data files.

6.14 Financial flows from Development Assistance Committee members

Net disbursements

$ millions	Total net flows[a] 2008	Official development assistance[a] Total 2008	Bilateral grants 2008	Bilateral loans 2008	Contributions to multilateral institutions 2008	Other official flows[a] 2008	Private flows[a] Total 2008	Foreign direct investment 2008	Bilateral portfolio investment 2008	Multilateral portfolio investment 2008	Private export credits 2008	Net grants by NGOs[a] 2008
Australia	3,997	2,954	2,600	53	301	59	314	1,673	−1,223	0	−136	670
Austria	11,302	1,714	1,275	−42	480	103	9,348	7,532	0	0	1,817	137
Belgium	4,425	2,386	1,404	−28	1,010	−138	1,816	1,617	0	0	199	361
Canada	24,068	4,785	3,396	−39	1,428	1,608	16,184	14,872	988	0	324	1,491
Denmark	5,150	2,803	1,853	−25	975	−84	2,303	2,303	0	0	0	129
Finland	−222	1,166	681	13	473	22	−1,422	−32	−1,390	0	0	13
France	40,641	10,908	5,980	481	4,446	−229	29,962	24,609	6,098	0	−745	0
Germany	33,395	13,981	9,392	−329	4,918	−462	18,251	9,598	5,218	−275	3,708	1,626
Greece	1,166	703	312	0	391	1	460	460	0	0	0	2
Ireland	6,101	1,328	931	0	397	0	4,500	0	4,500	0	0	273
Italy	5,581	4,861	1,919	−81	3,022	408	207	1,544	−1,339	0	2	105
Japan	31,783	9,579	7,764	−940	2,756	−1,986	23,738	25,710	3,952	−1,046	−4,878	452
Luxembourg	426	415	279	0	136	0	0	0	0	0	0	11
Netherlands	−14,022	6,993	5,312	−112	1,793	0	−21,345	−24,523	3,365	−169	−18	330
New Zealand	433	348	278	0	70	8	29	29	0	0	0	48
Norway	3,963	3,963	2,941	95	928	0	0	0	0	0	0	0
Portugal	1,528	620	238	136	247	0	906	341	−95	0	660	1
Spain	30,087	6,867	4,776	25	2,065	0	23,220	23,334	0	0	−114	0
Sweden	5,896	4,732	3,086	57	1,589	31	1,108	−314	0	0	1,422	25
Switzerland	12,923	2,038	1,536	14	487	0	10,487	11,432	0	−274	−671	398
United Kingdom	41,878	11,500	7,064	303	4,133	−22	29,938	23,783	2,223	0	3,932	462
United States	14,084	26,842	24,825	−965	2,982	−1,100	−28,781	54,172	−75,801	−8,220	1,068	17,122
Total	**264,581**	**121,483**	**87,839**	**−1,384**	**35,029**	**−1,782**	**121,224**	**178,140**	**−53,504**	**−9,983**	**6,572**	**23,655**

Official development assistance

	Commitments[b] $ millions 2000	2008	Gross disbursements[b] $ millions 2000	2008	Net disbursements $ millions[b] 2000	2008	Per capita[b] $ 2000	2008	% of GNI[a] 2000	2008	% of general government disbursements[a] 2000	2008
Australia	2,141	4,698	1,845	2,834	1,845	2,834	96	133	0.27	0.32	0.73	0.88
Austria	956	1,693	738	1,631	734	1,585	90	190	0.23	0.43	0.46	0.86
Belgium	1,451	2,949	1,451	2,319	1,413	2,219	138	208	0.36	0.48	0.74	0.96
Canada	3,282	5,343	2,908	4,673	2,867	4,635	93	139	0.25	0.32	0.60	0.81
Denmark	2,732	2,298	2,914	2,631	2,883	2,573	540	467	1.06	0.82	1.96	1.62
Finland	574	1,221	614	1,073	603	1,072	116	201	0.31	0.44	0.64	0.89
France	8,066	14,861	8,601	11,637	7,062	10,122	120	163	0.30	0.39	0.62	0.74
Germany	9,183	16,864	9,321	14,910	8,076	13,060	98	159	0.27	0.38	0.57	0.89
Greece	415	645	415	645	415	645	38	57	0.20	0.21	0.42	0.42
Ireland	430	1,272	430	1,272	430	1,272	114	293	0.29	0.59	0.87	1.20
Italy	2,869	5,158	2,838	4,655	2,443	4,440	43	75	0.13	0.22	0.28	0.44
Japan	14,388	18,425	13,704	15,491	11,357	8,502	89	67	0.28	0.19	0.86	0.53
Luxembourg	227	388	227	388	227	388	515	792	0.70	0.97	1.76	1.94
Netherlands	6,072	9,010	5,694	6,792	5,532	6,522	347	396	0.84	0.80	1.86	1.77
New Zealand	235	456	221	357	221	357	58	84	0.25	0.30	0.57	0.68
Norway	2,189	4,489	2,471	3,635	2,459	3,635	548	757	0.76	0.88	1.83	2.22
Portugal	764	582	764	582	497	576	48	56	0.26	0.27	0.60	0.56
Spain	2,717	6,015	2,717	6,864	2,339	6,304	59	137	0.22	0.45	0.57	1.07
Sweden	2,189	4,018	2,739	4,513	2,738	4,510	309	487	0.80	0.98	1.35	1.93
Switzerland	1,359	1,891	1,339	1,824	1,335	1,813	186	235	0.34	0.42	1.11	1.29
United Kingdom	7,224	12,825	7,224	12,825	7,144	12,315	122	202	0.32	0.43	0.80	0.92
United States	15,108	33,919	13,015	27,210	11,928	26,254	43	86	0.10	0.19	0.31	0.48
Total	**84,571**	**149,021**	**82,188**	**128,762**	**74,548**	**115,632**	**88**	**129**	**0.22**	**0.31**	**0.60**	**0.73**

Note: Components may not sum to totals because of gaps in reporting.
a. At current prices and exchange rates. b. At 2007 prices and exchange rates.

About the data

The flows of official and private financial resources from the members of the Development Assistance Committee (DAC) of the Organisation for Economic Co-operation and Development (OECD) to developing economies are compiled by DAC, based principally on reporting by DAC members using standard questionnaires issued by the DAC Secretariat.

The table shows data reported by DAC member economies and does not include aid provided by the European Commission—a multilateral member of DAC.

DAC exists to help its members coordinate their development assistance and to encourage the expansion and improve the effectiveness of the aggregate resources flowing to recipient economies. In this capacity DAC monitors the flow of all financial resources, but its main concern is official development assistance (ODA). Grants or loans to countries and territories on the DAC list of aid recipients have to meet three criteria to be counted as ODA. They are undertaken by the official sector. They promote economic development and welfare as the main objective. And they are provided on concessional financial terms (loans must have a grant element of at least 25 percent, calculated at a discount rate of 10 percent). The DAC Statistical Reporting Directives provide the most detailed explanation of this definition and all ODA-related rules.

This definition excludes nonconcessional flows from official creditors, which are classified as "other official flows," and aid for military purposes. Transfer payments to private individuals, such as pensions, reparations, and insurance payouts, are in general not counted. In addition to financial flows, ODA includes technical cooperation, most expenditures for peacekeeping under UN mandates and assistance to refugees, contributions to multilateral institutions such as the United Nations and its specialized agencies, and concessional funding to multilateral development banks.

A DAC revision of the list of countries and territories counted as aid recipients has governed aid reporting for the three years starting in 2005. In the past DAC distinguished aid going to Part I and Part II countries. Part I countries, the recipients of ODA, comprised many of the countries classified by the World Bank as low- and middle-income economies. Part II countries, whose assistance was designated official aid, included the more advanced countries of Central and Eastern Europe, countries of the former Soviet Union, and certain advanced developing countries and territories. This distinction has been dropped. ODA recipients now comprise all low- and middle-income countries except those that are members of the Group of Eight or the European Union (including countries with a firm date for EU accession). The content and structure of tables 6.14–6.17 were revised to reflect this change. Because official aid flows are quite small relative to ODA, the net effect of these changes is believed to be minor.

Flows are transfers of resources, either in cash or in the form of commodities or services measured on a cash basis. Short-term capital transactions (with one year or less maturity) are not counted. Repayments of the principal (but not interest) of ODA loans are recorded as negative flows. Proceeds from official equity investments in a developing country are reported as ODA, while proceeds from their later sale are recorded as negative flows.

The table is based on donor country reports and does not provide a complete picture of the resources received by developing economies for two reasons. First, flows from DAC members are only part of the aggregate resource flows to these economies. Second, the data that record contributions to multilateral institutions measure the flow of resources made available to those institutions by DAC members, not the flow of resources from those institutions to developing and transition economies.

Aid as a share of gross national income (GNI), aid per capita, and ODA as a share of the general government disbursements of the donor are calculated by the OECD. The denominators used in calculating these ratios may differ from corresponding values elsewhere in this book because of differences in timing or definitions.

Definitions

• **Net disbursements** are gross disbursements of grants and loans minus repayments of principal on earlier loans. • **Total net flows** are ODA or official aid flows, other official flows, private flows, and net grants by nongovernmental organizations. • **Official development assistance** refers to flows that meet the DAC definition of ODA and are made to countries and territories on the DAC list of aid recipients. • **Bilateral grants** are transfers of money or in kind for which no repayment is required. • **Bilateral loans** are loans extended by governments or official agencies with a grant element of at least 25 percent (at a 10 percent discount rate). • **Contributions to multilateral institutions** are concessional funding received by multilateral institutions from DAC members as grants or capital subscriptions. • **Other official flows** are transactions by the official sector whose main objective is other than development or whose grant element is less than 25 percent. • **Private flows** are flows at market terms financed from private sector resources in donor countries. They include changes in holdings of private long-term assets by reporting country residents. • **Foreign direct investment** is investment by residents of DAC member countries to acquire a lasting management interest (at least 10 percent of voting stock) in an enterprise operating in the recipient country. The data reflect changes in the net worth of subsidiaries in recipient countries whose parent company is in the DAC source country. • **Bilateral portfolio investment** is bank lending and the purchase of bonds, shares, and real estate by residents of DAC member countries in recipient countries. • **Multilateral portfolio investment** is transactions of private banks and nonbanks in DAC member countries in the securities issued by multilateral institutions. • **Private export credits** are loans extended to recipient countries by the private sector in DAC member countries to promote trade; they may be supported by an official guarantee. • **Net grants by nongovernmental organizations (NGOs)** are private grants by NGOs, net of subsidies from the official sector. • **Commitments** are obligations, expressed in writing and backed by funds, undertaken by an official donor to provide specified assistance to a recipient country or multilateral organization. • **Gross disbursements** are the international transfer of financial resources, goods, and services, valued at the cost to the donor.

Data sources

Data on financial flows are compiled by OECD DAC and published in its annual statistical report, *Geographical Distribution of Financial Flows to Developing Countries*, and its annual *Development Co-operation Report*. Data are available electronically on the OECD-DAC's *International Development Statistics* CD-ROM and at www.oecd.org/dac/stats/idsonline.

6.15 Allocation of bilateral aid from Development Assistance Committee members

6.15a Aid by purpose

	Net disbursements				Share of bilateral ODA net disbursements									
					%									
	$ millions[a]		Development projects, programs, and other resource provisions		Technical cooperation[b]		Debt-related aid		Humanitarian assistance		Administrative costs			
	2000	2008	2000	2008	2000	2008	2000	2008	2000	2008	2000	2008		
Australia	758	2,653	27.8	41.2	55.1	34.0	1.1	9.7	9.7	11.3	6.2	3.8		
Austria	273	1,234	28.7	12.2	41.8	21.5	20.4	59.4	2.7	3.6	6.4	3.3		
Belgium	477	1,376	33.6	25.5	46.9	52.9	6.6	7.3	5.4	9.2	7.5	5.1		
Canada	1,160	3,357	39.6	28.5	43.0	49.3	1.1	4.0	5.0	10.7	11.4	7.5		
Denmark	1,024	1,828	65.8	67.9	25.3	10.0	1.0	5.3	0.0	9.2	8.0	7.6		
Finland	217	693	40.8	33.7	41.4	42.3	0.0	0.3	10.5	12.9	7.2	10.8		
France	2,829	6,461	25.4	33.2	50.6	45.0	17.0	15.1	0.4	0.4	6.7	6.4		
Germany	2,687	9,063	16.8	17.9	63.8	47.2	6.6	28.3	4.1	3.3	8.7	3.3		
Greece	99	312	69.6	16.4	23.8	70.6	0.0	0.0	6.4	5.5	0.2	7.5		
Ireland	154	931	79.1	71.1	0.4	4.4	0.0	0.0	15.5	19.1	5.1	5.4		
Italy	377	1,838	10.2	32.3	8.1	9.2	57.5	48.4	18.3	6.5	5.9	3.6		
Japan	9,768	6,823	60.4	28.8	24.9	28.7	4.2	25.0	0.9	3.8	9.5	13.8		
Luxembourg	99	279	84.4	76.8	3.2	3.6	0.8	0.0	10.4	12.1	1.2	7.5		
Netherlands	2,243	5,200	41.1	71.1	33.7	12.6	6.8	2.4	9.1	7.7	9.4	6.2		
New Zealand	85	278	39.7	56.4	48.1	25.7	0.0	0.0	3.4	9.4	8.8	8.4		
Norway	934	3,036	57.9	56.0	23.0	23.8	1.0	1.4	11.3	11.9	6.9	6.9		
Portugal	179	373	30.4	53.0	50.4	42.3	14.6	0.1	1.9	0.3	2.7	4.3		
Spain	720	4,802	69.3	54.3	17.9	25.3	2.3	7.1	3.7	9.0	6.8	4.3		
Sweden	1,242	3,142	60.9	62.5	13.6	18.7	3.1	0.0	14.6	11.6	7.7	7.2		
Switzerland	627	1,550	58.6	46.3	19.4	27.6	0.9	6.4	20.2	10.7	0.9	9.1		
United Kingdom	2,710	7,367	47.7	61.5	25.5	15.7	5.7	7.5	12.7	9.1	8.4	6.3		
United States	7,405	23,860	14.6	70.0	64.4	5.4	1.7	0.9	9.6	18.4	9.7	5.3		
Total	**36,064**	**86,455**	**40.5**	**50.4**	**39.4**	**23.0**	**5.4**	**10.2**	**6.1**	**10.2**	**8.6**	**6.2**		

a. At current exchange rates and prices. b. Includes aid for promoting development awareness and aid provided to refugees in donor economies.

About the data

Aid can be used in many ways. The sector to which aid goes, the form it takes, and the procurement restrictions attached to it are important influences on aid effectiveness. The data on allocation of official development assistance (ODA) in the table are based principally on reporting by members of the Organisation for Economic Co-operation and Development (OECD) Development Assistance Committee (DAC). For more detailed explanation of ODA, see *About the data* for table 6.14.

The form in which an ODA contribution reaches the benefiting sector or the economy is important. A distinction is made between resource provision and technical cooperation. Resource provision involves mainly cash or in-kind transfers and financing of capital projects, with the deliverables being financial support and the provision of commodities and supplies. Technical cooperation includes grants to nationals of aid-recipient countries receiving education or training at home or abroad, and payments to consultants, advisers, and similar personnel and to teachers and administrators serving in recipient countries. Technical cooperation is spent mostly in the donor economy.

Two other types of aid are presented because they serve distinctive purposes. Debt-related aid aims to provide debt relief on liabilities that recipient countries have difficulty servicing. Thus, this type of aid may not provide a full value of new resource flows for development, in particular for heavily indebted poor countries. Humanitarian assistance provides relief following sudden disasters and supports food programs in emergency situations. This type of aid does not generally contribute to financing long-term development.

Definitions

• **Net disbursements** are gross disbursements of grants and loans minus repayments of principal on earlier loans • **Development projects, programs, and other resource provisions** are aid provided as cash transfers, aid in kind, development food aid, and the financing of capital projects, intended to increase or improve the recipient's stock of physical capital and to support recipient's development plans and other activities with finance and commodity supply. • **Technical cooperation** is the provision of resources whose main aim is to augment the stock of human intellectual capital, such as the level of knowledge, skills, and technical know-how in the recipient country (including the cost of associated equipment). Contributions take the form mainly of the supply of human resources from donors or action directed to human resources (such as training or advice). Also included are aid for promoting development awareness and aid provided to refugees in the donor economy. Assistance specifically to facilitate a capital project is not included. • **Debt-related aid** groups all actions relating to debt, including forgiveness, swaps, buybacks, rescheduling, and refinancing. • **Humanitarian assistance** is emergency and distress relief (including aid to refugees and assistance for disaster preparedness). • **Administrative costs** are the total current budget outlays of institutions responsible for the formulation and implementation of donor's aid programs and other administrative costs incurred by donors in aid delivery.

Data sources

Data on aid flows are published by OECD DAC in its annual statistical report, *Geographical Distribution of Financial Flows to Developing Countries*, and its annual *Development Co-operation Report*. Data are available electronically on the OECD DAC's *International Development Statistics* CD-ROM and at www.oecd.org/dac/stats/idsonline.

6.15b   Aid by sector

Share of bilateral ODA commitments (%)	Total sector-allocable aid 2008	Social infrastructure and services Total 2008	Education 2008	Health 2008	Population 2008	Water supply and sanitation 2008	Government and civil society 2008	Economic infrastructure, services, and production sector Total 2008	Transport and communication 2008	Agriculture 2008	Multi-sector or cross-cutting 2008	Untied aid[a] 2008
Australia	70.9	45.3	10.4	5.5	2.3	0.5	23.1	11.3	5.2	3.9	14.3	96.7
Austria	33.0	24.9	12.6	3.4	0.4	2.8	4.9	5.6	0.3	0.9	2.5	82.3
Belgium	71.7	45.5	12.2	11.4	0.6	5.8	11.8	17.9	3.1	6.8	8.3	91.9
Canada	63.1	41.9	7.5	9.7	1.7	1.2	20.3	14.1	2.9	7.1	7.1	90.8
Denmark	64.9	34.9	3.9	1.2	1.7	1.2	23.3	15.9	1.3	3.6	14.0	98.5
Finland	73.9	37.2	7.9	3.8	1.4	5.6	12.9	21.7	1.3	9.6	15.0	92.3
France	66.2	29.7	18.6	1.9	0.1	3.8	1.6	25.8	15.1	5.6	10.6	81.9
Germany	66.2	35.6	13.7	2.4	1.4	7.2	9.6	23.3	1.8	1.9	7.3	98.2
Greece	71.8	63.3	27.7	2.5	1.9	0.2	19.8	4.9	2.0	1.3	3.7	37.9[b]
Ireland	65.4	53.1	12.8	13.3	3.6	3.0	16.3	8.2	0.4	6.0	4.1	100.0[b]
Italy	42.5	24.1	3.5	5.3	0.4	7.0	6.2	11.7	1.7	3.2	6.7	78.0
Japan	68.8	17.4	4.4	1.3	0.2	9.3	1.5	48.7	25.3	5.8	2.7	96.5
Luxembourg	70.4	46.7	10.2	13.3	7.1	6.8	4.0	14.5	1.8	6.2	9.2	100.0[b]
Netherlands	74.6	58.5	13.2	5.1	4.9	5.7	27.2	10.2	1.6	1.7	5.9	94.5
New Zealand	54.5	41.8	17.5	5.3	1.6	1.2	14.7	9.4	1.8	3.1	3.3	92.7
Norway	67.2	42.1	8.7	6.0	2.3	1.5	20.4	14.0	0.4	4.1	11.1	100.0
Portugal	65.8	48.9	19.1	2.1	0.1	0.1	21.3	14.0	12.9	0.8	2.9	29.1[b]
Spain	65.0	43.4	9.4	5.2	2.1	10.7	9.9	15.0	4.2	3.7	6.6	69.1
Sweden	51.3	30.4	3.9	4.8	2.0	2.4	14.8	11.7	1.5	3.0	9.2	99.9
Switzerland	45.9	21.8	3.2	3.1	0.2	3.2	11.3	13.9	1.3	5.0	10.3	97.3
United Kingdom	62.7	42.4	7.4	7.0	5.5	2.0	17.3	16.4	1.5	1.2	3.9	100.0[b]
United States	74.9	51.8	3.5	3.9	19.4	2.7	15.4	20.3	5.8	5.1	2.8	75.0
Total	**67.8**	**39.2**	**8.0**	**4.0**	**6.6**	**4.8**	**12.2**	**22.9**	**7.8**	**4.3**	**5.7**	**87.3**

a. Excludes technical cooperation and administrative costs. b. Gross disbursements.

About the data

The Development Assistance Committee (DAC) records the sector classification of aid using a three-level hierarchy. The top level is grouped by themes, such as social infrastructure and services; economic infrastructure, services, and production; and multisector or cross-cutting areas. The second level is more specific. Education and health and transport and storage are examples. The third level comprises subsectors such as basic education and basic health. Some contributions are reported as non-sector-allocable aid.

Reporting on the sectoral destination and the form of aid by donors may not be complete. Also, measures of aid allocation may differ from the perspectives of donors and recipients because of difference in classification, available information, and recording time.

The proportion of untied aid is reported because tying arrangements may prevent recipients from obtaining the best value for their money. Tying requires recipients to purchase goods and services from the donor country or from a specified group of countries. Such arrangements prevent a recipient from misappropriating or mismanaging aid receipts, but they may also be motivated by a desire to benefit donor country suppliers.

Definitions

• **Bilateral official development assistance (ODA) commitments** are firm obligations, expressed in writing and backed by the necessary funds, undertaken by official bilateral donors to provide specified assistance to a recipient country or a multilateral organization. Bilateral commitments are recorded in the full amount of expected transfer, irrespective of the time required for completing disbursements. • **Total sector-allocable aid** is the sum of aid that can be assigned to specific sectors or multisector activities. • **Social infrastructure and services** refer to efforts to develop the human resources potential of aid recipients. • **Education** refers to general teaching and instruction at all levels, as well as construction to improve or adapt educational establishments. Training in a particular field is reported for the sector concerned. • **Health** refers to assistance to hospitals, clinics, other medical and dental services, public health administration, and medical insurance programs. • **Population** refers to all activities related to family planning and research into population problems. • **Water supply and sanitation** refer to assistance for water supply and use, sanitation, and water resources development (including rivers). • **Government and civil society** refer to assistance to strengthen government administrative apparatus and planning and activities promoting good governance and civil society. • **Economic infrastructure, services, and production sector** group assistance for networks, utilities, services that facilitate economic activity, and contributions to all directly productive sectors. • **Transport and communication** refer to road, rail, water, and air transport; post and telecommunications; and television and print media. • **Agriculture** refers to sector policy, development, and inputs; crop and livestock production; and agricultural credit, cooperatives, and research. • **Multisector or cross-cutting** refers to support for projects that straddle several sectors. • **Untied aid** is ODA not subject to restrictions by donors on procurement sources.

Data sources

Data on aid flows are published annually by the Organisation for Economic Co-operation and Development (OECD) DAC in *Geographical Distribution of Financial Flows to Developing Countries* and *Development Co-operation Report*. Data are available electronically on the OECD DAC's *International Development Statistics* CD-ROM and at www.oecd.org/dac/stats/idsonline.

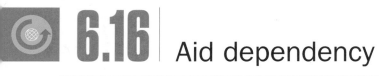
| | Net official development assistance (ODA) | | | | Aid dependency ratios | | | | | | | |
| | Total $ millions | | Per capita $ | | Net ODA as % of GNI | | Net ODA as % of gross capital formation | | Net ODA as % of imports of goods, services, and income | | Net ODA as % of central government expense | |
	2000	2008	2000	2008	2000	2008	2000	2008	2000	2008	2000	2008
Afghanistan	136	4,865	6	168	..	45.8	..	165.8	..	..	..	196.1
Albania	317	386	103	123	8.4	3.0	34.8	9.7	21.0	5.1	..	..
Algeria	200	316	7	9	0.4	0.2	1.5	0.6	..	..	..	0.8
Angola	302	369	21	20	4.1	0.5	22.0	3.5	4.1	0.6	..	..
Argentina	52	131	1	3	0.0	0.0	0.1	0.2	0.1	0.2	..	..
Armenia	216	303	70	98	11.0	2.4	60.6	6.2	21.2	5.7	..	12.3
Australia												
Austria												
Azerbaijan	139	235	17	27	2.8	0.6	12.8	2.5	5.8	1.4	..	3.3
Bangladesh	1,172	2,061	8	13	2.4	2.4	10.8	10.7	11.7	7.8	..	23.9
Belarus	..	110	..	11	..	0.2	..	0.5	..	0.3	1.3	0.5
Belgium												
Benin	241	641	36	74	10.7	9.6	56.4	46.3	32.4	..	..	64.3
Bolivia	482	628	58	65	5.9	3.9	31.6	21.5	19.7	9.6	..	..
Bosnia and Herzegovina	737	482	199	128	12.4	2.5	65.1	10.7	17.4	3.6	..	6.7
Botswana	31	716	18	373	0.5	5.4	1.4	16.5	1.0	10.9	..	..
Brazil	231	460	1	2	0.0	0.0	0.2	0.2	0.2	0.2	..	0.1
Bulgaria	..	..	..	..	..	..	..	..	..	..	..	..
Burkina Faso	338	998	29	66	13.0	12.6	77.2	..	48.9	..	..	98.2
Burundi	93	509	14	63	12.9	43.9	213.8	..	56.5	93.4	..	..
Cambodia	396	743	31	51	11.2	7.5	61.8	..	16.1	9.2	..	..
Cameroon	377	525	24	27	4.0	2.3	22.4	..	12.7	6.0	..	..
Canada												
Central African Republic	75	256	20	59	8.0	13.0	82.4	111.2	..	..	..	..
Chad	130	416	15	38	9.5	6.2	40.4	32.8	..	..	..	..
Chile	49	73	3	4	0.1	0.0	0.3	0.2	0.2	0.1	0.3	0.2
China	1,712	1,489	1	1	0.1	0.0	0.4	0.1	0.6	0.1	..	..
Hong Kong SAR, China	..	..	..	..	..	..	..	..	..	..	..	..
Colombia	186	972	5	22	0.2	0.4	1.3	1.6	1.0	1.7	..	1.7
Congo, Dem. Rep.	177	1,610	3	25	4.5	15.5	119.1	57.8	..	..	15.2	..
Congo, Rep.	32	505	11	140	1.4	6.6	4.4	22.6	1.6	..	..	..
Costa Rica	10	66	2	15	0.1	0.2	0.4	0.9	0.1	0.4	..	1.0
Côte d'Ivoire	351	617	20	30	3.6	2.7	31.2	26.0	7.9	5.9	..	14.7
Croatia	66	397	15	90	0.3	0.6	1.6	1.9	0.6	1.0	0.8	..
Cuba	44	127	4	11	..	..	..	..	..	..	..	..
Czech Republic	..	..	..	..	..	..	..	..	..	..	..	..
Denmark												
Dominican Republic	56	153	6	15	0.2	0.3	1.0	1.8	0.5	0.7	..	..
Ecuador	146	231	12	17	1.0	0.4	4.6	1.5	2.3	1.0	..	..
Egypt, Arab Rep.	1,327	1,348	19	17	1.3	0.8	6.8	3.7	5.6	2.0	..	2.7
El Salvador	180	233	30	38	1.4	1.1	8.1	7.1	3.0	2.0	..	49.9
Eritrea	176	143	48	29	27.7	8.7	116.6	..	34.4	..	..	..
Estonia	..	..	..	..	..	..	..	..	..	..	..	..
Ethiopia	686	3,327	10	41	8.4	13.0	41.4	64.7	41.0	34.5	..	..
Finland												
France												
Gabon	12	55	9	38	0.3	0.4	1.1	1.5	0.5	..	..	..
Gambia, The	50	94	38	57	12.4	12.3	67.8	46.2	..	22.8	..	..
Georgia	169	888	36	206	5.3	7.0	20.8	22.9	13.6	10.9	47.9	23.8
Germany												
Ghana	598	1,293	31	55	12.4	8.6	50.0	21.6	17.2	10.0	..	..
Greece												
Guatemala	263	536	23	39	1.4	1.4	7.6	7.8	4.4	3.1	12.5	11.7
Guinea	153	319	18	32	5.0	9.1	24.9	54.2	15.7	16.7	..	..
Guinea-Bissau	80	132	62	84	39.5	31.6	329.8	123.3	..	..	..	..
Haiti	208	912	24	92	..	..	20.8	49.3	15.1	31.5	..	..
Honduras	448	564	72	77	6.4	4.3	22.3	12.6	8.9	4.7	..	18.4

	Net official development assistance (ODA)				Aid dependency ratios							
	Total $ millions		Per capita $		Net ODA as % of GNI		Net ODA as % of gross capital formation		Net ODA as % of imports of goods, services, and income		Net ODA as % of central government expense	
	2000	2008	2000	2008	2000	2008	2000	2008	2000	2008	2000	2008
Hungary	..	..	..	..	..	..	..	..	..	..	..	..
India	1,457	2,108	1	2	0.3	0.2	1.3	0.5	1.8	0.5	2.0	1.1
Indonesia	1,651	1,225	8	5	1.1	0.3	4.5	0.9	2.5	0.7	..	..
Iran, Islamic Rep.	130	98	2	1	0.1	..	0.4	..	0.7	..	0.2	0.1
Iraq	100	9,870	4	321	..	..	..	..	..	..	..	..
Ireland												
Israel	..	..	..	..	..	..	..	..	..	..	..	..
Italy												
Jamaica	9	79	3	30	0.1	0.6	..	..	0.2	0.7	..	1.6
Japan												
Jordan	552	742	115	126	6.4	3.3	29.2	13.7	8.7	3.8	..	9.6
Kazakhstan	189	333	13	21	1.1	0.3	5.7	0.7	1.8	0.5	7.5	1.7
Kenya	509	1,360	16	35	4.1	4.5	23.0	23.4	12.9	10.6	23.9	20.9
Korea, Dem. Rep.	73	218	3	9	..	..	..	..	..	..	..	..
Korea, Rep.	..	..	..	..	..	..	..	..	..	..	..	..
Kosovo					..	..	..	..	..	..	..	..
Kuwait	..	..	..	..	..	..	..	..	..	..	..	..
Kyrgyz Republic	215	360	44	68	16.7	7.2	78.3	29.3	28.5	7.4	99.2	41.8
Lao PDR	281	496	52	80	16.9	9.3	57.2	24.1	44.0	..	..	..
Latvia	..	..	..	..	..	..	..	..	..	..	..	..
Lebanon	199	1,076	53	257	1.1	3.7	5.7	12.0	..	3.3	3.8	12.1
Lesotho	37	143	19	70	3.6	7.0	11.1	31.4	4.4	8.2	..	17.2
Liberia	67	1,250	24	330	17.4	185.8	..	742.0	..	41.4	..	..
Libya	..	60	..	10	..	0.1	..	0.2	..	0.2	..	..
Lithuania	..	..	..	..	..	..	..	..	..	..	..	..
Macedonia, FYR	251	221	125	108	7.1	2.3	31.5	8.4	10.5	2.8	..	7.4
Madagascar	320	841	21	44	8.4	8.9	54.9	25.0	20.2	..	77.8	..
Malawi	446	913	38	61	26.1	21.2	188.6	80.6	65.6	..	..	..
Malaysia	45	158	2	6	0.1	0.1	0.2	..	0.0	0.1	0.3	..
Mali	359	964	34	76	15.0	11.4	60.4	..	34.4	..	127.8	..
Mauritania	216	311	83	97	19.8	..	103.3	..	..	..	..	..
Mauritius	20	110	17	86	0.4	1.2	1.7	4.3	0.7	1.6	2.2	6.1
Mexico	−58	149	−1	1	0.0	0.0	0.0	0.1	0.0	0.0	−0.1	..
Moldova	123	299	30	82	9.4	4.5	39.7	13.4	11.2	5.0	32.9	15.1
Mongolia	217	246	91	93	20.0	4.8	68.6	12.1	27.4	..	85.2	17.8
Morocco	419	1,217	15	39	1.2	1.4	4.4	3.8	3.1	2.5	..	4.6
Mozambique	903	1,994	49	89	22.5	22.0	68.7	109.4	51.2	38.3	..	..
Myanmar	106	534	2	11	..	..	..	..	..	4.0	..	..
Namibia	152	207	84	97	3.9	2.4	22.8	9.1	8.2	4.4	13.7	..
Nepal	387	716	16	25	7.0	5.6	29.0	17.9	21.2	16.1	..	..
Netherlands												
New Zealand												
Nicaragua	560	741	110	131	15.0	11.5	47.2	..	23.5	13.4	86.4	57.3
Niger	208	605	19	41	11.7	11.3	101.4	..	43.0	..	..	..
Nigeria	174	1,290	1	9	0.4	0.7	..	..	1.1	2.1	..	..
Norway												
Oman	45	32	19	11	0.2	..	1.9	..	0.6	0.1	0.9	..
Pakistan	700	1,539	5	9	1.0	0.9	5.5	4.3	4.8	2.9	5.7	5.7
Panama	15	29	5	8	0.1	0.1	0.5	0.5	0.1	0.1	0.6	..
Papua New Guinea	275	304	51	46	8.3	4.0	35.7	19.0	13.7	..	26.2	..
Paraguay	82	134	15	21	1.1	0.8	6.1	4.1	2.3	1.3	..	5.0
Peru	397	466	15	16	0.8	0.4	3.7	1.4	3.4	1.1	4.2	2.2
Philippines	572	61	7	1	0.7	0.0	3.6	0.2	1.1	0.1	4.3	0.2
Poland	..	..	..	..	..	..	..	..	..	..	..	..
Portugal												
Puerto Rico	..	..	..	..	..	..	..	..	..	..	..	..
Qatar	..	..	..	..	..	..	..	..	..	..	..	..

	Net official development assistance (ODA)				Aid dependency ratios							
	Total $ millions		Per capita $		Net ODA as % of GNI		Net ODA as % of gross capital formation		Net ODA as % of imports of goods, services, and income		Net ODA as % of central government expense	
	2000	2008	2000	2008	2000	2008	2000	2008	2000	2008	2000	2008
Romania	..	..	..	..	..	..	..	..	..	..	..	..
Russian Federation	..	..	..	..	..	..	..	..	..	..	..	..
Rwanda	321	931	40	96	18.7	19.3	101.2	86.7	71.2	63.6	..	..
Saudi Arabia	22	..	1	..	0.0	..	0.1	..	0.0	..	..	..
Senegal	424	1,058	43	87	..	8.0	44.2	26.4	22.0	..	71.1	..
Serbia	1,134[a]	1,047	151[a]	142	12.6[a]	2.1	150.1[a]	8.9	..	3.6	..	5.6
Sierra Leone	181	367	43	66	29.3	19.2	413.2	127.5	68.8	53.3	98.8	..
Singapore	..	..	..	..	..	..	..	..	..	..	..	..
Slovak Republic	..	..	..	..	..	..	..	..	..	..	..	..
Slovenia	61	..	31	..	0.3	..	1.1	..	0.5	..	0.8	..
Somalia	101	758	14	85	..	..	..	..	..	..	..	..
South Africa	486	1,125	11	23	0.4	0.4	2.3	1.8	1.3	0.9	1.3	1.3
Spain	..	..	..	..	..	..	..	..	..	..	..	..
Sri Lanka	275	730	15	36	1.7	1.8	6.0	6.6	3.2	4.3	7.3	..
Sudan	220	2,384	6	58	1.9	4.8	9.7	18.0	8.5	17.1	..	..
Swaziland	13	67	12	58	0.9	2.3	5.1	14.4	0.9	..	..	..
Sweden	..	..	..	..	..	..	..	..	..	..	..	..
Switzerland	..	..	..	..	..	..	..	..	..	..	..	..
Syrian Arab Republic	158	136	10	7	0.9	0.3	4.7	1.8	2.4	..	..	..
Tajikistan	124	291	20	43	15.8	5.8	125.1	28.2	..	6.9	160.3	..
Tanzania	1,035	2,331	30	55	11.6	11.7	64.7	..	46.4	28.2	..	..
Thailand	697	−621	11	−9	0.6	−0.2	2.5	−0.8	0.9	−0.3	..	−1.2
Timor-Leste	231	278	284	253	71.6	9.5	285.9	..	..	..	..	..
Togo	70	330	13	51	5.4	11.4	29.4	..	10.5	..	..	75.3
Trinidad and Tobago	−2	12	−1	9	0.0	0.1	−0.1	0.4	0.0	..	..	..
Tunisia	222	479	23	46	1.2	1.3	4.2	4.4	2.1	1.6	4.1	3.9
Turkey	327	2,024	5	27	0.1	0.3	0.6	1.3	0.5	0.9	..	1.2
Turkmenistan	31	18	7	4	1.2	0.1	3.1	1.8	..	..	..	..
Uganda	844	1,657	35	52	13.9	11.8	70.0	49.1	53.6	29.4	95.5	76.3
Ukraine	..	618	..	13	..	0.3	..	1.4	..	0.6	..	0.9
United Arab Emirates	..	..	..	..	..	..	..	..	..	..	..	..
United Kingdom	..	..	..	..	..	..	..	..	..	..	..	..
United States	..	..	..	..	..	..	..	..	..	..	..	..
Uruguay	17	33	5	10	0.1	0.1	0.5	0.5	0.3	0.3	0.3	0.4
Uzbekistan	186	187	8	7	1.4	0.7	8.3	2.9	..	..	..	..
Venezuela, RB	76	59	3	2	0.1	0.0	0.3	0.1	0.3	0.1	0.3	..
Vietnam	1,681	2,552	22	30	5.5	2.9	18.2	6.8	9.3	2.9	..	..
West Bank and Gaza	637	2,593	212	659	13.3	..	47.4	..	18.0	..	..	..
Yemen, Rep.	263	305	14	13	3.0	1.3	14.3	..	6.2	2.2	..	..
Zambia	795	1,086	76	86	25.8	8.4	140.8	34.1	53.1	15.8	..	..
Zimbabwe	176	611	14	49	2.5	..	17.5	..	..	..	..	..
World	**49,791 s**	**128,609 s**	**8 w**	**19 w**	**0.2 w**	**0.2 w**	**0.7 w**	**.. w**	**0.5 w**	**0.6 w**	**.. w**	**.. w**
Low income	15,018	41,380	18	42	6.5	7.4	30.3	27.3	18.4	13.6	..	..
Middle income	22,711	50,070	5	11	0.4	0.3	1.6	1.0	1.3	0.9	..	..
Lower middle income	16,814	37,094	5	10	0.6	0.4	2.2	1.2	2.1	1.3	..	..
Upper middle income	5,182	11,825	6	12	0.2	0.1	0.8	0.6	0.5	0.4	..	..
Low & middle income	49,488	128,113	10	23	0.8	0.7	3.4	2.4	2.7	2.1	..	..
East Asia & Pacific	8,563	9,118	5	5	0.5	0.2	1.6	0.4	1.4	0.4	..	..
Europe & Central Asia	4,462	8,241	10	19	0.5	0.2	2.4	0.8	1.4	0.5	..	..
Latin America & Carib.	4,838	9,299	9	16	0.2	0.2	1.2	1.0	0.9	0.8	..	..
Middle East & N. Africa	4,472	23,624	16	73	1.0	1.9	4.0	..	3.3	6.0	..	..
South Asia	4,199	12,318	3	8	0.7	0.8	3.0	2.3	3.6	2.5	..	..
Sub-Saharan Africa	13,245	40,090	20	49	4.1	4.3	23.1	21.9	11.0	9.2	..	..
High income	304	496	0	0	0.0	0.0	0.0	..	0.0	0.0	..	..
Euro area	..	..	..	..	..	..	..	..	..	..	..	..

Note: Regional aggregates include data for economies not listed in the table. World and income group totals include aid not allocated by country or region—including administrative costs, research on development issues, and aid to nongovernmental organizations. Thus regional and income group totals do not sum to the world total.
a. Includes Montenegro.

About the data

Unless otherwise noted, aid includes official development assistance (ODA; see *About the data* for table 6.14). The data cover loans and grants from Development Assistance Committee (DAC) member countries, multilateral organizations, and non-DAC donors. They do not reflect aid given by recipient countries to other developing countries. As a result, some countries that are net donors (such as Saudi Arabia) are shown in the table as aid recipients (see table 6.16a). Aid given before 2005 to countries that were Part II recipients (see *About the data* for table 6.14 for more information) is defined as official aid.

The table does not distinguish types of aid (program, project, or food aid; emergency assistance; postconflict peacekeeping assistance; or technical cooperation), which may have different effects on the economy. Expenditures on technical cooperation do not always directly benefit the economy to the extent that they defray costs incurred outside the country on salaries and benefits of technical experts and overhead costs of firms supplying technical services.

Ratios of aid to gross national income (GNI), gross capital formation, imports, and government spending provide measures of recipient country dependency on aid. But care must be taken in drawing policy conclusions. For foreign policy reasons some countries have traditionally received large amounts of aid. Thus aid dependency ratios may reveal as much about a donor's interests as about a recipient's needs. Ratios are generally much higher in Sub-Saharan Africa than in other regions, and they increased in the 1980s. High ratios are due only in part to aid flows. Many African countries saw severe erosion in their terms of trade in the 1980s, which, along with weak policies, contributed to falling incomes, imports, and investment. Thus the increase in aid dependency ratios reflects events affecting both the numerator (aid) and the denominator (GNI).

Because the table relies on information from donors, it is not necessarily consistent with information recorded by recipients in the balance of payments, which often excludes all or some technical assistance—particularly payments to expatriates made directly by the donor. Similarly, grant commodity aid may not always be recorded in trade data or in the balance of payments. Moreover, DAC statistics exclude purely military aid.

The nominal values used here may overstate the real value of aid to recipients. Changes in international prices and exchange rates can reduce the purchasing power of aid. Tying aid, still prevalent though declining in importance, also tends to reduce its purchasing power (see *About the data* for table 6.15).

The aggregates refer to World Bank definitions. Therefore the ratios shown may differ from those of the Organisation for Economic Co-operation and Development (OECD).

Definitions

• **Net official development assistance** is flows (net of repayment of principal) that meet the DAC definition of ODA and are made to countries and territories on the DAC list of aid recipients. See *About the data* for table 6.14. • **Net official development assistance per capita** is net ODA divided by midyear population. • **Aid dependency ratios** are calculated using values in U.S. dollars converted at official exchange rates. Imports of goods, services, and income refer to international transactions involving a change in ownership of general merchandise, goods sent for processing and repairs, nonmonetary gold, services, receipts of employee compensation for nonresident workers, and investment income. For definitions of GNI, gross capital formation, and central government expense, see *Definitions* for tables 1.1, 4.8, and 4.10.

Official development assistance from non-DAC donors, 2004–08 — 6.16a

Net disbursements ($ millions)

	2004	2005	2006	2007	2008
OECD members (non-DAC)					
Czech Republic	108	135	161	179	249
Hungary	70	100	149	103	107
Iceland	21	27	41	48	48
Korea, Rep.[a]	423	752	455	696	802
Poland	118	205	297	363	372
Slovak Republic	28	56	55	67	92
Turkey	339	601	714	602	780
Arab countries					
Kuwait	161	218	158	110	283
Saudi Arabia	1,734	1,005	2,095	2,079	5,564
United Arab Emirates	181	141	219	429	88
Other donors					
Israel[b]	84	95	90	111	138
Taiwan, China	421	483	513	514	435
Thailand	..	..	74	67	178
Others	22	86	121	188	343
Total	3,712	3,905	5,142	5,558	9,481

Note: The table does not reflect aid provided by several major emerging non–Organisation for Economic Co-operation and Development donors because information on their aid has not been disclosed.
a. The Republic of Korea became a DAC member in November 2009. Its disbursements will be reflected in DAC data beginning with 2010 flows. b. Includes $47.9 million in 2004, $49.2 million in 2005, $45.5 million in 2006, $42.9 million in 2007, and $43.0 million in 2008 for first-year sustenance expenses for people arriving from developing countries (many of which are experiencing civil war or severe unrest) or people who have left their country for humanitarian or political reasons. *Source:* Organisation for Economic Co-operation and Development.

Data sources

Data on financial flows are compiled by OECD DAC and published in its annual statistical report, *Geographical Distribution of Financial Flows to Developing Countries,* and in its annual *Development Co-operation Report.* Data are available electronically on the OECD DAC's *International Development Statistics* CD-ROM and at www.oecd.org/dac/stats/idsonline. Data on population, GNI, gross capital formation, imports of goods and services, and central government expense used in computing the ratios are from World Bank and International Monetary Fund databases.

	Total $ millions 2008	United States 2008	Germany 2008	European Commission 2008	United Kingdom 2008	France 2008	Japan 2008	Netherlands 2008	Spain 2008	Sweden 2008	Canada 2008	Other DAC donors $ millions 2008
				Ten major DAC donors $ millions								
Afghanistan	4,300.1	2,111.6	294.0	349.3	322.3	19.9	208.0	112.0	71.8	73.9	207.9	529.4
Albania	352.2	35.9	44.7	84.6	2.8	4.4	−2.5	18.3	16.9	11.3	0.0	135.8
Algeria	325.9	9.1	12.5	84.7	2.1	121.8	4.0	0.0	64.2	2.1	2.9	22.6
Angola	233.3	42.7	11.7	49.4	9.6	2.9	17.8	−2.7	13.6	5.0	0.4	83.1
Argentina	103.8	7.2	22.1	16.6	1.0	12.8	5.9	0.3	29.7	0.2	1.9	6.3
Armenia	225.1	93.8	27.9	16.3	6.6	5.5	57.7	0.2	0.7	2.7	0.3	13.4
Australia												
Austria												
Azerbaijan	129.2	42.0	26.4	13.0	1.9	28.2	−2.8	0.0	0.4	1.0	0.2	19.0
Bangladesh	1,009.0	93.2	65.9	194.5	252.5	−3.7	41.1	84.7	9.4	38.1	82.1	151.1
Belarus	75.3	8.9	21.3	17.4	1.1	1.5	0.4	0.0	0.1	14.8	0.0	9.6
Belgium												
Benin	429.6	34.6	46.6	127.1	0.0	66.4	27.2	35.3	2.0	0.5	7.0	83.0
Bolivia	539.1	123.8	52.7	43.8	1.0	13.9	35.5	41.4	93.0	27.6	21.5	84.9
Bosnia and Herzegovina	426.7	26.4	46.9	105.2	9.3	6.3	10.6	31.3	42.4	28.7	5.0	114.6
Botswana	709.4	231.9	439.0	26.7	1.1	2.4	−2.1	0.0	0.0	4.3	1.4	4.8
Brazil	427.0	12.3	126.7	48.6	13.5	41.0	93.3	0.5	36.8	3.2	11.4	39.7
Bulgaria												
Burkina Faso	620.6	19.4	44.9	145.5	0.2	142.0	21.0	88.9	2.9	23.0	29.9	102.9
Burundi	339.7	30.2	23.1	84.6	14.2	17.4	23.3	32.3	1.9	7.0	4.2	101.4
Cambodia	462.5	69.8	33.8	37.5	30.4	35.2	114.8	1.9	11.8	16.1	11.5	99.8
Cameroon	357.6	16.1	110.0	59.9	2.9	113.2	15.6	0.6	12.6	0.7	11.9	14.0
Canada												
Central African Republic	170.4	34.2	6.8	41.9	5.7	26.4	12.2	2.9	2.2	6.4	2.9	29.1
Chad	423.0	80.7	32.6	145.6	11.5	39.5	14.4	7.5	10.9	10.1	6.3	64.0
Chile	58.3	1.0	20.1	6.5	0.5	9.1	6.6	0.2	7.1	0.6	2.5	4.2
China	1,477.7	65.2	411.9	124.7	174.9	207.5	278.3	16.7	43.0	14.8	54.3	86.3
Hong Kong SAR, China												
Colombia	955.2	636.1	42.1	57.0	3.3	22.7	−6.9	32.6	85.0	26.3	14.4	42.8
Congo, Dem. Rep.	1,168.7	196.6	61.2	224.3	192.9	30.5	51.2	47.8	0.7	68.0	22.9	272.7
Congo, Rep.	449.3	0.3	−0.3	28.5	0.0	368.0	10.6	0.0	39.3	1.6	0.8	0.6
Costa Rica	66.9	−0.1	29.7	5.9	−0.2	6.6	−1.2	4.7	15.5	1.0	2.9	2.1
Côte d'Ivoire	337.2	88.8	17.5	144.3	0.3	39.5	19.5	0.1	5.2	0.0	3.4	18.6
Croatia	387.3	7.4	21.2	337.0	1.4	4.3	0.0	0.1	0.9	2.7	0.2	12.0
Cuba	94.4	12.0	2.6	2.6	0.2	3.0	4.0	0.1	45.8	0.9	8.3	14.9
Czech Republic												
Denmark												
Dominican Republic	136.6	24.8	8.1	57.7	1.5	9.9	1.6	0.0	32.1	0.7	1.6	−1.4
Ecuador	232.8	46.4	24.7	40.4	−0.6	−0.8	−5.7	3.3	87.9	0.7	4.5	32.1
Egypt, Arab Rep.	1,167.5	470.8	170.3	207.7	8.8	142.0	11.6	19.7	15.6	2.2	14.5	104.4
El Salvador	232.3	42.4	13.4	28.4	0.0	3.4	30.6	0.3	83.6	3.6	3.6	23.0
Eritrea	69.4	3.4	1.3	16.9	5.6	0.8	17.7	3.9	1.8	1.9	0.1	16.1
Estonia												
Ethiopia	2,299.8	811.4	98.3	460.8	253.7	18.7	47.1	113.6	60.5	46.9	152.6	236.2
Finland												
France												
Gabon	44.3	0.5	−3.0	6.7	0.0	37.4	1.8	0.0	0.5	0.0	0.7	−0.2
Gambia, The	37.7	12.0	0.8	9.9	3.8	0.5	1.1	3.9	2.2	0.9	0.8	1.9
Georgia	691.9	402.1	70.7	113.4	12.8	5.4	2.4	8.9	2.7	27.3	3.8	42.5
Germany												
Ghana	839.1	79.5	71.7	115.9	150.8	43.0	54.0	120.2	16.1	1.3	74.0	112.5
Greece												
Guatemala	504.7	70.4	18.8	39.1	0.7	2.6	10.6	27.4	255.9	27.3	15.0	37.0
Guinea	243.9	43.3	23.7	35.0	1.2	73.0	16.9	0.0	2.9	0.7	6.5	40.7
Guinea-Bissau	101.0	0.7	0.6	48.4	0.1	5.6	5.8	0.0	16.4	0.1	0.5	22.9
Haiti	673.3	259.1	5.7	117.2	0.0	38.4	11.7	4.6	45.5	9.1	147.6	34.5
Honduras	369.7	96.3	32.2	23.8	0.0	1.4	40.9	1.2	117.6	17.5	14.2	24.8

Ten major DAC donors

	Total $ millions 2008	United States 2008	Germany 2008	European Commission 2008	United Kingdom 2008	France 2008	Japan 2008	Netherlands 2008	Spain 2008	Sweden 2008	Canada 2008	Other DAC donors $ millions 2008
Hungary												
India	1,669.2	52.1	147.7	122.3	613.1	−27.2	599.8	4.9	14.0	12.3	13.3	116.8
Indonesia	628.9	115.1	29.7	54.5	100.7	103.5	−284.9	75.5	9.5	12.2	82.4	330.7
Iran, Islamic Rep.	64.8	2.7	42.7	1.8	1.7	15.6	−16.7	4.5	0.7	0.0	0.2	11.6
Iraq	9,780.9	2,742.0	1,854.3	38.0	639.0	315.0	1,755.2	81.8	129.0	26.7	142.0	2,057.8
Ireland												
Israel												
Italy												
Jamaica	68.8	−0.9	−7.8	74.3	6.0	−0.8	−3.7	−5.3	2.0	0.1	3.4	1.5
Japan												
Jordan	539.0	384.1	21.7	122.5	4.5	3.3	−50.1	0.3	12.7	0.1	7.7	32.3
Kazakhstan	245.8	157.6	18.4	16.2	5.4	3.4	37.9	0.0	0.1	0.3	0.2	6.3
Kenya	1,042.7	439.4	85.3	91.3	91.4	55.7	8.8	15.9	38.6	65.9	26.2	124.3
Korea, Dem. Rep.	207.8	152.4	5.5	18.2	0.3	1.2	0.0	1.0	0.4	5.8	2.4	20.6
Korea, Rep.												
Kosovo												
Kuwait												
Kyrgyz Republic	175.2	63.6	21.3	33.4	13.7	1.0	12.4	0.1	3.3	8.7	0.3	17.4
Lao PDR	232.4	3.2	28.8	18.7	0.3	25.4	66.3	0.0	0.2	20.8	1.7	67.0
Latvia												
Lebanon	865.7	209.6	36.4	121.6	1.0	305.8	13.8	2.5	51.8	1.8	16.2	105.1
Lesotho	91.5	13.7	7.4	25.6	7.9	−1.8	13.2	0.0	1.5	0.2	0.7	23.3
Liberia	858.4	276.0	316.6	49.5	32.4	26.8	14.0	20.0	24.3	26.3	2.0	70.6
Libya	56.0	14.3	3.4	4.3	1.1	29.0	0.2	0.0	0.0	0.0	0.0	3.7
Lithuania												
Macedonia, FYR	202.6	32.1	24.8	61.6	2.1	3.8	21.4	20.2	4.1	11.3	0.0	21.3
Madagascar	414.0	83.9	17.7	139.9	2.4	88.4	20.4	4.2	14.6	0.6	3.1	39.0
Malawi	562.2	87.7	29.6	130.5	146.9	0.9	30.8	0.1	2.9	14.5	16.3	102.1
Malaysia	152.4	5.6	10.8	0.3	18.9	−9.2	117.5	0.0	0.0	0.4	0.3	7.8
Mali	680.1	53.3	39.4	149.0	0.0	81.9	34.5	79.6	31.2	29.3	99.1	82.9
Mauritania	179.5	25.6	17.4	40.4	0.0	29.4	14.5	0.2	34.1	1.1	1.5	15.2
Mauritius	111.1	0.2	0.8	95.0	0.6	15.8	0.4	0.0	0.0	0.0	0.3	−2.0
Mexico	126.1	102.5	39.2	21.7	6.8	10.8	−54.7	−0.3	−15.1	0.0	5.9	9.4
Moldova	197.2	35.9	10.7	83.1	6.1	7.3	9.6	6.9	1.8	13.5	0.2	22.1
Mongolia	171.6	35.4	32.4	10.6	1.2	0.9	60.7	6.6	4.1	1.2	1.8	16.9
Morocco	1,095.5	5.7	90.6	483.8	6.7	163.2	105.8	0.6	117.4	0.0	10.3	111.5
Mozambique	1,501.7	226.7	74.9	161.4	197.9	12.3	23.7	105.7	78.5	119.6	77.2	423.8
Myanmar	475.9	71.6	14.3	58.4	82.4	5.8	42.5	15.8	9.2	21.6	22.3	131.9
Namibia	173.2	71.0	22.2	23.3	1.0	1.9	9.7	0.3	15.1	2.3	1.1	25.5
Nepal	497.2	77.7	62.3	46.2	98.6	−2.8	33.9	2.4	2.9	2.5	9.4	164.2
Netherlands												
New Zealand												
Nicaragua	566.1	103.5	26.1	34.8	10.7	1.4	43.8	37.0	125.4	33.5	16.8	133.3
Niger	420.6	45.9	21.0	151.5	7.4	67.8	16.9	0.1	24.0	1.6	15.3	69.2
Nigeria	727.5	363.9	27.5	91.1	47.2	11.9	29.0	1.7	25.4	1.0	26.7	102.2
Norway												
Oman	3.8	1.4	0.5	0.0	0.6	0.7	0.5	0.1	0.0	0.0	0.0	0.0
Pakistan	979.4	350.6	89.0	62.7	260.3	9.4	34.2	31.1	3.3	9.0	41.6	88.2
Panama	30.2	13.7	1.2	2.8	0.0	0.2	4.1	0.0	7.4	0.2	0.6	−0.1
Papua New Guinea	288.8	2.0	0.1	25.4	1.1	−0.1	−82.6	0.0	0.0	0.2	0.7	342.0
Paraguay	115.2	29.7	7.0	17.5	0.1	0.9	30.9	0.0	23.0	1.9	1.0	3.3
Peru	437.1	94.0	93.6	52.4	−11.6	9.3	−17.9	−1.4	131.5	3.0	15.6	68.6
Philippines	32.2	71.3	31.6	58.2	1.3	−5.6	−284.4	1.2	35.3	6.2	15.5	101.6
Poland												
Portugal												
Puerto Rico												
Qatar												

	Total $ millions 2008	Ten major DAC donors $ millions										Other DAC donors $ millions 2008
		United States 2008	Germany 2008	European Commission 2008	United Kingdom 2008	France 2008	Japan 2008	Netherlands 2008	Spain 2008	Sweden 2008	Canada 2008	
Romania												
Russian Federation												
Rwanda	553.4	117.4	24.5	103.2	99.9	4.0	17.8	38.8	24.9	14.4	14.3	94.4
Saudi Arabia												
Senegal	678.8	71.6	27.8	134.7	1.0	189.0	25.1	37.9	59.1	0.3	73.3	59.0
Serbia	932.8	94.5	107.8	392.6	12.1	17.8	5.9	6.1	16.3	39.4	4.5	235.9
Sierra Leone	219.0	15.8	14.9	44.2	92.6	1.3	14.1	0.0	3.4	2.3	4.2	26.4
Singapore												
Slovak Republic												
Slovenia												
Somalia	704.7	242.7	10.1	139.3	76.1	8.5	23.3	18.7	14.6	25.0	21.8	124.7
South Africa	1,045.3	378.7	150.1	164.0	113.5	32.9	3.7	36.3	0.6	12.6	14.7	138.3
Spain												
Sri Lanka	497.4	51.8	11.1	111.6	1.8	19.6	96.7	19.8	26.0	15.5	42.1	101.5
Sudan	2,096.1	848.2	47.3	277.8	199.2	11.2	109.6	157.6	37.7	65.0	83.9	258.6
Swaziland	28.8	8.7	−1.0	11.2	2.5	0.3	3.2	0.0	0.0	0.0	0.6	3.3
Sweden												
Switzerland												
Syrian Arab Republic	106.2	16.2	27.0	51.6	2.3	26.7	−56.7	2.9	7.5	0.0	1.9	26.8
Tajikistan	174.3	59.9	22.2	31.1	7.7	5.9	8.1	0.8	2.5	12.5	5.7	17.9
Tanzania	1,551.6	247.0	87.4	185.9	254.2	4.8	71.0	114.9	3.4	125.5	44.7	412.9
Thailand	−673.4	39.6	−19.2	27.2	2.2	−2.9	−748.5	1.1	0.1	7.7	1.2	18.1
Timor-Leste	255.4	32.7	6.7	27.4	0.2	0.5	26.5	0.0	14.0	6.0	1.8	139.7
Togo	215.0	3.0	8.4	39.0	9.0	127.7	0.3	13.2	3.5	0.8	2.6	7.5
Trinidad and Tobago	11.6	0.3	0.3	7.7	0.9	1.7	0.0	0.0	0.0	0.0	0.7	0.1
Tunisia	478.6	−8.1	27.4	230.2	1.5	160.5	54.0	−1.3	16.2	0.1	2.5	−4.4
Turkey	1,991.4	−5.4	−50.1	1,342.5	4.6	293.8	285.9	−0.6	92.1	7.3	−2.3	23.7
Turkmenistan	2.4	−3.4	1.8	3.5	0.4	0.3	−1.5	0.0	0.0	0.0	0.0	1.2
Uganda	1,280.1	352.9	37.8	275.1	65.7	17.4	57.0	82.9	11.5	64.1	21.2	294.6
Ukraine	527.2	98.9	77.1	242.3	3.2	25.0	8.4	0.0	0.3	21.5	18.7	31.7
United Arab Emirates												
United Kingdom												
United States												
Uruguay	24.2	1.0	−0.5	11.3	0.1	1.4	1.0	0.0	9.4	0.2	1.1	−0.7
Uzbekistan	119.9	18.0	29.5	10.6	1.0	3.0	48.6	0.0	0.4	0.1	0.0	8.8
Venezuela, RB	53.4	9.6	8.2	6.8	0.5	6.6	2.8	0.2	15.5	0.1	0.6	2.6
Vietnam	1,664.2	62.6	115.0	68.0	125.9	165.6	619.0	40.6	49.5	37.6	37.6	342.8
West Bank and Gaza	2,043.6	490.6	77.4	661.3	102.6	74.2	30.3	75.1	103.2	71.8	44.3	312.9
Yemen, Rep.	224.4	25.5	67.2	17.7	33.2	4.7	12.0	37.8	1.9	1.2	1.3	22.0
Zambia	812.8	226.5	45.5	109.7	61.6	1.2	37.1	85.1	1.0	51.5	14.3	179.5
Zimbabwe	592.2	222.9	24.9	62.0	89.2	7.4	10.0	29.8	4.8	25.7	21.1	94.5
World	100,882.5 s	23,859.6 s	9,062.7 s	14,427.7 s	7,366.8 s	6,461.3 s	6,823.3 s	5,199.6 s	4,801.6 s	3,142.3 s	3,356.7 s	16,381.0 s
Low income	29,256.8	7,152.3	2,060.2	4,472.9	2,835.3	1,507.0	1,929.7	1,405.5	703.2	983.2	1,295.7	4,911.8
Middle income	42,807.3	9,982.7	5,122.7	7,431.6	2,554.4	3,615.3	2,700.6	916.8	2,278.5	623.5	872.6	6,708.7
Lower middle income	30,905.9	7,734.7	3,708.6	4,054.3	2,301.8	2,055.2	2,115.1	663.3	1,517.1	449.8	713.3	5,592.8
Upper middle income	10,837.8	2,184.5	1,242.5	2,938.9	229.9	1,482.4	584.9	195.1	690.1	165.9	118.4	1,005.2
Low & middle income	100,440.2	23,850.3	9,040.7	14,069.3	7,363.8	6,450.3	6,822.0	5,199.3	4,786.7	3,134.1	3,355.3	16,368.5
East Asia & Pacific	6,695.7	943.2	725.9	599.6	545.0	691.8	86.7	171.7	189.3	165.7	280.1	2,296.7
Europe & Central Asia	6,867.0	1,353.2	547.6	2,636.0	91.5	426.0	505.4	94.4	185.2	205.9	37.2	784.7
Latin America & Carib.	8,059.3	1,870.7	818.1	1,102.2	167.0	211.4	268.7	230.2	1,975.6	200.4	480.6	734.5
Middle East & N. Africa	17,614.1	4,701.8	2,499.9	2,174.0	843.2	1,449.9	1,874.7	224.6	596.3	129.6	272.1	2,848.1
South Asia	9,186.2	2,813.1	676.3	912.8	1,552.7	16.0	1,044.6	297.5	128.0	156.1	400.7	1,188.4
Sub-Saharan Africa	29,656.6	6,691.1	2,353.5	4,849.5	2,507.0	2,681.5	1,391.9	1,496.6	846.6	1,015.6	1,302.5	4,520.9
High income	442.4	9.3	22.0	358.4	3.1	11.0	1.3	0.3	14.9	8.3	1.3	12.5
Euro area	..	..	..	..	..	..	..	..	..	..	..	..

Note: Regional aggregates include data for economies not specified elsewhere. World and income group totals include aid not allocated by country or region.

The table shows net bilateral aid to low- and middle-income economies from members of the Development Assistance Committee (DAC) of the Organisation for Economic Co-operation and Development (OECD). The data include aid to some countries and territories not shown in the table and aid to unspecified economies recorded only at the regional or global level. Aid to countries and territories not shown in the table has been assigned to regional totals based on the World Bank's regional classification system. Aid to unspecified economies is included in regional totals and, when possible, income group totals. Aid not allocated by country or region—including administrative costs, research on development, and aid to nongovernmental organizations—is included in the world total. Thus regional and income group totals do not sum to the world total.

The table is based on donor country reports of bilateral programs, which may differ from reports by recipient countries. Recipients may lack access to information on such aid expenditures as development-oriented research, stipends and tuition costs for aid-financed students in donor countries,

and payment of experts hired by donor countries. Moreover, a full accounting would include donor country contributions to multilateral institutions, the flow of resources from multilateral institutions to recipient countries, and flows from countries that are not members of DAC. Previous editions of the table included only DAC member economies. The table also includes net aid from the European Commission—a multilateral member of DAC.

The expenditures that countries report as official development assistance (ODA) have changed. For example, some DAC members have reported as ODA the aid provided to refugees during the first 12 months of their stay within the donor's borders.

Some of the aid recipients shown in the table are also aid donors. See table 6.16a for a summary of ODA from non-DAC countries.

- **Net aid** refers to net bilateral official development assistance that meets the DAC definition of official development assistance and is made to countries and territories on the DAC list of aid recipients. See *About the data* for table 6.14. • **Other DAC donors** are Australia, Austria, Belgium, Denmark, Finland, Greece, Ireland, Italy, Luxembourg, New Zealand, Norway, Portugal, and Switzerland.

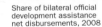 

Share of bilateral official development assistance net disbursements, 2008

- East Asia & Pacific
- Middle East & North Africa
- Europe & Central Asia
- South Asia
- Latin America & Caribbean
- Sub-Saharan Africa

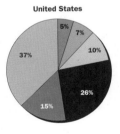

United States
37%, 5%, 7%, 10%, 26%, 15%

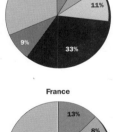

Germany
9%, 7%, 11%, 31%, 9%, 33%

European Commission
40%, 5%, 21%, 9%, 7%, 18%

United Kingdom
44%, 9%, 2%, 3%, 15%, 27%

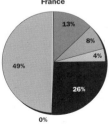

France
49%, 13%, 8%, 4%, 26%, 0%

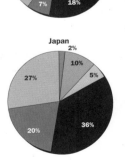

Japan
27%, 2%, 10%, 5%, 20%, 36%

In 2008 Sub-Saharan Africa received 38 percent of total bilateral net official development assistance disbursements from Development Assistance Committee (DAC) donors, and the Middle East and North Africa received 22 percent. However, destinations of aid vary by donor.

Note: Data are the distribution of bilateral aid from the top six DAC donors in 2008 and exclude aid to high-income economies (less than 1 percent of bilateral aid) and aid unallocated by region.
Source: Organisation for Economic Co-operation and Development, Development Assistance Committee.

Data on financial flows are compiled by OECD DAC and published in its annual statistical report, *Geographical Distribution of Financial Flows to Developing Countries,* and its annual *Development Co-operation Report.* Data are available electronically on the OECD DAC's *International Development Statistics* CD-ROM and at www.oecd.org/dac/stats/idsonline.

6.18 Movement of people

	Net migration		International migrant stock		Refugees				Workers' remittances and compensation of employees			
					thousands				$ millions			
					By country of origin		By country of asylum		Received		Paid	
	thousands		thousands									
	1990–95	2000–05	1995	2005	1995	2008	1995	2008	1995	2008	1995	2008
Afghanistan	3,266	805	70	86	2,679.1	2,833.1	19.6	0.0	..	..	..	..
Albania	–423	–100	71	83	5.8	15.0	4.7	0.1	427	1,495	..	16
Algeria	–50	–140	299	242	1.5	9.1	192.5	94.1	1,120[a]	2,202[a]	..	..
Angola	143	175	38	56	246.7	171.4	10.9	12.7	5	82	210	669
Argentina	120	–100	1,588	1,494	0.3	1.0	10.3	2.8	64	694	195	596
Armenia	–500	–100	682	493	201.4	16.3	219.0	4.0	65	1,062	17	185
Australia	371	641	3,854	4,336	0.0	0.0	62.1	20.9	1,651	4,713	700	3,049
Austria	234	220	989	1,156	0.0	0.0	34.4	37.6	1,012	3,239	346	3,446
Azerbaijan	–116	–100	525	255	200.5	16.3	233.7	2.1	3	1,554	9	593
Bangladesh	–500	–700	1,006	1,032	57.0	10.1	51.1	28.4	1,202	8,995	1	15
Belarus	0	20	1,185	1,107	0.1	5.4	29.0	0.6	29	443	12	141
Belgium	85	196	916	882	0.0	0.1	31.7	17.0	4,937	10,425	3,252	4,240
Benin	105	99	146	188	0.1	0.3	23.8	6.9	100	271[a]	26	115[a]
Bolivia	–100	–100	70	114	0.2	0.5	0.7	0.7	7	1,144	9	106
Bosnia and Herzegovina	–1,025	62	73	35	769.8	74.4	40.0	7.3	..	2,735	..	70
Botswana	14	20	39	80	0.0	0.0	0.3	3.0	59	114	200	145
Brazil	–184	–229	731	686	0.1	1.4	2.1	3.9	3,315	5,089	347	1,191
Bulgaria	–349	–41	47	104	4.2	3.0	1.3	5.1	42	2,634	34	74
Burkina Faso	–128	100	464	773	0.1	0.7	29.8	0.6	80[a]	50[a]	51	44[a]
Burundi	–250	192	295	82	350.6	281.6	173.0	21.1	..	4	5	0
Cambodia	150	10	116	304	61.2	17.3	0.0	0.2	12	325	52	187
Cameroon	–5	–12	246	212	2.0	13.9	45.8	81.0	11	145	22	42
Canada	643	1,089	5,047	6,304	0.0	0.1	152.1	173.7	..	..	..	..
Central African Republic	37	–45	67	76	0.2	125.1	33.9	7.4	0	..	27	..
Chad	–10	219	78	358	59.7	55.1	0.1	330.5	1	..	15	..
Chile	90	30	136	231	14.3	1.0	0.3	1.6	..	3	7[a]	6
China	–829[b]	–2,058[b]	437[b]	590[b]	124.7[c]	195.3[c]	288.3	301.0	878[a]	48,524[a]	19	5,737
Hong Kong SAR, China	300	113	2,431	2,721	0.2	0.0	1.5	0.1	..	355	..	393
Colombia	–250	–120	109	110	1.9	373.5	0.2	0.2	815	4,884	150	88
Congo, Dem. Rep.	1,208	–237	1,919	480	89.7	368.0	1,433.8	155.2	..	..	..	..
Congo, Rep.	–14	4	131	129	0.2	19.9	19.4	24.8	4	15[a]	27	102[a]
Costa Rica	62	84	228	443	0.2	0.4	24.2	18.1	123	605	36	269
Côte d'Ivoire	375	–339	1,985	2,371	0.2	22.2	297.9	24.8	151	195	457	21
Croatia	153	–13	721	661	245.6	97.0	198.6	1.6	544	1,602	16	116
Cuba	–120	–163	25	15	24.9	7.9	1.8	0.5	..	..	..	..
Czech Republic	8	67	454	453	2.0	1.4	2.7	2.1	191	1,415	101	3,826
Denmark	58	46	297	421	0.0	0.0	64.8	23.4	523	890	209	3,222
Dominican Republic	–129	–148	322	393	0.0	0.3	1.0	..	839	3,556	7	29
Ecuador	–50	–400	88	124	0.2	1.1	0.2	101.4	386	2,828	4	66
Egypt, Arab Rep.	–498	–291	174	247	0.9	6.8	5.4	97.9	3,226	8,694	223	241
El Salvador	–249	–340	28	36	23.5	5.2	0.2	0.0	1,064	3,804	1	19
Eritrea	–359	229	12	15	286.7	186.4	1.1	4.9	..	..	..	..
Estonia	–108	1	309	202	0.4	0.2	..	0.0	1	398	3	105
Ethiopia	768	–340	795	554	101.0	63.9	393.5	83.6	27	387	0	21
Finland	43	33	103	171	0.0	0.0	10.2	6.6	74	828	54	457
France	239	761	6,085	6,479	0.0	0.1	155.2	171.2	4,640	15,908	4,935	6,247
Gabon	20	10	164	245	0.0	0.1	0.8	9.0	4	11[a]	99	186[a]
Gambia, The	45	31	148	232	0.2	1.4	6.6	14.8	19[a]	67	..	3
Georgia	–544	–309	250	191	0.3	12.6	0.1	1.0	284	732	12	47
Germany	2,649	930	8,992	10,598	0.4	0.2	1,267.9	582.7	4,523	11,064	11,348	14,976
Ghana	40	12	1,038	1,669	13.6	13.2	83.2	18.2	17	126	5	6[a]
Greece	470	154	549	975	0.2	0.1	4.4	2.2	3,286	2,687	300	1,912
Guatemala	–360	–300	46	53	42.9	5.9	1.5	0.1	358	4,460	8	26
Guinea	350	–425	814	401	0.4	9.5	672.3	21.5	1	72	10	56
Guinea-Bissau	20	1	32	19	0.8	1.1	15.4	7.9	2	30[a]	3	..[a]
Haiti	–133	–140	22	30	13.9	23.1	..	0.0	109[a]	1,410	..	117
Honduras	–120	–150	31	26	1.2	1.1	0.1	0.0	124	2,869	8	5

	Net migration		International migrant stock		Refugees				Workers' remittances and compensation of employees			
							thousands			$ millions		
					By country of origin		By country of asylum		Received		Paid	
	thousands		thousands									
	1990–95	2000–05	1995	2005	1995	2008	1995	2008	1995	2008	1995	2008
Hungary	104	70	293	333	2.3	1.6	11.4	7.8	152	2,631	146	1,562
India	–960	–1,540	7,022	5,887	5.0	19.6	227.5	184.5	6,223	49,941	419	3,815[a]
Indonesia	–725	–1,000	219	136	9.8	19.3	0.0	0.4	651	6,794	..	1,971
Iran, Islamic Rep.	–1,164	–993	3,016	2,062	112.4	69.1	2,072.0	980.1	1,600[a]	1,115[a]	..	..
Iraq	–154	–224	134	128	718.7	1,903.5	116.7	39.5	..	3[a]	..	17[a]
Ireland	–1	230	264	618	0.0	0.0	0.4	9.7	347	646	173	2,829
Israel	484	115	1,919	2,661	0.9	1.5	..	9.1	701	1,422	1,407	3,550
Italy	294	1,750	1,723	3,068	0.1	0.1	74.3	47.1	2,364	3,139	1,824	12,716
Jamaica	–113	–76	22	27	0.0	0.8	0.0	..	653	2,180	74	419
Japan	474	82	1,363	1,999	0.0	0.2	5.4	2.0	1,151	1,929	1,820	4,743
Jordan	509	104	1,608	2,345	0.5	1.9	1,288.9[d]	2,452.0[d]	1,441	3,794	107	472
Kazakhstan	–1,509	–200	3,295	2,974	0.1	4.8	15.6	4.4	116	192	503	3,559
Kenya	222	25	528	790	9.3	9.7	234.7	320.6	298[a]	1,692[a]	4	65
Korea, Dem. Rep.	0	0	35	37	0.0	0.9	0.0	..	..	..	..	..
Korea, Rep.	–627	–65	584	551	0.0	1.1	0.0	0.2	1,080	3,062	634	1,973
Kosovo	..	..	..	..	..	..	..	..	..	..	..	..
Kuwait	–598	264	1,090	1,870	0.8	0.9	3.3	38.2	..	..	1,354	5,559
Kyrgyz Republic	–273	–75	482	288	0.0	2.5	13.4	0.4	1	1,232	41	196
Lao PDR	–30	–115	23	20	58.2	8.6	..	..	22	1[a]	9	1[a]
Latvia	–134	–20	527	380	0.2	0.8	..	0.0	41	601	1	58
Lebanon	230	100	656	721	13.5	13.0	348.0[d]	472.6[d]	1,225[a]	7,180	..	4,028
Lesotho	–84	–36	6	6	0.0	0.0	0.1	..	411	439	75	13
Liberia	–523	62	199	97	744.6	75.2	120.1	10.2	..	58	..	0
Libya	10	14	506	618	0.6	2.1	4.0	6.7	..	16[a]	222	964
Lithuania	–99	–36	272	165	0.1	0.5	0.0	0.8	1	1,460	1	615
Macedonia, FYR	–27	–10	115	120	12.9	7.5	9.0	1.7	68	407	1	33
Madagascar	–7	–5	44	40	0.1	0.3	0.1	..	14	11[a]	11	21[a]
Malawi	–920	–30	325	279	0.0	0.1	1.0	4.2	1	1[a]	1[a]	1[a]
Malaysia	287	150	1,193	2,029	0.1	0.6	5.3	36.7	716[a]	1,920[a]	1,329	6,385
Mali	–260	–134	174	165	77.2	1.8	17.9	9.6	112	344[a]	42	83[a]
Mauritania	–15	30	118	66	84.3	45.6	34.4	27.0	5	2[a]	14	..
Mauritius	–7	0	18	41	0.0	0.0	..	..	132	215	1	14
Mexico	–1,364	–2,702	458	605	0.4	6.2	38.7	1.1	4,368	26,304	..	..
Moldova	–121	–320	473	440	0.5	5.6	..	0.1	1	1,897	1	115
Mongolia	–173	17	7	9	0.0	1.3	..	0.0	..	200[a]	..	77[a]
Morocco	–450	–550	55	51	0.3	3.5	0.1	0.8	1,970	6,895	20	58
Mozambique	650	–20	246	406	125.6	0.2	0.1	3.2	59	116	21	57
Myanmar	–126	–1,000	114	93	152.3	184.4	..	..	81	150[a]	..	32[a]
Namibia	–13	–1	118	132	0.0	1.0	1.7	6.8	16	14	11	43
Nepal	–101	–100	625	819	0.0	4.2	124.8	124.8	57	2,727	9	5
Netherlands	191	110	1,387	1,735	0.1	0.0	80.0	77.6	1,359	3,299	2,802	8,280
New Zealand	143	103	594	858	..	0.0	3.8	2.7	1,652	626	427	1,202
Nicaragua	–114	–206	27	35	23.9	1.5	0.6	0.1	75	818	..	..
Niger	–3	–28	171	183	10.3	0.8	27.6	0.3	8	79[a]	29	18[a]
Nigeria	–96	–170	582	972	1.9	14.2	8.1	10.1	804[a]	9,980[a]	5	103[a]
Norway	42	84	237	371	0.0	0.0	47.6	36.1	239	685	603	4,776
Oman	23	–50	582	666	0.0	0.1	..	0.0	39	39	1,537	5,181
Pakistan	–2,611	–1,239	4,077	3,554	5.3	32.4	1,202.5	1,780.9	1,712	7,039	4	2[a]
Panama	8	8	73	102	0.2	0.1	0.9	16.9	112	196	20	198
Papua New Guinea	0	0	31	25	2.0	0.0	9.6	10.0	16	13[a]	16	135[a]
Paraguay	–30	–45	183	168	0.1	0.1	0.1	0.1	287	503	..	..
Peru	–300	–525	51	42	5.9	7.3	0.6	1.1	599	2,437	34	133
Philippines	–900	–900	210	375	0.5	1.4	0.8	0.1	5,360	18,643	151	44
Poland	–77	–200	964	825	19.7	2.4	0.6	12.8	724	10,447	262	1,717
Portugal	0	291	528	764	0.0	0.0	0.2	0.4	3,953	4,057	527	1,410
Puerto Rico	–4	–27	339	352	0.0	..	..	..	..	..	..	..
Qatar	14	219	406	713	0.0	0.1	..	0.0	..	..	..	..

6.18 Movement of people

	Net migration		International migrant stock		Refugees				Workers' remittances and compensation of employees			
	thousands		thousands		thousands				$ millions			
					By country of origin		By country of asylum		Received		Paid	
	1990–95	2000–05	1995	2005	1995	2008	1995	2008	1995	2008	1995	2008
Romania	−529	−270	135	133	17.0	4.8	0.2	1.6	9	9,381	2	664
Russian Federation	2,220	964	11,707	12,080	207.0	103.1	246.7	3.5	2,502	6,033	3,938	26,145
Rwanda	−1,681	6	337	436	1,819.4	72.5	7.8	55.1	21	68	1	70
Saudi Arabia	−500	285	4,611	6,337	0.3	0.7	13.2	240.6	..	216	16,594	21,696
Senegal	−100	−100	291	220	17.6	16.0	66.8	33.2	146	1,288[a]	76	143[a]
Serbia	451	−339	874	675	86.1[e]	185.9	650.7[e]	96.7	1,295[a,e]	5,538[a,e]	..	138
Sierra Leone	−450	336	101	152	379.5	32.5	4.7	7.8	24	150[a]	..	3
Singapore	250	139	992	1,494	0.0	0.1	0.1	0.0	..	..	..	..
Slovak Republic	−3	10	114	124	0.0	0.3	2.3	0.3	26	1,973	3	144
Slovenia	38	23	200	167	12.9	0.1	22.3	0.3	272	343	31	353
Somalia	−893	−200	19	21	638.7	561.2	0.6	1.8	..	..	..	..
South Africa	900	700	1,098	1,249	0.5	0.5	101.4	43.5	105	823	629	1,133
Spain	324	2,504	1,041	4,608	0.0	0.0	5.9	4.7	3,237	11,776	868	14,659
Sri Lanka	−256	−442	426	366	107.6	137.8	0.0	0.3	809	2,947	16	385
Sudan	−168	−532	1,111	640	445.3	419.2	674.1	181.6	346	3,100	1	2[a]
Swaziland	−38	−46	35	39	0.0	0.0	0.7	0.8	83	100[a]	4	8[a]
Sweden	151	186	906	1,113	0.0	0.0	199.2	77.0	288	822	336	854
Switzerland	227	200	1,471	1,660	0.0	0.0	82.9	46.1	1,473	2,200	10,114	19,022
Syrian Arab Republic	−70	300	817	1,326	8.0	15.2	373.5[d]	1,567.6[d]	339	850[a]	15	252[a]
Tajikistan	−296	−345	305	306	59.0	0.5	0.6	1.8	..	2,544	..	199
Tanzania	591	−345	1,134	798	0.1	1.3	829.7	321.9	1	19	1	54
Thailand	−39	1,411	549	982	0.2	1.8	106.6	112.9	1,695	1,898	..	..
Timor-Leste	0	41	10	12	..	0.0	..	0.0	..	..	..	..
Togo	−122	−4	169	183	93.2	16.8	10.9	9.4	15	284[a]	47[a]	..
Trinidad and Tobago	−24	−20	46	38	0.0	0.2	..	0.0	32	109[a]	14	..
Tunisia	−43	−81	38	35	0.3	2.3	0.2	0.1	680	1,977	36	16
Turkey	−70	−71	1,212	1,334	44.9	214.4	12.8	11.1	3,327	1,360	..	111
Turkmenistan	50	−25	260	224	0.0	0.7	23.3	0.1	4	..	7	..
Uganda	120	−5	661	652	24.2	7.5	229.4	162.1	..	724	..	364
Ukraine	100	−173	6,172	5,391	1.7	28.4	5.2	7.2	6	5,769	1	54
United Arab Emirates	340	577	1,716	2,863	0.0	0.3	0.4	0.2	..	..	..	..
United Kingdom	167	948	4,191	5,838	0.1	0.2	90.9	292.1	2,469	7,861	2,581	4,633
United States	6,565	5,676	28,522	39,266	0.2	2.1	623.3	279.5	2,179	3,045	22,181	48,187
Uruguay	−20	−104	93	84	0.3	0.2	0.1	0.1	..	108	..	5
Uzbekistan	−340	−400	1,474	1,268	0.1	6.3	2.6	0.8	..	..	..	..
Venezuela, RB	40	40	1,019	1,011	0.5	5.8	1.6	201.2	2	137	203	860
Vietnam	−840	−200	39	55	543.5	328.2	34.4	2.4	..	7,200[a]	..	..
West Bank and Gaza	1	11	1,201	1,661	72.8	340.0	1,201.0[d]	1,836.1[d]	582	630[a]	..	..
Yemen, Rep.	650	−100	378	455	0.4	1.8	53.5	140.2	1,081	1,411	19	18[a]
Zambia	−11	−82	271	287	0.0	0.2	130.0	83.5	..	68	59	337
Zimbabwe	−192	−700	433	391	0.0	16.8	0.5	3.5	44	..	7	139
World	..[f] s	..[f] s	165,659[g] s	194,797[g] s	18,068.7[d,h] s	15,161.6[d,h] s	18,068.7[d] s	15,161.6[d] s	101,963 s	443,392 s	100,821 s	288,361 s
Low income	−344	−3,728	15,731	14,820	8,552.0	5,386.1	4,882.4	2,024.9	3,525	31,917	431	2,400
Middle income	−12,982	−14,512	62,754	62,860	3,719.2	4,672.9	9,932.2	10,916.7	53,106	303,872	10,282	65,441
Lower middle income	−11,033	−11,119	33,284	32,088	2,490.7	3,629.0	8,477.2	9,826.5	31,986	203,769	1,959	15,361
Upper middle income	−1,949	−3,393	29,471	30,772	1,228.5	1,043.9	1,455.1	1,090.2	21,121	100,103	8,323	50,080
Low & middle income	−13,325	−18,240	78,485	77,680	12,271.2	10,059.0	14,814.7	12,941.6	56,631	335,789	10,714	67,841
East Asia & Pacific	−3,285	−3,722	3,047	4,739	952.9	761.1	447.0	463.6	9,525	86,060	1,617	14,551
Europe & Central Asia	−3,597	−2,138	31,097	28,924	1,631.5	712.5	1,221.9	187.7	7,206	57,516	4,770	34,731
Latin America & Carib.	−3,388	−5,738	5,440	5,951	155.7	446.6	93.9	350.2	13,427	64,438	1,123	4,258
Middle East & N. Africa	−1,044	−1,850	8,985	10,002	948.0	2,368.9	5,683.0	7,696.9	13,275	34,798	722	6,156
South Asia	−1,262	−3,181	13,257	11,785	2,958.7	3,142.1	1,625.5	2,119.0	10,005	71,652	476	4,352
Sub-Saharan Africa	−749	−1,611	16,659	16,279	5,624.4	2,627.7	5,743.4	2,124.1	3,193	21,324	2,006	3,794
High income	13,308	18,091	87,174	117,117	267.3	109.4	3,254.1	2,220.0	45,332	107,603	90,107	220,520
Euro area	4,604	7,269	23,080	31,629	13.9	1.0	1,690.4	966.3	30,826	71,436	28,737	83,142

a. World Bank estimates. b. Includes Taiwan, China. c. Includes Tibetans, who are listed separately by the UN Refugee Agency (UNHCR). d. Includes Palestinian refugees under the mandate of the United Nations Relief and Works Agency for Palestine Refugees in the Near East (UNRWA), who are not included in data from the UNHCR. e. Includes Montenegro. f. World totals computed by the United Nations sum to zero, but because the aggregates refer to World Bank definitions, regional and income group totals do not. g. World totals are computed by the World Bank and include only economies covered by *World Development Indicators*, so data may differ from what is published by the United Nations Population Division. h. Includes refugees without specified country of origin and Palestinian refugees under the mandate of the UNRWA, so regional and income group totals do not sum to the world total.

Movement of people, most often through migration, is a significant part of global integration. Migrants contribute to the economies of both their host country and their country of origin. Yet reliable statistics on migration are difficult to collect and are often incomplete, making international comparisons a challenge.

The United Nations Population Division provides data on net migration and migrant stock. To derive estimates of net migration, the organization takes into account the past migration history of a country or area, the migration policy of a country, and the influx of refugees in recent periods. The data to calculate these official estimates come from a variety of sources, including border statistics, administrative records, surveys, and censuses. When no official estimates can be made because of insufficient data, net migration is derived through the balance equation, which is the difference between overall population growth and the natural increase during the 1990–2000 intercensal period.

The data used to estimate the international migrant stock at a particular time are obtained mainly from population censuses. The estimates are derived from the data on foreign-born population—people who have residence in one country but were born in another country. When data on the foreign-born population are not available, data on foreign population—that is, people who are citizens of a country other than the country in which they reside—are used as estimates.

After the breakup of the Soviet Union in 1991 people living in one of the newly independent countries who were born in another were classified as international migrants. Estimates of migrant stock in the newly independent states from 1990 on are based on the 1989 census of the Soviet Union.

For countries with information on the international migrant stock for at least two points in time, interpolation or extrapolation was used to estimate the international migrant stock on July 1 of the reference years. For countries with only one observation, estimates for the reference years were derived using rates of change in the migrant stock in the years preceding or following the single observation available. A model was used to estimate migrants for countries that had no data.

Registrations, together with other sources—including estimates and surveys—are the main sources of refugee data. But there are difficulties in collecting accurate statistics. Although refugees are often registered individually, the accuracy of registrations varies greatly. Many refugees may not be aware of the need to register or may choose not to do so. And administrative records tend to overestimate the number of refugees because it is easier to register than to de-register. The UN Refugee Agency (UNHCR) collects and maintains data on refugees, except for Palestinian refugees residing in areas under the mandate of the United Nations Relief and Works Agency for Palestine Refugees in the Near East (UNRWA). The UNRWA provides services to Palestinian refugees who live in certain areas and who register with the agency. Registration is voluntary, and estimates by the UNRWA are not an accurate count of the Palestinian refugee population. The table shows estimates of refugees collected by the UNHCR, complemented by estimates of Palestinian refugees under the UNRWA mandate. Thus, the aggregates differ from those published by the UNHCR.

Workers' remittances and compensation of employees are World Bank staff estimates based on data from the International Monetary Fund's (IMF) *Balance of Payments Statistics Yearbook*. The IMF data are supplemented by World Bank staff estimates for missing data for countries where workers' remittances are important. The data reported here are the sum of three items defined in the fifth edition of the IMF's *Balance of Payments Manual*: workers' remittances, compensation of employees, and migrants' transfers.

The distinction among these three items is not always consistent in the data reported by countries to the IMF. In some cases countries compile data on the basis of the citizenship of migrant workers rather than their residency status. Some countries also report remittances entirely as workers' remittances or compensation of employees. Following the fifth edition of the *Balance of Payments Manual* in 1993, migrants' transfers are considered a capital transaction, but previous editions regarded them as current transfers. For these reasons the figures presented in the table take all three items into account.

• **Net migration** is the net total of migrants during the period. It is the total number of immigrants less the total number of emigrants, including both citizens and noncitizens. Data are five-year estimates. • **International migrant stock** is the number of people born in a country other than that in which they live. It includes refugees. • **Refugees** are people who are recognized as refugees under the 1951 Convention Relating to the Status of Refugees or its 1967 Protocol, the 1969 Organization of African Unity Convention Governing the Specific Aspects of Refugee Problems in Africa, people recognized as refugees in accordance with the UNHCR statute, people granted refugee-like humanitarian status, and people provided temporary protection. Asylum seekers—people who have applied for asylum or refugee status and who have not yet received a decision or who are registered as asylum seekers—are excluded. Palestinian refugees are people (and their descendants) whose residence was Palestine between June 1946 and May 1948 and who lost their homes and means of livelihood as a result of the 1948 Arab-Israeli conflict. • **Country of origin** refers to the nationality or country of citizenship of a claimant. • **Country of asylum** is the country where an asylum claim was filed and granted. • **Workers' remittances and compensation of employees** received and paid comprise current transfers by migrant workers and wages and salaries earned by nonresident workers. Remittances are classified as current private transfers from migrant workers resident in the host country for more than a year, irrespective of their immigration status, to recipients in their country of origin. Migrants' transfers are defined as the net worth of migrants who are expected to remain in the host country for more than one year that is transferred to another country at the time of migration. Compensation of employees is the income of migrants who have lived in the host country for less than a year.

Data sources

Data on net migration are from the United Nations Population Division's *World Population Prospects: The 2008 Revision*. Data on migration stock are from the United Nations Population Division's *Trends in Total Migrant Stock: The 2008 Revision*. Data on refugees are from the UNHCR's *Statistical Yearbook 2008*, complemented by statistics on Palestinian refugees under the mandate of the UNRWA as published on its website. Data on remittances are World Bank staff estimates based on IMF balance of payments data.

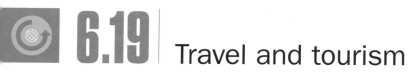

	International tourists				Inbound tourism expenditure				Outbound tourism expenditure			
	thousands				$ millions		% of exports		$ millions		% of imports	
	Inbound		Outbound									
	1995	**2008**	**1995**	**2008**	**1995**	**2008**	**1995**	**2008**	**1995**	**2008**	**1995**	**2008**
Afghanistan	..	..	..	..	..	..	..	..	..	..	..	..
Albania	304[a]	2,675[a]	12	3,716	70	1,849	23.2	48.2	19	1,644	2.3	22.6
Algeria	520[a,b]	1,772[a,b]	1,090	1,539	32[c]	325[c]	..	..	186[c]	469[c]	..	..
Angola	9	294	3	..	27	293	0.7	0.5	113	447	3.2	1.0
Argentina	2,289	4,665	3,815	4,611	2,550	5,308	10.2	6.5	4,013	5,971	15.4	8.8
Armenia	12	558	..	516	14	377	4.7	21.5	12	383	1.7	8.1
Australia	3,726[a]	5,586[a]	2,519	5,808	11,915	28,470	17.1	12.2	7,260	24,903	9.7	10.3
Austria	17,173[d]	21,935[d]	3,713	9,876	14,529	24,343	16.2	10.1	11,686	13,988	12.7	6.3
Azerbaijan	..	1,409	432	2,162	87	381	11.1	1.2	165	454	12.8	4.0
Bangladesh	156	467	830	875	25[e]	91[e]	0.6	0.5	234[e]	918	3.1	3.6
Belarus	161	91	626	380	28	585	0.5	1.6	101	812	1.8	1.9
Belgium	5,560[d]	7,165[d]	5,645	8,887	4,548[e]	13,063	2.4	2.8	8,115[e]	20,883	4.5	4.4
Benin	138	186	..	..	85[e]	206	13.8	15.3	48	107	5.4	5.1
Bolivia	284	594	249	589	92	302	7.5	4.3	72	381	4.6	6.7
Bosnia and Herzegovina	115[d]	322[d]	..	..	257	920	22.9	13.4	97	274	2.4	2.1
Botswana	521	1,500	..	..	176	515[e]	7.3	9.2	153	490[e]	7.5	8.4
Brazil	1,991	5,050	2,600	4,936	1,085	6,109	2.1	2.7	3,982	13,269	6.3	6.0
Bulgaria	3,466	5,780	3,524	5,727	662	4,831	9.8	15.8	312	3,380	4.8	8.0
Burkina Faso	124[f]	226[f]	..	..	..	57	..	..	..	91	..	..
Burundi	34[b]	201[b]	36	..	2	2	1.9	1.2	25[e]	98	9.7	18.5
Cambodia	..	2,001	31	786	71	1,300	7.3	20.5	22	191	1.6	2.5
Cameroon	100[f]	185[f]	..	..	75	165	3.7	2.2	140	502	8.7	6.0
Canada	16,932	17,142	18,206	27,037	9,176	17,771	4.2	3.4	12,658	34,007	6.3	7.0
Central African Republic	26[g]	14[g]	..	11	4[c]	..	..	..	43[c]	..	..	..
Chad	19[f]	25[f]	..	..	43[c]	..	..	..	38[c]	..	..	..
Chile	1,540	2,699	1,070	3,061	1,186	2,632	6.1	3.4	934	1,788	5.1	2.6
China	20,034	53,049	4,520	45,844	8,730[e]	44,130	5.9	2.8	3,688[e]	40,987	2.7	3.3
Hong Kong SAR, China	7,137	17,319	..	81,911	9,604[c,e]	20,413[c]	3.5	4.5	10,497[c,e]	15,888[c,e]	6.5	3.7
Colombia	1,433[a]	1,222[a]	1,057	2,041	887	2,499	7.2	5.9	1,162	2,337	7.3	5.2
Congo, Dem. Rep.	35[g]	47[g]	50	..	..	..	..	..	..	..	..	..
Congo, Rep.	37[f]	43[f]	..	..	15	54	1.1	0.9	69	168	5.1	2.6
Costa Rica	785	2,089	273	519	763	2,526	17.1	18.5	336	718	7.1	4.4
Côte d'Ivoire	188	..	..	..	103	114[e]	2.4	1.0	312	380[e]	8.2	4.1
Croatia	1,485[d]	9,415[d]	..	..	1,349[e]	11,668	19.3	39.4	422[e]	1,152	4.6	3.3
Cuba	742[d]	2,316[g]	72	202	1,100[c]	2,548	..	..	..	..	..	..
Czech Republic	3,381[d]	6,649[d]	..	..	2,880[e]	8,728	10.2	5.2	1,635[e]	4,731	5.4	3.0
Denmark	2,124[d]	4,503[d]	5,035	6,347	3,691[e]	6,686[e]	5.6	3.6	4,288[e]	9,678[e]	7.4	5.4
Dominican Republic	1,776[b,g]	3,980[b,g]	168	413	1,571[e]	4,176[e]	27.4	35.1	267	522[e]	4.4	2.9
Ecuador	440[a,h]	1,005[a,h]	271	815	315	745	6.1	3.6	331	790	5.8	3.8
Egypt, Arab Rep.	2,871	12,296	2,683	4,531	2,954	12,104	22.3	22.1	1,371	3,390	8.0	5.0
El Salvador	235	1,385	348	1,012	152	1,180	7.5	19.3	99	709	2.7	6.4
Eritrea	315[a,b]	81[a,b]	..	..	58[c]	60	43.1	..	..	..	..	..
Estonia	530	1,970	1,764	..	452	1,662	17.6	9.4	121	938	4.2	5.0
Ethiopia	103[g]	330[b]	120	..	177	1,184	23.1	33.7	30	156[e]	2.1	1.6
Finland	2,644	3,583	5,147	5,854	2,383	4,861	5.0	3.8	2,853	5,534	7.6	4.7
France	60,033	78,449	18,686	23,347	31,295	66,821	8.6	8.7	20,699	52,135	6.2	6.2
Gabon	125[g]	..	203	..	94	13	3.2	0.2	182	346	10.6	14.4
Gambia, The	45	147	..	307	28[e]	83	15.8	30.8	16	8	6.9	2.2
Georgia	85[a]	1,290[a]	228	..	75	505	13.1	13.7	171	338	12.1	4.5
Germany	14,847[d]	24,884[d]	55,800	73,000	24,052	51,225	4.0	2.9	66,527	103,386	11.3	6.8
Ghana	286[b]	587[b]	..	..	30	970	1.9	13.7	74	870	3.5	6.9
Greece	10,130	15,939	..	..	4,182	17,586	26.9	22.1	1,495	3,946	6.0	3.3
Guatemala	563[a]	1,715[a]	333	1,277	216	1,068[e]	7.7	11.1	167	750	4.5	4.8
Guinea	12[g]	46[g]	..	..	1	2	0.1	0.2	29	30	2.9	1.7
Guinea-Bissau	..	30	..	..	3	3	5.3	..	6	16	6.7	..
Haiti	145	304	..	..	90[e]	279	46.8	33.5	35[e]	383	4.4	13.3
Honduras	271	899	149	387	85	622	5.2	8.9	99	421	5.3	3.6

	International tourists				Inbound tourism expenditure				Outbound tourism expenditure			
	thousands				$ millions		% of exports		$ millions		% of imports	
	Inbound		Outbound									
	1995	2008	1995	2008	1995	2008	1995	2008	1995	2008	1995	2008
Hungary	..	8,814	13,083	18,471	2,938	7,112	14.9	5.6	1,501	4,637	7.5	3.7
India	2,124[h]	5,367[h]	3,056	10,647	2,582[e]	12,461	6.8	4.3	996[e]	12,081	2.1	3.3
Indonesia	4,324	6,234	1,782	5,486	5,229[e]	8,150	9.9	5.3	2,172[e]	8,547	4.0	5.9
Iran, Islamic Rep.	489	2,034	1,000	..	205	2,196	1.1	..	247	9,482	1.6	..
Iraq	61[a]	..	..	..	18[e]	555	..	1.4	117[e]	705	..	3.3
Ireland	4,818	8,026	2,547	7,713	2,698	9,953	5.5	4.5	2,034[e]	10,551	4.8	5.4
Israel	2,215[h]	2,572[h]	2,259	4,207	3,491	4,807	12.7	5.9	2,626	4,445	7.4	5.3
Italy	31,052	42,734	18,173	28,284	30,426	48,793	10.3	7.3	17,219	37,728	6.9	5.6
Jamaica	1,147[b,g]	1,767[b,g]	..	..	1,199	2,222	35.3	42.0	173	312	4.6	3.1
Japan	3,345[a,h]	8,351[a,h]	15,298	15,987	4,894	13,781	1.0	1.5	46,966	38,976	11.2	4.4
Jordan	1,075[h]	3,729[b]	1,128	2,288	973	3,539	28.0	28.6	719	1,140	14.7	5.9
Kazakhstan	..	3,447	523	5,243	155	1,255	2.6	1.6	296	1,305	4.9	2.6
Kenya	896	1,644	..	..	590	1,398	16.7	16.9	183	266[e]	3.1	2.1
Korea, Dem. Rep.	..	..	..	..	..	..	..	..	..	..	..	..
Korea, Rep.	3,753[a,b]	6,891[a,b]	3,819	11,996	6,670	12,783	4.5	2.5	6,947	19,512	4.5	3.8
Kosovo	..	..	..	..	..	..	..	..	..	..	..	..
Kuwait	72[f]	293[f]	878	2,649	307	610	2.2	0.6	2,514	8,341	19.9	22.0
Kyrgyz Republic	36	2,435	42	1,521	5[e]	569	1.1	20.7	7[e]	451	1.0	9.5
Lao PDR	60	1,295	..	..	52	276[e]	12.8	19.4	34	..	4.5	..
Latvia	539	1,684	1,812	3,782	37	1,134	1.8	8.0	62	1,250	2.8	6.6
Lebanon	450	1,333	..	..	710	7,690	..	32.0	..	4,297	..	14.5
Lesotho	87	285	..	..	29	34[e]	14.6	3.6	17	19	1.6	1.1
Liberia	..	..	..	..	..	158[e]	..	24.9	..	58	..	2.5
Libya	56	..	484	..	4	99	0.1	0.2	493	1,339	8.6	5.1
Lithuania	650	1,611	1,925	2,847	102	1,406	3.2	4.9	107	1,533	2.7	4.5
Macedonia, FYR	147[d]	255[d]	..	..	19[e]	262	2.7	5.3	27[e]	190	1.7	2.5
Madagascar	75[g]	375[g]	39	..	106	620	14.2	21.8	79	143[e]	8.0	3.9
Malawi	192	742	..	..	22	48	4.7	..	53	84	8.0	..
Malaysia	7,469	22,052	20,642	..	5,044	18,553	6.1	8.1	2,722	7,724	3.1	4.3
Mali	42[f,g]	190[f,g]	..	..	26	227	4.9	11.7	74	201	7.5	7.7
Mauritania	..	..	..	..	11[e]	..	2.2	..	30	..	5.9	..
Mauritius	422	930	107	226	616	1,823	26.2	36.9	184	489	7.5	7.7
Mexico	20,241[b]	22,637[b]	8,450	14,450	6,847	14,647	7.7	4.7	3,587	10,185	4.4	3.1
Moldova	32	7	71	85	71	289	8.0	11.6	73	345	7.3	6.1
Mongolia	108	446	..	..	33	261	6.5	12.9	22	212	4.2	11.3
Morocco	2,602[b]	7,879[b]	1,317	3,058	1,469	8,885	16.2	26.3	356	1,910	3.2	4.1
Mozambique	..	771	..	..	49	213	10.2	6.6	68	241	6.6	5.5
Myanmar	117	193	..	..	169	59	12.9	1.2	18[e]	40	0.9	1.4
Namibia	272	929	..	..	278[e]	382	16.0	10.4	90[e]	92	4.3	2.1
Nepal	363	500	100	561	232	353	22.5	20.6	167	545	10.3	12.5
Netherlands	6,574[d]	10,104[d]	12,313	18,458	10,611	20,526	4.4	3.2	13,151	22,212	6.1	3.9
New Zealand	1,475	2,411	920	1,965	2,318[e]	5,030[e]	13.0	12.5	1,259[e]	2,991[e]	7.3	7.0
Nicaragua	281	858	255	1,100	51	276[e]	7.7	9.4	56	218	4.9	4.1
Niger	35	48	10	..	7[e]	45	2.2	5.9	26	49	5.7	3.7
Nigeria	656	1,111	..	..	47	586	0.4	0.7	939	4,774	7.3	10.0
Norway	2,880	4,440	590	3,395	2,730	5,559	4.9	2.5	4,481	15,932[e]	9.6	12.2
Oman	279[f]	1,273[f]	..	..	193	1,111	2.5	2.8	349[e]	1,199	6.3	4.5
Pakistan	378	823	..	..	582	915	5.7	3.6	654	2,035	4.6	4.3
Panama	345	1,293	185	369	372	2,223	4.9	13.8	181	560	2.3	3.2
Papua New Guinea	42	114	51	..	25[e]	4	0.8	0.1	58[e]	56	3.0	2.1
Paraguay	438[h]	428[h]	427	278	162	128	3.4	1.4	173	210	3.3	2.2
Peru	479	2,058	508	1,971	521	2,396	7.9	6.8	428	1,353	4.5	4.0
Philippines	1,760[b]	3,139[b]	1,615	2,745	1,141	4,990	4.3	8.5	551	2,778	1.7	4.0
Poland	19,215	12,960	36,387	47,561	6,927	12,841	19.4	6.0	5,865	10,381	17.3	4.4
Portugal	9,511[h]	12,321[b]	..	20,989	5,646	14,047	17.5	17.0	2,540	5,283	6.4	5.1
Puerto Rico	3,131[g]	3,894[g]	1,237	1,493	1,828[c]	3,645[c]	..	..	1,155[c]	1,834[c]	..	..
Qatar	309[f]	1,405[f]	..	..	..	874[c]	..	..	..	3,751[c]	..	..

	International tourists				Inbound tourism expenditure				Outbound tourism expenditure			
	thousands				$ millions		% of exports		$ millions		% of imports	
	Inbound		Outbound									
	1995	**2008**	**1995**	**2008**	**1995**	**2008**	**1995**	**2008**	**1995**	**2008**	**1995**	**2008**
Romania	5,445[a]	8,862[a]	5,737	13,072	689	2,627	7.3	4.2	749	2,411	6.6	2.7
Russian Federation	10,290[a]	23,676[a]	21,329	36,538	4,312[e]	15,923	4.6	3.0	11,599[e]	28,122	14.0	7.6
Rwanda	..	981	..	..	4	202	5.4	30.4	13	104	3.5	7.4
Saudi Arabia	3,325	14,757	..	4,087	..	7,227[c]	..	2.2	..	16,666[c]	..	9.5
Senegal	..	875	..	..	168	622	11.2	21.6	154	352	8.5	6.5
Serbia	..	646	..	..	..	1,113	..	7.4	..	1,435	..	5.4
Sierra Leone	38[g]	36[g]	6	73	57[e]	34[e]	44.4	10.2	51	24	19.4	4.1
Singapore	6,070	7,778	2,867	6,828	7,611[e]	10,583[e]	4.8	2.5	4,663[e]	14,189[e]	3.2	3.6
Slovak Republic	903[d]	1,767[d]	218	23,837	630	3,004	5.7	3.8	338	2,596	3.2	3.2
Slovenia	732[d]	1,771[d]	..	2,459	1,128	3,115	10.9	8.4	606	1,567	5.6	4.1
Somalia	..	..	..	..	..	..	..	..	..	..	..	..
South Africa	4,488	9,592	2,520	4,429	2,655	8,861	7.7	9.0	2,414	6,792	7.2	6.3
Spain	34,920	57,316	3,648	11,229	27,369	70,234	20.4	16.4	5,826	26,829	4.3	5.2
Sri Lanka	403[h]	438[h]	504	966	367	803	7.9	7.9	279	777	4.7	5.0
Sudan	29	436	195	..	8[e]	331[e]	1.2	2.7	43[e]	1,188[e]	3.5	11.0
Swaziland	300[i]	754[f]	..	1,177	54	32	5.3	1.5	45	63	3.5	2.5
Sweden	2,310[d]	3,434[d]	10,127	12,681	4,390	14,399	4.6	5.6	6,816	17,310	8.4	7.8
Switzerland	6,946[f]	8,608[f]	11,148	..	11,354	17,573	9.2	5.5	9,478	13,407	8.7	5.1
Syrian Arab Republic	815[d]	5,430[d]	1,746	5,253	1,258[e]	2,972	21.9	19.0	498[e]	710	9.0	4.6
Tajikistan	..	..	..	..	..	24	..	1.4	..	11[e]	..	0.3
Tanzania	285	750	157	..	502[e]	1,358	39.7	26.1	360[e]	746	16.8	9.3
Thailand	6,952[b]	14,536	1,820	4,018	9,257	21,980	13.2	10.5	4,791	6,963	5.8	3.4
Timor-Leste	..	..	..	..	..	..	..	..	..	..	..	..
Togo	53[f]	74[f]	..	..	13[e]	38	2.8	4.2	40	59	6.0	4.3
Trinidad and Tobago	260[g]	433[g]	261	..	232	615	8.3	4.3	91	204	4.3	1.9
Tunisia	4,120[h]	7,049[h]	1,778	3,118	1,838	3,909	23.0	15.5	294	555	3.3	2.1
Turkey	7,083	24,994	3,981	9,873	4,957[e]	25,019	13.6	14.2	911[e]	4,031	2.3	1.9
Turkmenistan	218	8	21	38	13	..	0.7	..	74	..	4.1	..
Uganda	160	844	148	337	78[e]	531	11.7	15.5	80[e]	314	5.4	6.0
Ukraine	3,716	25,449	6,552	15,499	191[e]	6,722	1.1	7.9	210[e]	4,585	1.1	4.6
United Arab Emirates	2,315[b,i]	7,126[b,i]	..	..	632	7,162[c]	..	..	..	13,288[c]	..	..
United Kingdom	21,719	30,142	41,345	69,011	27,577	45,345	8.6	6.0	30,749	84,218	9.4	10.0
United States	43,490	57,938	51,285	63,549	93,700	166,530	11.8	9.1	60,924	117,969	6.8	4.7
Uruguay	2,022	1,938	562	734	725	1,180	20.7	12.6	332	487	9.3	4.8
Uzbekistan	92	1,069	246	1,150	15	64[c]	..	..	..	..	..	..
Venezuela, RB	700	745	534	1,745	995	984	4.8	1.0	1,852	2,566	11.0	4.3
Vietnam	1,351[a]	4,254[a]	..	..	..	3,926[c]	..	5.6	..	..	..	..
West Bank and Gaza	220[f]	387[f]	..	..	255[e]	212	33.4	22.9	162[e]	376	5.8	8.5
Yemen, Rep.	61[f]	404[f]	..	..	50[e]	886[e]	2.3	8.7	76[e]	246	3.1	2.1
Zambia	163	812	..	..	29	146	2.4	2.8	83	107	6.2	2.0
Zimbabwe	1,416[a]	2,508[a]	256	..	145	365[c]	..	..	106[c]	..	..	..
World	**536,909 t**	**927,848 t**	**576,560 t**	**1,027,062 t**	**486,780 t**	**1,139,379 t**	**7.6 w**	**5.8 w**	**458,837 t**	**1,028,751 t**	**7.4 w**	**5.3 w**
Low income	8,001	23,743	..	..	..	..	10.6	9.1	..	..	5.0	..
Middle income	157,253	345,869	175,694	363,133	88,430	305,501	8.1	5.5	65,704	227,180	5.8	4.3
Lower middle income	57,366	166,594	36,710	142,650	39,463	146,807	8.2	4.9	20,472	111,854	3.9	3.9
Upper middle income	100,145	179,371	124,078	208,648	48,963	158,652	7.9	6.0	45,510	115,055	7.4	4.9
Low & middle income	167,692	375,532	195,002	413,087	92,494	323,111	8.1	5.6	69,333	239,061	5.8	4.3
East Asia & Pacific	43,653	109,209	36,055	..	31,197	104,753	7.8	4.5	14,769	70,557	3.5	3.7
Europe & Central Asia	54,490	123,198	86,619	149,215	19,155	81,028	8.4	5.9	22,399	68,075	9.5	4.9
Latin America & Carib.	38,965	60,922	21,780	41,578	21,591	55,179	7.5	5.3	18,751	44,731	6.5	4.5
Middle East & N. Africa	13,349	42,820	13,407	25,352	9,771	43,878	13.0	16.7	4,844	19,782	5.7	5.7
South Asia	3,819	8,472	5,151	15,005	4,016	15,342	6.8	4.4	2,393	16,660	3.0	3.5
Sub-Saharan Africa	12,954	29,153	..	..	6,729	22,956	7.6	6.0	6,761	22,119	6.7	5.9
High income	364,532	546,528	337,054	531,446	394,244	816,408	7.5	5.8	388,810	790,377	7.8	5.7
Euro area	202,533	290,386	140,127	232,712	164,023	356,496	7.8	6.3	154,993	312,836	7.8	5.6

Note: Aggregates are based on World Bank country classifications and differ from those of the World Tourism Organization. Regional and income group totals include countries not shown in the table for which data are available.
a. Arrivals of nonresident visitors at national borders. b. Includes nationals residing abroad. c. Country estimates. d. Arrivals in all types of accommodation establishments. e. Expenditure of travel related items only; excludes passenger transport items. f. Arrivals in hotels and similar establishments. g. Arrivals by air only. h. Excludes nationals residing abroad. i. Arrivals in hotels only.

About the data

Tourism is defined as the activities of people traveling to and staying in places outside their usual environment for no more than one year for leisure, business, and other purposes not related to an activity remunerated from within the place visited. The social and economic phenomenon of tourism has grown substantially over the past quarter century.

Statistical information on tourism is based mainly on data on arrivals and overnight stays along with balance of payments information. These data do not completely capture the economic phenomenon of tourism or provide the information needed for effective public policies and efficient business operations. Data are needed on the scale and significance of tourism. Information on the role of tourism in national economies is particularly deficient. Although the World Tourism Organization reports progress in harmonizing definitions and measurement, differences in national practices still prevent full comparability.

The data in the table are from the World Tourism Organization, a United Nations agency. The data on inbound and outbound tourists refer to the number of arrivals and departures, not to the number of people traveling. Thus a person who makes several trips to a country during a given period is counted each time as a new arrival. Unless otherwise indicated in the footnotes, the data on inbound tourism show the arrivals of nonresident tourists (overnight visitors) at national borders. When data on international tourists are unavailable or incomplete, the table shows the arrivals of international visitors, which include tourists, same-day visitors, cruise passengers, and crew members.

Sources and collection methods for arrivals differ across countries. In some cases data are from border statistics (police, immigration, and the like) and supplemented by border surveys. In other cases data are from tourism accommodation establishments. For some countries number of arrivals is limited to arrivals by air and for others to arrivals staying in hotels. Some countries include arrivals of nationals residing abroad while others do not. Caution should thus be used in comparing arrivals across countries.

The World Tourism Organization is improving its coverage of tourism expenditure data, using balance of payments data from the International Monetary Fund (IMF) supplemented by data from individual countries. These data, shown in the table, include travel and passenger transport items as defined in the IMF's (1993) *Balance of Payments Manual*. When the IMF does not report data on passenger transport items, expenditure data for travel items are shown.

The aggregates are calculated using the World Bank's weighted aggregation methodology (see *Statistical methods*) and differ from the World Tourism Organization's aggregates.

Definitions

• **International inbound tourists** (overnight visitors) are the number of tourists who travel to a country other than that in which they usually reside, and outside their usual environment, for a period not exceeding 12 months and whose main purpose in visiting is other than an activity remunerated from within the country visited. When data on number of tourists are not available, the number of visitors, which includes tourists, same-day visitors, cruise passengers, and crew members, is shown instead. • **International outbound tourists** are the number of departures that people make from their country of usual residence to any other country for any purpose other than an activity remunerated in the country visited. • **Inbound tourism expenditure** is expenditures by international inbound visitors, including payments to national carriers for international transport. These receipts include any other prepayment made for goods or services received in the destination country. They may include receipts from same-day visitors, except when these are important enough to justify separate classification. For some countries they do not include receipts for passenger transport items. Their share in exports is calculated as a ratio to exports of goods and services (all transactions between residents of a country and the rest of the world involving a change of ownership from residents to nonresidents of general merchandise, goods sent for processing and repairs, nonmonetary gold, and services). • **Outbound tourism expenditure** is expenditures of international outbound visitors in other countries, including payments to foreign carriers for international transport. These expenditures may include those by residents traveling abroad as same-day visitors, except when these are important enough to justify separate classification. For some countries they do not include expenditures for passenger transport items. Their share in imports is calculated as a ratio to imports of goods and services (all transactions between residents of a country and the rest of the world involving a change of ownership from nonresidents to residents of general merchandise, goods sent for processing and repairs, nonmonetary gold, and services).

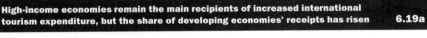

High-income economies remain the main recipients of increased international tourism expenditure, but the share of developing economies' receipts has risen **6.19a**

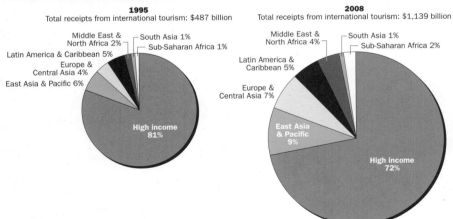

1995
Total receipts from international tourism: $487 billion

Middle East & North Africa 2%
Sub-Saharan Africa 1%
South Asia 1%
Latin America & Caribbean 5%
Europe & Central Asia 4%
East Asia & Pacific 6%
High income 81%

2008
Total receipts from international tourism: $1,139 billion

Middle East & North Africa 4%
South Asia 1%
Sub-Saharan Africa 2%
Latin America & Caribbean 5%
Europe & Central Asia 7%
East Asia & Pacific 9%
High income 72%

Although more than 70 percent of international tourism expenditures went to high-income economies in 2008, the share of developing economies' receipts has increased since 1995. The share of receipts by East Asia and Pacific and Europe and Central Asia increased the most—about 3 percentage points.

Source: World Bank staff calculations based on World Tourism Organization data.

Data sources

Data on visitors and tourism expenditure are from the World Tourism Organization's *Yearbook of Tourism Statistics* and *Compendium of Tourism Statistics 2010*. Data in the table are updated from electronic files provided by the World Tourism Organization. Data on exports and imports are from the IMF's *Balance of Payments Statistics Yearbook* and data files.

PRIMARY DATA DOCUMENTATION

As a major user of socioeconomic data, the World Bank recognizes the importance of data documentation to inform users of differences in the methods and conventions used by primary data collectors—usually national statistical agencies, central banks, and customs services—and by international organizations, which compile the statistics that appear in the World Development Indicators database. These differences may give rise to significant discrepancies over time both within countries and across them. Delays in reporting data and the use of old surveys as the base for current estimates may further compromise the quality of data reported here.

The tables in this section provide information on sources, methods, and reporting standards of the principal demographic, economic, and environmental indicators in *World Development Indicators*. Additional documentation is available from the World Bank's Country Statistical Information Database at www. worldbank.org/data.

The demand for good-quality statistical data is increasing. Timely and reliable statistics are key to the broad development strategy often referred to as "managing for results." Monitoring and reporting on publicly agreed indicators are central to implementing poverty reduction strategies and lie at the heart of the Millennium Development Goals and the new Results Measurement System adopted for the 14th replenishment of the International Development Association.

A global action plan to improve national and international statistics was agreed on during the Second Roundtable on Managing for Development Results in February 2004 in Marrakech, Morocco. The plan, now referred to as the Marrakech Action Plan for Statistics, or MAPS, has been widely endorsed and forms the overarching framework for statistical capacity building. The third roundtable conference, held in February 2007 in Hanoi, Vietnam, reaffirmed MAPS as the guiding strategy for improving the capacity of the national and international statistical systems. See www.mfdr.org/RT3 for reports from the conference.

PRIMARY DATA DOCUMENTATION

	Currency	Base year	Reference year	System of National Accounts	SNA price valuation	Alternative conversion factor	PPP survey year	Balance of Payments Manual in use	External debt	System of trade	Accounting concept	IMF data dissemination standard
				National accounts				**Balance of payments and trade**			**Government finance**	**IMF data dissemination standard**
Afghanistan	Afghan afghani	2002/03			VAB				Actual	G	C	G
Albania	Albanian lek	a	1996	b	VAB		2005	BPM5	Actual	G	C	G
Algeria	Algerian dinar	1980			VAB			BPM5	Actual	S	B	G
American Samoa	U.S. dollar											
Andorra	Euro									G		
Angola	Angolan kwanza	1997			VAP	1991–96	2005	BPM5	Actual	S		G
Antigua and Barbuda	East Caribbean dollar	1990			VAB			BPM5		G		G
Argentina	Argentine peso	1993		b	VAB	1971–84	2005	BPM5	Actual	C	C	S
Armenia	Armenian dram	a	1996	b	VAB	1990–95	2005	BPM5	Actual	S	C	G
Aruba	Aruban florin	1995								S		
Australia	Australian dollar	a	2007	b	VAB		2005	BPM5		G	C	S
Austria	Euro	2000		b	VAB		2005	BPM5		S	C	S
Azerbaijan	New Azeri manat	a	2003	b	VAB	1992–95	2005	BPM5	Actual	G	C	G
Bahamas, The	Bahamian dollar	2006		b	VAB			BPM5		G	B	G
Bahrain	Bahraini dinar	1985			VAP		2005	BPM5		G	C	G
Bangladesh	Bangladeshi taka	1995/96		b	VAB		2005	BPM5	Preliminary	G	C	G
Barbados	Barbados dollar	1974			VAB			BPM5		G	C	G
Belarus	Belarusian rubel	a	2000	b	VAB	1990–95	2005	BPM5	Actual	G	C	S
Belgium	Euro	2000		b	VAB		2005	BPM5		S	C	S
Belize	Belize dollar	2000		b	VAB			BPM5	Actual	G	B	G
Benin	CFA franc	1985			VAP	1992	2005	BPM5	Preliminary	S	B	G
Bermuda	Bermuda dollar	1996			VAB							
Bhutan	Bhutanese ngultrum	2000		b	VAB		2005		Actual		C	
Bolivia	Bolivian Boliviano	1990		b	VAB	1960–85	2005	BPM5	Actual	S	C	G
Bosnia and Herzegovina	Bosnia and Herzegovina convertible mark	a	1996	b	VAB		2005	BPM5	Actual	G	C	
Botswana	Botswana pula	1993/94		b	VAB		2005	BPM5	Preliminary	G	B	G
Brazil	Brazilian real	2000		b	VAB		2005	BPM5	Actual	S	C	S
Brunei Darussalam	Brunei dollar	2000			VAP		2005			G		G
Bulgaria	Bulgarian lev	a	2002	b	VAB	1978–89, 1991–92	2005	BPM5	Actual	G	C	S
Burkina Faso	CFA franc	1999			VAB	1992–93	2005	BPM4	Actual	G	B	G
Burundi	Burundi franc	1980			VAB		2005	BPM5	Actual	S	C	
Cambodia	Cambodian riel	2000			VAB		2005	BPM5	Actual	G	C	G
Cameroon	CFA franc	2000		b	VAB		2005	BPM5	Actual	S	C	G
Canada	Canadian dollar	2000		b	VAB		2005	BPM5		G	C	S
Cape Verde	Cape Verde escudo	1980			VAP		2005	BPM5	Actual	S		G
Cayman Islands	Cayman Islands dollar											
Central African Republic	CFA franc	2000			VAB		2005	BPM4	Preliminary	S	B	G
Chad	CFA franc	1995		b	VAB		2005	BPM5	Actual	S		G
Channel Islands	Jersey pound and Guernsey pound	2007, 2003	2007	b	VAB							
Chile	Chilean peso	2003		b	VAB		2005	BPM5	Actual	S	C	S
China	Chinese yuan	2000		b	VAP	1978–93	2005	BPM5	Preliminary	S	B	G
Hong Kong SAR, China	Hong Kong dollar	2006		b	VAB		2005	BPM5		G	C	S
Colombia	Colombian peso	2000		b	VAB	1992–94	2005	BPM5	Actual	S	B	S
Comoros	Comorian franc	1990			VAP		2005		Preliminary			
Congo, Dem. Rep.	Congolese franc	1987		b	VAB	1999–2001	2005	BPM5	Estimate	S	C	G
Congo, Rep.	CFA franc	1978			VAP	1993	2005	BPM5	Preliminary	S	C	G
Costa Rica	Costa Rican colon	1991		b	VAB			BPM5	Actual	S	C	S
Côte d'Ivoire	CFA franc	1996			VAP		2005	BPM5	Actual	S	C	G
Croatia	Croatian kuna	a	1997	b	VAB		2005	BPM5		G	C	S
Cuba	Cuban peso	1984			VAP					G		
Cyprus	Euro	a	2000		VAB		2005	BPM5		G	C	S
Czech Republic	Czech koruna	2000	1995	b	VAB		2005	BPM5		G	C	S
Denmark	Danish krone	2000		b	VAB		2005	BPM5		G	C	S
Djibouti	Djibouti franc	1990			VAB		2005		Actual			

	Latest population census	Latest demographic, education, or health household survey	Source of most recent income and expenditure data	Vital registration complete	Latest agricultural census	Latest industrial data	Latest trade data	Latest water withdrawal data
Afghanistan	1979	MICS, 2003					2008	2000
Albania	2001	MICS, 2005	LSMS, 2005	Yes	1998	2005	2008	2000
Algeria	2008	MICS, 2006	IHS, 1995		2001		2007	2000
American Samoa	2000			Yes				
Andorra	c			Yes			2006	
Angola	1970	MICS, 2001; MIS, 2006/07	IHS, 2000		1964–65		1991	2000
Antigua and Barbuda	2001			Yes			2007	1990
Argentina	2001		IHS, 2006	Yes	2002	2001	2008	2000
Armenia	2001	DHS, 2005	IHS, 2007	Yes			2008	2000
Aruba	2000						2008	
Australia	2006		ES/BS, 1994	Yes	2001	2004	2008	2000
Austria	2001		IS, 2000	Yes	1999–2000	2004	2008	2000
Azerbaijan	2009	DHS, 2006	ES/BS, 2005	Yes		2005	2008	2005
Bahamas, The	2000					1997	2008	
Bahrain	2001			Yes			2007	2003
Bangladesh	2001	DHS, 2007	IHS, 2005		2005	1997	2007	2000
Barbados	2000			Yes			2008	2000
Belarus	1999	MICS, 2005	ES/BS, 2007	Yes	1994		2008	2000
Belgium	2001		IHS, 2000	Yes	1999–2000d	2004	2008	
Belize	2000	MICS, 2006	ES/BS, 1995				2008	2000
Benin	2002	DHS, 2006	CWIQ, 2003		1992		2005	2001
Bermuda	2000			Yes			2008	
Bhutan	2005		IHS, 2003		2000		2008	2000
Bolivia	2001	DHS, 2008	IHS, 2007		1984–88	2000	2008	2000
Bosnia and Herzegovina	1991	MICS, 2006	LSMS, 2007	Yes			2008	
Botswana	2001	MICS, 2000	ES/BS, 1993/94		1993	2005	2008	2000
Brazil	2000	DHS, 1996	LFS, 2007		1996	2004	2008	2000
Brunei Darussalam	2001			Yes			2006	
Bulgaria	2001		ES/BS, 2003	Yes		2005	2008	2000
Burkina Faso	2006	MICS, 2006	CWIQ, 2003		1993		2005	2000
Burundi	1990	MICS, 2005	CWIQ, 2006				2008	2000
Cambodia	2008	DHS, 2005	IHS, 2007			1999	2004	2000
Cameroon	1987	MICS, 2006	PS, 2001		1984		2006	2000
Canada	2006		LFS, 2000	Yes	1996/2001	2001	2008	2000
Cape Verde	2000		ES/BS, 2001	Yes	2004		2008	
Cayman Islands	1999			Yes				
Central African Republic	2003	MICS, 2006	PS, 2003		1985		2005	2000
Chad	1993	DHS, 2004	PS, 2002–03				1996	2000
Channel Islands	2001			Yes				
Chile	2002		IHS, 2006	Yes	1997	2005	2008	2000
China	2000	NSS, 2007	IHS, 2005		1997	2005	2008	2000
Hong Kong SAR, China	2006			Yes			2008	
Colombia	2005	DHS, 2005	IHS, 2006		2001	2004	2008	2000
Comoros	2003	MICS, 2000	IHS, 2004				2007	
Congo, Dem. Rep.	1984	DHS, 2007	1-2-3, 2005–06		1990		1986	2000
Congo, Rep.	1996	DHS, 2005	CWIQ/PS, 2005		1985–86		1995	2002
Costa Rica	2000	RHS, 1993	LFS, 2007	Yes	1973		2008	2000
Côte d'Ivoire	1998	MICS, 2006	IHS, 2002		2001		2008	
Croatia	2001		ES/BS, 2005	Yes	2003		2008	
Cuba	2002	MICS, 2006		Yes			2006	2000
Cyprus	2001			Yes		2005	2008	2000
Czech Republic	2001	RHS, 1993	IS, 1996	Yes	2000	2005	2008	2000
Denmark	2001		ITR, 1997	Yes	1999–2000	2004	2008	2000
Djibouti	2009	MICS, 2006	PS, 2002				1998	2000

	Currency	Base year	Reference year	System of National Accounts	SNA price valuation	Alternative conversion factor	PPP survey year	Balance of Payments Manual in use	External debt	System of trade	Accounting concept	IMF data dissemination standard
Dominica	East Caribbean dollar	1990		b	VAB			BPM5	Actual	G		G
Dominican Republic	Dominican peso	1991			VAB			BPM5	Actual	G	C	G
Ecuador	U.S. dollar	2000		b	VAB		2005	BPM5	Actual	S	B	S
Egypt, Arab Rep.	Egyptian pound	1991/92			VAB		2005	BPM5	Actual	S	B	S
El Salvador	U.S. dollar	1990			VAB			BPM5	Actual	S	C	S
Equatorial Guinea	CFA franc	2000			VAB	1965–84	2005					
Eritrea	Eritrean nakfa	1992			VAB			BPM4	Actual	G		
Estonia	Estonian kroon	2000		b	VAB	1987–95	2005	BPM5		G	C	S
Ethiopia	Ethiopian birr	1999/2000		b	VAB		2005	BPM5	Actual	G	C	G
Faeroe Islands	Danish krone				VAB			BPM5		G		
Fiji	Fijian dollar	1995			VAB		2005	BPM4	Actual	G	B	G
Finland	Euro	2000		b	VAB		2005	BPM5		G	C	S
France	Euro	a	2000	b	VAB		2005	BPM5		S	C	S
French Polynesia	CFP franc									G		
Gabon	CFA franc	1991			VAP	1993	2005	BPM5	Preliminary	S		G
Gambia, The	Gambian dalasi	1987			VAB		2005	BPM5	Estimate	G	C	G
Georgia	Georgian lari	a	1996	b	VAB	1990–95	2005	BPM5	Actual	G	C	G
Germany	Euro	2000		b	VAB		2005	BPM5		S	C	S
Ghana	New Ghanaian cedi	1975			VAP	1973–87	2005	BPM5	Actual	S	B	G
Greece	Euro	a	2000		VAB		2005	BPM5		S	C	S
Greenland	Danish krone									G		
Grenada	East Caribbean dollar	1990			VAB			BPM5	Actual	G	B	G
Guam	U.S. dollar											
Guatemala	Guatemalan quetzal	2001		b	VAB			BPM5	Actual	S	B	G
Guinea	Guinean franc	1996			VAB		2005	BPM5	Estimate	S	C	G
Guinea-Bissau	CFA franc	1986			VAB		2005	BPM5	Actual	G		G
Guyana	Guyana dollar	1988			VAB			BPM5	Actual	S		
Haiti	Haitian gourde	1986/87			VAB	1991		BPM5	Preliminary	G		
Honduras	Honduran lempira	2000		b	VAB	1988–89		BPM5	Actual	S	B	G
Hungary	Hungarian forint	a	2000	b	VAB		2005	BPM5		S	C	S
Iceland	Iceland krona	2000			VAB		2005	BPM5		G	C	S
India	Indian rupee	1999/2000		b	VAB		2005	BPM5	Actual	G	C	S
Indonesia	Indonesian rupiah	2000			VAP		2005	BPM5	Actual	S	C	S
Iran, Islamic Rep.	Iranian rial	1997/98			VAB	1980–2002	2005	BPM5	Actual	G	C	
Iraq	Iraqi dinar	1997			VAB	1997, 2004	2005	BPM5		S		G
Ireland	Euro	2000		b	VAB		2005	BPM5		G	C	S
Isle of Man	Manx pound	2005	2003									
Israel	Israeli new shekel	2005		b	VAP		2005	BPM5		S	C	S
Italy	Euro	2000		b	VAB		2005	BPM5		S	C	S
Jamaica	Jamaican dollar	2003			VAB			BPM5	Actual	G	C	G
Japan	Japanese yen	2000			VAB		2005	BPM5		G	C	S
Jordan	Jordanian dinar	1994			VAB		2005	BPM5	Actual	G	B	S
Kazakhstan	Kazakh tenge	a	1995	b	VAB	1987–95	2005	BPM5	Actual	S	C	S
Kenya	Kenyan shilling	2001		b	VAB		2005	BPM5	Actual	G	B	G
Kiribati	Australian dollar	1991			VAB					G		G
Korea, Dem. Rep.	Democratic People's Republic of Korean won							BPM5				
Korea, Rep.	Korean won	2000		b	VAB		2005	BPM5		S	C	S
Kosovo	Euro											
Kuwait	Kuwaiti dinar	1995			VAP		2005	BPM5		S	C	G
Kyrgyz Republic	Kyrgyz som	a	1995	b	VAB	1990–95	2005	BPM5	Actual	G	C	S
Lao PDR	Lao kip	1990			VAB		2005	BPM5	Preliminary	G		
Latvia	Latvian lats	2000		b	VAB	1987–95	2005	BPM5	Actual	S	C	S
Lebanon	Lebanese pound	1997			VAB		2005	BPM5	Actual	G	B	G
Lesotho	Lesotho loti	1995		b	VAB		2005	BPM5	Actual	G	C	G
Liberia	Liberian dollar	1992			VAP		2005	BPM5	Estimate			G

PRIMARY DATA DOCUMENTATION

	Latest population census	Latest demographic, education, or health household survey	Source of most recent income and expenditure data	Vital registration complete	Latest agricultural census	Latest industrial data	Latest trade data	Latest water withdrawal data
Dominica	2001			Yes			2008	
Dominican Republic	2002	DHS, 2007	IHS, 2005		1971		2008	2000
Ecuador	2001	RHS, 2004	LFS, 2005		1999–2000	2004	2008	2000
Egypt, Arab Rep.	2006	DHS, 2008	ES/BS, 2004–05	Yes	1999–2000	2001	2008	2000
El Salvador	2007	RHS, 2008	IHS, 2007	Yes	1970–71		2008	2000
Equatorial Guinea	2002							2000
Eritrea	1984	DHS, 2002				2005	2003	2004
Estonia	2000		ES/BS, 2004	Yes	2001	2005	2008	2000
Ethiopia	2007	DHS, 2005	ES/BS, 2005		2001–02	2005	2008	2002
Faeroe Islands	c						2005	
Fiji	2007			Yes		2003	2007	2000
Finland	2000		IS, 2000	Yes	1999–2000	2004	2008	2000
France	2006e		ES/BS, 1994/95	Yes	1999–2000	2004	2008	2000
French Polynesia	2007			Yes			2008	
Gabon	2003	DHS, 2000	CWIQ/IHS, 2005		1974–75		2006	2000
Gambia, The	2003	MICS, 2005/06	IHS, 2003		2001–02		2008	2000
Georgia	2002	MICS, 2005; RHS, 2005	IHS, 2007	Yes	2004	2005	2008	2005
Germany	2001		IHS, 2000	Yes	1999–2000	2004	2008	2000
Ghana	2000	DHS, 2008	LSMS, 2006		1984	2002	2008	2000
Greece	2001		IHS, 2000	Yes	1999–2000	2003	2008	2000
Greenland	c			Yes			2007	
Grenada	2001						2008	
Guam	2000			Yes				
Guatemala	2002	RHS, 2002	LSMS, 2006	Yes	2003		2008	2000
Guinea	1996	DHS, 2005	CWIQ, 2003		2000–01		2008	2000
Guinea-Bissau	2009	MICS, 2006	CWIQ, 2002		1988		2005	2000
Guyana	2002	MICS, 2006	IHS, 1998				2008	2000
Haiti	2003	DHS, 2005/06	IHS, 2001		1971		1997	2000
Honduras	2001	DHS, 2005/06	IHS, 2006		1993		2007	2000
Hungary	2001		ES/BS, 2004	Yes	2000	2004	2008	2000
Iceland	c			Yes		2004	2008	2000
India	2001	DHS, 2005/06	IHS, 2004/05		1995–96/ 2000–01	2003	2008	2000
Indonesia	2000	DHS, 2007	IHS, 2007		2003	2004	2008	2000
Iran, Islamic Rep.	2006	DHS, 2000	ES/BS, 2005	Yes	2003	2004	2006	2004
Iraq	1997	MICS, 2006			1981	1996	2008	2000
Ireland	2006		IHS, 2000	Yes	2000	2004	2008	2000
Isle of Man	2006			Yes				
Israel	2008		ES/BS, 2001	Yes	1981	2004	2008	2004
Italy	2001		ES/BS, 2000	Yes	2000	2004	2008	2000
Jamaica	2001	MICS 2005	LSMS, 2004		1996		2008	2000
Japan	2005		IS, 1993	Yes	2000	2004	2008	2000
Jordan	2004	DHS, 2007	ES/BS, 2006		1997	2005	2008	2005
Kazakhstan	1999	MICS, 2006	ES/BS, 2007	Yes			2008	2000
Kenya	1999	DHS, 2003; SPA, 2004	IHS, 2005–06		1977–79	2005	2008	2003
Kiribati	2005						2005	
Korea, Dem. Rep.	2008	MICS, 2000						2000
Korea, Rep.	2005		ES/BS, 1998	Yes	2000	2005	2008	2000
Kosovo	1981							
Kuwait	2005	FHS, 1996		Yes	1970		2007	2002
Kyrgyz Republic	2009	MICS 2005/06	ES/BS, 2007	Yes	2002	2004	2007	2000
Lao PDR	2005	MICS, 2006	ES/BS, 2002–03		1998–99	1998	1975	2000
Latvia	2000		IHS, 2007	Yes	2001	2005	2008	2000
Lebanon	1970	MICS, 2000			1998–99	1997	2008	2005
Lesotho	2006	DHS, 2004	ES/BS, 2002–03		1999–2000		2004	2000
Liberia	2008	DHS, 2007; MIS, 2008/09	CWIQ, 2007				1985	2000

	Currency	National accounts						Balance of payments and trade			Government finance	IMF data dissemination standard
		Base year	Reference year	System of National Accounts	SNA price valuation	Alternative conversion factor	PPP survey year	Balance of Payments Manual in use	External debt	System of trade	Accounting concept	
Libya	Libyan dinar	1999			VAB	1986		BPM5		G		G
Liechtenstein	Swiss franc				VAB					S		
Lithuania	Lithuanian litas	2000		[b]	VAB	1990–95	2005	BPM5	Actual	G	C	S
Luxembourg	Euro		2000		VAB		2005	BPM5		S	C	S
Macau SAR, China	Macao pataca	2002			VAB		2005	BPM5		G	C	G
Macedonia, FYR	Macedonian denar	1997	1995	[b]	VAB		2005	BPM5	Actual	G		G
Madagascar	Malagasy ariary	1984			VAB		2005	BPM5	Actual	G	C	G
Malawi	Malawi kwacha	1994			VAB		2005	BPM5	Actual	G		G
Malaysia	Malaysian ringgit	2000			VAP		2005	BPM5	Estimate	G	C	S
Maldives	Maldivian rufiyaa	1995			VAB		2005	BPM5	Actual	G	C	
Mali	CFA franc	1987			VAB		2005	BPM4	Actual	G	B	G
Malta	Euro (data reported in Maltese liri)	1973			VAB		2005	BPM5		G	C	S
Marshall Islands	U.S. dollar	1991			VAB							
Mauritania	Mauritanian ouguiya	1998			VAB		2005	BPM4	Actual	G		G
Mauritius	Mauritian rupee	2006			VAB		2005	BPM5	Actual	G	C	G
Mayotte	Euro											
Mexico	Mexican peso	2003		[b]	VAB		2005	BPM5	Actual	G	C	S
Micronesia, Fed. Sts.	U.S. dollar	1998			VAB							
Moldova	Moldovan leu	[a]	1996	[b]	VAB	1990–95	2005	BPM5	Actual	G	C	S
Monaco	Euro											
Mongolia	Mongolian tugrik	2005		[b]	VAB		2005	BPM5	Estimate	S	C	G
Montenegro	Euro	2000		[b]	VAB		2005		Actual			
Morocco	Moroccan dirham	1998			VAB		2005	BPM5	Actual	S	C	S
Mozambique	New Mozambican metical	2003			VAB	1992–95	2005	BPM5	Actual	S		G
Myanmar	Myanmar kyat	1985/86			VAP			BPM5	Estimate	G	C	
Namibia	Namibian dollar	2004/05		[b]	VAB		2005	BPM5		G	B	G
Nepal	Nepalese rupee	2000/01			VAB		2005	BPM5	Actual	S	C	G
Netherlands Antilles	Netherlands Antilles guilder							BPM5		S		
Netherlands	Euro	[a]	2000	[b]	VAB		2005	BPM5		S	C	S
New Caledonia	CFP franc									S		
New Zealand	New Zealand dollar	2000/01			VAB		2005	BPM5		G	C	
Nicaragua	Nicaraguan gold cordoba	1994		[b]	VAB	1965–95		BPM5	Actual	S	B	G
Niger	CFA franc	1987			VAP	1993	2005	BPM5	Preliminary	S		G
Nigeria	Nigerian naira	2002			VAB	1971–98	2005	BPM5	Preliminary	G		
Northern Mariana Islands	U.S. dollar											
Norway	Norwegian krone	[a]	2000	[b]	VAB		2005	BPM5		G	C	S
Oman	Rial Omani	1988			VAP		2005	BPM5		G	B	G
Pakistan	Pakistani rupee	1999/2000		[b]	VAB		2005	BPM5	Actual	G	C	G
Palau	U.S. dollar	1995			VAB							
Panama	Panamanian balboa	1996		[b]	VAB			BPM5	Actual	S	C	G
Papua New Guinea	Papua New Guinea kina	1998			VAB	1989		BPM5	Actual	G	B	
Paraguay	Paraguayan guarani	1994			VAP		2005	BPM5	Actual	S	C	G
Peru	Peruvian new sol	1994			VAB	1985–90	2005	BPM5	Actual	S	C	S
Philippines	Philippine peso	1985			VAP		2005	BPM5	Actual	G	B	S
Poland	Polish zloty	[a]	2002	[b]	VAB		2005	BPM5	Actual	S	C	S
Portugal	Euro	2000		[b]	VAB		2005	BPM5		S	C	S
Puerto Rico	U.S. dollar	1954			VAP					G		
Qatar	Qatari riyal	2001			VAP		2005				B	G
Romania	New Romanian leu	[a]	2005	[b]	VAB	1987–89, 1992	2005	BPM5	Actual	S	C	S
Russian Federation	Russian ruble	2000		[b]	VAB	1987–95	2005	BPM5	Preliminary	G	C	S
Rwanda	Rwandan franc	1995			VAP	1994	2005	BPM5	Estimate	G	C	G
Samoa	Samoan tala	2002			VAB			BPM5	Preliminary	G		

PRIMARY DATA DOCUMENTATION

	Latest population census	Latest demographic, education, or health household survey	Source of most recent income and expenditure data	Vital registration complete	Latest agricultural census	Latest industrial data	Latest trade data	Latest water withdrawal data
Libya	1995	MICS, 2000			2001		2004	2000
Liechtenstein	2000			Yes				
Lithuania	2001		ES/BS, 2004	Yes	2003	2005	2008	2000
Luxembourg	2001			Yes	1999–2000[d]	2004	2008	
Macau SAR, China	2006			Yes			2008	
Macedonia, FYR	2002	MICS, 2005	ES/BS, 2006	Yes	1994	2000	2008	
Madagascar	1993	DHS, 2003/04	PS, 2005		2004	2005	2008	2000
Malawi	2008	MICS 2006	LSMS, 2004–05		1993	2000	2008	2000
Malaysia	2000		ES/BS, 2004	Yes		2004	2008	2000
Maldives	2006	MICS, 2001		Yes			2008	
Mali	1998	DHS, 2006	IHS, 2006		1984		2008	2000
Malta	2005			Yes	2001	2004	2008	2000
Marshall Islands	1999							
Mauritania	2000	MICS, 2007	IHS, 2000		1984–85		2008	2000
Mauritius	2000			Yes		2003	2008	2003
Mayotte	2007						2007	
Mexico	2005	ENPF, 1995	LFS, 2008		1991	1999	2008	2000
Micronesia, Fed. Sts.	2000							
Moldova	2004	DHS, 2005	ES/BS, 2007	Yes		2004	2008	2000
Monaco	2008							
Mongolia	2000	MICS, 2005	LSMS, 2006–08	Yes		1999	2007	2000
Montenegro	2003	MICS, 2005/06	ES/BS, 2007	Yes				
Morocco	2004	MICS, 2006	ES/BS, 2007		1996	2005	2008	2000
Mozambique	2007	DHS, 2003	ES/BS, 2002/03		1999–2000		2008	2000
Myanmar	1983	MICS, 2000			2003		2001	2000
Namibia	2001	DHS, 2006/07	ES/BS, 1993/94		1996–97		2008	2000
Nepal	2001	DHS, 2006	LSMS, 2003/04		2002	2001	2002	2000
Netherlands Antilles	2001			Yes			2008	2000
Netherlands	2001		IHS, 1999	Yes	1999–2000[d]	2004	2008	
New Caledonia	2009			Yes			2008	
New Zealand	2006		IS, 1997	Yes	2002	2003	2008	2000
Nicaragua	2005	RHS, 2006/07	LSMS, 2005		2001		2007	2000
Niger	2001	DHS/MICS, 2006	QWIC/PS, 2005		1980		2008	2000
Nigeria	2006	DHS, 2008	IHS, 2003–04		1960		2008	2000
Northern Mariana Islands	2000							
Norway	2001		IS, 2000	Yes	1999	2003	2008	2000
Oman	2003	FHS, 1995			1978–79	2005	2008	2003
Pakistan	1998	DHS, 2006/07	LSMS, 2004/05		2000		2008	2000
Palau	2005			Yes				
Panama	2000	LSMS, 2003	LFS, 2006		2001	2000	2008	2000
Papua New Guinea	2000	DHS, 1996	IHS, 1996				2004	2000
Paraguay	2002	RHS, 2004	IHS, 2007		1991		2008	2000
Peru	2007	DHS, 2007/08	LSMS, 2007		1994	2006	2008	2000
Philippines	2007	DHS, 2008	ES/BS, 2006	Yes	2002	2004	2008	2000
Poland	2002		ES/BS, 2005	Yes	1996/2002	2004	2008	2000
Portugal	2001		IS, 1997	Yes	1999	2004	2008	2000
Puerto Rico	2000	RHS, 1995/96		Yes	1997/2002			
Qatar	2004			Yes	2000–01	2005	2008	2005
Romania	2002	RHS, 1999	LFS, 2007	Yes	2002	2005	2008	2000
Russian Federation	2002	RHS, 1996	IHS, 2007	Yes	1994–95	2005	2008	2000
Rwanda	2002	DHS, 2007/08	IHS, 2000		1984	1998	2008	2000
Samoa	2006				1999		2008	

	Currency	Base year	Reference year	System of National Accounts	SNA price valuation	Alternative conversion factor	PPP survey year	Balance of Payments Manual in use	External debt	System of trade	Accounting concept	IMF data dissemination standard
		National accounts						**Balance of payments and trade**			**Government finance**	**IMF data dissemination standard**
San Marino	Euro	1995	2000	b	VAB					S	C	G
São Tomé and Príncipe	São Tomé and Principe dobra	2001			VAP		2005		Preliminary	S		G
Saudi Arabia	Saudi Arabian riyal	1999			VAP		2005	BPM4		G		G
Senegal	CFA franc	1999	1987	b	VAB		2005	BPM5	Actual	S	B	G
Serbia	Serbian dinar	a	2002	b	VAB		2005		Actual	G	C	G
Seychelles	Seychelles rupee	1986			VAP			BPM5	Actual	G	C	S
Sierra Leone	Sierra Leonean leone	1990		b	VAB		2005	BPM5	Preliminary	S	B	G
Singapore	Singapore dollar	2000		b	VAB		2005	BPM5		G	C	S
Slovak Republic	Euro	2000	1995	b	VAB		2005	BPM5		G	C	S
Slovenia	Euro	a	2000	b	VAB		2005	BPM5		S	C	S
Solomon Islands	Solomon Islands dollar	2004			VAB			BPM5	Actual			
Somalia	Somali shilling	1985			VAB	1977–90			Estimate			
South Africa	South African rand	2000		b	VAB		2005	BPM5	Preliminary	G	C	S
Spain	Euro	2000		b	VAB		2005	BPM5		S	C	S
Sri Lanka	Sri Lankan rupee	2002			VAP		2005	BPM5	Actual	G	B	G
St. Kitts and Nevis	East Caribbean dollar	1990		b	VAB			BPM5	Preliminary	G	C	G
St. Lucia	East Caribbean dollar	1990			VAB			BPM5	Actual	G		G
St. Vincent & Grenadines	East Caribbean dollar	1990			VAB			BPM5	Preliminary	G	C	G
Sudan	Sudanese pound	1981/82[f]	1996		VAB		2005	BPM5	Actual	G	B	G
Suriname	Suriname dollar	1990		b	VAB			BPM5		G		G
Swaziland	Swaziland lilangeni	2000			VAB		2005		Preliminary	G	C	G
Sweden	Swedish krona	a	2000		VAB		2005	BPM5		G	C	S
Switzerland	Swiss franc	2000			VAB		2005	BPM5		S	C	S
Syrian Arab Republic	Syrian pound	2000			VAB	1970–2008	2005	BPM5		S	C	G
Tajikistan	Tajik somoni	a	2000	b	VAB	1990–95	2005	BPM5	Preliminary	G	C	G
Tanzania	Tanzanian shilling	1992			VAB		2005	BPM5	Actual	S		G
Thailand	Thai baht	1988			VAP		2005	BPM5	Estimate	G	C	S
Timor-Leste	U.S. dollar	2000			VAP							
Togo	CFA franc	1978			VAP		2005	BPM5	Actual	S	B	G
Tonga	Tongan pa'anga	2000/01			VAB			BPM5	Actual			G
Trinidad and Tobago	Trinidad and Tobago dollar	2000		b	VAB			BPM5		S	C	G
Tunisia	Tunisian dinar	1990			VAP		2005	BPM5	Actual	G	C	S
Turkey	New Turkish lira	1998			VAB		2005	BPM5	Actual	S	B	S
Turkmenistan	New Turkmen manat	a	2007	b	VAB	1987–95, 1997–2007		BPM5	Estimate	G		
Uganda	Ugandan shilling	2001/02			VAB		2005	BPM5	Actual	G	B	G
Ukraine	Ukrainian hryvnia	a	2003	b	VAB	1987–95	2005	BPM5	Actual	G	C	S
United Arab Emirates	U.A.E. dirham	1995			VAB			BPM4		G	C	G
United Kingdom	Pound sterling	2000		b	VAB		2005	BPM5		G	C	S
United States	U.S. dollar	a	2000		VAB		2005	BPM5		G	C	S
Uruguay	Uruguayan peso	2005			VAB		2005	BPM5	Actual	S	C	S
Uzbekistan	Uzbek sum	a	1997	b	VAB	1990–95		BPM5	Actual	G		
Vanuatu	Vanuatu vatu	1983			VAP			BPM5	Estimate		C	G
Venezuela, RB	Venezuelan bolivar fuerte	1997			VAB		2005	BPM5	Actual	G	C	G
Vietnam	Vietnamese dong	1994		b	VAP	1991	2005	BPM4	Estimate	G	C	G
Virgin Islands (U.S.)	U.S. dollar	1982								G		
West Bank and Gaza	Israeli new shekel	1997			VAB						B	G
Yemen, Rep.	Yemeni rial	1990			VAP	1990–96	2005	BPM5	Actual	G	B	G
Zambia	Zambian kwacha	1994			VAB	1990–92	2005	BPM5	Preliminary	G	B	G
Zimbabwe	Zimbabwe dollar	1990			VAB	1991, 1998	2005	BPM5	Actual	G	C	G

PRIMARY DATA DOCUMENTATION

	Latest population census	Latest demographic, education, or health household survey	Source of most recent income and expenditure data	Vital registration complete	Latest agricultural census	Latest industrial data	Latest trade data	Latest water withdrawal data
San Marino	c			Yes				
São Tomé and Príncipe	2001		PS, 2000–01				2008	
Saudi Arabia	2004	Demographic survey, 2007			1999	2005	2007	2006
Senegal	2002	DHS, 2005; MIS, 2008–09	PS, 2005		1998–99	2001	2008	2002
Serbia	2002	MICS, 2005–06		Yes			2008	
Seychelles	2002			Yes	1998		2008	2003
Sierra Leone	2004	DHS, 2008	IHS, 2003		1984–85		2002	2000
Singapore	2000	General household, 2005		Yes		2005	2008	
Slovak Republic	2001		IS, 1996	Yes	2001	2004	2008	
Slovenia	2002		ES/BS, 2004	Yes	2000	2005	2008	
Solomon Islands	1999						2007	
Somalia	1987	MICS, 2006					1982	2003
South Africa	2001	DHS, 2003	ES/BS, 2000		2000	2005	2008	2000
Spain	2001		IHS, 2000	Yes	1999	2004	2008	2000
Sri Lanka	2001	DHS, 1987	ES/BS, 2002	Yes	2002	2005	2008	2000
St. Kitts and Nevis	2001						2007	
St. Lucia	2001		IHS, 1995	Yes			2008	
St. Vincent & Grenadines	2001			Yes			2008	
Sudan	2008	MICS-PAPFAM, 2006			2000		2008	2000
Suriname	2004	MICS, 2000	ES/BS, 1999	Yes			2008	2000
Swaziland	2007	DHS, 2006/07	ES/BS, 2000/01		2003		2007	2000
Sweden	c		IS, 2000	Yes	1999–2000	2004	2008	2000
Switzerland	2000		ES/BS, 2000	Yes	2000		2008	2000
Syrian Arab Republic	2004	MICS, 2006			1981		2007	2003
Tajikistan	2000	MICS, 2005	LSMS, 2004		1994		2000	2000
Tanzania	2002	DHS, 2004/05; AIS, 2007/08	ES/BS, 2000/01		2002–03		2007	2002
Thailand	2000	MICS, 2005/06	IHS, 2004		2003	1999	2008	2000
Timor-Leste	2004	DGHS, 2003	LSMS, 2007				2005	
Togo	1981	MICS, 2006	CWIQ, 2006		1996		2007	2002
Tonga	2006			Yes	2001		2007	
Trinidad and Tobago	2000	MICS, 2006	IHS, 1992	Yes	2004	2005	2008	2000
Tunisia	2004	MICS, 2006	IHS, 2000		2004		2008	2000
Turkey	2000	DHS, 2003	LFS, 2006		2001	2000	2008	2003
Turkmenistan	1995	MICS, 2006	LSMS, 1998	Yes			2000	2000
Uganda	2002	DHS, 2006; SPA, 2007	PS, 2005		1991	2001	2008	
Ukraine	2001	DHS, 2007	ES/BS, 2008	Yes			2008	2000
United Arab Emirates	2005				1998		2008	2005
United Kingdom	2001		IS, 1999	Yes	1999–2000[d]	2004	2008	2000
United States	2000	CPS (monthly)	LFS, 2000	Yes	1997/2002	2004	2008	2000
Uruguay	2004		IHS, 2007	Yes	2000	2004	2008	2000
Uzbekistan	1989	MICS, 2006	ES/BS, 2003	Yes				2000
Vanuatu	2009						2007	
Venezuela, RB	2001	MICS, 2000	IHS, 2003	Yes	1997		2008	
Vietnam	2009	MICS, 2006	IHS, 2006		2001	1999	2008	2000
Virgin Islands (U.S.)	2000			Yes				
West Bank and Gaza	2007	PAPFAM, 2006			1971			
Yemen, Rep.	2004	MICS, 2006	ES/BS, 2005		2002	2005	2008	2000
Zambia	2000	DHS, 2007	IHS, 2004–05		1990		2008	2000
Zimbabwe	2002	DHS, 2005/06			1960	1995	2008	2002

Note: For explanation of the abbreviations used in the table see notes following the table.
a. Original chained constant price data are rescaled. b. Country uses the 1993 System of National Accounts methodology. c. Register based. d. Conducted annually. e. Rolling. f. Reporting period switch from fiscal year to calendar year from 1996. Pre-1996 data converted to calendar year.

• **Base year** is the base or pricing period used for constant price calculations in the country's national accounts. Price indexes derived from national accounts aggregates, such as the implicit deflator for gross domestic product (GDP), express the price level relative to base year prices. • **Reference year** is the year in which the local currency, constant price series of a country is valued. The reference year is usually the same as the base year used to report the constant price series. However, when the constant price data are chain linked, the base year is changed annually, so the data are rescaled to a specific reference year to provide a consistent time series. When the country has not rescaled following a change in base year, World Bank staff rescale the data to maintain a longer historical series. To allow for cross-country comparison and data aggregation, constant price data reported in *World Development Indicators* are rescaled to a common reference year (2000) and currency (U.S. dollars). • **System of National Accounts** identifies countries that use the 1993 System of National Accounts (1993 SNA), the terminology applied in *World Development Indicators* since 2001, to compile national accounts. Although more countries are adopting the 1993 SNA, many still follow the 1968 SNA, and some low-income countries use concepts from the 1953 SNA. • **SNA price valuation** shows whether value added in the national accounts is reported at basic prices (VAB) or producer prices (VAP). Producer prices include taxes paid by producers and thus tend to overstate the actual value added in production. However, VAB can be higher than VAP in countries with high agricultural subsidies. See *About the data* for tables 4.1 and 4.2 for further discussion of national accounts valuation. • **Alternative conversion factor** identifies the countries and years for which a World Bank–estimated conversion factor has been used in place of the official exchange rate (line rf in the International Monetary Fund's [IMF] *International Financial Statistics*). See *Statistical methods* for further discussion of alternative conversion factors. • **Purchasing power parity (PPP) survey year** is the latest available survey year for the International Comparison Program's estimates of PPPs. See *About the data* for table 1.1 for a more detailed description of PPPs. • **Balance of Payments Manual in use** refers to the classification system used to compile and report data on balance of payments items in table 4.15. BPM4 refers to the 4th edition of the IMF's *Balance of Payments Manual* (1977), and BPM5 to the 5th edition (1993). • **External debt** shows debt reporting status for 2008 data. *Actual* indicates that data are as reported, *preliminary* that data are based on reported or collected information but include an

element of staff estimation, and *estimate* that data are World Bank staff estimates. • **System of trade** refers to the United Nations general trade system (G) or special trade system (S). Under the general trade system goods entering directly for domestic consumption and goods entered into customs storage are recorded as imports at arrival. Under the special trade system goods are recorded as imports when declared for domestic consumption whether at time of entry or on withdrawal from customs storage. Exports under the general system comprise outward-moving goods: (a) national goods wholly or partly produced in the country; (b) foreign goods, neither transformed nor declared for domestic consumption in the country, that move outward from customs storage; and (c) nationalized goods that have been declared for domestic consumption and move outward without being transformed. Under the special system of trade, exports are categories a and c. In some compilations categories b and c are classified as re-exports. Direct transit trade—goods entering or leaving for transport only—is excluded from both import and export statistics. See *About the data* for tables 4.4, 4.5, and 6.2 for further discussion. • **Government finance accounting concept** is the accounting basis for reporting central government financial data. For most countries government finance data have been consolidated (C) into one set of accounts capturing all central government fiscal activities. Budgetary central government accounts (B) exclude some central government units. See *About the data* for tables 4.10, 4.11, and 4.12 for further details. • **IMF data dissemination standard** shows the countries that subscribe to the IMF's Special Data Dissemination Standard (SDDS) or General Data Dissemination System (GDDS). S refers to countries that subscribe to the SDDS and have posted data on the Dissemination Standards Bulletin Board at http://dsbb.imf.org. G refers to countries that subscribe to the GDDS. The SDDS was established for member countries that have or might seek access to international capital markets to guide them in providing their economic and financial data to the public. The GDDS helps countries disseminate comprehensive, timely, accessible, and reliable economic, financial, and sociodemographic statistics. IMF member countries elect to participate in either the SDDS or the GDDS. Both standards enhance the availability of timely and comprehensive data and therefore contribute to the pursuit of sound macroeconomic policies. The SDDS is also expected to improve the functioning of financial markets. • **Latest population census** shows the most recent year in which a census was conducted and in which at least preliminary results have been released.

The preliminary results from the very recent censuses could be reflected in timely revisions if basic data are available, such as population by age and sex, as well as the detailed definition of counting, coverage, and completeness. Countries that hold register-based censuses produce similar census tables every 5 or 10 years. Germany's 2001 census is a register-based test census using a sample of 1.2 percent of the population. A rare case, France has been conducting a rolling census every year since 2004; the 1999 general population census was the last to cover the entire population simultaneously (www.insee.fr/en/recensement/page_accueil_rp.htm). • **Latest demographic, education, or health household survey** indicates the household surveys used to compile the demographic, education, and health data in section 2. AIS is HIV/AIDS Indicator Survey, CPS is Current Population Survey, DGHS is Demographic and General Health Survey, DHS is Demographic and Health Survey, ENPF is National Family Planning Survey (Encuesta Nacional de Planificacion Familiar), FHS is Family Health Survey, LSMS is Living Standards Measurement Survey, MICS is Multiple Indicator Cluster Survey, MIS is Malaria Indicator Survey, NSS is National Sample Survey on Population Change, PAPFAM is Pan Arab Project for Family Health, RHS is Reproductive Health Survey, and SPA is Service Provision Assessments. Detailed information for AIS, DHS, MIS, and SPA are available at www.measuredhs.com/aboutsurveys; for MICS at www.childinfo.org; and for RHS at www.cdc.gov/reproductivehealth/surveys. • **Source of most recent income and expenditure data** shows household surveys that collect income and expenditure data. Names and detailed information on household surveys can be found on the website of the International Household Survey Network (www.surveynetwork.org). Core Welfare Indicator Questionnaire Surveys (CWIQ), developed by the World Bank, measure changes in key social indicators for different population groups—specifically indicators of access, utilization, and satisfaction with core social and economic services. Expenditure survey/budget surveys (ES/BS) collect detailed information on household consumption as well as on general demographic, social, and economic characteristics. Integrated household surveys (IHS) collect detailed information on a wide variety of topics, including health, education, economic activities, housing, and utilities. Income surveys (IS) collect information on the income and wealth of households as well as various social and economic characteristics. Labor force surveys (LFS) collect information on employment, unemployment, hours of work, income, and wages. Living Standards Measurement Studies (LSMS), developed by the World Bank, provide a comprehensive picture of household welfare and the factors that affect it; they typically incorporate data collection at the individual, household, and community levels. Priority surveys (PS) are a light monitoring survey, designed by the World Bank, for collecting data from a large number of households cost-effectively and quickly. Income tax registers (ITR) provide information on a population's income and allowance, such as gross income, taxable income, and taxes by socioeconomic group. 1-2-3 surveys (1-2-3) are implemented in three phases and collect sociodemographic and employment data, data on the informal sector, and information on living conditions and household consumption. • **Vital registration complete** identifies countries judged to have at least 90 percent complete registries of vital (birth and death) statistics by the United Nations Statistics Division and reported in Population and Vital Statistics Reports. Countries with complete vital statistics registries may have more accurate and more timely demographic indicators than other countries. • **Latest agricultural census** shows the most recent year in which an agricultural census was conducted and reported to the Food and Agriculture Organization of the United Nations. • **Latest industrial data** show the most recent year for which manufacturing value added data at the three-digit level of the International Standard Industrial Classification (ISIC, revision 2 or 3) are available in the United Nations Industrial Development Organization database. • **Latest trade data** show the most recent year for which structure of merchandise trade data from the United Nations Statistics Division's Commodity Trade (Comtrade) database are available. • **Latest water withdrawal data** show the most recent year for which data on freshwater withdrawals have been compiled from a variety of sources. See *About the data* for table 3.5 for more information.

Exceptional reporting periods

In most economies the **fiscal year** is concurrent with the calendar year. Exceptions are shown in the table at right. The ending date reported here is for the fiscal year of the central government. Fiscal years for other levels of government and reporting years for statistical surveys may differ. And some countries that follow a fiscal year report their national accounts data on a calendar year basis as shown in the *reporting period* column.

The **reporting period for national accounts data** is designated as either calendar year basis (CY) or fiscal year basis (FY). Most economies report their

national accounts and balance of payments data using calendar years, but some use fiscal years. In *World Development Indicators* fiscal year data are assigned to the calendar year that contains the larger share of the fiscal year. If a country's fiscal year ends before June 30, data are shown in the first year of the fiscal period; if the fiscal year ends on or after June 30, data are shown in the second year of the period. Balance of payments data are reported in *World Development Indicators* by calendar year and so are not comparable to the national accounts data of the countries that report their national accounts on a fiscal year basis.

Economies with exceptional reporting periods

Economy	Fiscal year end	Reporting period for national accounts data
Afghanistan	Mar. 20	FY
Australia	Jun. 30	FY
Bangladesh	Jun. 30	FY
Botswana	Jun. 30	FY
Canada	Mar. 31	CY
Egypt, Arab Rep.	Jun. 30	FY
Ethiopia	Jul. 7	FY
Gambia, The	Jun. 30	CY
Haiti	Sep. 30	FY
India	Mar. 31	FY
Indonesia	Mar. 31	CY
Iran, Islamic Rep.	Mar. 20	FY
Japan	Mar. 31	CY
Kenya	Jun. 30	CY
Kuwait	Jun. 30	CY
Lesotho	Mar. 31	CY
Malawi	Mar. 31	CY
Myanmar	Mar. 31	FY
Namibia	Mar. 31	CY
Nepal	Jul. 14	FY
New Zealand	Mar. 31	FY
Pakistan	Jun. 30	FY
Puerto Rico	Jun. 30	FY
Sierra Leone	Jun. 30	CY
Singapore	Mar. 31	CY
South Africa	Mar. 31	CY
Swaziland	Mar. 31	CY
Sweden	Jun. 30	CY
Thailand	Sep. 30	CY
Uganda	Jun. 30	FY
United States	Sep. 30	CY
Zimbabwe	Jun. 30	CY

Revisions to national accounts data

National accounts data are revised by national statistical offices when methodologies change or data sources improve. National accounts data in *World Development Indicators* are also revised when data sources change. The following notes, while not comprehensive, provide information on revisions from previous data.

• **Antigua and Barbuda.** The government has revised national accounts data for 1998–2008. • **Bahamas.** The government has revised national accounts data for 1997–2007. The new base year is 2006. • **Belize.** The government has revised national accounts data for 1991–2008. • **Bermuda.** The Statistical Office has revised national accounts data for 1996–2007. • **Croatia.** The Statistical Bureau has revised main GDP aggregates for 1995–2005. • **Guatemala.** The government has revised national accounts data to conform to the 1993 SNA methodology. The new base year is 2001. • **Haiti.** The government has revised national accounts data following changes in the methodology. Current price series since 1991 and constant price series since 1996 have been revised. The new base year is 1986/87. • **Kiribati.** The government statistical office has revised national accounts data for 1970–2008. • **Lebanon.** The government has revised national accounts data for 1997–2007. The new base year is 1997. • **Maldives.** National accounts data for 2001–08 have been revised to reflect a change in source from the Asian Development Bank to the Maldives Planning Department. • **Mauritius.** National accounts now reflect fiscal year data rather than calendar year data. The new base year is 2006. • **Micronesia, Fed. Sts.** The government statistical office has revised national accounts data for 1995–2008. • **Namibia.** The government has revised national accounts data since 2000. The new base year is 2004/05. • **Serbia.** The Statistical Bureau has revised current and constant GDP for 1997–2006. • **St. Lucia.** The government has revised national accounts data for 1998–2008. • **Uruguay.** The government has revised national accounts data for 1997–2008. The new base year is 2005.

Changes to national currencies

• **Slovak Republic.** On January 1, 2009, the euro replaced the Slovak koruna as the Slovak Republic's currency. • **Turkmenistan.** On January 1, 2009, the Turkmen manat was redenominated (1 new manat = 5,000 old manats).

STATISTICAL METHODS

This section describes some of the statistical procedures used in preparing *World Development Indicators*. It covers the methods employed for calculating regional and income group aggregates and for calculating growth rates, and it describes the *World Bank Atlas* method for deriving the conversion factor used to estimate gross national income (GNI) and GNI per capita in U.S. dollars. Other statistical procedures and calculations are described in the *About the data* sections following each table.

Aggregation rules

Aggregates based on the World Bank's regional and income classifications of economies appear at the end of most tables. The countries included in these classifications are shown on the flaps on the front and back covers of the book. Most tables also include the aggregate euro area. This aggregate includes the member states of the Economic and Monetary Union (EMU) of the European Union that have adopted the euro as their currency: Austria, Belgium, Cyprus, Finland, France, Germany, Greece, Ireland, Italy, Luxembourg, Malta, Netherlands, Portugal, Slovak Republic, Slovenia, and Spain. Other classifications, such as the European Union and regional trade blocs, are documented in *About the data* for the tables in which they appear.

Because of missing data, aggregates for groups of economies should be treated as approximations of unknown totals or average values. Regional and income group aggregates are based on the largest available set of data, including values for the 154 economies shown in the main tables, other economies shown in table 1.6, and Taiwan, China. The aggregation rules are intended to yield estimates for a consistent set of economies from one period to the next and for all indicators. Small differences between sums of subgroup aggregates and overall totals and averages may occur because of the approximations used. In addition, compilation errors and data reporting practices may cause discrepancies in theoretically identical aggregates such as world exports and world imports.

Five methods of aggregation are used in *World Development Indicators:*

- For group and world totals denoted in the tables by a *t*, missing data are imputed based on the relationship of the sum of available data to the total in the year of the previous estimate. The imputation process works forward and backward from 2000. Missing values in 2000 are imputed using one of several proxy variables for which complete data are available in that year. The imputed value is calculated so that it (or its proxy) bears the same relationship to the total of available data. Imputed values are usually not calculated if missing data account for more than a third of the total in the benchmark year. The variables used as proxies are GNI in U.S. dollars, total population, exports and imports of goods and services in U.S. dollars, and value added in agriculture, industry, manufacturing, and services in U.S. dollars.
- Aggregates marked by an *s* are sums of available data. Missing values are not imputed. Sums are not computed if more than a third of the observations in the series or a proxy for the series are missing in a given year.
- Aggregates of ratios are denoted by a *w* when calculated as weighted averages of the ratios (using the value of the denominator or, in some cases, another indicator as a weight) and denoted by a *u* when calculated as unweighted averages. The aggregate ratios are based on available data, including data for economies not shown in the main tables. Missing values are assumed to have the same average value as the available data. No aggregate is calculated if missing data account for more than a third of the value of weights in the benchmark year. In a few cases the aggregate ratio may be computed as the ratio of group totals after imputing values for missing data according to the above rules for computing totals.
- Aggregate growth rates are denoted by a *w* when calculated as a weighted average of growth rates. In a few cases growth rates may be computed from time series of group totals. Growth rates are not calculated if more than half the observations in a period are missing. For further discussion of methods of computing growth rates see below.
- Aggregates denoted by an *m* are medians of the values shown in the table. No value is shown if more than half the observations for countries with a population of more than 1 million are missing.

Exceptions to the rules occur throughout the book. Depending on the judgment of World Bank analysts, the aggregates may be based on as little as 50 percent of the available data. In other cases, where missing or excluded values are judged to be small or irrelevant, aggregates are based only on the data shown in the tables.

Growth rates

Growth rates are calculated as annual averages and represented as percentages. Except where noted, growth rates of values are computed from constant price series. Three principal methods are used to calculate growth rates: least squares, exponential endpoint, and geometric endpoint. Rates of change from one period to the next are calculated as proportional changes from the earlier period.

Least squares growth rate. Least squares growth rates are used wherever there is a sufficiently long time series to permit a reliable calculation. No growth rate is calculated if more than half the observations in a period are missing. The least squares growth rate, *r*, is estimated by fitting a linear regression trend line to the logarithmic annual values of the variable in the relevant period. The regression equation takes the form

$$\ln X_t = a + bt$$

which is the logarithmic transformation of the compound growth equation,

$$X_t = X_o (1 + r)^t.$$

In this equation X is the variable, t is time, and $a = \ln X_o$ and $b = \ln (1 + r)$ are parameters to be estimated. If b^* is the least-squares estimate of b, then the average annual growth rate, *r*, is obtained as $[\exp(b^*) - 1]$ and is multiplied by 100 for expression as a percentage. The calculated growth rate is an average rate that is representative of the available observations over the entire period. It does not necessarily match the actual growth rate between any two periods.

Exponential growth rate. The growth rate between two points in time for certain demographic indicators, notably labor force and population, is calculated from the equation

$$r = \ln(p_n/p_0)/n$$

where p_n and p_0 are the last and first observations in the period, n is the number of years in the period, and ln is the natural logarithm operator. This growth rate is based on a model of continuous, exponential growth between two points in time. It does not take into account the intermediate values of the series. Nor does it correspond to the annual rate of change measured at a one-year interval, which is given by $(p_n - p_{n-1})/p_{n-1}$.

Geometric growth rate. The geometric growth rate is applicable to compound growth over discrete periods, such as the payment and reinvestment of interest or dividends. Although continuous growth, as modeled by the exponential growth rate, may be more realistic, most economic phenomena are measured only at intervals, in which case the compound growth model is appropriate. The average growth rate over n periods is calculated as

$$r = \exp[\ln(p_n/p_0)/n] - 1.$$

Like the exponential growth rate, it does not take into account intermediate values of the series.

World Bank *Atlas* method

In calculating GNI and GNI per capita in U.S. dollars for certain operational purposes, the World Bank uses the *Atlas* conversion factor. The purpose of the *Atlas* conversion factor is to reduce the impact of exchange rate fluctuations in the cross-country comparison of national incomes.

The *Atlas* conversion factor for any year is the average of a country's exchange rate (or alternative conversion factor) for that year and its exchange rates for the two preceding years, adjusted for the difference between the rate of inflation in the country and that in Japan, the United Kingdom, the United States, and the euro area. A country's inflation rate is measured by the change in its GDP deflator.

The inflation rate for Japan, the United Kingdom, the United States, and the euro area, representing international inflation, is measured by the change in the "SDR deflator." (Special drawing rights, or SDRs, are the International Monetary Fund's unit of account.) The SDR deflator is calculated as a weighted average of these countries' GDP deflators in SDR terms, the weights being the amount of each country's currency in one SDR unit. Weights vary over time because both the composition of the SDR and the relative exchange rates for each currency change. The SDR deflator is calculated in SDR terms first and then converted to U.S. dollars using the SDR to dollar *Atlas* conversion factor. The *Atlas* conversion factor is then applied to a country's GNI. The resulting GNI in U.S. dollars is divided by the midyear population to derive GNI per capita.

When official exchange rates are deemed to be unreliable or unrepresentative of the effective exchange rate during a period, an alternative estimate of the exchange rate is used in the *Atlas* formula (see below).

The following formulas describe the calculation of the *Atlas* conversion factor for year t:

$$e_t^* = \frac{1}{3}\left[e_{t-2}\left(\frac{p_t}{p_{t-2}} \Big/ \frac{p_t^{S\$}}{p_{t-2}^{S\$}} \right) + e_{t-1}\left(\frac{p_t}{p_{t-1}} \Big/ \frac{p_t^{S\$}}{p_{t-1}^{S\$}} \right) + e_t \right]$$

and the calculation of GNI per capita in U.S. dollars for year t:

$$Y_t^\$ = (Y_t/N_t)/e_t^*$$

where e_t^* is the *Atlas* conversion factor (national currency to the U.S. dollar) for year t, e_t is the average annual exchange rate (national currency to the U.S. dollar) for year t, p_t is the GDP deflator for year t, $p_t^{S\$}$ is the SDR deflator in U.S. dollar terms for year t, $Y_t^\$$ is the *Atlas* GNI per capita in U.S. dollars in year t, Y_t is current GNI (local currency) for year t, and N_t is the midyear population for year t.

Alternative conversion factors

The World Bank systematically assesses the appropriateness of official exchange rates as conversion factors. An alternative conversion factor is used when the official exchange rate is judged to diverge by an exceptionally large margin from the rate effectively applied to domestic transactions of foreign currencies and traded products. This applies to only a small number of countries, as shown in *Primary data documentation*. Alternative conversion factors are used in the *Atlas* methodology and elsewhere in *World Development Indicators* as single-year conversion factors.

CREDITS

1. World view

Section 1 was prepared by a team led by Eric Swanson. Sarwar Lateef and Eric Swanson wrote the introduction with input from Sulekha Patel, Uranbileg Batjargal, and Masako Hiraga. Bhaskar Naidu Kalimili coordinated tables 1.1 and 1.6. Shota Hatakeyama, Mehdi Akhlagi, Raymond Muhula, and Masako Hiraga prepared tables 1.2, 1.3, and 1.5. Uranbileg Batjargal prepared table 1.4, with valuable assistance from Azita Amjadi. Yuri Dikhanov and the International Comparison Program team provided the new estimates of purchasing power parities (PPP), and Sup Lee prepared the special PPP table. Changqing Sun prepared the estimates of gross national income in PPP terms. Luca Bandiera of the World Bank's Economic Policy and Debt Department provided the estimates of debt relief for the Heavily Indebted Poor Countries Debt Initiative and Multilateral Debt Relief Initiative.

2. People

Section 2 was prepared by Sulekha Patel and Shota Hatakeyama in partnership with the World Bank's Human Development Network and the Development Research Group in the Development Economics Vice Presidency. Masako Hiraga and William Prince provided invaluable assistance in data and table preparation, and Kiyomi Horiuchi prepared the demographic estimates and projections. The introduction was written by Sulekha Patel with valuable inputs and comments from Albert Motivans of the United Nations Educational, Scientific, and Cultural Organization Institute for Statistics. Carla AbouZahr from the World Health Organization provided comments during initial discussions, and Sarwar Lateef provided comments on the first draft. The poverty estimates were prepared by Shaohua Chen and and Prem Sangraula of the World Bank's Poverty Monitoring Group and Changquin Sun. The data on children at work were prepared by Lorenzo Guarcello and Furio Rosati from the Understanding Children's Work project. Other contributions were provided by Eduard Bos, Charu Garg, and Emi Suzuki (population, health, and nutrition); Montserrat Pallares-Miralles and Carolina Romero Robayo (vulnerability and security); Lawrence Jeffrey Johnson and Sara Elder of the International Labour Organization (labor force); Juan Cruz Perusia and Olivier Labe of the United Nations Educational, Scientific, and Cultural Organization Institute for Statistics (education and literacy); the World Health Organization's Chandika Indikadahena (health expenditure), Monika Bloessner and Mercedes de Onis (malnutrition and overweight), Neeru Gupta and Teena Kunjument (health workers), Jessica Ho (hospital beds), Rifat Hossain (water and sanitation) and Philippe Glaziou (tuberculosis); Delice Gan of International Diabetes Federation (diabetes); and Nyein Nyein Lwin of the United Nations Children's Fund (health). Eric Swanson provided valuable comments and suggestions on the introduction and at all stages of production.

3. Environment

Section 3 was prepared by Mehdi Akhlaghi in partnership with the World Bank's Sustainable Development Network. Important contributions were made by Carola Fabi and Edward Gillin of the Food and Agriculture Organization of the United Nations; Ricardo Quercioli of the International Energy Agency; Amy Cassara, Christian Layke, Daniel Prager, and Robin White of the World Resources Institute; Laura Battlebury of the World Conservation Monitoring Centre; and Gerhard Metchies of German Technical Cooperation (GTZ). The World Bank's Environment Department devoted substantial staff resources to the book, for which the team is very grateful. Mehdi Akhlaghi wrote the introduction with valuable comments from Sarwar Lateef, Bruce Ross-Larson, and Eric Swanson. Other contributions were made by Susmita Dasgupta, Kirk Hamilton, Craig Meisner, Brian Blankespoor, Olivier Dupriz, Akiko Saesaka, Kiran Pandey, Giovanni Ruta, and Lopamudra Chakraborti.

4. Economy

Section 4 was prepared by Bala Bhaskar Naidu Kalimili and Soong Sup Lee in close collaboration with the Sustainable Development and Economic Data Team of the World Bank's Development Data Group, led by Soong Sup Lee. Soong Sup Lee wrote the introduction with valuable suggestions from Sarwar Lateef and Eric Swanson, and with assistance from Uranbileg Batjargal and Olga Akcadag. Contributions to the section were provided by Azita Amjadi (trade). The national accounts data for low- and middle-income economies were gathered by the World Bank's regional staff through the annual Unified Survey. Maja Bresslauer, Mahyar Eshragh-Tabary, Victor Gabor, Bala Bhaskar Naidu Kalimili, and Raymond Muhula worked on updating, estimating, and validating the databases for national accounts. The team is grateful to the International Monetary Fund, Organisation for Economic Co-operation and Development, United Nations Industrial Development Organization, and World Trade Organization for access to their databases.

5. States and markets

Section 5 was prepared by David Cieslikowski and Raymond Muhula, in partnership with the World Bank's Financial and Private Sector Development Network, Poverty Reduction and Economic Management Network, Sustainable Development Network, the International Finance Corporation, and external partners. David Cieslikowski wrote the introduction with input from Eric Swanson. Gary Milante and Nadia F. Pittaretti gave valuable advice on the development of the fragile situations table. Other contributors include Ada Karina Izaguirre (privatization and infrastructure projects); Leora Klapper (business registration); Federica Saliola (Enterprise Surveys); Sylvia Solf (Doing Business); Alka Banerjee, Isilay Cabuk, and Nabeel Gadit (Standard & Poor's global stock market indexes); Jeff Wagland of KPMG (tax rates); Satish Mannan (public policies and institutions); Nigel Adderley of the International Institute for Strategic Studies (military personnel); Bjorn Hagelin and Sam Perlo-Freeman of the Stockholm International Peace Research Institute (military expenditures and arms transfers); Kacem Iaych of the International Road Federation, Ananthanaryan Sainarayan of the Internataional Civil Aviation Organization, and Helene Stephan (transport); Jane Degerlund of Containerisation International (ports); Vanessa Grey and Esperanza Magpantay of the International Telecommunication Union; Ernesto Fernandez Polcuch and Georges Boade of the United Nations Educational, Scientific, and Cultural

Organization Institute for Statistics (research and development, researchers, and technicians); Anders Halvorsen of the World Information Technology and Services Alliance (information and communication technology expenditures); and Ryan Lamb of the World Intellectual Property Organization (patents and trademarks).

6. Global links

Section 6 was prepared by Uranbileg Batjargal in partnership with the Financial Data Team of the World Bank's Development Data Group, Development Research Group (trade), Development Prospects Group (commodity prices and remittances), International Trade Department (trade facilitation), and external partners. Uranbileg Batjargal wrote the introduction, with valuable comments from Eric Swanson. Substantial input for the data and tables came from Azita Amjadi (trade and tariffs) and Yasue Sakuramoto (external debt and financial data). Eric Swanson provided guidance on table contents and organization. Other contributors include Frederic Docquier (emigration rates); Flavine Creppy and Yumiko Mochizuki of the United Nations Conference on Trade and Development, and Francis Ng (trade); Betty Dow (commodity prices); Ciara Browne and Thierry Geiger of the World Economic Forum, Jean François Arvis, Monica Alina Mustra, Philip Schuler, and Vera Wen (trade facilitation); Christine Nashick, Jeff Reynolds, and Joe Siegel of DHL (freight costs); Yasmin Ahmad, Elena Bernaldo, and Aimee Nichols of the Organisation for Economic Co-operation and Development (aid); Akane Hanai and Ibrahim Levent (external debt); Henrik Pilgaard of the United Nations Refugee Agency (refugees); Costanza Giovannelli and Bela Hovy of the United Nations Population Division (migration); Sanket Mohapatra and Ani Rudra Silwal (remittances); and Teresa Ciller of the World Tourism Organization (tourism). Ramgopal Erabelly, Shelley Lai Fu, and William Prince provided valuable technical assistance.

Other parts of the book

Jeff Lecksell of the World Bank's Map Design Unit coordinated preparation of the maps on the inside covers. David Cieslikowski prepared *Users guide*. Eric Swanson wrote *Statistical methods*. Maja Bresslauer, Buyant Erdene Khaltarkhuu, and William Prince prepared *Primary data documentation*. Richard Fix and Alison Kwong prepared *Partners* and *Index of indicators*.

Database management

Mehdi Akhlaghi and William Prince coordinated management of the integrated World Development Indicators database. Operation of the database management system was made possible by Ramgopal Erabelly, Shelley Fu, and Shahin Outadi in the Data and Information Systems Team under the leadership of Reza Farivari.

Design, production, and editing

Richard Fix and Alison Kwong coordinated all stages of production with Communications Development Incorporated, which provided overall design direction, editing, and layout, led by Meta de Coquereaumont, Bruce Ross-Larson, and Christopher Trott. Elaine Wilson created the cover and graphics and typeset the book.

Joseph Caponio provided production assistance. Communications Development's London partner, Peter Grundy of Peter Grundy Art & Design, designed the report. Staff from External Affairs oversaw printing and dissemination of the book.

Client services

The Development Data Group's Client Services and Communications Team (Azita Amjadi, Richard Fix, Buyant Erdene Khaltarkhuu, Alison Kwong, Beatriz Prieto-Oramas, and Vera Wen) contributed to the design and planning and helped coordinate work with the Office of the Publisher.

Administrative assistance, office technology, and systems support

Awatif Abuzeid and Estela Zamora provided administrative assistance. Jean-Pierre Djomalieu, Gytis Kanchas, and Nacer Megherbi provided information technology support. Ramvel Chandrasekaran, Ugendran Makhachkala, and Malarvizhi Veerappan provided systems support on the Development Data Platform application.

Publishing and dissemination

The Office of the Publisher, under the direction of Carlos Rossel, provided valuable assistance throughout the production process. Denise Bergeron, Stephen McGroarty, and Nora Ridolfi coordinated printing and supervised marketing and distribution. Merrell Tuck-Primdahl of the Development Economics Vice President's Office managed the communications strategy.

World Development Indicators CD-ROM

Programming was carried out under the management of Vilas Mandlekar by Abarna Panchapakesan and Sujay Ramasamy. System testing was carried out under the guidance of Azita Amjadi and Vilas Mandlekar and included Buyant Erdene Khaltarkhuu, Parastoo Oloumi, William Prince, and Vera Wen. Systems development was undertaken in the Data and Information Systems Team lead by Reza Farivari. Masako Hiraga produced the social indicators tables. Kiyomi Horiuchi produced the population projection tables. William Prince coordinated user interface design and overall production and provided quality assurance, with assistance from Jomo Tariku. Photo credits belong to the World Bank photo library.

WDI Online

Design, programming, and testing were carried out by Reza Farivari and his team: Azita Amjadi, Ying Chi, Ramgopal Erabelly, Shelley Fu, and Buyant Erdene Khaltarkhuu. William Prince coordinated production and provided quality assurance. Malika Khek and Devika Levy of the Office of the Publisher were responsible for implementation of *WDI Online* and management of the subscription service.

Client feedback

The team is grateful to the many people who have taken the time to provide assistance on its publications. Their feedback and suggestions have helped improve this year's edition.

BIBLIOGRAPHY

Abadzi, Helen. 2007. "Absenteeism and Beyond: Instructional Time Loss and Consequences." Policy Research Working Paper 4376. World Bank, Washington, D.C.

Abdul Latif Jameel Poverty Action Lab. 2009. "Showing Up Is the First Step: Addressing Provider Absence in Education and Health." *Fighting Poverty: What Works?* Issue 2.

Africa Union and United Nations Economic Commission for Africa. 2005. "Transport and the Millennium Development Goals in Africa." Background document for the meeting of experts preceding the meeting of African transport ministers on the role of transport in achieving the Millennium Development Goals, April 4–5, Addis Ababa.

Agénor, Pierre-Richard, and Blance Moreno-Dodson. 2006. "Public Infrastructure and Growth: New Channels and Policy Implications." Policy Research Working Paper 4604. World Bank, Washington, D.C.

Aminian, Nathalie, K.C. Fung, and Francis Ng. 2008. "Integration of Markets vs. Integration by Agreements." Policy Research Working Paper 4546. World Bank, Development Research Group, Washington, D.C.

Anderson, Kym, Marianne Kurzweil, Will Martin, Damiano Sandri, and Ernesto Valenzuela. 2008. "Measuring Distortions to Agricultural Incentives, Revisited." Policy Research Working Paper 4612. World Bank, Development Research Group, Washington, D.C.

Arnold, John. 2006. "Best Practices in Management of International Trade Corridors." Transport Paper 13. World Bank, Transport Sector Board, Washington, D.C.

Arvis, Jean-François, Monica Alina Mustra, Lauri Ojala, Ben Shepherd, and Daniel Saslavsky. 2010. *Connecting to Compete 2010: Trade Logistics in the Global Economy: The Logistics Performance Index and Its Indicators.* Washington, D.C.: World Bank, International Trade Department.

Arvis, Jean-François, Monica Alina Mustra, John Panzer, Lauri Ojala, and Tapio Naula. 2007. *Connecting to Compete 2007: Trade Logistics in the Global Economy: The Logistics Performance Index and Its Indicators.* Washington, D.C.: World Bank, International Trade Department.

Arvis, Jean-François, Gael Raballand, and Jean-François Marteau. 2007. "The Cost of Being Landlocked: Logistics Costs and Supply Chain Reliability." Policy Research Working Paper 4258. World Bank, Development Research Group, Washington, D.C.

Asian Development Bank. 2009. "The GMS Program." [www.adb.org/GMS/Program]. Manila.

Babinard, Julie, and Peter Roberts. 2006. "Maternal and Child Mortality Development Goals: What Can the Transport Sector Do?" Transport Paper 12. World Bank, Transport Sector Board, Washington, D.C.

Bagai, Shweta, Richard Newfarmer, and John S. Wilson. 2004. "Trade Facilitation: Using WTO Disciplines to Promote Development." Trade Note 15. World Bank, International Trade Department, Washington, D.C.

Bagai, Shweta, and John S. Wilson. 2006. "The Data Chase: What's Out There on Trade Costs and Nontariff Barriers?" Policy Research Working Paper 3899. World Bank, Development Research Group, Washington, D.C.

Ball, Nicole. 1984. "Measuring Third World Security Expenditure: A Research Note." *World Development* 12 (2): 157–64.

Barnes, Douglas F. 2009. "Indoor Air Pollution and Improved Stoves: what Have We Learned, How Do We Move Forward?" Seminar presentation, November 12. World Bank, Development Research Group. Washington, D.C.

Bates, Bryson, Zbigniew Kundzewicz, Shaohong Wu, and Jean Palutikof, eds. 2008. *Climate Change and Water.* Technical Paper IV. Geneva: Intergovernmental Panel on Climate Change.

Beck, Thorsten, and Ross Levine. 2001. "Stock Markets, Banks, and Growth: Correlation or Causality?" Policy Research Working Paper 2670. World Bank, Development Research Group, Washington, D.C.

Behrman, Jere R. 2008. "What Have We Learned and What's Next?" In John Cockburn and Martin Valdivia, eds., *Reaching the MDGs: An International Perspective.* Dakar: Poverty and Economic Policy Research Network. Berg, Andrew, and Anne Kruger. 2003. "Trade, Growth, and Poverty: A Selective Survey." Working Paper 03/30. International Monetary Fund, Washington, D.C.

Billmeier, Andreas, and Tommaso Nannicini. 2007. "Trade Openness and Growth: Pursuing Empirical Glasnost." Working Paper 07/156. International Monetary Fund, Washington, D.C.

Blonigen, Bruce, and Wilson, Wesley W. 2008. "Port Efficiency and Trade Flows." *Review of International Economies* 16 (1): 21–36.

Bourzac, Katherine. 2010. "Bacteria Make Diesel from Biomass." *Technology Review,* January 28.

Bown, Chad P. 2009. "The Pattern of Antidumping and Other Types of Contingent Protection." *PREMnotes* 144. World Bank, Poverty Reduction and Economic Management Network, Washington, D.C.

Bruns, Barbara, Alain Mingat, and Ramahatra Rakotomalala. 2003. *A Chance for Every Child: Achieving Universal Primary Education by 2015.* Washington, D.C.: World Bank.

Buys, Piet, Uwe Deichmann, and David Wheeler. 2006. "Road Network Upgrading and Overland Trade Expansion in Sub-Saharan Africa." Policy Research Working Paper 4097. World Bank, Development Research Group, Washington, D.C.

Caiola, Marcello. 1995. *A Manual for Country Economists.* Training Series 1, Vol. 1. Washington, D.C.: International Monetary Fund.

Calderon, César. 2009. "Infrastructure and Growth in Africa." Policy Research Working Paper 4712. World Bank, Africa Region, Washington, D.C.

Calderon, César, and Luis Serven. 2008. "Infrastructure and Economic Development in Sub-Saharan Africa. Policy Research Working Paper 4712. World Bank, Development Research Group, Macroeconomics and Growth Team, Washington, D.C.

Chen, Shaohua, and Martin Ravallion. 2008. "The Developing World Is Poorer than We Thought, but No Less Successful in the Fight Against Poverty." Policy Research Working Paper 4703. World Bank, Washington, D.C.

Chomitz, Kenneth M., Piet Buys, and Timothy S. Thomas. 2005. "Quantifying the Rural-Urban Gradient in Latin America and the Caribbean." Policy Research Working Paper 3634. World Bank, Development Research Group, Washington, D.C.

CIESIN (Center for International Earth Science Information Network). 2005. Gridded Population of the World. Columbia University and Centro Internacional de Agricultura Tropical. [http://sedac.ciesin.columbia.edu/gpw/].

CIIFAD (Cornell International Institute for Food, Agriculture and Development). n.d. "The System of Rice Intensification." [http://ciifad.cornell.edu/sri/index.html]. Ithaca, N.Y.

Claessens, Stijn, Daniela Klingebiel, and Sergio L. Schmukler. 2002. "Explaining the Migration of Stocks from Exchanges in Emerging Economies to International Centers." Policy Research Working Paper 2816. World Bank, Washington, D.C.

Clark, Ximena, David Dollar, and Alejandro Micco. 2004. "Port Efficiency, Maritime Transport Costs and Bilateral Trade." NBER Working Paper 10353. Cambridge, Mass.: National Bureau of Economic Research.

Commission on Growth and Development. 2008. The Growth Report: Strategies for Sustainable Growth and Inclusive Development. Washington, D.C.: World Bank.

Containerisation International. 2009. Containerisation International Yearbook 2009. London: Informa Maritime and Transport.

Corrao, Marlo Ann, G. Emmanuel Guindon, Namita Sharma, and Dorna Fakhrabadi Shokoohi. 2000. Tobacco Control Country Profile. Atlanta, Ga.: American Cancer Society.

De Onis, Mercedes, and Monika, Blössner. 2000. "The WHO Global Database on Child Growth and Malnutrition: Methodology and Applications." International Journal of Epidemiology 32: 518–26.

De Onis, Mercedes, Adelheid W. Onyango, Elaine Borghi, Cutberto Garza, and Hong Yang. 2006. "Comparison of the World Health Organization (WHO) Child Growth Standards and the National Center for Health Statistics/WHO International Growth Reference: Implications for Child Health Programmes." Public Health Nutrition 9 (7): 942–47.

Dennis, Allen, and Ben Shepherd. 2007. "Trade Costs, Barriers to Entry, and Export Diversification in Developing Countries." Policy Research Working Paper 4368. World Bank, Development Research Group, Washington, D.C.

Demirgüç-Kunt, Asli, and Ross Levine. 1996. "Stock Market Development and Financial Intermediaries: Stylized Facts." World Bank Economic Review 10 (2): 291–321.

DHL. 2010. "DHL Express Standard Rate Guideline 2010." Bonn, Germany.

Djankov, Simeon, Caroline L. Freund, and Cong S. Pham. 2010, "Trading on Time." Review of Economics and Statistics 92 (1): 166–73.

Docquier, Frédéric, Abdeslam Marfouk, and B. Lindsay Lowell. 2007. "A Gendered Assessment of the Brain Drain." Washington, D.C.

Eckert, Erin, Neeru Gupta, Michael Edwards, Randy Kolstad, and Aliou Barry. 2002. "Guinea Health Facility Survey 2001." MEASURE Evaluation Technical Report 11. University of North Carolina at Chapel Hill, Carolina Population Center, Chapel Hill, N.C.

Egyptian Ministry of Health and Population, El-Zanaty Associates, and ORC Macro. 2005. Egypt Service Provision Assessment Survey, 2004. Calverton, Md.: Egyptian Ministry of Health and ORC Macro.

Estache, Antonio, Marianela Gonzalez, and Lourdes Trujillo. 2007. "Government Expenditures on Education, Health, and Infrastructure: A Naïve Look at Levels, Outcomes, and Efficiency." Policy Research Working Paper 4129. World Bank, Washington, D.C.

Eurostat (Statistical Office of the European Communities). n.d. Demographic Statistics. [http://epp.eurostat.ec.europa.eu/portal/page/portal/eurostat/home/]. Luxembourg.

———. Various years. Statistical Yearbook. Luxembourg.

Fankhauser, Samuel. 1995. Valuing Climate Change: The Economics of the Greenhouse. London: Earthscan.

FAO (Food and Agriculture Organization of the United Nations). 2001. "Global Estimates of Gaseous Emissions of NH3, N0 and N20 from Agricultural Land, 2001." Food and Agriculture Organization of the United Nations, Rome.

———. 2003. "How the World Is Fed." In Agriculture, Food and Water. Rome: Food and Agriculture Organization.

———. 2005. Global Forest Resources Assessment 2005. Rome: Food and Agriculture Organization.

———. 2007. Coping with Water Scarcity: Challenge of the Twenty-First Century. Report for World Water Day 2007. Rome: Food and Agriculture Organization.

———. 2008a. "Climate Change Adaptation and Mitigation in the Food and Agriculture Sector." Technical background document from the expert consultation, March 5–7, Rome.

———. 2008b. "Climate Change and Food Security: A Framework Document." Food and Agriculture Organization, Rome.

———. 2009a. "2050: A Third More Mouths to Feed." Press release, September 23. Food and Agriculture Organization, Rome.

———. 2009b. "More People Than Ever Are Victims of Hunger." Press release, June 19. Food and Agriculture Organization, Rome.

———. 2010. "Water and Poverty: An Issue of Life and Livelihoods." [www.fao.org/nr/water/issues/scarcity.html]. Rome.

———. n.d. FAOSTAT database. [http://faostat.fao.org/default.aspx]. Rome.

———. Various years. The State of Food Insecurity in the World. Rome: Food and Agriculture Organization.

Faurèsa, Jean-Marc, Jippe Hoogeveena, and Jelle Bruinsmab. 2004. "The FAO Irrigated Area Forecast for 2030." Food and Agriculture Organization, Rome.

Filmer, Deon, Amer Hasan, and Lant Pritchett. 2006. "A Minimum Learning Goal: Measuring Real Progress in Education." Working Paper 97. Center for Global Development, Washington, D.C.

Finger, J. Michael, and John S. Wilson. 2006. "Implementing a WTO Agreement on Trade Facilitation: What Makes Sense?" Policy Research Working Paper 3971. World Bank, Development Research Group, Washington, D.C.

Foster, Vivien, and Jevgenijs Steinbuks. 2009. "Paying the Price for Unreliable Power Supplies: In-House Generation of Electricity by Firms in Africa." Policy Research Working Paper 4913. World Bank, Africa Region, Sustainable Development Front Office, Washington, D.C.

BIBLIOGRAPHY

Fredricksen, Birger. 1993. *Statistics of Education in Developing Countries: An Introduction to Their Collection and Analysis.* Paris: United Nations Educational, Scientific, and Cultural Organization.

Froese, R., and D. Pauly, eds. n.d. FishBase database. [www.fishbase.org]. Manila.

Gauthier, Bernard, Tessa Bold, Jakob Svensson, and Waly Wane. 2009. "Delivering Service Indicators in Africa: Education and Health." Revised Concept Paper. African Economic Research Consortium, Hewlett Foundation, and World Bank, Washington, D.C.

Geneva Declaration. 2008. *Global Burden of Armed Violence.* Geneva: Geneva Declaration.

Ghana Statistical Service, Ghana Ministry of Health, and ORC Macro. 2002. *Ghana Service Provision Assessment Survey, 2002.* Accra.

Glasier, Anna, A. Metin Gulmezoglu, George P. Schmid, Claudia Garcia Moreno, and Paul F. A. van Look. 2006. "Sexual and Reproductive Health: A Matter of Life and Death." *Lancet* 368 (9547): 1595–1607.

Global Transport Knowledge Partnership. 2008. "Transport and the Millennium Development Goals." [www.gtkp.com]. Geneva.

Grigoriou, Christopher. 2007. "Landlockedness, Infrastructure and Trade: New Estimates for Central Asian Countries." Policy Research Working Paper 4335. World Bank, Development Research Group, Washington, D.C.

GTZ (Deutsche Gesellschaft für Technische Zusammenarbeit). 2005. "Why Transport Matters: Contributions of the Transport Sector towards Achieving the Millennium Development Goals." Deutsche Gesellschaft für Technische Zusammenarbeit, Eschborn, Germany.

Gwatkin, Davidson R., Shea Rutstein, Kiersten Johnson, Eldaw Suliman, Adam Wagstaff, and Agbessi Amouzou. 2007. *Socio Economic Differences in Health, Nutrition, and Population.* Washington, D.C.: World Bank.

Hamilton, Kirk, and Michael Clemens. 1999. "Genuine Savings Rates in Developing Countries." *World Bank Economic Review* 13 (2): 333–56.

———. 2006. *Where Is the Wealth of Nations? Measuring Capital for the 21st Century.* Washington, D.C.: World Bank.

Hamilton, Kirk, and Giovanni Ruta. 2008. "Wealth Accounting, Exhaustible Resources and Social Welfare." *Environmental and Resource Economics* 42 (1): 53–64.

Hanushek, A. Eric. 2002. *The Long-Run Importance of School Quality.* NBER Working Paper 9071. Cambridge, Mass.: National Bureau of Economic Research.

Hanushek, A. Eric, and Wössman, Ludger. 2007. *Education Quality and Economic Growth.* Washington, D.C.: World Bank.

Happe, Nancy, and John Wakeman-Linn. 1994. "Military Expenditures and Arms Trade: Alternative Data Sources." Working Paper 94/69. International Monetary Fund, Policy Development and Review Department, Washington, D.C.

Hatzichronoglou, Thomas. 1997. "Revision of the High-Technology Sector and Product Classification." STI Working Paper 1997/2. Organisation for Economic Co-operation and Development, Directorate for Science, Technology, and Industry, Paris.

Hausman, Warren H., Hau L. Lee, and Uma Subramanian. 2005. "Global Logistics Indicators, Supply Chain Metrics, and Bilateral Trade Patterns." Policy Research Working Paper 3773. World Bank, Development Research Group, Washington, D.C.

Haver Analytics. n.d. Thomson Reuters Datastream. [www.haver.com]. New York.

Helble, Matthias, Catherine Mann, and John S. Wilson. 2009. "Aid for Trade Facilitation." Policy Research Working Paper 5064. World Bank, Development Research Group, Washington, D.C.

Helble, Matthias, Ben Shepherd, and John S. Wilson. 2007. "Transparency and Trade Facilitation in the Asia Pacific: Estimating the Gains from Reform." Asia Pacific Economic Cooperation and World Bank, Washington, D.C.

Hertel, Thomas W., Terrie Walmsley, and Ken Itakura. 2001. "Dynamic Effects of the 'New Age' Free Trade Agreement between Japan and Singapore." Purdue University, Center for Global Trade Analysis, West Lafayette, Ind.

Heston, Alan. 1994. "A Brief Review of Some Problems in Using National Accounts Data in Level of Output Comparisons and Growth Studies." *Journal of Development Economics* 44 (1): 29–52.

Hettige, Hemamala, Muthukumara Mani, and David Wheeler. 1998. "Industrial Pollution in Economic Development: Kuznets Revisited." Policy Research Working Paper 1876. World Bank, Development Research Group, Washington, D.C.

Hinz. Richard P., Montserrat Pallares-Miralles, Carolina Romero, and Edward Whitehouse. Forthcoming. "International Patterns of Pension Provision II: Facts and Figures of the 2000s." Social Protection Discussion Paper. World Bank, Washington, D.C.

Hoekman, Bernard, Will Martin, and Aaditya Mattoo. 2009. "Conclude Doha: It Matters!" Policy Research Working Paper 5135. World Bank, Poverty Reduction and Economic Management Network, International Trade Department, and Development Research Group, Washington, D.C.

Hummels, David. 2007. "Transportation Costs and International Trade in the Second Era of Globalization," *Journal of Economic Perspectives* 21 (3): 131–54.

ICAO (International Civil Aviation Organization). 2009. *Civil Aviation Statistics of the World.* Montreal: International Civil Aviation Organization.

IEA (International Energy Agency). 2009. "World Energy Outlook 2009 Fact Sheet: Why Is Our Current Energy Pathway Unsustainable?" International Energy Agency, Paris.

———. Various years. *Energy Balances of OECD Countries.* Paris: International Energy Agency.

———. Various years. *Energy Statistics and Balances of Non-OECD Countries.* Paris: International Energy Agency.

———. Various years. *Energy Statistics of OECD Countries.* Paris: International Energy Agency.

ILO (International Labour Organization). 2009a. *Guide to the New Millennium Development Goals Employment Indicators.* Geneva: International Labour Office.

———. 2009b. Resolution concerning statistics of child labour. Resolution II, Rpt. ICLS/18/2008/IV/FINAL, 18th International Conference of Labour Statisticians, Geneva.

———. Various years. *Key Indicators of the Labour Market*. Geneva: International Labour Organization.

———. Various years. *Yearbook of Labour Statistics*. Geneva: International Labour Organization.

IMF (International Monetary Fund). 1977. *Balance of Payments Manual*. 4th ed. Washington, D.C.: International Monetary Fund.

———. 1993. *Balance of Payments Manual*. 5th ed. Washington, D.C.: International Monetary Fund.

———. 1995. *Balance of Payments Compilation Guide*. Washington, D.C.: International Monetary Fund.

———. 1996. *Balance of Payments Textbook*. Washington, D.C.: International Monetary Fund.

———. 2000. *Monetary and Financial Statistics Manual*. Washington, D.C.: International Monetary Fund.

———. 2001. *Government Finance Statistics Manual*. Washington, D.C.: International Monetary Fund.

———. 2004. *Compilation Guide on Financial Soundness Indicators*. Washington, D.C.: International Monetary Fund.

———. 2009a. *Global Financial Stability Report*. Washington, D.C.: International Monetary Fund.

———. 2009b. *World Economic Outlook: Sustaining the Recovery*. Washington, D.C.: International Monetary Fund.

———. Various issues. *Direction of Trade Statistics Quarterly*. Washington, D.C.: International Monetary Fund.

———. Various issues. *Government Finance Statistics Yearbook*. Washington, D.C.: International Monetary Fund.

———. Various issues. *International Financial Statistics*. Washington, D.C.: International Monetary Fund.

———. Various years. *Balance of Payments Statistics Yearbook. Parts 1 and 2*. Washington, D.C.: International Monetary Fund.

———. Various years. *Direction of Trade Statistics Yearbook*. Washington, D.C.: International Monetary Fund.

———. Various years. *International Financial Statistics Yearbook*. Washington, D.C.: International Monetary Fund.

Inter-agency Group for Child Mortality Estimation. n.d. Child Mortality Estimation Info database. [www.childmortality.org]. New York.

Internal Displacement Monitoring Centre. 2009. *Internal Displacement: Global Overview of Trends and Developments in 2008*. Geneva: Internal Displacement Monitoring Centre.

International Diabetes Federation. Various years. *Diabetes Atlas*. Brussels: International Diabetes Federation.

International Institute for Strategic Studies. 2010. *The Military Balance 2010*. London: Oxford University Press.

International Trade Centre, UNCTAD (United Nations Conference on Trade and Development), and WTO (World Trade Organization). n.d. The Millennium Development Goals database. [www.mdg-trade.org]. Geneva.

International Working Group of External Debt Compilers. 1987. *External Debt Definitions*. Washington, D.C.: International Working Group of External Debt Compilers.

IPCC (Intergovernmental Panel on Climate Change). 2007. *Climate Change 2007: The Physical Science Basis. Contribution of Working Group I to the Fourth Assessment Report of the Intergovernmental Panel on Climate Change*. Cambridge, U.K.: Cambridge University Press.

IRF (International Road Federation). 2009. *World Road Statistics 2009*. Geneva: International Road Federation.

ITU (International Telecommunication Union). 2007. *ICTs and Climate Change*. ITU-T Technology Watch Report 3. Geneva: International Telecommunication Union.

———. n.d. World Telecommunication Indicators database. Geneva: International Telecommunication Union.

IUCN (World Conservation Union). 2008. *2008 IUCN Red List of Threatened Species*. Gland, Switzerland: World Conservation Union.

Ivanic, Maros, and Will Martin. 2008. "Implications of Higher Global Food Prices for Poverty in Low-Income Countries." Policy Research Working Paper 4594. World Bank, Development Research Group, Washington, D.C.

Kee, Hiau Looi, Alessandro Nicita, and Marcelo Olarreaga. 2006. "Estimating Trade Restrictiveness Indices." Policy Research Working Paper 3840. World Bank, Development Research Group, Washington, D.C.

Kenyan National Coordinating Agency for Population and Development of Kenya, Kenyan Ministry of Health, Kenyan Central Bureau of Statistics, and ORC Macro. 2005. *Kenya Service Provision Assessment Survey 2004*. Nairobi: Kenyan National Coordinating Agency for Population and Development, Kenyan Ministry of Health, Kenyan Central Bureau of Statistics, and ORC Macro.

Khandker, Shahidur, Zaid Bakht, and Gayatri B. Koolwal. 2006. "The Poverty Impact of Rural Roads: Evidence from Bangladesh." Policy Research Working Paper 3875. World Bank, Washington, D.C.

KPMG. 2009a. *Corporate and Indirect Tax Rate Survey 2009*. KPMG: New York.

———. 2009b. *Individual Income Tax and Social Security Rate Survey 2009*. KPMG: New York.

Kremer, Michael, and Eric Maskin. 2006. "Globalization and Inequality." Harvard University, Cambridge, Mass., and Institute for Advanced Study, Princeton, N.J.

Kundzewicz, Zbigniew W., and Luis José Mata. 2007. "Freshwater Resources and Their Management." In S. Solomon, D. Qin, M. Manning, Z. Chen, M. Marquis, K.B. Averyt, M. Tignor and H. L. Miller, eds., *Climate Change 2007: Climate Change Impacts, Adaptation and Vulnerability. Working Group II Contribution to the Fourth Assessment Report of the Intergovernmental Panel on Climate Change*. Cambridge, U.K.: Cambridge University Press.

Kunte, Arundhati, Kirk Hamilton, John Dixon, and Michael Clemens. 1998. "Estimating National Wealth: Methodology and Results." Environmental Economics Series 57. World Bank, Environment Department, Washington, D.C.

Labonne, Julien, and Robert S. Chase. 2009. "The Power of Information: The Impact of Mobile Phones on Farmer's Welfare in the Philippines." World Bank,

BIBLIOGRAPHY

Sustainable Development Network, Social Development Department, Washington, D.C.

Leipziger, Danny, Marianne Fay, Quentin Wodon, and Tito Yepes. 2003. "Achieving the Millennium Development Goals: The Role of Infrastructure." Policy Research Working Paper 3163. World Bank, Latin American and the Caribbean Region, Finance, Private Sector, and Infrastructure Department, Washington, D.C.

Lewis, Maureen. 2006. "Governance and Corruption in Public Health Care Systems." Working Paper 78. Center for Global Development, Washington, D.C.

Limao, Nuno, and Anthony J. Venables. 2001 "Infrastructure, Geographical Disadvantage, Transport Cost, and Trade." *World Bank Economic Review* 15 (3): 451–79.

Lin, Justin Yifu. 2010. "Stimulus in a Volatile Financial World." World Bank, Washington, D.C.

Lloyd, Peter J., Johanna L. Croser, and Kym Anderson. 2009. "Global Distortions to Agricultural Markets New Indicators of Trade and Welfare Impacts,1955 to 2007." Policy Research Working Paper 4865. World Bank, Development Research Group, Washington, D.C.

Loskshin, Michael, and Ruslan Yemtsov. 2004. "Evaluating the Impact of Infrastructure Rehabilitation Projects on Household Welfare in Rural Georgia." World Bank, Washington, D.C.

Luxembourg Income Study. n.d. Online database. [www.lisproject.org]. Luxembourg.

Macro International. Various years. *Demographic and Health Surveys.* [www.measuredhs.com]. Calverton, Md.: Macro International.

Manning, Richard. 2009. "Using Indicators to Encourage Development: Lessons from the Millennium Development Goals. Report 2009:01. Danish Institute for International Studies, Copenhagen.

MDG Africa Steering Group. 2008. *Achieving the Millennium Development Goals in Africa.* New York: MDG Africa Steering Group.

Melhem, Samia, Claudia Morrel, and Nidhi Tandon. 2009. *Information and Communication Technologies for Women's Socioeconomic Empowerment.* Working Paper 176. Washington, D.C.: World Bank.

Mishra, Prachi, and David Newhouse. 2007. "Health Aid and Infant Mortality." Working Paper 07/100. International Monetary Fund, Fiscal Affairs and Research Departments, Washington, D.C.

Modi, Vijay, Susan McDade, Dominique Lallement, and Jamal Saghir. 2005. *Energy Services for the Millennium Development Goals.* New York: Energy Sector Management Assistance Programme, United Nations Development Programme, UN Millennium Project, and World Bank.

Morgenstern, Oskar. 1963. *On the Accuracy of Economic Observations.* Princeton, N.J.: Princeton University Press.

National Science Board. 2008. *Science and Engineering Indicators 2008.* Arlington, Va.: National Science Foundation.

Netcraft. 2009. "Netcraft Secure Server Survey." [www.netcraft.com].

Njinkeu, Dominique, John S. Wilson, and Bruno Powo Fosso. 2008. "Expanding Trade within Africa: The Impact of Trade Facilitation." Policy Research

Working Paper 4790. World Bank, Development Research Group, Washington, D.C.

Noumba Um, Paul, Stephane Straub, and Charles Vellutini. 2009. "Infrastructure and Economic Growth in the Middle East and North Africa." Policy Research Working Paper 5105. World Bank, Middle East and North Africa Region, Sustainable Development Department, Washington, D.C.

Odoki, Jennaro B., Farhad Ahmed, Gary Taylor, and Sunday A. Okello. 2008. "Towards the Mainstreaming of an Approach to Include Social Benefits within Road Appraisal: A Case Study from Uganda." Transport Paper 17. World Bank, Transport Sector Board, Washington, D.C.

OECD (Organisation for Economic Co-operation and Development). 2005. *Guide to Measuring the Information Society.* DSTI/ICCP/ISS (2005)/6. Paris: Organisation for Economic Co-operation and Development.

————. 2009a. *Agricultural Policies in OECD Countries: Monitoring and Evaluation.* Paris: Organisation for Economic Co-operation and Development.

————. 2009b. "Trading out of Poverty: How Aid for Trade Can Help." *OECD Journal on Development* 10 (1): 1–38.

————. 2010a. *OECD Economic Surveys: China 2010.* Paris: Organisation for Economic Co-operation and Development.

————. 2010b *Restoring Fiscal Sustainability: Lessons for the Public Sector.* Paris: Organisation for Economic Co-operation and Development.

————. n.d. Producer and Consumer Support Estimates. Online database. [www.oecd.org/tad/support/psecse]. Paris.

————. Various issues. *Main Economic Indicators.* Paris: Organisation for Economic Co-operation and Development.

————. Various years. *National Accounts.* Vol. 1, Main Aggregates. Paris: Organisation for Economic Co-operation and Development.

————. Various years. *National Accounts.* Vol. 2, Detailed Tables. Paris: Organisation for Economic Co-operation and Development.

————. Various years. *OECD Health Data.* Paris: Organisation for Economic Co-operation and Development.

OECD (Organisation for Economic Co-operation and Development) DAC (Development Assistance Committee). 1996. *Shaping the 21st Century: The Contribution of Development Cooperation.* Paris: Organisation for Economic Co-operation and Development.

————. Various years. *Development Cooperation Report.* Paris: Organisation for Economic Co-operation and Development.

————. Various years. *Geographical Distribution of Financial Flows to Developing Economies.* Paris: Organisation for Economic Co-operation and Development.

————. Various years. International Development Statistics. CD-ROM. Paris: Organisation for Economic Co-operation and Development.

Pandey, Kiran D., Piet Buys, Kenneth Chomitz, and David Wheeler. 2006a. "Biodiversity Conservation Indicators: New Tools for Priority Setting at the Global Environmental Facility." World Bank, Development Economics Research Group and Environment Department, Washington, D.C.

Pandey, Kiran D., David Wheeler, Bart Ostro, Uwe Deichmann, Kirk Hamilton, and Katie Bolt. 2006b. "Ambient Particulate Matter Concentrations in Residential and Pollution Hotspots of World Cities: New Estimates Based on the Global Model of Ambient Particulates (GMAPS)." World Bank, Development Economics Research Group and Environment Department, Washington, D.C.

Pandey, Kiran D., Katharine Bolt, Uwe Deichmann, Kirk Hamilton, Bart Ostro, and David Wheeler. 2006c. "The Human Cost of Air Pollution: New Estimates for Developing Countries." World Bank, Development Research Group and Environment Department, Washington, D.C.

PARIS21 (The Partnership in Statistics for Development in the 21st Century). 2009. "PARIS21 at Ten: Improvements in Statistical Capacity since 1999." The Partnership in Statistics for Development in the 21st Century, Paris.

Partnership on Measuring ICT for Development. 2008. The Global Information Society: A Statistical View. Santiago: United Nations.

Pricewaterhouse Coopers. 2009. Worldwide Summaries Online. [www.pwc.com]. New York.

Raballand, Gaël, Patricia Macchi, Dino Merotto, and Carly Petracco. 2009. "Revising the Roads Investment Strategy in Rural Areas: An Application for Uganda." Policy Research Working Paper 5036. World Bank, Africa Region, Transport Unit, Washington, D.C.

RAMSI (Regional Assistance Mission to Solomon Islands). 2010. "Fact Sheets." [www.ramsi.org]. Honiara.

Ravallion, Martin, and Shaohua Chen. 1996. "What Can New Survey Data Tell Us about the Recent Changes in Living Standards in Developing and Transitional Economies?" Policy Research Working Paper 16943. World Bank, Development Research Group, Washington, D.C.

Ravallion, Martin, Shaohua Chen, and Prem Sangraula. 2008. "Dollar a Day Revisited." Policy Research Working Paper 4620. World Bank, Development Research Group, Washington, D.C.

Ravallion, Martin, Gaurav Datt, and Dominique van de Walle. 1991. "Quantifying Absolute Poverty in the Developing World." Review of Income and Wealth 37(4): 345–61.

Ruggles, Robert. 1994. "Issues Relating to the UN System of National Accounts and Developing Countries." Journal of Development Economics 44 (1): 77–85.

Rwandan National Institute of Statistics, Rwandan Ministry of Health, and Macro International Inc. 2008. Rwanda Service Provision Assessment Survey 2007. Calverton, Md.: Rwandan National Institute of Statistics, Rwandan Ministry of Health, and Macro International Inc.

Ryten, Jacob. 1998. "Fifty Years of ISIC: Historical Origins and Future Perspectives." ECA/STAT.AC. 63/22. United Nations Statistics Division, New York.

Schwartz, Jordan, Luis Andres, and Georgeta Dragoiu. 2009. "Crisis in Latin America: Infrastructure Investment, Employment and the Expectations of Stimulus." Policy Research Working Paper 5009. World Bank, Washington, D.C.

Seethepalli, Kalpana, Maria Caterina Bramati, and David Veredas. 2008. "How Relevant Is Infrastructure to Growth in East Asia?" Policy Research Working Paper 4597. World Bank, East Asia and Pacific Region, Sustainable Development Department, Washington, D.C.

Shankar, Anuraj, Linda Bartlett, Vincent Fauveau, Monir Islam, and Nancy Terreri. 2008. "Delivery of MDG 5 by Active Management with Data." Lancet 371(9620): 12–18.

Shepherd, Ben, and John S. Wilson. 2007. "Road Infrastructure in Europe and Central Asia: Does Network Quality Affect Trade?" Policy Research Working Paper 4104. World Bank, Development Research Group, Washington, D.C.

Singh, R.B., P. Kumar, and T. Woodhead. 2002. "Smallholder Farmers in India: Food Security and Agricultural Policy." Food and Agriculture Organization, Regional Office for Asia and the Pacific, Bangkok.

SIPRI (Stockholm International Peace Research Institute). 2009. SIPRI Yearbook 2009: Armaments, Disarmament, and International Security. Oxford, U.K.: Oxford University Press.

Smith, Lisa, and Laurence Haddad. 2000. "Overcoming Child Malnutrition in Developing Countries: Past Achievements and Future Choices." 2020 Brief 64. International Food Policy Research Institute, Washington, D.C.

SPC (Secretariat of the Pacific Community). n.d. Online Statistics and Demography. [www.spc.int]. Nouméa.

Srinivasan, T. N. 1994. "Database for Development Analysis: An Overview." Journal of Development Economics 44 (1): 3–28.

Standard & Poor's. 2000. The S&P Emerging Market Indices: Methodology, Definitions, and Practices. New York: Standard & Poor's.

———. 2009. Global Stock Markets Factbook 2009. New York: Standard & Poor's.

Stiglitz, Joseph E., Amartya Sen, and Jean-Paul Fitoussi. 2009. Report by the Commission on the Measurement of Economic Performance and Social Progress. Paris: Commission on the Measurement of Economic Performance and Social Progress.

Straub, Stéphane. 2008. "Infrastructure and Development: A Critical Appraisal of the Macro Level Literature." Policy Research Working Paper 4590. World Bank, East Asia and Pacific Region, Sustainable Development Department, Washington, D.C.

Straub, Stéphane, Charles Vellutini, and Michael Warlters. 2008. "Infrastructure and Economic Growth in East Asia." Policy Research Working Paper 4589. World Bank, East Asia and Pacific Region, Sustainable Development Department, Washington, D.C.

Takle, Eugene, and Don Hofstrand. 2008. "Global Warming: Agriculture's Impact on Greenhouse Gas Emissions." Ag Decision Maker, April.

Taylor, Benjamin J., and John S. Wilson. 2009. "The Crisis and Beyond: Why Trade Facilitation Matters." Research at the World Bank: A Brief from the Development Research Group. World Bank, Washington, D.C.

UCDP (Upsalla Conflict Data Program). n.d. UCDP database. [www.ucdp.uu.se/database]. Upsalla, Sweden.

UNAIDS (Joint United Nations Programme on HIV/AIDS) and WHO (World Health Organization). Various years. Report on the Global AIDS Epidemic. Geneva: Joint United Nations Programme on HIV/AIDS.

BIBLIOGRAPHY

UNCTAD (United Nations Conference on Trade and Development). 2001. *Electronic Commerce and Development Report 2001*. New York and Geneva: United Nations Conference on Trade and Development.

———— 2007. *Trade and Development Report 2007: Regional Cooperation for Development*. New York and Geneva: United Nations Conference on Trade and Development.

———— 2008. *Trade and Development Report 2008: Commodity Prices, Capital Flows and the Financing of Investment*. New York and Geneva: United Nations Conference on Trade and Development.

————. 2009. *Transport Newsletter*. Issue 43.

————. Various years. *Handbook of Statistics*. New York and Geneva: United Nations Conference on Trade and Development.

UNCTAD (United Nations Conference on Trade and Development) and UNEP (United Nations Environment Programme). 2008. *Organic Agriculture and Food Security in Africa*. UNCTAD-UNEP Capacity Building Task Force on Trade, Environment and Development. New York: United Nations.

Understanding Children's Work (UCW). n.d. Online database. [www.ucw-project.org]. Rome.

UNDP (United Nations Development Programme). 1990. *Human Development Report 1990*. New York: Oxford University Press.

————. 2005. *Human Development Report 2005: International Cooperation at a Crossroads: Aid, Trade and Security in an Unequal World*. New York: United Nations Development Programme.

————. 2006. *Asia-Pacific Human Development Report 2006: Trade on Human Terms: Transforming Trade for Human Development in Asia and the Pacific*. Colombo: Macmillan India Ltd.

United Nations Department of Peacekeeping Operations. n.d. "Current Operations." [www.un.org/en/peacekeeping/currentops.shtml]. New York.

UNESCO (United Nations Educational, Scientific, and Cultural Organization). 1997. *International Standard Classification of Education*. Paris: United Nations Educational, Scientific, and Cultural Organization.

————. 2009. *World Water Development Report 3: Water in a Changing World. 2009*. Paris: United Nations Educational, Scientific, and Cultural Organization.

————. Various years. *EFA Global Monitoring Report*. Paris: United Nations Educational, Scientific, and Cultural Organization.

UNESCO (United Nations Educational, Scientific, and Cultural Organization) Institute for Statistics. 2008a. "A Typology of Out-of-School Children to Improve Policies that Address Exclusion." Background document for the 48th Session of the International Conference on Education, November 25–28, Geneva.

————. 2008b. *A View Inside Primary Schools*. A World Education Indicators Cross-National Study. Montreal, Canada: United Nations Educational, Scientific, and Cultural Organization Institute for Statistics.

————. n.d. Online database. [www.uis.unesco.org]. Montreal.

————. Various years. *Global Education Digest*. Paris.

UNHCR (The UN Refugee Agency). Various years. *Statistical Yearbook*. Geneva: The UN Refugee Agency.

UNICEF (United Nations Children's Fund). Various years. Multiple Indicator Cluster Surveys. [www.childinfo.org]. New York.

————. Various years. *The State of the World's Children*. New York: Oxford University Press.

UNICEF (United Nations Children's Fund), WHO (World Health Organization), World Bank, and United Nations Population Division. 2007. "Levels and Trends of Child Mortality in 2006: Estimates Developed by the Inter-Agency Group for Child Mortality Estimation." Working Paper. United Nations, New York.

UNIDO (United Nations Industrial Development Organization). Various years. *International Yearbook of Industrial Statistics*. Vienna: United Nations Industrial Development Organization.

UNIFEM (United Nations Development Fund for Women). 2005. *Progress of the World's Women*. New York: United Nations Development Fund for Women.

United Nations. 1990. *International Standard Industrial Classification of All Economic Activities, Third Revision*. Statistical Papers Series M, No. 4, Rev. 3. New York: United Nations.

————. 1992. "Kyoto Protocol to the United Nations Framework Convention on Climate Change. United Nations, New York.

————. 2001. *UN Secretary-General's Road Map towards the Implementation of the Millennium Declaration*. New York: United Nations.

————. 2009a. *The Millennium Development Goals Report 2009*. New York: United Nations.

————. 2009b. "Fact Sheet: Stepping Up International Action on Climate Change: The Road to Copenhagen. United Nations Framework Convention on Climate Change, New York.

————. 2009c. "Copenhagen Accord." December 18. United Nations Framework Convention on Climate Change, Copenhagen.

————. 2009d. *World Economic and Social Survey 2009: Promoting Development, Saving the Planet*. New York: United Nations, Department of Economic and Social Affairs.

United Nations Population Division. 2006. *World Population Prospects: The 2004 Revision. Vol. III. Analytical Report*. New York: United Nations, Department of Economic and Social Affairs.

————. 2009a. *World Population Prospects: The 2008 Revision*. New York: United Nations, Department of Economic and Social Affairs.

————. 2009b. *Trends in Total Migrant Stock: 2008 Revision*. New York: United Nations, Department of Economic and Social Affairs.

————. Various years. *World Urbanization Prospects*. New York: United Nations, Department of Economic and Social Affairs.

United Nations Statistics Division. n.d. Cement Manufacturing Data Set. New York: United Nations.

————. n.d. Comtrade database. New York.

———. n.d. *International Standard Industrial Classification of All Economic Activities, Third Revision*. [http://unstats.un.org/unsd/cr/registry/]. New York.

———. n.d. World Energy Data Set. New York: United Nations.

———. Various issues. *Monthly Bulletin of Statistics*. New York: United Nations.

———. Various issues. *Population and Vital Statistics Report*. New York: United Nations.

———. Various years. *Demographic Yearbook*. New York: United Nations.

———. Various years. *International Trade Statistics Yearbook*. New York: United Nations.

———. Various years. *Energy Statistics Yearbook*. New York: United Nations.

———. Various years. *National Accounts Statistics: Main Aggregates and Detailed Tables. Parts 1 and 2*. New York: United Nations.

———. Various years. *National Income Accounts*. New York: United Nations.

———. Various years. *Statistical Yearbook*. New York: United Nations.

University of California, Berkeley, and Max Planck Institute for Demographic Research. n.d. Human Mortality Database. [www.mortality.org or www.humanmortality.de]. Berkeley, Calif., and Rostock, Germany.

UNODC (United Nations Office on Drugs and Crime). 2007. *9th UN Survey of Crime Trends*. Vienna: United Nations Office on Drugs and Crime.

———. 2008. *10th UN Survey of Crime Trends*. Vienna: United Nations Office on Drugs and Crime.

———. 2009. *International Homicide Statistics*. Vienna: United Nations Office on Drugs and Crime.

———. n.d. International Homicide Statistics database. Vienna: United Nations Office on Drugs and Crime.

USAID (U.S. Agency for International Development). 2007. "Calculating Tariff Equivalents for Time in Trade." U.S. Agency for International Development, Washington, D.C.

U.S. Census Bureau. n.d. International Data Base (IDB). [www.census.gov/ipc/www/idb/]. Washington, D.C.

U.S. Center for Disease Control and Prevention. Various years. *International Reproductive Health Surveys*. [www.cdc.gov/reproductivehealth/Surveys/]. Atlanta, Ga.

U.S. National Science Board. 2008. *Science and Engineering Indicators 2008*. Arlington, Va.: National Science Foundation.

U.S. President. 2010. *Economic Report of the President*. Washington, D.C.: U.S. Government Printing Office.

Vandermoortele, Jan. 2009. "Taking the MDGs Beyond 2015: Hasten Slowly." European Association for Development Research and Training Institutes, Bonn, Germany.

Watkins, Kevin. 2008. *The Millennium Development Goals: Three Proposals for Renewing the Vision and Reshaping the Future*. Paris: United Nations Educational, Scientific, and Cultural Organization.

WHO (World Health Organization). 2008a. *Health Metrics Network Framework and Standards for Country Health Information Systems*. Geneva: World Health Organization.

———. 2008b. "Measuring Health System Strengthening and Trends: A Toolkit for Countries." World Health Organization, Geneva.

———. 2008c. *The World Health Report: Primary Health Care*. Geneva: World Health Organization.

———. 2008d. *Worldwide Prevalence of Anemia 1993–2005*. Geneva: World Health Organization.

———. 2009. *WHO Report on the Global Tobacco Epidemic 2009: Implementing Smoke-Free Environments*. Geneva: World Health Organization.

———. n.d. Global Database on Child Growth and Malnutrition. [www.who.int/nutgrowthdb]. Geneva.

———. n.d. National Health Account database. [www.who.int/nha/en/]. Geneva.

———. Various years. *World Health Report*. Geneva: World Health Organization.

———. Various years. *World Health Statistics*. Geneva: World Health Organization.

———. Various years. *Global Tuberculosis Control Report*. Geneva: World Health Organization.

WHO (World Health Organization) and UNICEF (United Nations Children's Fund). 2008. *Progress on Drinking Water and Sanitation*. Geneva: World Health Organization.

———. Various years. WHO-UNICEF estimates of national immunization coverage database. [www.who.int/immunization_monitoring/routine/immunization_coverage/en/index4.html]. Geneva.

WHO (World Health Organization), UNICEF (United Nations Children's Fund), UNFPA (United Nations Population Fund), and World Bank. 2007. *Maternal Mortality in 2005: Estimates Developed by WHO, UNICEF, UNFPA, and the World Bank*. Geneva: World Health Organization.

Willoughby, Christopher. 2004. "Infrastructure and the Millennium Development Goals." Paper presented at the Session on Complementarity of Infrastructure for Achieving the MDGs, October 27, Berlin.

Wilson, John S. 2003. "Trade Facilitation: New Issues in a Development Context." Trade Note 12. World Bank, International Trade Department, Washington, D.C.

Wilson, John S., Catherine L. Mann, and Tsunehiro Otsuki. 2003. "Trade Facilitation and Economic Development: A New Approach to Measuring the Impact." *World Bank Economic Review 17(3): 367–89*.

———. 2004. "Assessing the Potential Benefit of Trade Facilitation: A Global Perspective." Policy Research Working Paper 3224. World Bank, Development Research Group, Washington, D.C.

Wilson, John S., and Tsunehiro Otsuki. 2007. "Regional Integration in South Asia: What Role for Trade Facilitation?" Policy Research Working Paper 4423. World Bank, Development Research Group, Washington, D.C.

WIPO (World Intellectual Property Organization). 2009. *WIPO Patent Report: Statistics on Worldwide Patent Activity*. Geneva: World Intellectual Property Organization.

WITSA (World Information Technology and Services Alliance). 2009. *Digital Planet 2009: The Global Information Economy*. Vienna, Va.: World Information Technology and Services Alliance.

BIBLIOGRAPHY

World Bank. 1990. *World Development Report 1990: Poverty.* Washington, D.C.: World Bank.

———. 2000a. *Making Transition Work for Everyone: Poverty and Inequality in Europe and Central Asia.* Washington, D.C.: World Bank.

———. 2000b. *Trade Blocs.* New York: Oxford University Press.

———. 2001. *World Development Report 2000/2001: Attacking Poverty.* New York: Oxford University Press.

———. 2002. *Global Economic Prospects 2002: Making Trade Work for the World's Poor.* Washington, D.C.: World Bank.

———. 2007a. *Healthy Development: The World Bank Strategy for Health, Nutrition, and Population Results.* Washington, D.C.: World Bank.

———. 2007b. *Sanitation and Water Supply: Improving Services for the Poor.* IDA at Work. Washington, D.C.: World Bank, Sustainable Development Network.

———. 2008a. "Brazil Country Partnership Strategy 2008–2011." World Bank, Latin America and the Caribbean Region, Washington, D.C.

———. 2008b. "Improving Trade and Transport for Landlocked Developing Countries: World Bank Contributions to Implementing the Almaty Programme of Action: A Report for the Mid-Term Review October 2008." World Bank, International Trade Department, Washington, D.C.

———. 2008c. "Safe, Clean, and Affordable . . . Transport for Development: The World Bank Group's Transport Business Strategy for 2008–2012." World Bank, Transport Sector Board, Washington, D.C.

———. 2008d. *World Development Report 2009: Reshaping Economic Geography.* Washington, D.C.: World Bank.

———. 2009a. *Africa's Development in a Changing Climate: Act Now, Act Together, Act Differently.* Washington, D.C.: World Bank.

———. 2009b. "Air Freight: A Market Study with Implications for Landlocked Countries." Transport Paper 26. World Bank, Washington, D.C.

———. 2009c. *Development Outreach.* October.

———. 2009d. *Doing Business 2010.* Washington, D.C.: World Bank.

———. 2009e. *Energy: Improving Services for the Poor.* IDA at Work. Washington, D.C.: World Bank, Sustainable Development Network.

———. 2009f. "Infrastructure Financing Gap Endangers Development Goals." Press release, April 23. World Bank, Washington, D.C.

———. 2009g. "Private Activity in Infrastructure Down, But Still Around Peak Levels." Private Participation in Infrastructure Data Update Note 28. World Bank, Washington, D.C.

———. 2009h. *Protecting Progress: The Challenge Facing Low-Income Countries in the Global Recession.* Washington, D.C.: World Bank.

———. 2009i. "Reduced Emissions and Enhanced Adaptation in Agricultural Landscapes." *Agriculture and Rural Development Notes,* Issue 50.

———. 2009j. "World Bank to Invest $45 Billion in Infrastructure to Help Create Jobs and Speed Crisis Recovery." Press release, April 23. World Bank, Washington, D.C.

———. 2009k. *World Development Report 2010: Development and Climate Change.* Washington, D.C.: World Bank.

———. 2009l. *Information and Communications for Development: Extending Reach and Increasing Impact.* Washington, D.C.: World Bank.

———. 2010. *Global Economic Prospects 2010: Crisis, Finance, and Growth.* Washington, D.C.: World Bank.

———. n.d. Enterprise Surveys Online. [www.enterprisesurveys.org]. Washington, D.C.

———. n.d. Performance Assessments and Allocation of IDA Resources Online database. [www.worldbank.org/ida]. Washington, D.C.

———. n.d. PovcalNet online database. [http://iresearch.worldbank.org/PovcalNet]. Washington, D.C.

———. n.d. Private Participation in Infrastructure Database. [http://ppi.worldbank.org/]. Washington, D.C.

———. n.d. World Trade Indicators Online database. [www.worldbank.org/wti]. Washington, D.C.

———. Various issues. *Commodity Market Review.* Washington, D.C.: World Bank, Development Prospects Group

———. Various issues. *Commodity Price Data.* Washington, D.C.: World Bank, Development Prospects Group.

———. Various issues. *Migration and Development Briefs.* Washington, D.C.: World Bank, Development Prospects Group.

———. Various years. *Global Development Finance: Volumes I and II.* Washington, D.C.: World Bank.

———. Various years. *World Development Indicators.* Washington, D.C.: World Bank.

———. Various years. *World Debt Tables.* Washington, D.C.: World Bank.

World Bank, Agence Françaisede Développement, Bundesministerium für Wirtschaftliche Zusammenarbeit und Entwicklung, Kreditanstalt für Wiederaufbau Entwicklungsbank, Deutsche Gesellschaft für Technische Zusammenarbeit, and Department for International Development. 2005. *Pro-Poor Growth in the 1990s: Lessons and Insights from 14 Countries.* Washington, D.C.: World Bank.

World Bank and IFPRI (International Food Policy Research Institute). 2006. *Agriculture and Achieving the Millennium Development Goals.* Report 32729-GLB. Washington, D.C.: World Bank.

World Bank and IMF (International Monetary Fund). 2007. *Global Monitoring Report 2007: Millennium Development Goals: Confronting the Challenges of Gender Equality and Fragile States.* Washington, D.C.: World Bank.

———. 2008. *Global Monitoring Report 2008: MDGs and the Environment.* Washington, D.C.: World Bank.

———. 2009a. "Heavily Indebted Poor Countries (HIPC) Initiative and Multilateral Debt Relief Initiative (MDRI)—Status of Implementation." Washington, D.C.

———. 2009b. *Global Monitoring Report 2009: A Development Emergency.* Washington, D.C.: World Bank.

World Economic Forum. 2009. *The Global Competitiveness Report 2009–2010.* Geneva: World Economic Forum.

World Tourism Organization. Various years. *Compendium of Tourism Statistics.* Madrid: World Tourism Organization.

————. Various years. *Yearbook of Tourism Statistics. Vols. 1 and 2.* Madrid: World Tourism Organization.

WTO (World Trade Organization). n.d. Regional Trade Agreements Gateway. [www.wto.org/english/tratop_e/region_e/region_e.htm]. Geneva.

————. n.d. Regional Trade Agreements Information System. Online database. [http://rtais.wto.org/]. Geneva.

————. Various years. *Annual Report.* Geneva.

Yepes, Tito, Justin Pierce, and Vivien Foster. 2009. "Making Sense of Africa's Infrastructure Endowment: A Benchmarking Approach." Policy Research Working Paper 4912. World Bank, Africa Region, Sustainable Development Front Office, Washington, D.C.

Zambian Ministry of Health and World Health Organization. 2006. "Service Availability Mapping." World Health Organization, Geneva.

INDEX OF INDICATORS

References are to table numbers.

B

C

INDEX OF INDICATORS

INDEX OF INDICATORS

INDEX OF INDICATORS

INDEX OF INDICATORS

INDEX OF INDICATORS

INDEX OF INDICATORS

INDEX OF INDICATORS